JOURNAL OF THE GENERAL CONVENTION

Of the Protestant Episcopal Church in the United States of America Otherwise known as

THE EPISCOPAL CHURCH

2003

Being the 74th General Convention, held in Minneapolis, Minneapolis from July Thirtieth to August Eighth Inclusive, in the Year of Our Lord, Two Thousand and Three.

The General Convention Office
Episcopal Church Center
815 Second Avenue
New York, New York 10017

TABLE OF CONTENTS

PART I
DIRECTORY
The General Convention	3
Officers	5
Committees, Commissions, Agencies and Boards	6
The Courts	38
The Provinces	39
The House of Bishops	
Officers	40
Roster	41
The House of Deputies	
Officers	45
Roster	46

PART II
THE GENERAL CONVENTION, MINNEAPOLIS, 2003
Minutes of the House of Bishops	67
Minutes of the House of Deputies	357

PART III
THE HOUSE OF BISHOPS INTERIM MEETINGS
Hendersonville, North Carolina, March 9–14, 2001	705
Burlington, Vermont, September 20–26, 2001	720
Navasota, Texas, March 7–12, 2002	737
Cleveland, Ohio, September 30–October 1, 2002	742
Hendersonville, North Carolina, March 14–20, 2003	765

PART IV
APPENDICES
Budget	791
Report of the Registrar	847
Report of the Recorder	863

INDEXES
Index of Resolution Actions	999
Index of the Journal	1009

Printed separately
PART IV—SUPPLEMENTS
  Constitution and Canons 2003: Together with the Rules of Order
  The Blue Book 2003: Reports of the Committees, Commissions, Agencies and Boards to the General Convention

The Most Reverend Frank T. Griswold
Primate and Presiding Bishop

The Rt. Rev. Arthur B. Williams, Jr.
Vice-President of the House of Bishops

The Very Rev. George L. Werner
President of the House of Deputies

Mr. Vincent C. Currie, Jr.
Vice-President of the House of Deputies

PART I

DIRECTORY

THE GENERAL CONVENTION
2004–2006

COMMITTEES, COMMISSIONS, AGENCIES AND BOARDS

Standing Commissions
- On Anglican and International Peace with Justice Concerns
- On Communication
- On Constitution and Canons
- On Domestic Mission and Evangelism
- On Ecumenical and Interreligious Relations
- On Health
- On Liturgy and Music
- On Ministry Development
- On National Concerns
- For Small Congregations
- On Stewardship and Development
- On Structure of the Church
- On World Mission

Joint Standing Committees
- On Nominations
- On Planning and Arrangements
- On Program, Budget and Finance

Boards and Agencies
- Board of the Archives of the Episcopal Church
- Board for Church Deployment
- Board of Trustees for the Church Pension Fund
- Episcopal Church Building Fund Board
- Episcopal Relief and Development
- Forward Movement Publications
- General Board of Examining Chaplains
- General Theological Seminary Board
- Historical Society of the Episcopal Church

JOURNAL

Executive Council and Committees
Executive Council
Anti-Racism
Audit
Criminal Justice
Economic Justice Loan
HIV/AIDS
Episcopal Council of Indigenous Ministries
Investment
Jubilee Ministries Advisory
Science, Technology and Faith
Social Responsibility in Investments
Status of Women

Committees Reporting to the House of Bishops
Committee on Pastoral Development
Planning Committee
Presiding Bishop's Council of Advice
Committee on Religious Communities
Committee on Theology

Committees Reporting to the House Of Deputies
President's Council of Advice
Committee on the State of the Church

Committees Reporting to General Convention
Disciplinary Policy and Procedure (Title IV Revisions)
Joint Nominating Committee for the Election of the Presiding Bishop
Institutional Wellness and the Prevention of Sexual Misconduct
Title IV Review Committee

THE COURTS

Court for the Trial of a Bishop
Court of Review for the Trial of a Bishop

THE PROVINCES

THE HOUSE OF BISHOPS

THE HOUSE OF DEPUTIES

DIRECTORY

OFFICERS OF THE GENERAL CONVENTION

Presiding Bishop, Chief Pastor and Primate
The Most Rev. Frank T. Griswold, D.D.
815 Second Avenue, New York, NY 10017

President of the House of Deputies
The Very Rev. George L. Werner
815 Second Avenue, New York, NY 10017

Vice-President of the House of Deputies
Mr. Vincent C. Currie, Jr.
815 Second Avenue, New York, NY 10017

Executive Officer and Secretary
The Rev. Rosemari G. Sullivan
815 Second Avenue, New York, NY 10017

Treasurer
Mr. Thomas Hershkowitz
815 Second Avenue, New York, NY 10017

Custodian of the Standard Book of Common Prayer
The Rev. Canon Gregory M. Howe
815 Second Avenue, New York, NY 10017

Custodian of the Archives
The Archives of the Episcopal Church
606 Rathervue Place, PO Box 2247, Austin, TX 78768
Mr. Mark J. Duffy, Canonical Archivist

Recorder of Ordination
The Church Pension Fund
445 Fifth Avenue, New York, NY 10016

STANDING COMMISSION ON ANGLICAN AND INTERNATIONAL PEACE WITH JUSTICE CONCERNS [1]

The Rev. Randolph K. Dales, *Chair*
2006, *New Hampshire, I*

Mrs. Mary H. Miller, *Vice-Chair*
2006, *Maryland, III*

Ms. Jacqueline Scott, *Secretary*
2006, *Colorado, VI*

The Rev. Theodora N. Brooks
2006, *New York, II*

Mr. Dennis G. Case
2006, *Southwestern Virginia, III*

The Very Rev. Allen W. Farabee
2009, *Western New York, II*

The Rt. Rev. Carol Joy Gallagher
2009, *Southern Virginia, III*

The Rt. Rev. J. Gary Gloster
2006, *North Carolina, IV*

The Rev. Edward E. Godden
Executive Council Liaison
Delaware, III

The Rt. Rev. James L. Jelinek
2009, *Minnesota, VI*

The Rev. Michael Kinman
2009, *Missouri, V*

The Rt. Rev. John B. Lipscomb
2006, *Southwest Florida, IV*

Dr. K. Tyler Miller
2009, *Newark, II*

Mrs. Guadalupe Moriel-Guillen
2009, *Los Angeles, VIII*

Ms. Michele K. Spike
2009, *Churches in Europe, II*

STANDING COMMISSION ON COMMUNICATION

The Rev. W. Nicholas Knisely
Chair
2009, *Bethlehem, III,*

Mrs. Cynthia Wilson McFarland, *Vice-Chair*
2009, *Central New York, II*

The Rev. Mary L. Allen
2006, *Utah, VIII*

Mr. Douglas R. Briggs
2006, *Missouri, V*

The Rev. Jon Paul Davidson
2006, *Nevada, VIII*

Ms. Dorothy J. Fuller
Executive Council Liaison
El Camino Real, VIII

The Rt. Rev. Paul V. Marshall
2006, *Bethlehem, III*

Mr. Sean Meade
2006, *Northern Indiana, V*

---

[1]The Episcopal Church website: http://www.episcopalchurch.org/gc.htm has additional contact information.

STANDING COMMISSIONS   DIRECTORY

The Rev. Brenda Monroe
2009, Atlanta, IV

Mr. Brian K. Reid
2009, California, VIII

The Rt. Rev. Kirk Smith
2009, Arizona, VIII

Mr. Ralph Spence Jr.
2006, Montana, VI

Ms. Richelle Thompson
2009, Southern Ohio, V

The Rt. Rev. Pierre Whalon
2009, Churches in Europe, II

The Rt. Rev. Geralyn Wolf
2006, Rhode Island, I

Staff/Consultants
Mrs. Barbara C. Caum, *Consultant*

Mr. Dan England, *Director*
Office of Communication

Mr. James R. McMahon
Special Representative for HD President
New Hampshire, I

Consultant
The Rev. Mark Seitz

STANDING COMMISSION ON CONSTITUTION AND CANONS

Mr. Duncan A. Bayne, *Chair*
2006, Olympia, VIII

Matthew Livingood, Esq., *Vice-Chair*
2009, Oklahoma, VII

Mr. William Fleener, Jr., *Secretary*
2006, Western Michigan, V

Rosalie Simmonds Ballentine, Esq.
2006, Virgin Islands, II

The Rt. Rev. Dorsey F. Henderson, Jr.
2009, Upper South Carolina, IV

Lawrence R. Hitt II, Esq.
2009, Colorado, VI

The Rev. Gregory A. Jacobs
2006, Ohio, V

The Rt. Rev. Charles E. Jenkins, III
2006, Louisiana, IV

Thomas A. Little, Esq.
2009, Vermont, I

The Rev. R. Stan Runnels
2006, Mississippi, IV

The Rt. Rev. Stacy F. Sauls
2006, Lexington, IV
Member and Executive Council Liaison

The Rev. Ward H. Simpson
2009, Eau Claire, V

Ms. Anne Karoly, *Staff*

STANDING COMMISSION ON DOMESTIC MISSION AND EVANGELISM

Ms. Sarah Elizabeth Lawton, *Chair*
2006 California, VIII

Ms. Lallie B. Lloyd, *Vice-Chair*
2009 Massachusetts, I

Mr. Michael Allen
2006 Kentucky, IV

The Rev. Dr. James H. Cooper
2006 Florida, IV

Ms. Angelica L. Duque
2009, Colombia, IX

The Rt. Rev. Daniel W. Herzog
2006 Albany, II

The Rev. Mary E. Hileman
2006 Oklahoma, VII

The Rev. Colenzo Hubbard
2006 West Tennessee, IV

The Rt. Rev. David C. Jones
2009 Virginia, III

Mr. David H. Keller
2006 Upper South Carolina, IV

Ms. Kirstin Nielsen
2009 Idaho, VIII

Ms. Joanne O'Donnell
2009 Los Angeles, VIII

Ms. Elizabeth Panilaitis
2009 Connecticut, I

The Rev. Bonnie A. Perry
2009 Chicago, V

The Rev. Silvestre E. Romero
2009 El Camino Real, VIII

The Rev. Sandra A. Wilson
2009 Minnesota, VI

Executive Council Liaison
The Rev. Kwasi A. Thornell,
2006 Southern Ohio, V

Staff
The Rev. Charles N. Fulton,
New York, II

STANDING COMMISSION ON ECUMENICAL AND INTERRELIGIOUS RELATIONS

The Rt. Rev. William O. Gregg, *Chair*
2006 Eastern Oregon, VIII

The Very Rev. Donald G. Brown,
Vice-Chair
2006 Northern California, VIII

The Rev. Daniel S. Appleyard
2009 Michigan, V

The Very Rev. C.B. Baker
2009 West Tennessee, IV

Dr. Roderick B. Dugliss
2009 California, VIII

The Rev. Dr. M. David Eckel
2006 Massachusetts, I

Ms. Janet Farmer
2009 Texas, VII

James R. Foster Esq.
2006 Eastern Oregon, VIII

Ms. Elaine C. Francis
2009 Virgin Islands, II

The Rt. Rev. Edwin F. Gulick, Jr.
2009 Kentucky, IV

Ms. Diane L. Knippers
2006 Virginia, III

The Rev. Lorraine Mills-Curran
2009 Rhode Island, I

The Rt. Rev. William D. Persell
2006 Chicago, V

The Rt. Rev. Alan Scarfe
2009 Iowa, VI

The Rt. Rev. Douglas E. Theuner
2006 New Hampshire, I

Ms. Alice Roberta Webley
2006 Western Michigan, V

The Rt. Rev. Pierre Whalon
2009 Churches in Europe, II

The Rev. Dr. Ellen K. Wondra
2006 Rochester, II

Executive Council Liaison
The Rev. Canon Tim E. Vann
2006 Nebraska, VI

Ex Officio Members
Mr. Arthur J. Geissler, *EDEO Liaison*

The Rev. Dr. Randall Lee, *ELCA Liaison*

The Rev. Canon Dr. J. Robert Wright
Theological Consultant
New York, II

Staff/Consultants
The Rt. Rev. C. Christopher Epting
New York, II

Dr. Thomas Ferguson
New York, II

STANDING COMMISSION ON HEALTH

Members to be appointed.

STANDING COMMISSION ON LITURGY AND MUSIC

The Rt. Rev. John Neil Alexander, *Chair*
2009 Atlanta, IV

Ms. Judith Dodge, *Vice-Chair*
2006 Washington, III

The Rev. Susan Anslow Williams, *Secretary*
2006 Western New York, II

The Rt. Rev. Wendell N. Gibbs, Jr.
2006 Michigan, V

The Rt. Rev. Barry R. Howe
2006 West Missouri, VII

Ms. Julia Huttar Bailey
2009 Michigan, V

Mr. R.C. Laird
2006 Minnesota, VI

Dr. Carl Maultsby
2009 New York, II

JOURNAL

The Very Rev. Ernesto R. Medina
2009 Los Angeles, VIII

Miss Marcia S. Pruner
2006 Northern Michigan, V

The Rev. John W. Ruder
2006 Olympia, VIII

The Rt. Rev. George Wayne Smith
2009 Missouri, V

Mrs. Mildred Springer
2009 Nevada, VIII

The Rev. H. Lawrence Thompson
2009 Pittsburgh, III

Ms. Jessica Wilkerson
2009 Montana, VI

Mr. Ted M. Yumoto
2006 San Joaquin, VIII

Executive Council Liaison
The Very Rev. Cynthia L. Black
2006 Western Michigan, V

Ex Officio Members
The Rev. Canon Gregory M. Howe
Custodian of the Standard Book
2006 Delaware, III

Staff/Consultants
The Rev. Devon Anderson
Special Rep, PHOD
2009 Minnesota, VI

The Rev. Dr. Clayton L. Morris
DFMS Liturgical Officer
California, VIII

The Rt. Rev. Jeffery W. Rowthorn
Special Rep, PB
2006 Connecticut, I

Mr. Frank Tedeschi
V.P. & E.D., Church Publishing

The Rev. Dr. Louis Weil
Special Rep, PB, 2006

STANDING COMMISSION ON MINISTRY DEVELOPMENT

The Rt. Rev. John P. Croneberger, *Chair*
2006 Newark, II

Ms. Ellen W. Bruckner, *Vice-Chair*
2006 Iowa, VI

The Rev. Jennifer L. Adams
2006 Western Michigan, V

Mr. Aldin Barnes
2009 Montana, VI

Mrs. Stephanie Cheney, *Province IV Rep.*
2009 West Tennessee, IV

Mrs. Janet B. Farnsworth, *Province II Rep.*
2006 Rochester, II

The Rev. Warren Frelund
2006 Iowa, VI

Dr. Rosemary Gooden
2009 Chicago, V

The Rev. Canon Richard A. Halladay
Province V Rep.
2006 Indianapolis, V

The Ven. Joyce Hardy
2009 Arkansas, VII

Ms. Thurma Hilton, *Province VII Rep.*
2006 Texas, VII

STANDING COMMISSIONS   DIRECTORY

The Rt. Rev. James A. Kelsey
2006 Northern Michigan, V

Mrs. Christine D. Keyser-Ball
2006 Florida, IV

Canon Emily Morales, *Province IX Rep.*
Puerto Rico, IX

Dr. Donn F. Morgan
2009 California, VIII

Mr. Bruce T. Swan
2009 Connecticut, I

The Rev. Ellen L. Tillotson, *Province I Rep.*
2003 Connecticut, I

Ms. Eve Van Sice
2006 Missouri, V

The Rev. Winnie S. Varghese
2009 New York, II

The Rev. Canon Jenny Vervynck
Province VIII Rep.
2009 San Diego, VIII

The Rev. Roy C. Walworth,
Province VI Rep.
2006 Wyoming, VI

The Rt. Rev. Keith B. Whitmore
2009 Eau Claire, V

Mr. Timothy D. Wittlinger
2006 Michigan, V

Executive Council Liaison
The Rev. Brian N. Prior
2006 Spokane, VIII

Ministry Development Staff
The Rev. Lynne A. Grifo
Connecticut, I

The Rev. Melford E. Holland
Pennyslvania, III

Ms. Molly A. Shaw
2006 New York, II

Ms. Margaret Stevens
2006 Pennsylvania, III

STANDING COMMISSION ON NATIONAL CONCERNS

The Rev. Canon Michael L. Barlowe, *Chair*
2006 California, VIII

The Hon. Marge Kilkelly, *Vice-Chair*
2006 Maine, I

Ms. Karen O. Patterson, *Secretary*
2006 Southwest Florida, IV

The Rev. Richard J. Aguilar
2009 Southern Ohio, V

Ms. Linda L. Anderson
2009 Minnesota, VI

Dr. Thomas R. Bates
2009 Central Florida, IV

The Hon. James E. Bradberry
2009 Southern Virginia, III

The Rt. Rev. John B. Chane
2009 Washington, III

The Rev. Barbara T. Cheney
2009 Connecticut, I

The Rev. Jan Davey
2009 Rio Grande, VII

Ms. Lillian Davis-Wilson
2006 Western New York, II

Mr. Erin A. Ferguson
2009 Southeast Florida, IV

JOURNAL

Mrs. Georgette Forney
2006 Pittsburgh, III

The Rev. Dr. Eugene C. McDowell
2006 Western North Carolina, IV

The Rt. Rev. M. Thomas Shaw III, SSJE
2006 Massachusetts, I

The Rev. Dr. Richard L. Tolliver
2006 Chicago, V

Executive Council Liaison
Ms. D. Rebecca Snow
2006 Alaska, VIII

STANDING COMMISSION FOR SMALL CONGREGATIONS

The Rt. Rev. Larry E. Maze, *Convenor*
2006 Arkansas, VII

Ms. Ramona Burroughs
2006 South Dakota, VI

Mr. Frank Connizzo
2009 Kansas, VII

Mrs. Karen DuPlantier
2006 Southern Ohio, V

The Rt. Rev. Thomas Clark Ely
2009 Vermont, I

The Very Rev. Canon H. W. Herrmann SSC
2006 Quincy, V

The Rev. Canon Kristi Philip
2009 Spokane, VIII

The Rt. Rev. James J. Shand
2009 Easton, III

Ms. Bonnie Studdiford
2006 Maine, I

Mr. Lonell Wright
2009 Louisiana, IV

Executive Council Liaison
Ms. Terry Roberts
2006 Minnesota, VI

STANDING COMMISSION ON STEWARDSHIP AND DEVELOPMENT

Mrs. Angela M. Daniel, *Co-Chair*
2009 Upper South Carolina, IV

The Very Rev. Dr. W. Richard Hamlin
Co-Chair
2006 Central New York, II

Ms. Susan T. Erdey, *Secretary*
2006 New York, II

Ms. Patricia Abrams
2009 Chicago, V

The Rt. Rev. J. Jon Bruno
2009 Los Angeles, VIII

Canon Sharon L. Davenport
2006 Northwestern Pennsylvania, III

The Rev. John Fritschner, *Chaplain*
2009 Alabama, IV

Ms. Kelsey Kemp
2009 Northwest Texas, VII

STANDING COMMISSIONS | DIRECTORY

Mrs. Joan O. Kline
2006 Southwest Florida, IV

Ms. Blanca Rivera
2006 Milwaukee, V

The Rt. Rev. Gordon Paul Scruton
Co-Facilitator
2006 Western Massachusetts, I

Mrs. Pamela S. Wesley Gomez
Co-Facilitator
2009 Connecticut, I

Other Participants
Mr. Thomas R. Gossen
Executive Council Liaison
2006 Kansas, VII

Ms. Terry Parsons, *Congregational Dev. Office*

STANDING COMMISSION ON THE STRUCTURE OF THE CHURCH

John Wood Goldsack Esq., *Chair*
2006 New Jersey, II

The Rt. Rev. James Elliot Curry, *Vice-Chair*
2009 Connecticut, I

The Rev. S. Brooks Keith, *Secretary*
2009 Colorado, VI

The Rev. H. Jay Atwood
2006 Fort Worth, VII

Mr. Justin Chapman
2006 Minnesota, VI

JoAnn B. Jones Esq.
2009 Pennsylvania, III

The Rev. John David Lane
2006 Southwestern Virginia, III

Ms. Barbara G. Mann
2009 South Carolina, IV

The Rt. Rev. V. Gene Robinson
2006 New Hampshire, I

Ms. Margaret N. Tinsman
2006 Iowa, VI

Ms. Mary Ann Weiss
2009 Lexington, IV

Executive Council Liaison
Dr. Delbert C. Glover
2006 Western Massachusetts, I

Ex Officio Members
Mr. David R. Pitts
Special Rep. PHOD
2006 Louisiana, IV

STANDING COMMISSION ON WORLD MISSION

Mrs. Helena Mbele-Mbong, *Chair*
2006 Churches in Europe, II

The Rt. Rev. Wilfrido Ramos-Orench
Vice-Chair
Member and Executive Council Liaison
2006 Connecticut, I

Ms. Martha Bedell Alexander, *Secretary*
2009 North Carolina, IV

Mr. Saulo Salvador, *Treasurer*
2009 Southeast Florida, IV

The Rev. Katharine Babson
2009 Virginia, III

Ms. Diana Dillenberger-Frade
2006 Southeast Florida, IV

The Rt. Rev. Jean Zaché Duracin
2006 Haiti, II

The Rev. Canon Mark Harris
2009 Delaware, III

The Rt. Rev. Julio Cesar Holguín
2009 Dominican Republic, IX

Mr. Willis J. Jenkins
2006 Oklahoma, VII

Maria L. Mendez, M.D.
2009 Puerto Rico, IX

The Very Rev. Robert S. Munday, Ph.D.
2006 Quincy, V

Executive Council Liaison
The Very Rev. Titus L. Presler
2006 Texas, VII

Staff
The Rev. Canon J. Patrick Mauney
Rhode Island, I

JOINT COMMITTEES — DIRECTORY

JOINT STANDING COMMITTEE ON NOMINATIONS

The Rt. Rev. Don E. Johnson, *Convenor*
West Tennessee, IV

The Rev. John A. Baldwin
Southern Virginia, III

The Rt. Rev. Michael Bruce Curry
North Carolina, IV

Mrs. Patricia B. Kilpatrick
Ohio, V

The Rt. Rev. Mark L. MacDonald
Alaska, VIII

The Rev. Canon David L. Seger
Northern Indiana, V

Ms. Pamela Stewart
Long Island, II

Mrs. Deborah J. Stokes
Southern Ohio, V

Mr. Daniel Valdez
Los Angeles, VIII

Mrs. Kathryn W. Weathersby
Mississippi, IV

The Rev. Vicki D. Zust
Southern Ohio, V

JOINT STANDING COMMITTEE ON PLANNING AND ARRANGEMENTS

The Most Rev. Frank T. Griswold, *Chair*
Presiding Bishop & Primate
Chicago, V

Ms. Bonnie Anderson, *HD Vice-President*
2006, Michigan, V

Mr. N. Kurt Barnes, *Treasurer & CFO,*
DFMS
New York, II

The Rev. Joan Beilstein, *Clergy Representative*
2006, Washington, III

Mr. J. P. Causey, Jr.
HD Dispatch of Business Chair
2006, Virginia, III

The Rt. Rev. Richard S.O. Chang
HB Vice-Chair
2006, Hawaii, VIII

Mr. Owen Cope, *Lay Representative*
2006, Louisiana, IV

Ms. Lori M. Ionnitiu
General Convention Manager

Ms. Harriett M. Neer
ECW President
2006, Arkansas, VII

Mrs. Karyl F. Otten,
ECW Vice-President
2006, Utah, VIII

The Rt. Rev. Kenneth L. Price, Jr.
HB Secretary
2006, Southern Ohio, V

The Rev. Canon Anne W. Robbins
Host Diocese Rep.
2006, Southern Ohio, V

JOURNAL

The Rev. Rosemari G. Sullivan
GC Executive Officer & Sec'y
2006, Virginia, III

The Rt. Rev. Herbert Thompson, Jr.
Bishop of Host Diocese
2006, Southern Ohio, V

The Very Rev. George L.W. Werner
HD President
2006, Pittsburgh, III

The Rt. Rev. Wayne P. Wright
HB Dispatch of Business Chair
2006, Delaware, III

Staff
Mrs. Nancy Caparulo
HD Special Ass't to HD Pres.
New Jersey, II

JOINT STANDING COMMITTEE ON PROGRAM, BUDGET AND FINANCE

Ms. Pan Adams, *Chair*
Arkansas, VII

The Rt. Rev. Andrew D. Smith, *Vice-Chair*
Connecticut, I

The Hon. Byron Rushing, *Secretary*
Massachusetts, I

The Rt. Rev. Lloyd Allen
Honduras, IX

The Rev. Howard R. Anderson
Minnesota, VI

Mr. Sunand Bal
Arizona, VIII

Ms. Anne Bardol
Northwestern Pennsylvania, III

Mr. Arthur M. Bjontegard, Jr.
Upper South Carolina, IV

Mr. Jon B. Boss
Southern Ohio, V

The Rt. Rev. C. Franklin Brookhart, Jr.
Montana, VI

The Rt. Rev. George E. Councell
New Jersey, II

Mr. Pete Dawson
Eau Claire, V

The Rt. Rev. Robert Gepert
Western Michigan, V

Ms. Lyn Headley-Moore
Newark, II

The Rev. Gerald W. Keucher
New York, II

The Rt. Rev. W. Michie Klusmeyer
West Virginia, III

Ms. Darling Martinez
Puerto Rico, IX

The Rev. Kathleen S. Milligan
Iowa, VI

The Rev. Altagracia Perez
Los Angeles, VIII

Mrs. Jennifer M. Railing
Central Pennsylvania, III

The Rev. Sandino Augusto Sanchez
Dominican Republic, IX

The Rev. Canon Jo Ann T. Smith
Kansas, VII

BOARDS AND AGENCIES   DIRECTORY

Mr. Dennis Stark
Rhode Island, I

The Rt. Rev. James Edward Waggoner, Jr.
Spokane, VIII

The Rt. Rev. Dean Wolfe
Kansas, VII

Ex Officio Members
Mr. N. Kurt Barnes
DFMS Treasurer & CFO
New York, II

The Most Rev. Frank T. Griswold
Presiding Bishop & Primate
Chicago, V

Mr. Russell V. Palmore, Jr., *A&F Chair*
Virginia, III

The Rev. Rosemari G. Sullivan
GC Executive Officer & Sec'y
Virginia, III

The Very Rev. George L.W. Werner
House of Deputies President
Pittsburgh, III

Staff
Mrs. Nancy Caparulo
New Jersey, II

BOARD OF THE ARCHIVES OF THE EPISCOPAL CHURCH

The Rt. Rev. Larry E. Maze, *Chair*
2009, Arkansas, VII

The Rev. Canon Robert G. Carroon
Secretary, 2009, Connecticut, I

The Rt. Rev. John Neil Alexander
2009, Atlanta, IV

Mr. R.P.M. Bowden
2006, Atlanta, IV

Ms. Judy Dailey
2009, Maryland, III

Ms. Michelle A. Francis
2006, Western North Carolina, IV

Ms. Michaela French
2009, Maryland, III

The Rev. Canon John E. Kitagawa
2009, Arizona, VIII

Ms. Margaret D. Lewis
2006, Washington, III

The Rev. Canon Edward W. Rodman
2006, Massachusetts, I

Mr. Newland F. Smith III
2006, Chicago, V

Ex Officio Members
Mr. Mark J. Duffy
Canonical Archivist of the Episcopal Church
Texas, VII

The Very Rev. Titus L. Presler
ETSS Dean, Texas, VII

BOARD FOR CHURCH DEPLOYMENT

The Rev. John F. Koepke III, *Chair*
2006, *Southern Ohio, V*

Canon Roberta Fairman, *Vice-Chair*
2006, *New Hampshire, I*

The Rt. Rev. Richard S.O. Chang
2006, *Hawaii, VIII*

Canon Alice R. Clayton
2009, *East Tennessee, IV*

The Rt. Rev. Wendell N. Gibbs, Jr.
2009, *Michigan, V*

The Rt. Rev. Katharine Jefferts Schori
2009, *Nevada, VIII*

The Rev. Canon David W. Kent
2006, *Kansas, VII*

Ms. Emily Peach
2009, *Missouri, V*

The Rt. Rev. F. Neff Powell
2006, *Southwestern Virginia, III*

The Rev. Janice M. Robinson
2006, *Washington, III*

The Rev. Canon Matthew Stockard
2009, *East Carolina, IV*

Canon Jill Swans
2009, *Pennsylvania, III*

Staff/Consultants
The Rev. Nancy Miller
Interim Assistant Director

Mrs. Pamela A. Ramsden
Associate Director

BOARD OF TRUSTEES FOR THE CHURCH PENSION FUND

Mr. David R. Pitts, *Chair*
Louisiana, IV, 2009

The Rt. Rev. Gayle E. Harris, *Vice-Chair*
Massachusetts, I, 2009

The Rt. Rev. Peter James Lee, *Vice-Chair*
Virginia, III, 2006

The Very Rev. Martin L. Agnew, Jr.
Western Louisiana, VII, 2009

Mr. James E. Bayne
Dallas, VII, 2009

Mr. Sheridan C. Biggs
Albany, II, 2009

The Rev. A. Thomas Blackmon
Dallas, VII, 2006

Mr. Alan F. Blanchard, *President, CPF*
New York, II

Mr. David L. Brigham
Vermont, I, 2009

The Rev. Randall Chase, Jr.
Rhode Island, I, 2006

Barbara B. Creed Esq.
El Camino Real, VIII, 2006

Ms. Amy L. Domini
Massachusetts, I, 2006

BOARDS AND AGENCIES DIRECTORY

The Rev. Canon Carlson Gerdau
Chicago, V, 2009

Dr. Deborah Harmon Hines
Western Massachusetts, I, 2006

The Rt. Rev. Robert H. Johnson
Western North Carolina, IV, 2009

The Rt. Rev. Chilton R. Knudsen
Maine, I, 2006

Mr. Arthur K. Kusumoto
Hawaii, VIII, 2006

Ms. Joon D. Matsumura
Los Angeles, VIII, 2009

Ms. Virginia A. Norman
Dominican Republic, IX, 2009

The Rt. Rev. Claude E. Payne
Texas, VII, 2006

Mr. Quintin E. Primo III
Chicago, V, 2006

The Rt. Rev. V. Gene Robinson
New Hampshire, I, 2009

Mrs. Katherine Tyler Scott
Indianapolis, V, 2006

Cecil Wray Esq.
New York, II, 2006

The Rt. Rev. Wayne P. Wright
Delaware, III, 2009

EPISCOPAL CHURCH BUILDING FUND BOARD

The Rt. Rev. Gethin B. Hughes, *Chair*
San Diego, VIII

Mr. Stanley I. Garnett, *Vice-Chair*
Newark, II

Mr. Thomas D. Haines, *Treasurer*
Long Island, II

Mrs. Joyce Phillips Austin, *Asst. Treasurer*
New York, II

The Rev. Canon Christoph Keller III
Secretary
Arkansas, VII

Mr. William M. Barnum
Rhode Island, I

Mr. Brewster Caesar
Colorado, VI

Ms. Marina Carrott
Chicago, V

The Rev. Charles N. Fulton, *President*
New York, II

Mr. Lawrence M. Knapp
Pittsburgh, III

The Rev. Eliza M. Linley
California, VIII

Ms. Barbara Losse
Utah, VIII

The Rev. Richard F. Milwee
Arkansas, VII

The Rev. Richard J. Petranek
Texas, VII

Phoebe A. Roaf, Esq.

Robert C. Royce Esq., *Legal Counsel*
East Carolina, IV

The Rev. Martini Shaw

JOURNAL

The Rev. Ralph R. Warren, Jr.
Southeast Florida, IV

Other Participants
Ms. Sarah O'Brien, *ECBF Vice-President*

EPISCOPAL RELIEF AND DEVELOPMENT BOARD OF DIRECTORS

The Rt. Rev. Harry B. Bainbridge III, *Chair*
Idaho, VIII, 2006

The Rev. Dr. William Robert Abstein II
Vice-Chair
Tennessee, IV, 2007

Mrs. Patricia C. Mordecai, *Treasurer*
New York, II

The Rev. Dr. Canon David W. Perry
Secretary
Oregon, VIII, 2006

Mr. N. Kurt Barnes
DFMS Treasurer & CFO

Ms. Margaret Boeth
New York, II, 2005

Mr. Jacob F. Bryan IV
Florida, IV, 2007

The Rev. Gwen Buehrens
Massachusetts, I, 2007

Mr. Kurt DelBene
Olympia, VIII

The Most Rev. Frank T. Griswold
Presiding Bishop & Primate
Chicago, V

Mr. Edwin K. Hall
Washington, III, 2005

Mr. Gerald Harner
El Camino Real, VIII, 2004

The Rev. Dr. J. Barney Hawkins
Maryland, III, 2005

Dr. Lawrence C. Howard
Pittsburgh, III, 2006

Dr. Bessie Lyman
Massachusetts, I, 2004

Mr. Witney W. Schneidman
Virginia, III, 2005

Dr. Stan Shaffer
Kansas, VII, 2005

Mrs. Sandra Swan, *ERD President*
Connecticut, I

Mrs. Gilda Wray
New York, II, 2005

FORWARD MOVEMENT PUBLICATIONS EXECUTIVE COMMITTEE

Ms. Margaret G. Beers, *Chair*
Washington, III

The Rt. Rev. J. Clark Grew II, *Vice-Chair*
Ohio, V

Ms. Janet K. Simpkinson, *Treasurer*

The Rev. Edward S. Gleason, *Secretary*
Editor & Director, FMP
Southern Ohio, V

The Rev. James Lee Burns
New York, II

The Rt. Rev. Edward W. Jones
Indianapolis, V

The Rt. Rev. Stacy F. Sauls
Lexington, IV

Dr. Cynthia Shattuck

Ms. Naomi T. Stoehr
Southern Ohio, V

The Rev. Robert H. Thompson
Southern Ohio, V

Ms. Phyllis Alexander Tickle

The Rev. Lorentho Wooden
Southern Ohio, V

GENERAL BOARD OF EXAMINING CHAPLAINS

Dr. Leonard Johnson, *Chair*
California, VIII, 2009

The Rt. Rev. Edward L. Lee, Jr., *Vice-Chair*
Western Michigan, V, 2006

The Rev. Dr. Katharine C. Black
Massachusetts, I, 2006

Dr. Mary C. Callaway
New York, II, 2009

Mr. Philip Clark
Northern California, VIII, 2006

The Rev. Mark Taylor Crawford
Texas, VII, 2009

The Rev. Susan Dolan-Henderson
ETSS Representative
Texas, VII, 2009

The Rt. Rev. Philip M. Duncan II
Central Gulf Coast, IV, 2009

Mrs. Jo Ann Giannini
Indianapolis, V, 2009

The Rev. F. Scott Hennessy
Virginia, III, 2006

The Rt. Rev. Barry R. Howe
West Missouri, VII, 2009

The Rev. Robert D. Hughes III
Sewanee Representative
Southern Ohio, V, 2009

The Rev. Lloyd A. Lewis, Jr.
Long Island, II, 2006

Dr. Susan Hill Lindley
Minnesota, VI, 2006

JOURNAL

The Rev. John H. Loving
Northwest Texas, VII, 2006

The Rev. Dr. Richard McCall
Massachusetts, I, 2006

The Rev. Stephen E. Moore
Olympia, VIII, 2009

The Rev. Dr. Frederick W. Schmidt
Perkins Representative
Washington, III, 2009

The Rt. Rev. Katharine Jefferts Schori
Nevada, VIII, 2009

The Rev. Harmon L. Smith
North Carolina, IV, 2006

The Rev. Mary C. Sulerud
Washington, III, 2009

Dr. Peter W. Williams
Southern Ohio, V, 2006

Other Participants
The Rev. Richard F. Tombaugh
Executive Secretary
Connecticut, I

BOARD OF TRUSTEES OF THE GENERAL THEOLOGICAL SEMINARY OF THE EPISCOPAL CHURCH

The Very Rev. Robert E. Giannini, *Chair*
Indianapolis, V, 2006

Ms. Juli S. Towell, *Vice-Chair*
New Jersey, II, 2006

Mr. Richard Pivirotto, *Second Vice-Chair*
Connecticut, I, 2007

Dr. Frederick W. Gerbracht, Jr., *Treasurer*
Long Island, II, 2007

Miss Gwendolyn Simmons, *Secretary*
New York, II, 2005

The Rev. Lauren Ackland
Newark, II, 2006

The Rt. Rev. John Neil Alexander
Atlanta, IV, 2007

The Rev. Yamily Bass-Choate
Mississippi, IV, 2007

The Rt. Rev. G.P. Mellick Belshaw
New Jersey, II, 2007

Mrs. Marjorie L. Christie
Newark, II, 2007

The Rt. Rev. Michael Bruce Curry
North Carolina, IV, 2007

Dr. Pamela W. Darling
2007

Duncan N. Darrow, Esq.
Long Island, II, 2006

Mr. Joseph A. Davenport III
Louisiana, IV, 2006

Gabrielle P. Dennison, Esq.
2005

The Rt. Rev. Philip M. Duncan II
Central Gulf Coast, IV, 2006

Mr. William B. Eagleson, Jr.

Dr. Michael Gilligan
2006

Dr. Warren F. Ilchman
New York, II, 2005

BOARDS AND AGENCIES

The Rt. Rev. James L. Jelinek
Minnesota, VI

Mr. Gary Johnson
2006

Mrs. Patricia B. Kilpatrick
Ohio, V, 2005

The Rev. Paula Lawrence-Wehmiller
*Diocese of Pennsylvania, III
2007*

Ms. Janet Louard
2007

The Rev. Dr. William C. Lutz
Central New York, II, 2005

The Rev. Denis O'Pray
Los Angeles, VIII, 2006

Canon Diane M. Porter
Long Island, II, 2005

The Rt. Rev. Wilfrido Ramos-Orench
Connecticut, I, 2005

The Rev. James C. Ransom
Maryland, III, 2007

The Rev. Douglas E. Remer
Southwest Florida, IV, 2007

The Rev. Nancy A. Roosevelt
Ohio, V, 2005

The Rt. Rev. Catherine S. Roskam
New York, II, 2006

The Rev. Mark A. Santucci
Connecticut, I, 2007

Ms. Cynthia H. Schwab
West Missouri, VII, 2006

The Rev. Jeffrey H. Walker
Connecticut, I, 2005

Mrs. Caroline Keller Winter
2005

Mr. Robert E. Wright
North Carolina, IV, 2007

Ex Officio Members
The Very Rev. Ward B. Ewing
*GTS Dean & President
Western New York, II*

The Most Rev. Frank T. Griswold
*Presiding Bishop & Primate
Chicago, V*

The Rt. Rev. Mark S. Sisk
*Bishop of New York
New York, II*

HISTORICAL SOCIETY OF THE EPISCOPAL CHURCH

Professor Thad W. Tate, *President*
Southern Virginia, III

The Rev. Dr. Alfred A. Moss, Jr.
*First Vice-President
Virginia, III*

The Rev. Dr. Eugene Y. Lowe, Jr.
*Second Vice-President
New York, II*

Dr. Frederick W. Gerbracht, Jr., *Treasurer*
Long Island, II

JOURNAL

Dr. Thomas A. Mason, *Secretary*
Indianapolis, V

The Rev. Canon Dr. J. Robert Wright
Episcopal Church Historiographer
New York, II

Mr. Mark J. Duffy
Episcopal Church Archivist
Texas, VII

Dr. Pamela W. Darling
2004

Ms. Alexandra S. Gressitt
2004, Virginia, III

The Rt. Rev. David B. Joslin
2004, New Jersey, II

Dr. Henry W. Bowden
2005, New Jersey, II

Dr. Allen C. Guelzo
2005

Dr. Fredrica Harris Thompsett
2005

The Rev. Dr. Norman Brooks Graebner
2006, North Carolina, IV

The Rev. Canon J. Patrick Mauney
2006, Rhode Island, I

Dr. Alda M. Morgan
2006, California, VIII

Dr. James E. Bradley, *Book Review Editor*

Professor Alan L. Hayes, *Church Review Editor*

The Rev. Dr. Grant LeMarquand
International Editor
Pittsburgh, III

Dr. J. Barrett Miller
Book Review Editor

The Rev. Dr. John F. Woolverton
Editor-in-Chief
New Hampshire, I

Dr. Robert Bruce Mullin
The African-American History Project
New York, II

The Rev. Bindy Snyder, *EWHP President*

The Rev. Dr. Gregory S. Straub
NEHA President
Easton, III

Staff/Consultants
Ms. May D. Lofgreen, *Business Manager*
Texas, VII

Ex Officio Members
Mr. N. Kurt Barnes,
DFMS Treasurer & CFO

The Most Rev. Frank T. Griswold
Presiding Bishop & Primate

The Rt. Rev. Kenneth L. Price, Jr.
HB Secretary
Southern Ohio, V

The Rev. Rosemari G. Sullivan
GC Executive Officer & Sec'y
Virginia, III

The Very Rev. George L.W. Werner
House of Deputies President
Pittsburgh, III

EXECUTIVE COUNCIL

The Most Rev. Frank T. Griswold, *Chair*
Presiding Bishop & Primate
Chicago, V

The Very Rev. George L.W. Werner
Vice-Chair
President, House of Deputies
Pittsburgh, III

Elected by GC Until 2006
The Very Rev. Cynthia L. Black
Western Michigan, V

Dr. Louie Crew
Newark, II

The Rt. Rev. Theodore A. Daniels
Texas, VII

The Rev. Anthony Guillen
Los Angeles, VIII

Ms. Sarah Taylor Harte
Long Island, II

Mr. Frank L. Oberly
Oklahoma, VII

Mr. Russell V. Palmore, Jr.
Virginia, III

Ms. Diane B. Pollard
New York, II

The Rt. Rev. Catherine S. Roskam
New York, II

Ms. D. Rebecca Snow
Alaska, VIII

Elected By Province Until 2006
I: The Rev. Ann S. Coburn
Massachusetts

II: The Rev. Canon Stephen T. Lane
Rochester

III: The Rev. Edward E. Godden
Delaware

IV: Dr. Lillian E. Yeager
Kentucky

V: The Rev. Kwasi A. Thornell
Southern Ohio

VI: The Rev. Canon Tim E. Vann
Nebraska

VII: The Rev. Kenneth W. Kesselus
Texas

VIII: The Rev. Brian N. Prior
Spokane

IX: Mrs. Carmen Brooks
Honduras

Elected by GC Until 2009
Mr. R.P.M. Bowden
Atlanta, IV

Ms. Dorothy J. Fuller
El Camino Real, VIII

Mr. Thomas R. Gossen
Kansas, VII

Ms. Josephine H. Hicks
North Carolina, IV

Ms. Sandra F. McPhee
Chicago, V

Mr. Albert T. Mollegen, Jr.
Connecticut, I

The Very Rev. Titus L. Presler
Texas, VII

JOURNAL

The Rt. Rev. Wilfrido Ramos-Orench
Connecticut, I

The Rev. Canon Edward W. Rodman
Massachusetts, I

The Rt. Rev. Stacy F. Sauls
Lexington, IV

Elected by Province Until 2009
I: Dr. Delbert C. Glover
Western Massachusetts

II: Edgar K. Byham Esq.
Newark

III: Mr. John Vanderstar
Washington

IV: The Rev. Timothy E. Kimbrough
North Carolina

V: Ms. Bonnie Anderson
Vice-President, House of Deputies
Michigan

VI: Ms. Terry Roberts
Minnesota

VII: Mrs. Sharon F. Denton
Western Kansas

VIII: Mr. Ted M. Yumoto
San Joaquin

IX: The Rt. Rev. Julio Cesar Holguín
Dominican Republic

Ex Officio Members
Mr. N. Kurt Barnes, *Treasurer*
DFMS Treasurer & CFO
New York, II

Mrs. Patricia C. Mordecai
DFMS Chief Operating Officer
New York, II

The Rev. Rosemari G. Sullivan, *Secretary*
GC Executive Officer & Sec'y
Virginia, III

Other Participants
Mr. David Booth Beers
Chancellor to the PB
Washington, III

The Ven. James B. Boyles
Anglican Church of Canada Rep.

Ms. Marian Conboy, *Staff*

Ms. Cheryl J. Dawkins, *Staff*

The Rev. Helena Rose Houldcroft
Canadian Partner

EXECUTIVE COUNCIL COMMITTEE ON ANTI-RACISM

The Rev. Dr. Sheryl A. Kujawa-Holbrook
Chair
Massachusetts, I

Mr. Hilario Albert
New York, II

Mr. R.P.M. Bowden
Executive Council Liaison
Atlanta, IV

Dr. Anita George
Mississippi, IV

The Rev. John E. Kitagawa
Arizona, VIII

The Rev. Anna B. Lange-Soto
El Camino Real, VIII

EXECUTIVE COUNCIL DIRECTORY

The Rt. Rev. John L. Rabb
Maryland, III

The Rev. William H. Stokes
Southeast Florida, IV

Staff Consultant
The Rev. Jayne Oasin
New Jersey, II

EXECUTIVE COUNCIL AUDIT COMMITTEE

Mr. Andrew G. McMaster, Jr., *Chair*

Ms. Anne Bardol, *PB&F Member*
Northwestern Pennsylvania, III

Mr. N. Kurt Barnes
DFMS Treasurer
New York, II

The Rev. Ann S. Coburn, *A&F Member*
Massachusetts, I

Ms. Josephine H. Hicks, *A&F Member*
North Carolina, IV

The Rev. Gerald W. Keucher, *PB&F Member*
New York, II

Mrs. Patricia C. Mordecai
DFMS Chief Operating Officer
New York, II

Mr. Ernest Q. Petrey, Jr.

Other Participants
Mrs. Nancy Caparulo, *Staff*
New Jersey, II

Controllers/Treasurer's Office Staff
Ms. Julie Castillo, *Assistant Treasurer*

Mr. Jose Gonzalez, *Grants Auditor*
New York, II

Mr. Tom Hershkowitz, *Controller*

EXECUTIVE COUNCIL COMMITTEE ON CRIMINAL JUSTICE

The Rev. Rodgers Wood, *Chair*

The Rt. Rev. J. Jon Bruno
Los Angeles, VIII

The Rt. Rev. J. Gary Gloster
North Carolina, IV

Mr. Ike Griffin

The Rev. Canon Anthony Jewiss, *Staff*
Los Angeles, VIII

The Rev. Jackie Means, *Staff*
Indianapolis, V

Ms. Ellen Morell

Mr. Frank L. Oberly
Oklahoma, VII

The Rt. Rev. Victor A. Scantlebury
Chicago, V

The Rev. Thomas M. Van Culin
Hawaii, VIII

The Very Rev. C. David Williams
Newark, II

JOURNAL

EXECUTIVE COUNCIL ECONOMIC JUSTICE LOAN COMMITTEE

Mr. W. B. McKeown, *Chair*
New York, II

Ms. Maria B. Campbell
Investment Committee Rep.

Mrs. Toni H. McGauley
East Tennessee, IV

Ms. Lindsey W. Parker
Massachusetts, I

The Rev. Canon Edward W. Rodman
Executive Council Member
Massachusetts, I

EXECUTIVE COUNCIL STANDING COMMITTEE ON HIV/AIDS

The Rt. Rev. Rodney R. Michel, *Convenor*
Long Island, II

The Rev. Billy J. Alford
Georgia, IV

The Very Rev. Rich Demarest
Idaho, VIII

Mrs. Sharon F. Denton
Executive Council Liaison
Western Kansas, VII

Mr. Christopher M. Haley-Walden
Minnesota, VI

Mr. Elton M. Hartney
Western New York, II

Mr. Brian Hughes

The Rev. Carlos Sandoval MD
Southeast Florida, IV

The Rev. Trudie Smither
Dallas, VII

EPISCOPAL COUNCIL ON INDIGENOUS MINISTRIES

Mr. Frank L. Oberly, *Chair*
2006, Oklahoma, VII

The Rt. Rev. Carol Joy Gallagher, *Secretary*
2006, Southern Virginia, III

The Rev. Malcolm N. Chun
2009, Hawaii, VIII

Ms. Becky Clark
2009, Olympia, VIII

The Rt. Rev. Mark L. MacDonald
Alaska, VIII

Mr. Robert McGhee
2006, Alabama, IV

The Rt. Rev. Steven T. Plummer
Navajoland Area Mission, VIII

The Rt. Rev. Creighton L. Robertson
South Dakota, VI

Ms. Debbie Royals
2006

Mrs. Carol Smith
2009

EXECUTIVE COUNCIL DIRECTORY

The Rev. Michael G. Smith
Minnesota, VI

The Rev. Robert Two Bulls, Jr.
2009, Los Angeles, VIII

EXECUTIVE COUNCIL INVESTMENT COMMITTEE

Mr. Richard H. Gillons, *Chair*

Ms. Maria B. Campbell, *Vice-Chair*

Ms. Bonnie Anderson
Michigan, V

Mr. N. Kurt Barnes
DFMS Treasurer
New York, II

Mr. Arthur M. Bjontegard, Jr.
2006, Upper South Carolina, IV

Mr. James S. Clarke

Ms. Catherine A. Lynch
2005

The Rev. William D. Nix, Jr.
2004, Northwest Texas, VII

Ms. Jean E. Sheridan
2005

Mr. Robert C. Wilkins
2005

Ms. Sally M. Zimmerman
2006

Staff
Ms. Julie Castillo, *Assistant Treasurer*
Ms. Denise Coy, *Administrative Assistant*
Mr. Lloyd Mondal, *Investment Accountant*

EXECUTIVE COUNCIL JUBILEE ADVISORY COMMITTEE

The Rt. Rev. Charles G. vonRosenberg
Chair
2006, East Tennessee, IV

Ms. Dawn E. Conley
2006, Chicago, V

The Rev. Hayden G. Crawford
2006, Southwest Florida, IV

Mr. Jack Hanstein
2006, Northern California, VIII

Ms. Iris E. Harris
2006, Washington, III

The Rev. Aiden Koe
2006, Los Angeles, VIII

Mr. Frank L. Oberly
Executive Council Liaison
2006, Oklahoma, VII

The Rev. Becca Stevens-Hummon
2006, Tennessee, IV

The Very Rev. Pascual Torres
2006, Honduras, IX

Other Participants
The Rev. Canon Carmen B. Guerrero
Jubilee Ministry Officer
Los Angeles, VIII

EXECUTIVE COUNCIL COMMITTEE ON SCIENCE, TECHNOLOGY AND FAITH

Dr. Robert J. Schneider, *Co-Chair*
Western North Carolina, IV

The Rev. Barbara Smith-Moran S.O.Sc.,
Co-Chair
Massachusetts, I

The Rev. Dr. Norman J. Faramelli
Massachusetts, I

Dr. Neil James
Florida, IV

Dr. James A. Jordan, Jr.
Northern California, VIII

Dr. Paul S. Julienne
Virginia, II

The Rev. Dr. Thomas Lindell S.O.Sc.
Arizona, VIII

Dr. Sandra Michael
Central New York, II

Dr. John Miers
Washington, III

The Rev. Canon Johnnie E. Ross
Lexington, IV

Dr. Stephen Stray
Oklahoma, VII

Ms. Susan Youmans
Massachusetts, I

Staff
The Rev. Canon Anthony Jewiss
Los Angeles, VIII

EXECUTIVE COUNCIL COMMITTEE ON SOCIAL RESPONSIBILITY IN INVESTMENTS

Ms. Lindsey W. Parker, *Chair*
Massachusetts, I

Mr. Larry J. Bingham
Kansas, VII

Edgar K. Byham Esq.
Executive Council Liaison
Newark, II

The Rev. Canon Kathleen J. Cullinane
Indianapolis, V

The Rev. Peter T. Elvin
Western Massachusetts, I

The Rev. Elizabeth McWhorter
Washington, III

The Rev. Edward Miller, Jr.
Virginia, III

The Rt. Rev. Orris G. Walker, Jr.
Long Island, II

Mr. Warren J. Wong
California, VIII

Ms. Sally M. Zimmerman
Investment Committee Rep.

HB COMMITTEES　　　　　　　　　　　　　　　　　DIRECTORY

EXECUTIVE COUNCIL COMMITTEE ON THE STATUS OF WOMEN

The Rev. Barbara H. Schlachter, *President*
Iowa, VI

The Rev. Catherine Munz, *Vice-President*
Pittsburgh, III

The Rt. Rev. Mark Andrus, *Secretary*
Alabama, IV

Mrs. Cynthia S. Bartol
Virginia, III

The Rev. Robert W. Cowperthwaite
Tennessee, IV

Ms. Lyn Headley-Moore
Newark, II

Ms. Nicole S. Janelle
Maine, I

The Rev. Mary Moreno Richardson
San Diego, VIII

Mrs. Constance Ott
Milwaukee, V

Ms. Stephanie Rhodes
Missouri, V

Ms. Kim Robey
Long Island, II

Mrs. Margaret Slingluff
Central Gulf Coast, IV

HOUSE OF BISHOPS COMMITTEE ON PASTORAL DEVELOPMENT

The Rt. Rev. Robert H. Johnson, *Chair*
Western North Carolina, IV

The Rt. Rev. J. Gary Gloster
Vice-Chair & Secretary
North Carolina, IV

The Rt. Rev. Bruce Caldwell
Wyoming, VI

The Rt. Rev. Clarence N. Coleridge
Pennsylvania, III

The Rt. Rev. Theodore A. Daniels
Texas, VII

The Rt. Rev. Katharine Jefferts Schori
Nevada, VIII

Ms. Ira P. Leidel
Eastern Michigan, V

The Rt. Rev. F. Clayton Matthews
Office for Pastoral Development
Virginia, III

The Rt. Rev. Larry E. Maze
Arkansas, VII

The Rt. Rev. Jack M. McKelvey
Rochester, II

Ms. Jamel Shimpfky
El Camino Real, VIII

The Rt. Rev. Vincent W. Warner
Olympia, VIII

JOURNAL

HOUSE OF BISHOPS PLANNING COMMITTEE

The Rt. Rev. Mark S. Sisk, *Chair*
2009, New York, II

The Rt. Rev. Lloyd Allen
2009, Honduras, IX

The Rt. Rev. David C. Bane, Jr.
2006, Southern Virginia, III

The Rt. Rev. Thomas Clark Ely
2009, Vermont, I

The Rt. Rev. Daniel W. Herzog
2006, Albany, II

The Rt. Rev. Rayford B. High, Jr.
2009, Texas, VII

The Rt. Rev. Katharine Jefferts Schori
2009, Nevada, VIII

The Rt. Rev. Edward S. Little II
2006, Northern Indiana, V

The Rt. Rev. Henry N. Parsley, Jr.
2006, Alabama, IV

The Rt. Rev. Victor A. Scantlebury
2009, Chicago, V

The Rt. Rev. Geralyn Wolf
2009, Rhode Island, I

Ex Officio Members

The Rt. Rev. Richard S.O. Chang
HB Vice-Chair
Hawaii, VIII

The Most Rev. Frank T. Griswold
Presiding Bishop & Primate
Chicago, V

The Rt. Rev. Kenneth L. Price, Jr.
HB Secretary
Southern Ohio, V

Staff/Consultants
The Rev. Dr. Michael Battle, *Chaplain*
North Carolina, IV

Mrs. Barbara L. Braver
Ass't to PB for Communication

The Rev. Canon Carlson Gerdau
Canon to PB & Primate
Chicago, V

The Rt. Rev. F. Clayton Matthews
Office for Pastoral Development
Virginia, III

The Rev. Dr. Mark McIntosh, *Chaplain*
Chicago, V

Ms. Susan H. Miller, *Consultant*
Florida, IV

PRESIDING BISHOP'S COUNCIL OF ADVICE

I: The Rt. Rev. Chilton R. Knudsen
Maine

II: The Rt. Rev. Jack M. McKelvey
Rochester

III: The Rt. Rev. Robert W. Ihloff
Maryland

IV: The Rt. Rev. Charles E. Jenkins III
Chair
Louisiana

V: The Rt. Rev. Wendell N. Gibbs, Jr.
Michigan

HB COMMITTEES   DIRECTORY

VI: The Rt. Rev. James L. Jelinek
Minnesota

VII: The Rt. Rev. D. Bruce MacPherson
Western Louisiana

VIII: The Rt. Rev. Harry B. Bainbridge III
Idaho

IX: The Rt. Rev. Lloyd Allen
Honduras

Other Participants
Mrs. Barbara L. Braver
Ass't to PB for Communication

The Rt. Rev. Richard S.O. Chang
HB Vice-Chair
Hawaii, VIII

The Rev. Canon Carlson Gerdau
Canon to PB & Primate
Chicago, V

The Most Rev. Frank T. Griswold
Presiding Bishop & Primate
Chicago, V

The Rt. Rev. F. Clayton Matthews
Office for Pastoral Development
Virginia, III

HOUSE OF BISHOPS COMMITTEE ON RELIGIOUS COMMUNITIES

The Rt. Rev. Rodney R. Michel, *Chair*
Long Island, II

The Rt. Rev. James Mark Dyer
Virginia, III

The Rt. Rev. Dorsey F. Henderson, Jr.
Upper South Carolina, IV

The Rt. Rev. Robert L. Ladehoff
Oregon, VIII

The Rt. Rev. Jerry A. Lamb
Northern California, VIII

The Rt. Rev. F. Clayton Matthews
Virginia, III

The Rt. Rev. Geralyn Wolf
Rhode Island, I

HOUSE OF BISHOPS COMMITTEE ON THEOLOGY

The Rt. Rev. Henry N. Parsley, Jr., *Chair*
Alabama, IV, 2006

The Rev. Dr. Michael Battle
North Carolina, IV

The Rt. Rev. Joe G. Burnett
Nebraska, VI

Professor Ellen Charry
New Jersey, II

The Rt. Rev. Theodore A. Daniels
Texas, VII

The Rev. Dr. Ian T. Douglas
Massachusetts, I

The Rt. Rev. William O. Gregg
Eastern Oregon, VIII

The Rev. Dr. A. Katherine Grieb
Virginia, III

The Rt. Rev. Robert W. Ihloff
Maryland, III

The Rt. Rev. John B. Lipscomb
Southwest Florida, IV

The Rev. Dr. Mark McIntosh
Chicago, V

The Rt. Rev. Catherine S. Roskam
New York, II

Professor Kathy Tanner
Chicago, V

Ex Officio Members
The Most Rev. Frank T. Griswold
Presiding Bishop & Primate
Chicago, V

Consultant
Ms. Jacqueline B. Winter
Asst. to the Canon Theologian & Comm. Coord.
Chicago, V

HOUSE OF DEPUTIES PRESIDENT'S COUNCIL OF ADVICE

The Very Rev. George L.W. Werner, *Chair*
House of Deputies President
Pittsburgh, III

Ms. Bonnie Anderson, *HD Vice-President*
Michigan, V

Mrs. Carmen Brooks
Honduras, IX

Mr. J. P. Causey, Jr.
Virginia, III

Mr. Vincent Currie, Jr.
Central Gulf Coast, IV

Mrs. Pauline Getz
San Diego, VIII

The Very Rev. H. Scott Kirby
Eau Claire, V

The Rev. Canon Stephen T. Lane
Rochester, II

The Rev. Brian N. Prior
Spokane, VIII

GC COMMITTEES DIRECTORY

The Rev. Canon Anne W. Robbins
Southern Ohio, V

Robert C. Royce Esq.
East Carolina, IV

The Rev. James B. Simons
Pittsburgh, III

The Rev. Rosemari G. Sullivan
GC Executive Officer & Sec'y, HD Sec'y
Virginia, III

The Rev. Helen C. Svoboda-Barber
Kansas, VII

The Rev. Kwasi A. Thornell
Southern Ohio, V

Mrs. Katherine Tyler Scott
Indianapolis, V

The Rev. Francis H. Wade
Washington, III

The Rev. Sandra A. Wilson
Minnesota, VI

Staff
Mrs. Nancy Caparulo
Special Ass't to HD Pres.

HOUSE OF DEPUTIES COMMITTEE ON THE STATE OF THE CHURCH

The Rev. Reynolds S. Cheney II, *Chair*
West Tennessee, IV

Mr. Alfred D. Price, *Vice-Chair*
Western New York, II

The Rev. Nancy A. Ferriani, *Secretary*
Indianapolis, V

The Rev. Ronald Abrams
East Carolina, IV

The Rev. Canon Augusta R. Anderson
Western North Carolina, IV

Ms. Anne C. Brown
Vermont, I

Dr. Harold H. Brown
Maine, I

The Rev. Dr. Robert G. Certain
San Diego, VIII

The Rev. Andrew A. Cooley
Colorado, VI

Ms. Hillary Dowling
Bethlehem, III

Mrs. Debby Melnyk
Florida, IV

Mr. Richard E. Miller
Southeast Florida, IV

The Rev. Shaw Mudge, Jr.
Albany, II

Ms. Kathy Pluhar
Minnesota, VI

INSTITUTIONAL WELLNESS AND THE PREVENTION OF SEXUAL MISCONDUCT TASK FORCE

Members to be appointed.

TASK FORCE ON DISCIPLINARY POLICY AND PROCEDURE

The Rt. Rev. Catherine M. Waynick, *Chair*
2006, Indianapolis, V

The Rev. Canon Margo E. Maris
2006, Minnesota, VI

Mr. Les Alvis
2006, Mississippi, IV

The Rt. Rev. F. Clayton Matthews
2006, Virginia, III

Mr. Duncan A. Bayne
2006, Olympia, VIII

The Rt. Rev. C. Wallis Ohl, Jr.
2006, Northwest Texas, VII

The Rev. Virginia N. Herring
2006, North Carolina, IV

Ms. Woodi Sprinkel
2006, Virginia, III

Mr. Stephen F. Hutchinson
2006, Utah, VIII

Mr. Timothy D. Wittlinger
2006, Michigan, V

Sally A. Johnson Esq.
2006, Minnesota, VI

The Very Rev. Dr. Guy F. Lytle III
2006, Tennessee, IV

JOINT NOMINATING COMMITTEE FOR THE ELECTION OF THE PRESIDING BISHOP

The Rt. Rev. Peter James Lee, *Co-Chair*
Virginia, III

Mr. Don Betts
Nebraska, VI

Ms. Diane B. Pollard, *Co-Chair*
New York, II

The Rt. Rev. Bruce Caldwell
Wyoming, VI

The Rev. Thomas J. Brown, *Secretary*
Vermont, I

Mrs. Jane R. Cosby
Pennsylvania, III

The Rt. Rev. Gladstone B. Adams III
Central New York, II

Mr. Vincent Currie, Jr.
Central Gulf Coast, IV

The Rt. Rev. David Alvarez
Puerto Rico, IX

The Rev. Jeannette DeFriest
Newark, II

GC COMMITTEES DIRECTORY

Ms. Blanca Lucia Echeverry
Colombia, IX

Dr. Scott E. Evenbeck
Indianapolis, V

The Rev. Ann K. Fontaine
Wyoming, VI

The Rt. Rev. Duncan Montgomery Gray III
Mississippi, IV

The Rev. James P. Haney V
Kansas, VII

Mrs. Bettye Jo Harris
Hawaii, VIII

The Rt. Rev. Gayle E. Harris
Massachusetts, I

The Rev. Canon Mark Harris
Delaware, III

The Rev. E. Claiborne Jones
Atlanta, IV

Ms. Sarah J. Knoll
Kansas, VII

The Rt. Rev. Jerry A. Lamb
Northern California, VIII

Mr. Albert T. Mollegen, Jr.
Connecticut, I

The Rt. Rev. Kenneth L. Price, Jr.
Southern Ohio, V

The Rev. Bavi E. Rivera
California, VIII

The Rev. Luis F. Ruiz
Colombia, IX

The Rev. Dr. Richard L. Tolliver
Chicago, V

Ms. Sierra Wilkinson, *Youth Rep.*
Georgia, IV

The Rt. Rev. Don A. Wimberly
Texas, VII

Mr. Bradley A. Woodall, *Youth Rep.*
West Missouri, VII

TITLE IV REVIEW COMMITTEE

The Rt. Rev. Charles L. Keyser, *Chair*
2006, Montana, VI

Mr. J. P. Causey, Jr.
2006, Virginia, III

The Rt. Rev. Michael W. Creighton
2006, Central Pennsylvania, III

The Rt. Rev. Barbara C. Harris
2006, Massachusetts, I

The Rt. Rev. Dorsey F. Henderson, Jr.
2006, Upper South Carolina, IV

The Rev. Carolyn S. Keil-Kuhr
2006, Montana, VI

The Very Rev. H. Scott Kirby
2006, Eau Claire, V

Mrs. Deborah J. Stokes
2006, Southern Ohio, V

The Rt. Rev. James Edward Waggoner, Jr.
2006, Spokane, VIII

THE COURT FOR THE TRIAL OF A BISHOP

The Rt. Rev. Bruce Caldwell
2012, Wyoming, VI

The Rt. Rev. J. Clark Grew II
2006, Ohio, V

The Rt. Rev. Sam B. Hulsey
2006, Northwest Texas, VII

The Rt. Rev. Henry Louttit, Jr.
2009, Georgia, IV

The Rt. Rev. Mary Adelia R. McLeod
2006, Central Florida, IV

The Rt. Rev. Stacy F. Sauls
2012, Lexington, IV

The Rt. Rev. Victor A. Scantlebury
2009, Chicago, V

The Rt. Rev. Mark S. Sisk
2009, New York, II

The Rt. Rev. Andrew D. Smith
2012, Connecticut, I

COURT OF REVIEW FOR THE TRIAL OF A BISHOP

The Rt. Rev. Clifton Daniel III
2009, East Carolina, IV

The Rt. Rev. Duncan Montgomery Gray III
2012, Mississippi, IV

The Rt. Rev. Daniel W. Herzog
2012, Albany, II

The Rt. Rev. Katharine Jefferts Schori
2012, Nevada, VIII

The Rt. Rev. John B. Lipscomb
2009, Southwest Florida, IV

The Rt. Rev. D. Bruce MacPherson
2009, Western Louisiana, VII

The Rt. Rev. Chester L. Talton
2006, Los Angeles, VIII

The Rt. Rev. Franklin D. Turner
2006, Pennsylvania, III

The Rt. Rev. O'Kelley Whitaker
2006, Southern Virginia, III

PROVINCIAL PRESIDENTS AND VICE-PRESIDENTS

PROVINCE I

The Rt. Rev. Chilton R. Knudsen
President
Maine

Ms. Marge Burke
Vice-President
New Hampshire

PROVINCE II

The Rt. Rev. Jack M. McKelvey
President, Rochester

Michael Rehill, Esq.
Vice-President, Newark

PROVINCE III

The Rt. Rev. Robert W. Ihloff
President, Maryland

Ms. Ruby M. VanCroft
Vice-President, Washington

PROVINCE IV

The Rev. Robert Sessum
President, Lexington

The Rt. Rev. Charles E. Jenkins
Vice-President, Louisiana

PROVINCE V

The Rt. Rev. Wendell N. Gibbs, Jr.
President, Michigan

The Rev. Marion Luckey
Vice-President, Northern Michigan

PROVINCE VI

The Rt. Rev. James Jelinek *(Interim)*
President, Minnesota

The Rev. Marianne Ell *(Interim)*
Vice-President, North Dakota

PROVINCE VII

Ms. Shelly Simpson Vescovo
President, Dallas

The Rt. Rev. D. Bruce MacPherson
Vice-President, Western Louisiana

PROVINCE VIII

The Rt. Rev. Harry Bainbridge
President, Idaho

The Rev. Dr. John H. Eastwood
Vice-President, California

PROVINCE IX

The Rt. Rev. Lloyd E. Allen
President, Honduras

The Rt. Rev. Julio C. Holguín
Vice-President, Dominican Republic

OFFICERS OF THE HOUSE OF BISHOPS

President
The Most Rev. Frank T. Griswold

Vice-President
The Rt. Right Rev. Arthur B. Williams, Jr.

Secretary
The Rt. Rev. Richard S. O. Chang

Assistant Secretaries
The Reverend John A. Lawrence, Legislative Secretary
Ms. Lynn Bates, Administrative Secretary
Mrs. Sue Wood, Recording Secretary

HOUSE OF BISHOPS DIRECTORY

ROSTER OF THE HOUSE OF BISHOPS 2003
(In Order of Consecration)

An asterisk indicates that the Bishop was in attendance at the 2003 Convention

Bishop Hatch–0504 (Res.)
Bishop Richards–0508 (Res.)
Bishop Murray–0521 (Res.)
Bishop Cadigan–0563 (Res.)
Bishop Millard–0565 (Res.)
Bishop Sanders–0586 (Res.)
Bishop Montgomery–0587 (Res.)
* Bishop Putnam–0595 (Res.)
* Bishop Reed–0603 (Res.)
Bishop Bailey–0604 (Res.)
Bishop Reus-Froylan–0608 (Res.)
Bishop Martin–0620 (Res.)
Bishop Burt–0621 (Res.)
Bishop Wyatt–0623 (Res.)
Bishop Spears–0624 (Res.)
Bishop Wood–0625 (Res.)
Bishop Frey–0627 (Res.)
Bishop Browning–0630 (Res.)
Bishop Rivera–0635 (Res.)
Bishop Leighton–0639 (Res.)
Bishop Haynsworth–0640 (Res.)
Bishop Spofford–0643 (Res.)
Bishop Reeves–0646 (Res.)
Bishop Smith–0647 (Res.)
Bishop Folwell–0648 (Res.)
Bishop Hobgood–0656 (Res.)
Bishop Caceres–0657 (Res.)
* Bishop Stough–0658 (Res.)
Bishop Vogel–0662 (Res.)
Bishop Henton–0663 (Res.)
* Bishop Charles–0665 (Res.)
* Bishop McGehee–0667 (Res.)
Bishop Porteus–0668 (Res.)
Bishop Trelease–0669 (Res.)
* Bishop Righter–0671 (Res.)
Bishop Hillestad–0674 (Res.)
Bishop Sims–0676 (Res.)
Bishop Isaac–0678 (Res.)
Bishop Sheridan–0682 (Res.)

Bishop Cox–0684 (Res.)
Bishop Atkinson–0687 (Res.)
Bishop Weinhauer–0690 (Res.)
Bishop Parsons–0691 (Res.)
* Bishop Wolterstorff–0697 (Res.)
Bishop Gray–0698 (Res.)
Bishop Cerveny–0699 (Res.)
Bishop Belshaw–0702 (Res.)
Bishop Witcher–0703 (Res.)
Bishop Jones–0704 (Res.)
Bishop Cochrane–0709 (Res.)
Bishop Brown–0711 (Res.)
Bishop Vaché–0712 (Res.)
Bishop Spong–0713 (Res.)
Bishop Heistand–0714 (Res.)
Bishop Coburn–0715 (Res.)
* Bishop Warner–0717 (Res.)
* Bishop McAllister–0718 (Res.)
Bishop Jones–0719 (Res.)
Bishop Jones–0721 (Res.)
* Assistant Bp. of Los Angeles–0722
Bishop Pina-Lopez–0725 (Res.)
*Bishop Thompson–0726 (Res.)
Bishop Wallace–0727 (Res.)
*Bishop Schofield–0728 (Res.)
* Bishop Light–0729 (Res.)
Bishop Merino–0730 (Res.)
* Bishop of California–0732
Bishop Beckham–0733 (Res.)
* Bishop Walmsley–0736 (Res.)
Bishop Black–0737 (Res.)
Bishop Hopkins–0740 (Res.)
Bishop Estill–0741 (Res.)
Bishop Hunt–0744 (Res.)
Bishop Kimsey–0745 (Res.)
Bishop Benitez–0747 (Res.)
* Bishop Donovan–0748 (Res.)
Bishop Allison–0749 (Res.)
* Bishop Wantland–0750 (Res.)

JOURNAL

Bishop Mallory–0751 (Res.)
Bishop McNutt–0752 (Res.)
Bishop Hulsey–0753 (Res.)
Bishop Wolfrum–0754 (Res.)
* Bishop Duvall–0755 (Res.)
Bishop Whitaker–0756 (Res.)
* Bishop Grein–0758 (Res.)
* Bishop Hathaway–0761 (Res.)
* Assisting in Pennsylvania–0763
Bishop Hultstrand–0766 (Res.)
* Bishop Eastman–0767 (Res.)
Bishop Birney–0768 (Res.)
Bishop Ray–0769 (Res.)
* Assisting in Texas–0770
Bishop Dyer–0772 (Res.)
Bishop Dickson–0773 (Res.)
Bishop Moodey–0774 (Res.)
Bishop Sorge–0775 (Res.)
Bishop Patterson–0776 (Res.)
Bishop Shipps–0778 (Res.)
* Assistant Bp. of Southeast Florida–0779
* Bishop of Southeast Florida–0780
Bishop Pettit–0781 (Res.)
Bishop Ball–0782 (Res.)
Bishop Wissemann–0783 (Res.)
Bishop Burrill–0784 (Res.)
* Bishop of Virginia–0785
* Headmaster, St. Paul's School–0786
Bishop White–0787 (Res.)
* Bishop of Texas–0789
Bishop Meeks–0790 (Res.)
* Bishop Pope–0791 (Res.)
* Presiding Bishop–0794
* Bishop Harris–0795 (Res.)
* Bishop Vest–0796 (Res.)
Bishop Carr–0798 (Res.)
* Bishop of Oregon–0801
Bishop MacNaughton–0802 (Res.)
* Assistant Bp. of Washington–0804
* Bishop of New Hampshire–0805
* Assisting in Minnesota–0806)
Bishop Bowman–0811 (Res.)
* Bishop Williams–0812 (Res.)
Bishop Haines–0814 (Res.)
* Assistant Bp. of Virginia–0815
* Bishop Tennis–0816 (Res.)
Bishop Hart–0817 (Res.)
Bishop Allan–0818 (Res.)
* Assistant Bp. of New York–0819
* Bishop Rowthorn–0821 (Res.)
Bishop McArthur–0822 (Res.)
Bishop MacBurney–0823 (Res.)
* Bishop of Oklahoma–0824
Bishop Chien–0825 (Res.)
* Bishop of Long Island–0826
* Bishop Borsch–0828 (Res.)
* Bishop of Southern Ohio–0829
* Ecumenical Officer–0830
* Bishop Turner–0831 (Res.)
* Bishop of San Joaquin–0832
Bishop Wood–0833 (Res.)
* Bishop Harris–0834 (Res.)
* Bishop Buchanan–0835 (Res.)
* Bishop of Rio Grande–0836
* Bishop of Western North Carolina–0837
* Bishop Hampton–0838 (Res.)
* Bishop of Central Florida–0839
* Bishop of Northwestern Pennsylvania–0840
Bishop Smith–0841 (Res.)
Bishop Hargrove–0842 (Res.)
Bishop of Olympia–0843
*Assistant Bp. of Los Angeles–0844
Bishop Sterling–0845 (Res.)
* Bishop of Nebraska–0846
Bishop Lee–0847 (Res.)
Bishop Longest–0848 (Res.)
* Bishop of North Dakota–0850
* Bishop Smalley–0851 (Res.)
* Bishop of South Carolina–0852
* Bishop of Navajoland Area Mission–0853
* Assisting in Georgia–0854
* Bishop Williams–0855 (Res.)
Bishop of Central Ecuador–0856
* Bishop Thornton–0857 (Res.)
* Bishop of El Camino Real–0858
* Bishop of Colorado– 0860
* Bishop Suffragan of Los Angeles–0861
Bishop Wiedrich–0862 (Res.)
* Bishop Rockwell–0863 (Res.)
* Assistant Bp. of Chicago–0864
* Bishop Charleston–0865 (Res.)
* Bishop of Rochester–0866

HOUSE OF BISHOPS   DIRECTORY

* Bishop of Northern California–0868
* Bishop Marble–0869 (Res.)
* Bishop of Dominican Republic–0870
* Bishop Joslin–0871 (Res.)
* Bishop of Springfield–0872
* Bishop of San Diego–0874
* Bishop of Arizona–0875
* Bishop Dixon–0876 (Res.)
Bishop Townsend–0877 (Res.)
* Bishop of Dallas–0879
* Bishop of Fort Worth–0880
* Bishop of Haiti–0881
* Bishop of Tennessee–0882
* Bishop for Pastoral Development–0883
* Bishop Payne–0884 (Res.)
* Bishop of Minnesota–0885
* Bishop Doss–0886 (Res.)
Bishop McLeod–0887 (Res.)
Bishop Coleman–0888 (Res.)
* Bishop of West Texas–0889
* Bishop of Ohio–0890
* Bishop of Kentucky–0891
* Bishop of Florida–0892
* Bishop Johnson–0893 (Res.)
* Bishop of Fond Du Lac–0894
* Bishop of Arkansas–0895
* Bishop of South Dakota–0896
* Bishop of Quincy–0897
* Bishop of Massachusetts–0898
* Bishop of Litoral–0899
* Bishop Suffragan of Southern Ohio–0900
* Bishop of Georgia–0901
* Bishop of Upper South Carolina–0902
Bishop Said–0903 (Res.)
Bishop Strickland–0904 (Res.)
Assistant Bishop of Alabama–0906
* Bishop Suffragan of Virginia–0907
* Bishop of Central Pennsylvania–0910
* Bishop Hibbs–0911 (Res.)
* Bishop Suffragan of New York–0912
* Bishop of Rhode Island–0913
* Bishop of Southwest Florida–0914
* Bishop Suffragan of South Carolina–0915
* Bishop of Pittsburgh–0916
* Bishop of Connecticut–0917

* Bishop of Utah–0918
* Bishop of Bethlehem–0919
* Bishop Suffragan of North Carolina–0920
* Bishop of Eastern Michigan–0921
* Bishop of East Carolina–0922
* Bishop of Alabama–0923
* Bishop of Western Massachusetts–0924
* Bishop of Southwestern Virginia–0925
* Bishop of Hawaii–0926
* Bishop of Pennsylvania–0927
* Bishop Suffragan of Long Island–0928
* Bishop of Indianapolis–0929
* Bishop of Northwest Texas–0930
* Bp. of the Virgin Islands–0931
* Bishop of Southern Virginia–0932
* Bishop of Alaska–0933
* Bishop of Wyoming–0934
* Bishop of Albany–0935
* Bishop of Louisiana–0936
* Bishop of West Missouri–0937
* Bishop of Maine–0938
* Bishop of New York–0939
* Bishop of Idaho–0940
* Bishop of Delaware–0941
* Bishop Suffragan of Maryland–0942
* Bishop of Newark–0943
* Bishop of East Tennessee–0944
* Bishop of Chicago–0945
* Bishop of Eau Claire–0946
* Bishop of Western New York–0947
* Bishop of Northern Michigan–0948
* Bishop of Western Louisiana–0949
* Bishop of Michigan–0950
* Bishop Suffragan for Chaplaincies–0951
* Bishop of Northern Indiana–0952
* Bishop of Los Angeles–0953
* Bishop Suffragan of Albany–0954
* Bishop of North Carolina–0955
* Bishop of Mississippi–0956
* Bishop of Eastern Oregon–0957
* Bishop of Lexington–0958
* Bishop Suffragan of Connecticut–0959
* Bishop Suffragan of Connecticut–0960
* Bishop of Spokane–0961
* Bishop of Taiwan–0962
* Bishop of Nevada–0963

JOURNAL

* Bishop Suffragan of Massachusetts—0964
* Bishop of Vermont—0965
* Bishop of Central Gulf Coast—0966
* Bishop of West Tennessee—0967
* Bishop of Atlanta—0968
* Bishop of Colombia—0969
* Bishop of West Virginia—0970
* Bishop of Honduras—0971
* Bishop of Central New York—0972
* Bishop Suffragan of American Churches in Europe—0973
* Bishop Suffragan of Alabama—0974
* Bishop of Missouri—0975
* Bishop Suffragan of Southern Virginia—0977
* Bishop of Western Michigan—0978
* Bishop of Washington—0979
* Assistant Bp. of Pittsburgh—0980a
* Bishop Suffragan of Massachusetts—0981
* Bishop of Easton—0982
* Bishop of Iowa—0983
* Bishop of Western Kansas—0976
* Bishop of Puerto Rico—0984

HOUSE OF DEPUTIES — DIRECTORY

OFFICERS OF THE HOUSE OF DEPUTIES

President
The Very Rev. George L.W. Werner

Vice-President
Mr. Vincent C. Currie, Jr.

Secretary
The Rev. Rosemari Sullivan

Assistant Secretaries
The Rev. Saundra D. Richardson, Recording Secretary
Mr. Willie Smith, Assistant Recording Secretary
The Rev. Dr. Gregory S. Straub, Voting Secretary

DEPUTIES TO THE 2003 GENERAL CONVENTION

An asterisk indicates the deputation chair(s)
Clerical deputies are listed in the left column, lay deputies are listed in the right.

Alabama (Province IV)

The Rev. Robert T. J. Childers.
The Rev. Douglas M. Carpenter*
The Rev. John Breckinridge Fritschner
The Rev. William M. King

Mrs. Elouisa S. Stokes
Mr. Paul T. Thibodaux
Ms. Cecil P. Williamson
Mr. Marcellus L. Smith

Alaska (Province VIII)

The Rev. James N. Hunter II
The Rev. Michael Burke*
The Rev. Hunter Silides
The Rev. David Elsensohn

Ms. D. Rebecca Snow
Ms. Amanda Frank
Ms. Stacy Thorpe
Mr. Clarence Bolden

Albany (Province II)

The Rev. Shaw Mudge, Jr.
The Rev. Canon Charles B. King, Jr.*
The Rev. John L. Scott III
The Rev. Dr. Carola von Wrangel

Mr. Scott A. Garno
Mr. George J. Marshall, Sr.
Mr. James H.K. Bruner
Ms. Doris E. Bedell

Arizona (Province VIII)

The Ven. Paul William Greeley
The Very Rev. Rebecca L. McClain
The Rev. Elizabeth Huskey Simmons
The Rev. Carol S. Hosler

Mrs. Lucille Miner Geib
Mrs. Virginia V. Washington
Mr. Matthew K. Chew*
Mr. Sunand Bal

Arkansas (Province VII)

The Rev. Lowell Grisham*
The Rev. Susan Payne
The Rev. Canon Dr. Peggy Bosmyer
The Rev. JoAnn D. Barker

Ms. Pan Adams
Mrs. Elizabeth P. Matthews
Mr. Don Edgington
Mr. William M. Hawkins

HOUSE OF DEPUTIES DIRECTORY

Atlanta (Province IV)

The Rev. E. Claiborne Jones
The Very Rev. Samuel G. Candler
The Rev. Richard H. Callaway
The Rev. G. Porter Taylor

Richard P. Perry Esq.*
Mr. R.P.M. Bowden
Mrs. Janet W. Patterson
Mrs. Angela Williamson

Bethlehem (Province III)

The Ven. Richard I. Cluett*
The Rev. Cn. Jane B. Teter
The Rev. W. Nicholas Knisely
The Rev. Cn. Donald J. Muller

Mrs. Janet G. Charney
Mrs. Barbara C. Caum
Mr. Mark Edward Laubach
Ms. Hillary Stevens Dowling

California (Province VIII)

The Rev. Katherine M. Lehman*
The Rev. Bavi E. Rivera
The Rev. George S. Sotelo
The Rev. Katherine E. Salinaro

Canon Holly McAlpen*
Mr. Nigel A. Renton
Mr. Warren J. Wong
Ms. Mary Louise Gotthold

Central Florida (Province IV)

The Rev. Canon Ernest L. Bennett*
The Rev. Donald Curran
The Rev. Dr. Dabney T. Smith
The Rev. Lorne Coyle

Mrs. Phyllis Bartle
Dr. Thomas R. Bates
Mrs. Anneke Bertsch
Mr. Edgar Spalding

Central Gulf Coast (Province IV)

The Rev. Canon T. Mark Dunnam
The Rev. Dr. W. Kenneth Cumbie
The Rev. Albert W. Pruitt
The Rev. Teresa B. Leifur

Mr. Vincent Currie, Jr.*
Ms. Margaret Slingluff
Dr. William Hamilton, Jr.
Mr. Robert C. McMillan

Central New York (Province II)

The Very Rev. Dr. W. Richard Hamlin*
The Rev. David T. Andrews, Jr.
The Very Rev. David G. Bollinger
The Rev. Douglas Taylor-Weiss

Dr. Sandra Michael
Ms. Cynthia Wilson McFarland
Mr. Milton Harris Coleman
Prof. John W. Chaffee

Central Pennsylvania (Province III)

The Rev. Katherine G.L. Harrigan*
The Ven. Paul C. Donecker
The Rev. Canon Mark A. Scheneman
The Rev. Marjorie A. Menaul

Mr. Brian A. Amato
Mrs. Jennifer M. Railing
Dr. George H. Love
Mrs. Carol Fish

Chicago (Province V)

The Rev. Bonnie A. Perry*
The Very Rev. James B. Lemler
The Rev. Dr. Richard L. Tolliver
The Rev. Canon Shawn M. Schreiner

Mrs. Anne Lea Tuohy
Ms. Tessa Craib-Cox
Mr. Newland F. Smith III
Ms. Patricia Abrams

Churches in Europe (Province II)

The Rev. Kempton Baldridge
The Rev. Peter F. Casparian
The Rev. Karl Bell
The Rev. Allan Sandlin

Mr. Charles Trueheart
Mr. Peter John Handford
Mr. Richard Cole
Mrs. Nell Seymour Toensmann

Colorado (Province VI)

The Rev. Canon Ephraim Radner
The Rev. Robert Davidson
The Rev. John R. Johanssen
The Rev. Andrew A. Cooley*

Mrs. Deborah Hogue
Mr. Gary W. Thompson
Lawrence R. Hitt II, Esq.
Ms. Jacqueline B. Scott

Connecticut (Province I)

The Rev. Canon Robert G. Carroon*
The Rev. Barbara T. Cheney
The Rev. Ellen L. Tillotson
The Rev. Dr. James G. Bradley

Mr. Albert T. Mollegen, Jr.
Mr. Eugene D. Lattimer
Ms. Elizabeth Panilaitis
Ms. Rose Fichera Eagen

Dallas (Province VII)

The Rev. Canon Paul E. Lambert*
The Rev. David H. Roseberry
The Rev. Mark S. Anschutz
The Rev. William C. Treadwell III

Mrs. Laura Julian Allen
Mr. Neil D. Anderson
Mr. Rodney Maceo Williams Sr.
Mrs. Judie H. Firmin

Delaware (Province III)

The Rev. Canon Lloyd S. Casson
The Rev. Canon Mark Harris
The Rev. Gary L. Rowe
The Rev. Edward E. Godden

Ms. Cynthia Primo Martin*
Mrs. Margaret Ann Delaplane
Mrs. Barbara Krieger
Mr. William S. Hitch Sr.

Dominican Republic (Province IX)

The Rev. Ramon A. Garcia
The Rev. Mercedes Julian
The Rev. Augusto Sandino Sanchez

Mr. Alexander Romero
Mrs. Ana Lidia Toribio
Mr. Enriquillo Fernandez

East Carolina (Province IV)

The Rev. Fredricka Steenstra*
The Rev. Joseph W. Cooper
The Rev. Charles Gill
The Rev. Ronald Abrams

Mr. Larry S. Overton
Mrs. Nancy W. Broadwell
Mrs. Joan Geiszler-Ludlum
Mr. John Becker

East Tennessee (Province IV)

The Rev. Joseph H. Ballard, Jr.
The Rev. Dan Matthews, Jr.
The Rev. Suzanne N. Smitherman
The Rev. Frank M. Cooper IV

Ms. Alice R. Clayton*
Mr. Richard Govan
Ms. Lynn Schmissrauter
Mr. Jim Shearouse

Eastern Michigan (Province V)

The Very Rev. Charles E. N. Hoffacker*
The Rev. Mary J. Shortt
The Rev. J. Thomas Downs
The Rev. Elizabeth Morris Downie

Dr. Jerald Kabell
Ms. Joyce B. Thewalt
Ms. Beverly Shortt
Mrs. Sharon Huitema

Eastern Oregon (Province VIII)

The Rev. William R. Ellis, Jr.*
The Rev. Tracy M Browning
The Rev. Larry E. Harrelson
The Rev. Daniel W. Gardner

James R. Foster Esq.
Mr. John C. Adams
Ms. Jean C. Gillespie
Ms. Jean Gardner

(Province III)

The Rev. Charles E. Osberger *
The Rev. Dr. Gregory S. Straub
The Rev. Dr. M. Douglas Girardeau
The Rev. Sheila Nelson-McJilton

Mr. Eddie Vance
Mr. Ray H. Zeigler
Mrs. Kathleen Wise
Dr. Granville Blades Esq

Eau Claire (Province V)

The Rev. John E. Rasmus*
The Very Rev. H. Scott Kirby
The Rev. Ward H. Simpson
The Rev. Alan P. Coudriet

Mr. Pete Dawson *
Mr. Gregg Westigard
Ms. Barbara Gaynor
Dr. Paul Chase

El Camino Real (Province VIII)

The Rev. Ernest W. Cockrell
The Rev. Wendy Smith PhD
The Rev. Thomas B. Woodward
The Rev. Martin I. Yabroff

Ms. Dorothy J. Fuller*
Dr. Gordon W. Gritter
Mr. Franklin D. Snow
Mr. J. Patrick Waddell

Florida (Province IV)

The Rev. Cn. Ellis English Brust
The Rev. Dr. James H. Cooper
The Rev. Canon Robert F. Marsh
The Rev. Gilbert T. Crosby

Mr. Fred C. Isaac*
Mr. Calvin Williams
Dr. Shirleen S. Wait
Mrs. Deborah D Melnyk

Fond Du Lac (Province V)

The Rev. Wilson K. Roane*
The Rev. David L. Klutterman
The Rev. William L. Bippus
The Rev. Ed Smith

Mrs. Sandra Muinde
Mrs. Blanche A. Powless
Mr. Hugh T. Nolin
Mr. Richard Wilson

Fort Worth (Province VII)

The Rev. Canon Charles Albert Hough III *
The Very Rev. Christopher T. Cantrell SSC
The Rev. H. Jay Atwood
The Rev. Thomas E. Hightower

Mrs. Judy R. Mayo
Mr. Anthony J. Clark
Dr. Franklin Salazar
Mrs. Jo Ann Patton

HOUSE OF DEPUTIES — DIRECTORY

Georgia (Province IV)

The Rev. Billy J. Alford*
The Rev. Canon Robert Carter
The Very Rev. H. Neal Phelps
The Rev. William Willoughby III

Mr. William Buck Crosby
Mrs. Joy Fisher
Ms. Edna Jean Drazdowski
Mrs. Vera Pryor

Haiti (Province II)

The Rev. MacDonald Jean*
The Rev. David Cesar

Mrs. Esther Juste*
Mrs. Marie Josee Joseph

Hawaii (Province VIII)

The Rev. Canon Robert L. Fitzpatrick*
The Rev. Carol M. Arney
The Rev. Morley E. Frech, Jr.
The Rev. Darrow L.K. Aiona

Mr. Arthur K. Kusumoto*
Dr. James D. Putnam
Mrs. Bettye Jo Harris
Ms. Cynthia M. Salley

Honduras (Province IX)

The Very Rev. Pascual Torres
The Rev. Francisco Pena
The Ven. John H. Park
The Rev. Oscar O. Lopez

Mrs. Rosa Martinez de Allen
Mrs. Consuelo Coindet
Mr. Jorge Calderon
Mrs. Susan Delgado-Park

Idaho (Province VIII)

The Rev. Brian Thom*
The Rev. Brian Baker
The Ven. Eileen O'Shea
The Rev. Doug Yarbrough

Ms. Joanne B. Galbraith
Mr. Garre L. Biladeau
Mr. Lance Nielsen
Ms. Kirstin Nielsen

Indianapolis (Province V)

The Rev. Nancy A. Ferriani
The Rev. Canon David Shoulders
The Rev. Canon Kathleen J. Cullinane
The Rev. Charles Carpenter

Dr. Scott E. Evenbeck
Dr. Katherine Tyler Scott
Ms. Sally A. Pedersen
Mr. Donald L. Sodrel

Iowa (Province VI)

The Rev. Willa Marie Goodfellow*
The Rev. Kathleen S. Milligan
The Rev. John Harper
The Rev. Canon Robert E. Holzhammer

Ms. Ellen W. Bruckner*
Ms. Margaret N. Tinsman
Ms. Raisin Horn
Ms. Nancylee Ziese

Kansas (Province VII)

The Rev. James P. Haney V
The Rev. Dr. Robert C. Lord
The Ven. James E. Upton
The Rev. Canon Jo Ann T. Smith

Mr. Larry J. Bingham *
Mr. Frank Connizzo
Ms. Sarah J. Knoll
Mr. Mike Morrow

Kentucky (Province IV)

The Rev. Lucinda R. Laird*
The Rev. Paul Jeanes
The Rev. Cynthia R. Banks
The Very Rev. Keith A. Marsh

Dr. Lillian E. Yeager
Mr. Michael Allen
Dr. Mary Abrams
Ms. Carol A. Trevathan

Lexington (Province IV)

The Rev. Cn. Johnnie E. Ross *
The Rev. Alan Sutherland
The Rev. Robert L. Sessum
The Rev. Anisa Cottrell-Willis

Ms. Therese Yeiser
Mrs. Carolyn C. Ware
Mr. David Davidson
Ms. Juanita Betz Peterson

Litoral (Province IX)

The Rev. Hector Perez*

Mr. Santiago Gomez

Long Island (Province II)

The Rev. Canon Dr. Johncy Itty *
The Rev. Cecily P. Broderick y Guerra
The Rev. Dr. Elizabeth Anne Belasco
The Very Rev. William M. Viola

Ms. Valarie H. Crosdale
Mr. James N. Tempro
Ms. June S. Gerbracht
Mr. William A.G. Hogg

Los Angeles (Province VIII)

The Rev. Anthony Guillen
The Very Rev. Ernesto R. Medina
The Rev. Altagracia Perez
The Very Rev. Canon Mary June Nestler

Canon Jenny Ladefoged*
Mr. Daniel Valdez
Ms. Harriet Rodiger
Mr. James White

Louisiana (Province IV)

The Rev. Ralph F. Howe, Jr.*
The Rev. Fred Devall
The Rev. Charles Dana Krutz
The Rev. Susan Gaumer

Ms. Harriet H. Murrell
Mr. David R. Pitts
Mr. Owen Cope
Mr. Lonell Wright

HOUSE OF DEPUTIES DIRECTORY

Maine (Province I)

The Rev. Holly Lyman Antolini
The Rev. Linton H. Studdiford
The Rev. Christopher John Chornyak
The Rev. Anne Stanley

The Hon. Marge Kilkelly*
Ms. Nicole S. Janelle
Ms. Rita Tams Redfield
Dr. Harold H. Brown

Maryland (Province III)

The Rev. Mary D. Glasspool*
The Rev. Eddie M. Blue
The Rev. Angela F. Shepherd
The Rev. William P. Baxter, Jr.

Ms. Alma Thompson Bell
Ms. Marjorie J. Mack
Mr. Russell R. Reno, Jr.
Mr. David G. Mallery

Massachusetts (Province I)

The Rev. Jane Soyster Gould*
The Rev. Dr. Ian T. Douglas
The Ven. Mark Hollingsworth, Jr.
The Rev. Jurgen W. Liias

Mr. Byron Rushing*
Ms. Betsy Ridge Madsen
Ms. Rebecca A. Alden
Mr. John R. Roberts

Michigan (Province V)

The Rev. Susan E. McGarry
The Rev. Barbara Cavin
The Rev. Canon John F Keydel, Jr.
The Rev. Daniel S. Appleyard

Mr. G. Herb Gunn*
Ms. Edwina Moore Simpson
Ms. Bonnie Anderson
Reid D. Ferrall Esq.

Milwaukee (Province V)

The Rev. Gary P Lambert*
The Ven. Thomas F. Winslow
The Rev. Martha Berger
The Rev. Laura L. Norby

Mrs. Carlynn Higbie
Mrs. Wendy Wastcoat Sopkovich
Ms. Constance Ott
Mr. Michael Lyon

Minnesota (Province VI)

The Rev. Howard R. Anderson*
The Rev. Grant Abbott
The Rev. Mariann Edgar Budde
The Rev. Canon Michael G. Smith

Dr. Susan Hill Lindley
Sally A. Johnson Esq.
Ms. Kathy Pluhar
Ms. Terry Roberts

Mississippi (Province IV)

The Very Rev. Zabron A. Davis III*
The Rev. R. Stan Runnels
The Rev. Canon David H. Johnson
The Rev. David A. Elliott III

Dr. Anita George
Mr. Michael J. Chaney
Canon Kathryn W. Weathersby
Dr. Edward B. Sisson

Missouri (Province V)

The Rev. Michael Kinman*
The Rev. Tamsen E. Whistler
The Rev. Jason Samuel
The Rev. Frederick W. Thayer

Mr. Lawrence George*
Ms. Stephanie Rhodes
Mr. Michael Thomas Clark
Dr. James Hood

Montana (Province VI)

The Rev. Jean Griffin Collins
The Rev. Carolyn S. Keil-Kuhr
The Rev. John F. Naumann
The Rev. Gary Waddingham

Ms. Jessica L. Wilkerson
Mr. Ralph Spence, Jr.*
Mr. Aldin Barnes
Mrs. Sandra L Williams

Navajoland Area Mission (Province VIII)

The Rev. Carol R. Tookey

Ms. Rosella A. Jim

Nebraska (Province VI)

The Rev. Canon Tim E. Vann*
The Rev. Tim Anderson
The Very Rev. Richard Martindale
The Very Rev. Thomas J. Hurley

Mr. D. C. Bradford III*
Mr. Don Betts
Mr. John M. Brightman
Mrs. Margaret Schaefer

Nevada (Province VIII)

The Rev. Britt Olson
The Rev. Elizabeth Ann Tattersall
The Ven. Eric V. Heidecker
The Rev. Delany Armistead

Mr. Lawrence M. Kirk*
Ms. Virginia J. Hastings
Mrs. Betty-Jeanne Cousins
Mrs. Mildred Springer

New Hampshire (Province I)

The Rev. Canon Gene Robinson*
The Rev. Hays M. Junkin
The Rev. Canon Marthe Fillman Dyner
The Rev. Randolph K. Dales

Canon Roberta Fairman
Ms. Debra L. Harris
Ms. Alice Crapser
Ms. Susan Langle

HOUSE OF DEPUTIES — DIRECTORY

New Jersey (Province II)

The Rev. Peter K. Stimpson*
The Rev. Dr. Virginia M. Sheay
The Rev. Leroy A. Lyons
The Rev. John V Zamboni

Mr. Peter J. Hausman
Mrs. Cora M. Gaines*
John Wood Goldsack Esq.
Mr. Charles H. Perfater

New York (Province II)

The Rev. Theodora N. Brooks
The Rev. Dr. Roger Ferlo
The Rev. Gerald W. Keucher
The Rev. Sr. Jean Campbell OSH

Ms. Diane B. Pollard*
Mr. Fred Wibiralske
Mrs. Dorothy M. Smith
Mrs. Nell Braxton Gibson

Newark (Province II)

The Rev. Elizabeth Kaeton
The Rev. Edward M. Hasse
The Rev. Jeannette DeFriest
The Rev. Geoffrey B. Curtiss

Ms. Lyn Headley-Moore*
Dr. Louie Crew
Mr. Michael F. Rehill
Ms. Martha S. Gardner

North Carolina (Province IV)

The Rev. Timothy E. Kimbrough
The Rev. Dr. Winston B. Charles
The Rev. Ida Louise Johnson
The Rev. Donald Goodheart

The Hon. Martha Bedell Alexander
Mr. C. Thomas Fennimore
Mr. Joseph S. Ferrell
Ms. Judith B. Lane*

North Dakota (Province VI)

The Rev. Marianne Ell*
The Rev. John Floberg
The Rev. W. Duane Fox
The Rev. Michael J Horn

Mrs. Donna Lee Pettit
Ms. Sandra Holbrook
Mr. Robert Fox
Mr. Dennis Potter

Northern California (Province VIII)

The Ven. Ernestina Rodriguez Campbell*
The Rev. Mark F. Allen
The Very Rev. Donald G. Brown
The Rev. Stephen M. Carpenter

Mr. Dustin Spence
Mrs. Beatryce Clark
Mr. L. Miles Snyder
Mr. Jack Hanstein

Northern Indiana (Province V)

The Rev. Brian G. Grantz*
The Rev. Margaret Griggs Harker
The Rev. David K. Ottsen
The Very Rev. Frederick E. Mann

Canon Nancy Moody
Mrs. Charlotte A. Strowhorn
Ms. Arlyne N. Black
Mrs. Anne E. Donnelly

Northern Michigan (Province V)

The Rev. Rayford Ray
The Rev. Bonnie Turner
The Rev. Kevin L. Thew Forrester
The Rev. Dr. Mark C. Engle Sr.

Ms. Arlene Gordanier*
Marcia S. Pruner
Mr. Richard M. Graybill
Mrs. Katherine Walsh Carrigan

Northwest Texas (Province VII)

The Rev. Jacob Clemmens
The Rev. James P. Haney*
The Rev. Canon William Dale Nix
The Rev. J. Scott Mayer

Ms. Claire Cowden
Mrs. Jackie B. Batjer
Mr. Richard H. Davis
Mr. Cliff Craig

Northwestern Pennsylvania (Province III)

The Ven. Dennis A. Blauser*
The Rev. Sean W. Rowe
The Rev. Douglas K. Dayton
The Very Rev. John P. Downey

Miss Erin Blauser
Canon Sharon L. Davenport
Mr. Gary C. Yaeger
Ms. Anne Bardol

Ohio (Province V)

The Rev. Gregory A. Jacobs
The Rev. Gay C. Jennings
The Rev. Stephen Smith
The Rev. Dr. Patricia L. Hanen

Mrs. Patricia B. Kilpatrick*
Ms. Susannah W. Perkinson
Mr. Sam McDonald
Ms. Beverly Y. Scipio

Oklahoma (Province VII)

The Rev. Kenneth L. Armstrong*
The Rev. Noel J. Doherty
The Rev. Dr. Mary E. Hileman
The Rev. Stanny Joris

William R. Cathcart Esq.
Matthew Livingood Esq.
Dr. Timothy R. Bridges
Mrs. Glennes T. Clifford

HOUSE OF DEPUTIES DIRECTORY

Olympia (Province VIII)

The Rev. Stephen E. Moore
The Rev. John P. Lambert
The Rev. Dr. Peter M. Strimer
The Rev. Robert L. Christie

Ms. Hisako M. Beasley*
Mr. Duncan A. Bayne
Mr. James F. Church
Mrs. Linda L. Potter

Oregon (Province VIII)

The Rev. Linda Potter*
The Rev. Robert P. Morrison
The Rev. Sherman Hesselgrave
The Rev. John S. Scannell

Mrs. Judith C. Cato
Mrs. Barbara Ross
Mr. Francis Whitaker
Ms. Alice Speers

Pennsylvania (Province III)

The Rev. John E. Midwood*
The Rev. Mary Laney
The Rev. Rodger C. Broadley
The Rev. Canon Nancy H. Wittig

Mr. Christopher Hart*
JoAnn B. Jones Esq.
Mrs. Jane R. Cosby
Mrs. Ginger Goodrich

Pittsburgh (Province III)

The Very Rev. George L.W. Werner
The Rev. Canon Mary Maggard Hays*
The Rev. James B. Simons
The Rev. Scott T. Quinn

Mr. Donald W. Bushyager*
Mrs. Joan Malley
Mr. William F. Roemer
Mrs. Elizabeth V. Hobbs

Puerto Rico (Province IX)

Wilner Millien
Rafael Lebron
Rosali Fernandez-Pola
Emily Morales

Francisco Quirones
Miguel Ponce-Lopez
Lucy Linares
Rebecca Tirado-Muniz

Quincy (Province V)

The Rev. Dr. Robert S. Munday Ph.D.
The Very Rev. Canon H. W. Herrmann SSC
The Very Rev. Michael J. McKinnon
The Rev. Margaret Lee

Ms. Lynn J. Funk*
Talmadge Brenner Esq.
Mrs. Joan C. Quigg
Ms. Crystal Jeanne Gabelhausen

Rhode Island (Province I)

The Rev. Canon Randall Chase, Jr.* Mrs. Caryl S. Frink
The Rev. Dr. R. Craig Burlington Ms. Elizabeth Fornal
The Rev. Canon John Van Siclen Mr. Dennis E. Stark
The Rev. Mark Galloway Mr. Mr. Harry Sacchetti

Rio Grande (Province VII)

The Rev. Dr. Colin P. Kelly III Canon Robert E. Sutton
The Rev. Jan Davey Mr. George Du Sang
The Very Rev. Arthur Tripp Ms. Marjorie Lemon
The Very Rev. Ronald R. Thomson* Mr. Kay L. Fancher

Rochester (Province II)

The Rev. Canon Stephen T. Lane Ms. Josephine Dewey*
The Very Rev. Jorge M. Gutierrez Ms. Nancy Bell
The Very Rev. David Robinson Ms. Dawn C. Wilkins
The Very Rev. Mark Lattime Ms. Bonnie Tyo

San Diego (Province VIII)

The Rev. Joseph Acton Pauline H. Getz, Esq.
The Rev. Dr. Robert G. Certain Mr. Larry Salvadori
The Rev. Gary G. Nicolosi Mrs. Camilla Levien
The Rev. Lawrence D. Bausch Mrs. Catherine F. Martensen*

San Joaquin (Province VIII)

The Very Rev. Canon James Snell Mr. Ted M. Yumoto
The Very Rev. Mark Lawrence Charles L. Reed, Esq.
The Rev. Richard Bruce Matters Mrs. Debra Cavanagh
The Rev. Daniel Martins Mrs. Nancy T. Salmon

South Carolina (Province IV)

The Very Rev. John B. Burwell Col. Robert S. Bell
The Rev. Dr. Kendall Harmon Mrs. Lydia Evans
The Rev. Jennie C. Olbrych Mr. Lonnie Hamilton III
The Rev. Canon Michael T. Malone Mr. Wade H. Logan III

HOUSE OF DEPUTIES DIRECTORY

South Dakota (Province VI)

The Rev. Webster Two Hawk
The Rev. Virginia Bird
The Rev. David A. Cameron
The Very Rev. Marcia Hunter

Mr. Kenneth Owens
Ms. Virginia Slechta
Mrs. Marjorie D. Gross
Ms. Caitlin Collier

Southeast Florida (Province IV)

The Rev. Mary Gray-Reeves
The Rev. Bryan A. Hobbs
The Ven. Paul A. Rasmus
The Rev. Horace David Ward

Mr. Richard E. Miller*
Mr. Manuel G. Mesa
Ms. Lynne Libby
Mr. Ted Burnett

Southern Ohio (Province V)

The Rev. Canon Anne W. Robbins*
The Rev. Canon Kwasi A. Thornell
The Rev. Vicki Diane Zust
The Rev. Benjamin E.K. Speare-Hardy II

Mr. Jon B. Boss
Mr. John K. Webster
Mr. Andrew E. Figueroa
Ms. Deborah J. Stokes

Southern Virginia (Province III)

The Rev. Joy E. Walton*
The Rev. Dr. Paul Hogg, Jr.
The Rev. Mark S. Delcuze
The Rev. John A. Baldwin

Mrs. Frances S. Barber
The Hon. James E. Bradberry
Mrs. Sue E. Wilder
Mrs. Sara Mueller

Southwest Florida (Province IV)

The Rev. Hayden G. Crawford*
The Rev. Sharon L. Lewis
The Very Rev. Barry P. Kubler
The Rev. John D. Hiers

Mrs. Joan O. Kline
Mr. Roger D. Schwenke
Mr. Donald J. Scott
Ms. Karen O. Patterson

Southwestern Virginia (Province III)

The Rev. John David Lane
The Rev. Clare Fischer-Davies
The Rev. Deborah Hentz Hunley
The Rev. Christine Payden-Travers

Mr. Jack Barrow
Ms. Frances C. Marshall
Mr. Robert K. Miller
Mr. Calvert G deColigny Jr

Spokane (Province VIII)

The Rev. Canon Mart K. Craft*
The Rev. Canon Kristi Philip
The Rev. Brian N. Prior
The Rev. Steven Woolley

Mrs. Gloria N. Lund
Mr. Thomas Robison
Mrs. Marcia O'Leary
Mrs. Margaret Rehberg

Springfield (Province V)

The Very Rev. Christopher L. Ashmore
The Ven. Shawn W. Denney
The Rev. Dr. Virginia L. Bennett
The Rev. James O. Cravens

Mr. Kevin James Babb*
Mrs. Marilynn S. Belleville
Dr. Arthur Larkin Casebeer
Mr. David Wakefield

Taiwan (Province VIII)

The Rev. Peter T. P. Chen
The Rev. Elizabeth Wei

Mr. Herbert H. P. Ma*
Mr. Pao-Sheng Hu

Tennessee (Province IV)

The Rev. Eugene F. Wise, Jr.*
The Very Rev. Kenneth B. Swanson
The Rev. Becca Stevens-Hummon
The Rev. Robert W. Cowperthwaite

David B. Herbert Esq.
Mr. Warner A. (Pete) Stringer III
Ms. Karen Keele
Mrs. Martha Bennett

Texas (Province VII)

The Rev. Dena A. Harrison*
The Rev. Canon Rayford B. High, Jr.
The Rev. Kenneth W. Kesselus
The Rev. Uriel Osnaya-Jimenez

Mr. Ronald D. Null
Mrs. Mary M. MacGregor
Mr. William Gammon III
Mr. John Bennet Waters, Sr.

Upper South Carolina (Province IV)

The Rev. Donald A. Lowery*
The Rev. Calvin R. Griffin
The Rev. Dr. Robert S. Dannals
The Rev. Timothy M. Dombek

Mr. Arthur M. Bjontegard, Jr.*
Mrs. Angela M. Daniel
Mr. Jimmy Hartley
Mr. David H. Keller

Utah (Province VIII)

The Rev. James R. Tendick*
The Rev. Canon David E. Bailey
The Rev. Canon Pablo Ramos
The Rev. W. Lee Shaw

Mr. Russell C. Babcock
Ms. Karen Cramer
Ms. Ann B. Ellingson
Mr. Stephen F. Hutchinson

HOUSE OF DEPUTIES   DIRECTORY

Vermont (Province I)

The Rev. Gordon A. Bardos
The Rev. Thomas J Brown
The Rev. Dr. Lee Alison Crawford
The Rev. Diane E. Root

Mr. James Larkin*
Thomas A. Little, Esq.
Ms. Anne C. Brown
Mr. Peter D Galbraith

Virgin Islands (Province II)

The Rev. E. Ambrose Gumbs
The Very Rev. Ashton J. Brooks
The Rev. Wilfred Daniel
The Rev. Rawle C. Belle

Canon Rosalie Simmonds Ballentine, Esq.
Mrs. Judithann H. Gardine*
Mrs. Aida R. Nieves
Mrs. Gloria Carlos

Virginia (Province III)

The Rev. Susan Ellyn Goff
The Very Rev. Susan N. Eaves
The Rev. Jeffrey O Cerar
The Rev. Jim Papile

Mr. Russell V. Palmore, Jr.*
Mr. Jack W. Burtch, Jr.
Mr. Russell Vance Randle
Mr. J. P. Causey, Jr.

Washington (Province III)

The Rev. Dr. Francis H. Wade*
The Rev. Margaret M. Graham
The Rev. Dr. David S. Pollock
The Rev. Joan Elizabeth Beilstein

Mr. Paul E. Cooney
Mr. John Vanderstar
Ms. Iris E. Harris
Dr. Linda R. Freeman

West Missouri (Province VII)

The Rev. Ross W. Stuckey*
The Rev. Constance F. Tyndall
The Rev. Kenneth L. Chumbley
The Ven. John H. McCann

Ms. Cynthia H. Schwab
Mrs. Carolyn B. Phelps
Ms. Shirley Bolden
Mr. Channing Horner

West Tennessee (Province IV)

The Rev. Reynolds S. Cheney II*
The Rev. Rene Somodevilla
The Rev. Colenzo Hubbard
The Rev. Jeffery W. Marx

Charles M. Crump, Esq.
The Hon. James F. Russell
Mr. Theodore B. Sloan
Miss. Carolyn Corum

West Texas (Province VII)

The Rev. Gary Lillibridge
The Rev. James Murguia
The Rev. Ned F. Bowersox
The Rev. Nancy Coon

Mr. John C. Brooke
Mr. Robert L. Browning
Ms. Priscilla Murguia
Mrs. Susan Hardaway

West Virginia (Province III)

The Rev. Cheryl Winter*
The Rev. Mark Seitz
The Rev. Arthur L. Bennett III
The Rev. Karl D. Ruttan

Ms. Deborah A. Short
Mrs. Ruth T. Foose
Mr. Thomas D. Miller
Mr. Harold Stewart

Western Kansas (Province VII)

The Rev. Michael P. Milliken*
The Very Rev. Timothy E. Kline
The Rev. Dennis Gilhousen
The Rev. Kevin Schmidt

Mr. Zeltus J. Ford
Mr. Robert L. Carson
Mrs. Sharon F. Denton
Miss Linda S. Boone

Western Louisiana (Province VII)

The Rev. William Bryant*
The Very Rev. Martin L. Agnew, Jr.
The Very Rev. Michael K Adams
The Rev. James E. Flowers

Mr. R. Thad Andress
Mrs. Carolyn Ledet
Mr. Norman Parker
Mr. John H. Robert

Western Massachusetts (Province I)

The Very Rev. Canon Sarah Shofstall
The Rev. Len Cowan
The Rev. Canon Dr. Paul Taylor
The Rev. Nancy Baillie Strong

Dr. Delbert C. Glover
Dr. Margo E. McMahon
Dr. Deborah Harmon Hines
Mrs. Kathleen T. Randall

Western Michigan (Province V)

The Rev. D. Edward Emenheiser
The Rev. Jennifer L. Adams
The Rev. C. Mark Rutenbar
The Rev. Charles Peyton McCabe III

Ms. Netty Cove
Mrs. Barbara K. Coulter
Dr. Lawrence W. Manglitz
Ms. Pamela B. Chapman

HOUSE OF DEPUTIES   DIRECTORY

Western New York (Province II)

The Rev. Susan Anslow Williams*
The Very Rev. Allen W. Farabee
The Very Rev. Charles W. Whitmore
The Rev. Earle C. King, Jr.

Mr. Elton M. Hartney
Mr. Alfred D. Price
Mrs. Particia Gail Zebrowski
Ms. Lillian Davis-Wilson

Western North Carolina (Province IV)

The Rev. Tim McRee*
The Rev. William A. Whisenhunt
The Rev. Eugene C. McDowell
i The Rev. Canon Augusta R. Anderson

Ms. Diane Mance
Mrs. Matilda O. Kistler
Mr. Lawrence E. Thompson
Mr. Cobb Milner, Jr.

Wyoming (Province VI)

The Very Rev. Marilyn J. Engstrom
The Rev. Warren Murphy
The Rev. Ann K. Fontaine
The Rev. Roy Walworth

Ms. Laurie Kadrich*
Mr. John Masters
Mr. Norm Peterson
Ms. Mary Ellen Honsaker

PART II

GENERAL CONVENTION 74th SESSION

HOUSE OF BISHOPS MINUTES

FIRST DAY

Wednesday
July 30, 2003

MORNING SESSION

This being the day and place designated by the Presiding Bishop, with the advice and consent of the Executive Council, pursuant to Article 1, Section 6 of the Constitution, for the Seventy-fourth Regular Meeting of the General Convention, the House of Bishops assembled in the Minneapolis Convention Center, Minneapolis, Minnesota, in the Diocese of Minnesota, on Wednesday, July 30, 2003, with the Presiding Bishop in the Chair.

Call to Order
The Presiding Bishop called the House of Bishops to order at 11:13 a.m.
Conversation time of 20 minutes began at 11:15 a.m.

Message from the House of Deputies
The Presiding Bishop announced the arrival of a delegation from the House of Deputies, and introduced Deputy Crump of West Tennessee and Deputy Perez from Los Angeles, who addressed the House and informed the House of Bishops that the House of Deputies has been duly organized with the Very Rev. George L. Werner of the Diocese of Pittsburgh as President, Mr. Vincent C. Currie, Jr., of the Diocese of Central Gulf Coast as Vice-President, and the Rev. Rosemari G. Sullivan of the Diocese of Virginia as Secretary and that it is now ready to proceed to business.

The deputies then withdrew.

Agenda of the Day
The House of Bishops Committee on Dispatch of Business moved to adopt the agenda of the day.

Motion carried
Agenda adopted

Quorum
Following the roll call, the Secretary announced that the current membership of the House, pursuant to Article 1, Section 2, was 288 bishops entitled to vote, of which number 155 being retired are not to be counted in computing a quorum. (See Appendix A–Day 1 for Make-Up of the House of Bishops) On the basis of 133 members, therefore, a quorum was 67 active bishops entitled to vote. There being 124 such bishops present, an undoubted quorum existed, and the Secretary so certified.

House Organized
The Secretary of the House moved that the House of Deputies be notified that the

House of Bishops was organized and ready to proceed to business, with the Most Rev. Frank T. Griswold, Primate, in the Chair, with the retired Suffragan Bishop of Ohio as Vice-Chair, and with the Bishop of Hawaii as Secretary.

Motion carried
(Communicated to the House of Deputies in HB Message #1)

A delegation of the Bishop of California and the Junior Suffragan Bishop of Massachusetts delivered HB Message #1 to the House of Deputies.

Dispatch of Business
The Secretary of the House moved the minutes of the Spring Meeting of 2003 be accepted by title.

Motion carried

Welcome from Host Bishop
The Bishop of Minnesota, the Rt. Rev. James L. Jelinek, addressed the House.

Appointment of Assistant Secretaries
The Secretary of the House appointed the following Assistant Secretaries:
  Ms. Lynn Bates–Administration
  The Rev. John A. Lawrence–Legislation
  Mrs. Sue Wood–Recording

Introduction of New Members
The Rt. Rev. Alan Scarfe, Bishop of Iowa, was introduced.

Introduction of Visiting Bishops
The Presiding Bishop introduced the visiting bishops:
  The Rt. Rev. Justice Akrofi, Bishop of Accra, West Africa
  The Rt. Rev. Riah Hanna Abu El-Assal, Bishop in Jerusalem
  The Most Rev. Josiah Idowu-Fearon, Archbishop, Kaduna, Nigeria
  The Rt. Rev. Nudal Alves Gomes, Bishop Suffragan of Curitiba, Brazil
  The Rt. Rev. Orlando Guerreo-Torres, Bishop of Venezuela
  The Most Rev. Clive Hanford, Primate, Cyprus and the Gulf
  The Rt. Rev. Joseph Noriaka Iida, Retired Bishop of Kyushu, Japan
  The Rt. Rev. Carlos Lopez-Lozano, Bishop, Spanish Reformed Church
  The Rt. Rev. Michael Nazir-Ali, Bishop of Rochester, England
  The Most Rev. Njongonkulu Winston Hugh Ndungane, Primate, South Africa
  The Rt. Rev. Jubal Pereira Neves, Bishop of South Western Brazil
  The Most Rev. Livingston Mpalayuni-Nkoyoyo, Primate of Uganda
  The Rt. Rev. Filadelfo Oliveria Neto, Bishop Suffragan, Recife, Brazil
  The Most Rev. Orlando Santos de Oliveira, Primate, Southern Brazil
  The Most Rev. Michael Geoffrey Peers, Primate, Canada
  The Rt. Rev. Mano Rumalshah, Secretary General of the USPG
  The Most Rev. Ignacio Capuyan Soliba, Primate, Philippines
Bishops from former ECUSA dioceses with covenants for autonomy:
  The Rt. Rev. Hector Monterroso, Bishop of Costa Rica

The Rt. Rev. Julio Murray, Bishop of Panama
The Rt. Rev. Edward W. Neufville, Bishop of Liberia
The Rt. Rev. Carlos Touche-Porter, Bishop of Mexico

Introduction of Bishops who are former members of the House:
The Most Rev. Martin de Jesus Barahona, Bishop of El Salvador and Primate of Igesia Anglicana de la Region Central de America (IARCA)
The Rt. Rev. Martiniano M. Garcia, Acting Primate of Mexico
The Rt. Rev. Armando Guerra Sorias, Bishop of Guatemala

Necrology
The Presiding Bishop announced members who died since the preceding meeting:

November 12, 2002
The Rt. Rev. Harold S. Jones
Retired Bishop Suffragan of South Dakota

January 11, 2003
The Rt. Rev. Reginald H. Gooden
Retired Bishop of the Republic of Panama

March 22, 2003
The Rt. Rev. Walter H. Jones
Retired Archbishop of Rupert's Land, formerly Bishop of South Dakota

May 2, 2003
The Rt. Rev. Paul Moore, Jr.
Retired Bishop of New York

May 30, 2003
The Rt. Rev. Robert Tharp
Retired Bishop of East Tennessee

June 21, 2003
The Rt. Rev. A. Ervine Swift
Retired Bishop of Puerto Rico and Virgin Islands

Election of Vice-Chair
The House of Bishops Committee on Nominations and Elections nominated retired Bishop Suffragan of Ohio, the Rt. Rev. Arthur B. Williams, Jr., as Vice-Chair of the House. There being no further nominations, the House cast a unanimous vote for Bishop Williams.

Motion carried

Communications from the Presiding Bishop
The Presiding Bishop appointed the Rev. Dr. Michael Battle and the Rev. Mark McIntosh as chaplains of the House.

Consent Process
The Presiding Bishop proposed an outline for the Consent Process. The House accepted the process as presented by the Presiding Bishop.

Motion carried

Report of the Nominations Committee
The Chair of the House of Bishops Nominations and Elections Committee moved the Readmission of the Rt. Rev. Sergio Carranza, Assistant Bishop of Los Angeles, to the House.
Motion carried
(Communicated to the House of Deputies in HB Message #7)

Election of the Court for the Trial of a Bishop
The House of Bishops Nominations and Elections Committee nominated to the Court for Trial of a Bishop until 2012:
   The Rt. Rev. Bruce Caldwell, Bishop of Wyoming
   The Rt. Rev. Stacy Sauls, Bishop of Lexington
   The Rt. Rev. Andrew Smith, Bishop of Connecticut

Election of the Court of Review of the Trial of a Bishop
The House of Bishops Nominations and Elections Committee nominated to the Court of Review for the Trial of a Bishop until 2012:
   The Rt. Rev. Duncan Gray, III, Bishop of Mississippi
   The Rt. Rev. Daniel Herzog, Bishop of Albany
   The Rt. Rev. Katharine Jefferts Schori, Bishop of Nevada
There being no further nominations, a unanimous ballot was cast for the nominees.
Motion carried
(Communicated to the House of Deputies in HB Message #7)

Personal Privilege
The Bishop of Oregon introduced the Rev. Richard Tombaugh, Executive Secretary of the General Board of Examining Chaplains.

Noonday Prayers
Noonday prayers were led by the Chaplain, the Rev. Michael Battle.

RECESS
Following announcements by the Secretary, the House of Bishops Committee on Dispatch of Business moved that the House stand in recess until 4:15 p.m.
Motion carried

The House recessed at 12:24 p.m.

AFTERNOON SESSION

The House reconvened at 4:15 p.m. and was called to order by the Presiding Bishop.
There was reflection by the Chaplain, the Rev. Mark McIntosh, and conversation for 30 minutes.
The House resumed at 4:45 p.m.

Appointments by the Presiding Bishop
The Presiding Bishop announced the following appointments:
Board of Archives
The Rt. Rev. Neil Alexander, Bishop of Atlanta
The Rt. Rev. Wayne Wright, Bishop of Delaware
Motion carried
(Communicated to the House of Deputies in HB Message #2)

The Presiding Bishop announced the following appointments:
Church Deployment Board
The Rt. Rev. Wendell Gibbs, Bishop of Michigan
The Rt. Rev. Katharine Jefferts Schori, Bishop of Nevada
Motion carried
(Communicated to the House of Deputies in HB Message #3)

Nominations by the Presiding Bishop
The Presiding Bishop nominated the Rev. Dr. Robert Wright as Historiographer.
Motion was made to approve the nomination.
Motion carried
(Communicated to the House of Deputies in HB Message #4)

The Presiding Bishop nominated the Rev. Canon Carlson Gerdau as Registrar.
Motion was made to approve the nomination.
Motion carried
(Communicated to the House of Deputies in HB Message #5)

The Presiding Bishop nominated the Church Pension Fund as Recorder of Ordinations.
Motion was made to approve the nomination.
Motion carried
(Communicated to the House of Deputies in HB Message #6)

Appointments by the Presiding Bishop
The Presiding Bishop announced the following appointments:
Title IV Review Committee
 The Rt. Rev. Michael Creighton, Bishop of Central Pennsylvania
 The Rt. Rev. Francis Gray, Assistant Bishop of Virginia
 The Rt. Rev. Barbara Harris, Retired Bishop Suffragan of Massachusetts
 The Rt. Rev. Dorsey Henderson, Bishop of Upper South Carolina
 The Rt. Rev. Charles Keyser, Retired Bishop of the Armed Services
(Communicated to the House of Deputies in HB Message #2)

Dispatch of Business

Dispatch of Business reminded Committees that Report #1 is to be committee organization and to use printed amendment forms.

The House of Bishops Committee on Dispatch of Business presented its Report #7 on HD Message #1 on Resolution A156 (2003 General Convention Daily Agenda) and moved concurrence.

The House concurred
(Communicated to the House of Deputies in HB Message #8)

Final Text of Resolution:

(A156)
Resolved, That the 2003 General Convention function through the following activities:
1. formal legislative sessions of the two Houses;
2. a joint session for presentation of the budget proposal;
3. meetings of the legislative committees of the two Houses; and
4. open hearings to be conducted as needed by all legislative committees; and be it further

Resolved, That the schedule and the daily timetable of the 74th General Convention held in Minneapolis, Minnesota be:

Sunday, July 27, 2003
11:00 a.m.–2:30 p.m.	Volunteer Supervisors Gathering
4:00–6:00 p.m.	HD Secretariat and Committee on Dispatch of Business Orientation

Monday, July 28, 2003
9:30 a.m.–5:00 p.m.	Registration
9:30 a.m.–5:00 p.m.	Deputy Certification
2:00 p.m.–6:00 p.m.	Legislative Committee Officers Orientation

Tuesday, July 29, 2003
9:30 a.m.–5:30 p.m.	Registration
9:00 a.m.–12:00 noon	Legislative Committee Meetings
9:30 a.m.–1:45 p.m.	Deputy Certification
2:00 p.m.–3:00 p.m.	PB/Pres HD Presentation to GC
3:00 p.m.–5:00 p.m.	Orientation
3:30 p.m.–5:30 p.m.	Deputy Certification
8:00 p.m.	Legislative Committee Meetings

Wednesday, July 30, 2003—First Legislative Day
7:30 a.m.–9:00 am	Legislative Committee Meetings
8:00 a.m.–5:00 p.m.	Registration
8:30 a.m.–9:30 a.m.	Deputy Certification
9:30 a.m.–10:45 p.m.	Eucharist and Scripture Reflection
11:00 a.m.–12:30 p.m.	Legislative Session

12:30 p.m.–1:15 p.m.	Deputy Certification
2:00 p.m.–4:00 p.m.	Legislative Committee Meetings
4:15 p.m.–6:00 p.m.	Legislative Session
8:00 p.m.	Conversations

Thursday, July 31, 2003—Second Legislative Day

7:30 a.m.–9:00 a.m.	Legislative Committee Meetings
8:00 a.m.–5:00 p.m.	Registration
8:30 a.m.–9:30 a.m.	Deputy Certification
9:30 a.m.–10:45 a.m.	Eucharist and Scripture Reflection
11:00 a.m.–12:30 p.m.	Legislative Session
12:30–1:15 p.m.	Deputy Certification
2:00 p.m.–3:30 p.m.	Legislative Committee Hearings
3:45 p.m.–6:00 p.m.	Legislative Session
5:00 p.m.	Resolution Filing Deadline
7:00 - 9:00 p.m.	Presiding Bishop's Forum–Global Reconciliation
8:00 p.m.	PB&F Hearing

Friday, August 1, 2003—Third Legislative Day

7:00 a.m.–8:30 a.m.	Legislative Committee Meetings
9:00 a.m.–1:00 p.m.	Morning of Prayer
12:00 noon–5:00 p.m.	Registration
1:00 p.m.–1:45 p.m.	Deputy Certification
2:30 p.m.–6:00 p.m.	Legislative Session
8:00 p.m.	PB&F Hearing

Saturday, August 2, 2003—Fourth Legislative Day

7:30 a.m.–9:00 a.m.	Legislative Committee Meetings
8:00 a.m.–1:00 p.m.	Registration
8:30 a.m.–9:30 a.m.	Deputy Certification
9:30 a.m.–10:45 a.m.	Eucharist and Scripture Reflection
11:00 a.m.–1:00 p.m.	Legislative Session
Evening	Seminary Dinners

Sunday, August 3, 2003—Fifth Legislative Day

10:00 a.m.	UTO In-gathering and Eucharist
12:30 p.m.–5:00 p.m.	Registration
1:15 p.m.–2:00 p.m.	Deputy Certification
2:30 p.m.–6:00 p.m.	Legislative Session
5:00 p.m.	Bishops' Dinner
8:00 p.m.	Anti-Racism Program

Monday, August 4, 2003—Sixth Legislative Day

7:30 a.m.–9:00 a.m.	Legislative Committee Meetings
8:00 a.m.–5:00 p.m.	Registration
8:30 a.m.–9:30 a.m.	Deputy Certification
9:30 a.m.–10:45 a.m.	Eucharist and Scripture Reflection
11:00 a.m.–1:00 p.m.	Legislative Session (Provincial Caucuses)

12:30 p.m.–1:15 p.m.	Deputy Certification
2:30 p.m.–6:00 p.m.	Legislative Session

Tuesday, August 5, 2003—Seventh Legislative Day

7:30 a.m.–9:00 a.m.	Legislative Committee Meetings
8:00 a.m.–5:00 p.m.	Registration
8:30 a.m.–9:30 a.m.	Deputy Certification
9:30 a.m.–10:45 a.m.	Eucharist and Scripture Reflection
11:00 a.m.–1:00 p.m.	Legislative Session
12:30 p.m.–1:15 p.m.	Deputy Certification
2:30 p.m.–6:00 p.m.	Legislative Session
Evening	Provincial Dinners

Wednesday, August 6, 2003—Eighth Legislative Day

7:30 a.m.–9:00 a.m.	Legislative Committee Meetings
8:00 a.m.–5:00 p.m.	Registration
8:30 a.m.–9:30 a.m.	Deputy Certification
9:30 a.m.–10:45 a.m.	Eucharist and Scripture Reflection
11:00 a.m. - 1:00 p.m.	Legislative Session (Provincial Caucuses)
12:30 p.m.–1:15 p.m.	Deputy Certification
2:30 p.m.	Joint Session–Program, Budget & Finance
2:30 p.m.–6:00 p.m.	Legislative Session (Includes Joint Session: PB&F Budget)
8:00 p.m.–10:00 p.m.	Reserved for Legislation

Thursday, August 7, 2003—Ninth Leglisative Day

7:30 a.m.–9:00 a.m.	Legislative Committee Meetings
8:00 a.m.–5:00 p.m.	Registration
8:30 a.m.–9:30 a.m.	Deputy Certification
9:30 a.m.–10:45 a.m.	Eucharist and Scripture Reflection
11:00 a.m.–1:00 p.m.	Legislative Session
12:30 p.m.–1:15 p.m.	Deputy Certification
2:30 p.m.–6:00 p.m.	Legislative Session
8:00 p.m.–10:00 p.m.	Reserved for Legislation

Friday, August 8, 2003—Tenth Legislative Day

9:00 a.m.–10:15 am	Eucharist and Scripture Reflection
8:00 a.m.–2:00 p.m.	Registration
8:30 a.m.–9:30 a.m.	Deputy Certification
10:30 a.m.–1:00 p.m.	Legislative Session
12:30 p.m.–1:15 p.m.	Deputy Certification
2:30 p.m.–6:00 p.m.	Legislative Session
6:00 p.m.	Joint Adjournment Sine Die

Rules of Order

The House of Bishops Committee on Rules of Order presented its Report #1 on Resolution B011 (Amend Rules pertaining to 2/3rds Votes) and moved adoption.

Final Text of Resolution:

(B011)
Resolved, That the Rules of Order of the House of Bishops be amended to change every reference of a qualified two-thirds vote to an unqualified two-thirds vote, i.e., "two-thirds vote of those present and voting."

Motion carried
Resolution adopted
(Communicated to the House of Deputies in HB Message #9)

The House of Bishops Committee on Rules of Order presented its Report #2 on Resolution B012 (Amend House of Bishops Rule XXIV) and moved adoption.

Final Text of Resolution:

(B012)
Resolved, That Rule XXIV (General Rules General Convention Constitution and Canons 2000, pg. 185) be amended as follows:
"Any Bishop of a Church in the Anglican Communion who is in exile from a Diocese, or is without membership in a House of Bishops because the Diocese is temporarily in an extra-provincial status, and who is resident in any jurisdiction in this Church, *or any other Bishop of a Church in the Anglican Communion who has resigned his or her position in that Church, who has made his or her primary residence in any jurisdiction in this Church,* may be admitted to this House as a collegial member..."

Motion carried
Resolution adopted
(Communicated to the House of Deputies in HB Message #10)

The House of Bishops Committee on Rules of Order presented its Report #3 on Resolution B013 (Amend House of Bishops Rule II–First Day) and moved adoption.

Final Text of Resolution:

(B013)
Resolved, That the first two sentences of Rule II shall be deleted and replaced by the following two sentences:
"*The House shall then proceed to elect a Secretary if the office is vacant; and the person elected shall serve until the end of that meeting of the Convention. At the end of each meeting of the Convention, the House shall proceed to elect a Secretary who shall continue in office until the conclusion of the triennial*

meeting of the Convention following that election..."

Motion carried
Resolution adopted
(Communicated to the House of Deputies in HB Message #11)

The House of Bishops Committee on Rules of Order presented its Report #4 on Resolution B014 (Amend House of Bishops Rule VI–First Day) and moved adoption.

Final Text of Resolution:

(B014)
Resolved, **That the first sentence of Rule VI shall be deleted and replaced by the following two sentences:**
The House shall then proceed to elect a Vice-Chair, if the office is then vacant, after hearing the report of the nominating committee of the House and after receiving any other nominations from the floor; and the person elected shall serve until the conclusion of that meeting. At the conclusion of each meeting of the Convention, the House, using the same procedure, shall proceed to elect a Vice-Chair who shall continue in office until the conclusion of the triennial meeting of the Convention following that election.

Motion carried
Resolution adopted
(Communicated to the House of Deputies in HB Message #12)

The House of Bishops Committee on Rules of Order presented its Report #5 on Resolution B015 (Amend House of Bishops Rule X) and moved adoption.

Original Text of Resolution:

(B015)
Resolved, That Rule X (Standing Orders General Convention Constitution and Canons 2000, pg.189) be amended as follows:
Whenever the House shall make a determination under Article I.2 of the Constitution that a resigned Bishop shall or shall not retain a seat and vote in the House, the following understanding of the intent of the pertinent terms of that provision of the Constitution shall apply: (a) "advanced age" shall mean at least 62 years of age; (b) "bodily infirmity" shall mean either a condition for which one is eligible for disability retirement benefits from the Church Pension Fund or Social Security Administration, or a physical or mental impairment that a physician or psychiatrist (approved by the Presiding Bishop) certifies would likely result in eligibility for such disability retirement benefits should the Bishop continue in active episcopal ministry; (c) "office created by the General Convention" shall mean a ministry funded by the General Convention Budget and approved by the Presiding Bishop; and (d) "mission strategy" shall mean a strategy that would allow the election of an indigenous member of the clergy of a non-domestic diocese as Bishop, or that would allow a diocese to implement a new mission strategy as determined by the Presiding Bishop, or that would allow a transition in episcopal leadership after a Diocesan Bishop or Bishop Suffragan has served 10 or more years in either or both of those offices.

It was moved to amend the resolution.

Proposed Amendment:
Delete "amended" and insert "added" in the first sentence.

Motion carried

Final Text of Resolution:
Resolved, **That Rule X (Standing Orders General Convention Constitution and Canons 2000, pg.189) be added as follows:**
Whenever the House shall make a determination under Article I.2 of the Constitution that a resigned Bishop shall or shall not retain a seat and vote in the House, the following understanding of the intent of the pertinent terms of that provision of the Constitution shall apply: (a) "advanced age" shall mean at least 62 years of age; (b) "bodily infirmity" shall mean either a condition for which one is eligible for disability retirement benefits from the Church Pension Fund or Social Security Administration, or a physical or mental impairment that a physician or psychiatrist (approved by the Presiding Bishop) certifies would likely result in eligibility for such disability retirement benefits should the Bishop continue in active episcopal ministry; (c) "office created by the General Convention" shall mean a ministry funded by the General Convention Budget and approved by the Presiding Bishop; and (d) "mission strategy" shall mean a strategy that would allow the election of an indigenous member of the clergy of a non-domestic diocese as Bishop, or that would allow a diocese to implement a new mission strategy as determined by the Presiding Bishop, or that would allow a transition in episcopal leadership after a Diocesan Bishop or Bishop Suffragan has served 10 or more years in either or both of those offices.

Motion carried
Resolution adopted with amendment
(Communicated to the House of Deputies in HB Message #13)

Committee on Constitution

The House of Bishops Committee on Constitution presented its Report #1 on Resolution A108 (Constitution Article X, Second Reading) and moved the resolution, recommending rejection.

Original Text of Resolution:
(A108)
Resolved, the House of Deputies concurring, That Article X of the Constitution be amended to include the following sentence at the end of the second paragraph:
Provide for use of other forms for the renewal and enrichment of the common worship of this church for such periods of time and upon such terms and conditions as the General Convention may provide; and be it further
Resolved, That this resolution be sent within six months to the Secretary of the Convention of every Diocese to be made known to the Diocesan Convention at its

next meeting.

Motion defeated
Resolution rejected
(Communicated to the House of Deputies in HB Message #14)

The House of Bishops Committee on Constitution presented its Report #2 on Resolution A112 (Amend Constitution Article I.4) and moved the resolution, recommending rejection.

Original Text of Resolution:
(A112)
Resolved, the House of Deputies concurring, That Article I.4 be amended to read as follows:
...and not more than four Lay Persons, *confirmed* adult communicants of this Church, in good standing in the Diocese....

Motion defeated
Resolution rejected
(Communicated to the House of Deputies in HB Message #15)

The House of Bishops Committee on Constitution presented its Report #3 on Resolution A143 (Amend Constitution Article I.7) and moved adoption with amendment.

Original Text of Resolution:
(A143)
Resolved, the House of Deputies concurring, That Article I.7 of the Constitution be amended to read:
Section 7. The General Convention shall meet not less than once in each three years, at a time and place appointed by ~~a preceding Convention; but if there shall appear to the Presiding Bishop, acting with the advice and consent of the Executive Council of the Church or of a successor canonical body having substantially the powers now vested in the Executive Council, sufficient cause for changing the place or date so appointed, the Presiding Bishop, with the advice and consent of such body, shall appoint another place or date, or both, for such meeting.~~ *the Joint Standing Committee on Planning and Arrangements.* Special meetings may be provided for by Canon.

Committee Amendment:
Resolved, the House of Deputies concurring, That Article I.7 of the Constitution be amended to read:
Section 7. The General Convention shall meet not less than once in each three years, at a time and place appointed ~~by a preceding Convention; but if there shall appear to the Presiding Bishop, acting with the advice and consent of the Executive Council of the Church or of a successor canonical body having substantially the powers now vested in the Executive Council, sufficient cause for changing the~~

~~place or date so appointed, the Presiding Bishop, with the advice and consent of such body, shall appoint another place or date, or both, for such meeting.~~ *the Joint Standing Committee on Planning and Arrangements.* Special meetings may be provided for by Canon.
And be it further
Resolved, <u>That this resolution be sent within six months to the Secretary of the Convention of every Diocese to be made known to the Diocesan Convention at its next meeting.</u>

Motion carried
Resolution adopted with amendment
(Communicated to the House of Deputies in HB Message #16)

The House of Bishops Committee on Constitution presented its Report #4 on Resolution A039 (Amend Constitution Article II.2, First Reading) and moved adoption with amendment.

Original Text of Resolution:

(A039)
Resolved, the House of Deputies concurring, That the second sentence of Article II, Section 2 of the Constitution be amended to read as follows:
Section 2. ...But if the election shall have taken place within ~~three months next~~ *120 days* before the meeting of General Convention, the consent of the House of Deputies shall be required in place of that of a majority of the Standing Committees. No one shall be ordained and consecrated Bishop by fewer than three Bishops.

Committee Amendment:

Resolved,, the House of Deputies concurring, That the second sentence of Article II, Section 2 of the Constitution be amended to read as follows:
Section 2. No one shall be ordained and consecrated Bishop until the attainment of thirty years of age; nor without the consent of a majority of the Standing Committees of all the Dioceses, and the consent of a majority of the Bishops of this Church exercising jurisdiction. But if the election shall have taken place within ~~three months next~~ *120 days* before the meeting of General Convention, the consent of the House of Deputies shall be required in place of that of a majority of the Standing Committees. No one shall be ordained and consecrated Bishop by fewer than three Bishops.
And be it further
Resolved, <u>That this resolution be sent within six months to the Secretary of the Convention of every Diocese to be made known to the Diocesan Convention at its next meeting.</u>

Motion carried
Resolution adopted with amendment
(Communicated to the House of Deputies in HB Message #17)

Special Order of Business
Sandra Swan, Director of Episcopal Relief and Development Fund, addressed the House.

Erin Ferguson, Youth Representative from the Diocese of Southeast Florida, accompanied by other youth representatives, addressed the House.

Privilege and Courtesy
The Chair of the House of Bishops Committee on Privilege and Courtesy made a motion to grant seat and voice to the following bishops because of the Covenants Agreements between ECUSA and their Provinces adopted by the General Convention:

   The Most Rev. Martin Barahona, Primate of IARCA and Bishop of El Salvador
   The Rt. Rev. Mariniano Garcia, Acting Primate of Mexico
   The Rt. Rev. Armando Guerra, Bishop of Guatemala
   The Rt. Rev. Hector Monterroso, Bishop of Costa Rica
   The Rt. Rev. Julio Murray, Bishop of Panama
   The Rt. Rev. Edward Neufville, Bishop of Liberia
   The Rt. Rev. Carlos Touches-Porter, Bishop of Mexico

Motion carried
(Communicated to the House of Deputies in HB Message #18)

Committee on Canons
The House of Bishops Committee on Canons presented its Report #1 on Resolution A041 (Ratify Actions of Standing Commission on Liturgy and Music) and moved adoption.

Original Text of Resolution:
(A041)
Resolved, the House of Deputies concurring, That all actions taken by and in the name of the Standing Commission on Liturgy and Music since the adjournment *sine die* of the 72nd General Convention, be and the same hereby are ratified in all respects.

Motion carried
Resolution adopted
(Communicated to the House of Deputies in HB Message #19)

The House of Bishops Committee on Canons presented its Report #2 on Resolution A114 (Amend Canon I.2.5) and moved the resolution, recommending rejection.

Original Text of Resolution:
(A114)
Resolved, the House of Deputies concurring, That Canon I.2.5 be amended to read as follows:
The Presiding Bishop may appoint, as Chancellor to the Presiding Bishop, a*nconfirmed* adult communicant of the Church in good standing who is learned in both ecclesiastical and secular law....

Motion defeated
Resolution rejected
(Communicated to the House of Deputies in HB Message #20)

The House of Bishops Committee on Canons presented its Report #3 on Resolution A144 (Amend Canon I.1.14) and moved adoption.

Original Text of Resolution:
(A144)
Resolved, the House of Deputies concurring, That Canon I.1.14 be amended to read as follows:

(a) At each meeting of the General Convention the Joint Standing Committee on Planning and Arrangements shall submit to the General Convention its recommendations for sites for the meeting of the General Convention to be held as the ~~second~~ *third* succeeding General Convention following the General Convention at which the report is made. Approval of sites. In making such recommendations, the Committee shall certify to the Convention the willingness of the Dioceses within which recommended sites are located to have the General Convention meet within their jurisdictions.

(b) From the sites recommended by the Joint Committee, the General Convention shall approve no fewer than three nor more than five sites as possible for such meeting of the General Convention.

(c) From the sites approved by the General Convention, the Joint Committee, with the advice and consent of a majority vote of the following: The Presidents and the Vice-Presidents of both Houses of Convention, the Presidents of the Provinces and the Executive Council, shall determine the site for such General Convention and proceed to make all reasonable and necessary arrangements and commitments for that meeting of the General Convention. ~~The site shall be recommended before the meeting of the General Convention next preceding that Convention.~~

~~(d)~~ ~~Subject to the Constitution, the General Convention shall appoint a site at the General Convention next preceding such Convention.~~

(c)(d) Upon the final selection of and the arrangements for the site for that General Convention, the Joint Committee shall advise the Secretary of General Convention, who shall communicate the determination to the Dioceses.

(f) ~~In the event of a change of circumstances indicating the necessity or advisability of changing the site of a future meeting of the General Convention previously determined by action of the General Convention, the Joint Committee shall investigate and make recommendations to the Presiding Bishop, to the President of the House of Deputies, and to the Executive Council if such Convention is the next succeeding meeting or to the General Convention with respect to any later meeting of the Convention.~~

(g)(e) Within such guidelines as may have been established by the General Convention regarding the date and length of future General Conventions, and pursuant to the reasonable and necessary arrangements and commitments with the Dioceses and operators of facilities within the Diocese in which the next General Convention will be held, the Joint Committee shall fix the date and the length of the next succeeding Convention, report the same to the Secretary of the General Convention and include the same in its report to the Convention. In the event of a change of circumstances indicating the necessity or advisability of changing the date or length previously fixed, the Joint Committee shall investigate and make recommendations to the Presiding Bishop and the President of the House of Deputies, who, with the advice and consent of the Executive Council, may fix a different date or length or both.

Motion carried
Resolution adopted
(Communicated to the House of Deputies in HB Message #21)

The House of Bishops Committee on Canons presented its Report #4 on Resolution A049 (Amend Canon IV.2(A)(2)) and moved adoption.

Original Text of Resolution:
(A049)
Resolved, the House of Deputies concurring, That Canon IV.2(A)(2) be amended to read as follows:
Sec. 2. The Waiver and Voluntary Submission shall be evidenced by a written instrument, which shall contain: (i) the name of the Priest or Deacon, (ii) a reference to the Canon specifying the Offense, (iii) general information sufficient to identify the Offense, and (iv) a statement that the Priest or Deacon is aware of the Sentence to be imposed and the effect thereof, and shall be signed and Acknowledged by the Priest or Deacon, after opportunity to consult with and obtain advice from independent legal counsel of the Priest or Deacon's choosing. If the Priest or Deacon has so consulted with legal counsel, that counsel shall also be identified in the Waiver and Voluntary Submission. Legal counsel shall not be a

Chancellor, a Vice Chancellor, the Church Attorney or a Lay Assessor in that Diocese. The Waiver and Voluntary Submission may be withdrawn by the Priest or Deacon within three days of execution by the Priest or Deacon and thereafter shall be effective and irrevocable. The Church Attorney, each Complainant and Victim shall be given an opportunity to be heard *on the Sentence* by the Bishop who is to impose and pronounce Sentence prior to the execution of the Waiver and Voluntary Submission.

Motion carried
Resolution adopted
(Communicated to the House of Deputies in HB Message #22)

The House of Bishops Committee on Canons presented its Report #5 on Resolution A045 (Amend Canon I.17.2) and moved adoption.

Original Text of Resolution:
(A045)
Resolved, the House of Deputies concurring, That Canon I.17.2 be amended to read as follows:
(a) *All members of this Church who have received Holy Communion in this Church at least three times during the preceding year are to be considered communicants of this Church.*
(b) For the purposes of statistical consistency throughout the Church, communicants sixteen years of age and over are to be considered adult communicants.

Motion carried
Resolution adopted
(Communicated to the House of Deputies in HB Message #23)

The House of Bishops Committee on Canons presented its Report #6 on Resolution A050 (Amend Canon IV.2(B)(10)) and moved adoption.

Original Text of Resolution:
(A050)
Resolved, the House of Deputies concurring, That Canon IV.2(B)(10) be amended to read as follows:
Sec.10. The Waiver and Voluntary Submission shall be evidenced by a written instrument, which shall contain (i) the name of the Bishop, (ii) a reference to the Canon specifying the Offense, (iii) general information sufficient to identify the Offense, and (iv) a statement that the Bishop is aware of the Sentence to be imposed and the effect thereof, and shall be signed and Acknowledged by the Bishop, after opportunity to consult with and obtain advice from independent legal counsel of the Bishop's choosing. If the Bishop has so consulted with legal counsel, that counsel shall also be identified in the Waiver and Voluntary Submission. Legal counsel shall not be the Presiding Bishop's Chancellor. The Waiver and Voluntary Submission may be withdrawn by the Bishop within three days of execution by the

Bishop and thereafter shall be effective and irrevocable. The Church Attorney, each Complainant and Victim shall be given an opportunity to be heard *on the Sentence* by the Presiding Bishop who is to impose and pronounce Sentence prior to the execution of the Waiver and Voluntary Submission.

Motion carried
Resolution adopted
(Communicated to the House of Deputies in HB Message #24)

The House of Bishops Committee on World Mission presented its Report #1 on Resolution A152 (Episcopal Partnership for Global Mission) and moved adoption.

Original Text of Resolution:
(A152)
Resolved, the House of Deputies concurring, That the 74th General Convention commend the Executive Council of The Episcopal Church for its collaboration with the Episcopal Partnership for Global Mission (EPGM) and for its recognition of missionaries from EPGM agencies at its January 2003 meeting in the Dominican Republic.

Motion carried
Resolution adopted
(Communicated to the House of Deputies in HB Message #25)

RECESS

Following announcements by the Secretary, the House of Bishops Committee on Dispatch of Business moved that the House stand in recess until 11:00 a.m. on the Second Legislative Day.

Motion carried

The House recessed at 5:53 p.m. with prayer led by Chaplain Battle.

Appendix A
Day 1

Make-Up of the House of Bishops

Diocesan Bishops	100
Coadjutor Bishops	0
Suffragan Bishops	17
Presiding Bishop	1
Assistant Bishops	8
Assisting Bishops	3
Resigned Bishops	146
Resigned with Seat and Voice	2
Special Ministries	2
Total Membership	277

Note: A quorum is defined by Article 1, Section 2 of the Constitution as "a majority of all bishops entitled to vote (279), exclusive of bishops who have resigned their jurisdictions or positions (148)" Thus the present quorum is 75.

Appendix B
Day 1

House of Bishops Legislative Committees

01   **Dispatch of Business**
Price Jr., The Rt. Rev. Kenneth L., Chair (Southern Ohio, V)
Wright, The Rt. Rev. Wayne P., Vice-Chair (Delaware, III)
Chang, The Rt. Rev. Richard S.O., Secretary (Hawaii, VIII)
Johnson, The Rt. Rev. Don E. (West Tennessee, IV)

02   **Certification of Minutes**
Rabb, The Rt. Rev. John L., Chair (Maryland, III)
Bena, The Rt. Rev. David John (Albany, II)

03   **Rules of Order**
Herlong, The Rt. Rev. Bertram N., Chair (Tennessee, IV)
Price Jr., The Rt. Rev. Kenneth L., Vice-Chair (Southern Ohio, V)
Powell, The Rt. Rev. F. Neff, Secretary (Southwestern Virginia, III)
Chang, The Rt. Rev. Richard S.O. (Hawaii, VIII)

04   **Constitution**
Sauls, The Rt. Rev. Stacy F., Chair (Lexington, IV)
Lamb, The Rt. Rev. Jerry A. (Northern California, VIII)
Shand, The Rt. Rev. James J. (Easton, III)

05   **Canons**
Walker Jr., The Rt. Rev. Orris G., Chair (Long Island, II)
Henderson Jr., The Rt. Rev. Dorsey F. (Upper South Carolina, IV)
McKelvey, The Rt. Rev. Jack M. (Rochester, II)
Scantlebury, The Rt. Rev. Victor A. (Chicago, V)

06   **Structure**
Wimberly, The Rt. Rev. Don A., Chair (Texas, VII)
MacPherson, The Rt. Rev. D. Bruce, Vice-Chair (Western Louisiana, VII)
Whitmore, The Rt. Rev. Keith B., Secretary (Eau Claire, V)
Duncan, II, The Rt. Rev. Philip M. (Central Gulf Coast, IV)
Hughes, The Rt. Rev. Gethin B. (San Diego, VIII)
Shahan, The Rt. Rev. Robert R. (Arizona, VIII)

07   **Consecration of Bishops**
      Talton, The Rt. Rev. Chester L., Chair (Los Angeles, VIII)
      Bane Jr., The Rt. Rev. David C., Vice-Chair (Southern Virginia, III)
      Herzog, The Rt. Rev. Daniel W., Secretary (Albany, II)
      Knudsen, The Rt. Rev. Chilton R. (Maine, I)
      Lai, The Rt. Rev. David Jung-Hsin (Taiwan, VIII)
      Swing, The Rt. Rev. William E. (California, VIII)

08   **World Mission**
      Daniel, III, The Rt. Rev. Clifton, Chair (East Carolina, IV)
      Skilton, The Rt. Rev. William J., Vice-Chair (South Carolina, IV)
      Ramos-Orench, The Rt. Rev. Wilfrido, Secretary (Connecticut, I)
      Bena, The Rt. Rev. David John (Albany, II)
      Duncan Jr., The Rt. Rev. Robert W. (Pittsburgh, III)
      Duque Gómez, The Rt. Rev. Francisco (Colombia, IX)
      Fairfield, The Rt. Rev. Andrew H. (North Dakota, VI)
      Gray Jr., The Rt. Rev. Francis C. (Virginia, III)
      Wolf, The Rt. Rev. Geralyn (Rhode Island, I)

09   **National and International Concerns**
      Shaw III, SSJE, The Rt. Rev. M. Thomas, Chair (Massachusetts, I)
      Chane, The Rt. Rev. John B. (Washington, III)
      Charleston, The Rt. Rev. Steven (Massachusetts, I)
      Gloster, The Rt. Rev. J. Gary (North Carolina, IV)
      Lipscomb, The Rt. Rev. John B. (Southwest Florida, IV)
      MacDonald, The Rt. Rev. Mark L. (Alaska, VIII)
      Packard, The Rt. Rev. George E. (New York, II)
      Persell, The Rt. Rev. William D. (Chicago, V)
      Taylor, The Rt. Rev. E. Don (New York, II)
      vonRosenberg, The Rt. Rev. Charles G. (East Tennessee, IV)

10   **Social and Urban Affairs**
      Ihloff, The Rt. Rev. Robert W., Chair (Maryland, III)
      Adams III, The Rt. Rev. Gladstone B. (Central New York, II)
      Gallagher, The Rt. Rev. Carol Joy (Southern Virginia, III)
      MacDonald, The Rt. Rev. Mark L. (Alaska, VIII)
      Shimpfky, The Rt. Rev. Richard L. (El Camino Real, VIII)
      Sisk, The Rt. Rev. Mark S. (New York, II)
      Stanton, The Rt. Rev. James M. (Dallas, VII)

11	**Church in Small Communities**	

        Maze, The Rt. Rev. Larry E., Chair (Arkansas, VII)
        Caldwell, The Rt. Rev. Bruce, Vice-Chair (Wyoming, VI)
        Powell, The Rt. Rev. F. Neff, Secretary (Southwestern Virginia, III)
        Ely, The Rt. Rev. Thomas Clark (Vermont, I)
        Klusmeyer, The Rt. Rev. W. Michie (West Virginia, III)
        Plummer, The Rt. Rev. Steven T. (Navajoland Area Mission, VIII)

12   **Evangelism**

        Curry, The Rt. Rev. Michael Bruce, Chair (North Carolina, IV)
        Creighton, The Rt. Rev. Michael W., Vice-Chair (Central Pennsylvania, III)
        Ladehoff, The Rt. Rev. Robert L., Secretary (Oregon, VIII)
        Daniels, The Rt. Rev. Theodore A. (Virgin Islands, II)
        Garrison, The Rt. Rev. J. Michael (Western New York, II)
        Jenkins III, The Rt. Rev. Charles E. (Louisiana, IV)
        Smith, The Rt. Rev. George Wayne (Missouri, V)
        Winterrowd, The Rt. Rev. William J. (Colorado, VI)

13   **Prayer Book, Liturgy and Music**

        Louttit Jr., The Rt. Rev. Henry, Chair (Georgia, IV)
        Roskam, The Rt. Rev. Catherine S., Vice-Chair (New York, II)
        Howe, The Rt. Rev. Barry R., Secretary (West Missouri, VII)
        Alexander, The Rt. Rev. John Neil (Atlanta, IV)
        Cederholm Jr., The Rt. Rev. Roy Frederick (Massachusetts, I)
        Gibbs Jr., The Rt. Rev. Wendell N. (Michigan, V)
        Gregg, The Rt. Rev. William O. (Eastern Oregon, VIII)
        Ladehoff, The Rt. Rev. Robert L. (Oregon, VIII)
        Marshall, The Rt. Rev. Paul V. (Bethlehem, III)
        Schoefield, The Rt. Rev. John-David M., Secretary (San Joaquin, VIII)

14   **Ministry**

        Croneberger, The Rt. Rev. John P., Chair (Newark, II)
        Kelsey, The Rt. Rev. James A., Vice-Chair (Northern Michigan, V)
        Jefferts Schori, The Rt. Rev. Katharine, Secretary (Nevada, VIII)
        Gray III, The Rt. Rev. Duncan Montgomery (Mississippi, IV)
        Jecko, The Rt. Rev. Stephen H. (Florida, IV)
        Johnson, The Rt. Rev. Robert H. (Western North Carolina, IV)
        Leidel Jr., The Rt. Rev. Edwin M. (Eastern Michigan, V)
        Warner, The Rt. Rev. Vincent W. (Olympia, VIII)
        Waynick, The Rt. Rev. Catherine M. (Indianapolis, V)

15   **Education**
      Smalley, The Rt. Rev. William E., Chair (Kansas, VII)
      Hibbs, The Rt. Rev. Robert B., Vice-Chair (West Texas, VII)
      Adams Jr., The Rt. Rev. James M., Secretary (Western Kansas, VII)
      Anderson, The Rt. Rev. Craig B. (New Hampshire, I)
      Andrus, The Rt. Rev. Mark (Alabama, IV)
      Bainbridge III, The Rt. Rev. Harry B. (Idaho, VIII)
      Curry, The Rt. Rev. James Elliot (Connecticut, I)
      Irish, The Rt. Rev. Carolyn T. (Utah, VIII)
      Rabb, The Rt. Rev. John L. (Maryland, III)

16   **Church Pension Fund**
      Folts, The Rt. Rev. James E., Chair (West Texas, VII)
      Beckwith, The Rt. Rev. Peter H., Vice-Chair (Springfield, V)
      Michel, The Rt. Rev. Rodney R., Secretary (Long Island, II)
      Beckwith, Allen, The Rt. Rev. Lloyd (Honduras, IX)
      Moody, The Rt. Rev. Robert M. (Oklahoma, VII)

17   **Stewardship and Development**
      Scruton, The Rt. Rev. Gordon Paul, Chair (Western Massachusetts, I)
      Parsley Jr., The Rt. Rev. Henry N., Vice-Chair (Alabama, IV)
      Johnson, The Rt. Rev. Don E., Secretary (West Tennessee, IV)
      Bruno, The Rt. Rev. Joseph Jon (Los Angeles, VIII)
      Grew II, The Rt. Rev. J. Clark (Ohio, V)
      Thompson Jr., The Rt. Rev. Herbert (Southern Ohio, V)

18   **Ecumenical Relations**
      Gulick Jr., The Rt. Rev. Edwin F., Chair (Kentucky, IV)
      Theuner, The Rt. Rev. Douglas E., Vice-Chair (New Hampshire, I)
      Frade, The Rt. Rev. Leopold (Southeast Florida, IV)
      Robertson, The Rt. Rev. Creighton L. (South Dakota, VI)
      Rowley Jr., The Rt. Rev. Robert D. (Northwestern Pennsylvania, III)
      Scarfe, The Rt. Rev. Alan (Iowa, VI)
      Whalon, The Rt. Rev. Pierre (Churches in Europe, II)

19   **Communications**
      Jones, The Rt. Rev. David C., Chair (Virginia, III)
      Little II, The Rt. Rev. Edward S., Secretary (Northern Indiana, V)
      Harris, The Rt. Rev. Gayle E. (Massachusetts, I)
      Howe, The Rt. Rev. John W. (Central Florida, IV)
      Marshall, The Rt. Rev. Paul V. (Bethlehem, III)

20	**Miscellaneous Resolutions**	

20 **Miscellaneous Resolutions**
  Ottley, The Rt. Rev. James H., Chair (Southeast Florida, IV)
  Swing, The Rt. Rev. William E. (California, VIII)

21 **Privilege and Courtesy**
  Ottley, The Rt. Rev. James H., Chair (Southeast Florida, IV)
  Swing, The Rt. Rev. William E. (California, VIII)

22 **Committees and Commissions**
  Salmon Jr., The Rt. Rev. Edward L., Chair (South Carolina, IV)
  McKelvey, The Rt. Rev. Jack M., Vice-Chair (Rochester, II)
  Michel, The Rt. Rev. Rodney R., Secretary (Long Island, II)

25 **Program, Budget and Finance**
  Jacobus, The Rt. Rev. Russell E., Vice-Chair (Fond Du Lac, V)
  Bennison Jr., The Rt. Rev. Charles E. (Pennsylvania, III)
  Holguín, The Rt. Rev. Julio Cesar (Dominican Republic, IX)
  Joslin, The Rt. Rev. David B. (New Jersey, II)
  Krotz, The Rt. Rev. James E. (Nebraska, VI)
  Ohl Jr., The Rt. Rev. C. Wallis (Northwest Texas, VII)
  Smith, The Rt. Rev. Andrew D. (Connecticut, I)
  vonRosenberg, The Rt. Rev. Charles G. (East Tennessee, IV)
  Waggoner Jr., The Rt. Rev. James Edward (Spokane, VIII)

A **House of Bishops Pastoral Letter**
  Sisk, The Rt. Rev. Mark S., Chair (New York, II)
  Howe, The Rt. Rev. Barry R. (West Missouri, VII)
  Parsley Jr., The Rt. Rev. Henry N. (Alabama, IV)
  Waynick, The Rt. Rev. Catherine M. (Indianapolis, V)

B **House of Bishops Committee on Resignation of Bishops**
  Knudsen, The Rt. Rev. Chilton R., Chair (Maine, I)
  Sauls, The Rt. Rev. Stacy F., Vice-Chair (Lexington, IV)
  Powell, The Rt. Rev. F. Neff, Secretary (Southwestern Virginia, III)
  Duracin, The Rt. Rev. Jean Zaché, (Haiti, II)
  Ohl Jr., The Rt. Rev. C. Wallis (Northwest Texas, VII)
  Shahan, The Rt. Rev. Robert R. (Arizona, VIII)

C	**House of Bishops Committee on Religious Communities**
	Michel, The Rt. Rev. Rodney R., Chair (Long Island, II)
	Dyer, The Rt. Rev. J. Mark (Bethlehem, resigned, III)
	Henderson Jr., The Rt. Rev. Dorsey F. (Upper South Carolina, IV)
	Knudsen, The Rt. Rev. Chilton R. (Maine, I)
	Ladehoff, The Rt. Rev. Robert L. (Oregon, VIII)
	Lamb, The Rt. Rev. Jerry A. (Northern California, VIII)
	Roskam, The Rt. Rev. Catherine S. (New York, II)
D	**House of Bishops Committee on Nominations and Elections**
	Howe, The Rt. Rev. Barry R., Chair (West Missouri, VII)
	Jefferts Schori, The Rt. Rev. Katharine, Secretary (Nevada, VIII)
	Alard, The Rt. Rev. Leopoldo J. (Texas, VII)
	Salmon Jr., The Rt. Rev. Edward L. (South Carolina, IV)
	Taylor, The Rt. Rev. E. Don (New York, II)

MINNEAPOLIS MEETING   HOUSE OF BISHOPS

SECOND DAY

Thursday
July 31, 2003

MORNING SESSION

The House reconvened at 11:02 a.m. with the Presiding Bishop in the chair.

Official Acts
The Presiding Bishop laid official acts, by title, before the House. (See Appendix C–Day 2 for Official Acts of the Presiding Bishop)

Consecration of Bishops
The Presiding Bishop read HD Message #9 on Resolution C039 and HD Message #5 on Resolution C040 regarding consent for the consecrations of the Rev. George Edward Councell, Bishop-elect of the Diocese of New Jersey and the Rev. Joe Goodwin Burnett, Bishop-elect of the Diocese of Nebraska.

The House of Bishops Committee on Consecration of Bishops found all to be in order regarding these candidates. Ballot #1 on the consent to the consecration of the Rev. George Edward Councell, Bishop-elect of the Diocese of New Jersey, was taken and the resolution was moved.

Ballot #1 taken

Special Order of Business
The Most Rev. Michael G. Peers, Primate of the Anglican Church of Canada, addressed the House.
The Secretary asked for late arrivals to report at the end of the session.

Previous Day's Minutes
The House of Bishops Committee on Dispatch of Business moved to dispense with the reading of the previous day's minutes.

Motion carried

Introduction of Visiting Bishops
The Presiding Bishop welcomed the Most Rev. Ignacio Soliba, Primate of the Philippines, the Rt. Rev. Hector Monterroso, Bishop of Costa Rica, and the Rt. Rev. Armando Guerra, Bishop of Guatemala.

Messages from the House of Deputies
The Secretary announced that the following messages had been received from the House of Deputies.

HD Message #1:   A156 (2003 General Convention Daily Agenda)
The House of Deputies adopted the resolution with amendment.

HD Message #2:	A149 (Special Legislative Committees)
	The House of Deputies rejected the resolution with amendment.
HD Message #3:	Special Order for Election of President and Vice-President.
	The House of Deputies adopted the resolution.
HD Message #4:	A009 (Amend Canon I.4.2(b))
	The House of Deputies adopted the resolution.
HD Message #5:	C040 (Consent to the Election of the Rev. Joe Goodwin Burnett as Bishop of the Diocese of Nebraska)
	The House of Deputies adopted the resolution.
HD Message #6:	Special Order for Election of Trustees of the Church Pension Fund.
	The House of Deputies adopted the resolution.
HD Message #7:	A148 (Amend HDRO Article VI)
	The House of Deputies rejected the resolution.
HD Message #8:	A040 (Amend Canon I.1.2(n)(6))
	The House of Deputies adopted the resolution.
HD Message #9:	C039 (Consent to the Election of the Rev. George Edward Councell as Bishop of the Diocese of New Jersey)
	The House of Deputies adopted the resolution.
HD Message #10:	A008 (Repeal Mandatory Federal Sentencing Guidelines)
	The House of Deputies adopted the resolution with amendment.
HD Message #11:	A124 (Standing Commission on Health and a Staff Position in Health Care)
	The House of Deputies adopted the resolution with amendment.

Resignation of Bishops

The House of Bishops Committee on Resignation of Bishops presented its report.

    The Rt. Rev. Leopoldo J. Alard, Bishop Suffragan of Texas, August 11, 2003

    The Rt. Rev. Robert L. Ladehoff, Bishop of Oregon, September 20, 2003

    The Rt. Rev. Andrew H. Fairfield, Bishop of North Dakota, August 15, 2003

    The Rt. Rev. Alfred Clark Marble, Bishop of Mississippi, April 4, 2003

    The Rt. Rev. Theodore A. Daniels, Bishop of Virgin Islands, August 31, 2003

    The Rt. Rev. James E. Krotz, Bishop of Nebraska, September 1, 2003

    The Rt. Rev. Roger J. White, Bishop of Milwaukee, January 31, 2003

    The Rt. Rev. Claude E. Payne, Bishop of Texas, December 31, 2003

    The Rt. Rev. Robert B. Hibbs, Bishop Suffragan of West Texas, December 31, 2003

    The Rt. Rev. Robert H. Johnson, Bishop of Western North Carolina, October 1, 2004

    The Rt. Rev. William E. Smalley, Bishop of Kansas, January 1, 2004

    The Rt. Rev. Douglas Theuner, Bishop of New Hampshire, March 7, 2004

A motion was made to accept the report of the committee.

Motion carried
(Communicated to the House of Deputies in HB Message #26)

The Presiding Bishop yielded the chair to the Vice–Chair.

Noonday Prayers
Noonday prayers were led by Chaplain McIntosh.

Church in Small Communities
The House of Bishops Committee on Church in Small Communities presented its Report #1 on Resolution A133 (Adopt "Expanding Mission and Vitality in Small Congregations") and moved adoption with amendment.

Original Text of Resolution:
(A133)
Resolved, the House of Deputies concurring, That the 74th General Convention adopt "Expanding Mission and Vitality in Small Congregations: A Framework Affirming and Strengthening the Ministry of Small Churches" offered by the Standing Commission for Small Congregations; and be it further
Resolved, That the Office of Congregational Development and the Missioner for Rural and Small Communities be directed to print and distribute this document throughout The Episcopal Church.

Committee Amendment:
Resolved, the House of Deputies concurring, That the 74th General Convention adopt "Expanding Mission and Vitality in Small Congregations: A Framework Affirming and Strengthening the Ministry of Small Churches" offered by the Standing Commission for Small Congregations; and be it further
Resolved, That the Office of Congregational Development and the Missioner for Rural and Small Communities be directed to print, distribute *and promote* this document throughout The Episcopal Church.

Motion carried
Resolution adopted with amendment
(Communicated to the House of Deputies in HB Message #27)

Prayer Book, Liturgy and Church Music
The House of Bishops Committee on Prayer Book, Liturgy and Church Music presented its Report #1 on Resolution A091 (Continue Use of Enriching Our Worship 1 & 2) and moved adoption.

Original Text of Resolution:
(A091)
Resolved, the House of Deputies concurring, That the 74th General Convention authorize continuing use of *Enriching Our Worship Volume 1: The Daily Office, Great Litany, and Eucharist* and *Enriching Our Worship Volume 2: Ministry with the Sick and Dying, and Burial of a Child* during the 2004–2006 triennium, under the direction of the diocesan bishop or ecclesiastical authority.

Motion carried
Resolution adopted
(Communicated to the House of Deputies in HB Message #28)

The House of Bishops Committee on Prayer Book, Liturgy and Church Music presented its Report #2 on Resolution A093 (Approve Liturgical Calendar Commemorations) and moved adoption.

Original Text of Resolution:
(A093)
Resolved, the House of Deputies concurring, That the commemorations of Enmegahbowh, Florence Nightingale, and Philip the Deacon, proposed by the 73rd General Convention (Journal, page 473) and approved for trial use, be now finally approved and entered in the Calendar of the Church Year (Book of Common Prayer, pages 15–30).

Motion carried
Resolution adopted
(Communicated to the House of Deputies in HB Message #29)

The House of Bishops Committee on Prayer Book, Liturgy and Church Music presented its Report #3 on Resolution A094 (Church Year Calendar Inclusions) and moved adoption.

Original Text of Resolution:
(A094)
Resolved, the House of Deputies concurring, That the 74th General Convention propose additional commemorations for inclusion in the Calendar of the Church Year and authorize trial use thereof for the triennium 2004–2006, as follows:
February 17 - Janani Luwum, Archbishop of Uganda, and Martyr, 1977
November 6 - William Temple, Archbishop of Canterbury, 1944
November 22 - Clive Staples Lewis, Apologist and Spiritual Writer, 1963

Motion carried
Resolution adopted
(Communicated to the House of Deputies in HB Message #30)

MINNEAPOLIS MEETING   HOUSE OF BISHOPS

The House of Bishops Committee on Prayer Book, Liturgy and Church Music presented its Report #4 on Resolution A095 (Authorize Trial Use of Commemorations) and moved adoption.

Original Text of Resolution:
(A095)
Resolved, the House of Deputies concurring, That the 74th General Convention authorize, for trial use until the 2006 General Convention, the commemorations proposed by this Convention, with the following propers:

February 17
Janani Luwum Archbishop of Uganda, and Martyr, 1977
I. O God, whose Son the Good Shepherd laid down his life for the sheep: We give thee thanks for thy faithful shepherd, Janani Luwum, who after his Savior's example gave up his life for the people of Uganda. Grant us to be so inspired by his witness that we make no peace with oppression, but live as those who are sealed with the cross of Christ, who died and rose again, and now liveth and reigneth with thee and the Holy Spirit, one God, for ever and ever. *Amen.*
II. O God, whose Son the Good Shepherd laid down his life for the sheep: We give you thanks for your faithful shepherd, Janani Luwum, who after his Savior's example gave up his life for the people of Uganda. Grant us to be so inspired by his witness that we make no peace with oppression, but live as those who are sealed with the cross of Christ, who died and rose again, and now lives and reigns with you and the Holy Spirit, one God, for ever and ever. *Amen.*
Psalm - 119:41-48
Lesson - Ecclesiasticus 4:20-28
Gospel - John 12: 24-32
Preface of Holy Week

November 6
William Temple
Archbishop of Canterbury, 1944
I. O God of light and love, who illumined thy Church through the witness of thy servant William Temple: Inspire us, we pray, by his teaching and example, that we may rejoice with courage, confidence and faith in the Word made flesh, and may be led to establish that city which has justice for its foundation and love for its law; through Jesus Christ, the light of the world, who liveth and reigneth with thee and the Holy Spirit, one God, now and for ever. *Amen.*
II. O God of light and love, you illumined your Church through the witness of your servant William Temple: Inspire us, we pray, by his teaching and example, that we may rejoice with courage, confidence and faith in the Word made flesh, and may be led to establish that city which has justice for its foundation and love for its law; through Jesus Christ, the light of the world, who lives and reigns with you and the Holy Spirit, one God, now and for ever. *Amen.*
Psalm - 119: 97-104
Lesson - Ephesians 3:7-12
Gospel - John 1:9-18
Preface of the Epiphany

JOURNAL SECOND DAY

November 22
Clive Staples Lewis
Apologist and Spiritual Writer, 1963
I. O God of searing truth and surpassing beauty, we give thee thanks for Clive Staples Lewis whose sanctified imagination lighteth fires of faith in young and old alike; Surprise us also with thy joy and draw us into that new and abundant life which is ours in Christ Jesus, who liveth and reigneth with thee and the Holy Spirit, one God, now and for ever. *Amen.*
II. O God of searing truth and surpassing beauty, we give you thanks for Clive Staples Lewis whose sanctified imagination lights fires of faith in young and old alike; Surprise us also with your joy and draw us into that new and abundant life which is ours in Christ Jesus, who lives and reigns with you and the Holy Spirit, one God, now and for ever. *Amen.*
Psalm -139:1-9
Lesson - 1 Peter 1:3-9
Gospel - John 16:7-15
Preface of a Saint (3)

Motion carried
Resolution adopted
(Communicated to the House of Deputies in HB Message #31)

The House of Bishops Committee on Prayer Book, Liturgy and Church Music presented its Report #5 on Resolution A096 (Inclusion in the Church Year Calendar) and moved adoption.

Original Text of Resolution:
(A096)
Resolved, the House of Deputies concurring, That the 74th General Convention propose an additional commemoration for inclusion in the Calendar of the Church Year and authorize trial use thereof for the triennium 2004–2006, as follows:
September 22 - Philander Chase, Bishop of Ohio, and of Illinois, 1852

Motion carried
Resolution adopted
(Communicated to the House of Deputies in HB Message #32)

The House of Bishops Committee on Prayer Book, Liturgy and Church Music presented its Report #6 on Resolution A097 (Authorize Trial Use of Commemoration) and moved adoption.

Original Text of Resolution:
(A097)
Resolved, the House of Deputies concurring, That the 74th General Convention authorize, for trial use until the General Convention of 2006, the commemoration proposed by this Convention, with the following propers:

September 22
Philander Chase
Bishop of Ohio, and of Illinois, 1852
I. Almighty God, whose Son Jesus Christ is the pioneer and perfecter of our faith We give thee heartfelt thanks for the pioneering spirit of thy servant Philander Chase, and for his zeal in opening new frontiers for the ministry of thy Church. Grant us grace to minister in Christ's name in every place, led by bold witnesses to the Gospel of the Prince of Peace, even Jesus Christ our Lord, who liveth and reigneth with thee and the Holy Spirit, one God, for ever and ever. *Amen.*
II. Almighty God, whose Son Jesus Christ is the pioneer and perfecter of our faith: We give you heartfelt thanks for the pioneering spirit of your servant Philander Chase, and for his zeal in opening new frontiers for the ministry of your Church. Grant us grace to minister in Christ's name in every place, led by bold witnesses to the Gospel of the Prince of Peace, Jesus Christ our Lord, who lives and reigns with you and the Holy Spirit, one God, for ever and ever. *Amen.*
Psalm -108:1-6 or 16:5-11
Lesson-Isaiah 44:1-6, 8
Gospel-Luke 9:1-6
Preface of a Saint(1)

Motion carried
Resolution adopted
(Communicated to the House of Deputies in HB Message #33)

The House of Bishops Committee on Prayer Book, Liturgy and Church Music presented its Report #7 on Resolution C010 (Liturgical Commemoration of King Charles the Martyr) and moved the resolution, recommending rejection.

Original Text of Resolution:
(C010)
Resolved, the House of Deputies concurring, That The Episcopal Church commemorate on 30 January the life and ministry of Charles I, King of England and Scotland, adding his name to the Liturgical Calendar; and be it further
Resolved, That his name be included in the next and subsequent volumes of *Lesser Feasts and Fasts* along with appropriate collects, scripture readings, and commentary on his life and ministry.

Motion defeated
Resolution rejected
(Communicated to the House of Deputies in HB Message #34)

The House of Bishops Committee on Prayer Book, Liturgy and Church Music presented its Report #8 on Resolution C009 (Liturgical Commemoration of Tikhon, Russian Orthodox Bishop of Alaska and North America) and moved to refer the resolution to the Standing Commission on Liturgy and Music.

Original Text of Resolution:
(C009)
Resolved, the House of Deputies concurring, That Tikhon be added to *Lesser Feasts and Fasts*; and be it further
Resolved, That since he served faithfully as Russian Orthodox Bishop of Alaska and California and then Bishop of New York, as a close friend of The Episcopal Church, and finally as Patriarch of Moscow, the Diocese of New York petition the Standing Commission on Liturgy and Music to move a resolution to the General Convention of 2003 commemorating Tikhon on April 7th in The Episcopal Church's *Lesser Feasts and Fasts* and the calendar of the Book of Common Prayer.

Motion carried
Resolution referred to a Standing Commission
(Communicated to the House of Deputies in HB Message #35)

The House of Bishops Committee on Prayer Book, Liturgy and Church Music presented its Report #9 on Resolution C013 (Liturgical Commemoration of The Rev. Dr. John Roberts) and moved to refer the resolution to the Standing Commission on Liturgy and Music.

Original Text of Resolution:
(C013)
Resolved, the House of Deputies concurring, That the 74th General Convention direct the Standing Commission on Liturgy and Music to add the Rev. Dr. John Roberts, (born March 31, 1853) Missionary to the Wind River Indian Reservation and western Wyoming, pastor and teacher, founder of the Shoshone Episcopal Mission, churches on the Wind River Reservation and surrounding area, to the Calendar of Lesser Feasts and Fasts, with appropriate Propers and biographical materials.

Motion carried
Resolution referred to a Standing Commission
(Communicated to the House of Deputies in HB Message #36)

Ministry
The House of Bishops Committee on Ministry presented its Report #1 on Resolution A119 (Role of Deacons) and moved adoption with amendment.

Original Text of Resolution:
(A119)
Resolved, the House of Deputies concurring, That the Standing Commission on Ministry Development in consultation with the North American Association of the Diaconate will continue the study of the role of deacons in the councils of the church, in the dioceses and in congregations. A report on this work will be submitted to the 75th General Convention.

Committee Amendment:
Resolved, the House of Deputies concurring, That the Standing Commission on Ministry Development in consultation *with the dioceses of the church and* the North American Association of the Diaconate will continue the study of the role of deacons in the councils of the church, in the dioceses and in congregations. A report on this work will be submitted to the 75th General Convention.

Motion carried
Resolution adopted with amendment
(Communicated to the House of Deputies in HB Message #37)

The House of Bishops Committee on Ministry presented its Report #2 on Resolution A121 (Clergy and Lay Professional Continuing Education) and moved adoption with amendment.

Original Text of Resolution:
(A121)
Resolved, the House of Deputies concurring, That the 74th General Convention direct each Diocese to develop a plan and make provisions for the continuing education of all clergy and lay professionals in its jurisdiction, such plan and its progress to be reported annually to the Standing Commission on Ministry Development; and be it further
Resolved, That dioceses that do not have continuing education policies or programs be urged to participate in a pilot program for the development of a diocesan continuing education policy and program sponsored by the Office for Ministry Development and Miller and Associates; and be it further
Resolved, That the 74th General Convention authorize $46,000 to support the participation of up to 20 dioceses in the above mentioned pilot program.

Committee Amendment:
Resolved, the House of Deputies concurring, That the 74th General Convention *encourage* ~~direct~~ each Diocese to develop a plan and make provisions for the continuing education of all clergy and lay professionals in its jurisdiction, such plan and its progress to be reported annually to the Standing Commission on Ministry Development; and be it further
Resolved, That dioceses that do not have continuing education policies or programs be urged to participate in a pilot program for the development of a diocesan continuing education policy and program sponsored by the Office for Ministry Development ~~and Miller and Associates~~; and be it further
Resolved, That the 74th General Convention ~~authorize $46,000 to support the participation of up to 20 dioceses in the above mentioned pilot program.~~ request the Joint Standing Committee on Program, Budget and Finance to consider a budget allocation of $46,000 for implementation of this resolution.

JOURNAL SECOND DAY

The Bishop of Rhode Island moved to amend the resolution.

Proposed Amendment:
Delete "the 74th General Convention direct" and substitute "that each diocese develop a plan and make provisions for."

Motion defeated
Amendment defeated

The Bishop of Ohio moved to amend the resolution.

Proposed Amendment:
Delete the second resolve.

Motion defeated
Amendment defeated

A vote was taken on Resolution A121 as amended.

Motion carried
Resolution adopted with amendment
(Communicated to the House of Deputies in HB Message #38)

Recess

Following announcements by the Secretary, the House of Bishops Committee on Dispatch of Business moved that the House stand in recess until 3:45 p.m.
The House recessed at 12:35 p.m. with prayers led by Chaplain McIntosh.

AFTERNOON SESSION

The House was reconvened by the Vice-Chair at 3:45 p.m
Thirty minutes was allowed for reflection by the Chaplain and conversation.
The House resumed at 4:17 p.m.

Consecration of Bishops

The House of Bishops Committee on Consecration of Bishops read the results of Ballot #1 on the consent to the consecration of Bishop-elect Councell of the Diocese of New Jersey. Of 106 bishops with jurisdiction, 99 have given consent.

The House concurred
(Communicated to the House of Deputies in HB Message #51)

The House of Bishops Committee on Consecration of Bishops moved the resolution for the consent to the consecration of the Rev. Joe Goodwin Burnett, Bishop-elect of the Diocese of Nebraska, and Ballot #2 was taken.

Ballot #2 taken

Ministry

The House of Bishops Committee on Ministry presented its Report #3 on Resolution A060 (Contemporary Language Competency) and moved adoption of a substitute.

Original Text of Resolution:
(A060)
Resolved, the House of Deputies concurring, That the 74th General Convention direct the Standing Commission on Ministry Development to prepare revisions of the ordination canons to require competency in a contemporary language other than English or a culture other than the candidate's native culture, and require intercultural field education experience of all candidates.

Committee Substitute:
Resolved, the House of Deputies concurring, That the 74th General Convention recommend that all dioceses strongly encourage those preparing for ordination to study a contemporary language other than their native language and to participate in an intentional cross-cultural program.

The Bishop of East Carolina moved to amend the substitute resolution.

Proposed Amendment:
Replace "strongly encourage" with "urge."

Motion carried
Amendment adopted

The Bishop of Connecticut moved to return to the original resolution with a friendly amendment.

Proposed Amendment:
Replace the Committee substitute with the original text of the resolution. Insert "the study of a contemporary language other than their native language" and delete "competency in a contemporary language other than English" in the original text.

The question was called to terminate debate.

Motion carried
Debate terminated

A vote was taken on Resolution A060 as amended.

Motion carried
Resolution adopted with amendment
(Communicated to the House of Deputies in HB message #39)

Ecumenical Relations

The House of Bishops Committee on Ecumenical Relations presented its Report #1 on Resolution C031 (Waging Reconciliation) and moved adoption.

Original Text of Resolution:
(C031)
Resolved, the House of Deputies concurring, That the General Convention of The Episcopal Church speak out for an end to all forms of religious persecution and war by instituting, recognizing, supporting, and encouraging the yearly celebration of interfaith worship services (like the World Sabbath of Religious Reconciliation) in all communities across America and around the world.

The Bishop of Northern Indiana moved to refer the resolution to the Standing Commission on Ecumenical Relations.

Motion defeated
Referral defeated

A vote was taken on Resolution C031.

Motion carried
Resolution adopted
(Communicated to the House of Deputies in HB Message #40)

The House of Bishops Committee on Ecumenical Relations presented its Report #2 on Resolution A085 (ELCA Member Reception) and moved adoption.

Original Text of Resolution:
(A085)
Resolved, the House of Deputies concurring, That the rubrics concerning Confirmation with forms for Reception and the Reaffirmation of Baptismal Vows (BCP, 412) allow such reception of members of the Evangelical Lutheran Church in America.

The Bishop of Atlanta moved to amend the resolution.

Proposed Amendment:
Add "that the Canons on Church Membership (Title I, Can. 17) allows such reception of members of the ELCA" and delete "that the rubrics concerning Confirmation with forms for Reception and the Reaffirmation of Baptismal Vows (BCP, 412).

Motion carried
Amendment adopted

The Bishop of Virginia moved to amend the amended resolution.

Proposed Amendment:
At the end, add "who have made a mature public affirmation of faith" and delete "such."

The question was called to terminate debate.

Motion carried
Debate terminated

MINNEAPOLIS MEETING   HOUSE OF BISHOPS

A vote was taken on the proposed amendment.

Motion carried
Amendment adopted

The Bishop of New Hampshire moved to table the resolution.

Motion defeated

The Bishop of Southwest Florida moved to table the resolution to a time certain when the Committee on Theology brings its report on confirmation.

Motion carried
Consideration postponed

[Consideration of Resolution A085 resumed on Day 3. See Page 117. *Ed.*]

The House of Bishops Committee on Ecumenical Relations presented its Report #3 on Resolution A090 (Christian-Muslim Dialogue) and moved adoption with amendment.

Original Text of Resolution:
(A090)
Resolved, the House of Deputies concurring, That the 74th General Convention reaffirm Resolution 1997-D069 on "Substantive Dialogue Between Christian and Muslim Communities," which calls for a "dialogue that maintains the theological integrity of both faith communities and commitment to genuine human rights and religious freedom as affirmed by the 71st General Convention (1994-D015);" and be it further

Resolved, That the General Convention direct current and future ECUSA efforts at Christian-Muslim dialogue and education to embody and strengthen that resolution's commitments to dialogue founded on "genuine human rights and religious freedom," as embodied in the United Nations Declaration on Human Rights (1948), Article 18, which states that "everyone has the right to freedom of thought, conscience, and religion; this right includes freedom to change his religion or belief, and freedom, either alone or in community with others and in public or private, to manifest his religion or belief in teaching, practice, worship, and observance;" and be it further

Resolved, That the General Convention direct that such efforts strengthen the peaceful and secure religious witness of other Christians around the world in their ministry among Muslim neighbors, particularly in areas of experienced religious oppression.

Committee Amendment:
Resolved, the House of Deputies concurring, That the 74th General Convention reaffirm Resolution 1997-D069 on "Substantive Dialogue Between Christian and Muslim Communities," which calls for a "dialogue that maintains the theological integrity of both faith communities and commitment to genuine human rights and religious freedom as affirmed by the 71st General Convention (1994-D015);" and be it further

Resolved, That the General Convention direct current and future ECUSA efforts at

Christian-Muslim dialogue and education to embody and strengthen that resolution's commitments to dialogue, *in cooperation with other Christian bodies*, founded on "genuine human rights and religious freedom," as embodied in the United Nations Declaration on Human Rights (1948), Article 18, which states that "everyone has the right to freedom of thought, conscience, and religion; this right includes freedom to change his religion or belief, and freedom, either alone or in community with others and in public or private, to manifest his religion or belief in teaching, practice, worship, and observance;" and be it further
Resolved, That the General Convention direct that such efforts strengthen the peaceful and secure religious witness of other Christians around the world in their ministry among Muslim neighbors, particularly in areas of experienced religious oppression.

Motion carried
Resolution adopted with amendment
(Communicated to the House of Deputies in HB Message #41)

Canons

The House of Bishops Committee on Canons presented its Report #7 on Resolution A046 (Amend Canon III.22.1(e)) and moved adoption with amendment.

Original Text of Resolution:
(A046)
Resolved, the House of Deputies concurring, That Canon III.22.1(e) be amended as follows:

(e) The Secretary of the *body* (Convention) electing a Bishop Diocesan, Bishop Coadjutor, or Bishop Suffragan, shall inform the Presiding Bishop promptly of the name of the person elected. It shall be the duty of the Bishop-elect to notify the Presiding Bishop of his acceptance or declination of the election, at the same time as the Bishop-elect notifies the electing diocese.

Committee Amendment:
Resolved, the House of Deputies concurring, That Canon III.22.1(e) be amended as follows:

(e) The Secretary of the *body* ~~(Convention)~~ electing a Bishop Diocesan, Bishop Coadjutor, or Bishop Suffragan, shall inform the Presiding Bishop promptly of the name of the person elected. It shall be the duty of the Bishop-elect to notify the Presiding Bishop of his acceptance or declination of the election, at the same time as the Bishop-elect notifies the electing diocese.

The Bishop of Northwest Texas moved to amend the resolution.

Proposed Amendment:
Delete "his."

MINNEAPOLIS MEETING　　　　　　　HOUSE OF BISHOPS

A vote was taken on the amendment.

Motion carried
Amendment adopted

A vote was taken on Resolution A046 as amended.

Motion carried
Resolution adopted with amendment
(Communicated to the House of Deputies in HB Message #42)

The House of Bishops Committee on Canons presented its Report #8 on Resolution A048 (Amend Canon IV.4.16(d)) and moved adoption of a substitute.

Original Text of Resolution:
(A048)
Resolved, the House of Deputies concurring, That Canon IV.4.16(d) be amended to read as follows:
(d) If the Respondent fails or refuses to answer or otherwise enter an appearance, except for reasonable cause to be allowed by the Court, the Church Attorney may, no sooner than thirty days after the answer is due, move for Summary Judgment of Offense in accordance with the Rules of Procedure. If the motion is granted *the Bishop shall be notified, and* the Respondent shall be given notice that Sentence of Admonition, Suspension or Deposition will be adjudged and pronounced by the ~~Court~~ *Bishop* at the expiration of thirty days after the date of the Notice of Sentence, or at such convenient time thereafter as the ~~Court~~ *Bishop* shall determine....

Committee Substitute:
Resolved, the House of Deputies concurring, That Canon IV.4.16(d) be amended to read as follows:
(d) If the Respondent fails or refuses to answer or otherwise enter an appearance, except for reasonable cause to be allowed by the Court, the Church Attorney may, no sooner than thirty days after the answer is due, move for Summary Judgment of Offense in accordance with the Rules of Procedure. If the motion is granted *the Bishop shall be notified, and* the Respondent shall be given notice that Sentence of Admonition, Suspension or Deposition will be adjudged *by the Court* and pronounced by the ~~Court~~ *Bishop* at the expiration of thirty days after the Notice of Sentence, or at such convenient time thereafter as the ~~Court~~ *Bishop* shall determine. Sentence of Admonition, Suspension or of Deposition from the Ordained Ministry may, thereafter, be adjudged *by the Court* and pronounced by the ~~Court~~ *Bishop*.

Motion carried
Substitute resolution adopted
(Communicated to the House of Deputies in HB Message #43)

Prayer Book, Liturgy and Church Music
The Committee on Prayer Book, Liturgy and Church Music presented its Report #11 on Resolution A098 (Church Year Calendar Inclusion) and moved adoption.

Original Text of Resolution:
(A098)
Resolved, the House of Deputies concurring, That the 74th General Convention propose an additional commemoration for inclusion in the Calendar of the Church Year and authorize trial use for the triennium 2004–2006, as follows:
January 24 - Ordination of Florence Li Tim-Oi, First Woman Priest in the Anglican Communion, 1944

Motion carried
Resolution adopted
(Communicated to the House of Deputies in HB Message #44)

The House of Bishops Committee on Prayer Book, Liturgy and Church Music presented its Report #10 on Resolution A099 (Authorize Trial Use of Commemoration) and moved adoption.

Original Text of Resolution:
(A099)
Resolved, the House of Deputies concurring, That the 74th General Convention authorize, for trial use until the General Convention of 2006, the above-listed commemoration proposed by this Convention, with the following propers:
January 24
Ordination of Florence Li Tim-Oi
First Woman Priest in the Anglican Communion, 1944
I. Gracious God, we thank thee for calling Florence Li Tim-Oi, much-beloved daughter, to be the first woman to exercise the office of a priest in our Communion; By the grace of thy Spirit inspire us to follow her example, serving thy people with patience and happiness all our days, and witnessing in every circumstance to our Savior Jesus Christ, who liveth and reigneth with thee and the same Spirit, one God, for ever and ever. *Amen.*
II. Gracious God, we thank you for calling Florence Li Tim-Oi, much-beloved daughter, to be the first woman to exercise the office of a priest in our Communion; By the grace of your Spirit inspire us to follow her example, serving your people with patience and happiness all our days, and witnessing in every circumstance to our Savior Jesus Christ, who lives and reigns with you and the same Spirit, one God, for ever and ever. *Amen.*
Psalm - 116:1-2
Lesson - Galatians 3:23-28
Gospel - Luke 10:1-9
Preface of a Saint(2)

Motion carried
Resolution adopted
(Communicated to the House of Deputies in HB Message #45)

Ministry
The House of Bishops Committee on Ministry presented its Report #4 on Resolution A064 (Seminarian Expenses) and moved adoption of a substitute.

Original Text of Resolution:
(A064)
Resolved, the House of Deputies concurring, That The Episcopal Church as a national body move towards paying for seminarians' expenses in preparation for ministry; and be it further
Resolved, That the Church Pension Fund be urged to examine the feasibility of a program to underwrite the loan costs for seminarians of the church exploring such possibilities as:
> determining the feasibility of amortizing seminary loan payments over the course of a cleric's career;
> including seminary debt in the pension premium of parochial/institutional clergy, distributed over the course of a cleric's career; and be it further

Resolved, That dioceses and congregations commit a greater proportion of income to the support of candidates preparing for ordination and lay professionals; and be it further
Resolved, That The Episcopal Church seek funding support for the debt reduction of newly ordained persons who serve in priority mission areas that are under-served and under-funded, including new church plants, multi-cultural and specialized cultural ministries and rural areas; and be it further
Resolved, That The Episcopal Church encourage the development of a fund to defray the educational expenses of seminarians through a partnership with the Episcopal Church Foundation, Society for the Increase of the Ministry, Episcopal Evangelical Education Society, and the Church Pension Fund.

Committee Substitute:
Resolved, the House of Deputies concurring, That the 74th General Convention direct the Standing Commission on Ministry Development to convene a partnership including members from the Church Pension Fund, the Episcopal Church Foundation, the Society for the Increase of the Ministry, the Episcopal Evangelical Education Society, the Council of Seminary Deans, and any other appropriate groups to address the urgent issue of seminarian debt and report back to the 75th General Convention with recommendations. This committee will include in its consideration the following points:
> determining the feasibility of amortizing seminary loan payments over the course of a cleric's career;
> including seminarian debt in the pension premium of parochial/institutional clergy, distributed over the course of a cleric's career;
> dioceses and congregations committing a greater proportion of income to the support of people preparing for ordination and lay professions;
> seeking funding support for the debt reduction of newly ordained persons who serve in priority mission areas that are under-served and under-funded, including new church plants, multicultural and specialized cultural ministries

and rural areas; and

the development of a fund to defray the educational expenses of seminarians through partnerships.

Motion carried
Substitute resolution adopted
(Communicated to the House of Deputies in HB Message #46)

Education

The House of Bishops Committee on Education presented its Report #1 on Resolution A038 (Peace and Justice Studies and Training) and moved adoption.

Original Text of Resolution:
(A038)
Resolved, the House of Deputies concurring, That the 74th General Convention of The Episcopal Church commend to Episcopal colleges and schools the inclusion in their curriculum of peace and justice studies and education and training for service and careers in non-governmental organizations and civil society.

Motion carried
Resolution adopted
(Communicated to the House of Deputies in HB Message #47)

The House of Bishops Committee on Education presented its Report #2 on Resolution A007 (Aging Task Force) and moved adoption with amendment.

Original Text of Resolution:
(A007)
Resolved, the House of Deputies concurring, That the 74th General Convention authorize the creation of a six-person Task Force of the Executive Council, coordinated through the Office of Ministry Development and the Office of the Bishop of the Armed Services, Health Care and Prison Ministries, to assess ministry opportunities with and for an aging population both within and outside the church; and be it further
Resolved, That $10,000 be allocated for this purpose.

Committee Amendment:
Resolved, the House of Deputies concurring, That the 74th General Convention authorize the creation of a six-person Task Force of the Executive Council, coordinated through the Office of Ministry Development and the Office of the Bishop of the Armed Services, Health Care and Prison Ministries, to assess ministry opportunities with and for an aging population both within and outside the church; and be it further
Resolved, That ~~$10,000 be allocated for this purpose.~~ *the General Convention request the Joint Standing Committee on Program, Budget and Finance to consider a budget allocation of $10,000 for implementation of this resolution.*

A friendly amendment was moved to delete the words "and the Office of the Bishop of the Armed Services, Health Care and Prison Ministries."
Amendment adopted
A vote was taken on Resolution A007 as amended.
Motion carried
Resolution adopted with amendment
(Communicated to the House of Deputies in HB Message #48)

The House of Bishops Committee on Education presented its Report #3 on Resolution A013 (The Church's Role in Counseling and Education on Biomedical Ethics) and moved adoption with amendment.

Original Text of Resolution:
(A013)
Resolved, the House of Deputies concurring, That the 74th General Convention, recognizing the changing world in which we live, continue a program of sustained study in bioethics to inform and educate members of congregations and clergy about the expanding range of issues and choices they and their children will face throughout life. To this end, we commend study of "A Christian Response to our New Genetic Powers;" and be it further
Resolved,, That the Church:
- Call on provinces and dioceses to work with congregations to encourage local education and to provide resource teams.
- Devise a way to sustain initiative and development of expertise in biomedical ethics in the national church through the continued work of an Executive Council Task Force with a budget of $36,000 for the triennium.
- Stress the importance of basic education about science and biomedicine among the people of God and encourage and support the teaching of biomedical ethics in its seminaries.
- Commit itself to ecumenical and interfaith discussion of questions of biomedical ethics and be prepared to join with other groups in such interfaith educational ventures.

Committee Amendment:
Resolved, the House of Deputies concurring, That the 74th General Convention, recognizing the changing world in which we live, continue a program of sustained study in bioethics to inform and educate members of congregations and clergy about the expanding range of issues and choices they and their children will face throughout life. To this end, we commend study of "A Christian Response to ~~our~~ *the* New Genetic*s* ~~Powers~~;" and be it further
Resolved, That the Church:
- Call on provinces and dioceses to work with congregations to encourage local education and to provide resource teams.
- Devise a way to sustain initiative and development of expertise in biomedical ethics in the national church through the *continuation* ~~continued work~~ of an

Executive Council Task Force *on Ethics and New Genetics* ~~with a budget of $36,000 for the triennium.~~

Stress the importance of basic education about science and biomedicine among the people of God and encourage and support the teaching of biomedical ethics in its seminaries.

Commit itself to ecumenical and interfaith discussion of questions of biomedical ethics and be prepared to join with other groups in such interfaith educational ventures; and be it further

Resolved, That the General Convention request the Joint Standing Committee on Program, Budget and Finance to consider a budget allocation of $36,000 for implementation of this resolution.

The Committee agreed to a friendly amendment from the floor to amend their report by deleting the words "Ethics and" in the name of the task force.

Motion carried
Resolution adopted with amendment
(Communicated to the House of Deputies in HB Message #49)

The House of Bishops Committee on Education presented its Report #4 on Resolution A030 (21st Century Survey Resources) and moved adoption with amendment.

Original Text of Resolution:
(A030)

Resolved, the House of Deputies concurring, That the 74th General Convention direct the Episcopal Church Center staff to use data from the 21st Century Survey and other sources to develop educational resources on issues of violence, poverty, justice, and inclusion, particularly as these issues pertain to women; and be it further

Resolved, That $8,000 be allocated from the Program Budget for this work.

Committee Amendment:

Resolved, the House of Deputies concurring, That the 74th General Convention direct the Episcopal Church Center staff to use data from the 21st Century Survey and other sources to develop educational resources *on the church's responses* to issues of violence, poverty, *in*justice, and *exclusion* ~~inclusion~~, particularly as these issues pertain to women; and be it further

Resolved, That *the General Convention request the Joint Standing Committee on Program, Budget and Finance to consider a budget of* $8,000 ~~be allocated from the Program Budget~~ *for implementation of this resolution's work.*

Motion carried
Resolution adopted with amendment
(Communicated to the House of Deputies in HB Message #50)

The House of Bishops Committee on Education presented its Report #5 on Resolution A029 (Open Dialogue on Difficult Issues) and moved adoption with amendment.
A motion was made to table the resolution until the following day.
Motion carried
Consideration postponed

Dispatch of Business
The House of Bishops Committee on Dispatch of Business reminded committee chairs to get committee reports in early in the day.

Procedures
The Chair reminded the House of procedures for bringing messages to bishops on the floor via pages.

Consecration of Bishops
The House of Bishops Committee on Consecration of Bishops read the results of Ballot #2 for the consent to the consecration of Bishop-elect Burnett of the Diocese of Nebraska. Of the 106 bishops with jurisdiction, 102 have given consent.
The House concurred
(Communicated to the House of Deputies in HB Message #52)

Recess
Following announcements by the Secretary, the House of Bishops Committee on Dispatch of Business moved that the House stand in recess until 2:30 p.m. on the Third Legislative Day.
Motion carried

The House recessed at 5:52 p.m. with prayers led by Chaplin McIntosh.

Appendix C
Day Two

Official Acts of the Presiding Bishop

CONSECRATIONS
William Otis Gregg, Bishop of Eastern Oregon
    September 23, 2000
Don Edward Johnson, Bishop of West Tennessee
    June 30, 2001
John Neil Alexander, Bishop of Atlanta
    July 7, 2001
Francisco Jose Duque, Bishop Coadjutor of Columbia
    July 14, 2001
William Michie Klusmeyer, Bishop of West Virginia
    October 13, 2001
Pierre Welte Whalon, Bishop Suffragan in charge of the
    Convocation of American Churches in Europe
    November 18, 2001
Mark Handley Andrus, Bishop Suffragan of Alabama
    February 7, 2002
John Byson Chane, Bishop of Washington DC
    June 1, 2002

CONFIRMATIONS, RECEPTIONS, AND REAFFIRMATIONS
The Church of St. Luke in-the-Fields *Easter Vigil*
    March 30, 2002

CONFIRMATIONS
   Matthew Vaughan Barton
   Philip Andrew Calkins
   Sally Harper Swigert Hamilton
   Jerry W. James
   Grant Michael Paul Nichols
   Gordon Travers
   Elizabeth Louise Ward
   Matthew Blake Whitenack

RECEPTION
   Reynaldo Alonso
   Mary Margaret Collins
   Charles Arthur Keenan, Jr.
   Alicia Ann Mathewson
   Stephen E. Novak
   Kevin Joseph Reilly

Kimberly Anne Stein
Lathleen Yaccarino

REAFFIRMATIONS
William D. Hawkins
Alexander Wishart Tooker III
Evelyn Childress Wellons

INHIBITION
Signed by Presiding Bishop against The Rt. Rev. Charles I. Jones
July 30, 2002

BAPTISMS
St. John's Church, Cold Spring Harbor, NY
September 8, 2002
Isabelle Lydia Grace
Hannah Catherine Quinn

WEDDING
St. Ann's Episcopal Church, Bridgehampton, New York
September 14, 2002
Daphne Lynch
Jason Firfield

CONFIRMATIONS
Church of the Transfiguration, New York, New York
January 19, 2003
Amelia Ramroop
Scott Quentin Roberts

THIRD DAY

Friday
August 1, 2003

AFTERNOON SESSION

The House reconvened at 2:30 p.m. with the Presiding Bishop in the chair. Thirty minutes was allowed for reflections by the Chaplain and conversation. The House resumed at 3:00 p.m.

Agenda of the Day
The House of Bishops Committee on Dispatch of Business moved to adopt the agenda of the day.

Motion carried
Agenda adopted

Late Arrivals
The Secretary informed the House of nine additional late arrivals.

Previous Day's Minutes
The House of Bishops Committee on Dispatch of Business moved to dispense with the reading of the previous day's minutes.

Motion carried

Consecration of Bishops
The Presiding Bishop read HD Message #18 on C041 and HD Message #19 on C042 regarding consent for the consecrations of the Rev. Samuel Johnson Howard, Bishop Coadjutor-elect of the Diocese of Florida, and the Rev. C. Franklin Brookhart, Jr., Bishop-elect of the Diocese of Montana.

The House of Bishops Committee on Consecration of Bishops found all to be in order regarding these candidates. Ballot #3 was taken on the consent to the consecration of the Rev. Samuel Johnson Howard, Bishop Coadjutor-elect of the Diocese of Florida and the resolution was moved.

Ballot #3 taken

Messages from the House of Deputies
The Secretary announced that the following messages had been received from the House of Deputies.

HD Message #12:	Special Order for Election of Trustees of Church Pension Fund.
	The House of Deputies adopted the resolution.
HD Message #13:	A148 (Amend HDRO Article VI)
	The House of Deputies rejected the resolution.

HD Message #14:	[Duplicate of HD Message #7. *Ed.*] C040 (Consent to the Election of the Rev. Joe Goodwin Burnett as Bishop of the Diocese of Nebraska) The House of Deputies adopted the resolution. [Duplicate message for HD Message #5, see House of Bishops Day 2 Messages from the House of Deputies. *Ed.*]
HD Message #15:	A141 (Admit Diocese of Puerto Rico) The House of Deputies adopted the resolution with amendment.
HD Message #16:	A120 (Theological Education Committee) The House of Deputies adopted the resolution with amendment.
HD Message #17:	A145 (General Convention Model) The House of Deputies adopted the resolution.
HD Message #18:	C041 (Consent to the Election of The Rev. Samuel Johnson Howard as Bishop Coadjutor of the Diocese of Florida) The House of Deputies adopted the resolution.
HD Message #19:	C042 (Consent to the Election of The Rev. C. Franklin Brookhart, Jr. as Bishop of the Diocese of Montana) The House of Deputies adopted the resolution.
HD Message #20:	A026 (Baptismal Parity) The House of Deputies adopted the resolution with amendment.
HD Message #21:	A083 (Articulate Faith Story) The House of Deputies adopted the resolution with amendment.
HD Message #22:	C027 (AV Materials of the Episcopal Church) The House of Deputies adopted the resolution.
HD Message #23:	A082 (Multilingual Publications) The House of Deputies adopted a substitute resolution.
HD Message #24:	A027 (Use of Titles) The House of Deputies adopted a substitute resolution.
HD Message #25:	A154 (75th General Convention Site) The House of Deputies adopted the resolution.

Ecumenical Relations

The Parliamentarian changed his ruling on the tabling of Resolution A085. Debate resumed on Resolution A085.

The Bishop of Southwest Florida proposed a substitute.

Proposed Substitute:

(A085)
Resolved, the House of Deputies concurring, That the rubrics of the Book of Common Prayer and the Constitution and Canons of The Episcopal Church allow

JOURNAL   **THIRD DAY**

reception of members of the Evangelical Lutheran Church in America.
Motion carried
Substitute resolution adopted
(Communicated to the House of Deputies in HB Message #53)

Consecration of Bishops

The House of Bishops Committee on the Consecration of Bishops moved the resolution on the consent for the consecration of the Rev. C. Franklin Brookhart, Jr., Bishop-elect of the Diocese of Montana, and Ballot #4 was taken.
Ballot #4 taken

Education

The House of Bishops Committee on Education presented its Report #5 on Resolution A029 (Open Dialogue on Difficult Issues) moved adoption with amendment.

Original Text of Resolution:
(A029)
Resolved, the House of Deputies concurring, That the 74th General Convention of The Episcopal Church commit itself to foster moral deliberation on social questions, seeking to be a community where open, passionate, and respectful deliberation of challenging, contemporary issues is expected and encouraged; engage those of diverse classes, genders, ages, races, cultures and perspectives in the deliberation process so that our limited horizons might be expanded and our witness in the world enhanced; address the issues faced by the people of God, in order to equip them for their discipleship and citizenship in the world; and be it further
Resolved, That the 74th General Convention direct the Peace and Justice Ministries Office and Ethnic and Women's Ministries to collaborate in developing models and trainers, lay and ordained, across the Church to guide conversations on difficult issues facing Americans today; and be it further
Resolved, That up to $28,000 be allocated from the Program Budget for this work including $6,000 for planning the process and printing materials; $20,000 to bring trainers from dioceses and provinces together to learn the process and $2,000 to sustain the process.

Committee Amendment:
Resolved, the House of Deputies concurring, That the 74th General Convention of The Episcopal Church commit itself to foster moral deliberation on social questions, seeking to be a community where open, passionate, and respectful deliberation of challenging, contemporary issues is expected and encouraged; engage those of diverse classes, genders, ages, races, *disabilities, engaging* cultures, *sexual orientation,* and perspectives ~~in the deliberation process~~ so that our limited horizons might be expanded and our witness in the world enhanced; address the

MINNEAPOLIS MEETING   HOUSE OF BISHOPS

issues faced by the people of God, in order to equip them for their discipleship and citizenship in the world; and be it further

Resolved, That the 74th General Convention direct the Peace and Justice Ministries Office and Ethnic and Women's Ministries *and, where appropriate, the Committee on Anti-Racism of the Executive Council and other groups* to collaborate in developing models and trainers, lay and ordained, ~~across the Church~~ to guide conversations on difficult issues facing ~~Americans~~ *our church and societies* today; and be it further

Resolved, That *the General Convention request the Joint Standing Committee on Program, Budget, and Finance to consider a budget allocation of* $28,000 ~~up to be allocated from the Program Budget for this work~~ *for implementation of this resolution,* including $6,000 for planning the process and printing materials; $20,000 to bring trainers from dioceses and provinces together to learn the process and $2,000 to sustain the process.

The Bishop Suffragan of New York, withdrew her amendment from the previous day and proposed a new amendment to replace the second resolve.

Proposed Amendment:

Resolved, That in addition to the curricula identified and developed in accordance with Resolution A009 of the 73rd General Convention which provide guided conversation around sexual orientation, in particular "Room For Grace Dialogue", the 74th General Convention direct the Peace and Justice Ministries Office and Ethnic and Women's Ministries and, where appropriate, Committee on Anti-Racism of the Executive Council and other groups to collaborate in further developing models and trainers, lay and ordained, to guide conversations on difficult issues facing our church and societies today and to promulgate their use; and be it further

Motion carried
Amendment adopted

A vote was taken on Resolution A029.

Motion carried
Resolution adopted with amendment
(Communicated to the House of Deputies in HB Message #54)

Stewardship and Development

The House of Bishops Committee on Stewardship and Development presented its Report #1 on Resolution A135 (Holy Habits) and moved adoption with amendment.

Original Text of Resolution:

(A135)
Resolved, the House of Deputies concurring, That in recognition of the church's tradition of calling us to work, pray, and give for the spread of God's kingdom, all members of The Episcopal Church be encouraged to develop a personal spiritual discipline that includes, at a minimum, the holy habits of tithing, daily personal prayer and study, Sabbath time, and regular corporate worship; and be it further

Resolved, That the Bishops and Deputies of the 74th General Convention be given

an opportunity to sign the following declaration:
> As Christian stewards and leaders of The Episcopal Church, we affirm that we are tithing, or have adopted a plan to work toward tithing; and that, if we are not already doing so, we are committed to give priority to corporate worship, personal daily prayer and study, and Sabbath time in our own lives; and we invite all members of the Episcopal Church to join us in these holy habits; and be it further

Resolved, That the Secretary publish a list of these signatories in the Journal of the 74th General Convention and provide the same to Episcopal Life for publication of the statement and the list of signatories.

Committee Amendment :

Resolved, the House of Deputies concurring, That in recognition of the church's tradition of calling us to work, pray, and give for the spread of God's kingdom, all members of The Episcopal Church be encouraged to develop a personal spiritual discipline that includes, at a minimum, the holy habits of tithing, daily personal prayer and study, Sabbath time, and regular corporate worship; and be it further

Resolved, That the Bishops and Deputies of the 74th General Convention be given an opportunity to sign the following declaration:
> As Christian stewards and leaders of The Episcopal Church, we affirm that we are tithing, or have adopted a plan to work toward tithing as *a minimum standard for our giving,* and that, if we are not already doing so, we are committed to give priority to corporate worship, personal daily prayer and study, and Sabbath time in our own lives; and we invite all members of the Episcopal Church to join us in these holy habits; and be it further

Resolved, That we commit ourselves to present this declaration to our diocesan conventions for adoption and signature, and in turn to the vestries and people of our parishes, missions, and university centers; and be it further

Resolved, That the Secretary publish a list of ~~these~~ *the General Convention* signatories in the Journal of the 74th General Convention and provide the same to *Episcopal Life* for publication of the statement and the list of signatories.

Bishop Hampton moved to amend the amended resolution.

Proposed Amendment:

Delete the word, "minimum" before "standard for our giving."

The question was called to terminate debate.

Motion carried
Debate terminated

A vote was taken on the proposed amendment.

Motion defeated
Amendment defeated

The Bishop of Albany moved to amend the amended resolution.

Proposed Amendment:
Delete "regular" and insert "weekly" before "corporate worship" in the first resolve clause.

Motion carried
Amendment adopted

A vote was taken on Resolution A135 as amended.

Motion carried
Resolution adopted with amendment
(Communicated to the House of Deputies in HB Message #55)

The House of Bishops Committee on Stewardship and Development presented its Report #2 on Resolution A134 (Implement Alleluia Fund) and moved adoption with amendment.

Original Text of Resolution:
(A134)
Resolved, the House of Deputies concurring, That the 74th General Convention commend those dioceses that have already implemented Resolution A036 of the 73rd General Convention, The Alleluia Fund–Build My Church; and be it further
Resolved, That all dioceses be encouraged to engage in this process of planning, giving, and spiritual transformation as a part of their 20/20 initiative in order to develop and maintain relationships with individual members of their dioceses and to fund new mission opportunities; and be it further
Resolved, That all dioceses are encouraged to designate a tithe of their Alleluia Fund offerings to mission beyond the diocese.

Committee Amendment:
Resolved, the House of Deputies concurring, That the 74th General Convention commend those dioceses that have already implemented Resolution A036 of the 73rd General Convention, The Alleluia Fund–Build My Church *and other similar funds*; and be it further
Resolved, That all dioceses, *as a part of their 20/20 initiative,* be encouraged *to articulate a vision* and engage in ~~this~~ *the Alleluia Fund* process of planning, giving, and spiritual transformation as a part of their 20/20 initiative in order to ~~develop and maintain relationships with individual members of their dioceses and to~~ fund new mission opportunities; ~~and be it further~~
~~*Resolved,* That all dioceses are encouraged to designate a tithe of their Alleluia Fund offerings to mission beyond the diocese~~.

Motion carried
Resolution adopted with amendment
(Communicated to the House of Deputies in HB Message #56)

The House of Bishops Committee on Stewardship and Development presented its Report #3 on Resolution A138 (50/50 Outreach for Congregations) and moved adoption with amendment.

Original Text of Resolution:
(A138)
Resolved, the House of Deputies concurring, That the 74th General Convention urge congregations to adopt the principle of devoting as much of their resources of time, talent, and treasure outside of the congregation as on itself. Part of the 50/50 sharing should include adoption of the 1% giving to seminaries, the .7% giving to international development programs that address root causes of ill health, illiteracy, and economic justice, and other worthwhile causes.

Committee Amendment:
Resolved, the House of Deputies concurring, That the 74th General Convention urge congregations to adopt the principle of devoting as much of their resources of time, talent, and treasure outside of the congregation as on itself. Part of the 50/50 sharing should include adoption of the 1% giving to seminaries, the .7% giving to international development programs that address root causes of ill health, illiteracy, and economic justice, and other worthwhile causes; and be it further
Resolved, That each diocese be urged to adopt the principle of 50/50 sharing of its resources through budgetary allocation for outreach, aided congregations, support to the Domestic and Foreign Missionary Society, and other mission efforts beyond diocesan administrative commitments, and then to establish a 3-year plan to move toward the accomplishment of that 50/50 sharing goal.

The Bishop of Northwestern Pennsylvania moved to amend the amended resolution.

Proposed Amendment:
Insert "on the same basis as congregations" after "resources" in the second resolve clause.

Motion carried
Amendment adopted

A vote was taken on Resolution A138 as amended.

Motion carried
Resolution adopted with amendment
(Communicated to the House of Deputies in HB Message #57)

Ecumenical Relations
The House of Bishops Committee on Ecumenical Relations presented its Report #4 on Resolution B003 (Study and Present the Reuilly Accord) and moved adoption with amendment.

Original Text of Resolution:
(B003)
Resolved, the House of Deputies concurring, That the 74th General Convention direct the Standing Commission on Ecumenical Relations to study and present the Reuilly Accord between the French Reformed and Lutheran Churches and the Church of England for signature by the 75th General Convention.

Committee Amendment:
Resolved, the House of Deputies concurring, That the 74th General Convention direct the Standing Commission on Ecumenical Relations to study and present the Reuilly Accord *of 1998* between the *French Reformed Church, the French Lutheran Church*, and the Church of England for *possible* signature by the 75th General Convention.

Motion carried
Resolution adopted with amendment
(Communicated to the House of Deputies in HB Message #58)

The House of Bishops Committee on Ecumenical Relations presented its Report #5 on Resolution B006 (Dialogue with Reformed Episcopal Church) and moved adoption.

Original Text of Resolution:
(B006)
Resolved, the House of Deputies concurring, That the General Convention receive with thanksgiving the start of ecumenical dialogue with the Reformed Episcopal Church (REC) and the Anglican Province of America (APA), occasioned by Resolution D047 of the 73rd General Convention; and be it further,

Resolved, That the 1940 Report of the Committee on Approaches to Unity of the Episcopal Church and the Report submitted to the Bishops of the Anglican Communion by this Church concerning the validity of Holy Orders of the Reformed Episcopal Church be referred to the Standing Commission on Ecumenical Relations for study during the 2004–2006 triennium and that the Commission report back to the 2006 General Convention on the validity of Holy Orders of the Reformed Episcopal Church.

Motion carried
Resolution adopted
(Communicated to the House of Deputies in HB Message #59)

The House of Bishops Committee on Ecumenical Relations presented its Report #6 on Resolution A087 (Interim Eucharistic Sharing with the Moravian Church in America, Northern and Southern Provinces) and moved adoption.

Original Text of Resolution:
(A087)
Resolved, the House of Deputies concurring, That the 74th General Convention meeting in Minneapolis, MN, July 30–August 8, 2003 with concurrent action by the Synods of the Moravian Church in America (Northern and Southern Provinces), authorize continuing dialogue with the Moravian Church in America (Northern and Southern Provinces) which may lead to a future proposal of Full Communion including interchangeability of clergy for ministry of Word and Sacrament; and be it further
Resolved, That the 74th General Convention of The Episcopal Church, meeting in Minneapolis, MN, July 30-August 8, 2003, establish Interim Eucharistic Sharing between The Episcopal Church and the Moravian Church under the following guidelines:
1. Moravian Provincial Elders' Conferences and Episcopal diocesan authorities are hereby encouraged to authorize joint celebrations of the Eucharist.
2. An authorized liturgy of the host church must be used, with ordained ministers of both churches standing at the Communion Table for the Great Thanksgiving.
3. The Preacher may be from either church.

Motion carried
Resolution adopted
(Communicated to the House of Deputies in HB Message #60)

Introduction of Visiting Bishops
The Ecumenical Officer made introductions of visiting bishops: the Rt. Rev. Hopeton Clennon and the Rt. Rev. Dr. Otto Dreydoppel of the Moravian Church in America.

Constitution
The House of Bishops Committee on Constitution presented its Report #5 on Resolution D028 (Amend Constitution Article X [The Book of Common Prayer–Second Reading]) and moved that the Committee be discharged as the matter is considered in Resolution A108.

Motion carried
Committee discharged
(Communicated to the House of Deputies in HB Message #61)

Canons
The House of Bishops Committee on Canons presented its Report #10 on Resolution D018 (Amend Canon I.6.1) and moved the resolution, recommending rejection.

Original Text of Resolution:
(D018)
Resolved, the House of Deputies concurring, That Canon I.6.1 be amended to include a new subsection as follows:
(3) the ethnic origin of all clergy on staff, in such categories as Executive Council shall, from time to time, determine; and an estimate by percentage, according to the same categories, of all members of the congregation.
And be it further
Resolved, That the existing subsection (3) be re-numbered (4).

Motion defeated
Resolution rejected
(Communicated to the House of Deputies in HB Message #62)

Structure
The House of Bishops Committee on Structure presented its Report #1 on HD Message #4 on Resolution A009 (Amend Canon I.4.2(b)) and moved concurrence.

The House concurred
(Communicated to the House of Deputies in HB Message #63)

Final Text of Resolution:
(A009)
Resolved, That Canon I.4.2(b) be amended to read as follows:
(b) Except in the case of members initially elected for shorter terms in order to achieve rotation of terms, the terms of office of the members of the Council (other than ex officiis members) shall be equal to twice the interval between regular meetings of the General Convention. The terms of office of all members shall commence immediately upon the adjournment of the General Convention at which they were elected or, in the case of election by a Synod, upon adjournment of the first regular meeting of General Convention following such election. *The term of a member shall become vacant in the event of two absences from meetings of the Council in the interval between successive regular meetings of the General Convention unless excused by the Chair for good cause.* Members shall remain in office until their successors are elected and qualified. No person who has served at least three consecutive years on the Executive Council shall be eligible for immediate re-election for a term of more than three years. After any person shall have served six consecutive years on the Executive Council, a period of three years shall elapse before such person shall be eligible for re-election to the Council.

World Mission
The House of Bishops Committee on World Mission presented its Report #2 on Resolution A151 (World Mission Funds) and moved adoption with amendment.

Original Text of Resolution:
(A151)
Resolved, the House of Deputies concurring, That the 2003 General Convention adopt the principle that world mission funds historically committed to the church's global engagement through financial covenants to former international jurisdictions of the church be re-deployed in other areas of the church's global engagement, and especially to world mission, as such funds become available through incrementally diminishing levels of support to the autonomous jurisdictions; and be it further
Resolved, That a detailed financial plan for the re-deployment of such funds be presented by the Standing Commission on World Mission to the 2006 General Convention.

Committee Amendment:
Resolved, the House of Deputies concurring, That the 2003 General Convention adopt the principle that world mission funds historically committed to the church's global engagement through financial covenants to former international jurisdictions of the church be re-deployed in other areas of the church's global engagement, and especially to world mission, as such funds become available through incrementally diminishing levels of support to the autonomous jurisdictions; and be it further
Resolved, That a detailed financial plan ~~for the re-deployment of such funds~~ *in consultation between the Standing Commission on World Mission and the Joint Standing Committee on Program, Budget, and Finance be developed and* be presented by the Standing Commission on World Mission to the 2006 General Convention.

Motion carried
Resolution adopted with amendment
(Communicated to the House of Deputies in HB Message #64)

Social and Urban Affairs
The House of Bishops Committee on Social and Urban Affairs presented its Report #1 on HD Message #10 on Resolution A008 (Repeal Mandatory Federal Sentencing Guidelines) and moved concurrence.

The House concurred
(Communicated to the House of Deputies in HB Message #65)

Final Text of Resolution:
(A008)
Resolved, **That the 74th General Convention urge the Congress of the United States to repeal the mandatory Federal sentencing guidelines used in federal**

criminal matters, and direct the Office of Government Relations to work for such repeal in order to give federal judges more discretion in sentencing offenders, and to overcome the current racially discriminatory impact of these guidelines.

Ministry
The House of Bishops Committee on Ministry presented its Report #5 on Resolution C019 (Direct Ordination) and moved adoption with amendment.

Original Text of Resolution:
(C019)
Resolved, the House of Deputies concurring, That the 74th General Convention adopt canonical revisions allowing bishops, with the consent of the Standing Committee, to ordain candidates for the priesthood directly to the priesthood.

Committee Amendment:
Resolved, the House of Deputies concurring, That the 74th General Convention ~~adopt~~ *direct its ministry committees to propose* canonical revisions ~~allowing bishops, with the consent of the Standing Committee, to ordain~~ *for ordination of* candidates for the priesthood directly to the priesthood.

The Presiding Bishop moved at 3:57 p.m. that the House recess for ten minutes for the purpose of table discussion.

Motion carried

The Bishop of Pennsylvania moved to amend the amended resolution.

Proposed Amendment:
Add "prepare a theological rationale for and against the ordination" and delete "propose canonical revisions for."
The question was called to terminate debate.

Motion carried
Debate terminated

A vote was taken on the proposed amendment.

Motion defeated
Amendment defeated

The question was called to terminate debate.

Motion carried
Debate terminated

A vote was taken on Resolution C019.

Motion defeated
Resolution rejected

(Communicated to the House of Deputies in HB Message #66)

The House of Bishops Committee on Ministry presented its Report #6 on Resolution A063 (Ethnic Specific Discernment Committees) and moved adoption with amendment.

Original Text of Resolution:
(A063)
Resolved, the House of Deputies concurring, That the 74th General Convention encourage bishops and commissions on ministry to designate ethnic-specific discernment committees to identify, support, and retain individuals for ministry from communities not well represented within a diocese's current leadership.

Committee Amendment:
Resolved, the House of Deputies concurring, That the 74th General Convention encourage bishops and commissions on ministry ~~to designate ethnic-specific discernment committees~~ to identify, support, and retain individuals for ministry from *specific cultural* communities *within the diocese* not well represented ~~within~~ *in a the* diocese's current leadership.

Motion carried
Resolution adopted with amendment
(Communicated to the House of Deputies in HB Message #67)

Consecration of Bishops
The Presiding Bishop read the results of Ballot #3 on the consent of the consecration of Bishop Coadjutor-elect Howard of the Diocese of Florida. Of 106 bishops with jurisdiction, 103 have given consent.

The House concurred
(Communicated to the House of Deputies in HB Message #68)

The Presiding Bishop read the results of Ballot #4 on the consent of the consecration of Bishop-elect Brookhart of the Diocese of Montana. Of 106 bishops with jurisdiction, 103 have given consent.

The House concurred
(Communicated to the House of Deputies in HB Message #69)

The Presiding Bishop yielded the chair to the Vice-Chair.

Stewardship and Development
The Committee on Stewardship and Development presented its Report #4 on Resolution A139 (Affirm the Work of TENS) and moved adoption with amendment.

Original Text of Resolution:
(A139)
Resolved, the House of Deputies concurring, That the 74th General Convention commend the transforming ministry of The Episcopal Network for Stewardship (TENS), a ministry that invites individuals, congregations, and dioceses to grow

into a new understanding of Christian stewardship theology that transforms us from selfishness and fear to love and giving, and we invite all dioceses and congregations to become members of TENS not only to support this important ministry but also to receive the many resources TENS is developing and making available to the church.

Committee Amendment:
Resolved, the House of Deputies concurring, That the 74th General Convention commend the transforming ministry of The Episcopal Network for Stewardship (TENS), a ministry that invites individuals, congregations, and dioceses to grow into a new understanding of Christian stewardship theology that transforms us from selfishness and fear to love and giving ~~, and we invite all dioceses and congregations to become members of TENS~~; and be it further
Resolved, That all dioceses and congregations are encouraged to accept the invitation to become members of The Episcopal Network of Stewardship not only to support this important ministry but also to receive the many resources TENS is developing and making available to the church.

Motion carried
Resolution adopted with amendment
(Communicated to the House of Deputies in HB Message #70)

The House of Bishops Committee on Stewardship and Development presented its Report #5 on Resolution A140 (Mission Funding) and moved adoption with amendment.

Original Text of Resolution:
(A140)
Resolved, the House of Deputies concurring, That the 74th General Convention direct:
- the beginning of a discernment process for a church-wide major mission funding effort;
- and the immediate creation of a Mission Funding Office for The Episcopal Church, grounded in the stewardship theology of this church.

Committee Amendment:
Resolved, the House of Deputies concurring, That *in recognition of the 20/20 initiatives, creating a need to raise large sums of money for mission, and the very real potential for major gifts that parish and diocesan funding efforts do not attract;* ~~the~~ the 74th General Convention ~~direct~~ *urge the Presiding Bishop and Executive Council to establish*:
- ~~the beginning of a discernment process for a church-wide major mission funding effort;~~
- ~~and the immediate creation of~~ a Mission Funding Office for The Episcopal Church, grounded in the stewardship theology of this church; *and be it further*
Resolved, That this office initiate a discernment process for a church-wide mission funding effort focused on, but not limited to, the 20/20 initiatives and on fostering cooperative seeking of new

funds at all levels of the church.

Motion carried
Resolution adopted with amendment
(Communicated to the House of Deputies in HB Message #71)

Personal Privilege
The Bishop of Kansas commended the work of The Episcopal Network for Stewardship (TENS) and its Executive Director, Tom Gossen.

Ecumenical Relations
The Committee on Ecumenical Relations presented its Report #8 on Resolution A086 (Lutheran Ordination Bylaw) and moved adoption with amendment.

Original Text of Resolution:
(A086)
Resolved, the House of Deputies concurring, That the House of Bishops is hereby requested to establish a committee to monitor the ways and extent to which the ELCA ordination bylaw exception may cause any additional limitations upon the full communion that has been jointly established and to report their findings and any recommendations to the next General Convention.

Committee Amendment:
Resolved, the House of Deputies concurring, That ~~the House of Bishops~~ *the Standing Commission on Ecumenical Relations* is hereby requested ~~to establish a committee~~ *to be in conversation with representatives of the ELCA* to monitor the ways and extent to which the ELCA ordination bylaw exception may cause any additional limitations upon the full communion that has been jointly established, *to clarify the intent and meaning of paragraph 20 of "Called to Common Mission" and the ELCA bylaw 7.31.17 "Ordination Under Unusual Circumstances,"* and to report their findings and any recommendations to the next General Convention.

Motion carried
Resolution adopted with amendment
(Communicated to the House of Deputies in HB Message #72)

Miscellaneous Resolutions
The House of Bishops Committee on Miscellaneous Resolutions presented its Report #1 on Resolution B001 (Endorse Certain Historic Anglican Doctrines and Policies) and moved the resolution, recommending rejection.

Original Text of Resolution:
(B001)
Resolved, the House of Deputies concurring, That the 74th General Convention affirm that "Holy Scripture containeth all things necessary to salvation: so that whatsoever is not read therein, nor may be proved thereby, is not to be required of

any man, that it should be believed as an article of the Faith, or be thought requisite or necessary to salvation," as set forth in Article VI of the Articles of Religion established by the General Convention on September 12, 1801; and be it further
Resolved, That the 74th General Convention re-affirm that "it is not lawful for the Church to ordain [that is, establish or enact] any thing that is contrary to God's Word written, neither may it so expound one place of Scripture, that it be repugnant to another," as set forth in Article XX of the Articles of Religion established by the General Convention on September 12, 1801; and be it further
Resolved, That the 74th General Convention affirm that every member of this Church is conscience-bound first of all to obey the teaching and direction of Our Lord Jesus Christ as set forth in Holy Scripture in any matter where a decision or action of this Church, or this General Convention, may depart from that teaching; and be it further
Resolved, That the 74th General Convention reaffirm that the statements known as the Chicago-Lambeth Quadrilaterial of 1886, 1888, as set forth in the Book of Common Prayer, 1979 continue to be true and accurate statements of the faith and policy of this Church, and the Anglican Communion; and be it further
Resolved, That the 74th General Convention affirm that councils of the Church have, and sometimes will, err but that Our Lord Jesus Christ, present through the person of the Holy Spirit, can and will correct such error; and be it further
Resolved, That the 74th General Convention direct the Office of the Presiding Bishop to forward a copy of this resolution to every diocese within The Episcopal Church.

The Retired Bishop Suffragan of Massachusetts moved to table the resolution.
Motion defeated

There was a request for division.
Motion defeated

Roll Call
There was a request by five bishops for a roll call vote on Resolution B001.

RECESS
The Chair called a ten-minute recess at 5:05 p.m.
The House of Bishops resumed at 5:15 p.m.

Roll Call Vote on Resolution B001

| 66 | yes | 84 | no | 8 | abstain |

(See Appendix D–Day 3 for the record of the Roll Call Vote.)
Motion defeated
Resolution rejected
(Communicated to the House of Deputies in HB Message #73)

Executive Council
Ballots were distributed for the election of members to Executive Council.

Canons
The House of Bishops Committee on Canons presented its Report #11 on Resolution D013 (Annotated Constitution and Canons, known as White and Dykman) and moved adoption with amendment.

Original Text of Resolution:
(D013)
Resolved, the House of Deputies concurring, That the 74th General Convention direct that during the next triennium the Standing Committee on Constitution and Canons be authorized to initiate the editing, revising, and updating of the *Annotated Constitution and Canons for the Government of the Protestant Episcopal Church in the United States of America otherwise known as the Episcopal Church (1954 edition),* more familiarly known as White and Dykman, and all subsequent supplemental editions, for the purpose of creating a new and complete edition of the *Annotated Constitution and Canons;* and be it further

Resolved, That the Standing Committee on Constitution and Canons be authorized to arrange for the publication, distribution, and sale of this new edition of the *Annotated Constitution and Canons;* and be it further

Resolved, That there be appropriated from the budget of General Convention the sum of $45,000 during the triennium for this work.

Committee Amendment:
Resolved, the House of Deputies concurring, That the 74th General Convention direct that during the next triennium the Standing ~~Committee~~ Commission on Constitution and Canons be authorized to initiate the editing, revising, and updating of the *Annotated Constitution and Canons for the Government of the Protestant Episcopal Church in the United States of America otherwise known as the Episcopal Church (1954 edition),* more familiarly known as White and Dykman, and all subsequent supplemental editions, for the purpose of creating a new and complete edition of the *Annotated Constitution and Canons;* and be it further

Resolved, That the Standing ~~Committee~~ Commission on Constitution and Canons be authorized to arrange for the publication, distribution, and sale of this new edition of Annotated Constitution and Canons; and be it further

Resolved, That *the General Convention request the Joint Standing Committee on Program, Budget and Finance to consider a budget allocation of $45,000 for implementation of this resolution.* ~~there be appropriated from the Budget of General Convention the sum of $45,000 during the triennium for this work.~~

Motion carried
Resolution adopted with amendment
(Communicated to the House of Deputies in HB Message #74)

Structure

The House of Bishops Committee on Structure presented its Report #2 on Resolution A040 (Amend Canon l.1.2(n)(6)) and moved concurrence.

The House concurred
(Communicated to the House of Deputies in HB Message #75)

Final Text of Resolution:

(A040)
Resolved, That Canon I.1.2(n) be amended by adding this subsection:
(6) A Standing Commission on Liturgy and Music consisting of 16 members (4 Bishops, 4 Priests and/or Deacons and 8 Lay Persons). In addition, the Custodian of the Book of Common Prayer shall be a member *ex officio* with voice, but without vote. The Standing Commission shall:

(i) Discharge such duties as shall be assigned to it by the General Convention as to policies and strategies concerning the common worship of this Church.

(ii) Collect, collate and catalogue material bearing upon possible future revisions of The Book of Common Prayer.

(iii) Cause to be prepared and to present to the General Convention recommendations concerning the Lectionary, Psalter, and offices for special occasions as authorized or directed by the General Convention or House of Bishops.

(iv) Recommend to the General Convention authorized translations of the Holy Scripture from which the Lessons prescribed in the Book of Common Prayer are to be read.

(v) Receive and evaluate requests for consideration of individuals or groups to be included in the Calendar of the Church year and make recommendations thereon to the General Convention for acceptance or rejection.

(vi) Collect, collate and catalogue material bearing upon possible future revisions of The Hymnal 1982 and other musical publications regularly in use in this Church and encourage the composition of new musical materials.

(vii) Cause to be prepared and present to the General Convention recommendations concerning the musical settings of liturgical texts and rubrics, and norms as to liturgical music and the manner of its rendition.

(viii) At the direction of General Convention, serve the Church in matters pertaining to policies and strategies concerning Church music.

Church in Small Communities

The House of Bishops Committee on Church in Small Communities presented its Report #2 on Resolution B010 (Continue Leadership Program for Musicians Serving Small Congregations) and moved adoption with amendment.

Original Text of Resolution:
(B010)
Resolved, the House of Deputies concurring, That the 74th General Convention endorse the continuation of the Leadership Program for Musicians Serving Small Congregations, which provides musicians who serve small congregations with continuing education for musical leadership in liturgy; and be it further
Resolved, That the General Convention request the Joint Standing Committee on Program, Budget and Finance to consider a budget allocation of $75,000 for implementation of this resolution.

Committee Amendment:
Resolved, the House of Deputies concurring, That the 74th General Convention endorse the continuation of the Leadership Program for Musicians Serving Small Congregations, which provides musicians who serve small congregations with continuing education for musical leadership in liturgy; and be it further
Resolved, That the program staff at the Church Center promote and distribute information about this program to all congregations with average Sunday attendance of 150 and fewer, and to all dioceses; and be it further
Resolved, That the General Convention request the Joint Standing Committee on Program, Budget and Finance to consider a budget allocation of $75,000 for implementation of this resolution.

Motion carried
Resolution adopted with amendment
(Communicated to the House of Deputies in HB Message #76)

The House of Bishops Committee on Prayer Book, Liturgy and Church Music presented its Report #12 on Resolution A100 (Revise *Lesser Feasts and Fasts 2000*) and moved adoption of a substitute.

Original Text of Resolution:
(A100)
Resolved, the House of Deputies concurring, That the 74th General Convention direct the Standing Commission on Liturgy and Music to undertake a revision of *Lesser Feasts and Fasts 2000*, and to report on the progress of this revision to the 75th General Convention; and be it further
Resolved, That the sum of $18,000.00 be appropriated for support of this undertaking during the triennium 2004–2006; this appropriation to be administered by the Office of Liturgy and Music.

Committee Substitute:
Resolved, the House of Deputies concurring, That the 74th General Convention direct the Standing Commission on Liturgy and Music to undertake a revision of *Lesser Feasts and Fasts 2000*, to reflect our increasing awareness of the importance of the ministry of all the people of God and of the cultural diversity of The Episcopal Church, of the wider Anglican Communion, of our ecumenical partners, and of our lively experience of sainthood in local communities; and be it further
Resolved, That the SCLM produce a study of the significance of that experience of local sainthood in encouraging the living out of baptism; and be it further
Resolved, That the General Convention request the Joint Standing Committee on Program, Budget, and Finance to consider a budget allocation of $20,000 for implementation of this resolution.

Motion carried
Substitute resolution adopted
(Communicated to the House of Deputies in HB Message #77)

Prayer Book, Liturgy and Church Music
The Committee on Prayer Book, Liturgy and Church Music presented its Report #13 on Resolution A092 (Reauthorize Enriching Our Worship work) and moved adoption of a substitute.

Original Text of Resolution:
(A092)
Resolved, the House of Deputies concurring, That the 74th General Convention direct the Standing Commission on Liturgy and Music to continue to develop expansive language liturgies for the Pastoral Offices of the Book of Common Prayer 1979; and be it further
Resolved, That the Office for Liturgy and Music, in consultation with the Standing Commission on Liturgy and Music, create a Task Force of six people to engage the work; and be it further
Resolved, That the sum of $14,400 be appropriated for the work of the Task Force.

Committee Substitute:
Resolved, the House of Deputies concurring, That the 74th General Convention direct the Standing Commission on Liturgy and Music (SCLM) to further develop *Enriching Our Worship* and *Enriching Our Music,* preparing and collecting rites and music that are culturally diverse for use in a wide range of settings to advance the goals of 20/20. These rites may include, but not be limited to, pastoral rites to celebrate specific events grounded in the many cultures in our Church, such as:
    Pastoral offices of the Book of Common Prayer 1979;
    Rites of Passage, such as Quinceañeras (e.g. Latin American); Naming of Elders (e.g. Korean); Day of the Dead (e.g. Latin American); Honoring of Ancestors (e.g. Chinese); Adoption Rites (e.g. Native American); and Journey to Adulthood Rites;

Mission and evangelism-based prayers;
Creative worship resources for multi-sensory worship;
And Spanish music resources; and be it further

Resolved, That the development of these rites and resources be designed and implemented using models which would innovatively draw on and reflect our Church's liturgical, cultural, racial, generational, gender, and ethnic diversity; and be it further

Resolved, That the SCLM begin to develop a network for sharing these learnings and resources and report on their progress to the 75th General Convention; and be it further

Resolved, That the General Convention request the Joint Standing Committee on Program, Budget, and Finance to consider a budget allocation of $130,000 for implementation of this resolution.

The Bishop of the Convocation of American Churches in Europe moved to amend the substitute resolution.

Proposed Amendment:
Add "and French" before "music resources."
The question was called to terminate debate.

> **Motion carried**
> **Debate terminated**

A vote was taken on the proposed amendment.

> **Motion carried**
> **Amendment adopted**

Bishop of Michigan moved to amend the substitute resolution.

Proposed Amendment:
Insert "and music" after "these rites."

> **Motion carried**
> **Amendment adopted**

A vote was taken on Resolution A092 as amended.

> **Motion carried**
> **Resolution adopted with amendment**
> (Communicated to the House of Deputies in HB Message #78)

The House of Bishops Committee on Prayer Book, Liturgy and Church Music presented its Report #14 on Resolution A071 (Mission-based Prayers) and moved that the Committee be discharged.

> **Motion carried**
> **Committee discharged**
> (Communicated to the House of Deputies in HB Message #79)

MINNEAPOLIS MEETING　　　　　　　　　HOUSE OF BISHOPS

The House of Bishops Committee on Prayer Book, Liturgy and Church Music presented its Report #15 on Resolution A070 (Creative Worship Resources) and moved that the Committee be discharged.

Motion carried
Committee discharged
(Communicated to the House of Deputies in HB Message #80)

The House of Bishops Committee on Prayer Book, Liturgy and Church Music presented its Report #16 on Resolution A069 (Spanish Music Resources) and moved that the Committee be discharged.

Motion carried
Committee discharged
(Communicated to the House of Deputies in HB Message #81)

The House of Bishops Committee on Prayer Book, Liturgy and Church Music presented its Report #17 on Resolution A102 (Culturally Sensitive Rites) and moved that the Committee be discharged.

Motion carried
Committee discharged
(Communicated to the House of Deputies in HB Message #82)

The House of Bishops Committee on Prayer Book, Liturgy and Church Music presented its Report #18 on Resolution A104 (Facilitate the Enrichment of Worship with Evangelism Focus) and moved that the Committee be discharged.

Motion carried
Committee discharged
(Communicated to the House of Deputies in HB Message #83)

The House of Bishops Committee on Prayer Book, Liturgy and Church Music presented its Report #19 on Resolution A105 (Resources for Liturgical Education) and moved that the Committee be discharged.

Motion carried
Committee discharged
(Communicated to the House of Deputies in HB Message #84)

Recess

Following announcements by the Secretary, the House of Bishops Committee on Dispatch of Business moved that the House stand in recess until 11:00 a.m. on the Fourth Legislative Day.

Motion carried

The House recessed at 5:50 p.m. with prayer led by Chaplain McIntosh.

Appendix D
Day 3

Vote on Resolution B001

		Yea	Nay	Abstain
Bishop R. Hatch	0504			
Bishop D. Richards	0508			
Bishop W. Crittenden	0514			
Bishop G. Murray	0521			
Bishop G. Cadigan	0563			
Bishop G. Millard	0565			
Bishop C. Bennison	0567			
Bishop R. De Witt	0573			
Bishop J. Montomery	0587			
Bishop J. Burgess	0590			
Bishop F. Putnam	0595	x		
Bishop D. Reed	0603	x		
Bishop S. Bailey	0604			
Bishop R. Martain	0620			
Bishop J. Burt	0621			
Bishop J. Wyatt	0623			
Bishop R. Spears	0624			
Bishop M. Wood	0625			
Bishop W. Frey	0627			
Bishop E. Browning	0630			
Bishop V. Rivera	0635			
Bishop D. Leighton	0639			
Bishop G. Haynsworth	0640			
Bishop W. Spofford	0643			
Bishop P. Reeves	0646			
Bishop P. Smith	0647			
Bishop W. Folwell	0648			
Bishop C. Hobgood	0656			
Bishop A. Caceres	0657			
Bishop F. Stough	0658			
Bishop A. Vogel	0662			
Bishop W. Henton	0663			
Bishop O. Charles	0665		x	
Bishop C. McGehee	0667			
Bishop M. Potreus	0668			
Bishop R. Trelease	0669			
Bishop W. Righter	0671		x	

		Yea	Nay	Abstain
Bishop A. Hillestad	0674			
Bishop B. Simes	0676			
Bishop T. Isaac	0678			
Bishop W. Sheridan	0682			
Bishop W. Cox	0684			
Bishop R. Atkinson	0687			
Bishop W. Weinhauer	0690			
Bishop D. Parsons	0691			
Bishop R. Wolterstorff	0697	x		
Bishop D. Gray	0698			
Bishop F. Cerveny	0699			
Bishop M. Belshaw	0702			
Bishop R. Witcher	0703			
Bishop W. Jones	0704			
Bishop R. Cochrane	0709			
Bishop J. Brown	0711			
Bishop C. Vaché	0712			x
Bishop J. Spong	0713			
Bishop J. Heistand	0714			
Bishop J. Coburn	0715			
Bishop J. Warner	0717			x
Bishop G. McAllister	0718			
Bishop E. Jones	0719			
Bishop B. Jones	0721			
Bishop R. Anderson	0722		x	
Bishop C. Child	0723			
Bishop C. Burgreen	0724			
Bishop H. Pina-Oplez	0725			
Bishop J. Thompson	0726			
Bishop L. Wallace	0727			
Bishop C. Schofield	0728			
Bishop H. Light	0729			
Bishop B. Merino	0730			
Bishop W. Swing	0732		x	
Bishop W. Beckham	0733			
Bishop W. Sanders	0735			
Bishop A. Walmsley	0736		x	
Bishop W. Black	0737			
Bishop H. Hopkins	0740			
Bishop R. Estill	0741			
Bishop G. Hunt	0744			
Bishop R. Kimsey	0745			

MINNEAPOLIS MEETING   HOUSE OF BISHOPS

		Yea	Nay	Abstain
Bishop M. Benitez	0747			
Bishop H. Donovan	0748			x
Bishop F. Allison	0749			
Bishop W. Wantland	0750	x		
Bishop S. Mallory	0751			
Bishop C. McNutt	0752			
Bishop S. Hulsey	0753			
Bishop W. Wolfrum	0754			
Bishop C. Duvall	0755			
Bishop O'Kelley Whitaker	0756			
Bishop R. Grein	0758			x
Bishop A. Hathaway	0761	x		
Bishop C. Coleridge	0763	x		
Bishop D. Hultstrand	0766			
Bishop T. Eastman	0767			
Bishop D. Birney	0768			
Bishop T. Ray	0769			
Bishop G. Charlton	0770	x		
Bishop J. Dyer	0772			
Bishop A. Dickson	0773			
Bishop J. Moodey	0774			
Bishop E. Sorge	0775			
Bishop D. Patterson	0776			
Bishop H. Shipps	0778			
Bishop J. Ottley	0779		x	
Bishop L. Frade	0780	x		
Bishop V. Pettit	0781			
Bishop D. Ball	0782			
Bishop A. Wissemann	0783			
Bishop W. Burrill	0784			
Bishop P.J. Lee	0785			x
Bishop C. Anderson	0786			
Bishop R. White	0787			
Bishop D. Wimberly	0789	x		
Bishop H. Meeks	0790			
Bishop C. Pope	0791			
Bishop F. Griswold	0794			
Bishop R. Harris	0795			x
Bishop F. Vest	0796		x	
Bishop W. Carr	0798			
Bishop R. Ladehoff	0801		x	
Bishop J. MacNaughton	0802			

		Yea	Nay	Abstain
Bishop A. Bartlett	0804		x	
Bishop D. Theuner	0805			
Bishop D. Swenson	0806		x	
Bishop R. Miller	0808			
Bishop D. Bowman	0811			
Bishop A. Williams	0813		x	
Bishop R. Haines	0814			
Bishop F. Gray	0815	x		
Bishop C. Tennis	0816		x	
Bishop D. Hart	0817			
Bishop F. Allan	0818			
Bishop D. Taylor	0819			
Bishop J. Rowthorn	0821	x		
Bishop E. McArthur	0822			
Bishop MacBurney	0823			
Bishop R. Moody	0824	x		
Bishop J. Chien	0825			
Bishop O. Walker	0826		x	
Bishop F. Borsch	0828			x
Bishop H. Thompson	0829	x		
Bishop C. Epting	0830	x		
Bishop F. Turner	0831		x	
Bishop J D Schofield	0832			
Bishop S. Wood	0833			
Bishop B. Harris	0834		x	
Bishop J. Buchanan	0835			x
Bishop T. Kelshaw	0836			
Bishop R. Johnson	0837		x	
Bishop S. Hampton	0838		x	
Bishop J. Howe	0839	x		
Bishop R. Rowley	0840		x	
Bishop J. Smith	0841			
Bishop R. Hargrove	0842			
Bishop V. Warner	0843			
Bishop S. Carranza-Gomez	0844		x	
Bishop W. Sterling	0845			
Bishop J. Krotz	0846		x	
Bishop E. Lee	0847			
Bishop C. Longest	0848			
Bishop A. Fairfield	0850	x		
Bishop W. Smalley	0851		x	
Bishop E. Salmon	0852	x		

MINNEAPOLIS MEETING — HOUSE OF BISHOPS

		Yea	Nay	Abstain
Bishop S. Plummer	0853	x		
Bishop C. Keyser	0854		x	
Bishop H. Williams	0855		x	
Bishop N. Larrea	0856			
Bishop J. Thornton	0857			
Bishop R. Shimpfky	0858		x	
Bishop W Winterrowd	0860		x	
Bishop C. Talton	0861		x	
Bishop W. Wiedrich	0862			
Bishop H. Rockwell	0863			
Bishop V. Scantlebury	0864		x	
Bishop S. Charleston	0865		x	
Bishop J. McKelvey	0866		x	
Bishop J. Lamb	0868	x		
Bishop A. Marble	0869		x	
Bishop J. Holguín	0870	x		
Bishop D. Joslin	0871			
Bishop P. Beckwith	0872	x		
Bishop G. Hughes	0874	x		
Bishop R. Shahan	0875		x	
Bishop J. Dixon	0876		x	
Bishop M. Townsend	0877			
Bishop J. Stanton	0879	x		
Bishop J. Iker	0880	x		
Bishop J. Duracin	0881	x		
Bishop B. Herlong	0882	x		
Bishop C. Matthews	0883		x	
Bishop C. Payne	0884			
Bishop J. Jelinek	0885		x	
Bishop J. Doss	0886		x	
Bishop M.A. McLeod	0887			
Bishop J. Coleman	0888			
Bishop J. Folts	0889	x		
Bishop C. Grew	0890		x	
Bishop E. Gulick	0891		x	
Bishop S. Jecko	0892	x		
Bishop R. Johnson	0893		x	
Bishop R. Jacobus	0894	x		
Bishop L. Maze	0895		x	
Bishop C. Robertson	0896			
Bishop K. Ackerman	0897	x		
Bishop T. Shaw	0898		x	

		Yea	Nay	Abstain
Bishop A Morante	0899		x	
Bishop K. Price	0900		x	
Bishop H. Louttit	0901	x		
Bishop D. Henderson	0902	x		
Bishop J. Said	0903			
Bishop V. Strickland	0904			
Bishop O. Soto	0906			
Bishop D. Jones	0907	x		
Bishop L. Alard	0908			
Bishop R. Ihloff	0909		x	
Bishop M Creighton	0910		x	
Bishop R. Hibbs	0911	x		
Bishop C. Roskam	0912		x	
Bishop G. Wolf	0913	x		
Bishop J. Lipscomb	0914	x		
Bishop W. Skilton	0915	x		
Bishop R. Duncan	0916	x		
Bishop A. Smith	0917		x	
Bishop C. Irish	0918		x	
Bishop P. Marshall	0919		x	
Bishop G. Gloster	0920		x	
Bishop E. Leidel	0921		x	
Bishop C. Daniel	0922		x	
Bishop H. Parsley	0923	x		
Bishop G. Scruton	0924	x		
Bishop N. Powell	0925		x	
Bishop R. Chang	0926		x	
Bishop C. Bennison	0927	x		
Bishop R. Michel	0928		x	
Bishop C. Waynick	0929		x	
Bishop W. Ohl	0930	x		
Bishop T. Daniels	0931	x		
Bishop D. Bane	0932	x		
Bishop M. MacDonald	0933	x		
Bishop B. Caldwell	0934		x	
Bishop D. Herzog	0935	x		
Bishop C. Jenkins	0936	x		
Bishop B. Howe	0937		x	
Bishop C. Knudsen	0938		x	
Bishop M. Sisk	0939	x		
Bishop H. Bainbridge	0940		x	
Bishop W. Wright	0941		x	

MINNEAPOLIS MEETING   HOUSE OF BISHOPS

		Yea	Nay	Abstain
Bishop J. Rabb	0942		x	
Bishop J. Croneberger	0943		x	
Bishop C. vonRosenberg	0944	x		
Bishop W. Persell	0945		x	
Bishop K. Whitmore	0946	x		
Bishop M. Garrison	0947		x	
Bishop J. Kelsey	0948		x	
Bishop B. MacPherson	0949	x		
Bishop W. Gibbs	0950	x		
Bishop G. Packard	0951	x		
Bishop E. Little	0952	x		
Bishop J. Bruno	0953		x	
Bishop D. Bena	0954	x		
Bishop M. Curry	0955		x	
Bishop D. Gray	0956	x		
Bishop W. Gregg	0957	x		
Bishop S. Sauls	0958		x	
Bishop J. Curry	0959		x	
Bishop W. Ramos-Orench	0960		x	
Bishop J. Waggoner	0961		x	
Bishop D. Lai	0962		x	
Bishop K. Jefferts Schori	0963		x	
Bishop R. Cederholm	0964		x	
Bishop T. Ely	0965		x	
Bishop P. Duncan	0966	x		
Bishop D. Johnson	0967	x		
Bishop N. Alexander	0968		x	
Bishop F. Duque	0969	x		
Bishop W. Klusmeyer	0970	x		
Bishop L. Allen	0971	x		
Bishop G. Adams	0972		x	
Bishop P. Whalon	0973	x		
Bishop M. Andrus	0974		x	
Bishop G. W. Smith	0975		x	
Bishop J. Adams	0976	x		
Bishop C. Gallagher	0977		x	
Bishop R. Gepert	0978		x	
Bishop J. Chane	0979		x	
Bishop H. Scriven	0980a	x		
Bishop G. Harris	0981		x	
Bishop J. Shand	0982	x		
Bishop A. Scarfe	0983		x	

The following Bishops have requested to state their reasons for their no vote:

This resolution raises the status of the Articles of Religion to a confessional document. *Bishop Stacy Sauls*

It raises the 39 Articles to the level of doctrine. *Bishop Gladstone Adams*

This resolution raises the Articles of Religion to the status of a confessional document. *Bishop Edwin Gulick*

The undersigned respectfully states his opposition to B001 on the following grounds: The 1978 Lambeth Conference, and indeed the Mother Church do not require subscription to the Articles of Religion; The Resolution specifically seeks to bind my conscience; I confess to being in direct violation of the Articles regulating sacramental practice, and would not wish to accord authority to them. *Bishop Paul Marshall*

The resolution raises the Articles of Religion from historical documents for our study and instruction to "confessional documents," contrary to the historic witness and long-standing tradition of the Episcopal Church. My reason has no ground with the named position on Holy Scripture, the theology of the Book of Common Prayer 1979, or the Chicago-Lambeth Quadrilateral. *Bishop J. Neil Alexander*

In my ordinations to Diaconate, Priesthood, and Episcopacy I articulated and signed the oath of conformity. I see no need to "sign on" to a list of historical understandings, many of which are not required of clergy even in the Church of England. *Bishop Catherine Waynick*

It was unclear to me why these pieces of our Anglican tradition, and no others which also slipped into "historical status," had been chosen for affirmation. Failing a compelling rationale for selection, it seemed best to vote in the negative. *Bishop Mark Hadley Andrus*

While adhering to the scriptures as pertaining to all things necessary for salvation and believing that all members of the church are bound as followers of Christ to the teaching and direction of Christ as both Lord and Savior and God's Living Word, I also believe that we are conscience bound to follow Christ using not only scriptures but tradition and reason as God's spirit directs. The resolution was too narrow in its focus. For this reason I registered my vote as no. The 39 Articles are historical signposts for our church. They do not posses for us the elevated position of a confessional creed. *Bishop Alan Scarfe*

The language of B001 does not reflect most recent gender inclusive language as required for all resolutions of General Convention (see line 3) making it out of order. *Bishop Carol Gallagher*

Appendix E
Day 3

Signatures Collected in Affirmation of Resolution A135 on Holy Habits

Resolved, the House of Deputies concurring, That in recognition of the church's tradition of calling us to work, pray, and give for the spread of God's kingdom, all members of The Episcopal Church be encouraged to develop a personal spiritual discipline that includes, at a minimum, the holy habits of tithing, daily personal prayer and study, Sabbath time, and weekly corporate worship; and be it further
Resolved, That the Bishops and Deputies of the 74th General Convention be given an opportunity to sign the following declaration:

> As Christian stewards and leaders of The Episcopal Church, we affirm that we are tithing, or have adopted a plan to work toward tithing as a minimum standard for our giving; and that, if we are not already doing so, we are committed to give priority to corporate worship, personal daily prayer and study, and Sabbath time in our own lives; and we invite all members of The Episcopal Church to join us in these holy habits; and be it further

Resolved, That we commit ourselves to present this declaration to our diocesan conventions for adoption and signature, and in turn to the vestries and people of our parishes, missions, and university centers; and be it further
Resolved, That the Secretary publish a list of the General Convention signatories in the Journal of the 74th General Convention and provide the same to *Episcopal Life* for publication of the statement and the list of signatories.

Signed in Minneapolis, Minnesota at General Convention by:

Gladstone B. Adams III (Central New York)
Lloyd E. Allen (Hondoras)
Harry B. Bainbridge (Idaho)
David C. Bane, Jr. (Southern Virginia)
David J. Bena (Albany)
Charles E. Bennison, Jr. (Pennsylvania)
Roy F. Cederholm (Massachusetts)
Richard S.O. Chang (Hawaii)
Michael W. Creighton (Central Pennsylvania)
John Palmer Croneberger (Newark)
James E. Curry (Connecticut)
Michael B. Curry (North Carolina)
Theodore A. Daniels (Virgin Islands)
Philip M. Duncan, II (Central Gulf Coast)
Robert Wm. Duncan (Pittsburgh)
Thomas C. Ely (Vermont)
C. Christopher Epting (New York)
Andrew A. Fairfield (North Dakota)
James E. Folts (West Texas)
Leopold Frade (Southeast Florida)
J. Michael Garrison (Western New York)
Robert R. Gepert (Western Michigan)
Wendell N. Gibbs, Jr. (Michigan)
J. Gary Gloster (North Carolina)
William O. Gregg (Eastern Oregon)
Barry R. Howe (West Missouri)
John W. Howe (Central Florida)
Robert W. Ihloff (Maryland)
Carolyn T. Irish (Utah)
Russell E. Jacobus (Fond du Lac)
Katharine Jefferts (Nevada)
Don E. Johnson (West Tennessee)
Robert H. Johnson (Western North Carolina)
David C. Jones (Virginia)

David B. Joslin (New Jersey)
W. Michie Klusmeyer (West Virginia)
Chilton R. Knudsen (Maine)
Robert L. Ladehoff (Oregon)
Peter James Lee (Virginia)
John B. Lipscomb (Southwest Florida)
Edward S. Little (Northern Indiana)
Mark MacDonald (Alaska)
D. Bruce MacPherson (Western Louisiana)
Paul V. Marshall (Bethlehem)
F. Clayton Matthews (Virginia)
Larry E. Maze (Arkansas)
Jack M. McKelvey (Rochester)
Henry N. Parsley, Jr. (Alabama)
William D. Persell (Chicago)
Kenneth L. Price, Jr. (Southern Ohio)
John L. Rabb (Maryland)
Creighton L. Robertson (South Dakota)
Robert D. Rowley, Jr. (Northwest Penn)
Alan Scarfe (Iowa)
Gordon P. Scruton (Western Massachusetts)
Robert R. Shahan (Arizona)
James J. Shand (Easton)
M. Thomas Shaw, III, SSJ (Massachusetts)
William E. Smalley (Kansas)
Andrew D. Smith (Connecticut)
George Wayne Smith (Missouri)
James M. Stanton (Dallas)
Charles G. von Rosenberg (East Tennessee)
James E. Waggoner, Jr. (Spokane)
Oris G. Walker, Jr. (Long Island)
Arthur E. Walmsley (Retired, Connecticut)
William C. Wantland (Retired, Eau Claire)
Catherine Waynick (Indianapolis)
Pierre Whalon (Europe)
Keith Whitmore (Eau Claire)
Hunt Williams (Retired, North Carolina)
Don A. Wimberly (Texas)

MINNEAPOLIS MEETING — HOUSE OF BISHOPS

FOURTH DAY

Saturday
August 2, 2003

MORNING SESSION

The House of Bishops reconvened at 11:07 a.m. with the Presiding Bishop in the chair.

Conversation time of twenty minutes was allowed beginning at 11:08 a.m.

The House resumed at 11:22 a.m. and the Secretary made announcements.

Agenda of the Day

The House of Bishops Committee on Dispatch of Business moved to adopt the agenda of the day.

Motion carried
Agenda adopted

Previous Day's Minutes

The House of Bishops Committee on Dispatch of Business moved to dispense with the reading of the previous day's minutes.

Motion carried

Introduction of Visiting Bishops

The Presiding Bishop introduced the Most Rev. Josiah Idowu-Fearson, Archbishop, Kaduna, Nigeria and the Rt. Rev. Mano Rumalshah, Secretary General of the United Society for the Propogation of the Gospel.

The Presiding Bishop asked the Bishop of Indianapolis to introduce the Rev. Mauricio José Araújo de Andrade, Bishop-elect of Brasilia.

Consecration of Bishops

The Presiding Bishop read HD Message #34 on HD Resolution C043 and HD Message #35 on Resolution C044 regarding consent for the consecrations of the Rev. Canon Johncy Itty, Bishop-elect of the Diocese of Oregon; and the Rev. Steven Andrew Miller, Bishop-elect of the Diocese of Milwaukee.

The House of Bishops Committee on Consecration of Bishops found all to be in order regarding these candidates. Ballot #5 was taken on the consent to the consecration of the Rev. Canon Johncy Itty, Bishop-elect of the Diocese of Oregon and the resolution was moved.

Ballot #5 taken

Messages from the House of Deputies
The Secretary announced that the following messages had been received from the House of Deputies.

HD Message #26:	Secretary of House of Deputies Made Secretary of General Convention.
	The House of Deputies adopted the resolution.
HD Message #27:	Election of Treasurer of General Convention.
	The House of Deputies adopted the resolution.
HD Message #28:	D032 (Courtesy for Gail Courtney Rittgers)
	The House of Deputies adopted the resolution.
HD Message #29:	A127 (Mandatory Sentencing Guidelines)
	The House of Deputies discharged the resolution for other reasons.
HD Message #30:	A015 (Jubilee Ministry Thanksgiving)
	The House of Deputies adopted the resolution.
HD Message #31:	A155 (76th General Convention Site)
	The House of Deputies adopted the resolution.
HD Message #32:	D039 (Priorities for Triennial Budget Decisions)
	The House of Deputies adopted the resolution.
HD Message #33:	A146 (Provincial Coordinators Funding)
	The House of Deputies adopted the resolution.
HD Message #34:	C043 (Consent to the Election of the Rev. Canon Johncy Itty as Bishop of the Diocese of Oregon)
	The House of Deputies adopted the resolution.
HD Message #35:	C044 (Consent to the Election of the Rev. Steven A. Miller as Bishop of the Diocese of Milwaukee)
	The House of Deputies adopted the resolution.
HD Message #36:	D007 (Episcopal Election Reform)
	The House of Deputies adopted the resolution with amendment.
HD Message #37:	C022 (Explosion of AIDS Worldwide/Continuing Epidemic in the United States)
	The House of Deputies adopted the resolution.
HD Message #38:	A024 (Support for CEDAW)
	The House of Deputies discharged the resolution.
HD Message #39:	A019 (Continue Standing Committee on HIV/AIDS)
	The House of Deputies adopted the resolution with amendment.
HD Message #40:	A010 (Continue Anti-Racism Mandate)
	The House of Deputies adopted the resolution with amendment.
HD Message #41:	A014 (Approve Research on Human Stem Cells)
	The House of Deputies adopted a substitute resolution.

HD Message #42:	C015 (Ethnic Desks at the National Church Office) The House of Deputies adopted the resolution with amendment.
HD Message #43:	A073 (Plant New Churches) The House of Deputies adopted the resolution with amendment.
HD Message #44:	A081 (National Ad Campaign) The House of Deputies adopted the resolution with amendment.
HD Message #45:	Special Order for Election of Members of Executive Council. The House of Deputies adopted the resolution.
HD Message #46:	C029 (Translation of Documents into Spanish) The House of Deputies adopted a substitute resolution with floor amendment.

Consecration of Bishops
The House of Bishops Committee on Consecration of Bishops moved the resolution for the consent to the consecration of the Rev. Steven A. Miller, Bishop-elect of the Diocese of Milwaukee, and Ballot #6 was taken.

Ballot #6 taken

President of House of Deputies
The Presiding Bishop informed the House that the Rev. George Werner has been elected President of the House of Deputies.

Structure
The House of Bishops Committee on Structure presented its Report #15 on HD Message #85 on Resolution A141 (Admit Diocese of Puerto Rico) and moved concurrence.

The House concurred
(Communicated to the House of Deputies in HB Message #85)

Final Text of Resolution:
(A141)
Resolved, **That the 2003 General Convention admit the Diocese of Puerto Rico to The Episcopal Church USA and recognize it as a diocese in union with General Convention;** and be it further
Resolved, **That Canon I.9.1 be amended to delete "and" before Honduras and insert "*and Puerto Rico*" after Honduras.** And be it further
Resolved, **That this amendment become effective immediately;** and be it further
Resolved, **That the Diocese of Puerto Rico be entitled to all rights pertaining to membership in The Episcopal Church as provided in the Constitution and Canons, including, but not limited to, voice and vote in the House of**

Bishops and House of Deputies, in accordance with the rules of those houses; and be it further

Resolved, That the Diocese of Puerto Rico be obligated to undertake all responsibilities pertaining to diocesan membership in The Episcopal Church as provided in the Constitution and Canons, including, but not limited to, conforming its constitution and canons to the provisions of the Constitution and Canons of the Episcopal Church; submitting annual diocesan and parochial reports to the General Convention Office; contributing annually to the apportionment budget of the Domestic and Foreign Missionary Society; and reporting fully on any financial assistance it receives from the General Convention budget; and be it further

Resolved, That the Convention affirm that the clergy and lay employees of the Diocese of Puerto Rico will be eligible to participate in companion pension plans administered by the Church Pension Fund, with benefits adapted to the particular needs of the Diocese and consistent with applicable law; and be it further

Resolved, That the Convention urge the Church Pension Fund to work with the Diocese of Puerto Rico to develop a plan to cover the unfunded period of time for those of its clergy who previously participated in the Church Pension Fund when the Diocese was a member of The Episcopal Church; and be it further

Resolved, That the portion of this resolution accepting the Diocese of Puerto Rico into union with the General Convention become effective immediately upon concurrence of the House of Deputies and the House of Bishops; and be it further

Resolved, That the Convention reaffirm the principle that dioceses of this church that are not located within the United States may seek autonomy according to the procedures set forth in Resolution 235a of the 1991 General Convention or may join other provinces of the Anglican Communion.

The House of Bishops Committee on Structure presented its Report #3 on HD Message #32 on Resolution D039 (Priorities for Triennial Budget Decisions) and moved concurrence.

The House concurred
(Communicated to the House of Deputies in HB Message #86)

Final Text of Resolution:
(D039)
Resolved, That the 74th General Convention endorse the following statement of priorities in rank order for the budget of the next triennium and direct the Joint Standing Committee on Program Budget and Finance to use these priorities in forming the Budget of The Episcopal Church 2004-2006.

PRIORITIES
We offer these mission priorities as an expression of our commitment to Jesus Christ.

We are committed to the importance of our ministry of reconciliation and communion at every level of our common life.

We embrace diversity and seek to promote inclusion and power sharing which underlie and inform all priorities, decisions, and all that we do. In faithfulness to these commitments, we continue to honor our covenants and partnerships with overseas dioceses.

We affirm the work of the Executive Council in identifying the following priorities for the mission of the church for the next triennium.

1. **YOUNG ADULTS AND YOUTH:** Reaching out to young adults and youth through intentional inclusion and full incorporation in the thinking, work, worship and structure of the Church.
2. **RECONCILIATION AND EVANGELISM:** Reconciling and engaging those who do not know Christ by participating in God's mission of reconciling all things to Christ and proclaiming the Gospel to those who are not yet members of the Church.
3. **CONGREGATIONAL TRANSFORMATION:** Revitalizing and transforming congregations through commitment to leadership development, spiritual growth, dynamic and inclusive worship, greater diversity, and mission.
4. **JUSTICE AND PEACE:** Promoting justice and peace for all of God's creation and reaching out to the dispossessed, imprisoned and otherwise voiceless needy.
5. **PARTNERSHIPS:** Reaffirming the importance of our partnerships with provinces of the Anglican Communion and beyond and our relationships with ecumenical and interfaith partners.

Prayer Book, Liturgy and Church Music

The House of Bishops Committee on Prayer Book, Liturgy and Church Music presented its Report #20 on Resolution A101 (Church Planting Liturgies) and moved adoption with amendment.

Original Text of Resolution:

(A101)
Resolved, the House of Deputies concurring, That the 74th General Convention approve for publication and distribution by Church Publishing, Inc., these liturgies: Discernment for a New Church Mission; A Liturgy for Commissioning a Church Planter, Missioner or Mission Team; A Liturgy for the Opening of a New Congregation; Setting Apart Secular Space for Sacred Use; A Litany for the Mission of the Church; A Variety of Church Planting Collects, Blessings and other Prayers; and Hymn Suggestions for Church Planting Liturgies; and be it further
Resolved, That these liturgies be printed side-by-side in English and Spanish.

Committee Amendment:

Resolved, the House of Deputies concurring, That the 74th General Convention approve for publication and distribution by Church Publishing, Inc., these liturgies: Discernment for a New Church Mission; A Liturgy for Commissioning a Church

Planter, Missioner or Mission Team; A Liturgy for the Opening of a New Congregation; Setting Apart Secular Space for Sacred Use; A Litany for the Mission of the Church; A Variety of Church Planting Collects, Blessings and other Prayers; and Hymn Suggestions for Church Planting Liturgies; and be it further

Resolved, That these liturgies be printed side-by-side in English and Spanish; and be it further

Resolved, That the proposed liturgies be changed as follows:

1. That the following rubric be added at the end of the introductory rubrics of each of the services [Blue Book pages 164,172,186, and 192]: "It is appropriate to adapt this rite to local custom, language, dialect, and idiom."
2. That the first rubric heading [Blue Book page 164], Concerning the Celebration, be changed to "Concerning the Service."
3. That in the first sentence of that rubric [Blue Book page 164] the words "congregations, dioceses, or other church bodies" be changed to "congregations and dioceses."
4. That the Collect for Raising Up of People with Skills Needed for a Church Planting [Blue Book page 168] be changed to the following:
   "Holy Spirit, you delight in equipping us with all the gifts of service (especially____) to extend the Realm of God: raise up and empower those among us whom you call to this new work, that the Body of Christ may grow in strength and health, for the transforming of the world; through Jesus Christ our Lord. Amen."
5. That the second word of the Collect for Apostolic-model Church Planting [Blue Book page 174] be changed from "Father" to "God."
6. In the Liturgy for Commissioning, in The Commissioning [Blue Book page 178], after the people's response "We will", add the following rubric: "Appropriate symbols of the new ministry may be given."
7. That the rubric beginning "Following Communion" [Blue Book page 184] be deleted.
8. That the rubric concerning the post-communion prayer [Blue Book page 184] be changed from "the following is said" to "the following may be said."
9. That the immediately following rubric, reading "Celebrant," [Blue Book page 184] be changed to read "Celebrant or other person appointed".
10. That the following rubric be added after the post-communion prayer [Blue Book page 184]: The Bishop or Celebrant may bless the people.
11. That the rubric beginning "The Bishop or the Bishop's representative" and the two following lines beginning "Receive" be deleted [Blue Book page 184].
12. That the Dismissal [Blue Book page 184] be changed to the following:
    Deacon: Go forth into the world, sharing the Good News of God's love. [Alleluia, alleluia.]
    People: We go in the Name of Christ. [Alleluia, alleluia.]
13. That in the collect in the liturgy for Setting Apart Secular Space for

Sacred Use that begins "Blessed are you, O God" [Blue Book page 194] the phrase "we dedicate this space" be changed to "we dedicate our use of this space" and in the last sentence the word "always" be deleted.

14. That the sixth prayer of A Variety of Church Planting Collects, Blessings and Other Prayers, beginning "Most Holy and life-giving God," [Blue Book page 202] be changed to the following:

> Most Holy and life-giving God: the friends of Jesus carried your good news, each to a different place according to their gifts and calling. Bless N. (and N.) as they carry your word of love, making disciples for your service and building up your Church, through the power of your Spirit and in the Name of Jesus. Amen.

15. In the several Dismissals in these liturgies add the words, "Deacon, or the Celebrant, dismisses the people."

And be it further
Resolved, That appropriate corrections to the Spanish rites be made.

The Retired Bishop of Kentucky moved to delete in the first resolve clause "A Litany for the Mission of Church."

Motion failed
Amendment defeated

A vote was taken on Resolution A101 as amended.

Motion carried
Resolution adopted with amendment
(Communicated to the House of Deputies in HB Message #87)

Education
The House of Bishops Committee on Education presented its Report #8 on Resolution A021 (Broadening HIV Prevention Methods) and moved adoption with amendment.

Original Text of Resolution:
(A021)
Resolved, the House of Deputies concurring, That The Episcopal Church, through its General Convention, call upon its African-American members and its congregations with larger populations of African-Americans to take the lead in insuring that all methods used to prevent the spread of HIV are taught in school curricula, Church School curricula and in other educational settings. Educational efforts shall be intentionally directed toward the prevention of HIV among men who have sex with other men.

Committee Amendment:
Resolved, the House of Deputies concurring, That The Episcopal Church, through its General Convention, call upon its ~~African-American~~ members and its

congregations ~~with larger populations of African-Americans~~ to take the lead in insuring that all methods used to prevent the spread of HIV are taught in school curricula, Church School curricula and in other educational settings. ~~Educational efforts shall be intentionally directed toward the prevention of HIV among men who have sex with other men.~~

Motion carried
Resolution adopted with amendment
(Communicated to the House of Deputies in HB Message #88)

The House of Bishops Committee on Education presented its Report #10 on Resolution A065 (Leadership Programs for 18–25 Year-Olds) and moved adoption of a substitute.

Original Text of Resolution:
(A065)
Resolved, the House of Deputies concurring, That The Episcopal Church encourage dioceses to explore and develop exciting internships and leadership development programs aimed at 18–25 year-olds, with a focus on social justice, discipleship, simple living, intentional community, spiritual formation, theological reflection, and vocational discernment.

Committee Substitute:
Resolved, the House of Deputies concurring, That the Ministries with Young People Cluster be directed to review and identify existing internships and leadership programs for 18–30 year-old members of our church, particularly seeking programs that focus on social justice, discipleship, simple living, intentional community, spiritual formation, theological reflection, and vocational discernment; and be it further

Resolved, That the 74th General Convention of The Episcopal Church encourage dioceses, congregations, educational institutions, and other organizations of our church to explore and develop new internships and leadership development programs for 18–30 year-old members of our church, including programs that send young people into mission fields to do the work of the church; and to seek funding from additional sources to support this work; and be it further

Resolved, That the Ministries with Young People Cluster be directed to support these efforts, and to hold these programs up to dioceses, congregations, institutions, and other organizations of our church, so that they may be shared and implemented throughout our church; and be it further

Resolved, That the General Convention request the Joint Standing Committee on Program, Budget and Finance to consider a budget allocation of $500,000 per year, for a total of $1,500,000 during the next triennium, for implementation of this resolution, and that this allocation be used to support young adults' participation in these programs and the development efforts that are encouraged in this resolution.

Motion carried
Substitute resolution adopted
(Communicated to the House of Deputies in HB Message #89)

Church Pension Fund

The House of Bishops Committee on Church Pension Fund presented its Report #1 on Resolution D042 (Amend Canon I.8.2, Regarding Election of Church Pension Fund Trustees) and moved adoption of a substitute.

Original Text of Resolution:

(D042)

Resolved, the House of Deputies concurring, That Canon I.8.2 be amended to read as follows:

That the General Convention at each regular meeting shall elect, on the nomination of a Joint Committee thereof, ~~twelve~~ nine persons to serve as Trustees of The Church Pension Fund for a term of six years and until their successors shall have been elected and have qualified, and shall also fill such vacancies as may exist on the Board of Trustees. *At the first meeting following the General Convention, the Trustees of The Church Pension Fund shall elect three persons for a term of six years and until their successors shall have been elected.* ~~Effective January 1, 1989, a~~ Any person who has been elected as a Trustee by General Convention for twelve or more consecutive years shall not be eligible for reelection until the next regular General Convention following the one in which that person was not eligible for reelection to the Board of Trustees. Any vacancy which occurs at a time when the General Convention is not in session may be filled by the Board of Trustees by appointment, *ad interim,* of a Trustee who shall serve until the next session of the General Convention thereafter shall have elected a Trustee to serve for the remainder of the unexpired term pertaining to such vacancy.

Committee Substitute:

Resolved, the House of Deputies concurring, That Canon I.8.2 be amended to read as follows:

The General Convention at each regular meeting shall elect, on the nomination of a Joint Committee thereof, twelve persons to serve as Trustees of The Church Pension Fund for a term of six years and until their successors shall have been elected and have qualified, and shall also fill such vacancies as may exist on the Board of Trustees. *At a meeting following the General Convention, the Trustees of the Church Pension Fund may elect up to three (3) additional persons to serve until the next General Convention if the Trustees believe there are particular areas of expertise that need strengthening on the Board of Trustees.* ~~Effective January 1, 1989,~~ Any person who has been elected as a Trustee by General Convention for twelve ~~or more~~ consecutive years shall not be eligible for reelection until the next regular General Convention following the one in which that person was not eligible for reelection to the Board of Trustees. Any vacancy which occurs at a time when the General Convention is not in session may be filled by the Board of Trustees by appointment,*ad interim,* of a Trustee who shall serve until the next session of the General Convention thereafter shall have elected a Trustee to serve for the remainder of the unexpired term pertaining to such vacancy.

Motion carried
Substitute resolution adopted
(Communicated to the House of Deputies in HB Message #90)

Reconsider Resolution A101
The Bishop of Haiti moved to reconsider Resolution A101.

Proposed Amendment
Amend the adopted resolution by adding the words "and French" to the second resolve clause so that all services will be published in French.

Motion carried
Amendment adopted

A vote was taken on Resolution A101 as amended.

Motion carried
Resolution adopted with amendment
(Communicated to the House of Deputies in HB Message #87)

Stewardship and Development
The House of Bishops Committee on Stewardship and Development presented its Report #7 on Resolution A136 (National Mission Narrative/Annual Report) and moved adoption with amendment.

Original Text of Resolution:
(A136)
Resolved, the House of Deputies concurring, That the 74th General Convention direct the Episcopal Church Center staff to develop, produce, publish, and distribute to The Episcopal Church at-large an annual report that describes, in word and image, the good works that are being accomplished throughout our church in this country and in the world.

Committee Amendment:
Resolved, the House of Deputies concurring, *That as responsible stewards we are called to communicate the use of and to be accountable for the resources provided to accomplish the mission and ministry of The Episcopal Church. In the spirit of this responsibility,* That the 74th General Convention direct *the Executive Council and* the Episcopal Church Center staff to develop ~~produce, publish,~~ and distribute, *in a variety of media forms, a yearly report* ~~to the Episcopal Church at large an annual report~~ that describes, in word and image *what has been accomplished through the Domestic and Foreign Missionary Society budget in that prior year. This report will include a thorough financial overview of the expenditures of our budget presented in a manner that measures our success in fulfilling our mission priorities.* ~~the good works that are being accomplished throughout our church in this country and in the world.~~

Motion carried
Resolution adopted with amendment
(Communicated to the House of Deputies in HB Message #91)

Consecration of Bishops
The Presiding Bishop read the results of Ballot #5 on the consent to the consecration of Bishop-elect Itty of the Diocese of Oregon. Of 106 bishops with jurisdiction, 103 have given consent.

The House concurred
(Communicated to the House of Deputies in HB Message #92)

Executive Council
The Secretary announced the results of the election of Bishops for the Executive Council. There were 149 ballots cast and the Bishop of Lexington and the Bishop Suffragan of Connecticut, received a majority and were elected.
(Communicated to the House of Deputies in HB Message #96)

Ecumenical Relations
The House of Bishops Committee on Ecumenical Relations presented its Report #10 on Resolution A088 (Response to Gift of Authority) and moved adoption.

Original Text of Resolution:
(A088)
Resolved, the House of Deputies concurring, That the affirmations noted and the questions raised in the report of the Standing Commission on Ecumenical Relations be referred to ARCIC for further dialogue; and be it further
Resolved, That the Report of the Standing Commission on Ecumenical Relations on the Gift of Authority be transmitted to the Anglican Communion Office as the official response of this Church.

Motion carried
Resolution adopted
(Communicated to the House of Deputies in HB Message #93)

The House of Bishops Committee on Ecumenical Relations presented its Report #11 on Resolution A089 ("Open Communion") and moved adoption with amendment.

Original Text of Resolution:
(A089)
Resolved, the House of Deputies concurring, That the 74th General Convention of the Episcopal Church establish a task force to study the matter of the increasingly common practice of open communion to report back to the 2006 General Convention; and be it further
Resolved, That this task force shall be comprised of Bishops, Priests, Deacons, and lay persons with representation from the Standing Commission on Ecumenical Relations, the Standing Commission on Liturgy and Music, and the Standing Commission on Constitution and Canons, as proposed by the Chairs of those Commissions.
The Bishop of South Carolina moved to refer the resolution to the House of Bishops Committee on Theology.

Motion carried
Resolution referred
(Communicated to the House of Deputies in HB Message #94)

Consent Calendar
The Secretary laid the Consent Calendar on the table for the Fifth Legislative Day.

Canons
The House of Bishops Committee on Canons presented its Report #12 on Resolution A047 (Amend Canon IV.14.13) and moved adoption of a substitute.

Original Text of Resolution:
(A047)
Resolved, the House of Deputies concurring, That Canon IV.14.13 be amended to add "
(a)" to the title of the existing section, and add a new subparagraph (b) to read as follows:
(b) Any Bishop exercising authority as provided in this Title (i) who is related by blood or marriage to the Respondent or any alleged victim, or (ii) who reasonably believes himself or herself unable to render a fair and independent sentence, shall be disqualified and excused from service in connection with the matter.

Committee Substitute:
Resolved, the House of Deputies concurring, That Canon IV.14.13 be amended to read as follows:
Sec. 13. ~~Relationship to parties~~ *Disqualification of Bishop, Judge, or Member of a Review Committee.*
~~Any member of any Diocesan Review Committee, Review Committee or any Court provided for in this Title (i) who is related to the Respondent by blood or marriage, (ii) who has knowledge of essential facts involved in the matter, (iii) who has a close personal or professional relationship with the Respondent, any alleged Victim, or~~

~~any witness in the matter, or (iv) who reasonably believes himself or herself unable to render a fair and independent judgment, shall be disqualified and excused from service in connection with the matter.~~

(a) Any Bishop exercising authority as provided in this Title shall disqualify himself or herself in any proceeding in which the Bishop's impartiality may reasonably be questioned. The Bishop shall also disqualify himself or herself when the Bishop, the Bishop's spouse, or a person within the third degree of relationship to either of them, or the spouse of such person, (1) is the Respondent, alleged Victim, or Complainant, or (2) is likely to be a witness in the proceeding.

(b) Any member of any Diocesan Review Committee, Review Committee, or any Ecclesiastical Court provided for in this Title, shall disqualify himself or herself in any proceeding in which the member's impartiality may reasonably be questioned. The member shall also disqualify himself or herself when the member, the member's spouse, any person within the third degree of relationship to either of them, or the spouse of such person, (1) is the Respondent, alleged Victim, or Complainant, (2) is likely to be a witness in the proceeding, (3) has a personal bias or prejudice concerning the Respondent, alleged Victim, or Complainant, (4) has personal knowledge of disputed evidentiary facts concerning the proceeding, (5) has a personal financial interest in the outcome of the proceeding or in the Respondent, alleged Victim, Complainant, or any other interest that could be substantially affected by the outcome, or (6) is a member of the same congregation or otherwise has a close personal or professional relationship with the Respondent, any alleged Victim, Complainant, or any witness in the matter.

(c) No Bishop, Ecclesiastical Court, Diocesan Review Committee, or Review Committee shall accept from the parties to the proceeding any waiver of any ground for disqualification enumerated in this Section unless preceded by full disclosure of the basis for the disqualification, on the record, to all parties.

The Bishop of Lexington moved to amend the resolution.

Proposed Amendment:
Substitute the original text of the resolution for the Committee substitute.
The Chair suspended debate on this matter to be reconsidered at another time.

Consideration postponed

[Consideration of Resolution A047 resumed on Day 5. See Page 165. *Ed.*]

Consecration of Bishops
The Presiding Bishop read the results of Ballot #6 on the consent to the consecration of Bishop-elect Miller of the Diocese of Milwaukee. Of 106 bishops with jurisdiction, 102 have given consent.

The House concurred
(Communicated to the House of Deputies in HB Message #95)

Recess

Following announcements by the Secretary, the House of Bishops Committee on Dispatch of Business moved that the House stand in recess until 2:30 p.m. on the Fifth Legislative Day.

Motion carried

The House recessed at 12:59 p.m. with prayer led by Chaplain Battle.

MINNEAPOLIS MEETING   HOUSE OF BISHOPS

FIFTH DAY

Sunday
August 3, 2003

AFTERNOON SESSION

The House of Bishops reconvened at 2:30 p.m. with the Presiding Bishop in the chair.

Reflections were led by the Chaplain and forty minutes were allowed for conversation.

The House resumed at 3:17 p.m.

Agenda of the Day
The House of Bishops Committee on Dispatch of Business moved to adopt the agenda of the day.

Motion carried
Agenda adopted

Previous Day's Minutes
The House of Bishops Committee on Dispatch of Business moved to dispense with the reading of the previous day's minutes.

Motion carried

Messages from the House of Deputies
The Secretary announced that the following messages had been received from the House of Deputies:

HD Message #47:	D053 (Honor John Kemper Cannon) The House of Deputies adopted the resolution with amendment.
HD Message #48:	C026 (Reduce the Use of Toxic Chemicals) The House of Deputies rejected the resolution.
HD Message #49:	C017 (Global Warming/Energy Conservation for National Church Headquarters) The House of Deputies adopted the resolution with amendment.
HD Message #50:	Special Order for Consideration of C045 (Consent to the Election of The Rev. Canon V. Gene Robinson as Bishop Coadjutor of the Diocese of New Hampshire) The House of Deputies adopted the resolution with amendment.
HD Message #51:	A039 (Amend Constitution Article II.2, First Reading) The House of Deputies concurred.
HD Message #52:	A045 (Amend Canon I.17.2) The House of Deputies concurred.

HD Message #53:	A049 (Amend Canon IV.2(A)(2))
	The House of Deputies concurred.
HD Message #54:	A050 (Amend Canon IV.2(B)(10))
	The House of Deputies concurred.
HD Message #55:	A072 (Amend Canon I.6.1)
	The House of Deputies adopted the resolution with amendment.
HD Message #56:	C034 (Length of General Convention)
	The House of Deputies discharged the resolution.
HD Message #57:	A152 (Episcopal Partnership for Global Mission)
	The House of Deputies concurred.
HD Message #58:	A133 (Adopt "Expanding Mission and Vitality in Small Congregations")
	The House of Deputies concurred.
HD Message #59:	A035 (Implement Humanitarian Goals in Africa)
	The House of Deputies adopted the resolution with amendment.

Consent Calendar
The Secretary moved to accept the Consent Calendar.

Motion carried

Stewardship and Development
The House of Bishops Committee on Stewardship and Development presented its Report #8 on Resolution B022 (Celebration of African Martyrs) and moved adoption.

Original Text of Resolution:
(B022)
Resolved, the House of Deputies concurring, That the 74th General Convention encourage congregations to take a special offering on occasions when martyrs of Africa are being commemorated, and that such offerings be sent to Episcopal Relief and Development to support Anglican Provinces in Africa; and be it further *Resolved,* That educational materials about African Anglican Provinces be provided at every level of the church.

Motion carried
Resolution adopted
(Communicated to the House of Deputies in HB Message #97)

Communications

The House of Bishops Committee on Communications presented its Report #5 on Resolution D021 (Support for Church Publishing Inc.'s Revised Strategy) and moved adoption.

Original Text of Resolution:
(D021)
Resolved, the House of Deputies concurring, That the 74th General Convention of The Episcopal Church endorse the Church Pension Fund's goal of firmly establishing Church Publishing Incorporated as a significant provider of books, software, and related services to The Episcopal Church's institutions and individuals; and be it further
Resolved, That we thank The Rt. Rev. Hays Rockwell for his willingness to serve as chairperson of the reconstituted Board of Directors of Church Publishing Incorporated; and be it further
Resolved, That we encourage all the member organizations of the Episcopal Publishing Ministries to work together to provide members of the Anglican Communion and others with materials to strengthen them spiritually and theologically; to increase their knowledge of the history and traditions of their Church; and to facilitate Christian worship and witness.

Motion carried
Resolution adopted
(Communicated to the House of Deputies in HB Message #98)

Canons

The House of Bishops Committee on Canons resumed its Report #12 on Resolution A047 (Amend Canon IV.14.13) and moved adoption of a substitute.

The Bishop of Lexington moved to amend the resolution.

Proposed Amendment:
Substitute the original text of the resolution for the committee substitute.

A vote was taken on the motion. There were 63 "yes" votes and 67 "no" votes.

Motion defeated
Amendment defeated

The Bishop of Southwest Florida moved to amend the resolution.

Proposed Amendment:
Delete the first sentence in Sec. 13(a) and in the same section, delete the word "also" in the second sentence. Delete the first sentence in Sec. 13(b), and in the same section, delete the word "also" in the second sentence.

The question was called to terminate debate on the amendment.
> Motion carried
> Debate terminated

A vote was taken on the proposed amendment.
> Motion defeated
> Amendment defeated

A vote was taken on substitute Resolution A047.
> Motion carried
> Substitute resolution adopted
> (Communicated to the House of Deputies in HB Message #99)

General Board Examining Chaplains and Trustees of General Theological Seminary

Ballots were distributed to elect members to the General Board of Examining Chaplains and to elect Trustees of General Theological Seminary.

Canons

The House of Bishops Committee on Canons presented its Report #13 on Resolution A051 (Amend Canon IV.4.14) and moved adoption of a substitute.

Original Text of Resolution:

(A051)
Resolved, the House of Deputies concurring, That Canon IV.4.14 be amended by numbering the existing section as *(a)*, and adding a new section *(b)* as follows:
(b) The record shall be in the custody of the Clerk and kept in the depository of the Registrar of the General Convention, and in the Archives of The Episcopal Church.

Committee Substitute:

Resolved, the House of Deputies concurring, That Canon IV.4.14 be amended to read as follows:
Sec. 14. (a) The Ecclesiastical Trial Court shall keep a *complete and accurate record* of ~~the~~ *its* proceedings. ~~in each case brought before it and the record shall be certified by the Presiding Judge of the Court. If the record cannot be authenticated by the Presiding Judge by reason of the Presiding Judge's death, disability or absence, it shall be authenticated by a member of the Court designated for that purpose by majority vote of the Court.~~ *When all proceedings on a Presentment have been concluded, including any and all appeals, the Presiding Judge shall certify the record. If the Presiding Judge did not participate in the proceeding for any reason, by majority vote the Court shall designate another member to certify the record.*
(b) The Court shall promptly deliver the original certified record of the proceedings to the Archives of The Episcopal Church.
And be it further
Resolved, That Canon IV.4.31 be amended to read as follows:
Sec. 31. During the period between General Conventions, each Provincial Synod shall elect the Judges of the Court of Review in the Province. The Synod shall

prescribe the time and the manner in which such Judges shall be elected. The persons so elected, except in case of death, resignation, or declination to serve, shall continue to be members of the Court for such terms as the Synod may set and until their successors shall be elected. The Bishop elected by the Synod shall be the Presiding ~~Officer~~ *Judge* of the Court.

And be it further

Resolved, That Canon IV.4.48 be amended to read as follows:

Sec. 48. *(a)* The Court of Review shall keep a *complete and accurate record* of all *its* proceedings. *When all proceedings on an appeal have been concluded, the Presiding Judge shall certify the record. If the Presiding Judge did not participate in the proceeding for any reason, by majority vote the Court shall designate another member to certify the record.*

(b) The Court shall promptly deliver the original certified record of the proceedings to the Archives of The Episcopal Church.

And be it further

Resolved, That Canon IV.5.29 be amended to read as follows:

Sec. 29(a) The Court *for the Trial of a Bishop* shall keep a *complete and accurate* record of ~~all~~ *its* proceedings. *When all proceedings on a Presentment have been concluded, including any and all appeals, the Presiding Judge shall certify the record. If the Presiding Judge did not participate in the proceeding for any reason, by majority vote the Court shall designate another member to certify the record.*

(b) ~~The record shall be kept by the Clerk, inserted in a book and be attested by the signature of the Presiding Judge and Clerk. The record shall be in the custody of the Clerk and kept in the depository of the Registrar of the General Convention, and in the Archives of the Episcopal Church and shall be open to the inspection of every member of this Church.~~ The Court shall promptly deliver the original certified record of the proceedings to the Archives of The Episcopal Church.

And be it further

Resolved, That a new section be added to Canon IV.6, numbered 22 to read as follows, and that the existing Section 22 of Canon IV.6 be renumbered Section 23:

Sec. 22 (a) The Court of Review of a Trial of a Bishop shall keep a complete and accurate record of its proceedings. When all proceedings on an appeal have been concluded, the Presiding Judge shall certify the record. If the Presiding Judge did not participate in the proceeding for any reason, by majority vote the Court shall designate another member to certify the record.

(b) The Court shall promptly deliver the original certified record of the proceedings to the Archives of The Episcopal Church.

Sec ~~22~~23. The reasonable and necessary expenses of the Court of Review of the Trial of a Bishop, including but not limited to the fees, costs, disbursements and expenses of the Judges, Church Attorneys, Clerks, Reporters and Lay Assessors, shall be charged upon the General Convention and shall be paid by the Treasurer of General Convention upon the order of the Presiding Judge of the Court. The Court shall have the authority to contract for and bind the General Convention to payment of these expenses.

And be it further

Resolved, That Canon IV.4.51 be amended by striking the last two sentences thereof, to read as follows:

Sec. 51. The concurrence of five members of a Court of Review shall be necessary to pronounce a judgment. The judgment or decision of the Court shall be in writing, signed by the members of the Court concurring therein, and shall distinctly specify the grounds of the decision and shall be attached to the record. If the concurrence of five of the members cannot be obtained, that fact shall be stated in the record, and the determination or Judgment of the Trial Court shall stand as affirmed except as to any reversal in part in which there has been concurrence. Immediately after the determination of the appeal, the Presiding Judge of the Court shall give notice thereof in writing to the appellant and appellee and to the Bishop and the Diocesan Review Committee of the Diocese in which the Trial was had. ~~Upon the determination of the appeal, the original record upon which the appeal was heard, together with the record of the Court of Review, certified by the Presiding Judge and the Secretary or Clerk, shall be remitted to the Bishop or the Diocesan Review Committee of the jurisdiction in which the Trial was had and to the Archives of The Episcopal Church. All records remitted as herein provided shall be deposited and be preserved among the Archives of the jurisdiction to which they are sent.~~

And be it further

Resolved, That a new section be added to Canon IV.14, numbered 29, to read as follows

Sec. 29. Record of Certain Title IV Proceedings and Actions.

(a) Each Ecclesiastical Court shall keep a complete and accurate record of its proceedings. When all proceedings on a Presentment or other matter have been concluded, including any and all appeals, the Presiding Judge shall certify the record. If the Presiding Judge did not participate in the proceeding for any reason, the Court, by majority vote, shall designate another member to certify the record.

(b) A Court may make provision for the preservation and storage of a copy of the record of each proceeding in the Diocese in which the Presentment or other proceeding originated.

(c) A Court shall promptly deliver the original certified record of its proceedings to the Archives of The Episcopal Church.

(d) A Bishop, including the Presiding Bishop, who pronounces a Sentence shall deliver a copy of the notice of the Sentence to the Archives of The Episcopal Church.

(e) In the case of a Waiver and Voluntary Submission to discipline of a Deacon, Priest or Bishop, the Ecclesiastical Authority with jurisdiction shall promptly deliver a copy of the required written instrument to the Archives of The Episcopal Church

(f) Bishops, including the Presiding Bishop, shall promptly deliver a record of any action of remission or modification of a Sentence to the Archives of The Episcopal Church.

And be it further

Resolved, That the definition of "Sentence" in Canon IV.15 be amended to read as follows:

Sentence shall mean the sentence adjudged by an Ecclesiastical Court after a finding of a commission of an Offense or the lesser Sentence to be pronounced by a Bishop or the Presiding Bishop, as the case may be. *The Sentence, whether Admonition, Suspension or Deposition, shall specify the Canon or Canons under which the action is being taken.*

And be it further
Resolved, That the Standing Commission on Constitution and Canons be directed during the next triennium to consider any further canonical changes that may be appropriate in light of the changes made in this Resolution, and to report on its work to the 75th General Convention.

Motion carried
Substitute resolution adopted
(Communicated to the House of Deputies in HB Message #100)

World Mission

The House of Bishops Committee on World Mission presented its Report #3 on Resolution D009 (Support 2008 Anglican Gathering) and moved adoption.

Original Text of Resolution:
(D009)
Resolved, the House of Deputies concurring, That the 74th General Convention enthusiastically support and affirm the call of the Anglican Consultative Council meetings XI (Scotland 1999) and XII (Hong Kong 2002), and of the Joint Standing Committee of the Primates and Anglican Consultative Council, that there be an Anglican congress of lay people, priests, deacons, and bishops from every diocese in the Anglican Communion described as the "Anglican Gathering" and tentatively planned to be held in South Africa in mid-2008; and be it further
Resolved, That every diocese of The Episcopal Church begin to plan and make financial provisions for representation at the 2008 Anglican Gathering; and be it further
Resolved, That the Standing Commission on World Mission work cooperatively with the Executive Council and the Joint Standing Committee on Program, Budget and Finance to prepare during the next triennium a financial provision for the 75th General Convention to support the 2008 Anglican Gathering; and be it further
Resolved, That the department of Anglican and Global Relations at the Episcopal Church Center, working in consultation with the Standing Commission on World Mission, be directed to assist the wider Anglican Communion in every way possible in the development of the 2008 Anglican Gathering; and be it further
Resolved, That the Presiding Bishop communicate The Episcopal Church's enthusiastic support for the 2008 Anglican Gathering to the Archbishop of Canterbury and the Primates of the Anglican Communion; and be it further
Resolved, That the Secretary of the General Convention, along with The Episcopal Church's members of the Anglican Consultative Council, communicate the substance of this resolution to the General Secretary of the Anglican Communion, the Anglican Consultative Council, and the staff and leadership of the Inter-Anglican Standing Commission on Mission and Evangelism.

Motion carried
Resolution adopted
(Communicated to the House of Deputies in HB Message #101)

The House of Bishops Committee on World Mission presented its Report #5 on Resolution A137 (Accountability Of Mission Partners) and moved adoption of a substitute.

Original Text of Resolution:
(A137)
Resolved, the House of Deputies concurring, That the 74th General Convention require that recipients of grants or gifts from the Domestic and Foreign Missionary Society maintain appropriate accounting records and controls over such grants and gifts.

Committee Substitute:
Resolved, the House of Deputies concurring, That the 74th General Convention affirm the action of the Executive Council taken at its January 2003 meeting requiring that recipients of grants or gifts from the Domestic and Foreign Missionary Society maintain appropriate accounting records and controls over such grants and gifts; and be it further
Resolved, That the Domestic and Foreign Missionary Society continue to provide technical support, when necessary, for preparing these reports.

Motion carried
Substitute resolution adopted
(Communicated to the House of Deputies in HB Message #102)

Education
The House of Bishops Committee on Education presented its Report #11 on Resolution B024 (Task Force on Lifelong Christian Education and Formation) and moved adoption.

Original Text of Resolution:
(B024)
Resolved, the House of Deputies concurring, That the 74th General Convention authorize the creation of a nine-year Task Force of Executive Council on Lifelong Christian Education and Formation that will
- Develop a comprehensive vision and strategy to strengthen Lifelong Christian Education and Formation throughout The Episcopal Church and equip people of all ages to experience, to tell about, and to invite others into the Good News of the Gospel;
- Integrate Christian Formation into every area of the church's mission and ministry, recognizing that learning occurs in multiple ways throughout the entire life cycle;
- Identify and communicate resources and models that support the gifts and needs of a church of great diversity and that promote outcomes recommended by the 20/20 Strategy Group;
- Encourage conversation and collaboration among the many entities in the

church that address specific aspects of Christian Education and Formation for mission and ministry;

Provide international and ecumenical links for Christian Education and Formation; and be it further

Resolved, That this Task Force be composed of sixteen members: four bishops; four clergy; and eight lay persons; that the Task Force will meet at least two times a year, commencing in 2004, with additional small gatherings for conversation with selected groups involved in lifelong learning and formation; and that the Task Force will report on its work beginning at the 75th General Convention in 2006; and be it further

Resolved, That the General Convention request the Joint Standing Committee on Program, Budget and Finance to consider a budget allocation of $120,000 for implementation of this resolution for the next three years.

Motion carried
Resolution adopted
(Communicated to the House of Deputies in HB Message #103)

The House of Bishops Committee on Education presented its Report #12 on Resolution D075 (Holistic Christian Education Study) and moved that the Committee be discharged.

Motion carried
Committee discharged
(Communicated to the House of Deputies in HB Message #104)

Stewardship and Development

The House of Bishops Committee on Stewardship and Development presented its Report #9 on Resolution B004 (Mission Funding Task Force) and moved adoption of a substitute.

Original Text of Resolution:

(B004)

Resolved, the House of Deputies concurring, That a task force consisting of twelve persons, to be appointed jointly by the Presiding Bishop and the President of the House of Deputies, is directed to study the system of funding the budget of The Episcopal Church, such study to include facilitating mission at the global, national, diocesan, and parish and community levels and the encouragement of mutual responsibility, equity, and accountability among the dioceses of this church. The task force will report its findings and recommendations to the 75th General Convention; and be it further

Resolved, That the task force shall be named the Mission Funding Task Force, and be allocated funding to enable the deliberations of the Task Force in the amount of $60,000 for the triennium.

Committee Substitute:
Resolved, the House of Deputies concurring, That in light of the need for resources to fulfill the 20/20 initiatives and to more fully address the many issues facing The Episcopal Church at all levels, the 74th General Convention direct the Presiding Bishop and the President of the House of Deputies to appoint a task force of 12 people, including, among others, members of the Standing Commission on Stewardship and Development, the Joint Standing Committee on Program, Budget and Finance and the House of Deputies Committee on the State of the Church. This task force is to be named the Mission Funding Task Force; and be it further
Resolved, That the Mission Funding Task Force will undertake a comprehensive study on the systems and procedures for funding, budgeting, and expenditure of the Domestic and Foreign Missionary Society; and be it further
Resolved, That this study include, but not be limited to the following issues:
   The level of the church at which mission support is most efficient
   The best use of resources and the possible need for redirection of resources
   The effectiveness in supporting our stated priorities
   Possible unexplored efficiencies
   The review of existing commitments with quantification of the discretionary funding amount remaining after funding those commitments
   The most efficient and equitable method of funding the budget
   The encouragement of mutual responsibility, equity and accountability to and among the dioceses of the church.
The Task Force will report its findings and recommendations for consideration at the 75th General Convention; and be it further
Resolved, That the General Convention request the Joint Standing Committee on Program, Budget and Finance to consider a budget allocation of $75,000 for the implementation of this resolution.

Motion carried
Substitute resolution adopted
(Communicated to the House of Deputies in HB Message #105)

The House of Bishops Committee on Stewardship and Development presented its Report #10 on Resolution A066 (Campus Ministry Allocation) and moved adoption of a substitute.

Original Text of Resolution:
(A066)
Resolved, the House of Deputies concurring, That the 74th General Convention call upon all dioceses of The Episcopal Church to allocate a meaningful proportion of budgeted income to campus ministry as a form of mission to the next generation.

Committee Substitute:
Resolved, the House of Deputies concurring, That the 74th General Convention call upon the Executive Council, the dioceses and congregations of The Episcopal Church to affirm existing campus ministries and explore new and creative forms of

campus ministry, new sources of funding and to commit adequate resources in time, talent, and treasure to ensure a significant and effective ministry at each campus.

Motion carried
Substitute resolution adopted
(Communicated to the House of Deputies in HB Message #106)

Social and Urban Affairs
The House of Bishops Committee on Social and Urban Affairs presented its Report #2 on HD Message #40 on Resolution A010 (Continue Anti-Racism Mandate) and moved concurrence.

The House concurred
(Communicated to the House of Deputies in HB Message #107)

Final Text of Resolution:
(A010)
Resolved, That The Episcopal Church reaffirm its historic commitment to eradicate racial injustice in the Church and in secular society, and that the Executive Council continue the anti-racism program with appropriate staffing and budget, as approved by the 73rd General Convention (A047) and recommend the National Dialogues on Anti-Racism methodology; and be it further

Resolved, That the emerging provincial network of anti-racism trainers be recognized as an important resource, and its utilization commended to the several provinces, dioceses, and affiliated organizations of the Church; and be it further

Resolved, That the 74th General Convention extend its appreciation to the organizers and participants of the anti-racism hearings and call upon the anti-racism committee (Anti-Racism Advisory Committee of the Executive Council and the Office of Social Justice) to implement a program that responds to the issues raised at the hearings, as appropriate; and be it further

Resolved, That all persons seeking election or appointment to the several standing commissions, other committees of Executive Council, related boards and auxiliary organizations must have had anti-racism training as required by the 73rd General Convention (B049) or agree to have this training within a year of their appointment; and be it further

Resolved, That the Office of Peace and Justice be commended for its "Stop the Hate" Campaign, and be encouraged to develop similar programs that address the issues of racial profiling and other abuses of the criminal justice system that have emerged in this post 9/11 environment; and be it further

Resolved, **That the Anti-Racism Committee of Executive Council be directed to prepare a report for the other standing committees and commissions of the Church that inform them of the several issues emerging from the anti-racism hearings, and specify what actions each might take to ameliorate the impact of racism in their area of concern.**

The House of Bishops Committee on Social and Urban Affairs presented its Report #3 on HD Message #41 on Resolution A014 (Approve Research on Human Stem Cells) and moved concurrence.

The Bishop of Pittsburgh moved to refer the resolution to the House of Bishops Committee on Theology.

Motion failed

The Bishop Suffragan of New York moved to amend the resolution.

Proposed Amendment:
Delete section A and renumber sections B and C.

Motion carried
Amendment adopted

A vote was taken on Resolution A014 as amended.

Motion carried
The House concurred with amendment
(Communicated to the House of Deputies in HB Message #108)

RECESS

Following announcements by the Secretary, the House Committee on Dispatch of Business moved that the House stand in recess until 11:00 a.m. on the Sixth Legislative Day.

Motion carried

The House recessed at 4:34 p.m. with prayer led by Chaplain Battle.

MINNEAPOLIS MEETING　　　　　　　　　　HOUSE OF BISHOPS

SIXTH DAY

Monday
August 4, 2003

MORNING SESSION

The House reconvened at 11:00 a.m. with the Presiding Bishop in the chair.
The House spent ten minutes in table conversations.
The Presiding Bishop yielded the chair to the Vice-Chair.
The House resumed at 11:11 a.m.

Agenda of the Day
The House of Bishops Committee on Dispatch of Business moved to adopt the agenda of the day.

Motion carried
Agenda adopted

Previous Day's Minutes
The House of Bishops Committee on Dispatch of Business moved to dispense with the reading of the previous day's minutes.

Motion carried

Messages from the House of Deputies
The Secretary announced that the following messages had been received from the House of Deputies.

HD Message #60:	A119 (Role of Deacons)
	The House of Deputies concurred.
HD Message #61:	A006 (Employment Policies Task Group)
	The House of Deputies adopted the resolution with amendment.
HD Message #62:	C012 (Church's Ethnic Desks and 20/20)
	The House of Deputies discharged the resolution.
HD Message #63:	A091 (Continue use of Enriching Our Worship 1&2)
	The House of Deputies concurred.
HD Message #64	A093 (Approve Liturgical Calendar Commemorations)
	The House of Deputies concurred.
HD Message #65:	A094 (Church Year Calendar Inclusions)
	The House of Deputies concurred.
HD Message #66:	A095 (Authorize Trial Use of Commemorations)
	The House of Deputies concurred.
HD Message #67:	A096 (Inclusion in the Church Year Calendar)
	The House of Deputies concurred.
HD Message #68:	A097 (Authorize Trial Use of Commemoration)
	The House of Deputies concurred.

HD Message #69:	C009 (Liturgical Commemoration of Tikhon, Russian Orthodox Bishop of Alaska and North America) The House of Deputies referred the resolution to a Standing Commission.
HD Message #70:	C013 (Liturgical Commemoration of The Rev. Dr. John Roberts) The House of Deputies referred the resolution to a Standing Commission.
HD Message #71:	D024 (Thanksgiving for the Ministry of The Episcopal Church and Visual Arts) The House of Deputies adopted the resolution.
HD Message #72:	Presiding Bishop's Appointments. The House of Deputies concurred.
HD Message #73:	Presiding Bishop's Appointments. The House of Deputies concurred.
HD Message #74:	Presiding Bishop's Appointments. The House of Deputies concurred.
HD Message #75:	Presiding Bishop's Appointments. The House of Deputies concurred.
HD Message #76:	A017 (National Conversation on Women's Ordination) The House of Deputies adopted the resolution with amendment.
HD Message #77:	A041 (Ratify Actions of Standing Commission on Liturgy and Music) The House of Deputies concurred.
HD Message #78:	A023 (Establish Institutional Wellness and the Prevention of Sexual Misconduct Task Force) The House of Deputies adopted the resolution with amendment.
HD Message #79:	A151 (World Mission Funds) The House of Deputies concurred.
HD Message #80:	A123 (Diocesan Alcohol and Drug Dependency Policies) The House of Deputies adopted the resolution with amendment.
HD Message #81:	C045 (Consent to the Election of The Rev. Canon V. Gene Robinson as Bishop Coadjutor of the Diocese of New Hampshire) The House of Deputies adopted the resolution.

Special Order of Business

The Ecumenical Officer introduced the Rev. Mark Hanson, Presiding Bishop of the Evangelical Lutheran Church in America.

Bishop Hanson addressed the House.

The Ecumenical Officer introduced Ecumenical visitors to the House of Bishops.
Representing the Evangelical Lutheran Church in America
    Presiding Bishop Mark S. Hanson
    Mrs. Ione Hanson
    Rev. Lowell Almen
    Rev. Robert Brusic
    Rev. Duane Larson
    Rev. Randall Lee
    Bishop Peter Rogness
    Rev. Dr. Merlyn E. Satrom
Representing Mar Thoma Syrian Church
    The Rt. Rev. Dr. Euyakim Mar Coorilos
Representing the Moravian Church
    The Rt. Rev. Graham Rights
    Mrs. Peggy Cartner
    The Rt. Rev. Hopeton Clennon
    The Rev. Dr. Otto Dreydoppel
    The Rev. Burke Johnson
    Mrs. Eleanor Johnson
    The Rev. Robert Sawyer
    Mrs. Jill Sawyer
Representing the American Baptist Church USA
    Rev. Rothang Chhangte
Representing the Disciples of Christ Church
    The Rev. Mark MacWhorter
Representing the International Council of Community Churches
    The Rev. Herman Harmelink, III
    The Rev. Michael E. Livingston
Representing the Presbyterian Church USA
    Elder Freda Gardner
    The Rev. Richard Headen
Representing the United Church of Christ
    The Rev. Dr. Elizabeth Nordbeck
    The Rev. Lydia Veliko
Representing the United Methodist Church
    Bishop Wayne K. Clymer
Representing the Roman Catholic Church
    The Most Rev. Stephen Blaire
    Dr. John Borelli
    Archbishop William Levada
    The Rev. Lee A. Piche
Representing the Antiochian Orthodox Archdiocese of North America
    The Rev. William Olnhausen

Representing Diocese of the Armenian Church in America
   The Rt. Rev. Vicken Aykazian
Representing the Greek Orthodox Church
   The Rev. Dr. Harry Pappas
Representing the Orthodox Church in America
   The Very Rev. Andrew Morbey
Representing the Patriarchal Parishes of the Russian Orthodox Church
   The Rev. Alexander Abramov
Representing the National Council of Churches of Christ
   Elenie Huszagh, Esq.
Representing Churches Uniting in Christ
   The Rev. Dr. Bertrice Wood
Representing the Minnesota Council of Churches
   The Rev. Peg Chemberlin

Bishop Clennon of the Moravian Church addressed the House.

Election for Trustees of The General Theological Seminary

The Secretary announced the results of the election for Trustees of the General Theological Seminary.

    The House of Bishops elected two bishops for three-year terms:
        The Rt. Rev. J. Neil Alexander
        The Rt. Rev. Michael Bruce Curry
            (Communicated to the House of Deputies in HB Message #117)

Election for The General Board of Examining Chaplains

The Secretary announced the results of the election for members to the General Board of Examining Chaplains.

    The House of Bishops elected one bishop for a three-year term:
        The Rt. Rev. Philip M. Duncan.

    The House of Bishops elected two bishops for six-year terms:
        The Rt. Rev. Barry R. Howe
        The Rt. Rev. Katharine Jefferts Schori

    The House of Bishops elected three lay persons for six-year terms:
        Dr. Mary Chilton Callaway
        Ms. Josephine R. Giannini
        Mr. Leonard Wilkie Johnson

    The House of Bishops elected three faculty for six-year terms:
        The Rev. Susan M. Dolan-Henderson
        The Rev. Robert Davis Hughes
        The Rev. Frederick W. Schmidt

The House of Bishop elected two priests for six-year terms:
The Rev. Mark T. Crawford
The Rev. Mary Catherine Miller Suleru
(Communicated to the House of Deputies in HB Message #116)

Recess

Following announcements by the Secretary, the House of Bishops Committee on Dispatch of Business moved that the House stand in recess until 2:30 p.m.

Motion carried

The House recessed at 11:50 a.m. with prayer led by Chaplain McIntosh.

AFTERNOON SESSION

The House reconvened at 2:30 p.m. with the Presiding Bishop in the chair. Reflections were led by the Chaplain and conversation was held for one hour. The House resumed at 3:30 p.m.

Consecration of Bishops

The Presiding Bishop read a statement (see Appendix F–Day 6) regarding allegations against the Bishop-elect of New Hampshire.
1. Questions have been raised and a thorough investigation will be made.
2. The Bishop of Western Massachusetts will chair the committee to investigate this matter.
3. The balloting for consents will not take place at this time. The process is suspended pending the investigation.

The Bishop of New Hampshire read a statement (see Appendix G–Day 6) expressing that he and the diocese had asked for the investigation and have confidence in both the Bishop-elect of New Hampshire and in the Presiding Bishop's commitment to investigate fully these matters.

Ecumenical Relations

The House of Bishops Committee on Ecumenical Relations presented its Report #12 on Resolution D010 (Amend Canons I.1.2 (n) (5), HBRO: General I(18) & HDRO IV.7(18)) and moved adoption with amendment.

Original Text of Resolution:

(D010)
Resolved, the House of Deputies concurring, That Canon I.1.2 (n) (5) be amended to read:
A Standing Commission on Ecumenical *and Interfaith* Relations consisting of 18 members (6 Bishops, 6 Priests and/or Deacons and 6 Lay Persons) *some of whom would have specific knowledge and experience in interfaith matters.* Its duties shall be to recommend to the General Convention a comprehensive and coordinated policy

and strategy on relations between this Church and other Churches, *and this Church and other religions*, to make recommendations to General Convention concerning interchurch cooperation and unity, *and interfaith dialogue and action*, and to carry out such instructions on ecumenical *and interfaith* matters as may be given it from time to time by the General Convention. It shall also nominate for appointment by the Presiding Bishop, with the advice and consent of the Executive Council, persons to serve on the governing bodies of ecumenical *and interfaith* organizations to which this Church belongs by action of the General Convention, who shall report to the Presiding Bishop, Executive Council and the Standing Commission on Ecumenical *and Interfaith* Relations.

And be it further

Resolved, That the "Rules of Order" of the House of Bishops on "General Rules for the Meetings of This House" I(18) be amended to read: Ecumenical *and Interfaith* Relations.

And be it further

Resolved, That the "Rules of Order" of the House of Deputies on "Legislative Committees" IV.7(18) be amended to read: Ecumenical *and Interfaith* Relations.

Committee Amendment:

Resolved, the House of Deputies concurring, That Canon I.1.2 (n) (5) be amended to read:

A Standing Commission on Ecumenical *and* ~~Interfaith~~ Interreligious Relations consisting of 18 members (6 Bishops, 6 Priests and/or Deacons and 6 Lay Persons) ~~some of whom would have specific knowledge and experience in interfaith matters~~. Its duties shall be to recommend to the General Convention a comprehensive and coordinated policy and strategy on relations between this Church and other Churches, *and this Church and other religions*, to make recommendations to General Convention concerning interchurch cooperation and unity, *and* ~~interfaith~~ interreligious *dialogue and action*, and to carry out such instruction on ecumenical *and* ~~interfaith~~ interreligious matters as may be given it from time to time by the General Convention. It shall also nominate for appointment by the Presiding Bishop, with the advice and consent of the Executive Council, persons to serve on the governing bodies of ecumenical *and* ~~interfaith~~ interreligious organizations to which this Church belongs by action of the General Convention, who shall report to the Presiding Bishop, Executive Council and the Standing Commission on Ecumenical *and* ~~Interfaith~~ Interreligious Relations. ~~And be it further~~

~~*Resolved*, That the "Rules of Order" of the House of Bishops on "General Rules for the Meetings of This House" I(18) be expanded to read: Ecumenical *and Interfaith* Relations; and be it further~~

~~*Resolved*, That the "Rules of Order" of the House of Deputies on "Legislative Committees" IV.7(18) be expanded to read: Ecumenical *and Interfaith* Relations.~~

Motion carried
Resolution adopted with amendment
(Communicated to the House of Deputies in HB Message #118)

Communications

The House of Bishops Committee on Communications presented its Report #1 on HD Message #22 on Resolution C027 (AV Materials of The Episcopal Church) and moved concurrence.

The House concurred
(Communicated to the House of Deputies in HB Message #119)

Final Text of Resolution:

(C027)
Resolved, That the 74th General Convention require all audio-visual materials produced by and for the General Convention, and programs of the Executive Council and staff, be made accessible to all people:
> by providing closed captioning in English for deaf and hard-of-hearing people, as well as subtitling or dubbing in Spanish and other languages where appropriate, and
> by urging all producers of religious audio-visual materials to do the same.

The House of Bishops Committee on Communications presented its Report #2 on HD Message #23 on Resolution A082 (Multilingual Publications) and moved concurrence.

The House concurred
(Communicated to the House of Deputies in HB Message #123)

Final Text of Resolution:

(A082)
Resolved, That the 74th General Convention, consistent with the Executive Council's June 2002 mandate that materials issued by the Church Center be multilingual when appropriate, ask the Executive Council, in coordination with the Church Center staff, to develop a strategy to utilize existing multilingual resources and to consider the employment of translation services; and be it further
Resolved, That the 74th General Convention request the Joint Standing Committee on Program, Budget and Finance to consider a budget allocation of $85,000 per year for the triennium for implementation of this resolution.

The House of Bishops Committee on Communications presented its Report #3 on HD Message #24 on Resolution A027 (Use of Titles) and moved concurrence.

The House concurred
(Communicated to the House of Deputies in HB Message #120)

Final Text of Resolution:
(A027)
Resolved, That the 74th General Convention strongly encourage bodies of The Episcopal Church to respect and reflect the equality of men and women in the Church bestowed by Baptism by (1) addressing individuals by the form of address each one prefers, and (2) addressing groups by forms of address that include everyone equally.

The House of Bishops Committee on Communications presented its Report #4 on HD Message #20 on Resolution A026 (Baptismal Parity) and moved concurrence.
The House concurred
(Communicated to the House of Deputies in HB Message #121)

Final Text of Resolution:
(A026)
Resolved, That the 74th General Convention commit itself to using language and visual images that reflect the diversity of age, sex, ethnicity, disability, and race among the baptized membership of The Episcopal Church; and be it further
Resolved, That the 74th General Convention direct the Executive Council to appoint a task force to (1) explore ways to include all who are created in God's image in our use of biblical and theological language and our use of visual images, (2) create guidelines that assure inclusion of persons of both sexes, and all ages, ethnicities and races, and (3) encourage incorporation of these guidelines in the everyday worship, music, education, preaching, written materials, and visual art used at the congregational, diocesan, and national levels of The Episcopal Church; and be it further
Resolved, That the task force include theologians, members of the Standing Commission on Liturgy and Music, the Committee on the Status of Women, the House of Bishops Theology Committee, representatives of the ethnic desks, and the Episcopal News Service; and be it further
Resolved, That the 74th General Convention request the Joint Standing Committee on Program, Budget and Finance to consider a budget allocation of $35,500 ($34,000 for two meetings of the Task Force and $1,500 for communication of these guidelines) for implementation of this resolution.

Miscellaneous Resolutions
The Hosue of Bishops Committee on Miscellaneous Resolutions presented its Report #2 on Resolution B009 (Request for Faith and Order Commission) and moved adoption with amendment.

Original Text of Resolution:
(B009)
Resolved, the House of Deputies concurring, That the 74th General Convention recognize the complexity of the theological issues pertaining to human sexuality and the divisions present in our church and other parts of the Anglican Communion about these matters, and call upon the Archbishop of Canterbury to appoint a Commission on Faith and Order charged to study the issues before us and to make a comprehensive report to the Lambeth Conference which will enable the conference fully to engage these matters and offer guidance to our churches; and be it further

Resolved, That such Faith and Order Commission will receive all relevant documents on these matters from The Episcopal Church and other constituent churches, consult with the church at a variety of levels, including appropriate ecumenical consultation, and issue its report at least nine months prior to the 2008 Lambeth Conference.

Committee Amendment:
Resolved, the House of Deputies concurring, That the 74th General Convention recognize the complexity of the theological issues pertaining to human sexuality and the divisions present in our church and *between and in* other parts of the Anglican Communion about these matters, and call upon the *Anglican Consultative Council* ~~Archbishop of Canterbury~~ to appoint a Commission on Faith and Order charged to study the issues before us and to make a comprehensive report to the Lambeth Conference which will enable the conference fully to engage these matters and offer guidance to our churches; and be it further

Resolved, That such Faith and Order Commission will receive all relevant documents on these matters from The Episcopal Church and other constituent churches, *fulfill the promise of Resolution 10 of the 1998 Lambeth Conference to listen to the voices of homosexual persons in each province in the Communion,* consult with the church at a variety of levels, including appropriate ecumenical consultation, and issue its report at least nine months prior to the 2008 Lambeth Conference.

The Bishop of Vermont moved to postpone the consideration of Resolution B009 until after the consideration of Resolution C051.

Motion carried
Consideration postponed

The House of Bishops Committee on Miscellaneous Resolutions presented its Report #3 on Resolution D041 (Service Animals Welcome) and moved adoption.

Original Text of Resolution:
(D041)
Resolved, the House of Deputies concurring, That the 74th General Convention of The Episcopal Church support congregations working toward becoming welcoming and safe places for all people; and be it further

Resolved, That, as some people need the assistance of trained, certified service animals to function in daily life, all congregations and institutions of The Episcopal Church open their buildings and facilities to trained, certified service animals, so that no one is excluded from worshiping and otherwise participating in the life of the church.

> Motion carried
> Resolution adopted
> (Communicated to the House of Deputies in HB Message #122)

Pastoral Letter
The Bishop of New York presented a draft of the pastoral letter.

Original Text of Resolution:
(B027)
Resolved, the House of Bishops offers the following letter:

A Pastoral Letter From the Bishops of the Episcopal Church
To be read in every parish, mission, preaching station, and church-related institution which works with children and youth.

Dear Brothers and Sisters in Christ,

We your bishops are steadfastly committed to seeing that the Episcopal Church is a community of safety and health for all people. The Body of Christ, the Church, must be a place where adults, children, and young people find the love and blessing of God, and where no one is hurt.

We are all aware of the reports in the media during the past year and more of incidents of sexual misconduct in churches. Many of these tragedies have involved children and young people. While the Roman Catholic Church has most often been mentioned in news reports and accusations, the rest of the Church and many secular agencies have also been caught up in trying to address the damage done to our children by sexual predators. The Episcopal Church is not immune to this scourge in our society and we must respond to it honestly and forthrightly.

Our Church has repeatedly upheld our mandate to be a haven of safety for all. The Scriptures teach us that every human being is made in the image of God; and our Lord enjoins us to receive and serve the least among us as we would receive and serve him. The mandates of our baptismal covenant include seeking and serving Christ in all persons, loving our neighbors as ourselves, striving for justice and peace for all people, and respecting the dignity of every human being.

Because of these mandates of love, respect, service, and justice, we have acknowledged our obligation to articulate clear standards about sexual harassment and misconduct, and to ensure that all our work and ministry is guided by them. We have been committed to sexual conduct training and abuse prevention for all our clergy and lay leaders. We have been clear that exploitation and abusiveness are always unacceptable in our common life. We have made efforts to become aware of the spiritual and emotional damage that is done by sexual misconduct, and to do our best to guarantee that none who come to us will suffer such harm. In spite of our best efforts, it is sad when we discover that we have not done enough.

While we were in conference together at Kanuga, North Carolina, in the spring many of us had the opportunity to learn more about pedophilia, a form of predatory sexual behavior that has caused untold harm in our society and in the Body of Christ. It is especially important that we as a church focus on understanding and preventing pedophilia.

While we need to be aware that pedophilia is a reality in our society, which can be manifest in the church, we must be very clear about the nature of this tragic problem. Pedophilia is pervasive; one in eight males and one in four females will be molested before they reach the age of eighteen. Of reported cases in the general population, sixty percent (60%) of abusers are known to their victims, thirty percent (30%) are family members or relatives, and ten percent (10%) are strangers. We must be aware that the Church is a community which offers predators the opportunity to become known and trusted by parents and their children.

We also know that offenders are predominantly male and heterosexual. We must take great care not to equate pedophilia with homosexuality in out minds or our conversation, and we must never assume that only men molest children in this way.

What we have learned most recently about the repetitive nature of pedophilia makes it imperative that we take very clear steps together to do the screening necessary to ensure that our children encounter God's love among us, and that we do all in our power to protect them from the distorted perceptions of love offered by predators.

In a Mind of The House resolution passed at Kanuga in March of 2003, we committed ourselves to support the development of church-wide policies to safeguard our children; and until such time as these policies are adopted, to revisit and revise our diocesan policies to ensure that ministries provided to the children among us will be life-giving and free from abusiveness of any kind.

Among the basic provisions we have committed to implement are:
1. Thorough *screening and selection* of clergy, lay employees and volunteers who work with children and youth;
2. Articulation of clear behavioral standards for interactions between clergy, lay employees, volunteers and children and youth;
3. Careful, *continuous monitoring of all programs and interactions* involving children and youth;
4. Provision for (of mandatory) *education and training of clergy, lay employees and volunteers* for work with children and youth; and
5. Guidelines for responding to concerns about behavior or allegations of abuse.

In addition we asked the Presiding Bishop to create a working group from among our members to partner with the Church Pension Group, the Church Insurance Corporation and other agencies and appropriate organizations to develop the materials necessary to provide the Church with consistent expectations and standards.

We realize that in many of our congregations, persons who offer to take on ministries with children and youth are a blessing to an understaffed education or formation program for children or youth. The overwhelming majority are trustworthy and caring persons whose ministry will bear great good fruit.

But we must acknowledge that there are times when predators use the church as an opportunity for sexual abuse of children and adolescents, who can suffer severe spiritual, emotional, and sometimes physical damage as a result. In response to such times we are called to acknowledge two truths: that human sin and failure are very real, and that God's grace, mercy and power are always strong enough to heal and transform our pain.

[Our doors must always be open to anyone who comes to us. Without such inclusiveness our mission falls short of calling all people to know the reconciling love of God. We must be willing to receive all persons as gifts to us from God, and to encourage their ministries - even when it means taking on the enormously challenging task of incorporating those who have been involved in pedophilia. At the same time, we must be sure that the ministries of all our members are faithful and life-giving.]

We have no intention to call our members to suspicion and mistrust. We do recognize the need to call our members beyond the naiveté of unquestioning confidence and into the care and discipline which must characterize our choices where children are concerned. Jesus called us to be as wise as serpents and as gentle as doves. In the case of pedophilia, our consistency in carefully screening, choosing and training *all* who work with children and youth will serve to allay any concerns about favoritism or carelessness, while providing the ability to firmly guide those who might harm children into other areas of ministry which serve the Church and contribute to our mission.

Some helpful materials will be available through your diocesan office by the first of November. We ask that as you make use of them you will remember the challenge our Lord provided to his followers, "unless you become as children you cannot enter the kingdom of God." We renew our commitment to ensure that our church is a community of love and care for every person. We ask that you join us in doing all in our power to see that all our members find among us a safe place where they can be open and trusting and able to know the reconciling love of God in Christ that makes all things new.

A Collect for the Care of Children

Almighty God, heavenly Father, you have blessed us with the joy and care of children: Give us calm strength and patient wisdom as we bring them up, that we may teach them to love whatever is just and true and good, following the example of our Savior Jesus Christ. Amen. (BCP 829)

Bishops of The Episcopal Church
Gathered at General Convention, Minneapolis, MN
August 6, 2003
The Feast of the Transfiguration

The Senior Suffragan of Massachusetts moved to strike the third sentence of the bracketed paragraph.

Motion carried
Amendment adopted

The Bishop of San Diego moved to strike the entire paragraph.

The Bishop of Connecticut moved to table consideration until all have had the opportunity to read the text.

Motion carried
Consideration postponed

The General Board of Examining Chaplains
The House Committee on Dispatch of Business distributed ballots for the election of one priest for a six-year term to the General Board of Examining Chaplains.

Evangelism
The House of Bishops Committee on Evangelism presented its Report #1 on HD Message #42 on Resolution C015 (Ethnic Desks at the National Church Office) and moved concurrence.

The House concurred
(Communicated to the House of Deputies in HB Message #124)

Final Text of Resolution:
(C015)
Resolved, **That The Episcopal Church Center develop new, creative ways of welcoming and incorporating people of diverse ethnic backgrounds into The Episcopal Church;** and be it further
Resolved, **That the Asiamerica Ministries, Black Ministries, Hispanic Ministries, and Native American Ministries desks of the Episcopal Church Center be retained, holding advocacy and congregational development as equal responsibilities, and be given the budget and resources they need in order to function as an integral part of the work of the church's work of evangelism to double the average Sunday attendance by 20/20.**

The House of Bishops Committee on Evangelism presented its Report #2 on HD Message #21 on Resolution A083 (Articulate Faith Story) and moved concurrence.

The House concurred
(Communicated to the House of Deputies in HB Message #125)

Final Text of Resolution:
(A083)
Resolved, **That the 74th General Convention call every Episcopalian to be able to articulate his or her faith story; and urge dioceses and congregations to create opportunities for these stories to be told.**

Prayer Book, Liturgy and Church Music
The House of Bishops Committee on Prayer Book, Liturgy and Church Music presented its Report #21 on Resolution A103 (Adopt the Revised Common Lectionary) and moved adoption with amendment.

Original Text of Resolution:
(A103)
Resolved, the House of Deputies concurring, That the 74th General Convention authorize the *Revised Common Lectionary,* as amended in General Convention Resolution A063, affirmed by the 73rd General Convention; and be it further
Resolved, That substitution of the *Revised Common Lectionary* for the table of readings currently printed in the Book of Common Prayer take effect on the first day of Advent in the year 2003; and be it further
Resolved, That the Standing Commission on Liturgy and Music make available the table of readings and suggestion for its use to the congregations of The Episcopal Church.

Committee Amendment:
Resolved, the House of Deputies concurring, That the 74th General Convention authorize the *Revised Common Lectionary, for liturgical use* as amended in General Convention Resolution A063, affirmed by the 73rd General Convention; and be it further
Resolved, That substitution of the *Revised Common Lectionary* for the table of readings currently printed in the Book of Common Prayer take effect on the first day of Advent in the year 2004 ~~2003~~; and be it further
Resolved, That the Standing Commission on Liturgy and Music make available the table of readings and suggestions for its use to the congregations of The Episcopal Church.

The Bishop of Alabama moved to amend the resolution.

Proposed Amendment:
Delete "for liturgical use" and substitute "for trial use."
The question was called to terminate debate on the resolution.

Motion carried
Debate terminated

A vote was taken on the proposed amendment.

Motion defeated
Amendment defeated

A vote was taken on Resolution A103 as amended.

Motion carried
Resolution adopted with amendment
(Communicated to the House of Deputies in HB Message #126)

Ministry

The House of Bishops Committee on Ministry presented its Report #7 on Resolution B020 (Family Survivors of Murder Victims and the Impact of Executions on Healing and Pastoral Care) and moved adoption.

Original Text of Resolution:
(B020)
Resolved, the House of Deputies concurring, That the 74th General Convention call for and support an interdenominational and interdisciplinary study entitled "Surviving Loved Ones of Murder Victims: The Impact of Executions on Healing and Pastoral Care," to be conducted through the International Center for Healing and Law by Mark Umbreit, Ph.D., a professor at the University of Minnesota School of Social Work, and a continuing team of colleagues, coordinated through the Office of Peace and Justice of The Episcopal Church; and be it further
Resolved, That the General Convention request the Joint Standing Committee on Program, Budget, and Finance to consider a budget allocation of $50,000 for implementation of the resolution.

Motion carried
Resolution adopted
(Communicated to the House of Deputies in HB Message #127)

The House of Bishops Committee on Ministry presented its Report #8 on Resolution D060 (Education about Ordained and Licensed Ministries) and moved adoption.

Original Text of Resolution:
(D060)
Resolved, the House of Deputies concurring, That the Standing Commission on Ministry Development be directed to develop educational resources on the roles and responsibilities of the ordained and licensed members of the church; and be it further
Resolved, That these resources be made readily available to any community of faith, through multiple forms of media.

Motion carried
Resolution adopted
(Communicated to the House of Deputies in HB Message #128)

The General Board of Examining Chaplains
The Secretary announced there was no election for the General Board of Examining Chaplains. Balloting will be held again.

RECESS
The Presiding Bishop announced a recess of fifteen minutes at 4:39 p.m.

Resume
The House resumed at 5:07 p.m.

The General Board of Examining Chaplains
The Secretary announced the election result for the General Board of Examining Chaplains. The Rev. Stephen E. Moore was elected for a six-year term.

Stewardship and Development
The House of Bishops Committee on Stewardship and Development presented its Report #6 on Resolution D001 (Funding Implications of a 10% Tithe) and moved that the Committee be discharged.

Motion carried
Committee discharged
(Communicated to the House of Deputies in HB Message #129)

Communications
The House of Bishops Committee on Communications presented its Report #6 on HD Message #46 on Resolution C029 (Translation of Documents into Spanish) and moved concurrence.

The House concurred
(Communicated to the House of Deputies in HB Message #130)

Final Text of Resolution:
(C029)
Resolved, **That the 74th General Convention direct that all official documents, publications, and digital publications produced by the Domestic and Foreign Missionary Society be issued in Spanish and French no later than 2006, and in other languages used in The Episcopal Church as soon as possible;** and be it further
Resolved, **That translated materials shall include, but are not limited to the following: Episcopal News Service (ENS) press releases, the Presiding Bishop's monthly message, Pastoral Letters of the House of Bishops, Summary Reports of the actions of General Convention, Executive Council resolutions and actions, and official communications from The Episcopal Church;** and be it further
Resolved, **That materials produced in Spanish and French be published on The Episcopal Church website after review by the Office of Ethnic Congregational Development;** and be it further
Resolved, **That *Episcopal Life* be urged to publish a section of the newspaper in Spanish and French;** and be it further
Resolved, **That the 74th General Convention encourage dioceses, congregations, and other agencies and institutions related to The Episcopal Church to make available, as appropriate, materials in Spanish and French**

or other languages of its constituents; and be it further
Resolved, That the 74th General Convention request the Joint Standing Committee on Program, Budget and Finance to consider a budget allocation of $85,000 per year for the triennium for the implementation of this resolution.

Miscellaneous Resolutions
The House of Bishops Committee on Miscellaneous Resolutions presented its Report #4 on Resolution A154 (75th General Convention Site).

The Bishop of Northwestern Pennsylvania moved to postpone consideration of the resolution until August 8, 2003.

Motion carried
Consideration postponed

[Note: Consideration of Resolution A154 resumed on Day 9. See page 249. *Ed.*]

World Mission
The House of Bishops Committee on World Mission presented its Report #6 on Resolution A150 (World Mission Vision) and moved adoption with amendment.

Original Text of Resolution:
(A150)
Resolved, the House of Deputies concurring, That the 2003 General Convention call the church to study, during the 2004–2006 triennium, the vision for world mission contained in the document, "Companions in Transformation: The Episcopal Church's World Mission in a New Century," prepared by the Standing Commission on World Mission; and be it further

Resolved, That the Convention call on parishes, dioceses, voluntary mission agencies, seminaries, mission networks, and Episcopal Church Center agencies to consider the statement's proposals and reflect on the feasibility of initiating their implementation during the 2007–2009 triennium; and be it further

Resolved, That the Convention request the Standing Commission on World Mission to gather and interpret responses from around the church and make specific programmatic and budgetary proposals to the 2006 General Convention.

Committee Amendment:
Resolved, the House of Deputies concurring, That the 2003 General Convention call the church to study, during the 2004–2006 triennium, the vision for world mission contained in the document, "Companions in Transformation: The Episcopal Church's World Mission in a New Century," prepared by the Standing Commission on World Mission; and be it further

Resolved, That a study group in each diocese be designated to make a critical study of the Vision statement, this group to include diocesan representatives of groups such as Companion Diocese Committees, the Global Mission Network, United Thank Offering, Episcopal Relief and Development and other member groups of the Episcopal Partnership for Global Mission (EPGM) and others as may be available, and that a report from each diocese be forwarded to the

Standing Commission on World Mission by World Mission Sunday in January 2005; and be it further
Resolved, That the Convention call on parishes, dioceses, voluntary mission agencies, seminaries, mission networks, and Episcopal Church Center agencies to ~~consider the statement's proposals and reflect on the feasibility of initiating their implementation during the 2007-2009 triennium~~ *participate in the outlined process during the triennium;* and be it further
Resolved, That the Convention request the Standing Commission on World Mission to gather and interpret responses from around the church and make specific programmatic and budgetary proposals to the 2006 General Convention.

Motion carried
Resolution adopted with amendment
(Communicated to the House of Deputies in HB Message #131)

Prayer Book, Liturgy and Church Music
The House of Bishops Committee on Prayer Book, Liturgy and Church Music presented its Report #26 on Resolution D047 (Post-Abortion Healing Service) and moved adoption of a substitute.

Original Text of Resolution:
(D047)
Resolved, the House of Deputies concurring, That the 74th General Convention direct the Office for Liturgy and Music to invite abortion recovery programs and the National Organization of Episcopalians for Life to participate in the development of a liturgy for a healing/memorial service that specifically ministers to the special needs of those who are suffering from post-abortion stress, consistent with Resolution D083 (Ministry to Men and Women Suffering From Post-Abortion Stress), passed at the 73rd General Convention, which acknowledges the post-abortion suffering of some persons; and be it further
Resolved, that the Office for Liturgy and Music publish the newly developed liturgy, making it available both on the church's website and in print.

Committee Substitute:
Resolved, the House of Deputies concurring, That the 74th General Convention direct the Standing Commission on Liturgy and Music to develop liturgies supplemental to "Burial of a Child" (Enriching Our Worship 2), that respond to the pastoral needs of women and men who have experienced miscarriage, abortion, or other trauma in the childbearing or childbirth process, for presentation to and consideration by the 75th General Convention.

The Bishop of Quincy moved to amend the substitute resolution.

Proposed Amendment:
Add "Book of Occasional Services" in place of "Enriching Our Worship 2."

The question was called to terminate debate on the amendment.

Motion carried
Debate terminated

A vote was taken on the proposed amendment.

Motion defeated
Amendment defeated

A vote was taken on substitute Resolution D047.

Motion carried
Substitute resolution adopted
(Communicated to the House of Deputies in HB Message #132)

The House of Bishops Committee on Prayer Book, Liturgy and Church Music presented its Report #29 on Resolution A044 (Amend Canon I.17.1(c)) and moved adoption.

Original Text of Resolution:
(A044)
Resolved, the House of Deputies concurring, That Canon I.17.1(c) be amended to read as follows:
(c) It is expected that all adult members of this Church, after appropriate instruction, will have made a mature public affirmation of their faith and commitment to the responsibilities of their Baptism and will have been confirmed or received *by the laying on of hands* by a Bishop of this Church or by a Bishop of a Church in communion with this Church. Those who have previously made a mature public commitment in another Church may be received *by the laying on of hands by a Bishop of this Church*, not confirmed.

The Committee agreed to amend their report at the suggestion of Bishop Bartlett by deleting the word "not" and replacing it with "rather than" before the word "confirmed" in the last sentence.

The Bishop of Pennsylvania moved to refer the resolution to the House of Bishops Committee on Theology for its report on confirmation.

Motion defeated

The Bishop Suffragan of Virginia moved to amend the resolution.

Proposed Amendment:
Delete "rather than confirmed" and end the last sentence at "this Church."
The question was called to terminate debate.

Motion carried
Debate terminated

A vote was taken on the proposed amendment.

Motion defeated
Amendment defeated

A vote was taken on Resolution A044.

Motion carried
Resolution adopted
(Communicated to the House of Deputies in HB Message #133)

Recess

Following announcements by the Secretary, the House of Bishops Committee on Dispatch of Business moved that the House stand in recess until 11:00 a.m. on the Seventh Legislative Day.

Motion carried

The House recessed at 5:46 p.m. with reflections by Chaplain McIntosh.

Appendix F
Day 6

Statement from the Presiding Bishop

August 4, 2003

Questions have been raised and brought to my attention regarding the Bishop-Elect of the Diocese of New Hampshire. The Standing Committee and Bishop of New Hampshire, together with the Bishop-Elect, Canon Robinson, have asked that a thorough investigation be undertaken before we proceed with seeking the consent of the Bishops with jurisdiction. The investigation will be overseen by the Bishop of Western Massachusetts, the Rt. Rev. Gordon P. Scruton. I will advise the Bishops with jurisdiction as to when we might proceed.

The Most Rev. Frank T. Griswold
Presiding Bishop and Primate
Episcopal Church, USA

Appendix G
Day 6

Statement from the Bishop of New Hampshire and Standing Committee of New Hampshire

August 4, 2003

The Bishop and the President of the Standing Committee of New Hampshire have requested that the Presiding Bishop investigate two concerns raised about Canon Robinson after the House of Deputies voted yesterday:
1. His relationship to a website of outright.org, a secular outreach program for gay and bisexual youth.
2. An email accusation of inappropriate conduct circulated to a group of bishops.

The Bishop and the President of the Standing Committee of the Diocese of New Hampshire express continued confidence in Canon Robinson. We also continue to maintain an open, prayerful, transparent, and spirit-led process. We have full confidence in the Presiding Bishop's commitment to fully investigate these matters.

MINNEAPOLIS MEETING   HOUSE OF BISHOPS

SEVENTH DAY

Tuesday
August 5, 2003

MORNING SESSION

The House reconvened at 11:05 a.m. with the Presiding Bishop in the chair. Conversation time was held for five minutes. The House resumed at 11:10 a.m.

Agenda of the Day
The House of Bishops Committee on Dispatch of Business moved to adopt the agenda of the day.

Motion carried
Agenda adopted

Previous Day's Minutes
The House of Bishops Committee on Dispatch of Business moved to dispense with the reading of the previous day's minutes.

Motion carried

Special Order of Business
The Presiding Bishop introduced the Rt. Rev. Michael Nazir-Ali, Bishop of Rochester, England.

Announcements
The Secretary gave announcements.

Messages from the House of Deputies
The Secretary announced that the following messages had been received from the House of Deputies.

HD Message #82:	Special Order for Election of Members of Joint Nominating Committee for Election of the Presiding Bishop. The House of Deputies adopted the resolution.
HD Message #83:	Special Order for Election of Trustees of General Theological Seminary. The House of Deputies adopted the resolution with amendment.
HD Message #84:	A122 (Improving Health Care for Children) The House of Deputies adopted the resolution with amendment.
HD Message #85:	A020 (HIV Medications Availability) The House of Deputies adopted the resolution with amendment.
HD Message #86:	A018 (HIV/AIDS Drugs Full Inclusion)

	The House of Deputies adopted the resolution with amendment.
HD Message #87:	A130 (Establish Living Wage)
	The House of Deputies adopted the resolution with amendment.
HD Message #88:	C021 (Stem Cell Research and Alleviation of Pain)
	The House of Deputies discharged the resolution.
HD Message #89:	C020 (Stem Cell Research)
	The House of Deputies discharged the resolution.
HD Message #90:	D046 (Stewardship of Water)
	The House of Deputies adopted the resolution.
HD Message #91:	A005 (Continue Forward Movement Publications)
	The House of Deputies adopted the resolution.
HD Message #92:	A042 (Amend Canon I.1.9)
	The House of Deputies adopted the resolution.
HD Message #93:	C008 (Episcopal Council of Indigenous Ministries Funding)
	The House of Deputies adopted the resolution with amendment.
HD Message #94:	C006 (Evangelism to the New Majority)
	The House of Deputies adopted a substitute resolution.
HD Message #95:	A064 (Seminarian Expenses)
	The House of Deputies concurred.
HD Message #96:	A013 (The Church's Role in Counseling and Education on Biomedical Ethics)
	The House of Deputies concurred.
HD Message #97:	A030 (21st Century Survey Resources)
	The House of Deputies concurred.
HD Message #98:	A007 (Aging Task Force)
	The House of Deputies concurred.
HD Message #99:	A038 (Peace and Justice Studies and Training)
	The House of Deputies concurred.
HD Message #100:	C031 (Waging Reconciliation)
	The House of Deputies concurred.
HD Message #101:	A090 (Christian-Muslim Dialogue)
	The House of Deputies concurred.
HD Message #102:	D044 (Election Clarification)
	The House of Deputies adopted the resolution with amendment.
HD Message #103:	A147 (Legislative Committee Membership)
	The House of Deputies adopted a substitute resolution.
HD Message #104:	A043 (Amend Canon I.6.1)
	The House of Deputies discharged the resolution.
HD Message #105:	D005 (Amend Canons I.2.4(c) & I.4.3)
	The House of Deputies rejected the resolution.

HD Message #106:	A011 (Ethical Guidelines for Gene Transfer and Germline Interventions) The House of Deputies adopted the resolution with amendment.
HD Message #107:	D016 (The Protection of Animals from Cruel Treatment) The House of Deputies adopted a substitute resolution.
HD Message #108:	A012 (Caring for Children in the Face of the New Genetics) The House of Deputies adopted the resolution with amendment.
HD Message #109:	B010 (Continue Leadership Program for Musicians Serving Small Congregations) The House of Deputies concurred.
HD Message #110:	A084 (20/20 Vision Reporting) The House of Deputies adopted a substitute resolution.
HD Message #111:	A098 (Church Year Calendar Inclusion) The House of Deputies concurred.
HD Message #112:	A099 (Authorize Trial Use of Commemoration) The House of Deputies concurred.
HD Message #113:	A121 (Clergy and Lay Professional Continuing Education) The House of Deputies concurred.

Presiding Bishop
The Presiding Bishop yielded the chair to the Vice-Chair.

Dispatch of Business
The House of Bishops Committee on Dispatch of Business asked for five minutes for committees to pick up reports and to submit reports expeditiously.

Ministry
The House of Bishops Committee on Ministry presented its Report #9 on Resolution C023 (Direct Ordination to the Priesthood) and moved the resolution, recommending rejection.

Original Text of Resolution:
(C023)
Resolved, the House of Bishops concurring, That the 74th General Convention adopt canonical revisions allowing bishops, with the consent of the Standing Committee, to ordain candidates for the priesthood directly to the priesthood.

The question was called to terminate debate on the resolution.

Motion carried
Debate terminated

A vote was taken on Resolution C023.

Motion defeated
Resolution rejected
(Communicated to the House of Deputies in HB Message #134)

The House of Bishops Committee on Ministry presented its Report #10 on Resolution C032 (Direct Ordination to the Priesthood) and moved the resolution, recommending rejection.

Original Text of Resolution:
(C032)
Resolved, the House of Deputies concurring, That revisions to the Canons be adopted that would allow Bishops, with the consent of the diocesan standing committees, to ordain candidates for the priesthood directly to the priesthood.

Motion defeated
Resolution rejected
(Communicated to the House of Deputies in HB Message #135)

The House of Bishops Committee on Ministry presented its Report #11 on Resolution A118 (Amend Canon IV.3.27) and moved the resolution, recommending rejection.

Original Text of Resolution:
(A118)
Resolved, the House of Deputies concurring, That Canon IV.3.27 be amended to read: "There shall be a Review Committee consisting of five Bishops of this Church, two Priests, and two ~~confirmed~~ adult lay communicants in good standing...."

Rules of Order
A motion was made to suspend the rules to consider Reports #11–15 on Resolution A118, Resolution A117, Resolution A116, Resolution A115, and Resolution A113 as a group.

Motion carried
Rules suspended

Bishop Doss moved to table consideration until after the luncheon recess.

Motion defeated

The question was called to terminate debate.

Motion carried
Debate terminated

A vote was taken on Resolution A118.

Motion defeated
Resolution rejected
(Communicated to the House of Deputies in HB Message #136)

The House of Bishops Committee on Ministry presented its Report #12 on Resolution A117 (Amend Canon I.9.7) and moved the resolution, recommending rejection.

Original Text of Resolution:
(A117)
Resolved, the House of Deputies concurring, That Canon I.9.7 be amended to read as follows:
"... resident in the Diocese or Area Mission, and Lay Persons, ~~confirmed~~ adult communicants of this Church in good standing...."

Motion defeated
Resolution rejected
(Communicated to the House of Deputies in HB Message #137)

The House of Bishops Committee on Ministry presented its Report #13 on Resolution A116 (Amend Canon I.4.3(d)) and moved the resolution, recommending rejection.

Original Text of Resolution:
(A116)
Resolved, the House of Deputies concurring, That Canon I.4.3(d) be amended to read as follows:
"The Presiding Bishop shall appoint, with the advice and consent of a majority of the Executive Council, an executive director, who shall be an adult ~~confirmed~~ communicant in good standing...."

Motion defeated
Resolution rejected
(Communicated to the House of Deputies in HB Message #138)

The House of Bishops Committee on Ministry presented its Report #14 on Resolution A115 (Amend Canon I.4.1(c)) and moved the resolution, recommending rejection.

Original Text of Resolution:
(A115)
Resolved, the House of Deputies concurring, That Canon I.4.1(c) be amended to read as follows:
"...and by one Lay Person who is ~~a confirmed~~ *an* adult communicant in good standing of a Diocese...."

Motion defeated
Resolution rejected
(Communicated to the House of Deputies in HB Message #139)

The House of Bishops Committee on Ministry presented its Report #15 on Resolution A113 (Amend Canon I.1.2(a)) and moved the resolution, recommending rejection.

Original Text of Resolution:
(A113)
Resolved, the House of Deputies concurring, That Canon I.1.2(a) be amended to read as follows:
"...and Lay Persons, who shall be ~~confirmed~~ adult communicants of this Church in good standing...."

Motion defeated
Resolution rejected
(Communicated to the House of Deputies in HB Message #140)

Education
The House of Bishops Committee on Education presented its Report #9 on Resolution A059 (Design New Resources) and moved adoption of a substitute.

Original Text of Resolution:
(A059)
Resolved, the House of Deputies concurring, That the seminaries and diocesan schools for ministry of The Episcopal Church be urged to review curriculum resources and design new resources that focus on:
    intercultural leadership
    contemporary foreign language courses
    anti-racism education
    church planting
    congregational revitalization
    evangelism
    management of change
    negotiation of conflict.

Committee Substitute:
Resolved, the House of Deputies concurring, That in support of this church's 20/20 program for evangelism, and in recognition of the joys and challenges of 21st century ministry, and in acknowledgment that this ministry requires specific strategies and skills in:
    intercultural leadership
    contemporary foreign language courses
    anti-racism education
    church planting
    congregational revitalization
    evangelism
    management of change
    negotiation of conflict; and be it further

Resolved, That the 74th General Convention strongly urge that dioceses carry out recruitment, discernment, and evaluation of persons for lay and ordained ministries which consider these strategies and skills as integral aspects of church leadership; that the seminaries and diocesan schools for ministry of The Episcopal Church be urged to review and renew curricula, providing inclusion of these strategies and skills; and that opportunities across the church for continuing education, focus on these strategies and skills, most especially in the coming triennium, in order to lay a strong foundation for 20/20 evangelism.

Motion carried
Substitute resolution adopted
(Communicated to the House of Deputies in HB Message #141)

The House of Bishops Committee on Education presented its Report #6 on Resolution A061 (Continuing Education Scholarships) and moved that the Committee be discharged.

Motion carried
Committee discharged
(Communicated to the House of Deputies in HB Message #142)

The House of Bishops Committee on Education presented its Report #13 on Resolution D033 (Encourage Basic Financial Teaching) and moved adoption of a substitute.

Original Text of Resolution:
(D033)
Resolved, the House of Deputies concurring, That the 74th General Convention strongly encourage all clergy in charge of congregations to make available instruction in basic financial teaching, including, but not limited to, budgeting, saving, responsible handling of debt, the making of wills, and Biblical teaching regarding financial matters; and be it further
Resolved, That Dioceses assist congregations by recommending appropriate materials.

Committee Substitute:
Resolved, the House of Deputies concurring, That the 74th General Convention, mindful of the rubric found on page 445 of The Book of Common Prayer,* direct every congregation to provide educational opportunities and other resources for Christians of all ages that promote understanding the role of money in our lives; Biblical teachings about financial and material matters; and good stewardship relating to budgeting, saving, responsible handling of debt, life planning and the making of wills, recognizing that from the earliest years and throughout life, attitudes toward money influence who we are and the choices we make, and that the spiritual practice of stewardship begins with a joyous awareness of God's love for us and a gratitude for the abundance of God's gifts; and be it further
Resolved, That the Office of Stewardship of the Episcopal Church Center and

Dioceses assist congregations by recommending appropriate materials.

*From Thanksgiving for the Birth or Adoption of a Child, The Book of Common Prayer, page 445, "The Minister of the Congregation is directed to instruct the people, from time to time, about the duty of Christian parents to make prudent provision for the well-being of their families, and of all persons to make wills, while they are in health, arranging for the disposal of their temporal goods, not neglecting, if they are able, to leave bequests for religious and charitable uses."

Motion carried
Substitute resolution adopted
(Communicated to the House of Deputies in HB Message #143)

Committees and Commissions

The House of Bishops Committee on Committees and Commissions presented its Report #1 on HD Message #11 on Resolution A124 (Standing Commission on Health and a Staff Position in Health Care) and moved concurrence.

The Bishop of Upper South Carolina moved to refer the resolution to the Committee on Canons.

Motion carried
Resolution re-referred to a Legislative Committee

Constitution

The House of Bishops Committee on Constitution presented its Report #6 on Resolution B005 (Amend Constitution Article I.2) and moved adoption of a substitute.

Original Text of Resolution:

(B005)

Resolved, the House of Deputies concurring, That Article 1, Section 2 of the Constituition be amended as follows:

All Bishops, unless under discipline, have seat and voice in the House of Bishops. Each Bishop of this Church having jurisdiction, every Bishop Coadjutor, every Suffragan Bishop, every Assistant Bishop, and every Bishop ~~who by reason of advanced age or bodily infirmity, or~~ who, under an election to an office created by the General Convention, or for reasons of mission strategy determined by action of the General Convention or the House of Bishops, has resigned a jurisdiction, shall have a seat, *voice,* and a vote in the House of Bishops. A majority of all Bishops entitled to vote, ~~exclusive of Bishops who have resigned their jurisdiction or positions~~, shall be necessary to constitute a quorum for the transaction of business.

Committee Substitute:

Resolved, the House of Deputies concurring, That Article 1, Section 2 of the Constitution be amended to read as follows:

~~Each Bishop of this Church having jurisdiction, every Bishop Coadjutor, every Suffragan Bishop, every Assistant Bishop, and every Bishop who by reason of~~

MINNEAPOLIS MEETING — HOUSE OF BISHOPS

~~advanced age or bodily infirmity, or who, under an election to an office created by the General Convention, or for reasons of mission strategy determined by action of the General Convention or the House of Bishops, has resigned a jurisdiction, shall have a seat, and a vote in the House of Bishops. A majority of all Bishops entitled to vote, exclusive of Bishops who have resigned their jurisdiction or positions, shall be necessary to constitute a quorum for the transaction of business.~~

All Bishops of this Church shall have seat and voice in the House of Bishops. Each Bishop of this Church having jurisdiction, Bishop Coadjutor, Bishop Suffragan, Assistant Bishop, and every Bishop holding an office created by General Convention shall have a vote in the House of Bishops. A majority of all Bishops entitled to vote shall be necessary to constitute a quorum for transaction of business.

Bishop Charlton moved to amend the resolution.

Proposed Amendment:

Following the words "House of Bishops" in the second sentence, add the sentence "Resigned Bishops shall be entitled to vote on all Mind of the House resolutions and upon those resolutions which have been determined, by a Mind of the House resolution, to be concerned with the Faith and/or of the order of the church."

The question was called to terminate debate on the proposed amendment.

Motion carried
Debate terminated

A vote was taken on the proposed amendment.

Motion defeated
Amendment defeated

The question was called to terminate debate on the main motion.

Motion carried
Debate terminated

Bishop Eastman and five other bishops requested a roll call vote.

Roll Call Vote on B005

| 127 | yes | 30 | no | 7 | abstain |

(See Appendix H–Day 7 for the record of the Roll Call Vote)

Motion carried
Substitute resolution adopted
(Communicated to the House of Deputies in HB Message #144)

Personal Privilege

The Bishop of El Camino Real asked for Personal Privilege.
The Ecumenical Officer asked for Personal Privilege.
Bishop Eastman asked for Personal Privilege.

Constitution

The House of Bishops Committee on Constitution presented its Report #7 on Resolution D027 (Amend Constitution Article II.1 [Election of Bishops–Second Reading]) and moved adoption.

Original Text of Resolution:
(D027)
Resolved, the House of Deputies concurring, That Article II, Sec. 1 of the Constitution of the General Convention be amended to read:
Sec. 1. In every Diocese the Bishop or the Bishop Coadjutor shall be chosen agreeably to rules prescribed by the Convention of that Diocese, *provided that the retirement date of the Bishop Diocesan shall not be more than thirty-six months after the consecration of the Bishop Coadjutor.* Bishops of Missionary Dioceses shall be chosen in accordance with the Canons of the General Convention.
And be it further
Resolved, That this resolution be sent within six months to the Secretary of the Convention of every Diocese to be made known to the Diocesan Convention at its next meeting.
The question was called to terminate debate on the resolution.

Motion carried
Debate terminated

A vote was taken on Resolution D027.

Motion carried
Resolution adopted
(Communicated to the House of Deputies in HB Message #145)

The House of Bishops Committee on Constitution presented its Report #9 on Resolution D062 (Amend Constitution Article IX [Second Reading]) and moved adoption.

Original Text of Resolution:
(D062)
Resolved, That the first paragraph of Article IX of the Constitution be amended to read as follows:
The General Convention may, by Canon, establish *one or more* a Court *courts* for the Trial of Bishops, ~~which shall be composed of Bishops only~~.
Resolved, That this resolution be sent within six months to the Secretary of the Convention of every Diocese to be made known to the Diocesan Convention at its next meeting.

Motion carried
Resolution adopted
(Communicated to the House of Deputies in HB Message #146)

National and International Concerns
The House of Bishops Committee on National and International Concerns presented its Report #1 on Resolution D020 (Opposition to Sharia Law) and moved adoption of a substitute.

Original Text of Resolution:
(D020)
Resolved, the House of Bishops concurring, That because certain aspects of Sharia law violate fundamental human rights when imposed by the state, it is the policy of The Episcopal Church to oppose, through all available means, the governmental imposition or continuation in any country of those aspects of Sharia law providing for:
 subjugation of women;
 denial of full rights of citizenship to Christians, Jews, and to members of other non-Islamic faiths, while imposing blasphemy laws on non-Muslims;
 prohibitions on peaceful Christian evangelism and voluntary Muslim conversion to other faiths.

Committee Substitute:
Resolved, the House of Deputies concurring, That the 74th General Convention support the Archbishop of Canterbury and other Anglican leaders who have jointly affirmed with Islamic leaders in various countries our shared desire to honor those teachings in our respective traditions which work to avoid coercion and respect individual liberty; and be it further
Resolved, That in further dialogue, particular attention be paid to vigorously oppose any nation's or other governmental body's imposition or continuation of a legal system which violates fundamental human rights; and be it further
Resolved, That General Convention urge the application of these principles by the United States government to the reconstruction underway in Iraq and Afghanistan, in peace negotiations in Sudan, and in ongoing discussions with Nigeria and Indonesia, with particular attention to the rights of religious minorities, women, and those seeking to change their faith.

Motion carried
Substitute resolution adopted
(Communicated to the House of Deputies in HB Message #147)

Bishop of the Polish National Catholic Church
The Chair recognized the Rt. Rev. Thomas Gnat, the Polish National Catholic Church Bishop of the Eastern Diocese of the PNCC of the United States and Canada, who was in the gallery.

Personal Privilege
The Bishop of Southern Ohio commended Bishop Rockwell who will serve on the Board of Church Publishing, Inc., as its chair.

Bishop Rockwell addressed the House.

Presiding Bishop

The Presiding Bishop returned to the chair.

The Presiding Bishop announced that the report from the Bishop of Western Massachusetts regarding the Bishop-elect of New Hampshire will be received at the beginning of the afternoon session.

RECESS

Following announcements by the Secretary, the House of Bishops Committee on Dispatch of Business moved that the House stand in recess until 2:30 p.m.

Motion carried

Personal Privilege

Bishop Hampton spoke to the House regarding the Peace Cranes to be distributed the following day, August 6, commemorating the bombing of Hiroshima, Japan.

The House recessed at 12:55 p.m. with prayers led by Chaplain Battle.

AFTERNOON SESSION

The House reconvened at 2:30 p.m. with the Presiding Bishop in the chair.

A period of one hour and fifteen minutes was allowed for the Chaplain's reflections and conversation.

The House resumed at 3:50 p.m.

Presiding Bishop

The Presiding Bishop asked the gallery and press for quiet. He requested that there be no recording of table conversations and no show of approval or disapproval following the investigative report.

The Presiding Bishop announced to the gallery that prayer, reconciliation, and anointing had been held in closed session.

Consecration of Bishops

The Bishop of Western Massachusetts read the report pertaining to the allegations against the Bishop-elect of New Hampshire. (See Appendix I–Day 7 for the Report from the Bishop of Western Massachusetts)

Discussion

A one-hour period of comments by the House followed.

By show of hands the discussion was concluded.

Reflections

Chaplain Battle led reflections followed by fifteen minutes of silence at 5:40 pm.

Consecration of Bishops

The House of Bishops Committee on Consecration of Bishops moved the resolution on the consent to the consecration of the Rev. Canon V. Gene Robinson, Bishop Coadjutor-elect of the Diocese of New Hampshire, and Ballot #7 was taken.

Ballot #7 taken

RECESS

The Presiding Bishop declared a ten minute recess at 5:55 p.m.

Social and Urban Affairs

The House of Bishops Committee on Social and Urban Affairs presented its Report #4 on HD Message #108 on Resolution A012 (Caring for Children in the Face of the New Genetics) and moved concurrence.

The House concurred
(Communicated to the House of Deputies in HB Message #148)

Final Text of Resolution:

(A012)
Resolved, That the 74th General Convention reaffirm that children are entrusted to us as gifts from God to be nurtured toward maturity. Therefore:
- Genetic testing of children can be an important part of parental responsibility, and may be carried out if it is clearly in the child's best interests to be tested;
- Treatment for genetic diseases and the use of somatic gene transfer therapies may be used if they are proven safe and effective;
- New genetic techniques may be used in conjunction with in vitro fertilization to avoid procreation of human beings with clearly serious disorders of their DNA or chromosomes;
- It is not morally acceptable to use reproductive cloning, and it is therefore morally irresponsible for physicians, scientists, and prospective parents to engage in it.

Consent Calendar

The Secretary laid the Consent Calendar for the Eighth Legislative Day on the table.

Evangelism

The House of Bishops Committee on Evangelism presented its Report #3 on HD Message #93 on Resolution C008 (Episcopal Council of Indigenous Ministries Funding) and moved concurrence.

The House concurred
(Communicated to the House of Deputies in HB Message #149)

Final Text of Resolution:

(C008)
Resolved, That The Episcopal Church of the United States of America in the 74th General Convention of The Episcopal Church, meeting in Minneapolis in July, 2003, reaffirm the 72nd General Convention's designation of the decade 1997–2007 as the "Decade of Remembrance, Recognition, and Reconciliation" during which each diocese will take such steps as necessary to fully recognize and welcome Native Peoples into congregational life, which will include a special effort toward developing an outreach partnership among urban Native Peoples; and be it further
Resolved, That the 74th General Convention of The Episcopal Church request the Joint Standing Committee on Program, Budget and Finance to consider and adopt a budget allocation for Native American ministries, working with the Episcopal Council of Indigenous Ministries, of $1,500,000 funding for the triennium, for grants for projects which seek to welcome Native Peoples into congregational life, providing leadership training programs for young adults, evangelism programs for youth, and mission among urban and rural Native Peoples; and that progress reports be presented at the 75th General Convention. This proposed funding allocation is in addition to proposed funding allocations as found in the Budget Proposal of the Presiding Bishop and the Executive Council to the 74th General Convention on pages 30 (Domestic Appropriations) and 26 (Ethnic Congregational Development—Native American Ministries).

The House of Bishops Committee on Evangelism presented its Report #4 on HD Message #94 on Resolution C006 (Evangelism to the New Majority) and moved concurrence.

The House concurred
(Communicated to the House of Deputies in HB Message #150)

Final Text of Resolution:

(C006)
Resolved, That in implementing the 20/20 goal of focusing The Episcopal Church on domestic mission and evangelism, this church reach out to groups not traditionally within the scope of these efforts, which include persons who have felt unwelcome or alienated by the church, particularly, though not limited to, those who identify themselves as the "new majority" characterized by diversity of race, ethnicity, language, disability, and sexual orientation; and be it further
Resolved, That the 74th General Convention affirm the work of the Congregational Development Unit of the Church Center, already begun in these efforts, and urge them to continue to include and expand, as components of their ongoing and future programs, elements of diversity, including but not limited to the groups listed above.

MINNEAPOLIS MEETING					HOUSE OF BISHOPS

Prayer Book, Liturgy and Church Music
The House of Bishops Committee on Prayer Book, Liturgy and Church Music presented its Report #30 on Resolution A109 (International Anglican Liturgical Consultation) and moved adoption of a substitute.

Original Text of Resolution:
(A109)
Resolved, the House of Deputies concurring, That the 74th General Convention appropriate $25,000.00 to support the church's participation in and support of the Consultation; and be it further
Resolved, That this appropriation be administered by the Office for Liturgy and Music.

Committee Substitute:
Resolved, the House of Deputies concurring, That the 74th General Convention reaffirm and support the Church's participation in and support of the International Anglican Liturgical Consultation; and be it further
Resolved, That the General Convention request the Joint Standing Committee on Program, Budget and Finance to consider a budget allocation of $25,000 for implementation of this resolution.

Motion carried
Substitute resolution adopted
(Communicated to the House of Deputies in HB Message #151)

The House of Bishops Committee on Prayer Book, Liturgy and Church Music presented its Report #31 on Resolution A107 (Renewal and Enrichment of Common Worship) and moved that the Committee be discharged.

Motion carried
Committee discharged
(Communicated to the House of Deputies in HB Message #152)

The House of Bishops Committee on Prayer Book, Liturgy and Church Music presented its Report #32 on Resolution A131 (Worker's Prayer) and moved the resolution, recommending rejection.

Original Text of Resolution:
(A131)
Resolved, the House of Deputies concurring, That the 74th General Convention recommend to the Standing Commission on Liturgy and Music to include the prayer, "A Worker's Prayer" in the Book of Common Prayer in the "Prayers for the Social Order" section.

Lord, we pray today for all who work and all who are seeking work. As You looked at the work You had done and saw that it was good, help us to value all work performed with diligence, care and honesty. Help us to seek rewards for our work not only in the wages we receive, but also in stewardship of Your creation and justice toward all persons. Help us to recognize that we cannot do our work alone, but depend upon the work of many others, some of whom we do not even know. Help us to remember that it is Your gift to find, even in the inevitable routine, occasions of interest and joy. Help us to remember that laborers are worthy not only of their hire, but of their rest. Help us to say "Well done" to others, as we hope to hear the same. Finally, when we cannot see the direction to go, give us faith that you can always work for good through us. We ask these things in the name of Him who promised to be with us always. *Amen.*

Motion defeated
Resolution rejected
(Communicated to the House of Deputies in HB Message #153)

The House of Bishops Committee on Prayer Book, Liturgy and Church Music presented its Report #33 on Resolution C035 (Publish Lectionary for Lesser Feasts and Fasts) and moved the resolution, recommending rejection.

Original Text of Resolution:
(C035)
Resolved, the House of Deputies concurring, That the 74th General Convention direct the Standing Liturgical Commission to develop and publish a lectionary volume to accompany *Lesser Feasts and Fasts*, and that said lectionary volume be updated following each revision of the Calendar; and be it further
Resolved, That the General Convention request the Joint Standing Committee on Program, Budget, and Finance to consider a budget allocation of $10,000 for implementation of this resolution.

Motion defeated
Resolution rejected
(Communicated to the House of Deputies in HB Message #154)

The House of Bishops Committee on Prayer Book, Liturgy and Church Music presented its Report #34 on Resolution D003 (Revision of the Catechism) and moved to refer the resolution to the Standing Commission on Liturgy and Music.

Original Text of Resolution:
(D003)
Resolved, the House of Deputies concurring, That the catechism be changed in The Book of Common Prayer (page 847) to quote Micah 6:8 correctly:
"Question: What response did God require from the chosen people? Answer: God required the chosen people to be faithful; ~~to love justice, to do mercy,~~ *to do justice, to love mercy* and to walk humbly with their God."

And be it further
Resolved, That all future printings of The Book of Common Prayer include this correction in an erratum until a new edition is approved.

Motion carried
Resolution referred to a Standing Commission
(Communicated to the House of Deputies in HB Message #155)

The House of Bishops Committee on Prayer Book, Liturgy and Church Music presented its Report #35 on Resolution D035 (To Transfer the Comemoration of Harriet Tubman from July 20 to March 10) and moved to refer the resolution to the Standing Commission on Liturgy and Music.

Original Text of Resolution:
(D035)
Resolved, the House of Deputies concurring, That the commemoration of Harriet Ross Tubman Davis be observed on March 10 in the Calendar of Lesser Feasts and that her name be removed from the commemorations of July 20.

Motion carried
Resolution referred to a Standing Commission
(Communicated to the House of Deputies in HB Message #156)

The House of Bishops Committee on Prayer Book, Liturgy and Church Music presented its Report #37 on Resolution D049 (First Communion on the Moon) and moved to refer the resolution to the Standing Commission on Liturgy and Music.

Original Text of Resolution:
(D049)
Resolved, the House of Deputies concurring, That the 74th General Convention promote local commemoration of the 35th anniversary of "The First Communion on the Moon," July 20, 2004, in worship and teaching; and be it further
Resolved, That the 74th General Convention direct the Standing Commission on Liturgy and Music to prepare propers and collects for churchwide observance of the 40th anniversary of the event, July 20, 2009; and be it further
Resolved, That the General Convention direct the Standing Commission on Liturgy and Music to prepare to include "The First Communion on the Moon" in The Episcopal Church's *Lesser Feasts and Fasts* and on the calendar in the Book of Common Prayer for July 20.

Motion carried
Resolution referred to a Standing Commission
(Communicated to the House of Deputies in HB Message #157)

Consent Calendar
The Bishop of Kansas asked to restore Resolution A110 to the Consent Calendar.

Ecumenical Relations
The House of Bishops Committee on Ecumenical Relations presented its Report #7 on Resolution D004 (Evangelical Lutheran Church in America Ordination Practices) and moved that the Committee be discharged.

Motion carried
Committee discharged
(Communicated to the House of Deputies in HB Message #158)

The House of Bishops Committee on Ecumenical Relations presented its Report #9 on Resolution C011 (Evangelical Lutheran Church in America—Change in Ordination Policy) and moved that the Committee be discharged.

Motion carried
Committee discharged
(Communicated to the House of Deputies in HB Message #159)

Constitution
The House of Bishops Committee on Constitution presented its Report #8 on Resolution B023 (Change Consent Process to Provinces) and moved the resolution, recommending rejection.

Original Text of Resolution:
(B023)
Resolved, the House of Deputies concurring, That the 74th General Convention amend the Constitution of the General Convention, Article II, Section 2, 1st sentence, so as to read:
No one shall be ordained and consecrated Bishop until the attainment of thirty years of age; nor without the consent of a majority of the Standing Committees of all the Dioceses *within the Province where the election has occurred,* and the consent of a majority of the Bishops of this Church exercising jurisdiction *in said Province.* But if the election shall have taken place within three months next before the meeting of the General Convention, the consent of the House of Deputies shall be required in place of that of a majority of the Standing Committees. No one shall be ordained and consecrated Bishop by fewer than three Bishops.
And be it further
Resolved, That Title III, Canon 22, Sections 4(a) and (b) be amended so as to correspond to the change in the Constitution.

The Bishop of Connecticut moved to refer the resolution to the Standing Commission on Constitution and Canons.

Motion carried
Resolution referred to a Standing Commission
(Communicated to the House of Deputies in HB Message #160)

Structure

The House of Bishops Committee on Structure presented its Report #5 on HD Message #33 on Resolution A146 (Provincial Coordinators Funding) and moved concurrence.

The House concurred
(Communicated to the House of Deputies in HB Message #161)

Final Text of Resolution:
(A146)
Resolved, **That the 74th General Convention continue to appropriate sufficient funds to ensure the continuation of Provincial Coordinators.**

The House of Bishops Committee on Structure presented its Report #6 on HD Message #55 on Resolution A072 (Amend Canon I.6.1) and moved concurrence.

The House concurred
(Communicated to the House of Deputies in HB Message #162)

Final Text of Resolution:
(A072)
Resolved, **That Canon I.6.1 be amended to read as follows:**
A report of every Parish and other Congregation of this Church shall be prepared annually for the year ending December 31 preceding, in the form authorized by the Executive Council and approved by the Committee on the State of the Church, and shall be filed not later than March 1 with the Bishop of the Diocese, or, where there is no Bishop, with the ecclesiastical authority of the Diocese. The Bishop or the ecclesiastical authority, as the case may be, shall keep a copy and submit the report to the Executive Council not later than May 1. In every Parish *and other Congregation* **the preparation and filing of this report shall be the joint duty of the Rector** *or Member of the Clergy in charge thereof* **and** ~~Vestry; and in every other Congregation the duty of the Member of the Clergy in charge thereof~~ *the lay leadership; and before the filing thereof the report shall be approved by the Vestry or bishop's committee or mission council.* **This report shall include the following information:...**

The House of Bishops Committee on Structure presented its Report #7 on HD Message #17 on Resolution A145 (General Convention Model) and moved concurrence.

The House concurred
(Communicated to the House of Deputies in HB Message #163)

Final Text of Resolution:
(A145)
Resolved, **That the Presiding Bishop and the President of the House of Deputies appoint a Joint Task Force consisting of members of the Standing Commission on Structure of the Church and the Joint Standing Committee on Planning and Arrangements to prepare a comprehensive model for General Convention with respect to the structure of General Convention and the General Convention agenda to be considered for implementation by the 75th General Convention.**

The House of Bishops Committee on Structure presented its Report #8 on HD Message #39 on Resolution A019 (Continue Standing Committee on HIV/AIDS) and moved concurrence.

The House concurred
(Communicated to the House of Deputies in HB Message #164)

Final Text of Resolution:
(A019)
Resolved, **That the 74th General Convention authorize the continuation of the Executive Council Standing Committee on HIV/AIDS for the 2004–2006 Triennium;** and be it further
Resolved, **That the Standing Committee on HIV/AIDS for the next triennium focus on the "quiet voices of AIDS" in our church and in our nation and in the world, those whom we are called to serve but may overlook;** and be it further
Resolved, **That the Standing Committee undertake a survey of HIV/AIDS ministries at all levels of the church;** and be it further
Resolved, **That the Standing Committee on HIV/AIDS report at least annually to the Executive Council of the General Convention on the state of the church's response to the HIV/AIDS pandemic, with particular attention to the implementation of pertinent resolutions of General Convention.**

The House of Bishops Committee on Structure presented its Report #9 on HD Message #78 on Resolution A023 (Institutional Wellness and the Prevention of Sexual Misconduct Task Force) and moved concurrence.

The House concurred
(Communicated to the House of Deputies in HB Message #165)

Final Text of Resolution:
(A023)

Resolved, That the General Convention establish, pursuant to Joint Rule 23, a Task Force of not less than ten nor more than fifteen persons. These persons should be laity, bishops, priests, and deacons with experience and expertise in dealing with sexual misconduct in church settings. Membership should include, but not be limited to representatives from the Standing Commission on Ministry Development, the Council of Seminary Deans, the Nathan Network, the National Network of Episcopal Clergy Associations, the Task Force on Disciplinary Policy and Procedures, and the National Network of Lay Professionals; and be it further

Resolved, That the Task Force shall study and gather information concerning matters of institutional wellness for the prevention of sexual misconduct. Its study shall include such concerns as screening, selection and training of clergy, lay employees and volunteers; monitoring and supervision; behavior management; incident investigation; and the articulation of pastoral standards and codes of ethical behavior; and be it further

Resolved, That each body named shall recommend Task Force members from its own membership, and the appointments shall be overseen by the Bishop of the Office of Pastoral Development. Additional members shall then be appointed by the Bishop of the Office of Pastoral Development, and the entire Task Force shall include at least two bishops, two clergy, and two laity. The Task Force shall have the services of the Office of Pastoral Development and a Church Pension staff person; and be it further

Resolved, That a report be made to the Standing Commission on Ministry Development, as well as to the 2006 General Convention; and be it further

Resolved, That the General Convention request the Joint Standing Committee on Program, Budget and Finance to consider the allocation of $50,000 for the implementation of this resolution.

The House of Bishops Committee on Structure presented its Report #10 on HD Message #16 on Resolution A120 (Theological Education Committee) and moved concurrence.

The House concurred
(Communicated to the House of Deputies in HB Message #166)

Final Text of Resolution:
(A120)

Resolved, That the 74th General Convention direct the Standing Commission on Ministry Development, contingent upon finding funding from other sources outside of General Convention, to convene a Strategic Planning Committee, consisting of bishops, seminary deans, and provincial representatives; and be it further

Resolved, That this Committee is to function in a broad collaborative manner for six years to prepare an in-depth study that will chart the future of

theological education in the Church; and be it further
Resolved, That the Standing Commission on Ministry Development will report on the work of this Strategic Planning Committee to the 75th General Convention and will deliver its final report to the 76th General Convention.

Evangelism

The House of Bishops Committee on Evangelism presented its Report #5 on HD Message #110 on Resolution A084 (20/20 Vision Reporting) and moved concurrence.

The House concurred
(Communicated to the House of Deputies in HB Message #167)

Final Text of Resolution:

(A084)
Resolved, That the 74th General Convention direct the Standing Commission on Domestic Mission and Evangelism (SCDME) in consultation with other committees and commissions to develop strategic plans in accomplishing measurable goals of the 20/20 vision in the next triennium and urge individuals, congregations, dioceses, provinces, and the Church Center staff to accomplish those goals; and be it further
Resolved, That the SCDME annually report to the Executive Council and Episcopal Church at-large through its means of communication such as Episcopal Life and our website on how the whole Church is progressing toward the 20/20 vision as articulated in the SCDME report and the 20/20 Task Force report to the 74th General Convention in each of the nine areas: leadership, spirituality, prayer and worship, research, new congregation development, vital congregations, next generations, communication, funding, and reporting.

Ministry

The House of Bishops Committee on Ministry presented its Report #17 on Resolution A022 (Nathan Network Funding) and moved adoption.

Original Text of Resolution:

(A022)
Resolved, the House of Deputies concurring, That the sum of $49,000 be appropriated for the next triennium to provide start-up funding for a national network of diocesan personnel working with sexual misconduct in the Church.

Motion carried
Resolution adopted
(Communicated to the House of Deputies in HB Message #168)

| MINNEAPOLIS MEETING | HOUSE OF BISHOPS |

The House of Bishops Committee on Ministry presented its Report #19 on Resolution A062 (Diversity in Leadership Recruitment) and moved that the Committee be discharged.

Motion carried
Committee discharged
(Communicated to the House of Deputies in HB Message #169)

The House of Bishops Committee on Ministry presented its Report #20 on Resolution A067 (Fund for Theological Education) and moved adoption of a substitute.

Original Text of Resolution:
(A067)
Resolved, the House of Deputies concurring, That The Episcopal Church allocate $300,000 to be matched by the Lilly Endowment's $2.3 million to be a full partner and participant in the Fund for Theological Education's pastoral leadership search effort (Pulse Project) which will identify, cultivate, and recruit exceptional candidates under age 35 for ordination by developing materials, a database, and a website, this project being in conjunction with the Presbyterian Church (USA), the United Methodist Church, and the Evangelical Lutheran Church in America.

Committee Substitute:
Resolved, the House of Deputies concurring, That the 74th General Convention affirm the participation of The Episcopal Church as a full partner in the Fund for Theological Education's Pastoral Leadership Search Effort (PLSE Project) which will identify, cultivate, and recruit exceptional candidates under age 35 representing the multicultural diversity of society for ordination by developing materials, a database, and a website; this project being in conjunction with the Presbyterian Church (USA), the United Methodist Church, and the United Church of Christ; and that the Convention encourage broad-based Episcopal Church funding support to provide $300,000 for three years as the Episcopal denomination's match for the Lilly Endowment's $2.3 million grant to the FTE for this project.

Motion carried
Substitute resolution adopted
(Communicated to the House of Deputies in HB Message #170)

The House of Bishops Committee on Ministry presented its Report #21 on Resolution B017 (Fresh Start) and moved adoption with amendment.

Original Text of Resolution:
(B017)
Resolved, the House of Deputies concurring, That the 74th General Convention commend the use of Fresh Start, a resource for congregations and clergy in transition, as a program of The Episcopal Church; and be it further
Resolved, That the General Convention affirm the collaborative partnership of the

Office for Ministry Development and Church Deployment Office of The Episcopal Church, The Episcopal Church Foundation, the dioceses, and the National Fresh Start Committee, in the development and on-going support of Fresh Start; and be it further
Resolved, That the Fresh Start partners report back to the 75th General Convention regarding the program's impact upon clergy, congregations, and dioceses.

Committee Amendment:
Resolved, the House of Deputies concurring, That the 74th General Convention commend the use of Fresh Start, a resource for congregations and clergy in transition, as a program of The Episcopal Church; and be it further
Resolved, That the General Convention affirm the collaborative partnership of the Office for Ministry Development and Church Deployment Office of The Episcopal Church, The Episcopal Church Foundation, the dioceses, and the National Fresh Start Committee, in the development and on-going support of Fresh Start; and be it further
Resolved, That Fresh Start adapt this material in order to provide for its use in culturally diverse settings; and be it further
Resolved, That the Fresh Start partners report back to the 75th General Convention regarding the program's impact upon clergy, congregations, and dioceses.

Motion carried
Resolution adopted with amendment
(Communicated to the House of Deputies in HB Message #171)

The House of Bishops Committee on Ministry presented its Report #22 on Resolution B018 (Families of Clergy United in Support) and moved adoption with amendment.

Original Text of Resolution:
(B018)
Resolved, the House of Deputies concurring, That the 74th General Convention recognize that healthy families of clergy promote the well-being of clergy and congregations, and thus deserve spiritual and institutional support; and be it further
Resolved, That the 74th General Convention encourage the effort of Families of Clergy United in Support (FOCUS) in their work of advocacy and awareness of clergy, in efforts to promote the following:
1. Provide a chaplain in each diocese for families of clergy.
2. Provide education for each search committee regarding the special needs and concerns of families of clergy in transition, and about the expectations placed on family by congregations.
3. Provide support by seminaries for spouses, partners, and children of postulants and candidates in the process of ordination; and be it further

Resolved, That the General Convention request the Joint Standing Committee on Program, Budget and Finance to consider a budget allocation of $75,000 for implementation of this resolution.

Committee Amendment:
Resolved, the House of Deputies concurring, That the 74th General Convention recognize that healthy families of clergy promote the well-being of clergy and congregations, and thus deserve spiritual and institutional support; and be it further *Resolved,* That the 74th General Convention *commend and* encourage the effort of Families of Clergy United in Support (FOCUS) in their work of advocacy and *education for* awareness of clergy *family needs,* in efforts to promote the following:
1. Provide a chaplain in each diocese for families of clergy.
2. Provide education for each search committee regarding the special needs and concerns of families of clergy in transition, and about the expectations placed on family by congregations.
3. Provide support by seminaries for spouses, partners, and children of postulants and candidates in the process of ordination; and be it further

Resolved, That the Office of Ministry Development provide oversight and coordination with FOCUS and other programs that support the well-being of clergy and clergy families, and assist in seeking funding for such programs, including for Families of Clergy United in Support, and be it further

Resolved, That the General Convention request the Joint Standing Committee on Program, Budget and Finance to consider a budget allocation of $75,000 for implementation of this resolution.

Motion carried
Resolution adopted with amendment
(Communicated to the House of Deputies in HB Message #172)

Communications
The House of Bishops Committee on Communications presented its Report #7 on Resolution C037 (Facilitating International Communications within The Episcopal Church) and moved adoption of a substitute.

Original Text of Resolution:
(C037)
Resolved, the House of Deputuies concurring, That The Episcopal Church exists beyond the national boundaries of the United States of America; and be it further
Resolved, That a number of its members either reside within Dioceses or Convocations located in Columbia, the Dominican Republic, Ecuador, El Salvador, Europe, Guatemala, Haiti, Micronesia, Nicaragua, Litoral Honduras, Panama, Taiwan or the Virgin Islands, or serve in various locations around the world within the Armed Forces of the United States of America; and be it further
Resolved, That the various church bodies and affiliated organizations, agencies and publishers be made aware of this international distinction when producing information material, documentation, advertisements, and publications; and be it further
Resolved, That advertisements that appear in Episcopal publications offer information to readers that contains methods of contact that are not limited to a

1-800 telephone number; and be it further
Resolved, That websites which offer the possibility to input and revise data online be designed to include international as well as U.S. data. These changes might allow for longer addresses, accurate entry of postal codes, the addition of the country code with more space for longer telephone numbers, and the opportunity to add other titles, job descriptions, mission opportunities, or additional comments; and be it further
Resolved, That websites which offer the possibility to acquire items online make every effort to facilitate the purchase of these items by persons residing outside of the 50 states, including members of the Armed Forces using APO addresses, and that the maximum amount of contact information for these organizations be available on their websites.

Committee Substitute:

Resolved, the House of Deputies concurring, That the 74th General Convention urge all church bodies and affiliated organizations, agencies, and publishers to recognize The Episcopal Church's international membership beyond the boundaries of the United States when producing informational material, documentation, publications, websites, and advertisements; and be it further
Resolved, That the Domestic and Foreign Missionary Society provide methods of contact that allow for international and military postal addresses and telephone numbers for online purchase and information collection.

Motion carried
Substitute resolution adopted
(Communicated to the House of Deputies in HB Message #173)

The House of Bishops Committee on Communications presented its Report #9 on HD Message #76 on Resolution A017 (National Conversation on Women's Ordination) and moved concurrence.

The House concurred
(Communicated to the House of Deputies in HB Message #174)

Final Text of Resolution:

(A017)
Resolved, **That the 74th General Convention give thanks for the work of the Holy Spirit within our communion through the life-giving ministry of ordained women.**

Consecration of Bishops

The Presiding Bishop read the results of Ballot #7 for the consent to the consecration of Bishop Coadjutor-elect Robinson of the Diocese of New Hampshire. Of 107 bishops with jurisdiction, 62 have given consent.

The House concurred
(Communicated to the House of Deputies in HB Message #175)

The Bishop of Pittsburgh and others came forward. The Bishop of Pittsburgh read a statement on behalf of the group. The Bishop Suffragan of South Carolina, read the statement in Spanish (see Appendix J–Day 7 for Statement of Bishops upon the Confirmation of Gene Robinson).

Recess

The House recessed with prayers led by Chaplain Battle.

The House recessed at 7:07 p.m. until 11:00 a.m. on the Eighth Legislative Day.

Appendix H
Day 7

Vote on Resolution B005 (Proposed Substitute Resolution)

		Yea	Nay	Abstain
Bishop F. Putnam	0595	x		
Bishop D. Reed	0603	x		
Bishop F. Stough	0658			
Bishop O. Charles	0665		x	
Bishop C. McGehee	0667			
Bishop M. Potreus	0668			
Bishop W. Righter	0671		x	
Bishop R. Wolterstorff	0697		x	
Bishop C. Vaché	0712			x
Bishop J. Warner	0717			
Bishop G. McAllister	0718	x		
Bishop R. Anderson	0722	x		
Bishop H. Light	0729			
Bishop W. Swing	0732	x		
Bishop A. Walmsley	0736	x		
Bishop H. Donovan	0748	x		
Bishop W. Wantland	0750		x	
Bishop C. Duvall	0755			
Bishop R. Grein	0758	x		
Bishop A. Hathaway	0761			
Bishop C. Coleridge	0763	x		
Bishop T. Eastman	0767	x		
Bishop G. Charlton	0770			x
Bishop J. Ottley	0779	x		
Bishop L. Frade	0780		x	
Bishop V. Pettit	0781			
Bishop P.J. Lee	0785	x		
Bishop C. Anderson	0786			
Bishop D. Wimberley	0789	x		
Bishop C. Pope	0791	x		
Bishop F. Griswold	0794			
Bishop R. Harris	0795	x		
Bishop F. Vest	0796		x	
Bishop R. Ladehoff	0801	x		
Bishop A. Bartlett	0804	x		
Bishop D. Theuner	0805	x		
Bishop D. Swenson	0806	x		

MINNEAPOLIS MEETING   HOUSE OF BISHOPS

		Yea	Nay	Abstain
Bishop A. Williams	0812	x		
Bishop F. Gray	0815	x		
Bishop C. Tennis	0816	x		
Bishop D. Taylor	0819	x		
Bishop J. Rowthorn	0821		x	
Bishop R. Moody	0824	x		
Bishop O. Walker	0826		x	
Bishop F. Borsch	0828			
Bishop H. Thompson	0829	x		
Bishop C. Epting	0830	x		
Bishop F. Turner	0831	x		
Bishop J. D. Schofield	0832	x		
Bishop B. Harris	0834	x		
Bishop J. Buchanan	0835			x
Bishop T. Kelshaw	0836	x		
Bishop R. Johnson	0837	x		
Bishop S. Hampton	0838	x		
Bishop J. Howe	0839		x	
Bishop R. Rowley	0840	x		
Bishop S. Carranza-Gomez	0844	x		
Bishop J. Krotz	0846	x		
Bishop A. Fairfield	0850			x
Bishop W. Smalley	0851	x		
Bishop E. Salmon	0852	x		
Bishop S. Plummer	0853	x		
Bishop C. Keyser	0854		x	
Bishop H. Williams	0855			x
Bishop J. Thornton	0857	x		
Bishop R. Shimpfky	0858	x		
Bishop W Winterrowd	0860	x		
Bishop C. Talton	0861	x		
Bishop H. Rockwell	0863	x		
Bishop V. Scantlebury	0864	x		
Bishop S. Charleston	0865	x		
Bishop J. McKelvey	0866	x		
Bishop J. Lamb	0868	x		
Bishop A. Marble	0869	x		
Bishop J. Holguin	0870		x	
Bishop D. Joslin	0871	x		
Bishop P. Beckwith	0872		x	
Bishop G. Hughes	0874	x		
Bishop R. Shahan	0875	x		

		Yea	Nay	Abstain
Bishop J. Dixon	0876	x		
Bishop J. Stanton	0879		x	
Bishop J. Iker	0880		x	
Bishop J. Duracin	0881		x	
Bishop B. Herlong	0882		x	
Bishop C. Matthews	0883	x		
Bishop C. Payne	0884			x
Bishop J. Jelinek	0885	x		
Bishop J. Doss	0886	x		
Bishop J. Folts	0889	x		
Bishop C. Grew	0890	x		
Bishop E. Gulick	0891	x		
Bishop S. Jecko	0892		x	
Bishop R. Johnson	0893	x		
Bishop R. Jacobus	0894	x		
Bishop L. Maze	0895			
Bishop C. Robertson	0896	x		
Bishop K. Ackerman	0897		x	
Bishop T. Shaw	0898	x		
Bishop A Morante	0899		x	
Bishop K. Price	0900	x		
Bishop H. Louttit	0901	x		
Bishop D. Henderson	0902		x	
Bishop D. Jones	0907	x		
Bishop R. Ihloff	0909	x		
Bishop M Creighton	0910	x		
Bishop R. Hibbs	0911		x	
Bishop C. Roskam	0912	x		
Bishop G. Wolf	0913	x		
Bishop J. Lipscomb	0914	x		
Bishop W. Skilton	0915	x		
Bishop R. Duncan	0916	x		
Bishop A. Smith	0917	x		
Bishop C. Irish	0918	x		
Bishop P. Marshall	0919		x	
Bishop G. Gloster	0920	x		
Bishop E. Leidel	0921	x		
Bishop C. Daniel	0922	x		
Bishop H. Parsley	0923	x		
Bishop G. Scruton	0924			
Bishop N. Powell	0925	x		
Bishop R. Chang	0926	x		

MINNEAPOLIS MEETING   HOUSE OF BISHOPS

		Yea	Nay	Abstain
Bishop C. Bennison	0927	x		
Bishop R. Michel	0928		x	
Bishop C. Waynick	0929	x		
Bishop W. Ohl	0930	x		
Bishop T. Daniels	0931	x		
Bishop D. Bane	0932	x		
Bishop M. MacDonald	0933		x	
Bishop B. Caldwell	0934	x		
Bishop D. Herzog	0935		x	
Bishop C. Jenkins	0936	x		
Bishop B. Howe	0937	x		
Bishop C. Knudsen	0938	x		
Bishop M. Sisk	0939	x		
Bishop H. Bainbridge	0940	x		
Bishop W. Wright	0941	x		
Bishop J. Rabb	0942	x		
Bishop J. Croneberger	0943	x		
Bishop C. vonRosenberg	0944	x		
Bishop W. Persell	0945	x		
Bishop K. Whitmore	0946	x		
Bishop M. Garrison	0947	x		
Bishop J. Kelsey	0948	x		
Bishop B. MacPherson	0949	x		
Bishop W. Gibbs	0950	x		
Bishop G. Packard	0951			x
Bishop E. Little	0952		x	
Bishop J. Bruno	0953	x		
Bishop D. Bena	0954		x	
Bishop M. Curry	0955	x		
Bishop D. Gray	0956	x		
Bishop W. Gregg	0957	x		
Bishop S. Sauls	0958	x		
Bishop J. Curry	0959	x		
Bishop W. Ramos-Orench	0960	x		
Bishop J. Waggoner	0961	x		
Bishop D. Lai	0962	x		
Bishop K. Jefferts Schori	0963	x		
Bishop R. Cederholm	0964	x		
Bishop T. Ely	0965			
Bishop P. Duncan	0966	x		
Bishop D. Johnson	0967	x		
Bishop J. Alexander	0968	x		

		Yea	Nay	Abstain
Bishop F. Duque	0969		x	
Bishop W. Klusmeyer	0970	x		
Bishop L. Allen	0971	x		
Bishop P. Whalon	0973		x	
Bishop M. Andrus	0974	x		
Bishop G. W. Smith	0975	x		
Bishop J. Adams	0976	x		
Bishop C. Gallagher	0977	x		
Bishop R. Gepert	0978	x		
Bishop J. Chane	0979	x		
Bishop H. Scriven	0980a	x		
Bishop G. Harris	0981		x	
Bishop J. Shand	0982	x		
Bishop A. Scarfe	0983	x		
Bishop D. Alvarez	0984	x		

Appendix I
Day 7

Report on Bishop-elect of New Hampshire

Report to the House of Bishops
The Rt. Rev. Gordon P. Scruton, Diocese of Western Massachusetts
August 5, 2003

A. Introduction

On Monday, August 4, 2003, the Bishop, the President of the Standing Committee, and the Bishop-elect of the Diocese of New Hampshire asked the Presiding Bishop to investigate two matters concerning the Bishop-elect which had come to light Sunday evening. The Presiding Bishop asked me to conduct the investigation, the focus of which was to determine if either or both of the concerns raised constitute cause for further investigation and thus sufficient reason to postpone the process of seeking consents to the election of the Rev. Canon V. Gene Robinson.

The Gospel of Jesus Christ and our Canons require us to hold each other accountable for our character and behavior. The Episcopal Church has clear policies in place to guide our response in such instances. These policies ensure that truth can be pursued and respect and care can be shown for all parties involved.

B. First Concern

Late Sunday evening, August 3, 2003, an adult member of a Vermont Episcopal congregation sent an E-mail to the Rt. Rev. Thomas C. Ely, Bishop of Vermont. The E-mail stated that "I am a straight man reporting homosexual harassment by a gay male priest from another Diocese." Bishop Ely contacted the individual that evening and the following morning to inquire further about the concern being raised and to assure the individual that the Church takes such concerns seriously. The individual then indicated to Bishop Ely that he had sent the E-mail to many bishops. Bishop Ely then informed the Bishop of New Hampshire and the Presiding Bishop of the concern being raised.

On Monday afternoon, I spoke by speaker phone with the individual in the presence of Bishop Ely, his Chancellor, Thomas Little, and the Rev. Hays Junkin, President of the Standing Committee of the Diocese of New Hampshire.

I asked the individual to tell the story of his experience that caused him to raise his concerns. According to the individual, the events took place at a Province I convocation in November of 1999, at Mont Marie Conference Center in Holyoke, Massachusetts. There were two exchanges between the individual and Canon Robinson at the convocation.

In the first, the individual was seated at the beginning of a plenary session. As Canon Robinson was passing by him, the individual asked Canon Robinson a question about the order of events or the schedule or convocation procedure, or something of that nature. Canon Robinson put his left hand on the individual's arm and his right hand on the individual's upper back as he listened to his questions and answered them. This incident was in public view and was brief. The individual said Canon Robinson answered his questions and spoke no inappropriate words. The second incident occurred later in the convocation while the two were standing in proximity. During a light moment in the convocation, the individual turned to Canon Robinson to make a comment. In response, Canon Robinson touched the individual's forearm and back while responding with his own comment.

The individual then described to me the feelings he had during these two exchanges. He said that in his opinion, Canon Robinson's placement of his hands seemed inappropriate to him, given that they did not know each other, and presumed a far greater familiarity or intimacy than was the case. The individual said these incidents made him feel uncomfortable. He said he has never said anything to anyone about this, but did mention it to his wife but not at the time. He acknowledged that other people could have seen the exchange as natural and normal.

He said he had not thought that the House of Deputies was going to consent to Canon Robinsons' election; and when he learned consent had been given, he found himself late Sunday night needing to tell someone of his experience. He observed that when he wrote the E-mail, he was feeling upset, in part because he expected his concern to be brushed under the rug. He thought the Church would close ranks and not listen to him. I asked him whether he wanted to bring a formal charge of harassment. He said very clearly, no. He regretted having used the word "harassment" in his E-mail.

The Title IV disciplinary process for priests was then explained to the individual, and I asked him again if he wished to proceed to file a written complaint. Again, he indicated that he had no desire to pursue the matter any further. He said he was thankful the Church has taken this seriously and that he felt "listened to." He also indicated that he was not seeking any personal attention or notoriety and regrets that it has been taken this way by some.

Bishop Ely knows the individual and is maintaining ongoing pastoral contact with him and his family, both personally and through their parish priest.

C. Second Concern

The second focus of my investigation involved concerns about a pornographic web site. Two bishops brought the website to the attention of the parliamentarian of the House of Deputies who reviewed the material and contacted the Chancellor to the Presiding Bishop on Sunday evening.

The concern expressed has been the involvement or lack of involvement of Canon Robinson with the website. The website in question could be reached through a link from the Concord, New Hampshire Chapter of an organization known as Outright. Canon Robinson has referred to his involvement with this organization in his resume, which is on the Diocese of New Hampshire website. He has also referred to his involvement with that organization in hearings during this Convention as an example of his work with youth.

In my investigation, I have consulted with Canon Robinson and I have reviewed the website of Concord Outright. At the formal request of an American Anglican Council representative, who this morning provided the Presiding Bishop with a disk prepared on August 2, I have reviewed a downstream link site which showed graphic sexual materials. I have also had communications from Outright in

Portland, Maine, where the website is based, and from representatives of Outright in Concord and I have carefully reviewed them.

What appears to be beyond dispute is that Canon Robinson helped to found Concord Outright in 1995. Investigation shows that the organization was founded to provide support and counseling for young people concerned about their sexuality. Canon Robinson's role in the Concord Chapter of Outright was primarily to provide training to insure that appropriate boundaries were observed for the protection of both young people and those working with them.

Canon Robinson ended his involvement in Outright in 1998 and has not been associated with Outright since that time. The website was established in 2002. Canon Robinson was not aware that the organization has a website until this Convention. The response of Outright emphasized to me that Canon Robinson has had no part in the creation of the website.

I see no evidence that Canon Robinson was aware of or associated with the website or its contents.

D. Conclusion

In both allegations, it is my conclusion that there is no necessity to pursue further investigation and no reason on these grounds to prevent the Bishops with jurisdiction from going forward with their voting about whether or not to consent to Canon Robinson's consecration.

The Standing Committee of the Diocese of New Hampshire concurs in these conclusions and continues to seek the required consents.

Appendix J
Day 7

Statement of Bishops upon the Confirmation of Gene Robinson

August 4, 2003

The bishops who stand before you are filled with sorrow. This body, in willfully confirming the election of a person sexually active outside of holy matrimony, has departed from the historic faith and order of the Church of Jesus Christ. This body has denied the plain teaching of Scripture and the moral consensus of the Church throughout the ages. This body has divided itself from millions of Anglican Christians around the world, brothers and sisters who have pleaded with us to maintain the Church's traditional teaching on marriage and sexuality.

With grief too deep for words, the bishops who stand before you must reject this action of the 74th General Convention of the Episcopal Church. As faithful Episcopalians and members of this house, we are calling upon the Primates of the Anglican Communion, under the presidency of the Archbishop of Canterbury, and in accordance with Lambeth Resolution III.6 (b), to intervene in the pastoral emergency that has overtaken us. Most Reverend sir, we must go to take counsel with our people and minister to them.

May God have mercy on His Church.

Apéndice J
Día 7
Declaración de Obispos sobre la Confirmación de la Elección de Gene Robinson

4 de agosto de 2003

Los Obispos que estamos de pie frente a ustedes nos sentimos muy entristecidos. Este cuerpo, al confirmar deliberadamente la elección de una persona activa sexualmente fuera del Santo Matrimonio se ha apartado de la fe y del orden histórico de la Iglesia de Jesucristo. Este cuerpo ha rechazado la clara enseñanza de las Sagradas Escrituras y el consenso moral de la iglesia mantenido a través de los siglos. Este cuerpo se ha separado de los millones de cristianos anglicanos de todas partes del mundo; los hermanos y hermanas que nos han rogado mantener las enseñanzas tradicionales sobre el matrimonio y la sexualidad.

Con una tristeza tan profunda que nos es imposible expresar en palabras, los obispos que se encuentran ante ustedes rechazan este acto de la 74ª Convención de la Iglesia Episcopal. Como fieles episcopales y miembros de esta Cámara, apelamos a los Primados de la Comunión Anglicana, bajo la presidencia del Arzobispo de Canterbury, y de acuerdo con la resolución de Lambeth III.6 (b), para solicitarles que intervengan en esta emergencia pastoral en la que nos encontramos. Su gracia Reverendísima, ahora debemos partir para deliberar junto con nuestro pueblo y para ministrarles.

Que Dios tenga misericordia de su Iglesia.

MINNEAPOLIS MEETING　　　　　　　　　HOUSE OF BISHOPS

EIGHTH DAY

Wednesday
August 6, 2003

MORNING SESSION

The House convened at 11:00 a.m. with the Presiding Bishop in the chair.
Table conversation was held for twenty-five minutes.
The House resumed at 11:25 a.m.

Personal Privilege
The Presiding Bishop called on the following bishops who addressed the House.
- The Assistant Bishop of Chicago
- The Bishop of Mississippi
- Bishop Coleridge
- Bishop Reed
- The Bishop Suffragan of New York
- The Bishop Suffragan of Alabama
- The Bishop Suffragan of South Carolina
- The Bishop of Western Kansas
- The Assistant Bishop of Virginia
- The Bishop of Central Pennsylvania
- The Junior Bishop Suffragan of Connecticut
- The Bishop of Honduras
- The Bishop of Washington
- The Bishop of New Hampshire
- The Senior Bishop Suffragan of Connecticut
- The Bishop of Rochester

Agenda of the Day
The House of Bishops Committee on Dispatch of Business moved to adopt the agenda of the day.

Motion carried

Previous Day's Minutes
The House of Bishops Committee on Dispatch of Business moved to dispense with the reading of the previous day's minutes.

Motion carried

Consecration of Bishops
The Secretary announced a correction to the Report on the Consecration of Bishops for Ballot #7.

The vote of the Bishop of Western Massachusetts was incorrectly reported as a "yes." The bishop did not vote. This correction does not affect the report's total.

Consecration of Bishops

The Presiding Bishop read HD Message #118 on Resolution C046, HD Message #119 on Resolution C047, and HD Message #120 on Resolution C048 regarding consent to the consecrations of the Rev. Canon Rayford B. High, Bishop Suffragan-elect of the Diocese of Texas, the Rev. Robert J. O'Neill, Bishop Coadjutor-elect of the Diocese of Colorado, and the Rev. Dean Elliot Wolfe, Bishop Coadjutor-elect of the Diocese of Kansas.

The House of Bishops Committee on Consecration of Bishops found all to be in order regarding this candidate. Ballot #8 was taken on the consent to the consecration of the Rev. Rayford B. High, Bishop Suffragan-elect of the Diocese of Texas and the resolution was moved.

Ballot #8 taken

The House of Bishops Committee on Consecration of Bishops found all to be in order regarding this candidate. Ballot #9 was taken on the consent to the consecration of the Rev. Robert John O'Neill, Bishop Coadjutor-elect of the Diocese of Colorado and the resolution was moved.

Ballot #9 taken

The House of Bishops Committee on Consecration of Bishops found all to be in order regarding this candidate. Ballot #10 was taken on the consent to the consecration of the Rev. Dean E. Wolfe, Bishop Coadjutor-elect of the Diocese of Kansas and the resolution was moved.

Ballot #10 taken

Messages from the House of Deputies

The Secretary announced that the following messages had been received from the House of Deputies.

HD Message #114: A142 (Admit Diocese of Venezuela)
The House of Deputies adopted the resolution with amendment.

HD Message #115: A060 (Contemporary Language Competency)
The House of Deputies concurred with substitute resolution.

HD Message #116: Special Order for Consideration of Specific Matters.
The House of Deputies adopted the Special Order with amendment.

HD Message #117: A143 (Amend Constitution Article I.7)
The House of Deputies adopted a substitute resolution.

HD Message #118: C046 (Consent to the Election of The Rev. Rayford B. High as Bishop Suffragan of the Diocese of Texas)
The House of Deputies adopted the resolution.

HD Message #119: C047 (Consent to the Election of The Rev. Robert John O'Neill as Bishop Coadjutor of the Diocese of Colorado)

	The House of Deputies adopted the resolution.
HD Message #120:	C048 (Consent to the Election of The Rev. Dean E. Wolfe as Bishop Coadjutor of the Diocese of Kansas)
	The House of Deputies adopted the resolution.
HD Message #121:	A132 (Christian Responses to Warfare)
	The House of Deputies adopted the resolution with amendment.
HD Message #122:	D006 (Supporting International Relief and Development)
	The House of Deputies adopted the resolution with amendment.
HD Message #123:	A025 (Trafficking of Women, Girls and Boys)
	The House of Deputies adopted a substitute resolution.
HD Message #124:	C033 (Immigration and Undocumented Workers)
	The House of Deputies adopted a substitute resolution.
HD Message #125:	A036 (Korean Peninsula and the Democratic Peoples Republic of Korea)
	The House of Deputies adopted the resolution with amendment.
HD Message #126:	D023 (U.S. Support for the People of Liberia)
	The House of Deputies adopted the resolution with amendment.
HD Message #127:	B008 (Protection of Children and Youth from Abuse)
	The House of Deputies adopted the resolution.
HD Message #128:	A129 (Dismantling Racial Profiling)
	The House of Deputies adopted the resolution with amendment.
HD Message #129:	C004 (Reparative Therapies)
	The House of Deputies adopted a substitute resolution.
HD Message #130:	C036 (Spirituality of Food Production)
	The House of Deputies adopted the resolution with amendment.
HD Message #131:	A125 (Ministry to Prisoners and Their Families)
	The House of Deputies adopted the resolution with amendment.
HD Message #132:	D015 (COSE Materials Available on the Web)
	The House of Deputies adopted the resolution with amendment.
HD Message #133:	A126 (Youth Charged and Convicted as Adults)
	The House of Deputies adopted the resolution with amendment.
HD Message #134:	C030 (The Working Poor)
	The House of Deputies adopted the resolution with amendment.
HD Message #135:	D077 (Post 9/11 Racial Hatred And Incarcerations)

	The House of Deputies adopted the resolution with amendment.
HD Message #136:	Special Order of Debate.
	The House of Deputies adopted the Special Order.
HD Message #137:	A077 (Trained Leadership)
	The House of Deputies adopted a substitute resolution.
HD Message #138:	A101 (Church Planting Liturgies)
	The House of Deputies concurred with amendment.
HD Message #139:	A080 (Episcopal Church Website)
	The House of Deputies adopted a substitute resolution.

Committee of Conference

A message was received from the House of Deputies on Resolution A060 (Contemporary Language Competency). The President of the House of Deputies has requested a Committee of Conference to bring forward a mutually acceptable resolution because the House of Deputies has adopted a substitute to the text adopted by the House of Bishops.

Deputy Cluett of Bethlehem and Deputy Snow of Alaska were appointed for the House of Deputies.

The Presiding Bishop appointed the Bishop of Newark and the Bishop of Northern Michigan for the House of Bishops.

Structure

The House of Bishops Committee on Structure presented its Report #11 on HD Message #114 on A142 (Admit Diocese of Venezuela) and moved concurrence.

The House concurred
(Communicated to the House of Deputies in HB Message #177)

Final Text of Resolution:

(A142)

Resolved, **That the 74th General Convention admit the Diocese of Venezuela to The Episcopal Church USA and recognize it as a diocese in union with General Convention;** and be it further

Resolved, **That the General Convention designate the Diocese of Venezuela as a member diocese of Province IX of The Episcopal Church;** and be further

Resolved, **That the Diocese of Venezuela be entitled to all rights pertaining to membership in The Episcopal Church as provided in the Constitution and Canons, including, but not limited to, voice and vote in the House of Bishops and House of Deputies, in accordance with the rules of those houses;** and be it further

Resolved, **That the Diocese of Venezuela be obligated to undertake all responsibilities pertaining to diocesan membership in The Episcopal Church as provided in the Constitution and Canons, including, but not**

limited to, conforming its constitution and canons to the provisions of the Constitution and Canons of The Episcopal Church; submitting annual diocesan and parochial reports to the General Convention Office; contributing annually to the apportionment budget of the Domestic and Foreign Missionary Society; and reporting fully on any financial assistance it receives from the General Convention budget; and be it further

Resolved, That the Convention affirm that the clergy and lay employees of the Diocese of Venezuela will be eligible to participate in companion pension plans administered by the Church Pension Fund, subject to the rules of the Church Pension Fund; and be it further

Resolved, That the Convention urge the Church Pension Fund to work with the Diocese of Venezuela to develop a plan to cover its clergy; and be it further

Resolved, That the portion of this resolution accepting the Diocese of Venezuela into union with the General Convention shall become effective on such date as the Executive Council adopts a resolution accepting and approving a certification to it by the Secretary of the General Convention that she has received from the Diocese the following:

1. A certified copy of the Constitution of the Diocese that contains an unqualified accession to the Constitution and canons of The Episcopal Church and otherwise conforms in essential part to such Constitution and canons;
2. A certified copy of the canons of the Diocese that conform in essential part to the canons of The Episcopal Church;
3. An annual diocesan report and annual parochial reports required by Canon I.6 for the last full year prior to compliance with this resolution;
4. A commitment by the Diocese to a contribution to the budget of The Episcopal Church for the year in which the Diocese is to come into union with the General Convention; and
5. An audited accounting of any funds received by the Diocese from the General Convention budget in the last full year prior to compliance with this resolution;and be it further

Resolved, That the Convention reaffirm the principle that dioceses of this church that are not located within the United States may seek autonomy according to the procedures set forth in Resolution 235a of the 1991 General Convention or may join other provinces of the Anglican Communion.

RECESS

Following announcements by the Secretary, the House of Bishops Committee on Dispatch of Business moved that the House stand in recess until after the Joint Session with the House of Deputies.

Motion carried

The House recessed at 12:50 p.m. with prayer led by Chaplain McIntosh.

Personal Privilege
Bishop Hampton made remarks encouraging leaving gratuities for the housekeepers in the hotels.

AFTERNOON SESSION

The House resumed at 2:30 p.m. in Joint Session with the House of Deputies for the presentation of the budget.

The House of Bishops resumed at 3:25 p.m. with the Presiding Bishop in the chair.

The Chaplain led the House in reflections and one hour was allowed for conversation.

The House resumed at 4:16 p.m.

Consent Calendar
The House of Bishops Committee on Dispatch of Business moved adoption of the Consent Calendar.

Motion carried

Ministry
The House of Bishops Committee on Ministry presented its Report #16 on Resolution A110 (Complete Title III Revisions) and moved adoption.

Original Text of Resolution:
(A110)

Resolved, the House of Deputies concurring, That the Standing Commission on Ministry Development complete its revisions of the present Title III Canons 10, 11, 12, and 22–32, and report to the 75th General Convention.

Motion carried
Resolution adopted
(Communicated to the House of Deputies in HB Message #178)

Communications
The House of Bishops Committee on Communications presented its Report #8 on HD Message #91 on Resolution A005 (Continue Forward Movement Publications) and moved concurrence.

The House concurred
(Communicated to the House of Deputies in HB Message #179)

Final Text of Resolution:
(A005)

Resolved, **That the Presiding Bishop be authorized to continue Forward Movement Publications under his supervision and to appoint such staff members and commission as may be required to maintain its work.**

Joint Nominating Committee for the Election of the Presiding Bishop
Ballots were collected for the Joint Nominating Committee for the Election of the Presiding Bishop.

Introduction of Visiting Bishops
The Presiding Bishop introduced the Rt. Rev. William Anderson, Bishop of the Diocese of New Caledonia, Canada, who was in the gallery.

Consecration of Bishops
The Presiding Bishop read the results of Ballot #8 on the consent to the consecration of Bishop Suffragan-elect High of the Diocese of Texas. Of 107 bishops with jurisdiction, 93 have given consent.
The House concurred
(Communicated to the House of Deputies in HB Message #180)

The Presiding Bishop read the results of Ballot #10 on the consent to the consecration of Bishop Coadjutor-elect Wolfe of the Diocese of Kansas. Of 107 bishops with jurisdiction, 93 have given consent.
The House concurred
(Communicated to the House of Deputies in HB Message #181)

The Presiding Bishop read the results of Ballot #9 on the consent to the consecration of Bishop Coadjutor-elect O'Neill of the Diocese of Colorado. Of 107 bishops with jurisdiction, 93 have given consent.
The House concurred
(Communicated to the House of Deputies in HB Message #182)

Special Order of Business
The Presiding Bishop introduced the newly elected ECW President, Ms. Harriett Neer, who addressed the House.

Prayer Book, Liturgy and Church Music
The House of Bishops Committee on Prayer Book, Liturgy and Church Music presented its Report #25 on Resolution C051 (Blessing of Committed Same-Gender Relationships) and moved adoption of a substitute.

Original Text of Resolution:
(C051)
Resolved, the House of Deputies concurring, That the 74th General Convention approve the liturgical blessing of the committed relationship of two adults of the

same-gender and authorize the inclusion of a text of such blessing in "The Book of Occasional Services."

Committee Substitute:
Resolved, the House of Deputies concurring, That the 74th General Convention affirm the following:
1. That our life together as a community of faith is grounded in the saving work of Jesus Christ and expressed in the principles of the Chicago-Lambeth Quadrilateral: Holy Scripture, the historic Creeds of the Church, the two dominical sacraments, and the historic episcopate.
2. That we reaffirm Resolution A069 of the 65th General Convention (1976) that "homosexual persons are children of God who have a full and equal claim with all other persons upon the love, acceptance, and pastoral concern and care of the Church."
3. That, in our understanding of homosexual persons, differences exist among us about how best to care pastorally for those who intend to live in monogamous, non-celibate unions; and what is, or should be, required, permitted, or prohibited by the doctrine, discipline, and worship of The Episcopal Church concerning the blessing of the same.
4. That we reaffirm Resolution D039 of the 73rd General Convention (2000), that "We expect such relationships will be characterized by fidelity, monogamy, mutual affection, and respect, careful, honest communication, and the holy love which enables those in such relationships to see in each other the image of God," and that such relationships exist throughout the church.
5. That, in keeping with the Pastoral Letter from the Primates of the Anglican Communion (5/27/2003) "acknowledging the responsibility of Christian leaders to attend to the pastoral needs of minorities in their care;" we recognize that local faith communities are operating within the bounds of our common life as they explore and experience liturgies celebrating and blessing same-sex unions.
6. That we commit ourselves, and call our church, in the spirit of Resolution A104 of the 70th General Convention (1991), to continued prayer, study, and discernment, to include:
    1. The preparation by the Standing Commission on Liturgy and Music, for study and consideration by the 75th General Convention, rites for possible inclusion in *Enriching Our Worship* by means of which support and blessing may be expressed for same-sex relationships with the permission of the ecclesiastical authority.
    2. The compilation and development of resources to facilitate as wide a conversation of discernment as possible throughout the church.
7. That our baptism into Jesus Christ is inseparable from our communion with one another, and we commit ourselves to that communion despite our diversity of opinion and, among dioceses, a diversity of pastoral practice with homosexual persons.
8. That it is a matter of faith that our Lord longs for our unity as his disciples, and for us this entails living within the boundaries of the Constitution and

Canons of The Episcopal Church. We believe this discipline expresses faithfulness to our polity and that it will facilitate the conversation we seek, not only in The Episcopal Church, but also in the wider Anglican Communion and beyond.

The Bishop of Virginia moved to amend the substitute resolution.

Proposed Amendment:
Delete all the words in section (a) of paragraph 6 and delete the letter (b) so that the text of paragraph 6 reads "That we commit ourselves, and call our church, in the spirit of Resolution A104 of the 70th General Convention (1991) to continued prayer, study, and discernment, to include the compilation and development of resources to facilitate as wide a conversation of discernment as possible throughout the church."

The Bishop Suffragan of Maryland made a friendly amendment to the Bishop of Virginia's amendment.

Proposed Amendment:
Insert "on the pastoral care for gay and lesbian persons" after the words "study and discernment" in paragraph six.

Motion carried
Amendment carried

The Committee agreed to amend their report at the suggestion of the Bishop of the Diocese of Missouri by deleting "homosexual persons" and adding "the gay men and lesbians among us."

The Bishop of Pennsylvania moved to amend the substitute resolution.

Proposed Amendment:
In paragraph six, insert "by the Standing Commission on Liturgy and Music" before "of resources."

Motion carried
Amendment carried

The Bishop of Pennsylvania moved to amend the previous amendment.

Proposed Amendment:
Delete the previous amendment to paragraph six, "by the Standing Commission on Liturgy and Music" and insert "by a special commission organized and appointed by the Presiding Bishop."

Motion carried
Amendment carried

The Presiding Bishop moved to amend the substitute resolution.

Proposed Amendment:
Delete in paragraph 5, "in keeping with the Pastoral Letter from the Primates of the Anglican Communion (5/27/2003) "acknowledging the responsibility of Christian leaders to attend to the pastoral needs of minorities in their care;"

Motion carried
Amendment carried

The Bishop of Tennessee moved to substitute Resolution B007 for Resolution C051.

Proposed Amendment
The Bishop Suffragan of Alabama moved to amend B007 to insert paragraph 6 from Resolution C051 as amended to this resolution as point 6, "That we commit ourselves, and call on church, in the spirit of Resolution (A104) of the 70th General Convention (1991), to continued prayer, study, and discernment to include the compilation and development of resources to facilitate as wide a conversation as possible throughout the church" and after point 5, add the words, "under direction of Presiding Bishop".

The Bishop of Tennesse accepted the Bishop Suffragan of Alabama's amendment to Resolution B007 in his motion to substitute Resolution B007 for Resolution C051.

A vote was taken to substitute Resolution B007 as amended for Resolution C051.

Motion defeated
Substitute defeated

A vote was taken on Resolution C051 as amended.

Motion carried
Substitute resolution adopted with amendment
(Communicated to the House of Deputies in HB Message #183)

[See Appendix K for Minority Report on Resolution C051.]

Dispatch of Business
The House of Bishops Committee on Dispatch of Business made announcements regarding committee work and calendar for the Ninth Legislative Day.

Joint Nominating Committee for the Election of the Presiding Bishop

The Secretary announced the results of the election of bishops on the Joint Nominating Committee for the Election of the Presiding Bishop:

Province I	The Rt. Rev. Gayle Harris
Province II	The Rt. Rev. Gladstone Adams
Province III	The Rt. Rev. Peter Lee
Province IV	The Rt. Rev. Duncan Gray
Province V	The Rt. Rev. Kenneth Price
Province VI	The Rt. Rev. Bruce Caldwell
Province VII	The Rt. Rev. Don Adger Wimberly
Province VIII	The Rt. Rev. Jerry Lamb
Province IX	The Rt. Rev. David Alvarez

(Communicated to the House of Deputies in HB Message #184)

RECESS

Following announcements by the Secretary, the House of Bishop Committee on Dispatch of Business moved that the House stand in recess until 11:00 a.m. on the Ninth Legislative Day.

Motion carried

The House recessed at 5:55 p.m. with prayer led by Chaplain McIntosh.

Appendix K
Day 8

Minority Report separately distributed in the House of Bishops regarding the Substitute Resolution Adopted by the House of Bishops

We, the undersigned, believe that the Substitute Resolution offered by the Prayer Book, Liturgy and Church MusicCommittee should not be passed for the following five reasons:

1. On point number three, the resolution conflates two very different issues. While we acknowledge that differences do exist in how to faithfully and effectively provide pastoral care for people who believe themselves to be homosexual persons, we also affirm that those pastoral concerns, skills, and techniques are very different from developing rites for same-sex unions. We are also concerned that in this paragraph the phrase "...and what is, or should be, required, permitted, or prohibited by the doctrine, discipline and worship..." [of this church] is deeply troubling. We question why is this phrase "or should be" is included. Why can we not simply say, as our ordination vows require us to say, "what is required, permitted or prohibited..."
2. On point number four, we happily acknowledge that relationships characterized by fidelity, monogamy, mutual affection and respect, careful and honest communication, and holy love which enables those in such relationships to see in each other the image of God. They are called "holy marriage" and they have been part of the life of the church for 2,000 years. But this resolution is not about marriage relationships between a man and a woman, it is about creating something new in the life of the church.
3. On point five, we wish to state in the strongest possible terms that, far from being consonant with the Primate's Pastoral Letter, this is a denial of it. We quote from that letter, "The Archbishop of Canterbury spoke for us all when he said that it is through liturgy that we express what we believe, and that there is no theological consensus about same-sex unions. Therefore, we as a body cannot support the authorization of such rites." Thus, the Primate's letter, in the strongest language and with a clear intent, implored this church not to develop such rites. This resolution is a complete and arrogant repudiation of the clear intention of the leaders of our church.
4. On point five, we ask the question, "What does it mean 'to experience' such liturgies?" A simple reading of this language flies in the face of the intention of the Primate's letter as it raises the question of how one can "experience" a liturgy without actually performing such a liturgy. Thus, this resolution has the effect of authorizing the performing of (quoting the resolution) "celebrating and blessing same-sex unions."
5. On point six, we note the seemingly conciliatory and congenial dilution of the language of the previous resolutions. But this resolution has the same effect in the life of the church as those more forthright resolutions.

We note the language specifying "possible inclusion" and the change from the *Book of Occasional Services* to *Enriching Our Worship*. We note, however, that the reality that (a) once these rites are published by the Church Publishing Company they carry the implicit imprimatur of the Church. Thus (b) people both in and outside of the church can reasonably conclude that these rites of blessing are themselves blessed by the church itself. That is because (c) the subtleties which mark the distinctions between the *Book of Common Prayer*, the *Book of Occasional Services*, and *Enriching Our Worship* are lost on the vast majority of men and women in and outside the church. The reality is that no one outside a close coterie of canon lawyers and liturgical scholars will make a distinction between including these rites in *Enriching Our Worship* and the *Book of Common Prayer*.

We note that the stated purpose of *Enriching Our Worship* (preface p. 13) is that it "contains texts intended to be explorations for the development of liturgical materials...[and] looking forward to the[ir] dissemination throughout the Church..." Publication by the Church for propagation by the Church for use in the Church of rites of same-sex blessings is the true intent of this resolution.

We note that the preface of *Enriching Our Worship* goes on to say (p. 17) "Whatever we imagine the future of the *Book of Common Prayer* to be, the task of the months and years to come is to compose, use, evaluate and distribute a wide variety of emerging resources." The intention of this resolution becomes clear if we substitute in that sentence the phrase from the substitute resolution "celebrating and blessing same-sex unions." Thus, we could reasonably read the preface of the *Enriching Our Worship* to read as follows: "Whatever we imagine the future of the *Book of Common Prayer* to be, the task of the months and years to come is to compose, use, evaluate and distribute liturgies for the celebration and blessing of same-sex unions."

Thus, while the proposed change from the *Book of Occasional Services* to *Enriching Our Worship* seems conciliatory and congenial, the actual difference is insignificant and the end result is the same as the previous resolutions.

Respectfully Submitted,
The Rev. Dr. Kendall Harmon

NINTH DAY

Thursday
August 7, 2003

MORNING SESSION

The House reconvened at 11:08 a.m. with the Vice-Chair in the chair.
Table conversation was allowed for ten minutes.
The Presiding Bishop returned to the chair.
The House resumed at 11:23 a.m.

Agenda of the Day
The House of Bishops Committee on Dispatch of Business moved to adopt the agenda of the day.

Motion carried

Previous Day's Minutes
The House of Bishops Committee on Dispatch of Business moved to dispense with the reading of the previous day's minutes.

Motion carried

Messages from the House of Deputies
The Secretary announced that the following messages had been received from the House of Deputies:

HD Message #140: Appointment of Deputy Members for Committee on Conference for Resolution A060.
The House of Deputies adopted the resolution.

HD Message #141: D051 (Full Accessibility at General Convention)
The House of Deputies adopted the resolution with amendment.

HD Message #142: A079 (General Convention Deputies)
The House of Deputies adopted the resolution with amendment.

HD Message #143: C026 (Reduce the Use of Toxic Chemicals)
The House of Deputies adopted the resolution with amendment.

HD Message #144: B026 (Criminal Justice Committee)
The House of Deputies adopted the resolution with amendment.

HD Message #145: A033 (Just and Unjust Wars)
The House of Deputies adopted the resolution with amendment.

HD Message #146: C003 (In Support of Representative John Conyers' H.R. 40)
The House of Deputies rejected the resolution.

HD Message #147:	A089 ("Open Communion")
	The House of Deputies concurred.
HD Message #149:	C024 (Nonviolent United States Foreign Policy)
	The House of Deputies adopted the resolution with amendment.
HD Message #150:	D008 (Demolition of Palestinian Homes)
	The House of Deputies adopted the resolution with amendment.
HD Message #151:	D061 (Jubilee Ministry Funding)
	The House of Deputies adopted the resolution with amendment.
HD Message #152:	D025 (Continuation of Efforts to End Racism)
	The House of Deputies adopted the resolution with amendment.
HD Message #153:	A128 (Ministering to "At Risk" Youth)
	The House of Deputies adopted a substitute resolution.
HD Message #154:	D043 (Elimination of Barriers)
	The House of Deputies adopted the resolution with amendment.
HD Message #155:	A032 (Youth Study)
	The House of Deputies adopted the resolution with amendment.
HD Message #156:	D057 (General Convention)
	The House of Deputies adopted the resolution with amendment.
HD Message #157:	D080 (Courtesy Resolution—Alan Blanchard)
	The House of Deputies adopted a substitute resolution.
HD Message #158:	Special Order of Debate on Report of Program, Budget and Finance.
	The House of Deputies adopted the Special Order.
HD Message #159:	A075 (Diocese Mission Perspective)
	The House of Deputies adopted the resolution with amendment.
HD Message #160:	A074 (Congregational Annual Study)
	The House of Deputies adopted the resolution with amendment.
HD Message #161:	C052 (Transfer of Diocesan Territories)
	The House of Deputies adopted the resolution.
HD Message #161:	General Board of Examining Chaplains.
	The House of Deputies concurred.
	[Note: HD Message #161 was used for Resolution C052 (see above) and for the election of the General Board of Examining Chaplains. For the GBEC, the message replaced HD Message #148. *Ed.*]

HD Message #162:	D072 (Amendment Canon III.22.3 (a)) The House of Deputies adopted the resolution with amendment.
HD Message #163:	D031 (Culture of Nonviolence) The House of Deputies adopted the resolution with amendment.
HD Message #164:	D066 (Declaration on Sustainable Development) The House of Deputies adopted the resolution with amendment.
HD Message #165:	D068 (Response To New War Situations) The House of Deputies adopted a substitute resolution.
HD Message #166:	D063 (Civil Liberties and the USA Patriot Act) The House of Deputies adopted a substitute resolution.
HD Message #167:	A144 (Amend Canon I.1.14) The House of Deputies concurred with amendment.
HD Message #168:	D081 (Israeli Security Wall) The House of Deputies adopted the resolution with amendment.
HD Message #169:	D034 (Sex Trafficking) The House of Deputies adopted the resolution with amendment.
HD Message #170:	D014 (Japanese-American Internment in World War II: A Call for Accountability) The House of Deputies adopted a substitute resolution.
HD Message #171:	A037 (Status of Forces Agreement with Korea) The House of Deputies adopted the resolution with amendment.
HD Message #172:	D054 (HIV/AIDS Keeping America's Promise to Africa) The House of Deputies adopted a substitute resolution.
HD Message #173:	A028 (Palestinian and Afghani Women Support) The House of Deputies adopted a substitute resolution.
HD Message #174:	D070 (Water Policy) The House of Deputies adopted the resolution.
HD Message #175:	Consent to the Election of The Rev. Canon Rayford B. High as Bishop Suffragan of the Diocese of Texas. The House of Deputies adopted the resolution. [Duplicate message sent for HD Message #118. *Ed.*]
HD Message #176:	D071 (Oppose Federally Sponsored Marriage Promotion) The House of Deputies adopted a substitute resolution.
HD Message #177:	D036 (Marriage) The House of Deputies adopted a substitute resolution.
HD Message #178:	D045 (Withdraw From the Religious Coalition for Reproductive Choice) The House of Deputies referred to a Standing Commission.

HD Message #179:   D040 (Invest in Housing for the Poor)
The House of Deputies adopted the resolution with amendment.

HD Message #180:   D062 (Amend Constitution Article IX [Second Reading])
The House of Deputies concurred.

HD Message #181:   D056 (Amend Canons on Court for Trial of a Bishop)
The House of Deputies adopted the resolution with amendment.

HD Message #182:   D069 (Standing Commission On Episcopal Church Communication)
The House of Deputies adopted the resolution with amendment.

HD Message #183:   C028 (Immigrant Workers Freedom Ride)
The House of Deputies adopted the resolution.

HD Message #184:   D073 (Formation of Episcopal Community Services In America)
The House of Deputies adopted the resolution.

HD Message #185:   A076 (Transformation Resources)
The House of Deputies adopted the resolution with amendment.

HD Message #186:   D011 (Appending "Anglican Communion" to materials)
The House of Deputies adopted the resolution.

HD Message #187:   D017 (Promoting Reconciliation and Minimizing the Likelihood of Schism)
The House of Deputies referred the resolution to a Standing Commission.

Special Order of Business

The President of the House of Deputies and the General Convention Manager were recognized.

The President of the House of Deputies addressed the House regarding General Convention planning and site selection for 2006.

The Bishop of Fond du Lac moved to take Resolution A154 from the table.

Motion carried

Miscellaneous Resolutions

The House of Bishops Committee on Miscellaneous Resolutions presented its Report #4 on HD Message #25 on Resolution A154 (75th General Convention Site) and moved concurrence.

The House concurred
(Communicated to the House of Deputies in HB Message #185)

Final Text of Resolution:
(A154)
Resolved, That Columbus, Ohio, be selected as the site for the 75th General Convention in 2006.

Social and Urban Affairs
The House of Bishops Committee on Social and Urban Affairs presented its Report #13 on HD Message #151 on Resolution D061 (Jubilee Ministry Funding) and moved concurrence.

Motion defeated
Resolution rejected
(Communicated to the House of Deputies in HB Message #186)

New Resolutions
The House of Bishops Committee on Dispatch of Business reminded the House this is the last day to consider new resolutions. Tomorrow's agenda will only have messages and concurrences.

Miscellaneous Resolutions
The House of Bishops Committee on Miscellaneous Resolutions resumed presentation of its Report #2 on Resolution B009 (Request for Faith and Order Commission) and moved adoption with amendment.

The question was called to terminate debate on the resolution.

Motion carried
Debate terminated

A vote was taken on Resolution B009 as amended.

Motion carried
Resolution adopted with amendment
(Communicated to the House of Deputies in HB Message #187)

Prayer Book, Liturgy and Church Music
The House of Bishops Committee on Prayer Book, Liturgy and Church Music presented its Report #22 on Resolution B007 (Affirmations for Facilitating Emergence of Consensus) and moved that the Committee be discharged.

Motion carried
Committee discharged
(Communicated to the House of Deputies in HB Message #188)

MINNEAPOLIS MEETING   HOUSE OF BISHOPS

The House of Bishops Committee on Prayer Book, Liturgy and Church Music presented its Report #23 on Resolution C005 (Rites for Blessing and Supporting Committed Relationships) and moved that the Committee be discharged.
Motion carried
Committee discharged
(Communicated to the House of Deputies in HB Message #189)

The House of Bishops Committee on Prayer Book, Liturgy and Music presented its Report #24 on Resolution D022 (Resolution on Rites Supporting Life-long Relationshops) and moved that the Committee be discharged.
Motion carried
Committee discharged
(Communicated to the House of Deputies in HB Message #190)

Committees and Commissions
The House of Bishops Committee on Committees and Commissions resumed its presentation on its Report #1 on HD Message #11 on Resolution A124 (Standing Commission on Health and a Staff Position in Health Care) and moved concurrence with a substitute resolution.

Committee Substitute:
Resolved, the House of Bishops concurring, That the 74th General Convention reaffirm the commitment of The Episcopal Church in providing a Christian response to the health care needs of those within our nation, as expressed in the 1991 and 1994 Blue Book reports of the Standing Commission on Health and the 2000 Blue Book Report of the Standing Commission on National Concerns; and be it further
Resolved, That the 74th General Convention reestablish a Standing Commission on Health and that it direct Executive Council to appoint a person to the staff at The Episcopal Church Center with background in and knowledge about health care policy to assist this commission, and that their joint duties include:

- Articulating and communicating positions adopted by The Episcopal Church on health care policy to Episcopalians, the public, and public policy makers;
- Advocating, in cooperation with the Office of Government Relations, for a health care system in which all may be guaranteed decent and appropriate primary health care during their lives and as they approach death;
- Bringing together those within The Episcopal Church who develop, provide, and/or teach health care and health care policy to continue to develop a Christian approach to pressing issues that affect the health care system of this nation;
- Understanding and keeping abreast of the rapidly changing health care market and developments in biomedical research that affect health policy;
- Collecting and developing resources and teaching materials related to access to health care for the use of dioceses, congregations, and individuals;

Advocating health ministry in and through local Episcopal congregations; and be it further

Resolved, That the 74th General Convention direct the Executive Council to report to the 75th General Convention about this appointment; and be it further

Resolved, That the General Convention request the Joint Standing Committee on Program, Budget and Finance to consider a budget allocation of $200,000 for implementation of this resolution; and be it further

Resolved, That Canon I.1.2(n) be amended to add a subsection (6), appropriately renumbering the renaming subsections thereafter, reading as follows:

(6) A Standing Commission on Health consisting of 11 members (3 Bishops, 3 Priests and/or Deacons, and 5 Lay Persons). It shall be the duty of the Commission to:

(a) *Articulate and communicate positions adopted by The Episcopal Church on health care policy to Episcopalians, the public, and public policy makers;*

(b) *Advocate, in cooperation with the Office of Government Relations, for a health care system in which all may be guaranteed decent and appropriate primary health care during their lives and as they approach death;*

(c) *Bring together those within The Episcopal Church who develop, provide and/or teach health care and health policy to continue to develop a Christian approach to pressing issues that affect the health care system of this nation;*

(d) *Understand and keep abreast of the rapidly changing health care market and developments in biomedical research that affect health policy;*

(e) *Collect and develop resources and teaching materials related to access to health care for the use of dioceses, congregations, and individuals;*

(f) *Advocate health ministry in and through local Episcopal congregations; and*

(g) *Discharge such other duties as shall be assigned by the General Convention.*

Motion carried
The House concurred with a substitute resolution
(Communicated to the House of Deputies in HB Message #191)

Communications

The House of Bishops Committee on Communications presented its Report #10 on Resolution D026 (Commendation of www.ExploreFaith.org) and moved that the Committee be discharged.

Motion carried
Committee discharged
(Communicated to the House of Deputies in HB Message #192)

The House of Bishops Committee on Communications presented its Report #11 on HD Message #44 on Resolution A081 (National Ad Campaign) and moved concurrence.

The House concurred
(Communicated to the House of Deputies in HB Message #193)

Final Text of Resolution:
(A081)
Resolved, That the 74th General Convention direct the Office of Communication to develop a multilingual national advertising campaign, with radio and television advertisements reflecting the multicultural nature of The Episcopal Church; and that the General Convention urge congregations and dioceses to offer training in welcoming and incorporating newcomers who may come in response to the advertising campaign; and be it further

Resolved, That the 74th General Convention request the Joint Standing Committee on Program, Budget and Finance to consider a total budget allocation of not less than $1,500,000 for the triennium for the implementation of this resolution.

Social and Urban Affairs

The House of Bishops Committee on Social and Urban Affairs presented its Report #5 on HD Message #107 on Resolution D016 (The Protection of Animals from Cruel Treatment) and moved concurrence.

The House concurred
(Communicated to the House of Deputies in HB Message #194)

Final Text of Resolution:
(D016)
Resolved, **That the 74th General Convention recognize that responsible care of animals falls within the stewardship of creation;** and be it further

Resolved, **That The Episcopal Church encourage its members to ensure that husbandry methods for captive and domestic animals would prohibit suffering in such conditions as puppy mills, and factory-farms;** and be it further

Resolved, **That The Episcopal Church's Peace and Justice Office identify existing guidelines to educate its members to adhere to ethical standards in the care and treatment of animals;** and be it further

Resolved, **That The Episcopal Church, through its Office of Government Relations, identify and advocate for legislation protecting animals and effective enforcement measures.**

The House of Bishops Committee on Social and Urban Affairs presented its Report #6 on HD Message #131 on Resolution A125 (Ministry to Prisoners and Their Families) and moved concurrence.

The House concurred
(Communicated to the House of Deputies in HB Message #195)

Final Text of Resolution:
(A125)
Resolved, That the 74th General Convention of The Episcopal Church, through the Executive Council, urge dioceses and congregations to become familiar with the criminal justice system and establish ministries which assist prisoners and their families during sentencing, while in prison, and during their readjustment period; and be it further

Resolved, That the 74th General Convention support the establishment and/or expansion of occupational, therapeutic treatment, and academic programs in prisons where prisoners may be prepared for re-entry into society; and be it further

Resolved, That the 74th General Convention ask the Office of Peace and Justice to identify training programs for volunteers who work both inside prisons and with post-release programs and to assist dioceses and congregations with this work; and be it further

Resolved, That the 74th General Convention ask the Office of Peace and Justice to identify religious education programs that can be, or have been, adapted for the cultures of particular prison populations and when appropriate, to provide training in such programs for dioceses and congregations.

The House of Bishops Committee on Social and Urban Affairs presented its Report #7 on HD Message #106 on Resolution A011 (Ethical Guidelines for Gene Transfer and Germline Interventions) and moved concurrence.

The House concurred
(Communicated to the House of Deputies in HB Message #196)

Final Text of Resolution:
(A011)
Resolved, That the 74th General Convention recognize that God has entrusted us to use our medical and other capabilities to work toward healing and restoring creation where it has gone awry. Therefore, the General Convention sets forth the following guidelines for genetic research and interventions:

It is morally acceptable, in principle, to engage in experimental somatic cell human gene transfer for therapeutic purposes, in an effort to treat or prevent disease.

All experimental genetic interventions in human beings must meet ethical standards of research, which require that investigators demonstrate the scientific merit of their research, protect the health and welfare of human volunteers, while ensuring their volunteers' choice to participate without conflicts of interest or undue financial influence.

Until there is strong scientific evidence that the use of germline procedures is safe, effective, and stable across generations and that guidelines have been established for their use before they are employed, we should not consider the use of germline interventions in human beings.

Ongoing public oversight of research into both somatic cell and germline interventions, in both the public and private sectors, is essential. Members of a federally appointed interdisciplinary review body should be chosen by publicly accountable methods.

The House of Bishops Committee on Social and Urban Affairs presented its Report #8 on HD Message #135 on Resolution A126 (Youth Charged and Convicted as Adults) and moved concurrence.

The House concurred
(Communicated to the House of Deputies in HB Message #197)

Final Text of Resolution:
(A126)
Resolved, That the 74th General Convention of The Episcopal Church direct the Office of Government Relations to work for legislation that provides alternatives to sentencing for juveniles, offers creative programs for rehabilitation, and establishes separate intermediary facilities for incarceration for juveniles convicted of serious crimes; and be it further

Resolved, That the 74th General Convention call upon dioceses, congregations, and individual Episcopalians to promote reforms in state juvenile justice systems that focus on justice, human dignity, and rehabilitation; and be it further

Resolved, That the 74th General Convention encourage defense attorneys to offer pro bono services to alleviate the growing epidemic of inadequate counsel and express gratitude for those who provide these services.

The House of Bishops Committee on Social and Urban Affairs presented its Report #9 on HD Message #127 on Resolution B008 (Protection of Children and Youth from Abuse) and moved concurrence.

The House concurred
(Communicated to the House of Deputies in HB Message #198)

Final Text of Resolution:
(B008)
Resolved, That the 74th General Convention of The Episcopal Church recommit itself to the vision of the role of children in the church as articulated in *A Children's Charter for the Church* as adopted by the 72nd General Convention in 1997. The *Charter,* among other things, calls the church to:

Receive, nurture, and treasure each child as a gift from God;

Love, shelter, protect, and defend children within its own community and in the world, especially those who are abused, neglected, or in danger; and

Advocate for the integrity of childhood and the dignity of all children at every level of our religious, civic, and political structures; and be it further

Resolved, That this Church acknowledge that the times and circumstances demand that the church articulate a clear and firm commitment to the safety of all, especially children; that we support this commitment with clear and firm policies and procedures for the well-being of all; and that we commit this Church to being and becoming a place where children and youth are safe, especially from abuse and neglect; and be it further

Resolved, That each diocese develop and adopt policies for the protection of children and youth from abuse that address the following:

1. A screening and selection process for all clergy, lay employees, and volunteers who regularly work with children or youth. Dioceses are encouraged to consider:

   a. A written application
   b. A public records check
   c. An interview
   d. Reference checks
   e. A general provision that volunteers not work with children or youth until they have been known to the clergy or congregation for at least six months

2. The articulation of behavioral standards for clergy, lay employees, and volunteers working with children or youth. Dioceses are encouraged to consider:

   a. Respect for the privacy and dignity of children and youth by not putting them in inappropriate unmonitored one-to-one situations
   b. Age-appropriate arrangements for sleeping, bathing, dressing, or showering
   c. The prohibition of dating, romantic involvements, or sexual contact with a child or youth
   d. The prohibition of any sexually oriented materials (magazines, cards, videos, films, clothing, etc.) in the presence of children and youth except as expressly permitted as part of a pre-authorized educational program
   e. Guidelines for physical contact and expressions of affection that define appropriate and inappropriate behaviors
   f. The prohibition of discussing their own sexual activities and fantasies with children or youth
   g. The prohibition of the non-sacramental use, possession, distribution or being under the influence of alcohol, illegal drugs, or the misuse of legal drugs

3. The monitoring of programs and interaction with children and youth.

Dioceses are encouraged to consider:

a. The prohibition of the development or initiation of new activities for children or youth without prior approval from the appropriate decision-maker(s)

b. The recognition that the ordinary standard is the presence of two unrelated adults for any activities involving children or youth

4. Education and training. Dioceses are encouraged to consider:

a. Child abuse prevention for clergy, lay employees, and volunteers who regularly work with children or youth

b. Specialized training for those who recruit, screen, or select persons to work with children or youth

5. Guidelines for responding to concerns. Dioceses are encouraged to consider:

a. Inappropriate behavior with children or youth
b. Violation of policies for the protection of children or youth
c. Suspected abuse of children or youth; and be it further

Resolved, That each diocese shall report to the House of Bishops Committee on Pastoral Development prior to the Spring 2006 meeting of the House of Bishops with a copy of its adopted and implemented policy and an evaluation of the history of its use. A summary report shall be made to the House of Bishops Spring 2006 meeting and a full report made to the 75th General Convention.

Personal Privilege
The Bishop of New York asked for Personal Privilege.

Pastoral Letter
The Bishop of New York returned to the discussion of the Pastoral Letter.

Bishop R Anderson moved to amend the Pastoral Letter.

Proposed Amendment
Delete the balance of bracketed words in the third paragraph from the end of the letter.

Motion carried
Amendment adopted

The Bishop of Western North Carolina moved to amend the Pastoral Letter.

Proposed Amendment
In Paragraph one add in the last line "where no one might be hurt and where their hurts may be healed."

Motion carried
Amendment adopted

The Senior Bishop Suffragan of Massachusetts moved to amend the Pastoral Letter.

Proposed Amendment
After the words "favoritism or carelessness," in the second to last paragraph add "prohibiting those who have harmed children from ministries involving children,".

Motion carried
Amendment adopted

The Bishop of North Carolina moved to amend the Pastoral Letter.

Proposed Amendment
In the tenth paragraph, after the words "Among the basic provisions we have committed to implement" and before the word "are" add "as delineated in Resolution B008 (Protection of Children and Youth from Abuse), of the 74th General Convention in 2003."

Motion carried
Amendment adopted

A vote was taken on the Pastoral Letter as amended.

Motion carried
Letter adopted with amendment
(Communicated to the House of Deputies in HB Message #199)

Final Text of Resolution:
(B027)

A Pastoral Letter From the Bishops of the Episcopal Church
To be read or cause to be distributed in every parish, mission, preaching station, and church-related institution which works with children and youth.

Dear Brothers and Sisters in Christ,

We your bishops are steadfastly committed to seeing that the Episcopal Church is a community of safety and health for all people. The Body of Christ, the Church, must be a place where adults, children, and young people find the love and blessing of God, and where no one might be hurt and where their hurts may be healed.

We are all aware of the reports in the media, during the past year and more, of incidents of sexual misconduct in churches. Many of these tragedies have involved children and young people. While the Roman Catholic Church has most often been mentioned in news reports and accusations, the rest of the Church and many secular agencies have also been caught up in trying to address the damage done to our children by sexual predators. The Episcopal Church is not immune to this scourge in our society and we must respond to it honestly and forthrightly.

Our Church has repeatedly upheld our mandate to be a haven of safety for all. The Scriptures teach us that every human being is made in the image of God; and our Lord enjoins us to receive and serve the least among us as we would receive and serve him. The mandates of our baptismal covenant include seeking and serving Christ in all persons, loving our neighbors as ourselves, striving for justice and peace for all people, and respecting the dignity of every human being.

Because of these mandates of love, respect, service, and justice, we have acknowledged our obligation to articulate clear standards about sexual harassment and misconduct and to ensure that all our work and ministry is guided by them. We have been committed to sexual conduct training and abuse prevention for all our clergy and lay leaders. We have been clear that exploitation and abusiveness are always unacceptable in our common life. We have made efforts to become aware of the spiritual and emotional damage that is done by sexual misconduct and to do our best to guarantee that none who come to us will suffer such harm. In spite of our best efforts, it is sad when we discover that we have not done enough.

While we were in conference together at Kanuga, North Carolina, in the spring, many of us had the opportunity to learn more about pedophilia, a form of predatory sexual behavior that has caused untold harm in our society and in the Body of Christ. It is especially important that we as a church focus on understanding and preventing pedophilia.

While we need to be aware that pedophilia is a reality in our society, which can be manifest in the church, we must be very clear about the nature of this tragic problem. Pedophilia is pervasive; one in eight males and one in four females will be molested before they reach the age of eighteen. Of reported cases in the general population, sixty percent (60%) of abusers are known to their victims, thirty percent (30%) are family members or relatives, and ten percent (10%) are strangers. We must be aware that the Church is a community which offers predators the opportunity to become known and trusted by parents and their children.

We also know that offenders are predominantly male and heterosexual. We must take great care not to equate pedophilia with homosexuality in our minds or our conversation, and we must never assume that only men molest children in this way.

What we have learned most recently about the repetitive nature of pedophilia makes it imperative that we take very clear steps together to do the screening necessary to ensure that our children encounter God's love among us and that we do all in our power to protect them from the distorted perceptions of love offered by predators.

In a Mind of The House resolution passed at Kanuga in March of 2003, we committed ourselves to support the development of church-wide policies to safeguard our children; and until such time as these policies are adopted, to revisit and revise our diocesan policies to ensure that ministries provided to the children among us will be life-giving and free from abusiveness of any kind.

Among the basic provisions we have committed to implement, delineated in Resolution B008 on the "Protection of Children and Youth from Abuse" adopted at the 74th General Convention in 2003, are:

1. Thorough *screening and selection* of clergy, lay employees and volunteers who work with children and youth;
2. Articulation of clear behavioral standards for interactions between clergy, lay employees, volunteers and children and youth;
3. Careful, *continuous monitoring of all programs and interactions* involving children and youth;
4. Provision for *education and training of clergy, lay employees and volunteers* for work with children and youth; and
5. Guidelines for responding to concerns about behavior or allegations of abuse.

In addition, we asked the Presiding Bishop to create a working group from among our members to partner with the Church Pension Group, the Church Insurance Corporation and other agencies and appropriate organizations to develop the materials necessary to provide the Church with consistent expectations and standards.

We realize that in many of our congregations, persons who offer to take on ministries with children and youth are a blessing to an understaffed education or formation program for children or youth. The overwhelming majority are trustworthy and caring persons whose ministry will bear great good fruit.

But we must acknowledge that there are times when predators use the church as an opportunity for sexual abuse of children and adolescents who can suffer severe spiritual, emotional, and sometimes physical damage as a result. In response to such times, we are called to acknowledge two truths: that human sin and failure are very real, and that God's grace, mercy, and power are always strong enough to heal and transform our pain.

We have no intention to call our members to suspicion and mistrust. We do recognize the need to call our members beyond the naiveté of unquestioning confidence and into the care and discipline which must characterize our choices where children are concerned. Jesus called us to be as wise as serpents and as gentle as doves. In the case of pedophilia, our consistency in carefully screening, choosing and training *all* who work with children and youth will serve to allay any concerns about favoritism or carelessness, prohibiting those who have harmed children from ministries involving children, while providing the ability to firmly guide those who might harm children into other areas of ministry which serve the Church and contribute to our mission.

Some helpful materials will be available through your diocesan office by the first of November. We ask that, as you make use of them, you will remember the challenge our Lord provided to his followers, "unless you become as children you cannot enter the kingdom of God." We renew our commitment to ensure that our church is a community of love and care for every person. We ask that you join us in doing all in our power to see that all our members find among us a safe place where they can be open and trusting and able to know the reconciling love of God in Christ that makes all things new.

A Collect for the Care of Children
Almighty God, heavenly Father, you have blessed us with the joy and care of children: Give us calm strength and patient wisdom as we bring them up, that we may teach them to love whatever is just and true and good, following the example of our Savior Jesus Christ. Amen. (BCP 829)
Bishops of the Episcopal Church
Gathered at General Convention, Minneapolis, Minnesota
August 6, 2003—The Feast of the Transfiguration

RECESS

Following announcements by the Secretary, the House of Bishops Committee on Dispatch of Business moved that the House stand in recess until 2:30 p.m.
Motion carried

The House recessed at 12:51 p.m. with prayers led by Chaplain Battle.

AFTERNOON SESSION

The Presiding Bishop called the House to order at 2:35 p.m.

The Chaplain offered reflections and fifteen minutes were allowed for table conversation.

The House resumed at 3:01 p.m.

Social and Urban Affairs

The House of Bishops Committee on Social and Urban Affairs presented its Report #10 on HD Message #129 on Resolution C004 (Reparative Therapies) and moved concurrence.

The Bishop of Minnesota moved to amend the title to delete "Reparative" to "Helpful Therapies for Change."
Motion defeated
Amendment defeated

A vote was taken on Resolution C004.
The House concurred
(Communicated to the House of Deputies in HB Message #200)

Final Text of Resolution:
(C004)
Resolved, That the 74th General Convention of The Episcopal Church affirm that sexuality is a gift of God and insists that any religious, spiritual, psychological, or psychiatric treatment which seeks to assist those who are confused about or unhappy with their sexual orientation not be coercive or manipulative; and be it further
Resolved, That this Church oppose any religious, spiritual, psychological, or psychiatric consulting or treatment which compromises our baptismal covenant to respect the dignity of every human being, affirming that medical treatment, psychological therapy, and pastoral counseling should conform to the professional standards of the respective professions.

The House of Bishops Committee on Social and Urban Affairs presented its Report #11 on HD Message #134 on Resolution C030 (The Working Poor) and moved concurrence.

The House concurred
(Communicated to the House of Deputies in HB Message #201)

Final Text of Resolution:
(C030)
Resolved, That the 74th General Convention urge our elected congresspersons and U.S. senators to initiate or support legislation raising the federal minimum wage; to at least $8.70 an hour, this figure being the hourly equivalent of an annual wage at the current federal poverty line, $18,100 for a family of four persons.

The House of Bishops Committee on Social and Urban Affairs presented its Report #12 on HD Message #132 on Resolution D015 (Make COSE Materials Available on the Web) and moved concurrence.

The House concurred
(Communicated to the House of Deputies in HB Message #202)

Final Text of Resolution:
(D015)
Resolved, That the 74th General Convention of The Episcopal Church, recalling that the 71st General Convention, in Resolution B022a, commended the Manual and Training materials prepared by the Committee on Sexual Exploitation (entitled "Respecting the Dignity of Every Human Being"), "... for use by the dioceses and institutions of this Church ... in setting policies and procedures and in educating and training clergy and laity;" direct the Executive Council, to make available to all dioceses electronic copies of this Manual and Training materials; and be it further
Resolved, That the 74th General Convention direct the Executive Council, to

also make available to all dioceses electronic copies of the updates to the Manual and Training materials distributed at the 72nd General Convention, along with electronic copies of the pamphlets, including, but not limited to, "For Persons with Complaints: Information of the Episcopal Church Discipline," "A Diocesan Guide to Understanding Title IV," "A Clergy Guide to Understanding Title IV," "What a Congregation (and Vestry) Should Know about the Revised Disciplinary Canons of the Episcopal Church" and "Guidelines for Bishops Meeting with Complaints in Accordance with Title IV" as revised, and "Guidelines for Bishops Meeting with A Respondent in Accordance with Title IV" and "Suggested Standards for the Restoration of Rehabilitated Sexual Exploitative Clerics" when available; and be it further

Resolved, That the Executive Council be requested to also make the electronic copies available on The Episcopal Church national website; and be it further

Resolved, That the Title IV Revision Task Force explore the financial and logistical feasibility of offering one or more Response Teams on a national level to any diocese requesting their services (when invited by either the diocesan Ecclesiastical Authority or the Diocesan Review Committee).

Canons

The House of Bisohps Committee on Canons presented its Report #14 on Resolution D067 (Amend Canon II.2) and moved adoption with amendment.

Original Text of Resolution:

(D067)

Resolved, the House of Deputies concurring, That Canon 2, Title II be amended as follows:

The Lessons prescribed in the Book of Common Prayer shall be read from the translation of the Holy Scriptures commonly known as the King James or Authorized Version (which is the historic Bible of this Church) together with the Marginal Readings authorized for use by the General Convention of 1901; or from one of the three translations known as Revised Versions, including the English Revision of 1881, the American Revision of 1901, and the Revised Standard Version of 1952; from the Jerusalem Bible of 1966; from the New English Bible with the Apocrypha of 1970; or from The 1976 Good News Bible (Today's English Version) ~~and its corresponding Spanish version " Dios Habla Hoy,"~~ ; or from The New American Bible (1970); or from The Revised Standard Version, an Ecumenical Edition, commonly known as the "R.S.V. Common Bible" (1973); or from The New International Version (1978); or from The New Jerusalem Bible (1987); or from the Revised English Bible (1989); or from the New Revised Standard Version (1990); *or from translations of those approved versions published in any other language;* or from other versions of the Bible, including those in languages other than English, which shall be authorized by diocesan bishops for specific use in congregations or ministries within their dioceses.

Committee Amendment:
Resolved, the House of Deputies concurring, That Canon 2, Title II be amended as follows:
The Lessons prescribed in the Book of Common Prayer shall be read from the translation of the Holy Scriptures commonly known as the King James or Authorized Version (which is the historic Bible of this Church) together with the Marginal Readings authorized for use by the General Convention of 1901; or from one of the three translations known as Revised Versions, including the English Revision of 1881, the American Revision of 1901, and the Revised Standard Version of 1952; from the Jerusalem Bible of 1966; from the New English Bible with the Apocrypha of 1970; or from The 1976 Good News Bible (Today's English Version) ~~and its corresponding Spanish version " Dios Habla Hoy;"~~ ; or from The New American Bible (1970); or from The Revised Standard Version, an Ecumenical Edition, commonly known as the "R.S.V. Common Bible" (1973); or from The New International Version (1978); or from The New Jerusalem Bible (1987); or from the Revised English Bible (1989); or from the NewRevised Standard Version (1990); *or from translations,* authorized by the diocesan bishop, *of those approved versions published in any other language;* or from other versions of the Bible, including those in languages other than English, which shall be authorized by diocesan bishops for specific use in congregations or ministries within their dioceses.

Motion carried
Resolution adopted with amendment
(Communicated to the House of Deputies in HB Message #203)

The House of Bishops Committee on Canons presented its Report #15 on Resolution D012 (Amend Canons I.13, IV.3.42, 43, IV.14.2) and moved to refer the resolution to the Standing Commission on Constitutions and Canons.

Original Text of Resolution:
(D012)
Resolved, the House of Deputies concurring, That Canons I.13, IV.3.42, 43, IV.14.2 be amended as follows:
Canon IV.3.42. Within one hundred twenty days after receipt from the statement of the Review Committee, unless delayed for good and sufficient cause stated, the Church Attorney shall render a confidential report to the Review Committee of the findings of that investigation ~~and as to whether or not an offense may have been committed if the facts disclosed by the investigation be found to be true upon Trial, and with a recommendation as to the matter in the interest of justice and the good order and discipline of this Church and based upon such other matters as shall be pertinent~~. The report of the Church Attorney shall be confidential for all purposes as between the Church Attorney and the Review Committee. *Provided, however,* the Review Committee shall share the Report of the Church Attorney with the Presiding Bishop*, the Respondent, the alleged Victim and the Complainant.*
Canon IV.3.43(b) In its deliberations, the Review Committee may consider the

Church Attorney's report, responsible writings or sworn statements pertaining to the matter, including experts' statements, whether or not submitted by the Church Attorney. To assist in its deliberations, the Review Committee ~~may~~ *shall* provide an opportunity to be heard to the Respondent, the alleged Victim, *and* the Complainant or other persons and receive additional evidence *offered by the Respondent, the alleged Victim and/or the Complainant, and may provide an opportunity to be heard to other persons and receive additional evidence* which it in its sole discretion deems appropriate.

Canon IV.14.2. Resort to secular courts. No Member of the Clergy of this Church may resort to the secular courts for the purpose of interpreting the Constitution and Canons, or for the purpose of resolving any dispute arising thereunder, or for the purpose of delaying, hindering or reviewing or affecting in any way any proceeding under this Title. *Nothing in this Title, however, shall be construed as limiting or restricting the right of any Member of the Clergy to resort to the secular courts to seek compensation for breach of a contract of employment.*

Canon I.13. *Sec 4. No Parish or Congregation of this Church shall deny any Member of the Clergy the right to seek compensation in the secular courts for the breach of a contract of employment.*

Motion carried
Resolution referred to a Standing Commission
(Communicated to the House of Deputies in HB Message #204)

National and International Concerns

The House of Bishops Committee on National and International Concerns presented its Report #2 on HD Message #122 on Resolution D006 (Supporting International Relief and Development) and moved concurrence.

The House concurred
(Communicated to the House of Deputies in HB Message #205)

Final Text of Resolution:

(D006)
Resolved, **That the 74th General Convention endorse and embrace the achievement of the United Nations' Millennium Development Goals (MDGs) that pledge to:**
1. eradicate extreme poverty and hunger;
2. achieve universal primary education;
3. promote gender equality and empower women;
4. reduce child mortality;
5. improve maternal health;
6. combat **HIV/AIDS**, malaria, and other diseases;
7. ensure environmental stability; and
8. develop a global partnership for development; and be it further

Resolved, **That the Convention, recognizing that funding for nutritional, education, health care, and development programs is essential to achieve not**

only the MDGs, but also for recognizing the dignity of all human beings, reaffirm the 73rd General Convention's Resolutions A001 and D033 challenging all dioceses and congregations to contribute 0.7% of their annual budgets to fund international development programs; and be it further
Resolved, That the appropriate offices and staff of the Episcopal Church Center, in cooperation with Episcopal Relief and Development, promote among dioceses and congregations education about and participation in the 0.7% contribution for international development; and be it further
Resolved, That the Executive Council be directed to fulfill the 73rd General Convention's Resolution D033 requiring the Council to develop a process for an annual accounting of each diocese's progress toward living into the 0.7% contribution goal; and be it further
Resolved, That the Executive Council in cooperation with the Communications Office at the Episcopal Church Center publish annually the annual accounting of all dioceses' level of participation in the 0.7% contribution goal; and be it further
Resolved, That the Standing Commission on Anglican and International Peace with Justice present a full report to the 75th General Convention of the level of participation of all dioceses in the call to contribute 0.7% of their annual budgets to fund international development programs; and be it further
Resolved, That the United States government, as one of the 191 national signatories to the United Nations' Millennium Development Goals, be encouraged to provide appropriate leadership and resources toward international efforts to implement these and other internationally agreed development goals and that the Episcopal Office of Government Relations actively advocate that the United States government fulfill its commitment to funding international development aid at 0.7% of the U.S. Gross National Product (GNP); and be it further
Resolved, That all Episcopalians contact their elected representatives, urging them to support the United States government's fulfillment of its commitment to funding international development aid at 0.7% of the U.S. GNP.

The House of Bishops Committee on National and International Concerns presented its Report #4 on HD Message #126 on Resolution D023 (U.S. Support for the People of Liberia) and moved concurrence.

The House concurred
(Communicated to the House of Deputies in HB Message #206)

Final Text of Resolution:
(D023)
Resolved, That the 74th General Convention, in support of the Presiding Bishop's statement of July 22, 2003, urge the President of the United States to act immediately to deploy peacekeeping forces, after adequately assessing their support and relative security, to achieve a ceasefire in Liberia, and that

the Convention further support that presence, along with an international force, to remain at least until an orderly transition is made to a legitimate and stable government; and be it further

Resolved, That the Convention commend support from both government and nongovernment organizations to provide humanitarian aid and reconstruction including conflict resolution education from the United States, the United Nations, and other individual nations, and further urge our own congregations and dioceses to assist the Episcopal Church in Liberia with its efforts to restore pastoral care, health services, and education to the people; and be it further

Resolved, That Liberians residing temporarily in the United States be granted temporary protected status until such time as circumstances in Liberia permit their safe and orderly return; and be it further

Resolved, That Liberian refugees in adjacent West African countries who have prospects for U.S. resettlement be considered for resettlement, given the ongoing uncertainty of the political situation in Liberia; and be it further

Resolved, That the Convention send its warmest greetings to the Liberian people, especially its Episcopal members, through the delegation present at the 74th General Convention; and be it further

Resolved, That the Convention urge all Episcopalians to pray for the Bishop, clergy, Episcopal Church, and people of Liberia for a swift resolution of this conflict and the restoration of peace.

Visiting Bishop
The Bishop of Liberia addressed the House.

Prayer Book, Liturgy and Church Music
The House of Bishops Committee on Prayer Book, Liturgy and Church Music presented its Report #38 on Resolution C025 (Lifting Up of the Ministry of the Baptized in Ordinations) and moved adoption of a substitute.

Original Text of Resolution:
(C025)
Resolved, the House of Deputies concurring, That the 74th General Convention direct the Standing Commission on Liturgy and Music to develop supplemental liturgical materials that include various measures to hold up the ministry of the baptized and to reflect the role of the laity in the selection and presentation of the candidate, for the Episcopal Services of the Book of Common Prayer and to present those materials to the 75th General Convention.

Committee Substitute:
Resolved, the House of Deputies concurring, That the 74th General Convention direct the Standing Commission on Liturgy and Music to collect, develop, and

distribute supplemental materials in which the roles of the baptized in the discernment, selection, and presentation of priests, deacons, and bishops, be more fully reflected in the liturgical rites celebrating those occasions, and to present these materials to the 75th General Convention.

Motion carried
Substitute resolution adopted
(Communicated to the House of Deputies in HB Message #207)

The House of Bishops Committee on Prayer Book, Liturgy and Church Music presented its Report #39 on Resolution A106 (Liturgical Development and Episcopal Authority) and moved adoption of a substitute.

Original Text of Resolution:
(A106)
Resolved, the House of Deputies concurring, That the Standing Commission on Liturgy and Music direct the Office of Liturgy and Music to invite bishops and the larger church into dialogue about the relation between local liturgical initiatives and ordered authority; and be it further
Resolved, That the SCLM be directed to develop frameworks for resolving the theological, pastoral, canonical, and liturgical issues involved in the creation of new rites, and to provide facilitated conversations at the meetings of Provincial Synods in which bishops and the larger church enter into dialogue about the relation between liturgical initiatives and ordered authority; and be it further
Resolved, That the SCLM in consultation with the Commission on Constitution and Canons examine canons and rubrics that govern the development and use of liturgical materials and propose amendments authorizing appropriate local and regional liturgical initiatives; and be it further
Resolved, That the Office for Liturgy and Music be directed to establish a website for collecting, cataloguing, editing, and offering locally developed explanatory materials, strategies, and processes; and be it further
Resolved, That the sum of $15,000.00 be appropriated to provide for the costs of consultation and communication necessary in the completion of these tasks, this appropriation to be administered by the Office for Liturgy and Music.

Committee Substitute:
Resolved, the House of Deputies concurring, That as this Church expresses its theology best in the context of worship, it is important that our liturgies reflect the varied roles and diverse cultures of the baptized; and be it further
Resolved, That the Standing Commission on Liturgy and Music, in consultation with the Standing Commission on Ministry Development and other concerned committees and groups, invite the bishops and larger church into conversation about our life in Christ as expressed in the rites of this Church, the possibility for local liturgical initiatives in this expression, and the role of the bishop in such undertakings; and be it further
Resolved, That the Standing Commission on Liturgy and Music develop and implement a framework for conversations within the Church regarding the

theological, pastoral, canonical, and liturgical issues involved in the creation of new rites; and be it further

Resolved, That the Standing Commission on Liturgy and Music, in consultation with the Standing Commission on Constitution and Canons, examine canons and rubrics that govern the development and use of liturgical materials, and propose amendments authorizing appropriate local and regional liturgical initiatives; and be it further

Resolved, That the Office for Liturgy and Music be directed to establish a website for collecting, cataloguing, editing, and offering locally developed liturgies authorized by the ecclesiastical authority, explanatory materials, strategies, and processes; and be it further

Resolved, That the General Convention request the Joint Standing Committee on Program, Budget and Finance to consider a budget allocation of $15,000 for the implementation of this resolution.

Motion carried
Substitute resolution adopted
(Communicated to the House of Deputies in HB Message #208)

Special Order of Business

The Joint Standing Committee on Program, Budget and Finance was greeted and addressed the House. The Chair, Deputy Anderson from Michigan, stated that the Budget has been adopted by the House of Deputies.

The Bishop of Fond du Lac moved concurrence with the House of Deputies on Resolution D086 (Budget for the Episcopal Church 2004–2006).

The House concurred
(Communicated to the House of Deputies in HB Message #209)

Final Text of Resolution:

(D086)
*Resolved,*That the 74th General Convention adopt the Budget for The Episcopal Church for the next triennium as set forth below:

1.0   The Budget for The Episcopal Church for the period January 1, 2004 through December 31, 2006, which shall be a unified budget including Canonical, Corporate, and Program (mission) portions, is adopted at a total of $146,395,000.00.

    1.1   The Canonical portion, providing for the contingent expenses of the General Convention, the stipend of the Presiding Bishop and the expenses of that office, the expenses of the President of the House of Deputies, and Church Pension Fund assessments is adopted at a total of $28,115,000.00 as follows:

        For the year 2004 $ 8,474,000.00
        For the year 2005 $ 8,618,000.00

For the year 2006 $ 11,023,000.00

1.2 The Corporate portion, providing for the requirements for the administrative support of the Domestic and Foreign Missionary Society offices, is adopted at a total of $25,567,000.00 as follows:
For the year 2004 $ 8,225,000.00
For the year 2005 $ 8,577,000.00
For the year 2006 $ 8,765,000.00

1.3 The Program (mission) portion, providing for support for the mission and ministry (restricted and unrestricted) of the Church, is adopted at a total of $92,713,000.00 as follows:
For the year 2004 $ 30,510,000.00
For the year 2005 $ 30,821,000.00
For the year 2006 $ 31,382,000.00

2.0 The funding policy for the period January 1, 2004 through December 31, 2006 is adopted, based on a single Asking (apportioned share) of the dioceses. After a $100,000 exemption from total income, a single asking shall be applied at a flat rate of 21% of the balance of income to the diocese, reported in the diocesan financial statements for the year two years prior to the year to which the pledge is applied [e.g.: 2004 Askings (apportioned share) are to be based on 2002 actual income figures]. "Income" includes (1) all congregational giving to the diocese, (2) all unrestricted investment and endowment income to the diocese, (3) restricted investment and endowment income to the diocese which covers costs in the operating budget, and (4) other earnings from investments or enterprises. It is intended that income shall include revenues that fund normal operating and program expenses of the dioceses. It is not intended to include pass-through income that is used for expenses for programming that are simply administered by the dioceses, or that would not be otherwise funded by contributions from parishes or out of investment income.

2.1 We rejoice with dioceses that have moved toward, and those that give at and above, the 21% Asking. Such giving creates a strong financial basis for vital mission and witness of The Episcopal Church. We encourage all our dioceses to adopt the 21% Asking; then we could allocate an additional 4.7 million dollars each year toward fulfilling the mission priorities which we have embraced in this 74th General Convention.

2.2 For the budgetary period income from diocesan commitments, totaling $90,487,000.00 is anticipated as follows:

For the year 2004 $ 29,473,000.00
For the year 2005 $ 30,062, 000.00
For the year 2006 $ 30,952,000.00

2.3 For the budgetary period 2004–2006, payment by the dioceses of the Askings shall be made in twelve equal monthly payments.

2.4 All additional income, other than from the Askings of the dioceses, totaling $55,908,000.00, is projected as follows:

For the year 2004 $ 18,554,000.00
For the year 2005 $ 18,382,000.00
For the year 2006 $ 18,972,000.00

2.5 A General Ordination fee is hereby authorized, which fees shall be added to the funding from dioceses and applied to the expenses of examination as appropriated in the budget. A candidate for Holy Orders eligible for examination and so certified by the diocesan bishop shall not be disqualified for examination because the fee has not been paid.

2.6 General Convention registration and exhibitors fees are hereby authorized, which fees shall be added to the funding from dioceses and applied to the expenses of the 2006 General Convention, and for no other purpose.

3.0 In the exercise of their respective authorities, the Executive Council of the General Convention and the Joint Standing Committee on Program, Budget and Finance shall be subject to the following policies:

3.1 Each year, the Executive Council, with the advice of the Joint Standing Committee on Program, Budget and Finance, shall adjust the budget to the assured income of the Executive Council so as to carry out the Budget for The Episcopal Church for that year on a balanced budget basis.

3.2 The fiscal year shall begin January 1.

3.3 If in any year the total anticipated income for budget support is less than the amount required to support the budget approved by the General Convention, the Canonical portion of the Budget for The Episcopal Church shall have funding priority over any other budget areas.

3.4 Net surpluses that are realized in any year of the triennium are to be allocated in the subsequent years of the triennium in the following rank order, as needed, to:

Ministries With Young People
Ethnic Congregational Development
Congregational Development

3.5 Undesignated bequests and legacies received during the budgetary period shall be set aside in the general endowment fund of which only the income shall be used for the general purposes of the Society.

3.6 Designated bequests and legacies received during the budgetary period shall be set aside in specific funds of which only the income shall be used for the purposes so designated.

3.7 Each Committee, Commission, Agency and Board (CCAB) proposing to the General Convention any resolution with funding implications shall present to the Joint Standing Committee on Program, Budget and Finance a detailed budget in support of its plan(s), including cost estimates from contractors and suppliers for all goods and services, by no later than six months before the opening day of the General Convention

3.8 Subsequent editions of the *Report and Proposal of the Presiding Bishop and Executive Council to the General Convention* contain the following information for each year of the preceding triennium:
- A description of the actual income and expenditures of the DFMS, relating the expenditures to the Church's priorities with accompanying narrative.
- Endowment balance and total investment return, with accompanying narrative.
- Posting of this report on the DFMS website when it is released to the Bishops and Deputies.

Presiding Bishop

The Presiding Bishop yielded the chair to the Vice-Chair.

The Bishop of Western North Carolina moved that a letter be sent from the House of Bishops to the Executive Council urging their consideration of Resolution A022 (Nathan Network Funding) and Resolution A023 (Establish Institutional Wellness and the Prevention of Sexual Misconduct Task Force). "For the Secretary of the House of Bishops to write a letter to the Executive Council urging support for the fundings of the Nathan Network (A022) and ask the Executive Council to call on the Bishop of the Office of Pastoral Development to explain the pressing need for these funds for the church."

Motion carried

Ministry

The House of Bishops Committee on Ministry presented its Report #24 on Resolution A111 (Title III Proposed Canons) and moved adoption of a substitute.

Original Text of Resolution:
(A111)
[Note: See *The Blue Book* Report of Standing Commission on Ministry Development, pp. 220-237. The *italized text* in the Committee Substitute are proposed changes to the original text of the resolution. *Ed.*]

Committee Substitute:
Resolved, the House of Deputies concurring, That Canons III.1–9, 13 ~~21~~ *17, and 19* be deleted and replaced by the following ~~proposed~~ *amended* Canons III.1–9, *with all remaining Canons renumbered as appropriate.*

CANON 1: Of the Ministry of All Baptized Persons

Sec.1. Each Diocese shall make provision for the affirmation and development of the ministry of all baptized persons, including:

(a) Assistance in understanding that all baptized persons are called to minister in Christ's name, to identify their gifts with the help of the Church and to serve Christ's mission at all times and in all places.

(b) Assistance in understanding that all baptized persons are called to sustain their ministries through commitment to life-long Christian formation.

Sec. 2. No person shall be denied access to or the exercise of any ministry, lay or ordained, in this Church because of race, color, ethnic origin, national origin, sex, marital status, sexual orientation, disabilities or age, except as otherwise provided by these Canons. No right to licensing, ordination, or election is hereby established.

CANON 2: Commissions on Ministry

Sec. 1. In each Diocese there shall be a Commission on Ministry ("Commission") consisting of Priests, Deacons, if any, and Lay Persons. The Canons of each Diocese shall provide for the number of members, terms of office, and manner of selection to the Commission.

Sec. 2. The Commission shall advise and assist the Bishop:

(a) In the implementation of Title III of these Canons.

(b) In the determination of present and future opportunities and needs for the ministry of all baptized persons.

(c) In the design and oversight of the ongoing process for discernment, formation *for ministry* and assessment *of readiness therefor.*

Sec. 3. The Commission may adopt rules for its work, subject to the approval of the Bishop; Provided that they are not inconsistent with the Constitution and Canons of this Church and of the Diocese.

Sec. 4. The Commission may establish committees consisting of members and other persons to report to the Commission or to act on its behalf.

Sec. 5. The Bishop and Commission shall ensure that the members of the

Commission and its committees receive ongoing education and training for their work.

CANON 3: Of Discernment

Sec 1. The Bishop and Commission shall provide encouragement, training and necessary resources to assist each congregation in developing an ongoing process of community discernment appropriate to the cultural background, age and life experiences of all persons seeking direction in their call to ministry.

Sec 2. The Bishop, in consultation with the Commission, may ~~designate~~ *utilize* college and university campus ministry centers and other communities of faith as additional ~~discernment~~ communities *where discernment takes place. In cases where these discernment communities are located in another jurisdiction, the Bishop will consult with the bishop where the discernment community is located.*

Sec 3. The Bishop and Commission shall actively solicit from congregations, schools and other youth organizations, college and university campus ministry centers, seminaries, and other communities of faith, names of persons whose *demonstrated qualities of Christian commitment and* potential for leadership and vision mark them as desirable candidates for positions of leadership in the Church.

Sec. 4. The Bishop, Commission, and the discernment community shall assist persons engaged in a process of ministry discernment to determine appropriate avenues for the expression and support of their ministries, either lay or ordained.

CANON 4: Of Licensed Ministries

Sec. 1.

(a) A confirmed communicant in good standing or, *in extraordinary circumstances,* subject to guidelines established by the Bishop, a communicant in good standing, may be ~~authorized or~~ licensed by the Ecclesiastical Authority to serve as Pastoral Leader, Worship Leader, Preacher, Eucharistic Minister, Eucharistic Visitor, or Catechist~~, or in other licensed ministries. The Bishop, or Ecclesiastical authority, in consultation with the Commission on Ministry, may determine other licensed ministries~~. Requirements and guidelines for the selection, training, continuing education, and deployment of such persons *and the duration of licenses* shall be established by the Bishop in consultation with the Commission on Ministry.

(b) The Presiding Bishop or the Bishop Suffragan for the Armed ~~Services~~ *Forces*~~, Healthcare and Prison Ministries~~ may authorize a member of the Armed ~~Services~~ *Forces* to exercise one or more of these ministries in the Armed ~~Services~~ *Forces* in accordance with the provisions of this Canon. Requirements and guidelines for the selection, training, continuing education, and deployment of such persons shall be established by the Bishop granting the license.

Sec. 2.

(a) The ~~Priest-in-Charge~~ *Member of the Clergy* or other leader exercising oversight of the congregation or other community of faith may request the Ecclesiastical Authority *with jurisdiction* to license persons within that congregation *or other community of faith* to exercise such ministries. The license shall be issued for a period of time to be determined under Canon III.4.1(a) and may be renewed. The license may be revoked by the Ecclesiastical Authority upon request of or upon notice to the ~~Priest-in-Charge~~ *Member of the Clergy* or other leader exercising oversight of the congregation or other community of faith. ~~The Ecclesiastical Authority shall communicate the reasons for revocation or non-renewal to the person whose license is being revoked or not renewed.~~

(b) In renewing the license, the Ecclesiastical Authority shall consider the performance of the ministry by the person licensed, continuing education in the licensed area, and the endorsement of the ~~Priest-in-Charge~~ *Member of the Clergy* or other leader exercising oversight of the congregation or other community of faith in which the person is serving.

(c) A person licensed in any Diocese under the provisions of this Canon may serve in another congregation or other community of faith in the same or another Diocese only at the invitation of the ~~Priest-in-Charge~~ *Member of the Clergy* or other leader exercising oversight, and with the consent of the Ecclesiastical Authority in whose jurisdiction the service will occur.

Sec. 3. A Pastoral Leader is a lay person authorized to exercise pastoral or administrative responsibility in a congregation under special circumstances, as defined by the Bishop.

Sec. 4. A Worship Leader is a lay person who regularly leads public worship under the direction of the ~~Priest-in-Charge~~ *Member of the Clergy* or other leader exercising oversight of the congregation or other community of faith.

Sec. 5. A Preacher is a lay person authorized to preach. Persons so authorized shall only preach in congregations under the direction of the ~~Priest-in-Charge~~ *Member of the Clergy* or other leader exercising oversight of the congregation or other community of faith.

Sec. 6. A Eucharistic Minister is a lay person authorized to administer the ~~Consecrated Elements~~ *Chalice* at a Celebration of Holy Eucharist. A Eucharistic Minister ~~shall~~ *should normally* act under the direction of a Deacon, if any*, or otherwise, the Member of the Clergy or other leader exercising oversight of the congregation or other community of faith*.

Sec. 7. A Eucharistic Visitor is a lay person authorized to take the Consecrated Elements in a timely manner following a Celebration of Holy Eucharist to members of the congregation who, by reason of illness or infirmity, were unable to be present at the Celebration. A Eucharistic Visitor ~~shall~~ *should normally* act under the direction of a Deacon, if any*, or otherwise, the Member of the Clergy or other leader exercising oversight of the congregation or other community of faith*.

Sec. 8. A Catechist is a lay person authorized to prepare persons for Baptism, Confirmation, Reception, and the Reaffirmation of Baptismal Vows*, and shall function under the direction of the* ~~Priest-in-Charge~~ *Member of the Clergy or other leader exercising oversight of the congregation or other community of faith*.

CANON 5: Of General Provisions Respecting Ordination

Sec. 1.

(a) The canonical authority assigned to the Bishop Diocesan by this Title may be exercised by a Bishop Coadjutor, when so empowered under Canon III.25, by a Bishop Suffragan when requested by the Bishop Diocesan, or by any other Bishop of the Anglican Communion canonically in charge of a Diocese, at the request of the ordinand's Bishop.

(b) The Council of Advice of the Convocation of American Churches in Europe, and the board appointed by a Bishop having jurisdiction in an Area Mission in accordance with the provisions of Canon I.11.2*(c)*, shall, for the purpose of this and other Canons of Title III have the same powers as the Standing Committee of a Diocese.

(c) In case of a vacancy in the episcopate in a Diocese, the Ecclesiastical Authority may authorize and request the President of the House of Bishops of the Province to take order for an ordination.

Sec. 2.

~~(a)~~ ~~All certificates and testimonials required by this Title shall be in the form provided by this Title, and shall be signed and dated.~~

~~(b)~~(a) No *Nominee,* Applicant, Postulant or Candidate for ordination shall sign any of the certificates ~~prescribed~~ *required* by this Title.

~~(c)~~(b) Testimonials required of the Standing Committee by this Title must be signed by a majority of the whole Committee, at a meeting duly convened, except that testimonials may be executed in counterparts, each of which shall be deemed an original.

~~(d)~~(c) Whenever the ~~certificate~~ *letter of support* of a Vestry is required, ~~such certificate~~ *the letter* must be signed *and dated* by at least two-thirds of all of the members of the Vestry, at a meeting duly convened, and by the Rector or Priest-in-Charge of the Parish, and attested by the Clerk of the Vestry. Should there be no Rector or Priest-in-Charge, the ~~certificate~~ *letter* shall be signed by a Priest of the Diocese acquainted with the ~~applicant~~ *nominee* and the Parish, the reason for the substitution being stated in the attesting clause.

~~(e)~~(d) If the congregation or other discernment community ~~of faith~~ of which the ~~applicant~~ nominee is a member is not a Parish, the ~~certification~~ letter of support required by Canon III.6 or Canon III.8 shall be ~~given~~ signed and dated by the ~~Priest-in-Charge~~ *Member of the Clergy* and the ~~local~~ council of the congregation or other community of faith ~~to which the applicant belongs~~, and shall be attested by the secretary of the meeting at which the ~~certification~~ *letter* was approved. Should there be no ~~Priest-in-Charge~~*Member of the Clergy*, the ~~certification~~ *letter* shall be signed *and dated* by a Priest of the Diocese acquainted with the ~~applicant~~ *nominee* and the congregation or other community of faith, the reason for the substitution being stated in the attesting clause.

(f)(e) If the applicant is a member of a Religious Order or Christian Community recognized by Canon III.30 the ~~certificates~~ *letters of support* referred to in Canon III.6 or Canon III.8 and any other requirements imposed on a congregation or ~~Priest-in-Charge~~ *Member of the Clergy,* may be given by the Superior or person in charge, and Chapter, or other comparable body of the Order or Community.

Sec. ~~53~~. An application for any dispensation permitted by this Title from any of the requirements for ordination must first be made to the Bishop, and if approved, referred to the Standing Committee for its advice and consent.

CANON 6: Of the Ordination of Deacons

Sec. 1. Selection

The Bishop, in consultation with the Commission, shall establish procedures to identify and select persons *with evident gifts and fitness* for ordination to the Diaconate.

(a) Nomination. A confirmed adult communicant in good standing, who has been a member of the Episcopal Church for the preceding three years, may be ~~n~~Nominated ~~to be a Postulant~~ for ordination to the diaconate by the person's congregation or other community of faith. The ~~n~~Nomination shall be in writing, ~~signed by the Rector or Priest-in-Charge and at least two-thirds of the Vestry or comparable body,~~ *and shall include:*

(1) *Full name and date of birth.*

(2) *The length of time resident in the Diocese.*

(3) *Evidence of Baptism and Confirmation.*

(4) *Whether an application has been made previously for Postulancy or the person has been Nominated in any diocese.*

(5) *A description of the process of discernment by which the applicant has been identified for ordination to the Diaconate.*

(6) *The level of education attained and, if any, the degrees earned and areas of specialization.*

(7) *A letter of support by the applicant's discernment community, including a statement committing the discernment community to involve itself in the applicant's preparation for ordination to the Diaconate. If it be a congregation, the letter shall be signed by a two-thirds majority of the Vestry or comparable body, and the Member of the Clergy or leader exercising oversight.*

(8) *An acceptance in writing by the nominated person.*

~~and~~ The nomination shall be submitted to the Bishop~~. Upon acceptance in writing by the nominated person, the Bishop~~ , *who* may admit the person as a ~~Postulant~~ *Nominee* for ordination to the ~~d~~Diaconate.

(b) ~~Postulancy~~*Admission*. ~~Postulancy~~ *Admission* is ~~a~~*the* time ~~between nomination and candidacy and includes a process~~ of exploration of and decision on the ~~Postulant's~~ *Nominee's* call to the diaconate.

(1) ~~During Postulancy t~~There shall be a thorough investigation of the ~~Postulant~~ *Nominee* which shall include:
 (i) a background check, and
 (ii) medical and *complete* psychological ~~examination~~*evaluation* by professionals approved by the Bishop, using forms prepared for ~~that~~*the* purpose by The Church Pension Fund, *and if desired or necessary, psychiatric referral.*
 (iii) Reports of all investigations and examinations shall be kept on file by the Bishop. ~~The Bishop, with regard for confidentiality, may make information from the reports available to the Commission.~~

(2) The Bishop, or the Bishop's designee, may interview the ~~Postulant~~ *Nominee*. The Commission or a designated committee shall interview the ~~Postulant~~ *Nominee*, and the Commission or designated committee shall submit a recommendation to the Bishop.

(3) The Bishop may then admit the ~~Postulant~~ *Nominee* as a Candidate, informing the Candidate and the ~~Candidate's Rector or Priest-in-Charge~~ *Member of the Clergy or other leader of the Candidate's discernment community* in writing.

Sec. 2. Candidacy

(a) Candidacy is a time, no less than one year in length, of formation in preparation for ordination to the Diaconate, *established by a formal commitment by the Candidate, the Bishop, the Commission and the congregation or other community of faith.*

(b) The Bishop may assign the Candidate to any congregation of the diocese or other community of faith after consultation with the ~~Rector~~ *Member of the Clergy* or other leader exercising oversight.

(c) At the Bishop's sole discretion, any Candidate may be removed from the list of Candidates, with reasons given to the Candidate and written notice of the removal being given to the Candidate and the ~~Rector~~*Member of the Clergy* or other leader exercising oversight of the nominating congregation or other community of faith and the Commission.

Sec. 3. Preparation for Ordination

(a) The Bishop, in consultation with the Commission, shall determine the length of time and extent of formation needed to prepare each Candidate for ordination. ~~Formation shall reflect the local culture and each Candidate's background, age, occupation, and ministry. Prior education and learning from life experience may be considered as part of the formation required for ordination.~~

(b) Before ordination each Candidate shall be prepared in and demonstrate basic competence in five general areas:

(1) *Academic studies including, The Holy Scriptures, theology and the tradition of the Church.*
~~(1)~~(2) Diakonia and the diaconate.
~~(2)~~(3) Human awareness and understanding.
~~(3)~~(4) Spiritual development and discipline.
~~(4)~~(5) Practical training and experience.
~~(5)~~ ~~Academic study and education.~~

~~(c)~~ ~~Wherever possible, formation shall take place in community, including persons in preparation for the diaconate, or others preparing for ministry.~~

(c)~~(d)~~ The formation process shall include sexual misconduct prevention training, training regarding Title IV of these Canons, and anti-racism training.

(d)~~(e)~~ *Formation shall reflect the local culture and each Candidate's background, age, occupation, and ministry. Prior education and learning from life experience may be considered as part of the formation required for ordination.*

(e) *Wherever possible, formation shall take place in community, including persons in preparation for the diaconate, or others preparing for ministry.*

(f)~~(e)~~ Each Candidate shall communicate with the Bishop in person or by letter, four times a year, in the Ember Weeks, reflecting on the Candidate's *academic*, diaconal, human, spiritual, and practical, ~~and academic~~ development.

(g)~~(f)~~ During Candidacy each Candidate's progress shall be evaluated from time to time, and there shall be a written report of the evaluation *by those authorized by the Commission to be in charge of the evaluation program.* Upon certification by those in charge of the Candidate's program of preparation that the Candidate has successfully completed preparation and is ready for ordination, a final written assessment of readiness for ordination to the Diaconate shall be prepared as determined by the Bishop in consultation with the Commission. *This report shall include a recommendation from the Commission regarding the readiness of the Candidate for ordination.* Records shall be kept of all evaluations, and assessments, *and the recommendation,* and shall be made available to the Standing Committee.

(h)~~(g)~~ *If the medical examination, psychological examination, or background check have taken place more than 36 months prior to ordination, they must be updated.*

(i)~~(h)~~ *Before ordination each Candidate must have reached the age of twenty-four, and made application for ordination.*

(j)~~(i)~~ Upon certification in writing by the Standing Committee that all canonical requirements have been met, *and that there is no sufficient objection on medical, psychological, moral, doctrinal, or spiritual grounds and that they recommend ordination,* the Bishop may ordain the Candidate a Deacon.

~~Sec. 4. A person previously ordained a Priest or a Bishop, and not previously ordained a Deacon, may be nominated to be a Postulant for the diaconate and shall fulfill the requirements of this Canon. Upon completion of these requirements, the Priest or Bishop may be ordained a Deacon.~~

CANON 7: Of the Life and Work of Deacons

Sec. ~~1~~ 1. Deacons serve directly under the authority of and are accountable to the Bishop.

Sec. ~~3~~ 2. Deacons canonically resident in each Diocese constitute a Community of Deacons, which shall meet from time to time. The Bishop may appoint one or more of such Deacons as Archdeacon(s) to assist the Bishop in the formation, deployment, supervision, and support of the Deacons or those in preparation to be Deacons, and in the implementation of this canon.

Sec. 3. The Bishop may establish a ~~c~~Council *on Deacons ("Council")* to oversee, study, and promote the diaconate.

Sec. 4. The Bishop, after consultation with *the Deacon* and the ~~Rector~~ *Member of the Clergy* or other leader exercising oversight, may assign a Deacon to one or more congregations, other communities of faith or non-parochial ministries. Deacons assigned to a congregation or other community of faith act under the authority of the ~~Rector~~ *Member of the Clergy* or other leader exercising oversight in all matters concerning the congregation.

~~(a)~~ ~~Deacons may have a letter of agreement, subject to the Bishop's approval, setting forth mutual responsibilities in the assignment.~~

(a)~~(b)~~ Deacons shall report annually to the Bishop or the Bishop's designee on their life and work.

(b)~~(c)~~ Deacons may serve as administrators of congregations or other communities of faith, but no Deacon shall be in charge of a congregation or other community of faith.

(c)~~(d)~~ Deacons may accept ~~a chaplaincy~~ *chaplaincies* in any hospital, prison, or other institution, or serve as Deacons in the Armed ~~Services~~ *Forces*.

Sec. 5. The Bishop and Commission shall require and provide for the continuing education of Deacons and keep a record of such education.

Sec. 6.(a)~~After consultation among all affected parties, a Bishop may license Deacons canonically resident in another diocese to serve in that Bishop's diocese.~~ A Deacon ~~without such a written license~~ may not serve as Deacon for more than two months in any diocese *other than* ~~outside~~ the diocese in which the Deacon is canonically resident unless the Bishop of the other diocese shall have granted a license to the Deacon to serve in that diocese.

(b) (1) A Deacon desiring to become canonically resident within a Diocese shall *request* ~~present to the Ecclesiastical Authority~~ a testimonial from the Ecclesiastical Authority of the

Diocese in which the Deacon is canonically resident *to present to the receiving diocese,* which testimonial, *if granted,* shall be given by the Ecclesiastical Authority to the applicant, and a duplicate thereof may be sent to the Ecclesiastical Authority of the Diocese to which transfer is proposed. The testimonial shall be in the following words:

I hereby certify that A.B., who has signified to me the desire to be transferred to the Ecclesiastical Authority of _____, is a Deacon of _____ in good standing, and has not, so far as I know or believe, been justly liable to evil report, for error in religion or for viciousness of life, for the last three years.

(Date) _____

(Signed) _____

(2) Such testimonial shall be called Letters Dimissory. If the Ecclesiastical Authority ~~is moved to~~ accepts the Letters Dimissory, the canonical residence of the Deacon so transferred shall date from the acceptance of the Letters Dimissory, of which prompt notice shall be given both to the applicant and to the Ecclesiastical Authority from which it came.

(3) Letters Dimissory not presented within six months from the date of ~~their~~ transmission to the applicant shall become void.

(4) A statement of the record of payments to The Church Pension Fund by or on behalf of the Deacon concerned shall accompany Letters Dimissory.

Sec. 7. A Deacon may retire from active service *for reasons of age or infirmity with the consent of the Bishop* at any time *and shall retire for reasons of age or infirmity at the request of the Bishop* ~~mutually acceptable to the Deacon and the Bishop, or at any time for reasons of health~~. The Bishop may, *with the consent of the Deacon,* assign a retired Deacon to any congregation, other community of faith or non-parochial ministry, for a period not to exceed twelve months, and this period may be renewed.

~~Sec. 8. (a) A Deacon of this Church not subject to the provisions of Canon IV.8 may declare, in writing, to the Ecclesiastical Authority of the Diocese of canonical residence, a renunciation of the Diaconate of this Church, and a desire to be removed therefrom. Upon receipt of such declaration, the Bishop shall record it. The Bishop, upon determining that the person is not subject to the provisions of Canon IV.8 but is acting voluntarily and for causes that do not affect the Deacon's moral character, shall present the declaration to the clerical members of the Standing Committee. With the advice and consent of a majority of such members, the Bishop may pronounce that such renunciation is accepted, and the Deacon is released from the obligations of the office and deprived of the rights conferred in ordination. The Bishop shall also declare that the renunciation was for causes that do not affect the person's moral character and, if requested, shall give a certificate~~

~~to this effect to the person so removed from the Diaconate.~~

~~(b) If a Deacon making the declaration provided in the preceding section of this Canon is under Presentment for any canonical Offense, or has been placed on Trial for the same, the Ecclesiastical Authority to whom such declaration is made shall not consider or act upon such declaration until after the Presentment is dismissed or the Trial concluded and the Deacon judged not to have committed an Offense.~~

~~(c) If a renunciation is accepted, the Bishop shall pronounce a declaration of removal in the presence of two or more Deacons or members of the Standing Committee and shall enter it in the official records of the Diocese of canonical residence. The Bishop who pronounces the declaration of removal shall give notice thereof in writing to every Member of the Clergy, each Vestry, the Secretary of the Convention and the Standing Committee of the Diocese in which the Deacon was canonically resident, and to all Bishops of this Church, the Ecclesiastical Authority of each Diocese of this Church, the Presiding Bishop, the Recorder, the Secretary of the House of Bishops, the Secretary of the House of Deputies, the Church Pension Fund, and the Church Deployment Board.~~

~~(d) In case of a vacancy in the episcopate in a Diocese, the Ecclesiastical Authority may request the President of the House of Bishops of the Province, or the President's designee, to exercise the canonical authority assigned to the Bishop by this section.~~

~~(e) A person removed from the Diaconate pursuant to this section may apply to the Bishop in writing for restoration to the Diaconate, and the Bishop, with the consent of the Standing Committee, may restore the person as a Deacon.~~

CANON 8: Of the Ordination of Priests

Sec. 1. The Bishop, in consultation with the Commission, shall establish procedures to identify and select persons *with evident gifts and fitness* for ordination to the Priesthood.

Sec 2. Of General Provisions concerning Postulancy and Candidacy

(a) Postulancy is a time, no less than six months in length, for the exploration of and decision on the Postulant's call to the Priesthood.

(b) Candidacy is a time of formation in preparation for ordination to the Priesthood, established by a formal commitment by the Candidate, the Bishop, the Commission and the congregation or other community of faith. The period of Candidacy shall be no less than six months.

(c) The combined period for Postulancy~~, and~~ Candidacy *and Diaconate* under this Canon shall ~~last~~*be* no less than 18 months.

(d) The responsibilities for the formation and preparation of Postulants and Candidates shall include the following:

(1) Each Postulant or Candidate for ordination to the Priesthood shall communicate with the Bishop in person or by letter, four times a year, in the Ember Weeks, reflecting on the individual's academic experience and personal and spiritual development.

(2) The congregation or other community of faith shall nominate appropriate persons for the ordination process, nurture them in their faith, and provide continuing support for such persons through Postulancy, Candidacy, and ordination.

(3) The Bishop and the Commission shall work closely with the Postulant or Candidate to develop and monitor a program of preparation for ordination to the Priesthood in accordance with Canon III.8.4 and to ensure that pastoral guidance is provided throughout the period of preparation.

(4) The Standing Committee shall certify that all canonical requirements for ordination have been met *and make a recommendation regarding ordination.*

(5) The seminary or other formation program shall provide for, monitor and report on the academic performance and personal qualifications of the Candidate or Postulant for ordination. These reports will be made upon request of the Bishop and Commission, but at least once per year.

(e) Prior to ordination *as a deacon under this canon*, the following must be accomplished:

(1) a thorough background check of the applicant.

(2) sexual misconduct prevention training, training regarding Title IV of these Canons, and anti-racism training.

~~(3)~~ ~~consultation by the Bishop with the applicant regarding financial resources available for the support of the applicant throughout preparation for ordination, and~~

(3)~~(4)~~ thorough examinations, both ~~physical~~ *medical* and psychological, by professionals ~~appointed~~ *approved* by the Bishop~~,~~ ~~The appointed professionals shall use~~ *using* the forms ~~for medical and psychological or psychiatric reports~~ prepared by the Church Pension Fund for this purpose*, and if desired or necessary, psychiatric referral.* These reports shall be kept on file by the Bishop. ~~When deemed appropriate the Bishop may make available information from the reports to the Commission with proper regard for confidentiality.~~

(4) *If the medical examination, psychological examination, or background check have taken place more than 36 months prior to*

ordination as a Deacon under this canon, they must be updated.

Sec. 3. Postulancy

(a) A person *nominated* ~~desiring to be considered~~ for admission as a Postulant for ordination to the Priesthood shall *provide* ~~apply~~ to the Bishop. ~~Such application shall include~~ the following:

(1) Full name and date of birth.
(2) The length of time resident in the Diocese.
(3) Evidence of Baptism and Confirmation.
(4) Whether an application has been made previously for Postulancy in any diocese.
(5) A description of the process of discernment by which the ~~applicant~~*nominee* has been identified for ordination to the Priesthood.
(6) The level of education attained and, if any, the degrees earned and areas of specialization.
(7) A letter of support by the ~~applicant's~~ *nominee's* congregation or other community of faith, including a statement committing the congregation or other community of faith to involve itself in the ~~applicant's~~*nominee's* preparation for ordination to the Priesthood. If it be a congregation, the letter shall be signed by a two-thirds majority of the Vestry ~~or comparable body~~, and the ~~Rector~~*Member of the Clergy* or leader exercising oversight.
(8) A written request from the nominee for admission to Postulancy.

(b) Before granting admission as a Postulant, the Bishop:

(1) shall determine that the person is a confirmed adult communicant in good standing of a congregation or other community of faith, and has been a member of the Episcopal Church for the preceding three years, and
(2) shall confer in person with the ~~applicant~~*nominee*,
(3) shall consult with the nominee regarding financial resources which will be available for the support of the Postulant throughout preparation for ordination. During Postulancy and later Candidacy, the Bishop or someone appointed by the Bishop shall review periodically the financial condition and plans of the Postulant.

(c) On the basis of the application and the personal interview, the Bishop shall notify the ~~applicant~~ *nominee* and the Commission whether the application process may proceed.

(d) If the Bishop approves proceeding, the Commission, or a committee of the Commission, shall meet with the ~~applicant~~ *nominee* to review the application and prepare an evaluation of the

(e) The Bishop may admit the ~~applicant~~ *nominee* as a Postulant for ordination to the Priesthood. The Bishop shall record the Postulant's name and date of admission in a Register kept for that purpose. The Bishop shall inform the Postulant, the ~~Rector~~ *Member of the Clergy* or other leader exercising oversight of the Postulant's congregation or other community of faith, the Commission, the Standing Committee, and the Dean of the seminary the Postulant may be attending or proposes to attend, or the director of Postulant's program of preparation, of the fact and date of such admission.

(f) Any Postulant may be removed as a Postulant at the sole discretion of the Bishop, ~~who shall give the reasons to the Postulant~~. The Bishop shall give written notice of the removal to the ~~Rector~~ *Candidate and the Member of the Clergy* or other leader exercising oversight of the Postulant's congregation or other community of faith, the Commission, the Standing Committee, and the Dean of the seminary the Postulant may be attending or the director of the program of preparation.

(g) No Bishop shall consider accepting as a Postulant any person who has been refused admission as a Candidate for ordination to the Priesthood in any other Diocese, or who, having been admitted, has afterwards ceased to be a Candidate, until receipt of a letter from the Bishop of the Diocese refusing admission, or in which the person has been a Candidate, declaring the cause of refusal or of cessation. If the Bishop decides to proceed the Bishop shall send the letter to the Commission.

Sec. 4. Formation. Postulants shall pursue the program of preparation for ordination to the Priesthood developed by the Bishop and Commission. The program shall include theological training, practical experience, emotional development, and spiritual formation.

(a) If the Postulant has not previously obtained a baccalaureate degree, the Commission, Bishop and Postulant shall, ~~as necessary,~~ design a program of *such* additional academic work to prepare the Postulant to undertake a program of theological education.

(b) Prior education and learning from life experience may be considered as part of the formation required for the Priesthood.

(c) Whenever possible, formation for the Priesthood shall take place in community, including other persons in preparation for the Priesthood, a ministry team, or others preparing for ministry.

(d) Formation shall take into account the local culture and each Candidate's background, age, occupation, and ministry.

(e) Subject areas for study during this program of preparation shall

include:
- (1) The Holy Scriptures;
- (2) Church History, including the Ecumenical Movement;
- (3) Christian Theology, including Missionary Theology and Missiology;
- (4) Christian Ethics and Moral Theology;
- (5) Studies in contemporary society, including racial and minority groups;
- (6) Liturgics and Church Music; Christian Worship and Music according to the contents and use of the Book of Common Prayer and the Hymnal, ~~respectively;~~ *and authorized supplemental texts;* and
- (7) Theory and practice of ministry.

Sec. 5. Candidacy

(a) A person desiring to be considered as a Candidate for ordination to the Priesthood shall apply to the Bishop. Such application shall include the following:
- (1) the Postulant's date of admission to Postulancy, and
- (2) a letter of support by the Postulant's congregation ~~or an authorized representative of the Postulant's congregation~~ or other community of faith. If it be a congregation, the letter shall be signed by at least two-thirds of the Vestry and the ~~Rector~~ *Member of the Clergy* or other leader exercising oversight.

(b) Upon compliance with these requirements, and receipt of a statement from the Commission attesting to the continuing formation of the Postulant, the Bishop may admit the applicant as a Candidate for ordination to the Priesthood. The Bishop shall record the Candidate's name and date of admission in a Register kept for that purpose. The Bishop shall inform the Candidate, the ~~Rector~~ *Member of the Clergy* or leader exercising oversight of the Candidate's congregation or other community of faith, the Commission, the Standing Committee, and the Dean of the seminary the Candidate may be attending or proposes to attend, or the director of the Candidate's program of preparation, of the fact and date of such admission.

(c) A Candidate must remain in canonical relationship with the Diocese in which admission has been granted until ordination to the ~~Priesthood~~ *Diaconate under this Canon*, except as provided in Canon III.8.5(d).

(d) For reasons satisfactory to the Bishop, the Candidate may be transferred to another Diocese upon request, provided that the Bishop of the receiving Diocese is willing to accept the Candidate.

(e) Any Candidate may be removed as a Candidate at the sole discretion of the Bishop, who shall give the reasons to the Candidate. The Bishop shall give written notice of the removal to the ~~Rector~~ *Member of the Clergy* or other leader exercising oversight of the Candidate's congregation or other community of faith, the Commission, the Standing Committee, and the Dean of the seminary the Candidate may be attending or the director of the program of preparation.

(f) If a Bishop has removed the Candidate's name from the list of Candidates, except by transfer, or the Candidate's application for ordination has been rejected, no other Bishop may ordain the person without readmission to Candidacy for a period of at least twelve months.

Sec. 6. *Ordination to the Diaconate*

(a) *A Candidate must first be ordained Deacon before being ordained Priest.*

(b) *To be ordained Deacon under this canon, a person must be at least twenty-one years of age.*

(c) *No one shall be ordained Deacon under this canon within six months of admission as a Candidate nor within one year of admission as Postulant*

(d) *The Bishop shall obtain in writing:*

    (1) *an application from the Candidate requesting ordination as a Deacon under this canon, including the Candidate's dates of admission to Postulancy and Candidacy;;*

    (2) *letter of support from the Candidate's congregation or other community of faith, signed and dated by at least two-thirds of the Vestry and the Member of the Clergy or other leader exercising oversight;*

    (3) *a certificate from the seminary or other program of preparation, showing the Candidate's scholastic record in the subjects required by the Canons, and giving an evaluation with recommendation as to the Candidate's other personal qualifications for ordination together with a recommendation regarding ordination to the Diaconate under this canon.*

(e) *The Standing Committee shall obtain:*

    (1) *the application for ordination to the Diaconate under this canon specified in Canon III.8.6(d)(1), including the accompanying letter of support by the Candidate's congregation or other community of faith specified in Canon III.8.6(d)(2),*

    (2) *certificates from the Bishop who admitted the Candidate to Postulancy and Candidacy, giving the dates of admission, and*

    (3) *a certificate from the Commission giving a recommendation regarding ordination to the Diaconate under this canon.*

(f) *On the receipt of such certificates, the Standing Committee, a majority of all the* members consenting, shall certify that the canonical requirements for ordination to the Diaconate under this canon have been met and there is no sufficient objection on medical, psychological, moral, doctrinal, or spiritual grounds and that they recommend ordination, by a testimonial addressed to the Bishop in the form specified below and signed by the consenting members of the Standing Committee.

To the Right Reverend _____, Bishop of _____ We, the Standing Committee of _____, having been duly convened at _____, do testify that A.B., desiring to be ordained to the Diaconate and Priesthood under Canon III.8, has presented to us the certificates as required by the Canons indicating A.B.'s preparedness for ordination to the Diaconate under Canon III.8; and we certify that all canonical requirements for ordination to the Diaconate under Canon III.8 have been met; and we find no sufficient objection to ordination. Therefore, we recommend A. B. for ordination. In witness whereof, we have hereunto set our hands this _____ day of _____, in the year of our Lord _____ (Signed) _____

(g) The testimonial having been presented to the Bishop, and there being no sufficient objection on medical, psychological, moral, doctrinal, or spiritual grounds, the Bishop may ordain the Candidate to the Diaconate under this canon; and at the time of ordination the Candidate shall subscribe publicly and make, in the presence of the Bishop, the declaration required in Article VIII of the Constitution.

Sec. 67. Ordination to the Priesthood

(a) A person may be ordained Priest

    (1) after at least six months as a ~~Candidate~~ Deacon under this canon , and

    (2) upon attainment of at least twenty-four years of age.

    (3) *If the medical examination, psychological examination, and background check have taken place or been updated within 36 months prior to ordination as a Priest.*

(b) The Bishop shall obtain in writing and provide to the Standing Committee:

    (1) an application from the ~~Candidate~~ Deacon requesting ordination as a Priest, including the ~~Candidate's~~ Deacon's dates of admission to Postulancy and Candidacy,

    (2) a letter of support from the ~~Candidate's~~ Deacon's congregation *or other community of faith*, signed by at least two-thirds of the Vestry and the ~~Rector~~ *Member of the Clergy* or other leader exercising oversight~~, or from an authorized representative of the Candidate's congregation or other community of faith~~,

    (3) *evidence of admission to Postulancy and Candidacy, including dates of admission, and ordination to the Diaconate,*

    (4)~~(3)~~ a certificate from the seminary or other program of preparation, showing the ~~Candidate's~~ *Deacon's* scholastic record in the subjects required by the Canons, and giving an evaluation with recommendation as to the ~~Candidate's~~ *Deacon's* other personal qualifications for ordination together with a recommendation regarding ordination *to the Priesthood*, and

(5)~~(4)~~ a statement from the Commission attesting to the successful completion of the program of formation designed during Postulancy under Canon III.8.4, *and recommending the Deacon for ordination to the Priesthood.*

~~(c)~~ ~~The Standing Committee shall obtain:~~

~~(1)~~ ~~the application for ordination specified in Canon III.8.6(b)(i), including the accompanying letter of support by the Candidate's congregation or community of faith specified in Canon III.8.6(b)(ii);~~

~~(2)~~ ~~certificates from the Bishop who admitted the Candidate to Postulancy and Candidacy, giving the dates of admission, and~~

~~(3)~~ ~~a certificate from the Commission attesting to successful completion of the program of formation designed during Postulancy under Canon III.8.4, and recommending the Candidate for ordination to the Priesthood.~~

~~(d)~~(c) On the receipt of such certificates, the Standing Committee, *a majority of all the members consenting,* shall certify that the canonical requirements for ordination to the Priesthood have been met, *and there is no sufficient objection on medical, psychological, moral, doctrinal, or spiritual grounds and that they recommend ordination,* by a testimonial addressed to the Bishop in the form specified below and signed by the ~~President~~ *consenting members* of the Standing Committee.

To the Right Reverend _____, Bishop of _____ We, the Standing Committee of _____, having been duly convened at _____, do testify that A.B., desiring to be ordained to the Priesthood, has presented to us the certificates as required by the Canons indicating A.B.'s preparedness for ordination *to the Priesthood have been met*; and we certify that all canonical requirements for ordination *to the Priesthood* have been met, *and we find no sufficient objection to ordination. Therefore, we recommend A. B. for ordination.* In witness whereof, we have hereunto set our hands this _____ day of _____, in the year of our Lord _____.

(Signed) _____

~~(e)~~(d) The testimonial having been presented to the Bishop, and there being no sufficient objection on medical, psychological, moral, doctrinal, or spiritual grounds, the Bishop may ordain the ~~Candidate~~ *Deacon* to the Priesthood; and at the time of ordination the ~~Candidate~~ *Deacon* shall subscribe publicly and make, in the presence of the Bishop, the declaration required in Article VIII of the Constitution.

(f)(e) No ~~Candidate~~ *Deacon* shall be ordained to the Priesthood until having been appointed to serve in a Parochial Cure within the jurisdiction of this Church, or as a Missionary under the Ecclesiastical Authority of a Diocese, or as an officer of a Missionary Society recognized by the General Convention, or as a Chaplain of the Armed Services of the United States, or as a Chaplain in a recognized hospital or other welfare institution, or as a Chaplain or instructor in a school, college, or other seminary, or with other opportunity for the exercise of the office of Priest within the Church judged appropriate by the Bishop.

~~(g)~~(f) A person ordained to the Diaconate *under Canon III.6* who is subsequently called to the Priesthood shall fulfill the Postulancy and Candidacy requirements set forth in this canon. Upon completion of these requirements, the Deacon may be ordained to the Priesthood.

CANON 9: Of the Life and Work of Priests
Sec. 1. The Bishop and Commission shall require and provide for the continuing education of Priests and keep a record of such education.
Of Mentoring for Newly Ordained Priests
Sec. 2. Each newly ordained priest, whether employed or not, shall be assigned a mentor priest by the Bishop in consultation with the Commission on Ministry. The mentor and new priest shall meet regularly for at least a year to provide guidance, information and a sustained dialogue about priestly ministry.
Of the Appointment of Priests
Sec. ~~2~~3. (a) Rectors.

(1) When a Parish is without a Rector, the Wardens or other officers shall promptly notify the Ecclesiastical Authority in writing. If the Parish shall for thirty days fail to provide services of public worship, the Ecclesiastical Authority shall make provision for such worship.

(2) No Parish may elect a Rector until the names of the proposed nominees have been forwarded to the Ecclesiastical Authority and a time, not exceeding thirty days, given to the Ecclesiastical Authority to communicate with the Vestry, nor until any such communication, has been considered by the Vestry at a meeting duly called and held for that purpose.

(3) Written notice of the election of a Rector, signed by the Wardens, shall be forwarded to the Ecclesiastical Authority. If the Ecclesiastical Authority is satisfied that the person so elected is a duly qualified Priest and that such Priest has accepted the office to which elected, the notice shall be sent to the Secretary of the Convention,

who shall record it. Race, color, ethnic origin, sex, national origin, marital status, sexual orientation, disabilities or age, except as otherwise specified by these Canons, shall not be a factor in the determination of the Ecclesiastical Authority as to whether such person is a duly qualified Priest. The recorded notice shall be sufficient evidence of the relationship between the Priest and the Parish.

(4) ~~Rectors may have a letter of agreement with the Parish setting forth mutual responsibilities, subject to the Bishop's approval~~

(b) Priests-in-Charge. *After consultation with the Vestry,* ~~T~~*t*he Bishop may appoint a Priest to serve as Priest-in-Charge of any congregation in which there is no Rector. In such congregations, the Priest-in-Charge shall exercise the duties of Rector outlined in Canon III.9.4 subject to the authority of the Bishop.

(c) Assistants. A Priest serving as an assistant in a Parish, by whatever title designated, shall be selected by the Rector, and when required by the Canons of the Diocese, subject to the approval of the Vestry, and shall serve under the authority and direction of the Rector. Before the selection of an assistant the name of the Priest proposed for selection shall be made known to the Bishop and a time, not exceeding thirty days, given for the Bishop to communicate with the Rector and Vestry on the proposed selection. Any assistant shall serve at the pleasure of the Rector and may not serve beyond the period of service of the Rector, except that pending the call of a new Rector, an assistant may continue in the service of the Parish if requested to do so by the Vestry under such conditions as the Bishop and Vestry shall determine. *An assistant may continue to serve at the request of a new Rector.* ~~Assistants may have a letter of agreement with the Rector and the Vestry setting forth mutual responsibilities subject to the Bishop's approval.~~

(d) Chaplains.

(1) A Priest may be given ecclesiastical endorsement for service as a Chaplain in the Armed Services of the United States of America or as a Chaplain for the Veterans' Administration, or in any Federal Correctional Institution, by the Office of the Bishop Suffragan for the Armed ~~Services~~ *Forces*, ~~Health Care Ministries and Prison Ministries~~ subject to the approval of the Ecclesiastical Authority of the Diocese in which the Priest is canonically resident.

(2) Any Priest serving on active duty with the Armed Services shall retain the Priest's canonical residence and shall be subject to the ecclesiastical supervision of the

Bishop of the Diocese of which the Priest is canonically resident, even though the Priest's work as a Chaplain shall be subject to the general supervision of the Office of the Bishop Suffragan for the Armed ~~Services~~ *Forces*, ~~Health Care Ministries and Prison Ministries,~~ or such other Bishop as the Presiding Bishop may designate.

(3) Any Priest serving on a military installation or at a Veterans' Administration facility or Federal Correctional Institution shall not be subject to Canons ~~III.9.2(f)(1)~~ *III.9.3.(e)(1)* or ~~III.10.3(a)~~ *III.9.4(a)*. When serving other than on a military installation or at a Veterans' Administration facility, or Federal Correctional Institution, a Chaplain shall be subject to these Sections.

(e) Non-ecclesiastical or Non-parochial Employment of Priests

(1) Any Priest who has left a position in this Church without having received a call to a new *ecclesiastical* position and who desires to continue the exercise of the office of Priest shall notify the Ecclesiastical Authority of the Diocese in which the Priest is canonically resident and shall advise the Bishop that reasonable opportunities for the exercise of the office of Priest exist and that use will be made of such opportunities. After having determined that the person will have and use opportunities for the exercise of the office of Priest, the Bishop, with the advice and consent of the Standing Committee, may approve the Priest's continued exercise of the office on condition that the Priest report annually in writing, in a manner prescribed by the Bishop, as provided in Canon I.6.2.

(2) A Priest who would be permitted under Canon III.~~9.7~~ *18* to renounce the exercise of ordained office, who desires to enter into other than ecclesiastical employment, may declare in writing to the Ecclesiastical Authority of the Diocese in which the Priest is canonically resident a desire to be released from the obligations of the office and a desire to be released from the exercise of the office of Priest. Upon receipt of such declaration, the Ecclesiastical Authority shall proceed in the same manner as if the declaration was one of renunciation of the ordained Priesthood under Canon III.~~9.7~~ *18*.

(3) (i). A Priest not in parochial employment moving to another jurisdiction shall report to the Bishop of that jurisdiction within sixty days of such move.

(ii). The Priest:

(a) May officiate or preach in that

jurisdiction only under the terms of Canon III.9.5(a).

(b) Shall provide notice of such move, in writing and within sixty days, to the Ecclesiastical Authority of the Diocese in which the Priest is canonically resident.

(c) Shall forward a copy of the report required by Canon I.6.2 to the Ecclesiastical Authority to whose jurisdiction the Priest has moved.

(iii). Upon receipt of the notice required by Canon III.9.2(d)(iii)(b)(2), the Ecclesiastical Authority shall provide written notice thereof to the Ecclesiastical Authority into whose jurisdiction the person has moved.

(4) If the Priest fails to comply with the provisions of this Canon, the Bishop of the Diocese in which the Priest is canonically resident may proceed in accordance with Canon IV.11.

Of Letters Dimissory
Sec. 34.

(a) A Priest desiring to become canonically resident within a Diocese shall present to the Ecclesiastical Authority a testimonial from the Ecclesiastical Authority of the Diocese of current canonical residence, which testimonial shall be given by the Ecclesiastical Authority to the applicant, and a duplicate thereof may be sent to the Ecclesiastical Authority of the Diocese to which transfer is proposed. The testimonial shall be accompanied by a statement of the record of payments to The Church Pension Fund by or on behalf of the Priest concerned and shall be in the following words:
I hereby certify that A.B., who has signified to me the desire to be transferred to the Ecclesiastical Authority of _____, is a Priest of _____ in good standing, and has not, so far as I know or believe, been justly liable to evil report, for error in religion or for viciousness of life, for the last three years.

(Date) _____   (Signed) _____

(b) Such a testimonial shall be called Letters Dimissory. If the Ecclesiastical Authority accepts the Letters Dimissory, the canonical residence of the Priest transferred shall date from such acceptance, and prompt notice of acceptance shall be given to the applicant and to the Ecclesiastical Authority issuing the Letters Dimissory.

(c) Letters Dimissory not presented within six months of their date of

(d) receipt by the applicant shall become void.

If a Priest has been called to a Cure in a congregation in another Diocese, the Priest shall present Letters Dimissory. The Ecclesiastical Authority of the Diocese shall accept Letters Dimissory within three months of their receipt unless the Bishop or Standing Committee has received credible information concerning the character *or behavior* of the Priest concerned which would form grounds for canonical inquiry and presentment. In such a case, the Ecclesiastical Authority shall notify the Ecclesiastical Authority of the Diocese in which the Priest is canonically resident and need not accept the Letters Dimissory unless and until the Priest shall be exculpated. The Ecclesiastical Authority shall not refuse to accept Letters Dimissory based on the applicant's race, color, ethnic origin, sex, national origin, marital status, sexual orientation, disabilities or age.

(e) A Priest shall not be in charge of any congregation in the Diocese to which the person moves until obtaining from the Ecclesiastical Authority of that Diocese a certificate in the following words:

I hereby certify that A.B., has been canonically transferred to my jurisdiction and is a Priest in good standing.

(Date) _____ (Signed) _____

(f) (a) No person who has been refused ordination or reception as a Candidate in any Diocese, and is thereafter ordained in another Diocese, shall be transferred to the Diocese in which such refusal has occurred without the consent of its Ecclesiastical Authority.

Of ~~the~~ Priests and Their Duties
Sec. 45.

(a) (1) The Rector shall have full authority and responsibility for the conduct of the worship and the spiritual jurisdiction of the Parish, subject to the Rubrics of the Book of Common Prayer, the Constitution and Canons of this Church, and the pastoral direction of the Bishop.

(2) For the purposes of the office and for the full and free discharge of all functions and duties pertaining thereto, the Rector shall at all times be entitled to the use and control of the Church and Parish buildings together with all appurtenances and furniture.

(b) (1) It shall be the duty of the Priest to ensure all persons in their charge receive i*I*nstruction in the Holy Scriptures; in the subjects contained in An Outline of the Faith, commonly called the Catechism; in the doctrine, discipline and worship of this Church; and in the exercise of their ministry as baptized persons.

(2) It shall be the duty of Priests to ensure that all persons in their charge are instructed concerning Christian stewardship, including:

    (i) reverence for the creation and the right use of God's gifts;

    (ii) generous and consistent offering of time, talent, and treasure for the mission and ministry of the Church at home and abroad;

    (iii) the biblical standard of the tithe for financial stewardship; and

    (iv) the responsibility of all persons to make a will as prescribed in the Book of Common Prayer~~, page 445~~.

(3) It shall be the duty of Priests to ensure that persons be prepared for Baptism. Before baptizing infants or children, Priests shall ensure that sponsors be prepared by instructing both the parents and the Godparents concerning the significance of Holy Baptism, the responsibilities of parents and Godparents for the Christian training of the baptized child, and how these obligations may properly be discharged.

(4) It shall be the duty of Priests to encourage and ensure the preparation of persons for Confirmation, Reception, and the Reaffirmation of Baptismal Vows, and to be ready to present them to the Bishop with a list of their names.

(5) On notice being received of the Bishop's intention to visit any congregation, the Rector shall announce the fact to the congregation. At every visitation it shall be the duty of the Rector and the Wardens, Vestry or other officers, to exhibit to the Bishop the Parish Register and to give information as to the state of the congregation, spiritual and temporal, in such categories as the Bishop shall have previously requested in writing.

(6) The Alms and Contributions, not otherwise specifically designated, at the Administration of the Holy Communion on one Sunday in each calendar month, and other offerings for the poor, shall be deposited with the Rector or with such Church officer as the Rector shall appoint to be applied to such pious and charitable uses as the Rector shall determine. When a Parish is without a Rector or Priest-in-Charge, the Vestry shall designate a member of the Parish to fulfill this function.

(7) Whenever the House of Bishops shall publish a Pastoral Letter, it shall be the duty of the Rector to read it to the congregation on some occasion of public worship on a

		Lord's Day, or to cause copies of the same to be distributed to the members of the congregation, not later than thirty days after receipt.
	(8)	Whenever the House of Bishops shall adopt a Position Paper, ~~it may~~ and require communication of the content of the Paper to the membership of the Church, *the Rector shall so communicate the Paper* in the manner set forth in the preceding section of this Canon.
(c)	(1)	It shall be the duty of the Rector to record in the Parish Register all Baptisms, Confirmations (including the canonical equivalents in Canon I.17.1(d)), Marriages and Burials.
	(2)	The registry of each Baptism shall be signed by the officiating Member of the Clergy.
	(3)	The Rector shall record in the Parish Register all persons who have received Holy Baptism, all communicants, all persons who have received Confirmation (including the canonical equivalents in Canon I.17.1(d)), all persons who have died, and all persons who have been received or removed by letter of transfer. The Rector shall also designate in the Parish Register the names of (1) those persons whose domicile is unknown, (2) those persons whose domicile is known but are inactive, and (3) those families and persons who are active within the congregation. The Parish Register shall remain with the congregation at all times.

Of Licenses
Sec. 56.

(a)		No Priest shall preach, minister the Sacraments, or hold any public service, within the limits of any Diocese other than the Diocese in which the Priest is canonically resident for more than two months without a license from the Ecclesiastical Authority of the Diocese in which the Priest desires to so officiate. No Priest shall be denied such a license on account of the Priest's race, color, ethnic origin, sex, national origin, marital status, sexual orientation, disabilities or age, except as otherwise provided in these Canons.
(b)		No Priest shall preach, read prayers in public worship, or perform any similar function, in a congregation without the consent of the Rector or Priest-in-Charge of that congregation, except as follows:
	(1)	In the absence or disability of the Rector or Priest-in-Charge, and if provision has not been made for the stated services of the congregation or other community of faith, a Warden may give such consent.
	(2)	(1) If there be two or more congregations or Churches in

one Cure, as provided by Canon I.13.3(b), consent may be given by the majority of the Priests-in-Charge of such congregations, or by the Bishop; Provided, that nothing in this Section shall prevent any Member of the Clergy of this Church from officiating, with the consent of the Rector or Priest-in-Charge, in the Church or place of public worship used by the congregation of the consenting Rector or Priest-in-Charge, or in private for members of the congregation; or in the absence of the Rector or Priest-in-Charge, with the consent of the Wardens or Trustees of the congregation; Provided further, that the license of the Ecclesiastical Authority provided in Canon III.9.5(a), if required, be obtained.

(3) This Canon shall not apply to any Church, Chapel, or Oratory, which is part of the premises of an incorporated institution created by legislative authority, provided that such place of worship is designated and set apart for the convenience and use of such institution, and not as a place for public or parochial worship.

(c) No Rector or Priest-in-Charge of any congregation of this Church, or if there be none, no Wardens, Members of the Vestry, or Trustees of any congregation, shall permit any person to officiate in the congregation without sufficient evidence that such person is duly licensed and ordained and in good standing in this Church; Provided, nothing in these Canons shall prevent:

(1) The General Convention, by Canon or otherwise, from authorizing persons to officiate in congregations in accordance with such terms as it deems appropriate; or

(2) The Bishop of any Diocese from giving permission

(i) To a Member of the Clergy of this Church, to invite Clergy of another Church to assist in the Book of Common Prayer Offices of Holy Matrimony or of the Burial of the Dead, or to read Morning or Evening Prayer, in the manner specified in Canon III.9.5; or

(ii) To Clergy of any other Church to preach the Gospel, or in ecumenical settings to assist in the administration of the sacraments; or

(iii) To godly persons who are not Clergy of this Church to address the Church on special occasions.

(iv) To the ~~Rector~~*Member of the Clergy* or Priest-in-Charge of a congregation or if there be none, to the Wardens, to invite Clergy ordained in another Church in communion with this Church to officiate on an occasional basis, provided that such clergy are instructed to teach and act *in a manner* consistent with the Doctrine, Discipline, and Worship of this Church.

(d) If any ~~Rector~~*Member of the Clergy* or Priest-in-Charge, as a result of disability or any other cause, shall neglect to perform regular services in the congregation, and refuse, without good cause, to consent to any other duly qualified Member of the Clergy to perform such services, the Wardens, Vestry, or Trustees of the congregation shall, upon providing evidence to the Ecclesiastical Authority of the Diocese of such neglect or refusal and with the written consent of the Ecclesiastical Authority, have the authority to permit any duly qualified Member of the Clergy to officiate.

(e) (1) Any Priest desiring to officiate temporarily outside the jurisdiction of this Church but in a Church in communion with this Church, shall obtain from the Ecclesiastical Authority of the Diocese in which the person is canonically resident, a testimonial which shall set forth the person's official standing, and which may be in the following words:

I hereby certify that A.B., who has signified to me the desire to be permitted to officiate temporarily in churches not under the jurisdiction of The Episcopal Church, yet in communion with this Church, is a Priest of _____ in good standing, and as such is entitled to the rights and privileges of that Order.

(Date) _____ (Signed) _____

Such testimonial shall be valid for one year and shall be returned to the Ecclesiastical Authority at the end of that period.

(2) The Ecclesiastical Authority giving such testimonial shall record its issuance, the name of the Priest to whom issued, its date and the date of its return.

~~Of Disagreements Affecting Pastoral Relation~~
~~Sec. 6. (a)~~

~~(a)~~ ~~Reconciliation. In a Parish, when the pastoral relationship between a Rector and the Vestry or congregation is imperiled by disagreement or dissension, and the issues are deemed serious by the Rector or by a majority vote of the Vestry, either party may petition the Ecclesiastical Authority, in writing, to intervene and assist the parties in their efforts to resolve the disagreement. The Ecclesiastical Authority shall initiate appropriate proceedings under the circumstances, which may include the appointment of a~~

~~consultant. The parties to the disagreement, following the recommendations of the Ecclesiastical Authority, shall labor in good faith to reconcile their differences. Whenever the Standing Committee is the Ecclesiastical Authority, it shall request the Bishop of a neighboring Diocese to perform the duties of the Ecclesiastical Authority under this Canon.~~

~~(b)~~ ~~Dissolution~~

~~(1)   Except upon mandatory resignation by reason of age, a Rector may not resign as Rector of a Parish without the consent of its Vestry, nor may any Rector canonically or lawfully elected and in charge of a Parish be removed by the Vestry without the consent of the Rector, except as hereinafter provided.~~

~~(2)   If for any urgent reason a Rector or Vestry desires a dissolution of the pastoral relation, and the parties cannot agree, either party may give notice in writing to the Ecclesiastical Authority of the Diocese. Whenever the Standing Committee is the Ecclesiastical Authority of the Diocese, it shall request the Bishop of another Diocese to perform the duties of the Ecclesiastical Authority under this Canon.~~

~~(3)   Within sixty days of receipt of the written notice the Bishop, as chief pastor of the Diocese, shall mediate the differences between Rector and Vestry in every informal way which the Bishop deems proper and may appoint a committee of at least one Presbyter and one Lay Person, none of whom may be members of the Parish involved, to make a report to the Bishop.~~

~~(4)   If the differences between the parties are not resolved after completion of the mediation, the Bishop shall proceed as follows:~~

~~(i)   The Bishop shall give notice to the Rector and Vestry that a godly judgment will be rendered after consultation with the Standing Committee and that either party has a right within ten days to request in writing an opportunity to confer with the Standing Committee before such consultation.~~

~~(ii)   If a timely request is made, the President of the Standing Committee shall set a date for a conference within thirty days of the request.~~

~~(iii)   At the conference each party shall be entitled to representation and to present its position fully.~~

~~(iv)   Within thirty days after the conference, or after the Bishop's notice if no conference is~~

~~requested, the Bishop shall confer with the Standing Committee, receive its recommendation and thereafter, as final arbiter and judge, render a godly judgment.~~

~~(v) Upon the request of either party the Bishop shall explain the reasons for the judgment. If the explanation is in writing, copies shall be delivered to both parties.~~

~~(vi) If the pastoral relation is to be continued, the Bishop shall require the parties to agree on definitions of responsibility and accountability for the Rector and the Vestry.~~

~~(vii) If the pastoral relation is to be dissolved:~~

~~(a) The Bishop shall direct the Secretary of the Convention to record the dissolution.~~

~~(b) The judgment shall include such terms and conditions including financial settlements as shall be deemed by the Bishop to be just and compassionate.~~

~~(5) In either event the Bishop shall offer supportive services to the Priest and the Parish.~~

~~(6) In the event of the failure or refusal of either party to comply with the terms of the judgment, the Bishop may impose such penalties as may be set forth in the Constitution and Canons of the Diocese, and in the absence thereof, may:~~

~~(i) In the case of a Rector, suspend the Rector from the exercise of the priestly office until the Priest shall comply with the judgment.~~

~~(ii) In the case of a Vestry, invoke any available sanctions including recommending to the Convention of the Diocese that the Parish be placed under the supervision of the Bishop as a Mission until it has complied with the judgment.~~

~~(7) The Bishop may extend the time periods provided by this Canon, for cause shown, provided that all be done to expedite these proceedings. All parties shall be notified in writing of the length of any extension.~~

~~(8) (a). Statements made during the course of proceedings under this Canon are not discoverable nor admissible in any proceedings under Title IV, provided that such does not require the exclusion of evidence in any proceeding under the Canons which is otherwise discoverable and~~

admissible. ~~(b). In the course of proceedings under this Canon, if a charge is made by the Vestry against the Rector that could give rise to a disciplinary proceeding under Canon IV.1, all proceedings under this Canon with respect to such charge shall be suspended until the charge has been resolved or withdrawn.~~

~~(9)~~ ~~This Canon shall not apply in any Diocese which has established, by Canon, a provision on this subject consistent with this Canon.~~

~~Of Renunciation~~
~~Sec. 7. (a)~~

~~(a)~~ ~~A Priest of this Church not subject to the provisions of Canon IV.8 may declare, in writing, to the Ecclesiastical Authority of the Diocese of canonical residence, a renunciation of the Priesthood of this Church, and a desire to be removed there from. Upon receipt of such declaration, the Bishop shall record it. The Bishop, upon determining that the person is not subject to the provisions of Canon IV.8 but is acting voluntarily and for causes that do not affect the Priest's moral character, shall present the declaration to the clerical members of the Standing Committee. With the advice and consent of a majority of such members, the Bishop may pronounce that such renunciation is accepted, and the Priest is released from the obligations of the office and deprived of the rights conferred in ordination. The Bishop shall also declare that the renunciation was for causes that do not affect the person's moral character and, if requested, shall give a certificate to this effect to the person so removed from the Priesthood.~~

~~(b)~~ ~~If a Priest making the declaration provided in the preceding Section of this Canon is under Presentment for any canonical Offense, or has been placed on Trial for the same, the Ecclesiastical Authority to whom such declaration is made shall not consider or act upon such declaration until after the Presentment is dismissed or the Trial concluded and the Priest judged not to have committed an Offense.~~

~~(c)~~ ~~If a renunciation is accepted, the Bishop shall pronounce a declaration of removal in the presence of two or more Priests, and shall enter it in the official records of the Diocese of canonical residence. The Bishop who pronounces the declaration of removal shall give notice thereof in writing to every Member of the Clergy, each Vestry, the Secretary of the Convention and the Standing Committee of the Diocese in which the Priest was canonically resident, and to all Bishops of this Church, the Ecclesiastical Authority of each Diocese of this Church, the Presiding Bishop, the Recorder, the Secretary of the House of Bishops, the Secretary of the House of Deputies, the Church Pension Fund, and the Church Deployment Board.~~

~~(d) A person removed from the Priesthood pursuant to this section may apply to the Bishop in writing for restoration to the Priesthood, and the Bishop, with the consent of the Standing Committee, may restore the person as a Priest.~~

~~(e) In case of a vacancy in the episcopate in a Diocese, the Ecclesiastical Authority may request the President of the House of Bishops of the Province, or the President's designee, to exercise the canonical authority assigned to the Bishop by this section.~~

Of Retirement

Sec. ~~87~~. Upon attaining the age of seventy-two years, a Priest occupying any position in this Church shall resign that position and retire from active service, and the resignation shall be accepted. Thereafter, the Priest may accept any position in this Church, except the position or positions from which resignation pursuant to this Section has occurred; Provided,

(a) tenure in the position shall be for a period of not more than one year, which period may be renewed from time to time,

(b) service in the position shall have the express approval of the Bishop and Standing Committee of the Diocese in which the service is to be performed, acting in consultation with the Ecclesiastical Authority of the Diocese in which the Priest is canonically resident.

(c) Anything in this Canon to the contrary notwithstanding, a Priest who has served in a non-stipendiary capacity in a position before retirement may, at the Bishop's request, serve in the same position for six months thereafter, and this period may be renewed from time to time.

The Bishop of North Carolina moved to amend the substitute resolution.

Proposed Amendment:

In Canon III.1, under Sec. 2, add the words "no person shall be denied access to the discernment process for any ministry, lay or ordained, in this church" and delete the words "exercise of any ministry".

Motion carried
Amendment adopted

The Bishop of North Carolina accepted to add "the discernment process" and delete "or the exercise of".

The ammendment reads as follows:

Sec. 2. No person shall be denied ~~the exercise of~~ access to the discernment process for any ministry, lay or ordained, in this Church because of race, color, ethnic origin, national origin, sex, marital status, sexual orientation, disabilities or age, except as otherwise provided by these Canons. No right to licensing, ordination, or election is hereby established.

The Bishop of Virginia moved to amend the substitute resolution.

Proposed Amendment:
In Canon III.4, under Sec. 6., delete "Chalice" and restore the words "consecrated elements".

Motion carried
Amendment adopted

The amendment reads as follows:
Sec. 6. A Eucharistic Minister is a lay person authorized to administer the Consecrated Elements ~~Chalice~~ at a Celebration of Holy Eucharist. A Eucharistic Minister ~~shall~~*should normally* act under the direction of a Deacon, if any, *or otherwise, the Member of the Clergy or other leader exercising oversight of the comgregation or other community of faith.*

Bishop Joslin moved to amend the substitute resolution.

Proposed Amendment:
In Canon III.5, under Sec. 1(c), after the words "Bishops of the Province", add "or some other bishop with the consent of the President of the House of Bishops of the Province".

Motion defeated
Amendment defeated

The Bishop of Kentucky moved to amend the substitute resolution.

Proposed Amendment:
In Canon III.6, under Sec. 1(a), delete the words "who has been a member of the Episcopal Church for the preceding three years."

Motion carried
Amendment adopted

The amendment reads as follows:
(a) Nomination. A confirmed adult communicant in good standing, ~~who has been a member of the Episcopal Church for the preceding three years,~~ may be ~~n~~Nominated ~~to be a Postulant~~ for ordination to the diaconate by the person's congregation or other communtiy of faith. The ~~n~~Nomination shall be in writing, ~~signed by the Rector or Priest-in-Charge and at least two thirds of the Vestry or comparable body,~~ and shall include:

The Bishop of Lexington moved to amend the substitute resolution.

Proposed Amendment:
In the first sentence of Canon III.6, under Sec. 6, delete "shall" and replace it with "may."

Motion defeated
Amendment defeated

The Bishop of Northern California moved to amend the substitute resolution.

Proposed Amendment:

In Canon III.6, under Sec.1(b), restore the term "postulancy" in place of "admission" and delete "nominee" and replace it with "postulant" in the entire section.

Motion carried
Amendment adopted

The amendment reads as follows:

Postulancy ~~Admission~~Postulancy ~~Admission~~ is a*the* time ~~between nomination and candidacy and includes a process~~ of exploration of and decision on the ~~Postulant's Nominee's~~ Postulant's call to the diaconate.

(1) ~~During~~ Postulancy t*T*here shall be a thorough investigation of the Postulant ~~Nominee~~ which shall include:

    (i) a background check, and

    (ii) medical and *complete* psychological ~~examination~~*evaluation* by professionals approved by the Bishop, using forms prepared for ~~that~~*the* purpose by The Church Pension Fund, *and if desired or necessary, psychiatric referral.*

    (iii) Reports of all investigations and examinations shall be kept on file by the Bishop. ~~The Bishop, with regard for confidentiality, may make information from the reports available to the Commission.~~

(2) The Bishop, or the Bishop's designee, may interview the Postulant ~~Nominee~~. The Commission or a designated committee shall interview the Postulant ~~Nominee~~, and the Commission or designated committee shall submit a recommendation to the Bishop.

(3) The Bishop may then admit the Postulant ~~Nominee~~ as a Candidate, informing the Candidate and the ~~Candidate's Rector or Priest-in-Charge~~ *Member of the Clergy or other leader of the Candidate's discernment community* in writing.

The Bishop of Tennessee moved to amend the substitute resolution.

Proposed Amendment:

In Canon III.7, under Sec. 7(c), add the words "and may" and, after the word "faith", add "under the direct supervision of the Bishop or the Bishop's designee". Delete "but no deacon shall".

The question was called to terminate debate.

Motion carried
Debate terminated

A vote was taken on the amendment.

Motion defeated
Amendment defeated

MINNEAPOLIS MEETING   HOUSE OF BISHOPS

The Bishop Suffragan for Chaplaincies moved to amend the substitute resolution.

Proposed Amendment:
Add words "under the guidance of the Presiding Bishop or the Bishop Suffragan of the Armed Forces."

Motion defeated
Amendment defeated

The Bishop of Northwestern Pennsylvania moved to amend the substitute resolution.

Proposed Amendment:
In Canon III.7, under Sec. 4(c), after "institution", delete the comma, insert a period and delete "or serve as Deacons in the Armed Forces".

Motion carried
Amendment adopted

The amendment reads as follows:
(c) Deacons may accept a~~chaplaincy~~ *chaplaincies* in any hospital, prison, or other institution~~, or serve as Deacons in the Armed Services~~ *Forces*.

The Bishop of Minnesota moved to amend the substitute resolution.

Proposed Amendment:
In Canon III.7, under Sec. 4, restore subsection (a) and re-number the subsequent subsections.

The question was called to terminate debate on the amendment.

Motion carried
Debate terminated

A vote was taken on the amendment.

Motion carried
Amendment adopted

The amendment reads as follows with the subsequent sections re-numbered:
(a) Deacons may have a letter of agreement, subject to the Bishop's approval, setting forth mutual responsibilites in the assignment.

The Bishop of Northern Indiana moved to amend the substitute resolution.

Proposed Amendment:
In Canon III.8, under Sec. 3(b)(1), delete "and has been a member of the Episcopal Church for the preceding three years".

The question was called to terminate debate.

Motion carried
Debate terminated

A vote was taken on the amendment.

Motion carried
Amendment adopted

The amendment reads as follows:
(b) Before granting admission as a Postulant, the Bishop:
(1) shall determine that the person is a confirmed adult communicant in good standing of a congregation or other community of faith, ~~and has been a member of the Episcopal Church for the preceeding three years~~, and
(2)....

The Bishop of Vermont moved to amend the substitute resolution.

Proposed Amendment:
In Canon III.8, under Sec. 2(d)(4), at the end of the sentence, add "as prescribed in Sec. 6 and 7 of this canon".
The question was called to terminate debate.

Motion carried
Debate terminated

A vote was taken on the proposed amendment.

Motion carried
Amendment adopted

The amendment reads as follows:
(4) The Standing Committee shall certify that all canonical requirements for ordination have been met *and make a recommendation regarding ordination* <u>as prescribed in Sec. 6 and 7 of this canon</u>.

The Bishop of Minnesota moved to amend the substitute resolution.

Proposed Amendment:
In Canon III.9, under Sec. 3(a)(2) and under Sec. 3(c), delete "thirty" and insert "sixty" before "days."

Motion carried
Amendment adopted

The amendment reads as follows:
Sec. 3(a)(2) No Parish may elect a Rector until the names of the proposed nominees have been forwarded to the Ecclesiastical Authority and a time, not exceeding ~~thirty~~ <u>sixty</u> days, given to the Ecclesiastical Authority to communicate with the Vestr, not until any such communication has been considered by the Vestry at a meeting fuly called and held for that purpose.
Sec. 3(c) Assistants. A Priest serving as an assistant in a Parish, by whatever title designated, shall be selected by the Rector, and when required by the Canons of the Diocese, subject to the approval of the Vestry, and shall serve under the authoriy and direction of the Rector. Before the selection of an assistant the name of the Priest proposed for selection shall be made known to the Bishop and a time, not exceeding ~~thirty~~ <u>sixty</u> days, given for the Bishop to communicate communicate with the Rector and Vestry on the proposed selection. Any assistant shall serve at the pleasure of the Rector and may not serve beyond the period of service of the Rector, except that pending the call of a new Rector, an assistant may continue in the service of the Parish if requested to do so by the Vestry under such conditions as the Bishop and Vestry shall determine. *An assistant may continue to serve at the request*

MINNEAPOLIS MEETING — HOUSE OF BISHOPS

of a new Rector. ~~Assistants may have a letter of agreement with the Rector and the Vestry setting forth mutual responsibilities subject to the Bishop's approval.~~"

The Bishop of Oregon moved to amend the substitute resolution.

Proposed Amendment:

In Canon III.9, under Sec. 3(a), restore subsection (4) and in Canon III.9, under Sec. 3(c), restore the last sentence of the subsection.

Motion carried
Amendment adopted

The amendment reads as follows:
Sec. 3(a) <u>(4) Rectors may have a letter of agreement with the Parish setting forth mutual responsibilities, subject to the Bishop's approval.</u>
Sec. 3(c) Assistants. A Priest serving as an assistant in a Parish, by whatever title designated, shall be selected by the Rector, and when required by the Canons of the Diocese, subject to the approval of the Vestry, and shall serve under the authoriy and direction of the Rector. Before the selection of an assistant the name of the Priest proposed for selection shall be made known to the Bishop and a time, not exceeding ~~thirty~~ <u>sixty</u> days, given for the Bishop to communicate communicate with the Rector and Vestry on the proposed selection. Any assistant shall serve at the pleasure of the Rector and may not serve beyond the period of service of the Rector, except that pending the call of a new Rector, an assistant may continue in the service of the Parish if requested to do so by the Vestry under such conditions as the Bishop and Vestry shall determine. *An assistant may continue to serve at the request of a new Rector.* <u>Assistants may have a letter of agreement with the Rector and the Vestry setting forth mutual responsibilities subject to the Bishop's approval.</u>

The Bishop of Upper South Carolina moved to amend the substitute resolution.

Proposed Amendment:

In Canon III.9.5, under subsection (a)(2), delete the period at the end of the sentence, add a comma and the words "and to access to all records and registers maintained by or on behalf of the congregation."

Motion carried
Amendment adopted

The amendment reads as follows:
(a)(2) For the purposes of the office and for the full and free discharge of all funtions and duties pertaining thereto, the Rector shall at all times be entitled to the use and control of the Church and Parish buildings together with all appurtenances and furniture<u>, and to access to all records and registers maintained by or on behalf of the congregation</u>.

The Bishop of Northwestern Pennsylvania moved to amend the substitute resolution.

JOURNAL NINTH DAY

Proposed Amendment:
In Canon III.9, under re-numbered Sec. 7, in the second sentence after "in this Church" add "including, with the permission of the ecclesiastical authority," Delete the word "except" in the same sentence.

Motion carried
Amendment adopted

The amendment reads as follows:
Sec. ~~8~~7. Upon attaining the age of seventy-two years, a Priest occupying any position in this Church shall resign that position and retire from active service, and the resignation shall be accepted. Thereafter, the Priest may accept any position in this Church, including, with the permission of the Ecclesiastical Authority ~~except~~ the position or positions from the resignation pursuant to this Section has occured; Provided,...

The Bishop of Atlanta moved to amend the substitute resolution.

Proposed Amendment:
In Canon III.9.7, under subsection (b), delete "and standing committee".

Motion carried
Amendment adopted

The amendment reads as follows:
(b) service in the position shall have the express approval of the Bishop ~~and Standing Committee~~ of the Diocese in which the service is to be performed, acting in consultation with the Ecclesiastical Authority of the Diocese in which the Priest is canonically resident.

The Bishop of Pennsylvania moved to amend the substitute resolution.

Proposed Amendment:
In Canon III.9.6, under subsection (a), at the end of the last sentence, add the sentence "Upon expiration or withdrawal of a license, a priest shall cease immediately to officiate."

Motion carried
Amendment adopted

The amendment reads as follows:
(a) No priest shall preach, minister the Sacraments, or hold any public service, within the limits of any Diocese other than the Diocese in which the Priest is canonically resident for more than two months without a license from the Ecclesiastical Authority for the Diocese in which the Priest desires to so officiate. No Priest shall be denied such a license on account of the Priest's race, color, ethnic origin, sex, national origin, marital status, sexual orientation, disabilities or age, except as otehrwise provided in these Canons. <u>Upon expiration or withdrawal of a license, a Priest shall cease immediately to officiate.</u>

A vote was taken on substitute Resolution A111 as amended.

Motion carried
Resolution adopted with amendment
(Communicated to the House of Deputies in HB Message #210)

National and International Concerns
The House of Bishops Committee on National and International Concerns presented its Report #5 on Resolution D050 (Cuba–Honoring Commitments) and moved adoption.

Original Text of Resolution:
(D050)
Resolved, the House of Deputies concurring, That the 74th General Convention, through both its national and diocesan leadership, request our federal legislative delegations in Washington, D.C. to encourage immediate action on the filed applications to release pension payments, restricted endowment, and trust income held by ECUSA for the Diocese of Cuba, and other grants the disbursement of which was stopped by the Patriot Act passed after September 11th by Congress; and be it further
Resolved, That we continue to work with the Anglican Church of Canada, which continues to provide oversight and assistance to the Cuban Church.

Motion carried
Resolution adopted
(Communicated to the House of Deputies in HB Message #211)

Recess
Following announcements by the Secretary, the House of Bishops Committee on Dispatch of Business moved that the House stand in recess until 10:30 a.m. on the Tenth Legislative Day.

Motion carried

The House recessed at 6:05 p.m. with prayers led by Chaplain Battle.

JOURNAL

TENTH DAY

TENTH DAY

Friday
August 8, 2003

MORNING SESSION

The House reconvened at 10:42 a.m. with the Presiding Bishop in the chair.
Table conversation was allowed for five minutes.
The House resumed at 10:49 a.m.

Choir
The Presiding Bishop thanked the Choir of Bishops and Spouses for their participation in today's Eucharist.

Announcement
The Bishop of Maryland spoke about Companion Diocese visitors at the General Convention.

Agenda of the Day
The House of Bishops Committee on Dispatch of Business moved to adopt the agenda of the day.

Motion carried

Previous Day's Minutes
The House of Bishops Committee on Dispatch of Business moved to dispense with the reading of the Previous Day's Minutes.

Motion carried

Messages from the House of Deputies
The Secretary announced that the following messages had been received from the House of Deputies.

HD Message #188: D052 (Rescind Policy of Disinvestment in Defense Contractors)
The House of Deputies adopted the resolution.

HD Message #189: A135 (Holy Habits)
The House of Deputies concurred.

HD Message #190: A138 (50/50 Outreach for Congregations)
The House of Deputies concurred.

HD Message #191: A139 (Affirm the Work of TENS)
The House of Deputies concurred.

HD Message #192: A140 (Mission Funding)
The House of Deputies concurred.

HD Message #193: B003 (Study and Present the Reuilly Accord)
The House of Deputies concurred.

HD Message #194: B006 (Dialogue with Reformed Episcopal Church)

MINNEAPOLIS MEETING HOUSE OF BISHOPS

	The House of Deputies concurred.
HD Message #195:	A087 (Interim Eucharistic Sharing with the Moravian Church in America, Northern and Southern Provinces)
	The House of Deputies concurred.
HD Message #196:	A086 (Lutheran Ordination Bylaw)
	The House of Deputies concurred.
HD Message #197:	D058 (Providing Assisted Hearing Devices)
	The House of Deputies discharged the resolution.
HD Message #198:	A034 (United Nations Millennium Development Goals)
	The House of Deputies discharged the resolution.
HD Message #199:	A092 (Reauthorize Enriching Our Worship work)
	The House of Deputies concurred.
HD Message #200:	A100 (Revise Lesser Feasts and Fasts 2000)
	The House of Deputies concurred.
HD Message #201:	A068 (Episcopal Church Website)
	The House of Deputies discharged the resolution.
HD Message #202:	A078 (Next Generation Mentoring)
	The House of Deputies discharged the resolution.
HD Message #203:	D084 (LISTSERV Appreciation)
	The House of Deputies adopted the resolution.
HD Message #204:	D085 (Gratitude to Church Periodical Club)
	The House of Deputies adopted the resolution.
HD Message #205:	D089 (Thanks to Bishop Jelinek and the Diocese of Minnesota)
	The House of Deputies adopted the resolution.
HD Message #206:	D090 (Nancy Piatkowski)
	The House of Deputies adopted the resolution.
HD Message #207:	D092 (Greetings to the Archbishop of Canterbury)
	The House of Deputies adopted the resolution.
HD Message #208:	D088 (Ministry to the Deaf)
	The House of Deputies adopted the resolution.
HD Message #209:	D087 (Evening of Conversations)
	The House of Deputies adopted the resolution.
HD Message #210:	D086 (Budget for The Episcopal Church 2004–2006)
	The House of Deputies adopted the resolution.
HD Message # 211:	A001 (Budget Appropriation for the Archives of the Episcopal Church)
	The House of Deputies discharged the resolution.
HD Message #212:	A002 (Budget Appropriation for the Board for Church Deployment)
	The House of Deputies discharged the resolution.
HD Message #213:	A003 (Budget Appropriation for the General Board of Examining Chaplains)
	The House of Deputies discharged the resolution.

HD Message #214:	A004 (General Ordination Exam Fee)
	The House of Deputies discharged the resolution.
HD Message #215:	A157 (Joint Standing Committee on Program, Budget and Finance Budget Appropriation)
	The House of Deputies discharged the resolution.
HD Message #216:	A158 (Title IV Budget Appropriation)
	The House of Deputies discharged the resolution.
HD Message #217:	A065 (Leadership Programs for 18–25 Year-Olds)
	The House of Deputies concurred.
HD Message #218:	A021 (Broadening HIV Prevention Methods)
	The House of Deputies concurred.
HD Message #219:	A088 (Response to Gift of Authority)
	The House of Deputies concurred.
HD Message #220:	D009 (Support 2008 Anglican Gathering)
	The House of Deputies concurred.
HD Message #221:	D030 (Funding Regional Ministry vs Political Advocacy)
	The House of Deputies rejected the resolution.
HD Message #222:	D059 (Justice for Juveniles)
	The House of Deputies discharged the resolution.
HD Message #223:	A014 (Approve Research on Human Stem Cells)
	The House of Deputies concurred.
HD Message #224:	C001 (Opposition to Reparative/Conversion Therapy)
	The House of Deputies discharged the resolution.
HD Message #225:	D029 (Reparative Therapy)
	The House of Deputies discharged the resolution.
HD Message #226:	C051 (Blessing of Committed Same–Gender Relationships)
	The House of Deputies concurred.
HD Message #227:	Special Order of Debate on C051.
	The House of Deputies adopted the Special Order with amendment.

Evangelism

The House of Bishops Committee on Evangelism presented its Report #6 on HD Message #43 on Resolution A073 (Plant New Churches) and moved concurrence.

The House concurred
(Communicated to the House of Deputies in HB Message #212)

Final Text of Resolution:

(A073)
Resolved, **That the 74th General Convention direct the Congregational Development Unit of the Episcopal Church Center to:**
develop a system for identifying persons with the skills and temperament to plant new churches and/or revitalize existing congregations;

in cooperation with the Office on Ministry Development, develop and recommend practices for recruiting, training, deploying, and retaining such persons;

develop and carry out events to include an annual national conference of church planters to share stories and resources;

develop training and mentoring programs for laypersons and congregations involved in church planting;

through the office of the Director of Research at the Episcopal Church Center, conduct and fund research into how other denominations plant and sustain new churches, with special emphasis on learning best practices for planting churches in less affluent areas or areas with negative population growth;

and make an annual report to the Executive Council and The Episcopal Church at-large on the net increase in new church starts; and be it further

Resolved, That we commend the work already begun by the Congregational Development Unit of the Episcopal Church Center.

The House of Bishops Committee on Evangelism presented its Report #7 on HD Message #137 on Resolution A077 (Trained Leadership) and moved concurrence.
                   The House concurred
(Communicated to the House of Deputies in HB Message #213)

Final Text of Resolution:
(A077)

Resolved, That the 74th General Convention adopt a vision as part of the 20/20 initiative that there shall be effective, well-organized ministries with children, youth, and young adults in every congregation where appropriate; and there shall be campus ministries in all colleges and universities where appropriate; and be it further

Resolved, That the 74th General Convention commend the work of the Ministries with Young People Cluster, which has three networks: (1) youth ministries, (2) Christian education ministries, and (3) higher education ministries; and be it further

Resolved, That the 74th General Convention direct the Ministries with Young People Cluster to create an additional network for young adult ministries; and be it further

Resolved, That in order to accomplish these training goals by 2009 the Youth Ministries Cluster, in coordination with the Standing Commission on Domestic Mission and Evangelism, call upon their provincial networks to develop and implement in the dioceses, training strategies that include, but are not limited to:

 education in leadership development;

 sharing of technology, training resources, curricula, theological, and multicultural resources;

practical application for life-long Christian formation;
the strengthening of the existing networks in dioceses and provinces; and be it further
Resolved, That the 74th General Convention, request the Joint Standing Committee on Program, Budget and Finance to consider a budget allocation of $250,000 per year for each of the four ministry networks (1) youth ministries, (2) Christian education ministries, (3) higher education ministries, and (4) young adult ministries for a budget allocation of $3,000,000 for implementation of this resolution; and be it further
Resolved, That the office of the Treasurer of the Episcopal Church Center in cooperation with the various dioceses as facilitated by the Provincial Leadership Conference establish a fair share strategy for fund distribution to be reported to the 75th General Convention.

Stewardship and Development
The House of Bishops Committee on Stewardship and Development presented its Report #11 on HD Message #90 on Resolution D046 (Stewardship of Water) and moved concurrence.
The House concurred
(Communicated to the House of Deputies in HB Message #214)

Final Text of Resolution:
(D046)
Resolved, That the 74th General Convention urge dioceses, congregations, and communicants to regard water resources as precious, and to recognize that the right use of water is an explicit means to show love for one's neighbor, since water connects people and all creatures throughout the global community; and be it further
Resolved, That the 74th General Convention encourage dioceses, congregations, and communicants to become active stewards of their water resources through conservation efforts including reduction of consumption; through examination of water discharge such that contaminated water does not improperly leave church grounds; and through the creation of environmental programs for stewardship of water and the whole of creation and for the education of congregants in regard to good and faithful stewardship of the earth's resources; and be it further
Resolved, That the General Convention encourage dioceses, congregations, and communicants to undertake one or more of the following four stewardship steps:
>When and where possible, install water-saving devices, such as low-flow commodes and aspirators on sink faucets.
>Replant church grounds and home gardens with plants and trees that are drought-tolerant and have low needs for water, and that are native to the region and therefore able to survive local climatic conditions.
>Devise drainage systems that allow rainwater to flow from gutters and

drain pipes to spread onto the lawn and landscaped areas of church grounds and home gardens, thereby reducing water lost to sewer systems.

Pave new or repave existing parking lots with materials that are pervious, so that water penetrates into soil beneath parking areas, thereby reducing the flow of oil and other auto fluids into streams.

Miscellaneous Resolutions

The House of Bishops Committee on Miscellaneous Resolutions presented its Report #5 on HD Message #71 on Resolution D024 (Thanksgiving for the Ministry of The Episcopal Church and Visual Arts) and moved concurrence.

The House concurred
(Communicated to the House of Deputies in HB Message #215)

Final Text of Resolution:

(D024)
Resolved, That the 74th General Convention of The Episcopal Church give special thanksgiving for The Episcopal Church and Visual Arts (ECVA). We praise God for the gifts of imagination, vision, and beauty that draw the community of faith deeper into the life of Christ.

The House of Bishops Committee on Miscellaneous Resolutions presented its Report #6 on HD Message #31 on Resolution A155 (76th General Convention Site) and moved concurrence.

The House concurred
(Communicated to the House of Deputies in HB Message #216)

Final Text of Resolution:

(A155)
Resolved, That the following five sites be considered for the 76th General Convention and that no less than three be selected for final consideration. The five sites are: Salt Lake City, Utah; Reno, Nevada; Portland, Oregon; Anaheim, California; and Charlotte, North Carolina.

The House of Bishops Committee on Miscellaneous Resolutions presented its Report #7 on HD Message #30 on Resolution A015 (Jubilee Ministry Thanksgiving) and moved concurrence.

The House concurred
(Communicated to the House of Deputies in HB Message #217)

Final Text of Resolution:
(A015)
Resolved, That the 74th General Convention acknowledge with thanks to God the ministry of Jubilee on its 21st anniversary; and be it further
Resolved, That this ministry of "joint discipleship in Christ with poor and oppressed people, wherever they are found, to meet basic human needs and to build a just society," continue to be "at the heart of the mission of the Church...;" and be it further
Resolved, That Jubilee Ministry be reaffirmed and commended to the whole Church.

The House of Bishops Committee on Miscellaneous Resolutions presented its Report #8 on HD Message #92 on Resolution A042 (Amend Canon I.1.9) and moved concurrence.
                The House concurred
(Communicated to the House of Deputies in HB Message #218)

Final Text of Resolution:
(A042)
Resolved, That Canon I.1.9 be amended as follows:
Sec. 9. The Treasurer *of the General Convention* shall have authority to borrow, in behalf and in the name of the General Convention, such a sum as may be judged by the Treasurer to be necessary to help defray the expense of the General Convention, with the approval of the Presiding Bishop and the Executive Council.

Privilege and Courtesy
The House of Bishops Committee on Privilege and Courtesy presented its Report #2 on HD Message #28 on Resolution D032 (Courtesy for Gail Courtney Rittgers) and moved concurrence.
                The House concurred
(Communicated to the House of Deputies in HB Message #219)

Final Text of Resolution:
(D032)
Resolved, That the 74th General Convention send its congratulations and best wishes to Gail Courtney Rittgers, a member of Grace Episcopal Church, Alexandria, Virginia, on the occasion today of her 101st birthday; and be it further
Resolved, That the Convention recognize that she has been a mainstay of her church community for many years; taught Sunday School until the age of 80; served on the vestry; and remains active in the women's Bible study group; and be it further

Resolved, That the Convention pray that Gail Courtney Rittgers may continue to inspire those around her to lives of loving and faithful service.

Structure

The House of Bishops Committee on Structure presented its Report #12 on HD Message #103 on Resolution A147 (Legislative Committee Membership) and moved concurrence.

The House concurred
(Communicated to the House of Deputies in HB Message #220)

Final Text of Resolution:

(A147)
Resolved, That it is the sense of the Convention that the work of Legislative Committees is facilitated when the membership includes deputies and bishops who are also members of the appropriate Standing Commissions or Committees, in order to provide continuity.

National and International Concerns

The House of Bishops Committee on National and International Concerns presented its Report #3 on HD Message #145 on Resolution A033 (Just and Unjust Wars) and moved concurrence.

The House concurred
(Communicated to the House of Deputies in HB Message #221)

Final Text of Resolution:

(A033)
Resolved, That the 74th General Convention call upon all members of The Episcopal Church, in discussions about war and especially the strategy of preemptive strikes, to seriously consider and utilize the Just War criteria developed over the centuries and generally expressed as follows. First, whether lethal force may be used is governed by the following criteria:

Just cause: Force may be used only to correct a grave, public evil, i.e., aggression or massive violation of the basic rights of whole populations.

Comparative justice: While there may be rights and wrongs on all sides of a conflict, to override the presumption against the use of force, the injustice suffered by one part must significantly outweigh that suffered by the other.

Legitimate authority: Only duly constituted public authorities may use deadly force or wage war.

Right intention: Force may be used only in a truly just cause and solely for that purpose.

Probability of success: Arms may not be used in a futile cause or in a case where disproportionate measures are required to achieve success.

Proportionality: The overall destruction expected from the use of force must be outweighed by the good to be achieved.

Last resort: Force may be used only after all peaceful alternatives have been seriously tried and exhausted.

These criteria taken as a whole must be satisfied in order to override the strong presumption against the use of force. Second, the Just War tradition seeks also to curb the violence of war through restraint on armed combat between the contending parties by imposing the following moral standards for the conduct of armed conflict:

Noncombatant immunity: Civilians may not be the objects of direct attack, and military personnel must take due care to avoid and minimize indirect harm to civilians.

Proportionality: In the conduct of hostilities, efforts must be made to attain military objectives with no more force than is militarily necessary and to avoid disproportionate collateral damage to civilian life and property.

Right intention: Even in the midst of conflict, the aim of political and military leaders must be peace with justice, so that acts of vengeance and indiscriminate violence, whether by individuals, military units or governments, are forbidden; and be it further

Resolved, That when legitimate civilian authority determines that war is justified, members of The Episcopal Church recall our Lord's teaching to love our enemies, counsel that participation in or refusal to participate in any war is a discernment process requiring deep reflection and prayer with humility, and acknowledge that one participates in war with great reluctance, always seeking God's mercy and forgiveness; and be it further

Resolved, That the 74th General Convention, recalling the longstanding Episcopal Church view, originally adopted by the 1930 Lambeth Conference and by the 1931 General Convention, that "war as a method of settling international disputes is incompatible with the teaching and example of our Lord Jesus Christ," urge dioceses and congregations to study and better understand Just War theory and pacifism as they apply to the situation of the United States in responding to contemporary international conflicts.

The House of Bishops Committee on National and International Concerns presented its Report #6 on HD Message #130 on Resolution C036 (Spirituality of Food Production) and moved concurrence.

The House concurred
(Communicated to the House of Deputies in HB Message #222)

Final Text of Resolution:
(C036)
Resolved, That the General Convention accept the Episcopal Ecological Network's offer to continually provide its bishops, clergy, and lay persons

with information and educational opportunities concerning the issues of food sources, biodiversity, genetic engineering, ownership and distribution of our food sources, and related issues concerning the health and well-being of ourselves and future generations and encourage them to work in conjunction with the Peace and Justice Ministries Office of the National Church Center in this regard; and be it further

Resolved, That the Office of Government Relations and other appropriate bodies will advise elected and appointed government officials and other secular and religious bodies of its concerns about food sources, biodiversity, genetic engineering, ownership and distribution of our food sources, and related issues concerning the health and well-being of ourselves and future generations; and be it further

Resolved, That the General Convention support the rights of consumers to know the source and content of their food stuffs; and that the farming and processing practices used are healthy and sustainable for all of creation and that The Episcopal Church is committed to making this a reality; and be it further

Resolved, That the General Convention refer this position to the Committee on Social Responsibility in Investments for consideration when developing and managing stock portfolios and for use in making shareholder resolutions.

The House of Bishops Committee on National and International Concerns presented its Report #7 on HD Message #124 on Resolution C033 (Immigration and Undocumented Workers) and moved concurrence.

The House concurred
(Communicated to the House of Deputies in HB Message #223)

Final Text of Resolution:

(C033)

Resolved, That the 74th General Convention urge that the Congress of the United States enact legislation to expand the temporary workers' programs to include all persons currently residing in the United States engaged in meaningful labor, as well as overseas workers offered employment in the United States through formal contractual arrangements in response to the labor needs of specific sectors of the economy; and be it further

Resolved, That such temporary workers receive such compensation and benefits for themselves and their dependents living with them that parallel those available to other legal residents such as the federally mandated minimum hourly wage, Social Security, driver's license, medical care and education; and be it further

Resolved, That based upon a specified period of residence in the United States, such workers have the option of adjusting to permanent resident status, which could lead to naturalization; and be it further

Resolved, That this resolution be sent to concerned members of Congress and state legislatures as an expression of The Episcopal Church.

The House of Bishops Committee on National and International Concerns presented its Report #8 on HD Message #123 on Resolution A025 (Trafficking of Women, Girls, and Boys) and moved concurrence.

The House concurred

(Communicated to the House of Deputies in HB Message #224)

Final Text of Resolution:

(A025)
Resolved, That the 74th General Convention recommend that the Executive Council provide $4,000 to the Committee on the Status of Women to enable identification and development of resource materials to be used by congregations and dioceses to address the domestic and international problem of trafficking in women, girls, and boys as well as any known local connections in trafficking; and be it further
Resolved, That the General Convention request the Joint Standing Committee on Program, Budget and Finance to consider a budget allocation of $4,000 for implementation of this resolution.

The House of Bishops Committee on National and International Concerns presented its Report #9 on HD Message #121 on Resolution A132 (Christian Responses to Warfare) and moved concurrence.

The House concurred

(Communicated to the House of Deputies in HB Message #225)

Final Text of Resolution:

(A132)
Resolved, That the 74th General Convention urge dioceses and congregations to study and better understand Just War theory and pacifism as they apply to the situation of the United States in responding to contemporary international conflicts; and be it further
Resolved, That we commend "Just Peace Readings" from the Office of the Bishop Suffragan for Chaplaincies of the Episcopal Church Center, and the website, www.episcopalchurch.org/chaplain, as an important resource in the continuing study of Just War.

The House of Bishops Committee on National and International Concerns presented its Report #10 on HD Message #150 on Resolution D008 (Demolition of Palestinian Homes) and moved concurrence.

The House concurred

(Communicated to the House of Deputies in HB Message #226)

Final Text of Resolution:
(D008)
Resolved, That the 74th General Convention recognize that Israeli demolition of Palestinian homes in the Gaza Strip and the Occupied Territories of the West Bank and East Jerusalem is illegal under international law and is a deterrent to the peace process, and therefore call upon the President and the U.S. government to urge the State of Israel to end its policy of the demolition of Palestinian homes.
[At the request of the House, the following reference is added: Geneva Convention for the Protection of Civilians, 1948. *Ed.*]

Social and Urban Affairs
The House of Bishops Committee on Social and Urban Affairs presented its Report #14 on HD Message #153 on Resolution A128 (Ministering to "At Risk" Youth) and moved concurrence.

The House concurred
(Communicated to the House of Deputies in HB Message #227)

Final Text of Resolution:
(A128)
Resolved, That the 74th General Convention of The Episcopal Church affirm that all young people are created in the image of God and possess potential to love and serve God. Further, the Convention recognizes that many aspects of our culture work to obscure the image of God in young people and render all young people "Youth At Risk"; and be it further
Resolved, That the Church reaffirm its commitment to support the development of caring, competent, faithful, and loving young people and provide sufficient human and financial resources in the Office of Youth Ministries to challenge, inspire, and support dioceses and parishes in their work with young people; and be it further
Resolved, That the 74th General Convention commend the following programs and educational possibilities for local implementation:
- Literacy programs, including reading, cultural, social, spiritual, and computer literacy
- Mentoring programs
- Conflict resolution and anger management programs
- Religious education programs and curricula that recognize the socio-economic, ethnic, racial, linguistic, and cultural diversity of our church
- After school programs
- Creation and maintenance of Episcopal schools that provide access to all youth
- Development of Episcopal camps to provide access to all youth.

Prayer Book, Liturgy and Church Music

The House of Bishops Committee on Prayer Book, Liturgy and Church Music presented its Report #40 on HD Message #138 on Resolution A101 (Church Planting Liturgies) and moved concurrence.

The House concurred
(Communicated to the House of Deputies in HB Message #228)

Final Text of Resolution:

(A101)
Resolved, That the 74th General Convention approve for publication and distribution by Church Publishing, Inc., these liturgies: Discernment for a New Church Mission; A Liturgy for Commissioning a Church Planter, Missioner or Mission Team; A Liturgy for the Opening of a New Congregation; Setting Apart Secular Space for Sacred Use; A Litany for the Mission of the Church; A Variety of Church Planting Collects, Blessings and other Prayers; and Hymn Suggestions for Church Planting Liturgies; and be it further
Resolved, That these bilingual liturgies be printed side-by-side in English and Spanish, and in English and French; and be it further
Resolved, That the proposed liturgies be changed as follows from the Blue Book report:

1. That the following rubric be added at the end of the introductory rubrics of each of the services [Blue Book pages 164,172,186, and 192]: "It is appropriate to adapt this rite to local custom, language, dialect, and idiom."
2. That the first rubric heading [Blue Book page 164], Concerning the Celebration, be changed to "Concerning the Service."
3. That in the first sentence of that rubric [Blue Book page 164] the words "congregations, dioceses, or other church bodies" be changed to "congregations and dioceses."
4. That the Collect for Raising Up of People with Skills Needed for a Church Planting (Blue Book page 168) be changed to the following:
   "Holy Spirit, you delight in equipping us with all the gifts of service (especially_____) to extend the Realm of God: raise up and empower those among us whom you call to this new work, that the Body of Christ may grow in strength and health, for the transforming of the world; through Jesus Christ our Lord. Amen."
5. That the second word of the Collect for Apostolic-model Church Planting [Blue Book page 174] be changed from "Father" to "God."
6. In the Liturgy for Commissioning, in The Commissioning (Blue Book page 178), after the people's response "We will", add the following rubric: "Appropriate symbols of the new ministry may be

given."
7. That the rubric beginning "Following Communion" [Blue Book page 184] be deleted.
8. That the rubric concerning the post-communion prayer [Blue Book page 184] be changed from "the following is said" to "the following may be said."
9. That the immediately following rubric, reading "Celebrant," [Blue Book page 184] be changed to read "Celebrant or other person appointed."
10. That the following rubric be added after the post-communion prayer [Blue Book page 184]: "The Bishop or Celebrant may bless the people."
11. That the rubric beginning "The Bishop or the Bishop's representative" and the two following lines beginning "Receive" be deleted [Blue Book page 184].
12. That the Dismissal [Blue Book page 184] be changed to the following: "Deacon: Go forth into the world, sharing the Good News of God's love. [Alleluia, alleluia.]
People: We go in the Name of Christ. [Alleluia, alleluia.]"
13. That in the collect in the liturgy for Setting Apart Secular Space for Sacred Use that begins "Blessed are you, O God" [Blue Book page 194] the phrase "we dedicate this space" be changed to "we dedicate our use of this space" and in the last sentence the word "always" be deleted.
14. That the sixth prayer of A Variety of Church Planting Collects, Blessings and Other Prayers, beginning "Most Holy and life-giving God," [Blue Book page 202] be changed to the following:
"Most Holy and life-giving God: the friends of Jesus carried your good news, each to a different place according to their gifts and calling. Bless N. (and N.) as they carry your word of love, making disciples for your service and building up your Church, through the power of your Spirit and in the Name of Jesus. Amen."
15. In the several Dismissals in these liturgies add the words, "Deacon, or the Celebrant, dismisses the people."
16. In the Dismissal [Blue Book page 190–191], to "officiant/celebrant" add "Deacon or."

And be it further
Resolved, That appropriate corrections to the Spanish rites be made.

Ministry

The House of Bishops Committee on Ministry presented its Report #25 on Resolution A060 (Contemporary Language Competency) and moved the resolution, recommending to concur with amendment.

Committee Amendment:
Resolved, the House of Deputies concurring, That the 74th General Convention recommend that all dioceses strongly encourage those preparing for ordination to study a contemporary language other than their native language and to participate in an intentional cross-cultural program; and be it further

Resolved, That the 74th General Convention direct the Standing Commission on Ministry Development to consider, in its continued revision of Title III, how to address the Church's need for multilingual and cross-cultural competency for many ordained and lay leaders in various mission contexts including possible canonical revisions regarding formation and continuing education, and report back to the 75th General Convention.

Motion carried
The House concurred with amendment
(Communicated to the House of Deputies in HB Message #229)

Communications
The House of Bishops Committee on Communications presented its Report #12 on HD Message #139 on Resolution A080 (Episcopal Church Website) and moved concurrence.

The House concurred
(Communicated to the House of Deputies in HB Message #230)

Final Text of Resolution:
(A080)

Resolved, That the 74th General Convention direct the Episcopal Church Center staff to:

- Continue to develop the Domestic and Foreign Missionary Society website in ways that are more highly visual and professional in their appearance, dynamic, interactive, easier to navigate, and constantly updated;
- Deploy user-profiling tools to deliver website material according to user preferences (such as seeker, lay, clergy, deputy, standing commission member);
- Include multilingual and next generations resources in all areas of the website;
- Collect and post on the website a variety of resources related to faith formation, ongoing spiritual growth, and education of both children and adults;
- Include resources on the website that are oriented to seekers from outside The Episcopal Church, and that assist in making disciples oriented to mission for the local context;

Devote a portion of the website to mentoring and relationship building among those who work with the next generations, including campus ministries, young adults ministries, youth ministries, and children's ministries;

Maintain a unity of design and ease of access including easy forward and backward mobility; and be it further

Resolved, That the Episcopal Church Center staff provide software and freeware resources for downloading.

Committees and Commissions

The House of Bishops Committee on Committees and Commissions presented its Report #2 on Resolution D074 (Name Change for Commission on Ecumenical Relations) and moved that the Committee be discharged as the matter is considered in Resolution D010.

Motion carried
Committee discharged
(Communicated to the House of Deputies in HB Message #231)

National and International Concerns

The House of Bishops Committee on National and International Concerns presented its Report #11 on HD Message #163 on Resolution D031 (Culture of Nonviolence) and moved concurrence.

The House concurred
(Communicated to the House of Deputies in HB Message #232)

Final Text of Resolution:

(D031)
Resolved, **That The Episcopal Church develop specific plans at national, provincial, and diocesan levels in the next triennium for the church to live into a culture of nonviolence which values love, compassion, and justice, and which rejects violence as a means of solving problems;** and be it further

Resolved, **That curricula in nonviolence awareness and training be promoted for use in dioceses and congregations;** and be it further

Resolved, **That the results of these plans be compiled by the Office of Peace and Justice and presented to the General Convention 2006.**

The House of Bishops Committee on National and International Concerns presented its Report #12 on HD Message #166 on Resolution D063 (Civil Liberties and the USA Patriot Act) and moved concurrence.

The House concurred
(Communicated to the House of Deputies in HB Message #233)

Final Text of Resolution:
(D063)
Resolved, That the 74th General Convention direct the Office of Government Relations to work to encourage the Congress of the United States to hold public hearings examining the relationship between the extension of police powers granted under HR 3162 RDS, the "Uniting and Strengthening America by Providing Appropriate Tools Required to Intercept and Obstruct Terrorism Act of 2001" (USA PATRIOT ACT), and the potential curtailing of civil liberties granted by the Constitution of the United States of America; and be it further
Resolved, That the 74th General Convention go on record as opposing the use of Federal legislation passed since 9/11 violating fundamental civil rights guaranteed by the United States Constitution.

The House of Bishops Committee on National and International Concerns presented its Report #13 on HD Message #170 on Resolution D014 (Japanese–American Internment in World War II: A Call for Accountability) and moved concurrence.

The House concurred
(Communicated to the House of Deputies in HB Message #234)

Final Text of Resolution:
(D014)
Resolved, That the 74th General Convention reaffirm previous actions taken by both Executive Council and General Conventions on the internment and redress of Japanese–Americans and Japanese Latin Americans during World War II; and be it further
Resolved, That The Episcopal Church, in reaffirming its baptismal covenant to "uphold the dignity of every human being," support the civil liberties of all, regardless of ethnicity and religious beliefs; and be it further
Resolved, That in this post 9/11 era, the Church call on the United States government to be mindful of the experience and treatment in the internment of Japanese-Americans; and be it further
Resolved, That the United States government be instructed by this deplorable history when it considers any reauthorization, expansion, or implementation of legislation or regulations relating to "The Patriot Act of 2001," H.R. 3162, which can be found at http://Thomas.loc.gov (please note no www) (click on: legislation related to the attacks of September 11, 2001).

The House of Bishops Committee on National and International Concerns presented its Report #14 on HD Message #183 on Resolution C028 (Immigrant Workers Freedom Ride) and moved concurrence.

The House concurred
(Communicated to the House of Deputies in HB Message #235)

Final Text of Resolution:
(C028)
Resolved, That the 74th General Convention actively work in support of the Immigrant Workers Freedom Ride (IWFR) by educating its members to the importance of immigration law reform, organizing local congregations to support the Freedom Ride both financially and by participating in activities to host and welcome the Freedom Riders on their national route to the nation's capital and calling on The Episcopal Church, USA to adopt this resolution in support of the IWFR.

The House of Bishops Committee on National and International Concerns presented its Report #15 on HD Message #173 on Resolution A028 (Palestinian and Afghani Women Support) and moved concurrence.

The House concurred
(Communicated to the House of Deputies in HB Message #236)

Final Text of Resolution:
(A028)
Resolved, That the 74th General Convention encourage dioceses to assist all Episcopalians to learn about the plight of and provide support for women and children of all faiths in war torn areas, recent examples including Israel/Palestine, Afghanistan, Iraq, Colombia, Sudan, and Liberia.

The House of Bishops Committee on National and International Concerns presented its Report #16 on HD Message #172 on Resolution D054 (HIV/AIDS Keeping America's Promise to Africa) and moved concurrence.

The House concurred
(Communicated to the House of Deputies in HB Message #237)

Final Text of Resolution:
(D054)
Resolved, That the 74th General Convention, through the Office of Government Relations, urge the United States government to keep America's "Promise to Africa" by fully funding the President's proposed five year, $15 billion budget request for HIV/AIDS relief for Africa and the Caribbean without cuts to current life-saving programs; and be it further
Resolved, That the 74th General Convention commend the President for the promise of significant new funding to combat the HIV/AIDS pandemic in Africa and now calls on the Administration to use the full influence of the Executive Office in order to press Congress to keep the "Promise to Africa;" and be it further
Resolved, That the Church encourage the government to continue to find new ways by which America can combat this deadly disease and promote human security, thereby waging global reconciliation; and be it further

Resolved, That the Church call on the United States government to honor and support trade policies that promote access to essential AIDS medicines for poor countries, and to make sustained commitment for a fair-share U.S. contribution to the "Global Fund to Fight AIDS, TB, and Malaria," an international public-private partnership world health campaign modeled on the world health campaigns which led to the successful eradication of polio and smallpox; and be it further

Resolved, That all Episcopalians take immediate action to contact their elected representatives, urging them to support funding for the "Promise to Africa" and the "Global Fund;" and be it further

Resolved, That all dioceses and communities of faith in The Episcopal Church be urged to examine and embrace ways by which they can join in the worldwide fight against HIV/AIDS.

The House of Bishops Committee on National and International Concerns presented its Report #17 on HD Message #171 on Resolution A037 (Status of Forces Agreement with Korea) and moved concurrence.

The House concurred
(Communicated to the House of Deputies in HB Message #238)

Final Text of Resolution:
(A037)

Resolved, That the 74th General Convention of The Episcopal Church in the United States of America urge the United States government in its renegotiation of the Status of Forces Agreement (SOFA) with the Republic of Korea to give special attention to the rights of Korean citizens to equal treatment and legal redress of grievances and adequate compensation to victims of weapons practice and testing; pollution of the environment; personal abuse, especially of a violent or sexual nature; and other negative effects of U.S. military presence and activity; and be it further

Resolved, That The Episcopal Church urge the U.S. government in all SOFA negotiations to recognize the rights of local people and assure their access to all mechanisms for redress of their grievances against U.S. military personnel; and be it further

Resolved, That the eventual goal be the phasing out of U.S. military bases in Korea.

The House of Bishops Committee on National and International Concerns presented its Report #18 on HD Message #168 on Resolution D081 (Israeli Security Wall) and moved concurrence.

The House concurred
(Communicated to the House of Deputies in HB Message #239)

Final Text of Resolution:
(D081)
Resolved, That the 74th General Convention recognize that the 360 kilometer long Israeli security wall currently under construction and the proposed additional 240 kilometer extension are impediments to the implementation of the performance-based roadmap leading to a final and comprehensive negotiated settlement of the Israeli-Palestinian conflict by 2005, as presented in President Bush's speech of 24 June 2002 and welcomed by the EU, Russia and the UN in the 16 July 2002 and 17 September 2002 Quartet Ministerial statements; and be it further
Resolved, That the 74th General Convention convey to the President, the Secretary of State and the National Security Advisor of the United States our support for their ongoing questioning of the construction of this wall.

The House of Bishops Committee on National and International Concerns presented its Report #19 on HD Message #HD Message #165 on Resolution D068 (Response to New War Situations) and moved concurrence.
The House concurred
(Communicated to the House of Deputies in HB Message #240)

Final Text of Resolution:
(D068)
Resolved, That the **Theology Committee of the House of Bishops be urged to prepare a study on new warfare situations which may not be adequately addressed by the Just War Theory, such as non-declared wars, asymmetric warfare, pre-emptive strikes, invitations to intervene by legitimate foreign authorities, international terrorism without boundaries, and other forms of military intervention not imagined in past centuries.**

The House of Bishops Committee on National and International Concerns presented its Report #20 on HD Message #164 on Resolution D066 (Declaration on Sustainable Development) and moved concurrence.
The House concurred
(Communicated to the House of Deputies in HB Message #241)

Final Text of Resolution:
(D066)
Resolved, That the 74th General Convention endorse and implement the four resolutions passed by the September 2002 Anglican Consultative Council (ACC) meeting in Hong Kong which
- ask all churches of the Anglican Communion to place environmental care on their agenda;
- ask all Anglicans to make their own personal commitment to care for God's world, respecting all life, for "the Earth is the Lord's and all that

is in it" (Psalm 24);
establish the Anglican Environmental Network as an official network of the Anglican Communion; and
endorse for immediate action the declaration of the Global Anglican Congress of the Stewardship of Creation.

The House of Bishops Committee on National and International Concerns presented its Report #21 on HD Message #149 on Resolution C024 (Nonviolent United States Foreign Policy) and moved concurrence.

The House concurred
(Communicated to the House of Deputies in HB Message #242)

Final Text of Resolution:
(C024)
Resolved, That the 74th General Convention support the World Council of Churches' Decade to Overcome Violence and its work with other faith communities—in this nation and around the world—to persuade governments to embrace less violent foreign policies, to encourage individuals and parishes to pray for peace, and to take political action to oppose foreign policies that are grounded in violence; and be it further
Resolved, That the 74th General Convention call on our nation to reconsider fundamentally the foreign policy it has thus far advanced, calling upon our leaders to employ diplomacy rather than warfare.

The House of Bishops Committee on National and International Concerns presented its Report #22 on HD Message #169 on Resolution D034 (Sex Trafficking) and moved concurrence.

The House concurred
(Communicated to the House of Deputies in HB Message #243)

Final Text of Resolution:
(D034)
Resolved, That the 74th General Convention condemn domestic and international trafficking in all persons for sexual purposes as an affront to human dignity and human rights; and be it further
Resolved, That the Executive Council request the appropriate Standing Committee to set up national and international plans of action for The Episcopal Church to prepare an educational campaign for parishes and dioceses on the topic of sex trafficking, and to prepare a model for a church initiative bringing together faith-based people with nongovernmental organizations, government, and law enforcement officials to create a victim-centered approach to anti-sex trafficking operations, finding ways to meet the medical, psychological, legal, and spiritual needs of persons who have been brought out of these horrendous circumstances; and be it further
Resolved, That this resolution be sent to every Province in the Anglican Communion.

The House of Bishops Committee on National and International Concerns presented its Report #23 on HD Message #188 on Resolution D052 (Rescind Policy of Disinvestment in Defense Contractors) and moved concurrence.
The question was called to terminate debate on the resolution.

Motion carried
Debate terminated

A vote was taken on Resolution D052.

Motion defeated
Resolution rejected
(Communicated to the House of Deputies in HB Message #244)

Social and Urban Affairs

The House of Bishops Committee on Social and Urban Affairs presented its Report #16 on HD Message #184 on Resolution D073 (Formation of Episcopal Community Services in America) and moved concurrence.

The House concurred
(Communicated to the House of Deputies in HB Message #245)

Final Text of Resolution:
(D073)
Resolved, **That the 74th General Convention of The Episcopal Church commend the formation of Episcopal Community Services in America as an umbrella organization for member organizations affiliated with The Episcopal Church that seek to serve those in need through health and social services.**

The House of Bishops Committee on Social and Urban Affairs presented its Report #17 on HD Message #174 on Resolution D070 (Water Policy) and moved concurrence.

The House concurred
(Communicated to the House of Deputies in HB Message #246)

Final Text of Resolution:
(D070)
Resolved, **That the 74th General Convention ask the Office of Government Relations to work on public policy to ensure that clean water is accessible and available to all;** and be it further
Resolved, **That the Standing Commission on Anglican and International Peace with Justice Concerns be urged to make water a priority.**

The House of Bishops Committee on Social and Urban Affairs presented its Report #18 on HD Message #176 on Resolution D071 (Oppose Federally Sponsored Marriage Promotion) and moved concurrence.

The House concurred
(Communicated to the House of Deputies in HB Message #247)

Final Text of Resolution:
(D071)
Resolved, **That the 74th General Convention express opposition to any effort by the Congress of the United States or the legislatures of any of the states that discriminate against single-parent households;** and be it further
Resolved, **That the Office of Government Relations is directed to advocate on the behalf of all needy families.**

The House of Bishops Committee on Social and Urban Affairs presented its Report #19 on HD Message #178 on Resolution D045 (Withdraw From the Religious Coalition for Reproductive Choice) and moved concurrence.

The Ecumenical Officer moved to refer the resolution to a Standing Commission on Health.

Motion defeated
Referral defeated

A vote was taken on Resolution D045.

Motion defeated
Resolution rejected
(Communicated to the House of Deputies in HB Message #248)

The House of Bishops Committee on Social and Urban Affairs presented its Report #20 on HD Message #179 on Resolution D040 (Invest in Housing for the Poor) and moved concurrence.

The House concurred
(Communicated to the House of Deputies in HB Message #249)

Final Text of Resolution:
(D040)
Resolved, **That the 74th General Convention reaffirm its commitment to providing rental and owner-occupied, housing that is safe, accessible, and affordable for low-income and moderate-income persons and their families, including persons with disabilities;** and be it further
Resolved, **That the Office of Governmental Relations urge the executive and legislative branches of the federal government and the dioceses to encourage state and local units of government to ensure that housing assistance programs are adequately funded to address the growing gap between the number of affordable housing units available and the number of renter**

households in the bottom quartile of income in this nation; and be it further
Resolved, That the Convention strongly encourage the local parish and interfaith community partnerships to address the lack of affordable housing for low- and moderate-income families including persons with disabilities throughout this nation; and be it further
Resolved, That the Convention urge the Episcopal Network for Economic Justice to identify existing and new opportunities for involvement in the creation and investment in affordable housing and to report through the Jubilee Ministries Advisory Committee on the status of this work to the 75th General Convention and on the opportunities for The Episcopal Church to become involved in the creation of affordable housing.

The House of Bishops Committee on Social and Urban Affairs presented its Report #21 on HD Message #177 on Resolution D036 (Marriage) and moved concurrence.

The House concurred
(Communicated to the House of Deputies in HB Message #250)

Final Text of Resolution:
(D036)
Resolved, That the 74th General Convention instruct the National Concerns Committee of Executive Council to report to the 75th General Convention on the responses by the dioceses of this Church to the charges and recommendations contained in Resolution D071 of the 72nd General Convention (Recognizing Lifelong Commitment and Fidelity in Marital Relationships) and Resolution A069 of the 67th General Convention (Encourage Dioceses to Establish Commissions on Marriage); and be it further
Resolved, That the National Concerns Committee of Executive Council make available to dioceses and congregations the developed programs for marriage enrichment and renewal and pre-marital counseling.

Evangelism
The House of Bishops Committee on Evangelism presented its Report #8 on HD Message #187 on Resolution D017 (Promoting Reconciliation and Minimizing the Likelihood of Schism) and moved concurrence with referral to a Standing Commission.

Final Text of Resolution:
(D017)
Resolved, That, the 2003 General Convention direct the Executive Council to lead and encourage reconciliation efforts throughout the Church; and be it further
Resolved, That the Executive Council report the results of those efforts in their annual report; and be it further

Resolved, That the reports include descriptions of the use of the Faith-Based Reconciliation model including:
1. acknowledgement of the wound
2. repentance
3. telling of stories
4. grief-sharing
5. making apologies to those adversely impacted
6. sharing of privilege
7. planning for and carrying out of changes
8. positively affirming and supporting multiculturalism, and
9. other, as those reporting deem appropriate; and be it further

Resolved, That the 2003 General Convention commend the leadership and ministry of the Presiding Bishop and the New Commandment Task Force in the work of reconciliation.

Motion carried
Resolution referred to a Standing Commission
(Communicated to the House of Deputies in HB Message #251)

The House of Bishops Committee on Evangelism presented its Report #9 on HD Message #186 on Resolution D011 (Appending "Anglican Communion" to materials) and moved concurrence.

The House concurred
(Communicated to the House of Deputies in HB Message #252)

Final Text of Resolution:
(D011)
Resolved, That the 74th General Convention encourage all Episcopal Church dioceses, congregations, and affiliate organizations to append the phrase, with appropriate connecting wording, "Anglican Communion" to their signage, publications, advertising, and communications so that churches and organizations of The Episcopal Church may be easily identified as part of the wider fellowship of churches in the Anglican Communion by persons of other member churches of the Communion.

The House of Bishops Committee on Evangelism presented its Report #10 on HD Message #185 on Resolution A076 (Transformation Resources) and moved concurrence.

The House concurred
(Communicated to the House of Deputies in HB Message #253)

Final Text of Resolution:
(A076)
Resolved, That Episcopal Church Center staff and specifically the ethnic ministries desks, be charged to:
- continue to develop strategic resources for transformation, such as: Transformation and Renewal (vitalization in Black congregations) and Start Up, Start Over (theory and best practices for congregational renewal)
- continue to hold up paradigmatic examples of transformation and resurrection, including those in multicultural congregations, via *Episcopal Life,* the national church website, etc.
- continue to develop and offer multicultural and multilingual resources for transforming congregations and leadership training
- develop a national consultancy gathering for leaders in multicultural congregations, for the purpose of networking, learning, and resource sharing
- continue to develop educational resources for transformation, such as Bible studies and small group resources for hospitality, mission, evangelism, and how to tell our own stories; resources that make liturgy more accessible, (e.g., the Rite series); resources for learning about culture and change
- continue to maintain awareness of opportunities for learning and transformation in congregational life (Congregational Development office).

The House of Bishops Committee on Evangelism presented its Report #11 on HD Message #160 on Resolution A074 (Congregational Annual Study) and moved concurrence.

The House concurred
(Communicated to the House of Deputies in HB Message #254)

Final Text of Resolution:
(A074)
Resolved, That every congregation of The Episcopal Church engage in annual (regular) study and review of its common life, asking the following questions:
Who are we? Who are we called to be?
Who is our neighbor? Are we meeting and learning about our neighbor?
What is our mission in this place? What ought it to be?
How are lives and communities being transformed?
How are people being equipped for Christ's ministry of reconciliation?
How is this community and congregation different from a year ago? Five years ago? Ten years ago?
How is leadership recognized, affirmed, and shared here?

The House of Bishops Committee on Evangelism presented its Report #12 on HD Message #159 on Resolution A075 (Diocese Mission Perspective) and moved concurrence.

The House concurred
(Communicated to the House of Deputies in HB Message #255)

Final Text of Resolution:
(A075)
Resolved, **That every diocese in The Episcopal Church be charged to:**
 foster a missional perspective or culture;
 foster a culture of partnering with others (congregations, denominations, etc.) for mission and ministry;
 equip people to facilitate congregational self-study and strategic planning, including the impact of the congregation's life-cycle in its transformation for mission;
 and that bishops organize visitations around these principles.

Communications
The House of Bishops Committee on Communications presented its Report #14 on HD Message #182 on Resolution D069 (Standing Commission on Church Communications) and moved concurrence.

The House concurred
(Communicated to the House of Deputies in HB Message #256)

Final Text of Resolution:
(D069)
Resolved, **That the 74th General Convention affirm the policy that broad, diverse, and multi-faceted communication is central to and essential for the mission of The Episcopal Church;** and be it further
Resolved, **That effective communication is an overarching ministry and cannot be fulfilled as either a list of tasks or an addendum to other facets of the Church's mission and ministries;** and be it further
Resolved, **That a national strategy for communication must meet the needs of, and be reflective of, a broad and diverse church;** and be it further
Resolved, **That Canon I.1.2(n) be amended by adding this subsection:**
(12) A Standing Commission on Episcopal Church Communication consisting of 14 members (4 Bishops, 4 Priests and/or Deacons, and 6 Lay Persons). It shall be the duty of the Commission to guide the policies, participate in the strategic planning, and share in the oversight of implementing a comprehensive communication strategy for the Episcopal Church.
And be it further
Resolved, **That the General Convention request that the Joint Standing Committee on Program, Budget and Finance consider a budget allocation of $0 for implementation of this resolution.**

Miscellaneous Resolutions

The House of Bishops Committee on Miscellaneous Resolutions presented its Report #9 on HD Message #142 on Resolution A079 (General Convention Deputies) and moved concurrence.

The House concurred
(Communicated to the House of Deputies in HB Message #257)

Final Text of Resolution:
(A079)
Resolved, That the 74th General Convention recommend that diocesan conventions nominate candidates for deputations to General Convention that incorporate the next generations, and also the multilingual, multicultural character of our churches and communities, so that deputations reflect the vision we have for the church we are; and be it further
Resolved, That the 74th General Convention recommend that all dioceses and congregations engage this vision when presenting candidates for all representative boards, including, but not limited to, vestries, delegations to diocesan conventions, and Standing Committees.

The House of Bishops Committee on Miscellaneous Resolutions presented its Report #11 on HD Message #141 on Resolution D051 (Full Accessibility at General Convention) and moved concurrence.

The House concurred
(Communicated to the House of Deputies in HB Message #258)

Final Text of Resolution:
(D051)
Resolved, That the 74th General Convention direct the Joint Standing Committee on Planning and Arrangements to recommend for future General Conventions, subsequent meetings of Executive Council, Standing Commissions, and Province meetings, only locations and schedules that provide full independent accessibility to all events, both official and ancillary, for all members of this Church including but not limited to the hearing impaired, sight impaired, and persons with other physical disabilities.

The House of Bishops Committee on Miscellaneous Resolutions presented its Report #10 on HD Message #161 on Resolution C052 (Transfer of Diocesan Territories) and moved concurrence.

The House concurred
(Communicated to the House of Deputies in HB Message #259)

Final Text of Resolution:
(C052)
Resolved, That the request of the Diocese of Wyoming and the Diocese of Idaho acting through their regularly convened conventions, and upon the approvals and consents of the respective Ecclesiastical authorities and of the standing committees of both dioceses that the territory generally described as the parish of Alta, Wyoming, and more particularly described as that portion of Teton County, Wyoming, lying west and north of the summit of the Teton Mountain Range, including the unincorporated community of Alta, be transferred from the Diocese of Wyoming to the Diocese of Idaho pursuant to Article V, Section 6 of the Constitution of the Protestant Episcopal Church.

The House of Bishops Committee on Miscellaneous Resolutions presented its Report #12 on HD Message #143 on Resolution C026 (Reduce the Use of Toxic Chemicals) and moved concurrence.

The House concurred
(Communicated to the House of Deputies in HB Message #260)

Final Text of Resolution:
(C026)
Resolved, That the 74th General Convention urge congregations, dioceses, provinces, and all church institutions to initiate a plan in the next triennium for the management of church buildings and grounds that phases out the use of unsafe pesticides, herbicides, and other toxic chemicals to control pests and undesirable plants, and institutes the use of alternatives, recognizing that children are the population most susceptible to toxins; and be it further
Resolved, That the appropriate standing committee report back to the 75th General Convention regarding the ongoing effectiveness of this work.

Committees and Commissions
The House of Bishops Committee on Committees and Commissions presented its Report #3 on HD Message #144 on Resolution B026 (Criminal Justice Committee) and moved concurrence.

The House concurred
(Communicated to the House of Deputies in HB Message #261)

Final Text of Resolution:
(B026)
Resolved, That the 74th General Convention recommend that, commencing with the triennium beginning in 2004, the Joint Committee on Criminal Justice be established as a Committee of the Executive Council called for

the purpose of fulfilling a revised mandate, convening two meetings of the Committee per year to implement the policy of the Committee, and accomplishing the work defined in the revised mandate. This work consists of the following tasks:

> Task 1—The establishing of a network of individuals and organizations involved in criminal justice that can assist the committee in accomplishing its purpose of achieving just reform; the work to be accomplished by committee members and the Church Center Officer for Criminal Justice Reform; $5,000 to be allocated for this work.
>
> Task 2—The preparing of an educational and consciousness-raising program to be presented to the Church; the work to be accomplished by a sub-committee convened by the Church Center Officer for Criminal Justice Reform; $15,000 to be allocated for this work.
>
> Task 3—The gathering and availability of a resource inventory of successful criminal justice programs dealing with advocacy, leadership, and program delivery; the work to be accomplished by committee members and the Church Center Officer for Criminal Justice Reform, and to be published as a web resource by the Communication department of the Church Center; $3,000 to be allocated for this work.
>
> Task 4—CCJI recognizes the need for development of worship materials specific to this ministry, and will undertake this work, which will be developed by committee members, the Church Center Officer for Criminal Justice Reform, and the Church Center Liturgical Officer as liaison to the Standing Commission on Liturgy and Music; and will be published in the forthcoming *Book of Occasional Services*, as well as being made widely available to both Episcopal and Ecumenical users via the web; $15,000 to be allocated for this work. A further $24,000 to be allocated for meetings, making a total of $62,000 that the General Convention request the Joint Standing Committee on Program, Budget and Finance to consider for the full implementation of this resolution.

Constitution

The House of Bishops Committee on Constitution presented its Report #10 on HD Message #117 on Resolution A143 (Amend Constitution Article I.7) and moved concurrence.

The House concurred
(Communicated to the House of Deputies in HB message #262)

Final Text of Resolution:

(A143)
Resolved, That Article I.7 of the Constitution be amended to read:
Section 7. The General Convention shall meet not less than once in each three years, at a time and place *determined in accordance with the Canons.* appointed by a preceding Convention; but if there shall appear to the

~~Presiding Bishop, acting with the advice and consent of the Executive Council of the Church or of a successor canonical body having substantially the powers now vested in the Executive Council, sufficient cause for changing the place or date so appointed, the Presiding Bishop, with the advice and consent of such body, shall appoint another place or date, or both, for such meeting.~~ Special meetings may be *held as* provided for by Canon.
And be it further
Resolved, That this resolution be sent within six months to the Secretary of the Convention of every Diocese to be made known to the Diocesan Convention at its next meeting.

National and International Concerns
The House of Bishops Committee on National and International Concerns presented its Report #24 on HD Message #59 on Resolution A035 (Implement Humanitarian Goals in Africa) and moved concurrence.

The House concurred
(Communicated to the House of Deputies in HB Message #263)

Final Text of Resolution:
(A035)
Resolved, That the 74th General Convention, in response to widespread humanitarian needs in Africa, commend those churches in Africa fighting AIDS, poverty and injustice, and call on The Episcopal Church at all levels to partner with the Anglican Churches in Africa and other agencies to implement the United Nations Millennium Development Goals in Africa; and be it further
Resolved, That the Convention commit $100,000 per year for three years through the Partnership Office for Africa to support a church-wide campaign to implement humanitarian development goals in Africa; and be it further
Resolved, That the General Convention request the Joint Standing Committee on Program, Budget and Finance to consider a budget allocation of $300,000 for implementation of this resolution.

The House of Bishops Committee on National and International Concerns presented its Report #25 on HD Message #80 on Resolution A123 (Diocesan Alcohol and Drug Dependency Policies) and moved concurrence.

The House concurred
(Communicated to the House of Deputies in HB Message #264)

Final Text of Resolution:
(A123)
Resolved, That the 74th General Convention call on all dioceses to establish Diocesan Committees on Alcoholism and Drug Dependency to provide educational programs for clergy, church staff, and congregations that take account of recent advances in treatment of alcohol and drug dependency, and that such committees address problems related to alcohol or drug dependency in clergy, church staff, and, when requested, laypersons; and be it further
Resolved, That dioceses make strong efforts to develop policies concerning treatment and future employment for diocesan clergy and church staff who are dependent on alcohol or drugs; and be it further
Resolved, That dioceses make strong efforts to ensure that health care insurance for diocesan clergy and church staff includes adequate coverage for mental health and addiction, particularly inpatient treatment for dependency on alcohol or drugs.

The House of Bishops Committee on National and International Concerns presented its Report #26 on HD Message #61 on Resolution A006 (Employment Policies Task Group) and moved concurrence.

The House concurred
(Communicated to the House of Deputies in HB Message #265)

Final Text of Resolution:
(A006)
Resolved, That the 74th General Convention authorize the Executive Council to appoint a Task Group in consultation with the Church Pension Fund to study employment policies and practices in the dioceses and parishes of the church and consider policy recommendations to the 75th General Convention that address issues of equity and justice for church employees working in circumstances of both affluence and poverty; and be it further
Resolved, That the General Convention request the Joint Standing Committee on Program, Budget and Finance to consider a budget allocation of $10,000 for implementation of this resolution.

The House of Bishops Committee on National and International Concerns presented its Report #27 on HD Message #87 on Resolution A130 (Establish Living Wage) and moved concurrence.

The House concurred
(Communicated to the House of Deputies in HB Message #266)

Final Text of Resolution:
(A130)
Resolved, That the 74th General Convention of The Episcopal Church,

through the Secretary of the Convention, call upon the President of the United States and members of Congress to establish a living wage including health benefits as the standard of compensation for all workers in the United States; and be it further
Resolved, That it is the policy of The Episcopal Church and its dioceses and congregations to provide employees with a living wage including health benefits and be a model for ethical labor practices; and be it further
Resolved, That it is the policy of The Episcopal Church to insist that companies in which the Church invests or with which it contracts provide their employees with a living wage and serve as a model for ethical labor practices; and be it further
Resolved, That the 74th General Convention continue to support living wage campaigns in the cities and counties of every diocese; and be it further
Resolved, That the 74th General Convention strongly affirm the right of workers to organize as protected by federal and state law especially in low wage industries and businesses and including the institutions of every diocese.

Social and Urban Affairs
The House of Bishops Committee on Social and Urban Affairs presented its Report #22 on HD Message #135 on Resolution D077 (Post 9/11 Racial Hatred and Incarcerations) and moved concurrence.
The House concurred
(Communicated to the House of Deputies in HB Message #267)

Final Text of Resolution:
(D077)
Resolved, That this Church affirm its abhorrence of all violence toward and racial profiling of Muslims and people of color done in the name of religion, especially toward our Muslim brothers and sisters; and be it further
Resolved, That all members of this Church be encouraged to reach out in friendship to our neighbors of all religions—especially at this time to Muslims—seeking mutual understanding and expressing support; and be it further
Resolved, That The Episcopal Church direct the Committee on National Concerns of Executive Council to examine and direct the Office of Government Relations to monitor governmental policies on the imprisonment and restrictions of American citizens or legal residents based solely on ethnicity; and be it further
Resolved, That the General Convention acknowledge the danger that in this post 9/11 era a repeat of racial hatred, terrorism, hysteria, and a failure of political leadership could result in governmental policies causing the incarceration of citizens and legal residents based solely on their ethnicity.

The House of Bishops Committee on Social and Urban Affairs presented its Report #23 on HD Message #152 on Resolution D025 (Committee on Racism) and moved concurrence.

The House concurred
(Communicated to the House of Deputies in HB Message #268)

Final Text of Resolution:
(D025)
Resolved, That the 74th General Convention call upon the Presiding Bishop and the Executive Council, working through its Anti-Racism Advisory Committee, to convene a series of conversations among various groups of people of color of all generations, to prepare a report to the 75th Convention on recommending substantive, systemic changes in the current norms of behavior and practice within The Episcopal Church that would enhance its inclusivity and authentically acknowledge and celebrate its diversity; and be it further
Resolved, That the Presiding Bishop and the Executive Council empower appropriate staff persons to work closely with Churches Uniting in Christ and other interreligious partners to fashion a mutually-agreed-upon anti-racism training modality that would permit coherent ecumenical dialogue on overcoming the sin of racism as an important step in furthering the quest for Christian unity.

RECESS
The Presiding Bishop called a ten minute recess at 11:54 a.m.

RESUME
The House resumed at 12:12 p.m.

Joint Nominating Committee for the Election of the Presiding Bishop
The Secretary read a message from the House of Deputies announcing that the following people have been elected to the Joint Nominating Committee for the Election of the Presiding Bishop.

Province I	Mr. A.T. Mollegen Jr., The Rev. Thomas J. Brown
Province II	Ms. Diane B. Pollard, The Rev. Jeannette DeFriest
Province III	Mrs. Jane R. Cosby, The Rev. Canon Mark Harris
Province IV	Mr. Vincent Currie Jr., The Rev. E. Claiborne Jones
Province V	Dr. Scott E. Evenbeck, The Rev. Dr. Richard L. Tolliver
Province VI	Mr. Don Betts, The Rev. Ann K. Fontaine

Province VII   Ms. Sarah J. Knoll, The Rev. James P. Haney, V
Province VIII   Mrs. Bettye Jo Harris, The Rev. Bavi E. Rivera
Province IX   Ms. Blanca Echeverry, The Rev. Luis F. Ruiz

The House of Bishops Committee on Dispatch of Business moved to concur.
The House concurred

Dispatch of Business

The House of Bishops Committee on Dispatch of Business presented its Report #13 on the Appointments by the President of the House of Deputies to the Board of Episcopal Church Archives and moved concurrence.
The House concurred
(Communicated to the House of Deputies in HB Message #269)

Final Text of Resolution:

Resolved, That the General Convention confirm the appointment by the President of the House of Deputies to the Board of the Episcopal Church Archives of:
     The Rev. Robert G. Carron of Connecticut
     The Rev. John Kitigawa of Arizona
     Ms. Judy Dailey of Easton
     Ms. Michaela French of Maryland

The House of Bishops Committee on Dispatch of Business presented its Report #14 on Resolution the Appointments by President of House of Deputies to Board for Church Deployment and moved concurrence.
The House concurred
(Communicated to the House of Deputies in HB Message #270)

Final Text of Resolution:

Resolved, That the General Convention confirm the appointment by the President of the House of Deputies to the Board for Church Deployment of:
     Clerical:
     The Rev. Canon Matthew Stockard of East Carolina
     Lay:
     Canon Jill Swans of Pennsylvania
     Canon Alice Clayton of East Tennessee
     Ms. Emily Peach of Missouri

Rules of Order

The House of Bishops Committee on Rules of Order presented its Report #6 on HD Message #102 on Resolution D044 (Election Clarification) and moved concurrence.
The House concurred
(Communicated to the House of Deputies in HB Message #271)

Final Text of Resolution:
(D044)
Resolved, That Joint Rule of Order 18.(c) be amended to read in part as follows:

(c)   The Secretary *of the House of Deputies* and the Treasurer of the General Convention under Canon I.1.*1(j).*

Privilege and Courtesy
The House of Bishops Committee on Privilege and Courtesy presented its Report #3 on HD Message #208 on Resolution D088 (Ministry to the Deaf) and moved concurrence.

The House concurred
(Communicated to the House of Deputies in HB Message #272)

Final Text of Resolution:
(D088)
Whereas, many in The Episcopal Church have been striving to make our church accessible to people whose primary language is American Sign Language; and

Whereas, St. Ann's Church for the Deaf, New York City, was organized in 1852 by the Rev. Thomas Gallaudet; and

Whereas, the Rev. Henry Winter Syle, the first deaf man ordained a priest (1853), brought the Gospel to deaf people in their own language; and

Whereas, this truly "silent minority" has had a presence at every General Convention since 1961, reminding the larger body that the churches of the Episcopal Conference of the Deaf are, indeed, part of The Episcopal Church and that it is necessary to facilitate understanding and communication in meetings of all levels of the Church; and

Whereas, an outward and visible sign of this ministry has been present in the 74th General Convention in the work of Rayelenn Casey of the Diocese of Central Pennsylvania, Donna Scarfe of the Diocese of Iowa, Kathy Beetham of the Diocese of North Carolina, Jan Williamson of the Diocese of San Diego, Nancy Diener of the Diocese of Minnesota, and Diane Lynch of the Diocese of New Jersey; now therefore be it

Resolved, That the 74th General Convention of the Episcopal Church commend the Episcopal Conference of the Deaf for its continued efforts to support deaf clergy and ministry in the deaf community so that the Good News may be brought to all of Jesus's sheep.

The House of Bishops Committee on Privilege and Courtesy presented its Report #4 on HD Message #207 on Resolution D092 (Greetings to the Archbishop of Canterbury) and moved concurrence.

The House concurred
(Communicated to the House of Deputies in HB Message #273)

Final Text of Resolution:
(D092)
Whereas, it has pleased Her Majesty Queen Elizabeth II to seek the advice of the Rt. Hon. Tony Blair, First Lord of the Treasury and Prime Minister, in the selection of the 104th Archbishop of Canterbury; and

Whereas, the Prime Minister advised Her Majesty to grant her license to the Dean and Chapter of Canterbury to elect the Most Rev. Rowan Williams, Bishop of Monmouth and Archbishop of the Church in Wales, to the See of Canterbury; and

Whereas, the Most Rev. Rowan Williams, having been installed in the Primatial Chair of St. Augustine of Canterbury as the Primate of All England, is the symbolic Head of the Anglican Communion; now therefore be it

Resolved, That the 74th General Convention send its respectful and affectionate greetings to His Grace, the Archbishop of Canterbury, to whom we say in his native tongue "*Cofion gynnes* (Warm greetings), *Pob hwyl* (Good luck), and *Yr Bendith Duw Hollalliog, yr Tad, yr Mab, yr Usprid Glad, a gydach ti, yn wastad* (God Almighty, the Father, the Son, and the Holy Spirit, go with you always)"; and be it further

Resolved, That the Secretary of the General Convention send a copy of this resolution to the Most Rev. Rowan Williams, Archbishop of Canterbury and Primate of All England, in token of the esteem of the General Convention for his office and our affection for his person, as we look forward to participation with him in the councils of the world-wide Anglican Communion.

The House of Bishops Committee on Privilege and Courtesy presented its Report #5 on HD Message #209 on Resolution D087 (Evening of Conversations) and moved concurrence.

The House concurred
(Communicated to the House of Deputies in HB Message #274)

Final Text of Resolution:
(D087)
Whereas, the Evening of Conversations provided members of this Convention an opportunity for exchanging ideas, experiences, and feelings about the challenging topics of Christian hope, interfaith dialogue, war and peace, 20/20, and engaging God's mission; now therefore be it

MINNEAPOLIS MEETING　　　　　　　　HOUSE OF BISHOPS

Resolved, That the 74th General Convention of The Episcopal Church express our gratitude to the planners, panelists, and participants in these stimulating conversations.

The House of Bishops Committee on Privilege and Courtesy presented its Report #7 on HD Message #206 on Resolution D090 (Nancy Piatkowski) and moved concurrence.

The House concurred
(Communicated to the House of Deputies in HB Message #275)

Final Text of Resolution:
(D090)
Whereas, Nancy Piatkowski served the Commission on the Status of Women; as Vice President of the Episcopal Women's History Project; and as Archivist for the Diocese of Western New York; and
Whereas, she was an educator, artisan, and friend who (in her own words) "marched to a different accordion;" and
Whereas, she died on July 12, 2003, after a short illness; now therefore be it
Resolved, That the 74th General Convention extend its sympathy to the family of Nancy Piatkowski, and that the Secretary be instructed to send a copy of this resolution to them.

The House of Bishops Committee on Privilege and Courtesy presented its Report #8 on HD Message #205 on Resolution D089 (Thanks to Bishop Jelinek and the Diocese of Minnesota) and moved concurrence.

The House concurred
(Communicated to the House of Deputies in HB Message #276)

Final Text of Resolution:
(D089)
Whereas, the Rt. Rev. James L. Jelinek and the people of the Diocese of Minnesota have offered gracious hospitality to the 74th General Convention by welcoming us at the convention center, and by providing assistance at the daily liturgies; and
Whereas, the Very Rev. Spenser Simrill, Dean of St. Mark's Cathedral, and the Rev. Dr. Sandye Wilson, Rector of Gethsemane Church, have made these churches available for creative worship, educational programs, and social events; now therefore be it
Resolved, That the 74th General Convention of the Episcopal Church give thanks and praise to God for the Rt. Rev. James Jelinek and the faithful people of the Diocese of Minnesota for their inclusive and generous hospitality.

JOURNAL   TENTH DAY

The House of Bishops Committee on Privilege and Courtesy presented its Report #9 on HD Message #204 on Resolution D085 (Gratitude to Church Periodical Club) and moved concurrence.

                                                    The House concurred
              (Communicated to the House of Deputies in HB Message #277)

Final Text of Resolution:

(D085)
Whereas, The Church Periodical Club continues to distribute "Energy Lift" candy to Deputies as it has done for ten successive General Conventions while engaging in the ministry of providing the printed word for more than a century; now therefore be it
Resolved, That the 74th General Convention of the Episcopal Church express appreciation to Priscilla Magar, the Church Periodical Club President, and to all the co-workers of the Church Periodical Club, for their traditional gift of succulent "Energy Lift" candy.

The House of Bishops Committee on Privilege and Courtesy presented its Report #10 on HD Message #203 on Resolution D084 (LISTSERV Appreciation) and moved concurrence.

                                                    The House concurred
              (Communicated to the House of Deputies in HB Message #278)

Final Text of Resolution:

(D084)
Whereas, the House of Bishops and the House of Deputies Listserv, lovingly created and maintained for General Convention by Dr. Louie Crew, was handed over in its adolescence to the gracious heart of Cynthia McFarland; and
Whereas, the ushers, better known as the "Keystone Kops," have saved us from repeating missteps and procedural errors; and
Whereas, we give special thanks for the ministry of Brian Reid, technical advisor to the listserv and world expert in internet technology; and
Whereas, this listserv enabled us to become better acquainted with each other as well as to discuss our differences and our commonalities; and
Whereas, the listserv was open to others as kibitzers, enabling the entire Church to observe our discussions and our frailties; now therefore be it
Resolved, That the 74th General Convention of The Episcopal Church give thanks for the ministry of communication of Brian Reid, Cynthia McFarland and her faithful ushers: Matt Chew, Ann Fontaine, Christopher Hart, Barbara Mann, Connie Ott, and Nigel Renton.

Elections

The Bishop of Hawaii was elected Vice-Chair of the House of Bishops.

The Bishop Suffragan of Southern Ohio was elected Secretary of the House of Bishops.

(Communicated to the House of Deputies in HB Message #279)

Resolution of Thanks

The House of Bishops Committee on Privilege and Courtesy presented its Report #11 on a Courtesy Resolution B028 (Gratitude to the Presiding Bishop) and moved adoption.

Final Text of Resolution:

(B028)

Resolved, **That the House of Bishops expressed deep gratitude to the Presiding Bishop, Frank T. Griswold, III, for his guidance throughout this 74th General Convention; and for his profound wisdom and spirituality.**

Motion carried
Resolution adopted
(Communicated to the House of Deputies in HB Message #280)

Secretariat Staff

The Presiding Bishop presented the House of Bishops Secretariat staff to the House.

RECESS

Following announcements by the Secretary, the House of Bishops Committee on Dispatch of Business moved that the House stand in recess until 2:30 p.m.

Motion carried

The House recessed at 12:36 p.m. with prayer led by Chaplain McIntosh.

AFTERNOON SESSION

The House reconvened at 2:30 p.m. with the Presiding Bishop in the chair.

Thirty minutes was allowed for the Chaplain's reflections and conversation.

The House resumed at 3:04 p.m.

Dispatch of Business

The House of Bishops Committee on Dispatch of Business presented its Report #15 on HD Message #248 on the Election of Trustees of the Church Pension Fund and moved concurrence.

The House concurred
(Communicated to the House of Deputies in HB Message #281)

Final Text of Resolution:
Resolved, That the following persons are elected as Trustees of the Church Pension Fund pursuant to Title I, Canon 8, Section 2:

To three-year terms:
Mrs. Barbara B. Creed
Mr. Cecil Wray

To six-year terms:
The Very Rev. M.L. Agnew Jr.
Mr. James E. Bayne
Mr. Sheridan C. Biggs
Mr. David L. Brigham
The Rev Canon Carlson Gerdau
The Rt. Rev. Gayle Elizabeth Harris
The Rt. Rev. Robert Hodges Johnson
Ms. Joon D. Matsumura
Mrs. Virginia A. Norman
Mr. David R. Pitts
The Rev. Canon V. Gene Robinson
The Rt. Rev. Wayne P. Wright

Canons
The House of Bishops Committee on Canons presented its Report #16 on HD Message #167 on Resolution A144 (Amend Canon I.1.14) and moved concurrence.

The House concurred
(Communicated to the House of Deputies in HB Message #282)

Final Text of Resolution:
(A144)
Resolved, **That Canon I.1.14 be amended to read as follows:**

(a) At each meeting of the General Convention the Joint Standing Committee on Planning and Arrangements shall submit to the General Convention its recommendations for sites for the meeting of the General Convention to be held as the ~~second~~ ***third*** succeeding General Convention following the General Convention at which the report is made. In making such recommendations, the Committee shall certify to the Convention the willingness of the Dioceses within which recommended sites are located to have the General Convention meet within their jurisdictions.

(b) From the sites recommended by the Joint Committee, the General Convention shall approve no fewer than three nor more than five sites as possible for such meeting of the General Convention.

(c) From the sites approved by the General Convention, the Joint

Committee, with the advice and consent of a majority vote of the following: The Presidents and the Vice-Presidents of both Houses of Convention, the Presidents of the Provinces and the Executive Council, shall determine the site for such General Convention and proceed to make all reasonable and necessary arrangements and commitments for that meeting of the General Convention. ~~The site shall be recommended before the meeting of the General Convention next preceding that Convention.~~ *The site and date thus selected shall be deemed to have been appointed by the General Convention, as provided in the Constitution.*

~~(d)~~ ~~Subject to the Constitution, the General Convention shall appoint a site at the General Convention next preceding such Convention.~~

~~(e)~~ (d) Upon the final selection of and the arrangements for the site for that General Convention, the Joint Committee shall advise the Secretary of General Convention, who shall communicate the determination to the Dioceses.

~~(f)~~ ~~In the event of a change of circumstances indicating the necessity or advisability of changing the site of a future meeting of the General Convention previously determined by action of the General Convention, the Joint Committee shall investigate and make recommendations to the Presiding Bishop, to the President of the House of Deputies, and to the Executive Council if such Convention is the next succeeding meeting or to the General Convention with respect to any later meeting of the Convention.~~

~~(g)~~ (e) Within such guidelines as may have been established by the General Convention regarding the date and length of future General Conventions, and pursuant to the reasonable and necessary arrangements and commitments with the Dioceses and operators of facilities within the Diocese in which the next General Convention will be held, the Joint Committee shall fix the date and the length of the next succeeding Convention, report the same to the Secretary of the General Convention and include the same in its report to the Convention. In the event of a change of circumstances indicating the necessity or advisability of changing the date or length previously fixed, the Joint Committee shall investigate and make recommendations to the Presiding Bishop and the President of the House of Deputies, who, with the advice and consent of the Executive Council, may fix a different date or length or both.

The House of Bishops Committee on Canons presented its Report #17 on HD Message #162 on Resolution D072 (Amendment Canon III.22.3 (a)) and moved concurrence.

The House concurred
(Communicated to the House of Deputies in HB Message #283)

Final Text of Resolution:
(D072)
Resolved, That Canon III.22.3(a) be amended to read in part as follows:
Sec. 3(a) When a Diocese desires the ordination of a Bishop-elect, if the date of the election occurs within ~~120 days~~ *three months* before a meeting of the General Convention, the Standing Committeeof the Diocese shall, by its President, or by some person or persons specially appointed, forward to the Secretary of the House of Deputies evidence of the election of the Bishop-elect by the Convention of the Diocese, together with evidence that the Bishop-elect has been duly ordered Deacon and Priest, evidence of acceptance of election, and a testimonial signed by a constitutional majority of the Convention, and a summary of biographical information relating to the Bishop-elect.
And be it further
Resolved, That Canon III.22.1 be amended by adding a new subsection (f):
Sec. 1(f) No Diocese shall elect a Bishop within thirty days before a meeting of the General Convention.

National and International Concerns
The House of Bishops Committee on National and International Concerns presented its Report #13 on HD Message #243 on Resolution C014 (Reaffirmation of Faith and Purpose) and moved concurrence with referral to a Standing Commission.

Final Text of Resolution:
(C014)
Resolved, That the 74th General Convention remain steadfast in seeking to encourage the strength and mission of the Episcopal Church and the Anglican Communion. This 74th General Convention is called to renew our commitment to the fullness of our Anglican Heritage. We are further called to act and legislate in ways that honor our Anglican traditions and Holy Scripture; and that unify our worldwide Christian witness and mission.

Motion carried
Resolution referred to a Standing Commission
(Communicated to the House of Deputies in HB Message #284)

Communications

The House of Bishops Committee on Communications presented its Report #13 on HD Message #156 on Resolution D057 (Use of Technology: General Convention) and moved concurrence.

The House concurred
(Communicated to the House of Deputies in HB Message #285)

Final Text of Resolution:

(D057)
Resolved, That the 74th General Convention express its gratitude to the Reverend Rosemari Sullivan, Secretary of the General Convention, and to her staff, for the use of technology to expedite and ease the work of the Convention. In particular we are thankful for the continued refinement of the electronic voting system, and for the use of the internet and computers in the processing and distribution of resolutions and the reporting of the action taken on the multitude of resolutions that come before the Convention; and be it further

Resolved, That the 74th General Convention commend the Very Reverend George Werner, President of the House of Deputies, on the creation of a task force on emerging technologies that explored and outlined avenues for expanded use of electronic technologies during the last triennium; and be it further

Resolved, That the Convention recommend the further development of such technologies for the 2006 General Convention that would facilitate the work of the convention, particularly in the areas of the electronic distribution of materials, electronic voting, electronic and real-time revisions of legislation, and others. The development of these technologies will be motivated and guided by a desire to speed the work of convention, reduce costs and the consumption of paper, and enhance the effective communication of the work of succeeding conventions; and be it further

Resolved, That an appropriate interim body investigate whether and how we might use technology to facilitate actions of General Convention between triennial sessions.

Messages from House of Deputies

The House of Bishops Committee on Dispatch of Business announced that there are no further messages from the House of Deputies.

Privilege and Courtesy

The House of Bishops Committee on Privilege and Courtesy presented its Report #27 on HD Message #289 on Resolution D093 (Honoring Sonia Francis) and moved concurrence.

The House concurred
(Communicated to the House of Deputies in HB Message #289)

Final Text of Resolution:
(D093)
Whereas, **Sonia Francis** was born in Honduras, emigrated to the United States, and joined the U.S. Army; and
Whereas, she then went to New York and joined the staff of the Episcopal Church Center as support staff for communications; and
Whereas, she became the Director of Communications and in 1997 was promoted to senior executive status as Deputy to the Presiding Bishop for **Program;** and
Whereas, she enjoyed singing duets with the President of the House of Deputies on the way to a conference; and
Whereas, she served the Church faithfully and effectively for 37 years, enjoying the respect and friendship of the Episcopal Church Center staff; and
Whereas, when she retired in March 2003 she had been the longest-serving member of the Episcopal Church Center staff; therefore be it
Resolved, That the 74th General Convention of The Episcopal Church recognize with great appreciation the faithful and dedicated service of Sonia Francis and wish her a long and happy retirement.

Prayer Book, Liturgy and Church Music
The Committee on Prayer Book, Liturgy and Church Music presented its Report #15 on HD Message #258 on Resolution A103 (Adopt the Revised Common Lectionary) and moved concurrence.

The House concurred

(Communicated to the House of Deputies in HB Message #287)

Final Text of Resolution:
(A103)
Resolved, That the 74th General Convention authorize the permissive use of the Revised Common Lectionary under the direction of the Bishop or Ecclesiastical authority of the Diocese.

Dispatch of Business
The House of Bishops Committee on Dispatch of Business moved that all legislation not handled at this Convention, be referred to Committees, Commissions, Agencies and Boards.

Motion carried

Thoughtful work
The Presiding Bishop thanked the House for its thoughtful and graceful work.

Adjourn
The House of Bishops Committee on Dispatch of Business moved that the House adjourn *sine die*.

Motion carried

The House adjourned at 3:30 p.m.

HOUSE OF DEPUTIES MINUTES

FIRST DAY

Wednesday
July 30, 2003

MORNING SESSION

This being the day and place designated for the meeting of the 74th General Convention, the President of the House of Deputies, the Very Rev. George Werner of Pittsburgh, called the House to order at 11:09 a.m. at the Minneapolis Convention Center in Minneapolis, in the Diocese of Minnesota.

The President spoke about the organization of the House of Deputies.

Appointment of the Chaplain
The President announced the appointment of the Rev. Brian N. Prior of Spokane as Chaplain of the House of Deputies for this Convention. The Chaplain led the House in opening prayers.

Appointment of Parliamentarian
The President announced the appointment of Mrs. Pauline Getz of San Diego as Parliamentarian of the House of Deputies. The President remarked on the untimely passing of John Cannon, Esq., the former Parliamentarian.

The President called on the Secretary for those for whom testimonials had been reported.

There were no objections.

Certification of Deputies
The House of Deputies Committee on Credentials presented its Report #1 and certified that a quorum was present for the transaction of business. For the morning of the First Legislative Day, there were 817 new deputies certified. At this legislative session there were 409 clerical deputies and 408 lay deputies certified and seated. The total count of the House is 825. The number of votes for a motion to prevail is 410.

Quorum
The President requested the Secretary to certify that a quorum was present.

The Secretary so certified:

> I hereby certify that, pursuant to Section 4, Article 1, of the Constitution, the clerical order being represented by at least one deputy in the majority of the dioceses entitled to representation in this Convention, and the lay order being likewise represented by at least one deputy in each of a majority of the dioceses entitled to representation, there is an undoubted quorum of this House present for the transaction of business.
>
> *The Rev. Rosemari G. Sullivan, Secretary*

The Chair of the House of Deputies Committee on Dispatch of Business moved that, since the Secretary had certified to this body the presence of a quorum, the House dispense with the calling of the roll, pursuant to the provisions of Canon I.1.1(a).

Motion carried

Election of the Secretary of the House of Deputies

The President called for nominations for Secretary of the House of Deputies. Deputy Palmore of Virginia placed in nomination the name of the Rev. Rosemari G. Sullivan of Virginia as Secretary of the House of Deputies.

The House of Deputies Committee on Dispatch of Business moved to close the nominations.

Motion carried

The House of Deputies Committee on Dispatch of Business moved for a single ballot.

Motion carried

The President called on the Vice-President of the House of Deputies, Deputy Currie of Central Gulf Coast, to cast a single ballot for the Rev. Rosemari G. Sullivan for Secretary of the House of Deputies.

Motion carried
Secretary of the House of Deputies elected

House of Deputies Organized

The President declared that the House of Deputies was now organized.

The President appointed Deputy Crump of West Tennessee and Deputy Perez of Los Angeles to so inform the House of Bishops.

Appointment of Assistant Secretaries

The Secretary announced pursuant to Canon I.1.1(d), subject to the approval of the House, the appointment of the following Assistant Secretaries:
1. Credentials and Voting Secretary: The Rev. Dr. Gregory S. Straub of Easton.
2. Assistant Credentials and Voting Secretary: The Rev. Gwen L. Buehrens of Massachusetts.
3. Recording Secretary: The Rev. Saundra Richardson of Michigan.
4. Assistant Recording Secretary: Mr. Willie Smith of Newark.

Approval received
Assistant Secretaries appointed

Legislative Committees

The Secretary announced the appointment of Legislative Committees, including Chairs and Vice-Chairs (See Appendix A–Day 1 for Legislative Committee Rosters).

Appointment of the Secretary of General Convention
The House of Deputies Committee on Dispatch of Business moved to elect the Rev. Rosemari Sullivan of Virginia as Secretary of the General Convention.

Motion carried
Secretary of General Convention elected
(Communicated to the House of Bishops in HD Message #26)

Election of the Treasurer of the General Convention
The President called for nominations for the Treasurer of the General Convantion. Deputy Anderson of Michigan nominated Mr. Thomas Herskowitz as Treasurer of the General Convention. The Chair of the House of Deputies Committee on Dispatch of Business moved for the Secretary to cast one ballot for Thomas Herskowitz.

Motion carried
Treasurer of General Convention elected
(Communicated to the House of Bishops in HD Message #27)

Dispatch of Business
The House of Deputies Committee on Dispatch of Business reminded the House that the Rules of Order limit floor access to Deputies only. The Chair of the House of Deputies Committee on Dispatch of Business moved to suspend the Rules of Order to allow pages, volunteers, and others needed for the conduct of business.

The President reminded the House that a two-thirds majority is required to suspend the Rules.

Motion carried
Rules suspended

Delegations with Seat and Voice
The President welcomed the delegation from Liberia, which has seat and voice in the House. The President welcomed two youth representatives from each Province, who have seat and voice in the House. The President called on the House of Deputies to welcome these delegations.

Dispatch of Business
The House of Deputies Committee on Dispatch of Business presented its Report #1 on Resolution A156 (2003 General Convention Daily Agenda) and moved adoption with amendment.

Original Text of Resolution:
(A156)
[Note: See *The Blue Book* Report of the Joint Standing Committee on Planning and Arrangements, pp. 330–332. *Ed.*]

Committee Amendment:

Resolved, the House of Bishops concurring, That the 2003 General Convention function through the following activities:
1. formal legislative sessions of the two Houses;
2. a joint session for presentation of the budget proposal;
3. meetings of the legislative committees of the two Houses; and
4. open hearings to be conducted as needed by all legislative committees; and be it further

Resolved, That the schedule and the daily timetable of the 74th General Convention held in Minneapolis, Minnesota be:

Sunday, July 27, 2003

11:00 a.m.–2:30 p.m.	Volunteer Supervisors Gathering
4:00 p.m.–6:00 p.m.	HD Secretariat and Committee on Dispatch of Business Orientation

Monday, July 28, 2003

9:30 a.m.–5:00 p.m.	Registration
9:30 a.m.–5:00 p.m.	Deputy Certification
2:00 p.m.–6:00 p.m.	Legislative Committee Officers Orientation

Tuesday, July 29, 2003

9:30 a.m.–5:30 p.m.	Registration
9:00 a.m.–12:00 noon	Legislative Committee Meetings
9:30 a.m.–1:45 p.m.	Deputy Certification
2:00 p.m.–3:00 p.m.	PB/Pres HD Presentation to GC
3:00 p.m.–5:00 p.m.	Orientation
3:30 p.m.–5:30 p.m.	Deputy Certification
8:00 p.m.	Legislative Committee Meetings

Wednesday, July 30, 2003—First Legislative Day

7:30 a.m.–9:00 a.m.	Legislative Committee Meetings
8:00 a.m.–5:00 p.m.	Registration
8:30 a.m.–9:30 a.m.	Deputy Certification
9:30 a.m.–10:45 p.m.	Eucharist and Scripture Reflection
11:00 a.m.–12:30 p.m.	Legislative Session
12:30 p.m. –1:*15* p.m.	Deputy Certification
2:00 p.m.–4:00 p.m.	Legislative Committee Meetings
4:15 p.m.–6:00 p.m.	Legislative Session
8:00 p.m.	Conversations

Thursday, July 31, 2003—Second Legislative Day

7:30 a.m.–9:00 a.m.	Legislative Committee Meetings
8:00 a.m.–5:00 p.m.	Registration
8:30 a.m.–9:30 a.m.	Deputy Certification
9:30 a.m.–10:45 a.m.	Eucharist and Scripture Reflection
11:00 a.m.–12:30 p.m.	Legislative Session

12:30 p.m.–1:*15* p.m.	Deputy Certification
2:00 p.m.–3:30 p.m.	Legislative Committee Hearings
3:45 p.m.–6:00 p.m.	Legislative Session
5:00 p.m.	Resolution Filing Deadline
7:00 p.m.–*9:00* p.m.	*Presiding Bishop's Forum–Global Reconciliation*
8:00 p.m.	PB&F and Hearing

Friday, August 1, 2003—Third Legislative Day

7:00 a.m.–8:30 a.m.	Legislative Committee Meetings
9:00 a.m.–1:00 p.m.	Morning of Prayer
12:00 noon–5:00 p.m.	Registration
1:00 p.m.–1:*45* p.m.	Deputy Certification
2:30 p.m.–6:00 p.m.	Legislative Session
8:00 p.m.	PB&F Hearing

Saturday, August 2, 2003—Fifth Legislative Day

7:30 a.m.–9:00 a.m.	Legislative Committee Meetings
8:00 a.m.–1:00 p.m.	Registration
8:30 a.m.–9:30 a.m.	Deputy Certification
9:30 a.m.–10:45 a.m.	Eucharist and Scripture Reflection
11:00 a.m.–1:00 p.m.	Legislative Session
Evening	*Seminary Dinners*

Sunday, August 3, 2003—Fifth Legislative Day

10:00 a.m.	UTO In-gathering and Eucharist
12:30 p.m.–5:00 p.m.	Registration
1:*15* p.m.–*2:00* p.m.	Deputy Certification
2:30 p.m.–6:00 p.m.	Legislative Session
5:00 p.m.	*Bishops' Dinner*
8:00 p.m.	Anti-Racism Program

Monday, August 4, 2003—Sixth Legislative Day

7:30 a.m.–9:00 a.m.	Legislative Committee Meetings
8:00 a.m.–5:00 p.m.	Registration
8:30 a.m.–9:30 a.m.	Deputy Certification
9:30 a.m.–10:45 a.m.	Eucharist and Scripture Reflection
11:00 a.m.–1:00 p.m.	Legislative Session (Provincial Caucuses)
12:30 p.m.–1:*15* p.m.	Deputy Certification
2:30 p.m.–6:00 p.m.	Legislative Session

Tuesday, August 5, 2003—Seventh Legislative Day

7:30 a.m.–9:00 a.m.	Legislative Committee Meetings
8:00 a.m.–5:00 p.m.	Registration
8:30 a.m.–9:30 a.m.	Deputy Certification
9:30 a.m.–10:45 a.m.	Eucharist and Scripture Reflection
11:00 a.m.–1:00 p.m.	Legislative Session
12:30 p.m.–1:*15* p.m.	Deputy Certification
2:30 p.m.–6:00 p.m.	Legislative Session

Evening	*Provincial Dinners*

Wednesday, August 6, 2003—Eighth Legislative Day

7:30 a.m.–9:00 a.m.	Legislative Committee Meetings
8:00 a.m.–5:00 p.m.	Registration
8:30 a.m.–9:30 a.m.	Deputy Certification
9:30 a.m.–10:45 a.m.	Eucharist and Scripture Reflection
11:00 a.m.–1:00 p.m.	Legislative Session (Provincial Caucuses)
12:30 p.m.–1:15 p.m.	Deputy Certification
2:30 p.m.	*Joint Session–Program, Budget & Finance*
2:30 p.m.–6:00 p.m.	Legislative Session (Includes Joint Session: Program, Budget & Finance)
8:00 p.m.–*10:00* p.m.	Reserved for Legislation

Thursday, August 7, 2003—Ninth Legislative Day

7:30 a.m.–9:00 a.m.	Legislative Committee Meetings
8:00 a.m.–5:00 p.m.	Registration
8:30 a.m.–9:30 a.m.	Deputy Certification
9:30 a.m.–10:45 a.m.	Eucharist and Scripture Reflection
11:00 a.m.–1:00 p.m.	Legislative Session
12:30 p.m.–1:15 p.m.	Deputy Certification
2:30 p.m.–6:00 p.m.	Legislative Session
8:00 p.m.–*10:00* p.m.	Reserved for Legislation

Friday, August 8, 2003—Tenth Legislative Day

9:00 a.m.–10:15 a.m.	Eucharist and Scripture Reflection
8:00 a.m.–2:00 p.m.	Registration
8:30 a.m.–9:30 *a.m.*	Deputy Certification
10:30 a.m.–1:00 p.m.	Legislative Session
12:30 p.m.–1:15 p.m.	Deputy Certification
2:30 p.m.–6:00 p.m.	Legislative Session
6:00 p.m.	*Joint Adjournment Sine Die*

Motion carried
Resolution adopted with amendment
(Communicated to the House of Bishops in HD Message #1)

Personal Privilege
The Secretary introduced the General Convention staff present on the platform.

Chancellor to the President of the House of Deputies
The President announced the appointment of Robert Royce, Esq., of South Carolina as Chancellor to the President.

Special Assistant to the President of the House of Deputies
The President announced the appointment of Ms. Debbie Robayo of Virginia as Special Assistant to the President of the House of Deputies.

Welcome by the President
The President addressed the House and reflected on the 1976 General Convention. The President recognized two senior deputies—Deputy Chew of Arizona and Deputy Moody of Northern Indiana—for their long service to the House. He asked deputies under the age of 35 to stand as he remarked on the increased involvement of young people in Convention. The President reminded the House that the Episcopal Church's membership extends beyond the continental United States to South America, Asia, Central America, Liberia, Europe and other countries. He stated that this diversity brings richness to the Church while making it an international church. The President asked the House to greet its brothers and sisters from around the world.

The President stated that laptop computers may be used in the House and that electronic communication is not allowed from the House floor.

Midday Prayers
The President called on the Chaplain for midday prayers.

House of Bishops Organized
The President welcomed and recognized visitors from the House of Bishops: Bishop Gayle Harris of Massachusetts and Bishop William Swing of California. Bishop Swing addressed the House and announced that the House of Bishops has a quorum and is organized for business. Bishop Harris announced that the House of Bishops is praying that God will grant both Houses the wisdom to live into our baptismal vows.

ECW President
President Stewart brought greetings from the 44th Triennial Meeting of the Women of the Church. The theme of the Triennial Meeting is "A New Light is Shining."

RECESS
Following announcements by the Secretary, the President announced that the House would stand in recess from 12:30 p.m. until 4:15 p.m.

AFTERNOON SESSION

Reconvene
The President reconvened the House at 4:19 p.m.

Mayor of Minneapolis

The President welcomed the Mayor of the City of Minneapolis, the Honorable R.T. Rybak, who is a life-long Episcopalian and a communicant of St. John's Church, Minneapolis. The Mayor welcomed the General Convention to Minneapolis.

Special Order of Business

The House of Deputies Committee on Dispatch of Business in its Report #2 moved to adopt a Special Order of Business:

Your Committee on Dispatch of Business, having been instructed by the President of the House to recommend an appropriate procedure for election, pursuant to Title I, Canon 1, Sec. 1(b), of a President and Vice-President, moves the adoption of the following resolutions:

Resolved, That the Secretary of the House prepare a form for nominations for President of the House and another form for nominations for Vice-President of the House, which shall contain blanks for the inclusion of:

1. Name of Nominee
2. Order
3. Diocese
4. Parish and City
5. Certification that if elected the nominee will accept the office
6. Signature of the nominator, his or her order and diocese; and that these forms shall be made available as soon as possible; and be it further

Resolved, That this House set a Special Order of Business at 11:30 a.m. the 2nd Legislative Day, Thursday, July 31, 2003 for the purpose of receiving nominations for President of this House, at which time all duly completed nomination forms shall be filed with the Secretary and each nominator shall have the privilege of speaking for not more than two minutes in support of the nominee, provided that not more than one nominator shall be recognized to speak on behalf of each nominee; and be it further

Resolved, That the Secretary be directed thereafter to prepare in uniform fashion a biographical sketch of each nominee, based on the information provided to the Secretary (by 1:00 p.m. Thursday, July 31), which sketches shall be limited to 150 words, arranged in alphabetical order by name of nominee, and distributed to the members of the House no later than 4:00 p.m. the 2nd Legislative Day, Thursday, July 31, 2003; and be it further

Resolved, That this House set a Special Order of Business at 11:30 a.m. the 4th Legislative Day, Saturday, August 2, 2003, for the purpose of electing a President of the House, to take office at the adjournment of the regular meeting at which elected pursuant to Canon I, Title 1, Sec. 1(b), provided that at the discretion of its presiding officer the House may proceed to conduct other business during the balloting for such election; and be it further

Resolved, That following the election of a President a similar procedure be followed for the election of a Vice-President of the House, with

1. A Special Order of Business at 2:45 p.m. the 5th Legislative Day, Sunday, August 3, 2003 for the purpose of receiving nominations under the same procedures,

2. The distribution of similar biographical sketches (delivered to the Secretary by 6:00 p.m. Sunday, August 3) prior to 11:30 a.m. the 6th Legislative Day, Monday, August 4, 2003, and
3. A Special Order of Business at 2:45 p.m. the 6th Legislative Day, Monday, August 4, 2003, to elect a Vice-President of the House for the same term under the same proviso; and be it further

Resolved, That the President of the House be requested to appoint a chairman and tellers of elections to serve the House on the occasions of each of its several elections.

A vote was taken on the Special Order of Business.

Motion carried
Special Order adopted
(Communicated to the House of Bishops in HD Message #3)

Rules of Order

The House of Deputies Committee on the Rules of Order presented its Report #1 on Resolution A149 (Special Legislative Committees) and moved the resolution, recommending rejection.

Original Text of Resolution:

(A149)
Resolved, the House of Bishops concurring, That Special Legislative Committees appointed to handle "hot button" issues be appointed sufficiently in advance of General Convention to ensure that existing Legislative Committees not lose vital members, and to allow scheduling of Special Hearings at times when members of Legislative Committees can attend.

Motion defeated
Resolution rejected
(Communicated to the House of Bishops in HD Message #2)

Structure

The House of Deputies Committee on Structure presented its Report #1 on Resolution A009 (Amend Canon I.4.2(b)) and moved adoption.

Original Text of Resolution:

(A009)
Resolved, the House of Bishops concurring, That Canon I.4.2(b) be amended to read as follows:
(b) Except in the case of members initially elected for shorter terms in order to achieve rotation of terms, the terms of office of the members of the Council (other than ex officiis members) shall be equal to twice the interval between regular meetings of the General Convention. The terms of office of all members shall

commence immediately upon the adjournment of the General Convention at which they were elected, or, in the case of election by a Synod, upon adjournment of the first regular meeting of General Convention following such election. *The term of a member shall become vacant in the event of two absences from meetings of the Council in the interval between successive regular meetings of the General Convention unless excused by the Chair for good cause.* Members shall remain in office until their successors are elected and qualified. No person who has served at least three consecutive years on the Executive Council shall be eligible for immediate re-election for a term of more than three years. After any person shall have served six consecutive years on the Executive Council, a period of three years shall elapse before such person shall be eligible for re-election to the Council.

Motion carried
Resolution adopted
(Communicated to the House of Bishops in HD Message #4)

The House of Deputies Committee on Structure presented its Report #2 on Resolution A040 (Amend Canon 1.1.2(n)(6)) and moved adoption.

Original Text of Resolution:

(A040)
Resolved, the House of Bishops concurring, That Canon I.1.2(n) be amended by adding this subsection:
(6) A Standing Commission on Liturgy and Music consisting of 16 members (4 Bishops, 4 Priests and/or Deacons and 8 Lay Persons). In addition, the Custodian of The Book of Common Prayer shall be a member ex officio, with voice, but without vote. The Standing Commission shall:

(I) Discharge such duties as shall be assigned to it by the General Convention as to policies and strategies concerning the common worship of this Church.

(ii) Collect, collate, and catalogue material bearing upon possible future revisions of The Book of Common Prayer.

(iii) Cause to be prepared and to present to the General Convention recommendations concerning the Lectionary, Psalter, and offices for special occasions as authorized or directed by the General Convention or House of Bishops.

(iv) Recommend to the General Convention authorized translations of the Holy Scripture from which the Lessons prescribed in The Book of Common Prayer are to be read.

(v) Receive and evaluate requests for consideration of individuals or groups to be included in the Calendar of the Church year, and make recommendations thereon to the General Convention for acceptance or rejection.

(vi) Collect, collate, and catalogue material bearing upon possible future revisions of The Hymnal 1982 and other musical publications

	regularly in use in this Church, and encourage the composition of new musical materials.
(vii)	Cause to be prepared and present to the General Convention recommendations concerning the musical settings of liturgical texts and rubrics, and norms as to liturgical music and the manner of its rendition.
(viii)	At the direction of General Convention, serve the Church in matters pertaining to policies and strategies concerning Church music.

Motion carried
Resolution adopted
(Communicated to the House of Bishops in HD Message #8)

Special Order of Business

The House of Deputies Committee on Dispatch of Business moved in its Report #4 to adopted a Special Order of Business:

The Joint Committee on Nominations having submitted names for election as Trustees of the Church Pension Fund, pursuant to Title I, Canon 8, Section 2, and Joint Rule of Order 18(a) [See *Blue Book*, pages 295-303], the Committee on Dispatch of Business moves the adoption of the following resolution:

Resolved, That the following procedures be followed in the election of Trustees of the Church Pension Fund at this General Convention pursuant to Title I, Canon 8, Section 2:

1. That nominations for election as Trustees of the Church Pension Fund be submitted to the Office of the Secretary on or before 6:15 p.m. Wednesday, July 30, 2003 the First Legislative day;
2. That this House set a Special Order of Business at 3:45 p.m. on the Second Legislative Day, Thursday, July 31, 2003, for the purpose of electing two Trustees of the Church Pension Fund to fill unexpired terms of three years each, and until his or her successor has been elected and qualified; and for electing twelve Trustees of the Church Pension Fund for a term of six years each, and until his or her successor has been elected and qualified. The Secretary shall prepare a ballot form listing alphabetically the names of all persons nominated. On each ballot, each member shall vote for the number of Trustees to be or remaining to be elected; any ballot with votes less than or in excess thereof shall be void. The person nominated for the unexpired term receiving the largest number of votes shall be deemed elected, and the twelve persons receiving the largest number of votes shall be deemed elected, provided that votes equal to or in excess of a majority of the ballots cast on any ballot shall be required for election;
3. Balloting shall continue until there shall be Trustees elected, provided that on the third and subsequent ballots there shall be retained on the ballot from those persons receiving the highest number of votes only that number of nominees equal to twice the number of Trustees then remaining to be elected;

4. In the event of a significant tie, election shall be by lot cast by the Secretary. The House may, at the discretion of its presiding officer, proceed to other business during the balloting for such election.

Motion carried
Special Order adopted
(Communicated to the House of Bishops in HD Message #6)

Rules of Order

The House of Deputies Committee on the Rules of Order presented its Report #2 on Resolution A148 (Amend HDRO Article VI) and moved adoption with amendment.

Original Text of Resolution:
(A148)
Resolved, the House of Bishops concurring, That Article VI, Resolutions and Memorials, Rule 21(e) of the Rules of Order, House of Deputies be amended to read:

(e) Any such Resolution received by the Secretary of the House of Deputies at least ~~ninety (90)~~ *thirty (30)* days prior to the opening date of the Convention shall be referred to the proper Legislative Committee or Special Committee Chair at least ~~sixty (60)~~ *fifteen (15)* days prior to the opening date of Convention. The Secretary shall acknowledge receipt of all such Resolutions to the proposer.

Committee Amendment:
Resolved, ~~the House of Bishops concurring,~~ That Article VI, Resolutions and Memorials, Rule 21(e) of the Rules of Order, House of Deputies be amended to read:

(e) Any such Resolution received by the Secretary of the House of Deputies at least ~~ninety (90)~~ *thirty (30)* days prior to the opening date of the Convention shall be referred to the proper Legislative Committee or Special Committee Chair at least ~~sixty (60)~~ *fifteen (15)* days prior to the opening date of Convention. The Secretary shall acknowledge receipt of all such Resolutions to the proposer.

Motion defeated
Resolution rejected
(Communicated to the House of Bishops in HD Message #7)

Consecration of Bishops

The House of Deputies Committee on the Consecration of Bishops presented its Report #1 on Resolution C040 (Consent to the Election of the Rev. Joe Goodwin Burnett as Bishop of the Diocese of Nebraska) and moved adoption.

Original Text of Resolution:
(C040)
Resolved, Pursuant to Article II, Section 2, and Canon III.22.3 of the Constitution and Canons, the House of Deputies consents to the ordination and consecration of the Rev. Joe Goodwin Burnett as Bishop of the Diocese of Nebraska.

Motion carried
Resolution adopted
(Communicated to the House of Bishops in HD Message #8)

The House of Deputies Committee on the Consecration of Bishops presented its Report #2 on Resolution C039 (Consent to the Election of the Rev. George Edward Councell as Bishop of the Diocese of New Jersey) and moved adoption.

Original Text of Resolution:
(C039)
Resolved, Pursuant to Article II, Section 2, and Canon III.22.3 of the Constitution and Canons, the House of Deputies consents to the ordination and consecration of the Rev. George Edward Councell as Bishop of the Diocese of New Jersey.

Motion carried
Resolution adopted
(Communicated to the House of Bishops in HD Message #9)

Social and Urban Affairs
The House of Deputies Committee on Social and Urban Affairs presented its Report #1 on Resolution A008 (Repeal Mandatory Federal Sentencing Guidelines) and moved adoption with amendment.

Original Text of Resolution:
(A008)
Resolved, the House of Bishops concurring, That the 74th General Convention urge the Congress of the United States to repeal the mandatory Federal sentencing guidelines used in federal criminal matters, and restore the discretion of federal trial judges.

Committee Amendment:

Resolved, the House of Bishops concurring, That the 74th General Convention urge the Congress of the United States to repeal the mandatory federal sentencing guidelines used in federal criminal matters, and ~~restore the discretion of federal trial judges~~ direct the *Office of Government Relations to work for such repeal in order to give federal judges more discretion in sentencing offenders, and to overcome the current racially discriminatory impact of these guidelines.*

Motion carried
Resolution adopted with amendment
(Communicated to the House of Bishops in HD Message #10)

Committees and Commissions

The House of Deputies Committee on Committees and Commissions presented its Report #1 on Resolution A124 (Standing Commission on Health and a Staff Position in Health Care) and moved adoption with amendment.

Original Text of Resolution:

(A124)
[Note: See *The Blue Book* Report of Standing Commission on National Concerns, pp. 257–258. *Ed.*]

Committee Amendment:

Resolved, the House of Bishops concurring, That the 74th General Convention reaffirm the commitment of The Episcopal Church in providing a Christian response to the health care needs of those within our nation, as expressed in the 1991 and 1994 Blue Book reports of the Standing Commission on Health and the 2000 Blue Book Report of the Standing Commission on National Concerns; and be it further

Resolved, That the 74th General Convention reestablish a Standing Commission on Health and that it direct Executive Council to appoint a person to the staff at The Episcopal Church Center with background in and knowledge about health care policy to assist this commission, and that their joint duties include:

- Articulating and communicating positions adopted by The Episcopal Church on health care policy to Episcopalians, the public, and public policy makers;
- Advocating, in cooperation with the Office of Government Relations, for a health care system in which all may be guaranteed decent and appropriate primary health care during their lives and as they approach death;
- Bringing together those within The Episcopal Church who develop, provide and/or teach health care and health care policy to continue to develop a Christian approach to pressing issues that affect the health care system of this nation;
- Understanding and keeping abreast of the rapidly changing health care market and developments in biomedical research that affect health policy;

Collecting and developing resources and teaching materials related to access to health care for the use of dioceses, congregations, and individuals;

Advocating health ministry in and through local Episcopal congregations; and be it further

Resolved, That the 74th General Convention direct the Executive Council to report to the 75th General Convention about this appointment; and be it further

Resolved, ~~That $200,000 be appropriated from the budget for the triennium.~~ *That the General Convention request the Joint Standing Committee on Program, Budget, and Finance to consider a budget allocation of $200,000 for implementation of this resolution.*

Motion carried
Resolution adopted with amendment
(Communicated to the House of Bishops in HD Message #11)

Dispatch of Business

The House of Deputies Committee on Dispatch of Business moved to suspend the rules for the Committee on Privilege and Courtesy to present a resolution regarding Gail Courtney Rittgers.

Motion carried
Rules suspended

Committee on Privilege and Courtesy

The House of Deputies Committee on Privilege and Courtesy presented its Report #2 on Resolution D032 (Gail Courtney Riggers) and moved adoption.

Original Text of Resolution:

(D032)

Resolved, the House of Bishops concurring, That the 74th General Convention send its congratulations and best wishes to Gail Courtney Rittgers, a member of Grace Episcopal Church, Alexandria, Virginia, on the occasion today of her 101st birthday;

Resolved, That the Convention recognize that she has been a mainstay of her church community for many years; taught Sunday School until the age of 80; served on the vestry; and remains active in the women's Bible study group; and be it further

Resolved, That the Convention pray that Gail Courtney Rittgers may continue to inspire those around her to lives of loving and faithful service.

Motion carried
Resolution adopted
(Communicated to the House of Bishops in HD Message #28)

Recess

The House recessed for a break at 5:20 p.m. to reconvene at 5:30 p.m.

Reconvene

MINNEAPOLIS MEETING — HOUSE OF DEPUTIES

The President called the House to order at 5:30 p.m.

Youth Presence Address

The President welcomed the Youth Presence and introduced its speaker, T.D. Smith of the Diocese of Iowa, who was accompanied by other members of the Youth Presence. Mr. Smith addressed the House and spoke about the need for for youth ministry resources. He asked, "Has our youth ministry failed?" and urged the removal of barriers which isolate youth ministry from the rest of the church.

Certification of Deputies

The Secretary reported that the House of Deputies Committee on Credentials had presented Report #2 for the afternoon session of the First Legislative Day. There were 6 new deputies certified, including 1 from the Diocese of Liberia. There were 10 changes in deputy status. There were at this legislative session 411 clerical deputies and 412 lay deputies certified and seated. The total count for the House of Deputies is 823. The number of votes for a motion to prevail is 413. The changes were as follows:

Diocese	*Alternate replacing*	*Deputy being replaced*
Arkansas	Gar Demo	Lowell Grisham
Minnesota	Michael Hanley	Howard Anderson
Mississippi	Suanna Smith	Anita George
Navajoland Area Mission	Maggie Brown	Anna Fowler
Newark	Marjorie Christie	Louie Crew
Rochester	Lesley Adams	Jorge Gutierrez
Southern Virginia	Stanley Sawyer	Paul Hogg
Upper South Carolina	Garfield Stuart	Angela Daniel
West Missouri	India Philley	Shirley Bolden
Western Massachusetts	Heidi Frantz-Dale	Len Cowan
Western New York	Alison Martin	Earle King

Search for New President of the Church Pension Fund

The President called upon David Pitts, Chair of the Search Committee for a New President of the Church Pension Fund, to talk about the selection process for the new President, which began more than a year ago. He reported that the Search Committee had consulted the Board of Trustees of the Church Pension Fund about the type of candidate needed and hired an outside firm to conduct the executive search. He added that Deputies were invited to submit nominees and a list of candidate qualifications would be distributed.

Announcements

The Secretary made announcements and noted that the UTO Boxes are now at every Deputation table.

RECESS

The President recessed the House at 5:55 p.m. to reconvene at 11:00 a.m. on Thursday, July 31, 2003.

Appendix A
Day 1

House of Deputies Legislative Committees

01 **Dispatch of Business**
Causey Jr., Mr. J. P., Chair (Virginia, III)
Simons, The Rev. James B., Vice-Chair (Pittsburgh, III)
Anderson, The Rev. Canon Augusta R., Secretary (Western North Carolina, IV)
Atwood, The Rev. H. Jay (Fort Worth, VII)
Biladeau, Mr. Garre L. (Idaho, VIII)
Blauser, Ms. Erin (Northwestern Pennsylvania, III)
Boone, Miss Linda S. (Western Kansas, VII)
Bowden, Mr. R.P.M., Ex-Officio (Atlanta, IV)
Brown, Dr. Harold H. (Maine, I)
Cole, Mr. Richard (Churches in Europe, II)
Cooper, The Rev. Frank M. (East Tennessee, IV)
Gill, The Rev. Charles (East Carolina, IV)
Glasspool, The Rev. Cn. Mary D. (Maryland, III)
Goodheart, The Rev. Donald (North Carolina, IV)
Horn, Ms. Raisin (Iowa, VI)
Kirby, The Very Rev. H. Scott (Eau Claire, V)
Lyons, The Rev. Leroy A. (New Jersey, II)
Matthews, Mrs. Elizabeth P. (Arkansas, VII)
Miller, Mr. Richard E. (Southeast Florida, IV)
Perry Esq., Richard P. (Atlanta, IV)
Rowe, The Rev. Gary L. (Delaware, III)
Shearouse, Mr. Jim (East Tennessee, IV)

02 **Certification of Minutes**
Foose, Mrs. Ruth T., Chair (West Virginia, III)
Williams Sr., Mr. Rodney Maceo, Vice-Chair (Dallas, VII)
Dewey, Ms. Josephine (Rochester, II)
Freeman, Dr. Linda R. (Washington, III)
Hesselgrave, The Rev. Sherman (Oregon, VIII)
Straub, The Rev. Dr. Gregory S. (Easton, III)

03 **Rules of Order**
Getz, Mrs. Pauline, Chair (San Diego, VIII)
Currie Jr., Mr. Vincent, Vice-Chair (Central Gulf Coast, IV)
Crump Esq., Charles M. (West Tennessee, IV)
Graham, The Rev. Margaret M., Secretary (Washington, III)
Holzhammer, The Rev. Canon Robert E. (Iowa, VI)
Isaac, Mr. Fred C. (Florida, IV)

Martindale, The Very Rev. Richard (Nebraska, VI)
Matthews, The Rev. Dan (East Tennessee, IV)
Valdez, Mr. Daniel (Los Angeles, VIII)
Werner, The Very Rev. George L.W. (Pittsburgh, III)
Yaeger, Mr. Gary C. (Northwestern Pennsylvania, III)

04 **Constitution**
Ballentine Esq., Rosalie Simmonds, Chair (Virgin Islands, II)
Moore, The Rev. Stephen E., Vice-Chair (Olympia, VIII)
Allen, Mrs. Laura Julian, Secretary (Dallas, VII)
Bradford III, Mr. D. C. Woody (Nebraska, VI)
Burtch Jr., Mr. Jack W. (Virginia, III)
Cathcart Esq., William R. (Oklahoma, VII)
Handford, Mr. Peter (Churches in Europe, II)
Kimbrough, The Rev. Timothy E. (North Carolina, IV)
Marshall Sr., Mr. George J. (Albany, II)
Overton, Mr. Larry S. (East Carolina, IV)
Rehill, Mr. Michael F. (Newark, II)
Root, The Rev. Diane E. (Vermont, I)
Russell, The Hon. James F. (West Tennessee, IV)
Toribio, Mrs. Ana Lidia (Dominican Republic, IX)

05 **Canons**
Palmore Jr., Mr. Russell V., Chair (Virginia, III)
Johnson Esq., Sally A., Vice-Chair (Minnesota, VI)
Anderson, Mr. Neil D. (Dallas, VII)
Babb, Mr. Kevin (Springfield, V)
Bayne, Mr. Duncan A. (Olympia, VIII)
Bennett, The Rev. Arthur L., Secretary (West Virginia, III)
Bradberry, The Hon. James E. (Southern Virginia, III)
Brenner Esq., Talmadge (Quincy, V)
Cooney, Mr. Paul E. (Washington, III)
Crosby, Mr. William (Georgia, IV)
Firmin, Mrs. Judie H. (Dallas, VII)
Herbert Esq., David B. (Tennessee, IV)
Hitt II, Esq., Lawrence R. (Colorado, VI)
Hutchinson, Mr. Stephen F. (Utah, VIII)
King Jr., The Rev. Canon Charles B. (Albany, II)
Little Esq., Thomas A. (Vermont, I))
Livingood Esq., Matthew (Oklahoma, VII)
Malone, The Rev. Canon Michael T. (South Carolina, IV)
Reno Jr., Mr. Russell R. (Maryland, III)
Rowe, The Rev. Sean W. (Northwestern Pennsylvania, III)
Runnels, The Rev. R. Stan (Mississippi, IV)

Simpson, The Rev. Ward H. (Eau Claire, V)
Smith, Mr. Marcellus L. (Alabama, IV)
Snyder, Mr. L. Miles (Northern California, VIII)
Tookey, The Rev. Carol R. (Navajoland Area Mission, VIII)
Tripp, The Very Rev. Arthur (Rio Grande, VII)
Waddell, Mr. J. Patrick (El Camino Real, VIII)
Wittlinger, Mr. Timothy D. (Michigan, V)

06 Structure

Pitts, Mr. David R., Chair (Louisiana, IV)
Carroon, The Rev. Canon Robert G., Vice-Chair (Connecticut, I)
Schwab, Ms. Cynthia H., Secretary (West Missouri, VII)
Alexander, Ms. Martha Bedell (North Carolina, IV)
Andress, Mr. R. Thad (Western Louisiana, VII)
Blue, The Rev. Eddie M. (Maryland, III)
Calderon, Jorge (Honduras, IX)
Chase Jr., The Rev. Randall (Rhode Island, I)
Davis, Mr. Richard H. (Northwest Texas, VII)
Eastwood Jr., The Rev. Dr. John H. (California, VIII)
Frank, Ms. Amanda (Alaska, VIII)
Garcia, The Rev. Ramon A. (Dominican Republic, IX)
Godden, The Rev. Edward E. (Delaware, III)
Juste, Mrs. Esther (Haiti, II)
Kesselus, The Rev. Kenneth W. (Texas, VII)
Kilpatrick, Mrs. Patricia B. (Ohio, V)
Marshall, Ms. Frances C. (Southwestern Virginia, III)
O'Shea, The Ven. Eileen (Idaho, VIII)
Rasmus, The Ven. Paul A. (Southeast Florida, IV)
Robinson, The Rev. V. Gene (New Hampshire, I)
Ross, The Rev. Canon Johnnie E. (Lexington, IV)
Thomson, The Very Rev. Ronald R. (Rio Grande, VII)
Tinsman, Ms. Margaret N. (Iowa, VI)
Vann, The Rev. Canon Tim E. (Nebraska, VI)
Whitmore, The Rev. Charles W. (Western New York, II)

07 Consecration of Bishops

Keil-Kuhr, The Rev. Carolyn S., Chair (Montana, VI)
Glover, Dr. Delbert C., Vice-Chair (Western Massachusetts, I)
Ferriani, The Rev. Nancy A., Secretary (Indianapolis, V)
Adams, Mr. John C. (Eastern Oregon, VIII)
Clark, Mr. Anthony J. (Fort Worth, VII)
Cowperthwaite, The Rev. Robert W. (Tennessee, IV)
Donecker, The Ven. Paul C. (Central Pennsylvania, III)
Hart, Mr. Christopher (Pennsylvania, III)

Jim, Ms. Rosella A. (Navajoland Area Mission, VIII)
Junkin, The Rev. Hays M. (New Hampshire, I)
Knoll, Ms. Sarah J. (Kansas, VII)
Lane, The Rev. John David (Southwestern Virginia, III)
Lawrence, The Very Rev. Mark (San Joaquin, VIII)
Lund, Mrs. Gloria N. (Spokane, VIII)
Masters, Mr. John (Wyoming, VI)
Murguia, The Rev. James (West Texas, VII)
Roberts, Ms. Terry (Minnesota, VI)
Robison, Mr. Thomas (Spokane, VIII)
Thompson Bell, Ms. Alma (Maryland, III)

08 World Mission

Broderick y Guerra, The Rev. Canon Cecily P., Chair (Long Island, II)
Moody, Canon Nancy, Vice-Chair (Northern Indiana, V)
Crawford, The Rev. Hayden G., Secretary (Southwest Florida, IV)
Bell, Col. Robert S. (South Carolina, IV)
Bowersox, The Rev. Ned F. (West Texas, VII)
Broadwell, Mrs. Nancy W. (East Carolina, IV)
Carpenter, The Rev. Douglas M. (Alabama, IV)
Carter, The Rev. Canon Robert (Georgia, IV)
Casparian, The Rev. Peter F. (Churches in Europe, II)
Crawford, The Rev. Dr. Lee Alison (Vermont, I)
Cullinane, The Rev. Canon Kathleen J. (Indianapolis, V)
Cumbie, The Rev. W. Kenneth (Central Gulf Coast, IV)
Dannals, The Rev. Dr. Robert S. (Upper South Carolina, IV)
Drazdowski, Ms. Edna Jean (Georgia, IV)
Gardine, Mrs. Judithann H. (Virgin Islands, II)
Harris, The Rev. Canon Mark (Delaware, III)
Hartley, Mr. Jimmy (Upper South Carolina, IV)
Hobbs, The Ven. Dr. Bryan A. (Southeast Florida, IV)
Hobbs, Mrs. Elizabeth V. (Pittsburgh, III)
Hunter II, The Rev. James N. (Alaska, VIII)
Jean, The Rev. MacDonald (Haiti, II)
Knisely, The Rev. W. Nicholas (Bethlehem, III)
Lambert, The Rev. John P. (Olympia, VIII)
Lord, The Rev. Robert C. (Kansas, VII)
Madsen, Ms. Betsy R. (Massachusetts, I)
Muinde, Mrs. Sandra (Fond Du Lac, V)
Osberger, The Rev. Charles E. (Easton, III)
Ramos, The Rev. Pablo (Utah, VIII)
Romero, Mr. Alexander (Dominican Republic, IX)
Ruttan, The Rev. Karl D. (West Virginia, III)

Spence, Mr. Dustin (Northern California, VIII)
Swanson, The Very Rev. Kenneth B. (Tennessee, IV)
Tolliver, The Rev. Dr. Richard L. (Chicago, V)

09 **National and International Concerns**
Cheney II, The Rev. Reynolds S., Chair (West Tennessee, IV)
Kinman, The Rev. Michael, Vice-Chair (Missouri, V)
Delaplane, Mrs. Margaret Ann, Secretary (Delaware, III)
Aiona, The Rev. Darrow L.K., Co Vice-Chair (Hawaii, VIII)
Bates, Dr. Thomas R. (Central Florida, IV)
Brooks, The Rev. Theodora N. (New York, II)
Cockrell, The Rev. Ernest W. (El Camino Real, VIII)
Coindet, Mrs. Consuelo (Honduras, IX)
Cope, Mr. Owen (Louisiana, IV)
Crosdale, Ms. Valarie H. (Long Island, II)
Douglas, The Rev. Dr. Ian T. (Massachusetts, I)
Dunnam, The Rev. Canon T. Mark (Central Gulf Coast, IV)
Harris, Mrs. Bettye Jo (Hawaii, VIII)
Harris, Ms. Iris E. (Washington, III)
Kilkelly, The Hon. Marge (Maine, I)
Melnyk, Mrs. Debby (Florida, IV)
Mesa, Mr. Manuel G. (Southeast Florida, IV)
Patterson, Ms. Karen O. (Southwest Florida, IV)
Redfield, Ms. Rita Tams (Maine, I)
Rhodes, Ms. Stephanie (Missouri, V)
Roemer, Mr. William F. (Pittsburgh, III)
Scott, Ms. Jacqueline (Colorado, VI)
Sessum, The Rev. Robert L. (Lexington, IV)
Smith III, Mr. Newland F. (Chicago, V)
Trueheart, Mr. Charles (Churches in Europe, II)
Wei, The Rev. Elizabeth (Taiwan, VIII)
Westigard, Mr. Gregg (Eau Claire, V)

10 **Social and Urban Affairs**
Dales, The Rev. Randolph K., Chair (New Hampshire, I)
Jones Esq., JoAnn B., Vice-Chair (Pennsylvania, III)
Alford, The Rev. Billy J. (Georgia, IV)
Bailey, The Rev. Canon David E. (Utah, VIII)
Batjer, Mrs. Jackie B. (Northwest Texas, VII)
Beasley, Ms. Hisako (Olympia, VIII)
Betts, Mr. Don (Nebraska, VI)
Bingham, Mr. Larry J. (Kansas, VII)
Brown, Ms. Anne C. (Vermont, I)
Casson, The Rev. Canon Lloyd S. (Delaware, III)

Cavanagh, Ms. Debra (San Joaquin, VIII)
Chaney, Mr. Michael J. (Mississippi, IV)
Chapman, Ms. Pamela B. (Western Michigan, V)
Cheney, The Rev. Barbara T. (Connecticut, I)
Church, Mr. James F. (Olympia, VIII)
Clark, Mr. Michael Thomas (Missouri, V)
Cottrell-Willis, The Rev. Anisa (Lexington, IV)
Davidson, The Rev. Robert (Colorado, VI)
Elliott III, The Rev. David A. (Mississippi, IV)
Farabee, The Very Rev. Allen W. (Western New York, II)
Gibson, Mrs. Nell Braxton (New York, II)
Gould, The Rev. Jane S. (Massachusetts, I)
Gritter, Dr. Gordon W. (El Camino Real, VIII)
Hamilton III, Mr. Lonnie (South Carolina, IV)
Honsaker, Ms. Mary Ellen (Wyoming, VI)
Janelle, Ms. Nicole S. (Maine, I)
Kaeton, The Rev. Canon Elizabeth (Newark, II)
Ladefoged, Canon Jenny (Los Angeles, VIII)
Lambert, The Rev. Canon Paul E. (Dallas, VII)
Lewis, The Rev. Sharon L. (Southwest Florida, IV)
Libby, Ms. Lynne (Southeast Florida, IV)
Martensen, Mrs. Catherine F. (San Diego, VIII)
McMahon, Dr. Margo E. (Western Massachusetts, I)
Ott, Mrs. Constance (Milwaukee, V)
Owens, Mr. Kenneth (South Dakota, VI)
Pruitt, The Rev. Albert W. (Central Gulf Coast, IV)
Rivera, The Rev. Bavi E. (California, VIII)
Salley, Ms. Cynthia M. (Hawaii, VIII)
Stevens-Hummon, The Rev. Becca (Tennessee, IV)
Stokes, Mrs. Deborah J. (Southern Ohio, V)
Thompson, Mr. Gary W. (Colorado, VI)
Thompson, Mr. Lawrence E. (Western North Carolina, IV)
Vanderstar, Mr. John (Washington, III)
Washington, Mrs. Virginia V. (Arizona, VIII)

11 **Church in Small Communities**
McGarry, The Rev. Susan E., Chair (Michigan, V)
Heidecker, The Ven. Eric V., Vice-Chair (Nevada, VIII)
Winter, The Rev. Cheryl, Secretary (West Virginia, III)
Blauser, The Ven. Dennis A. (Northwestern Pennsylvania, III)
Booth, The Rev. Cora (Rochester, II)
Collins, The Rev. Jean Griffin (Montana, VI)
Connizzo, Mr. Frank (Kansas, VII)

Davey, The Rev. Jan (Rio Grande, VII)
Ellis Jr., The Rev. William R. (Eastern Oregon, VIII)
Gilhousen, The Rev. Dennis (Western Kansas, VII)
Graybill, Mr. Richard M. (Northern Michigan, V)
Gumbs, The Rev. E. Ambrose (Virgin Islands, II)
Harker, The Rev. Margaret Griggs (Northern Indiana, V)
Harrigan, The Rev. Katherine G.L. (Central Pennsylvania, III)
Hawkins, Mr. William M. (Arkansas, VII)
Herrmann SSC, The Very Rev. Cn. H. W. (Quincy, V)
Horner, Mr. Channing (West Missouri, VII)
Miller, Mr. Thomas D. (West Virginia, III)
Murphy, The Rev. Warren (Wyoming, VI)
Pettit, Mrs. Donna Lee (North Dakota, VI)
Philip, The Rev. Canon Kristi (Spokane, VIII)
Pryor, Ms. Vera (Georgia, IV)
Ray, The Rev. Rayford (Northern Michigan, V)
Roane, The Rev. Wilson K. (Fond Du Lac, V)
Shortt, The Rev. Mary J. (Eastern Michigan, V)
Studdiford, The Rev. Linton H. (Maine, I)
Sutton, Canon Robert E. (Rio Grande, VII)
Teter, The Rev. Cn. Jane B. (Bethlehem, III)
Thorpe, Ms. Stacy (Alaska, VIII)
Two Hawk, The Rev. Webster (South Dakota, VI)

12 **Evangelism**
Lemler, The Very Rev. James B., Chair (Chicago, V)
Thornell, The Rev. Kwasi A., Vice-Chair (Southern Ohio, V)
Ottsen, The Rev. David K., Secretary (Northern Indiana, V)
Acton, The Rev. Joseph (San Diego, VIII)
Allen, Mr. Michael (Kentucky, IV)
Belleville, Mrs. Marilynn S. (Springfield, V)
Browning, Mr. Robert (West Texas, VII)
Burke, The Rev. Michael (Alaska, VIII)
Childers, The Rev. Robert T. J. (Alabama, IV)
Cooper, The Rev. Dr. James H. (Florida, IV)
Geib, Mrs. Lucille Miner (Arizona, VIII)
George, Mr. Lawrence (Missouri, V)
Hartney, Mr. Elton M. (Western New York, II)
Hileman, The Rev. Mary E. (Oklahoma, VII)
Howe Jr., The Rev. Ralph F. (Louisiana, IV)
Hubbard, The Rev. Colenzo (West Tennessee, IV)
Keller, Mr. David H. (Upper South Carolina, IV)
Kelly III, The Rev. Dr. Colin P. (Rio Grande, VII)

MacGregor, Mrs. Mary M. (Texas, VII)
Mayo, Mrs. Judy R. (Fort Worth, VII)
Mollegen Jr., Mr. Albert T. (Connecticut, I)
Mudge Jr., The Rev. Shaw (Albany, II)
Panilaitis, Ms. Elizabeth (Connecticut, I)
Potter, The Rev. Linda (Oregon, VIII)
Rasmus, The Rev. John E. (Eau Claire, V)
Roseberry, The Rev. David H. (Dallas, VII)
Ross, Mrs. Carole (Central Florida, IV)
Sheay, The Rev. Dr. Virginia M. (New Jersey, II)
Shepherd, The Rev. Angela F. (Maryland, III)
Smith, The Rev. Michael G. (Minnesota, VI)
Wait, Dr. Shirleen S. (Florida, IV)
Wong, Mr. Warren J. (California, VIII)
Yabroff, The Rev. Martin I. (El Camino Real, VIII)

13 Prayer Book, Liturgy and Music

Wade, The Rev. Francis H., Chair (Washington, III)
Medina, The Very Rev. Ernesto R., Vice-Chair (Los Angeles, VIII)
Charney, Mrs. Janet G., Secretary (Bethlehem, III)
Abrams, Dr. Mary (Kentucky, IV)
Antolini, The Rev. Holly Lyman (Maine, I)
Campbell OSH, The Rev. Sr. Jean (New York, II)
Candler, The Very Rev. Samuel G. (Atlanta, IV)
Clark, Mrs. Beatryce (Northern California, VIII)
Coleman, Mr. Milton Harris (Central New York, II)
Cooper, The Rev. Joseph W. (East Carolina, IV)
Coulter, Mrs. Barbara K. (Western Michigan, V)
Davis, The Very Rev. Zabron (Mississippi, IV)
Dowling, Ms. Hillary (Bethlehem, III)
Engstrom, The Rev. Marilyn J. (Wyoming, VI)
Fischer-Davies, The Rev. Clare (Southwestern Virginia, III)
Fox, The Rev. W. Duane (North Dakota, VI)
Garno, Mr. Scott A. (Albany, II)
Griffin, The Rev. Calvin R. (Upper South Carolina, IV)
Grisham, The Rev. Lowell (Arkansas, VII)
Guillen, The Rev. Anthony (Los Angeles, VIII)
Haney, V, The Rev. James P. (Kansas, VII)
Harmon, The Rev. Dr. Kendall (South Carolina, IV)
Hiers, The Rev. John D. (Southwest Florida, IV)
Johnson, The Rev. Ida Louise (North Carolina, IV)
Lehman, The Rev. Katherine M. (California, VIII)
Lowery, The Rev. Donald A. (Upper South Carolina, IV)

Marsh, The Very Rev. Keith A. (Kentucky, IV)
Morrison, The Rev. Robert P. (Oregon, VIII)
Phelps, The Very Rev. H. Neal (Georgia, IV)
Primo Martin, Ms. Cynthia (Delaware, III)
Pruner, Miss Marcia S. (Northern Michigan, V)
Schreiner, The Rev. Shawn M. (Chicago, V)
Shoulders, The Rev. Canon David (Indianapolis, V)
Slingluff, Mrs. Margaret (Central Gulf Coast, IV)
Smith, The Rev. Stephen (Ohio, V)
Wilkerson, Ms. Jessica (Montana, VI)
Williams, The Rev. Susan Anslow (Western New York, II)
Yumoto, Mr. Ted M. (San Joaquin, VIII)

14   Ministry

Robbins, The Rev. Canon Anne W., Chair (Southern Ohio, V)
Tyler Scott, Mrs. Katherine, Vice-Chair (Indianapolis, V)
Lane, The Rev. Canon Stephen T., Secretary (Rochester, II)
Abrams, The Rev. Ronald (East Carolina, IV)
Barnes, Mr. Aldin (Montana, VI)
Bird, The Rev. Virginia (South Dakota, VI)
Brightman, Mr. John (Nebraska, VI)
Bruckner, Ms. Ellen W. (Iowa, VI)
Burwell, The Very Rev. John B. (South Carolina, IV)
Cantrell, The Very Rev. Christopher T. (Fort Worth, VII)
Cluett, The Ven. Richard I. (Bethlehem, III)
Cowden, Ms. Claire (Northwest Texas, VII)
Emenheiser, The Rev. D. Edward (Western Michigan, V)
Fairman, Canon Roberta (New Hampshire, I)
Fontaine, The Rev. Ann K. (Wyoming, VI)
Fuller, Ms. Dorothy J. (El Camino Real, VIII)
Galbraith, Ms. Joanne B. (Idaho, VIII)
George, Dr. Anita (Mississippi, IV)
Gerbracht, Ms. June S. (Long Island, II)
Haney V, The Rev. James P. (Northwest Texas, VII)
Harrison, The Rev. Cn. Dena A. (Texas, VII)
Hays, The Rev. Canon Mary M. (Pittsburgh, III)
Hough III, The Rev. Canon Charles (Fort Worth, VII)
Hunley, The Rev. Deborah Hentz (Southwestern Virginia, III)
Laird, The Rev. Lucinda R. (Kentucky, IV)
Liias, The Rev. Jurgen W. (Massachusetts, I)
Mann, The Very Rev. Frederick E. (Northern Indiana, V)
Munday Ph.D., The Very Rev. Robert S. (Quincy, V)
Osnaya-Jimenez, The Rev. Uriel (Texas, VII)

Perry, The Rev. Bonnie A. (Chicago, V)
Pollock, The Rev. Dr. David S. (Washington, III)
Salmon, Mrs. Nancy T. (San Joaquin, VIII)
Scipio, Ms. Beverly Y. (Ohio, V)
Snow, Ms. D. Rebecca (Alaska, VIII)
Sotelo, The Rev. George S. (California, VIII)
Thom, The Rev. Brian (Idaho, VIII)
Tillotson, The Rev. Ellen L. (Connecticut, I)
Turner, The Rev. Bonnie (Northern Michigan, V)
Van Siclen, The Rev. Canon John (Rhode Island, I)
Winslow, The Ven. Thomas F. (Milwaukee, V)
Wittig, The Rev. Canon Nancy H. (Pennsylvania, III)

15   **Education**
Evenbeck, Dr. Scott E., Chair (Indianapolis, V)
Adams, The Rev. Jennifer L., Vice-Chair (Western Michigan, V)
Williamson, Mrs. Cecil P., Secretary (Alabama, IV)
Adams, The Very Rev. Michael K (Western Louisiana, VII)
Bausch, The Rev. Lawrence D. (San Diego, VIII)
Belasco, The Rev. Dr. Elizabeth A. (Long Island, II)
Betz Peterson, Ms. Juanita (Lexington, IV)
Bolden, Ms. Shirley (West Missouri, VII)
Broadley, The Rev. Rodger C. (Pennsylvania, III)
Cato, Mrs. Judith C. (Oregon, VIII)
Cramer, Ms. Karen (Utah, VIII)
Frink, Mrs. Caryl S. (Rhode Island, I)
Gordanier, Ms. Arlene (Northern Michigan, V)
Grantz, The Rev. Brian G. (Northern Indiana, V)
Hausman, Mr. Peter J. (New Jersey, II)
Hogg Jr., The Rev. Dr. Paul (Southern Virginia, III)
Julian, The Rev. Mercedes (Dominican Republic, IX)
Juste, Mrs. Esther (Haiti, II)
Klutterman, The Rev. David L. (Fond Du Lac, V)
Larkin, Mr. James (Vermont, I)
Lindley, Dr. Susan Hill (Minnesota, VI)
Love, Dr. George H. (Central Pennsylvania, III)
McClain, The Very Rev. Rebecca L. (Arizona, VIII)
McDonald, Mr. Sam (Ohio, V)
McDowell, The Rev. Dr. Eugene C. (Western North Carolina, IV)
Nestler, The Very Rev. Mary June (Los Angeles, VIII)
Rehberg, Mrs. Margaret (Spokane, VIII)
Smith, The Rev. Ed (Fond Du Lac, V)
Sopkovich, Ms. Wendy (Milwaukee, V)

Torres, The Very Rev. Pascual (Honduras, IX)
Tuohy, Mrs. Anne Lea (Chicago, V)
Wright, Mr. Lonell (Louisiana, IV)
Yeager, Dr. Lillian E. (Kentucky, IV)

16   Church Pension Fund
High Jr., The Rev. Rayford B., Chair (Texas, VII)
Pollard, Ms. Diane B., Vice-Chair (New York, II)
Baldwin, The Rev. John A., Secretary (Southern Virginia, III)
Agnew Jr., The Very Rev. Martin L. (Western Louisiana, VII)
Baxter Jr., The Rev. William P. (Maryland, III)
Beilstein, The Rev. Joan (Washington, III)
Brown, The Rev. Thomas J. (Vermont, I)
Chew, Mr. Matthew K. (Arizona, VIII)
DeFriest, The Rev. Jeannette (Newark, II)
Gutierrez, The Very Rev. Jorge M. (Rochester, II)
Harmon Hines, Dr. Deborah (Western Massachusetts, I)
Hurley, The Very Rev. Thomas J. (Nebraska, VI)
Kusumoto, Mr. Arthur K. (Hawaii, VIII)
Michael, Dr. Sandra (Central New York, II)
Price, Mr. Alfred D. (Western New York, II)
Weathersby, Mrs. Kathryn W. (Mississippi, IV)
Whisenhunt, The Rev. William A. (Western North Carolina, IV)
Wise Jr., The Rev. Eugene F. (Tennessee, IV)

17   Stewardship and Development
Anderson, The Rev. Howard R., Chair (Minnesota, VI)
Zust, The Rev. Vicki D., Vice-Chair (Southern Ohio, V)
Devall, The Rev. Fred, Secretary (Louisiana, IV)
Abrams, Ms. Patricia (Chicago, V)
Bedell, Ms. Doris E. (Albany, II)
Cosby, Mrs. Jane R. (Pennsylvania, III)
Davenport, Canon Sharon L. (Northwestern Pennsylvania, III)
Dyner, The Rev. Canon Marthe Fillman (New Hampshire, I)
Frech Jr., The Rev. Morley E. (Hawaii, VIII)
Gaines, Mrs. Cora M. (New Jersey, II)
Hamilton Jr., Dr. William (Central Gulf Coast, IV)
Hamlin, The Very Rev. Dr. W. Richard (Central New York, II)
Higbie, Mrs. Carlynn (Milwaukee, V)
Kline, Mrs. Joan O. (Southwest Florida, IV)
Midwood, The Rev. John E. (Pennsylvania, III)
Nolin, Mr. Hugh T. (Fond Du Lac, V)
Null, Mr. Ronald D. (Texas, VII)
Olbrych, The Rev. Jennie C. (South Carolina, IV)

Phelps, Mrs. Carolyn B. (West Missouri, VII)
Simpson, Ms. Edwina (Michigan, V)
Somodevilla, The Rev. Rene (West Tennessee, IV)
Speare-Hardy II, The Rev. Benjamin E.K. (Southern Ohio, V)
Stringer III, Mr. Warner A. (Pete) (Tennessee, IV)
Virden III, Mr. Walter (Fort Worth, VII)

18 Ecumenical Relations
Jacobs, The Rev. Gregory A., Chair (Ohio, V)
Gillespie, Ms. Jean C., Vice-Chair (Eastern Oregon, VIII)
Stuckey, The Rev. Ross W., Secretary (West Missouri, VII)
Abbott, The Rev. Grant (Minnesota, VI)
Alden, Ms. Rebecca A. (Massachusetts, I)
Appleyard, The Rev. Daniel S. (Michigan, V)
Armstrong, The Rev. Kenneth L. (Oklahoma, VII)
Bennett, The Rev. Dr. Virginia L. (Springfield, V)
Brown, The Very Rev. Donald G. (Northern California, VIII)
Cavin, The Rev. Barbara (Michigan, V)
Clifford, Mrs. Glennes T. (Oklahoma, VII)
Delcuze, The Rev. Mark S. (Southern Virginia, III)
Downey, The Very Rev. John P. (Northwestern Pennsylvania, III)
Ferlo, The Rev. Dr. Roger (New York, II)
Foster Esq., James R. (Eastern Oregon, VIII)
Gaumer, The Rev. Susan (Louisiana, IV)
Gross, Mrs. Marjorie D. (South Dakota, VI)
Hoffacker, The Very Rev. Charles E. N. (Eastern Michigan, V)
Holbrook, Ms. Sandra (North Dakota, VI)
King Jr., The Rev. Earle C. (Western New York, II)
Krutz, The Rev. Charles Dana (Louisiana, IV)
Murguia, Ms. Priscilla (West Texas, VII)
Nicolosi, The Rev. Gary G. (San Diego, VIII)
Norby, The Rev. Laura L. (Milwaukee, V)
Radner, The Rev. Canon Ephraim (Colorado, VI)
Vance, Mr. Eddie (Easton, III)

19 Communications
Jennings, The Rev. Gay C., Chair (Ohio, V)
Gunn, Mr. G. Herb, Vice-Chair (Michigan, V)
Caum, Mrs. Barbara C., Secretary (Bethlehem, III)
Clayton, Canon Alice R. (East Tennessee, IV)
Crew, Dr. Louie (Newark, II)
Daniel, The Rev. Wilfred (Virgin Islands, II)
Denton, Mrs. Sharon F. (Western Kansas, VII)
Downs, The Rev. J. Thomas (Eastern Michigan, V)

Goff, The Rev. Susan (Virginia, III)
Harris, Ms. Debra L. (New Hampshire, I)
Kirk, Mr. Lawrence M. (Nevada, VIII)
Mance, Ms. Diane (Western North Carolina, IV)
McFarland, Mrs. Cynthia Wilson (Central New York, II)
Nelson-McJilton, The Rev. Sheila (Easton, III)
Seitz, The Rev. Mark (West Virginia, III)
Silides, The Rev. Hunter (Alaska, VIII)
Spence Jr., Mr. Ralph (Montana, VI)
Stimpson, The Rev. Peter K. (New Jersey, II)
Thibodaux, Mr. Paul T. (Alabama, IV)
Toensmann, Mrs. Nell Seymour (Churches in Europe, II)
Webster, Mr. John K. (Southern Ohio, V)
Yeiser, Ms. Therese (Lexington, IV)

20 **Miscellaneous Resolutions**
Funk, Ms. Lynn J., Chair (Quincy, V)
Jones, The Rev. E. Claiborne, Vice-Chair (Atlanta, IV)
Walton, The Rev. Joy E., Secretary (Southern Virginia, III)
Olson, The Rev. Britt (Nevada, VIII)
Railing, Mrs. Jennifer M. (Central Pennsylvania, III)
Robert, Mr. John H. (Western Louisiana, VII)
Ward, The Rev. Horace David (Southeast Florida, IV)

21 **Privilege and Courtesy**
Renton, Mr. Nigel A., Chair (California, VIII)
Ziese, Ms. Nancylee, Vice-Chair (Iowa, VI)
Whistler, The Rev. Tamsen E., Secretary (Missouri, V)
Barrow, Mr. Jack (Southwestern Virginia, III)
Browning, The Rev. Tracy M. (Eastern Oregon, VIII)
Curran, The Rev. Donald (Central Florida, IV)
Ferrell, Mr. Joseph S. (North Carolina, IV)
Lane, Ms. Judith B. (North Carolina, IV)
Powless, Mrs. Blanche A. (Fond Du Lac, V)

22 **Committees and Commissions**
Campbell, The Rev. Deacon Tina, Chair (Northern California, VIII)
Goldsack Esq., John Wood, Vice-Chair (New Jersey, II)
Ell, The Rev. Marianne, Secretary (North Dakota, VI)
Bell, Ms. Nancy (Rochester, II)
Burlington, The Rev. R. Craig (Rhode Island, I)
Callaway, The Rev. Richard H. (Atlanta, IV)
Carpenter, The Rev. Stephen M. (Northern California, VIII)
Eaves, The Rev. Susan N. (Virginia, III)

MINNEAPOLIS MEETING   HOUSE OF DEPUTIES

Gaynor, Ms. Barbara (Eau Claire, V)
Jean, The Rev. MacDonald (Haiti, II)
Jeanes, The Rev. Paul (Kentucky, IV)
Kline, The Very Rev. Timothy E. (Western Kansas, VII)
Strowhorn, Mrs. Charlotte A. (Northern Indiana, V)

23   **Credentials**
Babcock, Mr. Russell C., Chair (Utah, VIII)
Hogue, Mrs. Deborah, Vice-Chair (Colorado, VI)
Baker, The Rev. Brian (Idaho, VIII)
Fancher, Mr. Kay L. (Rio Grande, VII)
Gammon III, Mr. William (Texas, VII)
Hasse, The Rev. Edward M. (Newark, II)
Quinn, The Rev. Scott T. (Pittsburgh, III)
Slechta, Ms. Virginia (South Dakota, VI)
Tattersall, The Rev. Elizabeth (Nevada, VIII)
Wilder, Mrs. Sue E. (Southern Virginia, III)
Williams, Mr. Calvin (Florida, IV)

24   **Sergeant-at-Arms**
Bowden, Mr. R.P.M., Chair (Atlanta, IV)

25   **Program, Budget and Finance**
Anderson, Ms. Bonnie, Chair (Michigan, V)
Nix Jr., The Rev. William D., Secretary (Northwest Texas, VII)
Adams, Ms. Pan (Arkansas, VII)
Bardol, Ms. Anne (Northwestern Pennsylvania, III)
Bennett, The Rev. Canon Ernest L. (Central Florida, IV)
Bjontegard Jr., Mr. Arthur M. (Upper South Carolina, IV)
Boss, Mr. Jon B. (Southern Ohio, V)
Bushyager, Mr. Donald W. (Pittsburgh, III)
Delgado-Park, Mrs. Susan (Honduras, IX)
Goodfellow, The Rev. Willa Marie (Iowa, VI)
Headley-Moore, Ms. Lyn (Newark, II)
Itty, The Rev. Johncy (Long Island, II)
McAlpen, Canon Holly (California, VIII)
Milligan, The Rev. Kathleen S. (Iowa, VI)
Perez, The Rev. Altagracia (Los Angeles, VIII)
Rushing, The Hon. Byron (Massachusetts, I)
Sanchez, The Rev. Sandino Augusto (Dominican Republic, IX)
Stark, Mr. Dennis (Rhode Island, I)

SECOND DAY

Thursday
July 31, 2003

MORNING SESSION

Reconvene
The Vice-President, Mr. Vincent Currie, Jr. of Central Gulf Coast, called the House to order at 11:10 a.m.

Prayers
The Vice-President called on the Chaplain for prayers.

Personal Privilege
The Vice-President introduced himself and offered remarks on the experience of the past three years.

Certification of Minutes
The House of Deputies Committee on Certification of Minutes presented its Report #1, stating that the Committee had met, read the minutes of the First Day, and certified that they were correct. The Chair moved adoption of the Report.

Motion carried
Minutes accepted

Certification of Deputies
The House of Deputies Committee on Credentials presented its Report #3. For the first session of the Second Legislative Day, there were 413 clerical deputies and 412 lay deputies certified and seated, bringing the total count of the House to 825. The number of votes for a motion to prevail is 414. There were 2 new deputies from the Diocese of Quincy certified and 26 changes on this day as follows:

Diocese	*Alternate replacing*	*Deputy being replaced*
Arkansas	Lowell Grisham	Gar Demo
Atlanta	John Andrews	Angela Williamson
Central Pennsylvania	John Hoover	Katherine Harrigan
East Tennessee	Jocelyn Bell	Frank Cooper
Iowa	Connie Whalen	Ellen Bruckner
Iowa	Sharon Mahood	Willa Goodfellow
Los Angeles	J. Edwin Bacon	Anthony Guillen
Maine	Paige Blair	Christopher Chornyak
Minnesota	Howard Anderson	Michael Hanley
Mississippi	Anita George	Suanna Smith
Newark	Louie Crew	Marjorie Christie
Northwest Texas	James Liggett	J. Mayer

Olympia	Mary Ellen Harris	Duncan Bayne
Rhode Island	Jennifer Phillips	Randall Chase
San Diego	Pauline Getz	John Witt
San Joaquin	James Snell	Richard Matters
Southern Virginia	Paul Hogg	Harold Cobb
Texas	James Cunningham	Mary MacGregor
Utah	Mark Brinkmann	David Bailey
Utah	Mary Allen	W. Lee Shaw
West Missouri	Shirley Bolden	India Philley
West Tennessee	Eugene Nobles	Charles Crump
Western Massachusetts	Len Cowan	Heidi Frantz-Dale
Western New York	Earle King	Susan Williams

Messages from the House of Bishops

The Secretary announced that the following messages had been received from the House of Bishops:

HB Message #1: The House of Bishops is organized and ready to proceed to business.

HB Message #2: Presiding Bishop's Appointments. Adopted.

HB Message #7: Report of the Nominations Committee. Adopted.

Dispatch of Business

The House of Deputies Committee on Dispatch of Business moved to suspend the rules for a Special Order of Business for a presentation on the 20/20 initiative and related resolutions at 4:15 p.m. today.

Motion carried
Special Order adopted

Voting

The Vice-President called on the Voting Secretary to clarify and remind the House that every member is required to vote on every issue.

Nominations for President of the House of Deputies

The Vice-President called for nominations for President of the House.
Deputy Moore of Newark nominated Dr. Louie Crew of Newark. Deputy Scott of Indianapolis nominated the Very Rev. George Werner of Pittsburgh.

The Vice-President seeing no further nominations declared the nominations closed and announced that the election for the President of the House of Deputies will take place on Saturday, August 2.

Structure

House of Deputies Committee on Structure presented its Report #3 on Resolution A141 (Admit Diocese of Puerto Rico) and moved adoption with amendment.

Original Text of Resolution:
(A141)
[Note: See *The Blue Book* Report of Standing Commission on Structure, pp. 278–279 or Report of Standing Commission on World Mission, pp. 287–288. *Ed.*]

Committee Amendment:
Resolved, the House of Bishops concurring, That the 2003 General Convention admit the Diocese of Puerto Rico to The Episcopal Church USA and recognize it as a diocese in union with General Convention; and be it further

Resolved, That the General Convention designate the Diocese of Puerto Rico as a member diocese of Province IX of The Episcopal Church; and be it further

Resolved, That the Diocese of Puerto Rico be entitled to all rights pertaining to membership in The Episcopal Church as provided in the Constitution and Canons, including, but not limited to, voice and vote in the House of Bishops and House of Deputies, in accordance with the rules of those houses; and be it further

Resolved, That the Diocese of Puerto Rico be obligated to undertake all responsibilities pertaining to diocesan membership in The Episcopal Church as provided in the Constitution and Canons, including, but not limited to, conforming its constitution and canons to the provisions of the Constitution and Canons of The Episcopal Church; submitting annual diocesan and parochial reports to the General Convention Office; contributing annually to the apportionment budget of the Domestic and Foreign Missionary Society; and reporting fully on any financial assistance it receives from the General Convention budget; and be it further

Resolved, That the Convention affirm that the clergy and lay employees of the Diocese of Puerto Rico will be eligible to participate in companion pension plans administered by the Church Pension Fund, with benefits adapted to the particular needs of the Diocese and consistent with applicable law; and be it further

Resolved, That the Convention urge the Church Pension Fund to work with the Diocese of Puerto Rico to develop a plan to cover the unfunded period of time for those of its clergy who previously participated in the Church Pension Fund when the Diocese was a member of The Episcopal Church; and be it further

Resolved, That the portion of this resolution accepting the Diocese of Puerto Rico into union with the General Convention become effective ~~by written directive by the Presiding Bishop to the Bishop of the Diocese on such date after January 1, 2004 on which the Secretary of the General Convention certifies to the Presiding Bishop that the Secretary has received from the Diocese written evidence that the Diocese has successfully undertaken all the foregoing responsibilities pertaining to membership in the Episcopal Church as provided in the Constitution and Canons~~ *immediately upon concurrence of the House of Deputies and the House of Bishops*; and be it further

Resolved, That the Convention reaffirm the principle that dioceses of this church that are not located within the United States may seek autonomy according to the procedures set forth in Resolution 235a of the 1991 General Convention or may join other provinces of the Anglican Communion.

Deputy Rehill of Newark moved to divide the Resolution, separating the second resolve from the rest of the resolution.

> **Motion carried**
> **Resolution divided**

Debate continued on the main part of the divided Resolution.

Deputy Hutchinson of Utah asked if a motion to suspend the Rules of Order to allow the consideration of a canonical matter without prior review by the Committee on Canons would be in order.

The Parliamentarian advised that such a motion would be in order.

Deputy Hutchinson of Utah moved to suspend the rules.

Debate followed on the motion to suspend the rules.

Deputy Hamilton of Central Gulf Coast moved to terminate debate on the motion to suspend the rules.

> **Motion carried**
> **Debate terminated**

A vote was taken to suspend the Rules of Order.

> **Motion failed**

Deputy Hart of Pennsylvania moved to terminate debate on the divided Resolution.

> **Motion carried**
> **Debate terminated**

The House voted on the divided Resolution A141, resolve clauses 1, and 3 through 8.

> **Motion carried**
> **Resolved clauses adopted**

The House then moved to a discussion of the second resolve clause.

Deputy Johnson of Minnesota moved that pursuant to Title V.1.1, to forego referring the current motion to the Committee on Canons.

> **Motion carried**

Deputy Johnson of Minnesota moved to amend the second resolve clause.

Proposed Amendment

That Canon I.9.1 be amended to delete "and" before Honduras and insert "and Puerto Rico" after Honduras. And that a new resolve clause be inserted with these words: "That this amendment become effective immediately."

> **Motion carried**
> **Resolved clauses adopted**

The House voted on the divided Resolution A141, the second resolve and a new clause.

> **Motion carried**
> **Resolved clauses adopted**
> **Resolution adopted with amendment**
> (Communicated to the House of Bishops in HD Message #15)

Midday Prayers
The Vice-President called upon the Chaplain for midday prayers.

Announcements
Deputy Wade of Washington, Chair of the House of Deputies Committee on Prayer Book, Liturgy and Church Music, explained the Committee's process for the special hearings on Resolutions C005, D022, and A007.

The Secretary announced that each Deputation table has the forms to be used by deputies when moving an amendment to a resolution.

The Secretary reminded the House that the rules of the House do not allow for the distribution of literature on the tables in the House of Deputies or in the Worship Hall.

The Secretary read a statement about expected demonstrations and urgently advised against interacting with the demonstrators in any fashion.

RECESS
At 12:45 p.m. the Vice President declared the House of Deputies in recess until 3:45 p.m.

AFTERNOON SESSION

Reconvene
The President reconvened the House at 3:50 p.m.

Rules of Order
Deputy Renton of California urged the Secretary of the House of Deputies to secure National and Church flags for the platform because they are required by the Rules of Orders. He added that the appropriate body might review this Rule and make recommendations accordingly.

Certification of Deputies
The House of Deputies Committee on Credentials presented its Report #4 for the afternoon session of the Second Legislative Day. There were no new deputies. There were 41 changes in deputy status. There were 413 clerical deputies and 412 lay deputies certified and seated. The total count for the House of Deputies is 825. There were 41 changes on this day as follows:

Diocese	Alternate replacing	Deputy being replaced
Arkansas	Teresa Cantrell	Pan Adams
Arkansas	Gar Demo	Susan Payne
Atlanta	C. Dean Taylor	G. Porter Taylor
Atlanta	Gini Peterson	Janet W. Patterson
Atlanta	Angela Williamson	John Andrews
California	John Eastwood	Katherine Salinaro

Central Pennsylvania	Katherine Harrigan	John Hoover
Delaware	Thomas Kerr	Gary Rowe
East Tennessee	Ed Cahill	Lynn Schmissrauter
Florida	Elizabeth Hobby	Deborah Melnyk
Hawaii	Linda Sproat	James Putnam
Iowa	Ellen Bruckner	Connie Whalen
Long Island	Bernice Coleman	Elizabeth Belasco
Milwaukee	Maurine Lewis	Gary Lambert
Mississippi	Janet Ott	David Elliott
Mississippi	Sissie Wile	Michael Chaney
Mississippi	Shannon Johnston	R. Runnels
Missouri	Marguerite Bowman	James Hood
Missouri	Larry Hooper	Michael Kinman
Northern California	Eric Duff	Stephen Carpenter
Pennsylvania	Ruth Kirk	Nancy Wittig
Rhode Island	Randall Chase	Jennifer Phillips
Rochester	Sarah Collins	Bonnie Tyo
Rochester	Jorge Gutierrez	Lesley Adams
Southern Virginia	Marion Wilson	Frances Barber
Southwest Florida	Paul Game	Roger Schwenke
Upper South Carolina	Angela Daniel	David Keller
Utah	David Bailey	Mark Brinkmann
Utah	W. Lee Shaw	Mary Allen
Washington	Geoffrey Cant	Paul Cooney
West Tennessee	Stephen Carpenter	Colenzo Hubbard
West Texas	Michael Chalk	Gary Lillibridge
West Texas	Amy Moehnke	Susan Hardaway
West Virginia	Sarah Bailey	Cheryl Winter
Western Michigan	Mary Jane Anderson	Netty Cove
Western Michigan	Alice Webley	Pamela Chapman
Western New York	Susan Williams	Alison Martin
Western North Carolina	Lauch Magruder	Lawrence Thompson
Western North Carolina	Houston Matthews	William Whisenhunt
Wyoming	Cliff Moore	Ann Fontaine
Wyoming	Vicki Gilmour	Mary Ellen Honsaker

Consent Calendar

Deputy Simons of Pittsburgh, the Vice-Chair of the House of Deputies Committee on Dispatch of Business, explained the Consent Calendar. Resolutions on the Consent Calendar are not subject to debate. A resolution may be withdrawn from the Consent Calendar prior to its consideration upon the request of any three deputies, or the resolution sponsor, or the Committee on Dispatch of Business.

Messages from the House of Bishops

The Secretary announced that the following messages had been received from the House of Bishops:

HB Message #14:	A108 (Amend Constitution Article X, Second Reading) Rejected.
HB Message #15:	A112 (Amend Constitution Article I.4) Rejected.
HB Message #8:	A156 (2003 General Convention Daily Agenda) Concurred.
HB Message #9:	B011 (Amend Rules pertaining to 2/3rds Votes) Adopted.
HB Message #10:	B012 (Amend House of Bishops Rule XXIV) Adopted.
HB Message #11:	B013 (Amend House of Bishops Rule II–First Day) Adopted.
HB Message #12:	B014 (Amend House of Bishops Rule VI–First Day) Adopted.
HB Message #13:	B015 (Amend House of Bishops Rule X) Adopted with Amendment.
HB Message #18:	Privilege and Courtesy. Adopted.
HB Message #20:	A114 (Amend Canon I.2.5) Rejected.
HB Message #26:	Resignation of Bishops. Adopted.
HB Message #34:	C010 (Liturgical Commemoration of King Charles the Martyr) Rejected.
HB Message #17:	A039 (Amend Constitution Article II.2, First Reading) Adopted with Amendment
HB Message #19:	A041 (Ratify Actions of Standing Commission on Liturgy and Music) Adopted.
HB Message #21:	A144 (Amend Canon I.I.14) Adopted.
HB Message #22:	A049 (Amend Canon IV.2(A)(2)) Adopted.
HB Message #23:	A045 (Amend Cannon I.17.2) Adopted.
HB Message #24:	A050 (Amend Canon IV.2(B)(10)) Adopted.
HB Message #25:	A152 (Episcopal Partnership for Global Mission) Adopted.
HB Message #27	A133 (Adopt "Expanding Mission and Vitality in Small Congregations") Adopted with Amendment.
HB Message #28:	A091 (Continue Use of Enriching Our Worship 1 & 2) Adopted.
HB Message #29:	A093 (Approve Liturgical Calendar Commemorations) Adopted.
HB Message #30:	A094 (Church Year Calendar Inclusions) Adopted.
HB Message #31	A095 (Authorize Trial Use of Commemorations) Adopted.
HB Message #32:	A096 (Inclusion in the Church Year Calendar) Adopted.
HB Message #33:	A097 (Authorize Trial Use of Commemoration) Adopted.
HB Message #35:	C009 (Liturgical Commemoration of Tikhon, Russian Orthodox Bishop of Alaska & North America) Referred to a Standing Commission.
HB Message #36:	C013 (Liturgical Commemoration of The Rev. Dr. John

	Roberts) Referred to a Standing Commission.
HB Message #37:	A119 (Role of Deacons) Adopted with Amendment.
HB Message #38:	A121 (Clergy and Lay Professional Continuing Education) Adopted with Amendment.

Dispatch of Business
The House of Deputies Committee on Dispatch of Business proposed a change in the afternoon schedule. The House will proceed to the Special Order of Business for the Election of Church Pension Fund Trustees, originally scheduled for 3:45 p.m. this afternoon, to be followed immediately by the Special Order of Business for the 20/20 initiative presentation, scheduled for 4:15 p.m. this afternoon.

Election of Church Pension Fund Trustees
The Secretary called upon the Voting Secretary to explain the distribution of Church Pension Fund Trustee ballots. Ballots would be distributed to each deputation based on the number of seated deputies.
Bishop Parsley of Alabama has withdrawn his name. Deputies are to vote for 12 candidates for six-year terms and 2 candidates for three-year terms.
Ballot #1 taken

20/20 Initiative Presentation
The Rev. John Guernsey of Virginia, Chair of the Standing Commission on Domestic Mission and Evangelism, and Ms. Sarah Lawton of California, Vice-Chair of the Standing Commission and Chair of the 20/20 Strategy Group, along with other members, spoke about the 20/20 initiative. They discussed the 20/20 initiative's broad-spectrum efforts to build up the body of Christ in ways which reflect the diversity of contemporary society, including taking on new forms of mission, courageous leadership, social justice and justice ministries, and community organizing, among other efforts.

Dispatch of Business
The President called upon the Chair of Dispatch of Business to return the House to the regular Calendar of Business.

Structure
The House of Deputies Committee on Structure presented its Report #4 on Resolution A120 (Theological Education Committee) and moved adoption with amendment.

Original Text of Resolution:
(A120)
Resolved, the House of Bishops concurring, That the 74th General Convention direct the Standing Commission on Ministry Development to convene a Strategic Planning Committee, consisting of three groups: a) 11 Bishops appointed by the Presiding Bishop, b) the 11 Seminary Deans or their appointees, and c) 18 Provincial Representatives, two to be elected from each province; and be it further

Resolved, That this Committee is to function in a broad collaborative manner for six years to prepare an in-depth study that will chart the future of theological education in the Church; and be it further
Resolved, That funding for the work of this Committee be sought from sources outside the General Convention and administered by the Standing Commission for Ministry Development; and be it further
Resolved, That the Standing Commission on Ministry Development will report on the work of this Strategic Planning Committee to the 75th General Convention and will deliver its final report to the 76th General Convention.

Committee Amendment:
Resolved, the House of Bishops concurring, That the 74th General Convention direct the Standing Commission on Ministry Development, *contingent upon finding funding from other sources outside of General Convention,* to convene a Strategic Planning Committee, consisting of *bishops, seminary deans, and Provincial representatives,* ~~three groups: a) 11 Bishops appointed by the Presiding Bishop, b) the 11 Seminary Deans or their appointees, and c) 18 Provincial Representatives, two to be elected from each province~~; and be it further
Resolved, That this Committee is to function in a broad collaborative manner for six years to prepare an in-depth study that will chart the future of theological education in the Church; and be it further
~~*Resolved,* That funding for the work of this Committee be sought from sources outside the General Convention and administered by the Standing Commission for Ministry Development; and be it further~~
Resolved, That the Standing Commission on Ministry Development will report on the work of this Strategic Planning Committee to the 75th General Convention and will deliver its final report to the 76th General Convention.

Motion carried
Resolution adopted with amendment
(Communicated to the House of Bishops in HD Message #16)

The House of Deputies Committee on Structure presented its Report #5 on Resolution A145 (General Convention Model) and moved adoption.

Original Text of Resolution:
(A145)
Resolved, the House of Bishops concurring, That the Presiding Bishop and the President of the House of Deputies appoint a Joint Task Force consisting of members of the Standing Commission on Structure of the Church and the Joint Standing Committee on Planning and Arrangements to prepare a comprehensive model for General Convention with respect to the Structure of General Convention and the General Convention Agenda to be considered for implementation by the 75th General Convention.

Motion carried
Resolution adopted
(Communicated to the House of Bishops in HD Message #17)

Consecration of Bishops

The House of Deputies Committee on the Consecration of Bishops presented its Report #3 on Resolution C041 (Consent to the Election of The Rev. Samuel Johnson Howard as Bishop Coadjutor of the Diocese of Florida) and moved adoption.

Original Text of Resolution:
(C041)
Resolved, Pursuant to Article II, Section 2, and Canon III.22.3 of the Constitution and Canons, the House of Deputies, consents to the ordination and consecration of the Rev. Samuel Johnson Howard as Bishop Coadjutor of the Diocese of Florida.

Motion carried
Resolution adopted
(Communicated to the House of Bishops in HD Message #18)

The House of Deputies Committee on the Consecration of Bishops presented its Report #4 on Resolution C042 (Consent to the Election of the Rev. C. Franklin Brookhart, Jr. as Bishop of the Diocese of Montana) and moved adoption.

Original Text of Resolution:
(C042)
Resolved, Pursuant to Article II, Section 2, and Canon III.22.3 of the Constitution and Canons, the House of Deputies, consents to the ordination and consecration of the Rev. C. Franklin Brookhart, Jr. as Bishop of the Diocese of Montana.

Motion carried
Resolution adopted
(Communicated to the House of Bishops in HD Message #19)

RECESS
The President called a ten minute recess at 5:00 p.m.

Reconvene
The President reconvened the House of Deputies at 5:10 p.m.

Social and Urban Affairs
The House of Deputies Committee on Social and Urban Affairs presented its Report #2 on Resolution C026 (Reduce the Use of Toxic Chemicals) and moved that the Committee be discharged and the resolution be re-referred to another Committee.

Motion carried
Committee discharged
Resolution re-referred to a Legislative Committee
(Communicated to the House of Bishops in HD Message #20)

Evangelism
The House of Deputies Committee on Evangelism presented its Report #1 on Resolution A083 (Articulate Faith Story) and recommended adoption with amendment.

Original Text of Resolution:
(A083)
Resolved, the House of Bishops concurring, That the 74th General Convention urge every Episcopalian to be able to articulate his or her faith story beginning with Epiphany 2004; and urge dioceses and congregations to create opportunities for these stories to be told.

Committee Amendment:
Resolved, the House of Bishops concurring, That the 74th General Convention call every Episcopalian to be able to articulate his or her faith story ~~beginning with Epiphany 2004~~; and urge dioceses and congregations to create opportunities for these stories to be told.

Deputy Shepherd of Maryland moved to amend the resolution.

Proposed Amendment:
Restore the original language of the resolution.

Motion defeated
Amendment defeated

A vote was taken on Resolution A083.

Motion carried
Resolution adopted with amendment
(Communicated to the House of Bishops in HD Message #21)

Communications

The House of Deputies Committee on Communications presented its Report #1 on Resolution C027 (AV Materials of The Episcopal Church) and moved adoption.

Original Text of Resolution:
(C027)
Resolved, the House of Bishops concurring, That the 74th General Convention require all audio-visual materials produced by and for the General Convention, and programs of the Executive Council and staff, be made accessible to all people:
> by providing closed captioning in English for deaf and hard-of-hearing people, as well as subtitling or dubbing in Spanish and other languages where appropriate, and
> by urging all producers of religious audio-visual materials to do the same.

Motion carried
Resolution adopted
(Communicated to the House of Bishops in HD Message #22)

The House of Deputies Committee on Communications presented its Report #2 on Resolution A082 (Multilingual Publications) and moved adoption of a substitute.

Original Text of Resolution:
(A082)
Resolved, the House of Bishops concurring, That the 74th General Convention, consistent with the Executive Council's June 2002 mandate that materials issued by the Church Center be multilingual, invest in additional linguistically and culturally skilled staff at the Church Center, the initial step being the employment of translation services; and that the General Convention direct the Church Center Staff to develop a strategy for multilingual publications and communication and report to Executive Council; and that $85,000 per year for the triennium be approved for this purpose.

Committee Substitute:
Resolved, the House of Bishops concurring, That the 74th General Convention, consistent with the Executive Council's June 2002 mandate that materials issued by the Church Center be multilingual when appropriate, ask the Executive Council, in coordination with the Church Center staff, to develop a strategy to utilize existing multilingual resources and to consider the employment of translation services; and be it further
Resolved, That the 74th General Convention request the Joint Standing Committee on Program, Budget and Finance to consider a budget allocation of $85,000 per year for the triennium for implementation of this resolution.

Motion carried
Substitute resolution adopted
(Communicated to the House of Bishops in HD Message #23)

The House of Deputies Committee on Communications presented its Report #3 on Resolution A027 (Use of Titles) and moved adoption of a substitute.

Original Text of Resolution:
(A027)
Resolved, the House of Bishops concurring, That the 74th General Convention direct all bodies of ECUSA to respect the baptismal parity of women and men in the church by consistently using language and titles that equally identify women (lay and ordained) with their male counterparts.

Committee Substitute:
Resolved, the House of Bishops concurring, That the 74th General Convention strongly encourages bodies of The Episcopal Church to respect and reflect the equality of men and women in the Church bestowed by Baptism by (1) addressing individuals by the form of address each one prefers, and (2) addressing groups by forms of address that include everyone equally.

Motion carried
Substitute resolution adopted
(Communicated to the House of Bishops in HD Message #24)

The House of Deputies Committee on Communications presented its Report #4 on Resolution A026 (Baptismal Parity) and moved adoption of a substitute.

Original Text of Resolution:
(A026)
Resolved, the House of Bishops concurring, That the 74th General Convention commit itself to baptismal parity for all members of all ages; and be it further
Resolved, That the 74th General Convention direct the Executive Council to appoint a special task force for (1) interpreting our biblical and theological language and heritage about God and people in ways that include all those created in God's image, (2) offer guidelines to assure linguistic visibility, and (3) introduce same in the everyday worship, music, education, preaching, written materials, and clip art used at the congregational, diocesan and national levels of The Episcopal Church; and be it further
Resolved, That the task force include theologians, members of the Standing Commission on Liturgy and Music, the Committee on the Status of Women, the House of Bishops Theology Committee, the Executive Council Anti-Racism Committee, and the Episcopal News Service; and be it further
Resolved, That the task force publish by 2006 those principles and guidelines with recommendations for introducing them to congregations, the Episcopal Church Center, church-related organizations, staff and media. Many Protestant denominations have such guidelines and stated commitments to linguistic inclusion, which encompass art work as well as language; and be it further
Resolved, That Baptismal parity is the welcoming of all baptized persons into the Body of Christ, where all are included equally and the grace and gifts bestowed by

God are recognized and fully utilized; and be it further
Resolved, That the Executive Council provide $34,000 for two meetings of the Task Force and $1,500 for publication of the principles and guidelines.

Committee Substitute:

Resolved, the House of Bishops concurring, That the 74th General Convention commit itself to using language and visual images that reflect the diversity of age, sex, ethnicity, and race among the baptized membership of The Episcopal Church; and be it further

Resolved, That the 74th General Convention direct the Executive Council to appoint a task force to (1) explore ways to include all who are created in God's image in our use of biblical and theological language and our use of visual images; (2) create guidelines that assure inclusion of persons of both sexes, and all ages; ethnicities and races; and (3) encourage incorporation of these guidelines in the everyday worship, music, education, preaching, written materials, and visual art used at the congregational, diocesan, and national levels of The Episcopal Church; and be it further

Resolved, That the task force include theologians, members of the Standing Commission on Liturgy and Music, the Committee on the Status of Women, the House of Bishops Theology Committee, the Executive Council Anti-Racism Committee, and the Episcopal News Service; and be it further

Resolved, That the 74th General Convention request the Joint Standing Committee on Program, Budget and Finance to consider a budget allocation of $35,500 ($34,000 for two meetings of the Task Force and $1,500 for communication of these guidelines) for implementation of this resolution.

Deputy Dombek of Upper South Carolina moved to amend the resolution.

Proposed Amendment:

Insert "those with disabilities" between the words "ethnicity" and "race" in the first resolve. Hearing no objection, the President ruled the acceptance of this amendment.

Motion carrried
Amendment adopted

Deputy Thornell of Southern Ohio moved to amend the resolution.

Proposed Amendment:

Substitute the phrase "representatives of the ethnic desks" for "the Executive Council Anti-Racism Committee."

Motion carried
Amendment adopted

A vote was taken on Resolution A026 as amended.

Substitute resolution adopted with amendment
(Communicated to the House of Bishops in HD Message #25)

Miscellaneous Resolutions
The House of Deputies Committee on Miscellaneous Resolutions presented its Report #2 on Resolution A154 (75th General Convention Site) and moved adoption.

Original Text of Resolution:
(A154)
Resolved, the House of Bishops concurring, That Columbus, Ohio be selected as the site for the 75th General Convention in 2006.

Deputy High of Texas moved to terminate debate.

Motion carried
Debate terminated

A vote was taken on Resolution A154.

Motion carried
Resolution adopted
(Communicated to the House of Bishops in HD Message #25)

Announcements
The Secretary read the announcements.

RECESS
The President recessed the House at 6:06 p.m. until 2:30 p.m. on Friday, August 1, 2003.

MINNEAPOLIS MEETING   HOUSE OF DEPUTIES

THIRD DAY

Friday
August 1, 2003

AFTERNOON SESSION

Reconvene
The President called the House to order at 2:32 p.m and made several announcements including that flags are now in place and that translators for Spanish-speaking deputies are available.

Prayers
The President called on the Chaplain for prayers.

Certification of Minutes
The House of Deputies Committee on Certification of Minutes presented its Report #2, stating that the Committee had met, read the minutes of the Second Day, and certified that they were correct. The Chair moved adoption of the Report.

Motion carried
Minutes accepted

Certification of Deputies
The House of Deputies Committee on Credentials presented its Report #5. For the first session on the Third Legislative Day, there were 412 clerical deputies and 413 lay deputies certified and seated, bringing the total count of the House to 825. There were no new deputies certified and 72 changes on this day as follows:

Diocese	*Alternate replacing*	*Deputy being replaced*
Arkansas	Susan Payne	Gar Demo
Arkansas	Pan Adams	Teresa Cantrell
Atlanta	Lori Lowe	E. Claiborne Jones
Atlanta	Janet W. Patterson	Gini Peterson
Atlanta	G. Porter Taylor	Richard Callaway
Atlanta	John Andrews	Richard Perry
Central Gulf Coast	Peter Wilson	William Hamilton
Central Pennsylvania	John Radomsky	Carol Fish
Central Pennsylvania	John Hoover	Marjorie Menaul
Chicago	James Steele	Bonnie Perry
Chicago	Richard Peete	Patricia Abrams
Colorado	Craig Moseley	Gary Thompson
Colorado	S. Brooks Keith	John Johanssen
Delaware	Gary Rowe	Thomas Kerr
Delaware	Herb Quick	William Hitch
East Carolina	Pamela Stringer	Joseph Cooper

East Tennessee	Lynn Schmissrauter	Ed Cahill
East Tennessee	Frank Cooper	Jocelyn Bell
El Camino Real	James Wilson	Dorothy Fuller
Florida	George Young	James Cooper
Florida	Deborah Melnyk	Shirleen Wait
Hawaii	James Putnam	Linda Sproat
Idaho	Margaret Babcock	Brian Thom
Iowa	Connie Whalen	Raisin Horn
Iowa	Willa Goodfellow	Sharon Mahood
Long Island	Elizabeth Belasco	Bernice Coleman
Maine	Christopher Chornyak	Paige Blair
Minnesota	Philip McNairy	Grant Abbott
Mississippi	David Elliott	Janet Ott
Mississippi	Danny Meadors	Kathryn Weathersby
Mississippi	Michael Chaney	Sissie Wile
Mississippi	Ruth Black	Zabron Davis
New Jersey	Terrence Rosheuvel	Leroy Lyons
New York	James Burns	Jean Campbell
Northern California	Barry Beisner	Mark Allen
Northwest Texas	J. Mayer	James Liggett
Oklahoma	Mary Gail Ruark	Glennes Clifford
Olympia	Duncan Bayne	Linda Potter
Oregon	James Boston	John Scannell
Oregon	Maron Van	Sherman Hesselgrave
Pennsylvania	Penelope Cutler	Jane Cosby
Pennsylvania	Robert Tate	Rodger Broadley
Pennsylvania	Nancy Wittig	Ruth Kirk
Pittsburgh	Stephen Stagnitta	Joan Malley
Pittsburgh	Thomas Moore	William Roemer
Rhode Island	Carol Bennett	Caryl Frink
Rhode Island	Jennifer Phillips	John Van Siclen
Rio Grande	Carole McGowan	Ronald Thomson
Rochester	Bonnie Tyo	Sarah Collins
San Joaquin	Nancy Salmon	Charles Reed
San Joaquin	Richard Matters	Ken Richards
Southern Virginia	Frances Barber	Marion Wilson
Southwest Florida	Fredrick Robinson	John Hiers
Tennessee	Langley Granbery	David Herbert
Texas	Mary MacGregor	William Gammon
Upper South Carolina	David Keller	Garfield Stuart
Upper South Carolina	Elizabeth Wickenberg Ely	Robert Dannals
Utah	Barbara Losse	Stephen Hutchinson
Washington	Paul Cooney	Geoffrey Cant

MINNEAPOLIS MEETING HOUSE OF DEPUTIES

Washington	Carolyn Feinglass	Iris Harris
Washington	Michael Hopkins	Margaret Graham
West Missouri	Bradley Woodall	Shirley Bolden
West Tennessee	Charles Crump	Eugene Nobles
West Texas	Susan Hardaway	Priscilla Murguia
West Texas	Kirk Mason	Robert Browning
West Virginia	Cheryl Winter	Karl Ruttan
Western Louisiana	Walter Baer	Martin Agnew
Western Massachusetts	Heidi Frantz-Dale	Sarah Shofstall
Western Michigan	Netty Cove	Mary Jane Anderson
Western North Carolina	William Whisenhunt	Houston Matthews
Wyoming	Ann Fontaine	Cliff Moore
Wyoming	Mary Ellen Honsaker	Vicki Gilmour

Voting Procedures

The President called upon the Voting Secretary, who apologized for the difficulties with the electronic voting instruments on the previous day and reported that all keypads have been tested.

Announcements

The Secretary announced the revised arrangements for witness registration at the Prayer Book, Liturgy and Music hearing, scheduled for this evening.

Messages from the House of Bishops

The Secretary announced that the following messages had been received from the House of Bishops:

HB Message #39:	A060 (Contemporary Language Competency) Adopted with Amendment.
HB Message #40:	C031 (Waging Reconciliation) Adopted.
HB Message #41:	A090 (Christian-Muslim Dialogue) Adopted with Amendment.
HB Message #42:	A046 (Amend Canon III.22.1(e)) Adopted with Amendment.
HB Message #43:	A048 (Amend Canon IV.4.16(d)) Adopted Substitute.
HB Message #44:	A098 (Church Year Calendar Inclusion) Adopted.
HB Message #45:	A099 (Authorize Trial Use of Commemoration) Adopted.
HB Message #46:	A064 (Seminarian Expenses) Adopted Substitute.
HB Message #47:	A038 (Peace and Justice Studies and Training) Adopted.
HB Message #48:	A007 (Aging Task Force) Adopted with Amendment.
HB Message #49:	A013 (The Church's Role in Counseling and Education on Biomedical Ethics) Adopted with Amendment.
HB Message #50:	A030 (21st Century Survey Resources) Adopted with Amendment.
HB Message #51:	Consent to the Election of the Rev. George Edward Councell as Bishop of the Diocese of New Jersey.

Concurred.

HB Message #52: Consent to the Election of the Rev. Joe Goodwin Burnett as Bishop of the Diocese of Nebraska. Concurred.

The President asked the Diocese of New Jersey deputation to escort Bishop-elect Councell to the podium to be introduced.

The President asked the Diocese of Nebraska deputation to escort Bishop-elect Burnett to the podium to be introduced.

Dispatch of Business
The House of Deputies Committee on Dispatch of Business reminded the House of a Special Order of Business for a John Cannon memorial on Saturday.

Consent Calendar

Social and Urban Affairs
The House of Deputies Committee on Social and Urban Affairs presented its Report #3 on Resolution A127 (Mandatory Sentencing Guidelines) and moved that the Committee be discharged.

Motion carried
Committee discharged
(Communicated to the House of Bishops in HD Message #29)

Miscellaneous Resolutions
The House of Deputies Committee on Miscellaneous Resolutions presented its Report #1 on Resolution A015 (Jubilee Ministry Thanksgiving) and moved adoption.

Original Text of Resolution:
(A015)
Resolved, the House of Bishops concurring, That the 74th General Convention acknowledge with thanks to God the ministry of Jubilee on its 21st anniversary; and be it further

Resolved, That this ministry of "joint discipleship in Christ with poor and oppressed people, wherever they are found, to meet basic human needs and to build a just society," continue to be "at the heart of the mission of the Church..."; and be it further

Resolved, That Jubilee Ministry be reaffirmed and commended to the whole Church.

Motion carried
Resolution adopted
(Communicated to the House of Bishops in HD Message #30)

The House of Deputies Committee on Miscellaneous Resolutions presented its Report #3 on Resolution A155 (76th General Convention Site) and moved adoption.

Original Text of Resolution:
(A155)
Resolved, the House of Bishops concurring, That the following five sites be considered for the 76th General Convention and that no less than three be selected for final consideration. The five sites are: Salt Lake City, Utah; Reno, Nevada; Portland, Oregon; Anaheim, California; and Charlotte, North Carolina.

Motion carried
Resolution adopted
(Communicated to the House of Bishops in HD Message #31)

(End of Consent Calendar)

Constitution

The House of Deputies Committee on Constitution presented its Report #1 on HB Message #16 on Resolution A143 (Amend Constitution Article I.7) and moved concurrence.

Deputy Rushing of Massachusetts moved to recommit the resolution to the legislative committee. Deputy Seitz of West Virginia moved the previous question to terminate debate.

Motion carried
Debate terminated

A vote was taken to refer Resolution A143 to the Legislative Committee.

Motion carried
Resolution referred to Legislative Committee
[Note: Consideration of Resolution A143 resumed on Day 7. See page 501. *Ed.*]

Structure

The House of Deputies Committee on Structure presented its Report #6 on Resolution D039 (Priorities for Triennial Budget Decisions) and moved adoption.

Original Text of Resolution:
(D039)
Resolved, the House of Bishops concurring, That the 74th General Convention endorse the following statement of priorities in rank order for the budget of the next triennium and direct the Joint Standing Committee on Program, Budget and Finance to use these priorities in forming the Budget of the Episcopal Church 2004–2006:
Priorities

We offer these mission priorities as an expression of our commitment to Jesus Christ.

We are committed to the importance of our ministry of reconciliation and communion at every level of our common life.

We embrace diversity and seek to promote inclusion and power sharing which underlie and inform all priorities, decisions, and all that we do. In faithfulness to these commitments, we continue to honor our covenants and partnerships with overseas dioceses. We affirm the work of the Executive Council in identifying the following priorities for the mission of the church for the next triennium.

1. YOUNG ADULTS AND YOUTH: Reaching out to young adults and youth through intentional inclusion and full incorporation in the thinking, work, worship, and structure of the Church.
2. RECONCILIATION AND EVANGELISM: Reconciling and engaging those who do not know Christ by participating in God's mission of reconciling all things to Christ and proclaiming the Gospel to those who are not yet members of the Church.
3. CONGREGATIONAL TRANSFORMATION: Revitalizing and transforming congregations through commitment to leadership development, spiritual growth, dynamic and inclusive worship, greater diversity, and mission.
4. JUSTICE AND PEACE: Promoting justice and peace for all of God's creation and reaching out to the dispossessed, imprisoned, and otherwise voiceless needy.
5. PARTNERSHIPS: Reaffirming the importance of our partnerships with provinces of the Anglican Communion and beyond and our relationships with ecumenical and interfaith partners.

Motion carried
Resolution adopted
(Communicated to the House of Bishops in HD Message #32)

The House of Deputies Committee on Structure presented its Report #7 on Resolution A147 (Legislative Committee Membership) and moved adoption.

Original Text of Resolution:
(A147)
Resolved, the House of Bishops concurring, That all Legislative Committees be appointed in such a manner to include a sufficient number of the members of the Standing Commission or Committee for such area of concern, together with a sufficient number of deputies not serving on the Standing Commission or Committee.

Deputy Ferrell of North Carolina moved that Resolution A147 be referred back to the House of Deputies Committee on Structure.

Motion carried
Resolution referred to Legislative Committee
[Note: Consideration of Resolution A147 resumed on Day 6. See page 480. *Ed.*]

MINNEAPOLIS MEETING   HOUSE OF DEPUTIES

The House of Deputies Committee on Structure presented its Report #8 on Resolution A146 (Provincial Coordinators Funding) and moved adoption.

Original Text of Resolution:
(A146)
Resolved, the House of Bishops concurring, That the 74th General Convention continue to appropriate sufficient funds to ensure the continuation of Provincial Coordinators.

Motion carried
Resolution adopted
(Communicated to the House of Bishops in HD Message #33)

The House of Deputies Committee on Structure presented its Report #9 on Resolution A019 (Continue Standing Committee on HIV/AIDS) and moved adoption with amendment.

Original Text of Resolution:
(A019)
Resolved, the House of Bishops concurring, That the 74th General Convention authorize the continuation of the Executive Council Standing Committee on HIV/AIDS for the 2004–2006 Triennium; and be it further
Resolved, That the Standing Committee on HIV/AIDS for the next triennium focus on the "quiet voices of AIDS" in our church and in our nation, those whom we are called to serve but may overlook; and be it further
Resolved, That the Standing Committee undertake a survey of HIV/AIDS ministries at all levels of the church; and be it further
Resolved, That the Standing Committee on HIV/AIDS report at least annually to the Executive Council of the General Convention on the state of the church's response to the HIV/AIDS pandemic, with particular attention to the implementation of pertinent resolutions of General Convention.

Committee Amendment:
Resolved, the House of Bishops concurring, That the 74th General Convention authorize the continuation of the Executive Council Standing Committee on HIV/AIDS for the 2004–2006 Triennium; and be it further
Resolved, That the Standing Committee on HIV/AIDS for the next triennium focus on the "quiet voices of AIDS" in our church and in our nation *and in the world*, those whom we are called to serve but may overlook; and be it further
Resolved, That the Standing Committee undertake a survey of HIV/AIDS ministries at all levels of the church; and be it further
Resolved, That the Standing Committee on HIV/AIDS report at least annually to the Executive Council of the General Convention on the state of the church's response to the HIV/AIDS pandemic, with particular attention to the implementation of pertinent resolutions of General Convention.

Deputy High of Texas moved to terminate debate.

Motion carried
Debate terminated

A vote was taken on Resolution A019 as amended.

Motion carried
Resolution adopted with amendment
(Communicated to the House of Bishops in HD Message #39)

Consecration of Bishops

The House of Deputies Committee on the Consecration of Bishops presented its Report #5 on Resolution C043 (Consent to the Election of the Rev. Canon Johncy Itty as Bishop of the Diocese of Oregon) and moved adoption.

Original Text of Resolution:
(C043)
Resolved, Pursuant to Article II, Section 2, and Canon III.22.3 of the Constitution and Canons, the House of Deputies consents to the ordination and consecration of the Rev. Canon Johncy Itty as Bishop of the Diocese of Oregon.

Motion carried
Resolution adopted
(Communicated to the House of Bishops in HD Message #34)

The House of Deputies Committee on the Consecration of Bishops presented its Report #6 on Resolution C044 (Consent to the Election of the Rev. Steven A. Miller as Bishop of the Diocese of Milwaukee) and moved adoption.

Original Text of Resolution:
(C044)
Resolved, Pursuant to Article II, Section 2, and Canon III.22.3 of the Constitution and Canons, the House of Deputies consents to the ordination and consecration of the Rev. Steven A. Miller as Bishop of the Diocese of Milwaukee.

Motion carried
Resolution adopted
(Communicated to the House of Bishops in HD Message #35)

The House of Deputies Committee on the Consecration of Bishops presented its Report #7 on Resolution D007 (Episcopal Election Reform) and moved adoption with amendment.

Original Text of Resolution:
(D007)
Resolved, the House of Bishops concurring, That an appropriate existing committee, commission, agency, or board (CCAB) be charged with the task of reviewing all

aspects of nominating, electing, and consecrating a bishop, and report to the 75th General Convention recommending ways for these processes to model ministry for this millennium, with the bishop seen less as prince and more as servant; and be it further

Resolved, That the group identify some of the conflicting and impossible expectations of nominees and of the one elected, and offer guidance regarding ways dioceses can be as clear and reasonable as possible in nominating, electing, consecrating, and holding those elected accountable; and be it further

Resolved, That the group imagine and identify ways local and diocesan communities can identify clergy who potentially have the gifts for episcopal ministry, and assist them in discerning whether or not they are being called to it; and be it further

Resolved, That the report include data on the costs of all episcopal elections over the two most recent triennia, reported within the context of the diocesan budgets to encourage good stewardship; and be it further

Resolved, That the report provide examples of ways that some have used these processes to model servanthood and celebrate diversity.

Committee Amendment:

Resolved, the House of Bishops concurring, That ~~an appropriate existing committee, commission, agency or board (CCAB)~~ *the Standing Commission on Ministry Development* be charged with the task of *gathering data and* reviewing all aspects of nominating, electing, and consecrating a bishop, and *present a* report to the 75th General Convention recommending ways for these processes to model ministry for *this present time* ~~millennium with the bishop seen less as prince and more as servant~~; and be it further

Resolved, That the *Standing Commission on Ministry Development* ~~group~~ identify some of the ~~conflicting and impossible~~ expectations of nominees and of the one elected, and offer guidance regarding ways dioceses can be as clear and reasonable as possible in nominating, electing, *and* consecrating~~, and holding those elected accountable~~; and be it further

~~*Resolved,* That the group imagine and identify ways local and diocesan communities can identify clergy who potentially have the gifts for episcopal ministry and assist them in discerning whether or not they are being called to it; and be it further~~

Resolved, That the report include data on the costs of all episcopal elections over the two most recent triennia~~, reported within the context of the diocesan budgets to encourage good stewardship~~; and be it further

Resolved, That the report provide examples of ways that some have used these processes to ~~model servanthood~~ *facilitate understanding of the ministry of all the baptized, model simplicity,* and celebrate diversity.

Motion carried
Resolution adopted with amendment
(Communicated to the House of Bishops in HD Message #36)

Election of Church Pension Fund Trustees
The Secretary read the results of Ballot #1 for Trustees of the Church Pension Fund.

Barbara B. Creed and Cecil Wray were elected to the two three-year unexpired terms.

M.L. Agnew Jr., James E. Bayne, Sheridan C. Biggs, David L. Brigham, Gayle Elizabeth Harris, Joon D. Matsumura, Virginia A. Norman, David R. Pitts, V. Gene Robinson, and Wayne P. Wright to ten of the twelve six-year terms.

A second ballot will be taken to elect persons to the remaining two six-year terms.

National and International Concerns
The House of Deputies Committee on National and International Concerns presented its Report #1 on Resolution C022 (Explosion of AIDS Worldwide/Continuing Epidemic in the United States) and moved adoption.

Original Text of Resolution:
(C022)
Resolved, the House of Bishops concurring, That each congregation is urged to designate annually an appropriate Sunday as Worldwide AIDS Sunday; and be it further

Resolved, That congregations dedicate this day to prayer for all people living with HIV/AIDS, and to learning more about this epidemic worldwide and ways to help; and be it further

Resolved, That congregations be urged to respond to AIDS in Africa and other heavily affected parts of the world by supporting AIDS service organizations in these areas that have proven records of success; and be it further

Resolved, That congregations be urged to respond to AIDS locally by supporting AIDS service organizations in their communities.

Motion carried
Resolution adopted
(Communicated to the House of Bishops in HD Message #37)

The House of Deputies Committee on National and International Concerns presented its Report #3 on Resolution A024 (Support for CEDAW) and moved that the Committee be discharged.

Motion carried
Committee discharged
(Communicated to the House of Bishops in HD Message #38)

Social and Urban Affairs
The House of Deputies Committee on Social and Urban Affairs presented its Report #4 on Resolution A010 (Continue Anti-Racism Mandate) and moved adoption with amendment.

Original Text of Resolution:
(A010)
Resolved, the House of Bishops concurring, That the Executive Council continue the anti-racism program with appropriate staffing and budget, under the mandate as defined by the committee recommendation regarding compliance; and be it further
Resolved, That the emerging provincial network of anti-racism trainers be recognized as an important resource, its utilization commended to the several provinces, dioceses, and affiliated organizations of the Church; and be it further
Resolved, That the 74th General Convention extend its appreciation to the organizers and participants of the anti-racism hearings, and call upon the anti-racism committee to implement a program that responds to the issues raised at the hearings, as appropriate; and be it further
Resolved, That all persons seeking election or appointment to the several standing commissions, other committees of Executive Council, related boards, and auxiliary organizations should have had the mandated anti-racism training as prescribed by this General Convention; and be it further
Resolved, That the Office of Peace and Justice be commended for its "Stop the Hate" Campaign and encourage it to develop similar programs that address the issues of racial profiling and other abuses of the criminal justice system that have emerged in this post 9/11 environment; and be it further
Resolved, That the Anti-Racism Committee of Executive Council be directed to prepare a report for the other standing committees and commissions of the Church that inform them of the several issues emerging from the anti-racism hearings and specify what actions each might take to ameliorate the impact of racism in their area of concern.

Committee Amendment:
Resolved, the House of Bishops concurring, That *The Episcopal Church reaffirm its historic commitment to eradicate racial injustice in the Church and in secular society, and that* the Executive Council continue the anti-racism program with appropriate staffing and budget, ~~under the mandate as defined by the committee recommendation regarding compliance~~ *as approved by the 73rd General Convention (A047), and recommend the National Dialogues on Anti-Racism methodology;* and be it further
Resolved, That the emerging provincial network of anti-racism trainers be recognized as an important resource, its utilization commended to the several provinces, dioceses, and affiliated organizations of the Church; and be it further
Resolved, That the 74th General Convention extend its appreciation to the organizers and participants of the anti-racism hearings and call upon the Anti-Racism Committee *(Anti-Racism Advisory Committee of the Executive Council and the Social Justice Department)* to implement a program that responds to the issues raised at the hearings, as appropriate; and be it further
Resolved, That all persons seeking election or appointment to the several standing commissions, other committees of Executive Council, related boards and auxiliary organizations ~~should have had the mandated~~ *must have* had anti-racism training ~~as prescribed by this General Convention~~ required *by the 73rd General Convention (B049) or agree to have this training within a year of their appointment;* and be it further

Resolved, That the Office of Peace and Justice be commended for its "Stop the Hate" Campaign and encourage it to develop similar programs that address the issues of racial profiling and other abuses of the criminal justice system that have emerged in this post 9/11 environment; and be it further
Resolved, That the Anti-Racism Committee of Executive Council be directed to prepare a report for the other standing committees and commissions of the Church that inform them of the several issues emerging from the anti-racism hearings and specify what actions each might take to ameliorate the impact of racism in their area of concern.

Motion carried
Resolution adopted with amendment
(Communicated to the House of Bishops in HD Message #40)

The House of Deputies Committee on Social and Urban Affairs presented its Report #5 on Resolution A014 (Approve Research on Human Stem Cells) and moved adoption of a substitute.

Original Text of Resolution:
(A014)
Resolved, the House of Bishops concurring, That the 74th General Convention support the choice of those who wish to donate their early embryos, remaining after in vitro fertilization (IVF) procedures have ended, for embryonic stem cell research, and urge the United States Congress to pass legislation that would authorize federally funded research for the derivation and use of human stem cells from early embryos that have been donated for such research by those who have completed IVF procedures, provided that:
- these early embryos are no longer required for procreation by those donating them;
- those donating early embryos have given their prior informed consent to their use in stem cell research;
- directors of fertility clinics from which early embryos are obtained certify that they were not deliberately created for research; and
- directors of fertility clinics and stem cell investigators certify that such early embryos have not been obtained through sale or purchase; and be it further

Resolved, That the 74th General Convention urge the Secretary of Health and Human Services to establish an interdisciplinary oversight body for all research in both the public and private sectors that involves stem cells from human embryos, parthenotes, sperm cells, or egg cells and have this body in place within six months of passing such legislation.

Committee Substitute:
Resolved, the House of Bishops concurring, that the 74th General Convention of The Episcopal Church, believing that a wider availability of embryonic stem cells for medical research holds the potential for discovery of effective treatment of a wide variety of diseases and other medical conditions;

(A) Urge that adult stem cell research continue;
(B) Support the choice of those who wish to donate their early embryos, remaining after in vitro fertilization (IVF) procedures have ended; and
(C) Urge that the United States Congress pass legislation that would authorize federal funding for derivation of and medical research on human embryonic stem cells that were generated for IVF and remain after fertilization procedures have been concluded, provided that:

1. These early embryos are no longer required for procreation by those donating them and would simply be discarded;
2. Those donating early embryos have given their prior informed consent to their use in stem cell research;
3. The embryos were not deliberately created for research purposes;
4. The embryos were not obtained by sale or purchase; and be it further

Resolved, That the 74th General Convention of the Episcopal Church urge the Secretary of Health and Human Services to establish an interdisciplinary oversight body for all research in both the public and private sectors that involves stem cells from human embryos, parthenotes, sperm cells, or egg cells, and have this body in place within six months of passing such legislation; and be it further

Resolved, That the 74th General Convention of the Episcopal Church direct the Secretary of General Convention to communicate this resolution to appropriate members and committees of the United States Congress and direct the Office of Government Relations to identify and advocate the legislation called for by this resolution.

Deputy Rehill of Newark moved to amend the substitute resolution.

Proposed Amendment:
Delete the word "adult" in the sentence: "Urge that adult stem cell research continue."

Motion carried
Amendment adopted

Deputy Simons of Pittsburgh moved to terminate debate.

Motion carried
Debate terminated

A vote was taken on substitute Resolution A014 as amended.

Motion carried
Substitute resolution adopted with amendment
(Communicated to the House of Bishops in HD Message #41)

Evangelism

The House of Deputies Committee on Evangelism presented its Report #2 on Resolution C015 (Ethnic Desks at the National Church Office) and moved adoption with amendment.

Original Text of Resolution:
(C015)
Resolved, the House of Bishops concurring, That the Episcopal Church Center develop new, creative ways of welcoming and incorporating people of diverse ethnic backgrounds into its fold by the year 2020; and be it further
Resolved, That the Asiamerica Ministries, Black Ministries, Hispanic Ministries, and Native American Ministries desks of the Episcopal Church Center be retained as they were originally chartered, in order to function as an integral part of the Church's work to double its Baptized membership by the year 2020.

Committee Amendment:
Resolved, the House of Bishops concurring, That the Episcopal Church Center develop new, creative ways of welcoming and incorporating people of diverse ethnic backgrounds into ~~its fold by the year 2020~~ *the Episcopal Church*; and be it further
Resolved, That the Asiamerica Ministries, Black Ministries, Hispanic Ministries, and Native American Ministries desks of the Episcopal Church Center be retained, ~~as they were originally chartered, in order to function as an integral part of the Church's work to double its Baptized membership by the year 2020~~ *holding advocacy and congregational development as equal responsibilities and be given the budget and resources they need in order to function as an integral part of the work of the church's work of evangelism to double the average Sunday attendance by 2020.*

Motion carried
Resolution adopted with amendment
(Communicated to the House of Bishops in HD Message #42)

The House of Deputies Committee on Evangelism presented its Report #3 on Resolution A073 (Plant New Churches) and moved adoption with amendment.

Original Text of Resolution:
(A073)
Resolved, the House of Bishops, That the 74th General Convention direct the Congregational Development Unit of the Episcopal Church Center to:
- develop a system for identifying persons with the skills and temperament to plant new churches and/or revitalize existing congregations;
- develop and carry out events to include an annual national conference of church planters to share stories and resources;
- develop training and mentoring programs for laypersons involved in church planting;
- through the office of the Director of Research at the Episcopal Church Center,

conduct and fund research into how other denominations plant and sustain new churches, with special emphasis on learning best practices for planting churches in less affluent areas or areas with negative population growth;

develop a 20/20 Resource Bank to support new church plants by creating a grassroots network that matches resources of all types with those that need them.

Committee Amendment:

Resolved, the House of Bishops concurring, That the 74th General Convention direct the Congregational Development Unit of the Episcopal Church Center to:

develop a system for identifying persons with the skills and temperament to plant new churches and/or revitalize existing congregations;

in cooperation with the Office on Ministry Development, develop and recommend practices for recruiting, training, deploying, and retaining such persons;

develop and carry out events to include an annual national conference of church planters to share stories and resources;

develop training and mentoring programs for laypersons *and congregations* involved in church planting;

through the office of the Director of Research at the Episcopal Church Center, conduct and fund research into how other denominations plant and sustain new churches, with special emphasis on learning best practices for planting churches in less affluent areas or areas with negative population growth;

~~develop a 20/20 Resource Bank to support new church plants by creating a grassroots network that matches resources of all types with those that need them~~ *and make an annual report to the Executive Council and The Episcopal Church at-large on the net increase in new church starts;* and be it further

Resolved, That we commend the work already begun by the Congregational Development Unit of the Episcopal Church Center.

Motion carried
Resolution adopted with amendment
(Communicated to the House of Bishops in HD Message #43)

Communications

The House of Deputies Committee on Communications presented its Report #5 on Resolution A081 (National Ad Campaign) and moved adoption with amendment.

Original Text of Resolution:

(A081)
Resolved, the House of Bishops concurring, That the 74th General Convention direct the Office of Communication to develop a national advertising campaign, with radio and television ads; and that the General Convention urge congregations and dioceses to offer training in welcoming and incorporating newcomers who may come in response to the advertising campaign; and that $750,000 be approved for this purpose.

Committee Amendment:
Resolved, the House of Bishops concurring, That the 74th General Convention direct the Office of Communication to develop a national advertising campaign, with radio and television ads; and that the General Convention urge congregations and dioceses to offer training in welcoming and incorporating newcomers who may come in response to the advertising campaign; ~~and that $750,000 be approved for this purpose~~; and be it further
Resolved, That the 74th General Convention request the Joint Standing Committee on Program, Budget and Finance to consider a total budget allocation of not less than $1,500,000 for the triennium for the implementation of this resolution.

Deputy Bacon of Los Angeles moved to amend the amended resolution.

Proposed Amendment:
Add the words "reflecting the multicultural nature of the church" after the word, "ads."

Motion carried
Amendment adopted

Deputy Renton of California moved to amend the resolution as amended.

Proposed Amendment:
Replace the word, "ads" with the word, "advertisements" in that same line. There being no objection, it was so ordered.

Motion carried
Amendment adopted

Deputy Mesa of Southeast Florida moved to amend the resolution as amended.

Proposed Amendment:
Insert the word, "multilingual" before the word "national" in the second line of the resolution.

Motion carried
Amendment adopted

Deputy Gunn of Michigan moved to amend the resolution as amended.

Proposed Amendment:
In the first resolve clause, delete "General Convention urge congregations and dioceses to offer training." In its place, insert "direct the Office of Communication to prepare and distribute materials for training."

Deputy Atwood of Fort Worth moved to terminate debate.

Motion carried
Debate terminated

A vote was taken on the Gunn amendment.

Motion defeated
Amendment defeated

A vote was taken on Resolution A081 as amended.

Motion carried
Resolution adopted with amendment
(Communicated to the House of Bishops in HD Message #44)

Special Order of Business

The House of Deputies Committee on Dispatch of Business directed the House to a Special Order to memorialize John Kemper Cannon, Esq., former Parliamentarian to four Presidents of the House of Deputies, a long-time Trustee of the Church Pension Fund, and Chair of the Board of the Episcopal Church Archives.

The President invited Yolanda Cannon, John's widow; Alan Blanchard, the President of the Church Pension Fund; Mark Duffy, the Archivist of the Episcopal Church; and Vincent Currie, Vice-President of the House of Deputies to the platform.

After several presentations were made, a time of silence was observed in John Cannon's memory.

Privilege and Courtesy

The House of Deputies Committee on Privilege and Courtesy presented its Report #2 on Resolution D053 (Honor John Kemper Cannon) and moved adoption.

Final Text of Resolution:

(D053)

Whereas, John Kemper Cannon, Esq., faithfully and ably served the House of Deputies for a quarter of a century as Parliamentarian, as Chancellor to the President, and as a member of the Council of Advice of four successive Presidents of the House of Deputies;

Whereas, he piloted the House through the often-stormy seas and hidden shoals of legislative procedure with consummate skill, grace, and good humor;

Whereas, he served The Episcopal Church as a member of the Executive Council, as chair of the Board of Trustees of the Church Pension Fund, as founding chair of CREDO Institute, Inc. and as chair of the Archives of the Episcopal Church;Now be it

Resolved, That the House of Deputies of the 74th General Convention render thanks and praise to Almighty God for the life and servanthood of John Kemper Cannon, cherish his memory, and extend condolences to his family, and especially to his beloved wife Yolanda.

Motion carried
Resolution adopted
(Communicated to the House of Bishops in HD Message #47)

JOURNAL THIRD DAY

Special Order of Business

The House of Deputies Committee on Dispatch of Business in its Report #11 moved to adopt a Special Order of Business:

The Joint Committee on Nominations having submitted names for election to The Executive Council, the House of Deputies Committee on Dispatch of Business moves the adoption of the following resolution:

Resolved, That the following procedures be followed in election of members of the Executive Council at this General Convention pursuant to the provisions of Title I, Canon 4:

1. That this House set a Special Order of Business at 12:00 noon on the 4th Legislative Day, Saturday, August 2, 2003, for the purpose of receiving nominations. The names of persons nominated by the Joint Committee on Nominations shall then be deemed to have been placed in nomination, and the biographical sketches printed on Pages 304 through 310 of the Blue Book shall be deemed to be the equivalent of nominating speeches, and no member of the House shall be recognized to speak further on behalf of any such nominee. Additional nominations may be made from the floor by name and diocese only, accompanied by a written nomination including (1) a biographical sketch of the nominee not longer than 150 words; (2) a certification that the nominee will serve if elected; and (3) the name and signature of the nominator, his or her order and diocese. All these documents shall be submitted to the Secretary at the time of nomination;

2. That the Secretary be directed to prepare a list of the names and biographical sketches as in the Committee's report or as filed in nominations from the floor of all nominees, arranged in alphabetical order by nominee's name, to be distributed to the House no later than 2:30 p.m. the 6th Legislative Day, Monday, August 4, 2003;

3. That this House set a Special Order of Business at 11:15 a.m. the 7th Legislative Day, Tuesday, August 5, 2003, for the purpose of electing two presbyters or deacons and six lay persons for a term equal to twice the interval between regular sessions of the General Convention each until his successor is elected. The Secretary shall prepare a ballot listing alphabetically by orders the names of all persons nominated. On each ballot, each member shall vote for the number of presbyters or deacons and lay persons to be or remaining to be elected, and any ballot with votes less than or in excess thereof shall be void. In the clerical order the two persons receiving the largest number of votes cast shall be deemed elected, and similarly in the lay order the six persons receiving the largest number of votes cast shall be deemed elected; provided that votes equal to or in excess of a majority of the ballots cast on any ballot shall be required for election. Balloting shall continue until the required number have been elected; provided that on the third ballot in each order there shall be retained on the ballot from those persons receiving the highest numbers of votes only that number of nominees equal to twice the number to be elected in such order. In the event

of a significant tie, election shall be by lot cast by the Secretary;
4. The House, at the discretion of its presiding officer, may proceed to other business during the balloting for these elections.

Motion carried
Resolution adopted
(Communicated to the House of Bishops in HD Message #45)

Communications

The House of Deputies Committee on Communications presented its Report #6 on Resolution C029 (Translation of Documents into Spanish) and moved adoption of a substitute.

Original Text of Resolution:

(C029)
Resolved, the House of Bishops concurring, That the 74th General Convention direct that all documents/announcements/cyber publications produced by the Domestic and Foreign Missionary Society/Episcopal Church will be provided no later than 2006 in both English and Spanish, including but not limited to the following:

Episcopal New Service (ENS) press releases
The Presiding Bishop's monthly message
House of Bishops pastoral letters
Summary reports of General Convention actions
Executive Council resolutions/actions
Official communications from the Episcopal Church Center; and be it further
Resolved, That all materials produced in Spanish be sent to the Hispanic Desk to be included in their website for easy retrieval or be mailed by them; and be it further
Resolved, That *Episcopal Life* be urged to provide a section in Spanish.

Committee Substitute:

(C029)
Resolved, the House of Bishops concurring, That the 74th General Convention direct that all official documents, publications, and digital publications produced by the Domestic and Foreign Missionary Society be issued in Spanish no later than 2006, and in other languages used in The Episcopal Church as soon as possible; and be it further
Resolved, That translated materials shall include, but are not limited to the following: Episcopal News Service (ENS) press releases, the Presiding Bishop's monthly message, Pastoral Letters of the House of Bishops, Summary Reports of the actions of General Convention, Executive Council resolutions and actions, and official communications from The Episcopal Church; and be it further
Resolved, That materials produced in Spanish be published on the Episcopal Church website after review by the Office of Ethnic Congregational Development; and be it further
Resolved, That *Episcopal Life* be urged to publish a section of the newspaper in Spanish; and be it further

JOURNAL   THIRD DAY

Resolved, That the 74th General Convention encourage dioceses, congregations, and other agencies and institutions related to The Episcopal Church to make available, as appropriate, materials in Spanish or other languages of its constituents; and be it further
Resolved, That the 74th General Convention request the Joint Standing Committee on Program, Budget and Finance to consider a budget allocation of $85,000 per year for the triennium for the implementation of this resolution.

Deputy Jean of Haiti moved an amendment to the substitute resolution.

Proposed Amendment:
Insert the words, "French and other languages" in the first resolve clause.

Deputy Allen of Kentucky moved to amend the substitute resolution by adding the words "and French" after "Spanish" in the third, fourth, and fifth resolve clauses.
Hearing no objection, the President ordered that this change be made to the Jean amendment.
Deputy Boston of Oregon moved to divide the resolve clause related to *Episcopal Life* from the rest of the resolution.

Motion defeated
Motion to divide rejected

Deputy Pollock of Washington moved to terminate debate on the Jean amendment and main motion.

Motion carried
Debate terminated

A vote was taken on the Jean amendment.

Motion carried
Amendment adopted

A vote was taken on substitute Resolution C029 as amended.

Motion carried
Substitute resolution adopted with amendment
(Communicated to the House of Bishops in HD Message #46)

Messages from the House of Bishops
The Secretary announced that the following messages had been received from the House of Bishops:

HB Message #61:	D028 (Amend Constitution Article X [The Book of Common Prayer—Second Reading]) Discharged.
HB Message #62:	D018 (Amend Canon I.6.1) Rejected.
HB Message #63:	A009 (Amend Canon I.4.2(b)) Concurred.
HB Message #65:	A008 (Repeal Mandatory Federal Sentencing Guidelines) Concurred.
HB Message #64:	A151 (World Mission Funds) Adopted with Amendment.
HB Message #59:	B006 (Dialogue with Reformed Episcopal Church) Adopted.

HB Message #60:	A087 (Interim Eucharistic Sharing with the Moravian Church in America, Northern & Southern Provinces) Adopted.
HB Message #54:	A027 (Use of Titles) Adopted with Amendment.
HB Message #55:	A135 (Holy Habits) Adopted with Amendment.
HB Message #56:	A134 (Implement Alleluia Fund) Adopted.
HB Message #57:	A138 (50/50 Outreach for Congregations) Adopted with Amendment.
HB Message #58:	B003 (Study and Present the Reuilly Accord) Adopted with Amendment.
HB Message #66:	C019 (Amend Canons: Direct Ordination) Rejected.
HB Message #68:	Consent to the Election of The Rev. Samuel Johnson Howard as Bishop Coadjutor of the Diocese of Florida. Concurred.
HB Message #69:	Consent to the Election of the The Rev. C. Franklin Brookhart, Jr. as Bishop of the Diocese of Montana. Concurred.
HB Message #67:	A063 (Ethnic Specific Discernment Committees) Adopt with Amendment.

Announcements
The Secretary read the announcements.

RECESS
The President recessed the House of Deputies at 6:10 p.m. to reconvene at 11:00 a.m. on Saturday, August 2, 2003.

FOURTH DAY

Saturday
August 2, 2003

MORNING SESSION

Reconvene
The Vice-President called the House to order at 11:10 a.m.

Morning Prayers
The Vice-President called on the Chaplain for prayers.

Certification of Minutes
The House of Deputies Committee on Certification of Minutes presented its Report #3 stating that the Committee had met, read the minutes of the Third Day, and certified that they were correct. The Chair moved adoption of the Report.

Motion carried
Minutes accepted

Personal Privilege
Deputy Gibson of New York requested that the voting totals from the election of the Trustees of the Church Pension Fund be read to the House. The Voting Secretary read the results.

Certification of Deputies
The House of Deputies Committee on Credentials presented its Report #6 for the morning session of the Fourth Legislative Day. There was 1 new deputy certified. There were 412 clerical deputies and 414 lay deputies certified and seated, bringing the total count of the House to 826. There were 72 changes on this day as follows:

Diocese	*Alternate replacing*	*Deputy being replaced*
Arkansas	Gar Demo	Lowell Grisham
Atlanta	Richard Perry	Angela Williamson
Atlanta	Richard Callaway	C. Dean Taylor
California	Sarah Lawton	Mary Gotthold
California	Kay Bishop	Warren Wong
Central Florida	Cathy Curran	Thomas Bates
Central Gulf Coast	William Hamilton	Peter Wilson
Central Pennsylvania	Marjorie Menaul	John Hoover
Central Pennsylvania	Carol Fish	John Radomsky
Chicago	Bonnie Perry	James Steele
Chicago	Patricia Abrams	Richard Peete
East Carolina	John Carter	Joan Geiszler-Ludlum
East Carolina	Joseph Cooper	Pamela Stringer

MINNEAPOLIS MEETING   HOUSE OF DEPUTIES

Eau Claire	Patrick Augustine	Alan Coudriet
Eau Claire	Guy Usher	Ward Simpson
El Camino Real	Dorothy Fuller	James Wilson
Florida	Shirleen Wait	Elizabeth Hobby
Idaho	Brian Thom	Margaret Babcock
Iowa	Raisin Horn	Connie Whalen
Los Angeles	Anthony Guillen	J. Edwin Bacon
Milwaukee	Ralph Modjeska	Wendy Sopkovich
Minnesota	Sandra Wilson	Mariann Budde
Minnesota	Grant Abbott	Philip McNairy
Mississippi	Kathryn Weathersby	Danny Meadors
Mississippi	Janet Ott	David Johnson
Mississippi	Zabron Davis	Ruth Black
Missouri	James Hood	Stephanie Rhodes
Nebraska	Beverly Whiteman	D. C. Bradford
Nebraska	Nancy Huston	Thomas Hurley
New Jersey	Joan Anders	Peter Stimpson
New Jersey	Leroy Lyons	Terrence Rosheuvel
New York	Jean Campbell	James Burns
Newark	Marjorie Christie	Michael Rehill
North Carolina	L. Murdock Smith	Timothy Kimbrough
Northern California	Mark Allen	Barry Beisner
Northern California	Stephen Carpenter	Eric Duff
Northern California	Craig Klein	L. Miles Snyder
Northwest Texas	Sue Veal	Richard Davis
Olympia	Linda Potter	Mary Ellen Harris
Oregon	John Scannell	James Boston
Oregon	Sherman Hesselgrave	Maron Van
Pennsylvania	Jane Cosby	Penelope Cutler
Pennsylvania	Rodger Broadley	Robert Tate
Pittsburgh	Joan Malley	Stephen Stagnitta
Pittsburgh	William Roemer	Thomas Moore
Rhode Island	Caryl Frink	Carol Bennett
Rhode Island	John Van Siclen	Jennifer Phillips
San Joaquin	Charles Reed	Suzette Peters
South Carolina	Margie Williams	Lydia Evans
Southern Virginia	Charles Pfeifer	Sara Mueller
Southern Virginia	Joy Walton	Stanley Sawyer
Southern Virginia	Joyce Moorman	Sue Wilder
Southwest Florida	Roger Schwenke	Paul Game
Southwest Florida	John Hiers	Sharon Lewis
Texas	James Nutter	Kenneth Kesselus
Upper South Carolina	Robert Dannals	Elizabeth Wickenberg Ely

JOURNAL   FOURTH DAY

Utah	Jay Stretch	Karen Cramer
Washington	Iris Harris	Carolyn Feinglass
Washington	Margaret Graham	Michael Hopkins
West Missouri	Shirley Bolden	Bradley Woodall
West Missouri	Robert Wood	Constance Tyndall
West Missouri	Kristina Coppinger	Ross Stuckey
West Tennessee	Colenzo Hubbard	Stephen Carpenter
West Texas	Sylvia Maddox	John Brooke
West Texas	Gary Lillibridge	Michael Chalk
West Texas	David Read	Ned Bowersox
West Texas	Alice Fischer	Susan Hardaway
West Virginia	Karl Ruttan	Sarah Bailey
Western Massachusetts	Sarah Shofstall	Heidi Frantz-Dale
Western Michigan	Pamela Chapman	Alice Webley
Western North Carolina	Lawrence Thompson	Lauch Magruder

Messages from the House of Bishops

The Secretary announced that the following messages had been received from the House of Bishops:

HB Message #68:	Consent to the Election of the Rev. Samuel Johnson Howard as Bishop Coadjutor of the Diocese of Florida. Concurred.
	The Vice-President asked the deputation of the Diocese of Florida to escort Bishop Coadjutor-elect Howard to the podium to be introduced.
HB Message #69:	Consent to the Election of the Rev. C. Franklin Brookhart, Jr. as Bishop of the Diocese of Montana. Concurred.
	The Vice-President asked the deputation of the Diocese of Montana to escort Bishop-elect Brookhart to the podium to be introduced.
HB Message #70:	A139 (Affirm the Work of TENS) Adopted with Amendment.
HB Message #71:	A140 (Mission Funding). Adopted with Amendment.
HB Message #72:	A086 (Lutheran Ordination Bylaw) Adopted with Amendment.
HB Message #73:	B001 (Endorse Certain Historic Anglican Doctrines and Policies) Rejected.
HB Message #74:	D013 (Annotated Constitution and Canons, known as White and Dykman) Adopted with Amendment.
HB Message #75:	A040 (Amend Canon l.1.2(n)(6)) Concurred.
HB Message #76:	B010 (Continue Leadership Program for Musicians Service Small Congregations) Adopted with Amendment.
HB Message #77:	A100 (Revise Lesser Feasts and Fasts 2000) Adopted Substitute.

HB Message #78: A092 (Reauthorize Enriching Our Worship Work) Adopted Substitute.

Dispatch of Business
The Chair of the House of Deputies Committee on Dispatch of Business advised the House that some resolutions had been reassigned to different committees and gave the schedule of Special Orders for this Morning:
11:30 a.m.: The Election of the President of the House of Deputies
11:40 a.m.: Balloting for Trustees of the Church Pension Fund—Second Ballot
12:15 p.m. Nominations for the Executive Council

Election of the President of the House of Deputies
Election Ballot #1 was taken for President of the House of Deputies.
Ballot #1 taken
The Secretary announced the results of Ballot #1 for President of the House of Deputies. The Very Rev. George Werner of Pittsburgh was reelected President of the House of Deputies.
The Vice-President asked the deputation from Pittsburgh to escort Deputy Werner to the platform. The President addressed the House and thanked the House for their confidence in him. He commended Deputy Crew of Newark for offering himself for servanthood as President, and invited the House to share in servanthood for the next three years.

Personal Privilege
Deputy Anderson of Michigan presented the President and his spouse with a floral tribute as a token of appreciation from the President's Council of Advice.
Deputy Crew of Newark congratulated the President and shared his joy in the President's election.

Election of Church Pension Fund Trustees
The Voting Secretary instructed the House regarding Ballot #2 for Church Pension Fund Trustees. The paper ballots were cast and collected for counting.
Ballot #2 taken

Dispatch of Business
The Chair of the House of Deputies Committee on Dispatch of Business instructed the House to turn to the supplemental daily calendar for the second legislative day.

Miscellaneous Resolutions
The House of Deputies Committee on Miscellaneous Resolutions presented its Report #4 on Resolution C017 (Global Warming/Energy Conservation for National Church Headquarters) and moved adoption with amendment.

Original Text of Resolution:
(C017)
Resolved, the House of Bishops concurring, That the General Convention authorize an energy audit at the Episcopal Church Center, with the audit process and results shared with the wider church through appropriate means; and be it further
Resolved, That those bodies overseeing the development of a new Church Center at General Seminary in New York incorporate in their architectural, financial, and operational plans measures to insure that the new headquarters functions in a manner that minimizes energy use and environmental impact, exploring options including but not limited to solar power, LEED certification, and Integrated Pest Management.

Committee Amendment:
Resolved, the House of Bishops concurring, That the General Convention authorize an energy audit at the Episcopal Church Center, with the audit process and results shared with the wider church through appropriate means; and be it further
Resolved, That those bodies overseeing the *renovation of the Episcopal* ~~development of a~~ ~~new~~ Church Center ~~at General Seminary~~ in New York incorporate in their architectural, financial and operational plans measures to insure that the *renovated* ~~new~~ headquarters functions in a manner that minimizes energy use and environmental impact, exploring options including but not limited to solar power, LEED certification and Integrated Pest Management.

Motion carried
Resolution adopted with amendment
(Communicated to the House of Bishops in HD Message #49)

Special Order of Business
The House of Deputies Committee on Dispatch of Business in its Report #10 moved adoption with amendment for a Special Order of Business for the consideration of Resolution C045:
Resolved, That this House set a Special Order of Business on the Fifth Legislative Day, Sunday, August 3, 2003, immediately following the nominations for Vice-President, for the purpose of considering and taking action with respect to the Report of Committee Seven on the Consecration of Bishops on Resolution C045; and be it further
Resolved, That in the consideration of the same the following rules of debate shall be followed:
1. The Committee Chair shall have two minutes to speak with respect to the report, and five minutes to respond to questions of information or clarification;
2. The entire debate of the report thereafter shall be limited to 45 additional minutes;
3. Each speaker shall be limited to two minutes and no speaker shall speak more than once on the same question;

4. The Chair shall designate two microphones, one for speakers in favor of the resolution and one for speakers in opposition to the resolution;
5. The Chair shall recognize only at those two microphones and, to the extent practicable speakers of opposite views in alternate succession;
6. Debate may be terminated prior to the expiration of the 45 minute period, or any extension thereof, or extended only by two-thirds vote of the House.
7. No amendments or procedural motions shall be entertained during the first 30 minutes of debate.

The Chair of the Committee on Dispatch of Business moved to amend the Special Order of Business.

Proposed Amendment:
Insert at the end of point one, "A filer of the Minority Report shall have two minutes to speak with respect to the minority report."

Motion carried
Amendment adopted

Deputy Seitz of West Virginia moved to amend the Special Order of Business.

Proposed Amendment:
Change the time stated in point two and six from 45 minutes to 60 minutes.
Deputy High of Texas moved to terminate debate on the amendment.

Motion carried
Debate terminated

A vote was taken on the Seitz amendment.

Motion defeated
Amendment defeated

Deputy Simons of Pittsburgh moved to amend the Special Order of Business.

Proposed Amendment:
Change the number of resolutions stated from two to three microphones. The third microphone to be for procedural motions.
Deputy Cravens of Springfield moved to terminate debate on the Simons amendment and the main motion.

Motion carried
Debate terminated

A vote was taken on the Simons amendment.

Motion carried
Amendment adopted

A vote was taken on the Special Order of Business as amended.

Motion carried
Special Order with amendment adopted

(Communicated to the House of Bishops in HD Message #50)

Special Order of Business—Final Text
Resolved, That this House set a Special Order of Business on the 5th Legislative Day, Sunday, August 3, 2003, immediately following the nominations for Vice-President,

for the purpose of considering and taking action with respect to the Report of Committee Seven on the Consecration of Bishops on Resolution C045; and be it further

Resolved, That in the consideration of the same the following rules of debate shall be followed:

1. The Committee Chair shall have two minutes to speak with respect to the report, and five minutes to respond to questions of information or clarification. A filer of the Minority Report shall then have two minutes to speak with respect to the minority report;
2. The entire debate of the report thereafter shall be limited to 45 additional minutes;
3. Each speaker shall be limited to two minutes and no speaker shall speak more than once on the same question;
4. The Chair shall designate three microphones, one for speakers in favor of the resolution and one for speakers in opposition to the resolution and one for procedural motions;
5. The Chair shall recognize only at those three microphones and, to the extent practicable speakers of opposite views in alternate succession;
6. Debate may be terminated prior to the expiration of the 45 minute period, or any extension thereof, or extended only by two-thirds vote of the House.
7. No amendments or procedural motions shall be entertained during the first 30 minutes of debate.

Nominations for Executive Council

The Vice-President called for nominations for Executive Council.

Deputy Ferlo of New York nominated Pamela Stewart of Long Island.

Deputy Tuohy of Chicago nominated the Rev. Bradley Dyche of Oklahoma.

Deputy Pollard of New York nominated the Rev. Canon Edward Rodman of Massachusetts.

Deputy Lowery of Upper South Carolina nominated Jimmy Hartley of Upper South Carolina.

Hearing no further nominations, the Vice-President moved the nominations be closed.

Constitution

The House of Deputies Committee on the Constitution presented its Report #2 on HB Message #17 on Resolution A039 (Amend Constitution Article II.2, First Reading) and moved concurrence.

The House concurred
(Communicated to the House of Bishops in HD Message #51)

Final Text of Resolution:

(A039)

Resolved, **That the second sentence of Article II, Section 2 of the Constitution be amended to read as follows:**

Section 2. No one shall be ordained and consecrated Bishop until the attainment of thirty years of age; nor without the consent of a majority of the Standing Committees of all the Dioceses, and the consent of a majority of the Bishops of this Church exercising jurisdiction. But if the election shall have taken place within ~~three months next~~ *120 days* before the meeting of General Convention, the consent of the House of Deputies shall be required in place of that of a majority of the Standing Committees. No one shall be ordained and consecrated Bishop by fewer than three Bishops.
And be it further
Resolved, That this resolution be sent within six months to the Secretary of the Convention of every Diocese to be made known to the Diocesan Convention at its next meeting.

Canons

The House of Deputies Committee on Canons presented its Report #1 on HB Message #23 on Resolution A045 (Amend Canon I.17.2) and moved concurrence.

The House concurred
(Communicated to the House of Bishops in HD Message #52)

Final Text of Resolution:
(A045)
Resolved, That Canon I.17.2 be amended to read as follows:

(a) *All members of this Church who have received Holy Communion in this Church at least three times during the preceding year are to be considered communicants of this Church.*

(b) For the purposes of statistical consistency throughout the Church, communicants sixteen years of age and over are to be considered adult communicants.

The House of Deputies Committee on Canons presented its Report #2 on HB Message #22 on Resolution A049 (Amend Canon IV.2(A)(2)) and moved concurrence.

The House concurred
(Communicated to the House of Bishops in HD Message #53)

Final Text of Resolution:
(A049)
Resolved, That Canon IV.2(A)(2) be amended to read as follows:
Sec.2. The Waiver and Voluntary Submission shall be evidenced by a written instrument, which shall contain: (i) the name of the Priest or Deacon, (ii) a reference to the Canon specifying the Offense, (iii) general information sufficient to identify the Offense, and (iv) a statement that the Priest or Deacon is aware of the Sentence to be imposed and the effect thereof, and

shall be signed and Acknowledged by the Priest or Deacon, after opportunity to consult with and obtain advice from independent legal counsel of the Priest or Deacon's choosing. If the Priest or Deacon has so consulted with legal counsel, that counsel shall also be identified in the Waiver and Voluntary Submission. Legal counsel shall not be a Chancellor, a Vice Chancellor, the Church Attorney or a Lay Assessor in that Diocese. The Waiver and Voluntary Submission may be withdrawn by the Priest or Deacon within three days of execution by the Priest or Deacon and thereafter shall be effective and irrevocable. The Church Attorney, each Complainant and Victim shall be given an opportunity to be heard *on the Sentence* by the Bishop who is to impose and pronounce Sentence prior to the execution of the Waiver and Voluntary Submission.

The House of Deputies Committee on Canons presented its Report #3 on HB Message #24 on Resolution A050 (Amend Canon IV.2(B)(10)) and moved concurrence.

The House concurred
(Communicated to the House of Bishops in HD Message #54)

Final Text of Resolution:
(A050)

Resolved, That Canon IV.2(B)(10) be amended to read as follows:
Sec.10. The Waiver and Voluntary Submission shall be evidenced by a written instrument, which shall contain (i) the name of the Bishop, (ii) a reference to the Canon specifying the Offense, (iii) general information sufficient to identify the Offense, and (iv) a statement that the Bishop is aware of the Sentence to be imposed and the effect thereof, and shall be signed and Acknowledged by the Bishop, after opportunity to consult with and obtain advice from independent legal counsel of the Bishop's choosing. If the Bishop has so consulted with legal counsel, that counsel shall also be identified in the Waiver and Voluntary Submission. Legal counsel shall not be the Presiding Bishop's Chancellor. The Waiver and Voluntary Submission may be withdrawn by the Bishop within three days of execution by the Bishop and thereafter shall be effective and irrevocable. The Church Attorney, each Complainant and Victim shall be given an opportunity to be heard *on the Sentence* by the Presiding Bishop who is to impose and pronounce Sentence prior to the execution of the Waiver and Voluntary Submission.

The House of Deputies Committee on Canons presented its Report #4 on HB Message #21 on Resolution A144 (Amend Canon I.1.14) and moved concurrence.
The Committee withdrew consideration of the resolution.

Consideration postponed
[Note: Consideration of Resolution A144 resumed on Day 8. See page 556. *Ed.*]

Structure

The House of Deputies Committee on Structure presented its Report #10 on Resolution A072 (Amend Canon I.6.1) and moved adoption with amendment.

Original Text of Resolution:

(A072)
Resolved, the House of Bishops concurring, That Canon I.6.1 be amended to read as follows:
A report of every Parish and other Congregation of this Church shall be prepared annually for the year ending December 31 preceding, in the form authorized by the Executive Council and approved by the Committee on the State of the Church, and shall be filed not later than March 1 with the Bishop of the Diocese, or, where there is no Bishop, with the ecclesiastical authority of the Diocese. The Bishop or the ecclesiastical authority, as the case may be, shall keep a copy and submit the report to the Executive Council not later than May 1. In every Parish *and other Congregation* the preparation and filing of this report shall be the joint duty of the Rector *or Member of the Clergy* and ~~Vestry, and in every other Congregation the duty of the Member of the Clergy in charge thereof~~ *the lay leadership; and before the filing thereof the report shall be approved by the Vestry or Bishop's committee or mission council.* This report shall include the following information:

Committee Amendment:

Resolved, the House of Bishops concurring, That Canon I.6.1 be amended to read as follows:
A report of every Parish and other Congregation of this Church shall be prepared annually for the year ending December 31 preceding, in the form authorized by the Executive Council and approved by the Committee on the State of the Church, and shall be filed not later than March 1 with the Bishop of the Diocese, or, where there is no Bishop, with the ecclesiastical authority of the Diocese. The Bishop or the ecclesiastical authority, as the case may be, shall keep a copy and submit the report to the Executive Council not later than May 1. In every Parish *and other Congregation* the preparation and filing of this report shall be the joint duty of the Rector *or Member of the Clergy* in charge thereof and ~~Vestry, and in every other Congregation the duty of the Member of the Clergy in charge thereof~~ *the lay leadership; and before the filing thereof the report shall be approved by the Vestry or Bishop's committee or mission council.* This report shall include the following information:

Motion carried
Resolution adopted with amendment
(Communicated to the House of Bishops in HD Message #55)

The House of Deputies Committee on Structure presented its Report #11 on Resolution A142 (Admit Diocese of Venezuela) and moved adoption with amendment.

Original Text of Resolution:
(A142)
[Note: See The Blue Book Report of Standing Commission on Structure, pp. 278–279 or Report of Standing Commission on World Mission, pp. 288–289. *Ed.*]

Committee Amendment:
Resolved, the House of Bishops concurring, That the 74th General Convention admit the Diocese of Venezuela to The Episcopal Church USA and recognize it as a diocese in union with General Convention; and be it further

Resolved, That the General Convention designate the Diocese of Venezuela as a member diocese of Province IX of The Episcopal Church; and be further

Resolved, That the Diocese of Venezuela be entitled to all rights pertaining to membership in The Episcopal Church as provided in the Constitution and Canons, including, but not limited to, voice and vote in the House of Bishops and House of Deputies, in accordance with the rules of those houses; and be it further

Resolved, That the Diocese of Venezuela be obligated to undertake all responsibilities pertaining to diocesan membership in The Episcopal Church as provided in the Constitution and Canons, including, but not limited to, conforming its constitution and canons to the provisions of the Constitution and Canons of The Episcopal Church; submitting annual diocesan and parochial reports to the General Convention Office; contributing annually to the apportionment budget of the Domestic and Foreign Missionary Society; and reporting fully on any financial assistance it receives from the General Convention budget; and be it further

Resolved, That the Convention affirm that the clergy and lay employees of the Diocese of Venezuela will be eligible to participate in *companion pension plans administered* by the Church Pension Fund, subject to the rules of the Church Pension Fund; and be it further

Resolved, That the Convention urge the Church Pension Fund to work with the Diocese of Venezuela to develop a plan to cover *its clergy* ~~the unfunded period of time for those of its clergy who previously participated in the Church Pension Fund when the diocese was a member of the Episcopal Church~~; and be it further

Resolved, That the Convention re-affirm the principle that dioceses of this Church that are not located within the United States may seek autonomy according to the procedures set forth in Resolution 235a of the 1991 General Convention or may join other provinces of the Anglican Communion; and be it further

Resolved, That the last sentence of Canon I.9.1 is hereby amended to read as follows: The Ninth Province shall consist of the Dioceses of this Church in Colombia, the Dominican Republic, Ecuador, Honduras, and Venezuela.

Motion withdrawn

[Note: Consideration of Resolution A142 resumed on Day 7. See page 493. *Ed.*]

The House of Deputies Committee on Structure presented its Report #12 on Resolution C034 (Length of General Convention) and moved that the Committee be discharged as the matter is considered in Resolution A145.

                Motion carried
              Committee discharged
(Communicated to the House of Bishops in HD Message #56)

World Mission

The House of Deputies Committee on World Mission presented its Report #1 on HB Message #25 on Resolution A152 (Episcopal Partnership for Global Mission) and moved concurrence.

              The House concurred
(Communicated to the House of Bishops in HD Message #57)

Final Text of Resolution:
(A152)
Resolved, **That the 74th General Convention commend the Executive Council of The Episcopal Church for its collaboration with the Episcopal Partnership for Global Mission (EPGM) and for its recognition of missionaries from EPGM agencies at its January 2003 meeting in the Dominican Republic.**

Church in Small Communities

The House of Deputies Committee on the Church in Small Communities presented its Report #1 on HB Message #27 on Resolution A133 (Adopt "Expanding Mission and Vitality in Small Congregations") and moved concurrence.

Deputy Mollegen of Connecticut moved an amendment to the resolution.

Proposed Amendment:
That the document mentioned in the resolution be posted on the DFMS website.

              Amendment withdrawn

A vote was taken on Resolution A152.

              The House concurred
(Communicated to the House of Bishops in HD Message #58)

Final Text of Resolution:
(A133)
Resolved, **That the 74th General Convention adopt "Expanding Mission and Vitality in Small Congregations: A Framework Affirming and Strengthening the Ministry of Small Churches" offered by the Standing Commission for Small Congregations;** and be it further

Resolved, **That the Office of Congregational Development and the Missioner** for Rural and Small Communities be directed to print, distribute, and promote this document throughout The Episcopal Church.

National and International Concerns
The House of Deputies Committee on National and International Concerns presented its Report #5 on Resolution A035 (Implement Humanitarian Goals in Africa) and moved adoption with amendment.

Original Text of Resolution:
(A035)
Resolved, the House of Bishops concurring, That the 74th General Convention, in response to widespread humanitarian needs in Africa, commend those churches in Africa fighting AIDS, poverty and injustice, and call on The Episcopal Church at all levels to partner with the Anglican Churches in Africa and other agencies to implement the United Nations Millennium Development Goals in Africa; and be it further
Resolved, That the Convention commit $100,000 per year for three years through the Partnership Office for Africa to support a church-wide campaign to implement humanitarian development goals in Africa.

Committee Amendment:
Resolved, the House of Bishops concurring, That the 74th General Convention, in response to widespread humanitarian needs in Africa, commend those churches in Africa fighting AIDS, poverty and injustice, and call on The Episcopal Church at all levels to partner with the Anglican Churches in Africa and other agencies to implement the United Nations Millennium Development Goals in Africa; and be it further
Resolved, That the Convention commit $100,000 per year for three years through the Partnership Office for Africa to support a church-wide campaign to implement humanitarian development goals in Africa; and be it further
Resolved, That the General Convention request the Joint Standing Committee on Program, Budget and Finance to consider a budget allocation of $300,000 for implementation of this resolution.

Motion carried
Resolution adopted with amendment
Communicated to the House of Bishops in HD Message #59)

Midday Prayers
The Vice-President called on the Chaplain for midday prayers.

Announcements
The Secretary read the announcements.

Recess
The Vice-President recessed the House at 1:19 p.m. to reconvene at 2:30 p.m. on Sunday, August 3, 2003.

MINNEAPOLIS MEETING HOUSE OF DEPUTIES

FIFTH DAY

Sunday
August 3, 2003

AFTERNOON SESSION

Reconvene
The President called the House to order at 2:34 p.m.

Afternoon Prayers
The President called on the Chaplain for prayers.

Certification of Minutes
The House of Deputies Committee on Certification of Minutes presented its Report #4, stating that the Committee had met, read the minutes of the Fourth Day, and certified that they were correct. The Chair moved adoption of the Report.

> Motion carried
> Minutes accepted

Certification of Deputies
The House of Deputies Committee on Credentials presented its Report #7 for the afternoon session of the Fifth Legislative Day, there were 412 clerical deputies and 415 lay deputies certified and seated, bringing the total count of the House to 827. There was 1 new deputy certified and 49 changes on this day, as follows:

Diocese	*Alternate replacing*	*Deputy being replaced*
Arkansas	Lowell Grisham	Gar Demo
Atlanta	Angela Williamson	John Andrews
Atlanta	E. Claiborne Jones	Lori Lowe
California	Joseph Lane	George Sotelo
California	Warren Wong	Kay Bishop
California	Bonita Palmer	Sarah Lawton
Central Florida	Carole Ross	Cathy Curran
Colorado	Gary Thompson	Craig Moseley
Colorado	John Johanssen	S. Brooks Keith
East Carolina	Joan Geiszler-Ludlum	John Carter
Eau Claire	Ward Simpson	John Rasmus
Eau Claire	Alan Coudriet	Patrick Augustine
Florida	James Cooper	George Young
Florida	Althea Hall	Shirleen Wait
Fort Worth	Ryan Reed	H. Jay Atwood
Georgia	Jane Pressly	Edna Drazdowski
Long Island	Richard Brewer	Cecily Broderick y Guerra
Maine	Paige Blair	Linton Studdiford

Massachusetts	Gale Davis Morris	Jurgen Liias
Milwaukee	Gary Lambert	Maurine Lewis
Milwaukee	Wendy Sopkovich	Ralph Modjeska
Minnesota	Mariann Budde	Sandra Wilson
Mississippi	David Johnson	Janet Ott
Mississippi	R. Runnels	Shannon Johnston
Missouri	Michael Kinman	Larry Hooper
Missouri	Stephanie Rhodes	Marguerite Bowman
Nebraska	D. C. Bradford	Beverly Whiteman
New Jersey	Peter Stimpson	Joan Anders
Newark	Michael Rehill	Marjorie Christie
Northern California	L. Miles Snyder	Craig Klein
Northwest Texas	Richard Davis	Sue Veal
Northwest Texas	James Liggett	William Nix
Oklahoma	Glennes Clifford	Mary Gail Ruark
Rio Grande	Ronald Thomson	Carole McGowan
South Carolina	Lydia Evans	Margie Williams
Southern Virginia	Sara Mueller	Charles Pfeifer
Southern Virginia	Sue Wilder	Joyce Moorman
Southwest Florida	Sharon Lewis	Fredrick Robinson
Texas	William Gammon	James Cunningham
Utah	Karen Cramer	Jay Stretch
West Missouri	Ross Stuckey	Kristina Coppinger
West Missouri	Constance Tyndall	Robert Wood
West Texas	Susan Hardaway	Alice Fischer
West Texas	Priscilla Murguia	Amy Moehnke
West Texas	Ned Bowersox	David Read
West Texas	Robert Browning	Kirk Mason
West Texas	John Brooke	Sylvia Maddox
Western Michigan	Cynthia Black	Charles McCabe

Messages from the House of Bishops

The Secretary announced that the following messages had been received from the House of Bishops:

HB Message #79:	A071 (Mission-based Prayers) Discharged.
HB Message #80:	A070 (Creative Worship Resources) Discharged.
HB Message #81:	A069 (Spanish Music Resources) Discharged.
HB Message #82:	A102 (Culturally Sensitive Rites) Discharged.
HB Message #83:	A104 (Facilitate the Enrichment of Worship with Evangelism Focus) Discharged.
HB Message #84:	A105 (Resources for Liturgical Education) Discharged.
HB Message #85:	A141 (Admit Diocese of Puerto Rico) Concurred.
HB Message #86:	D039 (Priorities for Triennial Budget Decisions) Concurred.

MINNEAPOLIS MEETING   HOUSE OF DEPUTIES

HB Message #87:   A101 (Church Planting Liturgies) Adopted with Amendment.
HB Message #88:   A021 (Broadening HIV Prevention Methods) Adopted with Amendment.
HB Message #89:   A065 (Leadership Programs for 18–25 Year-Olds) Adopted with Amendment.
HB Message #90:   D042 (Amend Canon I.8.2, Regarding Election of Church Pension Fund Trustees) Adopted Substitute.
HB Message #91:   A136 (National Mission Narrative/Annual Report) Adopted with Amendment.
HB Message #93:   A088 (Response to Gift of Authority) Adopted.
HB Message #94:   A089 (Open Communion) Refer to a Standing Commission.
HB Message #92:   Consent to the Election of the Rev. Canon Johncy Itty as Bishop of the Diocese of Oregon. Concurred.
HB Message #95:   Consent to the Election of the Rev. Steven Andrew Miller as Bishop of the Diocese of Milwaukee. Concurred.

The President asked the Diocese of Oregon deputation to escort Bishop-elect Itty to the podium to be introduced.

The President asked the Diocese of Milwaukee deputation to escort Bishop-elect Miller to the podium to be introduced.

Seating of the Deputation of the Diocese of Puerto Rico
The President suspended the Rules of Order against public demonstrations in for the House to welcome the Diocese of Puerto Rico deputation to the floor of the House and to the podium. Deputy Millien of Puerto Rico addressed the House with thanksgiving.

Dispatch of Business
The House of Deputies Committee on Dispatch of Business reminded the House of the scheduled Special Orders for nominations for Vice-President of the House of Deputies and for consideration of Resolution C045.

Nominations for Vice-President of the House of Deputies
The President called for nominations for Vice-President of the House.
Deputy Palmore of Virginia nominated Deputy Bonnie Anderson of Michigan.
Deputy Price of Western New York nominated Deputy James E. Bradberry of Southern Virginia.
The Chair of the Committee on Dispatch of Business moved that nominations be closed.

Motion carried
Nominations closed

Election of Church Pension Fund Trustees
The Secretary read the results of Ballot #2 for Church Pension Fund Trustees. No nominee received the requisite 413 votes. A third ballot will be taken at a later time.

Special Order of Business for Resolution CO45
The Chair of the House of Deputies Committee on Dispatch of Business read the adopted Special Order of Business for Resolution C045.

Consecration of Bishops
The House of Deputies Committee on the Consecration of Bishops presented its Report #8 on Resolution C045 (Consent to the Election of the Rev. Canon V. Gene Robinson as Bishop Coadjutor of the Diocese of New Hampshire) and moved adoption.

Original Text of Resolution:
(C045)
Resolved, Pursuant to Article II, Section 2, and Canon III.22.3 of the Constitution and Canons of the General Convention, the House of Deputies, consents to the ordination and consecration of the Rev. Canon V. Gene Robinson as Bishop Coadjutor of the Diocese of New Hampshire.

Minority Report
Believing that the work of Legislative Committee 07: Consecration of Bishops is, according to the Title III, Canon 22, more than merely a verification of correct procedure, but is equally concerned with the appropriateness of the candidate's wholesomeness of life (and consequently includes sexual behavior);
And that this wholesomeness is not merely a model for an individual diocese, but also for the entire One, Holy, Catholic and Apostolic Church to which he would be ordained and consecrated;
And whereas the approval of a bishop elect who is in a same-sex relationship, even if monogamous and loving, is in opposition to the clear teaching of Holy Scripture, the historic teaching of the church, and the promulgated teaching of this Body of Christ known as the Episcopal Church by previous General Conventions;
And whereas the approval of a bishop in said lifestyle would become a pretext upon which the church would de facto resolve the question of the appropriateness of homosexual behavior without due reordering of the church's teaching;
And whereas the approval of this consecration will bring profound consternation to many of our sisters and brothers at home and abroad, straining relationships within the Anglican Communion, and adversely affecting the mission and ministry of the church at home and abroad, the undersigned file this minority report and recommend rejection of C045.

Respectfully submitted,
(signed)
The Very Rev. Mark J. Lawrence
Anthony J. Clark
John E. Masters

The Chair of the House of Deputies Committee on the Consecration of Bishops described the Committee's process and recommendation to the House.

Deputy Lawrence of San Joaquin spoke on behalf of the Minority Report from the House of Deputies Committee on the Consecration of Bishops.

The President noted that the Special Order of Business called for up to five minutes of questions for the House of Deputies Committee on the Consecration of Bishops. There being no questions, the President addressed the House regarding consideration of Resolution C045, reminding those present of the need for courtesy and undergirding love. The President stated that no public demonstrations would be allowed and a recess would follow the voting results.

After thirty minutes of debate, the President called for procedural motions.

Deputy Ross of Florida, on behalf of the Clergy Deputation of Florida, the Lay Deputation of Fort Worth, and the Lay Deputation of San Joaquin, called for a vote by orders on Resolution C045. The President ruled that request to be in order.

Debate continued.

Deputy Logan of South Carolina moved to extend debate by 15 minutes.

Motion defeated

Debate continued.

Deputy Dales of New Hampshire moved to extend debate by 15 minutes.

Motion defeated

Deputy Smith of the Youth Delegation moved to terminate debate. The President ruled the motion was out of order until 45 minutes of debate had elapsed.

Debate continued.

The President announced that the time for debate under the Special Order of Business had expired.

Vote by Orders

The Voting Secretary explained the procedure for a vote by orders.

Deputy Masters of Wyoming asked if the Committee on Credentials had included the deputation from the Diocese of Puerto Rico in its report for today.

Certification of Deputies

The House of Deputies Committee on Credentials reported that Report #7 did not include the Puerto Rico deputation. The Voting Secretary updated the Credentials report, stating that there were 8 additional new deputies, 4 in the clerical order and 4 in the lay order, for a total of 9 new deputies, and a total of 416 clerical deputies and 419 lay deputies, and a total number of deputies of 835.

The President called on the Chaplain for prayer.

Ballot #1—Vote by Orders

A Vote by Orders on Resolution C045 was taken.

Ballot #1 taken by orders

Dispatch of Business
The House of Deputies Committee on Dispatch of Business moved to suspend the rules of order to take up the Consent Calendar for the Fifth Legislative Day.

Motion carried
Rules suspended

Consent Calendar

Dispatch of Business
The House of Deputies Committee on Dispatch of Business announced at the request of the Committee on Rules of Order that Resolution D048 has been withdrawn from the consent calendar.

The House of Deputies Committee on Dispatch of Business presented its Report #7 on Presiding Bishop's Appointments—Appointments to the Board for Clergy Deployment and moved concurrence.

Original Text of Resolution:
Resolved, the House of Bishops having elected the following bishops to be appointed to the Board for Clergy Deployment, the House of Deputies confirm the election of:
   The Rt. Rev. Wendell Gibbs, Bishop of Michigan
   The Rt. Rev. Katharine Jefferts Schori, Bishop of Nevada

Motion carried
Election confirmed
(Communicated to the House of Bishops in HD Message #72)

The House of Deputies Committee on Dispatch of Business presented its Report #8 on Presiding Bishop's Appointments—Historiographer and moved concurrence.

Original Text of Resolution:
Resolved, That the House of Bishops having nominated, the House of Deputies elect to the office of Historiographer:
   The Rev. Dr. Robert Wright

Motion carried
Historiographer elected
(Communicated to the House of Bishops in HD Message #73)

MINNEAPOLIS MEETING — HOUSE OF DEPUTIES

The House of Deputies Committee on Dispatch of Business presented its Report #9 on Presiding Bishop's Appointments—Registrar and moved concurrence.

Original Text of Resolution:
Resolved, The House of Bishops having nominated, the House of Deputies elect to the office of Registrar:
    The Rev. Canon Carl Gerdau

Motion carried
Registrar elected
(Communicated to the House of Bishops in HD Message #74)

The House of Deputies Committee on Dispatch of Business presented its Report #10 on Presiding Bishop's Appointments—Recorder of Ordinations and moved concurrence.

Original Text of Resolution:
Resolved, The House of Bishops having nominated, the House of Deputies elect to the office of Recorder of Ordinations:
    The Church Pension Fund

Motion carried
Recorder of Ordinations elected
(Communicated to the House of Bishops in HD Message #75)

Miscellaneous Resolutions
The House of Deputies Committee on Miscellaneous Resolutions presented its Report #6 on Resolution D024 (Thanksgiving for the Ministry of The Episcopal Church and Visual Arts) and moved adoption.

Original Text of Resolution:
(D024)
Resolved, the House of Bishops concurring, That the 74th General Convention of the Episcopal Church give special thanksgiving for The Episcopal Church and Visual Arts (ECVA). We praise God for the gifts of imagination, vision, and beauty that draw the community of faith deeper into the life of Christ.

Motion carried
Resolution adopted
(Communicated to the House of Bishops in HD Message #71)

(End of Consent Calendar)

Ministry

The House of Deputies Committee on Ministry presented its Report #1 on HB Message #37 on Resolution A119 (Role of Deacons) and moved concurrence.

The House concurred
(Communicated to the House of Bishops in HD Message #60)

Final Text of Resolution:
(A119)
Resolved, That the Standing Commission on Ministry Development in consultation with the dioceses of the church and the North American Association of the Diaconate will continue the study of the role of deacons in the councils of the church, in the dioceses, and in congregations. A report on this work will be submitted to the 75th General Convention.

National and International Concerns

The House of Deputies Committee on National and International Concerns presented its Report #6 on Resolution A006 (Employment Policies Task Group) and moved adoption with amendment.

Original Text of Resolution:
(A006)
Resolved, the House of Bishops concurring, That the 74th General Convention authorize the Executive Council to appoint a Task Group in consultation with the Church Pension Fund to study employment policies and practices in the dioceses and parishes of the church and consider policy recommendations to the 75th General Convention that address issues of equity and justice for church employees working in circumstances of both affluence and poverty; and be it further
Resolved, That $10,000 be allocated for this purpose.

Committee Amendment:
(A006)
Resolved, the House of Bishops concurring, That the 74th General Convention authorize the Executive Council to appoint a Task Group in consultation with the Church Pension Fund to study employment policies and practices in the dioceses and parishes of the church and consider policy recommendations to the 75th General Convention that address issues of equity and justice for church employees working in circumstances of both affluence and poverty; and be it further
Resolved, ~~That $10,000 be allocated for this purpose~~ *That the General Convention request the Joint Standing Committee on Program, Budget and Finance to consider a budget allocation of $10,000 for implementation of this resolution.*

Motion carried
Resolution adopted with amendment
(Communicated to the House of Bishops in HD Message #61)

Evangelism

The House of Deputies Committee on Evangelism presented its Report #4 on Resolution C012 (The Church's Ethnic Desks and 20/20) and moved that the Committee be discharged.

Motion carried
Committee discharged
(Communicated to the House of Bishops in HD Message #62)

Prayer Book, Liturgy and Church Music

The House of Deputies Committee on Prayer Book, Liturgy and Church Music presented its Report #1 on HB Message #28 on Resolution A091 (Continue use of Enriching Our Worship 1 & 2) and moved concurrence.

The House concurred
(Communicated to the House of Bishops in HD Message #63)

Final Text of Resolution:

(A091)
Resolved, That the 74th General Convention authorize continuing use of *Enriching Our Worship 1*: The Daily Office, Great Litany, and Eucharist and *Enriching Our Worship 2*: Ministry with the Sick and Dying, and Burial of a Child during the 2004–2006 triennium, under the direction of the diocesan bishop or ecclesiastical authority.

The House of Deputies Committee on Prayer Book, Liturgy and Church Music presented its Report #2 on HB Message #29 on Resolution A093 (Approve Liturgical Calendar Commemorations) and moved concurrence.

The House concurred
(Communicated to the House of Bishops in HD Message #64)

Final Text of Resolution:

(A093)
Resolved, That the commemorations of Enmegahbowh, Florence Nightingale, and Philip the Deacon, proposed by the 73rd General Convention (Journal, page 473) and approved for trial use, be now finally approved and entered in the Calendar of the Church Year (Book of Common Prayer, pages 15–30).

The House of Deputies Committee on Prayer Book, Liturgy and Church Music presented its Report #3 on HB Message #30 on Resolution A094 (Church Year Calendar Inclusions) and moved concurrence.

The House concurred
(Communicated to the House of Bishops in HD Message #65)

Final Text of Resolution:
(A094)
Resolved, That the 74th General Convention propose additional commemorations for inclusion in the Calendar of the Church Year and authorize trial use thereof for the triennium 2004–2006, as follows:
  February 17 - Janani Luwum, Archbishop of Uganda, and Martyr, 1977
  November 6 - William Temple, Archbishop of Canterbury, 1944
  November 22 - Clive Staples Lewis, Apologist and Spiritual Writer, 1963

The House of Deputies Committee on Prayer Book, Liturgy and Church Music presented its Report #4 on HB Message #31 on Resolution A095 (Authorize Trial Use of Commemorations) and moved concurrence.

The House concurred
(Communicated to the House of Bishops in HD Message #66)

Final Text of Resolution:
(A095)
Resolved, That the 74th General Convention authorize, for trial use until the 2006 General Convention, the commemorations proposed by this Convention, with the following propers:
February 17
Janani Luwum
Archbishop of Uganda, and Martyr, 1977
I. O God, whose Son the Good Shepherd laid down his life for the sheep: We give thee thanks for thy faithful shepherd, Janani Luwum, who after his Savior's example gave up his life for the people of Uganda. Grant us to be so inspired by his witness that we make no peace with oppression, but live as those who are sealed with the cross of Christ, who died and rose again, and now liveth and reigneth with thee and the Holy Spirit, one God, for ever and ever. *Amen.*
II. O God, whose Son the Good Shepherd laid down his life for the sheep: We give you thanks for your faithful shepherd, Janani Luwum, who after his Savior's example gave up his life for the people of Uganda. Grant us to be so inspired by his witness that we make no peace with oppression, but live as those who are sealed with the cross of Christ, who died and rose again, and now lives and reigns with you and the Holy Spirit, one God, for ever and ever. *Amen.*
Psalm - 119:41-48
Lesson - Ecclesiasticus 4:20-28
Gospel - John 12: 24-32
Preface of Holy Week
November 6
William Temple
Archbishop of Canterbury, 1944
I. O God of light and love, who illumined thy Church through the witness of

thy servant William Temple: Inspire us, we pray, by his teaching and example, that we may rejoice with courage, confidence and faith in the Word made flesh, and may be led to establish that city which has justice for its foundation and love for its law; through Jesus Christ, the light of the world, who liveth and reigneth with thee and the Holy Spirit, one God, now and for ever. *Amen.*

II. O God of light and love, you illumined your Church through the witness of your servant William Temple: Inspire us, we pray, by his teaching and example, that we may rejoice with courage, confidence and faith in the Word made flesh, and may be led to establish that city which has justice for its foundation and love for its law; through Jesus Christ, the light of the world, who lives and reigns with you and the Holy Spirit, one God, now and for ever. *Amen.*

Psalm - 119: 97-104
Lesson - Ephesians 3:7-12
Gospel - John 1:9-18
Preface of the Epiphany

November 22
Clive Staples Lewis
Apologist and Spiritual Writer, 1963

I. O God of searing truth and surpassing beauty, we give thee thanks for Clive Staples Lewis, whose sanctified imagination lighteth fires of faith in young and old alike; Surprise us also with thy joy and draw us into that new and abundant life which is ours in Christ Jesus, who liveth and reigneth with thee and the Holy Spirit, one God, now and for ever. *Amen.*

II. O God of searing truth and surpassing beauty, we give you thanks for Clive Staples Lewis, whose sanctified imagination lights fires of faith in young and old alike; Surprise us also with your joy and draw us into that new and abundant life which is ours in Christ Jesus, who lives and reigns with you and the Holy Spirit, one God, now and for ever. *Amen.*

Psalm -139:1-9
Lesson - 1 Peter 1:3-9
Gospel - John 16:7-15
Preface of a Saint (3)

The House of Deputies Committee on Prayer Book, Liturgy and Church Music presented its Report #5 on HB Message #32 on Resolution A096 (Inclusion in the Church Year Calendar) and moved concurrence.

The House concurred
(Communicated to the House of Bishops in HD Message #67)

Final Text of Resolution:
(A096)
Resolved, That the 74th General Convention propose an additional commemoration for inclusion in the Calendar of the Church Year and

authorize trial use thereof for the triennium 2004–2006, as follows:
September 22 - Philander Chase, Bishop of Ohio, and of Illinois, 1852

The House of Deputies Committee on Prayer Book, Liturgy and Church Music presented its Report #6 on HB Message #33 on Resolution A097 (Authorize Trial Use of Commemoration) and moved concurrence.

The House concurred
(Communicated to the House of Bishops in HD Message #68)

Final Text of Resolution:
(A097)
Resolved, That the 74th General Convention authorize, for trial use until the General Convention of 2006, the commemoration proposed by the Convention, with the following propers:
September 22
Philander Chase
Bishop of Ohio, and of Illinois, 1852
I. Almighty God, whose Son Jesus Christ is the pioneer and perfecter of our faith: We give thee heartfelt thanks for the pioneering spirit of thy servant Philander Chase, and for his zeal in opening new frontiers for the ministry of thy Church. Grant us grace to minister in Christ's name in every place, led by bold witnesses to the Gospel of the Prince of Peace, even Jesus Christ our Lord, who liveth and reigneth with thee and the Holy Spirit, one God, for ever and ever. *Amen.*
II. Almighty God, whose Son Jesus Christ is the pioneer and perfecter of our faith: We give you heartfelt thanks for the pioneering spirit of your servant Philander Chase, and for his zeal in opening new frontiers for the ministry of your Church. Grant us grace to minister in Christ's name in every place, led by bold witnesses to the Gospel of the Prince of Peace, Jesus Christ our Lord, who lives and reigns with you and the Holy Spirit, one God, for ever and ever. *Amen.*
Psalm-108:1-6 or 16:5-11
Lesson-Isaiah 44:1-6, 8
Gospel-Luke 9:1-6
Preface of a Saint(1)

The House of Deputies Committee on Prayer Book, Liturgy and Church Music presented its Report #7 on HB Message #35 on Resolution C009 (Liturgical Commemoration of Tikhon, Russian Orthodox Bishop of Alaska and North America) and moved concurrence with a referral to the Standing Commission on Liturgy and Music.

Final Text of Resolution:
(C009)
Resolved, **That Tikhon be added to lesser feasts;** and be it further

Resolved, That since he served faithfully as Russian Orthodox Bishop of Alaska and California and then Bishop of New York, as a close friend of the Episcopal Church, and finally as Patriarch of Moscow, the Diocese of New York petition the Standing Commission on Liturgy and Music to move a resolution to the General Convention of 2003 commemorating Tikhon on April 7th in the Episcopal Church's Lesser Feasts and Fasts and the calendar of the Book of Common Prayer.

Motion carried
Resolution referred to a Standing Commission
(Communicated to the House of Bishops in HD Message #69)

The House of Deputies Committee on Prayer Book, Liturgy and Church Music presented its Report #8 on Resolution C013 (Liturgical Commemoration of the Rev. Dr. John Roberts) and moved concurrence with a referral to the Standing Commission on Liturgy and Music.

Final Text of Resolution:
(C013)
Resolved, That the 74th General Convention direct the Standing Commission on Liturgy and Music to add the Rev. Dr. John Roberts, (born March 31, 1853) Missionary to the Wind River Indian Reservation and western Wyoming, pastor and teacher, founder of the Shoshone Episcopal Mission, churches on the Wind River Reservation and surrounding area, to the Calendar of Lesser Feasts and Fasts, with appropriate Propers and biographical materials.

Motion carried
Resolution referred to a Standing Commission
(Communicated to the House of Bishops in HD Message #70)

Communications
The House of Deputies Committee on Communications presented its Report #7 on Resolution A017 (National Conversation on Women's Ordination) and moved adoption with amendment.

Original Text of Resolution:
(A017)
Resolved, the House of Bishops concurring, That the 74th General Convention receive with thanks the report of the visitors representing the Executive Council in the implementation of Resolution A045 of the 73rd General Convention; and be it further
Resolved, That we give thanks for the work of the Holy Spirit within our communion through the life-giving ministry of ordained women; and be it further
Resolved, That, inasmuch as the 72nd General Convention in Resolution A052 clarified that the canons regarding the ordination of women are mandatory, we

engage in a national conversation drawing on the best theological resources available to assist the whole church to promote, explore, and develop ways to facilitate the ordination of women in every diocese and their full and equal deployment throughout the church; and be it further

Resolved, That such conversations be sponsored by the Executive Council of this Church and begin in the year following this General Convention in preparation for a day of dialogue and reflection to be held at the 75th General Convention in 2006; and be it further

Resolved, That the 2004–2006 Triennium budget include $50,000 for this national conversation.

Committee Amendment:

(A017)
Resolved, the House of Bishops concurring, That the 74th General Convention ~~receive with thanks the report of the visitors representing the Executive Council in the implementation of Resolution A045 of the 73rd General Convention; and be it further *Resolved,* That we~~ give thanks for the work of the Holy Spirit within our communion through the life-giving ministry of ordained women. ~~; and be it further *Resolved,* That, inasmuch as the 72nd General Convention in Resolution A052 clarified that the canons regarding the ordination of women are mandatory, we engage in a national conversation drawing on the best theological resources available to assist the whole church to promote, explore, and develop ways to facilitate the ordination of women in every diocese and their full and equal deployment throughout the church; and be it further *Resolved,* That such conversations be sponsored by the Executive Council of this Church and begin in the year following this General Convention in preparation for a day of dialogue and reflection to be held at the 75th General Convention in 2006; and be it further *Resolved,* That the 2004-2006 Triennium budget include $50,000 for this national conversation.~~

Deputy Cravens of Springfield moved to terminate debate.

Motion carried
Debate terminated

A vote was taken on Resolution A017 as amended.

Motion carried
Resolution adopted with amendment
(Communicated to the House of Bishops in HD Message #76)

Canons

The House of Deputies Committee on Canons presented its Report #5 on HB Message #19 on Resolution A041 (Ratify Actions of Standing Commission on Liturgy and Music) and moved concurrence.

The House concurred
(Communicated to the House of Bishops in HD Message #77)

Final Text of Resolution:
(A041)
Resolved, That all actions taken by and in the name of the Standing Commission on Liturgy and Music since the adjournment *sine die* of the 72nd General Convention, be and the same hereby are ratified in all respects.

Structure
The House of Deputies Committee on Structure presented its Report #13 on Resolution A023 (Establish Institutional Wellness and the Prevention of Sexual Misconduct Task Force) and moved adoption with amendment.

Original Text of Resolution:
(A023)
Resolved, the House of Bishops concurring, That the General Convention establish, pursuant to Joint Rule 23, a Task Force of not less than ten nor more than fifteen persons. These persons should be laity, bishops, priests, and deacons with experience and expertise in dealing with sexual misconduct in church settings. Membership should include, but not be limited to representatives from the Standing Commission on Ministry Development, the Council of Seminary Deans, the Nathan Network, the Committee on Sexual Exploitation, the National Network of Episcopal Clergy Associations, the A028 Task Force, and the National Network of Lay Professionals; and be it further

Resolved, That the Task Force shall study and gather information concerning matters of institutional wellness for the prevention of sexual misconduct. Its study shall include such concerns as screening, selection, and training of clergy, lay employees, and volunteers; monitoring and supervision; behavior management; incident investigation; and the articulation of pastoral standards and codes of ethical behavior; and be it further

Resolved, That each body named shall recommend Task Force members from its own membership, and the appointments shall be overseen by the Bishop of the Office of Pastoral Development. Additional members shall then be appointed by the Bishop of the Office of Pastoral Development, and the entire Task Force shall include at least two bishops, two clergy, and two laity. The Task Force shall have the services of the Office of Pastoral Development and a Church Pension staff person; and be it further

Resolved, That $50,000 be appropriated for the work of this Task Force for the next triennium.

Committee Amendment:
(A023)
Resolved, the House of Bishops concurring, That General Convention establish, pursuant to Joint Rule 23, a Task Force of not less than ten nor more than fifteen persons. These persons should be laity, bishops, priests, and deacons with experience and expertise in dealing with sexual misconduct in church settings. Membership should include, but not be limited to representatives from the

Standing Commission on Ministry Development, the Council of Seminary Deans, the Nathan Network, ~~the Committee on Sexual Exploitation~~, the National Network of Episcopal Clergy Associations, the ~~A028~~ Task Force *on Disciplinary Policy and Procedures,* and the National Network of Lay Professionals; and be it further

Resolved, That the Task Force shall study and gather information concerning matters of institutional wellness for the prevention of sexual misconduct. Its study shall include such concerns as screening, selection, and training of clergy, lay employees, and volunteers; monitoring and supervision; behavior management; incident investigation; and the articulation of pastoral standards and codes of ethical behavior; and be it further

Resolved, That each body named shall recommend Task Force members from its own membership, and the appointments shall be overseen by the Bishop of the Office of Pastoral Development. Additional members shall then be appointed by the Bishop of the Office of Pastoral Development, and the entire Task Force shall include at least two bishops, two clergy, and two laity. The Task Force shall have the services of the Office of Pastoral Development and a Church Pension staff person; and be it further

Resolved, That a report be made to the Standing Commission on Ministry Development, as well as to the 2006 General Convention; and be it further

Resolved, That ~~$50,000 be appropriated for the work of this Task Force for the next triennium~~ *the General Convention request the Joint Standing Committee on Program, Budget and Finance to consider the allocation of $50,000 for the implementation of this resolution.*

Motion carried
Resolution adopted with amendment
(Communicated to the House of Bishops in HD Message #78)

World Mission

The House of Deputies Committee on World Mission presented its Report #2 on HB Message #64 on Resolution A151 (World Mission Funds) and moved concurrence.

The House concurred
(Communicated to the House of Bishops in HD Message #79)

Final Text of Resolution:

(A151)

Resolved, **That the 2003 General Convention adopt the principle that world mission funds historically committed to the church's global engagement through financial covenants to former international jurisdictions of the church be re-deployed in other areas of the church's global engagement, and especially to world mission, as such funds become available through incrementally diminishing levels of support to the autonomous jurisdictions;** and be it further

Resolved, **That a detailed financial plan in consultation between the Standing Commission on World Mission and the Joint Standing Committee on**

Program, Budget, and Finance be developed and be presented by the Standing Commission on World Mission to the 2006 General Convention.

National and International Concerns

The House of Deputies Committee on National and International Concerns presented its Report #7 on Resolution A123 (Diocesan Alcohol and Drug Dependency Policies) and moved adoption.

Original Text of Resolution:

(A123)
Resolved, the House of Bishops concurring, That the 74th General Convention call on all dioceses to establish Diocesan Committees on Alcoholism and Drug Dependency to provide educational programs for clergy, church staff, and congregations that take account of recent advances in treatment of alcohol and drug dependency, and that such committees address problems related to alcohol or drug dependency in clergy, church staff, and, when requested, laypersons; and be it further
Resolved, That dioceses make strong efforts to develop policies concerning treatment and future employment for diocesan clergy and church staff who are dependent on alcohol or drugs; and be it further
Resolved, That dioceses make strong efforts to ensure that health care insurance for diocesan clergy and church staff includes coverage for mental health and addiction, particularly inpatient treatment for dependency on alcohol or drugs.
Deputy Alexander of North Carolina moved to amend the resolution.

Proposed Amendment:

Insert the word "adequate" before the word "coverage" in the third resolve clause.

Motion carried
Amendment adopted

Deputy Guillén of Los Angeles moved to amend the resolution.

Proposed Amendment:

Add the words "and other addictions" after the word "alcohol" in the first resolve clause.

Deputy Renton of California moved to terminate debate on the Guillén amendment and the main motion.

Motion carried
Debate terminated

Deputy Barnes of Montana rose to question if the Guillén amendment was germane to the motion.

The President ruled that the Guillén amendment was germane.

Deputy Rushing of Massachusetts rose to suggest that it was too late for Deputy Barnes to raise that question.

The President called this a teaching moment and asked if the House would sustain the President's ruling.

Motion carried

A vote was taken on the Guillén amendment.

Motion defeated
Amendment defeated

A vote was taken on Resolution A123 as amended.

Motion carried
Resolution adopted with amendment
(Communicated to the House of Bishops in HD Message #80)

Results of Ballot #1: Vote By Orders on Resolution C045

The Secretary read the results of no and divided votes on C045.
The President reminded the gallery that there would be no public demonstrations in the House.
The Secretary reported the results of Ballot #1 on Resolution C045.

Type	Total	Necessary	Yes	No	Divided	Results
Lay	108	55	63	32	13	Carried
Clerical	108	55	65	31	12	Carried

Motion carried
Resolution adopted
(Communicated to the House of Bishops in HD Message #81)

The President called on the Chaplain for prayers.

Messages from the House of Bishops

The Secretary announced that the following messages had been received from the House of Bishops:

HB Message #96:	Executive Council. Adopted
HB Message #97:	B022 (Celebration of African Martyrs) Adopted.
HB Message #98:	D021 (Support for Church Publishing Inc.'s Revised Strategy) Adopted.
HB Message #99:	A047 (Amend Canon IV.14.13) Adopted Substitute.
HB Message #100:	A051 (Amend Canon IV.4.14) Adopted Substitute.
HB Message #101:	D009 (Support 2008 Anglican Gathering) Adopted.
HB Message #102:	A137 (Accountability of Mission Partners) Adopted Substitute.
HB Message #103:	B024 (Task Force on Life-Long Christian Education and Formation) Adopted.

HB Message #105: B004 (Mission Funding Task Force) Adopted Substitute.
HB Message #106: A066 (Campus Ministry Allocation) Adopted Substitute.
HB Message #104: D075 (Holistic Christian Education Study) Discharged.
HB Message #107: A010 (Continue Anti-Racism Mandate) Concurred.

Announcements
The Secretary read the announcements.

RECESS

The President recessed the House at 5:36 p.m. until 11:00 a.m. on Monday, August 4, 2003.

SIXTH DAY

Monday
August 4, 2003

MORNING SESSION

Reconvene
The President called the House to order at 11:07 a.m.

Morning Prayers
The President called on the Chaplain for prayers.

Certification of Minutes
The House of Deputies Committee on Certification of Minutes presented its Report #5, stating that the Committee had met, read the minutes of the Fifth Day, and certified that they were correct. The Chair moved adoption of the Report.

Motion carried
Minutes accepted

Certification of Deputies
The House of Deputies Committee on Credentials presented it Report #8. For the first session of the Sixth Legislative Day there was 1 new deputy certified. There were 417 clerical deputies and 419 lay deputies certified and seated, bringing the total count of the House to 836. There were 52 changes on this day as follows:

Diocese	*Alternate replacing*	*Deputy being replaced*
Arkansas	Gar Demo	JoAnn Barker
Atlanta	Lori Lowe	Samuel Candler
California	Mary Gotthold	Bonita Palmer
California	Sarah Lawton	Holly McAlpen
California	George Sotelo	Joseph Lane
Central Florida	Thomas Bates	Carole Ross
East Tennessee	Ed Cahill	Richard Govan
East Tennessee	Jocelyn Bell	Suzanne Smitherman
Eau Claire	John Rasmus	Guy Usher
Eau Claire	Patrick Croy	Pete Dawson
El Camino Real	C. Jeff Kraemer	Thomas Woodward
Florida	Shirleen Wait	Althea Hall
Fort Worth	H. Jay Atwood	Ryan Reed
Hawaii	Alison Dingley	Carol Arney
Hawaii	Linda Sproat	Cynthia Salley
Idaho	Margaret Babcock	Brian Baker
Long Island	Bernice Coleman	Johncy Itty
Maine	Calvin Sanborn	Anne Stanley

MINNEAPOLIS MEETING — HOUSE OF DEPUTIES

Maine	Linton Studdiford	Paige Blair
Massachusetts	Miriam Gelfer	Mark Hollingsworth
Milwaukee	Ralph Modjeska	Carlynn Higbie
Mississippi	Sissie Wile	Anita George
Mississippi	Danny Meadors	Edward Sisson
Mississippi	Mike Dobrosky	Zabron Davis
New Jersey	Jean McFarland	Charles Perfater
New Jersey	Linda Gaither	John Goldsack
New Jersey	Terrence Rosheuvel	John Zamboni
New Jersey	Joan Anders	Virginia Sheay
New York	James Forde	Nell Gibson
New York	K. Dennis Winslow	Theodora Brooks
Newark	Kenneth Near	Edward Hasse
Newark	Marjorie Christie	Martha Gardner
Northern California	Craig Klein	Dustin Spence
Northwest Texas	William Nix	James Liggett
Ohio	Ann McConnell	Sam McDonald
Oklahoma	Dwight Helt	Noel Doherty
Olympia	Mary Ellen Harris	Hisako Beasley
Olympia	Dorsey McConnell	Stephen Moore
Oregon	Fred Terrill	Judith Cato
Pennsylvania	Karen Lash	JoAnn Jones
Pennsylvania	Glenn Matis	John Midwood
Pennsylvania	Ruth Kirk	Mary Laney
Quincy	Joan Quigg	Crystal Gabelhausen
Rochester	Lesley Adams	Mark Lattime
Southern Virginia	Harold Cobb	Mark Delcuze
Southern Virginia	David Teschner	Paul Hogg
Southwestern Virginia	Emily Fisher	Jack Barrow
Southwestern Virginia	Paul Fuller	John Lane
Spokane	Frank Storey	Margaret Rehberg
Tennessee	David Herbert	Langley Granbery
Texas	Kenneth Kesselus	James Nutter
Upper South Carolina	Garfield Stuart	David Keller
Vermont	Elizabeth Hall	Peter Galbraith
Vermont	John Morris	Thomas Brown
Virginia	Cynthia Bartol	Russell Randle
Washington	John Harmon	Margaret Graham
West Missouri	Robert Wood	John McCann
West Texas	David Read	Nancy Coon
Western Louisiana	Martin Agnew	Walter Baer
Western Michigan	Susan York	Cynthia Black
Western New York	Alison Martin	Earle King

Western North Carolina	Houston Matthews	Augusta Anderson
Wyoming	Vicki Gilmour	Laurie Kadrich
Wyoming	Cliff Moore	Marilyn Engstrom

Communications from the President

The President commended the House for accurately casting the first Vote by Orders and reminded the House not to be concerned about being behind schedule, noting that they were able to move through much of the legislation quickly and that there were fewer resolutions to consider than in years past. The President asked the Parliamentarian to remind the House of some basic rules and procedures.

Parlimentary Procedures

The Parliamentarian addressed the House on several procedures:

(1) All floor comments are to be directed to the Presiding Officer.
(2) It is not appropriate to offer comments prior to making a motion.
(3) Once a motion is made and seconded, that motion is in the hands of the House, and the deputy who made the motion no longer controls the motion.
(4) The House Rules of Order exist to protect the House and to ensure fairness.

Messages from the House of Bishops

The Secretary announced that the following messages had been received from the House of Bishops:

HB Message #108:   A014 (Approve Research on Human Stem Cells) Concurred with Amendment.

Dispatch of Business

The House of Deputies Committee on Dispatch of Business reported that a resolution had been reassigned to another Committee.

Special Order of Business

The House of Deputies Committee on Dispatch of Business moved a Special Order of Business for the Third Ballot for the Trustees of the Church Pension Fund prior to the Daily Calendar for the Sixth Legislative Day.

The House of Deputies Committee on Dispatch of Business moved a Special Order to reorder today's calendar:

1. Sandra Swan, Director of Episcopal Relief and Development, would address the House this morning.
2. Thereafter, the House would consider Special Order for Election of Members of Joint Nominating Committee for Election of the Presiding Bishop and Special Order for Election of Trustees of General Theological Seminary and then resume the daily calendar.
3. After the Consent Calendar this afternoon, the House would receive the

Ecumenical Visitors and be addressed by one of them.

Motion carried
Special Order adopted

Election of Trustees of the Church Pension Fund–Ballot #3

The Voting Secretary explained the procedures for the Third Ballot. The number of candidates is reduced to twice the number of positions still to be elected pursuant to the Special Order of Business passed on the First Legislative Day.
The previous vote totals of the four remaining candidates for two positions were shared with the House.

Ballot #3 taken

Episcopal Relief and Development

Sandra Swan, Executive Director of Episcopal Relief and Development, reported on the relief and development arm of the Episcopal Church, formerly known as the Presiding Bishop's Fund for World Relief. She described the programs goals and initiatives around the world and noted the passing of Bishop Robert Tharp, former Chair of ERD.

Special Order of Business

The House of Deputies Committee on Dispatch of Business in its Report #14 moved to adopt a Special Order of Business:
This General Convention being required to elect members of the Joint Nominating Committee for the Election of the Presiding Bishop pursuant to Title I, Canon 2, Section 1, your Committee on Dispatch of Business moves the adoption of the following resolutions:
Resolved, That the Clerical and Lay Deputies from each Province shall nominate two Clerical Deputies and two Lay Deputies at the Provincial Caucuses on the Sixth Legislative Day, Monday, August 4, 2003. Those eighteen persons constitute the only nominees upon which the House of Deputies shall vote in electing the members of the Joint Nominating Committee for the Election of the Presiding Bishop pursuant to Title I, Canon 2, Section 1; and be it further
Resolved, That the following procedures be followed in the election of the members of the Joint Nominating Committee for the Election of the Presiding Bishop pursuant to Title I, Canon 2, Section 1:

1. That the Secretary of the House prepare a form for nominations of the members of the Joint Nominating Committee for the Election of the Presiding Bishop, which shall contain blanks for the inclusion of:
   a. Name of Nominee
   b. Order
   c. Province
   d. Diocese
   e. Parish and City

f. Certification that the nominee has been duly nominated by another Deputy of the particular Province of the nominee
g. Certification that if elected the nominee will accept the office
h. Signature of an officer of the nominating Province, his or her title order and diocese
i. A biographical sketch of the nominee not longer than 150 words and which forms shall be made available and furnished to representative of each Province on or before the date of the Provincial Caucuses and returned to the Secretary or designated agent of the Secretary and distributed to the House of Deputies by 2:30 p.m. on the Eighth Legislative Day, Wednesday, August 6, 2003;

2. That this House set a Special Order of Business at 4:00 p.m. on the Ninth Legislative Day, Thursday, August 7, 2003, for the purpose of electing one Clerical Deputy and one Lay Deputy from each Province as members of the Joint Nominating Committee for the Election of the Presiding Bishop to remain in office until the sooner of the election of the next Presiding Bishop or the adjournment of the next General Convention. The Secretary shall prepare a ballot form listing numerically by Province and by Order within the Province the names of all persons nominated. On each ballot, each Deputy shall vote for one Clerical nominee and one Lay nominee from each Province; any ballot with votes less than or in excess thereof shall be void. The Clerical nominee and the Lay nominee in each Province receiving the largest number of votes shall be deemed elected, provided that votes equal to or in excess of a majority of the ballots cast on any ballot shall be required for election. Balloting shall continue until there shall be nine Clerical members and nine Lay members elected;
3. In the event of a significant tie, another ballot shall be required for election.
4. The House may, at the discretion of its presiding officer, proceed to other business during the balloting for such election.

The President recognized Deputy Renton of California to clarify the procedures for nominations by provinces.

A vote was taken on the Special Order of Business.

Motion carried
Special Order adopted
(Communicated to the House of Bishops in HD Message #82)

Dispatch of Business
The House of Deputies Committee on Dispatch of Business moved to adopt with amendment a Special Order of Business.

Proposed Amendment:
In the procedure numbered three (3), make the following corrections in the sentence:
That this House set a Special Order of Business immediately following the time for the ~~Consent Calendar~~ *joint session on the Budget* on the Eighth Legislative Day,

Wednesday, August 6, 2003, for the purpose of electing two Presbyters or Deacons and two lay persons as Trustees of the General Theological Seminary.

Special Order of Business

The Joint Standing Committee on Nominations having submitted nominees for election to the Board of Trustees of the General Theological Seminary, the Committee on Dispatch of Business moves the adoption of the following resolution:

Resolved, That the following procedures be followed in the election of Trustees of the General Theological Seminary:

1. That this House set a Special Order of Business at 2:50 p.m. on the Sixth Legislative Day, Monday, August 4, 2003, for the purpose of receiving nominations. The names of persons nominated by the Joint Standing Committee on Nominations shall then be deemed to have been placed in nomination, and the biographical sketches printed on Pages 318 through 322 of the Blue Book shall be deemed to be the equivalent of nominating speeches and no member of the House shall be recognized to speak further on behalf of any such nominee. Additional nominations may be made from the floor by name and diocese only, accompanied by a written nomination including (1) a biographical sketch of the nominee not longer than 150 words, (2) a certification that the nominee will serve if elected, and (3) the name and signature of the nominator, his or her order and diocese. All these documents shall be submitted to the Secretary at the time of nomination;
2. That the Secretary be directed to prepare a list of the names and biographical sketches as in the Committee's report or as filed in nominations from the floor of all nominees, arranged in alphabetical order by nominee's name, to be distributed to the House no later than 4:00 p.m. on the Seventh Legislative Day, Tuesday, August 5, 2003;
3. That this House set a Special Order of Business immediately following the time for the joint session on the Budget on the Eighth Legislative Day, Wednesday, August 6, 2003, for the purpose of electing two Presbyters or Deacons and two lay persons as Trustees of the General Theological Seminary. The Secretary shall prepare a ballot form listing by Order the names of all persons nominated. On each ballot, each Deputy shall vote for two Presbyter or Deacon nominees and two Lay nominees. Any ballot with votes less than or in excess thereof shall be void. The Presbyter or Deacon nominees and the Lay nominees receiving the largest number of votes shall be deemed elected, *provided* that votes equal to or in excess of a majority of the ballots cast on any ballot shall be required for election. Balloting shall continue until there shall be two Presbyter or Deacon Trustees and two Lay Trustees elected;
4. In the event of a significant tie, another ballot shall be required for election.
5. The House may, at the discretion of its presiding officer, proceed to other business during the balloting for such election.

A vote was taken on the Special Order of Business as amended.

Motion carried
Special Order with amendment adopted
(Communicated to the House of Bishops in HD Message #83)

National and International Concerns
The House of Deputies Committee on National and International Concerns presented its Report #8 on Resolution A122 (Improving Health Care for Children) and moved adoption with amendment.

Original Text of Resolution:
(A122)
Resolved, the House of Bishops concurring, That the 74th General Convention of The Episcopal Church encourage dioceses and congregations to establish programs to assist parents to apply for services for eligible children offered by Medicaid, the State Children's Health Insurance Program (SCHIP), and the Special Supplemental Nutrition Program for Women, Infants, and Children (WIC); and be it further
Resolved, That the Office of Government Relations of The Episcopal Church work with the Office of the Secretary of Health and Human Services and the Office of the Secretary of Agriculture, the White House, and Congress to ensure that these programs are adequately funded to meet the needs of the participants they serve; and be it further
Resolved, That the Office of Government Relations urge the Office of the Secretary of Health and Human Services, the White House, the United States Congress and state legislatures to provide more adequate access to mental health services for children in a form that does not require the separation of children from their families; and be it further
Resolved, That The Episcopal Church encourage congregations to become educated about and involved in the prevention of violence and maltreatment perpetrated upon children; and be it further
Resolved, That the Office of Government Relations of The Episcopal Church request the Office of the Secretary of Health and Human Services to make regulatory changes in Medicare and Medicaid health plans to enable terminally ill children to receive more adequate palliative care and pain relief services and their families to receive appropriate supportive services.

Committee Amendment:
Resolved, the House of Bishops concurring, That the 74th General Convention of The Episcopal Church encourage dioceses and congregations to establish programs to assist parents to apply for services for eligible children offered by Medicaid, the State Children's Health Insurance Program (SCHIP), and the Special Supplemental Nutrition Program for Women, Infants, and Children (WIC); and be it further
Resolved, That the Office of Government Relations of The Episcopal Church work with the Office of the Secretary of Health and Human Services and the Office of the Secretary of Agriculture, the White House, and Congress to ensure that these programs are adequately funded to meet the needs of the participants they serve;

and be it further

Resolved, That the Office of Government Relations urge the Office of the Secretary of Health and Human Services, the White House, the United States Congress and *that dioceses urge* state legislatures to provide more adequate access to mental health services for children in a form that does not require the separation of children from their families; and be it further

Resolved, That The Episcopal Church encourage congregations to become educated about and involved in the prevention of violence and maltreatment perpetrated upon children; and be it further

Resolved, That the Office of Government Relations of The Episcopal Church request the Office of the Secretary of Health and Human Services to make regulatory changes in Medicare and Medicaid health plans to enable terminally ill children to receive more adequate palliative care and pain relief services and their families to receive appropriate supportive services.

Deputy Wise of Easton moved to amend the amended resolution.

Proposed Amendment:
Insert after the word "establish," the words "or work with existing local" in the first resolve clause.

Motion carried
Amendment adopted

A vote was taken on Resolution A122 as amended.

Motion carried
Resolution adopted with amendment

(Communicated to the House of Bishops in HD Message #84)

The House of Deputies Committee on National and International Concerns presented its Report #9 on Resolution A020 (HIV Medications Availability) and moved adoption with amendment.

Original Text of Resolution:
(A020)

Resolved, the House of Bishops concurring, That The Episcopal Church through its General Convention, urge American pharmaceutical companies, the United States Food and Drug Administration, and the United States Patent Office to relinquish patent rights to pharmaceutical companies in developing countries to allow for the development of HIV medications and the creation of generic versions of those medications with the purpose of making those medications available to those who need them in those developing countries.

Committee Amendment:
Resolved, the House of Bishops concurring, That The Episcopal Church through its General Convention, urge American pharmaceutical companies, the United States Food and Drug Administration, and the United States Patent Office to relinquish

patent rights to pharmaceutical companies in developing countries to allow for the development of HIV medications *including antiretroviral drugs* and the creation of generic versions of those medications with the purpose of making those medications available to those who need them in those developing countries; and be it further
Resolved, That the General Convention direct the Social Responsibilities in Investments Committee of Executive Council and urge the Church Pension Fund to implement this resolution, especially through the influence of shareholder resolutions.
Motion carried
Resolution adopted with amendment
(Communicated to the House of Bishops in HD Message #85)

The House of Deputies Committee on National and International Concerns presented its Report #10 on Resolution A018 (HIV/AIDS Drugs Full Inclusion) and moved adoption with amendment.

Original Text of Resolution:
(A018)
Resolved, the House of Bishops concurring, That The Episcopal Church through the General Convention, urge American pharmaceutical companies and the United States Food and Drug Administration to increase their inclusion of women, African-Americans, and members of other communities of color in both the clinical drug trials for new HIV medications and the studies of the efficacy of new HIV medications to help insure that the medications perform effectively in all populations.

Committee Amendment:
Resolved, the House of Bishops concurring, That The Episcopal Church through the General Convention, urge American pharmaceutical companies and the United States Food and Drug Administration to increase their inclusion of women, African-Americans, and members of other communities of color in both the clinical drug trials for new HIV medications *including antiretroviral drugs* and the studies of the efficacy of new HIV medications to help insure that the medications perform effectively in all populations; and be it further
Resolved, That the General Convention direct the Social Responsibilities in Investments Committee of the Executive Council and urge the Church Pension Fund to implement this resolution, especially through the influence of shareholder resolutions.
Motion carried
Resolution adopted with amendment
(Communicated to the House of Bishops in HD Message #86)

| MINNEAPOLIS MEETING | HOUSE OF DEPUTIES |

The House of Deputies Committee on National and International Concerns presented its Report #11 on Resolution A130 (Establish Living Wage) and moved adoption with amendment.

Text of Original Resolution:
(A130)
Resolved, the House of Bishops concurring, That the 74th General Convention of The Episcopal Church, through the Secretary of the Convention, call upon the President of the United States and members of Congress to establish a living wage as the standard of compensation for all workers in the United States; and be it further

Resolved, That it is the policy of The Episcopal Church and its dioceses and congregations to provide employees with a living wage and be a model for ethical labor practices; and be it further

Resolved, That it is the policy of The Episcopal Church to insist that companies in which the Church invests or with which it contracts provide their employees with a living wage and serve as a model for ethical labor practices.

Committee Amendment:
Resolved, the House of Bishops concurring, That the 74th General Convention of The Episcopal Church, through the Secretary of the Convention, call upon the President of the United States and members of Congress to establish a living wage *including health benefits* as the standard of compensation for all workers in the United States; and be it further

Resolved, That it is the policy of The Episcopal Church and its dioceses and congregations to provide employees with a living wage and be a model for ethical labor practices; and be it further

Resolved, That it is the policy of The Episcopal Church to insist that companies in which the Church invests or with which it contracts provide their employees with a living wage and serve as a model for ethical labor practices; and be it further

Resolved, That the 74th General Convention continue to support living wage campaigns in the cities and counties of every diocese; and be it further

Resolved, That the 74th General Convention strongly affirm the right of workers to organize as protected by federal and state law especially in low wage industries and businesses and including the institutions of every diocese.

Deputy Robinson of Rochester moved an amendment.

Proposed Amendment:
Delete "as protected by federal and state law," in the final resolve clause and add "migrant farm workers."

Deputy Hart of Pennsylvania moved to terminate debate on the Robinson amendment only.

Motion carried
Debate terminated

A vote was taken on the Robinson amendment.

Motion defeated
Amendment defeated

Deputy Wade of Washington inquired why "including health benefits" had been inserted in the first resolve clause but not in the second resolve clause after "a living wage."

Proposed Amendment:
Hearing no objection, the President ordered such an amendment.

Motion carried
Amendment adopted

Deputy Renton of California moved to terminate debate.

Motion carried
Debate terminated

A vote was taken on Resolution A130 as amended.

Motion carried
Resolution adopted with amendment

(Communicated to the House of Bishops in HD Message #87)

Midday Prayers
The President called upon the Chaplain for midday prayers.

Announcements
The Secretary made announcements regarding the Provincial Caucuses.

RECESS
The President recessed the House at 12:39 p.m. until 2:30 p.m.

AFTERNOON SESSION

Reconvene
The President reconvened the House at 2:34 p.m.

Prayers
The President called upon the Chaplain for prayers.

Communication from the Presiding Bishop
The President read a statement from the Presiding Bishop, regarding an investigation to be undertaken regarding Bishop-elect V. Gene Robinson before the House of Bishops votes on Resolution C045 (see Appendix F—House of Bishops Day 6).

MINNEAPOLIS MEETING   HOUSE OF DEPUTIES

Statement from the Bishop of New Hampshire and the President of the Standing Committee of New Hampshire

Deputy Dales of New Hampshire read a statement read in the House of Bishops (See Appendix G—House of Bishops Day 6).

Certification of Deputies

The House of Deputies Committee on Credentials presented its Report #9. At the second legislative session on the Sixth Legislative Day there were no new deputies certified. There were at this session 417 clerical deputies and 419 lay deputies certified and seated. The total count for the House of Deputies is 836. There were 58 changes at this session, as follows:

Diocese	*Alternate replacing*	*Deputy being replaced*
Alabama	Tom Poynor	Cecil Williamson
Alabama	James Van Zandt	John Fritschner
Alabama	Sherry Travis	Robert Childers
Arkansas	Teresa Cantrell	Pan Adams
Arkansas	Joyce Hardy	Peggy Bosmyer
Atlanta	E. Bruce Garner	Angela Williamson
Atlanta	Gini Peterson	Janet W. Patterson
Atlanta	Lori Lowe	Samuel Candler
California	Kay Bishop	Mary Gotthold
Colorado	Zoe Cole	Jacqueline Scott
Colorado	Craig Moseley	Lawrence Hitt
Delaware	Margaret Patterson	Mark Harris
East Carolina	Pamela Stringer	Joseph Cooper
Eastern Michigan	Dokun Adewunmi	J. Thomas Downs
Fond Du Lac	Kay Drebert	William Bippus
Hawaii	Linda Sproat	Cynthia Salley
Idaho	Dean Hagerman	Joanne Galbraith
Iowa	Sharon Mahood	Kathleen Milligan
Iowa	Connie Whalen	Margaret Tinsman
Lexington	Janet Dunnavant	Alan Sutherland
Lexington	John Brantley	Therese Yeiser
Los Angeles	Joanna Satorius	Altagracia Perez
Maine	Calvin Sanborn	Anne Stanley
Maine	Paige Blair	Holly Antolini
Maine	Susan Partridge	Nicole Janelle
Michigan	Charles Tomlinson	G. Herb Gunn
Mississippi	Sissie Wile	Anita George
Mississippi	Edward Sisson	Danny Meadors
Mississippi	Ruth Black	David Elliott
Mississippi	Suanna Smith	Michael Chaney
Mississippi	Mike Dobrosky	Zabron Davis

Missouri	Larry Hooper	Jason Samuel
New Hampshire	William Exner	Gene Robinson
New Hampshire	Barbara Thrall	Hays Junkin
New Jersey	Virginia Sheay	Joan Anders
New York	Louise Jonsson	Fred Wibiralske
New York	Nell Gibson	James Forde
New York	Theodora Brooks	K. Dennis Winslow
Newark	Edward Hasse	Geoffrey Curtiss
Newark	Martha Gardner	Marjorie Christie
Oklahoma	Dwight Helt	Noel Doherty
Oregon	Marilynn Brown	Sherman Hesselgrave
Pennsylvania	Karen Lash	John Midwood
Pittsburgh	J. Douglas McGlynn	Scott Quinn
Puerto Rico	Emily Morales	Jose Emilio Figueroa
Rochester	Lesley Adams	Mark Lattime
Southern Ohio	Patricia Merchant	Benjamin Speare-Hardy
Southern Virginia	Harold Cobb	Mark Delcuze
Upper South Carolina	Garfield Stuart	David Keller
Vermont	Peter Galbraith	Elizabeth Hall
Virginia	Cynthia Bartol	Russell Randle
Washington	John Harmon	Margaret Graham
Washington	Salli Hartman	Paul Cooney
West Tennessee	Eugene Nobles	Carolyn Corum
Western Massachusetts	Heidi Frantz-Dale	Paul Taylor
Western New York	Earle King	Charles Whitmore
Wyoming	Laurie Kadrich	Norm Peterson
Wyoming	Marilyn Engstrom	Roy Walworth

Consent Calendar
Social and Urban Affairs

The House of Deputies Committee on Social and Urban Affairs presented its Report #7 on Resolution C021 (Stem Cell Research and Alleviation of Pain) and moved that the Committee be discharged.

Motion carried
Committee discharged
(Communicated to the House of Bishops in HD Message #88)

The House of Deputies Committee on Social and Urban Affairs presented its Report #8 on Resoluition C020 (Stem Cell Research) and moved that the Committee be discharged.

Motion carried
Committee discharged
(Communicated to the House of Bishops in HD Message #89)

Stewardship and Development

The House of Deputies Committee on Stewardship and Development presented its Report #3 on Resolution D046 (Stewardship of Water) and moved adoption.

Original Text of Resolution:
(D046)

Resolved, the House of Bishops concurring, That the 74th General Convention urge dioceses, congregations, and communicants to regard water resources as precious, and to recognize that the right use of water is an explicit means to show love for one's neighbor, since water connects people and all creatures throughout the global community; and be it further

Resolved, That the 74th General Convention encourage dioceses, congregations, and communicants to become active stewards of their water resources through conservation efforts including reduction of consumption; through examination of water discharge such that contaminated water does not improperly leave church grounds; and through the creation of environmental programs for stewardship of water and the whole of creation and for the education of congregants in regard to good and faithful stewardship of the earth's resources; and be it further

Resolved, That General Convention encourage dioceses, congregations, and communicants to undertake one or more of the following four stewardship steps:

- When and where possible, install water-saving devices, such as low-flow commodes and aspirators on sink faucets.
- Replant church grounds and home gardens with plants and trees that are drought-tolerant and have low needs for water, and that are native to the region and therefore able to survive local climatic conditions.
- Devise drainage systems that allow rainwater to flow from gutters and drain pipes to spread onto the lawn and landscaped areas of church grounds and home gardens, thereby reducing water lost to sewer systems.
- Pave new or repave existing parking lots with materials that are pervious, so that water penetrates into soil beneath parking areas, thereby reducing the flow of oil and other auto fluids into streams.

Motion carried
Resolution adopted
(Communicated to the House of Bishops in HD Message #90)

Communications

The House of Deputies Committee on Communications presented its Report #8 on Resolution A005 (Continue Forward Movement Publications) and moved adoption.

Original Text of Resolution:
(A005)
Resolved, the House of Bishops concurring, That the Presiding Bishop be authorized to continue Forward Movement Publications under his supervision and to appoint such staff members and commission as may be required to maintain its work.

Motion carried
Resolution adopted
(Communicated to the House of Bishops in HD Message #91)

Miscellaneous Resolutions
The House of Deputies Committee on Miscellaneous Resolutions presented its Report #9 on Resolution A042 (Amend Canon I.1.9) and moved adoption.

Original Text of Resolution:
(A042)
Resolved, the House of Bishops concurring, That Canon I.1.9 be amended as follows:
Sec. 9. The Treasurer *of the General Convention* shall have authority to borrow, in behalf and in the name of the General Convention, such a sum as may be judged by the Treasurer to be necessary to help defray the expense of the General Convention, with the approval of the Presiding Bishop and the Executive Council.

Motion carried
Resolution adopted
(Communicated to the House of Bishops in HD Message #92)

(End of Consent Calendar)
Messages from the House of Bishops
The Secretary announced that the following messages had been received from the House of Bishops:

HB Message #116:   General Board of Examining Chaplains. Adopted.
HB Message #117:   Trustees of the General Theological Seminary. Adopted.

Ecumenical Guests
Deputy Kirby of Eau Claire and the Eccumenical Officer, Bishop Epting, introduced the Ecumenical Guests.
The Rev. Robert Sawyer of the Moravian Church brought greetings on behalf of the ecumenical and interfaith guests:

Representing the Evangelical Lutheran Church in America
    Presiding Bishop Mark S. Hanson
    Mrs. Ione Hanson

Rev. Lowell Almen
Rev. Robert Brusic
Rev. Duane Larson
Rev. Randall Lee
Bishop Peter Rogness
Rev. Dr. Merlyn E. Satrom

Representing Mar Thoma Syrian Church
The Rt. Rev. Dr. Euyakim Mar Coorilos

Representing the Moravian Church
The Rt. Rev. Graham Rights
Mrs. Peggy Cartner
The Rt. Rev. Hopeton Clennon
The Rev. Dr. Otto Dreydoppel
The Rev. Burke Johnson
Mrs. Eleanor Johnson
The Rev. Robert Sawyer
Mrs. Jill Sawyer

Representing the American Baptist Church USA
The Rev. Rothang Chhangte

Representing the Disciples of Christ Church
The Rev. Mark MacWhorter

Representing the International Council of Community Churches
The Rev. Herman Harmelink, III
The Rev. Michael E. Livingston

Representing the Presbyterian Church USA
Elder Freda Gardner
The Rev. Richard Headen

Representing the United Church of Christ
The Rev. Dr. Elizabeth Nordbeck
The Rev. Lydia Veliko

Representing the United Methodist Church
Bishop Wayne K. Clymer

Representing the Roman Catholic Church
The Most Rev. Stephen Blaire
Dr. John Borelli
Archbishop William Levada
The Rev. Lee A. Piche

Representing the Antiochian Orthodox Archdiocese of North America
The Rev. William Olnhausen

Representing Diocese of the Armenian Church in America
The Rt. Rev. Vicken Aykazian

Representing the Greek Orthodox Church
The Rev. Dr. Harry Pappas

Representing the Orthodox Church in America
   The Very Rev. Andrew Morbey
Representing the Patriarchal Parishes of the Russian Orthodox Church
   The Rev. Alexander Abramov
Representing the National Council of Churches of Christ
   Elenie Huszagh, Esq.
Representing Churches Uniting in Christ
   The Rev. Dr. Bertrice Wood
Representing the Minnesota Council of Churches
   The Rev. Peg Chemberlin

Dispatch of Business

The House of Deputies Committee on Dispatch of Business announced that it was time for these Special Orders of Business:
1. The election of Vice-President of the House of Deputies, and
2. Nominations for the General Theological Seminary Board of Trustees.

Ballot #1 for Vice-President of the House of Deputies

Election Ballot #1 was taken for Vice President of the House of Deputies
Ballot #1 taken

Election of the Vice-President of the House of Deputies

The results of Ballot #1 for Vice-President of the House of Deputies were announced. Deputy Anderson of Michigan was elected.

The deputation of the Diocese of Michigan escorted Deputy Anderson to the platform. Deputy Anderson expressed her gratitude to the House upon her election.

Results of Ballot #3 for Trustees of the Church Pension Fund

The Secretary announced that Carlson Gerdau and Robert Hodges had been elected Trustees of the Church Pension Fund on the Third Ballot.
Trustees elected
(Communicated to the House of Bishops in HD Message #248)

Nominations for the General Theological Seminary Board of Trustees

Deputy Kinman of Missouri nominated Ronald Clingenpeel of Missouri.

The President opened nominations for the General Theological Seminary Board of Trustees.

The House of Deputies Committee on Dispatch of Business moved that nominations be closed.

Motion carried
Nominations closed

Dispatch of Business
The House of Deputies Committee on Dispatch of Business instructed the House to return to the daily calendar and announced that Resolution C030 has been withdrawn.

Personal Privilege
Deputy Guillén of Los Angeles asked the President to suspend the rules to allow deputies of color to join the deputation from Los Angeles for a greeting. Deputy Guillén, the deputation from Los Angeles, and deputies of color commended the Worship Committee for the inclusiveness of worship at this Convention.

Evangelism
The House of Deputies Committee on Evangelism presented its Report #5 on Resolution C008 (Episcopal Council of Indigenous Ministries Funding) and moved adoption with amendment.

Original Text of Resolution:
(C008)
Resolved, the House of Bishops concurring, That The Episcopal Church of the United States of America in its 74th General Convention of The Episcopal Church, meeting in Minneapolis in July, 2003, reaffirm the 72nd General Convention's designation of the decade 1997–2007 as the "Decade of Remembrance, Recognition, and Reconciliation" during which each diocese will take such steps as necessary to fully recognize and welcome Native Peoples into congregational life, which will include a special effort toward developing an outreach partnership among urban Native Peoples; and be it further
Resolved, That the 74th General Convention of The Episcopal Church appropriate for the Episcopal Council of Indigenous Ministries $900,000 funding for the triennium, and with the responsibility for awarding grants for projects which seek to welcome Native Peoples into congregational life, providing leadership training programs for young adults and evangelism programs for youth, and that progress reports be presented at the 75th General Convention.

Committee Amendment:
Resolved, the House of Bishops concurring, That The Episcopal Church of the United States of America in ~~it's~~ *the* 74th General Convention of The Episcopal Church, meeting in Minneapolis in July, 2003, reaffirm the 72nd General Convention's designation of the decade 1997–2007 as the "Decade of Remembrance, Recognition, and Reconciliation" during which each diocese will take such steps as necessary to fully recognize and welcome Native Peoples into congregational life, which will include a special effort toward developing an outreach partnership among urban Native Peoples; and be it further
Resolved, That the 74th General Convention of The Episcopal Church ~~appropriate for the Episcopal Council of Indigenous Ministries $900,000 funding for the triennium, and with the responsibility for awarding grants for projects which seek to welcome Native Peoples into congregational life, providing leadership training~~

JOURNAL SIXTH DAY

~~programs for young adults and evangelism programs for youth, and that progress reports be presented at the 75th General Convention.~~ *request The Joint Standing Committee on Program, Budget, and Finance to consider and adopt a budget allocation for Native American ministries, working with the Episcopal Council of Indigenous Ministries, of $1,500,000 funding for the triennium, for grants for projects which seek to welcome Native Peoples into congregational life, providing leadership training programs for young adults, evangelism programs for youth, and mission among urban and rural Native peoples; and that progress reports be presented at the 75th General Convention. This proposed funding allocation is in addition to proposed funding allocations as found in the Budget Proposal of the Presiding Bishop and the Executive Council to the 74th General Convention on pages 26 (Domestic Appropriations) and 30 (Ethnic Congregational Development—Native American Ministries).*

Deputy Cosby of Florida moved to terminate debate.

Deputy Roberts of Massachusetts noted two typographical errors. The page number references to the Budget proposal are reversed. The President accepted this correction.

A vote was taken to terminate debate.

Motion carried
Debate terminated

A vote was taken on Resolution C008 as amended.

Motion carried
Resolution adopted with amendment
(Communicated to the House of Bishops in HD Message #93)

The House of Deputies Committee on Evangelism presented its Report #6 on Resolution C006 (Evangelism to the New Majority) and moved adoption of a substitute.

Original Text of Resolution:
(C006)
Resolved, the House of Bishops concurring, That in implementing the 20/20 goal of focusing The Episcopal Church on mission, this church reach out to groups not traditionally within the scope of evangelism efforts, including those previously not affiliated with organized religion and those disaffected from their previous religious affiliations, particularly but not limited to those who identify themselves as part of the "new majority" characterized by diversity of race, ethnicity, language, disability, and sexual orientation; and be it further
Resolved, That the Office of Congregational Development, in consultation with dioceses and the Standing Commission on Domestic Mission and Evangelism, and after careful listening to and conscious accompaniment of these communities, and prayerful self-examination, prepare specific plans for mission and evangelism, including but not limited to the communities listed above, which shall be presented to Executive Council no later than the fall of 2004.

Committee Substitute:
Resolved, the House of Bishops concurring, That in implementing the 20/20 goal of focusing The Episcopal Church on domestic mission and evangelism, this church reach out to groups not traditionally within the scope of these efforts, which include persons who have felt unwelcome or alienated by the church, particularly though not limited to, those who identify themselves as the "new majority" characterized by diversity of race, ethnicity, language, disability, and sexual orientation; and be it further
Resolved, That the 74th General Convention affirm the work of the Congregational Development Unit of the Church Center, already begun in these efforts, and urge them to continue to include and expand, as components of their ongoing and future programs, elements of diversity, including but not limited to the groups listed above.

Motion carried
Substitute resolution adopted
(Communicated to the House of Bishops in HD Message #94)

Ministry
The House of Deputies Committee on Ministry presented its Report #2 on HB Message #46 on Resolution A064 (Seminarian Expenses) and moved concurrence.
The House concurred
(Communicated to the House of Bishops in HD Message #95)

Final Text of Resolution:
(A064)
Resolved, **That the 74th General Convention direct the Standing Commission on Ministry Development to convene a partnership including members from the Church Pension Fund, the Episcopal Church Foundation, the Society for the Increase of the Ministry, the Episcopal Evangelical Education Society, the Council of Seminary Deans, and any other appropriate groups to address the urgent issue of seminarian debt and report back to the 75th General Convention with recommendations. This committee will include in its consideration the following points:**
- determining the feasibility of amortizing seminary loan payments over the course of a cleric's career;
- including seminarian debt in the pension premium of parochial/institutional clergy, distributed over the course of a cleric's career;
- dioceses and congregations committing a greater proportion of income to the support of people preparing for ordination and lay professions;
- seeking funding support for the debt reduction of newly ordained persons who serve in priority mission areas that are under-served and under-funded, including new church plants, multicultural and

specialized cultural ministries and rural areas; and
the development of a fund to defray the educational expenses of seminarians through partnerships.

Education
The House of Deputies Committee on Education presented its Report #1 on HD Message #49 on Resolution A013 (The Church's Role in Counseling and Education on Biomedical Ethics) and moved concurrence.

The House concurred
(Communicated to the House of Bishops in HD Message #96)

[The final status of Resolution A013 is non-concurrence because the House of Bishops and the House of Deputies did not adopt the same text of the resolution. *Ed.*]

The House of Deputies Committee on Education presented its Report #2 on HB Message #50 on Resolution A030 (21st Century Survey Resources) and moved concurrence.

The House concurred
(Communicated to the House of Bishops in HD Message #97)

Final Text of Resolution:
(A030)
Resolved, That the 74th General Convention direct the Episcopal Church Center staff to use data from the 21st Century Survey and other sources to develop educational resources on the church's responses to issues of violence, poverty, injustice, and exclusion, particularly as these issues pertain to women; and be it further
Resolved, That the General Convention request the Joint Standing Committee on Program, Budget and Finance to consider a budget of $8,000 for implementation of this resolution.

The House of Deputies Committee on Education presented its Report #3 on HB Message #48 on Resolution A007 (Aging Task Force) and moved concurrence.

Final Text of Resolution:
(A007)
Resolved, That the 74th General Convention authorize the creation of a six-person Task Force of the Executive Council, coordinated through the Office of Ministry Development to assess ministry opportunities with and for an aging population both within and outside the church; and be it further
Resolved, That the General Convention request the Joint Standing Committee on Program, Budget and Finance to consider a budget allocation of $10,000 for implementation of this resolution.

The House of Deputies Committee on Education presented its Report #4 on HB Message #47 on Resolution A038 (Peace and Justice Studies and Training) and moved concurrence.

The House concurred
(Communicated to the House of Bishops in HD Message #99)

Final Text of Resolution:
(A038)
Resolved, That the 74th General Convention of The Episcopal Church commend to Episcopal colleges and schools the inclusion in their curriculum of peace and justice studies and education and training for service and careers in nongovernmental organizations and civil society.

Ecumenical Relationships
The House of Deputies Committee on Ecumenical Relationships presented its Report #1 on HB Message #40 on Resolution C031 (Waging Reconciliation) and moved concurrence.

The House concurred
(Communicated to the House of Bishops in HD Message #100)

Final Text of Resolution:
(C031)
Resolved, That the General Convention of The Episcopal Church speak out for an end to all forms of religious persecution and war by instituting, recognizing, supporting, and encouraging the yearly celebration of interfaith worship services (like the World Sabbath of Religious Reconciliation) in all communities across America and around the world.

The House of Deputies Committee on Ecumenical Relationships presented its Report #2 on HB Message #41 on Resolution A090 (Christian–Muslim Dialogue) and moved concurrence.

The House concurred
(Communicated to the House of Bishops in HD Message #101)

Final Text of Resolution:
(A090)
Resolved, That the 74th General Convention reaffirm Resolution 1997-D069 on "Substantive Dialogue Between Christian and Muslim Communities,"which calls for a "dialogue that maintains the theological integrity of both faith communities and commitment to genuine human rights and religious freedom as affirmed by the 71st General Convention (1994-D015);" and be it further

Resolved, That the General Convention direct current and future ECUSA efforts at Christian–Muslim dialogue and education to embody and strengthen that resolution's commitments to dialogue, in cooperation with other Christian bodies, founded on "genuine human rights and religious freedom," as embodied in the United Nations Declaration on Human Rights (1948), Article 18, which states that "everyone has the right to freedom of thought, conscience, and religion; this right includes freedom to change his religion or belief, and freedom, either alone or in community with others and in public or private, to manifest his religion or belief in teaching, practice, worship, and observance;" and be it further

Resolved, That the General Convention direct that such efforts strengthen the peaceful and secure religious witness of other Christians around the world in their ministry among Muslim neighbors, particularly in areas of experienced religious oppression.

Personal Privilege
Deputy Crump of West Tennessee remarked on the editorial oversight in the Church Pension Fund report in the *Blue Book*, which used bold type for the names of incumbent Trustees. The Secretary apologized for the oversight.

Rules of Order
The House of Deputies Committee on Rules of Order presented its Report #4 on Resolution D044 (Election Clarification) and moved adoption with amendment.

Original Text of Resolution:
(D044)
Resolved, the House of Bishops concurring, That Joint Rule of Order 18.(c) be amended to read in part as follows:

(c) The Secretary *of the House of Deputies* and the Treasurer of the General Convention under Canon I.1.

Committee Amendment:
Resolved, the House of Bishops concurring, That Joint Rule of Order 18.(c) be amended to read in part as follows:

(c) The Secretary *of the House of Deputies* and the Treasurer of the General Convention under Canon I.1.*1(j)*.

Motion carried
Resolution adopted with amendment
(Communicated to the House of Bishops in HD Message #102)

Canons

The House of Deputies Committee on Canons presented its Report #6 on Resolution D072 (Amendment Canon III.22.3(a)) and moved adoption with amendment.

Original Text of Resolution:
(D072)
Resolved, the House of Bishops concurring, That Canon III.22.3(a) be amended to read in part as follows:
When a Diocese desires the ordination of a Bishop-elect, if the date of election occurs within 120 days before a meeting of the General Convention, *provided, however, that no such election shall be held less than 30 days prior to the meeting of the General Convention,* the Standing Committee of the Diocese shall, by its President, or by some person or persons specially appointed, forward to the Secretary of the House of Deputies evidence of the election of the Bishop-elect by the Convention of the Diocese, together with evidence that the Bishop-elect has been duly ordered Deacon and Priest, evidence of acceptance of election, and a testimonial signed by a constitutional majority of the Convention, and a summary of biographical information relating to the Bishop-elect.

Committee Amendment:
Resolved, the House of Bishops concurring, That Canon III.22.3(a) be amended to read in part as follows:
When a Diocese desires the ordination of a Bishop-elect, if the date of election occurs within ~~120 days~~ three months before a meeting of the General Convention, *provided, however, that no such election shall be held less than 30 days prior to the meeting of the General Convention,* the Standing Committee of the Diocese shall, by its President, or by some person or persons specially appointed, forward to the Secretary of the House of Deputies evidence of the election of the Bishop-elect by the Convention of the Diocese, together with evidence that the Bishop-elect has been duly ordered Deacon and Priest, evidence of acceptance of election, and a testimonial signed by a constitutional majority of the Convention, and a summary of biographical information relating to the Bishop-elect.

Deputy Hart of Pennsylvania moved that the resolution be re-referred to the Committee on Canons.

Motion defeated
Referral to Legislative Committee failed

Deputy Rehill of Newark moved that the resolution be re-referred to the Committee on Constitution.

Deputy High of Texas moved to terminate debate.

Motion carried
Debate terminated

A vote was taken on re-referring Resolution D072 to the Committee on Constitution.

Motion carried
Resolution re-referred to a Legislative Committee

[Note: Consideration of Resolution D072 resumed on Day 8. See page 556. *Ed.*]

Structure

The House of Deputies Committee on Structure resumed its Report #14 on Resolution A147 (Legislative Committee Membership) and moved adoption of a substitute.

Committee Substitute:
(A147)
Resolved, the House of Bishops concurring, That it is the sense of the Convention that the work of Legislative Committees is facilitated when the membership includes deputies and bishops who are also members of the appropriate Standing Commissions or Committees, in order to provide continuity.

Motion carried
Substitute resolution adopted
(Communicated to the House of Bishops in HD Message #103)

The House of Deputies Committee on Structure presented its Report #15 on Resolution A043 (Amend Canon I.6.1) and moved that the Committee be discharged as the matter is considered in Resolution A072.

Motion carried
Committee discharged
(Communicated to the House of Bishops in HD Message #104)

The House of Deputies Committee on Structure presented its Report #16 on D005 (Amend Canons I.2.4(c) and I.4.3) and moved the resolution, recommending rejection.

Original Text of Resolution:
(D005)
Resolved, the House of Bishops concurring, That Canons I.2.4(c) and I.4.3 be amended as follows:
Canon I.2.4
(c) The Presiding Bishop shall perform such other functions as shall be prescribed in these Canons; and, to be enabled better to perform such duties and responsibilities, the Presiding Bishop may appoint, to positions established by the Executive Council of General Convention, officers, responsible to the Presiding Bishop, who may delegate such authority as shall seem appropriate.
Canon I.4.3
(d) *Upon the joint nomination of the Chair and Vice-Chair, the Executive Council* The

~~Presiding Bishop~~ shall appoint, ~~with the advice and consent of a majority of the Executive Council~~, an Executive Director, who shall be an adult confirmed communicant in good standing or a member of the clergy of this Church in good standing who shall be the chief operating officer and who shall serve at the pleasure of the ~~Presiding Bishop~~ *Executive Council* and be accountable to the ~~Presiding Bishop~~ *Executive Council.* If a vacancy shall occur in the office of the Executive Director, a successor shall be appointed in like manner.

(e) Upon the joint nomination of the Chair and Vice-Chair, the Executive Council shall appoint a Financial Officer of the Executive Council, who may, but need not, be the same person as the Treasurer of the General Convention and who shall report and be accountable to the ~~Chair of the~~ *Executive Council* and shall serve at the pleasure of the ~~Chair of the~~ *Executive Council.* If a vacancy shall occur in that office, a successor shall be appointed in like manner.

(h) *The Executive Director may appoint, to positions established by the Executive Council of General Convention, officers, responsible to the Executive Director, who may delegate such authority as shall seem appropriate.* The additional officers, agents and employees of the Council shall be such and shall perform such duties as the Council, upon the recommendation and under the authority and direction of the ~~Chair and President~~ *Executive Director*, may from time to time designate.

Motion defeated
Resolution rejected
(Communicated to the House of Bishops in HD Message #105)

Recess

The President recessed the House at 4:25 p.m. to reconvene at 4:45 p.m.

Reconvened
The Vice-President reconvened the House at 4:47 p.m.

Announcements
The Secretary read an announcement reminding the Press that this is a legislative body and requested that no interviews be conducted during the legislative session.

Social and Urban Affairs
The House of Deputies Committee on Social and Urban Affairs presented its Report #9 on Resolution A011 (Ethical Guidelines for Gene Transfer and Germline Interventions) and moved adoption with amendment.

Original Text of Resolution:
(A011)
Resolved, the House of Bishops concurring, That the 74th General Convention recognize that God has entrusted us to use our medical and other capabilities to work toward healing and restoring creation where it has gone awry. Therefore, that the General Convention set forth the following guidelines for genetic research and interventions:

- It is morally acceptable, in principle, to engage in experimental somatic cell human gene transfer for therapeutic purposes, in an effort to treat or prevent disease.
- All experimental genetic interventions in human beings must meet ethical standards of research, which require that investigators demonstrate the scientific merit of their research, protect the health and welfare of human volunteers, while ensuring their voluntary choice to participate.
- Until there is strong scientific evidence that the use of germline procedures is safe, effective, and stable across generations and that guidelines have been established for their use before they are employed, we should not consider the use of germline interventions in human beings.
- Ongoing public oversight of research into both somatic cell and germline interventions, in both the public and private sectors, is essential. Members of a federally appointed interdisciplinary review body should be chosen by publicly accountable methods.

Committee Amendment:

Resolved, the House of Bishops concurring, That the 74th General Convention recognize that God has entrusted us to use our medical and other capabilities to work toward healing and restoring creation where it has gone awry. Therefore, that the General Convention set forth the following guidelines for genetic research and interventions:
- It is morally acceptable, in principle, to engage in experimental somatic cell human gene transfer for therapeutic purposes, in an effort to treat or prevent disease.
- All experimental genetic interventions in human beings must meet ethical standards of research, which require that investigators demonstrate the scientific merit of their research, protect the health and welfare of human volunteers, while ensuring *their volunteers'* ~~their voluntary~~ choice to participate.
- Until there is strong scientific evidence that the use of germline procedures is safe, effective, and stable across generations and that guidelines have been established for their use before they are employed, we should not consider the use of germline interventions in human beings.
- Ongoing public oversight of research into both somatic cell and germline interventions, in both the public and private sectors, is essential. Members of a federally appointed interdisciplinary review body should be chosen by publicly accountable methods.

Deputy Black of Mississippi moved an amendment to the resolution.

Proposed Amendment:

Add "without undue financial influence or conflict of interest" at the end of the statement which begins, "All experimental genetic interventions."

Deputy Vanderstar of Washington suggested a rewording of the amendment to read: "without conflicts of interest or undue financial influence." That rewording became the Black amendment on the floor.

A vote was taken on the Black amendment.
Motion carried
Amendment adopted
A vote was taken on Resolution A011 as amended.
Motion carried
Resolution adopted with amendment
(Communicated to the House of Bishops in HD Message #106)

The House of Deputies Committee on Social and Urban Affairs presented its Report #10 on Resolution D016 (The Protection of Animals from Cruel Treatment) and moved adoption of a substitute.

Original Text of Resolution:
(D016)
Resolved, the House of Bishops concurring, That the 74th General Convention acknowledge as responsible stewards the Biblical call to respect and show concern for all God's creatures, recognize that animals have inherent worth and intrinsic value, and endorse as a basic guideline that no husbandry method for captive and domestic animals should deny the environmental requirements of the basic behavioral needs of these animals; and be it further
Resolved, That The Episcopal Church encourage its members to do whatever they can to reduce the suffering of animals in the United States, to foster good care and husbandry of animals, to promote improvements in legislation protecting animals, and to promote its more effective enforcement.

Committee Substitute:
Resolved, the House of Bishops concurring, That the 74th General Convention recognize that responsible care of animals falls within the stewardship of creation and expands our understanding of who is neighbor to include all animals; and be it further
Resolved, That The Episcopal Church encourage its members to insure that husbandry methods for captive and domestic animals would prohibit suffering in such conditions as puppy mills, factory-farmed, and laboratory animals; and be it further
Resolved, That The Episcopal Church's Peace and Justice Office undertake the task of developing appropriate guidelines to educate its members to adhere to ethical standards in the care and treatment of animals; and be it further
Resolved, That The Episcopal Church, through its Office of Government Relations, identify and advocate for legislation protecting animals and effective enforcement measures.
Deputy Martins of San Joaquin moved to amend the substitute resolution.

Proposed Amendment:
In the first resolve clause, delete the phrase "and expands our understanding of who is neighbor to include all animals."
Deputy Crew of Newark questioned the spelling of "insure." He believed the

committee must have meant "ensure."

The House voted on the Martins amendment.

Motion carried
Amendment adopted

Deputy Knoll of Kansas proposed an amendment to the resolution as amended.

Proposed Amendment:
In the second resolve clause, substitute the phrase "factory-farms and laboratories" for "factory-farmed and laboratory animals."

A vote was taken on the Knoll amendment.

Motion carried
Amendment adopted

Deputy Snow of Alaska proposed an amendment to the resolution as amended.

Proposed Amendment:
In the third resolve clause, replace the phrase "undertake the task of developing" with the phrase "identifying existing."

A vote was taken on the Snow amendment.

Motion carried
Amendment adopted

Deputy Moore of Atlanta proposed an amendment to the resolution as amended.

Proposed Amendment:
In the fourth resolve clause, add the words "educate and advocate for animals as a part of God's creation."

A vote was taken on the Moore amendment.

Motion defeated
Amendment defeated

Deputy Menaul of Central Pennsylvania moved an amendment to the resolution as amended.

Proposed Amendment:
In the second resolve clause, delete the words "and laboratories."

Deputy Perry of Chicago moved to terminate debate on the Menaul amendment and the main motion.

Deputy Rehill of Newark questioned whether the Menaul amendment was in order in that the previous Knoll amendment had carried. The Vice-President ruled that the Menaul amendment was in order.

The vote was taken on the motion to terminate debate.

Motion carried
Debate terminated

The Vice-President called for a vote on the Menaul amendment. Deputy Rehill of Newark raised a parliamentary inquiry on the Vice-President's ruling on the Menaul amendment.

Deputy Renton of California raised a parliamentary inquiry about Deputy Crew of Newark's earlier question about the word "insure."

The House voted on the ruling of the Chair.

Chair upheld

The vote was taken on the Menaul amendment.

Motion carried
Amendment adopted

The Secretary read the resolution with the Martins, Knoll, Snow, and Menaul amendments, noting that the Menaul amendment deleted the words "and laboratories" from the Knoll amendment.

The Vice-President called upon the House to vote on the substitute resolution as amended.

Motion carried
Substitute resolution as amended adopted
(Communicated to the House of Bishops in HD Message #107)

The House of Deputies Committee on Social and Urban Affairs presented its Report #11 on Resolution A012 (Caring for Children in the Face of the New Genetics) and moved adoption with amendment.

Original Text of Resolution:
(A012)
Resolved, the House of Bishops concurring, That the 74th General Convention reaffirm the church's traditional teaching about parenting and that children are trusts and gifts from God to be nurtured toward maturity. Therefore:
- Genetic testing of children can be an important part of parental responsibility, and may be carried out if it is clearly in the child's best interests to be tested.
- Parents should make responsible use of medical services, including treatment for genetic diseases and the use of somatic gene transfer therapies if they should be proven safe and effective.
- New genetic techniques may be used in conjunction with in vitro fertilization to avoid procreation of human beings with clearly serious disorders of their DNA or chromosomes.
- It is not morally acceptable to use reproductive cloning at this time for any reason, because the technique constitutes an unsafe form of experimentation on children. It is therefore morally irresponsible for physicians, scientists, and prospective parents to engage in it.

Committee Amendment:
Resolved, the House of Bishops concurring, That the 74th General Convention reaffirm ~~the church's traditional teaching about parenting and~~ that children are ~~trusts and~~ *entrusted to us as* gifts from God to be nurtured toward maturity. Therefore:
- Genetic testing of children can be an important part of parental responsibility, and may be carried out if it is clearly in the child's best interests to be tested.
- ~~Parents should make responsible use of medical services, including~~ Treatment for genetic diseases and the use of somatic gene transfer therapies *may be used*

if they ~~should be~~ *are* proven safe and effective.

New genetic techniques may be used in conjunction with in vitro fertilization to avoid procreation of human beings with clearly serious disorders of their DNA or chromosomes.

It is not morally acceptable to use reproductive cloning ~~at this time for any reason, because the technique constitutes an unsafe form of experimentation on children. It~~ *and it* is therefore morally irresponsible for physicians, scientists, and prospective parents to engage in it.

Deputy McGarry of Michigan moved an amendment to the resolution.

Proposed Amendment:
Insert the words "at this time" after the word "cloning."

Deputy Simons of Pittsburgh moved to terminate debate on the McGarry amendment and on the main motion.

> Motion carried
> Debate terminated

A vote was taken on the McGarry amendment.

> Motion defeated
> Amendment defeated

A vote was taken on Resolution A012 as amended.

> Motion carried
> Resolution adopted with amendment
> (Communicated to the House of Bishops in HD Message #108)

Church in Small Communities
The House of Deputies Committee on the Church in Small Communities presented its Report #3 on HB Message #76 on Resolution B010 (Continue Leadership Program for Musicians Serving Small Congregations) and moved concurrence.

> The House concurred
> (Communicated to the House of Bishops in HD Message #109)

Final Text of Resolution:
(B010)

Resolved, **That the 74th General Convention endorse the continuation of the Leadership Program for Musicians Serving Small Congregations, which provides musicians who serve small congregations with continuing education for musical leadership in liturgy;** and be it further

Resolved, **That the program staff at the Church Center promote and distribute information about this program to all congregations with average Sunday attendance of 150 and fewer, and to all dioceses;** and be it further

Resolved, **The General Convention request that the Joint Standing Committee on Program, Budget and Finance consider a budget allocation of $75,000 for implementation of this resolution.**

Evangelism

The House of Deputies Committee on Evangelism presented its Report #7 on Resolution A084 (20/20 Vision Reporting) and moved adoption of a substitute.

Original Text of Resolution:
(A084)
Resolved, the House of Bishops concurring, That the 74th General Convention direct the Standing Commission on Domestic Mission and Evangelism (SCDME):
- to report regularly to the Executive Council and the Episcopal Church at-large on how the whole church is living into the missional vision of 20/20;
- to facilitate communication among different agencies of the church that are carrying out parts of the 20/20 vision.

Committee Substitute:
Resolved, the House of Bishops concurring, That the 74th General Convention direct the Standing Commission on Domestic Mission and Evangelism in consultation with the 20/20 Task Force and other committees and commissions to develop strategic plans in accomplishing measurable goals of the 20/20 vision in the next triennium and urge individuals, congregations, dioceses, provinces, and the Church Center staff to accomplish those goals; and be it further
Resolved, That the SCDME annually report to the Executive Council and Episcopal Church at-large through its means of communication such as Episcopal Life and our website on how the whole Church is progressing toward the 20/20 vision as articulated in the SCDME report and the 20/20 Task Force report to the 74th General Convention in each of the nine areas: leadership, spirituality, prayer and worship, research, new congregation development, vital congregations, next generations, communication, funding, and reporting.

Deputy Lawton of California moved an amendment to the substitute resolution.

Proposed Amendment:
In the first resolve clause, delete the words "the 20/20 Task Force and."
Deputy Smith of the Youth Presence asked that 20/20 also be deleted in the second resolve clause. The Chair of the Committee on Evangelism stated that the report already existed.
The Chair called for a vote on the Lawton amendment.

Motion carried
Amendment adopted

A vote was taken on substitute Resolution A084 as amended.

Motion carried
Substitute resolution adopted with amendment
(Communicated to the House of Bishops in HD Message #110)

Prayer Book, Liturgy and Church Music
The House of Deputies Committee on the Prayer Book, Liturgy and Church Music presented its Report #9 on HB Message #44 on Resolution A098 (Church Year Calendar Inclusion) and moved concurrence.

The House concurred
(Communicated to the House of Bishops in HD Message #111)

Final Text of Resolution:
(A098)
Resolved, That the 74th General Convention propose an additional commemoration for inclusion in the Calendar of the Church Year and authorize trial use for the triennium 2004–2006, as follows:
   January 24 – Ordination of Florence Li Tim-Oi, First Woman Priest in the Anglican Communion, 1944

The House of Deputies Committee on the Prayer Book, Liturgy and Church Music presented its Report #10 on HB Message #45 on Resolution A099 (Authorize Trial Use of Commemoration) and moved concurrence.

The House concurred
(Communicated to the House of Bishops in HD Message #112)

Final Text of Resolution:
(A099)
Resolved, That the 74th General Convention authorize, for trial use until the General Convention of 2006, the above-listed commemoration proposed by the Convention, with the following propers:
January 24
Ordination of Florence Li Tim-Oi
First Woman Priest in the Anglican Communion, 1944
I. Gracious God, we thank thee for calling Florence Li Tim-Oi, much-beloved daughter, to be the first woman to exercise the office of a priest in our Communion; By the grace of thy Spirit inspire us to follow her example, serving thy people with patience and happiness all our days, and witnessing in every circumstance to our Savior Jesus Christ, who liveth and reigneth with thee and the same Spirit, one God, for ever and ever. *Amen.*
II. Gracious God, we thank you for calling Florence Li Tim-Oi, much-beloved daughter, to be the first woman to exercise the office of a priest in our Communion; By the grace of your Spirit inspire us to follow her example, serving your people with patience and happiness all our days, and witnessing in every circumstance to our Savior Jesus Christ, who lives and reigns with you and the same Spirit, one God, for ever and ever. *Amen.*

MINNEAPOLIS MEETING HOUSE OF DEPUTIES

Psalm–116:1-2
Lesson–Galatians 3:23-28
Gospel–Luke 10:1-9
Preface of a Saint (2)

Ministry

The House of Deputies Committee on Ministry presented its Report #3 on HB Message #38 on Resolution A121 (Clergy and Lay Professional Continuing Education) and moved concurrence.

The House concurred
(Communicated to the House of Bishops in HD Message #113)

Final Text of Resolution:

(A121)
Resolved, **That the 74th General Convention encourage each diocese to develop a plan and make provisions for the continuing education of all clergy and lay professionals in its jurisdiction, such plan and its progress to be reported annually to the Standing Commission on Ministry Development;** and be it further
Resolved, **That dioceses that do not have continuing education policies or programs be urged to participate in a pilot program for the development of a diocesan continuing education policy and program sponsored by the Office for Ministry Development;** and be it further
Resolved, **That the General Convention request the Joint Standing Committee on Program, Budget and Finance to consider a budget allocation of $46,000 for implementation of this resolution.**

The House of Deputies Committee on Ministry presented its Report #4 on HB Message #39 on Resolution A060 (Contemporary Language Competency) and moved concurrence, with a substitute.

Committee Substitute:

(A060)
Resolved, the House of Bishops concurring, That the 74th General Convention recommend that all dioceses strongly encourage those preparing for ordination to study a conteomporary language other than their native language and to participate in an intentional cross-cultural program.
Deputy Nestler of Los Angeles moved an amendment to the substitute resolution.

Proposed Amendment:

Add a second resolve clause:
Resolved, That the 74th General Convention of the Episcopal Church direct the Standing Commission on Ministry Development to prepare canonical revisions for consideration by the 75th General Convention that address the Church's need for multilingual and cross-cultural competency among clergy and lay leaders.

Deputy Alan of Kentucky moved to table consideration until the next legislative session.

The Vice-President ruled the motion out of order.

Deputy Renton of California moved to postpone discussion of Resolution A060 until 11:45 a.m. on Tuesday, August 5, 2003, the Seventh Legislative Day.

Motion carried
Consideration postponed

[Consideration of Resolution A060 resumed on Day 7. See page 495. *Ed.*]

Messages from the House of Bishops

The Secretary announced that the following messages had been received from the House of Bishops:

HB Message #118:	D010 (Amend Canons I.1.2(n) (5), HBRO: General I(18) & HDRO IV.7(18)) Adopted with Amendment.
HB Message #119:	C027 (AV Materials of The Episcopal Church) Concurred.
HB Message #120:	A027 (Use of Titles) Concurred.
HB Message #121:	A026 (Baptismal Parity) Concurred.
HB Message #122:	D041 (Invest in Housing for the Poor) Adopted.
HB Message #123:	A082 (Multilingual Publications) Concurred.
HB Message #124:	C015 (Ethnic Desks at the National Church Office) Concurred.
HB Message #125:	A083 (Articulate Faith Story) Concurred.
HB Message #126:	A103 (Adopt the Revised Common Lectionary) Adopted with Amendment.
HB Message #127:	B020 (Title III Revision—with Transitional Diaconate) Adopted Substitute.
HB Message #128:	D060 (Supporting International Relief and Development) Adopted.
HB Message #129:	D001 (Funding Implications of a 10% Tithe) Discharged.
HB Message #130:	C029 (Translation of Documents into Spanish) Concurred.
HB Message #131:	A150 (World Mission Funds) Adopted with Amendment.
HB Message #132:	D047 (Post-Abortion Healing Service) Adopted Substitute.
HB Message #133:	A044 (Amend Canon I.17.1(c)) Adopt with Amendment.

Announcements

The Secretary read the announcements.

Recess

The Vice-President recessed the House at 6:19 p.m. to reconvene at 11:00 a.m. on Tuesday, August 5, 2003.

MINNEAPOLIS MEETING   HOUSE OF DEPUTIES

SEVENTH DAY

Tuesday
August 5, 2003

MORNING SESSION

Reconvene
The President called the House to order at 11:07 a.m.

Morning Prayers
The President called on the Chaplain for prayers.

Certification of Minutes
The House of Deputies Committee on Certification of Minutes presented its Report #6 stating that the Committee had met, read the minutes of the Sixth Day, and certified that they were correct. The Chair moved adoption of the Report.

Motion carried
Minutes accepted

Certification of Deputies
The House of Deputies Committee on Credentials presented its Report #10 for the morning session of the Seventh Legislative Day. There were 417 clerical deputies and 419 lay deputies certified and seated, bringing the total count of the House to 836. There were no new deputies certified and 82 changes at this session, as follows:

Diocese	*Alternate replacing*	*Deputy being replaced*
Alaska	Virginia Doctor	Michael Burke
Arkansas	JoAnn Barker	Gar Demo
Atlanta	Samuel Candler	Lori Lowe
California	Katherine Salinaro	George Sotelo
Central Pennsylvania	John Hoover	Paul Donecker
Chicago	Graham Smith	Shawn Schreiner
Colorado	Jack Finlaw	Deborah Hogue
Colorado	Donald Armstrong	Ephraim Radner
Colorado	S. Brooks Keith	Robert Davidson
Connecticut	Mark Santucci	James Bradley
Delaware	William Hitch	Cynthia Primo Martin
Delaware	Lois Keen	Edward Godden
Delaware	Margaret Patterson	Lloyd Casson
East Tennessee	Richard Govan	Ed Cahill
East Tennessee	Suzanne Smitherman	Jocelyn Bell
Eau Claire	Pete Dawson	Barbara Gaynor
El Camino Real	Thomas Woodward	C. Jeff Kraemer

Fort Worth	Eugene Dugan	Anthony Clark
Georgia	Frank Logue	Robert Carter
Hawaii	Carol Arney	Alison Dingley
Hawaii	Cynthia Salley	Linda Sproat
Hawaii	Joseph Carr	Morley Frech
Idaho	Brian Baker	Margaret Babcock
Indianapolis	Sherry Mattson	Charles Carpenter
Long Island	Cecily Broderick y Guerra	Richard Brewer
Long Island	J. Vincent Welch	Valarie Crosdale
Maine	Anne Stanley	Calvin Sanborn
Maryland	Christine Kinard	Russell Reno
Massachusetts	Mark Hollingsworth	Miriam Gelfer
Milwaukee	Carlynn Higbie	Ralph Modjeska
Mississippi	Ruth Black	David Johnson
Mississippi	Edward Sisson	Kathryn Weathersby
Nebraska	Beverly Whiteman	Don Betts
New Jersey	Charles Perfater	Jean McFarland
New Jersey	John Zamboni	Terrence Rosheuvel
Newark	Joseph Pickard	Jeannette DeFriest
Northern California	Dustin Spence	L. Miles Snyder
Northern California	Eric Duff	Mark Allen
Northern California	Barry Beisner	Stephen Carpenter
Northwest Texas	Laura Deaderick	Jacob Clemmens
Northwest Texas	James Liggett	James Haney
Ohio	Sam McDonald	Ann McConnell
Olympia	Stephen Moore	Dorsey McConnell
Olympia	Hisako Beasley	Mary Ellen Harris
Oregon	Judith Cato	Alice Speers
Oregon	Marilynn Brown	John Scannell
Pennsylvania	Nokomis Wood	Christopher Hart
Pennsylvania	John Midwood	Glenn Matis
Pennsylvania	JoAnn Jones	Karen Lash
Pennsylvania	Mary Laney	Ruth Kirk
Rio Grande	David Basch	Kay Fancher
Rochester	Mark Lattime	Lesley Adams
San Diego	Amanda May	Gary Nicolosi
San Joaquin	Suzette Peters	Charles Reed
San Joaquin	Ken Richards	Richard Matters
Southern Ohio	Richard Jennings	Jon Boss
Southern Virginia	Paul Hogg	David Teschner
Southern Virginia	Mark Delcuze	Harold Cobb
Southern Virginia	Charles Pfeifer	James Bradberry
Southern Virginia	Joyce Moorman	Sara Mueller

Southwest Florida	Fredrick Robinson	Barry Kubler
Southwest Florida	Paul Game	Donald Scott
Southwestern Virginia	Jack Barrow	Calvert de Coligny
Southwestern Virginia	John Lane	Deborah Hunley
Spokane	Margaret Rehberg	Thomas Robison
Texas	James Cunningham	Mary MacGregor
Upper South Carolina	David Keller	Arthur Bjontegard
Vermont	Thomas Brown	John Morris
Virginia	Russell Randle	Cynthia Bartol
Virginia	Charles Alley	Jeffrey Cerar
Washington	Margaret Graham	David Pollock
Washington	Susan Blue	Joan Beilstein
Washington	Geoffrey Cant	John Vanderstar
West Missouri	John McCann	Robert Wood
West Tennessee	Jeff Garrety	Carolyn Corum
West Texas	Michael Chalk	James Murguia
West Texas	Kirk Mason	Robert Browning
Western Michigan	Charles McCabe	Susan York
Western North Carolina	Lauch Magruder	Matilda Kistler
Western North Carolina	Augusta Anderson	Tim McRee
Wyoming	Laurie Kadrich	Vicki Gilmour
Wyoming	Marilyn Engstrom	Warren Murphy

Communication from the President

The President reported that Resolution A142 (Admit Diocese of Venezuela) will soon be considered by the House. The President reminded the House that all resolutions initiated in the House of Deputies must be brought forward for action before the end of the following day. He commended the House for all its work thus far but urged the deputies to consider taking less time perfecting resolutions due to time constraints for the remainder of Convention.

Messages from the House of Bishops

The Secretary reported there were no messages from the House of Bishops.

Special Order of Business

The House of Deputies Committee on Dispatch of Business moved to suspend the rules for a Special Order of Business for the immediate consideration of Resolution A142 (Admit Diocese of Venezuela).

Motion carried
Rules suspended

Structure
The House of Deputies Committee on Structure resumed presentation of its Report #16 on Resolution A142 (Admit Diocese of Venezuela) and moved adoption with amendment.

Committee Amendment:
(A142)
Resolved, the House of Bishops concurring, That the 74th General Convention admit the Diocese of Venezuela to The Episcopal Church USA and recognize it as a diocese in union with General Convention; and be it further
Resolved, That the General Convention designate the Diocese of Venezuela as a member diocese of Province IX of The Episcopal Church; and be further
Resolved, That the Diocese of Venezuela be entitled to all rights pertaining to membership in The Episcopal Church as provided in the Constitution and Canons, including, but not limited to, voice and vote in the House of Bishops and House of Deputies, in accordance with the rules of those houses; and be it further
Resolved, That the Diocese of Venezuela be obligated to undertake all responsibilities pertaining to diocesan membership in The Episcopal Church as provided in the Constitution and Canons, including, but not limited to, conforming its constitution and canons to the provisions of the Constitution and Canons of The Episcopal Church; submitting annual diocesan and parochial reports to the General Convention Office; contributing annually to the apportionment budget of the Domestic and Foreign Missionary Society; and reporting fully on any financial assistance it receives from the General Convention budget; and be it further
Resolved, That the Convention affirm that the clergy and lay employees of the Diocese of Venezuela will be eligible to participate in *companion pension plans administered by* the Church Pension Fund, subject to the rules of the Church Pension Fund; and be it further
Resolved, That the Convention urge the Church Pension Fund to work with the Diocese of Venezuela to develop a plan to cover its clergy the unfunded period of time for those of its clergy who previously participated in the Church Pension Fund when the diocese was a member of The Episcopal Church ; and be it further
Resolved, That the portion of this resolution accepting the Diocese of Venezuela into union with the General Convention shall become effective on such date as the Executive Council adopts a resolution accepting and approving a certification to it by the Secretary of the General Convention that she has received from the Diocese the following:
1. *A certified copy of the Constitution of the Diocese that contains an unqualified accession to the Constitution and canons of The Episcopal Church and otherwise conforms in essential part to such Constitution and canons;*
2. *A certified copy of the canons of the Diocese that conform in essential part to the canons of The Episcopal Church;*
3. *An annual diocesan report and annual parochial reports required by Canon I.6 for the last full year prior to compliance with this resolution;*
4. *A commitment by the Diocese to a contribution to the budget of The Episcopal Church for the year in which the Diocese is to come into union with the General Convention; and*
5. *An audited accounting of any funds received by the Diocese from the General Convention*

budget in the last full year prior to compliance with this resolution.
Resolved, That the Convention reaffirm the principle that dioceses of this church that are not located within the United States may seek autonomy according to the procedures set forth in Resolution 235a of the 1991 General Convention or may join other provinces of the Anglican Communion. ~~, and be it further~~
~~*Resolved,* That the last sentence of Canon I.9.1 is hereby amended to read as follows: The Ninth Province shall consist of the Dioceses of this Church in Colombia, the Dominican Republic, Ecuador, Honduras, and Venezuela.~~

Motion carried
Resolution adopted with amendment
(Communicated to the House of Bishops in HD Message #114)

Welcome Deputy from Venezuela

The President welcomed the Deputy from Venezuela to the House of Deputies. The President stated that the process for the Diocese of Venezuela's entry into the Episcopal Church was not complete and asked the House to give seat and voice to the deputy. The House welcomed Deputy Salazar of Venezuela, and he addressed the House.

Dispatch of Business

The House of Deputies Committee on Dispatch of Business advised the House that the next business would be a Special Order for election of the Executive Council, followed by a Special Order for the continued consideration of Resolution A060.

Ballot #1 for Executive Council

Election Ballot #1 was taken for members of the Executive Council, six lay persons and two clergy persons, for six-year terms.

Ballot #1 taken

Reconsideration of Resolution A060

The House resumed consideration of Resolution A060.

The debate continued on the Nestler amendment.

The President noted that 15 minutes had expired from yesterday's debate and that speakers would be called upon based on their position at microphones at the previous session.

There were parliamentary inquiries to clarify the text of the resolution before the House. It was established that the House of Deputies Ministry Committee substitute resolution was before the House and that the Nestler amendment proposes to amend it.

[See House of Deputies, Sixth Legislative Day, page 489. *Ed.*]

Deputy Brown of Maine moved to terminate debate on the Nestler amendment.

Motion carried
Debate terminated

A vote was taken on the Nestler amendment.

Motion defeated
Amendment defeated

Deputy Rushing of Massachusetts moved to extend debate by 15 minutes.

Motion defeated

A vote was taken on Resolution A060 as substituted by the Committee.

Motion carried
Substitute resolution adopted

(Communicated to the House of Bishops in HD Message #115)

Committee of Conference

Deputy Snow of Alaska asked about forming a Committee of Conference on Resolution A060. The President will confer with the Chair of the House of Deputies Committee on Ministry and report to the House on the next business day.

Announcements

The Secretary read the announcements.

The President encouraged the submission of nominations for Committees, Commissions, Agencies and Boards.

Midday Prayers

The President called upon the Chaplain for midday prayers.

Messages from the House of Bishops

The Secretary announced that the following messages had been received from the House of Bishops:

HB Message #134:	C023 (Direct Ordination to the Priesthood) Rejected.
HB Message #135:	C032 (Direct Ordination to the Priesthood) Rejected.
HB Message #136:	A118 (Amend Canon IV.3.27) Rejected.
HB Message #137:	A117 (Amend Canon I.9.7) Rejected.
HB Message #138:	A116 (Amend Canon I.4.3(d)) Rejected.
HB Message #139:	A115 (Amend Canon I.4.1(c)) Rejected.
HB Message #140:	A113 (Amend Canon I.1.2(a)) Rejected.
HB Message #142:	A061 (Continuing Education Scholarships) Discharged.

Announcements

The Secretary announced that deputy certification would be open from 1:00 p.m. to 1:45 p.m. this afternoon.

RECESS

The President recessed the House at 12:54 p.m. until 2:30 p.m.

AFTERNOON SESSION

Reconvene
The President called the House to order at 2:34 p.m.

Prayers
The President called on the Chaplain for prayers.

Certification of Deputies
The House of Deputies Committee on Credentials presented its Report #11 for the afternoon session of the Seventh Legislative Day, and there was 1 new deputy from the Diocese of Quincy certified. There were 418 clerical deputies and 419 lay deputies certified and seated, bringing the total count of the House to 837. There were 67 changes on this day, as follows:

Diocese	*Alternate replacing*	*Deputy being replaced*
Alabama	James Van Zandt	John Fritschner
Arkansas	Joyce Hardy	Lowell Grisham
California	Kay Bishop	Warren Wong
Central Gulf Coast	Peter Wilson	Margaret Slingluff
Central Pennsylvania	John Radomsky	Brian Amato
Chicago	Shawn Schreiner	Richard Tolliver
Churches in Europe	Helena Mbele-Mbong	Charles Trueheart
Colorado	Robert Davidson	Andrew Cooley
Colorado	Deborah Hogue	Jack Finlaw
Delaware	Lloyd Casson	Margaret Patterson
Delaware	Cynthia Primo Martin	William Hitch
Eastern Michigan	Dokun Adewunmi	J. Thomas Downs
Eastern Oregon	Susan Powers	James Foster
Eau Claire	Patrick Augustine	Alan Coudriet
El Camino Real	Nayan McNeill	Martin Yabroff
Idaho	Margaret Babcock	Eileen O'Shea
Lexington	John Brantley	Carolyn Ware
Long Island	Richard Brewer	Elizabeth Belasco
Maryland	Edward Chapman	Angela Shepherd
Maryland	Russell Reno	Christine Kinard
Milwaukee	Ralph Modjeska	Carlynn Higbie
Minnesota	R.C. Laird	Kathy Pluhar
Minnesota	Michael Hanley	Mariann Budde
Minnesota	Sandra Wilson	Michael Smith
Minnesota	James Huber	Terry Roberts
Mississippi	Kathryn Weathersby	Danny Meadors
Mississippi	Anita George	Sissie Wile

New Hampshire	Barbara Thrall	Hays Junkin
New Jersey	John Goldsack	Linda Gaither
New York	William Augerson	Dorothy Smith
New York	Daniel Matthews	Roger Ferlo
Newark	Jeannette DeFriest	Joseph Pickard
Newark	Edward Hasse	Kenneth Near
Newark	Martha Gardner	Lyn Headley-Moore
Northern California	L. Miles Snyder	Craig Klein
Ohio	Bryan Gillooly	Stephen Smith
Oklahoma	Noel Doherty	Dwight Helt
Oregon	Alice Speers	Fred Terrill
Oregon	John Scannell	Marilynn Brown
Pennsylvania	Christopher Hart	Nokomis Wood
Pittsburgh	Joseph Sarria	Elizabeth Hobbs
Pittsburgh	J. Douglas McGlynn	Scott Quinn
Rochester	Sarah Collins	Bonnie Tyo
San Joaquin	Charles Reed	Suzette Peters
South Carolina	Mark Goodman	John Burwell
Southern Ohio	Jon Boss	Deborah Stokes
Southern Virginia	James Bradberry	Charles Pfeifer
Southern Virginia	David Teschner	Paul Hogg
Southern Virginia	Robert Lee	Sue Wilder
Southwestern Virginia	Deborah Hunley	Clare Fischer-Davies
Southwestern Virginia	Calvert de Coligny	Robert Miller
Upper South Carolina	Arthur Bjontegard	Jimmy Hartley
Utah	Stephen Hutchinson	Ann Ellingson
Vermont	John Morris	Thomas Brown
Virginia	Deborah Robayo	Russell Palmore
Virginia	Victoria Heard	Susan Eaves
Washington	Wesley Baldwin	Iris Harris
Washington	David Pollock	John Harmon
Washington	Joan Beilstein	Susan Blue
West Tennessee	Stephen Carpenter	Rene Somodevilla
West Texas	Nancy Coon	David Read
Western Louisiana	Reece Middleton	Norman Parker
Western Michigan	William Fleener	Barbara Coulter
Western New York	Earle King	Charles Whitmore
Western North Carolina	Matilda Kistler	Diane Mance

Personal Privilege

Deputy Bradberry of Southern Virginia thanked those who supported him for Vice-President of the House of Deputies. He said the Church would be richly rewarded by the leadership of Deputy Anderson of Michigan, who was elected Vice-President.

Dispatch of Business
The House of Deputies Committee on Dispatch of Business reminded the House that there was no Consent Calendar for the Seventh Legislative Day.

Forward Movement Publications
The Rev. Ted Gleason, Executive Director of Forward Movement Publications, addressed the House on the history, ministry, and future mission of Forward Movement Publications.

Special Order of Business
The House of Deputies Committee on Dispatch of Business presented its Report #16 on a Special Order of Business for Consideration of Specific Matter and moved adoption with amendment:
Resolved, That there be set at this time a Special Order of Business for the purpose of considering and taking action with respect to the Reports of Committees listed below:

Resolution	Report	Title	Calendar Page
Committee 4—Constitution			
Resolution A143	Report #3	Amend Constitution Art. I.7 (BB p. 279, C&C p. 3)	75
Committee 5—Canons			
Resolution D072	Report #6	Amend Canon III.22.3(a)	44
Committee 7—Consecration of Bishops			
Resolution C046	Report #9	Consent to the Election of The Rev. Rayford High	60
Resolution C047	Report #10	Consent to the Election of The Rev. Robert O'Neill	60
Resolution C048	Report #11	Consent to the Election of The Rev. Dean Wolfe	60
Committee 9—National and International Concerns			
Resolution A132	Report #13	Christian Responses to Warfare	54
Resolution A033	Report #14	Just and Unjust Wars	54
Resolution D006	Report #15	Supporting International Relief and Development	55
Resolution C036	Report #16	Spirituality of Food Production	56
Resolution A025	Report #4	Trafficking of Women, Girls, and Boys	61
Resolution C033	Report #17	Immigration and Undocumented Workers	77

Resolution A036	Report #18	Korean Peninsula and the Democratic Republic of Korea	62
Resolution D023	Report #19	US Support for People of Liberia	62

Committee 10–Social and Urban Affairs

Resolution B008	Report #13	Protection of Children and Youth from Abuse	64
Resolution A129	Report #16	Dismantling Racial Profiling	65
Resolution C004	Report #18	Reparative Therapies	66
Resolution C003	Report #19	In Support of Representative John Conyers' H.R. 40	66
Resolution A125	Report #20	Ministry to Prisoners and Their Families	67
Resolution D015	Report #22	Make COSE Materials Available on the Web	78
Resolution A126	Report #24	Youth Charged and Convicted as Adults	78
Resolution C030	Report #11	The Working Poor	56
Resolution D077	Report #25	Post-9/11 Racial Hatred and Incarcerations	79

Committee 12–Evangelism

Resolution A077	Report #8	Trained Leadership	68

Committee 17–Stewardship

Committee 19–Communications

Resolution A080	Report #9	Episcopal Church Website (BB p. 134)	77

Committee 20–Miscellaneous Resolutions

Resolution D051	Report #7	Full Accessibility at General Convention	51
Resolution A079	Report #10	General Convention Deputies	73
Resolution C026	Report #11	Reduce Use of Toxic Chemicals	74

Committee 22–Committees and Commissions

Resolution B026	Report #2	Criminal Justice Committee	74

The House of Deptuies Committee on Dispatch of Business moved an amendment to the Special Order of Business.

Proposed Amendment:
Delete Resolution D072 from the Special Order of Business.

A vote was taken on the Special Order of Business as amended.

**Motion carried
Special Order with amendment adopted**
(Communicated to the House of Bishops in HD Message #116)

Constitution

The House of Deputies Committee on Constitution resumed Report #3 on Resolution A143 (Amend Constitution Article I.7) and moved adoption of a substitute.

Committee Substitute:
(A143)
Resolved, the House of Bishops concurring, That Article I.7 of the Constitution be amended to read:
Section 7. The General Convention shall meet not less than once in each three years, at a time and place *determined in accordance with the Canons.* ~~appointed by a preceding Convention; but if there shall appear to the Presiding Bishop, acting with the advice and consent of the Executive Council of the Church or of a successor canonical body having substantially the powers now vested in the Executive Council, sufficient cause for changing the place or date so appointed, the Presiding Bishop, with the advice and consent of such body, shall appoint another place or date, or both, for such meeting.~~ Special meetings may be *held as* provided for by Canon.
And be it further
Resolved, That this resolution be sent within six months to the Secretary of the Convention of every Diocese to be made known to the Diocesan Convention at its next meeting.

**Motion carried
Substitute resolution adopted**
(Communicated to the House of Bishops in HD Message #117)

Consecration of Bishops

The House of Deputies Committee on the Consecration of Bishops presented its Report #9 on Resolution C046 (Consent to the Election of the Rev. Rayford B. High as Bishop Suffragan of the Diocese of Texas) and moved adoption.

Original Text of Resolution:
(C046)
Resolved, Pursuant to Article II, Section 2, and Canon III.22.3 of the Constitution and Canons, the House of Deputies consents to the ordination and consecration of the Rev. Rayford B. High as Bishop Suffragan of the Diocese of Texas.

Motion carried
Resolution adopted
(Communicated to the House of Bishops in HD Message #118)

The House of Deputies Committee on the Consecration of Bishops presented its Report #10 on Resolution C047 (Consent to the Election of the Rev. Robert John O'Neill as Bishop Coadjutor of the Diocese of Colorado) and moved adoption.

Original Text of Resolution:
(C047)
Resolved, Pursuant to Article II, Section 2, and Canon III.22.3 of the Constitution and Canons, the House of Deputies consents to the ordination and consecration of the Rev. Robert John O'Neill as Bishop Coadjutor of the Diocese of Colorado.

Motion carried
Resolution adopted
(Communicated to the House of Bishops in HD Message #119)

The House of Deputies Committee on the Consecration of Bishops presented its Report #11 on Resolution C048 (Consent to the Election of the Rev. Dean E. Wolfe as Bishop Coadjutor of the Diocese of Kansas) and moved adoption.

Original Text of Resolution:
(C048)
Resolved, Pursuant to Article II, Section 2, and Canon III.22.3 of the Constitution and Canons, the House of Deputies consents to the ordination and consecration of the Rev. Dean E. Wolfe as Bishop Coadjutor of the Diocese of Kansas.

Motion carried
Resolution adopted
(Communicated to the House of Bishops in HD Message #120)

National and International Concerns
The House of Deputies Committee on National and International Concerns presented its Report #13 on Resolution A132 (Christian Responses to Warfare) and moved adoption with amendment.

Original Text of Resolution:
(A132)
Resolved, the House of Bishops concurring, That the 74th General Convention urge dioceses and congregations to study and better understand just war theory and pacifism as they apply to the situation of the United States in responding to contemporary international conflicts.

Committee Amendment:
Resolved, the House of Bishops concurring, That the 74th General Convention urge dioceses and congregations to study and better understand just war theory and pacifism as they apply to the situation of the United States in responding to contemporary international conflicts; and be it further
Resolved, That we commend "Just Peace Readings" from the Office of the Bishop Suffragan for Chaplaincies of the Episcopal Church Center, and the website, www.episcopalchurch.org/chaplain, as an important resource in the continuing study of just war.

Motion carried
Resolution adopted with amendment
(Communicated to the House of Bishops in HD Message #121)

The House of Deputies Committee on National and International Concerns presented its Report #14 on Resolution A033 (Just and Unjust Wars) and moved adoption with amendment.

Original Text of Resolution:
(A033)
[Note: See *The Blue Book* Report of Standing Commission on Anglican and International Peace with Justice Concerns, pp. 97–98. *Ed.*]

Committee Amendment:
Resolved, the House of Bishops concurring, That the 74th General Convention, recalling the longstanding Episcopal Church view, originally adopted by the 1930 Lambeth Conference and by the 1931 General Convention, that "war as a method of settling international disputes is incompatible with the teaching and example of our Lord Jesus Christ," call upon all members of The Episcopal Church, in discussions about war and especially the strategy of preemptive strikes, to seriously consider and utilize the Just War criteria developed over the centuries and generally expressed as follows:
First, whether lethal force may be used is governed by the following criteria:
- Just cause: Force may be used only to correct a grave, public evil, i.e., aggression or massive violation of the basic rights of whole populations.
- Comparative justice: While there may be rights and wrongs on all sides of a conflict, to override the presumption against the use of force, the injustice suffered by one part must significantly outweigh that suffered by the other.
- Legitimate authority: Only duly constituted public authorities may use deadly force or wage war.

Right intention: Force may be used only in a truly just cause and solely for that purpose.

Probability of success: Arms may not be used in a futile cause or in a case where disproportionate measures are required to achieve success.

Proportionality: The overall destruction expected from the use of force must be outweighed by the good to be achieved.

Last resort: Force may be used only after all peaceful alternatives have been seriously tried and exhausted.

These criteria taken as a whole must be satisfied in order to override the strong presumption against the use of force. Second, the just war tradition seeks also to curb the violence of war through restraint on armed combat between the contending parties by imposing the following moral standards for the conduct of armed conflict:

Noncombatant immunity: Civilians may not be the objects of direct attack, and military personnel must take due care to avoid and minimize indirect harm to civilians.

Proportionality: In the conduct of hostilities, efforts must be made to attain military objectives with no more force than is militarily necessary and to avoid disproportionate collateral damage to civilian life and property.

Right intention: Even in the midst of conflict, the aim of political and military leaders must be peace with justice, so that acts of vengeance and indiscriminate violence, whether by individuals, military units or governments, are forbidden; and be it further

Resolved, That when legitimate civilian authority determines that war is justified, members of the Episcopal Church recall our Lord's teaching to love our enemies, counsel that participation in or refusal to participate in any war is a discernment process requiring deep reflection and prayer with humility, and acknowledge that one participates in war with great reluctance, always seeking God's mercy and forgiveness; and be it further

Resolved, That the 74th General Convention urge dioceses and congregations to study and better understand just war theory and pacifism as they apply to the situation of the United States in responding to contemporary international conflicts.

Deputy Papile of Virginia moved an amendment to the amended resolution.

Proposed Amendment:

In the first resolve clause, delete "recalling the longstanding Episcopal Church view, originally adopted by the 1930 Lambeth Conference and by the 1931 General Convention, that "war as a method of settling international disputes is incompatible with the teaching and example of our Lord Jesus Christ,".

In the last resolve clause, insert "recalling the longstanding Episcopal Church view, originally adopted by the 1930 Lambeth Conference and by the 1931 General Convention, that "war as a method of settling international disputes is incompatible with the teaching and example of our Lord Jesus Christ," before "urge dioceses and congregations."

The President ruled that consideration on Resolution A033 would be delayed until copies of the amendment were available.

Consideration postponed

[Note: Consideration of Resolution A033 resumed on Day 8. See page 538. *Ed.*]

The House of Deputies Committee on National and International Concerns presented its Report #15 on Resolution D006 (Supporting International Relief and Development) and moved adoption with amendment.

Original Text of Resolution:
(D006)

Resolved, the House of Bishops concurring, That the 74th General Convention endorse the United Nations' Millennium Development Goals (MDGs) that pledge to: (1) eradicate extreme poverty and hunger, (2) achieve universal primary education, (3) promote gender equality and empower women, (4) reduce child mortality, (5) improve maternal health, (6) combat HIV/AIDS, malaria and other diseases, (7) ensure environmental stability, and (8) develop a global partnership for development; and be it further

Resolved, That the Convention, recognizing that funding for nutritional, education, health care, and development programs is essential to achieve the MDGs, reaffirm the 73rd General Convention's Resolutions A001 and D033 challenging all dioceses and congregations to contribute 0.7% of their annual budgets to fund international development programs; and be it further

Resolved, That the appropriate offices and staff of the Episcopal Church Center, including Episcopal Relief and Development, promote among dioceses and congregations education about and participation in the 0.7% contribution for international development; and be it further

Resolved, That the Executive Council be directed to fulfill the 73rd General Convention's Resolution D033 requiring the Council to develop a process for an annual accounting of each dioceses progress toward living into the 0.7% contribution goal; and be it further

Resolved, That the Executive Council in cooperation with the Communications Office at the Episcopal Church Center publish annually the annual accounting of all dioceses' level of participation in the 0.7% contribution goal; and be it further

Resolved, That the Standing Commission on Anglican and International Peace with Justice present a full report to the 75th General Convention of the level of participation of all dioceses in the call to contribute 0.7% of their annual budgets to fund international development programs; and be it further

Resolved, That the Episcopal Office of Government Relations in Washington, DC lobby actively the United States government to fulfill its commitment to funding international development aid at 0.7% of U.S. Gross National Product (GNP); and be it further

Resolved, That the Episcopal Office of Government Relations urge all Episcopalians to press the United States government to fulfill its commitment to funding international development aid at 0.7% of U.S. Gross National Product (GNP).

Committee Amendment:

Resolved, the House of Bishops concurring, That the 74th General Convention endorse *and embrace the achievement of* the United Nations' Millennium Development Goals (MDGs) that pledge to:

(1) eradicate extreme poverty and hunger,
(2) achieve universal primary education,
(3) promote gender equality and empower women,
(4) reduce child mortality,
(5) improve maternal health,
(6) combat HIV/AIDS, malaria and other diseases,
(7) ensure environmental stability, and
(8) develop a global partnership for development; and be it further

Resolved, That the Convention, recognizing that funding for nutritional, education, health care, and development programs is essential to achieve *not only* the MDGs, *but also for recognizing the dignity of all human beings,* reaffirm the 73rd General Convention's Resolutions A001 and D033 challenging all dioceses and congregations to contribute 0.7% of their annual budgets to fund international development programs; and be it further

Resolved, That the appropriate offices and staff of the Episcopal Church Center, ~~including~~ *in cooperation with* Episcopal Relief and Development, promote among dioceses and congregations education about and participation in the 0.7% contribution for international development; and be it further

Resolved, That the Executive Council be directed to fulfill the 73rd General Convention's Resolution D033 requiring the Council to develop a process for an annual accounting of each diocese's progress toward living into the 0.7% contribution goal; and be it further

Resolved, That the Executive Council in cooperation with the Communications Office at the Episcopal Church Center publish annually the annual accounting of all dioceses' level of participation in the 0.7% contribution goal; and be it further

Resolved, That the Standing Commission on Anglican and International Peace with Justice present a full report to the 75th General Convention of the level of participation of all dioceses in the call to contribute 0.7% of their annual budgets to fund international development programs; and be it further

Resolved, That ~~the Episcopal Office of Government Relations in Washington, DC lobby actively~~ *the United States government, as one of the 191 national signatories to the United Nations Millennium Development Goals, be encouraged to provide appropriate leadership and resources toward international efforts to implement these and other internationally agreed development goals and that the Episcopal Office of Government Relations actively advocate* the United States government fulfill its commitment to funding international development aid at 0.7% of the U.S. Gross National Product (GNP); and be it further

Resolved, That *all Episcopalians contact their elected representatives, urging them to support* ~~the Episcopal Office of Government Relations urge all Episcopalians to press~~ the United States government*'s* ~~to fulfill~~ *fulfillment of* its commitment to funding international development aid at 0.7% of the U.S. *GNP*. ~~Gross National Product (GNP)~~.

Deputy Seitz of West Virginia moved to terminate debate.

Motion carried
Debate terminated

A vote was taken on Resolution D006 as amended.

Motion carried
Resolution adopted with amendment
(Communicated to the House of Bishops in HD Message #122)

The House of Deputies Committee on National and International Concerns presented its Report #16 on Resolution C036 (Spirituality of Food Production) and moved adoption with amendment.

Original Text of Resolution:
(C036)
Resolved, the House of Bishops concurring, That The Episcopal Church will continually provide its bishops, clergy, and lay persons with information and educational opportunities concerning the issues of food sources, biodiversity, genetic engineering, ownership, and distribution of our food sources, and related issues concerning the health and well-being of ourselves and future generations; and be it further

Resolved, That The Episcopal Church will advise elected and appointed government officials and other secular and religious bodies of its concerns about food sources, biodiversity, genetic engineering, ownership and distribution of our food sources, and related issues concerning the health and well-being of ourselves and future generations; and be it further

Resolved, That The Episcopal Church believes that consumers have a right to know the source and content of their food stuffs; and that the farming and processing practices used are healthy and sustainable for all of creation and The Episcopal Church is committed to making this a reality; and be it further

Resolved, That the General Convention refer this position to the Committee on Social Responsibility in Investment for consideration when developing stock portfolios.

Committee Amendment:
Resolved, the House of Bishops concurring, That ~~The Episcopal Church will~~ *the General Convention accept the Episcopal Ecological Network's offer to* continually provide its bishops, clergy, and lay persons with information and educational opportunities concerning the issues of food sources, biodiversity, genetic engineering, ownership, and distribution of our food sources, and related issues concerning the health and well-being of ourselves and future generations *and encourage them to work in conjunction with the Peace and Justice Ministries Office of the National Church Center in this regard*; and be it further

Resolved, That the ~~Episcopal Church~~ *Office of Government Relations and other appropriate*

bodies will advise elected and appointed government officials and other secular and religious bodies of its concerns about food sources, biodiversity, genetic engineering, ownership and distribution of our food sources, and related issues concerning the health and well-being of ourselves and future generations; and be it further

Resolved, That ~~The Episcopal Church believes that consumers have a right to know~~ *the General Convention support the rights of consumers to know* the source and content of their food stuffs; and that the farming and processing practices used are healthy and sustainable for all of creation and The Episcopal Church is committed to making this a reality; and be it further

Resolved, That the General Convention refer this position to the Committee on Social Responsibility in Investments for consideration when developing *and managing* stock portfolios *and for use in making shareholder resolutions.*

Motion carried
Resolution adopted with amendment
(Communicated to the House of Bishops in HD Message #130)

National and International Concerns

The House of Deputies Committee on National and International Concerns presented its Report #4 on Resolution A025 (Trafficking of Women, Girls, and Boys) and moved adoption of a substitute.

Original Text of Resolution:

(A025)
Resolved, the House of Bishops concurring, That the 74th General Convention recommend that every diocese bring to the attention of its members the domestic and international problem of trafficking in women, girls, and boys as well as any known local connections to trafficking; and be it further

Resolved, That the Executive Council provide $4,000 to the Committee on the Status of Women to enable identification and development of resource materials to be used by congregations and dioceses to address this problem; and be it further

Resolved, That the Office of Government Relations put trafficking—especially the sexual abuse of women and young girls—among its top priorities, including working with other denominations and alerting the Public Policy Network of opportunities to address trafficking in their home communities.

Committee Substitute:

Resolved, the House of Bishops concurring, That the 74th General Convention recommend that the Executive Council provide $4,000 to the Committee on the Status of Women to enable identification and development of resource materials to be used by congregations and dioceses to address the domestic and international problem of trafficking in women, girls, and boys as well as any known local connections in trafficking; and be it further

Resolved, That the General Convention request the Joint Standing Committee on Program, Budget and Finance to consider a budget allocation of $4,000 for implementation of this resolution.

Motion carried
Substitute resolution adopted
(Communicated to the House of Bishops in HD Message #123)

The House of Deputies Committee on National and International Concerns presented its Report #17 on Resolution C033 (Immigration and Undocumented Workers) and moved adoption of a substitute.

Original Text of Resolution:
(C033)
Resolved, the House of Bishops concurring, That the 74th General Convention urge the Congress of the United States to expand the Temporary Workers Program to cover all persons who enter this country to do legitimate work. Specifically, that the expanded program include the following benefit for the workers: Social Security numbers, workers' compensation, health and pension benefits, the right to change employers, as well as the options of applying for United States citizenship after a period of probation should they so choose. That this expansion of the Temporary Workers Program should include those who are currently here as undocumented workers; and be it further

Resolved, That the Convention further urge the Congress to provide access to education, and particularly post-secondary education, for the children of undocumented workers; and be it further

Resolved, That copies of this resolution be sent to all Representatives and Senators, serving in the Congress of the United States.

Committee Substitute:
Resolved, the House of Bishops concurring, That the 74th General Convention urge that the Congress of the United States enact legislation to expand the temporary workers' programs to include all persons currently residing in the United States engaged in meaningful labor, as well as overseas workers offered employment in the United States through formal contractual arrangements in response to the labor needs of specific sectors of the economy; and be it further

Resolved, That such temporary workers receive such compensation and benefits for themselves and their dependents living with them that parallel those available to other legal residents such as the federally mandated minimum hourly wage, social security, driver's license, medical care and education; and be it further

Resolved, That based upon a specified period of residence in the United States, such workers have the option of adjusting to permanent resident status, which could lead to naturalization; and be it further

Resolved, That this resolution be sent to concerned members of Congress and state legislatures as an expression of The Episcopal Church.

Motion carried
Substitute resolution adopted
(Communicated to the House of Bishops in HD Message #124)

The House of Deputies Committee on National and International Concerns presented its Report #18 on Resolution A036 (Korean Peninsula and the Democratic Peoples Republic of Korea) and moved adoption with amendment.

Original Text of Resolution:
(A036)
Resolved, the House of Bishops concurring, That the 74th General Convention of The Episcopal Church in the United States of America support the Anglican Church of Korea in its advocacy for the peaceful reunification of the Korean peninsula; and be it further
Resolved, That The Episcopal Church through its own offices and agencies and by appeal to the United States government urge special attention and aid to the relief of humanitarian needs and development of the Democratic Peoples Republic of Korea (North Korea) including poverty alleviation, food aid, energy development, transportation, education, and protection of human rights and the environment; and be it further
Resolved, That the Church urge the end of political demonization and militaristic rhetoric toward the Democratic Peoples Republic of Korea and its leaders in an effort to establish a more peaceful climate in the community of nations.

Committee Amendment:
Resolved, the House of Bishops concurring, That the 74th General Convention of The Episcopal Church in the United States of America support the Anglican Church of Korea in its advocacy for the peaceful reunification of the Korean peninsula; and be it further
Resolved, That the Episcopal Church through its own offices and agencies and by appeal to the United States government *to* urge *nongovernment organizations to* ~~special attention and~~ aid ~~to~~ the relief of humanitarian needs ~~and development of the Democratic Peoples Republic of Korea (North Korea)~~ including poverty alleviation, food ~~aid~~, *and* energy development, transportation, education, and protection of human rights and the environment; and be it further
~~*Resolved,* That the Church urge the end of political demonization and militaristic rhetoric toward the Democratic Peoples Republic of Korea and its leaders in an effort to establish a more peaceful climate in the community of nations.~~
Resolved, That the Church ask the United States to call on the People's Republic of China and Russia to allow entry in reasonable numbers of North Korean refugees and that the United States similarly move to welcome North Korean refugees into the United States.

Motion carried
Resolution adopted with amendment
(Communicated to the House of Bishops in HD Message #125)

The House of Deputies Committee on National and International Concerns presented its Report #19 on Resolution D023 (US Support for the People of Liberia) and moved adoption with amendment.

Text of Original Resolution:
(D023)
Resolved, the House of Bishops concurring, That the 74th General Convention, in support of the Presiding Bishop's statement of July 22, 2003, welcome the participation of U.S. peacekeepers in Liberia as part of an international force in order to bring an end to hostilities in that country, and that the Convention further support that presence there until an orderly transition is made to a legitimate and stable government, and that the Convention further support the departure of Charles Taylor from Liberia in conjunction with that international force; and be it further

Resolved, That the Convention commend support from both government and nongovernment organizations to provide humanitarian aid and reconstruction including conflict resolution education, particularly from the United States, but including the United Nations, and further urge our own congregations and dioceses to assist the Episcopal Church in Liberia with its efforts to restore pastoral care, health services, and education to the people; and be it further

Resolved, That Liberians residing temporarily in the United States be granted temporary protected status until such time as circumstances in Liberia permit their safe and orderly return; and be it further

Resolved, That Liberian refugees in adjacent West African countries who have prospects for U.S. resettlement be considered for resettlement, given the ongoing uncertainty of the political situation in Liberia; and be it further

Resolved, That the Convention send its warmest greetings to the Liberian people, especially its Episcopal members, through the delegation present at this 74th General Convention.

Committee Amendment:
Resolved, the House of Bishops concurring, That the 74th General Convention, in support of the Presiding Bishop's statement of July 22, 2003, ~~welcome the participation of U.S. peacekeepers in Liberia as part of an international force in order to bring an end to hostilities in that country, and that the Convention further support that presence there until an orderly transition is made to a legitimate and stable government, and that the Convention further support the departure of Charles Taylor from Liberia in conjunction with that international force;~~ *urge the President of the United States to act immediately to deploy peacekeeping forces, after adequately assessing their support and relative security to achieve a ceasefire in Liberia, and that the Convention further support that presence along with an international force, to remain at least until an orderly transition is made to a legitimate and stable government;* and be it further

Resolved, That the Convention commend support from both government and nongovernment organizations to provide humanitarian aid and reconstruction including conflict resolution education, ~~particularly~~ from the United States, ~~but including~~ the United Nations and *other individual nations*, and further urge our own congregations and dioceses to assist the Episcopal Church in Liberia with its efforts to restore pastoral care, health services, and education to the people; and be it further

Resolved, That Liberians residing temporarily in the United States be granted

temporary protected status until such time as circumstances in Liberia permit their safe and orderly return; and be it further
Resolved, That Liberian refugees in adjacent West African countries who have prospects for U.S. resettlement be considered for resettlement, given the ongoing uncertainty of the political situation in Liberia; and be it further
Resolved, That the Convention send its warmest greetings to the Liberian people, especially its Episcopal members, through the delegation present at this 74th General Convention; and be it further
Resolved, That the Convention urge all Episcopalians to pray for the Bishop, clergy, Episcopal Church and people of Liberia for a swift resolution of this conflict and the restoration of peace.
Deputy Simons of Pittsburgh moved to terminate debate.

Motion carried
Debate terminated

A vote was taken on Resolution D023 as amended.

Motion carried
Resolution adopted with amendment
(Communicated to the House of Bishops in HD Message #126)

Consecration of Bishops
Deputy Dales of New Hampshire read a statement from the Diocese of New Hampshire in regards to the consent to the election and consecration of V. Gene Robinson as Bishop Coadjutor-elect of the Diocese of New Hampshire. (See Appendix B–Day 8 for the Statement from the Diocese of Hampshire.)

Social and Urban Affairs
The House of Deputies Committee on Social and Urban Affairs presented its Report #13 on Resolution B008 (Protection of Children and Youth from Abuse) and moved adoption.

Original Text of Resolution:
(B008)
Resolved, the House of Bishops concurring, That the 74th General Convention of The Episcopal Church recommit itself to the vision of the role of children in the Church as articulated in *A Children's Charter for the Church* as adopted by the 72nd General Convention in 1997. The *Charter,* among other things, calls the Church to:
  Receive, nurture and treasure each child as a gift from God;
  Love, shelter, protect, and defend children within its own community and in the world, especially those who are abused, neglected, or in danger; and
  Advocate for the integrity of childhood and the dignity of all children at every level of our religious, civic, and political structures; and be it further
Resolved, That this Church acknowledge that the times and circumstances demand that the church articulate a clear and firm commitment to the safety of all, especially children; that we support this commitment with clear and firm policies and procedures for the well-being of all; and that we commit this Church to being

and becoming a place where children and youth are safe, especially from abuse and neglect; and be it further

Resolved, That each diocese develop and adopt policies for the protection of children and youth from abuse that address the following:

1. A screening and selection process for all clergy, lay employees, and volunteers who regularly work with children or youth. Dioceses are encouraged to consider:

    a. A written application
    b. A public records check
    c. An interview
    d. Reference checks
    e. A general provision that volunteers not work with children or youth until they have been known to the clergy or congregation for at least six months

2. The articulation of behavioral standards for clergy, lay employees, and volunteers working with children or youth. Dioceses are encouraged to consider:

    a. Respect for the privacy and dignity of children and youth by not putting them in inappropriate unmonitored one-to-one situations
    b. Age-appropriate arrangements for sleeping, bathing, dressing, or showering
    c. The prohibition of dating, romantic involvements, or sexual contact with a child or youth
    d. The prohibition of any sexually oriented materials (magazines, cards, videos, films, clothing, etc.) in the presence of children and youth except as expressly permitted as part of a pre-authorized educational program
    e. Guidelines for physical contact and expressions of affection that define appropriate and inappropriate behaviors
    f. The prohibition of discussing their own sexual activities and fantasies with children or youth
    g. The prohibition of the non-sacramental use, possession, distribution or being under the influence of alcohol, illegal drugs, or the misuse of legal drugs

3. The monitoring of programs and interaction with children and youth. Dioceses are encouraged to consider:

    a. The prohibition of the development or initiation of new activities for children or youth without prior approval from the appropriate decision-maker(s)
    b. The recognition that the ordinary standard is the presence of two unrelated adults for any activities involving children or youth

4. Education and training. Dioceses are encouraged to consider:
   a. Child abuse prevention for clergy, lay employees, and volunteers who regularly work with children or youth
   b. Specialized training for those who recruit, screen, or select persons to work with children or youth
5. Guidelines for responding to concerns. Dioceses are encouraged to consider:
   a. Inappropriate behavior with children or youth
   b. Violation of policies for the protection of children or youth
   c. Suspected abuse of children or youth; and be it further

Resolved, That each diocese shall report to the House of Bishops Committee on Pastoral Development prior to the Spring 2006 meeting of the House of Bishops with a copy of its adopted and implemented policy and an evaluation of the history of its use. A summary report shall be made to the House of Bishops Spring 2006 meeting and a full report made to the 75th General Convention.

Motion carried
Resolution adopted
(Communicated to the House of Bishops in HD Message #127)

The House of Deputies Committee on Social and Urban Affairs presented its Report #16 on Resolution A129 (Dismantling Racial Profiling) and moved adoption with amendment.

Original Text of Resolution:
(A129)
Resolved, the House of Bishops concurring, That the 74th General Convention deplore the immoral use of racial profiling unjustly to identify certain behaviors, and call for The Episcopal Church to recommit itself to being vigilant in speaking out against all negative profiling but especially racial profiling wherever it happens; and be it further
Resolved, That we renew our commitment to treat all people of color with honor and dignity, modeling the behavior that we commit to in our Baptismal Covenant: to strive for justice and peace among all people and respect the dignity of every human being; and be it further
Resolved, That each diocese be urged to commit funds specifically to help those who take action against racial profiling in their community; and be it further
Resolved, That the Anti-Racism Committee's diversity training be adjusted to include teaching about racial profiling, how to identify it, and various methods to end it.

Committee Amendment:
Resolved, the House of Bishops concurring, That the 74th General Convention deplore the immoral use of racial profiling *which* unjustly ~~to~~ *identifies* ~~identify~~ certain behaviors, and call for The Episcopal Church to recommit itself to being vigilant in speaking out against all negative profiling but especially racial profiling wherever it happens; and be it further
Resolved, That we renew our commitment to treat all people of color with honor and dignity, modeling the behavior that we commit to in our Baptismal Covenant: to strive for justice and peace among all people and respect the dignity of every human being; and be it further
Resolved, That each diocese be urged to commit funds specifically to help those who take action against racial profiling in their community; and be it further
Resolved, That the Anti-Racism Committee's diversity training be adjusted to include teaching about racial profiling, how to identify it, and various methods to end it.
Motion carried
Resolution adopted with amendment
(Communicated to the House of Bishops in HD Message #128)

The House of Deputies Committee on Social and Urban Affairs presented its Report #18 on Resolution C004 (Reparative Therapies) and moved adoption of a substitute.

Original Text of Resolution:
(C004)
Resolved, the House of Bishops concurring, That the 74th General Convention affirm that this Church does not insist that gay and lesbian people are in need of therapy to change their sexual orientation, nor should the church inhibit or discourage those who are unhappy with or confused about their sexual orientation from seeking therapy and/or pastoral counseling they believe would be helpful; and be it further
Resolved, That this Church oppose any religious, spiritual, psychological, or psychiatric counseling or treatment founded on the premise that homosexuality is a mental, spiritual, religious, or ethical disorder, affirming that medical treatment, psychological therapy, and pastoral counseling should conform to professional standards.

Committee Substitute:
Resolved, the House of Bishops concurring, That the 74th General Convention of The Episcopal Church affirm that sexual orientation is a gift of God and insists that any religious, spiritual, psychological, or psychiatric treatment known as "reparative," "conversion," "transformational" or "transformative" therapy which seeks to assist those who are confused about or unhappy with their sexual orientation not be coercive or manipulative; and be it further
Resolved, That this Church oppose any religious, spiritual, psychological, or psychiatric consulting or treatment which compromises our baptismal covenant to

respect the dignity of every human being, affirming that medical treatment, psychological therapy, and pastoral counseling should conform to the professional standards of the respective professions.

Deputy Randall of Western Massachusetts moved an amend the substitute resolution.

Proposed Amendment:
In the first resolve clause, delete "sexual orientation" and replace with "sexuality." Delete the words, "known as "reparative," "conversion," "transformational," or "transformative" therapy."

Motion carried
Amendment adopted

Deputy Simons of Pittsburgh moved to terminate debate.

Motion carried
Debate terminated

A vote was taken on substitute Resolution C004 as amended.

Motion carried
Substitute resolution adopted with amendment
(Communicated to the House of Bishops in HD Message #129)

Recess
The President announced a recess from 4:00 p.m. until 4:15 p.m.

Reconvene
The President called the House to order at 4:21 p.m.

Election of Executive Council—Ballot #1
The Secretary read the results of Election Ballot #1 for Executive Council. No members of the Clergy Order were elected on Ballot #1. Three of the six members were elected in the Lay Order. Newly-elected members of Executive Council:
In the Lay Order for six-year terms:
R.P.M. Bowden, Sr. of Atlanta
Thomas R. Gossen of Kansas
Albert Theodore Mollegen, Jr. of Connecticut

Ballot #2 taken

Consecration of Bishops
The Secretary read the report of Bishop Scruton to the House of Bishops on the investigation regarding the allegations concerning Bishop Coadjutor-elect Robinson of New Hampshire (See House of Bishops, Appendix I—Day 7 for Report on Bishop-elect of New Hampshire). Bishop Scruton found no grounds for the House of Bishops not to proceed to vote on the consent to the election and consecration of Bishop Coadjutor-elect Robinson.

Personal Privilege
Deputy Nagel of Central New York requested that the Chaplain lead the House in prayer for the deliberation of the House of Bishops.

Prayers
The President called upon the Chaplain for prayers.

Social and Urban Affairs
The House of Deputies Committee on Social and Urban Affairs presented its Report #19 on Resolution C003 (In Support of Representative John Conyers' H.R. 40) and moved adoption with amendment.

Original Text of Resolution:
(C003)
Resolved, the House of Bishops concurring, That pursuant to justice, human rights, and equity concerns, the 74th General Convention state its support for H.R. 40, a bill in the United States House of Representatives authored by Rep. John Conyers which calls for a congressional commission to be established to study the feasibility of restitution for Africans who were enslaved in America for 246 years.

Committee Amendment:
Resolved, the House of Bishops concurring, That pursuant to justice, human rights, and equity concerns, the 74th General Convention state its support for H.R. 40, a bill in the United States House of Representatives authored by Rep. John Conyers which calls for a congressional commission to be established to study the feasibility of restitution for Africans who were enslaved in America for 246 years; and be it further.
Resolved, That dioceses encourage their members to contact their congressmen in support of H.R. 40 or similar legislation with legislative intent.

Consideration was postponed until Wednesday, Augsut 6, 2003, the Eighth Legislative Day so that copies of H.R. 40 could be distributed to the House.

Consideration postponed

[Note: Consideration of Resolution C003 resumed on Day 8. See page 540. *Ed.*]

The House of Deputies Committee on Social and Urban Affairs presented its Report #20 on Resolution A125 (Ministry to Prisoners and Their Families) and moved adoption with amendment.

Original Text of Resolution:
(A125)
Resolved, the House of Bishops concurring, That the 74th General Convention of The Episcopal Church, through the Executive Council, urge dioceses and congregations to become familiar with the criminal justice system and form ministries which assist prisoners and their families during sentencing, while in prison, and during their readjustment period; and be it further
Resolved, That the 74th General Convention support the establishment and/or

expansion of occupational and academic programs in prisons where prisoners may be prepared for re-entry into society; and be it further

Resolved, That the 74th General Convention ask the Suffragan Bishop for Chaplaincies to identify training programs that will help dioceses and congregations support the post-release employment of convicted felons.

Committee Amendment:

Resolved, the House of Bishops concurring, That the 74th General Convention of The Episcopal Church, through the Executive Council, urge dioceses and congregations to become familiar with the criminal justice system and ~~form~~ *establish* ministries which assist prisoners and their families during sentencing, while in prison, and during their readjustment period; and be it further

Resolved, That the 74th General Convention support the establishment and/or expansion of occupational, *therapeutic treatment,* and academic programs in prisons where prisoners may be prepared for re-entry into society; and be it further

Resolved, That the 74th General Convention ask the ~~Suffragan Bishop for Chaplaincies~~ *Office of Peace and Justice* to identify training programs *for volunteers who work both inside prisons and with post-release programs and to assist* ~~that will help~~ dioceses and congregations ~~support the post-release employment of convicted felons~~ *with this work;* and be it further

Resolved, That the 74th General Convention ask the Office of Peace and Justice to identify religious education programs that can be, or have been, adapted for the cultures of particular prison populations and when appropriate, to provide training in such programs for dioceses and congregations.

Motion carried
Resolution adopted with amendment
(Communicated to the House of Bishops in HD Message #131)

The House of Deputies Committee on Social and Urban Affairs presented its Report #22 on Resolution D015 (COSE Materials Available on the Web) and moved adoption with amendment.

Original Text of Resolution:
(D015)
Resolved, the House of Bishops concurring, That the 74th General Convention of The Episcopal Church, recalling that the 71st General Convention in Resolution B022a, commended the manual and training materials prepared by the Committee on Sexual Exploitation (entitled "Respecting the Dignity of Every Human Being"), "...for use by the dioceses and institutions of this Church ... in setting policies and procedures and in educating and training clergy and laity;" direct the Secretary of the General Convention, to make available to all dioceses electronic copies of this manual and training materials; and be it further

Resolved, That the 74th General Convention direct the Secretary of the General Convention, to also make available to all dioceses electronic copies of the updates to the manual and training materials distributed at the 72nd General Convention, along with electronic copies of the pamphlets listed on page 390 of the 72nd

General Convention Blue Book; and be it further
Resolved, That the Secretary of the General Convention be requested to also make the electronic copies available on The Episcopal Church national website; and be it further
Resolved, That the Title IV Revision Task Force explore the feasibility of offering one or more Response Teams on a national level to any diocese requesting their services (when invited by either the diocesan Ecclesiastical Authority or the Diocesan Review Committee), with feasibility being understood to mean both financial and logistical.

Committee Amendment:

Resolved, the House of Bishops concurring, That the 74th General Convention of The Episcopal Church, recalling that the 71st General Convention in Resolution B022a, commended the manual and training materials prepared by the Committee on Sexual Exploitation (entitled "Respecting the Dignity of Every Human Being"), ... for use by the dioceses and institutions of this Church ... in setting policies and procedures and in educating and training clergy and laity;" direct the ~~Secretary of the General Convention~~ *Executive Council*, to make available to all dioceses electronic copies of this manual and training materials; and be it further
Resolved, That the 74th General Convention direct the ~~Secretary of the General Convention~~ *Executive Council*, to also make available to all dioceses electronic copies of the updates to the manual and training materials distributed at the 72nd General Convention, along with electronic copies of the pamphlets ~~listed on page 390 of the 72nd General Convention Blue Book~~ , *including, but not limited to, "For Persons with Complaints: Information of the Episcopal Church Discipline," "A Diocesan Guide to Understanding Title IV," "A Clergy Guide to Understanding Title IV," "What a Congregation (and Vestry) Should Know about the Revised Disciplinary Canons of the Episcopal Church" and "Guidelines for Bishops Meeting with Complaints in Accordance with Title IV" as revised, and "Guidelines for Bishops Meeting with A Respondent in Accordance with Title IV"* and *"Suggested Standards for the Restoration of Rehabilitated Sexual Exploitative Clerics" when available*; and be it further
Resolved, That the ~~Secretary of the General Convention~~ *Executive Council* be requested to also make the electronic copies available on the Episcopal Church national website; and be it further
Resolved, That the Title IV Revision Task Force explore the *financial and logistical* feasibility of offering one or more Response Teams on a national level to any diocese requesting their services—when invited by either the diocesan Ecclesiastical Authority or the Diocesan Review Committee. ~~, with feasibility being understood to mean both financial and logistical.~~

Motion carried
Resolution adopted with amendment
(Communicated to the House of Bishops in HD Message #132)

The House of Deputies Committee on Social and Urban Affairs presented its Report #24 on Resolution A126 (Youth Charged and Convicted as Adults) and moved adoption with amendment.

Original Text of Resolution:
(A126)
Resolved, the House of Bishops concurring, That the 74th General Convention of The Episcopal Church direct the Office of Government Relations to work for legislation that provides alternatives to sentencing for juveniles and establishes intermediary facilities for incarceration—between farm schools and adult prisons—for serious juvenile offenders; and be it further
Resolved, That the Peace and Justice Office explore, study, and make available to dioceses and congregations resources for ministering to families and juveniles who are heading toward or caught up in the U.S. criminal justice system.

Committee Amendment:
Resolved, the House of Bishops concurring, That the 74th General Convention of the Episcopal Church direct the Office of Government Relations to work for legislation that provides alternatives to sentencing for juveniles, *offers creative programs for rehabilitation,* and establishes *separate* intermediary facilities for incarceration ~~between farm schools and adult prisons~~ for ~~serious~~ juvenile*s* ~~offenders~~ *convicted of serious crimes*; and be it further
Resolved, ~~That the Peace and Justice Office explore, study, and make available to dioceses and congregations resources for ministering to families and juveniles who are heading toward or caught up in the U.S. criminal justice system.~~ *That the 74th General Convention call upon dioceses, congregations, and individual Episcopalians to promote reforms in state juvenile justice systems that focus on justice, human dignity, and rehabilitation;* and be it further
Resolved, That the 74th General Convention encourage defense attorneys to offer pro bono services to alleviate the growing epidemic of inadequate counsel and express gratitude for those who provide these services.

Motion carried
Resolution adopted with amendment
(Communicated to the House of Bishops in HD Message #133)

The House of Deputies Committee on Social and Urban Affairs presented its Report #11 on Resolution C030 (The Working Poor) and moved adoption with amendment.

Original Text of Resolution:
(C030)
Resolved, the House of Bishops concurring, That the 74th General Convention urge our elected congresspersons and U.S. senators to initiate or support legislation raising the federal minimum wage to at least $8.70 an hour, this figure being the hourly equivalent of an annual wage at the current federal poverty line, $18,100 for a family of four persons; and be it further
Resolved, That the 74th General Convention continue to support living wage campaigns in the cities and counties of every diocese; and be it further
Resolved, That the 74th General Convention strongly affirm the right of workers to

organize as protected by federal and state law, especially in low wage industries and businesses, and including the institutions of every diocese.

Committee Amendment:
Resolved, the House of Bishops concurring, That the 74th General Convention urge our elected congresspersons and U.S. senators to initiate or support legislation raising the federal minimum wage; ~~to at least $8.70 an hour, this figure being the hourly equivalent of an annual wage at the current federal poverty line, $18,100 for a family of four persons~~; and be it further
Resolved, That the 74th General Convention continue to support living wage campaigns in the cities and counties of every diocese, and be it further
Resolved, That the 74th General Convention ~~strongly affirm the~~ *reaffirm* The Episcopal Church commitment to the right of workers to organize as protected *and where permitted* by federal and state law, especially in low wage industries and businesses, and including the institutions of every diocese.

Deputy Curtis of Newark moved to amend the amended resolution.

Proposed Amendment:
Restore the deleted text in the first resolve clause in the Committee amendment.

Deputy Hart of Pennsylvania moved to terminate debate on the Curtis amendment and on the main motion.

The President asked to limit the vote to terminating the debate on the Curtis amendment only due to the limited debate and the number of people at microphones.

Motion carried
Debate terminated

A vote was taken on the Curtis amendment.

Motion carried
Amendment adopted

Deputy Lattime of Rochester moved to amend the amended resolution.

Proposed Amendment:
In the first resolve clause, add "and legislation that would provide equal labor rights and benefits, including the right to organize, to farm workers" after "federal minimum wage."

Deputy of Renton of California moved to terminate debate on the amendment and the main motion.

Motion carried
Debate terminated

A vote was taken on the Lattime amendment.

Motion defeated
Amendment defeated

A vote was taken on Resolution C030 as amended.

Motion carried
Resolution adopted with amendment
(Communicated to the House of Bishops in HD Message #134)

The House of Deputies Committee on Social and Urban Affairs presented its Report #25 on Resolution D077 (Post 9/11 Racial Hatred and Incarcerations) and moved adoption with amendment.

Original Text of Resolution:
(D077)
Resolved, the House of Bishops concurring, That this Church affirm its abhorrence of all violence toward and racial profiling of Muslims and people of color done in the name of religion, especially toward our Muslim brothers and sisters; and be it further
Resolved, That all members of this Church be encouraged to reach out in friendship to our neighbors of all religions—especially at this time to Muslims, seeking mutual understanding and expressing support; and be it further
Resolved, That The Episcopal Church direct the Committee on National Concerns of Executive Council to examine and direct the Office of Government Relations to monitor governmental policies on the imprisonment and restrictions of American citizens or legal residents who are of Southern Asian and Southwestern Asian ancestry; and be it further
Resolved, That the General Convention acknowledge the danger that in this post 9/11 era a repeat of racial hatred, terrorism, hysteria, and a failure of political leadership could result in governmental policies causing the incarceration of Southern Asian and Southwestern Asian citizens and legal residents based solely on their ethnicity; and be it further
Resolved, That the General Convention request the Joint Standing Committee on Program, Budget and Finance to consider a budget allocation of $25,000 for implementation of this resolution.

Committee Amendment:
Resolved, the House of Bishops concurring, That this Church affirm its abhorrence of all violence toward and racial profiling of Muslims and people of color done in the name of religion, especially toward our Muslim brothers and sisters; and be it further
Resolved, That all members of this Church be encouraged to reach out in friendship to our neighbors of all religions—especially at this time to Muslims, seeking mutual understanding and expressing support; and be it further
Resolved, That The Episcopal Church direct the Committee on National Concerns of Executive Council to examine and direct the Office of Government Relations to monitor governmental policies on the imprisonment and restrictions of American citizens or legal residents ~~who are of Southern Asian and Southwestern Asian ancestry~~ *based solely on ethnicity*; and be it further

Resolved, That the General Convention acknowledge the danger that in this post 9/11 era a repeat of racial hatred, terrorism, hysteria, and a failure of political leadership could result in governmental policies causing the incarceration of Southern Asian and Southwestern Asian citizens and legal residents based solely on their ethnicity; and be it further

Resolved, That the General Convention request the Joint Standing Committee on Program, Budget and Finance to consider a budget allocation of $25,000 for implementation of this resolution.

Deputy Hamilton of Central Gulf Coast moved to amend the amended resolution.

Proposed Amendment:
Remove the phrase "of Southern Asian and Southwestern Asian" to parallel the deletion in the earlier part of the committee's amendment.

Hearing no objections, the President ruled the acceptance of this amendment.

Deputy Logan of South Carolina moved to terminate debate.

Motion carried
Debate terminated

A vote was taken on Resolution D077 as amended.

Motion carried
Resolution adopted with amendment
(Communicated to the House of Bishops in HD Message #135)

Dispatch of Business
The House of Deputies Committee on Dispatch of Business in its Report #7 moved a Special Order of Business to suspend the Rules of Order:
Resolved, That there be set at this time a Special Order of Debate for the purpose of considering and taking action with respect to Reports of Committees, except reports presented under another Special Order of Business, as follows:
1. The Committee Chair or a designated member of the Committee shall have two minutes to speak with respect to the report;
2. The entire debate of the report thereafter shall be limited to ten additional minutes;
3. Each Speaker shall be limited to two minutes and no speaker shall speak more than once on the same question;
4. After three Deputies have spoken to the same point, pro or con, and no one is standing to speak to the contrary, debate on the matter shall terminate;
5. To the extent practicable the Chair shall recognize speakers of opposite views in alternate succession;
6. Debate may be terminated or extended by two-thirds vote of the House; and be it further

Resolved, That the Chair of Dispatch of Business is authorized to call up legislative matters at his discretion and as he deems beset in order to further the completion of business of this House.

Motion carried
Special Order adopted
(Communicated to the House of Bishops in HD Message #136)

Evangelism

The House of Deputies Committee on Evangelism presented its Report #8 on Resolution A077 (Trained Leadership) and moved adoption of a substitute.

Original Text of Resolution:
(A077)
Resolved, the House of Bishops concurring, That the 74th General Convention adopt a vision of a trained children's minister, a trained youth minister, and a trained young adult minister in every congregation; and an Episcopal ministry on every college campus; and be it further
Resolved, That the 74th General Convention authorize $4,000,000 for the next triennium to be dispersed among the provinces for the training and mentoring of those who minister with children, youth, young adults, and on college campuses; and be it further
Resolved, That provinces and dioceses be encouraged to match these funds.

Committee Substitute:
Resolved, the House of Bishops concurring, That the 74th General Convention adopt a vision as part of the 20/20 initiative that there shall be effective, well-organized ministries with children, youth, and young adults in every congregation where appropriate; and there shall be campus ministries in all colleges and universities where appropriate, and be it further
Resolved, That the 74th General Convention commend the work of the Ministries with Young People Cluster, which has three networks: (1) youth ministries, (2) Christian education ministries, and (3) higher education ministries; and be it further
Resolved, That the 74th General Convention direct the Ministries with Young People Cluster to create an additional network for young adult ministries; and be it further
Resolved, That in order to accomplish these training goals by 2009 the Youth Ministries Cluster, in coordination with the Standing Commission on Domestic Mission and Evangelism, call upon their provincial networks to develop and implement in the dioceses, training strategies that include, but are not limited to:
- education in leadership development
- sharing of technology, training resources, curricula, theological, and multicultural resources
- practical application for life-long Christian formation
- the strengthening of the existing networks in dioceses and provinces; and be it further

Resolved, That the 74th General Convention, request the Joint Standing Committee on Program, Budget and Finance consider a budget allocation of $250,000 per year

for each of the four ministry networks (1) youth ministries, (2) Christian education ministries, (3) higher education ministries, and (4) young adult ministries for a budget allocation of $3,000,000 for implementation of this resolution; and be it further
Resolved, That the office of the Treasurer of the Episcopal Church Center in cooperation with the various dioceses as facilitated by the Provincial Leadership Conference establish a fair share strategy for fund distribution to be reported to the 75th General Convention.

Motion carried
Substitute resolution adopted
(Communicated to the House of Bishops in HD Message #137)

Prayer Book, Liturgy and Church Music
The House of Deputies Committee on Prayer Book, Liturgy and Church Music presented its Report #14 on HB Message #87 on Resolution A101 (Church Planting Liturgies) and moved concurrence.

Deputy Hesselgrave of Oregon moved to amend the resolution.

Proposed Amendment:
Delete the words "side-by-side."

Motion defeated
Amendment defeated

Deputy Upton of Kansas moved to amend the resolution.

Proposed Amendment:
Insert, "deacon" for the the dismissal (Blue Book pages 190–191) instead of an officiant/celebrant.
Deputy Lane of South Western Virginia noted it should say deacon or officiant celebrant.
Deputy Upton agreed with this revision of his amendment.
The Chair called for the vote on the Upton amendment.

Motion carried
Amendment adopted

Deputy Toensmann of the Churches in Europe moved an amendment.

Proposed Amendment:
Amend the second resolve clause to read, "That these bilingual liturgies be printed side-by-side in English and Spanish, and English and French; and be it further".
The President noted that the time for debate had expired.
Deputy Barnes of Montana moved to extend debate by five minutes.

Motion defeated
Debate terminated

A vote was taken on the Toensmann amendment.

Motion carried
Amendment adopted

A vote was taken on Resolution A101 as amended.

Motion carried
The House concurred with amendment
(Communicated to the House of Bishops in HD Message #138)

Communications

The House of Deputies Committee on Communications presented its Report #9 on Resolution A080 (Episcopal Church Website) and moved adoption of a substitute.

Original Text of Resolution:
(A080)
Resolved, the House of Bishops concurring, That the 74th General Convention direct the Episcopal Church Center staff to develop and maintain a highly visual, dynamic, interactive, and constantly updated website that is professional in appearance and easy to navigate; to deploy user-profiling tools to deliver website material according to user preferences (such as seeker, lay, clergy, deputy, standing commission member); to include multilingual and next generations resources in all areas of the website; and to develop software and freeware resources for downloading.

Committee Substitute:
Resolved, the House of Bishops concurring, That the 74th General Convention direct the Episcopal Church Center staff to:
- Continue to develop the Domestic and Foreign Missionary Society website in ways that are more highly visual and professional in their appearance, dynamic, interactive, easier to navigate, and constantly updated;
- Deploy user-profiling tools to deliver website material according to user preferences such as seeker, lay, clergy, deputy, standing commission member;
- Include multilingual and next generations resources in all areas of the website;
- Collect and post on the website a variety of resources related to faith formation, ongoing spiritual growth, and education of both children and adults;
- Include resources on the website that are oriented to seekers from outside The Episcopal Church, and that assist in making disciples oriented to mission for the local context;
- Devote a portion of the website to mentoring and relationship building among those who work with the next generations, including campus ministries, young adults ministries, youth ministries, and children's ministries;
- Maintain a unity of design and ease of access including easy forward and backward mobility; and be it further

Resolved, That the Episcopal Church Center staff provide software and freeware resources for downloading.

**Motion carried
Substitute resolution adopted**
(Communicated to the House of Bishops in HD Message #139)

Miscellaneous Resolutions

The House of Deputies Committee on Miscellaneous Resolutions presented its Report #7 on Resolution D051 (Full Accessibility at General Convention) and moved adoption with amendment.

The President postponed consideration of Resolution D051 until the Eighth Legislative Day due to time for recess.

Consideration postponed

Messages from the House of Bishops

The Secretary announced that the following messages had been received from the House of Bishops:

HB Message #141:	A059 (Design New Resources) Adopted Substitute.
HB Message #143:	D033 (Encourage Basic Financial Teaching) Adopted Substitute.
HB Message #144:	B005 (Amend Constitution Article I.2) Adopt Substitute.
HB Message #145:	D027 (Amend Constitution Article II.1 [Election of Bishops–Second Reading]) Adopted.
HB Message #146:	D062 (Amend Constitution Article IX [Trial Court of Bishops–Second Reading]) Adopted.
HB Message #147:	D020 (Opposition to Sharia Law) Adopted Substitute.

Announcements

The President stated that the House of Bishops was about to vote on Resolution C045.

The Secretary read the announcements.

Recess

The President led the House in the Prayer of St. Francis. The House recessed at 6:04 p.m. to reconvene at 11:00 a.m. on Wednesday, August 6, 2003.

Appendix B
Day 7

A Statement from the Diocese of New Hampshire

Report of Action by the Standing Committee of the Diocese of New Hampshire:

(1) Having heard from Bishop Scruton regarding the allegations concerning Bishop Coadjutor-elect Robinson, the Standing Committee is satisfied that the investigation was full, complete, and transparent. They have full confidence in the Bishop-elect.

(2) The Standing Committee continues to request consent from the House of Bishops for Robinson's ordination and consecration as Bishop Coadjutor of New Hampshire.

MINNEAPOLIS MEETING   HOUSE OF DEPUTIES

EIGHTH DAY

Wednesday
August 6, 2003

MORNING SESSION

Reconvene
The President called the House to order at 11:05 a.m.

Morning Prayers
The President called on the Chaplain for prayers.

Certification of Minutes
The House of Deputies Committee on Certification of Minutes presented its Report #7, stating that the Committee had met, read the minutes of the Seventh Day, and certified that they were correct. The Vice-Chair moved adoption of the report.

Motion carried
Minutes accepted

Certification of Deputies
The House of Deputies Committee on Credentials presented its Report #12 for the first session of the Eighth Legislative Day, and there were no new deputies certified. There were 418 clerical deputies and 419 lay deputies certified and seated, bringing the total count of the House to 837. There were 101 changes on this day as follows:

Diocese	*Alternate replacing*	*Deputy being replaced*
Arkansas	Lowell Grisham	Joyce Hardy
Atlanta	Lori Lowe	E. Claiborne Jones
California	George Sotelo	Katherine Lehman
California	Holly McAlpen	Sarah Lawton
Central Florida	Carole Ross	Thomas Bates
Central Gulf Coast	Margaret Slingluff	Peter Wilson
Central Pennsylvania	Brian Amato	John Radomsky
Central Pennsylvania	Paul Donecker	Mark Scheneman
Chicago	Richard Tolliver	Graham Smith
Colorado	Ephraim Radner	Robert Davidson
Colorado	Andrew Cooley	S. Brooks Keith
Connecticut	James Bradley	Ellen Tillotson
Connecticut	John Sutton	Eugene Lattimer
Delaware	William Hitch	Herb Quick
Delaware	Edward Godden	Lois Keen
East Tennessee	Jocelyn Bell	Joseph Ballard

Eastern Oregon	James Foster	Susan Powers
Easton	Samuel Hartman	M. Douglas Girardeau
Eau Claire	Alan Coudriet	Patrick Augustine
Eau Claire	Barbara Gaynor	Paul Chase
El Camino Real	Martin Yabroff	Nayan McNeill
Florida	Elizabeth Hobby	Calvin Williams
Florida	John Palarine	Gilbert Crosby
Fort Worth	Anthony Clark	Eugene Dugan
Georgia	Robert Carter	H. Neal Phelps
Hawaii	Morley Frech	Joseph Carr
Idaho	Eileen O'Shea	Doug Yarbrough
Idaho	Dean Hagerman	Lance Nielsen
Indianapolis	Charles Carpenter	Sherry Mattson
Iowa	Sharon Mahood	Robert Holzhammer
Kansas	Larry Valentine	James Haney
Lexington	Janet Dunnavant	Anisa Cottrell-Willis
Lexington	Carolyn Ware	David Davidson
Long Island	Valarie Crosdale	J. Vincent Welch
Long Island	Elizabeth Belasco	Richard Brewer
Louisiana	Rex Perry	Ralph Howe
Maine	Paige Blair	Anne Stanley
Maine	Cyndy Anderson	Nicole Janelle
Maryland	Christine Kinard	Alma Bell
Maryland	Angela Shepherd	Edward Chapman
Massachusetts	Nadine Boakye	Byron Rushing
Milwaukee	Carlynn Higbie	Ralph Modjeska
Minnesota	Terry Roberts	James Huber
Minnesota	Mariann Budde	Michael Hanley
Minnesota	Kathy Pluhar	R.C. Laird
Mississippi	Zabron Davis	Mike Dobrosky
Nebraska	Don Betts	Margaret Schaefer
New York	Roger Ferlo	Daniel Matthews
New York	Dorothy Smith	William Augerson
Newark	Lyn Headley-Moore	Marjorie Christie
Northern California	Stephen Carpenter	Barry Beisner
Northern California	Mark Allen	Donald Brown
Northwest Texas	Sue Veal	Cliff Craig
Northwest Texas	James Haney	J. Mayer
Northwest Texas	Jacob Clemmens	Laura Deaderick
Ohio	Stephen Smith	Bryan Gillooly
Oklahoma	Dwight Helt	Kenneth Armstrong
Olympia	Mary Ellen Harris	James Church
Oregon	James Boston	Linda Potter

Pennsylvania	Peter Kreek	Ginger Goodrich
Pittsburgh	Elizabeth Hobbs	Joseph Sarria
Puerto Rico	Emily Morales	Wilner Millien
Rhode Island	Carol Bennett	Harry Sacchetti
Rhode Island	Jennifer Phillips	Mark Galloway
Rio Grande	Kay Fancher	George Du Sang
Rio Grande	Carole McGowan	Ronald Thomson
Rochester	Bonnie Tyo	Sarah Collins
San Diego	Gary Nicolosi	Amanda May
San Joaquin	Richard Matters	Ken Richards
South Carolina	John Burwell	Mark Goodman
Southeast Florida	William Stokes	Horace Ward
Southern Ohio	Deborah Stokes	Richard Jennings
Southern Virginia	Sara Mueller	Joyce Moorman
Southern Virginia	Sue Wilder	Robert Lee
Southwest Florida	Donald Scott	Joan Kline
Southwest Florida	Barry Kubler	John Hiers
Southwestern Virginia	Robert Miller	Emily Fisher
Upper South Carolina	Elizabeth Wickenberg Ely	Timothy Dombek
Utah	Ann Ellingson	Barbara Losse
Utah	Mary Allen	Pablo Ramos
Vermont	Thomas Brown	John Morris
Vermont	Peter Galbraith	Thomas Little
Virginia	Russell Palmore	Jack Burtch
Virginia	Susan Eaves	Victoria Heard
Washington	John Vanderstar	Geoffrey Cant
Washington	Iris Harris	Wesley Baldwin
West Tennessee	Carolyn Corum	Jeff Garrety
West Tennessee	Rene Somodevilla	Stephen Carpenter
West Texas	David Read	Gary Lillibridge
West Texas	Alice Fischer	John Brooke
West Texas	Sylvia Maddox	Kirk Mason
West Texas	James Murguia	Ned Bowersox
West Virginia	John Jeffries	Thomas Miller
Western Louisiana	Walter Baer	Martin Agnew
Western Louisiana	Norman Parker	Reece Middleton
Western New York	Linda Makson	Particia Zebrowski
Western New York	Charles Whitmore	Susan Williams
Western North Carolina	Tim McRee	Houston Matthews
Western North Carolina	Diane Mance	Lauch Magruder
Wyoming	Warren Murphy	Cliff Moore

Communications from the President
The President announced that permission had been granted to a deputy to read a statement following the Messages from the House of Bishops. After that, the President would call upon the Chaplain for prayers and the House would then return to regular business.

Messages from the House of Bishops
The Secretary announced that the following messages had been received from the House of Bishops:

HB Message #148:	A012 (Caring for Children in the Face of the New Genetics) Concurred.
HB Message #149:	C008 (Episcopal Council of Indigenous Ministries Funding) Concurred.
HB Message #150:	C006 (Evangelism to the New Majority) Concurred.
HB Message #151:	A109 (International Anglican Liturgical Consultation) Adopted Substitute.
HB Message #152:	A107 (Renewal and Enrichment of Common Worship) Discharged.
HB Message #153:	A131 (Worker's Prayer) Rejected.
HB Message #154:	C035 (Publish Lectionary for Lesser Feasts and Fasts) Rejected.
HB Message # 155:	D003 (Revision of the Catechism) Referred to a Standing Commission.
HB Message # 156:	D035 (To Transfer the Commemoration of Harriet Tubman from July 20 to March 10) Referred to a Standing Commission.
HB Message # 157:	D049 (First Communion on the Moon) Referred to a Standing Commission.
HB Message #158:	D004 (Evangelical Lutheran Church in America Ordination Practices) Discharged.
HB Message #159:	C011 (Evangelical Lutheran Church in America—Change in Ordination Policy) Discharged.
HB Message #160:	B023 (Change Consent Process to Provinces) Rejected.
HB Message #161:	A146 (Provincial Coordinators Funding) Concurred.
HB Message #162:	A072 (Amend Canon I.6.1) Concurred.
HB Message #163:	A145 (General Convention Model) Concurred.
HB Message #164:	A019 (Continue Standing Committee on HIV/AIDS) Concurred.
HB Message #165:	A023 (Establish Institutional Wellness and the Prevention of Sexual Misconduct Task Force) Concurred.
HB Message #166:	A120 (Theological Education Committee) Concurred.
HB Message #167:	A084 (20/20 Vision Reporting) Concurred.
HB Message # 168:	A022 (Nathan Network Funding) Adopted.
HB Message #169:	A062 (Diversity in Leadership Recruitment) Discharged.

HB Message # 170:	A067 (Fund for Theological Education) Adopted Substitute.
HB Message # 171:	B017 (Fresh Start) Adopted with Amendment.
HB Message # 172:	B018 (Families of Clergy United in Support—FOCUS) Adopted with Amendment.
HB Message # 173:	C037 (Facilitating International Communications within the Episcopal Church) Adopted Substitute.
HB Message #174:	A017 (National Conversation on Women's Ordination) Concurred.
HB Message #175:	Consent to the Election of the Rev. Canon V. Gene Robinson as Bishop Coadjutor of the Diocese of New Hampshire. Concurred.

The President asked the deputation of the Diocese of New Hampshire to escort Bishop Coadjutor-elect Robinson to the podium to be introduced.

Personal Privilege
Deputy Harmon of South Carolina spoke on behalf of members of the House who were against the consent to the election of Bishop Coadjutor-elect Robinson. Deputy Harmon stated that they disassociated themselves from the Church in this action, as they believed it was against the doctrine and discipline of this Church. He stated that they believed that the action violated the Thirty-nine Articles and that they joined the dissenting Bishops in asking the Archbishop of Canterbury to intervene. Deputy Harmon stated that they were not leaving the Episcopal Church, but rather, that the Episcopal Church was leaving them. He invited members of the House to sign their statement at the South Carolina deputation.

Prayers
The President called upon the Chaplain for prayers.

Personal Privilege
Deputy Anschutz of Dallas announced the resignation of Deputy Roseberry from the Dallas deputation and made some remarks.

Election of Executive Council—Ballot #2
The Secretary read Ballot #2 for Executive Council. No members of the Clergy Order or Lay Order were elected on Ballot #2.

Personal Privilege
Deputy Lopez of Honduras, as an overseas deputy, expressed distress upon the consent to the election of Bishop Coadjutor-elect Robinson of New Hampshire. Deputy Lopez stated that he did not know its effect upon his ministry in his diocese.

Parliamentary Inquiry
Deputy Hagerman of Idaho asked if voting tallies would reflect those who had absented themselves from the House.

Secretary of the House of Deputies
The President called upon the Secretary, who reported that all vote tallies represent those present and voting at the time the vote is taken.

Dispatch of Business
The House of Deputies Committee on Dispatch of Business reminded the House of a Special Order of Business at 2:30 p.m. for a presentation by the Joint Standing Committee on Program, Budget and Finance. A Special Order for the Election of Trustees of The General Theological Seminary would follow.

The President stated that the House needed to grant permission for the Presiding Bishop to speak at the Joint Session for the presentation by the Joint Standing Committee on Program, Budget and Finance. Hearing no objection, it was so ordered by the President.

The Chair of the House of Deputies Committee on Dispatch of Business spoke about expediting the work of the House after the Joint Session. The Order of Business would be the Special Order of Business passed on the Seventh Legislative Day beginning with Resolution D051.

Miscellaneous Resolutions
The House of Deputies Committee on Miscellaneous Resolutions presented its Report #7 on Resolution D051 (Full Accessibility at General Convention) and moved adoption with amendment.

Original Text of Resolution:
(D051)
Resolved, the House of Bishops concurring, That the 74th General Convention direct the Joint Standing Committee on Planning and Arrangements to recommend for future General Conventions, and subsequent triennium meetings of Executive Council, only locations that provide full independent accessibility to all scheduled events, both official and ancillary, for all members of this Church.

Committee Amendment:
Resolved, the House of Bishops concurring, That the 74th General Convention direct the Joint Standing Committee on Planning and Arrangements to recommend for future General Conventions, and subsequent ~~triennium~~ meetings of Executive Council, only locations *and schedules* that provide full independent accessibility to all ~~scheduled~~ events, both official and ancillary, for all members of this Church *including but not limited to the hearing impaired, sight impaired, and persons with physical disabilities.*

Deputy Sopkovich of Milwaukee moved to amend the resolution by deleting "and" between "General Conventions" and "subsequent," and after "of Executive

Council" add the words "standing commission meetings and Provincial meetings,". The President asked if this amendment might be added to the resolution. The Committee accepted the Sopkovich amendment.

A vote was taken on D051 as amended.

Motion carried
Resolution adopted with amendment
(Communicated to the House of Bishops in HD Message #141)

The House of Deputies Committee on Miscellaneous Resolutions presented its Report #10 on Resolution A079 (General Convention Deputies) and moved adoption.

Original Text of Resolution:
(A079)
Resolved, the House of Bishops concurring, That the 74th General Convention recommend that diocesan conventions elect deputations to General Convention that represent the next generations, and also the multilingual, multicultural character of our churches and communities, so that deputations reflect the vision we have for the church we would like to be in 2020.

Deputy Hartney of Western New York moved an amendment.

Proposed Amendment:
After "conventions" add "nominate candidates for" and delete "elect." After the second "that" add "incorporate" and delete "represent." After "we" add "are" and delete "would like to be in 2020."
Add a final resolve, "and be it further *Resolved,* That the 74th General Convention recommend that all dioceses and congregations engage the vision when presenting candidates for all representative boards, including, but not limited to, vestries, delegations to diocesan conventions, and standing committees."

A vote was taken on the Hartney amendment.

Motion carried
Amendment adopted

A vote was taken on Resolution A079 as amended.

Motion carried
Resolution adopted with amendment
(Communicated to the House of Bishops in HD Message #142)

The House of Deputies Committee on Miscellaneous Resolutions presented its Report #11 on Resolution C026 (Reduce the Use of Toxic Chemicals) and moved adoption with amendment.

Original Text of Resolution:
(C026)
Resolved, the House of Bishops concurring, That the 74th General Convention urge congregations, dioceses, provinces and all church institutions to initiate a plan in the next triennium for the management of Church buildings and grounds that phases out the use of pesticides and other toxic chemicals to control pests and institutes the use of alternatives, recognizing that children are the population most susceptible to toxins.

Committee Amendment:
Resolved, the House of Bishops concurring, That the 74th General Convention urge congregations, dioceses, provinces, and all church institutions to initiate a plan in the next triennium for the management of Church buildings and grounds that phases out the use of pesticides, *herbicides,* and other toxic chemicals to control pests *and undesirable plants,* and institutes the use of alternatives, recognizing that children are the population most susceptible to toxins; and be it further
Resolved, That the appropriate standing committee report back to the 75th General Convention regarding the ongoing effectiveness of this work.

Deputy Boalye of the Youth Presence moved an amendment.

Proposed Amendment:
Delete "phases out" and add "works to eliminate" and after "undesirable plants" add "cleaning products that contain toxic chemicals."

Deputy Ferrell of North Carolina moved to terminate debate on the amendment and on the main motion.

The President accepted the motion to terminate debate on the Boalye amendment only.

Motion carried
Debate terminated

A vote was taken on the Boalye amendment.

Motion defeated
Amendment defeated

Deputy Lyon of Milwaukee moved an amendment.

Proposed Amendment:
Add the word "unsafe" before the words: "pesticides, herbicides".

Deputy Hart of Pennsylvania moved to terminate debate on the Lyon amendment and on the main motion.

The President closed debate and called for a vote on the Lyon amendment.

Motion carried
Amendment adopted

A vote was taken on Resolution C026 as amended.

Motion carried
Resolution adopted with amendment
(Communicated to the House of Bishops in HD Message #143)

Committees and Commissions

The House of Deputies Committee on Committees and Commissions presented its Report #2 on Resolution B026 (Criminal Justice Committee) and moved adoption with amendment.

Original Text of Resolution:

(B026)

Resolved, the House of Bishops concurring, That the 74th General Convention direct that, commencing with the triennium beginning in 2004, the Joint Committee on Criminal Justice be designated a Committee of the Executive Council called for the purpose of fulfilling a revised mandate, convening two meetings of the Committee per year to implement the policy of the Committee, and accomplishing the work defined in the revised mandate. This work consists of the following tasks:

Task 1—The establishing of a network of individuals and organizations involved in criminal justice that can assist the committee in accomplishing its purpose of achieving just reform; the work to be accomplished by Committee Members and the Church Center Officer for Criminal Justice Reform; $5,000 to be allocated for this work.

Task 2—The preparing of an educational and consciousness-raising program to be presented to the Church; the work to be accomplished by a sub-committee convened by the Church Center Officer for Criminal Justice Reform; $15,000 to be allocated for this work.

Task 3—The gathering and availability of a resource inventory of successful criminal justice programs dealing with advocacy, leadership, and program delivery; the work to be accomplished by Committee Members and the Church Center Officer for Criminal Justice Reform, and to be published as a web resource by the Communication Department of the Church Center; $3,000 to be allocated for this work.

Task 4—CCJI recognizes the need for development of worship materials specific to this ministry, and will undertake this work, which will be developed by Committee Members, the Church Center Officer for Criminal Justice Reform, and the Church Center Liturgical Officer as liaison to the Standing Commission of Liturgy and Music; and will be published in the forthcoming Book of Occasional Services, as well as being made widely available to both Episcopal and Ecumenical users via the web; $15,000 to be allocated for this work. A further $24,000 to be allocated for meetings, making a total of $62,000 that the General Convention request the Joint Standing Committee on Program, Budget, and Finance to consider for the full implementation of this resolution.

Committee Amendment:
Resolved, the House of Bishops concurring, That the 74th General Convention ~~recommend~~ direct that, commencing with the triennium beginning in 2004, the Joint Committee on Criminal Justice be *established as* ~~designated~~ a Committee of the Executive Council called for the purpose of fulfilling a revised mandate, convening two meetings of the Committee per year to implement the policy of the Committee, and accomplishing the work defined in the revised mandate. This work consists of the following tasks:

- Task 1—The establishing of a network of individuals and organizations involved in criminal justice that can assist the committee in accomplishing its purpose of achieving just reform; the work to be accomplished by Committee Members and the Church Center Officer for Criminal Justice Reform; $5,000 to be allocated for this work.
- Task 2—The preparing of an educational and consciousness-raising program to be presented to the Church; the work to be accomplished by a sub-committee convened by the Church Center Officer for Criminal Justice Reform; $15,000 to be allocated for this work.
- Task 3—The gathering and availability of a resource inventory of successful criminal justice programs dealing with advocacy, leadership, and program delivery; the work to be accomplished by Committee Members and the Church Center Officer for Criminal Justice Reform, and to be published as a web resource by the Communication Department of the Church Center; $3,000 to be allocated for this work.
- Task 4—CCJI recognizes the need for development of worship materials specific to this ministry, and will undertake this work, which will be developed by Committee Members, the Church Center Officer for Criminal Justice Reform, and the Church Center Liturgical Officer as liaison to the Standing Commission of Liturgy and Music; and will be published in the forthcoming Book of Occasional Services, as well as being made widely available to both Episcopal and Ecumenical users via the web; $15,000 to be allocated for this work. A further $24,000 to be allocated for meetings, making a total of $62,000 that the General Convention request the Joint Standing Committee on Program, Budget, and Finance to consider for the full implementation of this resolution.

Motion carried
Resolution adopted with amendment
(Communicated to the House of Bishops in HD Message #144)

National and International Concerns
The House of Deputies Committee on National and International Concerns resumed presentation of its Report #14 on Resolution A033 (Just and Unjust Wars) and moved adoption with amendment.

Text of Resolution with Papile Amendment:
(A033)

Resolved, the House of Bishops concurring, That the 74th General Convention, ~~recalling the longstanding Episcopal Church view, originally adopted by the 1930 Lambeth Conference and by the 1931 General Convention, that "war as a method of settling international disputes is incompatible with the teaching and example of our Lord Jesus Christ,"~~ call upon all members of The Episcopal Church, in discussions about war and especially the strategy of preemptive strikes, to seriously consider and utilize the Just War criteria developed over the centuries and generally expressed as follows:

First, whether lethal force may be used is governed by the following criteria:

Just cause: Force may be used only to correct a grave, public evil, i.e., aggression or massive violation of the basic rights of whole populations.

Comparative justice: While there may be rights and wrongs on all sides of a conflict, to override the presumption against the use of force, the injustice suffered by one part must significantly outweigh that suffered by the other.

Legitimate authority: Only duly constituted public authorities may use deadly force or wage war.

Right intention: Force may be used only in a truly just cause and solely for that purpose.

Probability of success: Arms may not be used in a futile cause or in a case where disproportionate measures are required to achieve success.

Proportionality: The overall destruction expected from the use of force must be outweighed by the good to be achieved.

Last resort: Force may be used only after all peaceful alternatives have been seriously tried and exhausted.

These criteria taken as a whole must be satisfied in order to override the strong presumption against the use of force. Second, the just war tradition seeks also to curb the violence of war through restraint on armed combat between the contending parties by imposing the following moral standards for the conduct of armed conflict:

Noncombatant immunity: Civilians may not be the objects of direct attack, and military personnel must take due care to avoid and minimize indirect harm to civilians.

Proportionality: In the conduct of hostilities, efforts must be made to attain military objectives with no more force than is militarily necessary and to avoid disproportionate collateral damage to civilian life and property.

Right intention: Even in the midst of conflict, the aim of political and military leaders must be peace with justice, so that acts of vengeance and indiscriminate violence, whether by individuals, military units or governments, are forbidden; and be it further

Resolved, That when legitimate civilian authority determines that war is justified, members of the Episcopal Church recall our Lord's teaching to love our enemies, counsel that participation in or refusal to participate in any war is a discernment process requiring deep reflection and prayer with humility, and acknowledge that one participates in war with great reluctance, always seeking God's mercy and

forgiveness; and be it further
Resolved, That the 74th General Convention, recalling the longstanding Episcopal Church view, originally adopted by the 1930 Lambeth Conference and by the 1931 General Convention, that "war as a method of settling international disputes is incompatible with the teaching and example of our Lord Jesus Christ," urge dioceses and congregations to study and better understand just war theory and pacifism as they apply to the situation of the United States in responding to contemporary international conflicts.

Motion carried
Resolution adopted with amendment
(Communicated to the House of Bishops in HD Message #145)

Social and Urban Affairs

The House of Deputies Committee on Social and Urban Affairs resumed presenation of its Report #19 on Resolution C003 (In Support of Representative John Conyers' H.R. 40) and moved adoption with amendment.

The Chair of the Committee on Social and Urban Affairs asked that the word "congressmen" be corrected to "congressional representatives." The President accepted this as a grammatical correction.

Deputy Renton moved to terminate debate.

Motion carried
Debate terminated

A vote was taken on Resolution C003.

Motion defeated
Resolution rejected
(Communicated to the House of Bishops in HD Message #146)

Ballot #3 for Executive Council

Election Ballot #3 was taken for members of Executive Council, three lay persons and two clergy persons for six-year terms.

Ballot #3 taken

Personal Privilege

Deputy Ferguson of the Youth Presence stated that the matter of Resolution C003, slavery reparations, just defeated by the House, is a matter of deep concern to many members of the House.

Announcements

The Secretary read the announcements.

Midday Prayers

The President called upon the Chaplain for midday prayers.

Personal Privilege

Deputy Gardner of Newark advised the President that the sirens heard by the House during prayers were for the City of Minneapolis's observance of a minute of silence at 1:00 p.m. for the Hiroshima memorial and asked that the House might also observe a minute of silence.

The President asked the House to stand for a moment of silence.

RECESS

The President recessed the House at 1:10 p.m. to reconvene at 2:30 p.m. for the Joint Session on Program, Budget and Finance.

Joint Session for the Presentation by the Joint Standing Committee on Program, Budget and Finance

The President called the Joint Session to order at 2:34 p.m. The President welcomed the House of Bishops to the House of Deputies.

The Presiding Bishop addressed the Joint Session and spoke to the priorities set by the Joint Standing Committee on Program, Budget and Finance. All funding requests could be fulfilled if all dioceses met their apportionments.

Deputy Anderson of Michigan introduced the Joint Standing Committee on Program, Budget and Finance, who presented their Report.

RECESS

The President adjourned the Joint Session at 3:00 p.m. and recessed the House of Deputies until 3:25 p.m.

AFTERNOON SESSION

Reconvene

The President called the House to order at 3:27 p.m.

Prayers

The President called upon the Chaplain for prayers.

Certification of Deputies

The House of Deputies Committee on Credentials presented its Report #13, for the afternoon session of the Eighth Legislative Day. There was 1 new deputy certified from the Diocese of Venezuela. There were 418 clerical deputies and 420 lay deputies certified and seated, and a total count of the House of 438. There were 67 changes at this session, as follows:

Diocese	Alternate replacing	Deputy being replaced
Alabama	Tom Poynor	Cecil Williamson
Alabama	Sherry Travis	Robert Childers
Arkansas	Joyce Hardy	Lowell Grisham

Atlanta	E. Claiborne Jones	G. Porter Taylor
California	Warren Wong	Kay Bishop
Central Gulf Coast	Peter Wilson	Robert McMillan
Central Pennsylvania	Mark Scheneman	John Hoover
Chicago	Richard Peete	Tessa Craib-Cox
Churches in Europe	Charles Trueheart	Helena Mbele-Mbong
Colorado	Robert Davidson	Donald Armstrong
Colorado	S. Brooks Keith	Ephraim Radner
Connecticut	Eugene Lattimer	John Sutton
Connecticut	Ellen Tillotson	Mark Santucci
Dallas	James Biegler	David Roseberry
Delaware	Thomas Kerr	Lloyd Casson
East Carolina	Pamela Stringer	Ronald Abrams
East Tennessee	Ed Cahill	Alice Clayton
Eastern Oregon	Susan Powers	Jean Gardner
Idaho	Doug Yarbrough	Brian Baker
Lexington	David Davidson	John Brantley
Lexington	Anisa Cottrell-Willis	Robert Sessum
Louisiana	Kathleen Turner	Harriet Murrell
Louisiana	Ralph Howe	Rex Perry
Maine	Susan Partridge	Cyndy Anderson
Maine	Anne Stanley	Paige Blair
Maryland	Alma Bell	Christine Kinard
Massachusetts	Byron Rushing	Rebecca Alden
Milwaukee	Maurine Lewis	Thomas Winslow
Milwaukee	Ralph Modjeska	Wendy Sopkovich
Minnesota	Michael Smith	Grant Abbott
Minnesota	Philip McNairy	Howard Anderson
Mississippi	Suanna Smith	Michael Chaney
Mississippi	Shannon Johnston	Ruth Black
Mississippi	David Johnson	Zabron Davis
New Hampshire	Margaret Faulk	Debra Harris
New Hampshire	William Exner	Gene Robinson
New Hampshire	Debra Ogin	Susan Langle
New York	James Barba	Fred Wibiralske
New York	Tobias Haller	Jean Campbell
Northern California	Donald Brown	Eric Duff
Olympia	Dorsey McConnell	Robert Christie
Oregon	Fred Terrill	Barbara Ross
Oregon	Linda Potter	James Boston
Pittsburgh	Joseph Sarria	Joan Malley
Puerto Rico	Wilner Millien	Jose Emilio Figueroa
Rhode Island	Harry Sacchetti	Carol Bennett

Rochester	Sarah Collins	Josephine Dewey
San Joaquin	Suzette Peters	Debra Cavanagh
Southern Virginia	Paul Hogg	David Teschner
Southern Virginia	Charles Pfeifer	James Bradberry
Southwest Florida	John Hiers	Hayden Crawford
Southwestern Virginia	Clare Fischer-Davies	Paul Fuller
Texas	Mary MacGregor	James Cunningham
Upper South Carolina	Jimmy Hartley	Angela Daniel
Virginia	Jeffrey Cerar	Charles Alley
Virginia	Jack Burtch	Deborah Robayo
Virginia	Victoria Heard	Jim Papile
Washington	Salli Hartman	Paul Cooney
West Texas	John Brooke	Alice Fischer
West Texas	Robert Browning	Sylvia Maddox
Western Louisiana	Reece Middleton	Carolyn Ledet
Western Massachusetts	Heidi Frantz-Dale	Sarah Shofstall
Western Michigan	Kathleen Kingslight	C. Mark Rutenbar
Western Michigan	Barbara Coulter	William Fleener
Western New York	Particia Zebrowski	Lillian Davis-Wilson
Western North Carolina	Lauch Magruder	Lawrence Thompson

Election of Executive Council—Ballot #3

The President read the results of Election Ballot #3 for Executive Council. Newly-elected members of Executive Council:

In the Lay Order for six-year terms:
  Dorothy J. Fuller of El Camino Real
  Josephine H. Hicks of North Carolina
  Sandra Ferguson McPhee of Chicago

In the Clergy Order for six-year terms:
  Titus Presler of Texas
  Edward Rodman of Massachusetts

Messages from the House of Bishops

The Secretary announced that the following messages had been received from the House of Bishops:

HB Message #177:: A142 (Admit Diocese of Venezuela) Concurred.

Consent Calendar

Ecumenical Relations

The House of Deputies Committee on Ecumenical Relations presented its Report #9 on Resolution A089 ("Open Communion") and moved concurrence with referral to the Standing Commission on Ecumenical Relations.

Motion carried
Resolution referred to a Standing Commission
(Communicated to the House of Bishops in HD Message #147)

[Note: The final status of Resolution A089 is non-concurrence because the House of Bishops and the House of Deputies did not move the same action for the legislation. *Ed.*]

Nominations and Elections

The House of Deputies Committee on Nominations and Elections presented its Report #1 on General Board of Examining Chaplains and moved concurrence.

Original Text of Resolution:

Resolved, the House of Bishops having elected the following to the General Board of Examining Chaplains, the House of Deputies confirms the same pursuant to Title III, Canon 31, Section 1:

One Bishop (three-year term):
  The Rt. Rev. Philip M. Duncan, Central Gulf Coast
Two Bishops (six-year terms):
  The Rt. Rev. Barry R. Howe, West Missouri
  The Rt. Rev. Katharine Jefferts Schori, Nevada
Three Lay Persons (six-year terms):
  Mary Chilton Callaway, New York
  Josephine R. Giannini, Indianapolis
  Leonard Wilkie Johnson, California
Three Priests (six-year terms):
  The Rev. Mark T. Crawford, Texas
  The Rev. Mary Catherine Miller Sulerud, Washington
  The Rev. Stephen E. Moore, Olympia
Three Faculty (six-year terms):
  The Rev. Susan M. Dolan-Henderson, ETSS
  The Rev. Robert Davis Hughes, Sewanee
  The Rev. Frederick W. Schmidt, Perkins

Motion carried
Elections confirmed
(Communicated to the House of Bishops in HD Message #148)

(End of Consent Calendar)

Election of the General Theological Seminary Board of Trustees
Election Ballot #1 was taken for the General Theological Seminary Board of Trustees, two persons in the Lay Order and two persons in the Clergy Order for three-year terms.

Ballot #1 taken

Personal Privilege
Deputy Chew of Arizona, the Chair of the Joint Standing Committee on Nominations, spoke on the small number of nominees in recent years. He appealed to the House to submit nominees in summer 2004 when nominations begin for the next triennium.

Dispatch of Business
The Chair of the House of Deputies Committee on Dispatch of Business gave the order of business for the afternoon.

National and International Concerns
The House of Deputies Committee on National and International Concerns presented its Report #21 on Resolution C024 (Nonviolent United States Foreign Policy) and moved adoption.

Original Text of Resolution:
(C024)
Resolved, the House of Bishops concurring, That the 74th General Convention support the World Council of Churches' Decade to Overcome Violence and its work with other faith communities in this nation and around the world, to persuade governments to embrace less violent foreign policies, to encourage individuals and parishes to pray for peace and to take political action to oppose foreign policies that are grounded in violence; and be it further
Resolved, That the 74th General Convention call on our nation to reconsider fundamentally the foreign policy it has thus far advanced, calling upon our leaders to employ diplomacy rather than warfare, and specifically upon President Bush to cease aggression against other countries.

Deputy Downie of Eastern Michigan moved an amendment.

Proposed Amendment:
In the last resolve clause, delete "and specifically upon President Bush to cease aggression against other countries."

Motion carried
Amendment adopted

Deputy Cravens of Springfield moved to terminate debate.

Motion carried
Debate terminated

A vote was taken on Resolution C024 as amended.

Motion carried
Resolution adopted with amendment
(Communicated to the House of Bishops in HD Message #149)

The House of Deputies Committee on National and International Concerns presented its Report #26 on Resolution D008 (Demolition of Palestinian Homes) and moved adoption with amendment.

Original Text of Resolution:
(D008)
Resolved, the House of Bishops concurring, That the 74th General Convention recognize that Israeli demolition of Palestinian homes in the Gaza Strip and the Occupied Territories of the West Bank and East Jerusalem is illegal under international law and therefore calls upon the U.S. government to urge the State of Israel to end its policy of the demolition of Palestinian homes.

Committee Amendment:
Resolved, the House of Bishops concurring, That the 74th General Convention recognize that Israeli demolition of Palestinian homes in the Gaza Strip and the Occupied Territories of the West Bank and East Jerusalem is illegal under international law *and is a deterrent to the peace process,* and therefore call upon *the President and* the U.S. government to urge the State of Israel to end its policy of the demolition of Palestinian homes.

Deputy Simons of Pittsburgh moved to terminate debate.

Motion carried
Debate terminated

A vote was taken on Resolution D008 as amended.

Motion carried
Resolution adopted with amendment
(Communicated to the House of Bishops in HD Message #150)

Social and Urban Affairs
The House of Deputies Committee on Social and Urban Affairs presented its Report #26 on Resolution D061 (Jubilee Ministry Funding) and moved adoption.

Original Text of Resolution:
(D061)
Resolved, the House of Bishops concurring, That a Jubilee Ministries fund be established in order to enable the more than 600 Jubilee Centers to have the opportunity to apply for grant monies to further their ministries among the poor

and oppressed peoples of their neighborhoods; and be it further
Resolved, That the General Convention request the Joint Standing Committee on Program, Budget and Finance to consider a budget allocation of $1,000,000 for implementation of this resolution.

Deputy Curtis of Newark moved an amendment.

Proposed Amendment:
In the final resolve clause make these changes: insert "accept" in the place of "request," delete "to consider a" and "for implementation of this resolution." Insert "$150,000" in the place of "$1,000,000." At the end of the clause, add "and that Jubilee Ministry Centers will receive first funding priority of Episcopal Relief Development's Domestic Grant allocation of $600,000 and that ERD report to the 75th General Convention a report on grants given to Jubilee Ministry Centers."

Deputy Seitz of West Virginia moved to terminate debate on the amendment and the main motion.

The President asked for the vote only on the motion to terminate debate on the amendment.

Motion carried
Debate terminated

A vote was taken on the Curtis amendment.

Motion carried
Amendment adopted

Deputy Hart of Pennsylvania moved to terminate debate.

Motion carried
Debate terminated

A vote was taken on Resolution D061 as amended.

Motion carried
Resolution adopted with amendment
(Communicated to the House of Bishops in HD Message #151)

The House of Deputies Committee on Social and Urban Affairs presented its Report #27 on Resolution D025 (Continuation of Efforts to End Racism) and moved adoption with amendment.

Original Text of Resolution:
(D025)
Resolved, the House of Bishops concurring, That the 74th General Convention call upon the Presiding Bishop and the Executive Council, working through its Anti-Racism Committee, to convene a series of conversations among various groups of people of color, to prepare a report to the 75th Convention on recommending substantive, systemic changes in the current norms of behavior and practice within The Episcopal Church that would enhance its inclusivity and authentically acknowledge and celebrate its diversity; and be it further
Resolved, That the Presiding Bishop and the Executive Council empower

appropriate staff persons to work closely with the Churches Uniting in Christ to fashion a mutually-agreed-upon anti-racism training modality that would permit coherent ecumenical dialogue on overcoming the sin of racism as an important step in furthering the quest for Christian unity.

Committee Amendment:
Resolved, the House of Bishops concurring, That the 74th General Convention call upon the Presiding Bishop and the Executive Council, working through its Anti-Racism *Advisory* Committee, to convene a series of conversations among various groups of people of color *of all generations,* to prepare a report to the 75th Convention on recommending substantive, systemic changes in the current norms of behavior and practice within The Episcopal Church that would enhance its inclusivity and authentically acknowledge and celebrate its diversity; and be it further
Resolved, That the Presiding Bishop and the Executive Council empower appropriate staff persons to work closely with the Churches Uniting in Christ *and other interreligious partners* to fashion a mutually-agreed-upon anti-racism training modality that would permit coherent ecumenical dialogue on overcoming the sin of racism as an important step in furthering the quest for Christian unity.

Motion carried
Resolution adopted with amendment
(Communicated to the House of Bishops in HD Message #152)

The House of Deputies Committee on Social and Urban Affairs presented its Report #28 on Resolution A128 (Ministering to "At Risk" Youth) and moved adoption of a substitute.

Original Text of Resolution:
(A128)
Resolved, the House of Bishops concurring, That the 74th General Convention of The Episcopal Church recognize the value of young people and the problem of violence that pervades our society making all of our youth "at risk" youth; and be it further
Resolved, That the 74th General Convention of The Episcopal Church reaffirm the commitment of the Church to support the development of caring, competent, and loving young people; encourage dioceses and churches to offer ways to manage anger and teach the value of forgiveness to our young people; and recommend to dioceses and churches development of partnerships with community-based agencies, institutions, and schools to build an infrastructure that will permit outreach to "at risk" youth in every community.

Committee Substitute:
Resolved, the House of Bishops concurring, That the 74th General Convention of The Episcopal Church affirm that all young people are created in the image of God and possess potential to love and serve God. Further, that the Convention recognize that many aspects of our culture work to obscure the image of God in

young people and render all young people "Youth At Risk"; and be it further
Resolved, That the Church reaffirm its commitment to support the development of caring, competent, faithful, and loving young people and provide sufficient human and financial resources in the Office of Youth Ministries to challenge, inspire, and support dioceses and parishes in their work with young people; and be it further
Resolved, That the 74th General Convention commend the following programs and educational possibilities for local implementation:

- Literacy programs, including reading, cultural, social, spiritual, and computer literacy
- Mentoring programs
- Conflict resolution and anger management programs, especially "From Violence to Wholeness" produced by the Episcopal Peace Fellowship
- Religious education programs and curricula that recognize the socio-economic, ethnic, racial, linguistic, and cultural diversity of our church
- After school programs
- Creation and maintenance of Episcopal schools that provide access to all youth
- Development of Episcopal camps to provide access to all youth

Deputy Laird of Kentucky moved to amend the substitute resolution.

Proposed Amendment:
In the first resolve clause, delete the word "young" in the first sentence.

Motion defeated
Amendment defeated

Deputy Glasspool of Maryland moved to terminate debate.

Deputy Lane of Southwestern Virginia challenged the voice vote on the amendment. An electronic vote was taken and the rejection was sustained.

Chair's ruling sustained

The President called for a vote on the termination of debate.

Motion carried
Debate terminated

Deputy Engels of Northern Michigan inquired if the resolution should be considered, since "From Violence to Wholeness," mentioned in lines 24–25, has not been made available to the House.

The Chair of the House of Deputies Committee on Social and Urban Affairs stated that the reference to "From Violence to Wholeness" could be deleted from the resolution. There being no objections, it was so ordered.

Deputy Snow of Alaska moved to terminate debate.

Motion carried
Debate terminated

A vote was taken on substitute Resolution A128 as amended.

Motion carried
Substitute resolution adopted with amendment
(Communicated to the House of Bishops in HD Message #153)

Ministry

The House of Deputies Committee on Ministry presented its Report #5 on Resolution D043 (Elimination of Barriers) and moved adoption with amendment.

Original Text of Resolution:
(D043)
Resolved, the House of Bishops concurring, That the 74th General Convention of The Episcopal Church recognize and celebrate the blessings God has given the Church through the gifts of ordained persons of color and ordained women, while acknowledging that in many places the Church does not yet systematically recruit, train, and deploy such clergy; and be it further
Resolved, That each diocese shall assess the extent to which it has recruited, trained, and deployed women and persons of color for ordained ministries and report these data to the Office of the Assistant to the Presiding Bishop for Program by March 31, 2005; and be it further
Resolved, That each congregation and diocese shall complete by January 2006 a process of self-assessment to identify systemic barriers in its recruitment, training, and deployment of clergy of color and ordained women; and be it further
Resolved, That the Anti-Racism Desk and the Women's Desk at the Church Center shall assist dioceses and congregations by identifying available, appropriate self-assessment tools and other resources which could help the Church move toward elimination of such barriers to more inclusive ordination processes.

Committee Amendment:
Resolved, the House of Bishops concurring, That the 74th General Convention of The Episcopal Church recognize and celebrate the blessings God has given the Church through the gifts of ordained persons of color and ordained women, while acknowledging that in many places the Church does not yet systematically recruit, train, and deploy such clergy; and be it further
Resolved, That each diocese shall assess the extent to which it has recruited, trained, and deployed women and persons of color for ordained ministries and report these data to the Office of the Assistant to the Presiding Bishop for Program by March 31, 2005; and be it further
Resolved, That each congregation and diocese shall complete by January 2006 a process of self-assessment to identify systemic barriers in its recruitment, training, and deployment of clergy of color and ordained women; and be it further
Resolved, That the ~~Anti-Racism Desk~~ *Peace and Justice Ministries* and the Women's Desk at the Church Center shall assist dioceses and congregations by identifying available, appropriate self-assessment tools and other resources which could help the Church move toward elimination of such barriers to more inclusive ordination processes.

Motion carried
Resolution adopted with amendment
(Communicated to the House of Bishops in HD Message #154)

MINNEAPOLIS MEETING　　　　　　　　HOUSE OF DEPUTIES

The House of Deputies Committee on Ministry presented its Report #6 on Resolution A032 (Youth Study) and moved adoption with amendment.

Original Text of Resolution:
(A032)
Resolved, the House of Bishops concurring, That the 74th General Convention direct the Committee on the Status of Women, in cooperation with the 20/20 Committee and using a modified version of the 21st Century Survey, to study the attitudes, participation, and worship preferences of Episcopalians ages 15–30; and be it further
Resolved, That $10,000 for the survey and $1,500 for printing be allocated from the program budget for this work.

Committee Amendment:
Resolved, the House of Bishops concurring, That the 74th General Convention direct the Committee on the Status of Women, in cooperation with the 20/20 Committee and using a modified version of the 21st Century Survey, to study the attitudes, participation, and worship preferences of Episcopalians ages 15–30, *assuring that the survey participants reflect the multicultural diversity of the Church,* and be it further
Resolved, That *the General Convention request the Joint Standing Committee on Program, Budget and Finance to consider* $10,000 for the survey and $1,500 for printing be allocated from the program budget for this work.

Motion carried
Resolution adopted with amendment
(Communicated to the House of Bishops in HD Message #155)

Communications
The House of Deputies Committee on Communications presented its Report #10 on Resolution D057 (Use of Technology: General Convention) and moved adoption with amendment.

Original Text of Resolution:
(D057)
Resolved, the House of Bishops concurring, That the 74th General Convention express its gratitude to the Reverend Rosemari Sullivan, Secretary of the General Convention, and to her staff, for the use of technology to expedite and ease the work of this convention. In particular we are thankful for the continued refinement of the electronic voting system, and for the use of the internet and computers in the processing and distribution of resolutions and the reporting of the action taken on the multitude of resolutions that come before the Convention; and be it further
Resolved, That the 74th General Convention commend President George Werner on the creation of a task force on emerging technologies that explored and outlined avenues for expanded use of electronic technologies during the last triennium; and

be it further

Resolved, That the Convention recommend the further development of such technologies for the 2006 General Convention that would facilitate the work of the convention, particularly in the areas of the electronic distribution of materials, electronic voting, electronic and real-time revisions of legislation, and others. The development of these technologies will be motivated and guided by a desire to speed the work of convention, reduce costs, and the consumption of paper, and enhance the effective communication of the work of succeeding conventions.

Committee Amendment:

Resolved, the House of Bishops concurring, That the 74th General Convention express its gratitude to the Reverend Rosemari Sullivan, Secretary of the General Convention, and to her staff, for the use of technology to expedite and ease the work of this convention. In particular we are thankful for the continued refinement of the electronic voting system, and for the use of the internet and computers in the processing and distribution of resolutions and the reporting of the action taken on the multitude of resolutions that come before the Convention; and be it further

Resolved, That the 74th General Convention commend ~~President~~ *the Very Reverend* George Werner, *President of the House of Deputies* on the creation of a task force on emerging technologies that explored and outlined avenues for expanded use of electronic technologies during the last triennium; and be it further

Resolved, That the Convention recommend the further development of such technologies for the 2006 General Convention that would facilitate the work of the convention, particularly in the areas of the electronic distribution of materials, electronic voting, electronic and real-time revisions of legislation, and others. The development of these technologies will be motivated and guided by a desire to speed the work of convention, reduce costs, and the consumption of paper, and enhance the effective communication of the work of succeeding conventions; and be it further

Resolved, That an appropriate interim body investigate whether and how we might use technology to facilitate actions of General Convention between triennial sessions.

Motion carried
Resolution adopted with amendment
(Communicated to the House of Bishops in HD Message #156)

Privilege and Courtesy

The House of Deputies Committee on Privilege and Courtesy presented its Report #3 on Resolution D080 (Alan Blanchard) and moved adoption of a substitute.

Original Text of Resolution:

(D080)
Resolved, the House of Bishops concurring, That the 74th Convention of The Episcopal Church wishes to give thanks to God and to express our deep appreciation for the ministry of Alan Blanchard, President and CEO of the Church Pension Fund, on the eve of his retirement.

Final Text of Resolution:
Whereas, Alan F. Blanchard has faithfully and ably served the Church Pension Fund as President and Chief Executive Officer since 1991; and

Whereas, under his leadership the Church Pension Group has achieved excellence, dynamism, and vibrancy; and

Whereas, he has championed the CREDO Project (Clergy Reflection, Education, Discernment Opportunity), is a major wellness/development experience; and

Whereas, his accessibility, personal presence, and organizational skills have provided information, advice, and support to all who participate in and benefit from the Church Pension Fund; now therefore be it

Resolved, That the 74th General Convention render thanks to Alan F. Blanchard on the eve of his retirement for his faithful service and wish him a long and enjoyable life.

Motion carried
Substitute resolution adopted
(Communicated to the House of Bishops in HD Message #157)

Special Order of Business
The House of Deputies Committee of Dispatch of Business in its Report #18 moved to adopt a Special Order of Business for Debate on the Report of the Joint Standing Committee on Program, Budget, and Finance:

Resolved, That this House set a Special Order of Business for the purpose of considering and taking action with respect to the Report of the Joint Standing Committee on Program, Budget and Finance, to be implemented immediately following the Consent Calendar on the Ninth Legislative Day, Thursday, August 7, 2003; and be it further

Resolved, That in the consideration of the report of the Joint Standing Committee on Program, Budget and Finance, the following rules of debate shall be followed:
1. The Committee Chair shall have ten minutes to speak with respect to the report and ten minutes to respond to questions for information or clarification;
2. The entire debate of the report thereafter shall be limited to 45 minutes;
3. The sections of the report titled, respectively, "Revenues" and "Expenses" shall each be presented, debated and voted separately, and each paragraph, such as "Diocesan Commitments" under the section on Revenues or "Mission Program" under the section on Expenses, of each section shall be separately presented and debated sequentially in the order listed in the report. No more than 20 minutes shall be allotted for discussion and debate of the section on Revenues, with the time remaining of the 45 minutes for debate available for discussion and debate of the section on Expenses;
4. Each speaker shall be limited to two minutes and no speaker shall speak more than once on the same question;
5. Only motions to amend the paragraph of the section under debate shall be

entertained until debate on all paragraphs of the section under debate have been completed or until no member of the House desires to speak to the section, whichever shall first occur;
6. A motion to terminate debate on an amendment may not include termination of debate on the main motion;
7. Any amendment offered that would increase the proposed totals of either section of the budget must specify balancing adjustments of equal amount or the source of additional funds outside the budget;
8. No motion to lay on the table or otherwise terminate debate on a section of the report shall be entertained until the conclusion of the final discussion and debate on all paragraphs of the section under debate have been completed or until no member of the House desires to speak to the section, whichever shall first occur;
9. The provisions of this Special Order may only be amended by two-thirds vote of the House.

Motion carried
Special Order adopted
(Communicated to the House of Bishops in HD Message #158)

Evangelism

The House of Deputies Committee on Evangelism presented its Report #9 on Resolution A075 (Diocese Mission Perspective) and moved adoption with amendment.

Original Text of Resolution:

(A075)
Resolved, the House of Bishops concurring, That every diocese in The Episcopal Church be strongly encouraged to:
    foster a missional perspective or culture;
    foster a culture of partnering with others (congregations, denominations, etc.) for mission and ministry;
    equip people to facilitate congregational self-study;
    foster a culture in which transformation, death, and resurrection are the normal perspective on congregational life.

Committee Amendment:

Resolved, the House of Bishops concurring, That every diocese in The Episcopal Church be ~~strongly encouraged~~ *charged* to:
    foster a missional perspective or culture;
    foster a culture of partnering with others (congregations, denominations, etc.) for mission and ministry;
    equip people to facilitate congregational self-study *and strategic planning, including the impact of the congregation's life-cycle in its transformation for mission;*
    ~~foster a culture in which transformation, death, and resurrection are the normal perspective on congregational life.~~ *and that bishops organize visitations around these principles.*

Motion carried
Resolution adopted with amendment
(Communicated to the House of Bishops in HD Message #159)

The House of Deputies Committee on Evangelism presented its Report #10 on Resolution A074 (Congregational Annual Study) and moved adoption with amendment.

Original Text of Resolution:
(A074)
Resolved, the House of Bishops concurring, That every congregation of The Episcopal Church be strongly encouraged to engage in annual (regular) study and review of its common life.

Committee Amendment:
Resolved, the House of Bishops concurring, That every congregation of The Episcopal Church ~~be strongly encouraged to~~ engage in annual (regular) study and review of its common life, *asking the following questions:*
    Who are we? Who are we called to be?
    Who is our neighbor? Are we meeting and learning about our neighbor?
    What is our mission in this place? What ought it to be?
    How are lives and communities being transformed?
    How are people being equipped for Christ's ministry of reconciliation?
    How is this community and congregation different from a year ago? Five years ago? Ten years ago?
    How is leadership recognized, affirmed, and shared here?

Motion carried
Resolution adopted with amendment
(Communicated to the House of Bishops in HD Message #160)

Miscellaneous Resolutions
The House of Deputies Committee on Miscellaneous Resolutions presented its Report #14 on Resolution C052 (Transfer of Diocesan Territories) and moved adoption.

Original Text of Resolution:
(C052)
Resolved, the House of Bishops concurring, That the request of the Diocese of Wyoming and the Diocese of Idaho acting through their regularly convened conventions, and upon the approvals and consents of the respective Ecclesiastical authorities and of the standing committees of both dioceses that the territory generally described as the parish of Alta, Wyoming, and more particularly described as that portion of Teton County, Wyoming, lying west and north of the summit of the Teton Mountain Range, including the unincorporated community of Alta, be

transferred from the Diocese of Wyoming to the Diocese of Idaho pursuant to Article V, Section 6 of the Constitution of The Protestant Episcopal Church.

Motion carried
Resolution adopted
(Communicated to the House of Bishops in HD Message #161)

Canons

The House of Deputies Committee on Canons presented its Report #11 on Resolution D072 (Amendment Canon III.22.3(a)) and moved adoption with amendment.
[See Day 6 for Original Text of Resolution, pg 479. *Ed.*]

Committee Amendment:
(D072)
Resolved, the House of Bishops concurring, That Canon III.22.3(a) be amended to read in part as follows:
When a Diocese desires the ordination of a Bishop-elect, if the date of election occurs within ~~120 days~~ three months before a meeting of the General Convention, ~~provided, however, that no such election shall be held less than 30 days prior to the meeting of the General Convention~~, the Standing Committee of the Diocese shall, by its President, or by some person or persons specially appointed, forward to the Secretary of the House of Deputies evidence of the election of the Bishop-elect by the Convention of the Diocese, together with evidence that the Bishop-elect has been duly ordered Deacon and Priest, evidence of acceptance of election, and a testimonial signed by a constitutional majority of the Convention, and a summary of biographical information relating to the Bishop-elect.
And be it further
Resolved, That Canon II.22.1 be amended by adding the following subsection:
(f) No diocese shall elect a Bishop within thirty days before a meeting of the General Convention.

Motion carried
Resolution adopted with amendment
(Communicated to the House of Bishops in HD Message #162)

The House of Deputies Committee on Canons resumed its presention on Resolution A144 (Amend Canon I.1.14) on HB Message #21 in its Report #13 and moved concurrence with amendment.

Committee Amendment:
Resolved, the House of Bishops concurring, That Canon I.1.14 be amended to read as follows:

(a)   At each meeting of the General Convention the Joint Standing Committee on Planning and Arrangements shall submit to the

General Convention its recommendations for sites for the meeting of the General Convention to be held as the ~~second~~ *third* succeeding General Convention following the General Convention at which the report is made. In making such recommendations, the Committee shall certify to the Convention the willingness of the Dioceses within which recommended sites are located to have the General Convention meet within their jurisdictions.

(b) From the sites recommended by the Joint Committee, the General Convention shall approve no fewer than three nor more than five sites as possible for such meeting of the General Convention.

(c) From the sites approved by the General Convention, the Joint Committee, with the advice and consent of a majority vote of the following: The Presidents and the Vice-Presidents of both Houses of Convention, the Presidents of the Provinces and the Executive Council, shall determine the site for such General Convention and proceed to make all reasonable and necessary arrangements and commitments for that meeting of the General Convention. ~~The site shall be recommended before the meeting of the General Convention next preceding that Convention.~~ The site and date thus selected shall be deemed to have been appointed by the General Convention, as provided in the Constitution.

~~(d)~~ ~~Subject to the Constitution, the General Convention shall appoint a site at the General Convention next preceding such Convention.~~

~~(e)~~ (d) Upon the final selection of and the arrangements for the site for that General Convention, the Joint Committee shall advise the Secretary of General Convention, who shall communicate the determination to the Dioceses.

~~(f)~~ ~~In the event of a change of circumstances indicating the necessity or advisability of changing the site of a future meeting of the General Convention previously determined by action of the General Convention, the Joint Committee shall investigate and make recommendations to the Presiding Bishop, to the President of the House of Deputies, and to the Executive Council if such Convention is the next succeeding meeting or to the General Convention with respect to any later meeting of the Convention.~~

~~(g)~~ (e) Within such guidelines as may have been established by the General Convention regarding the date and length of future General Conventions, and pursuant to the reasonable and necessary arrangements and commitments with the Dioceses and operators of facilities within the Diocese in which the next General Convention will be held, the Joint Committee shall fix the date and the length of the next succeeding Convention, report the same to the Secretary of the General Convention and include the same in its report to the Convention. In the event of a change of circumstances indicating the necessity or advisability of changing the date or length previously fixed, the Joint Committee shall investigate and make recommendations to the Presiding Bishop and the President of the House of Deputies, who, with the advice and consent of the Executive Council, may fix a different date or length or both.

Motion carried
The House concurred with amendment
(Communicated to the House of Bishops in HD Message #167)

National and International Concerns

The House of Deputies Committee on National and International Concerns presented its Report #29 on Resolution D031 (Culture of Nonviolence) and moved adoption with amendment.

Original Text of Resolution:

(D031)
Resolved, the House of Bishops concurring, That The Episcopal Church develop on national, provincial, and diocesan levels specific plans in the next Triennium for the Church to become a culture of nonviolence which values love, compassion, and justice, and which rejects violence as a means of solving problems; and be it further
Resolved, That curricula in nonviolence awareness and training be promoted for use in dioceses and congregations; and be it further
Resolved, That the results of these plans be compiled and presented to the General Convention 2006.

Committee Amendment:

Resolved, the House of Bishops concurring, That The Episcopal Church develop *specific plans at* ~~on~~ national, provincial, and diocesan levels ~~specific plans~~ in the next triennium for the Church *to live into* ~~become~~ a culture of nonviolence which values love, compassion, and justice, and which rejects violence as a means of solving problems; and be it further
Resolved, That curricula in nonviolence awareness and training be promoted for use in dioceses and congregations; and be it further
Resolved, That the results of these plans be compiled *by the Office of Peace and Justice* and presented to the General Convention 2006.

Motion carried
Resolution adopted with amendment
(Communicated to the House of Bishops in HD Message #163)

The House of Deputies Committee on National and International Concerns presented its Report #30 on Resolution D081 (Israeli Security Wall) and moved adoption with amendment.

Original Text of Resolution:
(D081)
Resolved, the House of Bishops concurring, That the 74th General Convention recognize that the 360 kilometer long Israeli security wall currently under construction and the proposed additional 240 kilometer extension are impediments to the implementation of the performance-based roadmap leading to a final and comprehensive settlement of the Israeli-Palestinian conflict by 2005, as presented in President Bush's speech of 24 June 2002 and welcomed by the EU, Russia and the UN in the 16 July 2002 and 17 September 2002 Quartet Ministerial statements; and be it further
Resolved, That the 74th General Convention convey to President Bush and National Security Advisor Condoleezza Rice our support for their opposition to the construction of this wall.

Committee Amendment:
Resolved, the House of Bishops concurring, That the 74th General Convention recognize that the 360 kilometer long Israeli security wall currently under construction and the proposed additional 240 kilometer extension are impediments to the implementation of the performance-based roadmap leading to a final and comprehensive *negotiated* settlement of the Israeli-Palestinian conflict by 2005, as presented in President Bush's speech of 24 June 2002 and welcomed by the EU, Russia and the UN in the 16 July 2002 and 17 September 2002 Quartet Ministerial statements; and be it further
Resolved, That the 74th General Convention convey to *the* President ~~Bush~~ , *Secretary of State* and National Security Advisor ~~Condoleezza Rice~~ *of the United States* our support for their ~~opposition to~~ *ongoing questioning* of the construction of this wall.

Motion carried
Resolution adopted with amendment
(Communicated to the House of Bishops in HD Message #168)

The House of Deputies Committee on National and International Concerns presented its Report #31 on Resolution D066 (Declaration on Sustainable Development) and moved adoption with amendment.

Original Text of Resolution:
(D066)
Resolved, the House of Bishops concurring, That the 74th General Convention endorse and implement the four resolutions passed by the September 2002 Anglican Consultative Council (ACC) meeting in Hong Kong which
- ask all churches of the Anglican Communion to place environmental care on their agenda;
- ask all Anglicans to make their own personal commitment to care for God's world, respecting all life, for "the Earth is the Lord's and all that is in it" (Psalm 24);
- establish the Anglican Environmental Network as an official network of the

Anglican Communion; and

endorse for immediate action the declaration of the Anglican Congress to the Anglican Communion.

Committee Amendment:

Resolved, the House of Bishops concurring, That the 74th General Convention endorse and implement the four resolutions passed by the September 2002 Anglican Consultative Council (ACC) meeting in Hong Kong which

- ask all churches of the Anglican Communion to place environmental care on their agenda;
- ask all Anglicans to make their own personal commitment to care for God's world, respecting all life, for "the Earth is the Lord's and all that is in it" (Psalm 24);
- establish the Anglican Environmental Network as an official network of the Anglican Communion; and
- endorse for immediate action the declaration of the *Global* Anglican Congress *of the Stewardship of Creation* ~~to the Anglican Communion~~.

Motion carried
Resolution adopted with amendment
(Communicated to the House of Bishops in HD Message #164)

The House of Deputies Committee on National and International Concerns presented its Report #32 on Resolution D068 (Response to New War Situations) and moved adoption of a substitute.

Original Text of Resolution:

(D068)

Resolved, the House of Bishops concurring, That the Theology Committee of the House of Bishops be mandated to prepare a study on new warfare situations which may not be adequately addressed by the Just War theory and to report to both Houses at the General Convention of 2006.

Committee Substitute:

Resolved, the House of Bishops concurring, That the Theology Committee of the House of Bishops be urged to prepare a study on new warfare situations which may not be adequately addressed by the Just War Theory, such as non-declared wars, asymmetric warfare, pre-emptive strikes, invitations to intervene by legitimate foreign authorities, international terrorism without boundaries, and other forms of military intervention not imagined in past centuries.

Motion carried
Substitute resolution adopted
(Communicated to the House of Bishops in HD Message #165)

| MINNEAPOLIS MEETING | HOUSE OF DEPUTIES |

The House of Deputies Committee on National and International Concerns presented its Report #33 on Resolution D063 (Civil Liberties and the USA Patriot Act) and moved adoption with amendment.

Original Text of Resolution:
(D063)
Resolved, the House of Bishops concurring, That the 74th General Convention direct the Office of Government Relations to work to encourage the Congress of the United States to hold public hearings examining the relationship between the extension of police powers granted under HR 3162 RDS, the Uniting and Strengthening America by Providing Appropriate Tools Required to Intercept and Obstruct Terrorism Act of 2001 (USA PATRIOT Act), and the potential curtailing of civil liberties granted by the Constitution of the United States of America.

Committee Amendment:
Resolved, the House of Bishops concurring, That the 74th General Convention direct the Office of Government Relations to work to encourage the Congress of the United States to hold public hearings examining the relationship between the extension of police powers granted under HR 3162 RDS, the Uniting and Strengthening America by Providing Appropriate Tools Required to Intercept and Obstruct Terrorism Act of 2001 (USA PATRIOT Act), and the potential curtailing of civil liberties granted by the Constitution of the United States of America; and be it further
Resolved, That the 74th General Convention go on record as opposing the use of Federal legislation passed since 9/11 violating fundamental civil rights guaranteed by the United States Constitution.

Motion carried
Resolution adopted with amendment
(Communicated to the House of Bishops in HD Message #166)

Parliamentary Inquiry
Deputy Logan of South Carolina asked if the materials referenced in the resolution had been distributed to the House.
The Chair of the House of Deputies Committee on National and International Concerns referred to Resolution D014 on website information.
The President noted this could be added to the Archives.
Deputy Runnels of Mississippi stated that the Rules of Order do not currently apply to website references.
Deputy Kilkelly of Maine moved to suspend the rules to allow the website to be the source of information for this one time.

Motion carried
Rules suspended

The House of Deputies Committee on National and International Concerns presented its Report #36 on Resolution D034 (Sex Trafficking) and moved adoption with amendment.

Original Text of Resolution:
(D034)
Resolved, the House of Bishops concurring, That the 74th General Convention condemn domestic and international trafficking in all persons for sexual purposes as an affront to human dignity and human rights; and be it further
Resolved, That, recognizing that it is impossible to discern if a person's engaging in commercial sex is ever truly voluntary, we oppose any move by any government to legalize prostitution or so-called voluntary trafficking; and be it further
Resolved, That the Executive Council request the appropriate Standing Committee to set up national and international plans of action for the Church to prepare an educational campaign for parishes and dioceses on the topic of sex trafficking, and to prepare a model for a Church initiative bringing together faith-based people with nongovernmental organizations, government, and law enforcement officials to create a victim-centered approach to anti-sex trafficking operations, finding ways to meet the medical, psychological, legal, and spiritual needs of persons who have been brought out of these horrendous circumstances; and be it further
Resolved, That this resolution be sent to every Province in the Anglican Communion, along with relevant materials on sex trafficking and a request for information on any initiatives by the Church for combating this problem from each of those provinces.

Committee Amendment:
Resolved, the House of Bishops concurring, That the 74th General Convention condemn domestic and international trafficking in all persons for sexual purposes as an affront to human dignity and human rights; and be it further
Resolved, That recognizing that it is impossible to discern if a person's engaging in commercial sex is ever truly voluntary, we oppose any move by any government to legalize prostitution or so-called voluntary trafficking; and be it further
Resolved, That the Executive Council request the appropriate Standing Committee to set up national and international plans of action for The *Episcopal* Church to prepare an educational campaign for parishes and dioceses on the topic of sex trafficking, and to prepare a model for a church initiative bringing together faith-based people with nongovernmental organizations, government, and law enforcement officials to create a victim-centered approach to anti-sex trafficking operations, finding ways to meet the medical, psychological, legal, and spiritual needs of persons who have been brought out of these horrendous circumstances; and be it further
Resolved, That this resolution be sent to every Province in the Anglican Communion., along with relevant materials on sex trafficking and a request for information on any initiatives by the Church for combating this problem from each of those provinces.

Deputy Cheney of West Tennessee moved to amend the resolution.

Proposed Amendment:
Delete the second resolve clause.

Deputy Hart of Pennsylvania moved to terminate debate.

Motion carried
Debate terminated

A vote was taken on the Cheney amendment.

Motion carried
Amendment adopted

A vote was taken on Resolution D034 as amended.

Motion carried
Resolution adopted with amendment
(Communicated to the House of Bishops in HD Message #169)

The House of Deputies Committee on National and International Concerns presented its Report #37 on Resolution D054 (HIV/AIDS Keeping America's Promise to Africa) and moved adoption of a substitute.

Original Text of Resolution:
(D054)
Resolved, the House of Bishops concurring, That the 74th General Convention, through the Office of Government Relations, urge the United States government to keep America's promise to Africa by fully funding the President's $4.3 billion budget request for HIV/AIDS relief to Africa without cuts to current life-saving programs; and be it further
Resolved, That the 74th General Convention commend President George W. Bush for making the historic promise of $15 billion over five years in new funding to combat the HIV/AIDS pandemic in Africa, encourage him to use all the influence of his office to encourage Congress to keep this promise and further encourage him to continue to find new ways by which America can lead the way in this critical mission of mercy and global reconciliation; and be it further
Resolved, That all Episcopalians take immediate action to contact their elected representatives, urging them to support the full funding of President Bush's promise to Africa; and be it further
Resolved, That all dioceses and communities of faith in The Episcopal Church be urged to examine and embrace ways by which they can join in the worldwide fight against HIV/AIDS.

Committee Substitute:
Resolved, the House of Bishops concurring, That the 74th General Convention, through the Office of Government Relations, urge the United States government to keep America's "Promise to Africa" by fully funding the President's proposed 5-year, $15 billion budget request for HIV/AIDS relief for Africa and the Caribbean without cuts to current life-saving programs; and be it further
Resolved, That the 74th General Convention commend the President for the promise of significant new funding to combat the HIV/AIDS pandemic in Africa, and now call on the Administration to use the full influence of the Executive Office in order to press Congress to keep the Promise to Africa; and be it further

Resolved, That the Church encourage the government to continue to find new ways by which America can combat this deadly disease and promote human security, thereby waging global reconciliation; and be it further
Resolved, That the Church call on the United States government to honor and support trade policies that promote access to essential AIDS medicines for poor countries, and to make sustained commitment for a fair-share U.S. contribution to the Global Fund to Fight AIDS, TB, and Malaria, an international public-private partnership world health campaign, modeled on the world health campaigns which led to the successful eradication of polio and smallpox; and be it further
Resolved, That all Episcopalians take immediate action to contact their elected representatives, urging them to support funding for the Promise to Africa and the Global Fund; and be it further
Resolved, That all dioceses and communities of faith in the Episcopal Church be urged to examine and embrace ways by which they can join in the worldwide fight against HIV/AIDS.

Motion carried
Substitute resolution adopted
(Communicated to the House of Bishops in HD Message #172)

The House of Deputies Committee on National and International Concerns presented its Report #40 on Resolution A037 (Status of Forces Agreement with Korea) and moved adoption with amendment.

Original Text of Resolution:
(A037)
Resolved, the House of Bishops concurring, That the 74th General Convention of The Episcopal Church in the United States of America urge the United States government in its renegotiation of the Status of Forces Agreement (SOFA) with the Republic of Korea to give special attention to:
1. The rights of Korean citizens to equal treatment and legal redress of grievances and adequate compensation to victims of weapons practice and testing; pollution of the environment; personal abuse, especially of a violent or sexual nature; and other deleterious effects of U.S. military presence and activity; and
2. U.S. accountability for troops' misconduct and the right of victims to have U.S. troops tried in local courts, including the right to extradite personnel who have been removed from the host country; and be it further

Resolved, That The Episcopal Church urge the U.S. government in all SOFA negotiations to recognize the rights of local people and assure their access to all mechanisms for redress of their grievances against U.S. military personnel; and be it further
Resolved, That the eventual goal be the phasing out of U.S. military bases in Korea.

Committee Amendment:
Resolved, the House of Bishops concurring, That the 74th General Convention of The Episcopal Church in the United States of America urge the United States

MINNEAPOLIS MEETING   HOUSE OF DEPUTIES

government in its renegotiation of the Status of Forces Agreement (SOFA) with the Republic of Korea to give special attention ~~to:~~
1. ~~The rights of Korean citizens to equal treatment and legal redress of grievances and adequate compensation to victims of weapons practice and testing; pollution of the environment; personal abuse, especially of a violent or sexual nature; and other deleterious effects of U.S. military presence and activity; and~~
2. ~~U.S. accountability for troops' misconduct and the right of victims to have U.S. troops tried in local courts, including the right to extradite personnel who have been removed from the host country;~~

to the rights of Korean citizens to equal treatment and legal redress of grievances and adequate compensation to victims of weapons practice and testing; pollution of the environment; personal abuse, especially of a violent or sexual nature; and other negative effects of U.S. military presence and activity; and be it further

Resolved, That The Episcopal Church urge the U.S. government in all SOFA negotiations to recognize the rights of local people and assure their access to all mechanisms for redress of their grievances against U.S. military personnel; and be it further

Resolved, That the eventual goal be the phasing out of U.S. military bases in Korea.

Motion carried
Resolution adopted with amendment
(Communicated to the House of Bishops in HD Message #171)

The House of Deputies Committee on National and International Concerns presented its Report #41 on Resolution D014 (Japanese-American Internment in World War II: A Call for Accountability) and moved adoption of a substitute.

Original Text of Resolution:
(D014)
Resolved, the House of Bishops concurring, That the 74th General Convention affirm that the internment of Japanese-Americans during World War II was a tragedy that undermined civil liberties and God-given human dignity and freedom; and be it further

Resolved, That The Episcopal Church, in reaffirming its baptismal covenant to "uphold the dignity of every human being," seek continued healing for the consequences of Japanese-American internment in World War II; and be it further

Resolved, That The Episcopal Church call upon Representative Howard Coble (6th District, North Carolina) to retract in public his remarks made on February 4th of this year regarding Japanese-American internment and to issue a full, unequivocal apology to the Japanese-American community.

Committee Substitute:
Resolved, the House of Bishops concurring, That the 74th General Convention reaffirm previous actions taken by both Executive Council and General Conventions on the internment and redress of Japanese-Americans and Japanese Latin Americans during World War II; and be it further

Resolved, That The Episcopal Church, in reaffirming its baptismal covenant to "uphold the dignity of every human being," support the civil liberties of all, regardless of ethnicity and religious beliefs; and be it further

Resolved, That in this post 9/11 era, the Church call on the United States government to be mindful of the experience and treatment in the internment of Japanese-Americans; and be it further

Resolved, That the United States government be instructed by this deplorable history when it considers any reauthorization, expansion, or implementation of legislation or regulations relating to "USA PATRIOT Act," H.R. 3162, which can be found at http://Thomas.loc.gov (please note no www) (click on: legislation related to the attacks of September 11, 2001).

Motion carried
Substitute resolution adopted
(Communicated to the House of Bishops in HD Message #170)

The House of Deputies Committee on National and International Concerns presented its Report #42 on Resolution A028 (Palestinian and Afghani Women Support) and moved adoption of a substitute.

Original Text of Resolution:
(A028)
Resolved, the House of Bishops concurring, That the bishops and deputies of the 74th General Convention convey to their dioceses to reach out to Palestinian and Afghani women and children by using websites, such as, http://www.vitalvoices.org/programs/afghan_women or www.pcwf.org or earmarking contributions to Jerusalem 2000 or Episcopal Relief and Development.

Committee Substitute:
Resolved, the House of Bishops concurring, That the 74th General Convention encourage dioceses to assist all Episcopalians to learn about the plight of and provide support for women and children of all faiths in war torn areas, recent examples including Israel/Palestine, Afghanistan, Iraq, Colombia, Sudan, and Liberia; and be it further

Resolved, That the Convention commend such websites as: <www.vitalvoices.org/programs/afghan_women>, <www.pcwf.org>, or <www.er-d.org> (the website of Episcopal Relief and Development) resources in our education and action.

Deputy Seitz of West Virginia moved an amendment to the substitute.

Proposed Amendment:
Delete the second resolve clause.

Deputy High of Texas moved to terminate debate on the Seitz amendment and the main motion.

| MINNEAPOLIS MEETING | HOUSE OF DEPUTIES |

A vote was taken to terminate debate on the amendment and the main motion.
Motion carried
Debate terminated
A vote was taken on the Seitz amendment.
Motion carried
Amendment adopted
A vote was taken on substitute Resolution A028 as amended.
Motion carried
Substitute resolution adopted with amendment
(Communicated to the House of Bishops in HD Message #173)

Social and Urban Affairs
The House of Deputies Committee on Social and Urban Affairs presented its Report #29 on Resolution D070 (Water Policy) and moved adoption.

Original Text of Resolution:
(D070)
Resolved, the House of Bishops concurring, That the 74th General Convention ask the Office of Government Relations to work on public policy to ensure that clean water is accessible and available to all; and be it further
Resolved, That the Standing Commission on Anglican and International Peace with Justice Concerns be urged to make water a priority.
Motion carried
Resolution adopted
(Communicated to the House of Bishops in HD Message #174)

The House of Deputies Committee on Social and Urban Affairs presented its Report #31 on Resolution D071 (Oppose Federally Sponsored Marriage Promotion) and moved adoption of a substitute.

Original Text of Resolution:
(D071)
Resolved, the House of Bishops concurring, That the 74th General Convention urge the Congress of the United States to respect the act of marriage as a sacred and private covenant between the couple and God, and to reject the provisions of H.R. 4, "Personal Responsibility, Work, and Family Promotion Act of 2003," regarding marriage promotion.

Committee Substitute:
Resolved, the House of Bishops concurring, That the 74th General Convention express opposition to any effort by the Congress of United States or the legislatures of any of the states to divert Temporary Assistance to Needy Families (TANF) funds into government programs that discriminate against single-parent households or mandate that recipients of TANF be married; and be it further

Resolved, That the Office of Government Relations is directed to identify, and to advocate the defeat of, any such legislation.

Deputy Runnels of Mississippi moved to amend the substitute resolution.

Proposed Amendment:
In the first resolve clause, delete the words "to divert Temporary Assistance to Needy Families (TANF) funds into government programs" and delete the words "or mandate that recipients of TANF be married."
In the second resolve clause, delete the words "to identify, and to advocate the defeat of, any such legislation" and insert the words "to advocate on the behalf of all needy familites."
Deputy Seitz of West Virginia moved to terminate debate on the Runnels amendment.

> Motion carried
> Debate terminated

A vote was taken on the Runnels amendment.

> Motion carried
> Amendment adopted

A vote was taken on substitute Resolution D071 as amended.

> Motion carried
> Substitute resolution adopted with amendment
> (Communicated to the House of Bishops in HD Message #176)

The House of Deputies Committee on Social and Urban Affairs presented its Report #34 on Resolution D036 (Marriage) and moved adoption of a substitute.

Original Text of Resolution:
(D036)
Resolved, the House of Bishops concurring, That the 74th General Convention recognize the burgeoning marriage movement as a resource which provides new insight into building healthy marriages and strong families; and be it further
Resolved, That the General Convention instruct the National Concerns Committee to research and disseminate the social science findings of the marriage movement for use in parishes and dioceses in their own marriage programs.

Committee Substitute:
Resolved, the House of Bishops concurring, That the 74th General Convention instruct the National Concerns Committee of Executive Council to report to the 75th General Convention on the responses by the dioceses of this Church to the charges and recommendations contained in Resolution D071 of the 72nd General Convention (Recognizing Lifelong Commitment and Fidelity in Marital Relationships) and Resolution A069 of the 67th General Convention (Encourage Dioceses to Establish Commissions on Marriage); and be it further

Resolved, That the National Concerns Committee of Executive Council make available to dioceses and congregations the developed programs for marriage enrichment and renewal and pre-marital counseling.

Motion carried
Substitute resolution adopted
(Communicated to the House of Bishops in HD Message #177)

The House of Deputies Committee on Social and Urban Affairs presented its Report #35 on Resolution D045 (Withdraw From the Religious Coalition for Reproductive Choice) and moved to refer the resolution to the Standing Commission on National Concerns.

Original Text of Resolution:
(D045)
Resolved, the House of Bishops concurring, That the 74th General Convention of The Episcopal Church of the United States of America direct The Episcopal Church in the United States of America and its affiliate organizations, the Episcopal Urban Caucus and the Episcopal Women's Caucus, to immediately withdraw membership in and financial support for the Religious Coalition for Reproductive Choice (RCRC).

Motion carried
Referred to a Standing Commission
(Communicated to the House of Bishops in HD Message #178)

The House of Deputies Committee on Social and Urban Affairs presented its Report #36 on Resolution D040 (Invest in Housing for the Poor) and moved adoption with amendment.

Original Text of Resolution:
(D040)
Resolved, the House of Bishops concurring, That the 74th General Convention reaffirm its commitment to providing safe, affordable housing for low- and moderate-income persons and their families; and be it further
Resolved, That the office of Government Relations urge the Secretary of Housing and Urban Development, the White House, the United States Congress and state legislatures to ensure that housing assistance programs are adequately funded to address the growing gap between the number of affordable housing units available and the number of renter households in the bottom quartile of income in this nation; and be it further
Resolved, That the Convention encourage the development of local parish and interfaith community partnerships to address the lack of affordable housing for low- and moderate-income families throughout this great nation.

Committee Amendment:
Resolved, the House of Bishops concurring, That the 74th General Convention reaffirm its commitment to providing ~~safe~~ *rental and owner-occupied,* ~~affordable~~ housing *that is safe, accessible and affordable* for low-*income* and moderate-income persons and their families *including persons with disabilities*; and be it further
Resolved, That the Office of Government Relations urge the *Executive and Legislative branches of the federal government* ~~Secretary of Housing and Urban Development, the White House, the United States Congress and state legislatures~~ *and the dioceses to encourage state and local units of government* to ensure that housing assistance programs are adequately funded to address the growing gap between the number of affordable housing units available and the number of renter households in the bottom quartile of income in this nation; and be it further
Resolved, That the Convention ~~encourage~~ *strongly encourage* the ~~development of~~ local parish and interfaith community partnerships to address the lack of affordable housing for low- and moderate-income families *including persons with disabilities* throughout this ~~great~~ nation; and be it further
Resolved, That the Convention urge the Episcopal Network for Economic Justice to identify existing and new opportunities for involvement in the creation and investment in affordable housing and to report through the Jubilee Ministries Advisory Committee on the status of this work to the 75th General Convention and on the opportunities for The Episcopal Church to become involved in the creation of affordable housing.

Motion carried
Resolution adopted with amendment
(Communicated to the House of Bishops in HD Message #179)

Ministry
The House of Deputies Committee on Ministry presented its Report #7 on Resolution D056 (Amend Canons on Court for Trial of a Bishop) and moved adoption with amendment.
Rehill of Neward moved to table the resolution until after consideration of Resolution D062.

Motion carried
Consideration postponed

Constitution
The House of Deputies Committee on Constitution presented its Report #4 on HB Message #146 on Resolution D062 (Amend Constitution Article IX [Trial Court of Bishops–Second Reading]) and moved concurrence with amendment.

Committee Amendment:
(D062)
Resolved, That the first paragraph of Article IX of the Constitution be amended to read as follows:
The General Convention may, by Canon, establish *one or more* a Court *courts* for the Trial of Bishops, which shall be composed of Bishops only.
And be it further
Resolved, That this resolution be sent within six months to the Secretary of the Convention of every Diocese to be made known to the Diocesan Convention at its next meeting.

Ballot #2—Vote by Orders
Vote by Orders on Resolution D062 taken.

Ballot #2 taken by orders

Results of Ballot #2: Vote by Orders on Resolution D062

Type	Total	Necessary	Yes	No	Divided	Results
Clerical	106	54	103	2	1	Carried
Lay	106	54	104	2	0	Carried

The House concurred
(Communicated to the House of Bishops in HD Message #180)

Final Text of Resolution:
(D062)
Resolved, That the first paragraph of Article IX of the Constitution be amended to read as follows:
The General Convention may, by Canon, establish *one or more* a Court *courts* for the Trial of Bishops, which shall be composed of Bishops only.

Ministry
The House of Deputies Committee on Ministry presented Report #7 on Resolution D056 (Amend Canons on Court for Trial of a Bishop) and moved adoption with amendment.

Original Text of Resolution:
(D056)
Resolved, the House of Bishops concurring, That Canon IV.3.21(c) be amended to read as follows:
Sec. 21 (c) A Bishop may be Presented for an Offense under Canon IV.1.1(c) and any other Offenses arising out of acts alleged to be contrary to the doctrine of the Church which was the subject of the Statement of Disassociation only upon a written Presentment signed by any ten Bishops exercising jurisdiction in this Church. The Presentment shall be filed with the Presiding Bishop, together with a brief in support thereof, and a statement why the issuance of a Statement of Disassociation was not a sufficient response to the acts alleged, within six months

of the issuance of a Statement of Disassociation based upon the same doctrine as was alleged in the Request for a Statement of Disassociation. The Presiding Bishop shall thereupon serve a copy of the Presentment upon the Bishop presented, together with a copy of the supporting brief and statement. The Presiding Bishop shall fix a date for the filing of an answer, brief in support thereof, and statement why the issuance of a Statement of Disassociation was a sufficient response to the acts alleged, within three months from the date of service, and may extend the time for answering for not more than two additional months. Upon the filing of an answer, supporting brief, and statement, if any, or upon the expiration of the time fixed for an answer, if none be filed, the Presiding Bishop shall forthwith transmit copies of the Presentment, answer, briefs, and statements to each member of the House of Bishops. The written consent of one-third of the Bishops qualified to vote in the House of Bishops shall be required before the proceeding may continue. In case the Presiding Bishop does not receive the written consent of one-third of all the Bishops eligible to vote within sixty days of the date the notification by the Presiding Bishops was sent to them, the Presiding Bishop shall declare the Presentment dismissed and no further proceedings may be had thereon. If the Presiding Bishop receives the necessary written consents within sixty days as specified above, the Presiding Bishop shall forthwith forward the Presentment, answer, briefs, and statements to the Presiding Judge of The Court for the Trial of a Bishop *for an Offense of Doctrine.*

And be it further

Resolved, That Canon IV.5 sections 1–9 be amended to read as follows:

Sec. 1. The Court for the Trial of a Bishop is vested with jurisdiction to try a Bishop who is duly Presented for one or more Offenses *not including the Offense in Canon IV.1.1(c). The Court for the Trial of a Bishop for an Offense of Doctrine is vested with jurisdiction to try a Bishop who is duly Presented for one or more Offenses pursuant to Canon IV.3.21(c).*

Sec. 2. *The Court for the Trial of a Bishop shall consist of five Bishops of this Church, two Priests, and two confirmed adult lay communicants of this Church in good standing. Five Bishops shall be elected by the House of Bishops at each regular meeting of General Convention, to serve until the adjournment of the next regular meeting of General Convention. Two Priests and two confirmed adult lay communicants of this Church in good standing shall be elected by the House of Deputies at each regular meeting of General Convention, to serve until the adjournment of the next regular meeting of General Convention.*

Sec. 2 3. The Court for the Trial of a Bishop *for an Offense of Doctrine* shall consist of nine Bishops of this Church. Three Bishops shall be elected by the House of Bishops at each regular meeting of General Convention, to serve until the adjournment of the third succeeding regular meeting of General Convention.

Sec. 4. All judges shall serve until their successors are elected and qualify; Provided, however, there shall be no change in composition of a Court as to a proceeding pending before it, while that proceeding is unresolved except as specified in Canon IV.5.3.

Sec. 3 5 (a) No Judge shall sit as a member of a Court for the Trial of a Bishop who is a Complainant, or is related to the Respondent or Complainant by affinity or consanguinity, or who is excused pursuant to Canon IV.14.13; nor shall any Judge sit who, upon objection made by either party for any reason, is deemed by the other members of the Court to be disqualified.

(b) The death, permanent disability rendering the person unable to act, resignation or declination to serve as a member of ~~the~~ *a* Court ~~for the Trial of a Bishop~~ shall constitute a vacancy in ~~the~~ *that* Court. The recusal or disqualification of a member of ~~the~~ *a* Court from consideration of a particular Presentment shall constitute a temporary vacancy in ~~the~~ *that* Court.

(c) Notices of resignations or declinations to serve shall be given by any Bishop chosen to serve as a member of the Court for the Trial of a Bishop *or Court for the Trial of a Bishop for an Offense of Doctrine* by written notice sent to the Presiding Bishop.

(d) Notices of resignations or declinations to serve shall be given by any Priest or lay person chosen to serve as a member of the Court for the Trial of a Bishop by written notice sent to the President of the House of Deputies.

~~(d)~~*(e)* Notices of recusal shall be given by a Judge to the Presiding Judge.

Sec. ~~4~~ *6*. The Courts ~~for the Trial of a Bishop~~ shall from time to time elect from its own membership a Presiding Judge, who shall hold office until the expiration of the term for which chosen. If in any proceeding before ~~the~~ *a* Court the Presiding Judge is disqualified or is for any cause unable to act, ~~the~~ *that* Court shall elect from its members a Presiding Judge *pro tempore*.

Sec. ~~5~~ *7*. When ~~the~~ *a* Court is not in session, if there is a vacancy in the office of the Presiding Judge, the Bishop who is senior by consecration shall perform the duties of the office of Presiding Judge.

Sec. ~~6~~ *8*. Vacancies occurring in ~~the~~ *a* Court ~~for the Trial of a Bishop~~ shall be filled as follows:

(a) In the case of a temporary vacancy due to the recusal or disqualification of any Judge, the remaining Judges may appoint a Judge to take the place of the one so disqualified in that particular case. If the recused or disqualified Judge participated in any proceedings other than consideration of whether any Judge should be disqualified, the remaining Judges shall decide whether or not the Judge will be replaced for the remainder of that case.

(b) In the case of a vacancy in the Court, the remaining Judges shall have power to fill such vacancy until the next General Convention, when the House of Bishops shall choose a ~~person~~ *Bishop* to fill ~~such~~ a vacancy *of a Bishop and the House of Deputies shall choose a Priest or lay person, respectively, to fill a vacancy of a Priest or lay person*. The person so chosen shall serve during the remainder of the term.

Sec. ~~7~~ *9*. Not less than five of the Judges shall constitute a quorum, but any less number may adjourn the Court from time to time.

Sec. ~~8~~ *10*. (a) Upon receiving a Presentment, the Presiding Judge shall, within 30 days, send to each member of the Court a copy of the Presentment. If the Presentment is issued pursuant to Canon IV.2.31(c) the Presiding Judge shall also send a copy of the supporting briefs, answer, and statements.

(b) The Presiding Judge of the Court shall, within not more than three calendar
months from the Presiding Judge's receipt of the Presentment, summon the

Respondent to answer the Presentment in accordance with the Rules of Procedure.
(c) Court proceedings at which the Respondent and Church Attorney are to appear shall be held within the Diocese of the accused Bishop, or within the Diocese where the accused Bishops lives or serves, at the discretion of the Court. The Court may, for good cause, appoint another place for any such proceedings or conduct such proceedings by telephone conference provided that all participants can hear and be heard by all other participants in the telephone conference.

Sec. 9 *11.* Within three months following each regular meeting of General Convention, the Court for the Trial of a Bishop shall appoint a Church Attorney to serve until the next regular meeting of General Convention and until a successor is duly appointed and qualified, and from time to time for good cause and upon the request of the Church Attorney, appoint one or more assistant Church Attorneys to act for and in the place of the Church Attorney.

And be it further

Resolved, That Canon IV.6 sections 2 and 17 be amended to read as follows:

Sec. 2. The Court of Review of the Trial of a Bishop is vested with jurisdiction to hear and determine appeals from the determination of the Court for the Trial of a Bishop *and the Court for the Trial of a Bishop for an Offense of Doctrine.*

Sec. 17. An appeal shall be heard upon the Record on Appeal of the Court for the Trial of a Bishop *or the Court for the Trial of a Bishop for an Offense of Doctrine.* Except for the purpose of correcting the Record on Appeal, if defective, no new evidence shall be taken by the Court of Review.

And be it further

Resolved, That the definition of Ecclesiastical Trial Court in Canon IV.14 Sec. 23 be amended to read as follows:

Sec. 23. Expenses of Parties and Costs of Proceedings. Except as expressly provided in this Title, or applicable Diocesan canon, all costs, expenses and fees of the several parties shall be the obligation of the party incurring them. The record of proceedings of a Diocesan Ecclesiastical Trial Court shall be the expense of the Diocese. The record of proceedings of a Court of Review of a Trial of a Priest or Deacon shall be the expense of the Province. The Record of proceedings of a Review Committee, the Court for the Trial of a Bishop, *the Court for the Trial of a Bishop for an Offense of Doctrine* and the Court of Review of a Trial of a Bishop shall be the expense of the General Convention. Nothing in this Title precludes the voluntary payment of a Respondent's costs, expenses and fees by any other party or person, including a Diocese.

And be it further

Resolved, That Canon IV.15 be amended to read as follows:

Ecclesiastical Trial Court shall mean a Diocesan Court for the Trial of a Priest or Deacon established pursuant to Canon IV.4(a) and The Court for the Trial of a Bishop *and the Court for the Trial of a Bishop for an Offense of Doctrine* pursuant to Canon IV.5.1.

And be it further

Resolved, That the Title IV Appendix A be amended to read as follows:

Title IV Appendix A

Rules of Procedure of the Ecclesiastical Trial Courts and the Court for the Trial of

~~a Bishop~~

Committee Amendment:
Resolved, the House of Bishops concurring, That Canon IV.3.21(c) be amended to read as follows:
Sec. 21 (c) A Bishop may be Presented for an Offense under Canon IV.1.1(c) and any other Offenses arising out of acts alleged to be contrary to the doctrine of the Church which was the subject of the Statement of Disassociation only upon a written Presentment signed by any ten Bishops exercising jurisdiction in this Church. The Presentment shall be filed with the Presiding Bishop, together with a brief in support thereof, and a statement why the issuance of a Statement of Disassociation was not a sufficient response to the acts alleged, within six months of the issuance of a Statement of Disassociation based upon the same doctrine as was alleged in the Request for a Statement of Disassociation. The Presiding Bishop shall thereupon serve a copy of the Presentment upon the Bishop presented, together with a copy of the supporting brief and statement. The Presiding Bishop shall fix a date for the filing of an answer, brief in support thereof, and statement why the issuance of a Statement of Disassociation was a sufficient response to the acts alleged, within three months from the date of service, and may extend the time for answering for not more than two additional months. Upon the filing of an answer, supporting brief, and statement, if any, or upon the expiration of the time fixed for an answer, if none be filed, the Presiding Bishop shall forthwith transmit copies of the Presentment, answer, briefs, and statements to each member of the House of Bishops. The written consent of one-third of the Bishops qualified to vote in the House of Bishops shall be required before the proceeding may continue. In case the Presiding Bishop does not receive the written consent of one-third of all the Bishops eligible to vote within sixty days of the date the notification by the Presiding Bishops was sent to them, the Presiding Bishop shall declare the Presentment dismissed and no further proceedings may be had thereon. If the Presiding Bishop receives the necessary written consents within sixty days as specified above, the Presiding Bishop shall forthwith forward the Presentment, answer, briefs, and statements to the Presiding Judge of The Court for the Trial of a Bishop *for an Offense of Doctrine.*
And be it further
Resolved, That Canon IV.5 sections 1–9 be amended to read as follows:
Sec. 1. The Court for the Trial of a Bishop is vested with jurisdiction to try a Bishop who is duly Presented for one or more Offenses *not including the Offense in Canon IV.1.1(c). The Court for the Trial of a Bishop for an Offense of Doctrine is vested with jurisdiction to try a Bishop who is duly Presented for one or more Offenses pursuant to Canon IV.3.21(c).*
Sec. 2. *The Court for the Trial of a Bishop shall consist of five Bishops of this Church, two Priests* <u>or Deacons</u>*, and two confirmed adult lay communicants of this Church in good standing. Five Bishops shall be elected by the House of Bishops at each regular meeting of General Convention, to serve until the adjournment of the next regular meeting of General Convention. Two Priests* <u>or Deacons</u> *and two confirmed adult lay communicants of this Church in good standing shall be elected by the House of Deputies at each regular meeting of General Convention, to serve until the adjournment of the next regular meeting of General Convention.*

Sec. ~~2~~ 3. The Court for the Trial of a Bishop *for an Offense of Doctrine* shall consist of nine Bishops of this Church. Three Bishops shall be elected by the House of Bishops at each regular meeting of General Convention, to serve until the adjournment of the third succeeding regular meeting of General Convention.

Sec. 4. All judges shall serve until their successors are elected and qualify; Provided, however, there shall be no change in composition of a Court as to a proceeding pending before it, while that proceeding is unresolved except as specified in Canon IV.5.3.

Sec. ~~3~~ 5 (a) No Judge shall sit as a member of a Court for the Trial of a Bishop who is a Complainant, or is related to the Respondent or Complainant by affinity or consanguinity, or who is excused pursuant to Canon IV.14.13; nor shall any Judge sit who, upon objection made by either party for any reason, is deemed by the other members of the Court to be disqualified.

(b) The death, permanent disability rendering the person unable to act, resignation or declination to serve as a member of ~~the~~ *a* Court ~~for the Trial of a Bishop~~ shall constitute a vacancy in ~~the~~ *that* Court. The recusal or disqualification of a member of ~~the~~ *a* Court from consideration of a particular Presentment shall constitute a temporary vacancy in ~~the~~ *that* Court.

(c) Notices of resignations or declinations to serve shall be given by any Bishop chosen to serve as a member of the Court for the Trial of a Bishop *or Court for the Trial of a Bishop for an Offense of Doctrine* by written notice sent to the Presiding Bishop.

(d) Notices of resignations or declinations to serve shall be given by any Priest or lay person chosen to serve as a member of the Court for the Trial of a Bishop by written notice sent to the President of the House of Deputies.

~~(d)~~*(e)* Notices of recusal shall be given by a Judge to the Presiding Judge.

Sec. ~~4~~ 6. The Courts ~~for the Trial of a Bishop~~ shall from time to time elect from its own membership a Presiding Judge, who shall hold office until the expiration of the term for which chosen. If in any proceeding before ~~the~~ *a* Court the Presiding Judge is disqualified or is for any cause unable to act, ~~the~~ *that* Court shall elect from its members a Presiding Judge *pro tempore.*

Sec. ~~5~~ 7. When ~~the~~ *a* Court is not in session, if there is a vacancy in the office of the Presiding Judge, the Bishop who is senior by consecration shall perform the duties of the office of Presiding Judge.

Sec. ~~6~~ 8. Vacancies occurring in ~~the~~ *a* Court ~~for the Trial of a Bishop~~ shall be filled as follows:

(a) In the case of a temporary vacancy due to the recusal or disqualification of any Judge, the remaining Judges may appoint a Judge to take the place of the one so disqualified in that particular case. If the recused or disqualified Judge participated in any proceedings other than consideration of whether any Judge should be disqualified, the remaining Judges shall decide whether or not the Judge will be replaced for the remainder of that case.

(b) In the case of a vacancy in the Court, the remaining Judges shall have power to fill such vacancy until the next General Convention, when the House of Bishops shall choose a ~~person~~ *Bishop* to fill ~~such~~ a vacancy *of a Bishop and the House of Deputies shall choose a Priest* <u>or</u>

Deacon *or lay person, respectively, to fill a vacancy of a Priest* or Deacon *or lay person.* The person so chosen shall serve during the remainder of the term.

Sec. ~~7~~ *9.* Not less than five of the Judges shall constitute a quorum, but any less number may adjourn the Court from time to time.

Sec. ~~8~~ *10.* (a) Upon receiving a Presentment, the Presiding Judge shall, within 30 days, send to each member of the Court a copy of the Presentment. If the Presentment is issued pursuant to Canon IV.2.31(c) the Presiding Judge shall also send a copy of the supporting briefs, answer, and statements.

(b) The Presiding Judge of the Court shall, within not more than three calendar
months from the Presiding Judge's receipt of the Presentment, summon the Respondent to answer the Presentment in accordance with the Rules of Procedure.

(c) Court proceedings at which the Respondent and Church Attorney are to appear shall be held within the Diocese of the accused Bishop, or within the Diocese where the accused Bishops lives or serves, at the discretion of the Court. The Court may, for good cause, appoint another place for any such proceedings or conduct such proceedings by telephone conference provided that all participants can hear and be heard by all other participants in the telephone conference.

Sec. ~~9~~ *11.* Within three months following each regular meeting of General Convention, the Court for the Trial of a Bishop shall appoint a Church Attorney to serve until the next regular meeting of General Convention and until a successor is duly appointed and qualified, and from time to time for good cause and upon the request of the Church Attorney, appoint one or more assistant Church Attorneys to act for and in the place of the Church Attorney.

And be it further

Resolved, That Canon IV.6 sections 2 and 17 be amended to read as follows:

Sec. 2. The Court of Review of the Trial of a Bishop is vested with jurisdiction to hear and determine appeals from the determination of the Court for the Trial of a Bishop *and the Court for the Trial of a Bishop for an Offense of Doctrine.*

Sec. 17. An appeal shall be heard upon the Record on Appeal of the Court for the Trial of a Bishop *or the Court for the Trial of a Bishop for an Offense of Doctrine.* Except for the purpose of correcting the Record on Appeal, if defective, no new evidence shall be taken by the Court of Review.

And be it further

Resolved, That the definition of Ecclesiastical Trial Court in Canon IV.14 Sec. 23 be amended to read as follows:

Sec. 23. Expenses of Parties and Costs of Proceedings. Except as expressly provided in this Title, or applicable Diocesan canon, all costs, expenses and fees of the several parties shall be the obligation of the party incurring them. The record of proceedings of a Diocesan Ecclesiastical Trial Court shall be the expense of the Diocese. The record of proceedings of a Court of Review of a Trial of a Priest or Deacon shall be the expense of the Province. The Record of proceedings of a Review Committee, the Court for the Trial of a Bishop, *the Court for the Trial of a Bishop for an Offense of Doctrine* and the Court of Review of a Trial of a Bishop shall be the expense of the General Convention. Nothing in this Title precludes the

JOURNAL   **EIGHTH DAY**

voluntary payment of a Respondent's costs, expenses and fees by any other party or person, including a Diocese.
And be it further
Resolved, That Canon IV.15 be amended to read as follows:
Ecclesiastical Trial Court shall mean a Diocesan Court for the Trial of a Priest or Deacon established pursuant to Canon IV.4(a) and The Court for the Trial of a Bishop *and the Court for the Trial of a Bishop for an Offense of Doctrine* pursuant to Canon IV.5.1.
And be it further
Resolved, That the Title IV Appendix A be amended to read as follows:
Title IV Appendix A
Rules of Procedure of the Ecclesiastical Trial Courts ~~and the Court for the Trial of a Bishop~~.
Deputy Seitz of West Virginia moved to terminate debate.

Motion carried
Debate terminated

A vote was taken on Resolution D056 as amended.

Motion carried
Resolution adopted with amendment
(Communicated to the House of Bishops in HD Message #181)

Communications

The House of Deputies Committee on Communications presented its Report #13 on Resolution D069 (Standing Commission On Church Communications) and moved adoption with amendment.

Original Text of Resolution:

(D069)
Resolved, the House of Bishops concurring, That the 74th General Convention affirm the policy that broad, diverse, and multi-faceted communication is central to and essential for the mission of The Episcopal Church; and be it further
Resolved, That effective communication is an overarching ministry and cannot be fulfilled as either a list of tasks or an addendum to other facets of the Church's mission and ministries; and be it further
Resolved, That a national strategy for communication must meet the needs of, and be reflective of, a broad and diverse church; and be it further
Resolved, That the 74th General Convention establish a Standing Commission on Episcopal Church Communication that will guide the policies, participate in the strategic planning, and share in the oversight of implementing a comprehensive communication strategy for The Episcopal Church; and be it further
Resolved, That the General Convention request that the Joint Standing Committee on Program, Budget and Finance consider a budget allocation of $0 for implementation of this resolution.

Committee Amendment:
Resolved, the House of Bishops concurring, That the 74th General Convention affirm the policy that broad, diverse, and multi-faceted communication is central to and essential for the mission of The Episcopal Church; and be it further
Resolved, That effective communication is an overarching ministry and cannot be fulfilled as either a list of tasks or an addendum to other facets of the Church's mission and ministries; and be it further
Resolved, That a national strategy for communication must meet the needs of, and be reflective of, a broad and diverse church; and be it further
Resolved, That Canon I.1.2(n) be amended by adding this subsection:
(12) A Standing Commission on Episcopal Church Communication consisting of 14 members (4 Bishops, 4 Priests and/or Deacons, and 6 Lay Persons). It shall be the duty of the Commission to guide the policies, participate in the strategic planning, and share in the oversight of implementing a comprehensive communication strategy for the Episcopal Church.
And be it further
~~*Resolved,* That the 74th General Convention establish a Standing Commission on Episcopal Church Communication that will guide the policies, participate in the strategic planning, and share in the oversight of implementing a comprehensive communication strategy for the Episcopal Church; and be it further~~
Resolved, That the General Convention request that the Joint Standing Committee on Program, Budget and Finance consider a budget allocation of $0 for implementation of this resolution.

Motion carried
Resolution adopted with amendment
(Communicated to the House of Bishops in HD Message #182)

Special Order of Business
The House of Deputies Committee on Dispatch of Business moved a Special Order of Business to suspend the rules to consider five additional resolutions: C028, D073, A076, D011, and D017.

Motion carried
Special Order adopted

National and International Concerns
The House of Deputies Committee on National and International Concerns presented its Report #44 on Resolution C028 (Immigrant Workers Freedom Ride) and moved adoption.

Original Text of Resolution:
(C028)
Resolved, the House of Bishops concurring, That the 74th General Convention actively work in support of the Immigrant Workers Freedom Ride (IWFR) by educating its members to the importance of immigration law reform, organizing local congregations to support the Freedom Ride both financially and by

participating in activities to host and welcome the Freedom Riders on their national route to the nation's capital and calling on The Episcopal Church, USA to adopt this resolution in support of the IWFR.

Motion carried
Resolution adopted
(Communicated to the House of Bishops in HD Message #183)

Social and Urban Affairs
The House of Deputies Committee on Social and Urban Affairs presented its Report #37 on Resolution D073 (Formation of Episcopal Community Services in America) and moved adoption.

Original Text of Resolution:
(D073)
Resolved, the House of Bishops concurring, That the 74th General Convention of The Episcopal Church commend the formation of Episcopal Community Services in America as an umbrella organization for member organizations affiliated with The Episcopal Church that seek to serve those in need through health and social services.

Motion carried
Resolution adopted
(Communicated to the House of Bishops in HD Message #184)

Evangelism
The House of Deputies Committee on Evangelism presented its Report #11 on Resolution A076 (Transformation Resources) and moved adoption with amendment.

Original Text of Resolution:
(A076)
Resolved, the House of Bishops concurring, That Episcopal Church Center staff be charged to:
- continue to develop strategic resources for transformation, such as Transformation and Renewal (vitalization in Black congregations) and Start Up, Start Over (theory and best practices for congregational renewal)
- continue to hold up paradigmatic examples of transformation and resurrection, including those in multicultural congregations, via *Episcopal Life*, the national church website, etc.
- continue to develop and offer multicultural and multilingual resources for transforming congregations
- develop a national consultancy/gathering for leaders in multicultural congregations, for the purpose of networking, learning, and resource sharing
- continue to develop educational resources for transformation, such as Bible

studies and small group resources for hospitality, mission, evangelism, and how to tell our own stories; resources that make liturgy more accessible, (e.g., the Rite series); resources for learning about culture and change
continue to maintain awareness of opportunities for learning and transformation in congregational life (Congregational Development office).

Committee Amendment:
Resolved, the House of Bishops concurring, That Episcopal Church Center staff *and specifically the ethnic ministries desks,* be charged to:
continue to develop strategic resources for transformation, such as Transformation and Renewal (vitalization in Black congregations) and Start Up, Start Over (theory and best practices for congregational renewal).
continue to hold up paradigmatic examples of transformation and resurrection, including those in multicultural congregations, via *Episcopal Life,* the national church website, etc.
continue to develop and offer multicultural and multilingual resources for transforming congregations *and leadership training*
develop a national consultancy/gathering for leaders in multicultural congregations, for the purpose of networking, learning, and resource sharing
continue to develop educational resources for transformation, such as Bible studies and small group resources for hospitality, mission, evangelism, and how to tell our own stories; resources that make liturgy more accessible, (e.g., the Rite series); resources for learning about culture and change
continue to maintain awareness of opportunities for learning and transformation in congregational life (Congregational Development office).

Motion carried
Resolution adopted with amendment
(Communicated to the House of Bishops in HD Message #185)

The House of Deputies Committee on Evangelism presented its Report #13 on Resolution D011 (Appending "Anglican Communion" to materials) and moved adoption.

Original Text of Resolution:
(D011)
Resolved, the House of Bishops concurring, That the 74th General Convention encourage all Episcopal Church dioceses, congregations, and affiliate organizations to append the phrase, with appropriate connecting wording, "Anglican Communion" to their signage, publications, advertising and communications so that churches and organizations of The Episcopal Church may be easily identified as part of the wider fellowship of churches in the Anglican Communion by persons of other member churches of the Communion.

Motion carried
Resolution adopted
(Communicated to the House of Bishops in HD Message #186)

The House of Deputies Committee on Evangelism presented its Report #14 on Resolution D017 (Promoting Reconciliation and Minimizing the Likelihood of Schism) and moved adoption with amendment.

Original Text of Resolution:
(D017)
Resolved, the House of Bishops concurring, That, (a) in support of the 20/20 goal that the 2020 Episcopal Church "reflect the diversity of our society," (b) in response to the results of Resolution D023a of the 2000 General Convention, and (c) in proactive response to the hurts, tensions—and in some places conflict—among ECUSA progressives, moderates, and conservatives, regarding sexuality, potential schism, and other deep-felt issues, the 2003 General Convention direct the Presiding Bishop and Executive Council to include in their future triennial reports to General Convention descriptions of (a) their efforts at reconciliation among such Church groups and (b) results achieved in reconciling these groups; and be it further
Resolved, That the reports include descriptions of the use of the following strategies and tools of faith-based reconciliation particularly in regard to their effects on the Church's membership, mission, and ministry:
1. acknowledgement of the wound
2. repentance
3. telling of stories
4. grief-sharing
5. making apologies to those adversely impacted
6. sharing of privilege
7. planning for and carrying out of changes
8. positively affirming and supporting multiculturalism, and
9. other, as those reporting deem appropriate.

Committee Amendment:
Resolved, the House of Bishops concurring, That, the 2003 General Convention direct the Executive Council to lead and encourage reconciliation efforts throughout the Church; and be it further
Resolved, That the Executive Council report the results of those efforts in their annual report; and be it further
~~(a) in support of the 2020 goal that the 2020 Episcopal Church "reflect the diversity of our society," (b) in response to the results of Resolution D023a of the 2000 General Convention, and (c) in proactive response to the hurts, tensions -- and in some places conflict -- among ECUSA progressives, moderates and conservatives, regarding sexuality, potential schism, and other deep-felt issues, the 2003 General Convention directs the Presiding Bishop and Executive Council to include in their future triennial reports to General Convention descriptions of (a) their efforts at reconciliation among such Church groups and (b) results achieved in reconciling these groups; and be it further~~
Resolved, That the reports include descriptions of the use of the ~~following strategies and tools of faith-based reconciliation~~ *Faith-Based Reconciliation model* ~~particularly in~~

~~regard to their effects on the Church's membership, mission, and ministry~~ *including*:
1. acknowledgement of the wound
2. repentance
3. telling of stories
4. grief-sharing
5. making apologies to those adversely impacted
6. sharing of privilege
7. planning for and carrying out of changes
8. positively affirming and supporting multiculturalism, and
9. other, as those reporting deem appropriate; and be it further

Resolved, That the 2003 General Convention commend the leadership and ministry of the Presiding Bishop and the New Commandment Task Force in the work of reconciliation.

Deputy Rushing of Massachusetts moved to refer the resolution to Executive Council.

Motion carried
Resolution referred to Executive Council
(Communicated to the House of Bishops in HD Message #187)

Messages from the House of Bishops

The Secretary announced that the following messages had been received from the House of Bishops:

HB Message #178: A110 (Complete Title III Revisions) Adopted.
HB Message #179: A005 (Continue Forward Movement Publications) Concurred.
HB Message #180: Consent to the Election of the Rev. Canon Rayford B. High as Bishop Suffragan of the Diocese of Texas. Concurred.
HB Message #181: Consent to the Election of the Rev. Dean Elliot Wolfe as Bishop Coadjutor of the Diocese of Kansas. Concurred.
HB Message #182: Consent to the Election of the Rev. Robert John O'Neill as Bishop Coadjutor of the Diocese of Colorado. Concurred.

Announcements
The Secretary read the announcements.

RECESS
The President recessed the House at 6:38 p.m. to reconvene at 11:00 a.m. on Thursday, August 7, 2003.

NINTH DAY

Thursday
August 7, 2003

MORNING SESSION

Reconvene
The Vice-President called the House to order at 11:11 a.m.

Morning Prayers
The Vice-President called on the Chaplain for prayers.

Certification of Minutes
The House of Deputies Committee on Certification of Minutes presented its Report #8, stating that the Committee had met, read the minutes of the Eighth Day, and certified that they were correct. The Chair moved adoption of the report.

Motion carried
Minutes adopted

Certification of Deputies
The House of Deputies Committee on Credentials presented its Report #12 for the first session of the Ninth Legislative Day, and there was 1 new deputy certified from the Diocese of Venezuela.[1] There were 419 clerical deputies and 420 lay deputies certified and seated, bringing the total count of the House to 839. There were 93 changes on this day as follows:

Diocese	Alternate replacing	Deputy being replaced
Alabama	Tom Poynor	Cecil Williamson
Alabama	Sherry Travis	Robert Childers
Arkansas	Joyce Hardy	Lowell Grisham
Atlanta	E. Claiborne Jones	G. Porter Taylor
California	Warren Wong	Kay Bishop
Central Gulf Coast	Peter Wilson	Robert McMillan
Central Pennsylvania	Mark Scheneman	John Hoover
Chicago	Richard Peete	Tessa Craib-Cox
Churches in Europe	Charles Trueheart	Helena Mbele-Mbong
Colorado	Robert Davidson	Donald Armstrong
Colorado	S. Brooks Keith	Ephraim Radner
Connecticut	Eugene Lattimer	John Sutton
Connecticut	Ellen Tillotson	Mark Santucci
Dallas	James Biegler	David Roseberry
Delaware	Thomas Kerr	Lloyd Casson

[1] The certification of a new deputy from the Diocese of Venezuela is a duplication of the certification recorded on the Eighth Day for a deputy from the Diocese of Venezela. *Ed.*

East Carolina	Pamela Stringer	Ronald Abrams
East Tennessee	Ed Cahill	Alice Clayton
Eastern Oregon	Susan Powers	Jean Gardner
Idaho	Doug Yarbrough	Brian Baker
Lexington	David Davidson	John Brantley
Lexington	Anisa Cottrell-Willis	Robert Sessum
Louisiana	Kathleen Turner	Harriet Murrell
Louisiana	Ralph Howe	Rex Perry
Maine	Susan Partridge	Cyndy Anderson
Maine	Anne Stanley	Paige Blair
Maryland	Alma Bell	Christine Kinard
Massachusetts	Byron Rushing	Rebecca Alden
Milwaukee	Maurine Lewis	Thomas Winslow
Milwaukee	Ralph Modjeska	Wendy Sopkovich
Minnesota	Michael Smith	Grant Abbott
Minnesota	Philip McNairy	Howard Anderson
Mississippi	Suanna Smith	Michael Chaney
Mississippi	Shannon Johnston	Ruth Black
Mississippi	David Johnson	Zabron Davis
New Hampshire	Margaret Faulk	Debra Harris
New Hampshire	William Exner	Gene Robinson
New Hampshire	Debra Ogin	Susan Langle
New York	James Barba	Fred Wibiralske
New York	Tobias Haller	Jean Campbell
Northern California	Donald Brown	Eric Duff
Olympia	Dorsey McConnell	Robert Christie
Oregon	Fred Terrill	Barbara Ross
Oregon	Linda Potter	James Boston
Pittsburgh	Joseph Sarria	Joan Malley
Puerto Rico	Wilner Millien	Jose Emilio Figueroa
Rhode Island	Harry Sacchetti	Carol Bennett
Rochester	Sarah Collins	Josephine Dewey
San Joaquin	Suzette Peters	Debra Cavanagh
Southern Virginia	Paul Hogg	David Teschner
Southern Virginia	Charles Pfeifer	James Bradberry
Southwest Florida	John Hiers	Hayden Crawford
Southwestern Virginia	Clare Fischer-Davies	Paul Fuller
Texas	Mary MacGregor	James Cunningham
Upper South Carolina	Jimmy Hartley	Angela Daniel
Virginia	Jeffrey Cerar	Charles Alley
Virginia	Jack Burtch	Deborah Robayo
Virginia	Victoria Heard	Jim Papile
Washington	Salli Hartman	Paul Cooney

West Texas	John Brooke	Alice Fischer
West Texas	Robert Browning	Sylvia Maddox
Western Louisiana	Reece Middleton	Carolyn Ledet
Western Massachusetts	Heidi Frantz-Dale	Sarah Shofstall
Western Michigan	Kathleen Kingslight	C. Mark Rutenbar
Western Michigan	Barbara Coulter	William Fleener
Western New York	Particia Zebrowski	Lillian Davis-Wilson
Western North Carolina	Lauch Magruder	Lawrence Thompson

Messages from the House of Bishops

The Secretary announced that the following messages had been received from the House of Bishops:

HB Message #183: C051 (Blessing of Committed Same-Gender Relationships) Adopted Substitute.

HB Message #184: Election of Joint Nominating Committee for the Election of a Presiding Bishop. Adopted.

The Secretary read the names of the Bishops elected to the Joint Nominating Committee for the Election of a Presiding Bishop:
  Province I: Gayle Harris, Suffragan Bishop of Massachusetts
  Province II: Gladstone B Adams, III, Bishop of Central New York
  Province III: Peter J. Lee, Bishop of Virginia
  Province IV: Duncan M. Gray, III, Bishop of Mississippi
  Province V: Kenneth Price, Suffragan Bishop of Southern Ohio
  Province VI: Bruce Caldwell, Bishop of Wyoming
  Province VII: Don Adger Wimberly, Bishop of Texas
  Province VIII: Jerry Lamb, Bishop of Northern California
  Province IX: David Alvarez, Bishop of Puerto Rico

Election of the General Theological Seminary Board of Trustees—Ballot #1

The Secretary read the results of the first ballot for Trustees of the General Theological Seminary. Newly-elected members of the General Theological Seminary Board of Trustees:

Elected in the Lay Order for three-year terms:
  Marjorie Christie of Newark, and
  Robert E. Wright of North Carolina.

No members of the Clergy Order were elected on Ballot #1.

Messages from the House of Bishops
The Secretary announced that the following messages had been received from the House of Bishops:

HB Message #180: Consent to the Election of the Rev. Canon Rayford B. High as Bishop Suffragan of the Diocese of Texas. Concurred.

The Vice-President asked the deputation of the Diocese of Texas to escort Suffragan Bishop-elect High to the podium to be introduced.

HB Message #181: Consent to the Election of the Rev. Dean Elliot Wolfe as Bishop Coadjutor of the Diocese of Kansas. Concurred.

The Vice-President asked the deputation of the Diocese of Kansas to escort Bishop Coadjutor-elect Wolfe to the podium to be introduced.

HB Message #182: Consent to the Election of the Rev. Robert John O'Neill as Bishop Coadjutor of the Diocese of Colorado. Concurred.

The Vice-President asked the deputation of the Diocese of Colorado to escort Bishop Coadjutor-elect O'Neill to the podium to be introduced.

Dispatch of Business
The House of Deputies Committee on Dispatch of Business reminded the House of Special Orders set for today:
1. The budget will be presented by the Joint Standing Committee on Program, Budget and Finance immediately after the Consent Calendar at the afternoon session.
2. The election of the lay and clerical members of the Joint Nominating Committee for the Election of a Presiding Bishop will follow.

Rules of Order
The Chair of the House of Deputies Committee on Dispatch of Business moved the suspension of House of Deputies Rule 24 to give priority to legislation needing concurrence so that action can be taken by General Convention.

Motion carried
Rules suspended

National and International Concerns
The House of Deputies Committee on National and International Concerns presented its Report #28 on Resolution D052 (Rescind Policy of Disinvestment in Defense Contractors) and moved the resolution, recommending rejection.

Original Text of Resolution:
(D052)
Resolved, the House of Bishops concurring, That the 74th General Convention of The Episcopal Church reaffirm the resolutions of The Episcopal Church opposing war and support resolutions advocating world peace; and be it further
Resolved, That in order to ensure world peace and the protection of the United States from foreign hostile action, our armed forces must have the benefit of the most advanced research, technology, and production of military weapons,

ammunition, and other equipment; and be it further
Resolved, That the 74th General Convention disavow and hold for naught the resolution of the Executive Council of The Episcopal Church at its meeting of April 28–May 1, 2003 adopting a policy of disinvestment from certain categories of U.S. defense contractors; and be it further
Resolved, That copies of this resolution be sent by the Secretary to all parties to whom the above resolution of the Executive Council was sent; and be it further
Resolved, That other church investors including the Church Pension Fund, parishes, and dioceses are urged to refrain from adopting, or to rescind if adopted, any policies in support of the above Executive Council Resolution.

The Vice-President announced the time for debate had expired.
Deputy Snow of Alaska moved to extend debate by two minutes.

Motion defeated
Debate terminated

A vote was taken on Resolution D052.

Motion carried
Resolution adopted
(Communicated to the House of Bishops in HD Message #188)

Stewardship and Development
The House of Deputies Committee on Stewardship and Development presented its Report #1 on HB Message #55 on Resolution A135 (Holy Habits) and moved concurrence.

The House concurred
(Communicated to the House of Bishops in HD Message #189)

Final Text of Resolution:
(A135)
Resolved, **That in recognition of the church's tradition of calling us to work, pray, and give for the spread of God's kingdom, all members of The Episcopal Church be encouraged to develop a personal spiritual discipline that includes, at a minimum, the holy habits of tithing, daily personal prayer and study, Sabbath time, and weekly corporate worship;** and be it further
Resolved, **That the Bishops and Deputies of the 74th General Convention be given an opportunity to sign the following declaration:**
> As Christian stewards and leaders of The Episcopal Church, we affirm that we are tithing, or have adopted a plan to work toward tithing as a minimum standard for our giving; and that, if we are not already doing so, we are committed to give priority to corporate worship, personal daily prayer and study, and Sabbath time in our own lives; and we invite all members of The Episcopal Church to join us in these holy habits; and be it further

Resolved, **That we commit ourselves to present this declaration to our diocesan conventions for adoption and signature, and in turn to the vestries and**

people of our parishes, missions, and university centers; and be it further
Resolved, That the Secretary publish a list of the General Convention signatories in the Journal of the 74th General Convention and provide the same to *Episcopal Life* for publication of the statement and the list of signatories.
[See Appendix C–Day 9 for signatories.]

The House of Deputies Committee on Stewardship and Development presented its Report #2 on HB Message #57 on Resolution A138 (50/50 Outreach for Congregations) and moved concurrence.

The House concurred
(Communicated to the House of Bishops in HD Message #190)

Final Text of Resolution:
(A138)
Resolved, That the 74th General Convention urge congregations to adopt the principle of devoting as much of their resources of time, talent, and treasure outside of the congregation as on itself. Part of the 50/50 sharing should include adoption of the 1% giving to seminaries, the .7% giving to international development programs that address root causes of ill health, illiteracy, and economic justice, and other worthwhile causes; and be it further
Resolved, That each diocese be urged to adopt the principle of 50/50 sharing of its resources on the same basis as congregations through budgetary allocation for outreach, aided congregations, support to the Domestic and Foreign Missionary Society and other mission efforts beyond diocesan administrative commitments, and then to establish a 3-year plan to move toward the accomplishment of that 50/50 sharing goal.

The House of Deputies Committee on Stewardship and Development presented its Report #5 on HB Message #70 on Resolution A139 (Affirm the Work of TENS) and moved concurrence.

The House concurred
(Communicated to the House of Bishops in HD Message #191)

Final Text of Resolution:
(A139)
Resolved, That the 74th General Convention commend the transforming ministry of The Episcopal Network for Stewardship (TENS), a ministry that invites individuals, congregations, and dioceses to grow into a new understanding of Christian stewardship theology that transforms us from selfishness and fear to love and giving; and be it further
Resolved, That all dioceses and congregations are encouraged to accept the invitation to become members of The Episcopal Network of Stewardship

not only to support this important ministry but also to receive the many resources TENS is developing and making available to the church.

The House of Deputies Committee on Stewardship and Development presented its Report #6 on HB Message #71 on Resolution A140 (Mission Funding) and moved concurrence.

The House concurred
(Communicated to the House of Bishops in HD Message #192)

Final Text of Resolution:
(A140)
Resolved, That in recognition of the 20/20 initiatives, creating a need to raise large sums of money for mission and the very real potential for major gifts that parish and diocesan funding efforts do not attract; the 74th General Convention urge the Presiding Bishop and Executive Council to establish a Mission Funding Office for The Episcopal Church, grounded in the stewardship theology of this church; and be it further
Resolved, That this office initiate a discernment process for a church-wide mission funding effort focused on, but not limited to, the 20/20 initiatives and on fostering cooperative seeking of new funds at all levels of the church.

Reconsideration of Resolution C003
Deputy Tinsmann of Iowa, who had voted with the majority on C003, moved to suspend the rules to allow reconsideration of Resolution C003.

Motion defeated
Reconsideration failed

Ecumenical Relations
The House of Deputies Committee on Ecumenical Relations presented its Report #3 on HB Message #58 on Resolution B003 (Study and Present the Reuilly Accord) and moved concurrence.

Parlimentary Inquiry
Deputy Simons inquired whether the motion was out of order, because the House had not received the Reuilly Accord.
The Parliamentarian stated that the documents were not needed because the resolution called for a study on the Reuilly Accord.

Personal Privilege
Deputy Hunter of Alaska asked that prayers be offered because the motion to reconsider Resolution C003 was rejected.

MINNEAPOLIS MEETING   HOUSE OF DEPUTIES

Prayers
The Vice-President called upon the Chaplain for prayers.

A voted was taken on Resolution B003.
The House concurred
(Communicated to the House of Bishops in HD Message #193)

Final Text of Resolution:
(B003)
Resolved, **That the 74th General Convention direct the Standing Commission on Ecumenical Relations to study and present the Reuilly Accord of 1998 between the French Reformed Church, the French Lutheran Church, and the Church of England for possible signature by the 75th General Convention.**

The House of Deputies Committee on Ecumenical Relations presented its Report #4 on HB Message #59 on Resolution B006 (Dialogue with Reformed Episcopal Church) and moved concurrence.
The House concurred
(Communicated to the House of Bishops in HD Message #194)

Final Text of Resolution:
(B006)
Resolved, **That the General Convention receive with thanksgiving the start of ecumenical dialogue with the Reformed Episcopal Church (REC) and the Anglican Province of America (APA), occasioned by Resolution D047 of the 73rd General Convention;** and be it further
Resolved, **That the 1940 Report of the Committee on Approaches to Unity of the Episcopal Church and the Report submitted to the Bishops of the Anglican Communion by this Church concerning the validity of Holy Orders of the Reformed Episcopal Church be referred to the Standing Commission on Ecumenical Relations for study during the 2004–2006 triennium and that the Commission report back to the 2006 General Convention on the validity of Holy Orders of the Reformed Episcopal Church.**

The House of Deputies Committee on Ecumenical Relations presented its Report #5 on HB Message #60 on Resolution A087 (Interim Eucharistic Sharing with the Moravian Church in America, Northern and Southern Provinces) and moved concurrence.

Deputy Glasspool of Maryland moved to terminate debate.
Motion carried
Debate terminated

A vote was taken on Resolution A087.

The House concurred
(Communicated to the House of Bishops in HD Message #195)

Final Text of Resolution:
(A087)
Resolved, That the 74th General Convention meeting in Minneapolis, MN, July 30–August 8, 2003 with concurrent action by the Synods of the Moravian Church in America (Northern and Southern Provinces), authorize continuing dialogue with the Moravian Church in America (Northern and Southern Provinces) which may lead to a future proposal of Full Communion including interchangeability of clergy for ministry of Word and Sacrament; and be it further
Resolved, That the 74th General Convention of the Episcopal Church, meeting in Minneapolis, MN, July 30–August 8, 2003, establish Interim Eucharistic Sharing between the Episcopal Church and the Moravian Church under the following guidelines:
1. Moravian Provincial Elders' Conferences and Episcopal diocesan authorities are hereby encouraged to authorize joint celebrations of the Eucharist.
2. An authorized liturgy of the host church must be used, with ordained ministers of both churches standing at the Communion Table for the Great Thanksgiving.
3. The Preacher may be from either church.

The House of Deputies Committee on Ecumenical Relations presented its Report #6 on HB Message #72 on Resolution A086 (Lutheran Ordination Bylaw) and moved concurrence.

The House concurred
(Communicated to the House of Bishops in HD Message #196)

Final Text of Resolution:
(A086)
Resolved, That the Standing Commission on Ecumenical Relations is hereby requested to be in conversation with representatives of the ELCA to monitor the ways and extent to which the ELCA ordination bylaw exception may cause any additional limitations upon the full communion that has been jointly established, to clarify the intent and meaning of paragraph 20 of "Called to Common Mission" and the ELCA bylaw 7.31.17 "Ordination Under Unusual Circumstances," and to report their findings and any recommendations to the next General Convention.

Miscellaneous Resolutions
The Committee on Miscellaneous Resolutions presented its Report #8 on Resolution D058 (Providing Assisted Hearing Devices) and moved that the Committee be discharged.

> Motion carried
> Committee discharged
> (Communicated to the House of Bishops in HD Message #197)

National and International Concerns
The House of Deputies Committee on National and International Concerns presented its Report #12 on Resolution A034 (United Nations Millennium Development Goals) and moved that the Committee be discharged.

> Motion carried
> Committee discharged
> (Communicated to the House of Bishops in HD Message #198)

Prayer Book, Liturgy and Church Music
The House of Deputies Committee on Prayer Book, Liturgy and Church Music presented its Report #12 on HB Message #77 on Resolution A100 (Revise Lesser Feasts and Fasts 2000) and moved concurrence.

Deputy Ward of Iowa moved to terminate debate.

> Motion carried
> Debate terminated

A vote was taken on Resolution A100.

> The House concurred
> (Communicated to the House of Bishops in HD Message #200)

Final Text of Resolution:
(A100)
Resolved, **That the 74th General Convention direct the Standing Commission on Liturgy and Music to undertake a revision of** *Lesser Feasts and Fasts 2000,* **to reflect our increasing awareness of the importance of the ministry of all the people of God and of the cultural diversity of The Episcopal Church, of the wider Anglican Communion, of our ecumenical partners, and of our lively experience of sainthood in local communities;** and be it further
Resolved, **That the SCLM produce a study of the significance of that experience of local sainthood in encouraging the living out of baptism;** and be it further
Resolved, **That the General Convention request the Joint Standing Committee on Program, Budget, and Finance to consider a budget allocation of $20,000 for implementation of this resolution.**

The House of Deputies Committee on Prayer Book, Liturgy and Church Music presented its Report #13 on HB Messsage #78 on Resolution A092 (Reauthorize Enriching Our Worship Work) and moved concurrence.

Deputy Seitz of West Virginia moved to terminate debate.

Motion carried
Debate terminated

A vote was taken on Resolution A092.

The House concurred
(Communicated to the House of Bishops in HD Message #199)

Final Text of Resolution:
(A092)
Resolved, That the 74th General Convention direct the Standing Commission on Liturgy and Music (SCLM) to further develop **Enriching Our Worship** and **Enriching Our Music**, preparing and collecting rites and music that are culturally diverse for use in a wide range of settings to advance the goals of 20/20. These rites and music may include, but not be limited to, pastoral rites to celebrate specific events grounded in the many cultures in our Church, such as:
   Pastoral offices of the Book of Common Prayer 1979;
   Rites of Passage, such as Quinceañeras (e.g. Latin American); Naming of Elders (e.g. Korean); Day of the Dead (e.g. Latin American); Honoring of Ancestors (e.g. Chinese); Adoption Rites (e.g. Native American); and Journey to Adulthood Rites;
   Mission and evangelism-based prayers;
   Creative worship resources for multisensory worship;
   And Spanish and French music resources; and be it further
Resolved, That the development of these rites and resources be designed and implemented using models which would innovatively draw on and reflect our Church's liturgical, cultural, racial, generational, gender and ethnic diversity; and be it further
Resolved, That the SCLM begin to develop a network for sharing these learnings and resources and report on their progress to the 75th General Convention; and be it further
Resolved, That the General Convention request the Joint Standing Committee on Program, Budget and Finance to consider a budget allocation of $130,000 for implementation of this resolution.

Midday Prayers
The Vice-President called upon the Chaplain for midday prayers.

Announcements
The Secretary read announcements.

Personal Privilege
Deputy Harris of Washington asked that greetings be sent to Dr. Pamela Chinnis, former President of the House of Deputies.

RECESS
The Vice-President recessed the House at 1:10 p.m. to reconvene at 2:30 p.m.

AFTERNOON SESSION

Reconvene
The President called the House to order at 2:38 p.m.

Prayers
The President called upon the Chaplain for prayers.

Certfication of Deputies
The House of Deputies Committee on Credentials presented its Report #15 for the second legislative session of the Ninth Legislative Day, and there were 2 new deputies certified. There were 419 clerical deputies and 422 lay deputies certified and seated, bringing the total count of the House to 841. There were 62 changes on this day as follows:

Diocese	*Alternate replacing*	*Deputy being replaced*
Atlanta	Janet W. Patterson	E. Bruce Garner
Atlanta	Richard Perry	John Andrews
Atlanta	Richard Callaway	Lori Lowe
California	Mary Gotthold	Bonita Palmer
Central Gulf Coast	Robert McMillan	Peter Wilson
Colorado	Jack Finlaw	Jacqueline Scott
Connecticut	Barbara Cheney	Mark Santucci
Delaware	Gary Rowe	Margaret Patterson
East Carolina	Joseph Cooper	Pamela Stringer
Eastern Oregon	Jean Gardner	Susan Powers
Hawaii	Linda Sproat	Bettye Jo Harris
Hawaii	Robert Fitzpatrick	Joseph Carr
Idaho	Bruce Henne	Margaret Babcock
Indianapolis	Sally Pedersen	Donald Sodrel
Iowa	Connie Whalen	Raisin Horn
Los Angeles	Mary Nestler	Anthony Guillen
Los Angeles	Janis Jones	James White
Louisiana	Kathleen Turner	Lonell Wright
Maine	Holly Antolini	Paige Blair

Maryland	Marjorie Mack	Christine Kinard
Massachusetts	Nadine Boakye	Betsy Madsen
Massachusetts	Miriam Gelfer	Mark Hollingsworth
Milwaukee	Martha Berger	Maurine Lewis
Minnesota	Michael Hanley	Grant Abbott
Minnesota	Philip McNairy	Howard Anderson
Minnesota	Sandra Wilson	Mariann Budde
Mississippi	Edward Sisson	Danny Meadors
Mississippi	R. Runnels	Shannon Johnston
Missouri	Marguerite Bowman	Lawrence George
Missouri	Larry Hooper	Tamsen Whistler
New Hampshire	Susan Langle	Debra Ogin
New Jersey	Linda Gaither	Cora Gaines
New Jersey	Charles Perfater	Jean McFarland
New Jersey	Virginia Sheay	John Zamboni
New York	Tobias Haller	Gerald Keucher
New York	Theodora Brooks	K. Dennis Winslow
Newark	Marjorie Christie	Martha Gardner
Northern California	Jack Hanstein	Beatryce Clark
Oregon	John Scannell	James Boston
Pennsylvania	Karen Lash	JoAnn Jones
Pennsylvania	Mary Laney	Nancy Wittig
Pittsburgh	Joan Malley	Joseph Sarria
Rhode Island	Caryl Frink	Carol Bennett
Rochester	Dawn Wilkins	Nancy Bell
San Joaquin	Ken Richards	Mark Lawrence
Southeast Florida	William Stokes	Mary Gray-Reeves
Southern Virginia	Sue Wilder	Charles Pfeifer
Southern Virginia	David Teschner	Harold Cobb
Southern Virginia	Frances Barber	Joyce Moorman
Southern Virginia	Robert Lee	Sara Mueller
Texas	James Nutter	Kenneth Kesselus
Upper South Carolina	Robert Dannals	Calvin Griffin
Utah	Karen Cramer	Barbara Losse
Virginia	Susan Goff	Charles Alley
West Missouri	India Philley	Carolyn Phelps
West Missouri	Bradley Woodall	Margaret Heckendorn
West Tennessee	Jeff Garrety	James Russell
West Texas	Alice Fischer	Priscilla Murguia
West Virginia	Sarah Bailey	Cheryl Winter
West Virginia	Thomas Miller	Deborah Short
Western Louisiana	Carolyn Ledet	Reece Middleton
Western Massachusetts	Heidi Frantz-Dale	Nancy Strong

Messages from the House of Bishops
The Secretary announced that the following messages had been received from the House of Bishops:

HB Message #185:	A154 (75th General Convention Site) Concurred.
HB Message #186:	D061 (Jubilee Ministry Funding) Rejected.
HB Message #187:	B009 (Request for Faith and Order Commission) Adopted.
HB Message #188:	B007 (Affirmations for Facilitating Emergence of Consensus) Discharged.
HB Message #189:	C005 (Rites for Blessing and Supporting Committed Relationships) Discharged.
HB Message #190:	D022 (Resolution on Rites Supporting Life-long Relationships) Discharged.

Personal Privilege
Deputy Williams of Western New York, accompanied by Deputy Farabee of Western New York, expressed distress about the pain and disillusionment felt by deputies of color, due to the House's failure to reconsider Resolution C003. She expressed her own apologies and repentance for participating in that action.

Consent Calendar
Communications
The House of Deputies Committee on Communications presented its Report #11 on Resolution A068 (Episcopal Church Website) and moved that the Committee be discharged.

Motion carried
Committee discharged
(Communicated to the House of Bishops in HD Message #201)

The House of Deputies Committee on Communications presented its Report #12 on Resolution A078 (Next Generation Mentoring) and moved that the Committee be discharged.

Motion carried
Committee discharged
(Communicated to the House of Bishops in HD Message #202)

(End of Consent Calendar)

Personal Privilege
Deputy Stokes of Southern Ohio spoke in support of Resolution C003 for restitution for Africans enslaved in America. She stated that a petition would be made available, and the Secretary asked that copies be distributed to each deputation to sign and turn in at the Southern Ohio deputation.

Personal Privilege
Deputy Tolliver of Chicago expressed irritation that, unlike Resolution C003, there were many other resolutions related to governmental and legislative matters on which the House did not hesitate to take action.

Episcopal Church Women
The President invited Harriet Near, the new President of Episcopal Church Women, to address the House.

Dispatch of Business
The House of Deputies Committee on Dispatch of Business outlined the order of business for the afternoon:
1. Special Order of Business for Program, Budget and Finance Report;
2. Second Ballot for General Seminary Trustees;
3. Election of Presiding Bishop's Nominating Committee;
4. Special Order of Business to discuss Resolution C051; and once completed, the House will return to the Legislative Calendar.

Program, Budget and Finance
The Joint Standing Committee on Program, Budget and Finance presented its Report #1 on Resolution D086 (Budget for the Episcopal Church 2004–2006) and moved adoption.

Original Text of Resolution:
(D086)
Resolved, the House of Bishops concurring, That the 74th General Convention adopt the Budget for The Episcopal Church for the next triennium as set forth below:

1.0 The Budget for the Episcopal Church for the period January 1, 2004 through December 31, 2006, which shall be a unified budget including Canonical, Corporate, and Program (mission) portions, is adopted at a total of $146,395,000.00.

    1.1 The Canonical portion, providing for the contingent expenses of the General Convention, the stipend of the Presiding Bishop and the expenses of that office, the expenses of the President of the House of Deputies, and Church Pension Fund assessments is adopted at a total of $28,115,000.00 as follows:
        For the year 2004 $ 8,474,000.00
        For the year 2005 $ 8,618,000.00
        For the year 2006 $ 11,023,000.00

    1.2 The Corporate portion, providing for the requirements for the administrative support of the Domestic and Foreign Missionary Society offices, is adopted at a total of $25,567,000.00 as follows:
        For the year 2004 $ 8,225,000.00
        For the year 2005 $ 8,577,000.00

For the year 2006 $ 8,765,000.00

1.3 The Program (mission) portion, providing for support for the mission and ministry (restricted and unrestricted) of the Church, is adopted at a total of $92,713,000.00 as follows:
For the year 2004 $ 30,510,000.00
For the year 2005 $ 30,821,000.00
For the year 2006 $ 31,382,000.00

2.0 The funding policy for the period January 1, 2004 through December 31, 2006 is adopted, based on a single Asking (apportioned share) of the dioceses. After a $100,000 exemption from total income, a single asking shall be applied at a flat rate of 21% of the balance of income to the diocese, reported in the diocesan financial statements for the year two years prior to the year to which the pledge is applied [e.g.: 2004 Askings (apportioned share) are to be based on 2002 actual income figures]. "Income" includes (1) all congregational giving to the diocese, (2) all unrestricted investment and endowment income to the diocese, (3) restricted investment and endowment income to the diocese which covers costs in the operating budget, and (4) other earnings from investments or enterprises. It is intended that income shall include revenues that fund normal operating and program expenses of the dioceses. It is not intended to include pass-through income that is used for expenses for programming that are simply administered by the dioceses, or that would not be otherwise funded by contributions from parishes or out of investment income.

2.1 We rejoice with dioceses that have moved toward, and those that give at and above, the 21% Asking. Such giving creates a strong financial basis for vital mission and witness of The Episcopal Church. We encourage all our dioceses to adopt the 21% Asking; then we could allocate an additional 4.7 million dollars each year toward fulfilling the mission priorities which we have embraced in this 74th General Convention.

2.2 For the budgetary period income from diocesan commitments, totaling $90,487,000.00 is anticipated as follows:
For the year 2004 $ 29,473,000.00
For the year 2005 $ 30,062, 000.00
For the year 2006 $ 30,952,000.00

2.3 For the budgetary period 2004–2006, payment by the dioceses of the Askings shall be made in twelve equal monthly payments.

2.4 All additional income, other than from the Askings of the dioceses, totaling $55,908,000.00, is projected as follows:
For the year 2004 $ 18,554,000.00
For the year 2005 $ 18,382,000.00
For the year 2006 $ 18,972,000.00

2.5 A General Ordination fee is hereby authorized, which fees shall be added to the funding from dioceses and applied to the expenses of examination as appropriated in the budget. A candidate for Holy Orders eligible for examination and so certified by the diocesan bishop shall not be disqualified for examination because the fee has not been paid.

2.6 General Convention registration and exhibitors fees are hereby authorized, which fees shall be added to the funding from dioceses and applied to the expenses of the 2006 General Convention, and for no other purpose.

3.0 In the exercise of their respective authorities, the Executive Council of the General Convention and the Joint Standing Committee on Program, Budget and Finance shall be subject to the following policies:

3.1 Each year, the Executive Council, with the advice of the Joint Standing Committee on Program, Budget and Finance, shall adjust the budget to the assured income of the Executive Council so as to carry out the Budget for The Episcopal Church for that year on a balanced budget basis.

3.2 The fiscal year shall begin January 1.

3.3 If in any year the total anticipated income for budget support is less than the amount required to support the budget approved by the General Convention, the Canonical portion of the Budget for The Episcopal Church shall have funding priority over any other budget areas.

3.4 Net surpluses that are realized in any year of the triennium are to be allocated in the subsequent years of the triennium in the following rank order, as needed, to:
Ministries With Young People
Ethnic Congregational Development
Congregational Development

3.5 Undesignated bequests and legacies received during the budgetary period shall be set aside in the general endowment fund of which only the income shall be used for the general purposes of the Society.

3.6 Designated bequests and legacies received during the budgetary period shall be set aside in specific funds of which only the income shall be used for the purposes so designated.

3.7 Each Committee, Commission, Agency and Board (CCAB) proposing to the General Convention any resolution with funding implications shall present to the Joint Standing Committee on Program, Budget and Finance a detailed budget in support of its plan(s), including cost estimates from contractors and suppliers for all goods and services, by no later than six months before the opening day of the General Convention

3.8 Subsequent editions of the *Report and Proposal of the Presiding Bishop and Executive Council to the General Convention* contain the following information for each year of the preceding triennium:

MINNEAPOLIS MEETING HOUSE OF DEPUTIES

A description of the actual income and expenditures of the DFMS, relating the expenditures to the Church's priorities with accompanying narrative.

Endowment balance and total investment return, with accompanying narrative.

Posting of this report on the DFMS website when it is released to the Bishops and Deputies.

The House voted on the Revenue Section of the 2004–2006 Budget.
Motion carried
Resolution adopted

The House voted on the Expense Section of the 2004–2006 Budget.
Motion carried
Resolution adopted
(Communicated to the House of Bishops in HD Message #210)

The Chair of the Joint Standing Committee on Program, Budget and Finance moved that the Joint Committee be discharged from considering the following resolutions because they are in the adopted budget: Resolution A001 (Budget Appropriation for the Archives of the Episcopal Church), Resolution A002 (Budget Appropriation for the Board for Church Deployment), Resolution A003 (Budget Appropriation for the General Board of Examining Chaplains), Resolution A004 (General Ordination Exam Fee), Resolution A153 (House of Bishops Committee on Pastoral Development Budget Appropriation), Resolution A157 (Joint Standing Committee on Program, Budget and Finance Budget Appropriation), and Resolution A158 (Title IV Budget Appropriation).

Resolution A001 (Budget Appropriation for the Archives of the Episcopal Church)
Motion carried
Committee discharged
(Communicated to the House of Bishops in HD Message #211)

Resolution A002 (Budget Appropriation for the Board for Church Deployment)
Motion carried
Committee discharged
(Communicated to the House of Bishops in HD Message #212)

Resolution A003 (Budget Appropriation for the General Board of Examining Chaplains)

Motion carried
Committee discharged
(Communicated to the House of Bishops in HD Message #213)

Resolution A004 (General Ordination Exam Fee)

Motion carried
Committee discharged
(Communicated to the House of Bishops in HD Message #214)

Resolution A153 (House of Bishops Committee on Pastoral Development Budget Appropriation)

Motion carried
Committee discharged
(Communicated to the House of Bishops in HD Message #228)

Resolution A157 (Joint Standing Committee on Program, Budget and Finance Budget Appropriation)

Motion carried
Committee discharged
(Communicated to the House of Bishops in HD Message #215)

Resolution A158 (Title IV Budget Appropriation)

Motion carried
Committee discharged
(Communicated to the House of Bishops in HD Message #216)

The Chair of the Joint Standing Committee on Program, Budget and Finance reminded deputations about the Budget Covenants to be signed.

The President suspended the Rules for the House to express appreciation to the Joint Standing Committee on Program, Budget and Finance for their work.

Ballot #2 for the General Theological Seminary Board of Trustees

Election Ballot #2 was taken for the General Theological Seminary Board of Trustees, two clergy persons for three-year terms.

Ballot #2 taken

Privilege and Courtesy

The House of Deputies Committee on Privilege and Courtesy presented its Report #8 on Resolution D084 (LISTSERV Appreciation) and moved adoption.

Original Text of Resolution:
(D084)
Whereas, the House of Bishops and the House of Deputies Listserv, lovingly created and maintained for General Convention by Dr. Louie Crew, was handed over in its adolescence to the gracious heart of Cynthia McFarland; and

Whereas, the ushers, better known as the "Keystone Kops," have saved us from repeating missteps and procedural errors; and

Whereas, we give special thanks for the ministry of Brian Reid, technical advisor to the listserv and world expert in internet technology; and

Whereas, this listserv enabled us to become better acquainted with each other as well as to discuss our differences and our commonalities; and

Whereas, the listserv was open to others as kibitzers, enabling the entire Church to observe our discussions and our frailties; now therefore be it

Resolved, the House of Bishops concurring, that the 74th General Convention of The Episcopal Church give thanks for the ministry of communication of Brian Reid, Cynthia McFarland and her faithful ushers: Matt Chew, Ann Fontaine, Christopher Hart, Barbara Mann, Connie Ott, and Nigel Renton.

Motion carried
Resolution adopted
(Communicated to the House of Bishops in HD Message #203)

The House of Deputies Committee on Privilege and Courtesy presented its Report #9 on Resolution D085 (Gratitude to Church Periodical Club) and moved adoption.

Original Text of Resolution:
(D085)
Whereas, The Church Periodical Club continues to distribute "Energy Lift" candy to Deputies as it has done for ten successive General Conventions while engaging in the ministry of providing the printed word for more than a century; now therefore be it

Resolved, That the House of Deputies of the 74th General Convention of The Episcopal Church express appreciation to Priscilla Magar, the Church Periodical Club President, and to all the co-workers of the Church Periodical Club, for their traditional gift of succulent "Energy Lift" candy.

Motion carried
Resolution adopted
(Communicated to the House of Bishops in HD Message #204)

The House of Deputies Committee on Privilege and Courtesy presented its Report #13 on Resolution D089 (Thanks to Bishop Jelinek and the Diocese of Minnesota) and moved adoption.

Original Text of Resolution:
(D089)
Whereas, the Rt. Rev. James L. Jelinek and the people of the Diocese of Minnesota have offered gracious hospitality to the 74th General Convention by welcoming us at the convention center, and by providing assistance at the daily liturgies; and
Whereas, the Very Rev. Spenser Simrill, Dean of St. Mark's Cathedral, and the Rev. Dr. Sandye Wilson, Rector of Gethsemane Church, have made these churches available for creative worship, educational programs, and social events; now therefore be it
Resolved, the House of Bishops concurring, That the 74th General Convention of The Episcopal Church give thanks and praise to God for the Rt. Rev. James Jelinek and the faithful people of the Diocese of Minnesota for their inclusive and generous hospitality.

Motion carried
Resolution adopted
(Communicated to the House of Bishops in HD Message #205)

The House of Deputies Committee on Privilege and Courtesy presented its Report #14 on Resolution D090 (Nancy Piatkowski) and moved adoption.

Original Text of Resolution:
(D090)
Whereas, Nancy Piatkowski served the Commission on the Status of Women, as Vice-President of the Episcopal Women's History Project; and as Archivist for the Diocese of Western New York; and
Whereas, she was an educator, artisan, and friend who (in her own words) "marched to a different accordion;" and
Whereas, she died on July 12, 2003, after a short illness; now therefore be it
Resolved, That the 74th General Convention extend its sympathy to the family of Nancy Piatkowski, and that the Secretary be instructed to send a copy of this resolution to them.

Motion carried
Resolution adopted
(Communicated to the House of Bishops in HD Message #206)

The House of Deputies Committee on Privilege and Courtesy presented its Report #16 on Resolution D092 (Greetings to the Archbishop of Canterbury) and moved adoption.

Original Text of Resolution:
(D092)

Whereas, it has pleased Her Majesty Queen Elizabeth II to seek the advice of the Rt. Hon. Tony Blair, Prime Minister and First Lord of the Treasury, in the selection of the 104th Archbishop of Canterbury; and

Whereas, the Prime Minister advised Her Majesty to grant her license to the Dean and Chapter of Canterbury to elect the Most Rev. Rowan Williams, Bishop of Monmouth and Archbishop of the Church in Wales, to the See of Canterbury; and

Whereas, the Most Rev. Rowan Williams, having been installed in the Primatial Chair of St. Augustine of Canterbury as the Primate of All England, is the symbolic Head of the Anglican Communion; now therefore be it

Resolved, the House of Bishops concurring, That the 74th General Convention send its respectful and affectionate greetings to His Grace, the Archbishop of Canterbury, to whom we say in his native tongue "*Cofion gynnes* (Warm greetings), *Pob hwyl* (Good luck), and *Yr Bendith Duw Hollalliog, yr Tad, yr Mab, yr Usprid Glad, a gydach ti, yn wastad* (God Almighty, the Father, the Son, and the Holy Spirit, go with you always);" and be it further

Resolved, That the Secretary of the General Convention send a copy of this resolution to the Most Rev. Rowan Williams, Archbishop of Canterbury and Primate of All England, in token of the esteem of the General Convention for his office and our affection for his person, as we look forward to participation with him in the councils of the world-wide Anglican Communion.

Motion carried
Resolution adopted
(Communicated to the House of Bishops in HD Message #207)

The House of Deputies Committee on Privilege and Courtesy presented its Report #12 on Resolution D088 (Ministry to the Deaf) and moved adoption.

Original Text of Resolution:
(D088)

Whereas, many in The Episcopal Church have been striving to make our church accessible to people whose primary language is American Sign Language; and

Whereas, St. Ann's Church for the Deaf, New York City, was organized in 1852 by the Rev. Thomas Gallaudet; and

Whereas, the Rev. Henry Winter Syle, the first deaf man ordained a priest (1853), brought the Gospel to deaf people in their own language; and

Whereas, this truly "silent minority" has had a presence at every General Convention since 1961, reminding the larger body that the churches of the Episcopal Conference of the Deaf are, indeed, part of The Episcopal Church and that it is necessary to facilitate understanding and communication in meetings of all levels of the Church; and

Whereas, an outward and visible sign of this ministry has been present in the 74th General Convention in the work of Rayelenn Casey of the Diocese of Central Pennsylvania, Donna Scarfe of the Diocese of Iowa, Kathy Beetham of the

Diocese of North Carolina, Jan Williamson of the Diocese of San Diego, Nancy Diener of the Diocese of Minnesota, and Diane Lynch of the Diocese of New Jersey; now therefore be it

Resolved, the House of Bishops concurring, That the 74th General Convention of The Episcopal Church commend the Episcopal Conference of the Deaf for its continued efforts to support deaf clergy and ministry in the deaf community so that the Good News may be brought to all of Jesus's sheep.

Motion carried
Resolution adopted
(Communicated to the House of Bishops in HD Message #208)

The House of Deputies Committee on Privilege and Courtesy presented its Report #11 on Resolution D087 (Evening of Conversations) and moved adoption.

Original Text of Resolution:
(D087)
Whereas, the Evening of Conversations provided members of this Convention an opportunity for exchanging ideas, experiences, and feelings about the challenging topics of Christian hope, interfaith dialogue, war and peace, 20/20, and engaging God's mission; now therefore be it

Resolved, the House of Bishops concurring, That the 74th General Convention of The Episcopal Church express our gratitude to the planners, panelists, and participants in these stimulating conversations.

Motion carried
Resolution adopted
(Communicated to the House of Bishops in HD Message #209)

Ballot #1 for Joint Nominating Committee for the Election of the Presiding Bishop

Election Ballot #1 was taken for the Joint Nominating Committee for the Election of the Presiding Bishop.

The Secretary noted a typographical error in the Province Five nomination biographical information for the Rev. Richard Tolliver. He is Rector of St. Edmund's Church, not St. Edward's Church.

Ballot #1 taken

Personal Privilege

The Voting Secretary acknowledged the voting technicians who have so ably assisted with voting at Convention.

RECESS

The President recessed the House at 4:07 p.m. to reconvene at 4:20 p.m.

Reconvene
The President called the House to order at 4:25 p.m.

Appointments by President of the House of Deputies
Board of the Episcopal Church Archives
> The Rev. Robert G. Crew of Connecticut
> The Rev. John Kitigawa of Arizona
> Ms. Judy Dailey of Easton
> Ms. Michaela French of Maryland

Board for Church Deployment
Clerical:
> The Rev. Canon Matthew Stoddard of East Carolina

Lay:
> Canon Jill Swans of Pennsylvania
> Canon Alice Clayton of East Tennessee
> Ms. Emily Peach of Missouri

Title IV Review Committee
> Mr. J.P. Causey, Jr. of Virginia
> The Rev. Carolyn Kiel-Kuhr of Montana
> The Very Rev. Scott Kirby of Eau Claire
> Ms. Deborah J. Stokes of Southern Ohio

Special Order of Business
The House of Deputies Committee on Dispatch of Business moved a Special Order of Business for the immediate consideration of Resolution C051.

Your Committee on Dispatch of Business moves the adoption of the following resolutions:

Resolved, That this House set a Special Order of Business on the 9th Legislative Day, Thursday, August 7, 2003, immediately following the Nominations for Vice-President, for the purpose of considering and taking action with respect to the Report of Committee 7 on Resolution C051; and be it further

Resolved, That in the consideration of the same the following rules of debate shall be followed:
1. The Committee Chair shall have two minutes to speak with respect to the report, and five minutes to respond to questions of information or clarification; a filer of the Minority Report shall then have two minutes to speak with respect to the minority report;
2. The entire debate of the report thereafter shall be limited to 30 additional minutes;
3. Each speaker shall be limited to two minutes and no speaker shall speak more than once on the same question;
4. The Chair shall designate three microphones, one for speakers in favor of the resolution and one for speakers in opposition to the resolution and one for procedural motions;
5. The Chair shall recognize only those at the three microphones and, to the

extent practicable speakers of opposite views in alternate succession;
6. Debate may be terminated prior to the expiration of the 30 minute period, or any extension thereof, or extended only by two-thirds vote of the House.
7. No amendments or procedural motions shall be entertained during the first 15 minutes of debate, following the first 15 minute period, the Chair will recognize speakers at all other microphones for the purpose of speaking to amendments.

Deputy Glasspool of Maryland moved to amend the Special Order of Business.

Proposed Amendment:
Make all microphones available.

> Motion defeated
> Amendment defeated

Deputy Hitt of Colorado moved to amend the Special Order of Business.

Proposed Amendment:
Limit speakers to one minute.

> Motion carried
> Amendment adopted

Deputy Bradberry of Southern Virginia moved to amend the Special Order of Business.

Proposed Amendment:
That after 15 minutes all microphones be opened so persons may speak to amendments.

> Motion carried
> Amendment adopted

Deputy Ferrell of North Carolina moved to terminate debate on the Special Order of Business.

> Motion carried
> Debate terminated

A vote was taken on the Special Order of Business as amended.

> Motion carried
> Special Order adopted with amendments

Prayers
The President called on the Chaplain for prayers.

Prayer Book, Liturgy and Church Music
The Committee on Prayer Book, Liturgy and Church Music presented its Report #22 on HB Message #183 on Resolution C051 (Blessing of Committed Same-Gender Relationships) and moved concurrence.

Deputy Downie of Eastern Michigan moved to terminate debate.

> Motion carried
> Debate terminated

Vote by Orders
Deputy Cavanagh of San Joaquin, on behalf the clerical deputation of Florida, the lay and clerical deputations of San Joaquin, and the clerical deputation Central Florida asked for a vote by orders. The President ruled that request in order.

Ballot #3—Vote by Orders
Ballot #3 was taken on Resolution C051.
Ballot #3 taken by orders

Personal Privilege
Deputy Sanchez of the Dominican Republic expressed gratitude to the translators who have assisted deputies during Convention.

Dispatch of Business
The House of Deputies Committee on Dispatch of Business advised the House that the next Order of Business would be Resolution A065.

Education
The House of Deputies Committee on Education presented its Report #7 on HB Message #89 on Resolution A065 (Leadership Programs for 18–25 Year-Olds) and moved concurrence.
Deputy Kirby of Eau Claire moved to terminate debate.
Motion carried
Debate terminated

Special Order of Business
Deputy Dales of New Hampshire moved a procedural motion that for the remainder of this legislative day, all speakers, including committee chairs, be limited to one minute.
Motion carried
Special order adopted

The House proceeded to vote on Resolution A065.
The House concurred

(Communicated to the House of Bishops in HD Message #217)

Final Text of Resolution:
(A065)
Resolved, That the Ministries with Young People Cluster be directed to review and identify existing internships and leadership programs for 18–30 year-old members of our church, particularly seeking programs that focus on social justice, discipleship, simple living, intentional community, spiritual formation, theological reflection, and vocational discernment; and be it further
Resolved, That the 74th General Convention of The Episcopal Church

encourage dioceses, congregations, educational institutions, and other organizations of our church to explore and develop new internships and leadership development programs for 18–30 year-old members of our church, including programs that send young people into mission fields to do the work of the church; and to seek funding from additional sources to support this work; and be it further

Resolved, That the Ministries with Young People Cluster be directed to support these efforts, and to hold these programs up to dioceses, congregations, institutions, and other organizations of our church, so that they may be shared and implemented throughout our church; and be it further

Resolved, That the General Convention request the Joint Standing Committee on Program, Budget and Finance to consider a budget allocation of $500,000 per year, for a total of $1,500,000 during the next triennium, for implementation of this resolution, and that this allocation be used to support young adults' participation in these programs and the development efforts that are encouraged in this resolution.

The House of Deputies Committee on Education presented its Report #8 on HB Message #88 on Resolution A021 (Broadening HIV Prevention Methods) and moved concurrence.

The House concurred
(Communicated to the House of Bishops in HD Message #218)

Final Text of Resolution:
(A021)
Resolved, That The Episcopal Church through its General Convention call upon its members and its congregations to take the lead in insuring that all methods used to prevent the spread of HIV are taught in school curricula, church school curricula, and in other educational settings.

Ecumenical Relations

The House of Deputies Committee on Ecumenical Relations presented its Report #7 on HB Message #93 on Resolution A088 (Response to Gift of Authority) and moved concurrence.

The House concurred
(Communicated to the House of Bishops in HD Message #219)

Final Text of Resolution:
(A088)
Resolved, That the affirmations noted and the questions raised in the report of the Standing Commission on Ecumenical Relations be referred to **ARCIC** for further dialogue; and be it further

Resolved, That the report of the Standing Commission on Ecumenical Relations on the Gift of Authority be transmitted to the Anglican Communion Office as the official response of this Church.

World Mission

The House of Deputies Committee on World Mission presented its Report #3 on HB Message #101 on Resolution D009 (Support 2008 Anglican Gathering) and moved concurrence.

The House concurred
(Communicated to the House of Bishops in HD Message #220)

Final Text of Resolution:

(D009)
Resolved, That the 74th General Convention enthusiastically support and affirm the call of the Anglican Consultative Council meetings XI (Scotland 1999) and XII (Hong Kong 2002), and of the Joint Standing Committee of the Primates and Anglican Consultative Council, that there be an Anglican congress of lay people, priests, deacons, and bishops from every diocese in the Anglican Communion described as the "Anglican Gathering" and tentatively planned to be held in South Africa in mid–2008; and be it further

Resolved, That every diocese of The Episcopal Church begin to plan and make financial provisions for representation at the 2008 Anglican Gathering; and be it further

Resolved, That the Standing Commission on World Mission work cooperatively with the Executive Council and the Joint Standing Committee on Program, Budget and Finance to prepare during the next triennium a financial provision for the 75th General Convention to support the 2008 Anglican Gathering; and be it further

Resolved, That the department of Anglican and Global Relations at the Episcopal Church Center, working in consultation with the Standing Commission on World Mission, be directed to assist the wider Anglican Communion in every way possible in the development of the 2008 Anglican Gathering; and be it further

Resolved, That the Presiding Bishop communicate The Episcopal Church's enthusiastic support for the 2008 Anglican Gathering to the Archbishop of Canterbury and the Primates of the Anglican Communion; and be it further

Resolved, That the Secretary of the General Convention, along with The Episcopal Church's members of the Anglican Consultative Council, communicate the substance of this resolution to the General Secretary of the Anglican Communion, the Anglican Consultative Council, and the staff and leadership of the Inter-Anglican Standing Commission on Mission and Evangelism.

National and International Concerns

The House of Deputies Committee on National and International Concerns presented its Report #20 on Resolution D030 (Funding Regional Ministry vs Political Advocacy) and moved the resolution, recommending rejection.

Original Text of Resolution:
(D030)

Resolved, the House of Bishops concurring, That the 74th General Convention request the Executive Council, the Program, Budget and Finance Committee, and the Treasurer to reduce funding of the Washington office and staff to under $200,000 per year and to appropriate such funds in the manner set forth below; and be it further

Resolved, That these funds shall be used to provide members with "Action Alerts" on pending legislation, to respond to requests for information, and to publish internet resources to support grassroots political advocacy; and be it further

Resolved, That the resources saved through this action be offered to each of the nine Provinces of ECUSA and distributed annually in equal shares to those Provinces that accept this offer and agree to the conditions for their use; and be it further

Resolved, That the resources shall be used to provide "matching funds" for ministries chosen through a challenge process in each Province which shall include the review of diocesan as well as regional opportunities; and be it further

Resolved, That the ministries funded through this process shall be accountable to the sponsoring Provincial leadership, and each Province shall provide a report back to the next General Convention that includes a description of the distribution of funds as well as the ministry that was provided; and be it further

Resolved, That each Province, with the assistance of the Church Center staff, shall provide reports during the triennium to the membership through web pages and online bulletin boards that outline the challenge process, the ministry opportunities considered, and the allocation of funds; and be it further

Resolved, That the General Convention request the Joint Standing Committee on Program, Budget and Finance to consider the budget ramifications of this resolution.

Committee Amendment:

Resolved, the House of Bishops concurring, That the 74th General Convention request the Executive Council, the Program, Budget and Finance Committee, and the Treasurer to reduce funding of the Washington office and staff to under $200,000 per year and to appropriate such funds in the manner set forth below; and be it further

Resolved, That these funds shall be used to provide members with "Action Alerts" on pending legislation, to respond to requests for information, and to publish internet resources to support grassroots political advocacy; and be it further

Resolved, That the resources saved through this action be offered to each of the nine Provinces of ECUSA and distributed annually in equal shares to those Provinces that accept this offer and agree to the conditions for their use; and be it further

Resolved, That the resources shall be used to provide "matching funds" for ministries chosen through a challenge process in each Province which shall include the review of diocesan as well as regional opportunities; and be it further

Resolved, That the ministries funded through this process shall be accountable to the sponsoring Provincial leadership, and each Province shall provide a report back to the next General Convention that includes a description of the distribution of funds as well as the ministry that was provided; and be it further

Resolved, That each Province, with the assistance of the Church Center staff, shall provide reports during the triennium to the membership through web pages and online bulletin boards that outline the challenge process, the ministry opportunities considered, and the allocation of funds; and be it further

Resolved, That the General Convention request the Joint Standing Committee on Program, Budget and Finance to consider ~~the budget ramifications of this resolution~~ *reducing the budget allocation to under $200,000 for implementation of this resolution.*

Deputy Sessum of Lexington moved to terminate debate.

Motion carried
Debate terminated

A vote was taken on Resolution D030 as amended.

Motion defeated
Resolution rejected
(Communicated to the House of Bishops in HD Message #221)

Social and Urban Affairs

The House of Deputies Committee on Social and Urban Affairs presented its Report #14 on Resolution D059 (Justice For Juveniles) and moved that the Committee be discharged.

Motion carried
Committee discharged
(Communicated to the House of Bishops in HD Message #222)

The House of Deputies Committee on Social and Urban Affairs presented its Report #17 on HB Message #108 on Resolution A014 (Approve Research on Human Stem Cells) and moved concurrence.

The House concurred
(Communicated to the House of Bishops in HD Message #223)

Final Text of Resolution:
(A014)
Resolved, **That the 74th General Convention of The Episcopal Church, believing that a wider availability of embryonic stem cells for medical research holds the potential for discovery of effective treatment of a wide variety of diseases and other medical conditions;**

(A) Support the choice of those who wish to donate their early embryos, remaining after in vitro fertilization (IVF) procedures have ended; and
(B) Urge that the United States Congress pass legislation that would authorize federal funding for derivation of and medical research on human embryonic stem cells that were generated for IVF and remain after fertilization procedures have been concluded, provided that:
1. these early embryos are no longer required for procreation by those donating them and would simply be discarded;
2. those donating early embryos have given their prior informed consent to their use in stem cell research;
3. the embryos were not deliberately created for research purposes;
4. the embryos were not obtained by sale or purchase; and be it further

Resolved, That the 74th General Convention of The Episcopal Church urge the Secretary of Health and Human Services to establish an interdisciplinary oversight body for all research in both the public and private sectors that involves stem cells from human embryos, parthenotes, sperm cells, or egg cells, and have this body in place within six months of passing such legislation; and be it further

Resolved, That the 74th General Convention of The Episcopal Church direct the Secretary of General Convention to communicate this resolution to appropriate members and committees of the United States Congress and direct the Office of Government Relations to identify and advocate the legislation called for by this resolution.

The House of Deputies Committee on Social and Urban Affairs presented its Report #12 on Resolution C001 (Opposition to Reparative/Conversion Therapy) and moved that the Committee be discharged.

Motion carried
Committee discharged
(Communicated to the House of Bishops in HD Message #224)

The House of Deputies Committee on Social and Urban Affairs presented its Report #15 on Resolution D029 (Reparative Therapy) and moved that the Committee be discharged.

Motion carried
Committee discharged
(Communicated to the House of Bishops in HD Message #225)

Results of Ballot #3: Vote by Orders on Resolution C051

The Secretary read the results of Ballot #3 on Resolution C051.

Type	Total	Necessary	Yes	No	Divided	Results
Lay	108	55	58	38	12	Carried
Clergy	108	55	62	34	12	Carried

The House concurred
(Communicated to the House of Bishops in HD Message #226)

Final Text of Resolution:

(C051)

Resolved, That the 74th General Convention affirm the following:

1. That our life together as a community of faith is grounded in the saving work of Jesus Christ and expressed in the principles of the Chicago-Lambeth Quadrilateral: Holy Scripture, the historic Creeds of the Church, the two dominical Sacraments, and the Historic Episcopate.
2. That we reaffirm Resolution A069 of the 65th General Convention (1976) that "homosexual persons are children of God who have a full and equal claim with all other persons upon the love, acceptance, and pastoral concern and care of the Church."
3. That, in our understanding of homosexual persons, differences exist among us about how best to care pastorally for those who intend to live in monogamous, non-celibate unions; and what is, or should be, required, permitted, or prohibited by the doctrine, discipline, and worship of The Episcopal Church concerning the blessing of the same.
4. That we reaffirm Resolution D039 of the 73rd General Convention (2000), that "We expect such relationships will be characterized by fidelity, monogamy, mutual affection and respect, careful, honest communication, and the holy love which enables those in such relationships to see in each other the image of God," and that such relationships exist throughout the church.
5. That we recognize that local faith communities are operating within the bounds of our common life as they explore and experience liturgies celebrating and blessing same-sex unions.
6. That we commit ourselves, and call our church, in the spirit of Resolution A104 of the 70th General Convention (1991), to continued prayer, study, and discernment on the pastoral care for gay and lesbian persons, to include the compilation and development by a special commission organized and appointed by the Presiding Bishop of resources to facilitate as wide a conversation of discernment as possible throughout the church.
7. That our baptism into Jesus Christ is inseparable from our communion with one another, and we commit ourselves to that communion despite our diversity of opinion and, among dioceses, a diversity of pastoral

practice with the gay men and lesbians among us.
8. That it is a matter of faith that our Lord longs for our unity as his disciples, and for us this entails living within the boundaries of the Constitution and Canons of The Episcopal Church. We believe this discipline expresses faithfulness to our polity and that it will facilitate the conversation we seek, not only in The Episcopal Church, but also in the wider Anglican Communion and beyond.

[Note: For the Minority report distributed in the House of Bishops regarding Resolution C051, see House of Bishops Day 8, Appendix K. *Ed.*]

Appointments by the President

The President of the House of Deputies announced his appointments to the Board of the Episcopal Archives, the Church Deployment Board, and the Title IV Review Board and moved adoption.

Resolved, the House of Bishops concurring, That the General Convention confirm the appointment by the President of the House of Deputies to the Board of the Episcopal Church Archives of:
   The Rev. Robert G. Crew of Connecticut
   The Rev. John Kitigawa of Arizona
   Ms. Judy Dailey of Easton
   Ms. Michaela French of Maryland

Motion carried
Appointments confirmed
(Communicated to the House of Bishops in HD Message #229)

Resolved, the House of Bishops concurring, That the General Convention confirm the appointment by the President of the House of Deputies to the Board for Church Deployment of:
   Clerical:
   The Rev. Canon Matthew Stoddard of East Carolina
   Lay:
   Canon Jill Swans of Pennsylvania
   Canon Alice Clayton of East Tennessee
   Ms. Emily Peach of Missouri

Motion carried
Appointments confirmed
(Communicated to the House of Bishops in HD Message #230)

Resolved, That the House of Deputies confirm the appointment by the President of this House to the Title IV Review Committee of:
    Mr. J.P. Causey, Jr. of Virginia
    The Rev. Carolyn Kiel-Kuhr of Montana
    The Very Rev. Scott Kirby of Eau Claire
    Ms. Deborah J. Stokes of Southern Ohio

Motion carried
Appointments confirmed
(Communicated to the House of Bishops in HD Message #231)

Prayers
The President called on the Chaplain for prayers.

RECESS
The President recessed the House at 6:10 p.m. until 10:30 a.m. on Friday, August 8, 2003.

Appendix C
Day 9

Signatures Collected in Affirmation of Resolution A135 on Holy Habits

Resolved, That in recognition of the church's tradition of calling us to work, pray, and give for the spread of God's kingdom, all members of The Episcopal Church be encouraged to develop a personal spiritual discipline that includes, at a minimum, the holy habits of tithing, daily personal prayer and study, Sabbath time, and weekly corporate worship; and be it further
Resolved, That the Bishops and Deputies of the 74th General Convention be given an opportunity to sign the following declaration:
> As Christian stewards and leaders of The Episcopal Church, we affirm that we are tithing, or have adopted a plan to work toward tithing as a minimum standard for our giving; and that, if we are not already doing so, we are committed to give priority to corporate worship, personal daily prayer and study, and Sabbath time in our own lives; and we invite all members of The Episcopal Church to join us in these holy habits; and be it further

Resolved, That we commit ourselves to present this declaration to our diocesan conventions for adoption and signature, and in turn to the vestries and people of our parishes, missions, and university centers; and be it further
Resolved, That the Secretary publish a list of the General Convention signatories in the Journal of the 74th General Convention and provide the same to *Episcopal Life* for publication of the statement and the list of signatories.

Signed in Minneapolis, Minnesota at General Convention by:

Mary E. Abrams (Kentucky)
Ronald G. Abrams (East Carolina)
Jennifer L. Adams (Western Michigan)
Pan Adams (Arkansas)
Patricia Adams (Chicago)
Darrow L. K. Aiona (Hawaii)
Billy J. Alford (Georgia)
Laura Allen (Dallas)
Mark F. Allen (Northern California)
Michael Allen (Kentucky)
Martha Bedell Alexander (North Carolina)
Brian A. Amato (Central Pennsylvania)
Joan M. P. Anders (New Jersey)
Augusta A. Anderson (Western North Carolina)
Neil D. Anderson (Dallas)
Tim Anderson (Nebraska)
David T. Andrews, Jr. (Central New York)
John T. Andrews (Atlanta)
Mark S. Anschutz (Dallas)
Holly Lyman Antolini (Maine)
Kenneth L. Armstrong (Oklahoma)
Carol M. Arney (Hawaii)
Delaney W. Arstead (Nevada)
Kevin J. Babb (Springfield)
Margaret A. Babcock (Idaho)
Walter J. Baer (Oregon)
David E. Bailey (Utah)
Sarah E. Bailey (West Virginia)
Sunand Bal (Arizona)
Kempton Baldridge (Churches in Europe)
Joseph H. Ballard, Jr. (East Tennessee)
Rosalie Simmonds Ballentine (Virgin Islands)
Cynthia K.R. Banks (Kentucky)
Jo Ann Barker (Arkansas)

MINNEAPOLIS MEETING HOUSE OF DEPUTIES

Jack C. Barrow (Southwestern Virginia)
Phyllis Bartle (Central Florida)
William P. Baxter, Jr. (Maryland)
T. John F. Becker (East Carolina)
Doris E. Bedell (Albany)
Joan E. Beilstein (Washington)
Elizabeth A. Belasco (Long Island)
Alma T. Bell (Maryland)
Jocelyn J. Bell (East Tennessee)
Karl E. Bell (Churches in Europe)
Rawle C. Belle (Virgin Islands)
Marilynn Belleville (Springfield)
Arthur L. Bennett, III (West Virginia)
Carol Anne Bennett (Rhode Island)
Ernest L. Bennett (Central Florida)
Martha G. Bennett (Tennessee)
Virginia L. Bennett (Springfield)
Martha J. Berger (Milwaukee)
Anneke Bertsch (Central Florida)
Don Betts (Nebraska)
James C. Biegler (Dallas)
Garre L. Biladeau (Idaho)
Larry Bingham (Kansas)
William Bippos (Fond du Lac)
Arthur M. Bjontegard, Jr. (Upper South Carolina)
Arlyne N. Black (Northern Indiana)
G. Granville Blades (Easton)
Dennis A. Blauser (Northwestern Pennsylvania)
Eddie Blue (Maryland)
Clarence Bolden (Alaska)
Peggy Bosmyer (Arkansas)
Jon B. Boss (Southern Ohio)
R.P.M. Bowden (Atlanta)
Margie Bowman (Missouri)
Woody Bradford (Nebraska)
James Bradley (Connecticut)
T. Brenner (Quincy)
Timothy R. Bridges (Oklahoma)
Nancy W. Broadwell (East Carolina)
Cecily P. Broderick y Guerra (Long Island)
Ashton Jacinto Brooks (Virgin Islands)
Theodora N. Brooks (New York)
Anne Clarke Brown (Vermont)
Donald G. Brown (Northern California)
Maggie Morris Brown (Navajoland)

Thomas James Brown (Vermont)
William R. Bryant (Western Louisiana)
Gwen Buehrens (Massachusetts)
Ted R. Burnett (Southeast Florida)
Rick Callaway (Atlanta)
Jean Campbell, OSH (New York)
Sam G. Candler (Atlanta)
Teresa M. Cantrell (Arkansas)
Gloria E. Carlos (Virgin Islands)
Charles M. Carpenter (Indianapolis)
Douglas M. Carpenter (Alabama)
Stephen M. Carpenter (Northern California)
Robert G. Carroon (Connecticut)
Robert Carter (Georgia)
Arthur L. Casebeer (Springfield)
Peter F. Casparian (Churches in Europe)
Lloyd S. Casson (Delaware)
William R. Cathcart (Oklahoma)
Judith C. Cato (Oregon)
J. P. Causey, Jr. (Virginia)
Debra L. Cavanagh (San Joaquin)
Jeffrey O. Cerar (Virginia)
Robert G. Certain (San Diego)
Dr. John Chaffee (Central New York)
Pam Chapman (Western Michigan)
Winston B. Charles (North Carolina)
Janet Charney (Bethlehem)
Paul W. Chase (Eau Claire)
Randall Chase, Jr. (Rhode Island)
Barbara T. Cheney (Connecticut)
Reynolds S. Cheney III (West Tennessee)
Matt Chew (Arizona)
Robert T.J. Childers (Alabama)
Marge Christie (Newark)
Kenneth L. Chumbley (West Missouri)
Michael T. Clark (Missouri)
Alice Clayton (East Tennessee)
Jacob S. Clemmens (Northwest Texas)
Glennes Clifford (Oklahoma)
Richard I. Cluett (Bethlehem)
Ernest W. Cockrell (El Camino Real)
L. Zoe Cole (Colorado)
Richard Cole (Churches in Europe)
Bernice Coleman (Long Island)
Milton H. Coleman (Central New York)
Sarah H. Collins (Rochester)

Frank Connizzo (Kansas)
Andrew A. Cooley (Colorado)
Paul E. Cooney (Washington)
Frank Cooper (East Tennessee)
James H. Cooper (Florida)
Joseph W. Cooper (East Carolina)
Owen Cope (Louisiana)
Geoffrey B. Cortiss (Newark)
Carolyn Corum (West Tennessee)
Alan P. Coudriet (Eau Claire)
Barbara Coulter (Western Michigan)
Netty Cove (Western Michigan)
Claire Cowden (Northwest Texas)
D. Lorne Coyle (Central Florida)
Tessa Craib-Cox (Chicago)
Cliff Craig (Northwest Texas)
Karen Cramer (Utah)
Alice Crapser (New Hampshire)
James O. Cravens (Springfield)
Lee Alison Crawford (Vermont)
Louie Crew (Newark)
William W. "Buck" Crosby (Georgia)
Valarie H. Crosdale (Long Island)
Patrick G. Croy (Eau Claire)
Kate Cullinane (Indianapolis)
Walter K. Cumbie (Central Gulf Coast)
Donald J. Curran, Jr. (Central Florida)
Vincent Currie, Jr. (Central Gulf Coast)
Randolph K. Dales (New Hampshire)
Angela M. Daniel (Upper South Carolina)
Wilfred A. Daniel (Virgin Islands)
Robert S. Dannals (Upper South Carolina)
Sharon L. Davenport (Northwestern Pennsylvania)
David E. Davidson (Lexington)
Robert Davidson (Colorado)
Dick Davis (Northwest Texas)
Zabron Davis (Mississippi)
Lillian Davis-Wilson (Western New York)
Pete Dawson (Eau Claire)
Calvert G. de Coligny, Jr. (Southwestern Virginia)
Jeannette DeFriest (Newark)
Peggy Ann Delaplane (Delaware)
Mark S. Delcuze (Southern Virginia)
Shawn W. Denney (Springfield)
Elizabeth A. Dernier (Indianapolis)

Frederick D. Devall, IV (Louisiana)
Josephine Dewey (Rochester)
Ginny Doctor (Alaska)
Noel J. Doherty (Oklahoma)
Timothy M. Dombek (Upper South Carolina)
Anne E. Donnelly (Northern Indiana)
Hillary S. Dowling (Bethlehem)
Elizabeth Morris Downie (Eastern Michigan)
Tom Downs (Eastern Michigan)
Eric T. Duff (Northern California)
Marthe F. Dyner (New Hampshire)
Rose Fichera Eagen (Connecticut)
John H. Eastwood (California)
Don H. Edgington (Arkansas)
Marianne S. Ell (North Dakota)
Ann B. Ellingson (Utah)
David A. Elliott III (Mississippi)
D. Edward Emenheiser (Western Michigan)
Mark C. Engle (Northern Michigan)
Marilyn J. Engstrom (Wyoming)
Scott Evenbeck (Indianapolis)
William E. Exner (New Hampshire)
Roberta P. Fairman (New Hampshire)
Allen W. Farabee (Western New York)
C. Thomas Fennimore (North Carolina)
Dr. Roger A. Ferlo (New York)
Nancy A. Ferriani (Indianapolis)
Andrew Figueroa (Southern Ohio)
Jack D. Finlan (Colorado)
Clare Fischer-Davies (Southwestern Virginia)
Robert L. Fitzpatrick (Hawaii)
Joan F. Floberg (North Dakota)
Ann K. Fontaine (Wyoming)
Ruth T. Foose (West Virginia)
Elizabeth Fornal (Rhode Island)
Robert F. Fox (North Dakota)
Wesley D. Fox, Sr. (North Dakota)
Morley E. Frech, Jr. (Hawaii)
Caryl S. Frink (Rhode Island)
John B. Fritschner (Alabama)
L. Funk (Quincy)
Laura M. Gage (West Virginia)
Linda Gaither (New Jersey)

Joanne B. Galbraith (Idaho)
Mark R. Galloway (Rhode Island)
William Gammon III (Texas)
Judithann H. Gardine (Virgin Islands)
Martha Gardner (Newark)
Bruce Garner (Atlanta)
Scott A. Garno (Albany)
Jeff Garrety (West Tennessee)
Susan S. Gaumer (Louisiana)
Barbara A. Gaynor (Eau Claire)
Lucille Miner Geib (Arizona)
Anita P. George (Mississippi)
June S. Gerbracht (Long Island)
Pauline H. G. Getz (San Diego)
Nell Braxton Gibson (New York)
Charles E.B. Gill (East Carolina)
Betty Gilmore (Northwest Texas)
Giszler Joan C. Giszler-Ludlum (East Carolina)
Mary D. Glasspool (Maryland)
Edward E. Godden (Delaware)
Susan E. Goff (Virginia)
John Wood Goldsack (New Jersey)
Donald P. Goodheart (North Carolina)
Mary Louise Gotthold (California)
Rick Govan (East Tennessee)
P. William Greeley (Arizona)
Andrew Green (San Diego)
Lowell E. Grisham (Arkansas)
Gordon W. Gritter (El Camino Real)
Ambrose Gumbs (Virgin Islands)
Tobias S. Haler, BSG (New York)
William Hamilton Jr. (Central Gulf Coast)
W. Richard Hamlin, Ph.D. (Central New York)
Peter Handford (Churches in Europe)
Patricia Hanen (Ohio)
James P. Haney (Northwest Texas)
James P. Haney V (Kansas)
Michael Hanley (Minnesota)
Jack E. Hanstein (Northern California)
Katherine G.L. Harrigan (Central Pennsylvania)
Debra L. Harris (New Hampshire)
Iris E. Harris (Washington)
Mark Harris (Delaware)
Dena A. Harrison (Texas)
Jimmy Hartley (Upper South Carolina)
Samuel H. Hartman (Easton)
Matthew Hartney (Western New York)
Edward Hasse (Newark)
Billy Hawkins (Arkansas)
Lynn Headley-Moore (Newark)
Bruce Henne (Idaho)
David B. Herbert (Tennessee)
Canon H.W. "Sandy" Herrman (Quincy)
Sherman Hesselgrave (Oregon)
Carlynn N. Higbie (Milwaukee)
Rayford B. High, Jr. (Texas)
Mary E. Hileman (Oklahoma)
William S. Hitch (Delaware)
Lawrence R. Hitt (Colorado)
Bryan A. Hobbs (Southeast Florida)
Elizabeth Joy Hobby (Florida)
Charles Hoffacker (Eastern Michigan)
William Hogg (Long Island)
Deborah L. Hogue (Colorado)
Sandra Holbrook (North Dakota)
Mary Ellen Honsaker (Wyoming)
James F. Hood (Missouri)
Larry D. Hooper (Missouri)
Michael J. Horn (North Dakota)
Channing Horner (West Missouri)
Carol S. Hosler (Arizona)
Ralph Howe, Jr. (Louisiana)
Colenzo J. Hubbard (West Tennessee)
Sharon A. Huitema (Eastern Michigan)
Deborah Hentz Hunley (Southwestern Virginia)
James N. Hunter II (Alaska)
Stephen F. Hutchinson (Utah)
Fred C. Issac (Florida)
Gregory A. Jacobs (Ohio)
Paul Jeanes III (Kentucky)
John Jeffries (West Virginia)
Gay C. Jennings (Ohio)
Rosella A. Jim (Navajoland)
John R. Johanssen (Colorado)
David H. Johnson (Mississippi)
Ida Louise Johnson (North Carolina)
Sally Johnson (Minnesota)
Shannon Johnston (Mississippi)
E. Claiborne Jones (Atlanta)
Stanny Joris (Oklahoma)

Jerry Kabell (Eastern Michigan)
Laurie M. Kadrich (Wyoming)
Elizabeth Kaeton (Newark)
Stuart Brooks Keith III (Colorado)
Marge L. Kilkelly (Maine)
Patricia Kilpatrick (Ohio)
Timothy E. Kimbrough (North Carolina)
Charles B. King, Jr. (Albany)
Earle King (Western New York)
Sidney W. King, Jr. (Newark)
William King (Alabama)
Mike Kinman (Missouri)
H. Scott Kirby (Eau Claire)
Larry Kirk (Nevada)
Matilda O. Kistler (Western North Carolina)
Craig Klein (Northern California)
David Klutterman (Fond du Lac)
W. Nicholas Knisely (Bethlehem)
Sarah J. Knoll (Kansas)
C. Dana Krutz (Louisiana)
Arthur K. Kusumoto (Hawaii)
Lucinda Laird (Kentucky)
Gary Lambert (Milwaukee)
Paul E. Lambert (Dallas)
Judith B. Lane (North Carolina)
Stephen T. Lane (Rochester)
Susan Langle (New Hampshire)
Mark Lattime (Rochester)
Eugene D. Lattimer (Connecticut)
Mark Laubach (Bethlehem)
Sarah E. Lawton (California)
Teresa B. Leifur (Central Gulf Coast)
James B. Lemler (Chicago)
Carroll Levien (San Diego)
Susan H. Lindley (Minnesota)
James E. Lipton (Kansas)
Matthew Livingood (Oklahoma)
Frank Logue (Georgia)
Dr. George H. Love (Central Pennsylvania)
Lori M. Lowe (Atlanta)
Donald A. Lowery (Upper South Carolina)
Michael N. Lyon (Milwaukee)
Mary M. MacGregor (Texas)
Margie J. Mack (Maryland)

Linda A. Makson, AOJN (Western New York)
David G. Mallery (Maryland)
Diane Mance (Western North Carolina)
Lawrence W. Manglitz (Western Michigan)
Frederick E. Mann (Northern Indiana)
Keith A. Marsh (Kentucky)
Robert F. Marsh, Jr. (Florida)
Frances C. Marshall (Southwestern Virginia)
George J. Marshall (Albany)
Catherine F. Martensen (San Diego)
Cynthia Primo Martin (Delaware)
Richard Martindale (Nebraska)
Daniel H. Martins (San Joaquin)
Jeff Marx (West Tennessee)
John E. Masters (Wyoming)
Beth Mathews (Arkansas)
Richard Matters (San Joaquin)
J. Houston Matthews (Western North Carolina)
Sherry R. Mattson (Indianapolis)
Amanda G.R. May (San Diego)
J. Scott Mayer (Northwest Texas)
Holly McAlpen (California)
Charles P. McCabe III (Western Michigan)
John H. McCann (West Missouri)
Rebecca McClain (Arizona)
Samuel A. McDonald (Ohio)
Gene McDowell (Western North Carolina)
Cynthia McFarland (Central New York)
Michael J. McKinnon (Quincy)
Philip E. McNairy (Minnesota)
Timothy P. McRee (Western North Carolina)
Danny Ray Meadors (Mississippi)
Deborah D. Melnyk (Florida)
Dr. Sandra D. Michael (Central New York)
Richard E. Miller (Southeast Florida)
Robert K. Miller (Southwestern Virginia)
Tom Miller (West Virginia)
Cobb Milner (Western North Carolina)
Theodore Mollegen, Jr. (Connecticut)
Nancy L. Moody (Northern Indiana)
Robert P. Morrison (Oregon)
Mike Morrow (Kansas)
Craig Moseley (Colorado)

MINNEAPOLIS MEETING HOUSE OF DEPUTIES

Shaw Mudge, Jr. (Albany)
Sandra L. Muinde (Fond du Lac)
Donald J. Muller (Bethlehem)
Warren Murphy (Wyoming)
Harriet H. Murrell (Louisiana)
Virginia W. Nagel (Central New York)
Sheila Nelson-McJilton (Easton)
Gary G. Nicolosi (San Diego)
Kirstin J. Nielsen (Idaho)
Lance Nielsen (Idaho)
Aida R. Nieves (Virgin Islands)
William D. Nix (Northwest Texas)
Hugh Nolin (Fond du Lac)
Laura L. Norby (Milwaukee)
Ronald D. Null (Texas)
James W. Nutter (Texas)
Eileen E. O'Shea (Idaho)
Charlie Osberger (Easton)
Uriel Osnaya-Jimenez (Texas)
Constance K. Ott (Milwaukee)
David K. Ottsen (Northern Indiana)
Larry S. Overton (East Carolina)
John Palarine (Florida)
Russell Palmore (Virginia)
Elizabeth Panilaitis (Connecticut)
Janet W. Patterson (Atlanta)
Christine Payden-Travers (Southwestern Virginia)
Susan S. Payne (Arkansas)
Sally A. Pedersen (Indianapolis)
Charles Perfater (New Jersey)
Susanah W. Perkinson (Ohio)
Bonnie A. Perry (Chicago)
Gini Peterson (Atlanta)
Juanita Betz Peterson (Lexington)
Carolyn Phelps (West Missouri)
Neal Phelps (Georgia)
J.M. Philips (Rhode Island)
India Philley (West Missouri)
David R. Pitts (Louisiana)
Kathy Pluhar (Minnesota)
Diane B. Pollard (New York)
David S. Pollock (Washington)
Dennis W. Potter (North Dakota)
Linda Potter (Oregon)
Neff Powell (Southwestern Virginia)
Blanche Powless (Fond du Lac)

Alfred D. Price (Western New York)
Albert W. Pruitt (Central Gulf Coast)
Vera J. Pryor (Georgia)
James D. Putnam (Hawaii)
Joan Quigg (Quincy)
Pablo Ramos (Utah)
Russell V. Randle (Virginia)
John E. Rasmus (Eau Claire)
Paul A. Rasmus (Southeast Florida)
Rita Redfield (Maine)
Michael F. Rehill (Newark)
Ronnie Reno (Maryland)
Kenneth D. Richards (San Joaquin)
Bavi E. Rivera (California)
Wilson K. Roane (Fond du Lac)
Anne W. Robbins (Southern Ohio)
John H. Robert (Western Louisiana)
Terry Roberts (Minnesota)
David Robinson (Rochester)
Diane E. Root (Vermont)
Barbara T. Ross (Oregon)
Carole Ross (Central Florida)
Johnnie E. Ross (Lexington)
Gary L. Rowe (Delaware)
C. Mark Rutenbar (Western Michigan)
Karl D. Ruttan (West Virginia)
Harry Sacchetti (Rhode Island)
Cynthia Salley (Hawaii)
Nancy T. Salmon (San Joaquin)
Jason W. Samuel (Missouri)
Calvin F. Lyons Sanborn (Maine)
Allan Sandlin (Churches in Europe)
John S. Scannell (Oregon)
Lynn V. Schmissrauter (East Tennessee)
Shawn Schreiner (Chicago)
Cynthia H. Schwab (West Missouri)
Beverly Y. Scipio (Ohio)
Jacqueline B. Scott (Colorado)
John L. Scott, III (Albany)
Katherine Tyler Scott (Indianapolis)
Mark Seitz (West Virginia)
Robert Sessum (Lexington)
W. Lee Shaw (Utah)
Jim Shearouse (East Tennessee)
Virginia M. Sheay (New Jersey)
Angela F. Shepherd (Maryland)
Beverly Shortt (Eastern Michigan)

Mary Shortt (Eastern Michigan)
David I. Shoulders (Indianapolis)
Hunter P. Silides (Alaska)
Elizabeth H. Simmons (Arizona)
Ward H. Simpson (Eau Claire)
Edward B. Sisson (Mississippi)
Susan C. Skinner (Missouri)
Margaret McRae Slingluff (Central Gulf Coast)
Theodore B. Sloan (West Tennessee)
Dorothy M. Smith (New York)
Dr. Dabney T. Smith (Central Florida)
Edwin B. Smith (Fond du Lac)
JoAnn T. Smith (Kansas)
Marcellus Smith (Alabama)
Michael G. Smith (Minnesota)
Newland F. Smith, III (Chicago)
Stephen B. Smith (Ohio)
Suanna Smith (Mississippi)
Trudie Smither (Dallas)
Suzanne N. Smitherman (East Tennessee)
Jim Snell (San Joaquin)
D. Rebecca Snow (Alaska)
L. Miles Snyder (Northern California)
Rene Somodevilla (West Tennessee)
Wendy W. Sopkovich (Milwaukee)
George S. Sotelo (California)
Edgar J. Spalding (Central Florida)
Benjamin E.K. Speare-Hardy, II (Southern Ohio)
Alice C. Speers (Oregon)
Dustin C. Spence (Northern California)
Linda A. Sproat (Hawaii)
Anne G. Stanley (Maine)
D.E. Stark (Rhode Island)
Fredricka A. Steenstra (East Carolina)
Peter K. Stimpson (New Jersey)
Deborah J. Stokes (Southern Ohio)
Elouisa Stokes (Alabama)
William H. Stokes (Southeast Florida)
W.A. (Pete) Stringer, III (Tennessee)
Charlotte A. Strowhorn (Northern Indiana)
Garfield D. Stuart (Upper South Carolina)
Ross W. Stuckey (West Missouri)
Linton H. Studdiford (Maine)
Alan Sutherland (Lexington)

G. Porter Taylor (Atlanta)
Douglas Taylor-Weiss (Central New York)
James N. Tempro (Long Island)
James Tendick (Utah)
Jane B. Teter (Bethlehem)
Frederick W. Thayer (Missouri)
Joyce B. Thewalt (Eastern Michigan)
Paul T. Thibodaux (Alabama)
Gary W. Thompson (Colorado)
Larry Thompson (Western North Carolina)
Kwasi A. Thornell (Southern Ohio)
Stacy Thorpe (Alaska)
Ellen L. Tillotson (Connecticut)
Richard L. Tolliver (Chicago)
Carol R. Tookey (Navajoland)
Carol Trevathan (Kentucky)
Charles Trueheart (Churches Europe)
Anne Lea Tuohy (Chicago)
Kathleen C. Turner (Louisiana)
Constance F. Tyndall (West Missouri)
Larry E. Valentine (Kansas)
Charles E. Vance III (Easton)
John Vanderstar (Washington)
Julie A. Van Ham (Georgia)
Tim Vann (Nebraska)
John Van Siclen (Rhode Island)
Sue E. Veal (Northwest Texas)
William M. Viola (Long Island)
Francis H. Wade (Washington)
David H. Wakefield (Springfield)
Horace D. Ward (Southeast Florida)
Carolyn. C. Ware (Lexington)
Virginia Washington (Arizona)
John Bennet Waters (Texas)
Kathryn Weathersby (Mississippi)
John K. Webster (Southern Ohio)
Francis D. Whitaker (Oregon)
Charles W. Whitmore (Western New York)
Fred Wibiralske (New York)
Dawn C. Wilkins (Rochester)
Calvin E. Williams (Florida)
Rodney M. Williams, Sr. (Dallas)
Susan Anslow Williams (Western New York)
Angela Williamson (Atlanta)
Cecil P. Williamson (Alabama)

Anisa Cottrell Willis (Lexington)
Richard Wilson (Fond du Lac)
Sandye Wilson (Minnesota)
Thomas F. Winslow (Milwaukee)
Eugene Wise, Jr. (Tennessee)
Kathleen Wise (Easton)
Bradley Woodall (West Missouri)
Thomas B. Woodward (El Camino Real)
Carola von Wrangel (Albany)
Martin Yabroff (El Camino Real)
Gary C. Yaeger (Northwestern Pennsylvania)
Douglas W. Yarbrough (Idaho)
Dr. Lillian Yeager (Kentucky)
Therese G. Yeiser (Lexington)
George D. Young, III (Florida)
Ted M. Yumoto (San Joaquin)
Ray Zeigler (Easton)
Vicki D. Zust (Southern Ohio)

TENTH DAY

**Friday
August 8, 2003**

MORNING SESSION

Reconvene
The President called the House to order at 10:45 a.m.

Morning Prayers
The President called upon the Chaplain for prayers.

Certification of Minutes
The House of Deputies Committee on the Certification of Minutes presented its Report #9 stating that the Committee had met, read the Minutes of the Ninth Legislative Day, and certified that they were correct. The Chair moved adoption of the report.

Motion carried
Minutes accepted

Certification of Deputies
The House of Deputies Committee on Credentials presented its Report #16 for the first session of the Tenth Legislative Day. There were no new deputies certified. There were 419 clerical deputies and 422 lay deputies certified and seated, bringing the total count of the House to 841. There were 78 changes as follows:

Diocese	*Alternate replacing*	*Deputy being replaced*
Arizona	Pat Thompson	Sunand Bal
California	Robbins Clark	George Sotelo
Central Florida	Susan Hansell	Lorne Coyle
Central Pennsylvania	John Hoover	Marjorie Menaul
Churches in Europe	Helena Mbele-Mbong	Nell Toensmann
Colorado	Jacqueline Scott	Jack Finlaw
East Tennessee	Dan Matthews	Jocelyn Bell
Eastern Michigan	Cindy Kabell	Sharon Huitema
Eau Claire	Gregg Westigard	Patrick Croy
El Camino Real	Franklin Snow	James Wilson
El Camino Real	C. Jeff Kraemer	Thomas Woodward
Florida	Shirleen Wait	Fred Isaac
Fond Du Lac	Vicki Natzke	David Klutterman
Georgia	William Willoughby	Frank Logue
Hawaii	Alison Dingley	Carol Arney
Idaho	Margaret Babcock	Brian Baker
Idaho	Kirstin Nielsen	Dean Hagerman

MINNEAPOLIS MEETING — HOUSE OF DEPUTIES

Indianapolis	Donald Sodrel	Elizabeth Dernier
Indianapolis	Sherry Mattson	Kathleen Cullinane
Iowa	Raisin Horn	Connie Whalen
Kansas	Robert Erickson	Sarah Knoll
Lexington	Juanita Betz Peterson	John Brantley
Lexington	Janet Dunnavant	Johnnie Ross
Long Island	Richard Brewer	Elizabeth Belasco
Long Island	J. Vincent Welch	Valarie Crosdale
Los Angeles	James White	Janis Jones
Louisiana	Lonell Wright	Kathleen Turner
Maine	Christopher Chornyak	Calvin Sanborn
Maine	Harold Brown	Marge Kilkelly
Maryland	Christine Kinard	Russell Reno
Maryland	Edward Chapman	William Baxter
Massachusetts	Betsy Madsen	Byron Rushing
Minnesota	Grant Abbott	Michael Hanley
Mississippi	Shannon Johnston	David Elliott
Mississippi	Danny Meadors	Michael Chaney
Missouri	Tamsen Whistler	Larry Hooper
Missouri	Lawrence George	Marguerite Bowman
New Hampshire	Debra Ogin	Susan Langle
New Jersey	Jean McFarland	Peter Hausman
New Jersey	John Zamboni	Virginia Sheay
New York	Nell Gibson	James Forde
New York	Gerald Keucher	Roger Ferlo
Newark	Sidney King	Marjorie Christie
Northern California	Ernestina Campbell	Eric Duff
Northwest Texas	Jackie Batjer	Sue Veal
Ohio	Bryan Gillooly	Patricia Hanen
Oklahoma	Lillian R. Benefee	William Cathcart
Pennsylvania	JoAnn Jones	Karen Lash
Pittsburgh	Joseph Sarria	William Roemer
Rhode Island	Alcide Barnaby	Jennifer Phillips
Rochester	Jorge Gutierrez	Lesley Adams
Rochester	Nancy Bell	Sarah Collins
San Diego	Lawrence Bausch	Amanda May
San Diego	Joseph Acton	Gary Nicolosi
Southeast Florida	Mary Gray-Reeves	Horace Ward
Southern Virginia	Joy Walton	David Teschner
Southern Virginia	Harold Cobb	Paul Hogg
Southern Virginia	Sara Mueller	Robert Lee
Southwest Florida	Paul Game	Karen Patterson
Spokane	Thomas Robison	Gloria Lund

Texas	Kenneth Kesselus	James Nutter
Texas	Beth Null	Mary MacGregor
Texas	John Graham	Rayford High
Upper South Carolina	Calvin Griffin	Elizabeth Wickenberg Ely
Utah	Barbara Losse	Russell Babcock
Utah	Mark Brinkmann	W. Lee Shaw
Vermont	Elizabeth Hall	Peter Galbraith
Virgin Islands	Ashton Brooks	Lionel Rymer
Washington	Wesley Baldwin	Iris Harris
West Missouri	Carolyn Phelps	India Philley
West Tennessee	James Russell	Jeff Garrety
West Tennessee	Eugene Nobles	Theodore Sloan
West Texas	Michael Chalk	Gary Lillibridge
West Virginia	Deborah Short	John Jeffries
West Virginia	Harold Stewart	Laura Gage
West Virginia	Cheryl Winter	Sarah Bailey
Western Massachusetts	Nancy Strong	Len Cowan
Western New York	Elton Hartney	Lillian Davis-Wilson

Communications from the President

The President addressed the House in the light of this week's events. He stated that this Sunday will be one of the greatest missionary Sundays in the history of the Church. There is a great need for parish priests to preach the Gospel of Christ feeding the world. We can break open the Church to become what God calls it to be. The President reflected on the use, and on some of the realities of today and the 1979 Prayer Book. The President said we are called to speak the truth in love. We need each other. The President will continue to preach the Gospel of God's love.

Dispatch of Business

The House of Deputies Committee on Dispatch of Business moved to suspend the Rules of Order so as to not read the messages from the House of Bishops. Hearing no objections, the Chair so ordered the suspension of the Rules of Order.

Rules suspended

Messages from the House of Bishops

HB Message #185:	A154 (75th General Convention Site) Concurred.
HB Message #186:	D061 (Jubilee Ministry Funding) Not Concurred.
HB Message #188:	B007 (Affirmations for Facilitating Emergence of Consensus) Discharged.
HB Message #189:	C005 (Rites for Blessing and Supporting Committed Relationships) Discharged.
HB Message #190:	D022 (Resolution on Rites Supporting Life-long Relationships) Discharged.
HB Message #191:	A124 (Standing Commission on Health and a Staff Position

	in Health Care) Concurred with substitute resolution.
HB Message #192:	D026 (Commendation of www.ExploreFaith.org) Discharged.
HB Message #193:	A081 (National Ad Campaign) Concurred.
HB Message #194:	D016 (The Protection of Animals from Cruel Treatment) Concurred.
HB Message #195:	A125 (Ministry to Prisoners and Their Families) Concurred.
HB Message #196:	A011 (Ethical Guidelines for Gene Transfer and Germline Interventions) Concurred.
HB Message #197:	A126 (Youth Charged and Convicted as Adults) Concurred.
HB Message #198:	B008 (Protection of Children and Youth from Abuse) Concurred.
HB Message #199:	B027 (Pastoral Letter from the Bishops of The Episcopal Church) Adopted.
HB Message #200:	C004 (Reparative Therapies) Concurred.
HB Message #201:	C030 (The Working Poor) Concurred.
HB Message #202:	D015 (Make COSE Materials Available on the Web) Concurred.
HB Message #204:	D012 (Amend Canons I.13, IV.3.42, 43, IV.14.2) Referred to a Standing Commission.
HB Message #205:	D006 (Supporting International Relief and Development) Concurred.
HB Message #206:	D023 (US Support for the People of Liberia) Concurred.
HB Message #209:	D086 (Budget for the Episcopal Church 2004–2006) Concurred.

Election of the General Theological Seminary Board of Trustees—Ballot #2

The Secretary read the results of Ballot #2 for the General Theological Seminary Board of Trustees.

Newly-elected members of the General Theological Seminary Board of Trustees:

In the Clergy Order for three-year terms:
    Yamily Bass-Choate of Mississippi
    Paula Lawrence-Wehmiller of Pennsylvania

Election of the Joint Nominating Committee for the Presiding Bishop—Ballot #1

The Secretary read the results of Ballot #1 for the Joint Nominating Committee for the Presiding Bishop.

Newly-elected members of the Joint Nominating Committee for the Presiding Bishop:

Province I:	A.T. Mollegen Jr., Thomas J. Brown
Province II:	Diane B. Pollard, Jeannette De Friest
Province III:	Jane R. Cosby, Mark Harris
Province IV:	Vince Currie, Jr., (Elizabeth) Claiborne Jones
Province V:	Scott Evenbeck, Richard L. Tolliver
Province VI:	Don Betts, Ann K. Fontaine
Province VII:	Sarah Jacqueline Knoll, James P. Haney, V
Province VIII:	Bettye Jo Harris, Bavi Edna (Nedi) Rivera
Province IX:	Blanca Echeverry, Luis F. Ruiz

Dispatch of Business
The House of Deputies Committee on Dispatch of Business proposed the order in which the House would take up resolutions.

Education
The House of Deputies Committee on Education presented its Report #5 on HB Message #54 on Resolution A029 (Open Dialogue on Difficult Issues) and moved concurrence.

Special Order to Limit Debate
Deputy Atwood of Fort Worth moved to suspend the Rules of Order to limit debate to one minute.

Motion carried
Rules suspended

The House voted on Resolution A029.

The House concurred
(Communicated to the House of Bishops in HD Message #234)

Final Text of Resolution:
(A029)
Resolved, That the 74th General Convention of The Episcopal Church commit itself to foster moral deliberation on social questions, seeking to be a community where open, passionate, and respectful deliberation of challenging, contemporary issues is expected and encouraged; engage those of diverse classes, genders, ages, races, disabilities, engaging cultures, sexual orientation, and perspectives so that our limited horizons might be expanded and our witness in the world enhanced; address the issues faced by the people of God, in order to equip them for their discipleship and citizenship in the world; and be it further
Resolved, That in addition to the curricula identified and developed in accordance with Resolution A009 of the 73rd General Convention which

provide guided conversation around sexual orientation, in particular "Room for Grace Dialogue," the 74th General Convention direct the Peace and Justice Ministries Office and Ethnic and Women's Ministries and, where appropriate, the Committee on Anti-Racism of the Executive Council and other groups to collaborate in further developing models and trainers, lay and ordained, to guide conversations on difficult issues facing our church and societies today and to promulgate their use; and be it further

Resolved, That the General Convention request the Joint Standing Committee on Program, Budget, and Finance to consider a budget allocation of $28,000 for implementation of this resolution, including $6,000 for planning the process and printing materials, $20,000 to bring trainers from dioceses and provinces together to learn the process and $2,000 to sustain the process.

The House of Deputies Committee on Education presented its Report #9 on HB Message #103 on Resolution B024 (Task Force on Lifelong Christian Education and Formation) and moved concurrence.

The House concurred
(Communicated to the House of Bishops in HD Message #235)

Final Text of Resolution:

(B024)

Resolved, That the 74th General Convention authorize the creation of a nine year Task Force of Executive Council on Lifelong Christian Education and Formation that will

- Develop a comprehensive vision and strategy to strengthen Lifelong Christian Education and Formation throughout The Episcopal Church and equip people of all ages to experience, to tell about and to invite others into the Good News of the Gospel;
- Integrate Christian Formation into every area of the church's mission and ministry, recognizing that learning occurs in multiple ways throughout the entire life cycle;
- Identify and communicate resources and models that support the gifts and needs of a church of great diversity and that promote outcomes recommended by the 20/20 Strategy Group;
- Encourage conversation and collaboration among the many entities in the church that address specific aspects of Christian Education and Formation for mission and ministry;
- Provide international and ecumenical links for Christian Education and Formation; and be it further

Resolved, That this Task Force be composed of sixteen members: four bishops; four clergy; and eight lay persons; that the Task Force will meet at least two times a year, commencing in 2004, with additional small gatherings for conversation with selected groups involved in lifelong learning and formation; and that the Task Force will report on its work beginning at the 75th General Convention in 2006; and be it further

Resolved, That the General Convention request the Joint Standing Committee on Program, Budget and Finance to consider a budget allocation of $120,000 for implementation of this resolution for the next three years.

Death of Anglican Missionaries
Deputy Douglas of Massachusetts gave the House information on the death of Anglican Missionaries in the Solomon Islands. The President called on the Chaplain for prayers.

Stewardship and Development
The House of Deputies Committee on Stewardship and Development presented its Report #7 on HB Message #105 on Resolution B004 (Mission Funding Task Force) and moved concurrence.

The House concurred
(Communicated to the House of Bishops in HD Message #236)

Final Text of Resolution:
(B004)
Resolved, That in light of the need for resources to fulfill the 20/20 initiatives and to more fully address the many issues facing The Episcopal Church at all levels, this 74th General Convention direct the Presiding Bishop and the President of the House of Deputies to appoint a task force of 12 people, including, among others, members of the Standing Commission on Stewardship and Development, the Joint Standing Committee on Program, Budget and Finance and the Committee on the State of the Church. This task force is to be named the Mission Funding Task Force; and be it further

Resolved, That the Mission Funding Task Force will undertake a comprehensive study on the systems and procedures for funding, budgeting, and expenditure of the Domestic and Foreign Missionary Society; and be it further

Resolved That this study include, but not be limited to the following issues:
- The level of the church at which mission support is most efficient
- The best use of resources and the possible need for redirection of resources
- The effectiveness in supporting our stated priorities
- Possible unexplored efficiencies
- The review of existing commitments with quantification of the discretionary funding amount remaining after funding those commitments
- The most efficient and equitable method of funding the budget
- The encouragement of mutual responsibility, equity, and accountability to and among the dioceses of the church.

The Task Force will report its findings and recommendations for consideration at the 75th General Convention; and be it further

Resolved, That the General Convention request the Joint Standing Committee on Program, Budget and Finance to consider a budget allocation of $75,000 for the implementation of this resolution.

The House of Deputies Committee on Stewardship and Development presented its Report #8 on HB Message #91 on Resolution A136 (National Mission Narrative/Annual Report) and moved concurrence.

The House concurred
(Communicated to the House of Bishops in HD Message #237)

Final Text of Resolution:
(A136)
Resolved, **That as responsible stewards we are called to communicate the use of and to be accountable for the resources provided to accomplish the mission and ministry of The Episcopal Church. In the spirit of this responsibility, the 74th General Convention direct the Executive Council and the Episcopal Church Center staff to develop, and distribute, in a variety of media forms, a yearly report that describes, in word and image what has been accomplished through the Domestic and Foreign Missionary Society budget in that prior year. This report will include a thorough financial overview of the expenditures of our budget presented in a manner that measures our success in fulfilling our mission priorities.**

Miscellaneous Resolutions
The House of Deputies Committee on Miscellaneous Resolutions presented its Report #12 on Resolution C016 (Integrated Pest Management) and moved that the Committee be discharged as the matter is considered in Resolution C026.

Motion carried
Committee discharged
(Communicated to the House of Bishops in HD Message #300)

Dispatch of Business
The House of Deputies Committee on Dispatch of Business moved to suspend the Rules of Order so that all requests by committees to be discharged from considering a resolution may be grouped together on an ad hoc consent calendar unless inclusion of a particular resolution was objected to, according to the Rules of Order.

Motion carried
Rules suspended

World Mission

The House of Deputies Committee on World Mission presented its Report #4 on HB Message #102 on Resolution A137 (Accountability Of Mission Partners) and moved concurrence.

The House concurred
(Communicated to the House of Bishops in HD Message #238)

Final Text of Resolution:

(A137)
Resolved, That the 74th General Convention affirm the action of the Executive Council taken at its January 2003 meeting requiring that recipients of grants or gifts from the Domestic and Foreign Missionary Society maintain appropriate accounting records and controls over such grants and gifts; and be it further
Resolved, That the Domestic and Foreign Missionary Society continue to provide technical support, when necessary, for preparing these reports.

The House of Deputies Committee on World Mission presented its Report #6 on HB Message #131 on Resolution A150 (World Mission Vision) and moved concurrence.

The House concurred
(Communicated to the House of Bishops in HD Message #239)

Final Text of Resolution:

(A150)
Resolved, That the 2003 General Convention call the church to study, during the 2004–2006 triennium, the vision for world mission contained in the document, "Companions in Transformation: The Episcopal Church's World Mission in a New Century," prepared by the Standing Commission on World Mission; and be it further
Resolved, That a study group in each diocese be designated to make a critical study of the Vision statement, this group to include diocesan representatives of groups such as Companion Diocese Committees, the Global Mission Network, United Thank Offering, Episcopal Relief and Development, and other member groups of the Episcopal Partnership for Global Mission (EPGM) and others as may be available, and that a report from each diocese be forwarded to the Standing Commission on World Mission by World Mission Sunday in January 2005; and be it further
Resolved, That the Convention call on parishes, dioceses, voluntary mission agencies, seminaries, mission networks, and Episcopal Church Center agencies to participate in the outlined process during the triennium; and be it further
Resolved, That the Convention request the Standing Commission on World Mission to gather and interpret responses from around the Church and

make specific programmatic and budgetary proposals to the 2006 General Convention.

Prayer Book, Liturgy and Church Music
The House of Deputies Committee on Prayer Book, Liturgy and Church Music presented its Report #15 on HB Message #on Resolution A103 (Adopt the Revised Common Lectionary) and moved concurrence.
Deputy Renton of California moved to terminate debate.

Motion carried
Debate terminated

Parliamentary Inquiry
Deputy Crawford of Southwest Florida asked if Resolution 103 required a vote by orders at two Conventions and referred to the dioceses.
The Parliamentarian stated that action of one General Convention is necesarry because the resolution refers only to the liturgical reading; and it does requires a vote by orders in the House.

Ballot #4—Vote by Orders
Ballot #4 on Resolution A103 was taken.

Ballot #4 taken by orders

Joint Nominating Committee for the Election of the Presiding Bishop
The President announced the appointment of two youth members to the Joint Nominating Committee for the Election of the Presiding Bishop: Ciera Wilkerson of Province IV and Brad Westfall of Province IIV.

Dispatch of Business
The Chair of the Committee on Dispatch of Business moved a special order for the presentation of Resolution A111.

Rules suspended
Special Order adopted

Ministry
The House of Deputies Committee on Ministry presented its Report #13 on Resolution A111 (Title III Proposed Canons) and moved concurrence.

Consideration on Resolution A111 was postponed until after the midday recess so that the House would have time to study proposed text of the resolution.

Consideration postponed

Canons

The House of Deputies Committee on Canons presented its Report #6 on HB Message #99 on Resolution A047 (Amend Canon IV.14.13) and moved concurrence.

The House concurred
(Communicated to the House of Bishops in HD Message #241)

Final Text of Resolution:

(A047)
Resolved, That Canon IV.14.13 be amended to read as follows:
Sec. 13. ~~Relationship to parties.~~ Disqualification *of Bishop, Judge, or Member of a Review Committee.* ~~Any member of any Diocesan Review Committee, Review Committee or any Court provided for in this Title (i) who is related to the Respondent by blood or marriage, (ii) who has knowledge of essential facts involved in the matter, (iii) who has a close personal or professional relationship with the Respondent, any alleged Victim, or any witness in the matter, or (iv) who reasonably believes himself or herself unable to render a fair and independent judgment, shall be disqualified and excused from service in connection with the matter.~~
(a) Any Bishop exercising authority as provided in this Title shall disqualify himself or herself in any proceeding in which the Bishop's impartiality may reasonably be questioned. The Bishop shall also disqualify himself or herself when the Bishop, the Bishop's spouse, or a person within the third degree of relationship to either of them, or the spouse of such person, (1) is the Respondent, alleged Victim, or Complainant, or (2) is likely to be a witness in the proceeding.
(b) Any member of any Diocesan Review Committee, Review Committee, or any Ecclesiastical Court provided for in this Title, shall disqualify himself or herself in any proceeding in which the member's impartiality may reasonably be questioned. The member shall also disqualify himself or herself when the member, the member's spouse, any person within the third degree of relationship to either of them, or the spouse of such person, (1) is the Respondent, alleged Victim, or Complainant, (2) is likely to be a witness in the proceeding, (3) has a personal bias or prejudice concerning the Respondent, alleged Victim, or Complainant, (4) has personal knowledge of disputed evidentiary facts concerning the proceeding, (5) has a personal financial interest in the outcome of the proceeding or in the Respondent, alleged Victim, Complainant, or any other interest that could be substantially affected by the outcome, or (6) is a member of the same congregation or otherwise has a close personal or professional relationship with the Respondent, any alleged Victim, Complainant, or any witness in the matter.
(c) No Bishop, Ecclesiastical Court, Diocesan Review Committee, or Review Committee shall accept from the parties to the proceeding any waiver of any ground for disqualification enumerated in this Section unless preceded by full disclosure of the basis for the disqualification, on the record, to all parties.

National and International Concerns:
The House of Deputies Committee on National and International Concerns presented its Report #22 on Resolution D002 (International Peace Zone for the Jerusalem Area) and moved the resolution, recommending rejection.

Original Text of Resolution:
(D002)
Resolved, the House of Bishops concurring, That the 74th General Convention urge the United Nations, supported fully by the United States and international leaders, to establish an International Peace Zone for the Jerusalem Area; and be it further *Resolved,* That the 74th General Convention urge the United Nations to commit to the Peace Zone's endurance by moving its Headquarters to the Peace Zone.

Motion defeated
Resolution rejected
(Communicated to the House of Bishops in HD Message #242)

The House of Deputies Committee on National and International Concerns presented its Report #24 on Resolution C014 (Reaffirmation of Faith and Purpose) and moved to refer the resolution to the Standing Commission on Ministry Development.

Original Text of Resolution:
(C014)
Resolved, the House of Bishops concurring, That the 74th General Convention remain steadfast in seeking to encourage the strength and mission of The Episcopal Church and the Anglican Communion. The 74th General Convention is called to renew our commitment to the fullness of our Anglican Heritage. We are further called to act and legislate in ways that honor our Anglican traditions and Holy Scripture; and that unify our worldwide Christian witness and mission.

Motion carried
Resolution referred to a Standing Commission
(Communicated to the House of Bishops in HD Message #243)

Prayer Book, Liturgy and Church Music
The House of Deputies Committee on Prayer Book, Liturgy and Church Music presented its Report #16 on HB Message #133 on Resolution A044 (Amend Canon I.17.1(c)) and moved concurrence.

The House concurred
(Communicated to the House of Bishops in HD Message #244)

Final Text of Resolution:
(A044)
Resolved, That Canon I.17.1(c) be amended to read as follows:
(c) It is expected that all adult members of this Church, after appropriate instruction, will have made a mature public affirmation of their faith and commitment to the responsibilities of their Baptism and will have been confirmed or received *by the laying on of hands* by a Bishop of this Church or by a Bishop of a Church in communion with this Church. Those who have previously made a mature public commitment in another Church may be received *by the laying on of hands by a Bishop of this Church,* not *rather than* confirmed.

Ecumenical Relations
The House of Deputies Committee on Ecumenical Relations presented its Report #9 on HB Message #53 on Resolution A085 (ELCA Member Reception) and moved concurrence.

The House concurred

(Communicated to the House of Bishops in HD Message #245)

Final Text of Resolution:
(A085)
Resolved, That the rubrics of the Book of Common Prayer and the Constitution and Canons of The Episcopal Church allow reception of members of the Evangelical Lutheran Church in America.

Church Pension Fund
The House of Deputies Committee on the Church Pension Fund presented its Report #1 on HB Message #90 on Resolution D042 (Amend Canon I.8.2, Regarding Election of Church Pension Fund Trustees) and moved concurrence.

Deputy Renton of California moved to terminate debate.

Motion carried
Debate terminated

A vote was taken on Resolution D042.

Motion defeated
Resolution rejected

(Communicated to the House of Bishops in HD Message #246)

Results of Ballot #4: Vote by Orders on Resolution A103
The Secretary read the results of Ballot #4 including the no and divided votes.

Type	Total	Necessary	Yes	No	Divided	Results
Lay:	104	53	53	44	7	Carried
Clerical:	106	54	52	44	9	Failed

Resolution A103 carried in the lay order and failed in the clerical order.

Motion defeated
Resolution rejected
(Communicated to the House of Bishops in HD Message #217)

Announcements
The Secretary made the announcements.

Midday Prayers
The President called on the Chaplain for midday prayers.

RECESS
The President recessed the House at 1:10 p.m. to reconvene at 2:30 p.m.

AFTERNOON SESSION

Reconvene
The President called the House to order at 2:34 p.m.

Prayers
The President called upon the Chaplain for prayers.

Appreciation for Chaplain
The President excused the Chaplain who needed to leave to officiate at a wedding. The House recognized his spiritual guidance during Convention.

Certification of Deputies
The House of Deputies Committee on Credentials presented its Report #17 for the afternoon session of the Tenth Legislative Day, and there were no new deputies certified. There were 419 clerical deputies and 422 lay deputies certified and seated, bringing the total count of the House to 841. There were 35 changes on this day, as follows:

Diocese	*Alternate replacing*	*Deputy being replaced*
Atlanta	Lori Lowe	G. Porter Taylor
Central Florida	Lorne Coyle	Donald Curran
Central Pennsylvania	Marjorie Menaul	John Hoover
Chicago	Richard Peete	Anne Tuohy

Colorado	Zoe Cole	Gary Thompson
Colorado	Mary Kate Schroeder	Robert Davidson
El Camino Real	Nayan McNeill	Wendy Smith
Florida	Ellis Brust	George Young
Fond Du Lac	Kay Drebert	William Bippus
Kansas	Sarah Knoll	Robert Erickson
Lexington	Johnnie Ross	Janet Dunnavant
Los Angeles	Anthony Guillen	J. Edwin Bacon
Louisiana	Stephen Holmgren	Fred Devall
Massachusetts	Byron Rushing	Betsy Madsen
Michigan	Mark Jenkins	Susan McGarry
Minnesota	Michael Hanley	Philip McNairy
New Hampshire	Susan Langle	Debra Harris
Newark	Martha Gardner	Lyn Headley-Moore
Northern California	Eric Duff	Mark Allen
Oklahoma	Mary Gail Ruark	Timothy Bridges
Oregon	James Boston	John Scannell
Oregon	Maron Van	Sherman Hesselgrave
Pennsylvania	Nancy Wittig	Ruth Kirk
Rhode Island	Carol Bennett	Dennis Stark
Texas	James Cunningham	William Gammon
Utah	W. Lee Shaw	Mark Brinkmann
Vermont	Peter Galbraith	Elizabeth Hall
Washington	John Harmon	Margaret Graham
West Tennessee	Stephen Carpenter	Colenzo Hubbard
West Tennessee	Jeff Garrety	Eugene Nobles
Western Louisiana	Reece Middleton	Norman Parker
Western Massachusetts	Len Cowan	Heidi Frantz-Dale
Western Michigan	Alice Webley	Barbara Coulter
Western Michigan	LaRae Rutenbar	D. Emenheiser

Consent Calendar

Committees and Commissions

The House of Deputies Committee on Committees and Commissions presented its Report #3 on Resolution B025 (Criminal Justice Committee) and moved that the Committee be discharged.

Motion carried
Committee discharged
(Communicated to the House of Bishops in HD Message #314)

(End of Consent Calendar)

Debate Resumed on Resolution A111

Deputy Goodhart of North Carolina moved to recommit Resolution A111 to committee.

The President took a vote on whether the House would entertain a procedural motion at this time.

Motion defeated
Procedural motion rejected

Debate continued.

Deputy Kimble of North Carolina moved to recommit the resolution to the Standing Commission on Ministry Development.

Motion defeated
Recommit to Standing Commission failed

The President announced that the time for debate had expired.

Deputy Perry of Chicago moved to extend debate by 10 minutes.

Motion defeated
Debate terminated

A vote was taken on Resolution A111.

The House concurred
(Communicated to the House of Bishops in HD Message #249)

[The final text of Resolution A111 has not been *italized* because of its size and for ease of reading. *Ed.*]

Final Text of Resolution:

(A111)

Resolved, That Canons III.1-9, 13-17, and 19 be deleted and replaced by the following amended Canons III.1-9, with all remaining Canons renumbered as appropriate:

CANON 1: Of the Ministry of All Baptized Persons

Sec.1. Each Diocese shall make provision for the affirmation and development of the ministry of all baptized persons, including:

(a) Assistance in understanding that all baptized persons are called to minister in Christ's name, to identify their gifts with the help of the Church and to serve Christ's mission at all times and in all places.

(b) Assistance in understanding that all baptized persons are called to sustain their ministries through commitment to life-long Christian formation.

Sec. 2. No person shall be denied access to the discernment process for any ministry, lay or ordained, in this Church because of race, color, ethnic origin, national origin, sex, marital status, sexual orientation, disabilities, or age, except as otherwise provided by these Canons. No right to licensing, ordination, or election is hereby established.

CANON 2: Commissions on Ministry

Sec. 1. In each Diocese there shall be a Commission on Ministry ("Commission") consisting of Priests, Deacons, if any, and Lay Persons. The Canons of each Diocese shall provide for the number of members, terms of office, and manner of selection to the Commission.

Sec. 2. The Commission shall advise and assist the Bishop:

(a) In the implementation of Title III of these Canons.

(b) In the determination of present and future opportunities and needs for the ministry of all baptized persons.

(c) In the design and oversight of the ongoing process for discernment, formation for ministry and assessmentof readiness therefor.

Sec. 3. The Commission may adopt rules for its work, subject to the approval of the Bishop; Provided that they are not inconsistent with the Constitution and Canons of this Church and of the Diocese.

Sec. 4 The Commission may establish committees consisting of members and other persons to report to the Commission or to act on its behalf.

Sec. 5 The Bishop and Commission shall ensure that the members of the Commission and its committees receive ongoing education and training for their work.

CANON 3: Of Discernment

Sec 1. The Bishop and Commission shall provide encouragement, training and necessary resources to assist each congregation in developing an ongoing process of community discernment appropriate to the cultural background, age and life experiences of all persons seeking direction in their call to ministry.

Sec 2. The Bishop, in consultation with the Commission, may utilize college and university campus ministry centers and other communities of faith as additional communities where discernment takes place. In cases where these discernment communities are located in another jurisdiction, the Bishop will consult with the bishop where the discernment community is located.

Sec 3. The Bishop and Commission shall actively solicit from congregations, schools and other youth organizations, college and university campus ministry centers, seminaries, and other communities of faith, names of persons whose demonstrated qualities of Christian commitment and potential for leadership and vision mark them as desirable candidates for positions of leadership in the Church.

Sec. 4. The Bishop, Commission, and the discernment community shall assist persons engaged in a process of ministry discernment to determine appropriate avenues for the expression and support of their ministries, either lay or ordained.

CANON 4: Of Licensed Ministries

Sec. 1

(a) A confirmed communicant in good standing or, in extraordin-

	ary circumstances, subject to guidelines established by the Bishop, a communicant in good standing, may be licensed by the Ecclesiastical Authority to serve as Pastoral Leader, Worship Leader, Preacher, Eucharistic Minister, Eucharistic Visitor or Catechist. Requirements and guidelines for the selection, training, continuing education, and deployment of such persons and the duration of licenses shall be established by the Bishop in consultation with the Commission on Ministry.
(b)	The Presiding Bishop or the Bishop Suffragan for the Armed Forces may authorize a member of the Armed Forces to exercise one or more of these ministries in the Armed Forces in accordance with the provisions of this Canon. Requirements and guidelines for the selection, training, continuing education, and deployment of such persons shall be established by the Bishop granting the license.

Sec. 2

(a) The Member of the Clergy or other leader exercising oversight of the congregation or other community of faith may request the Ecclesiastical Authority with jurisdiction to license persons within that congregation or other community of faith to exercise such ministries. The license shall be issued for a period of time to be determined under Canon III.4.1(a) and may be renewed. The license may be revoked by the Ecclesiastical Authority upon request of or upon notice to the Member of the Clergy or other leader exercising oversight of the congregation or other community of faith.

(b) In renewing the license, the Ecclesiastical Authority shall consider the performance of the ministry by the person licensed, continuing education in the licensed area, and the endorsement of the Member of the Clergy or other leader exercising oversight of the congregation or other community of faith in which the person is serving.

(c) A person licensed in any Diocese under the provisions of this Canon may serve in another congregation or other community of faith in the same or another Diocese only at the invitation of the Member of the Clergy or other leader exercising oversight, and with the consent of the Ecclesiastical Authority in whose jurisdiction the service will occur.

Sec. 3. A Pastoral Leader is a lay person authorized to exercise pastoral or administrative responsibility in a congregation under special circumstances, as defined by the Bishop.

Sec. 4. A Worship Leader is a lay person who regularly leads public worship under the direction of the Member of the Clergy or other leader exercising oversight of the congregation or other community of faith.

Sec. 5. A Preacher is a lay person authorized to preach. Persons so authorized shall only preach in congregations under the direction of the Member of the Clergy or other leader exercising oversight of the congregation or other community of faith.

Sec. 6. A Eucharistic Minister is a lay person authorized to administer the Consecrated Elements at a Celebration of Holy Eucharist. A Eucharistic Minister should normally act under the direction of a Deacon, if any, or otherwise, the Member of the Clergy or other leader exercising oversight of the congregation or other community of faith.

Sec. 7. A Eucharistic Visitor is a lay person authorized to take the Consecrated Elements in a timely manner following a Celebration of Holy Eucharist to members of the congregation who, by reason of illness or infirmity, were unable to be present at the Celebration. A Eucharistic Visitor shall should normally act under the direction of a Deacon, if any, or otherwise, the Member of the Clergy or other leader exercising oversight of the congregation or other community of faith.

Sec. 8. A Catechist is a lay person authorized to prepare persons for Baptism, Confirmation, Reception, and the Reaffirmation of Baptismal Vows, and shall function under the direction of the Priest-in-Charge Member of the Clergy or other leader exercising oversight of the congregation or other community of faith.

CANON 5: Of General Provisions Respecting Ordination

Sec. 1.

(a) The canonical authority assigned to the Bishop Diocesan by this Title may be exercised by a Bishop Coadjutor, when so empowered under Canon III.25, by a Bishop Suffragan when requested by the Bishop Diocesan, or by any other Bishop of the Anglican Communion canonically in charge of a Diocese, at the request of the ordinand's Bishop.

(b) The Council of Advice of the Convocation of American Churches in Europe, and the board appointed by a Bishop having jurisdiction in an Area Mission in accordance with the provisions of Canon I.11.2(c), shall, for the purpose of this and other Canons of Title III have the same powers as the Standing Committee of a Diocese.

(c) In case of a vacancy in the episcopate in a Diocese, the Ecclesiastical Authority may authorize and request the President of the House of Bishops of the Province to take order for an ordination.

Sec. 2.

(a) No Nominee, Applicant, Postulant or Candidate for ordination shall sign any of the certificates prescribed required by this Title.

(b) Testimonials required of the Standing Committee by this Title must be signed by a majority of the whole Committee, at a

	meeting duly convened, except that testimonials may be executed in counterparts, each of which shall be deemed an original.
(c)	Whenever the letter of support of a Vestry is required, the letter must be signed and dated by at least two-thirds of all of the members of the Vestry, at a meeting duly convened, and by the Rector or Priest-in-Charge of the Parish, and attested by the Clerk of the Vestry. Should there be no Rector or Priest-in-Charge, the letter shall be signed by a Priest of the Diocese acquainted with the nominee and the Parish, the reason for the substitution being stated in the attesting clause.
(d)	If the congregation or other discernment community of which the nominee is a member is not a Parish, the letter of support required by Canon III.6 or Canon III.8 shall be signed and dated by the Member of the Clergy and the council of the that congregation or other community of faith, and shall be attested by the secretary of the meeting at which the letter was approved. Should there be no Member of the Clergy, the certification letter shall be signed and dated by a Priest of the Diocese acquainted with the applicant nominee and the congregation or other community of faith, the reason for the substitution being stated in the attesting clause.
(e)	If the applicant is a member of a Religious Order or Christian Community recognized by Canon III.30 the certificates letters of support referred to in Canon III.6 or Canon III.8 and any other requirements imposed on a congregation or Priest-in-Charge Member of the Clergy, may be given by the Superior or person in charge, and Chapter, or other comparable body of the Order or Community.

Sec. 3 An application for any dispensation permitted by this Title from any of the requirements for ordination must first be made to the Bishop, and if approved, referred to the Standing Committee for its advice and consent.

CANON 6: Of the Ordination of Deacons

Sec. 1. Selection

The Bishop, in consultation with the Commission, shall establish procedures to identify and select persons with evident gifts and fitness for ordination to the Diaconate.

(a)	Nomination. A confirmed adult communicant in good standing may be Nominated for ordination to the diaconate by the person's congregation or other community of faith. The Nomination shall be in writing, and shall include	
	(1)	Full name and date of birth.
	(2)	The length of time resident in the Diocese.
	(3)	Evidence of Baptism and Confirmation.
	(4)	Whether an application has been made previously

for Postulancy or the person has been Nominated in any diocese.

(5) A description of the process of discernment by which the applicant has been identified for ordination to the Diaconate.

(6) The level of education attained and, if any, the degrees earned and areas of specialization.

(7) A letter of support by the applicant's discernment community, including a statement committing the discernment community to involve itself in the applicant's preparation for ordination to the Diaconate. If it be a congregation, the letter shall be signed by a two-thirds majority of the Vestry or comparable body, and the Member of the Clergy or leader exercising oversight.

(8) An acceptance in writing by the nominated person.

The nomination shall be submitted to the Bishop, who may admit the person as a Nominee for ordination to the Diaconate.

(b) Admission to Postulancy. Postulancy is the time between nomination and candidacy and includes a process of exploration of and decision on the Postulant's call to the diaconate.

(1) There shall be a thorough investigation of the Postulant which shall include:

(i) a background check, and

(ii) medical and complete psychological evaluation by professionals approved by the Bishop, using forms prepared for the purpose by The Church Pension Fund, and if desired or necessary, psychiatric referral.

(iii) Reports of all investigations and examinations shall be kept on file by the Bishop.

(2) The Bishop, or the Bishop's designee, may interview the Postulant. The Commission or a designated committee shall interview the Postulant, and the Commission or designated committee shall submit a recommendation to the Bishop.

(3) The Bishop may then admit the Postulant as a Candidate, informing the Candidate and the Member of the Clergy or other leader of the Candidate's discernment community in writing.

Sec. 2. Candidacy

(a) Candidacy is a time, no less than one year in length, of formation in preparation for ordination to the Diaconate, established by a formal commitment by the Candidate, the Bishop, the Commission and the congregation or other community of faith.

(b) The Bishop may assign the Candidate to any congregation of the diocese or other community of faith after consultation with the Member of the Clergy or other leader exercising oversight.

(c) At the Bishop's sole discretion, any Candidate may be removed from the list of Candidates, with reasons given to the Candidate and written notice of the removal being given to the Candidate and the Member of the Clergy Rector or other leader exercising oversight of the nominating congregation or other community of faith and the Commission.

Sec. 3. Preparation for Ordination

(a) The Bishop, in consultation with the Commission, shall determine the length of time and extent of formation needed to prepare each Candidate for ordination.

(b) Before ordination each Candidate shall be prepared in and demonstrate basic competence in five general areas:

(1) Academic studies including, The Holy Scriptures, theology and the tradition of the Church.
(2) Diakonia and the diaconate,
(3) Human awareness and understanding,
(4) Spiritual development and discipline,
(5) Practical training and experience,

(c) The formation process shall include sexual misconduct prevention training, training regarding Title IV of these Canons, and anti-racism training.

(d) Formation shall reflect the local culture and each Candidate's background, age, occupation, and ministry. Prior education and learning from life experience may be considered as part of the formation required for ordination.

(e) Wherever possible, formation shall take place in community, including persons in preparation for the diaconate, or others preparing for ministry.

(f) Each Candidate shall communicate with the Bishop in person or by letter, four times a year, in the Ember Weeks, reflecting on the Candidate's academic, diaconal, human, spiritual, and practical, and academic development.

(g) During Candidacy each Candidate's progress shall be evaluated from time to time, and there shall be a written report of the evaluation by those authorized by the

Commission to be in charge of the evaluation program. Upon certification by those in charge of the Candidate's program of preparation that the Candidate has successfully completed preparation and is ready for ordination, a final written assessment of readiness for ordination to the Diaconate shall be prepared as determined by the Bishop in consultation with the Commission. This report shall include a recommendation from the Commission regarding the readiness of the Candidate for ordination. Records shall be kept of all evaluations, and assessments and the recommendation and shall be made available to the Standing Committee.

(h) If the medical examination, psychological examination, or background check have taken place more than 36 months prior to ordination, they must be updated.

(i) Before ordination each Candidate must have reached the age of twenty-four, and made application for ordination.

(j) Upon certification in writing by the Standing Committee that all canonical requirements have been met, and that there is no sufficient objection on medical, psychological, moral, doctrinal, or spiritual grounds and that they recommend ordination, the Bishop may ordain the Candidate a Deacon.

CANON 7: Of the Life and Work of Deacons

Sec. 1. Deacons serve directly under the authority of and are accountable to the Bishop.

Sec. 2. Deacons canonically resident in each Diocese constitute a Community of Deacons, which shall meet from time to time. The Bishop may appoint one or more of such Deacons as Archdeacon(s) to assist the Bishop in the formation, deployment, supervision, and support of the Deacons or those in preparation to be Deacons, and in the implementation of this canon..

Sec. 3. The Bishop may establish a Council on Deacons ("Council") to oversee, study, and promote the diaconate.

Sec. 4. The Bishop, after consultation with the Deacon and the Member of the Clergy or other leader exercising oversight, may assign a Deacon to one or more congregations, other communities of faith or non-parochial ministries. Deacons assigned to a congregation or other community of faith act under the authority of the Member of the Clergy or other leader exercising oversight in all matters concerning the congregation.

(a) Deacons may have a letter of agreement, subject to the Bishop's approval, setting forth mutual responsibilities in the assignment.

(b) Deacons shall report annually to the Bishop or the Bishop's designee on their life and work.

(c) Deacons may serve as administrators of congregations or other communities of faith, but no Deacon shall be in charge of a congregation or other community of faith.

(d) Deacons may accept chaplaincies in any hospital, prison, or other institution.

Sec. 5. The Bishop and Commission shall require and provide for the continuing education of Deacons and keep a record of such education.

Sec. 6.(a) A Deacon may not serve as Deacon for more than two months in any diocese other than the diocese in which the Deacon is canonically resident unless the Bishop of the other diocese shall have granted a license to the Deacon to serve in that diocese.

(b) (1) A Deacon desiring to become canonically resident within a Diocese shall request a testimonial from the Ecclesiastical Authority of the Diocese in which the Deacon is canonically resident to present to the receiving diocese, which testimonial, if granted, shall be given by the Ecclesiastical Authority to the applicant, and a duplicate thereof may be sent to the Ecclesiastical Authority of the Diocese to which transfer is proposed. The testimonial shall be in the following words:

I hereby certify that A.B., who has signified to me the desire to be transferred to the Ecclesiastical Authority of _____, is a Deacon of _____ in good standing, and has not, so far as I know or believe, been justly liable to evil report, for error in religion or for viciousness of life, for the last three years.

(Date)_____

(Signed) _____

(2) Such testimonial shall be called Letters Dimissory. If the Ecclesiastical Authority accepts the Letters Dimissory, the canonical residence of the Deacon so transferred shall date from the acceptance of the Letters Dimissory, of which prompt notice shall be given both to the applicant and to the Ecclesiastical Authority from which it came.

(3) Letters Dimissory not presented within six months from the date of transmission to the applicant shall become void.

(4) A statement of the record of payments to The Church Pension Fund by or on behalf of the Deacon concerned shall accompany Letters Dimissory.

Sec. 7. A Deacon may retire from active service for reasons of age or infirmity with the consent of the Bishop at any time and shall retire for reasons of age or infirmity at the request of the Bishop mutually acceptable to the Deacon and the Bishop, or at any time for reasons of health. The Bishop may, with the consent of the Deacon, assign a retired Deacon to any congregation, other community of faith or non-parochial ministry, for a period not to exceed twelve months, and this period may be renewed.

CANON 8: Of the Ordination of Priests

Sec. 1. The Bishop, in consultation with the Commission, shall establish procedures to identify and select persons with evident gifts and fitness for ordination to the Priesthood.

Sec 2. Of General Provisions concerning Postulancy and Candidacy

(a) Postulancy is a time, no less than six months in length, for the exploration of and decision on the Postulant's call to the Priesthood.

(b) Candidacy is a time of formation in preparation for ordination to the Priesthood, established by a formal commitment by the Candidate, the Bishop, the Commission and the congregation or other community of faith. The period of Candidacy shall be no less than six months.

(c) The combined period for Postulancy, Candidacy and Diaconate under this Canon shall be no less than 18 months.

(d) The responsibilities for the formation and preparation of Postulants and Candidates shall include the following:

(1) Each Postulant or Candidate for ordination to the Priesthood shall communicate with the Bishop in person or by letter, four times a year, in the Ember Weeks, reflecting on the individual's academic experience and personal and spiritual development.

(2) The congregation or other community of faith shall nominate appropriate persons for the ordination process, nurture them in their faith, and provide continuing support for such persons through Postulancy, Candidacy, and ordination.

(3) The Bishop and the Commission shall work closely with the Postulant or Candidate to develop and monitor a program of preparation for ordination to the Priesthood in accordance with Canon III.8.4 and to ensure that pastoral guidance is provided throughout the period of preparation.

(4) The Standing Committee shall certify that all canonical requirements for ordination have been met and make a recommendation regarding ordination as prescribed in sections 6 and 7 of this cannon.

(5) The seminary or other formation program shall provide for, monitor and report on the academic performance and personal qualifications of the Candidate or Postulant for ordination. These reports will be made upon request of the Bishop and Commission, but at least once per year.

(e)		Prior to ordination as a deacon under this canon, the following must be accomplished:
	(1)	a thorough background check of the applicant,
	(2)	sexual misconduct prevention training, training regarding Title IV of these Canons, and anti-racism training,
	(3)	thorough examinations, both medical and psychological, by professionals approved by the Bishop, using the forms prepared by the Church Pension Fund for this purpose, and if desired or necessary, psychiatric referral. These reports shall be kept on file by the Bishop.
	(4)	If the medical examination, psychological examination, or background check have taken place more than 36 months prior to ordination as a Deacon under this canon, they must be updated.

Sec. 3. Postulancy

(a) A person nominated for admission as a Postulant for ordination to the Priesthood shall provide to the Bishop the following:

    (1) Full name and date of birth.
    (2) The length of time resident in the Diocese.
    (3) Evidence of Baptism and Confirmation.
    (4) Whether an application has been made previously for Postulancy in any diocese.
    (5) A description of the process of discernment by which the nominee has been identified for ordination to the Priesthood.
    (6) The level of education attained and, if any, the degrees earned and areas of specialization.
    (7) A letter of support by the nominee's congregation or other community of faith, including a statement committing the congregation or other community of faith to involve itself in the nominee's preparation for ordination to the Priesthood. If it be a congregation, the letter shall be signed by a two-thirds majority of the Vestry, and the Member of the Clergy or leader exercising oversight.
    (8) A written request from the nominee for admission to Postulancy.

(b) Before granting admission as a Postulant, the Bishop:

    (1) shall determine that the person is a confirmed adult communicant in good standing of a congregation or

other community of faith, and
(2) shall confer in person with the nominee,
(3) shall consult with the nominee regarding financial resources which will be available for the support of the Postulant throughout preparation for ordination. During Postulancy and later Candidacy, the Bishop or someone appointed by the Bishop shall review periodically the financial condition and plans of the Postulant.

(c) On the basis of the application and the personal interview, the Bishop shall notify the nominee and the Commission whether the application process may proceed.

(d) If the Bishop approves proceeding, the Commission, or a committee of the Commission, shall meet with the nominee to review the application and prepare an evaluation of the nominee's qualifications to pursue a course of preparation for ordination to the Priesthood. The Commission shall present its evaluation and recommendations to the Bishop.

(e) The Bishop may admit the nominee as a Postulant for ordination to the Priesthood. The Bishop shall record the Postulant's name and date of admission in a Register kept for that purpose. The Bishop shall inform the Postulant, the Member of the Clergy or other leader exercising oversight of the Postulant's congregation or other community of faith, the Commission, the Standing Committee, and the Dean of the seminary the Postulant may be attending or proposes to attend, or the director of Postulant's program of preparation, of the fact and date of such admission.

(f) Any Postulant may be removed as a Postulant at the sole discretion of the Bishop. The Bishop shall give written notice of the removal to the Candidate and the Member of the Clergy or other leader exercising oversight of the Postulant's congregation or other community of faith, the Commission, the Standing Committee, and the Dean of the seminary the Postulant may be attending or the director of the program of preparation.

(g) No Bishop shall consider accepting as a Postulant any person who has been refused admission as a Candidate for ordination to the Priesthood in any other Diocese, or who, having been admitted, has afterwards ceased to be a Candidate, until receipt of a letter from the Bishop of the Diocese refusing admission, or in which the person has been a Candidate, declaring the cause of refusal or of cessation. If the Bishop decides to proceed the Bishop shall send the letter to the Commission.

Sec. 4. Formation. Postulants shall pursue the program of preparation for ordination to the Priesthood developed by the Bishop and Commission. The program shall include theological training, practical experience, emotional development, and spiritual formation.

- (a) If the Postulant has not previously obtained a baccalaureate degree, the Commission, Bishop and Postulant shall design a program of such additional academic work to prepare the Postulant to undertake a program of theological education.
- (b) Prior education and learning from life experience may be considered as part of the formation required for the Priesthood.
- (c) Whenever possible, formation for the Priesthood shall take place in community, including other persons in preparation for the Priesthood, a ministry team, or others preparing for ministry.
- (d) Formation shall take into account the local culture and each Candidate's background, age, occupation, and ministry.
- (e) Subject areas for study during this program of preparation shall include:
    - (1) The Holy Scriptures;
    - (2) Church History, including the Ecumenical Movement;
    - (3) Christian Theology, including Missionary Theology and Missiology;
    - (4) Christian Ethics and Moral Theology;
    - (5) Studies in contemporary society, including racial and minority groups;
    - (6) Liturgics and Church Music; Christian Worship and Music according to the contents and use of the Book of Common Prayer and the Hymnal; and authorized supplemental texts; and
    - (7) Theory and practice of ministry.

Sec. 5. Candidacy

- (a) A person desiring to be considered as a Candidate for ordination to the Priesthood shall apply to the Bishop. Such application shall include the following:
    - (1) the Postulant's date of admission to Postulancy, and
    - (2) a letter of support by the Postulant's congregation or other community of faith. If it be a congregation, the letter shall be signed by at least two-thirds of the Vestry and the Member of the Clergy or other leader exercising oversight.
- (b) Upon compliance with these requirements, and receipt of a

statement from the Commission attesting to the continuing formation of the Postulant, the Bishop may admit the applicant as a Candidate for ordination to the Priesthood. The Bishop shall record the Candidate's name and date of admission in a Register kept for that purpose. The Bishop shall inform the Candidate, the Member of the Clergy or leader exercising oversight of the Candidate's congregation or other community of faith, the Commission, the Standing Committee, and the Dean of the seminary the Candidate may be attending or proposes to attend, or the director of the Candidate's program of preparation, of the fact and date of such admission.

(c) A Candidate must remain in canonical relationship with the Diocese in which admission has been granted until ordination to the Diaconate under this Canon, except as provided in Canon III.8.5(d).

(d) For reasons satisfactory to the Bishop, the Candidate may be transferred to another Diocese upon request, provided that the Bishop of the receiving Diocese is willing to accept the Candidate.

(e) Any Candidate may be removed as a Candidate at the sole discretion of the Bishop. The Bishop shall give written notice of the removal to the Member of the Clergy or other leader exercising oversight of the Candidate's congregation or other community of faith, the Commission, the Standing Committee, and the Dean of the seminary the Candidate may be attending or the director of the program of preparation.

(f) If a Bishop has removed the Candidate's name from the list of Candidates, except by transfer, or the Candidate's application for ordination has been rejected, no other Bishop may ordain the person without readmission to Candidacy for a period of at least twelve months.

Sec. 6. Ordination to the Diaconate

(a) A Candidate must first be ordained Deacon before being ordained Priest.

(b) To be ordained Deacon under this canon, a person must be at least twenty-one years of age.

(c) No one shall be ordained Deacon under this canon within six months of admission as a Candidate nor within one year of admission as Postulant

(d) The Bishop shall obtain in writing:

(1) an application from the Candidate requesting ordination as a Deacon under this canon, including the Candidate's dates of admission to Postulancy and Candidacy;

(2) letter of support from the Candidate's congregation or other community of faith, signed and dated by at least two-thirds of the Vestry and the Member of the Clergy or other leader exercising oversight;

(3) a certificate from the seminary or other program of preparation, showing the Candidate's scholastic record in the subjects required by the Canons, and giving an evaluation with recommendation as to the Candidate's other personal qualifications for ordination together with a recommendation regarding ordination to the Diaconate under this canon.

(e) The Standing Committee shall obtain:

(1) the application for ordination to the Diaconate under this canon specified in Canon III.8.6(d)(1), including the accompanying letter of support by the Candidate's congregation or other community of faith specified in Canon III.8.6(d)(2),

(2) certificates from the Bishop who admitted the Candidate to Postulancy and Candidacy, giving the dates of admission, and

(3) a certificate from the Commission giving a recommendation regarding ordination to the Diaconate under this canon.

(f) On the receipt of such certificates, the Standing Committee, a majority of all the members consenting, shall certify that the canonical requirements for ordination to the Diaconate under this canon have been met and there is no sufficient objection on medical, psychological, moral, doctrinal, or spiritual grounds and that they recommend ordination, by a testimonial addressed to the Bishop in the form specified below and signed by the consenting members of the Standing Committee.

To the Right Reverend _____, Bishop of _____
We, the Standing Committee of _____, having been duly convened at _____, do testify that A.B., desiring to be ordained to the Diaconate and Priesthood under Canon III.8, has presented to us the certificates as required by the Canons indicating A.B.'s preparedness for ordination to the Diaconate under Canon III.8; and we certify that all canonical requirements for ordination to the Diaconate under Canon III.8 have been met; and we find no sufficient objection to ordination. Therefore, we recommend A. B. for ordination. In witness whereof, we have hereunto set our hands this _____ day of _____, in the year of our Lord _____ (Signed)

(g) The testimonial having been presented to the Bishop, and there being no sufficient objection on medical, psychological, moral, doctrinal, or spiritual grounds, the Bishop may ordain the Candidate to the Diaconate under this canon; and at the time of ordination the Candidate shall subscribe publicly and make, in the presence of the Bishop, the declaration required in Article VIII of the Constitution.

Sec. 67. Ordination to the Priesthood

(a) A person may be ordained Priest
  (1) after at least six months as a Deacon under this canon, and
  (2) upon attainment of at least twenty-four years of age.
  (3) If the medical examination, psychological examination, and background check have taken place or been updated within 36 months prior to ordination as a Priest.

(b) The Bishop shall obtain in writing and provide to the Standing Committee:
  (1) an application from the Deacon requesting ordination as a Priest, including the Deacon's dates of admission to Postulancy and Candidacy,
  (2) a letter of support from the Deacon's congregation or other community of faith, signed by at least two-thirds of the Vestry and the Member of the Clergy or other leader exercising oversight,
  (3) evidence of admission to Postulancy and Candidacy, including dates of admission, and ordination to the Diaconate,
  (4) a certificate from the seminary or other program of preparation, showing the Deacon's scholastic record in the subjects required by the Canons, and giving an evaluation with recommendation as to the Deacon's other personal qualifications for ordination together with a recommendation regarding ordination to the Priesthood, and
  (5) a statement from the Commission attesting to the successful completion of the program of formation designed during Postulancy under Canon III.8.4, and recommending the Deacon for ordination to the Priesthood.

(c) On the receipt of such certificates, the Standing Committee, a majority of all the members consenting, shall certify that the

canonical requirements for ordination to the Priesthood have been met, and there is no sufficient objection on medical, psychological, moral, doctrinal, or spiritual grounds and that they recommend ordination, by a testimonial addressed to the Bishop in the form specified below and signed by the consenting members of the Standing Committee.
To the Right Reverend _____, Bishop of _____
We, the Standing Committee of _____, having been duly convened at _____, do testify that A.B., desiring to be ordained to the Priesthood, has presented to us the certificates as required by the Canons indicating A.B.'s preparedness for ordination to the Priesthood have been met; and we certify that all canonical requirements for ordination to the Priesthood have been met, and we find no sufficient objection to ordination. Therefore, we recommend A. B. for ordination. In witness whereof, we have hereunto set our hands this _____ day of _____, in the year of our Lord _____
(Signed) _____

(d) The testimonial having been presented to the Bishop, and there being no sufficient objection on medical, psychological, moral, doctrinal, or spiritual grounds, the Bishop may ordain the Deacon to the Priesthood; and at the time of ordination the Deacon shall subscribe publicly and make, in the presence of the Bishop, the declaration required in Article VIII of the Constitution.

(e) No Deacon shall be ordained to the Priesthood until having been appointed to serve in a Parochial Cure within the jurisdiction of this Church, or as a Missionary under the Ecclesiastical Authority of a Diocese, or as an officer of a Missionary Society recognized by the General Convention, or as a Chaplain of the Armed Services of the United States, or as a Chaplain in a recognized hospital or other welfare institution, or as a Chaplain or instructor in a school, college, or other seminary, or with other opportunity for the exercise of the office of Priest within the Church judged appropriate by the Bishop.

(f) A person ordained to the Diaconate under Canon III.6 who is subsequently called to the Priesthood shall fulfill the Postulancy and Candidacy requirements set forth in this canon. Upon completion of these requirements, the Deacon may be ordained to the Priesthood.

CANON 9: Of the Life and Work of Priests
Sec. 1. The Bishop and Commission shall require and provide for the continuing education of Priests and keep a record of such education.
Of Mentoring for Newly Ordained Priests
Sec. 2. Each newly ordained priest, whether employed or not, shall be

assigned a mentor priest by the Bishop in consultation with the Commission on Ministry. The mentor and new priest shall meet regularly for at least a year to provide guidance, information and a sustained dialogue about priestly ministry.
Of the Appointment of Priests
Sec. 3. (a) Rectors.

    (1) When a Parish is without a Rector, the Wardens or other officers shall promptly notify the Ecclesiastical Authority in writing. If the Parish shall for thirty days fail to provide services of public worship, the Ecclesiastical Authority shall make provision for such worship.

    (2) No Parish may elect a Rector until the names of the proposed nominees have been forwarded to the Ecclesiastical Authority and a time, not exceeding sixty days, given to the Ecclesiastical Authority to communicate with the Vestry, nor until any such communication, has been considered by the Vestry at a meeting duly called and held for that purpose.

    (3) Written notice of the election of a Rector, signed by the Wardens, shall be forwarded to the Ecclesiastical Authority. If the Ecclesiastical Authority is satisfied that the person so elected is a duly qualified Priest and that such Priest has accepted the office to which elected, the notice shall be sent to the Secretary of the Convention, who shall record it. Race, color, ethnic origin, sex, national origin, marital status, sexual orientation, disabilities or age, except as otherwise specified by these Canons, shall not be a factor in the determination of the Ecclesiastical Authority as to whether such person is a duly qualified Priest. The recorded notice shall be sufficient evidence of the relationship between the Priest and the Parish.

    (4) Rectors may have a letter of agreement with the Parish setting forth mutual responsibilities, subject to the Bishop's approval.

(b) Priests-in-Charge. After consultation with the Vestry, the Bishop may appoint a Priest to serve as Priest-in-Charge of any congregation in which there is no Rector. In such congregations, the Priest-in-Charge shall exercise the duties of Rector outlined in Canon III.9.4 subject to the authority of the Bishop.

(c) Assistants. A Priest serving as an assistant in a Parish, by whatever title designated, shall be selected by the Rector, and when required by the Canons of the Diocese, subject to the approval of the Vestry, and shall serve under the authority and direction of the Rector. Before the selection of an assistant the name of the Priest proposed for selection shall be made known to the Bishop and a time, not exceeding sixty days, given for the Bishop to communicate with the Rector and Vestry on the proposed selection. Any assistant shall serve at the pleasure of the Rector and may not serve beyond the period of service of the Rector, except that pending the call of a new Rector, an assistant may continue in the service of the Parish if requested to do so by the Vestry under such conditions as the Bishop and Vestry shall determine. An assistant may continue to serve at the request of a new Rector. Assistants may have a letter of agreement with the Rector and the Vestry setting forth mutual responsibilities subject to the Bishop's approval.

(d) Chaplains.

    (1) A Priest may be given ecclesiastical endorsement for service as a Chaplain in the Armed Services of the United States of America or as a Chaplain for the Veterans' Administration, or in any Federal Correctional Institution, by the Office of the Bishop Suffragan for the Armed Forces, subject to the approval of the Ecclesiastical Authority of the Diocese in which the Priest is canonically resident.

    (2) Any Priest serving on active duty with the Armed Services shall retain the Priest's canonical residence and shall be subject to the ecclesiastical supervision of the Bishop of the Diocese of which the Priest is canonically resident, even though the Priest's work as a Chaplain shall be subject to the general supervision of the Office of the Bishop Suffragan for the Armed Forces, or such other Bishop as the Presiding Bishop may designate.

    (3) Any Priest serving on a military installation or at a Veterans' Administration facility or Federal Correctional Institution shall not be subject to Canons III.9.3.(e)(1) or III.9.4(a). When serving other than on a military installation or at a Veterans' Administration facility, or Federal Correctional Institution, a Chaplain shall be subject to these Sections.

(e) Non-ecclesiastical or Non-parochial Employment of Priests

    (1) Any Priest who has left a position in this Church without having received a call to a new ecclesiastical

position and who desires to continue the exercise of the office of Priest shall notify the Ecclesiastical Authority of the Diocese in which the Priest is canonically resident and shall advise the Bishop that reasonable opportunities for the exercise of the office of Priest exist and that use will be made of such opportunities. After having determined that the person will have and use opportunities for the exercise of the office of Priest, the Bishop, with the advice and consent of the Standing Committee, may approve the Priest's continued exercise of the office on condition that the Priest report annually in writing, in a manner prescribed by the Bishop, as provided in Canon I.6.2.

(2) A Priest who would be permitted under Canon III.18 to renounce the exercise of ordained office, who desires to enter into other than ecclesiastical employment, may declare in writing to the Ecclesiastical Authority of the Diocese in which the Priest is canonically resident a desire to be released from the obligations of the office and a desire to be released from the exercise of the office of Priest. Upon receipt of such declaration, the Ecclesiastical Authority shall proceed in the same manner as if the declaration was one of renunciation of the ordained Priesthood under Canon III.18.

(3)
- (i). A Priest not in parochial employment moving to another jurisdiction shall report to the Bishop of that jurisdiction within sixty days of such move.
- (ii). The Priest:
  - (a) May officiate or preach in that jurisdiction only under the terms of Canon III.9.5(a).
  - (b) Shall provide notice of such move, in writing and within sixty days, to the Ecclesiastical Authority of the Diocese in which the Priest is canonically resident.
  - (c) Shall forward a copy of the report required by Canon I.6.2 to the Ecclesiastical Authority to whose jurisdiction the Priest has moved.
- (iii). Upon receipt of the notice required by Canon III.9.2(d)(iii)(b)(2), the Ecclesiastical

Authority shall provide written notice thereof to the Ecclesiastical Authority into whose jurisdiction the person has moved.

(4) If the Priest fails to comply with the provisions of this Canon, the Bishop of the Diocese in which the Priest is canonically resident may proceed in accordance with Canon IV.11.

Of Letters Dimissory
Sec. 4.

(a) A Priest desiring to become canonically resident within a Diocese shall present to the Ecclesiastical Authority a testimonial from the Ecclesiastical Authority of the Diocese of current canonical residence, which testimonial shall be given by the Ecclesiastical Authority to the applicant, and a duplicate thereof may be sent to the Ecclesiastical Authority of the Diocese to which transfer is proposed. The testimonial shall be accompanied by a statement of the record of payments to The Church Pension Fund by or on behalf of the Priest concerned and shall be in the following words:
I hereby certify that A.B., who has signified to me the desire to be transferred to the Ecclesiastical Authority of _____, is a Priest of _____ in good standing, and has not, so far as I know or believe, been justly liable to evil report, for error in religion or for viciousness of life, for the last three years.

(Date) _____ (Signed) _____

(b) Such a testimonial shall be called Letters Dimissory. If the Ecclesiastical Authority accepts the Letters Dimissory, the canonical residence of the Priest transferred shall date from such acceptance, and prompt notice of acceptance shall be given to the applicant and to the Ecclesiastical Authority issuing the Letters Dimissory.

(c) Letters Dimissory not presented within six months of their date of receipt by the applicant shall become void.

(d) If a Priest has been called to a Cure in a congregation in another Diocese, the Priest shall present Letters Dimissory. The Ecclesiastical Authority of the Diocese shall accept Letters Dimissory within three months of their receipt unless the Bishop or Standing Committee has received credible information concerning the character or behavior of the Priest concerned which would form grounds for canonical inquiry and presentment. In such a case, the Ecclesiastical Authority shall notify the Ecclesiastical Authority of the Diocese in which the Priest is canonically resident and need not accept

(e) the Letters Dimissory unless and until the Priest shall be exculpated. The Ecclesiastical Authority shall not refuse to accept Letters Dimissory based on the applicant's race, color, ethnic origin, sex, national origin, marital status, sexual orientation, disabilities or age.

(e) A Priest shall not be in charge of any congregation in the Diocese to which the person moves until obtaining from the Ecclesiastical Authority of that Diocese a certificate in the following words:

I hereby certify that A.B. has been canonically transferred to my jurisdiction and is a Priest in good standing.

(Date) _____ (Signed) _____

(f) No person who has been refused ordination or reception as a Candidate in any Diocese, and is thereafter ordained in another Diocese, shall be transferred to the Diocese in which such refusal has occurred without the consent of its Ecclesiastical Authority.

Of Priests and Their Duties
Sec. 5.

(a) (1) The Rector shall have full authority and responsibility for the conduct of the worship and the spiritual jurisdiction of the Parish, subject to the Rubrics of the Book of Common Prayer, the Constitution and Canons of this Church, and the pastoral direction of the Bishop.

(2) For the purposes of the office and for the full and free discharge of all functions and duties pertaining thereto, the Rector shall at all times be entitled to the use and control of the Church and Parish buildings together with all appurtenances and furniture, and to access all records and registers maintained by or on behalf of the congregation.

(b) (1) It shall be the duty of the Priest to ensure all persons in their charge receive Instruction in the Holy Scriptures; in the subjects contained in An Outline of the Faith, commonly called the Catechism; in the doctrine, discipline and worship of this Church; and in the exercise of their ministry as baptized persons.

(2) It shall be the duty of Priests to ensure that all persons in their charge are instructed concerning Christian stewardship, including:

(i) reverence for the creation and the right use of God's gifts;

(ii) generous and consistent offering of time,

talent, and treasure for the mission and ministry of the Church at home and abroad;

(iii) the biblical standard of the tithe for financial stewardship; and

(iv) the responsibility of all persons to make a will as prescribed in the Book of Common Prayer, page 445.

(3) It shall be the duty of Priests to ensure that persons be prepared for Baptism. Before baptizing infants or children, Priests shall ensure that sponsors be prepared by instructing both the parents and the Godparents concerning the significance of Holy Baptism, the responsibilities of parents and Godparents for the Christian training of the baptized child, and how these obligations may properly be discharged.

(4) It shall be the duty of Priests to encourage and ensure the preparation of persons for Confirmation, Reception, and the Reaffirmation of Baptismal Vows, and to be ready to present them to the Bishop with a list of their names.

(5) On notice being received of the Bishop's intention to visit any congregation, the Rector shall announce the fact to the congregation. At every visitation it shall be the duty of the Rector and the Wardens, Vestry or other officers, to exhibit to the Bishop the Parish Register and to give information as to the state of the congregation, spiritual and temporal, in such categories as the Bishop shall have previously requested in writing.

(6) The Alms and Contributions, not otherwise specifically designated, at the Administration of the Holy Communion on one Sunday in each calendar month, and other offerings for the poor, shall be deposited with the Rector or with such Church officer as the Rector shall appoint to be applied to such pious and charitable uses as the Rector shall determine. When a Parish is without a Rector or Priest-in-Charge, the Vestry shall designate a member of the Parish to fulfill this function.

(7) Whenever the House of Bishops shall publish a Pastoral Letter, it shall be the duty of the Rector to read it to the congregation on some occasion of public worship on a Lord's Day, or to cause copies of the same to be distributed to the members of the congregation, not later than thirty days after receipt.

(8) Whenever the House of Bishops shall adopt a Position Paper, it may and require communication of the content of the Paper to the membership of the Church, the Rector shall so communicate the Paper in the manner set forth in the preceding section of this Canon.

(c) (1) It shall be the duty of the Rector to record in the Parish Register all Baptisms, Confirmations (including the canonical equivalents in Canon I.17.1(d)), Marriages and Burials.

(2) The registry of each Baptism shall be signed by the officiating Member of the Clergy.

(3) The Rector shall record in the Parish Register all persons who have received Holy Baptism, all communicants, all persons who have received Confirmation (including the canonical equivalents in Canon I.17.1(d)), all persons who have died, and all persons who have been received or removed by letter of transfer. The Rector shall also designate in the Parish Register the names of (1) those persons whose domicile is unknown, (2) those persons whose domicile is known but are inactive, and (3) those families and persons who are active within the congregation. The Parish Register shall remain with the congregation at all times.

Of Licenses
Sec. 6.

(a) No Priest shall preach, minister the Sacraments, or hold any public service, within the limits of any Diocese other than the Diocese in which the Priest is canonically resident for more than two months without a license from the Ecclesiastical Authority of the Diocese in which the Priest desires to so officiate. No Priest shall be denied such a license on account of the Priest's race, color, ethnic origin, sex, national origin, marital status, sexual orientation, disabilities or age, except as otherwise provided in these Canons. Upon expiration or withdrawal of a license, a priest shall cease immediately to officiate.

(b) No Priest shall preach, read prayers in public worship, or perform any similar function, in a congregation without the consent of the Rector or Priest-in-Charge of that congregation, except as follows:

(1) In the absence or disability of the Rector or Priest-in-Charge, and if provision has not been made for the stated services of the congregation or other community of faith, a Warden may give such

		consent.
(2)		(1) If there be two or more congregations or Churches in one Cure, as provided by Canon I.13.3(b), consent may be given by the majority of the Priests-in-Charge of such congregations, or by the Bishop; Provided, that nothing in this Section shall prevent any Member of the Clergy of this Church from officiating, with the consent of the Rector or Priest-in-Charge, in the Church or place of public worship used by the congregation of the consenting Rector or Priest-in-Charge, or in private for members of the congregation; or in the absence of the Rector or Priest-in-Charge, with the consent of the Wardens or Trustees of the congregation; Provided further, that the license of the Ecclesiastical Authority provided in Canon III,9.5(a), if required, be obtained.
(3)		This Canon shall not apply to any Church, Chapel, or Oratory, which is part of the premises of an incorporated institution created by legislative authority, provided that such place of worship is designated and set apart for the convenience and use of such institution, and not as a place for public or parochial worship.

(c) No Rector or Priest-in-Charge of any congregation of this Church, or if there be none, no Wardens, Members of the Vestry, or Trustees of any congregation, shall permit any person to officiate in the congregation without sufficient evidence that such person is duly licensed and ordained and in good standing in this Church; Provided, nothing in these Canons shall prevent:

(1) The General Convention, by Canon or otherwise, from authorizing persons to officiate in congregations in accordance with such terms as it deems appropriate; or

(2) The Bishop of any Diocese from giving permission

(i) To a Member of the Clergy of this Church, to invite Clergy of another Church to assist in the Book of Common Prayer Offices of Holy Matrimony or of the Burial of the Dead, or to read Morning or Evening Prayer, in the manner specified in Canon III.9.5; or

(ii) To Clergy of any other Church to preach the Gospel, or in ecumenical settings to assist in the administration of the sacraments; or

(iii) To godly persons who are not Clergy of this Church to address the Church on special occasions.

(iv) To the Member of the Clergy or Priest-in-Charge of a congregation or if there be none, to the Wardens, to invite Clergy ordained in another Church in communion with this Church to officiate on an occasional basis, provided that such clergy are instructed to teach and act in a manner consistent with the Doctrine, Discipline, and Worship of this Church.

(d) (a) If any Member of the Clergy or Priest-in-Charge, as a result of disability or any other cause, shall neglect to perform regular services in the congregation, and refuse, without good cause, to consent to any other duly qualified Member of the Clergy to perform such services, the Wardens, Vestry, or Trustees of the congregation shall, upon providing evidence to the Ecclesiastical Authority of the Diocese of such neglect or refusal and with the written consent of the Ecclesiastical Authority, have the authority to permit any duly qualified Member of the Clergy to officiate.

(e) (1) Any Priest desiring to officiate temporarily outside the jurisdiction of this Church but in a Church in communion with this Church, shall obtain from the Ecclesiastical Authority of the Diocese in which the person is canonically resident, a testimonial which shall set forth the person's official standing, and which may be in the following words:

I hereby certify that A.B., who has signified to me the desire to be permitted to officiate temporarily in churches not under the jurisdiction of The Episcopal Church, yet in communion with this Church, is a Priest of _____ in good standing, and as such is entitled to the rights and privileges of that Order.

(Date) _____ (Signed) _____

Such testimonial shall be valid for one year and shall be returned to the Ecclesiastical Authority at the end of that period.

(2) The Ecclesiastical Authority giving such testimonial shall record its issuance, the name of the Priest to whom issued, its date and the date of its return.

Of Retirement

Sec. 7. Upon attaining the age of seventy-two years, a Priest occupying any position in this Church shall resign that position and retire from active service, and the resignation shall be accepted. Thereafter, the Priest may accept any position in this Church, including, with permission of the ecclesiastical authority, the position or positions from which resignation pursuant to this Section has occurred; Provided,

- (a) tenure in the position shall be for a period of not more than one year, which period may be renewed from time to time,
- (b) service in the position shall have the express approval of the Bishop of the Diocese in which the service is to be performed, acting in consultation with the Ecclesiastical Authority of the Diocese in which the Priest is canonically resident.
- (c) Anything in this Canon to the contrary notwithstanding, a Priest who has served in a non-stipendiary capacity in a position before retirement may, at the Bishop's request, serve in the same position for six months thereafter, and this period may be renewed from time to time.

Reconsideration of Resolution A103

Deputy Wade of Washington moved to reconsider Resolution A103.
Deputy Seitz of West Virginia moved to terminate debate.

Motion carried
Debate terminated

A vote was taken to reconsider Resolution A103.

Motion carried
Resolution reconsidered

Parliamentary Procedures

The Parliamentarian clarified for the House that in vote by orders, the outcome is based on dioceses eligible for representation. Dioceses which are not now represented are nonetheless counted in the votes necessary for passage of a resolution.

Deputy Johnson of Minnesota moved a Substitute Resolution A103.

Substitute Resolution:

(A103)
Resolved, the House of Bishops concurring, That the 74th General Convention authorize the permissive use of the Revised Common Lectionary under the direction of the Bishop or Ecclesiastical authority of the diocese.

Deputy Seitz of West Virginia moved to terminate debate.

Vote by Orders

A deputy from Quincy moved on behalf of the clerical and lay orders of Forth Worth, the clerical and lay orders of Quincy, and the clerical order of South Carolina for a vote by orders on Resolution A103.

The vote was then taken on the motion to terminate debate.

Motion carried
Debate terminated

Ballot #5–Vote by Orders

Ballot #5 was taken on Resolution A103.

Ballot #5 taken by orders

Results of Ballot #5: Vote by Orders on Resolution A103

The Secretary read the results of Ballot #5.

Type	Total	Necessary	Yes	No	Divided	Results
Lay:	104	53	97	5	2	Carried
Clerical:	106	54	98	7	1	Carried

Motion carried
Substitute resolution adopted
(Communicated to the House of Bishops in HD Message #258)

Suspension of Personal Privilege

Deputy Blue of Washington moved to suspend personal privilege until business is completed.

Motion carried
Rules of Order suspended

Stewardship and Development

The House of Deputies Committee on Stewardship and Development presented its Report #9 on HB Message #56 on Resolution A134 (Implement Alleluia Fund) and moved concurrence.

The House concurred
(Communicated to the House of Bishops in HD Message #252)

Final Text of Resolution:

(A134)
Resolved, **That the 74th General Convention commend those dioceses that have already implemented Resolution A036 of the 73rd General Convention, The Alleluia Fund—Build My Church; and other similar funds;** and be it further
Resolved, **That all dioceses, as a part of their 20/20 initiative, be encouraged to articulate a vision and engage in the Alleluia Fund process of planning, giving, and spiritual transformation in order to fund new mission opportunities.**

The House of Deputies Committee on Stewardship and Development presented its Report #10 on HB Message #106 on Resolution A066 (Campus Ministry Allocation) and moved concurrence.

The House concurred
(Communicated to the House of Bishops in HD Message #250)

Final Text of Resolution:
(A066)
Resolved, **That the 74th General Convention call upon the Executive Council, the dioceses and congregations of The Episcopal Church to affirm existing campus ministries and explore new and creative forms of campus ministry, new sources of funding and to commit adequate resources in time, talent, and treasure to ensure a significant and effective ministry at each campus.**

The House of Deputies Committee on Stewardship and Development presented its Report #11 on HB Message #97 on Resolution B022 (Celebration of African Martyrs) and moved concurrence.

The House concurred
(Communicated to the House of Bishops in HD Message #251)

Final Text of Resolution:
(B022)
Resolved, **That the 74th General Convention encourage congregations to take a special offering on occasions when martyrs of Africa are being commemorated, and that such offerings be sent to Episcopal Relief and Development to support Anglican Provinces in Africa;** and be it further
Resolved, **That educational materials about African Anglican Provinces be provided at every level of the church.**

Constitution
The House of Deputies Committee on Constitution presented its Report #5 on HB Message #144 on Resolution B005 (Amend Constitution Article I.2) and moved concurrence.

The Chair of the Committee added a second resolve clause, "This resolution is to be sent to all dioceses within 6 months."

The President stated that this addition would not affect the concurrence.

Deputy Seitz of West Virginia moved to terminate debate.

Motion carried
Debate terminated

The vote was taken on Resolution B005.

The House concurred
(Communicated to the House of Bishops in HD Message #253)

Final Text of Resolution:
(B005)
Resolved, That Article 1, Section 2 of the Constitution be amended to read as follows:
~~Each Bishop of this Church having jurisdiction, every Bishop Coadjutor, every Suffragan Bishop, every Assistant Bishop, and every Bishop who by reason of advanced age or bodily infirmity, or who, under an election to an office created by the General Convention, or for reasons of mission strategy determined by action of the General Convention or the House of Bishops, has resigned a jurisdiction, shall have a seat, and a vote in the House of Bishops. A majority of all Bishops entitled to vote, exclusive of Bishops who have resigned their jurisdiction or positions, shall be necessary to constitute a quorum for the transaction of business.~~
All Bishops of this Church shall have seat and voice in the House of Bishops. Each Bishop of this Church having jurisdiction, Bishop Coadjutor, Bishop Suffragan, Assistant Bishop, and every Bishop holding an office created by General Convention shall have a vote in the House of Bishops. A majority of all Bishops entitled to vote shall be necessary to constitute a quorum for transaction of business.
And be it further
Resolved, That this resolution is to be sent to all dioceses within 6 months.

The House of Deputies Committee on Constitution presented its Report #6 on HB Message #145 on Resolution D027 (Amend Constitution Article II.1 [Election of Bishops–Second Reading]) and moved concurrence.

Ballot #6—Vote by Orders
Ballot #6 was taken on Resolution D027.

Ballot #6 taken by orders

Results of Ballot #6: Vote by Orders on Resolution D027
The Secretary reported the results on Ballot #6.

Type	Total	Necessary	Yes	No	Divided	Results
Lay:	104	53	101	2	1	Carried
Clergy:	100	51	97	1	2	Carried

The House concurred
(Communicated to the House of Bishops in HD Message #261)

Final Text of Resolution:
(D027)
Resolved, That Article II, Sec. 1 of the Constitution of the General Convention be amended to read:
Sec. 1. In every Diocese the Bishop or the Bishop Coadjutor shall be chosen agreeably to rules prescribed by the Convention of that Diocese, ***provided that the retirement date of the Bishop Diocesan shall not be more than***

thirty-six months after the consecration of the Bishop Coadjutor. Bishops of Missionary Dioceses shall be chosen in accordance with the Canons of the General Convention. And be it further
Resolved, That this resolution be sent within six months to the Secretary of the Convention of every Diocese to be made known to the Diocesan Convention at its next meeting.

The House of Deputies Committee on Constitution presented its Report #7 on HB Message #160 on Resolution B023 (Change Consent Process to Provinces) and moved concurrence with referral to the Standing Commission on Constitution and Canons.

Final Text of Resolution:
(B023)
Resolved, That the 74th General Convention amend the Constitution of the General Convention, Article II, Section 2, 1st sentence, so as to read:
No one shall be ordained and consecrated Bishop until the attainment of thirty years of age; nor without the consent of a majority of the Standing Committees of all the Dioceses *within the Province where the election has occurred*, and the consent of a majority of the Bishops of this Church exercising jurisdiction *in said Province*. But if the election shall have taken place within three months next before the meeting of the General Convention, the consent of the House of Deputies shall be required in place of that of a majority of the Standing Committees. No one shall be ordained and consecrated Bishop by fewer than three Bishops.
And be it further
Resolved, That Title III, Canon 22, Sections 4(a) and (b) be amended so as to correspond to the change in the Constitution.

Motion carried
Resolution referred to a Standing Commission
(Communicated to the House of Bishops in HD Message #265)

Canons
The House of Deputies Committee on Canons presented its Report #7 on HB Message #100 on Resolution A051 (Amend Canon IV.4.14) and moved concurrence.

The House concurred
(Communicated to the House of Bishops in HD Message #254)

Final Text of Resolution:
(A051)
Resolved, That Canon IV.4.14 be amended to read as follows:
Sec. 14. *(a)* The Ecclesiastical Trial Court shall keep a *complete and accurate* record of ~~the~~ *its* proceedings. ~~in each case brought before it and the record~~

~~shall be certified by the Presiding Judge of the Court. If the record cannot be authenticated by the Presiding Judge by reason of the Presiding Judge's death, disability or absence, it shall be authenticated by a member of the Court designated for that purpose by majority vote of the Court.~~ *When all proceedings on a Presentment have been concluded, including any and all appeals, the Presiding Judge shall certify the record. If the Presiding Judge did not participate in the proceeding for any reason, by majority vote the Court shall designate another member to certify the record.*
(b) The Court shall promptly deliver the original certified record of the proceedings to the Archives of the Episcopal Church.
And be it further
Resolved, That Canon IV.4.31 be amended to read as follows:
Sec. 31. During the period between General Conventions, each Provincial Synod shall elect the Judges of the Court of Review in the Province. The Synod shall prescribe the time and the manner in which such Judges shall be elected. The persons so elected, except in case of death, resignation, or declination to serve, shall continue to be members of the Court for such terms as the Synod may set and until their successors shall be elected. The Bishop elected by the Synod shall be the Presiding ~~Officer~~ *Judge* of the Court.
And be it further
Resolved, That Canon IV.4.48 be amended to read as follows:
Sec. 48. *(a)* The Court of Review shall keep a *complete and accurate* record of all ~~its~~ proceedings. *When all proceedings on an appeal have been concluded, the Presiding Judge shall certify the record. If the Presiding Judge did not participate in the proceeding for any reason, by majority vote the Court shall designate another member to certify the record.*
(b) The Court shall promptly deliver the original certified record of the proceedings to the Archives of the Episcopal Church.
And be it further
Resolved, That Canon IV.5.29 be amended to read as follows:
Sec. 29(a) The Court *for the Trial of a Bishop* shall keep a *complete and accurate* record of ~~all~~ *its* proceedings. *When all proceedings on a Presentment have been concluded, including any and all appeals, the Presiding Judge shall certify the record. If the Presiding Judge did not participate in the proceeding for any reason, by majority vote the Court shall designate another member to certify the record.*
(b) ~~The record shall be kept by the Clerk, inserted in a book and be attested by the signature of the Presiding Judge and Clerk. The record shall be in the custody of the Clerk and kept in the depository of the Registrar of the General Convention, and in the Archives of the Episcopal Church and shall be open to the inspection of every member of this Church.~~ *The Court shall promptly deliver the original certified record of the proceedings to the Archives of the Episcopal Church.*
And be it further
Resolved, That a new section be added to Canon IV.6, numbered 22 to read as

follows, and that the existing Section 22 of Canon IV.6 be renumbered Section 23:

Sec. 22 (a) The Court of Review of a Trial of a Bishop shall keep a complete and accurate record of its proceedings. When all proceedings on an appeal have been concluded, the Presiding Judge shall certify the record. If the Presiding Judge did not participate in the proceeding for any reason, by majority vote the Court shall designate another member to certify the record.

(b) The Court shall promptly deliver the original certified record of the proceedings to the Archives of the Episcopal Church.

Sec ~~22~~23. The reasonable and necessary expenses of the Court of Review of the Trial of a Bishop, including but not limited to the fees, costs, disbursements and expenses of the Judges, Church Attorneys, Clerks, Reporters and Lay Assessors, shall be charged upon the General Convention and shall be paid by the Treasurer of General Convention upon the order of the Presiding Judge of the Court. The Court shall have the authority to contract for and bind the General Convention to payment of these expenses.

And be it further

Resolved, That Canon IV.4.51 be amended by striking the last two sentences thereof, to read as follows:

Sec. 51. The concurrence of five members of a Court of Review shall be necessary to pronounce a judgment. The judgment or decision of the Court shall be in writing, signed by the members of the Court concurring therein, and shall distinctly specify the grounds of the decision and shall be attached to the record. If the concurrence of five of the members cannot be obtained, that fact shall be stated in the record, and the determination or Judgment of the Trial Court shall stand as affirmed except as to any reversal in part in which there has been concurrence. Immediately after the determination of the appeal, the Presiding Judge of the Court shall give notice thereof in writing to the appellant and appellee and to the Bishop and the Diocesan Review Committee of the Diocese in which the Trial was had. ~~Upon the determination of the appeal, the original record upon which the appeal was heard, together with the record of the Court of Review, certified by the Presiding Judge and the Secretary or Clerk, shall be remitted to the Bishop or the Diocesan Review Committee of the jurisdiction in which the Trial was had and to the Archives of the Episcopal Church. All records remitted as herein provided shall be deposited and be preserved among the Archives of the jurisdiction to which they are sent.~~

And be it further

Resolved, That a new section be added to Canon IV.14, numbered 29, to read as follows:

Sec. 29. Record of Certain Title IV Proceedings and Actions.

(a) Each Ecclesiastical Court shall keep a complete and accurate record of its proceedings. When all proceedings on a Presentment or other matter have been concluded, including any and all appeals, the Presiding Judge shall certify the record. If the Presiding Judge did not participate in the proceeding for any reason, the Court, by majority vote, shall designate another member to certify

the record.

(b) A Court may make provision for the preservation and storage of a copy of the record of each proceeding in the Diocese in which the Presentment or other proceeding originated.

(c) A Court shall promptly deliver the original certified record of its proceedings to the Archives of the Episcopal Church.

(d) A Bishop, including the Presiding Bishop, who pronounces a Sentence shall deliver a copy of the notice of the Sentence to the Archives of the Episcopal Church.

(e) In the case of a Waiver and Voluntary Submission to discipline of a Deacon, Priest or Bishop, the Ecclesiastical Authority with jurisdiction shall promptly deliver a copy of the required written instrument to the Archives of the Episcopal Church

(f) Bishops, including the Presiding Bishop, shall promptly deliver a record of any action of remission or modification of a Sentence to the Archives of the Episcopal Church.

And be it further

Resolved, That the definition of "Sentence" in Canon IV.15 be amended to read as follows:

Sentence shall mean the sentence adjudged by an Ecclesiastical Court after a finding of a commission of an Offense or the lesser Sentence to be pronounced by a Bishop or the Presiding Bishop, as the case may be. *The Sentence, whether Admonition, Suspension or Deposition, shall specify the Canon or Canons under which the action is being taken.*

And be it further

Resolved, That the Standing Commission on Constitution and Canons be directed during the next triennium to consider any further canonical changes that may be appropriate in light of the changes made in this Resolution, and to report on its work to the 75th General Convention.

The House of Deputies Committee on Canons presented its Report #8 on HB Message #43 on Resolution A048 (Amend Canon IV.4.16(d)) and moved concurrence.

The House concurred
(Communicated to the House of Bishops in HD Message #255)

Final Text of Resolution:

(A048)

Resolved, That Canon IV.4.16(d) be amended to read as follows:

(d) If the Respondent fails or refuses to answer or otherwise enter an appearance, except for reasonable cause to be allowed by the Court, the Church Attorney may, no sooner than thirty days after the answer is due, move for Summary Judgment of Offense in accordance with the Rules of Procedure. If the motion is granted *the Bishop shall be notified, and* the Respondent shall be given notice that Sentence of Admonition, Suspension or Deposition will be adjudged *by the Court* and pronounced by the ~~Court~~ *Bishop* at the expiration of thirty days after the Notice of Sentence, or at such convenient time thereafter as the ~~Court~~ *Bishop* shall determine. Sentence of Admonition, Suspension or of Deposition from the Ordained Ministry may, thereafter, be adjudged *by the Court* and pronounced by the ~~Court~~ *Bishop*.

The House of Deputies Committee on Canons presented its Report #9 on HB Message #42 on Resolution A046 (Amend Canon III.22.1(e)) and moved concurrence.

The House concurred
(Communicated to the House of Bishops in HD Message #256)

Final Text of Resolution:
(A046)
Resolved, That Canon III.22.1(e) be amended as follows:
(e) The Secretary of the *body* ~~Convention~~ electing a Bishop Diocesan, Bishop Coadjutor, or Bishop Suffragan, shall inform the Presiding Bishop promptly of the name of the person elected. It shall be the duty of the Bishop-elect to notify the Presiding Bishop of ~~his~~ acceptance or declination of the election, at the same time as the Bishop-elect notifies the electing diocese.

The House of Deputies Committee on Canons presented its Report #10 on HB Message #74 on Resolution D013 (Annotated Constitution and Canons, known as White and Dykman) and moved concurrence.

The House concurred
(Communicated to the House of Bishops in HD Message #257)

Final Text of Resolution:
(D013)
Resolved, That the 74th General Convention direct that during the next triennium the Standing Commission on Constitution and Canons be authorized to initiate the editing, revising, and updating of the *Annotated Constitution and Canons for the Government of the Protestant Episcopal Church in the United States of America otherwise known as The Episcopal Church (1954 edition)*, more familiarly known as *White and Dykman*, and all subsequent supplemental editions, for the purpose of creating a new and complete edition of the *Annotated Constitution and Canons*; and be it further
Resolved, That the Standing Commission on Constitution and Canons be authorized to arrange for the publication, distribution, and sale of this new edition of *Annotated Constitution and Canons*; and be it further
Resolved, That the General Convention request the Joint Standing Committee on Program, Budget and Finance to consider a budget allocation of $45,000 for implementation of this resolution.

JOURNAL   TENTH DAY

The House of Deputies Committee on Education presented its Report #10 on HB Message #141 on Resolution A059 (Design New Resources) and moved concurrence.

The House concurred
(Communicated to the House of Bishops in HD Message #259)

Final Text of Resolution:
(A059)
Resolved, That in support of this church's 20/20 program for evangelism, and in recognition of the joys and challenges of 21st century ministry, and in acknowledgment that this ministry requires specific strategies and skills in:
    intercultural leadership
    contemporary foreign language courses
    anti-racism education
    church planting
    congregational revitalization
    evangelism
    management of change
    negotiation of conflict; and be it further
Resolved, That the 74th General Convention strongly urge that dioceses carry out recruitment, discernment, and evaluation of persons for lay and ordained ministries which consider these strategies and skills as integral aspects of church leadership. That the seminaries and diocesan schools for ministry of The Episcopal Church be urged to review and renew curricula, providing inclusion of these strategies and skills; and that opportunities across the church for continuing education, focus on these strategies and skills, most especially in the coming triennium, in order to lay a strong foundation for 20/20 evangelism.

The House of Deputies Committee on Education presented its Report #11 on HB Message #143 on Resolution D033 (Encourage Basic Financial Teaching) and moved concurrence.

The House concurred
(Communicated to the House of Bishops in HD Message #260)

Final Text of Resolution:
(D033)
Resolved, That the 74th General Convention, mindful of the rubric found on page 445 of The Book of Common Prayer,* direct every congregation to provide educational opportunities and other resources for Christians of all ages that promote understanding the role of money in our lives; Biblical teachings about financial and material matters; and good stewardship relating to budgeting, saving, responsible handling of debt, life planning and the making of wills, recognizing that from the earliest years and throughout

life, attitudes toward money influence who we are and the choices we make, and that the spiritual practice of stewardship begins with a joyous awareness of God's love for us and a gratitude for the abundance of God's gifts; and be it further

Resolved, That the Office of Stewardship of the Episcopal Church Center and Dioceses assist congregations by recommending appropriate materials.

*From Thanksgiving for the Birth or Adoption of a Child, The Book of Common Prayer, page 445, "The Minister of the Congregation is directed to instruct the people, from time to time, about the duty of Christian parents to make prudent provision for the well-being of their families, and of all persons to make wills, while they are in health, arranging for the disposal of their temporal goods, not neglecting, if they are able, to leave bequests for religious and charitable uses."

The House of Deputies Committee on National and International Concerns presented its Report #38 on HB Message #147 on Resolution D020 (Opposition to Sharia Law) and moved concurrence.

The House concurred
(Communicated to the House of Bishops in HD Message #262)

Final Text of Resolution:
(D020)
Resolved, That the 74th General Convention support the Archbishop of Canterbury and other Anglican leaders who have jointly affirmed with Islamic leaders in various countries our shared desire to honor those teachings in our respective traditions which work to avoid coercion and respect individual liberty; and be it further

Resolved, That in further dialogue, particular attention be paid to vigorously oppose any nation's or other governmental body's imposition or continuation of a legal system which violates fundamental human rights; and be it further

Resolved, That the General Convention urge the application of these principles by the United States government to the reconstruction underway in Iraq and Afghanistan, in peace negotiations in Sudan, and in ongoing discussions with Nigeria and Indonesia, with particular attention to the rights of religious minorities, women, and those seeking to change their faith.

The House of Deputies Committee on Social and Urban Affairs presented its Report #32 on Resolution A016 (Food Security) and moved to refer the resolution to a Standing Commission.

Original Text of Resolution:
(A016)
Resolved, the House of Bishops concurring, That the mind of the 74th General Convention reflect the conclusions of the Executive Council Committee on

Science, Technology and Faith (ST&F) in its capacity of providing to the Church informed conclusions concerning the intersection of science and technology with the faith life of Episcopalians. Christians are called by God to be stewards of and delighters in God's world, and to protect the diversity of God's Creation. We urge Episcopalians in their corporate, community, and individual action to integrate national and international food security into their understanding of Christian responsibility; and be it further
Resolved, That in their understanding of Christian responsibility all Episcopalians support public policy and actions that foster research and development of the types of science and technology that preserve "biodiversity in food production", which refers to the maintenance of a healthy relationship among varieties of food crops and species on which they depend; and be it further
Resolved, That Episcopalians become informed about trade conditions and intellectual property practices that exacerbate the tendency of genetic modification technologies to reduce biodiversity in food production; and be it further
Resolved, That Episcopalians support and participate in programs that protect farming and farmlands and promote intentional purchases of food produced locally.

Motion carried
Resolution referred to a Standing Commission
(Communicated to the House of Bishops in HD Message #263)

Prayer Book, Liturgy and Church Music

The House of Deputies Committee on Prayer Book, Liturgy, and Music presented its Report #18 on HB Message #151 on Resolution A109 (International Anglican Liturgical Consultation) and moved concurrence.

The House concurred
(Communicated to the House of Bishops in HD Message #264)

Final Text of Resolution:

(A109)
Resolved, **That the 74th General Convention reaffirm and support the Church's participation in and support of the International Anglican Liturgical Consultation;** and be it further
Resolved, **That the General Convention request the Joint Standing Committee on Program, Budget and Finance to consider a budget allocation of $25,000 for implementation of this resolution.**

RECESS

The President recessed the House at 4:00 p.m. for a short break.

Reconvene

The House reconvened at 4:15 p.m.

Prayer Book, Liturgy and Church Music

The House of Deputies Committee on Prayer Book, Liturgy and Church Music presented its Report #19 on HB Message #157 on Resolution D049 (First Communion on the Moon) and moved concurrence with referral to the Standing Commission on Liturgy and Music.

Final Text of Resolution:

(D049)
Resolved, That the 74th General Convention promote local commemoration of the 35th anniversary of "The First Communion on the Moon," July 20, 2004, in worship and teaching; and be it further
Resolved, That the 74th General Convention direct the Standing Commission on Liturgy and Music to prepare propers and collects for churchwide observance of the 40th anniversary of the event, July 20, 2009; and be it further
Resolved, That the General Convention direct the Standing Commission on Liturgy and Music to prepare to include "The First Communion on the Moon" in the Episcopal Church's *Lesser Feasts and Fasts* and on the calendar in the Book of Common Prayer for July 20.

Motion carried
Resolution referred to a Standing Commission
(Communicated to the House of Bishops in HD Message #315)

The House of Deputies Committee on Prayer Book, Liturgy and Church Music presented its Report #20 on HB Message #155 on Resolution D003 (Revision of the Catechism) and moved concurrence with referral to the Standing Commission on Liturgy and Music.

Final Text of Resolution:

(D003)
Resolved, That the catechism be changed in The Book of Common Prayer (page 847) to quote Micah 6:8 correctly:
"Question: What response did God require from the chosen people? Answer: God required the chosen people to be faithful; ~~to love justice, to do mercy,~~ *to do justice, to love mercy* and to walk humbly with their God."; and be it further
Resolved, That all future printings of The Book of Common Prayer include this correction in an erratum until a new edition is approved.

Motion carried
Resolution referred to a Standing Commission
(Communicated to the House of Bishops in HD Message #267)

The House of Deputies Committee on Prayer Book, Liturgy and Church Music presented its Report #21 on HB Message #156 on Resolution D035 (To Transfer the Commemoration of Harriet Tubman from July 20 to March 10) and moved concurrence with referral to the Standing Commission on Liturgy and Music.

Final Text of Resolution:
(D035)
Resolved, That the commemoration of Harriet Ross Tubman Davis be observed on March 10 in the Calendar of Lesser Feasts and that her name be removed from the commemorations of July 20.

Motion carried
Resolution referred to a Standing Commission
(Communicated to the House of Bishops in HD Message #268)

Ecumenical Relations
The House of Deputies Committee on Ecumenical Relations presented its Report #10 on HB Message #118 on Resolution D010 (Amend Canons I.1.2 (n) (5), HBRO: General I(18) & HDRO IV.7(18)) and moved concurrence.

The House concurred
(Communicated to the House of Bishops in HD Message #269)

Final Text of Resolution:
(D010)
Resolved, That Canon I.1.2 (n) (5) be amended to read:
A Standing Commission on Ecumenical *and Interreligious* Relations consisting of 18 members (6 Bishops, 6 Priests and/or Deacons and 6 Lay Persons). Its duties shall be to recommend to the General Convention a comprehensive and coordinated policy and strategy on relations between this Church and other Churches, *and this Church and other religions;* to make recommendations to General Convention concerning interchurch cooperation and unity, *and interreligious dialogue and action,* and to carry out such instruction on ecumenical *and interreligious* matters as may be given it from time to time by the General Convention. It shall also nominate for appointment by the Presiding Bishop, with the advice and consent of the Executive Council, persons to serve on the governing bodies of of ecumenical *and interreligious* organizations to which this Church belongs by action of the General Convention, who shall report to the Presiding Bishop, Executive Council and the Standing Commission on Ecumenical *and Interreligious* Relations.

Communications
The House of Deputies Committee on Communication presented its Report #14 on HB Message #98 on Resolution D021 (Support for Church Publishing Inc.'s Revised Strategy) and moved concurrence.

The House concurred
(Communicated to the House of Bishops in HD Message #270)

Final Text of Resolution:
(D021)
Resolved, That the 74th General Convention of The Episcopal Church endorse the Church Pension Fund's goal of firmly establishing Church Publishing Incorporated as a significant provider of books, software, and related services to The Episcopal Church's institutions and individuals; and be it further
Resolved, That we thank the Rt. Rev. Hays Rockwell for his willingness to serve as chairperson of the reconstituted Board of Directors of Church Publishing Incorporated; and be it further
Resolved, That we encourage all the member organizations of the Episcopal Publishing Ministries to work together to provide members of the Anglican Communion and others with materials to strengthen them spiritually and theologically; to increase their knowledge of the history and traditions of their Church; and to facilitate Christian worship and witness.

The House of Deputies Committee on Communications presented its Report #15 on HB Message #173 on Resolution C037 (Facilitating International Communications within the Episcopal Church) and moved concurrence.
The House concurred
(Communicated to the House of Bishops in HD Message #271)

Final Text of Resolution:
(C037)
Resolved, That the 74th General Convention urge all church bodies and affiliated organizations, agencies, and publishers to recognize The Episcopal Church's international membership beyond the boundaries of the United States when producing informational material, documentation, publications, websites, and advertisements; and be it further
Resolved, That the Domestic and Foreign Missionary Society provide methods of contact that allow for international and military postal addresses and telephone numbers for online purchase and information collection.

Miscellaneous Resolutions
The House of Deputies Committee on Miscellaneous Resolutions presented its Report #13 on HB Message #122 on Resolution D041 (Service Animals Welcome) and moved concurrence.
The House concurred
(Communicated to the House of Bishops in HD Message #272)

Final Text of Resolution:
(D041)
Resolved, That the 74th General Convention of The Episcopal Church support

congregations working toward becoming welcoming and safe places for all people; and be it further

Resolved, That as some people need the assistance of trained, certified service animals to function in daily life, all congregations and institutions of The Episcopal Church open their buildings and facilities to trained, certified service animals, so that no one is excluded from worshiping and otherwise participating in the life of the church.

Canons

The House of Deputies Committee on Canons presented its Report #14 on HB Message #204 on Resolution D012 (Amend Canons I.13, IV.3.42, 43, IV.14.2) and moved concurrence with a referral to the Standing Commission on Constitution and Canons.

Final Text of Resolution:

(D012)
Resolved, That Canons I.13, IV.3.42, 43, IV.14.2 be amended as follows:
Canon IV.3.42. Within one hundred twenty days after receipt of the statement from the Review Committee, unless delayed for good and sufficient cause stated, the Church Attorney shall render a confidential report to the Review Committee of the findings of that investigation ~~and as to whether or not an offense may have been committed if the facts disclosed by the investigation be found to be true upon Trial, and with a recommendation as to the matter in the interest of justice and the good order and discipline of this Church and based upon such other matters as shall be pertinent~~. The report of the Church Attorney shall be confidential for all purposes as between the Church Attorney and the Review Committee, *Provided, however,* the Review Committee shall share the Report of the Church Attorney with the Presiding Bishop, *the Respondent, the alleged Victim and the Complainant.*
Canon IV.3.43(b) In its deliberations, the Review Committee may consider the Church Attorney's report, responsible writings or sworn statements pertaining to the matter, including experts' statements, whether or not submitted by the Church Attorney. To assist in its deliberations, the Review Committee ~~may~~ *shall* provide an opportunity to be heard to the Respondent, the alleged Victim, *and* the Complainant ~~or other persons~~ and receive additional evidence *offered by the Respondent, the alleged Victim and/or the Complainant, and may provide an opportunity to be heard to other persons and receive additional evidence* which it in its sole discretion deems appropriate.
Canon IV.14.2. Resort to secular courts. No Member of the Clergy of this Church may resort to the secular courts for the purpose of interpreting the Constitution and Canons, or for the purpose of resolving any dispute arising thereunder, or for the purpose of delaying, hindering or reviewing or affecting in any way any proceeding under this Title. *Nothing in this Title, however, shall be construed as limiting or restricting the right of any Member of*

the Clergy to resort to the secular courts to seek compensation for breach of a contract of employment.
Canon I.13. Sec 4. No Parish or Congregation of this Church shall deny any Member of the Clergy the right to seek compensation in the secular courts for the breach of a contract of employment.

Motion carried
Resolution referred to a Standing Commission
(Communicated to the House of Bishops in HD Message #273)

The House of Deputies Committee on Canons presented its Report #15 on HB Message #203 on Resolution D067 (Amend Canon 2, Title 2 of Translations of the Bible) and moved concurrence.

The House concurred
(Communicated to the House of Bishops in HD Message #274)

Final Text of Resolution:
(D067)
Resolved, That Canon 2, Title II be amended as follows:
The Lessons prescribed in the Book of Common Prayer shall be read from the translation of the Holy Scriptures commonly known as the King James or Authorized Version (which is the historic Bible of this Church) together with the Marginal Readings authorized for use by the General Convention of 1901; or from one of the three translations known as Revised Versions, including the English Revision of 1881, the American Revision of 1901, and the Revised Standard Version of 1952; from the Jerusalem Bible of 1966; from the New English Bible with the Apocrypha of 1970; or from The 1976 Good News Bible (Today's English Version) ~~and its corresponding Spanish version " Dios Habla Hoy;"~~; or from The New American Bible (1970); or from The Revised Standard Version, an Ecumenical Edition, commonly known as the "R.S.V. Common Bible" (1973); or from The New International Version (1978); or from The New Jerusalem Bible (1987); or from the Revised English Bible (1989); or from the New Revised Standard Version (1990); *or from translations, authorized by the diocesan bishop, of those approved versions published in any other language;* or from other versions of the Bible, including those in languages other than English, which shall be authorized by diocesan bishops for specific use in congregations or ministries within their dioceses.

National and International Concerns
The House of Deputies Committee on National and International Concerns presented its Report #47 on HB Message #211 on Resolution D050 (Cuba–Honoring Commitments) and moved concurrence.

The House concurred
(Communicated to the House of Bishops in HD Message #275)

Final Text of Resolution:
(D050)
Resolved, That the 74th General Convention, through both its national and diocesan leadership, request our federal legislative delegations in Washington, D.C. to encourage immediate action on the filed applications to release pension payments, restricted endowment, and trust income held by ECUSA for the Diocese of Cuba, and other grants the disbursement of which was stopped by the Patriot Act passed after September 11th by Congress; and be it further
Resolved, That we continue to work with the Anglican Church of Canada which continues to provide oversight and assistance to the Cuban Church.

Prayer Book, Liturgy and Church Music
The House of Deputies Committee on Prayer Book, Liturgy and Church Music presented its Report #17 on HB Message #132 on Resolution D047 (Post-Abortion Healing Service) and moved concurrence.
The House concurred
(Communicated to the House of Bishops in HD Message #276)

Final Text of Resolution:
(D047)
Resolved, That the 74th General Convention direct the Standing Commission on Liturgy and Music to develop liturgies supplemental to "Burial of a Child" (Enriching Our Worship 2), that respond to the pastoral needs of women and men who have experienced miscarriage, abortion, or other trauma in the childbearing or childbirth process, for presentation to and consideration by the 75th General Convention.

Prayer Book, Liturgy and Church Music
The House of Deputies Committee on Prayer Book, Liturgy and Church Music presented its Report #24 on HB Message #207 on Resolution C025 (Lifting Up of the Ministry of the Baptized in Ordinations) and moved concurrence.
The House concurred
(Communicated to the House of Bishops in HD Message #277)

Final Text of Resolution:
(C025)
Resolved, That the 74th General Convention direct the Standing Commission on Liturgy and Music to collect, develop, and distribute supplemental materials in which the roles of the baptized in the discernment, selection, and presentation of priests, deacons, and bishops, be more fully reflected in the liturgical rites celebrating those occasions, and to present these materials to the 75th General Convention.

The House of Deputies Committee on Prayer Book, Liturgy and Church Music presented its Report #25 on HB Message #208 on Resolution A106 (Liturgical Development and Episcopal Authority) and moved concurrence.

The House concurred
(Communicated to the House of Bishops in HD Message #278)

Final Text of Resolution:
(A106)
Resolved, That as this Church expresses its theology best in the context of worship, it is important that our liturgies reflect the varied roles and diverse cultures of the baptized; and be it further
Resolved, That the Standing Commission on Liturgy and Music, in consultation with the Standing Commission on Ministry Development and other concerned committees and groups, invite the bishops and larger church into conversation about our life in Christ as expressed in the rites of this Church, the possibility for local liturgical initiatives in this expression, and the role of the bishop in such undertakings; and be it further
Resolved, That the Standing Commission on Liturgy and Music develop and implement a framework for conversations within the Church regarding the theological, pastoral, canonical, and liturgical issues involved in the creation of new rites; and be it further
Resolved, That the Standing Commission on Liturgy and Music, in consultation with the Standing Commission on Constitution and Canons, examine canons and rubrics that govern the development and use of liturgical materials, and propose amendments authorizing appropriate local and regional liturgical initiatives; and be it further
Resolved, That the Office for Liturgy and Music be directed to establish a website for collecting, cataloguing, editing, and offering locally developed liturgies authorized by the ecclesiastical authority, explanatory materials, strategies, and processes; and be it further
Resolved, That the General Convention request the Joint Standing Committee on Program, Budget and Finance to consider a budget allocation of $15,000 for the implementation of this resolution.

Ministry
The House of Deputies Committee on Ministry presented its Report #10 on HB Message #178 on Resolution A110 (Complete Title III Revisions) and moved concurrence.

The House concurred
(Communicated to the House of Bishops in HD Message #279)

Final Text of Resolution:
(A110)
Resolved, That the Standing Commission on Ministry Development complete its revisions of the present Title III Canons 10, 11, 12, and 22–32, and report to the 75th General Convention.

The House of Deputies Committee on Ministry presented its Report #11 on HB Message #172 on Resolution B018 (Families of Clergy United in Support—FOCUS) and moved concurrence.

The House concurred
(Communicated to the House of Bishops in HD Message #280)

Final Text of Resolution:
(B018)
Resolved, That the 74th General Convention recognize that healthy families of clergy promote the well-being of clergy and congregations, and thus deserve spiritual and institutional support; and be it further
Resolved, That the 74th General Convention commend and encourage the effort of Families of Clergy United in Support (FOCUS) in their work of advocacy and education for awareness of clergy family needs, in efforts to promote the following:
1. Provide a chaplain in each diocese for families of clergy.
2. Provide education for each search committee regarding the special needs and concerns of families of clergy in transition, and about the expectations placed on family by congregations.
3. Provide support by seminaries for spouses, partners, and children of postulants and candidates in the process of ordination; and be it further

Resolved, That the Office of Ministry Development provide oversight and coordination with FOCUS and other programs that support the well-being of clergy and clergy families, and assist in seeking funding for such programs, including for Families of Clergy United in Support.

The House of Deputies Committee on Ministry presented its Report #12 on HB Message #127 on Resolution B020 (Family Survivors of Murder Victims and the Impact of Executions on Healing and Pastoral Care) and moved concurrence.

The House concurred
(Communicated to the House of Bishops in HD Message #281)

Final Text of Resolution:
(B020)
Resolved, That the 74th General Convention call for and support an interdenominational and interdisciplinary study entitled "Surviving Loved Ones of Murder Victims: The Impact of Executions on Healing and Pastoral Care," to be conducted through the International Center for Healing and

Law by Mark Umbreit, Ph.D., a professor at the University of Minnesota School of Social Work, and a continuing team of colleagues, coordinated through the Office of Peace and Justice of The Episcopal Church; and be it further
Resolved, That the General Convention request the Joint Standing Committee on Program, Budget and Finance to consider a budget allocation of $50,000 for implementation of the resolution.

The House of Deputies Committee on Ministry presented its Report #13 on HB Message #171 on Resolution B017 (Fresh Start) and moved concurrence.
The House concurred
(Communicated to the House of Bishops in HD Message #282)

Final Text of Resolution:
(B017)
Resolved, That the 74th General Convention commend the use of Fresh Start, a resource for congregations and clergy in transition, as a program of The Episcopal Church; and be it further
Resolved, That the General Convention affirm the collaborative partnership of the Office for Ministry Development and Church Deployment Office of The Episcopal Church, The Episcopal Church Foundation, the dioceses, and the National Fresh Start Committee, in the development and on-going support of Fresh Start; and be it further
Resolved, That Fresh Start adapt this material in order to provide for its use in culturally diverse settings; and be it further
Resolved, That the Fresh Start partners report back to the 75th General Convention regarding the program's impact upon clergy, congregations, and dioceses.

The House of Deputies Committee on Ministry presented its Report #14 on HB Message #170 on Resolution A067 (Fund for Theological Education) and moved concurrence.
The House concurred
(Communicated to the House of Bishops in HD Message #283)

Final Text of Resolution:
(A067)
Resolved, That the 74th General Convention affirm the participation of The Episcopal Church as a full partner in the Fund for Theological Education's Pastoral Leadership Search Effort (PLSE Project) which will identify, cultivate, and recruit exceptional candidates under age 35 representing the multicultural diversity of society for ordination by developing materials, a database, and a website; this project being in conjunction with the Presbyterian Church (USA), the United Methodist Church, and the United Church of Christ; and that the Convention encourage broad-based Episcopal

Church funding support to provide $300,000 for three years as the Episcopal denomination's match for the Lilly Endowment's $2.3 million grant to the FTE for this project.

The House of Deputies Committee on Ministry presented its Report #15 on HB Message #67 on Resolution A063 (Ethnic Specific Discernment Committees) and moved concurrence.

The House concurred
(Communicated to the House of Bishops in HD Message #284)

Final Text of Resolution:
(A063)
Resolved, **That the 74th General Convention encourage bishops and commissions on ministry to identify, support, and retain individuals for ministry from communities within the diocese not well represented in the diocese's current leadership.**

The House of Deputies Committee on Ministry presented its Report #16 on HB Message #168 on Resolution A022 (Nathan Network Funding) and moved concurrence with referral to a Standing Commission.

Motion carried
Resolution referred to a Standing Commission
(Communicated to the House of Bishops in HD Message #317)

[Note: The final status of Resolution A022 is non-concurrence because the House of Bishops and House of Deputies did not move the same action for the legislation. *Ed.*]

The House of Deputies Committee on Ministry presented its Report #17 on HB Message #128 on Resolution D060 (Education about Ordained and Licensed Ministries) and moved concurrence.

The House concurred
(Communicated to the House of Bishops in HD Message #285)

Final Text of Resolution:
(D060)
Resolved, **That the Standing Commission on Ministry Development be directed to develop educational resources on the roles and responsibilities of the ordained and licensed members of the church;** and be it further
Resolved, **That these resources be made readily available to any community of faith, through multiple forms of media.**

Ministry

The House of Deputies Committee on Ministry presented its Report #18 on HB Message #229 on Resolution A060 (Contemporary Language Competency) and moved concurrence.

The House concurred
(Communicated to the House of Bishops in HD Message #286)

Final Text of Resolution:
(A060)
Resolved, That the 74th General Convention recommend that all dioceses strongly encourage those preparing for ordination to study a contemporary language other than their native language and to participate in an intentional cross-cultural program; and be it further
Resolved, **That the 74th General Convention direct the Standing Commission on Ministry Development to consider, in its continued revision of Title III, how to address the Church's need for multilingual and cross-cultural competency for many ordained and lay leaders in various mission contexts including possible canonical revisions regarding formation and continuing education, and report back to the 75th General Convention.**

Miscellaneous Resolutions

The House of Deputies Committee on Miscellaneous Resolutions presented its Report #16 on HB Message #187 on Resolution B009 (Request for Faith and Order Commission) and moved concurrence.

Deputy Seitz moved to terminate debate.

Motion carried
Debate terminated

A vote was taken on Resolution B009.

Motion defeated
Resolution rejected
(Communicated to the House of Bishops in HD Message #287)

Committees and Commissions

The House of Deputies Committee on Committees and Commissions presented its Report #4 on HB Message #191 on Resolution A124 (Standing Commission on Health and a Staff Position in Health Care) and moved concurrence.

The House concurred
(Communicated to the House of Bishops in HD Message #290)

Final Text of Resolution:
(A124)

Resolved, That the 74th General Convention reaffirm the commitment of The Episcopal Church in providing a Christian response to the health care needs of those within our nation, as expressed in the 1991 and 1994 Blue Book reports of the Standing Commission on Health and the 2000 Blue Book Report of the Standing Commission on National Concerns, and be it further

Resolved, That the 74th General Convention reestablish a Standing Commission on Health and that it direct Executive Council to appoint a person to the staff at The Episcopal Church Center with background in and knowledge about health care policy to assist this commission, and that their joint duties include:

- Articulating and communicating positions adopted by The Episcopal Church on health care policy to Episcopalians, the public, and public policy makers;
- Advocating, in cooperation with the Office of Government Relations, for a health care system in which all may be guaranteed decent and appropriate primary health care during their lives and as they approach death;
- Bringing together those within The Episcopal Church who develop, provide, and/or teach health care and health care policy to continue to develop a Christian approach to pressing issues that affect the health care system of this nation;
- Understanding and keeping abreast of the rapidly changing health care market and developments in biomedical research that affect health policy;
- Collecting and developing resources and teaching materials related to access to health care for the use of dioceses, congregations, and individuals;
- Advocating health ministry in and through local Episcopal congregations; and be it further

Resolved, That the 74th General Convention direct the Executive Council to report to the 75th General Convention about this appointment; and be it further

Resolved, That the General Convention request the Joint Standing Committee on Program, Budget and Finance to consider a budget allocation of $200,000 for implementation of this resolution; and be it further

Resolved, That Canon I.1.2(n) be amended to add a subsection (6), appropriately renumbering the renaming subsections thereafter, reading as follows:

(6) A Standing Commission on Health consisting of 11 members (3 Bishops, 3 Priests and/or Deacons, and 5 Lay Persons). It shall be the duty of the Commission to:

> *(a)   Articulate and communicate positions adopted by The Episcopal Church on health care policy to Episcopalians, the public, and*

	public policy makers;
(b)	Advocate, in cooperation with the Office of Government Relations, for a health care system in which all may be guaranteed decent and appropriate primary health care during their lives and as they approach death;
(c)	Bring together those within The Episcopal Church who develop, provide and/or teach health care and health policy to continue to develop a Christian approach to pressing issues that affect the health care system of this nation;
(d)	Understand and keep abreast of the rapidly changing health care market and developments in biomedical research that affect health policy;
(e)	Collect and develop resources and teaching materials related to access to health care for the use of dioceses, congregations, and individuals;
(f)	Advocate health ministry in and through local Episcopal congregations; and
(g)	Discharge such other duties as shall be assigned by the General Convention.

Nominations and Elections

The House of Deputies Committee on Nominations and Elections presented its Report #2 on HB #117 on the election of Trustees of the General Theological Seminary by the House of Bishops and moved concurrence.

Final Text of Resolution:

Resolved, the House of Deputies confirming, That the following two bishops have been elected as Trustees of the General Theological Seminary for three-year terms:
    The Rt. Rev. Neil J. Alexander, Atlanta
    The Rt. Rev. Michael Bruce Curry, North Carolina

The House concurred
(Communicated to the House of Bishops in HD Message #288)

The House of Deputies Committee on Nominations and Elections presented its Report #3 on HB Message #96 on the election to Executive Council by the House of Bishops and moved concurrence.

Final Text of Resolution

Resolved, the House of Deputies confirming, That the following bishops have been elected to Executive Council:
    The Rt. Rev. Wilfrido Ramos-Orench, Bishop Suffragan of Connecticut
    The Rt. Rev. Stacy F. Sauls, Bishop of Lexington

The House concurred
(Communicated to the House of Bishops in HD Message #289)

JOURNAL   TENTH DAY

Dispatch of Business
The House of Deputies Committee on Dispatch of Business moved to suspend the Rules of Order so that all requests by Legislative Committees to be discharged from considering a resolution may be grouped together on an ad hoc consent calendar unless inclusion of a particular resolution was objected to; according to the Rules of Order.

Motion carried
Rules suspended

A vote was taken to discharge Committees from the following resolutions:

The House of Deputies Committee on Miscellaneous Resolutions presented its Report #12 on Resolution C016 (Integrated Pest Management) and moved that the Committee be discharged.

Motion carried
Committee discharged
(Communicated to the House of Bishops in HD Message #300)

The House of Deputies Committee on National and International Concerns presented its Report #25 on Resolution C007 (Ending the Cylce of Violence) and moved that the Committee be discharged.

Motion carried
Committee discharged
(Communicated to the House of Bishops in HD Message #303)

The House of Deputies Committee on National and International Concerns presented its Report #23 on Resolution C002 (Violence in the Name of Religion) and moved that the Committee be discharged.

Motion carried
Committee discharged
(Communicated to the House of Bishops in HD Message #304)

The House of Deputies Committee on Committees and Commissions presented its Report #3 on Resolution B025 (Criminal Justice Committee) and moved that the Committee be discharged.

Motion carried
Committee discharged
(Communicated to the House of Bishops in HD Message #314)

The House of Deputies Committee on National and International Concerns presented its Report #27 on Resolution C049 (Reversing the Trend in Declining US Foreign Aid to Developing Nations) and moved that the Committee be

discharged.
Motion carried
Committee discharged
(Communicated to the House of Bishops in HD Message #313)

The House of Deputies Committee on Canons presented its Report #12 on Resolution D064 (Amend Canon III.2.3(a)) and moved that the Committee be discharged.
Motion carried
Committee discharged
(Communicated to the House of Bishops in HD Message #305)

The House of Deputies Committee on National and International Concerns presented its Report #34 on Resolution D076 (Opposition to USA Patriot Act) and moved that the Committee be discharged.
Motion carried
Committee discharged
(Communicated to the House of Bishops in HD Message #302)

The House of Deputies Committee on National and International Concerns presented its Report #35 on Resolution C050 (International Family Planning) and moved that the Committee be discharged.
Motion carried
Committee discharged
(Communicated to the House of Bishops in HD Message #316)

The House of Deputies Committee on National and International Concerns presented its Report #39 on Resolution B016 (Human Rights in Afghanistan and Iraq) and moved that the Committee be discharged.
Motion carried
Committee discharged
(Communicated to the House of Bishops in HD Message #306)

The House of Deputies Committee on National and International Concerns presented its Report #43 on Resolution B019 (Crisis on Korean Penninsula) and moved that the Committee be discharged.
Motion carried
Committee discharged
(Communicated to the House of Bishops in HD Message #307)

The House of Deputies Committee on Social and Urban Affairs presented its Report #30 on Resolution C038 (Against Stigmatization and Spiritual Abuse of the Mentally Ill and Persons with Neurological Disorders) and moved that the Committee be discharged.

**Motion carried
Committee discharged**
(Communicated to the House of Bishops in HD Message #308)

The House of Deputies Committee on Social and Urban Affairs presented its Report #33 on Resolution D037 (Support for Pregnant Women) and moved that the Committee be discharged.

**Motion carried
Committee discharged**
(Communicated to the House of Bishops in HD Message #309)

The House of Deputies Committee on National and International Concerns presented its Report #45 on Resolution D065 (Funding for Global Engagement) and moved that the Committee be discharged.

**Motion carried
Committee discharged**
(Communicated to the House of Bishops in HD Message #310)

The House of Deputies Committee on National and International Concerns presented its Report #46 on Resolution D038 (Resolution on Liberia) and moved that the Committee be discharged.

**Motion carried
Committee discharged**
(Communicated to the House of Bishops in HD Message #311)

The House of Deputies Committee on Evangelism presented its Report #12 on Resolution A031 (A Multicultural, Multiracial Church) and moved that the Committee be discharged.

**Motion carried
Committee discharged**
(Communicated to the House of Bishops in HD Message #312)

Necrology
The Secretary read the Necrology of the House (see Appendix D–Day 10 for House of Deputies Necrology).

Privilege and Courtesy

The House of Deputies Committee on Privilege and Courtesy presented its Report #17 on Resolution D093 (Honoring Sonia Francis) and moved adoption.

Original Text of Resolution:

(D093)

Whereas, Sonia Francis was born in Honduras, emigrated to the United States, and joined the U.S. Army; and

Whereas, she then went to New York and joined the staff of the Episcopal Church Center as support staff for communications; and

Whereas, she became the Director of Communications and in 1997 was promoted to senior executive status as Deputy to the Presiding Bishop for Program; and

Whereas, she enjoyed singing duets with the President of the House of Deputies on the way to a conference; and

Whereas, she served the Church faithfully and effectively for 37 years, enjoying the respect and friendship of the Episcopal Church Center staff; and

Whereas, when she retired in March 2003 she had been the longest-serving member of the Episcopal Church Center staff; therefore be it

Resolved, the House of Bishops concurring, That the 74th General Convention of The Episcopal Church recognize with great appreciation the faithful and dedicated service of Sonia Francis and wish her a long and happy retirement.

Motion carried
Resolution adopted
(Communicated to the House of Bishops in HD Message #289)

The House of Deputies Committee on Privilege and Courtesy presented its Report #18 on Resolution D094 (Appreciation of Platform Party) and moved adoption.

Final Text of Resolution:

(D094)

Whereas, **The Rev. Rosemari Sullivan, in this her second General Convention, has performed her duties as Secretary to the House of Deputies with grace and clarity;** and

Whereas, **J. P. Causey, Jr. has been an efficient and flexible Chair of Dispatch;** and

Whereas, **The Rev. Gregory Straub has led us ably and clearly through a maze of voting procedures;** and

Whereas, **Our recording secretary and all other assistant secretaries have functioned quietly and effectively;** and

Whereas, **Pauline Getz, Esq. in her first convention as Parliamentarian, has persevered in holding the members of this House to its rules of order;** and

Whereas, **Vincent Currie, Jr. has shown us how an experienced Vice-President can help our business move right along;** and now therefore let it be

Resolved, **That the House of Deputies express its gratitude and appreciation to all those who have so ably served on the Platform with the Very Rev. George**

L. W. Werner, President of the House of Deputies, during the 74th General Convention.

Motion carried
Resolution adopted
(Communicated to the House of Bishops in HD Message #292)

The House of Deputies Committee on Privilege and Courtesy presented its Report #19 on Resolution D095 (Thanks for Worship) and moved adoption.

Final Text of Resolution:
(D095)
Resolved, That the 74th General Convention of the Episcopal Church give high praise and thanks to the numerous God-sent individuals who contributed their many and varied gifts to making our worship area spirit-filled; for the creative artists, musicians, ushers, presiders, preachers, deacons, readers and Communion ministers; for the Altar Guild and those involved in creating a truly godly peaceful setting for worship and prayer; and be it further
Resolved, That we express our grateful appreciation to the President of the House George Werner, Presiding Bishop Frank T. Griswold, Bishops Katharine Jefferts Schori, Catherine Roskam, and James Jelinek for speaking in languages other than their native tongue at General Convention Eucharists, together with those who read in languages other than English.

Motion carried
Resolution adopted
(Communicated to the House of Bishops in HD Message #293)

The House of Deputies Committee on Privilege and Courtesy presented its Report #20 on Resolution D096 (Thanks for Ministry with Young People Cluster Programs) and moved adoption.

Final Text of Resolution:
(D096)
Whereas, the 74th General Convention has adopted as its top priority ministries with children, youth, and young adults; and
Whereas, the Ministries with Young People Cluster trained and supported those young people who constitute the ongoing Official Youth Presence at this General Convention; and
Whereas, the Diocese of Minnesota, in partnership with the Office of Children's Ministries and Christian Education, has provided creative, engaging, and inclusive activities in special programs for children and youth at this Convention; and
Whereas, in offering these programs for the first time in any General Convention, the persons involved have intentionally lived out the 72nd and

73rd General Conventions' resolutions on the Children's Charter and demonstrated the 74th General Convention's commitment to the young people of this Church; now therefore be it
Resolved, That the 74th General Convention of The Episcopal Church give thanks to Almighty God for the presence and participation of children, youth, and young adults in the work and worship of this convention; and be it further
Resolved, That the General Convention commend the energy, effort, and vision of the planners, trainers, and leaders, and affirm the innovative partnership of diocesan, provincial, and National Church as a model for future General Conventions.

Motion carried
Resolution adopted
(Communicated to the House of Bishops in HD Message #294)

The House of Deputies Committee on Privilege and Courtesy presented its Report #21 on Resolution D097 (Thanks to Convention Volunteers) and moved adoption.

Final Text of Resolution:
(D097)
Resolved, That the House of Deputies of the 74th General Convention of The Episcopal Church express its thanks and appreciation to the countless volunteers from many dioceses throughout the Church who have offered their friendly assistance and gracious hospitality to all participants in this convention.

Motion carried
Resolution adopted
(Communicated to the House of Bishops in HD Message #295)

The House of Deputies Committee on Privilege and Courtesy presented its Report #22 on Resolution D098 (Behind the Scenes) and moved adoption.

Final Text of Resolution:
(D098)
Whereas, Those who work "behind the scenes" often toil for us without recognition; and
Whereas, Without the practiced hand of Lori Ionnitiu, General Convention Manager, at the tiller we might never have arrived in Minneapolis; and
Whereas, Communication to deputies in advance of the Convention has never been better; now, therefore be it

Resolved, That the House of Deputies of the 74th General Convention of the Episcopal Church express gratitude to the entire General Convention staff.

Motion carried
Resolution adopted
(Communicated to the House of Bishops in HD Message #296)

The House of Deputies Committee on Privilege and Courtesy presented its Report #15 on Resolution D091 (Thanks to Chaplain Brian Prior) and moved adoption with amendment.

Proposed Amendment:
Add the phrase "for the photography of the Rev. Cynthia Black."

Original Text of Resolution:
(D091)
Resolved, That the House of Deputies of the 74th General Convention give hearty thanks and praise to the Reverend Brian Prior for his comforting Godly encouragement, his very effective use of competent musicians, Aña Hernandez and Fran McKendree, his involvement of young people in Noonday Prayer, the use of creative artistic videos, and for his spiritual leadership of prayer throughout this "Camp Convention."

Final Text of Resolution:
(D091)
Resolved, **That the House of Deputies of the 74th General Convention give hearty thanks and praise to the Reverend Brian Prior for his comforting Godly encouragement, his very effective use of competent musicians, Aña Hernandez and Fran McKendree, his involvement of young people in Noonday Prayer, the use of creative artistic videos, for the photography of the Rev. Cynthia Black, and for his spiritual leadership of prayer throughout this "Camp Convention."**

Motion carried
Resolution adopted with amendment
(Communicated to the House of Bishops in HD Message #297)

The House of Deputies Committee on Privilege and Courtesy presented its Report #5 on Resolution D079 (Courtesy Resolution–Church Pension Fund Board of Trustees) and moved adoption.

Final Text of Resolution:
(D079)
Resolved, That the 74th Convention of The Episcopal Church wishes to give thanks to God and to express our deep appreciation for the ministry of The Church Pension Fund's Board of Trustees.

Motion carried
Resolution adopted
(Communicated to the House of Bishops in HD Message #298)

The House of Deputies Committee on Privilege and Courtesy presented its Report #7 on Resolution D083 (Expression of Gratitude to the Very Rev. George L. Werner) and moved adoption.

Final Text of Resolution:
(D083)
Whereas, The Very Reverend George L. Werner, President of the House of Deputies, has led us with wisdom, patience, courtesy, humility, and occasional glimpses of his marvelous sense of humor; and
Whereas, he has conducted himself with grace under pressure even though technologically challenged by the automated voting system; and
Whereas, he has distinguished himself in the service of the Church as a faithful member of Planning and Arrangements, Executive Council, Church Pension Fund, Chair of the Standing Committee on Health, and Chair of the Committee on the Status of the Church; now therefore be it;
Resolved, That the House of Deputies of the 74th General Convention of the Episcopal Church express its deep gratitude to the the Very Reverend George L. Werner for his exceptional service, and assure him of our prayerful support as he continues to fulfill his duties as President of the House.

Motion carried
Resolution adopted
(Communicated to the House of Bishops in HD Message #318)

The House of Deputies Committee on Privilege and Courtesy presented its Report #4 on Resolution D078 (Courtesy Resolution–David Hegg) and moved adoption.

Final Text of Resolution:
(D078)
Resolved, That the 74th Convention of The Episcopal Church wishes to give thanks to God and to express our deep appreciation for the ministry and life of the Rev. David Hegg, who faithfully served as Senior Vice-President (Pastoral Care and Education) of the Church Pension Fund from 1996–2002; and be it further

Resolved, That we give thanks for his life-long partner in this ministry, Judith Hegg, and extend to her our best wishes for her continued ministry to the wider church; and be it further
Resolved, That a copy of this resolution be forwarded to David's spouse, Judith, and to their family.

Motion carried
Resolution adopted

(Communicated to the House of Bishops in HD Message #299)

Personal Privilege
Deputy Crump of West Tennessee gave thanks for being able to serve at sixteen General Conventions and thanked the deputies for their courtesy to him.

Privilege and Courtesy
The House of Deputies Committee on Privilege and Courtesy presented its Report #6 on Resolution D082 (Gratitude to Minneapolis) and moved adoption.

Final Text of Resolution:
(D082)
Whereas, the city of Minneapolis has welcomed the 74th General Convention with warm hospitality; helpful people; sunny skies; and gentle rain; clean, well-planned streets, and convenient skyways; and a close proximity to Target; and
Whereas, the Honorable R.T. Rybak, mayor of Minneapolis, a life-long Episcopalian and mission-minded civic leader, has brought the House of Deputies his personal and friendly greetings; now, therefore, be it
Resolved, That the House of Deputies of the 74th General Convention express its gratitude to Mayor Rybak and to the good people of Minneapolis.

Motion carried
Resolution adopted

(Communicated to the House of Bishops in HD Message #301)

Dispatch of Business
The House of Deputies Committee on Dispatch of Business announced the House had completed its business and requested that it be discharged.

Prayers
The President called on the Secretary for prayers.

Adjournment
The President adjourned the House *sine die* at 5:12 p.m.

Appendix D
Day 10

House of Deputies Necrology

Diocese	Name
Albany	The Rev. Richard H. Frye
	Charles B. Kinly
Arkansas	The Rev. DeWayne Saba
Central Gulf Coast	The Rev. Benjamin A. Meginniss
Central New York	Dorothy Brittain
	The Rev. Stanley Gasek
	The Hon. Hugh R. Jones
	Dorothy Rose
Connecticut	The Very Rev. Robert Beecher
Delaware	The Rev. John C. Scobell
East Tennessee	James S. Morris
	The Rt. Rev. Robert Tharp
Idaho	Archie Biladeau
Michigan	John K. Cannon
Navajoland	The Rev. Margaret Hardy
Newark	Linda Strohmeier
New York	Gwendolyn Carter
Oklahoma	Duncan Brown
	Donald Gatchell
San Joaquin	Richard Foster
Springfield	David Heneghen
	Richard Milnes
South Dakota	Mary Loftesness
	Robert Maule
Southwestern Virginia	Purnell Eggleston
Western Kansas	T. David Russell
Wyoming	Dorothy Johnson

PART III

HOUSE OF BISHOPS INTERIM MEETINGS

MEETING OF THE HOUSE OF BISHOPS 2001

SPECIAL MEETING

Held at
Kanuga Conference Center

Hendersonville, North Carolina
March 9–14, 2001

SPECIAL MEETING OF THE HOUSE OF BISHOPS
Kanuga Conference Center
Hendersonville, North Carolina
March 9–14, 2001

FIRST DAY

Wednesday
March 14, 2001
Second Week of Lent

Call to Order
The House met in Special Session at the Kanuga Conference Center, Hendersonville, North Carolina on March 14, 2001.

The Presiding Bishop
The Presiding Bishop called the House to order in the Fireplace Lounge. Bishop Williams, Suffragan of Ohio, led the prayers.

Election of the Secretary of the House of Bishops
Bishop Harris, Suffragan of Massachusetts, placed in nomination Bishop Chang of Hawaii for Secretary of the House of Bishops.
It was moved, seconded, and carried that nominations be closed and that Bishop Chang be elected Secretary of the House of Bishops.

Motion carried

Appointment of Assistant Secretary
Bishop Chang of Hawaii announced the appointment of Bishop Henderson of Upper South Carolina and Bishop Waynick of Indianapolis as Assistants Secretaries of the House. The Presiding Bishop approved the appointments.

The Roll Call
It was moved, seconded, and carried to accept the registration as the record of attendance and quorum. Bishop Putnam, retired of Navajoland and former Suffragan of Oklahoma, was recognized as the senior bishop (#595) in attendance.

The Reading of the Minutes
It was moved, seconded, and carried that the reading of the minutes be dispensed.

Motion carried

Election of the Vice-Chair of the House of Bishops
Bishop Harris, Suffragan of Massachusetts, placed in nomination Bishop Williams, Suffragan of Ohio, for Vice-Chair of the House of Bishops.
It was moved, seconded, and carried that nominations be closed and that Bishop Williams be elected Vice-Chair of the House of Bishops.
Motion carried

Communications from the Presiding Bishop
The Presiding Bishop read a letter of greeting from the Most Rev. Michael Peers, Primate of Canada.

Report of the Committee on Dispatch of Business
Bishop Price, Suffragan of Southern Ohio, presented the orders for business.

Committee on Resignation of Bishops
Bishop Knudson of Maine reported that letters of resignation because of age were received from the following:
Bishop Grein of New York, effective July 1, 2001
Bishop Haines of Washington, effective December 31, 2001
Bishop Rockwell of Missouri, effective September 1, 2001
It was moved, second, and carried that the House approve the resignations of Bishops Grein, Haines, and Rockwell.
Motion carried
It was moved, second, and carried that Bishops Grein, Haines, and Rockwell, be granted seat, voice and vote in the House pursuant to Article I.2 of the Constitution.
Motion carried
Bishop Knudson of Maine reported on the resignation of Bishop Jones of Montana. In light of the case status, the Presiding Bishop reported only on the status of Bishop and Mrs. Jones.

Committee on Theology
Bishop Parsley of Alabama presented a report on the status of the work of the Committee on Theology on the charter of the Committee and the Mind of the House resolution on Human Sexuality from the meeting of the House at the 2000 General Convention.

Committee on Pastoral Development
Bishop Matthews of the Office for Pastoral Development reported on Episcopal Formation News, the College for Bishops, the Conference on Pastoral Standards, the Bishops Directory and a mailing of the Duke Divinity School study on ordination (Title III.21).
Bishop Warner of Olympia commended Bishop Matthews on his ministry and thanked the House for their support of the Office for Pastoral Development.

Workplace Standards
Bishop Roskam, Suffragan of New York, called the attention of the House to General Convention Resolution DO15.

Nominating Committee for Bishop Suffragan in Europe
Canon Gerdau, Canon to the Presiding Bishop and Primate, reported the status of the nominations for Bishop Suffragan in Europe.

Arctic Drilling
Bishop MacDonald of Alaska presented a status report on the Arctic National Wildlife Refuge and Congressional legislation to permit drilling for oil. The support of the House continues to be important.

Pastoral Letter Committee
Bishop Parsley of Alabama provided background before reading the proposed Pastoral Letter of the House.
It was moved, seconded, and carried that the Pastoral Letter be received by the House as read by Bishop Parsley of Alabama. Discussion of the Letter followed.
It was moved, seconded and carried that the Pastoral Letter be adopted as amended by the House of Bishops. Bishop Alard, Suffragan of Texas, requested that the Pastoral Letter be translated into Spanish.

Adjourn
It was moved, seconded, and carried that the meeting be adjourned.

Motion carried

Submitted by Richard S. O. Chang, Secretary
Certified by John L. Rabb, Chair, Committee on Certification of Minutes

Appendix A
Hendersonville, North Carolina

Meeting Agenda

Practical Approaches and Spiritual Disciplines for Mission Leadership

Friday, March 9, 2001
4:00 p.m.	*Invitation to the Work*
	(Most Rev. Frank T. Griswold)
5:15	Opening Eucharist
6:30	Supper and Small Group Connection

Saturday, March 10, 2001
7:30 a.m.	Morning Prayer
8:00	Breakfast
9:00	*Mission and the Adaptive Challenge*
	(Ronald Heifetz)
11:15	Break
11:45	Eucharist
12:45 p.m.	Lunch and Break
3:00	*Mission and the Adaptive Challenge 2*
	(Ronald Heifetz)
5:15	Break
5:45	Evening Prayer
6:15	Supper
8:00	Hospitality

Sunday, March 11, 2001
8:00 a.m.	Continental Breakfast
9:30	Holy Eucharist
10:30	Brunch and Free Afternoon
5:45 p.m.	Evening Prayer
6:15	Supper
7:15	Mini-Versity
9:30	Hospitality

Monday, March 12, 2001
7:30 a.m.	Morning Prayer
8:00	Breakfast
9:00	*Mission: Restoration of Relationships and Application of Learnings* (Most Rev. Frank T. Griswold)
11:15	Break
11:45	Eucharist
12:45 p.m.	Lunch and Break
3:00	Continued Group application, presentation of Group work (Most Rev. Frank T. Griswold)
5:15	Break
5:45	Evening Prayer
6:15	Supper
7:15	Optional Round 2 Mini-Versity
8:00	Hospitality opens

Tuesday, March 13, 2001
7:30 a.m.	Morning Prayer
8:00	Breakfast
9:00	*Practical Response to Adaptive Challenges* (Ronald Heifetz Most Rev. Frank T. Griswold)
11:15	Break
11:45	Eucharist
12:45 p.m.	Lunch and Break
3:00	*The Spiritual and Practical Disciplines of Leadership* (Roland Heifetz Most Rev. Frank T. Griswold)
5:15	Break
5:45	Evening Prayer
6:15	Banquet and Celebration

Wednesday, March 14, 2001
7:30 a.m.	Morning Prayer
8:30	*Mission: Beyond Ourselves* (Most Rev. Frank T. Griswold)
10:00	Break
10:30	Eucharist
11:30	Lunch and Departure Box lunches will be available for travel.

Appendix B
Hendersonville, North Carolina

Bishops Present at the Interim Meeting of March 2001

Alard, Leopoldo–Texas
Anderson, Robert–Los Angeles
Bainbridge, Harry B.–Idaho
Bane, David C.–Southern Virginia
Bartlett, Allen L.–Washington (Assisting Bishop)
Beckwich, Peter–Springfield
Bena, David J.–Albany
Bennison, Charles E.–Pennsylvania
Borsch, Frederick, H.–Los Angeles
Bowman, David C.–Central New York (Assisting Bishop)
Brown, James B.–Texas
Bruno, Jon–Los Angeles (Coadjutor)
Caldwell, Bruce–Wyoming
Chang, Richard–Hawaii
Charleston, Steven–Episcopal Divinity School
Chien, John–Taiwan
Coleridge, Clarence N.–Pennsylvania (Assisting Bishop)
Croneberger, John P.–Newark
Creighton, Michael–Central Pennsylvania
Curry, James E.–Connecticut
Curry, Michael B.–North Carolina
Daniel, Clifton–East Carolina
Daniels, Theodore–Virgin Islands
Dixon, Jane–Washington
Donovan, Herbert A.–Arkansas (Retired)
Duncan, Robert Wm.–Pittsburgh
Duracin, Jean Zaché–Haiti
Duvall, Charles–Central Gulf Coast
Ely, Thomas C.–Vermont
Epting, C. Christopher–Iowa
Folts, James E.–West Texas
Frade, Leo–Southeast Florida
Garrison, J. Michael–Western New York
Gibbs, Jr., Wendell N.–Michigan
Gloster, J. Gary–North Carolina
Gray, III, Duncan–Mississippi
Gray, Francis–Virginia (Assisting Bishop)
Gregg, William O.–Eastern Oregon

Grew, Clark–Ohio
Griswold, Frank–Presiding Bishop
Gulick, Edwin–Kentucky
Hargrove, Robert–Western Louisiana
Harris, Barbara–Massachusetts
Harris, Rogers S.–Southwest Florida (Retired)
Hart, Don – Southern Virginia (Assisting Bishop)
Haynsworth, George E.–South Carolina
Henderson, Dorsey–Upper South Carolina
Herlong, Bertram–Tennessee
Herzog, Daniel W.–Albany
Hibbs, Robert B.–West Texas
Holguín, Julio C.–Dominican Republic
Howe, Barry R.–West Missouri
Howe, John–Central Florida
Hughes, Gethin–San Diego
Iker, Jack–Fort Worth
Irish, Carolyn T.–Utah
Jacobus, Russell E.–Fond du Lac
Jecko, Stephen–Florida
Jefferts Schori, Katharine–Nevada
Jelinek, James L.–Minnesota
Jenkins, Charles E.–Louisiana
Johnson, Robert–Western North Carolina
Jones, David C.–Virginia
Joslin, David–New Jersey
Kelsey, James A.–Northern Michigan
Keyser, Charles–Armed Forces (Retired)
Knudsen, Chilton–Maine
Krotz, James A.–Nebraska
Ladehoff, Robert–Oregon
Lamb, Jerry A.–Northern California
Lee, Edward L.–Western Michigan
Leidel, Edwin–Eastern Michigan
Lipscomb, John B.–Southwest Florida
Little II, Edward S.–Northern Indiana
Louttit, Henry I.–Georgia
MacDonald, Mark L.–Alaska
MacPherson, D. Bruce–Dallas
Marble, Alfred C.–Mississippi

Matthews, F. Clayton–Office of Pastoral Development
Maze, Larry E.–Arkansas
McKelvey, Jack–Rochester
Michel, Rodney–Long Island
Moody, Robert–Oklahoma
Ohl Jr., Charles Wallis–Northwest Texas
Ottley, James H.–Honduras (Assisting Bishop)
Packard, George E.–Office of the Bishop for the Armed Services
Parsley, Henry N.–Alabama
Payne, Claude–Texas
Persell, William D.–Chicago
Powell, Neff –Southwestern Virginia
Price, Kenneth–Southern Ohio
Putnam, Frederick W.–Minnesota (Assisting Bishop)
Rabb, John–Maryland
Ramos–Orench, Wilfrido–Connecticut
Reed, David–Kentucky (Retired)
Rockwell, Hays–Missouri
Roskam, Catherine S.–New York
Rowley, Robert D.–Northwestern Pennsylvania
Rowthorn, Jeffery W.–Convocation of American Churches in Europe
Said, John–Southeast Florida
Salmon, Edward–South Carolina
Sauls, Stacy F.–Lexington
Scantlebury, Victor–Chicago (Assisting Bishop)
Schofield, John–David M.–San Joaquin
Scruton, Gordon P.–Western Massachusetts
Shahan, Robert R.–Arizona
Shaw, M. Thomas–Massachusetts
Shimpfky, Richard L.–El Camino Real
Sims, Bennett–Atlanta (Retired)
Sisk, Mark–New York (Coadjutor)
Skilton, William–South Carolina
Smalley, William E.–Kansas
Smith, Andrew D.–Connecticut
Soto, Onell–Alabama (Assisting Bishop)
Swenson, Daniel L.–Vermont (Retired)
Swing, William E.–California
Talton, Chester L.–Los Angeles
Taylor, Don–New York (Assisting Bishop)
Tennis, Cabell–Delaware (Retired)
Tharp, Robert G.–Atlanta (Assisting Bishop)
Theuner, Douglas–New Hampshire
Thompson, Herbert–Southern Ohio
Townsend, Martin G.–Easton
Vaché, Charles–West Virginia (Assisting Bishop)
Vest, Frank H.–Southern Virginia (Retired)
vonRosenberg, Charles–East Tennessee
Waggoner, James E.–Spokane
Walker, Orris G.–Long Island
Warner, Vincent W.–Olympia
Waynick, Catherine–Indianapolis
Whitmore, Keith B.–Eau Claire
Williams, Arthur–Ohio
Wimberly, Don A.–Texas (Assisting Bishop)
Winterrowd, William J.–Colorado
Wolf, Geralyn–Rhode Island
Wright, Wayne–Delaware

Honorary Members
Barahona, Martin–El Salvador

Collegial Members
Elder, Philip–Winward Islands (Retired)

Guests
Ayong, James–Papua New Guinea
Carey, George–Archbishop of Canterbury
Malango, Bernard A.–Northern Zambia

Appendix C
Hendersonville, North Carolina

Newly Consecrated Bishops

Bishops who have been consecrated since the meeting of the 73rd General Convention, held in Denver, July 16–25, 2000:

The Bishop of Eastern Oregon, September 23, 2000
William Otis Gregg (957)
Chief Consecrator:	Edmond Lee Browning, D.D., XXIV Presiding Bishop
Co-Consecrators:	Harry Brown Bainbridge
	Bishop of Idaho
	Rustin Ray Kimsey
	Bishop of Eastern Oregon, Resigned
	Robert Louis Ladehoff
	Bishop of Oregon
	Jerry Alban Lamb
	Bishop of Northern California

The Bishop of Lexington, September 30, 2000
Stacy Fred Sauls (958)
Chief Consecrator:	Robert Hodges Johnson
	Bishop of Western North Carolina
Co-Consecrators:	Don Adger Wimberly
	Bishop of Lexington, Resigned
	Edwin Funsten Gulick, Jr.
	Bishop of Kentucky
	Frank Kellogg Allan
	Bishop of Atlanta, Resigned
	Rogers Sanders Harris
	Bishop of Southwest Florida

The Bishop Suffragan of Connecticut, October 14, 2000
James Elliot Curry (959)
Chief Consecrator: Douglas Edwin Theuner
                     Bishop of New Hampshire
Co-Consecrators: Andrew Donnan Smith
                     Bishop of Connecticut
                     Clarence Nicholas Coleridge
                     Bishop of Connecticut, Resigned
                     Barbara Clementine Harris
                     Bishop Suffragan of Massachusetts
                     Chilton Abbie Richardson Knudsen
                     Bishop of Maine
                     Gordon Paul Scruton
                     Bishop of Western Massachusetts

The Bishop Suffragan of Connecticut, October 14, 2000
Wilfrido Ramos-Orench (960)
Chief Consecrator: Douglas Edwin Theuner
                     Bishop of New Hampshire
Co-Consecrators: Andrew Donnan Smith
                     Bishop of Connecticut
                     Clarence Nicholas Coleridge
                     Bishop of Connecticut, Resigned
                     José Antonio Ramos-Orench
                     Bishop of Costa Rica, Resigned
                     Francisco Reus-Froylan
                     Bishop of Puerto Rico, Resigned
                     Albert Irvine Swift
                     Bishop of Puerto Rico, Resigned

The Bishop of Spokane, October 21, 2000
James Edward Waggoner, Jr. (961)
Chief Consecrator: Jerry Alban Lamb
                     Bishop of Northern California
Co-Consecrators: Robert Poland Atkinson
                     Assistant Bishop of Virginia
                     Kenneth Lester Price, Jr.
                     Bishop Suffragan of Southern Ohio
                     Claude Charles Vaché
                     Bishop of Southern Virginia, Resigned
                     Leigh Allen Wallace, Jr.
                     Bishop of Spokane, Resigned
                     John Raymond Wyatt
                     Bishop of Spokane, Resigned

The Bishop Coadjutor of Taiwan, November 25, 2000
David Jung-Hsin Lai (962)
Chief Consecrator: Richard Sui On Chang
                        Bishop of Hawaii
Co-Consecrators: John Chih-Tsung Chien
                        Bishop of Taiwan
                        David Shoji Tani
                        Bishop of Okinawa
                        Michael C. Ingham
                        Bishop of New Westminster
                        Thomas Yee-po Soo
                        Bishop of Western Kowloon
                        John Chew
                        Bishop of Singapore

The Bishop of Nevada, February 24, 2001
Katharine Jefferts Schori (963)
Chief Consecrator: Jerry Alban Lamb
                        Bishop of Northern California
Co-Consecrators: Robert Louis Ladehoff
                        Bishop of Oregon
                        Carolyn Tanner Irish
                        Bishop of Utah

Resignations

Since the meeting of the General Convention, held in Denver, July 16–25, 2000, the Secretary has received notice of the intent of the following bishops to resign or retire:

July 1, 2001
The Rt. Rev. Richard F. Grein, Bishop of New York
Retirement
September 1, 2001
The Rt. Rev. Hays H. Rockwell, Bishop of Missouri
Retirement
December 31, 2001
The Rt. Rev. Ronald H. Haines, Bishop of Washington
Retirement

Necrology

Since the metting of the General Convention held in Denver, July 16–25, 2000, the following bishops have departed this life:

July 20, 2000
The Rt. Rev. James Duncan
Bishop of Southeasat Florida
August 17, 2000
The Rt. Rev. Robert H. Mize, Jr.
Assistant Bishop of San Joaquin
September 14, 2000
The Rt. Rev. Charles Gaskell
Bishop of Milwaukee
October 19, 2000
The Rt. Rev. Jackson Gilliam
Bishop of Montana
December 3, 2000
The Rt. Rev. George W. Barrett
Bishop of Rochester
December 7, 2000
The Rt. Rev. Charles G. Marmion, Jr.
Bishop of Kentucky

Appendix D
Hendersonville, North Carolina

Theological Calling
As Submitted by
The Committee on Theology of the House of Bishops

1. God's Plan of Salvation
   God has lovingly created the world and all this therein. Human beings are graciously created in the divine image, but we fail to live into the fullness of this gift and calling. In his life, death, and resurrection, Jesus Christ has restored us to unity with God and each other. Empowered by the Holy Spirit, we are called to grow into, revel in and herald God's grace for all creation.

2. The Great Tradition
   We believe that the Old and New Testaments are the revealed Word of God and contain all things necessary to salvation. We further believe that the Apostles' and Nicene Creeds are sufficient statements of the Christian faith. The Creeds and the Councils of the Church represent the Rule of Faith by which we interpret and live into the saving story of Scripture. These shape the inherited faith of the church universal in which we stand.

3. Baptism and Theology
   In baptism all Christians are incorporated into a disciplined life of faith found in worship and witness. Those who pray are theologians and theologians are those who pray. Theology is both derived from and informs our common life in prayer. As we pray so we believe, and as we believe so we pray.

4. The Teaching Charism
   As teachers, theologians aid the Church in its disciplined life of worship and witness through critical reflection and practice. This endeavor takes place in communion with those who have gone before and in conversation with those who are our contemporaries.

5. Theology in Community
   The task of theology is incarnate in our common life of word and sacrament that sends us into the world to participate in the mission of the Church: to restore all people to unity with God and each other in Christ (BCP p.855).

Appendix E
Hendersonville, North Carolina

Pastoral Letter to The Episcopal Church
The Fifth Sunday in Lent Sunday, April 1, 2001

The Bishops of the Episcopal Church meet twice each year for prayer, consultation, mutual support, and learning, for the good of the church and the world we are called to serve. We gathered for our spring retreat this year from March 9–14 in the ancient mountains of the Appalachian chain in Western North Carolina. Our meeting immediately followed the meeting of the Primates, the leaders of the 38 member churches of our Anglican Communion, presided over by the Archbishop of Canterbury. We were blessed by the presence of the Archbishop of Canterbury for two days, and by the participation of the Primates of Central Africa and Papua New Guinea. These brother Christians were a reminder of our participation in a 70-million-member worldwide Anglican family.

During these days we have been united through prayer to you, God's beloved people. With thankful hearts for the Spirit of Christ moving among us, we send you this pastoral letter, to be read in every congregation on Sunday, April 1.

Dearly Beloved in Christ:

Grace and peace be with you in these days of Lent as we journey with our Lord up to Jerusalem and through the cross into the joy of Easter and the new life of the resurrection.

Our retreat has made us freshly aware of the boundless love of God and the gift of our belovedness in Christ. We have become mindful of how God has been leading us into deeper communion as your bishops and into a renewed awareness of our call to mission. The words of the prophet Isaiah speak to us powerfully, "I am about to do a new thing, now it springs forth, do you not perceive it?"

We who are called as bishops to be a sign of unity, speak to you with minds and hearts being united and transformed by the love of God. Our unity does not mean we are in agreement about all of the difficult and complex questions before us. It means we have claimed our oneness in Christ.

We are heartened by the Primates' Pastoral Letter to the Anglican Communion and their conclusion that — though we live in enormously diverse settings, and hold a wide variety of perspectives — God means for us to remain united and to learn from one another in a spirit of unity and interdependence. The Primates have also called upon us to provide pastoral care for all in our Communion, as we grow in Christ's wisdom. We mean to respond faithfully to that call. We trust in the promise of God to lead us all the more deeply into the mind of Christ, whose dying and rising makes us free to live not for ourselves alone but for God.

Our Study together centered on leadership for the purpose of advancing the mission of the Church. This mission, as the Catechism of the Book of Common Prayer tells us, is "to restore all people to unity with God and each other in Christ." We live in a world urgently searching for such restoration: spiritually, socially, racially, and environmentally. As Christians we have been given a word to speak and a new life to live: God has "reconciled us to himself through Christ, and has given us the ministry of reconciliation" (II Corinthians 5:18). This is the Good News that we proclaim. This is the work God gives us to do.

Ronald Heifetz, the author of *Leadership Without Easy Answers*, was with us. He challenged us to help create an environment in our dioceses open to a variety of convictions so that faithful ministry and creative interaction can be sustained within a richness of diverse perspectives. The objective of such leadership is to build authentic community ready to be animated by the Spirit to go forward in mission.

We are under no illusions that leading in this way is simple. Each of us is keenly aware of our weakness and failure, such that repentance is the necessary preface to our leading. We are humbled by God's boundless mercy and promise. Our repentance renews us as we are encouraged by one another. As leaders we are convinced by the Gospel's deep assurance that every member of the Body of Christ is the beloved bearer of God's purposes in the world. We are grateful for the many gifts and capacities entrusted to our church. We are inspired by the faithful and sacrificial ministries of so many. We are sustained by your prayers.

As your servants we are determined to put our common call to serve the mission of Christ above all else. We pledge that we will give our best energies to the work of restoring all people to unity with God and one another, because we know that the reconciling power of God in Christ is ceaselessly at work to overcome all division. Every concern for truth finds its wellspring in God's love for the world. Every concern for justice finds its wellspring in God's love. Every concern for peace finds its wellspring there. We call upon you to grow in the unity of the Holy Spirit as we together claim the fullness of our calling to share in God's mission of reconciling love.

Forgetting what lies behind and straining forward to what lies ahead, let us press on toward the goal for the prize of the heavenly call of God in Christ Jesus (Philippians 3:13–14).

Your servants in Christ,

The Bishops of the Episcopal Church,
gathered for the Spring Meeting, March, 2001

MEETING OF THE HOUSE OF BISHOPS 2001

SPECIAL MEETING

Held at
The Radisson Hotel

Burlington, Vermont
September 20–26, 2001

SPECIAL MEETING OF THE HOUSE OF BISHOPS
Radisson Hotel
Burlington, Vermont
September 20–26, 2001

FIRST DAY

Tuesday
September 25, 2001
Sixteenth Week After Pentecost

Call to Order
The House of Bishops met September 25, 2001, at the Radisson Hotel, Burlington, Vermont. The Presiding Bishop called the House to order at 2:08 p.m. reminding the House of the work that had been done during the past week. He advised the House that it would meet in reflection groups in the course of the meeting.

The Report of the Committee on Dispatch of Business
Bishop Price, Bishop Suffragan of Southern Ohio, presented amended orders for business. The amended orders were moved, seconded and adopted.

Motion carried

The Appointment of the Secretary Pro-Tempore
Bishop Waynick of Indianapolis, Assistant Secretary, was appointed by the Presiding Bishop to serve as Secretary for this meeting.

Roll Call
It was moved, seconded, and carried to accept the registration for the Interim Meeting as the record of attendance and quorum. Bishop Putnam, retired of Navajoland and former Bishop Suffragan of Oklahoma, was warmly welcomed as the senior bishop (#595) in attendance.

Motion carried

The Reading of the Minutes
It was moved, seconded, and carried that the reading of the minutes for the Special Meeting of March 14, 2001, be dispensed.

Motion carried

Communications from the Presiding Bishop
The Presiding Bishop introduced Archbishop David Gitari, Primate of Kenya. The Archbishop conveyed a letter from a number of Primates of the Anglican

Communion that conveyed their greetings, their prayers, their stance regarding AMIA ordinations, and the pastoral care of congregations who feel uncared for because of their theology.

Committee on the Resignation of Bishops
Bishop Knudson of Maine presented the Committee Report and information to clarify the actions to be taken by the House regarding the seat, voice and vote of bishops who resign. Action is taken to determine the relationship of a bishop to the House as described in Article I.2 of the Constitution.

Change in Status
The House affirmed the retirement of Bishop Strickland of Western Kansas, who retains seat, voice and vote in the House. It was moved and carried that Bishop Doss of New Jersey and Bishop Townsend of Easton be granted seat and voice, but not vote, in the House.

No action was taken on the relationship of Bishop Jones in light of the current status of his case.

Other Reports

Task Force on General Convention Resolution A045
Bishop Lee of Virginia reported for the Task Force on Resolution AO45, regarding the work of visiting and assisting those dioceses not currently ordaining women to the priesthood. The other members of the Tasks Force are Bishop Lipscomb of Southwest Florida, Bishop Roskam, Bishop Suffragan of New York, the Rev. Scott Kirby, the Rev. Anne Colburn, the Rev. David Chi, Sarah Hart, Dianne Pollard, and Pauline Getz.

Ecumenical Relations
Bishop Epting reported on the status of our relationship with the ELCA with the "exception clause regarding presbyteral ordinations." Bishops are asked to report their participation in ELCA ordinations to Bishop Epting.

It was moved, seconded, and carried that the Presiding Bishop be empowered to speak with the new Presiding Bishop of the ELCA regarding the "exception provision" and its impact upon our relationships.

Motion carried

The General Board of Examining Chaplains
Bishop Ladehoff of Oregon reported on changes to questions in the General Ordination Examination, on the new method for reading of the exams, and the impending retirement of the Rev. Locke Bowman and the Rev. Tom Rightmyer.

It was moved, seconded, and carried that the House recognize the ministry of the Rev. Locke Bowman and the Rev. Tom Rightmeyer, and thank them for their devoted ministry.

Motion carried

It was moved, seconded, and carried to elect Susan Dolan Henderson, Professor Ethics at the Seminary of the Southwest, and Robert Hughes, who teaches theology at Sewanee, to the General Board of Examining Chaplains, to fill the vacancies created by the resignations of Ellen Wondra and Tom Bridenthal.

Bishop Lipscomb of Southwest Florida has also resigned from the Board, but no nomination has been made.

Theology Committee

Bishop Parsley of Alabama reported on the two meetings of the Committee that produced a document to be reviewed and discussed by the House prior to its affirmation. The Committee is currently working on Mind of the House Resolution B300 on Human Sexuality, and General Convention Resolutions A103 on confirmation, evangelism, baptism and adult leadership, and D023 on providing training for clergy and other leaders in contemporary methods of reconciliation.

Bishop Smalley of Kansas reminded the House that Kansas remains concerned about direct ordination to the priesthood and asked that it be addressed by the Committee and the House.

Gwi'chin Peoples

Bishop MacDonald of Alaska reported on a recent gathering of the Gwi'chin peoples who are grateful for the support of the Episcopal Church in helping them to retain their way of life.

Bishop MacDonald reported on two resolutions adopted at a meeting of Anglican Indigenous Nations in Australia. The first asks that the Anglican Communion at the ACC level and Lambeth Conference include representatives of the "Fourth World" as Indigenous Nations are sometimes being called. The second supports the Gwi'chin and denounces the drilling in the Alaskan National Wildlife Refuge.

Office for Pastoral Development

Bishop Matthews of the Office for Pastoral Development called the attention of the House to "Episcopal Formation News" which describes continuing education opportunities. He also commented on the election of bishops and appropriate letters to bishops-elect. The members of the Committee on Pastoral Development, including spouse members, were introduced to the House.

Church Pension Fund and Autonomous Provinces

Bishop Gray, Assistant Bishop of Virginia, reminded the House of unfulfilled commitments to the Church in the Philippines, Yarca, and Central America, to assist in the establishment of endowment funds for clergy pensions.

It was moved and seconded "That a base minimum pension for clergy in Province IX be established and funds made available from the Pension Fund 'abundance' to provide for that base to be established and carried forward." The motion was amended to include the Church in Liberia, Puerto Rico, Haiti, Cuba, and the Caribbean. The motion carried as amended.

Motion carried

Kanuga Greetings
Bishop Gloster, Bishop Suffragan of North Carolina, conveyed the greetings of Albert Gooch and the Kanuga Conference Center. The Board of Directors expressed their hope that the House would return to Kanuga for our meetings.

The Standing Commission on Liturgy and Music
Bishop Rowthorn, retired Bishop Suffragan of Europe and co-chair of the Commission, reported on the work of the Commission and conveyed the greetings of its members. Bishops Marshall of Bethlehem, Gibbs of Michigan, and Howe of West Missouri are members of the Commission. The Commission is working to develop a plan for liturgical renewal and enrichment of our worship. The collection of data for this process has not gone well, and bishops were asked for their support and cooperation.

General Convention Resolution A001
Bishop Rockwell of Missouri reminded the House of this resolution that obligates dioceses to commit .7% of their budgets to an International Development Fund in order to provide help and aid to the poorest of our brothers and sisters around the world. He asked how many dioceses have done this and what is happening to the funds collected.

"Manifesto to the Church"
Bishop Persell of Chicago reminded the House that the April 2001 "Manifesto to the Church" urges bishops and dioceses to make this ministry a priority. There will be a conference on Hispanic Ministry in Los Angeles on May 13–16, 2002. Bishop Hughes of San Diego noted that if we were to take 20/20 seriously, we would have to take Hispanic ministry seriously.

Recess
The Presiding Bishop declared the House in recess and reconvened the House after twenty minutes.

Announcements
Bishop Grey of Mississippi reminded the House of proposals for theological education in non-traditional settings and invited the House to sign up for a copy of material produced by him and the Rev. Ed DuBarry.
Bishop Bruno, Bishop Coadjutor of Los Angeles, invited the House to visit their website for information on ecumenical and interfaith dialogues.
Bishop Warner of Olympia described a model he has used for engaging public leaders in meaningful dialogue.
Bishop Thompson of Southern Ohio offered a statement that the Presiding Bishop indicated would be incorporated in some way in the overall statement of the House.

Reflection Group Discussions

The Presiding Bishop outlined these two questions to be addressed by members of the House for thirty minutes. First, given our discussions here, what needs to be offered to the Church and the world? What word needs to be spoken? Second, what do you see as a practical next step as we (the Church) move into the world in a new way in mission?

After more than thirty minutes, the Presiding Bishop reconvened the House to hear comments from the various reflection groups. The responses and comments will be incorporated into the Pastoral Letter of the House of Bishops.

Adjournment

The Presiding Bishop thanked the House for their participation in the meeting. At 5:23 p.m., it was moved, seconded, and carried that the meeting be adjourned.

Motion carried

Submitted by Catherine Waynick, Assistant Secretary
Certified by John L. Rabb, Chair, Committee on Certification of Minutes

Appendix A
Burlington, Vermont

Meeting Agenda

God's Mission in a Global Communion of Difference

Thursday, September 20, 2001
5:00 p.m.	Invitation to the Work (Most Rev. Frank T. Griswold)
6:00	Eucharist
7:00	Dinner in Conversation Groups

Friday, September 21, 2001
8:30am	Morning Prayer
9:00	"Engaging the Experience of Difference" Presentation, Group Conversation (Valerie Batts)
11:00	Reconvene
11:20	Break
11:35	Eucharist
12:30 p.m.	Lunch on your own
2:00	Bible Study
3:00	"God's Mission Through Scripture" Presentation, Group Conversation (Grant leMarquand)
5:00	Reconvene, response to questions, conversations
5:20	Reflections by the Chaplain *Class Dinner Night*

Saturday, September 22, 2001
8:30 a.m.	Morning Prayer
9:00	"Globalization and a World of Difference: The World of Economic Globalization" (Leng Lim, Richard Parker)
11:20	Break
11:35	Eucharist
12:30 p.m.	Box Lunch and Dialogue in Groups
2:30	Free Afternoon and Evening

Sunday, September 23, 2001
	Sabbath Time
8:00 p.m.	Evensong followed by Hospitality

Monday, September 24, 2001
8:30 a.m.	Morning Prayer
9:00	"Globalization and a World of Difference: God's Mission in a World of Suffering" Presentation, Group Conversation (Denise Ackerman)
11:00	Reconvene, response to questions, conversations
11:20	Breakfast
11:35	Eucharist
12:30 p.m.	Lunch on your own
2:00	Bible study
3:00	"Globalization and a World of Difference: The Plural World of a New Pentecost" (Christopher Duraisingh)
5:00	Reconvene, response to questions, conversations
5:20	Reflections by the chaplain
	Province Dinner Night

Tuesday, September 25, 2001
	House of Bishops Interim Meeting
8:30 a.m.	Morning Prayer
9:00	"Difference and God's Mission in the Anglican Communion" Presentation, Group Conversations (Ian Douglas)
11:00	Reconvene, response to questions, conversations
11:20	Break
11:35	Eucharist
12:30 p.m.	Lunch on your own
2:00	House of Bishops Interim Meeting–Business Session
5:00	End
6:30	Community Celebration Dinner

Wednesday, September 26, 2001
	Community of Bishops Re-gathered
8:30 a.m.	Morning Prayer
9:00	"Embracing the Fullness of God's Mission at Home" (Most Rev. Frank T. Griswold)
10:30	Break
11:00	Eucharist
Noon	End

Appendix B
Burlington, Vermont

Bishops Present at the Interim Meeting of September 2001

Ackerman, Keith L.
Adams III, Gladstone B.
Alexander, John Neil
Bainbridge, Harry B.
Ball, David S.
Bane Jr., David C.
Bartlett Jr., Allen L.
Beckwith, Peter H.
Bena, David John
Bennison Jr., Charles E.
Borsch, Frederick H.
Bruno, J. Jon
Buchanan, John C.
Caldwell, Bruce
Cederholm Jr., Roy Frederick
Charleston, Steven
Coleridge, Clarence N.
Creighton, Michael W.
Croneberger, John P.
Curry, James Elliot
Curry, Michael Bruce
Daniel III, Clifton
Daniels, Theodore A.
Dixon, Jane H.
Doss, Joe M.
Duncan II, Philip M.
Duncan Jr., Robert W.
Duracin, Jean Zaché
Ely, Thomas Clark
Epting, C. Christopher
Folts, James E.
Frade, Leopoldo
Garrison, J. Michael
Gibbs Jr., Wendell N.
Gloster, J. Gary
Gray III, Duncan Montgomery
Gray Jr., Francis C.
Gregg, William Otis
Grew II, J. Clark
Griswold, Frank T.
Gulick Jr., Edwin F.
Hargrove Jr., Robert J.

Harris, Barbara C.
Harris, Rogers S.
Hart, Donald P.
Henderson Jr., Dorsey F.
Herzog, Daniel W.
Hibbs, Robert B.
Howe, Barry R.
Hughes, Gethin B.
Ihloff, Robert W.
Irish, Carolyn T.
Jacobus, Russell E.
Jefferts Schori, Katharine
Jelinek, James L.
Jenkins, Charles E.
Johnson, Don E.
Johnson, Robert H.
Jones, David C.
Jones, Edward W.
Kelsey, James A.
Knudsen, Chilton R.
Ladehoff, Robert L.
Lamb, Jerry A.
Larrea, Neptalí
Lee Jr., Edward L.
Lee, Peter J.
Leidel Jr., Edwin M.
Lipscomb, John B.
Little II, Edward S.
Longest, Charles L.
Louttit, Henry
MacDonald, Mark L.
MacPherson, D. Bruce
Marble Jr., Alfred C.
Matthews, F. Clayton
McKelvey, Jack M.
Merino, Bernardo
Michel, Rodney R.
Moody, Robert M.
Ohl Jr., Charles Wallis
Packard, George E.
Parsley Jr., Henry N.
Payne, Claude E.

Persell, William D.
Pettit, Vincent K.
Powell, Neff
Price Jr., Kenneth L.
Putnam, Frederick W.
Rabb, John L.
Ramos-Orench, Wilfrido
Reed, David B.
Robertson, Creighton L.
Rockwell, Hays H.
Roskam, Catherine S.
Rowley Jr., Robert D.
Rowthorn, Jeffery W.
Salmon, Edward L.
Sauls, Stacy F.
Scantlebury, Victor A.
Scruton, Gordon Paul
Shahan, Robert R.
Shimpfky, Richard L.
Sisk, Mark S.
Skilton, William J.
Smalley, William E.
Smith, Andrew D.
Soto, Onell A.

Swing, William E.
Talton, Chester L.
Taylor, E. Don
Tennis, Cabell
Theuner, Douglas E.
Thompson Jr., Herbert
Townsend, Martin G.
Vaché, C. Charles
vonRosenberg, Charles G.
Waggoner, James Edward
Walker Jr., Orris G.
Walmsley, Arthur E.
Warner Jr., Vincent W.
Waynick, Catherine M.
White, Roger J.
Whitmore, Keith B.
Williams Jr., Arthur B.
Williams Jr., Huntington
Wolf, Geralyn Wright

Appendix C
Burlington, Vermont

Newly Consecrated Bishops

Bishops who have been consecrated since the meeting of the Interim Meeting of the House of Bishops, held at Kanuga Conference Center, Hendersonville, North Carolina, March 9–14, 2001:

The Bishop Suffragan of Massachusetts, March 24, 2001
Roy Frederick Cederholm, Jr. (964)
Chief Consecrator: Douglas Edwin Theuner
  Bishop of New Hampshire
Co-Consecrators: Marvil Thomas Shaw, SSJE
  Bishop of Massachusetts
  Barbara Clementine Harris
  Bishop Suffragan of Massachusetts
  Andrew Donnan Smith
  Bishop of Connecticut

The Bishop of Vermont, April 28, 2001
Thomas Clark Ely (965)
Chief Consecrator: Douglas Edwin Theuner
  Bishop of New Hampshire
Co-Consecrators: Andrew Donnan Smith
  Bishop of Connecticut
  Mary Adelia Rosamond McLeod
  Bishop of Vermont, Resigned
  Daniel Lee Swenson
  Bishop of Vermont, Resigned
  Morgan Porteus
  Bishop of Connecticut, Resigned
  Arthur Edward Walmsley
  Bishop of Connecticut, Resigned

The Bishop of the Central Gulf Coast, May 12, 2001
Philip Menzie Duncan (966)
Chief Consecrator: The Presiding Bishop
Co-Consecrators: Charles Farmer Duvall
  Bishop of Central Gulf Coast
  Barry Robert Howe
  Bishop Coadjutor of West Missouri
  Catherine Elizabeth Maples Waynick
  Bishop of Indianapolis
  David Bruce MacPherson
  Bishop Suffragan of Dallas

Rogers Sanders Harris
Bishop of Southwest Florida, Resigned
James Louis Jelinek
Bishop of Minnesota
Sam Byron Hulsey
Bishop of Northwest Texas, Resigned
Telesforo Alexander Isaac
Bishop of the Dominican Republic, Resigned

The Bishop of West Tennessee, June 30, 2001
Don Edward Johnson, (967)
Chief Consecrator: The Presiding Bishop
Co-Consecrators: William Evan Sanders
Bishop of East Tennessee, Resigned
Charles Glenn vonRosenberg
Bishop of East Tennessee
Duncan Montgomery Gray III
Bishop Coadjutor of Mississippi
James Malone Coleman
Bishop of West Tennessee

The Bishop of Atlanta, July 7, 2001
John Neil Alexander (968)
Chief Consecrator: The Presiding Bishop
Co-Consecrators: Frank Kellogg Allan
Bishop of Atlanta, Resigned
Charles Judson Child, Jr.
Bishop of Atlanta, Resigned
Bennett Jones Sims
Bishop of Atlanta, Resigned
Michael Bruce Curry
Bishop of North Carolina
Onell Asiselo Soto
Assistant Bishop of Atlanta
Ronald B. Warren
Bishop of Southeastern Synod, ELCA

Bishop Coadjutor of Colombia, July 14, 2001
Francisco José Duque-Gomez (969)
Chief Consecrator: El Obispo Primado
Co-Consecrators: Bernardo Merino Botero
Obispo de Colombia
Neptali Larrea-Moreno
Obispo de Ecuador, Diócesis Central
James Hamilton Ottley

Interino de Honduras
Alfredo Morante-España
Obispo de Ecuador, Diócesis de Litoral
Armando Guerra
Obispo de Venezuela

Change in Status

The following are changes in status received by the Secretary of the House of Bishops from the Presiding Bishop since the meeting of the Interim Meeting of the House of Bishops, held at Kanuga Conference Center, Hendersonville, North Carolina, March 9–14 2001:

April 15, 2001
The Rt. Rev. C. Christopher Epting
Bishop of Iowa
To Deputy for Ecumenical and Interfaith Relations

Resignations

Since the meeting of the Interim Meeting of the House of Bishops, held at Kanuga Conference Center, Hendersonville, North Carolina, March 9–14, 2001, the Secretary has received notice of the intent of the following bishops to resign or retire:

May 12, 2001
The Rt. Rev. Charles F. Duvall
Bishop of Central Gulf Coast

June 30, 2001
The Rt. Rev. John C.T. Chien
Bishop of Taiwan

August 1, 2001
The Rt. Rev. James M. Coleman
Bishop of West Tennessee

Necrology

Since the meeting of the Interim Meeting of the House of Bishops, held at Kanuga Conference Center, Hendersonville, North Carolina, March 9–14, 2001, the following bishops have departed this life:

May 10, 2001
The Rt. Rev. John Forsythe Ashby
Bishop of Western Kansas

July 18, 2001
The Rt. Rev. Gerald Francis Burrill
Retired Bishop of Chicago

Appendix D
Burlington, Vermont

The Theological Calling
A Reflective Framework to Guide the House of Bishops in our Vocation as Teachers

1. The Task of Theology
   Christian theology seeks to discern and articulate the grace and truth of God revealed in Jesus Christ and to guide the church in mission.
2. God's Plan of Salvation
   God, whom we know as Father, Son and Holy Spirit, has lovingly created the world and all that is therein. Human beings are graciously created in the divine image, but we have fallen into sin and fail to live into the fullness of this gift and calling. In his life, death, and resurrection, Jesus Christ, the incarnate Son of God, has restored us to unity with God and each other and calls us to reconciliation. Empowered by the Holy Spirit, we are called to grow in, rejoice in, and herald God's grace for all creation.
3. The Great Tradition
   We believe that the Old and New Testaments are the revealed Word of God and contain all things necessary to salvation. We further believe that the Apostles' and Nicene Creeds are sufficient statements of the essential of the Christian faith and express our basic beliefs about God and God's saving work. The truth of the Creeds is further expressed in the teaching, ascetical discipline, and ordering of the church in its pastoral ministry. The Creeds and the great Ecumenical Councils of the church thus help us to interpret and live into the saving story of Scripture. They shape the inherited faith of the church universal in which we stand as Anglicans.
4. Baptism and Theology
   In baptism all Christians are born anew by water and the Spirit, incorporated into the Body of Christ, and made part of the church's disciplined communal life of worship and witness. Theology is the way in which we speak of the mystery of God and express the faith of the church. Baptism calls us to be theologians; therefore from baptism we understand that those who pray are theologians and theologians are those who pray. Theology is both derived from and informs our common life in prayer and sacrament. As we pray so we believe, and as we believe so we pray.
5. The Teaching Charism
   The truth of God and the Gospel must be articulated faithfully and afresh for every generation. Guided by the Holy Spirit who leads the church into all truth, bishops in dialogue with academic theologians seek to discern and teach the wisdom of God. This is done *in colleguium*, in communion with the baptized who have gone before and in conversation with the faithful who are our contemporaries. The Committee on Theology of the House of Bishops, comprising bishops and consulting theologians, aids the church in this disciplined life of discernment and teaching through critical reflection and

practice.
6. Theology in Community
   The theological vocation is grounded in our common life as the Body of Christ and rooted in the ministry of Word and Sacrament. Discerning and articulating the grace and truth of God revealed in Jesus Christ empowers us to go out into the world to share in the mission of God: to restore all people to unity with God and each other in Christ (The Book of Common Prayer, page 855).

Submitted by the Theology Committee of the House of Bishops
May 2, 2001

Appendix E
Burlington, Vermont

On Waging Reconciliation
A Statement from Bishops of the Episcopal Church

September 26th, 2001

We, your bishops, have come together in the shadow of the shattering events of September 11. We in the United States now join that company of nations in which ideology disguised as true religion wreaks havoc and sudden death. Through this suffering, we have come into a new solidarity with those in other parts of the world for whom the evil forces of terrorism are a continuing fear and reality.

We grieve with those who have lost companions and loved ones, and pray for those who have so tragically died. We pray for the President of the United States, his advisors, and for the members of Congress that they may be given wisdom and prudence for their deliberations and measured patience in their actions. We pray for our military chaplains, and for those serving in the Armed Forces along with their families in these anxious and uncertain days. We also pray "for our enemies, and those who wish us harm; and for all whom we have injured or offended" (BCP, page 391).

At the same time we give thanks for the rescue workers and volunteers, and all those persons whose courageous efforts demonstrated a generosity and selflessness that bears witness to the spirit of our nation at its best. We give thanks too for all those who are reaching out to our Muslim brothers and sisters and others who are rendered vulnerable in this time of fear and recrimination.

We come together also in the shadow of the cross: that unequivocal sign that suffering and death are never the end but the way along which we pass into a future in which all things will be healed and reconciled. Through Christ "God was pleased to reconcile to himself all things whether on earth or in heaven, by making peace through the blood of his cross" (Col. 1:20). This radical act of peace-making is nothing less than the right ordering of all things according to God's passionate desire for justness, for the full flourishing of humankind and all creation.

This peace has already been achieved in Christ, but it has yet to be realized in our relationships with one another and the world around us. As members of a global community and the worldwide Anglican Communion, we are called to bear one another's burdens across the divides of culture, religion, and differing views of the world. The affluence of nations such as our own stands in stark contrast to other parts of the world wracked by the crushing poverty which causes the death of 6,000 children in the course of a morning.

We are called to self-examination and repentance: the willingness to change direction, to open our hearts and give room to God's compassion as it seeks to bind up, to heal, and to make all things new and whole. God's project, in which we participate by virtue of our baptism, is the ongoing work of reordering and transforming the patterns of our common life so they may reveal God's justness - not as an abstraction but in bread for the hungry and clothing for the naked. The mission of the Church is to participate in God's work in the world. We claim that mission.

"I have set before you life and death...choose life so that you and your descendants may live," declares Moses to the children to Israel. We choose life and immediately set ourselves to the task of developing clear steps that we will take personally and as a community of faith, to give substance to our resolve and embodiment to our hope. We do so not alone but trusting in your own faithfulness and your desire to be instruments of peace.

Let us therefore wage reconciliation. Let us offer our gifts for the carrying out of God's ongoing work of reconciliation, healing and making all things new. To this we pledge ourselves and call our church.

We go forth sober in the knowledge of the magnitude of the task to which we have all been called, yet confident and grounded in hope."And hope does not disappoint us, because God's love has been poured into our hearts through the Holy Spirit that has been given to us" (Romans 5:5).

"May the God of hope fill us with all joy and peace in believing through the power of the Holy Spirit" (Romans 15:13).

MEETING OF THE HOUSE OF BISHOPS 2002

SPECIAL MEETING

Held at
Camp Allen–The Diocese of Texas

Navasota, Texas
March 7–12, 2002

SPECIAL MEETING OF THE HOUSE OF BISHOPS
Camp Allen–The Diocese of Texas
Navasota, Texas
March 7–12, 2002

The House of Bishops met March 7–12, 2002 at Camp Allen in the Diocese of Texas. A legislative session of the House was not held, therefore there are no meeting minutes or other official documents from the gathering.
See Appendix A for members of the House present at the gathering.

Appendix A
Navasota, Texas

Bishops Present at the Interim Meeting of March 2002
Camp Allen–The Diocese of Texas

Ackerman, Keith–Quincy
Adams, Gladstone–Central New York
Adams, James–Western Kansas
Alard, Leopoldo–Texas
Alexander, John Neil–Atlanta
Allen, Lloyd–Honduras
Allison, Christopher–South Carolina
Anderson, Robert–Los Angeles
Andrus, Mark–Alabama
Bainbridge, Harry B.–Idaho
Bane, David C.–Southern Virginia
Bartlett, Allen L.–Washington (Assisting Bishop)
Beckwich, Peter–Springfield
Bena, David J.–Albany
Bennison, Charles E.–Pennsylvania
Bruno, Jon–Los Angeles
Caldwell, Bruce–Wyoming
Cederholm, Roy–Massachusetts
Chang, Richard S.O.–Hawaii
Charleston, Steven–Episcopal Divinity School
Creighton, Michael–Central Pennsylvania
Croneberger, John P.–Newark
Curry, James E.–Connecticut
Curry, Michael B.–North Carolina
Daniel, Clifton–East Carolina
Daniels, Theodore–Virgin Islands
Dixon, Jane–Washington
Donovan, Herbert A.–Arkansas (Retired)
Duncan, Phillip–Central Gulf Coast
Duncan, Robert Wm.–Pittsburgh
Duque, Francisco–Colombia
Duracin, Jean Zaché–Haiti
Ely, Thomas C.–Vermont
Epting, C. Christopher–Ecumenical Officer
Fairfield, Andrew–North Dakota
Folts, James E.–West Texas
Frade, Leopoldo–Southeast Florida
Frey, William–Colorado (Retired)
Gallagher, Carol–Southern Virginia
Garrison, J. Michael–Western New York
Gepert, Robert–Western Michigan
Gibbs, Jr., Wendell N.–Michigan
Gloster, J. Gary–North Carolina
Gray, III, Duncan–Mississippi
Gray, Francis–Virginia (Assisting Bishop)
Gregg, William O.–Eastern Oregon
Grew, Clark–Ohio
Griswold, Frank – Presiding Bishop
Gulick, Edwin–Kentucky
Haines, Ronald–Washington
Hargrove, Robert–Western Louisiana
Hathaway, Alden–Pittsburgh (Retired)
Henderson, Dorsey–Upper South Carolina
Herlong, Bertram–Tennessee
Herzog, Daniel W.–Albany
Hibbs, Robert B.–West Texas
Holguín, Julio C.–Dominican Republic
Howe, Barry R.–West Missouri
Howe, John–Central Florida
Hughes, Gethin–San Diego
Ihloff, Robert–Maryland
Irish, Carolyn T.–Utah
Jacobus, Russell E.–Fond du Lac
Jefferts Schori, Katharine–Nevada
Jenkins, Charles E.–Louisiana
Johnson, Don–West Tennessee
Johnson, Robert–Western North Carolina
Jones, David C.–Virginia
Joslin, David–New Jersey
Kelsey, James A.–Northern Michigan
Keyser, Charles–Montana

Klusmeyer, Michie–West Virginia
Knudsen, Chilton–Maine
Krotz, James A.–Nebraska
Ladehoff, Robert–Oregon
Lai, David–Taiwan
Lamb, Jerry A.–Northern California
Lee, Edward L.–Western Michigan
Lee, Peter–Virginia
Leidel, Edwin–Eastern Michigan
Lipscomb, John B.–Southwest Florida
Little, Edward–Northern Indiana
Louttit, Henry I.–Georgia
MacDonald, Mark L.–Alaska
MacPherson, D. Bruce–Dallas
Marble, Alfred C.–Mississippi
Marshall, Paul–Bethelem
Matthews, F. Clayton–Office of Pastoral Development
Maze, Larry E.–Arkansas
McKelvey, Jack–Rochester
Merino, Bernado–Colombia
Michel, Rodney–Long Island
Moody, Robert–Oklahoma
Moore, Paul–New York (Retired)
Ohl Jr., Charles Wallis–Northwest Texas
Ottley, James H.–Southeast Florida
Packard, George E.–Office of the Bishop for the Armed Services
Parsley, Henry N.–Alabama
Payne, Claude–Texas
Persell, William D.–Chicago
Plummer, Steven–Navajoland Area Mission
Price Jr., Kenneth–Southern Ohio
Putnam, Frederick W.–Minnesota (Assisting Bishop)
Rabb, John–Maryland
Ramos–Orench, Wilfrido–Connecticut
Reed, David–Kentucky (Retired)
Robertson, Creighton–South Dakota
Rockwell, Hays–Missouri
Roskam, Catherine S.–New York
Rowley, Robert D.–Northwestern Pennsylvania
Salmon, Edward–South Carolina
Sauls, Stacy F.–Lexington
Scantlebury, Victor–Chicago (Assisting Bishop)
Schofield, John–David M.–San Joaquin
Scruton, Gordon P.–Western Massachusetts
Shahan, Robert R.–Arizona
Shaw, M. Thomas–Massachusetts
Shimpfky, Richard L.–El Camino Real
Sisk, Mark–New York
Skilton, William–South Carolina
Smalley, William E. – Kansas
Smith, Andrew D.–Connecticut
Smith, Wayne–Missouri
Stanton, James–Dallas
Sterling, William–Texas (Retired)
Swing, William E.–California
Talton, Chester L.–Los Angeles
Taylor, Don–New York (Assisting Bishop)
Theuner, Douglas–New Hampshire
Thompson, Herbert–Southern Ohio
vonRosenberg, Charles–East Tennessee
Waggoner, James E.–Spokane
Walker, Orris G.–Long Island
Wallace, Leigh–Spokane (Retired)
Walmsley, Arthur–Connecticut (Retired)
Warner, Vincent W.–Olympia
Waynick, Catherine–Indianapolis
Whalon, Pierre–Convocation of American Churches in Europe
White, Roger–Milwaukee
Williams, Arthur–Ohio
Wimberly, Don A.–Texas (Assisting Bishop)
Winterrowd, William J.–Colorado
Wolf, Geralyn–Rhode Island
Wolfrum, William–Suffragan of Colorado (Retired)
Wright, Wayne–Delaware

Honorary Members
Alvarez, David–Puerto Rico
Neufville, Edward–Liberia

Guests
Akinola, Peter–Primate and Archbishop Nigeria and Abuja
Mottahedeh, Iraj–Primate of Jerusalem and the Middle East
Tutu, Desmond–Archbishop Emeritus of Cape Town, South Africa

MEETING OF THE HOUSE OF BISHOPS 2002

SPECIAL MEETING

Held at
The Marriott Hotel

Cleveland, Ohio
September 30–October 1, 2002

SPECIAL MEETING OF THE HOUSE OF BISHOPS
The Marriott Hotel
Cleveland, Ohio
September 30–October 1, 2002

FIRST DAY

Monday
September 30, 2002
Nineteenth Week After Pentecost

MORNING SESSION

Call to Order
The House of Bishops met September 30, 2002, at the Marriott Hotel, Cleveland, Ohio. The Presiding Bishop called the House to order at 9:20 a.m. The Call to Order was delayed by the distribution of materials to the bishops for the meeting.

The Roll Call
It was moved, seconded, and carried to accept the registration of 137 bishops for the Interim Meeting as the record of attendance and quorum. Bishop Putnam, Retired of Navajoland and former Bishop Suffragan of Oklahoma, was welcomed as the senior bishop (#595) in attendance at this Interim Meeting.

Motion carried

The Reading of the Minutes
It was moved, seconded, and carried that the reading of the minutes for the Interim Meeting of September 25, 2001, Burlington, VT, be dispensed.

Motion carried

Communications from the Presiding Bishop
The Presiding Bishop provided a status report on the proposal to relocate the Episcopal Church Center to General Theological Seminary. The process, that now is Phase One, will lead to a decision by the Executive Council was described.

The Presiding Bishop informed the House of the status of the Church Budget for the next Triennium citing possible shortfalls in endowment income and diocesan payments on askings.

The Presiding Bishop reported on Executive Council action to fund a feasibility study for a national fund raising campaign for mission.

Charles Fulton was introduced by the Presiding Bishop to make a presentation on a National Pilot Project on Church Development. Mr. Kirk Hadaway, Director of Research at the Church Center, will assist with this project to identify sites for building new church developments. The roles of the Domestic and Foreign Missionary Society and the Dioceses were described in terms of planning and funding. A brief question and answer period followed the presentation.

Committee on the Resignation of Bishops

Bishop Knudson of Maine informed the House that she would be leaving the meeting due to the death of her aunt. She cited Article I, Section 2 of the Constitution, noting the "advanced age", "bodily infirmity" and "mission strategy" criteria for resignation. The committee will present a report on "Missionary Strategy" to the House of Bishops at the March 2003 Spring Meeting. Bishop Rowley of Northwestern Pennsylvania will serve as a consultant to the committee.

It was moved and carried that pursuant to Article I, Section 2 of the Constitution the following bishops retain seat, voice and vote in the House of Bishops:

Ronald H. Haines	12/30/00
Bernardo Merino	05/13/02
Richard F. Grein	07/31/02
John L. Said	08/31/02
Jane H. Dixon	08/31/02
Hays Rockwell	09/01/02
Barbara C. Harris	11/01/02
Robert J. Hargrove	11/01/02
Arthur B. Williams	12/31/02

Committee on Nominations

Bishop Howe of West Missouri presented the Committee Report on the nomination of Henry Scriven, Assistant Bishop of Pittsburgh, including a brief resume.

It was moved and carried that the House of Bishops consent to the appointment of Henry Scriven as Assistant Bishop of Pittsburgh pursuant to Title III, Section 2(d), and to the granting of seat and vote in the House of Bishops pursuant to Article I, Section 2 of the Constitution.

Motion carried

Committee on Theology

Bishop Parsley of Alabama presented status reports on the several projects of the Committee after introducing the members of the Theology Committee. The papers on Reconciliation and on Human Sexuality will be distributed in the spring for discussion at the Spring Meeting of the House of Bishops in March 2003. The work on General Convention Resolution A103 on confirmation, evangelism, baptism and adult leadership continues.

"Mutual Responsibility and Collegiality"

Bishop Ilhoff of Maryland presented a resolution drafted from the reports from the reflection groups of the House that addressed the issues of respect, accountability, mutuality, and collegiality.

After lengthy discussion, including the adoption and defeat of several amendments, the amended resolution was adopted by the House of Bishops.

Mind of the House Resolution

Jesus prayed that we be one even as he and the Father are one. By God's grace, we continue to grow in community characterized by Christian reconciliation, peace, and collegiality. That growth, and our Episcopal vows, require that we confront instances of inappropriate behavior even as we strive to maintain our unity and our focus and energy on the mission of the Church.

We express our disappointment that the Bishop of Pennsylvania, clergy and lay leaders of Good Shepherd parish, various diocesan leaders, and others were unable to find a way to resolve the issues within the parish short of the difficulties in which we currently find ourselves.

We are also concerned that theological disputes not become the occasion for canonical violations or unilateral actions such as those taken by the Bishop of Pittsburgh; and furthermore, we deplore the extra-canonical action which he has taken.

Used properly, we believe the canons can be an instrument of grace and unifying factor in the life of the Church. We support the right of a bishop under the canons to depose a priest for the health and welfare of the diocese.

Furthermore, we expect that such depositions or other disciplinary actions be recognized by all bishops of the Episcopal Church and the Anglican Communion.

We lament the decisions on the part of the bishops of Kansas and Delaware which went beyond the consensus achieved by General Convention Resolution D039 when they formally authorized the blessing of same sex unions.

In order to support one another in waging reconciliation within the Body of Christ, and to enhance wider consultation and our role as guardians of the faith, unity, and discipline of the Church, we request that the Committee on Pastoral Care develop a mechanism for:
1. dealing with breaches of collegiality; and
2. providing assistance to bishops with diocesan situations which impact the larger church.

And that the report thereon be prepared and distributed to the members of the House of Bishops prior to the Spring meeting of 2003 and be considered at that meeting.

Motion carried
Resolution adopted

Recess
The Presiding Bishop recessed the meeting at 11:15 a.m. to allow the House to prepare for the celebration of the Eucharist. The meeting will reconvene at 2:00.

AFTERNOON SESSION

Reconvene
The Presiding Bishop reconvened the meeting of the House of Bishops at 2:12 p.m. in the Marriott Hotel, Cleveland, Ohio. The Presiding Bishop shared his reflections on the morning session. In the discussion the House was embodying reconciliation and expanding it. There was recognition of the tension between the realities of dioceses and the larger church.

Introduction of Guests
The Presiding Bishop introduced and welcomed the Most Rev. Michael Peers, Primate of Canada. Archbishop Peers addressed the House on the readmission of Cuba by the 2003 General Convention, the Anglican Consultative Council meeting in Hong Kong, the issue of residential schools, and the issues related to the Diocese of New Westminster. He concluded his remarks by asking for the continued support and prayers of ECUSA.

Global Reconciliation
Bishop Shaw of Massachusetts introduced the members of his committee. The committee had prepared a draft letter from the House of Bishops to the Congress of the United States. A statement entitled "Toward Reconciliation in the World" drafted by Bishop Gregg of Eastern Oregon was also distributed to the House. Bishop Shaw had a "Statement of Solidarity with the HIV/AIDS Initiative of the Council of Anglican Provinces in Africa" distributed to the House. All three documents would be considered by the House at 12:30 p.m. on October 1, 2002.

Office of Pastoral Development
Bishop Clay Matthews reported on the College for Bishops and programs of the Office of Pastoral Development. He announced a workshop on child abuse in March 2003 prior to the Spring Meeting. A brochure of the Pastoral Development Committee was circulated.

Arctic National Wildlife Refuge and the Gwi'chin People
Bishop MacDonald of Alaska presented a status report on the National Wildlife Refuge and oil exploration development. The resolution presented by Bishop MacDonald was moved, seconded, and carried as presented.

Mind of the House Resolution
Resolved, That the House of Bishops of The Episcopal Church, meeting in Cleveland, Ohio, September 30, 2002:
> Reaffirms its support of the Gwich'in People and Permanent Protection for the Arctic National Wildlife Refuge.

Expresses its opposition to any oil exploration and development in the Arctic National Wildlife Refuge.
Urges the rejection of H.R. 4 by Senate Conferees.

Motion carried
Resolution adopted

General Board of Examining Chaplains
Bishop Ladehoff of Oregon provided a status report on the Board and invited comments from the members of the House.

International Study Program at Canterbury
Bishop Lee of Virginia described the programs of the International Study Center at Canterbury Cathedral, stressing the summer program for seminarians.

Announcements
Bishop Hampton, Assistant of the Diocese of Olympia, reminded the members of the House about providing gratuities for the housekeepers and other staff of the Marriott Hotel.
The Secretary informed the House of future meeting dates in 2003 and 2004.

Recess
The Presiding Bishop declared the House in recess until 12:30 p.m. on October 1, 2002.

SECOND DAY

Tuesday
October 1, 2002
Nineteenth Week After Pentecost

MORNING SESSION

Call to Order
The Presiding Bishop called the House to order at 12:47 p.m. at the Marriott Hotel, Cleveland, Ohio. He informed the House that the agenda was limited to the consideration of three items: (1) the letter to Congress, (2) Toward Reconciliation in the World, and (3) the Statement on Solidarity with the HIV/AIDS Initiative of the Council of Anglican Provinces in Africa. These documents had been distributed to the House on the previous day.
The Presiding Bishop presented a gift to Archbishop Michael Peers and expressed appreciation for his presence. Archbishop Peers thanked the Presiding Bishop and the House in his final comments to the House.

Consideration of the Documents

The Presiding Bishop outlined the process that would be followed in the consideration of the documents on the agenda.

Following expanded group reports, Bishop Shaw of Massachusetts and the Presiding Bishop provided additional background on the letter to Congress.

After discussion, it was moved, seconded and carried that the draft letter be referred back to the original drafting committee for one hour so that they could incorporate the comments from the groups and discussion into the original draft letter.

Motion carried

Recess

At 1:25 p.m. the Presiding Bishop declared the House to be in recess until 2:45 p.m.

AFTERNOON SESSION

Reconvene

The Presiding Bishop reconvened the House of Bishops at 2:44 p.m.

"Letter to Congress"

Bishop Shaw of Massachusetts read the revised letter to the House. In the discussion that followed three amendments to the letter were adopted.

It was moved, seconded, and carried that the amended "Letter to Congress" be adopted by the House of Bishops.

Motion carried

It was moved, seconded, and carried that the letter be signed by the Presiding Bishop and the Secretary of the House and sent to the members of Congress. A list of the members of the House would be sent as a separate enclosure.

Motion carried

Several members of the House recommended that the members of the House contact the congressional delegations from their states to inform them about the letter.

Statement on Solidarity with the HIV/AIDS Initiative of the Council of Anglican Provinces in Africa

Bishop Shaw of Massachusetts moved the adoption of the Statement, and it carried.

Mind of the House Resolution

Nairobi, Kenya, August 19–22, 2002

Resolved, That the House of Bishops of the Episcopal Church renews its concern for all who suffer from the HIV/AIDS pandemic throughout the world, including those in our own dioceses, which are located within and outside the USA, and those in dioceses throughout the Anglican Communion; and be it further

Resolved, That the House renews the encouragement previously expressed by the House and by the General Convention that parishes, dioceses and church-wide bodies do all in their power to prevent the spread of HIV/AIDS and offer prayer and the compassionate ministry of Christ to all affected by HIV/AIDS; and be it further

Resolved, That the House congratulates the AIDS Board of the Council of Anglican Provinces in Africa (CAPA) on its second meeting held in Nairobi, Kenya, 19–22 August, 2002, and on the progress made since the first All Africa Anglican Conference on HIV/AIDS, held in Boksburg, South Africa, in August 2002, in addressing HIV/AIDS, on the continent most affected by the pandemic; and be it further

Resolved, That the House expresses its solidarity with CAPA's vision of "a generation without AIDS"; with the CAPA AIDS Board's insistence in Nairobi that debt cancellation in Africa is essential to addressing the pandemic on that continent; and with the board's six-fold call to responsibility on the part of the churches: Leadership, Care, Prevention, Counseling, Pastoral Care, and Death and Dying; and be it further

Resolved, That the House rejoices in the ministry of missionaries of the Domestic and Foreign Missionary Society in assisting African Anglican provinces in addressing the pandemic, noting the work of Douglas Huber, HIV/AIDS advisor to CAPA; Ted Karpf, canon for HIV/AIDS ministry in the Province of Southern Africa; Lin Parsons, HIV/AIDS educator in the Province of Central Africa; and others in diverse ministries that are affected by the pandemic; and be it further

Resolved, That the House expresses its gratitude for the significant financial contributions to HIV/AIDS work in Africa made by Episcopal parishes, dioceses and agencies, such as Episcopal Relief and Development, Trinity Grants, and the Jubilee groups of the dioceses of Massachusetts and New Hampshire; and be it further

Resolved, That in the spirit of God's Jubilee, the House as a body commits itself to CAPA's Partnership for Life by calling on each of the Episcopal Church's bishops to elicit a contribution of $1,000 from his or her diocese to enable the twelve member provinces of CAPA to establish early structures to implement the planning and capacity-building components of their AIDS responses, such contributions to be collected by the Secretary of the House and disbursed to CAPA through the Treasurer of the Domestic and Foreign Missionary Society; and be it further

Resolved, That the members of the House of Bishops commit themselves to prayer for CAPA and its AIDS board and for the bishops and dioceses of Anglican provinces in Africa as they address HIV/AIDS throughout the continent; and be it further

Resolved, That the members of the House of Bishops respond to the CAPA AIDS Board's desire for a closer relationship with this House by committing ourselves to support the work of the board and to stay informed of its progress during the coming year.

Motion carried
Resolution adopted

"Toward Reconciliation in the World"
Bishop Gregg of Eastern Oregon introduced the discussion. Following discussion, it was moved, seconded, and carried that "Toward Reconciliation" be referred to Dr. Ian Douglas and the original editorial committee for further work on the document and for report at the Spring Meeting of the House of Bishops in 2003.

Motion carried

Courtesy Resolutions
Bishop Daniels of the Virgin Islands moved the following resolution, and it was seconded and carried.

The House of Bishops expresses its thanks to:
- Chet Talton and the House of Bishops Planning Committee, the Spouses Planning Group, and their consultants, Susy Miller and Mary Williams;
- The Chaplains to the House, Michael Battle and Mark McIntosh; and the chaplain to the spouses, Sarah Buxton-Smith;
- Gerry Wolf for our liturgies and to Mark Johnson for our music;
- To our staff presenters this morning for being here and sharing with us some sense of the work that is going on for our behalf;
- To the staff who supported this meeting from the Presiding Bishop's Office, and from the General Convention Office; and
- To the Bishops of Ohio and the Diocese of Ohio.

Motion carried
Resolution adopted

Announcements
Bishop Payne of Texas shared comments on evangelism and the clear vision conferences. The Secretary reminded the members of the House that the memorials for George H. Quarterman, William Henry Marmion, D.D., David H. Lewis, Jr., and Anselmo Carral-Solar, have been distributed.

Adjournment
At 3:20 p.m., it was moved, seconded, and carried that the 2002 Interim Meeting of the House of Bishops be adjourned.

Motion carried

Submitted by, Richard S.O. Chang, Secretary of the House of Bishops
Certified by John L. Rabb, Chair, Committee on Certification of Minutes

Appendix A
Cleveland, Ohio

Meeting Agenda

Inhabiting Reconciliation: Living the Mystery

Thursday, September 26, 2002
2:00 p.m.	Opening Session (Most Rev. Frank T. Griswold)
2:45	Core Group Conversations
3:45	Break
4:00	Opening Eucharist
5:15	Hospitality
6:00	Community Supper
8:30	End of Day

Friday, September 27, 2002
8:30 a.m.	Morning Prayer
9:00	"Reconciliation Through the Lens of God's Love" (Mark McIntosh)
9:30	Core Group Conversations
11:30	Break
11:45	Eucharist
12:30 p.m.	Lunch on your own
2:00	"Repentance" (Michael Battle)
2:30	Core Group Conversations
4:30	End of Day Class Dinner Night

Saturday, September 28, 2002
8:30 a.m.	Morning Prayer
9:00	"Power, Influence and Authority" (Most Rev. Frank T. Griswold)
10:00	Core Group Conversation
11:30	Break
11:45	Eucharist
12:30 p.m.	Lunch on your own
2:00	Expanded Group Conversation
4:30	End of Day
5:30	Wine and Cheese Reception Evening "On The Town"

JOURNAL INTERIM MEETING

Sunday, September 29, 2002
11:00 a.m.	Worship
Noon	Lunch at Cathedral
	Sabbath time

Monday, September 30, 2002
8:30 a.m.	Morning Prayer
9:00	HOB Interim Meeting
11:30	Break
11:45	Eucharist
12:30 p.m.	Lunch on your own
2:00	"Reconciliation for the Sake of the World" (Most Rev. Frank T. Griswold)
2:45	Panel Discussion
3:45	Break
4:00	Expanded Group Conversation
5:00	End of Day
	Provincial Dinner Night

Tuesday, October 1, 2002
8:30 a.m.	Morning Prayer
9:00	Presenter
10:45	Break
11:00	"Full Circle: Personal, Communal and Global" (Most Rev. Frank T. Griswold)
11:30	Expanded Group Conversation with Lunch
1:30 p.m.	"Full Circle" Part Two (Most Rev. Frank T. Griswold)
2:00	Core Group Conversation
3:15	Closing Eucharist
5:30	Transportation
	Community Celebration
6:00	Supper

Appendix B
Cleveland, Ohio

Bishops Present at the Interim Meeting of Fall 2002

Adams III, Gladstone B.
Adams Jr., James M.
Alard, Leopoldo J.
Alexander, John Neil
Anderson, Robert M.
Andrus, Mark
Bainbridge, Harry B.
Bane Jr., David C.
Bartlett Jr., Allen L.
Beckwith, Peter H.
Bennison Jr., Charles E.
Black, William G.
Borsch, Frederick H.
Bowman, David C.
Bruno, J. Jon
Caldwell, Bruce
Cederholm Jr., Roy Frederick
Chane, John B.
Chang, Richard S.O.
Coleridge, Clarence N.
Creighton, Michael W.
Croneberger, John P.
Curry, James Elliot
Daniel III, Clifton
Daniels, Theodore A.
Doss, Joe M.
Duncan II, Philip M.
Duncan Jr., Robert W.
Duracin, Jean Zaché
Ely, Thomas Clark
Epting, C. Christopher
Folts, James E.
Frade, Leopoldo
Garrison, J. Michael
Gepert, Robert
Gibbs Jr., Wendell N.
Gloster, J. Gary
Gray III, Duncan Montgomery
Gray Jr., Francis C.
Gregg, William Otis
Grew II, J. Clark
Griswold, Frank T.
Gulick Jr., Edwin F.
Hampton, Sanford Z.K.
Hargrove Jr., Robert J.
Harris, Barbara C.
Hart, Donald P.
Henderson Jr., Dorsey F.
Herlong, Bertram N.
Herzog, Daniel W.
Hibbs, Robert B.
Holguín, Julio Cesar
Howe, Barry R.
Howe, John W.
Hughes, Gethin B.
Ihloff, Robert W.
Iker, Jack L.
Irish, Carolyn T.
Jacobus, Russell E.
Jecko, Stephen H.
Jefferts Schori, Katharine
Jelinek, James L.
Johnson, Robert H.
Johnson Jr., Robert C.
Jones, David C.
Joslin, David B.
Kelsey, James A.
Kelshaw, Terence
Keyser, Charles L.
Knudsen, Chilton R.
Krotz, James E.
Ladehoff, Robert L.
Lai, David Jung-Hsin
Lamb, Jerry A.
Lee, Peter J.
Leidel Jr., Edwin M.
Lipscomb, John B.
Little II, Edward S.
Louttit, Henry
MacDonald, Mark L.
MacPherson, D. Bruce
Marshall, Paul V.

Matthews, F. Clayton
Maze, Larry E.
McKelvey, Jack M.
Michel, Rodney R.
Moody, Robert M.
Ohl Jr., Charles Wallis
Ottley, James H.
Packard, George E.
Parsley Jr., Henry N.
Payne, Claude E.
Persell, William D.
Plummer, Steven T.
Powell, Neff
Price Jr., Kenneth L.
Putnam, Frederick W.
Rabb, John L.
Ramos-Orench, Wilfrido
Reed, David B.
Rowley Jr., Robert D.
Rowthorn, Jeffery W.
Salmon, Edward L.
Sauls, Stacy F.
Scantlebury, Victor A.
Schofield, John-David M.
Scriven, Henry W.
Scruton, Gordon Paul
Shahan, Robert R.
Shaw III, SSJE, M. Thomas

Shimpfky, Richard L.
Skilton, William J.
Smalley, William E.
Smith, George Wayne
Sterling Sr., William E.
Swenson, Daniel L.
Swing, William E.
Talton, Chester L.
Tennis, Cabell
Theuner, Douglas E.
Thompson Jr., Herbert
Vaché, C. Charles
vonRosenberg, Charles G.
Waggoner, James Edward
Walker Jr., Orris G.
Walmsley, Arthur E.
Waynick, Catherine M.
White, Roger J.
Whitmore, Keith B.
Williams Jr., Arthur B.
Wimberly, Don A.
Winterrowd, William J.
Wolf, Geralyn
Wright, Wayne P.

Appendix C
Cleveland, Ohio

Newly Consecrated Bishops

Bishops who have been consecrated since the Special Meeting of the House of Bishops, held at the Radisson Hotel, Burlington, Vermont, September 20–26, 2001:

Bishop of West Virginia, October 13, 2001
William Michie Klusmeyer (970)
Chief Consecrator: The Presiding Bishop
Co-consecrators: William Dailey Persell
Bishop of Chicago
Robert Poland Atkinson
Bishop of West Virginia, Resigned
Wendell Nathaniel Gibbs, Jr.
Bishop of Michigan
Claude Charles Vaché
Bishop of Southern Virginia, Resigned
James Winchester Montgomery
Bishop of Chicago, Resigned
Ralph William Dunkin
Bishop, West Virginia Synod, ELCA

Bishop of Honduras, October, 20, 2001
Lloyd Emmanuel Allen (971)
Chief Consecrator: James Hamilton Ottley
Bishop of Panama, Resigned
Co-Consecrators: Leopold Frade
Bishop of Southeast Florida
Francis Raymond Lyons III
Bishop of Bolivia
Julio Murray
Bishop of Panama
Sylvestre Donato Romero-Palma
Bishop of Belize

Bishop of Central New York, October 27, 2001
Gladstone Bailey Adams III, (972)
Chief Consecrator: Jack Marston McKelvey
                          Bishop of Rochester
Co-Consecrators: David Bruce Joslin
                          Assisting Bishop of New Jersey
                          Edwin Funsten Gulick, Jr.
                          Bishop of Kentucky
                          Martin deJesús Barahona
                          Bishop of El Salvador
                          David Charles Bowman
                          Assisting Bishop of Central New York
                          Lee M. Miller
                          Bishop, Upstate New York Synod, ELCA

Bishop Suffragan-in-Charge
of the Convocation of American Churches in Europe, November 18, 2001
Pierre Welte Whalon (973)
Chief Consecrator: The Presiding Bishop
Co-Consecrators: John Wadsworth Howe
                          Bishop of Central Florida
                          Jeffery William Rowthorn
                          Bishop-in-Charge
                          Convocation of American Churches in Europe
                          Geoffrey Rowell
                          Bishop of Basingstoke
                          Fernando da Luz Soares
                          Bishop of Portugal
                          Carlos Lopez Lozano
                          Bishop of the Spanish Reformed Church
                          Joachim Vobbe
                          Bishop of Germany, Old Catholic Church

Bishop Suffragan of Alabama, February 7, 2002
Mark Handley Andrus (974)
Chief Consecrator: The Presiding Bishop
Co-Consecrators: Henry Nutt Parsley, Jr.
                          Bishop of Alabama
                          Peter James Lee
                          Bishop of Virginia
                          David Colin Jones
                          Bishop Suffragan of Virginia
                          Creighton Leland Robertson
                          Bishop of South Dakota

Mary Adelia Rosamond McLeod
Bishop of Vermont, Resigned
Furman Charles Stough
Bishop of Alabama, Resigned
Robert Oran Miller
Bishop of Alabama, Resigned
Ronald B. Warren
Bishop, Southeast Synod, ELCA

Bishop Coadjutor of Missouri, March 2, 2002
George Wayne Smith (975)
Chief Consecrator: Joseph Clark Grew
                     Bishop of Ohio
Co-Consecrators: Hays Hamilton Rockwell
                     Bishop of Missouri
                     Carl Christopher Epting
                     Deputy for Ecumenical and Interfaith Relations
                     Philip Hougen
                     Bishop, Southeastern Iowa Synod, ELCA
                     Warren Freiheit
                     Bishop, Central/Southern Illinois Synod, ELCA

Bishop of Western Kansas, March 16, 2002
James Marshall Adams, Jr. (976)
Chief Consecrator: William Edward Smalley
                     Bishop of Kansas
Co-Consecrators: Vernon Edward Strickland
                     Bishop of Western Kansas
                     Russell Edward Jacobus
                     Bishop of Fond du Lac
                     Roger John White
                     Bishop of Milwaukee
                     Dorsey Felix Henderson, Jr.
                     Bishop of Upper South Carolina

Bishop Suffragan of Southern Virginia, April 6, 2002
Carol Joy W.T. Gallagher (977)
Chief Consecrator: Robert Deane Rowley
                     Bishop of Northwestern Pennsylvania
Co-Consecrators: David Conner Bane, Jr.
                     Bishop of Southern Virginia
                     Barbara Clementine Harris
                     Bishop Suffragan of Massachuestts
                     Donald Purple Hart
                     Assistant Bishop of Southern Virginia, Resigned

Wayne Parker Wright
Bishop of Delaware
Edmond Lee Browning
XXIV Presiding Bishop, Resigned
Mark Lawrence MacDonald, TSSF
Bishop of Alaska (Seal)

Bishop Coadjutor of Western Michigan, April 27, 2002
Ronald Gepert (978)
Chief Consecrator: Arthur Benjamin Williams, Jr.
                           Bishop Suffragan of Ohio
Co-Consecrators: Edward Lewis Lee, Jr.
                           Bishop of Western Michigan
                           James Michael Mark Dyer
                           Bishop of Bethlehem, Resigned
                           Robert Deane Rowley, Jr.
                           Bishop of Northwestern Pennsylvania

Bishop of Washington, June 1, 2002
John Bryson Chane (979)
Chief Consecrator: The Presiding Bishop
Co-Consecrators: Jane Holmes Dixon
                           Bishop of Washington, Pro-Tempore
                           Ronald Hayward Haines
                           Bishop of Washington, Resigned
                           Joseph Jon Bruno
                           Bishop of Los Angeles
                           Gethin Benwil Hughes
                           Bishop of San Diego
                           John Shelby Spong
                           Bishop of Newark, Resigned
                           Robert Munro Wolterstorff
                           Bishop of San Diego, Resigned

Newly Received Bishop

Bishops who have been received since the Special Meeting of the House of Bishops, held at The Radisson Hotel, Burlington, Vermont, September 20–26, 2001:

Assistant Bishop of Pittsburgh, September 1, 2002
Henry William Scriven (980-A)

Resignations

Since the Special Meeting of the House of Bishops held at The Radisson Hotel, Burlington, Vermont, September 20–26, 2001, the Secretary received notice of the intent of the following bishops to resign:

September 30, 2001
The Rt. Rev. Martin G. Townsend, Bishop of Easton
September 30, 2001
The Rt. Rev. Joe Morris Doss, Bishop of New Jersey
January 31, 2002
The Rt. Rev. Frederick H. Borsch, Bishop of Los Angeles
February 1, 2002
The Rt. Rev. Vernon E. Strickland, Bishop of Western Kansas
May 13, 2002
The Rt. Rev. Bernardo Merino-Botero, Bishop of Columbia
June 30, 2002
The Rt. Rev. Charles I. Jones, Bishop of Montana
June 30, 2002
The Rt. Rev. Edward L. Lee, Jr., Bishop of Western Michigan
August 31, 2002
The Rt. Rev. Jane Holmes Dixon, Bishop Suffragan of Washington
August 31, 2002
The Rt. Rev. John L. Said, Bishop Suffragan of Southeast Florida

Necrology

Since the Special Meeting of the House of Bishops, held at the Radisson Hotel, Burlington, Vermont, September 20–26, 2001, the following bishops have departed this life:

October 30, 2001
The Rt. Rev. David Rea Cochran
Retired Bishop of Alaska

May 14, 2002
The Rt. Rev. David Henry Lewis, Jr.
Retired Bishop Suffragan of Virginia

May 30, 2002
The Rt. Rev. William Henry Marmion
Retired Bishop of Southwestern Virginia

June 2, 2002
The Rt. Rev. Anselmo Carral-Solar
Retired Bishop of Guatemala

September 7, 2002
The Rt. Rev. George H. Quarterman
Retired Bishop Suffragan of Northwest Texas

Appendix D
Cleveland, Ohio

"Toward Reconciliation in the World"
Draft Document Presented to the House

Since September 11, 2001, the United States and many other nations have engaged in a concerted effort to enhance world security through focused activity against al Qaeda and other terrorist organizations and agents. We have rightly sought to bring to account those who would inflict random acts of violence on others as a means of achieving their particular agenda. The vicious deadly cycle of violent aggression spirals in a seemingly unending pattern and will continue to do so until the cycle is broken.

Thus far, our response as a nation has focused on military actions, enhancing homeland security, and developing a new foreign policy for dealing with the condition in which we find ourselves. We have sought to build relationships with countries through diplomatic work to form a common front against terrorism in an effort to secure ourselves against a repeat of September 11, 2001. Our efforts have met with limited success. There is not consensus at home or abroad with regard to the new Bush administration foreign policy.

At this point, the Bush administration has developed and seeks to implement a policy of pre-emptive war against what it believes to be the clear and present danger of Saddam Hussein and Iraq to the peace and common good of the United States and the world. The development of this foreign policy and its implementation raise profound questions and issues for all of us. For example, how do we determine who or what is in danger? How do we determine the appropriate, proportional response? How do we act in the larger international arena as a world citizen?

As bishops of the Episcopal Church, we affirm our statement of September 25, 2001. We affirm the need to enhance the security of our nation and that of the world. We affirm the decision of us all that those who would wreak the material destruction and human death through acts of violence should and ought to be brought to justice, especially as terrorist acts are frequently perpetrated against innocent men, women, and children. We affirm the decision to rid the world of the horror of terrorism. We grieve the further loss of life to those whom our country must send into harm's way. We grieve for those and for their families and friends.

We believe that we, as Christians, are called to more than to respond appropriately at the level of military responses, however necessary and appropriate they may be. We are called to be people of peace who make peace. We are sent as reconcilers, given by Christ the ministry of reconciliation. The task for us, and for the nation, is not merely to rid the world of the present perpetration of terrorism and other violence and destruction. Our call, and the work for which God equips us in the Spirit is to create a world environment in which the root causes of terrorism are overcome, to do the work of healing and reconciliation that unbinds all God's children and sets us free. The question for us, as Presiding Bishop Griswold has expressed it, is "What is our role in the community of nations? A super power, especially one that declares itself to be 'under God,' must exercise the role of super servant."

This immensely difficult and complex work will require of us commitment, perseverance and time. This work is the foundational work that addresses the condition that foments the anger, hostility, frustration, and hatred that erupt in the violence and destruction and death of war and terrorism. This work is slow, often tedious, and requires profound energy and creativity. The work is that of addressing concretely, the foundations of the relationships among people and nation, of the stewardship of our resources, of the values we hold, of our priorities, of our willingness to think globally, act globally, and to have the inherent connectedness opening all the parts of the created order, especially among people. It means, therefore, to live deeply into all the dimensions of our world effectively, constructively, and creatively.

Therefore, as Church and as individual Christians, we believe and call us and our government to commit to and expend the necessary time, energy, and other resources necessary, and to engage other churches, communities, and nations in order to seek, to develop and to implement strategies, policies and programs which are responsive and appropriate to the pressing needs in the arenas of political stability, economics, education, economic development, health and healthcare, World Bank and IMF policies and practices, environmental care and management, etc.

We believe that unless these fundamental areas are addressed with creativity, the reconciliation and peace of the world will not be possible. Unless the complex issues of human rights, oppression, and freedom are addressed, the human relationship is incapable of sustaining reconciliation and peace will not be possible. Until we rebuild the foundation in ways that respect and honor the diversities of the world, we will not learn how to be at unity and peace with one another. Until the foundations are laid new, the peace and security of the world will be hostage to the inevitability of another September 11th — we will condemn ourselves to live in the tension of anticipation of continued violence and terrorism.

For us Christians, this work means that we must renew our baptismal commitments: to believe in God, the Holy Trinity; to continue in the Apostles' teaching and fellowship; the prayer and the breaking of Bread; to repent and return to the Lord when we sin and seek God's forgiveness; to proclaim the Gospel in word and deed; to seek and serve Christ in all people; to respect the dignity of every human being; and to strive for justice and peace. Thus renewed, this commitment must be daily embodied by us as individuals, as Church, and as nation.

Appendix E
Cleveland, Ohio

A Letter from the House of Bishops to Congress

October 2, 2002

Dear Members of Congress:
The following is a letter written to you from the House of Bishops of the Episcopal Church on October 1 during our fall meeting in Cleveland, Ohio. It is my hope that you will receive this letter in the spirit in which it is offered.
Also included for your information is a listing of all bishops of the Episcopal Church in the United States.
Yours sincerely,
The Most Rev. Frank T. Griswold
Presiding Bishop and Primate

As you begin this critical debate on behalf of the citizens of this country over the resolution to authorize military action against Iraq, we, the bishops of The Episcopal Church, USA, meeting in Cleveland, Ohio, want you to know of our prayers and support as you make this difficult decision, not just for our country, but also for the people of Iraq and the peace of the world. We pray, as well, for members of the armed services and their families in the midst of international crisis and possible military action.

We deeply respect the seriousness of your responsibility to protect the lives of our citizens, and, with you, we condemn the brutality of Saddam Hussein and his regime.

As disciples of Jesus Christ, we abhor violence and war. Our faith requires us to strive always for justice and peace. We believe that restraint and the ongoing commitment to international cooperation are the means toward peace that we all desire.

With you, we recognize the possibility that war is sometimes unavoidable, but we do not believe that war with Iraq can be justified at this time.

Iraq has not attacked the United States.

Our nation has not exhausted all possibilities for a peaceful solution to this potential conflict, including a new vigorous arms inspection regime.

Our nation has not sufficiently garnered world support.

It is highly likely that the consequences of a war with Iraq will not be contained within its borders.

We believe a pre-emptive strike against Iraq, with the overwhelming force such a strike may require to attain an expedient victory, may have many unintended consequences, including unacceptable civilian casualties.

Further, in this instance, we do not support a decision to go to war without clear and convincing evidence of the need for us to defend ourselves against an imminent attack. The wisdom of our own Christian faith, as well as other religious traditions, teaches us to demonstrate the greatest prudence and caution when the lethal force of war is contemplated. We believe that writings on Just War are particularly helpful to our nation's ongoing deliberations. As we search for those responsible for the attacks of September 11, we must encourage such discernment that keeps our society civilized and free.

We stand with other Christian leaders who oppose a pre-emptive strike against Iraq. The leaders of the Evangelical Lutheran Church in America, the Presbyterian Church of the USA, the Orthodox Church in America, The Christian Church (The Disciples of Christ), The United Church of Christ, The African Methodist Episcopal Church, The Anglican Consultative Council, representing 70 million Anglicans around the world, and the United States Conference of Catholic Bishops, have all raised questions about the wisdom and morality of our country's pursuing this course of action.

Over the next weeks, as you debate our possible involvement in a war against Iraq, know that we are praying with you and for you.

The House of Bishops
The Episcopal Church
Cleveland, Ohio
October 1, 2002

MEETING OF THE HOUSE OF BISHOPS 2003

SPECIAL MEETING

Held at
Kanuga Conveference Center

Hendersonville, North Carolina
March 14–20, 2003

SPECIAL MEETING OF THE HOUSE OF BISHOPS
The Kanuga Conference Center
Hendersonville, North Carolina
March 14–20, 2003

FIRST DAY

Monday
March 17, 2003
Second Week of Lent

Call to Order
The House of Bishops met March 17, 2003, at the Kanuga Conference Center, Hendersonville, North Carolina. The Presiding Bishop called the House to order at 2:37 p.m.

The Roll Call
It was moved, seconded, and carried to accept the registration list of bishops for the Spring Meeting as the record of attendance and quorum. The Presiding Bishop recognized Charles Vache, Retired of Southern Virginia (#712) as the senior bishop in attendance at the meeting.

Motion carried

The Reading of the Minutes
It was moved, seconded, and carried that the reading of the minutes of the 2002 Interim Meeting of September 30 and October 1, 2002, be dispensed.

Motion carried

The Presentation of New Members
The Presiding Bishop introduced the new members since the 2002 Interim Meeting of the House of Bishops in Cleveland:
Gayle Harris, Bishop Suffragan of Massachusetts
James "Bud" Shand, Bishop of Easton
Alan Scarfe, Bishop-elect of Iowa.

Committee on the Dispatch of Business
Bishop Price of Southern Ohio presented the agenda for adoption. It was moved and carried that the agenda be adopted as amended with the addition of consideration of a resolution on worship at General Convention and that the Fund Raising Report be presented after the announcements.

Motion carried

Committee on the Resignation of Bishops

Bishop Knudsen of Maine presented the recommendations of their Committee to the Committee on the Rules of Order of the House on the definitions for "Advanced Age, Bodily Infirmity, Office Created by General Convention, and Mission Strategy" and "Honorary Bishops" in Rule 24. Discussion of the report led to the addition of the words, "or a psychiatrist approved by the Presiding Bishop" following "the bishop's physician(s)" at the end of the section on bodily infirmity. The words "at least" were inserted in the final sentence of the section on Mission Strategy after "Suffragan has served." The recommendations will be forwarded to the Committee on the Rules of Order.

The Committee on Resignation of Bishops recommends to the Rules Committee of the House of Bishops the following definitions:

Advanced Age = 62 +

Bodily Infirmity = eligible for a disability retirement from the Church Pension Fund and/or Social Security, or having a physical and/or mental impairment that will result in a disability if the bishop continues in active ministry, as certified by the bishop's physician(s) or a psychiatrist approved by the Presiding Bishop.

Office Created by General Convention = a ministry funded by the General Convention budget and approved by the Presiding Bishop.

Mission Strategy = to allow the election of an indigenous clergy of a non-domestic diocese as bishop; to allow a diocese to implement a new mission strategy as determined by the Presiding Bishop; and to allow a transition in Episcopal leadership after a Bishop Diocesan or Bishop Suffragan has served at least ten (10) or more years.

Honorary Bishop = from time to time, upon 30 days notice, a 2/3 vote of the House of Bishops will confer upon a Bishop status as an Honorary member.

The Rt. Rev. Chilton R. Knudsen, Chair
The Rt. Rev. C. Wallis Ohl, Jr.
The Rt. Rev. Neff Powell, Secretary
The Rt. Rev. Robert Shahan
The Rt. Rev. Stacy Sauls, Vice-Chair
The Rt. Rev. Jean Zaché Duracin

Committee on Pastoral Development

Bishop Warner of Olympia presented a report on the feedback from the expanded group discussions of the House on the Process for Accountability, and outlined the next steps for the Committee on Pastoral Development regarding the process. Bishop Matthews of the Office for Pastoral Development addressed the definition of covenant, the issues of confidentiality versus security, and the use of the Step One of the Process. Bishop Warner concluded the report by affirming the work of the spouses on the committee.

The African Chaplaincy Program
Benjamin Muskoe-Lubege from the Church Center staff was introduced by the Presiding Bishop. Father Muskoe-Lubege described his role as staff officer and resource to dioceses before introducing the Rev. Gordon Okunsanya, Chaplain to Africa Expatriates. Father Okunsanya outlined the benefits of the chaplaincy to ECUSA and African peoples in the United States. The members of the House were invited to offer comments on the Memorandum of Understanding on the Chaplaincy to Africa Expatriates.

Committee on Anti-Racism
Bishop Rabb of Maryland described the work of the committee and his vision for addressing the sin of racism. After introducing committee members, the objectives of the committee were outlined: the review and possible update of the 1994 Pastoral on the Sin of Racism; conduct personal evaluations that will lead to actions against racism with timelines; conduct anti-racism training and the report to the General Convention; and interact with the Interim Body on Racism. A video on racism will be shown at the General Convention.

Mind of the House Resolution on the Exploitation of Children and Youth
Bishop Gregg of Eastern Oregon introduced a resolution on the exploitation of children and youth. The resolution was result of the pre-meeting workshop organized by the Office on Pastoral Development. The resolution was moved, seconded and carried as presented.

Mind of the House Resolution
Brothers and Sister in Christ:
We are painfully aware of the fact that the problems of sexual abuse of children are not confined to the Roman Catholic Church. It is a major problem in all child-serving organizations and agencies; it is a problem in the Episcopal Church. The basic statistics of the general population are these: 1 in 8 males and 1 in 4 females are molested before they reach 18. Of reported cases in the general population, 60% of abusers are known to the victim, 30% are family/relative, and 10% are strangers. We, the undersigned members of this House, bring to you a proposal as a constructive response to a profound theological, pastoral, moral, and social matter. We are persuaded that the times and circumstances demand of us as Bishops of this Church to articulate a clear and firm stand that we support with clear and firm policies and procedures for the life of this faith community. The urgent issue is our continuing to work toward creating and sustaining a Church in which all God's children are secure and free from the threat and realities of sexual misconduct of all kinds, especially our children and youth. We commit ourselves to continue to lead the Church into being healthy and safe communities of God's people.

Be it Resolved, That the House of Bishops, through the Presiding Bishop, immediately create and charge a working group from this House to partner with the Church Pension Group (CPG) and the Church Insurance Corporation (CIC) and other agencies and appropriate organizations to develop a statement of general expectations[1] of behavior in this Church for ministry with children and youth be clergy, lay employees, and volunteers.[2]

Be it further Resolved, That the general expectations address these five areas:

1. Thorough screening and selection of clergy, lay employees and volunteers who work with children;
2. Articulation of clear behavioral standards for interactions between clergy, lay employees, volunteers and children;
3. Careful monitoring of programs and interaction with children and youth;
4. Provision for education and training of clergy, lay employees and volunteers for work with children and youth; and
5. Guidelines for responding to concerns about behavior or allegations of abuse.

Be it further Resolved, That while the church-wide expectations are being developed for implementations, we, the Bishops of this Church, do commit ourselves to develop and implement policies, procedures, and expectations for behaviors of clergy, lay employees, and volunteers working with children and youth in our dioceses. We commit to reviewing our current policies, procedures, and practices for adequacy and appropriateness, and to revise as may be needed. We commit to working together to provide appropriate training, education, and program/materials support for our dioceses in the context of the five areas of the second Resolve, above. We commit to be accountable to one another by reporting on our progress to the Presiding Bishop who will in turn report to the House of Bishops at our Spring, 2004, meeting.

Be it further Resolved, That the House of Bishops charge the Pastoral Letter Committee to write a Pastoral Letter to the Church, to be read in every parish, mission, preaching station, and church-related institutions which work with youth and children, on the prevention and response to child sexual abuse, and that this Letter address this issue from its moral and theological dimensions, evangelical implications, mission (God's Project), reconciliation, and our commitment to a healthy and secure environment for all persons, free from sexual misconduct, and

---

[1] It is the intention and expectation that these expectations be specific enough to serve as clear directions and guidelines, but general enough that each diocese would expand upon or develop them in terms of the specific content of policies and procedures and implementation according to the particularities of the diocese.

[2] This work is to include preparation of such resolutions to General Convention as may be necessary and appropriate, as well as coordinating this work with the appropriate legislative bodies and processes.

articulate the values of this Church and our expectations of ourselves as grounded in the Gospel, Baptism, the Ordinal, and moral commitment and leadership. And that this Letter be brought to the House of Bishops at the 74th General Convention (2003) for approval.

Be it further Resolved, That the House of Bishops, through the Presiding Bishop, appoint a separate working group to identify and make available resource for training and educating Bishops and clergy to respond to victims for the post-abuse care (pastoral, spiritual, therapeutic,) nurture, and healing of self and with others for the victim, family, and friends of the victim.

Motion carried
Resolution adopted

Mind of the House Resolution on General Convention Worship
The resolution on General Convention Worship presented by Bishop Roskam of New York and Bishop Howe of Central Florida was moved, seconded and carried.

Mind of the House Resolution
Resolved, That recognizing that Convention eucharists are the principal non-legislative gathering of the whole body of Convention and are for the express purpose of common worship, and in keeping with a spirit of collegiality, the bishops of this house agree to neither schedule nor encourage to be scheduled, nor attend nor celebrate any eucharist held at the same time as main Convention eucharists.

Motion carried
Resolution adopted

The Cambridge Consultation
Bishop Rowthorn distributed materials on the Cambridge Consultation and provided additional background information about the program.

The College of Bishops
Bishop Donovan announced that he had resigned as the coordinator for the College of Bishops. Bishop Borsch will fill the vacant position and be assisted by Carol Thomson.

The National Arctic Wildlife Refuge
After an update by Bishop MacDonald of Alaska, a resolution reaffirming the support of the House of Bishops of the Gwich'in People in their opposition to oil exploration in the Arctic National Wildlife Refuge was moved, seconded and carried.

Resolved, That the House of Bishops of the Episcopal Church, at its meeting on March 17th, 2003, at Kanuga Conference Center, North Carolina, reaffirms its support of the Gwich'in People in their opposition to oil exploration drilling in the Arctic National Wildlife Refuge. We urge The United States Senate and House of Representatives to reject any proposal that would permit oil exploration and drilling in the Arctic National Wildlife Refuge.

Motion carried
Resolution adopted

Fund Raising Survey Report

The Presiding Bishop introduced Dr. Kirk Hadaway, Director of Research at the Episcopal Church Center, and noted the importance of data collection as the first step of a capital campaign. Dr. Hadaway reported on the results of the fund raising survey from the eighty-two responding dioceses. In addition, he offered additional comments and observations about the data collected.

The Presiding Bishop reflected on future missional fund raising opportunities: seminary training for small church ministry, a Young Adult Service Corps, a long term development strategy for the Church, and Planned Giving.

Miscellaneous Announcements

Bishop Salmon of South Carolina informed the House about the water missions project. Bishops will receive a mailing from him with more information.

Bishop Scantlebury invited the House to discuss mission strategies in ethnic ministry at a future meeting.

Bishop Robert Anderson expressed appreciation on behalf of the House to Bishop Donovan for his ministry as the coordinator of the College for Bishops.

The Secretary noted that copies of the Memorials for Ned Cole and Hal Raymond Gross were available on the distribution table outside of the meeting room.

Adjournment

At 4:12 p.m., it was moved, seconded and carried that the meeting of the House be adjourned.

Motion carried

SECOND DAY

Tuesday
March 18, 2003
Second Week of Lent

Call to Order

The House of Bishops met March 18, 2003, at the Kanuga Conference Center, Hendersonville, North Carolina. The Presiding Bishop called the House to order at 4:50 p.m.

Theology Committee

Bishop Parsley of Alabama chaired the reporting from expanded group discussion of the report of the Theology Committee of the House of Bishops of the Episcopal Church, entitled, "The Gift of Sexuality: A Theological Perspective."

Bishop Little moved a resolution that the House receives the report of the Theology Committee. Bishop Jelineck asked that an amendment be added to express the appreciation of the House for the work of the Committee. His amendment was received as a friendly amendment by Bishop Little. Bishop Waynick of Indianapolis moved that "in all points" be added to the original resolution after "Though it does not reflect." The amendment carried. The amended resolution was adopted by the House of Bishops.

Motion carried
Resolution adopted

It was moved, seconded and carried that the House of Bishops request the Theology Committee to continue its work toward a fuller theology of body, sex, and sexuality, to be presented to the House of Bishops at a future meeting.

Motion carried

Pastoral Letter
Bishop Sisk of the Pastoral Letter Committee read "In the Shadow of War," a Pastoral Letter prepared by the Committee. The Pastoral Letter was adopted by the House with amendments. The sixth paragraph is amended to read, "In all times and circumstances, our faith is set upon the firm foundation of the love of Christ. We reaffirm our confidence that "neither death nor life...nor anything else in all creation, will be able to separate us from the love of God in Christ Jesus our Lord." (Romans 8:38–39). The page number in the Book of Common Prayer is to be inserted at the end of the collect.

Covenant for General Convention
Bishop Matthews reviewed the covenant adopted by the House of Bishops at the 2000 Spring Meeting of the House to form the basis of our preparation for and conduct at the 2000 General Convention in Denver. It was moved, seconded and carried that the covenant be adopted by the House for the 2003 General Convention in Minneapolis.

Motion carried

Adjournment
It was moved, seconded and carried that the meeting of the House of Bishops adjourn at 5:05 p.m.

Motion carried

Submitted by, Richard S.O. Chang, Secretary of the House of Bishops
Certified by John L. Rabb, Chair, Committee on Certification of Minutes

Appendix A
Hendersonville, North Carolina

Meeting Agenda

Monday, March 17 and Tuesday, March 18, 2003
The Call to Order
The Roll Call
The Minutes of the 2002 Interim Meeting
Presentation of New Members
Communications from the Presiding Bishop
Report of the Committee on Dispatch of Business
Reports of Committees of the House of Bishops
    Committee on Resignation of Bishops
    Committee on Pastoral Development
Other Reports
    Nigerian/African Chaplaincy Program
    Anti-Racism Committee
    Child AbuseWorkshop
    Resolution Fund Raising Survey Report
Announcements
Adjournment

Appendix B
Hendersonville, North Carolina

Bishops Present at the Interim Meeting of March 2003

Ackerman, Keith L.
Adams III, Gladstone B.
Adams Jr., James M.
Alexander, John Neil
Allen, Lloyd E.
Alvarez, David
Anderson, Robert M.
Andrus, Mark H.
Bainbridge, Harry B.
Bane Jr., David C.
Bartlett Jr., Allen L.
Beckwith, Peter H.
Benna, David J.
Bennison Jr., Charles E.
Bowman, David C.
Bruno, J. Jon
Buchanan, John C.
Caldwell, Bruce
Carranza-Gomez, Sergio
Cederholm Jr., Roy Frederick
Chane, John B.
Chang, Richard S.O.
Charleston, Steven
Coleridge, Clarence N.
Creighton, Michael W.
Croneberger, John P.
Curry, James Elliot
Curry, Michael B.
Daniel III, Clifton
Daniels, Theodore A.
Donovan, Herbert A.
Duncan II, Philip M.
Duracin, Jean-Zaché
Duque, Francisco
Duvall, Charles E.
Dyer, James Mark
Ely, Thomas Clark
Epting, C. Christopher
Fairfield, Andrew
Folts, James E.
Frade, Leopoldo

Gallagher, Carol J.
Garrison, J. Michael
Gepert, Robert
Gibbs Jr., Wendell N.
Gloster, J. Gary
Gray III, Duncan Montgomery
Gray Jr., Francis C.
Gregg, William Otis
Grew II, J. Clark
Griswold, Frank T.
Gulick Jr., Edwin F.
Harris, Gayle
Harris, Rogers
Henderson Jr., Dorsey F.
Herlong, Bertram N.
Herzog, Daniel W.
Hibbs, Robert B.
Holguín, Julio Cesar
Howe, Barry R.
Howe, John W.
Hughes, Gethin B.
Ihloff, Robert W.
Iker, Jack L.
Jacobus, Russell E.
Jecko, Stephen H.
Jefferts Schori, Katharine
Jelinek, James L.
Jenkins, Charles
Johnson, Don E.
Johnson, Robert H.
Joslin, David B.
Kelsey, James A.
Keyser, Charles L.
Klusmeyer, W. Michie
Knudsen, Chilton R.
Ladehoff, Robert L.
Lai, David Jung-Hsin
Lamb, Jerry A.
Lee, Peter J.
Leidel Jr., Edwin M.
Lipscomb, John B.

Little II, Edward S.
Louttit Jr, Henry
MacDonald, Mark L.
MacPherson, D. Bruce
Marble, Alfred C.
Matthews, F. Clayton
Maze, Larry E.
McKelvey, Jack M.
Michel, Rodney R.
Moody, Robert M.
Ottley, James H.
Packard, George E.
Parsley Jr., Henry N.
Payne, Claude E.
Persell, William D.
Plummer, Steven T.
Powell, Neff
Price Jr., Kenneth L.
Rabb, John L.
Ramos-Orench, Wilfrido
Reed, David B.
Roskam, Catherine
Rowley Jr., Robert D.
Rowthorn, Jeffery W.
Salmon, Edward L.
Sauls, Stacy F.
Scarfe, Alan
Scantlebury, Victor
Scriven, Henry W.
Shahan, Robert R.
Shand, James

Shaw III, SSJE, M. Thomas
Shimpfky, Richard L.
Sims, Bennett
Sisk, Mark S.
Skilton, William J.
Smalley, William E.
Smith, Andrew D.
Smith, G. Wayne
Stanton, James M.
Swing, William E.
Talton, Chester L.
Tharp, Robert G.
Theuner, Douglas E.
Thompson Jr., Herbert
Vaché, C. Charles
vonRosenberg, Charles G.
Waggoner, James Edward
Walker Jr., Orris G.
Warner, Vincent W.
Waynick, Catherine M.
Whalon, Pierre
Whitmore, Keith B.
Williams Jr., Arthur B.
Williams, Huntington
Wimberly, Don A.
Winterrowd, William J.
Wright, Wayne P.

Appendix C
Hendersonville, North Carolina

Newly Consecrated Bishops

Bishops who have been consecrated since the Special Meeting of the House of Bishops, held at Cleveland, Ohio, September 30-October 1, 2002:

Bishop Suffragan of Massachusetts, January 18, 2003
Gayle Elizabeth Harris (981)
    Chief Consecrator: Arthur Benjamin Williams, Jr.
        Bishop Suffragan of Ohio, Resigned
    Co-Consecrators: Marvil Thomas Shaw, S.S.J.E.
        Bishop of Massachusetts
        Barbara Clementine Harris
        Bishop Suffragan of Massachusetts, Resigned
        Roy Frederick Cederholm, Jr.
        Bishop Suffragan of Massachusetts
        Jack Marston McKelvey
        Bishop of Rochester
        Frederick Houk Borsch
        Bishop of Los Angeles, Resigned

Bishop of Easton, January 25, 2003
James Joseph Shand (982)
    Chief Consecrator: Robert Wilkes Ihloff
        Bishop of Maryland
    Co-Consecrators: Martin Gough Townsend
        Bishop of Easton, Resigned
        Elliott Lorenz Sorge
        Bishop of Easton, Resigned
        Robert William Duncan
        Bishop of Pittsburgh
        Charles Lindsay Longest
        Bishop Suffragan of Maryland, Resigned

Resignations

Since the Special Meeting of the House of Bishops held at Cleveland, Ohio, September 30–October 1, 2002, the Secretary received notice of the intent of the following bishops to resign:

November 1, 2002
The Rt. Rev. Robert J. Hargrove, Bishop of Western Louisiana
November 1, 2002
The Rt. Rev. Barbara C. Harris, Bishop Suffragan of Massachusetts
December 31, 2002
The Rt. Rev. Arthur B. Williams, Bishop Suffragan of Ohio

Necrology

Since the Special Meeting of the House of Bishops held at Cleveland, Ohio, September 30–October 1, 2002, the following bishops have departed this life:

October 13, 2002
The Rt. Rev. Hal Raymond Gross
Retired Bishop Suffragan of Oregon
November 11, 2002
The Rt. Rev. Harold S. Jones
Retired Bishop Suffragen of South Dakota
December 16, 2002
The Rt. Rev. Ned Cole, Jr.
Retired Bishop of Central New York
February 11, 2003
The Rt. Rev. Reginald Gooden
Retired Bishop of the Republic of Panama

Appendix D
Hendersonville, North Carolina

Process for Accountability
By the House through the Advisory Committee
Created by House of Bishops General Rule of Order XXVI[1]

In the case of alleged breaches of collegiality and church order that threaten to impact the larger Church, the Council of Advice, with the support of the Office of Pastoral Development, shall implement a process for engaging in conciliation among bishops.

1. Any Bishop may request a process of conciliation by the Council of Advice by a written request to the Presiding Bishop or to the President or Vice President of his/her Province (e.g., the Bishop of the Province who serves on the Council of Advice).
2. The Presiding Bishop, the Chair of the Council of Advice, the Bishop for the Office of Pastoral Development, and the Presiding Bishop's Chancellor shall review the issue(s) brought forward and assist the Presiding Bishop in determining whether or not the matter should be brought to the Council of Advice or to be addressed in a different way.
3. If a matter is referred to it by the Presiding Bishop, the Council of Advice shall determine a process by which the parties will be asked to share the history, facts, and perceived issues of the presenting situation. Such process may include, but not be limited to, a request that one or more of the Bishops in question meet with the Council of Advice (as a group or a sub-group) or be visited by one or more members of the Council of Advice.
4. The Council of Advice shall develop further steps following any such interviews that are consonant with a conciliation model, in which specific actions and accountability measures will be made clear by the Council of Advice.
5. The Council of Advice, in consultation with the bishops involved, shall determine an appropriate response to the presenting situation, including options for further conciliation, formal mediation, or voluntary binding arbitration.
6. In order to hold accountable the Bishops involved in this process, the Council of Advice shall, at a meeting of the House of Bishops, share, to the extent not confidential, the specific facts of the presenting situation, the actions taken, the results accomplished and any steps that remain to be taken.

---

[1] There shall be an Advisory Committee [commonly known as the Presiding Bishop's Council of Advice], composed of Bishops who are the Presidents or Vice Presidents of each Province, which will act as an advisory council to the Presiding Bishop between meetings of the House of Bishops. The committee shall elect its own officers. (House of Bishops General Rule of Order XXVI)

7. The agenda at each meeting of the House of Bishops, other than during its triennial meeting of the General Convention, shall include reports by the Council of Advice and time for appropriate House of Bishops conversation groups to reflect on the presenting situations pending before the Council of Advice. Such discussions are intended to be conducted without reference to personalities and without attempts to solve the issues involved.
8. Throughout this process, the Presiding Bishop shall be kept informed of the work done by the Council of Advice.
9. To prepare the Council of Advice for this work, the Office of Pastoral Development shall make arrangements for the members to receive conciliation/mediation training at the beginning of each Triennium (or at another time if needed) by a professionally-trained person who will be kept on retainer, to advise and train the Council as needed.

For the House of Bishop's Pastoral Development Committee
By the Rt. Rev'd. Jack M. McKelvey
25 November 2002

Adapted by the Rt. Rev'd. F. Clayton Matthews
Following the December meeting of the Presiding Bishop's Council of Advice and subsequent editing by the Presiding Bishop's Chancellor

Appendix E
Hendersonville, North Carolina

The Gift of Sexuality: A Theological Perspective

Report of the House of Bishops Theology Committee
Mind of the House Resolution

1. Preface

[1.0] The House of Bishops, meeting in the 73rd General Convention of the Episcopal Church, resolved to continue to study and be in conversation about issues of human sexuality. The resolution called for the Theology Committee of the House of Bishops, in consultation with the Pastoral Development Committee, to prepare a report on the matter, in the hope that a Mind of the House resolution will result.

[1.1] The following paper is the product of an eighteen-month study undertaken by the Theology Committee. The House of Bishops Theology Committee consists of six bishops and seven academic theologians of the Episcopal Church who represent diverse theological viewpoints. The Committee has not attempted to consider exhaustively all the issues related to the subject of human sexuality, but has focused primarily on those brought before the 73rd General Convention. The scope of this paper, therefore, has not included consideration of bisexual and transgendered persons or the broader range of heterosexuality. It has been our special concern to encourage the Church to think about how disagreement over issues of human sexuality may become open to God's grace.

[1.2] In our choice of language and approach we have attempted to respect the dignity of all persons whose lives and faith are affected by the complex subject of human sexuality. We have been sensitive to the cross-cultural issues of the Anglican Communion of which we are an integral part. For instance, we have consciously chosen to speak of "homosexual persons" rather than the self-appellation of "gay men and lesbians" as widely used in the United States of America. We have met in the context of corporate worship and prayer and have held our questions before God for guidance. We have sought wisdom from Scripture, reason, and tradition. We have been sustained by our mutual faith in Jesus Christ and our commitment to God's mission of reconciliation in the Church and the world.

[1.3] We offer this work to the House of Bishops and the Church, to the glory of God and in faith that, as our Lord promised, the Holy Spirit continues to guide the Church into all truth (John 16:13).

2. Introduction

[2.0] The Episcopal Church in the United States, the worldwide Anglican Communion, and many other Christian Churches and other faith traditions, are engaged in a debate over issues surrounding human sexuality. Our age has experienced new challenges in the understanding of the meaning of sexuality and its ordering for the good of persons and society. Scientific research into the complexities of human sexual behavior and technologies such as birth control and in vitro fertilization are changing how many in our world view human sexuality. We believe sexuality is one of God's wonderful, complex, confusing, and, sometimes, dangerous gifts. At the same time, we have been made freshly aware of how sexuality can be cheapened and exploited in human society and made an occasion of sin, hurt, and disorder, rather than the blessing God intends it to be.

[2.1] One of the more challenging areas of human sexuality in our Church is homosexuality. A certain percentage of human beings experience and understand themselves to be homosexually oriented. Homosexual persons are increasingly visible in our society, our churches, and our communities, bringing particular challenges and gifts to Christian ethical and theological understanding.

[2.2] The Christian community, from generation to generation, must address the new spiritual and moral concerns that emerge in the experience and understanding of God's people. The right ordering of human sexual behavior has always been an aspect of the Jewish and Christian visions of the good for human life and society. In relation to new and emerging learning about the experience of homosexually-oriented persons, our Church especially struggles with two related questions: (1) Is it ever appropriate to pronounce the Church's blessing on same-gender relationships as we do on heterosexual marriages and, if so, under what conditions? (2) Is it ever appropriate to ordain non-celibate homosexual persons, and thereby commend them as "wholesome examples" to the Church and society, and, if so, under what conditions?

3. The Theological Context

[3.0] Before addressing issues of homosexuality directly, it is important to reiterate the context within which this debate is taking place, namely that of Christian theology. Christian theology seeks to discern and articulate the grace and truth of God revealed in Jesus Christ and to guide the Church in mission. God, whom we know as Father, Son, and Holy Spirit, has lovingly created the world and all that is therein. Human beings are graciously created in the divine image (Gen. 1:26a), but we have fallen into sin and fail to live into the fullness of this gift and calling. In his life, death, resurrection, and ascension, Jesus Christ, the incarnate Son of God, has restored us to unity with God and each other and calls us to become agents of reconciliation (2 Cor. 5:18). Empowered by the Holy Spirit, we are called to grow into, rejoice in, and herald God's grace for all creation.

[3.1] We believe the Old and New Testaments are the revealed Word of God and contain all things necessary to salvation. We further believe that the Apostles and Nicene Creeds are enduring statements of the essentials of the Christian faith and express our basic beliefs about God and God's saving work. The truth of the Creeds is further expressed in the teaching, ascetical discipline, and ordering of the Church in its pastoral ministry. The Creeds and the great Ecumenical Councils of the Church thus help us to interpret and live into the saving story of Scripture. They shape the inherited faith of the Church in which we stand as Anglicans.

[3.2] In baptism all Christians are born anew by water and the Spirit (John 3:5), incorporated into the Body of Christ, and made part of the Church's disciplined communal life of worship and witness. Theology is the way in which we speak of the mystery of God and express the faith of the Church. Theology is both derived from and informs our common life in prayer and sacrament. As we pray so we believe, and as we believe so we pray.

[3.3] As Christians, we seek to hold all our thoughts before God for guidance and blessing. We know this is especially important in times of intense disagreement. We pray for God's wisdom, for the continual conversion and illumination of our minds and hearts. St. Paul teaches that the wisdom of God is the great reversal of strength and weakness, as the world understands these (1 Cor. 1:27–30). Political, military, economic, and social power often bespeak spiritual weakness. God's wisdom and strength is displayed in the humility of the Incarnation and cross. The cross unites enemies (Eph. 2:15–16) and reconciles those who are separated and divided by difference. Enmity and division ill befit the Church, and weaken its ministry and service to God's mission.

4. The Complex Gift of Human Sexuality

[4.0] Sexuality is a fundamental and complex aspect of human nature, which we both use and abuse. As Christians we believe it is part of God's good creation and intended to be a source of blessing and joy for human beings. We also believe sexual desire and behavior can be an occasion of sin leading to personal unhappiness and social disorder.

[4.1] The links between love and sexual pleasure testify to the way in which sexuality blesses human intimacy. Sexual intimacy has a public and social dimension as well. When healthy and well-ordered, our sexuality and sexual expressions contribute to the health and stability of individuals and society. Levels of sexuality and intimacy are factors in all human relationships and receive a range of expressions along a spectrum of relationships, from friendship to family in its various configurations. Within the context of marriage, healthy sexual intimacy supports the couple and the possibility of children and their care and nurture.

[4.2] Yet this great and mysterious gift is often the cause of pain to individuals and suffering throughout society. Human beings are most vulnerable in sexually intimate relationships. Our sexual lives can be very fragile and complex. When disordered, sexual behavior can destabilize human society and become a means of exploitation and damage. The staggering divorce rate in the United States, the proliferation of serial marriages, and the increase of promiscuity, especially among the young, attest to the varied struggles many experience around sexuality.

[4.4] Holy Scripture teaches that God gave sex as one of the means for married persons to share themselves with each other (1 Cor. 7:3–5); for procreation (Gen. 1:28); and to be an icon, on the human level, of the relationships between God and the people of Israel, and Christ and the Church (Eph. 5:25–33).

[4.5] We also recognize there is a range of sexual identities among human beings, and a portion of the population experiences itself as having a homosexual orientation. As Christians, we affirm that persons of all sexual orientations are created in the image of God, and they are full members of the human family. The Church vigorously denounces discrimination and violence based on sexual orientation, and we call upon all members of our society, and especially members of the body of Christ, to honor their baptismal vow to respect the full humanity and dignity of every human being (BCP 305).

[4.6] If we have correctly discerned God's purpose in giving us the gift of human sexuality, and if there are those both within and outside of the Church who experience themselves as exclusively homosexual in their sexual orientation, difficult questions inevitably arise as to what patterns of sexual intimacy are most congruent with the holiness of God's self-giving life. In particular, many are asking, with attendant pastoral concern, whether some forms of homosexual activity might be open to God's blessing in ways the Church has not previously recognized. Does the Church remain persuaded that all expressions of homosexual intimacy are sinful, or are there conditions under which we might be able to recognize that intimacy as a source of God's blessing, just as is true in some, though not all, expressions of heterosexual intimacy?

[4.9] These questions are controversial in part because they challenge the Church's traditional understanding of human sexuality which can be summarized as follows: Holy Scripture nowhere condones homosexual practice; in fact, a few passages of Hebrew Scripture and of letters of Paul explicitly proscribe homosexual acts; marriage is defined as the joining together of a man and a woman; marriage is the only appropriate setting for genital sexual intimacy; the norm for singleness, as for marriage, is chastity; but in the case of singleness that norm means abstinence.

5. Disagreement and Division

[5.0] The Episcopal Church, and the larger Anglican Communion, belongs to the tradition of the one, holy, catholic, and apostolic Church, and we are thereby bound by the decisions of the first Four Ecumenical Councils. These decided the Trinitarian identity of the one God, Father, Son and Holy Spirit, Creator of heaven and earth; and the full humanity and full divinity of Christ. These two great doctrines anchor the Church in orthodoxy. As Anglicans we further believe Christian unity is grounded in the principles of the Chicago-Lambeth Quadrilateral (BCP 876–878). It is our conviction that only those issues that undermine these foundational doctrines and commitments should constitute grounds for separation within the Church.

[5.1] We are aware, of course, that many other matters over the long course of Church history have in fact divided the Body of Christ. In many cases institutional arrogance, corruption, or timidity have underlain Church fracture. Other instances of Church division have been highly principled, including some over doctrinal issues that were never universally or even generally agreed upon at any council or public synod. Often such divisions are framed as a necessary pursuit of holiness.

[5.2] Nevertheless, authentic fidelity to Christ cannot posit the Church's unity and holiness over against one another, for they are integrally related marks of Christ's Body and only flourish as they are held together. It is a serious question whether the unity and catholicity of Christ's Body can ever rightly be held over against its holiness or apostolicity and vice versa. In other words, the holiness of the Church cannot be received from God and exercised apart from the continual conversion to Christ that the unity of the Church calls forth from us all. Apart from an abiding commitment to remain with one another in Christ, the desired holiness of one position or another may tend to fall into exclusivity and self-righteousness. Conversely, apart from a faithful desire to seek the holiness and moral goodness of Christ's Body, an intention to uphold the unity of the Church may lapse into unrooted toleration.

[5.3] We believe that disunity over issues of human sexuality in general, and homosexuality in particular, needs to be taken seriously by all members of the Church. And diverse opinion needs to be respected. But we do not believe these should be Church-dividing issues.

[5.4] There are those among us who believe that Scripture and/or the order of nature render all homosexual behavior intrinsically sinful, and therefore the normalization of any homosexual intimacy in liturgical and sacramental practice would so radically depart from the Church's historic teaching and practice that it would cut to the very integrity of the biblical historic Faith. Even though homosexuality has never been the subject of an ecumenical council or the cause of Church division, normalizing any homosexual behavior, and thus, arguably, changing the Church's understanding and teaching regarding marriage and sexual propriety, would be considered by some due cause for delegitimizing such a Church.

[5.5] There are others among us who believe that statements of Jesus and admonitions of Paul which call all within Christian community to lives of mutual upbuilding and fidelity open the door to reevaluating at least committed homosexual relationships. For some, the refusal to normalize those homosexual relationships that are intended to be "life-long committed relationships...characterized by fidelity, monogamy, mutual affection and respect, careful, honest communication and the holy love which enables those in such relationships to see in each other the image of God" (Resolution D039, from the 73rd General Convention) is the perpetuation of discrimination, prejudice, and injustice.

[5.6] Many Christians believe homosexual relationships as described in 5.5 to be holy and to indicate God's blessing on their unions. The Church's unwillingness to bless such unions or to accept individuals in such unions as appropriate candidates for ordination is seen as an oppressive betrayal of Christ's love and the denial of the unfolding of the Holy Spirit.

[5.7] The challenge we now face is how to maintain the unity of the Church in the face of such intense disagreement. Despite the common Faith that makes us one, we confess that on the issues surrounding human sexuality just now, we are of different minds. The depth and complexity of human sexuality are reflected in the multiple understandings and interpretations held by thoughtful people. There are at least three major perspectives: (1) Homosexuality is constitutional, i.e., an unchangeable given. Some believe this form of sexuality is a gift of God and therefore good in and of itself. As a gift of God, homosexuality is to be accepted and affirmed by those of this sexuality and those who support them. Others argue that even if a given, homosexual behavior is nonetheless an offense against nature and may be contrary to the will of God. (2) Homosexuality is a psychological reality that might be changed through therapy. (3) Homosexuality is a social construct of gender identification and therefore malleable.

[5.8] Regardless of the origin of homosexuality, there are at least two contrary positions regarding homosexual intimacy: (1) Homosexual genital expression is always sinful and is not acceptable within the Christian ethic. (2) Some homosexual genital expression is legitimate and Christians should lend pastoral support for such relationships. Neither the complexities nor the issues end here.

[5.9] Some understand the conflict sparked around homosexuality to be a matter of justice calling for redress of grievances and violence suffered by homosexual persons at the hands of both Church and society. Others see it as a pastoral issue, calling for compassion. Some believe that the intent of long-term faithful relationships among homosexual persons should be adequate grounds for normalizing them. For others intent does not address the issue. In a world in which all things have been corrupted by sin, neither our affections nor our intentions alone can be dispositive. Some see questions about homosexuality linked to questions about heterosexuality, while others object vigorously to making such connections. Some believe there is in homosexuality an inherent disposition to promiscuity, which undermines any argument that such unions should be blessed. Others are offended at this suggestion, and point to the high rate of heterosexual promiscuity in reply. Still others feel the Church is paralyzed by debates about this issue which distract us from pressing needs for attention to mission. Others would say this is an integral part of our mission.

[5.10] To overcome the painful disagreement present among us over these matters some believe compromise is necessary to preserve the unity and peace of the Church, while others believe that compromise with the truth as they understand it is not possible.

6. Questions about Same-Sex Blessings

[6.0] The question before the Church is whether some homosexual relationships are, like some heterosexual relationships, open to the blessing of God through the Church, or are they always inherently sinful? And for those who believe that at least certain homosexual practices are sinful, the question must be raised, "how sinful"?

[6.1] We have insisted there are no doctrinal grounds for inhospitality to homosexual persons as members of the Church. What then are the grounds for refusing to bless the relationships of homosexual couples who are prepared to commit themselves to the same standards and vows as do heterosexual couples?

[6.2] The Episcopal Church is committed "to support" those whose relationships of sexual intimacy are other than those of marriage. As noted above, it calls all such persons, whether heterosexual or homosexual, to standards of life-long commitment, "characterized by fidelity, monogamy, mutual affection and respect, careful, honest communication" and the kind of "holy love which enables those in such relationships to see in each other the image of God" (Resolution D039, from the 73rd General Convention). The question remains, does extending this support include pronouncing the Church's blessing on such relationships?

[6.5] Liturgy provides cohesion for the Anglican Communion, and it is through our liturgies that we define what we most deeply believe as Christians. Because at this time we are nowhere near consensus in the Church regarding the blessing of homosexual relationships, we cannot recommend authorizing the development of new rites for such blessings.

[6.6] For these reasons, we urge the greatest caution as the Church continues to seek the mind of Christ in these matters. This will require a diligent and perhaps painful willingness on the part of the Church to engage in focused conversation among all of us, and openness to the guidance and movement of the Holy Spirit. We urge the Church to cherish all members of the Body of Christ without fail, and to seek always for the fullness and diversity of that unity we are called to in Christ (Rom. 12:4–8).

[6.7] We call upon the Church to develop and provide pastoral support and spiritual guidance and specifically to provide prayers as we wrestle and discern the will of God with regard to human sexuality and its various expressions.

7. Questions about Ordination

[7.0] There is a subset of questions that needs further exploration. Chief among them is whether unmarried, non-celibate persons, heterosexual or homosexual, should be ordained. In our polity, ordination is at the discretion of the bishop as overseer in the community of faith with the advice and consent of the Standing Committee. Sexual discipline and holiness of life must be a very serious consideration for bishops, Standing Committees, and Commissions on Ministry as they discern what constitutes a "wholesome example to all people" (BCP 544).

[7.1] We affirm the responsibility of Dioceses to discern and raise up fit persons for the ministry of word and sacrament to build up the body of Christ in that place. We call on bishops and Standing Committees to be respectful of the ways in which decisions made in one Diocese have ramifications on others. We remind all that ordination is for the whole Church.

8. Living in Disagreement

[8.0] Our present conclusion is that equally sincere Christians, equally committed to an orthodox understanding of the Faith we share, equally looking to Scripture for guidance on this issue, are deeply divided regarding questions with respect to homosexuality. It will be crucial for all parties in this debate to ask God's blessing on their ever-deepening conversion in Christ, and to pray for God's love and forgiveness to be granted to all. Faithfulness and the courage to offer love and acceptance to those with whom we disagree is the great need of the moment.

[8.1] For these reasons, we believe it is imperative that the Episcopal Church refrain from any attempt to "settle" the matter legislatively. For a season at least, we must acknowledge and live with the great pain and discomfort of our disagreements. The act of trusting those with whom we disagree intensely bears witness to the reconciling power of God, which is always beyond our imagining. Sensitive restraint and mutual forbearance is needed rather than a vote that might "win" the argument for some and leave others seemingly rejected. "Let everyone be quick to listen, slow to speak, slow to anger; for your anger does not produce God's righteousness" (James 1:19–20).

[8.2] At the Lambeth Conference in 1998, the bishops of the Anglican Communion addressed questions of human sexuality. Although overshadowed by a controversial Resolution on Homosexuality, the report, *Human Sexuality*, was well crafted, and we believe it remains relevant to the present discussion. We share the principal conclusions of the report:

> Clearly some expressions of sexuality are inherently contrary to the Christian way and are sinful. Such unacceptable expressions of sexuality include promiscuity, prostitution, incest, pornography, pedophilia, predatory sexual behavior, and sadomasochism (all of which may be heterosexual and homosexual), adultery, violence against women and in families, rape and female circumcision. From a Christian perspective these forms of sexual expression remain sinful in any context. We are particularly concerned about the pressures on young people to engage in sexual activity at an early age, and we urge our churches to teach the virtue of abstinence.
>
> All human relationships need the transforming power of Christ which is available to all, and particularly when we fall short of biblical norms. We must confess that we are not of one mind about homosexuality. Our variety of understanding encompasses:
>
> i) Those who believe homosexual orientation is a disorder, but that through the grace of Christ people can be changed, although not without pain and struggle.
>
> ii) Those who believe that relationships between people of the same gender should not include genital expression, that this is the clear teaching of the Bible and of the Church universal, and that such activity (if unrepented of) is a barrier to the Kingdom of God.
>
> iii) Those who believe that committed homosexual relationships fall short of the biblical norm, but are to be preferred to relationships that are anonymous and transient.
>
> iv) Those who believe that the Church should accept and support or bless monogamous covenant relationships between homosexual people and that they may be ordained.
>
> We have prayed, studied and discussed these issues, and we are unable to reach a common mind on the scriptural, theological, historical, and scientific questions that are raised. There is much that we do not understand.

(*Called to Full Humanity*, Section 1 Report, pages, 16, 17)

[8.3] We encourage the continuing examination of God's gift of human sexuality. We urge Church leaders everywhere, both within our own household of faith and in other denominations, to join us in seeking the mind of Christ and the wisdom of God. But the responsibility for doing so is not reserved to theologians and ecclesiastical leaders alone. All those who bear the name of Christ share such responsibility. We believe that by patience, prayer, and continuing study, with forbearance and charity for all, God will guide the Church through this season of conflict to a place of reconciliation and peace for all. Let us support each other in love and prayer.

> *Guide us, O God, in our continuing consideration of human sexuality to be responsive to and respectful of all persons, their ideas and experience. Convert and empower us to listen penitently and, with humility, to speak honestly with one another. Set our disagreements within the mutual knowledge and love which we experience in you as Holy Trinity. Whenever we experience fear, anger, or mistrust with one another, gives us new hope and consolation in your never-failing love for your children. In all things, let us submit our ideas to your thoughts, our desires to your will, and our actions to your purpose. In our diversity as members of the Body of Christ, help us find our way, through Jesus Christ, Our Redeemer.*
> *Amen.*

PART IV

APPENDICES

BUDGET APPENDIX

THE BUDGET FOR THE EPISCOPAL CHURCH

2004–2006

ADOPTED AUGUST 7, 2003

THE BUDGET FOR THE EPISCOPAL CHURCH

2004–2006

TABLE OF CONTENTS

	Page(s)
A letter from the Joint Standing Committee on Program, Budget and Finance	793
Enabling Resolution	794
Mission Priorities Statement and Budget Report	797
Summary of Changes and Actions Taken	807
Budget Detail	809
2003 Diocesan Commitments	834
Resolution Disposition Table	838
Committee Roster	846

BUDGET   APPENDIX

THE GENERAL CONVENTION OF THE EPISCOPAL CHURCH

September, 2003

Dear Bishops and Deputies,

We are pleased to present The Budget for the Episcopal Church for the 2004-2006 Triennium, adopted by General Convention on August 7, 2003. In addition to the printed version, the budget will be published on our web site where any subsequent revisions, made by Executive Council during the triennium, as well as comparisons to actual results, will be published periodically. The enclosed package includes the commentary of the Joint Standing Committee on Program, Budget and Finance (PB&F), the enabling resolution and the budget priorities as adopted by General Convention.

In an unprecedented action, the General Convention endorsed mission budget priorities, in rank order, and further directed PB&F to use the priorities in forming the Budget for the Episcopal Church for 2004-2006. General Convention further stated that "We embrace diversity, promote inclusion and powersharing which underlie and inform all priorities, decisions and all that we do." The adopted budget reflects our priorities.

After the budget was adopted by General Convention, deputies from 81 dioceses signed a covenant pledging themselves to encourage their dioceses to support our common mission by giving a minimum of 21% or by intentionally working toward the 21% level. One deputation pledged at 25%.

We are the people of God filled with vision for ministry. As has been the situation in the past, the identified needs for ministry funding exceeded the amount of funds available. The Budget for the Episcopal Church incorporates many ministry initiatives agreed to by General Convention. In addition to diocesan commitments, the budget is premised upon the additional draw down of as much as $2.3 million (5.50% vs. 5.00% spending rate) from our endowment to support these new and expanded initiatives.

The budget is prepared and approved well in advance of the period to which it applies. With the passage of time, changes occur which affect not only our investment income, but also the ability of dioceses to provide the necessary amounts to support the budget. In addition, our mission strategies and tactics become more well defined as we move closer to the time of their implementation. As has been done in the past to accommodate these changes, each year during the triennium an annual budget, based upon the budget approved at General Convention, is reviewed and approved by Executive Council. Each such budget will be available on our web site and printed copies will be made available upon request. At all times, your comments are welcomed and encouraged.

General Convention identified important ministry we have to do together. We pray that each diocese will continue to meet, exceed or make significant efforts to strive toward meeting their full asking.

In peace,

Bonnie Anderson   *Thomas Hershkowitz*

Bonnie Anderson, Chair   Thomas Hershkowitz,
Joint Standing Committee on   Treasurer of the General Convention
Program, Budget and Finance

815 SECOND AVENUE NEW YORK, NY 10017 USA •212 716-6000 •800 334-7626 •www.episcopalchurch.org

Resolution D086: Budget for the Episcopal Church 2004–2006

Final Text of Resolution:

Resolved, That the 74th General Convention adopt the Budget for the Episcopal Church for the next triennium be adopted as set forth below:

1.0 The Budget for the Episcopal Church for the period January 1, 2004 through December 31, 2006, which shall be a unified budget including Canonical, Corporate, and Program (mission) portions, is adopted at a total of $146,395,000.00.

    1.1 The Canonical portion, providing for the contingent expenses of the General Convention, the stipend of the Presiding Bishop and the expenses of that office, the expenses of the President of the House of Deputies, and Church Pension Fund assessments is adopted at a total of $ 28,115,000.00 as follows:
        For the year 2004 $ 8,474,000.00
        For the year 2005 $ 8,618,000.00
        For the year 2006 $ 11,023,000.00

    1.2 The Corporate portion, providing for the requirements for the administrative support of the Domestic & Foreign Missionary Society offices, is adopted at a total of $ 25,567,000.00 as follows:
        For the year 2004 $ 8,225,000.00
        For the year 2005 $ 8,577,000.00
        For the year 2006 $ 8,765,000.00

    1.3 The Program (mission) portion, providing for support for the mission and ministry (restricted and unrestricted) of the Church, is adopted at a total of $92,713,000.00 as follows:
        For the year 2004 $ 30,510,000.00
        For the year 2005 $ 30,821,000.00
        For the year 2006 $ 31,382,000.00

2.0 The funding policy for the period January 1, 2004 through December 31, 2006 is adopted, based on a single Asking (apportioned share) of the dioceses. After a $100,000 exemption from total income, a single asking shall be applied at a flat rate of 21% of the balance of income to the diocese, reported in the diocesan financial statements for the year two years prior to the year to which the pledge is applied [e.g.: 2004 Askings (apportioned share) are to be based on 2002 actual income figures]. "Income" includes 1) all congregational giving to the diocese, 2) all unrestricted investment and endowment income to the diocese, 3) restricted investment and endowment income to the diocese which covers costs in the operating budget, and 4) other earnings from investments or enterprises. It is intended that income shall include revenues that fund normal operating and program expenses of the dioceses. It is not intended to include pass-through income that is used for expenses for programming that are simply administered by the dioceses, or that would not be otherwise funded by contributions from parishes or out of investment income.

2.1 We rejoice with dioceses that have moved toward, and those that give at and above, the 21% Asking. Such giving creates a strong financial basis for vital mission and witness of the Episcopal Church. We encourage all our dioceses to adopt the 21% Asking; then we could allocate an additional 4.7 million dollars each year toward fulfilling the mission priorities which we have embraced in this 74th General Convention.

2.2 For the budgetary period income from diocesan commitments, totaling $90,487,000.00 is anticipated as follows:
    For the year 2004 $ 29,473,000.00
    For the year 2005 $ 30,062,000.00
    For the year 2006 $ 30,952,000.00

2.3 For the budgetary period 2004-2006, payment by the dioceses of the Askings shall be made in twelve equal monthly payments.

2.4 All additional income, other than from the Askings of the dioceses, totaling $55,908,000.00, is projected as follows:
    For the year 2004 $ 18,554,000.00
    For the year 2005 $ 18,382,000.00
    For the year 2006 $ 18,972,000.00

2.5 A General Ordination fee is hereby authorized, which fees shall be added to the funding from dioceses and applied to the expenses of examination as appropriated in the budget. A candidate for Holy Orders eligible for examination and so certified by the diocesan bishop shall not be disqualified for examination because the fee has not been paid.

2.6 General Convention registration and exhibitors fees are hereby authorized, which fees shall be added to the funding from dioceses and applied to the expenses of the 2006 General Convention, and for no other purpose.

3.0 In the exercise of their respective authorities, the Executive Council of the General Convention and the Joint Standing Committee on Program, Budget and Finance shall be subject to the following policies:

    3.1 Each year, the Executive Council, with the advice of the Joint Standing Committee on Program, Budget and Finance, shall adjust the budget to the assured income of the Executive Council so as to carry out the Budget for the Episcopal Church for that year on a balanced budget basis.

    3.2 The fiscal year shall begin January 1.

    3.3 If in any year the total anticipated income for budget support is less than the amount required to support the budget approved by the General Convention, the Canonical portion of the Budget for the Episcopal Church shall have funding priority over any other budget areas.

    3.4 Net surpluses that are realized in any year of the triennium are to be allocated in the subsequent years of the triennium in the following rank order, as needed, to:
        Ministries With Young People
        Ethnic Congregational Development
        Congregational Development

    3.5 Undesignated bequests and legacies received during the budgetary period shall be set aside in the general endowment fund of which only the income shall be used for the general purposes of the Society.

    3.6 Designated bequests and legacies received during the budgetary period shall be set aside in specific funds of which only the income shall be used for the purposes so designated.

    3.7 Each Committee, Commission, Agency and Board (CCAB) proposing to the General Convention any resolution with funding implications shall present to the Standing Committee on Program, Budget and Finance a detailed budget in support of its plan(s), including cost estimates from contractors and suppliers for all goods and services, by no later than six months before the opening day of the General Convention.

    3.8 Subsequent editions of the *Report and Proposal of the Presiding Bishop and Executive Council to the General Convention* contain the following information for each year of the preceding triennium:
- A description of the actual income and expenditures of the DFMS, relating the expenditures to the Church's priorities with accompanying narrative.
- Endowment balance and total investment return, with accompanying narrative.
- Posting of this report on the DFMS website when it is released to the Bishops and Deputies.

BUDGET APPENDIX

The Joint Standing Committee on Program, Budget and Finance (PB&F) presents the Budget for the Episcopal Church for 2004-2006.

Introduction

The Mission Statement and Budget Proposal from the Presiding Bishop and the Executive Council to the 74th General Convention of the Episcopal Church reaches deputies' and bishops' hands in the spring of convention year. It is the starting place for in-depth deliberations before and during Convention.

As required by Canon, PB&F studied and discussed every aspect of the budget. Funding priorities were initially established by the Presiding Bishop and Executive Council. They were reviewed and modified by PB&F, and a final version was adopted by Convention. Open hearings on the spending and funding portions of the Budget were held on July 31st and August 1st.

Priorities

General Convention adopted the following priorities to guide the work of PB&F and to inform the entire Church of where we will engage mission in the next triennium. The resolution reads:

We offer these mission priorities as an expression of our commitment to Jesus Christ.

We are committed to the importance of our ministry of reconciliation and communion at every level of our communion.

We embrace diversity and seek to promote inclusion and power sharing which underlie and inform all priorities, decisions, and all that we do. In faithfulness to these commitments, we continue to honor our covenants and partnerships with overseas dioceses. We affirm the work of the Executive Council in identifying the following priorities for the mission of the Church for the next triennium.

1. **YOUNG ADULTS AND YOUTH**: Reaching out to young adults and youth through intentional inclusion and full incorporation in the thinking, work, worship and structure of the Church.
2. **RECONCILIATION AND EVANGELISM**: Reconciling and engaging those who do not know Christ by participating in God's mission of reconciling all things to Christ and proclaiming the Gospel to those who are not yet members of the Church.
3. **CONGREGATIONAL TRANSFORMATION**: Revitalizing and transforming congregations through commitment to leadership development, spiritual growth, dynamic and inclusive worship, greater diversity, and mission.
4. **JUSTICE AND PEACE**: Promoting justice and peace for all of God's creation and reaching out to the dispossessed, imprisoned and otherwise voiceless needy.
5. **PARTNERSHIPS**: Reaffirming the importance of our partnerships with provinces of the Anglican Communion and beyond and our relationships with ecumenical and interfaith partners.

20/20 Initiative

20/20 is a movement to transform the Church for the 21st century. The challenge of this bold vision requires new and innovative approaches in all aspects of ministry. It is a paradigm shift from our current response to mission and ministry to a new response to God's call.

The priorities are a visible sign that the principles of 20/20 have influenced the Church's thinking about how the Church organizes for mission. On the Resolution tracking sheet 20/20 resolutions with funding requests are identified by shading.

Overview of the Budget

In order to carry out the total mission activities that the General Convention identified, funding of $158,070,169 would be required. If every diocese would commit to and achieve 21% giving, the total amount available for ministry would be $160,056,769. The actual amount of revenue the Church anticipates for mission for the next three years is $146,395,000. This budget represents the Church's best response to all the ministry requests with the dollars available for work.

Figure 1

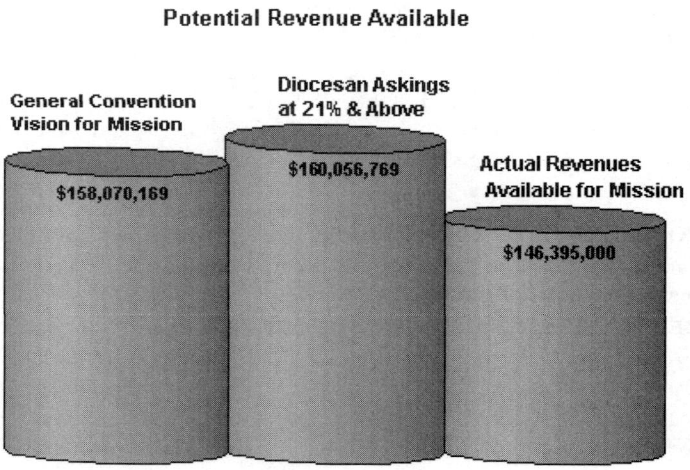

Potential Revenue Available

General Convention Vision for Mission: $158,070,169

Diocesan Askings at 21% & Above: $160,056,769

Actual Revenues Available for Mission: $146,395,000

BUDGET APPENDIX

Revenue for 2004-2006 is $146,395,000. Figure 2 illustrates total revenue and sources.

Figure 2

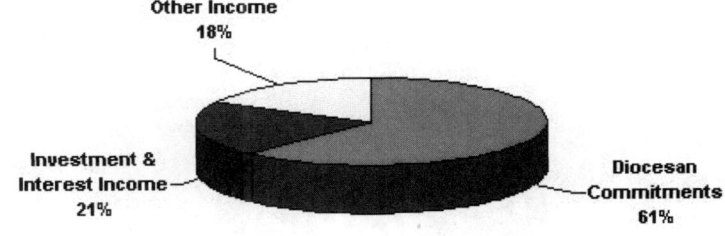

Summary
2004 - 2006 Revenues

Revenues	2004	2005	2006	Triennium
Diocesan Commitments	$29,473,000	$30,062,000	$30,952,000	$90,487,000
Investment & Interest Income	10,603,000	10,265,000	9,963,000	30,831,000
Other Income	7,951,000	8,117,000	9,009,000	25,077,000
Total Revenues	$48,027,000	$48,444,000	$49,924,000	$146,395,000

Figure 3 captures the **expenses** for the Episcopal Church for the next three years by category.

Figure 3

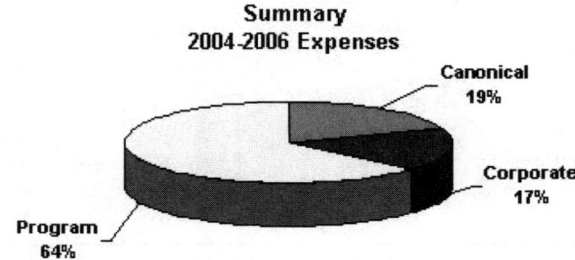

Expenses	2004	2005	2006	Triennium
Canonical	$8,474,000	$8,618,000	$11,023,000	$28,115,000
Corporate	8,225,000	8,577,000	8,765,000	25,567,000
Program	30,510,000	30,821,000	31,382,000	92,713,000
Total Expenses	$47,209,000	$48,016,000	$51,170,000	$146,395,000

Details of Revenue for 2004-2006

Diocesan Commitments

2003 Diocesan Askings are based on 2001 audited "income" as defined less a flat $100,000 optional exemption, times a rate of 21%. In total (see Figure 4), 5 dioceses have pledged more than 21%, 57 dioceses pledged at the 21% asking level, and 38 dioceses pledged below the 21% asking.

Figure 4

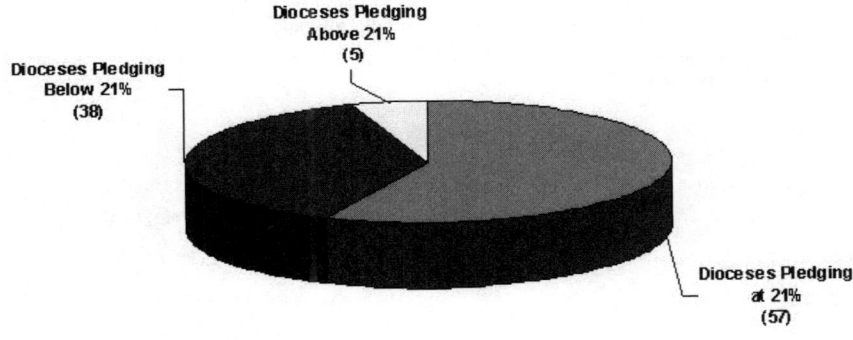

2003 Diocesan Pledge Acceptances

Estimates of diocesan commitments and payments for 2004 show a modest increase in 2005 and 2006. Actual pledge payments year-to-date in 2003 have been remarkably strong.

Estimated Diocesan Pledge Payments

2004	2005	2006	Triennium
$29,473,000	$30,062,000	$30,952,000	$90,487,000

Domestic & Foreign Missionary Society (DFMS) Investment Portfolio

Before setting an annual Payout Rate to support the DFMS Budget, a reduction must be made for the projected decline in purchasing power of the funds due to estimated inflation and for investment management expenses (see Figure 5).

The long-term investment objective of DFMS is to obtain an average annual total return, consisting of capital appreciation plus dividends and interest, of at least 8.5% over a rolling 5 year period. This allows a payout to the DFMS Budget of 5.5% after an allowance for inflation and investment fees averaging 3% annually.

Figure 5

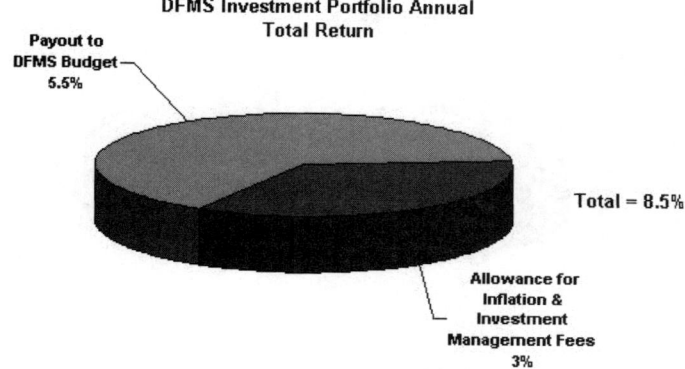

DFMS Investment Portfolio (continued)

Applying the 5.5% payout rate to the rolling 5 year portfolio average of $286,652,000 (see Figure 6) for the 5 year period 1998-2002 produces a projected payout of $15,765,000. However, 42% of these funds are held in custody for a third party or are unavailable to support the DFMS Budget, reducing the payout from the investment portfolio to $9,167,000 for 2004.

Calculating the 5 year rolling average for the last two years of the next triennium will require dropping the years 1998 and 1999, which were two of our "good" investment return years, as they will no longer be within the calculation period for the purposes of the Budget. Consequently, the estimated investment portfolio payout will be reduced to $8,673,000 and $8,311,000 in 2005 and 2006 respectively.

Figure 6

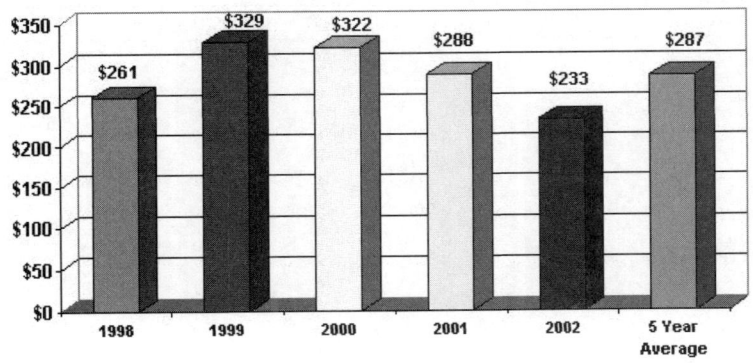

DFMS Investment Portfolio
Year End Market Values ($ in Millions)

In addition to the investment portfolio payouts, the DFMS earns interest income on its cash and other short term funds providing total investment and interest income for the Budget as follows:

	2004	2005	2006	Triennium
Portfolio Payout	9,167,000	8,673,000	8,311,000	26,151,000
Interest Income	1,436,000	1,592,000	1,652,000	4,680,000
Total	$10,603,000	$10,265,000	$9,963,000	$30,831,000

Other Income

The DFMS enjoys several smaller sources of revenue including Government Grants in support of Episcopal Migration Ministries, whose income is somewhat difficult to predict, and the Episcopal Life publication, the Episcopal Book and Resource Center, and Episcopal Parish Services.

Other Income	2004	2005	2006	Triennium
Government Grants (EMM)	$5,169,000	$5,180,000	$5,202,000	$15,551,000
Episcopal Life	1,856,000	1,989,000	2,112,000	5,957,000
Episcopal Parish Services & Episcopal Book & Resource Center	824,000	843,000	853,000	2,520,000
Other	102,000	105,000	842,000	1,049,000
Total Revenues	$7,951,000	$8,117,000	$9,009,000	$25,077,000

Details of Expenses for 2004-2006

Expenses

For purposes of this presentation of the Budget for the Episcopal Church for the 2004-2006 triennium and for the enabling resolution (D086), expenses are divided into the three portions identified in the Canons I.4.6. (b), (c): **Canonical**, **Corporate** and **Program**.

Figure 7

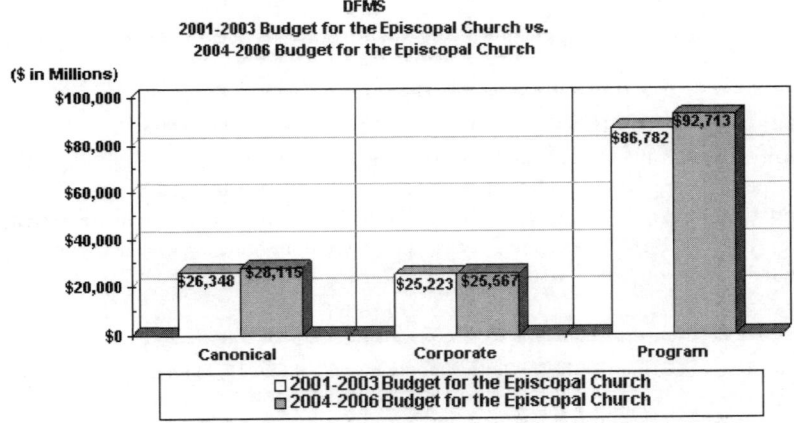

The **Canonical** portion provides for the expenses of the General Convention including Committees, Commissions, Agencies and Boards (CCAB'S), the stipend of the Presiding Bishop and the expenses of that office, the expenses of the President of the House of Deputies, and Church Pension Fund assessments. The **Corporate** portion provides for the administrative support of the Domestic & Foreign Missionary Society offices. The **Program** portion provides for support for the mission and ministry (restricted and unrestricted) of the Church. A significant segment (16.94%) of this portion is Communication. Another segment is Mission Block Grant Partnerships (32.78%), and Refugees/Episcopal Migration Ministries (16.77%).

While it is through the **Program** portion of the Budget that we carry out the *mission and ministry* adopted by General Conventions, it is through the **Canonical** and **Corporate** portions that such efforts obtain the administrative support so necessary for their day-to-day success. For example, this applies to the work of the Office of Ministry Development and the Standing Commission on Ministry Development, both of which are in the **Canonical** portion of the Budget. As the 20/20 movement and vision moves beyond the first step of "laying the foundation," even more of the mission and ministry of the **Canonical** and **Corporate** portions will be focused on step two, "gathering momentum."

Contributed Services to Episcopal Agencies

The DFMS provides office space as well as building, telephone and computer services in support of the mission and ministry of the following agencies which are housed in the Church Center in New York City:

- Episcopal Church Building Fund
- Episcopal Church Foundation
- Office of Anglican Observer at the UN
- Bible and Common Prayer Book Society
- Church Periodical Club
- Colleges and Universities of the Anglican Communion
- National Association of Episcopal Schools

The total amount of these contributed (or in-kind) services budgeted for the 2004-2006 triennium is $1,675,000.

Response to the 74th General Convention Priorities

More than **$57,495,000** of the 2004-2006 triennium's Budget for the Episcopal Church will be spent in support of the first three priorities: **Young Adults and Youth, Reconciliation and Evangelism**, and **Congregational Transformation**. That amount represents 44% of the Adopted Budget (excluding Episcopal Migration Ministries). The primary principles underlying the priorities are diversity, inclusion and power sharing.

Figure 8

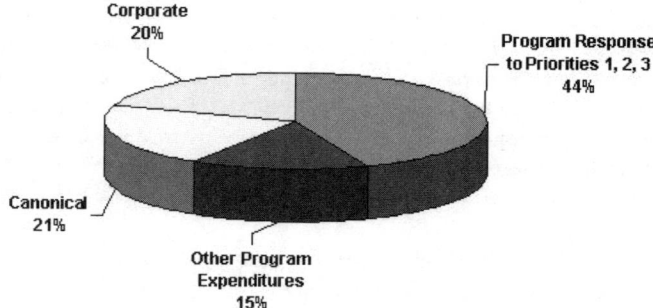

The Church has moved to greater clarity in responding to the call to engage God's mission. Priorities are now in place that pave the way for a dynamic transformation of the Church for the 21st century. Our work is not complete with the adoption of the Budget; our work has just begun.

SUMMARY OF CHANGES AND ACTIONS TAKEN

The following is a summary of actions taken in the Corporate & Canonical and Program sections of the Budget. During the last several days of Convention each section of PB&F developed its part of the Budget based upon the funding priorities. The results of this detailed review are measurable changes in allocations. These changes are the means to build capacity to meet our priorities. Such bold moves are not without sacrifice. Many traditional efforts, particularly in the Corporate and Canonical areas, will now be challenged to work with fewer financial resources.

The response to this Convention's priorities has resulted in the following actions:

CORPORATE AND CANONICAL

Reductions were made in the following areas of the **Canonical section** of the budget:
- Office of the Presiding Bishop - $50,000
- House of Bishops - $48,000
- House of Deputies - $25,000
- General Convention- site and facilities - $50,000
- Committees, Commissions, Agencies and Boards (CCABs) - $290,000
    - Review and individual decisions regarding funding levels of CCABs were made resulting in an approximate 10% reduction in the total allocation. Amount includes $25,000 for the establishment of a task force for the prevention of sexual misconduct
- Archives - $50,000
- Ecumenical and Interfaith Relations - $50,000
- Office of Pastoral Development - $41,000

Increases in the **Canonical Section** are as follows:
- General Board of Examining Chaplains - $24,000
    - Maintain the work of the group that administers the General Ordination Examinations (GOE)

Reductions were made in the following areas in the **Corporate section** of the Budget:
- Office of the Chief Operating Officer - $30,000
- Human Resources Department - $30,000
- Controller's Office - $15,000
- Treasurer's Office - $75,000
- Telecommunications - $100,000
- Building Services - $100,000

Contributed Services:
Episcopal Relief and Development (ERD) has been allocated $2,572,000 for contributed services by DFMS, which includes such items as postage, building services, telecommunications and other administrative and financial services.

PROGRAM (MISSION)
Reductions were made in the following areas of the **Program section** of the Budget:
- Program ministries support - $200,000
- Communication - $300,000

Increases in the **Program section** are:
- Ministries with Young People - $1,000,000
    - o Allocation of specific programs to be made by Executive Council and young people, together with the Church Center staff
- Overseas dioceses - $150,000
- Jubilee Ministries grants - $150,000
- Multi-cultural/multi-lingual liturgies for "new" populations - $130,000

Domestic and Foreign Missionary Society of the Protestant Episcopal Church in the United States of America

2004-2006 Budget: As adopted August 7, 2003

REVENUES	2004	2005	2006	Triennium
Diocesan Commitments	$29,473,000	$30,062,000	$30,952,000	$90,487,000
Investment & Interest Income	10,603,000	10,265,000	9,963,000	30,831,000
Episcopal Life	1,856,000	1,989,000	2,112,000	5,957,000
Government Grants (EMM)	5,169,000	5,180,000	5,202,000	15,551,000
Episcopal Parish Services & Episcopal Book and Resource Center	824,000	843,000	853,000	2,520,000
Other	102,000	105,000	842,000	1,049,000
GRAND TOTAL	**$48,027,000**	**$48,444,000**	**$49,924,000**	**$146,395,000**

EXPENSES	2004	2005	2006	Triennium
Canonical	$ 8,474,000	$ 8,618,000	$11,023,000	$28,115,000
Mission Program	15,324,000	15,563,000	15,731,000	46,618,000
Mission Block Grant Partnerships	10,210,000	10,140,000	10,043,000	30,393,000
Communication	4,976,000	5,118,000	5,608,000	15,702,000
Corporate (Reported as Mission Support in Pre-Convention Budget)	8,225,000	8,577,000	8,765,000	25,567,000
GRAND TOTAL	**$47,209,000**	**$48,016,000**	**$51,170,000**	**$146,395,000**

REVENUES

Diocesan Commitments	2004	2005	2006	Triennium
U.S. dioceses	$29,473,000	$30,062,000	$30,952,000	$90,487,000
Overseas dioceses (None assumed)	0	0	0	0
Total Diocesan Commitments	**$29,473,000**	**$30,062,000**	**$30,952,000**	**$90,487,000**

The funding policy for the period January 1, 2004 through December 31, 2006 is based on a single Asking of the Dioceses (apportioned share). After a $100,000 exemption from total income, a single asking shall be applied at a flat rate of 21% of the balance of income to the Diocese, as reported in the Diocesan Financial Statements for the year two years prior to the year to which the pledge is applied. For example, the 2004 Asking would be based on actual 2002 income. "Income" includes 1) all congregational giving to the Diocese, 2) all unrestricted investment and endowment income to the Diocese, 3) restricted investment and endowment income to the Diocese which covers costs in the operating budget, and 4) other earnings from investments or enterprises. It is intended that income shall include revenues that fund normal and programming expense of the dioceses. It is not intended to include pass-through income that is used for expenses for programming that is simply administered by the Dioceses or that would not be otherwise funded by contributions from parishes or out of investment income.

Investment and Interest Income	2004	2005	2006	Triennium
Interest Income (Non-Endowment Assets)	$1,436,000	$1,592,000	$1,652,000	$4,680,000
Unrestricted trust fund Income	4,624,000	4,389,000	4,219,000	13,232,000
Restricted trust fund Income	4,543,000	4,284,000	4,092,000	12,919,000
Total Investment & Interest Income	**$10,603,000**	**$10,265,000**	**$9,963,000**	**$30,831,000**

Investment income consists principally of income on the DFMS endowment, which represents both restricted and unrestricted income. This estimate assumes trust fund income at $1.079, $1.018, and $0.972 per share in 2004, 2005 and 2006 respectively, an estimate which in turn assumes a net 5% annual growth rate (net of distributions and management fees) in trust fund assets over that period and annual distributions set at approximately 5.50% of a five-year rolling average asset value. DFMS non-endowment assets are invested in short-term (usually 2-5 years to maturity) fixed income instruments.

Episcopal Life	2004	2005	2006	Triennium
Episcopal Life Subscription and Advertising Revenue	$1,856,000	$1,989,000	$2,112,000	$5,957,000
Total Episcopal Life	**$1,856,000**	**$1,989,000**	**$2,112,000**	**$5,957,000**

Episcopal Life costs are partially (86%) subsidized by revenues earned from advertising and subscription sales.

BUDGET APPENDIX

Government Grants (EMM)	2004	2005	2006	Triennium
Government Grants (EMM)	$5,169,000	$5,180,000	$5,202,000	$15,551,000
Total Government Grants	**$5,169,000**	**$5,180,000**	**$5,202,000**	**$15,551,000**

Episcopal Migration Ministries (the refugee program) is primarily supported by federal government contracts principally from the Reception and Placement Program funded by the State Department and the Department of Health and Human Services Matching Grant Program. It is estimated that DFMS and affiliated organizations will resettle 2200 refugees per year through the Reception and Placement Program, and 1000 refugees per year will qualify for participation in the Matching Grant Program. After withholding amounts necessary to cover administrative costs, these funds are passed to dioceses to fund local programs.

Episcopal Parish Services and Episcopal Book and Resource Center Revenues

Episcopal Parish Services (EPS) is a mail-order operation that sells and distributes printed and other materials produced by DFMS and others. The fulfillment and order processing operation is currently outsourced to Morehouse Publishing in Harrisburg, Pennsylvania.

The Episcopal Book and Resource Center (EBRC) specializes in books on congregational development, Christian education, theology, spirituality, pastoral care, and related subjects. It stocks a full spectrum of Bibles, the Book of Common Prayer, and Hymnals. The ministry of the bookstore is to serve the whole church (and beyond), by providing quality resources, knowledgeable service, and information to individuals, study groups, parishes/diocesan libraries, bookstores, and resource centers. Mailing, special ordering services, and an extensive online catalog, as well as a range of gifts are also offered.

	2004	2005	2006	Triennium
Episcopal Parish Services	$287,000	$296,000	$296,000	$879,000
Episcopal Book and Resource Center	537,000	547,000	557,000	1,641,000
Total EPS and EBRC	**$824,000**	**$843,000**	**$853,000**	**$2,520,000**
Other	**2004**	**2005**	**2006**	**Triennium**
General Convention fees	$0	$0	$400,000	$400,000
General Convention exhibits	0	0	330,000	330,000
GBEC Recovery fees	102,000	105,000	112,000	319,000
Total Other	**$102,000**	**$105,000**	**$842,000**	**$1,049,000**

EXPENSES

Canonical	2004	2005	2006	Triennium
Office of the Presiding Bishop	$1,772,000	$1,809,000	$1,860,000	$5,441,000
House of Bishops	251,000	250,000	251,000	752,000
House of Deputies	110,000	112,000	112,000	334,000
Office of the General Convention	1,184,000	1,223,000	1,283,000	3,690,000
General Convention-Site & Facilities	241,000	157,000	2,350,000	2,748,000
GC-Committees/Commissions Agencies & Boards	873,000	917,000	902,000	2,692,000
Office of the Suffragan Bishop for Chaplaincies	949,000	971,000	995,000	2,915,000
Office of Pastoral Development	391,000	402,000	410,000	1,203,000
Office for Ministry Development	521,000	536,000	549,000	1,606,000
Church Deployment Office	545,000	561,000	580,000	1,686,000
General Board of Examining Chaplains	178,000	184,000	193,000	555,000
Office for Liturgy and Music	203,000	209,000	221,000	633,000
Archives of the Episcopal Church	650,000	668,000	687,000	2,005,000
Ecumenical and Interfaith Relations	606,000	619,000	630,000	1,855,000
Canonical Total	**$8,474,000**	**$8,618,000**	**$11,023,000**	**$28,115,000**

Mission Program	2004	2005	2006	Triennium
Program Ministries Support	$453,000	$464,000	$477,000	$1,394,000
Anglican and Global Relations	3,052,000	3,097,000	3,143,000	9,292,000
Congregational Development	1,421,000	1,436,000	1,452,000	4,309,000
Ethnic Congregational Development and Women's Ministries	1,724,000	1,752,000	1,788,000	5,264,000
Peace and Justice Ministries	1,791,000	1,886,000	1,813,000	5,490,000
Ministries with Young People	1,743,000	1,744,000	1,830,000	5,317,000
Episcopal Migration Ministries	5,140,000	5,184,000	5,228,000	15,552,000
Mission Program Total	**$15,324,000**	**$15,563,000**	**$15,731,000**	**$46,618,000**

BUDGET   APPENDIX

Mission Block Grant Partnerships	2004	2005	2006	Triennium
Overseas Partnerships & Covenants	$4,915,000	$4,893,000	$4,838,000	$14,646,000
Domestic Mission Support	3,148,000	3,096,000	3,048,000	9,292,000
Support to Provinces	211,000	212,000	212,000	635,000
Ecumenical Appropriations (WCC & NCC)	529,000	532,000	537,000	1,598,000
Episcopal Relief and Development*	1,257,000	1,257,000	1,258,000	3,772,000
(*Including Contributed Services)				
Planned Giving	150,000	150,000	150,000	450,000
Mission Block Grant Partnerships Total	**$10,210,000**	**$10,140,000**	**$10,043,000**	**$30,393,000**

Office of Communication	2004	2005	2006	Triennium
Communication	$277,000	$285,000	$293,000	$855,000
Media Services	1,696,000	1,726,000	2,056,000	5,478,000
Episcopal Life	2,206,000	2,272,000	2,435,000	6,913,000
Episcopal Parish Services	263,000	288,000	264,000	815,000
Episcopal Book & Resource Center	534,000	547,000	560,000	1,641,000
Communication Total	**$4,976,000**	**$5,118,000**	**$5,608,000**	**$15,702,000**

Corporate (Reported as Mission Support in Pre-Convention Budget)

	2004	2005	2006	Triennium
Office of Chief Operating Officer	$480,000	$478,000	$515,000	$1,473,000
Treasurer's Office	1,695,000	1,737,000	1,782,000	5,214,000
Controller's Office	1,126,000	1,160,000	1,195,000	3,481,000
Human Resource Management	1,487,000	1,534,000	1,606,000	4,627,000
Management Information Systems	1,127,000	1,309,000	1,239,000	3,675,000
Purchasing	310,000	310,000	320,000	940,000
Mailing Center	705,000	720,000	747,000	2,172,000
Telecommunications	429,000	435,000	439,000	1,303,000
Building Services	1,723,000	1,751,000	1,780,000	5,254,000
Allocation of Contributed Services to ERD	(857,000)	(857,000)	(858,000)	(2,572,000)
Corporate Total	**$8,225,000**	**$8,577,000**	**$8,765,000**	**$25,567,000**

Note: "Staff Costs" in the following tables include salaries and benefits costs. "Other Costs," in the following tables includes staff expenses such as meetings, printing, and travel, which cannot be known with great certainty at this time but have been estimated based on past experience.

CANONICAL

Office of the Presiding Bishop

This Office supports the Presiding Bishop in his administrative and communication responsibilities as well as pastoral ministries. This includes working with and supporting the staff in carrying forth General Convention initiatives and policies, supporting the ecumenical initiatives and relationships of the Episcopal Church, and supporting pastoral relationships with the Bishops of this church. This office plans and coordinates the visits of the Presiding Bishop, as well as planning for meetings of the House of Bishops at General Convention and interim and special meetings. The office is responsible for the processes of election and consecration of bishops.

	2004	2005	2006	Triennium
Staff Costs	$1,148,000	$1,186,000	$1,227,000	$3,561,000
Council of Advice	30,000	30,000	30,000	90,000
Chancellor	55,000	55,000	55,000	165,000
Title IV Contingencies	200,000	200,000	200,000	600,000
Other Costs	339,000	338,000	348,000	1,025,000
Total Office of the Presiding Bishop	$1,772,000	$1,809,000	$1,860,000	$5,441,000

House of Bishops

The expenses in this area support the design and implementation of the annual Interim and Special Committee meetings of the House. Additional support is given to the planning group for the spouses meetings, which coincide with the House of Bishops meetings.

	2004	2005	2006	Triennium
Special Committee Meetings	$94,000	$94,000	$94,000	$282,000
Interim Meetings	$70,000	$70,000	$70,000	$210,000
Other Costs	87,000	86,000	87,000	260,000
Total House of Bishops	**$251,000**	**$250,000**	**$251,000**	**$752,000**

House of Deputies

In addition to that furnished by the Office of the General Convention, this line item provides support for the expenses of the President of the House of Deputies, who with the Presiding Bishop, appoints members of committees, commissions, agencies, boards and legislative committees, shares leadership of the Executive Council, serves ex officio as a member of all committees and commissions, represents the Episcopal Church in a variety of Anglican and ecumenical activities, and coordinates planning for the business of the House over which the President presides during the General Convention itself.

BUDGET APPENDIX

	2004	2005	2006	Triennium
Staff Costs	$47,000	$49,000	$51,000	$147,000
Other Costs	63,000	63,000	61,000	187,000
Total House of Deputies	**$110,000**	**$112,000**	**$112,000**	**$334,000**

Office of the General Convention

The General Convention Office, under the direction of the Executive Officer of the General Convention, undertakes the planning, logistical arrangements and staff support for the triennial Convention gatherings, the thrice-yearly Executive Council meetings, and the meetings and work of the Committees, Commissions, Agencies and Boards. It handles production of the *Reports to the General Convention*—known as the "Blue Book"—as well as the *Journal* and the updated *Constitution and Canons* issued after each Convention. It is also responsible for the collection, publication and analysis of annual Parochial Report and Diocesan Report data.

	2004	2005	2006	Triennium
Staff Costs	$1,037,000	$1,072,000	$1,108,000	$3,217,000
Other Costs	147,000	151,000	175,000	473,000
Total Office of the General Convention	**$1,184,000**	**$1,223,000**	**$1,283,000**	**$3,690,000**

General Convention

The General Convention is the governing body of the Episcopal Church in the USA. The Convention includes the House of Deputies, which has 800-plus members (up to four clergy and four lay persons from every diocese), and the House of Bishops, which consists of nearly 300 active and retired bishops.

The Convention meets every three years for a ten-day legislative session, and its powers are established by the first article of the Church's Constitution. The Houses meet and act separately, and both must concur in order to adopt legislation. Although bishops and deputies pay their own travel and lodging expenses, the planning, administrative, security and facilities costs are borne by this budget.

	2004	2005	2006	Triennium
Secretariat	$136,000	10,000	$300,000	$446,000
Site & Facilities:				
Site Expenses	105,000	117,000	830,000	1,052,000
Hall Expenses	0	30,000	832,000	862,000
Site Services	0	0	216,000	216,000
Site Personnel	0	0	172,000	172,000
Total General Convention - Site & Facilities	**$241,000**	**$157,000**	**$2,350,000**	**$2,748,000**

General Convention: Committees, Commissions, Agencies and Boards (CCABs)
Between the triennial meetings of the General Convention, various Committees, Commissions, Agencies, and Boards carry out the ongoing work of the Church.

Chief among these is the Executive Council, which includes a total of forty elected representatives who serve for staggered six-year terms: two persons elected from each of the Church's nine provinces, twenty people elected at–large by the General Convention, and the Presiding Bishop and the President of the House of Deputies. The Executive Council meets three times per year to carry out the program and policies adopted by the General Convention. The Executive Council has charge of the coordination, development, and implementation of the ministry and mission of the Church.

The other Committees, Commissions, Agencies and Boards were started at various times during the history of the Church to perform particular tasks. They are responsible for studying issues and making recommendations to the Convention. They report to each General Convention in writing, summarizing their work during the triennium and proposing legislation for Convention consideration. These reports are distributed in the *Blue Book* to all Bishops and Deputies for study before General Convention convenes.

Board of:	2004	2005	2006	Triennium
Archives	$15,000	$15,000	$15,000	$45,000
Church Deployment	22,000	21,000	22,000	65,000
General Board of Examining Chaplains	22,000	22,000	20,000	64,000
Subtotal Boards	**$59,000**	**$58,000**	**$57,000**	**$174,000**
Committees on:	2004	2005	2006	Triennium
Pastoral Development	$13,000	$16,000	$16,000	$45,000
State of the Church	12,000	14,000	20,000	46,000
Subtotal Committees	**$25,000**	**$30,000**	**$36,000**	**$91,000**
Joint Standing Committees on:	2004	2005	2006	Triennium
Nominations	$6,000	$14,000	$4,000	$24,000
Nominating Committee-PB	38,000	38,000	39,000	115,000
Planning and Arrangements	8,000	16,000	8,000	32,000
Program, Budget and Finance	13,000	28,000	49,000	90,000
Subtotal JSC	**$65,000**	**$96,000**	**$100,000**	**$261,000**
Standing Commissions on:	2004	2005	2006	Triennium
Anglican & International Concerns	$19,000	$29,000	$10,000	$58,000
Small Congregations	7,000	15,000	9,000	31,000
Constitution and Canons	6,000	13,000	29,000	48,000
Ecumenical Relations	30,000	29,000	31,000	90,000
Domestic Mission and Evangelism	37,000	37,000	22,000	96,000
Liturgy and Music	31,000	32,000	33,000	96,000
Ministry Development	30,000	48,000	51,000	129,000
National Concerns	22,000	23,000	26,000	71,000
Stewardship and Development	20,000	21,000	24,000	65,000

BUDGET APPENDIX

Structure of the Church	15,000	24,000	10,000	49,000
World Mission	24,000	37,000	28,000	89,000
Title IV Review Committee	21,000	20,000	19,000	60,000
Title III Revision	6,000	7,000	7,000	20,000
Subtotal SC	**$268,000**	**$335,000**	**$299,000**	**$902,000**
CCAB Chairs' Meetings	**$32,000**	**$0**	**$0**	**$32,000**
Executive Council Committees	2004	2005	2006	Triennium
Executive Council	$300,000	$300,000	$300,000	$900,000
Council Committees	69,000	44,000	53,000	166,000
Committee on the Status of Women	15,000	15,000	15,000	45,000
Committee on HIV/AIDS	14,000	14,000	16,000	44,000
Science, Technology and Faith	18,000	17,000	17,000	52,000
Sexual Misconduct Task Force	8,000	8,000	9,000	25,000
Task Force on Aging	0	0	0	0
National Conversation on Ordination of Women	0	0	0	0
Subtotal Executive Council	**$424,000**	**$398,000**	**$410,000**	**$1,232,000**

Total CCABs	**$873,000**	**$917,000**	**$902,000**	**$2,692,000**

Office of the Suffragan Bishop for Chaplaincies (OSBC) [2]

This Office has expanded and tailored its focus. The original offering of Armed Services, Healthcare and Prisons now includes that of "emergency responder" chaplains[3], e.g., police, fire, EMT, FBI, ATF, and Homeland Security. The necessity of this was apparent when chaplains from a variety of fields began to network in the support of the September 11th recovery. Under the statement, "*a new challenge requires ONE team*," chaplains from the federal ranks, for which this office has traditionally provided direct support, were joined by those of diocesan origins receiving indirect support. This relationship—with members of local clericuses—is not new since priests and deacons from state and local health and prison facilities have received such attention for some time. The key activity and clearer focus now is support of the bishop in local mission and as it might relate to a regional and national need. The core mission—though now to a variety of chaplaincies—remains recruitment, formation, and support. This Office continues support of programs vital to chaplains such as restorative justice, prison ministry and universal access to healthcare. There are 1200 clergy related to this episcopacy.

---

[2] Formerly The Office of the Bishop for the Armed Services, Healthcare and Prison Ministries.
[3] College and school chaplaincies come under the Office for Young Adult and Higher Education Ministries in Ministries with Young People.

The Suffragan Bishop of this Office, on behalf of the Presiding Bishop, has oversight of the missionary work in Micronesia.

	2004	2005	2006	Triennium
Staff Costs	$611,000	$633,000	$655,000	$1,899,000
Other Costs	338,000	338,000	340,000	1,016,000
Total OSBC	**$949,000**	**$971,000**	**$995,000**	**$2,915,000**

Office of Pastoral Development (OPD)

The Office of Pastoral Development of the House of Bishops provides direct support to the Presiding Bishop and the House of Bishops in the areas of episcopal formation and development, pastoral care of bishops, their families and diocesan systems, and mediation in Title IV (disciplinary) matters. Episcopal formation and development involves providing direct support for all episcopal elections, training and mentoring for all bishops, vocational assessment, retirement transitions, and deployment of bishops. Pastoral care means making residential care facility referrals for bishops and priests, planned interventions, and mediation within diocesan systems. Mediation within the Title IV disciplinary canons means providing a response from the Presiding Bishop's Office to complaints and formal charges against or concerning bishops. The intent of the response is to address satisfactorily the cause(s) of the complaint or charge in such a way that proceedings for a possible presentment and ecclesiastical trial do not have to occur.

This triennium (2004-2006), this office has also been given the new responsibility of providing full time administrative support to the College for Bishops as well as supervision for the administration of the work of Episcopal Visitors to Religious Orders and Communities.

	2004	2005	2006	Triennium
Staff Costs	$249,000	$258,000	$268,000	$775,000
Other Costs	142,000	144,000	142,000	428,000
Total OPD	**$391,000**	**$402,000**	**$410,000**	**$1,203,000**

Office for Ministry Development (OMD)

The Office for Ministry Development works to strengthen and support ministries of all baptized persons. The goal is to increase the capacity of the church to carry out effective mission in the world in response to the Gospel. To do this OMD forms collaborative relationships with:

- Ministry development specialists and practitioners around the church
- Leaders in theological education and continuing education
- Groups engaged in discernment, recruitment, training, education, and formation of leaders
- Fresh Start partners to strengthen the ministries of and build the relationships between clergy and congregations and the Bishop's office in the first two years of ministry together
- Those who are concerned with the health and wellness of church professionals and others

BUDGET APPENDIX

OMD also provides staff support to the Standing Commission on Ministry Development. SCMD works to invigorate and equip baptized persons in living the Baptismal Covenant by recommending policies and strategies to the General Convention, facilitating networks, and conducting surveys.

	2004	2005	2006	Triennium
Staff Costs	$370,000	$383,000	$395,000	$1,148,000
Fresh Start	30,000	32,000	32,000	94,000
Other Costs	121,000	121,000	122,000	364,000
Total OMD	**$521,000**	**$536,000**	**$549,000**	**$1,606,000**

Church Deployment Office (CDO)

The Church Deployment Office manages a personnel system for the clergy and lay professionals of the church and for dioceses, parishes and other institutions. It maintains computerized personnel profiles for clergy and lay persons and a searchable file of open positions. Both personnel and position databases are now available online to CDO's various users. CDO conducts computer searches on behalf of dioceses and parishes to identify candidates matching the ministry needs of open positions, and assists diocesan officials in conducting their own searches. CDO networks with and trains diocesan personnel and other users to facilitate their use of online and other services.

	2004	2005	2006	Triennium
Staff Costs	$462,000	$478,000	$496,000	$1,436,000
Other Costs	83,000	83,000	84,000	250,000
Total CDO	**$545,000**	**$561,000**	**$580,000**	**$1,686,000**

General Board of Examining Chaplains (GBEC)

The work of the GBEC is defined by Canon III.31. The Board, elected by the General Convention and responsible to the House of Bishops, consists of four bishops, six clergy with pastoral cures, six members of seminary faculties, and six lay persons. Its primary assignment is the annual General Ordination Examination, administered to seminary seniors and others pursuing Holy Orders, who are nominated by the bishops of the dioceses. The Board collaborates as needed with other General Convention groups devoted to the development and support of ordained ministry.

	2004	2005	2006	Triennium
Staff Costs	$42,000	$44,000	$45,000	$131,000
Other Costs	136,000	140,000	148,000	424,000
Total GBEC	**$178,000**	**$184,000**	**$193,000**	**$555,000**

Office for Liturgy and Music (LM)

The Liturgical Office supports the Presiding Bishop in his role as Chief Liturgical Officer of the Church, especially in organizing worship at General Convention, by assisting in planning occasional liturgical events for other national entities within the church, and by responding to questions about worship. This office supports the work of the Standing Commission on Liturgy and Music.

	2004	2005	2006	Triennium
Staff Costs	$156,000	$162,000	$168,000	$486,000
Other Costs	47,000	47,000	53,000	147,000
Total LM	**$203,000**	**$209,000**	**$221,000**	**$633,000**

Archives of the Episcopal Church

The Archives of the Episcopal Church is the national repository for documentation on the church, related Anglican bodies, and individual Episcopalians. The historical records office is located in Austin, Texas. Its mission is to preserve and make available evidence of the historic and contemporary ministry of the church. The Records Management and Information Services Office at the Episcopal Church Center works with office staff to improve record keeping and access to contemporary information in paper and digital formats.

	2004	2005	2006	Triennium
Staff Costs	$512,000	$530,000	$550,000	$1,592,000
Other Costs	138,000	138,000	137,000	413,000
Total Archives	**$650,000**	**$668,000**	**$687,000**	**$2,005,000**

Ecumenical and Interfaith Relations (EIR)

The Office of Ecumenical and Interfaith Relations coordinates, on behalf of the Presiding Bishop and the Episcopal Church, various bilateral and multilateral dialogues and conversations with other Christian communions working with the greater unity and common mission of the church. In an increasing multi-religious context, the office also works in the area of interfaith dialogue seeking greater understanding of and cooperation between the major religions of the world.

	2004	2005	2006	Triennium
Staff Costs	$336,000	$347,000	$359,000	$1,042,000
Other Costs	270,000	272,000	271,000	813,000
Total EIR	**$606,000**	**$619,000**	**$630,000**	**$1,855,000**

BUDGET APPENDIX

Mission Program

The Mission Program budget is an expression of the Episcopal Church's mission priorities as informed by the Baptismal Covenant, the priorities adopted by the Executive Council and General Convention, historic covenant and partnership commitments, new and prior actions of the General Convention.

Program Ministries Support

The Assistant to the Presiding Bishop for Program serves as a staff officer to the Presiding Bishop and is a member of the PB's Management Team at the Episcopal Church Center. Program Ministries Support serves the entire Program (Mission) Group in the accomplishment of its goals. Administrative costs for the Group include support for consultants, travel costs, and office expenses. Included in this section are the staff costs for the Assistant to the Presiding Bishop for Program. The work of this office consists of oversight, direction, coordination, and communication for the following:

- Anglican and Global Relations
- Congregational Development
- Ethnic Congregational Development
- Peace and Justice Ministries
- Women's Ministries
- Ministries With Young People
- Episcopal Migration Ministries
- Overseas Appropriations
- Domestic Appropriations

	2004	2005	2006	Triennium
Staff Costs	$263,000	$274,000	$288,000	$825,000
Other Costs	190,000	190,000	189,000	569,000
Total Program Ministries Support	**$453,000**	**$464,000**	**$477,000**	**$1,394,000**

Anglican and Global Relations (AGR)

The Anglican and Global Relations office makes possible a coordinated, comprehensive national response to the worldwide mission of the church by:
- Recruiting, training and supporting Appointed Missionaries and Volunteers who serve in approximately 30 countries, including the United States and around the globe
- Enabling Anglican Partner Provinces around the globe to participate effectively in the worldwide church through strong provincial secretariats
- Supporting theological education through scholarships both in the United States and overseas
- Developing and providing educational materials and curricula for world mission
- Servicing world mission networks
- Providing additional support to the Young Adult Service Corps to engage in servant ministry throughout the Anglican Communion
- Providing leadership support, direction and policy coordination for the Episcopal Church's relations with the 12 Anglican provinces in Africa (African Chaplaincy Program).

	2004	2005	2006	Triennium
Staff Costs	$1,217,000	$1,261,000	$1,307,000	$3,785,000
Anglican Partners:				
Africa	$141,000	$141,000	$141,000	$423,000

821

Asia/Pacific	17,000	17,000	17,000	51,000
Europe/Middle East	36,000	37,000	37,000	110,000
Caribbean/Latin America	99,000	98,000	99,000	296,000
Subtotal Anglican Partners	**$293,000**	**$293,000**	**$294,000**	**$880,000**
Partners Emerging Priorities	35,000	35,000	35,000	105,000
Mission Education Networks	126,000	126,000	126,000	378,000
Mission Personnel (Missionaries)	785,000	785,000	786,000	2,356,000
African Program Development	95,000	95,000	95,000	285,000
Volunteers for Mission	241,000	241,000	241,000	723,000
Young Adult Service Corps	103,000	103,000	103,000	309,000
Other Costs	157,000	158,000	156,000	471,000
Total AGR	**$3,052,000**	**$3,097,000**	**$3,143,000**	**$9,292,000**

Congregational Development

Congregational Development includes the work of Congregational Development and Redevelopment, Stewardship, and Research. The primary focus of this department is congregational growth and development, reaching the unchurched, and working toward more diversity within the congregations of the Episcopal Church. In addition to focusing on racial, ethnic and socio-economic diversity, special focus is given to generational diversity in congregations. Congregational Development, Ethnic Congregational Development, and Women's Ministries are responsible for developing a comprehensive strategy for congregational development for the Episcopal Church. The work involves planning and producing resources and national and regional training events, working with provinces, dioceses, and congregations of the Episcopal Church in the development and redevelopment of congregational ministries. Congregational Development contains the Office of Research which directs and coordinates an ongoing program of research and evaluation for the Episcopal Church.

	2004	2005	2006	Triennium
Staff Costs	$587,000	$602,000	$618,000	$1,807,000
Training: Congregational Development and Redevelopment	206,000	206,000	206,000	618,000
New Church Resources	65,000	65,000	65,000	195,000
Stewardship Resources	97,000	96,000	97,000	290,000
Resource Development	125,000	125,000	125,000	375,000
Consultation and Partnership	31,000	31,000	31,000	93,000
Research	90,000	90,000	90,000	270,000
Emerging Generation Program	117,000	117,000	116,000	350,000
Liturgies for "New" Populations	43,000	43,000	44,000	130,000
Other Costs	60,000	61,000	60,000	181,000
Total Congregational Development	**$1,421,000**	**$1,436,000**	**$1,452,000**	**$4,309,000**

Ethnic Congregational Development

Ethnic Congregational Development includes Asian American Ministries, Black Ministries, Hispanic Ministries, and Native American Ministries. A primary focus is congregational growth and development, reaching the unchurched in the expanding ethnic communities of our nation and working toward more diversity within the congregations of the Episcopal Church. Ethnic Congregational Development, Women's Ministries, and Congregational Development are responsible for developing a comprehensive strategy for congregational development for the Episcopal Church. This work involves planning and producing resources and national and regional training events, working with provinces, dioceses, and congregations of the Episcopal Church in the development and redevelopment of specific ethnic congregational ministries.

	2004	2005	2006	Triennium
Staff Costs	$633,000	$656,000	$679,000	$1,968,000
Asian American Ministries	167,000	167,000	167,000	501,000
Black Ministries	167,000	167,000	167,000	501,000
Hispanic Ministries	167,000	167,000	167,000	501,000
Native American Ministries	167,000	167,000	167,000	501,000
Other Costs	103,000	103,000	111,000	317,000
Total Ethnic Congregational Development	**$1,404,000**	**$1,427,000**	**$1,458,000**	**$4,289,000**

Peace and Justice Ministries (PJM)

The mandate of Peace and Justice Ministries is generated by the many social and programmatic policies established by General Convention and Executive Council. PJM works to equip Episcopalians to carry out their Baptismal Covenant to "strive for justice and peace among all people and respect the dignity of every human being" and to be faithful stewards of all God's creation. PJM includes the Office of Government Relations in Washington, D.C. and international Peace Ministries, domestic Social Justice, Jubilee Ministries, and environmental consultant's offices located at the Episcopal Church Center in New York. Some of the work is listed below but is only a partial description of the myriad projects undertaken during a triennium:

- Continuing the Church's second nine year phase (2000-2009) on anti-racism, providing training and resources for dioceses, congregations and national Church leadership
- Growing the number of Jubilee Centers and networks that serve and empower the poor and marginalized as well as providing grant support to Jubilee Centers
- Advocating Church policies to government with particular focus on civil rights, poverty reduction, environment, health, AIDS pandemic in Africa, globalization (especially debt reduction) and peacemaking in areas of conflict (with special attention to the Middle East)
- Growing the Public Policy Network so that the witness made in Washington and various state legislatures is strengthened
- Providing financial support and active participation in the Anglican Peace and Justice Network as well as working bilaterally with Anglican partners on various justice concerns
- Participating in the environmental ecumenical movement through the National

- Council of Churches, participating in the newly formed Anglican Environmental Network and providing appropriate resources to local Churches
- Monitoring the Church's investment portfolio for social responsibility in concert with established Church policy and managing the process for a $7 million alternative loan fund to empower marginalized communities
- Supporting the prophetic role and voice of the Presiding Bishop

	2004	2005	2006	Triennium
Staff Costs	$962,000	$995,000	$1,030,000	$2,987,000
Peace Ministries	156,000	111,000	111,000	378,000
Jubilee Ministries	126,000	241,000	136,000	503,000
Jubilee Grants	50,000	50,000	50,000	150,000
Social Justice	162,000	162,000	162,000	486,000
Office of Government Relations	260,000	251,000	248,000	759,000
Social Responsibility in Investments Committee	56,000	56,000	56,000	168,000
Other Costs	19,000	20,000	20,000	59,000
Total PJM	**$1,791,000**	**$1,886,000**	**$1,813,000**	**$5,490,000**

Women's Ministries

Women's Ministries serves the mission and ministry of all women in the Episcopal Church at every level—national, provincial, diocesan, and parochial—as well as the Anglican Communion. This department is responsive to the work of established women's organizations and networks in the church and identifies and communicates issues which affect the role of women in the life of the Episcopal Church and the Church's mission. Women's Ministries relates to: the Office of Research; Ethnic Congregational Development and Congregational Development to develop a comprehensive strategy for Congregational Development for the Episcopal Church; and works collaboratively with staff colleagues in the areas of leadership development, faith formation and spiritual development, justice and peace, and Anglican, ecumenical, and interfaith partnerships.

	2004	2005	2006	Triennium
Staff Costs	$162,000	$167,000	$173,000	$502,000
Other Costs	158,000	158,000	157,000	473,000
Total Women's Minitries	**$320,000**	**$325,000**	**$330,000**	**$975,000**

Ministries with Young People (MYP)

Ministries with Young People provides support to congregations, dioceses, and provinces in the areas of children's ministries, Christian education, youth ministries, and ministries with young adults and higher education. Through programs and special projects mandated by General Convention, MYP fulfills its mission through training events, conferences, consultations, network programs, and by producing basic and specialized resources for congregational use. MYP also works extensively with ecumenical partners and Episcopal curriculum developers in providing resources for the Church. The General Convention approved a $1,000,000 in additional funding for the Ministries with Young People Cluster with specific funding to be determined by Executive Council in consultation with young people and DFMS staff.

BUDGET APPENDIX

	2004	2005	2006	Triennium
Staff Costs	$678,000	$702,000	$727,000	$2,107,000
Children's Ministries and Christian Education	163,000	163,000	162,000	488,000
Youth Ministries	163,000	162,000	163,000	488,000
Young Adult and Higher Education Ministries	162,000	163,000	163,000	488,000
Expanded Campus Ministries	50,000	50,000	50,000	150,000
General Convention Youth Presence	0	0	60,000	60,000
Print and Electronic Resources	194,000	171,000	171,000	536,000
New and Expanded Initiatives	333,000	333,000	334,000	1,000,000
Total MYP	**$1,743,000**	**$1,744,000**	**$1,830,000**	**$5,317,000**

Episcopal Migration Ministries (EMM)

Episcopal Migration Ministries carries out the mission of the church to assist and advocate for refugees and immigrants and for all victims of persecution who have been violently uprooted from their homes. Through a network of diocesan programs, often involving parish sponsorship of refugees, EMM assists refugees' transition to life in the United States and helps them to become productive members of society. EMM promotes the protection and well being of immigrants and refugees in the United States and advocates for the just and humane treatment of forcibly displaced persons worldwide.

	2004	2005	2006	Triennium
Staff Costs	$1,152,000	$1,195,000	$1,240,000	$3,587,000
Grants	3,834,000	3,834,000	3,834,000	11,502,000
Other Costs	154,000	155,000	154,000	463,000
Total EMM	**$5,140,000**	**$5,184,000**	**$5,228,000**	**$15,552,000**

[These costs are supported through federal government contracts in the amounts of $5,169,000 in 2004, $5,180,000 in 2005, and $5,202,000 in 2006, for a total of $15,551,000 in the triennium.]

MISSION BLOCK GRANT PARTNERSHIPS

Church-wide Partnerships

The Executive Council is committed to sustaining relations with provinces and dioceses and to meeting the locally-established needs of our historic partners, including those dioceses within Domestic Missionary Partners (the former Coalition 14), overseas dioceses within ECUSA, and the three historically Black Episcopal Colleges. Supporting our Covenant Agreements provides a way for all Episcopalians to participate in the development and mission work of the church in Mexico, the Philippines, Central America, and Liberia. Working through provincial partnerships, the Council assists the church in understanding and responding to national and international public policy issues based on theological and ethical perspectives following the priorities established by the General Convention.

Overseas Covenants and Partnerships

The expenses here represent covenants and commitments with overseas partners, which have grown through historical development by General Convention mandates. Also reflected here is ECUSA's fair share of the Inter-Anglican budget (the Anglican Consultative Council).

Overseas Covenants	2004	2005	2006	Triennium
Central America	$1,009,000	$998,000	$991,000	$2,998,000
Liberia	228,000	221,000	214,000	663,000
Mexico	661,000	634,000	592,000	1,887,000
Philippines	266,000	267,000	267,000	800,000
Subtotal Overseas Covenants	**$2,164,000**	**$2,120,000**	**$2,064,000**	**$6,348,000**

Overseas Partnerships

Specific funding for overseas dioceses has yet to be determined and will be done on a year–to–year basis upon evaluation. Funds that become available in this category will be redistributed among the following dioceses by Executive Council; Cuba, Colombia, Dominican Republic, Ecuador Central, Ecuador Litoral, Haiti, Honduras, Micronesia(Guam), Puerto Rico, Taiwan, Venezuela and Virgin Islands.

Subtotal Overseas Dioceses	$2,173,000	$2,172,000	$2,173,000	$6,518,000
Anglican Consultative Council (ACC)	$578,000	$601,000	$601,000	$1,780,000
Total Overseas Partners and Covenants	$4,915,000	$4,893,000	$4,838,000	$14,646,000

BUDGET APPENDIX

Domestic Mission Support

These are block grant commitments paid monthly or quarterly to U.S. entities. The Executive Council is committed to sustaining relations with provinces and dioceses and to meeting the locally established needs of our historic partners, including those dioceses serving Native American congregations, dioceses within Domestic Missionary Partners (the former Coalition 14), and the three historically black Episcopal Colleges.

Block Grants:	2004	2005	2006	Triennium
Commission on Religion in Appalachia	$28,000	$28,000	$28,000	$84,000
Episcopal Appalachian Ministries	16,000	16,000	16,000	48,000
Domestic Missionary Partners (Eastern Oregon, Eau Claire, Western Kansas)	243,000	234,000	228,000	705,000
Native Americans (N. Dakota, S. Dakota, Navajoland, Alaska)	1,335,000	1,335,000	1,335,000	4,005,000
Indigenous Theological Training Institute	125,000	125,000	125,000	375,000
Historically Black Colleges (St. Paul's, St. Augustine's, Voorhees)	1,308,000	1,269,000	1,230,000	3,807,000
National Episcopal AIDS Coalition	73,000	71,000	68,000	212,000
Episcopal Conference of the Deaf	10,000	9,000	9,000	28,000
Ministries with the Disabled	10,000	9,000	9,000	28,000
Total Domestic Mission Support	**$3,148,000**	**$3,096,000**	**$3,048,000**	**$9,292,000**

Support to All Nine Provinces	2004	2005	2006	Triennium
Grant Support	$211,000	$212,000	$212,000	$635,000
Total Support to Provinces	**$211,000**	**$212,000**	**$212,000**	**$635,000**

Ecumenical Appropriations

The mission of the Ecumenical and Interfaith Relations Office is to promote the growth of visible unity in one Eucharistic fellowship, sustain, and strengthen dialogue for Christian unity with other churches. This section of the budget represents support for Episcopal Church participation in and with national and international councils, bodies, and communions seeking the unity of the church.

	2004	2005	2006	Triennium
National Council of Churches	$362,000	$363,000	$367,000	$1,092,000
World Council of Churches	167,000	169,000	170,000	506,000
Total Ecumenical Appropriations	**$529,000**	**$532,000**	**$537,000**	**$1,598,000**

Episcopal Relief and Development (ERD)

All activities of Episcopal Relief and Development are directed to fulfilling its mission: to be the primary means through which all Episcopalians can express their compassion for people in need throughout the world. ERD is the organized, tangible response to Christ's call to minister to the hungry and thirsty, the sick and the imprisoned, to clothe the naked and welcome the stranger. The amounts in the DFMS budget represent a block grant to support ERD domestic grants and administrative costs. In addition to direct support, DFMS provides indirect support in the form of space and utilities as well as accounting and administrative services shown as DFMS Contributed Services in the following table.

	2004	2005	2006	Triennium
Domestic Grant Support	$200,000	$200,000	$200,000	$600,000
Administrative Grant Support	200,000	200,000	200,000	600,000
DFMS Contributed Services	857,000	857,000	858,000	2,572,000
Total ERD	**$1,257,000**	**$1,257,000**	**$1,258,000**	**$3,772,000**

Planned Giving

The Planned Giving funds are used to support the Episcopal Church Foundation's (ECF) efforts at the parish and diocesan levels to build the church's financial strength at the grass-roots level.

	2004	2005	2006	Triennium
Episcopal Church Foundation Support	$150,000	$150,000	$150,000	$450,000
Total Planned Giving	**$150,000**	**$150,000**	**$150,000**	**$450,000**

COMMUNICATION

The Office of Communication (COMM) is a consultative service and strategy organization that interacts with four key constituents and audiences to help meet the communication needs of the church.
- Episcopal Church Center departments and other church agencies
- Churches, dioceses and provinces
- Church and other news organizations
- The general public

It provides breaking news through Episcopal News Service, feature and informational information through Episcopal Life, and web, video, satellite and other media services. The office also maintains an Information Desk and coordinates print production, as well as the resources provided through Episcopal Parish Services. The Director of Communication is a member of the Presiding Bishop's Management Team.

Depending on variables such as audience, message, timing and forum, the appropriate mix of these communication services can be deployed to serve the greater communication strategy which is to deliver timely, accurate and valuable information to the church and to the world, and to facilitate communication between constituents that intersect with The Episcopal Church.

	2004	2005	2006	Triennium
Staff Costs	$243,000	$251,000	$259,000	$753,000
Other Costs	34,000	34,000	34,000	102,000
Total COMM	**$277,000**	**$285,000**	**$293,000**	**$855,000**

Media Services	**2004**	**2005**	**2006**	**Triennium**
Staff Costs	$844,000	$874,000	$904,000	$2,622,000
News & Information	25,000	25,000	25,000	75,000
Radio /TV/ Multi-Media	105,000	105,000	105,000	315,000
Satellite/Cable/Webcast	95,000	95,000	95,000	285,000
Internet	255,000	255,000	255,000	765,000
Special Media Projects	85,000	85,000	85,000	255,000
Church Organizational Support	25,000	25,000	25,000	75,000
National Ad Campaign (Pilot/ Test Market)	250,000	250,000	250,000	750,000
Other Costs	12,000	12,000	312,000	336,000
Total Media Services	**$1,696,000**	**$1,726,000**	**$2,056,000**	**$5,478,000**

Episcopal Life	2004	2005	2006	Triennium
Staff Costs	$681,000	$705,000	$732,000	$2,118,000
Other Costs	1,525,000	1,567,000	1,703,000	4,795,000
Total Episcopal Life	**$2,206,000**	**$2,272,000**	**$2,435,000**	**$6,913,000**

[These costs are largely supported by advertising and subscription revenues, estimated at $1,856,000 in 2004, $1,989,000 in 2005, and $2,112,000 in 2006, for a total of $5,957,000 in the triennium.]

Episcopal Parish Services	2004	2005	2006	Triennium
Other Costs	$263,000	$288,000	$264,000	$815,000
Total Episcopal Parish Services	**$263,000**	**$288,000**	**$264,000**	**$815,000**

Episcopal Book and Resource Center (EBRC)

The Episcopal Book and Resource Center specializes in books on congregational development, Christian education, theology, spirituality, pastoral care, and related subjects. It stocks a full spectrum of Bibles, the Book of Common Prayer, and Hymnals. The ministry of EBRC is to serve the whole church (and beyond), by providing quality resources, knowledgeable service, and information to individuals, study groups, parishes/diocesan libraries, bookstores, and resource centers. Mailing, special ordering services, and an extensive online catalog, as well as a range of gifts are also offered.

Episcopal Book and Resource Center	2004	2005	2006	Triennium
Staff Costs	$190,000	$196,000	$204,000	$590,000
Other Costs	344,000	351,000	356,000	1,051,000
Total EBRC	**$534,000**	**$547,000**	**$560,000**	**$1,641,000**

BUDGET APPENDIX

CORPORATE (Reported as Mission Support in the Pre-Convention Budget)

The Corporate section includes all of the administrative and financial costs incurred for DFMS. Although these costs are incurred largely in support of all DFMS activities, they are currently presented on a gross cost (unallocated) basis.

Office of the Chief Operating Officer

Assisting the Presiding Bishop in his role as Chief Executive Officer, the Chief Operating Officer coordinates the work of the Management Team and the organization as a whole. This includes managing the internal organizational support functions, including human resources, building services, management information systems, telecommunications, mail and purchasing.

	2004	2005	2006	Triennium
Staff Costs	$387,000	$400,000	$415,000	$1,202,000
Other Costs	93,000	78,000	100,000	271,000
Total Chief Operating Officer	**$480,000**	**$478,000**	**$515,000**	**$1,473,000**

Treasurer's Office

The Office of the Treasurer is responsible for oversight of the financial functions and the investment assets of DFMS. This includes investment management of both the long-term assets, such as the endowment portfolio and charitable trusts, and short-term assets, such as DFMS operating cash and custodial accounts held for others; it also includes oversight of banking functions, such as electronic funds transfers, as well as financial management training and oversight of entities and activities funded throughout the budget.

	2004	2005	2006	Triennium
Staff Costs	$918,000	$951,000	$986,000	$2,855,000
Contingency	150,000	150,000	150,000	450,000
Other Costs	627,000	636,000	646,000	1,909,000
Total TREAS	**$1,695,000**	**$1,737,000**	**$1,782,000**	**$5,214,000**

Office of the Controller

The Office of the Controller is responsible for processing all of the financial transactions for DFMS and reporting, summarizing, and interpreting financial data for the use of management, creditors, boards and committees of the organization. As a unit of the Treasurer's Department, it helps to develop budgets and forecasts, measures actual performance against operating plans and interprets the results of operations to all levels of management. It performs all of the accounting functions for DFMS which includes cash receipts, accounts payable, payroll, cash disbursements, account and diocesan receivables, grants payable, etc. It also works closely with the Society's auditors to design and implement appropriate controls to safeguard assets and resources at DFMS.

	2004	2005	2006	Triennium
Staff Costs	$900,000	$934,000	$970,000	$2,804,000
Other Costs	226,000	226,000	225,000	677,000
Total CONT	**$1,126,000**	**$1,160,000**	**$1,195,000**	**$3,481,000**

Human Resource Management

The goal of Human Resource Management office is to have the best person in the right job at the right time, adequately prepared, effectively motivated, in compliance with moral and civil law, and reflective of the cultural diversity of the Church and society. In addition, the human resource management team ensures that all staff—both current and retired—are treated fairly in keeping with stated human resources policies and practices. Valuing responsibility over entitlement, partnership over dominance, self-management over control, and service over self-interest, the mission of this initiative is to partner with others in developing and realizing opportunities for enhancing the quality of effort and productivity in our mutual ministry.

	2004	2005	2006	Triennium
Staff Costs	$539,000	$558,000	$577,000	$1,674,000
Other Costs	328,000	317,000	332,000	977,000
Subtotal HRM	**$867,000**	**$875,000**	**$909,000**	**$2,651,000**
Retiree Health & Pension Costs	620,000	659,000	697,000	1,976,000
Total HRM	**$1,487,000**	**$1,534,000**	**$1,606,000**	**$4,627,000**

Management Information Systems

The MIS staff is responsible for all aspects of computer infrastructure at The Episcopal Church Center and DFMS satellite offices. Principal responsibilities include:

- Maintenance of computer network hardware, including a major upgrade or replacement of all personal computers approximately once a triennium
- Maintenance of wide area network connectivity to the Archives in Austin, Texas and the Office of Government Relations in Washington, D.C.
- Support for E-mail services including remote access worldwide for traveling employees, continuous Internet access, and maintenance of general software tools such as word processors and spreadsheet programs
- Assistance to other departments in the installation and maintenance of commercial software packages in specialized areas such as accounting, human resources, fund-raising, and grant management
- Development of custom software for individual departments, such as systems for transacting Parochial Report and Church Deployment activity over the World Wide Web, and approximately 30 local applications
- Hosting of web-enabled data base applications to permit continuous Internet access
- Strategic planning for the application of new technology to the Church's mission, in collaboration with other departments, Executive Council, and organizations such as the Church Pension Group
- Help-desk support and computer training for staff
- Selecting vendors in computer-related technologies (telecommunications, photocopying, etc.) and negotiating service contracts with them
- Special projects such as DFMS computer presence at General Convention

	2004	2005	2006	Triennium
Staff Costs	$635,000	$659,000	$683,000	$1,977,000
Other Costs	492,000	650,000	556,000	1,698,000
Total MIS	**$1,127,000**	**$1,309,000**	**$1,239,000**	**$3,675,000**

BUDGET APPENDIX

Purchasing

The Purchasing function for the procurement of supplies and equipment is carried out primarily through the Office of the Chief Operating Officer and Building Services. This includes the direct costs of stationery, office supplies, office equipment leases and maintenance costs.

	2004	2005	2006	Triennium
Other Costs	$310,000	$310,000	$320,000	$940,000
Total Purchasing Costs	**$310,000**	**$310,000**	**$320,000**	**$940,000**

Mailing Center (MC)

The Mailing Center handles all processing and mailing functions at the Episcopal Church Center for DFMS.

	2004	2005	2006	Triennium
Staff Costs	$263,000	$274,000	$284,000	$821,000
Other Costs	442,000	446,000	463,000	1,351,000
Total MC	**$705,000**	**$720,000**	**$747,000**	**$2,172,000**

Telecommunications (TELECOM)

Telecommunications operators are the first voices heard when calling the Episcopal Church Center. Telecommunications is responsible for answering inquiries and directing calls to the appropriate offices.

	2004	2005	2006	Triennium
Staff Costs	$124,000	$129,000	$134,000	$387,000
Other Costs	338,000	339,000	339,000	1,016,000
Recovery of Costs from Affiliated Agencies	(33,000)	(33,000)	(34,000)	(100,000)
Total TELECOM	**$429,000**	**$435,000**	**$439,000**	**$1,303,000**

Building Services

The Episcopal Church Center is open twenty-four hours a day, seven days a week. The Building Services staff manages all building functions, from utilities to cleaning, repairs, maintenance and security. The staff also handles the purchasing of furniture and fixtures, as well as all capital building improvements.

	2004	2005	2006	Triennium
Staff Costs	$335,000	$347,000	$360,000	$1,042,000
Utilities	291,000	291,000	291,000	873,000
Maintenance & Repairs	432,000	433,000	433,000	1,298,000
Cleaning	515,000	531,000	546,000	1,592,000
Security	117,000	118,000	118,000	353,000
Capital Projects	25,000	25,000	25,000	75,000
Other	8,000	6,000	7,000	21,000
Total Building Services	**$1,723,000**	**$1,751,000**	**$1,780,000**	**$5,254,000**
ERD Contributed Services	**2004**	**2005**	**2006**	**Triennium**
Allocation to ERD	($857,000)	($857,000)	($858,000)	($2,572,000)
ERD Contributed Services	**($857,000)**	**($857,000)**	**($858,000)**	**($2,572,000)**

Detail of Diocesan Commitments

Diocese	2003 Asking @ 21% of Income	2003 Actual Pledge	2003 % of Income Pledged	2003 Actual Pledge vs. 2003 Asking
Alabama	$481,616	$481,616	21%	$(0)
Alaska	143,797	69,660	10%	-74,137
Albany	155,159	135,215	18%	-19,944
Arizona	396,540	396,500	21%	0
Arkansas	271,122	258,211	20%	-12,911
Atlanta	597,812	597,812	21%	0
Bethlehem	196,464	25,000	3%	-171,464
California	609,904	610,000	21%	0
Central Florida	375,492	214,600	12%	-160,892
Central Gulf Coast	383,996	404,996	22%	+21,000
Central New York	294,124	294,124	21%	0
Central Pennsylvania	263,835	263,835	21%	0
Chicago	706,315	706,315	21%	0
Colorado	352,050	178,741	11%	-173,309
Connecticut	1,015,563	1,035,738	21%	+20,175
Dallas	681,972	511,344	16%	-170,628
Delaware	259,013	259,579	21%	566
East Carolina	244,699	244,700	21%	0
East Tennessee	297,361	297,361	21%	0
Eastern Michigan	155,480	97,647	13%	-57,833
Eastern Oregon	63,649	58,000	19%	-5,649
Easton	120,317	120,317	21%	0
Eau Claire	54,097	48,000	19%	-6,097
El Camino Real	287,047	287,047	21%	0
Florida	396,364	198,745	11%	-197,619
Fond du Lac	96,998	96,998	21%	0
Fort Worth	277,928	80,000	6%	-197,928
Georgia	325,182	325,182	21%	0
Hawaii	291,361	291,400	21%	0
Idaho	86,896	86,896	21%	0
Indianapolis	482,658	482,659	21%	0
Iowa	192,049	159,049	17%	-33,000
Kansas	261,366	261,366	21%	0
Kentucky	228,179	190,149	17%	-38,030
Lexington	185,386	185,386	21%	0
Long Island	571,592	420,000	15%	-151,592
Los Angeles	726,410	730,318	21%	+3,908

BUDGET APPENDIX

Detail of Diocesan Commitments

Diocese	2003 Asking @ 21% of Income	2003 Actual Pledge	2003 % of Income Pledged	2003 Actual Pledge vs. 2003 Asking
Louisiana	233,479	233,479	21%	0
Maine	253,003	253,003	21%	0
Maryland	547,208	456,500	18%	-90,708
Massachusetts	1,020,159	1,020,159	21%	0
Michigan	458,381	458,381	21%	0
Milwaukee	261,976	261,972	21%	0
Minnesota	468,975	468,975	21%	0
Mississippi	440,141	440,141	21%	0
Missouri	238,122	238,110	21%	0
Montana	83,414	80,000	20%	-3,414
Navajoland Area Mission	50,526	1,000	0%	-49,526
Nebraska	145,900	145,900	21%	0
Nevada	119,827	119,826	21%	0
New Hampshire	243,991	243,991	21%	0
New Jersey	560,449	400,000	15%	-160,449
New York	1,000,020	1,000,000	21%	0
Newark	595,287	710,250	25%	+114,963
North Carolina	770,451	770,451	21%	0
North Dakota	92,151	52,400	12%	-39,751
Northern California	314,470	314,469	21%	0
Northern Indiana	113,362	112,847	21%	-515
Northern Michigan	86,768	70,000	17%	-16,768
Northwestern Pennsylvania	107,450	107,448	21%	0
Northwest Texas	217,458	198,200	19%	-19,258
Ohio	568,864	568,864	21%	0
Oklahoma	378,404	378,404	21%	0
Olympia	553,803	553,802	21%	0
Oregon	397,312	397,312	21%	0
Pennsylvania	720,300	675,000	20%	-45,300
Pittsburgh	279,610	129,902	10%	-149,708
Quincy	35,923	21,503	13%	-14,420
Rhode Island	378,041	378,041	21%	0
Rio Grande	294,572	35,000	2%	-259,572
Rochester	314,037	314,037	21%	0
San Diego	256,733	144,669	12%	-112,064
San Joaquin	263,480	263,480	21%	0

Detail of Diocesan Commitments

Diocese	2003 Asking @ 21% of Income	2003 Actual Pledge	2003 % of Income Pledged	2003 Actual Pledge vs. 2003 Asking
South Carolina	417,333	151,347	8%	-265,986
South Dakota	91,035	69,360	16%	-21,675
Southeast Florida	478,860	478,860	21%	0
Southern Ohio	642,065	642,065	21%	0
Southern Virginia	326,707	200,000	13%	-126,707
Southwest Florida	470,606	470,606	21%	0
Southwestern Virginia	165,000	165,000	21%	0
Spokane	132,800	132,800	21%	0
Springfield	115,274	101,700	19%	-13,574
Tennessee	221,442	163,369	15%	-58,073
Texas	1,195,410	460,962	8%	-734,448
Upper South Carolina	384,978	384,978	21%	0
Utah	1,212,687	520,000	9%	-692,687
Vermont	138,099	80,000	12%	-58,099
Virginia	865,047	865,047	21%	0
Washington	483,835	580,030	25%	96,195
West Missouri	286,278	286,278	21%	0
West Tennessee	192,298	158,702	17%	-33,596
West Texas	665,207	601,860	19%	-63,347
West Virginia	147,418	147,418	21%	0
Western Kansas	42,047	42,047	21%	0
Western Louisiana	186,153	186,153	21%	0
Western Massachusetts	391,523	391,523	21%	0
Western Michigan	122,235	122,235	21%	0
Western New York	238,508	205,033	18%	-33,475
Western North Carolina	263,448	263,400	21%	0
Wyoming	141,612	141,612	21%	0
Total	$35,411,742	$31,134,407	18%	$(4,277,335)

BUDGET
APPENDIX

Notes:

Five dioceses exceeded the 21% asking for 2003 and as a Church we are especially grateful to the Dioceses of Newark, Washington, Central Gulf Coast, Connecticut, and Los Angeles for their leadership.

Several dioceses moved up to the 21% asking over the 2001-2003 triennium and as a Church we congratulate the Dioceses of Chicago, Northern Indiana, San Joaquin, Southwest Florida, and Wyoming.

The potential income from the 38 dioceses that were unable to meet the 21% asking could have resulted in an additional $4,500,000 being made available to the budget for 2003; if that 21% level of giving were attained over the 2004-2006 triennium, the resulting $13,700,000 would provide enough revenue to fund nearly all the requests to the DFMS for the triennium.

The above listing includes only pledges from domestic Dioceses. From time to time the DFMS receives payments from overseas Dioceses. For instance, in 2002 payments totaling $33,075 were received from the Dioceses of Taiwan, Haiti, Dominican Republic, Mexico and Honduras, and from the Convocation of American Churches in Europe. For 2003 DFMS received a pledge of $20,000 from the Bishop in charge of the Convocation of American Churches in Europe, this amount represents 20 % of the Convocation's annual income.

Shaded areas identify 20/20 resolutions					
RES#	TITLE	FUNDING REQUEST	PROPOSED BUDGET	ADOPTED BUDGET	ADDITIONAL COMMENTS
A001	Budget Appropriation for the Archives of the Episcopal Church	2,120,303	2,120,000	2,050,000	
A002	Budget Appropriation for the Board for Church Deployment	90,000	71,000	65,000	
A003	Budget Appropriation for the General Board of Examining Chaplains	650,169	602,000	619,000	
A004	General Ordination Exam Fee	n/a	n/a	n/a	
A006	Employment Policies Task Group	10,000	0	0	
A007	Aging Task Force	10,000	10,000	0	
A010	Continue Anti-Racism Mandate	Dollars Unknown		Same as Pre-Convention Budget	Already in budget
A013	The Church's Role in Counseling and Education on Biomedical Ethics	36,000	0	0	
A017	National Conversation on Women's Ordination	50,000	50,000	0	
A019	Continue Standing Committee on HIV/AIDS	44,000	44,000	44,000	
A022	Nathan Network Funding	49,000	41,000	0	

BUDGET   APPENDIX

Shaded areas identify 20/20 resolutions

RES#	TITLE	FUNDING REQUEST	PROPOSED BUDGET	ADOPTED BUDGET	ADDITIONAL COMMENTS
A023	Establish Institutional Wellness and the Prevention of Sexual Misconduct Task Force	50,000	0	25,000	
A025	Trafficking of Women, Girls and Boys	4,000	0	0	Already in budget
A026	Baptismal Parity	35,500	0	0	
A029	Open Dialogue on Difficult Issues	28,000	0	0	
A030	21st Century Survey Resources	8,000	0	0	Already in budget
A031	A Multicultural, Multiracial Church	20,000	0	0	Already in budget
A032	Youth Study	11,500	0	0	Already in budget
A035	Implement Humanitarian Goals in Africa	300,000	150,000	150,000	Already in budget
A061	Continuing Education Scholarships	0	0		Discharged by Committee
A065	Leadership Programs for 18-30 year olds	1,500,000	0	1,000,000	Partially funded by Adopted Budget, New and expanded initiative funding to be allocated by Executive Council in consultation with young people and staff.

839

JOURNAL REPORTS

Shaded areas identify 20/20 resolutions

RES#	TITLE	FUNDING REQUEST	PROPOSED BUDGET	ADOPTED BUDGET	ADDITIONAL COMMENTS
A067	Fund for Theological Education	300,000	0	0	
A069	Spanish Music Resources	0	0	0	Replaced by A092
A070	Creative Worship Resources	Dollars Unknown		0	Replaced by A092
A071	Mission-based Prayers	Dollars Unknown		0	Replaced by A092
A073	Plant New Churches	Dollars Unknown		0	Already in budget
A076	Transformation Resources	Dollars Unknown		0	Already in budget
A077	Trained Leadership	4,000,000	0	0	Initiatives to be determined by Executive Council in consultation with young people and staff. See A065 for new funding added to budget.
A081	National Ad Campaign	1,500,000	750,000	750,000	Pilot project in target markets Already in budget
A082	Multilingual Publications	255,000	100,000	100,000	Partially funded by Adopted Budget
A089	"Open Communion" Task Force	Dollars Unknown		0	

840

BUDGET APPENDIX

Shaded areas identify 20/20 resolutions

RES#	TITLE	FUNDING REQUEST	PROPOSED BUDGET	ADOPTED BUDGET	ADDITIONAL COMMENTS
A092	Reauthorize Enriching Our Worship work	130,000	0	130,000	Now called Multi-cultural, Multilingual Liturgies for "New" Populations
A100	Revise Lesser Feasts and Fasts 2000	20,000	0	0	
A101	Church Planting Liturgies	Dollars Unknown		0	
A102	Culturally Sensitive Rites	0	0	0	Replaced by A092
A104	Facilitate the Enrichment of Worship with Evangelism Focus	0	0	0	Replaced by A092
A105	Resources for Liturgical Education	Dollars Unknown		0	Replaced by A092
A106	Liturgical Development and Episcopal Authority	15,000	0	0	
A107	Renewal and Enrichment of Common Worship	300,000	0	0	
A109	International Anglican Liturgical Consultation	25,000	0	0	
A121	Clergy and Lay Professional Continuing Education	46,000	0	0	
A124	Standing Commission on Health and a Staff Position in Health Care	200,000	0	0	

Shaded areas identify 20/20 resolutions

RES#	TITLE	FUNDING REQUEST	PROPOSED BUDGET	ADOPTED BUDGET	ADDITIONAL COMMENTS
A126	Youth Charged and Convicted as Adults	Dollars Unknown		0	Already in budget
A133	Adopt "Expanding Mission and Vitality in Small Congregations"	Dollars Unknown		0	Already in budget
A136	National Mission Narrative/Annual Report	Dollars Unknown		0	Already in budget
A140	Mission Funding	Dollars Unknown		0	Recommended to Executive Council as priority
A146	Provincial Coordinators Funding	Dollars Unknown		Same as Pre-Convention Budget	Already in budget
A153	House of Bishops Committee on Pastoral Development Budget Appropriation	45,000	39,000	45,000	
A157	Joint Standing Committee on Program, Budget and Finance Budget Appropriation	106,000	67,000	90,000	Pre-Convention budget number in error
A158	Title IV Budget Appropriation	75,000	45,000	60,000	
B004	Mission Funding Task Force	75,000	0	0	
B006	Dialogue with Reformed Episcopal Church	Dollars Unknown		0	

BUDGET APPENDIX

Shaded areas identify 20/20 resolutions

RES#	TITLE	FUNDING REQUEST	PROPOSED BUDGET	ADOPTED BUDGET	ADDITIONAL COMMENTS
B010	Continue Leadership Program for Musicians Serving Small Congregations	75,000	60,000	60,000	
B018	Families of Clergy United in Support	75,000	0	0	
B020	Survivors of Murder Victims	50,000	0	0	
B024	Task Force on Life-Long Christian Education	120,000	0	0	
B026	Criminal Justice Committee	80,000	0	0	B025 Replaced by B026
C006	Evangelism to the New Majority	Dollars Unknown		0	Already in budget
C008	Episcopal Council of Indigenous Ministries Funding	1,500,000	0	0	
C016	Integrated Pest Management	Dollars Unknown		0	
C017	Global Warming/ Energy Conservation for National Church Headquarters	Dollars Unknown		0	
C025	Lifting Up of the Ministry of the Baptized in Ordinations	Dollars Unknown		0	
C027	Audio-Visual Materials of the Episcopal Church	Dollars Unknown		0	Already in budget
C029	Translation of Documents into Spanish	85,000	0	0	Partially funded by Adopted Budget
C035	Publish Lectionary for Lesser Feasts	10,000	0	0	

Shaded areas identify 20/20 resolutions					
RES#	TITLE	FUNDING REQUEST	PROPOSED BUDGET	ADOPTED BUDGET	ADDITIONAL COMMENTS
D001	Funding Implications of a 10% Tithe	Dollars Unknown		0	
D013	Annotated Constitution and Canons, known as White & Dykman	45,000	0	0	
D015	Make COSE Materials Available on the Web	Dollars Unknown		0	Already in budget
D022	Resolution on Rites Supporting Life-long Relationships	Dollars Unknown		0	Partially funded by Adopted Budget
D025	Continuation of Efforts to End Racism	Dollars Unknown		Same as Pre-Convention Budget	Already in budget
D030	Funding for Regional Ministry	Dollars Unknown		0	
D031	Develop plans for next Triennium	Dollars Unknown		0	Already in budget
D034	Sex Trafficking: Educational Material for Parishes & Dioceses	Dollars Unknown		0	
D036	Research & Disseminate Social Services Data on Marriage	Dollars Unknown		0	
D038	Resolution on Liberia	Dollars Unknown		0	
D047	Post Abortion Healing	Dollars Unknown		0	
D057	Use of Technology Task Force	Dollars Unknown		0	
D058	Provide Assistance Hearing Devices	Dollars Unknown		0	
D060	Education about Ordained and Licensed Ministries	Dollars Unknown		0	

BUDGET APPENDIX

RES#	TITLE	FUNDING REQUEST	PROPOSED BUDGET	ADOPTED BUDGET	ADDITIONAL COMMENTS
	Shaded areas identify 20/20 resolutions				
D061	Jubilee Ministries Funding	1,000,000	0	150,000	Partially funded by Adopted Budget
D068	Response to New War Situation	Dollars Unknown		0	
D069	SC on Church Communications	0	0	0	
D075	Holistic Christian Education Study	100,000		0	Replaced by B024 & A065
D077	Racial Hatred and Incarcerations	25,000		0	Already in budget
N/A	SC on Anglican and International Peace	72,000	66,000	58,000	
N/A	SC on Constitution and Canons	57,000	53,000	48,000	
N/A	SC on National Concerns	79,000	79,000	71,000	
N/A	SC on Stewardship and Development	68,000	68,000	65,000	
N/A	SC on Structure of the Church	49,000	49,000	49,000	
N/A	SC on World Mission	126,000	89,000	89,000	
N/A	SC on Nominations	33,000	27,000	24,000	
N/A	House of Deputies Committee-State of the Church	71,000	86,000	46,000	
N/A	Funding for Black Colleges	4,320,000	3,807,000	3,807,000	Already in budget
N/A	TOTALS	20,148,472	8,473,000	9,595,000	

845

THE JOINT STANDING COMMITTEE ON PROGRAM, BUDGET & FINANCE

Province I
Mr. Byron Rushing (Massachusetts)
The Right Reverend Andrew Smith (Connecticut)
Mr. Dennis Stark (Rhode Island)

Province II
Ms. Lyn Headley-Moore (Newark)
The Reverend Canon Dr. Johncy Itty, *Bishop Elect Oregon* (Long Island)
The Right Reverend David B. Joslin (New Jersey)

Province III
Ms. Anne Bardol (Northwestern Pennsylvania)
The Right Reverend Charles E. Bennison, Jr. (Pennsylvania)
Mr. Donald W. Bushyager (Pittsburgh)

Province IV
The Reverend Canon Ernest L. Bennett (Central Florida)
Mr. Arthur M. Bjontegard, Jr. (Upper South Carolina)
The Right Reverend Charles G. vonRosenberg (East Tennessee)

Province V
Ms. Bonnie Anderson, *Chair* (Michigan)
The Right Reverend Russell E. Jacobus, *Co-chair* (Fond du Lac)
Mr. Jon B. Boss (Southern Ohio)

Province VI
The Reverend Willa M. Goodfellow (Iowa)
The Reverend Kathleen S. Milligan (Iowa)
The Right Reverend James E. Krotz (Nebraska)

Province VII
Ms. Pan Adams (Arkansas)
The Reverend Canon William D. Nix (Northwest Texas)
The Right Reverend Wallis Ohl (Northwest Texas)

Province VIII
The Reverend Altagracia Perez (Los Angeles)
Canon Holly McAlpen (California)
The Right Reverend James E. Waggoner, Jr. (Spokane)

Province IX
The Right Reverend Julio Cesar Holguin (Dominican Republic)
The Reverend Augusto Sandino Sànchez (Dominican Republic)
Susan Delgado-Park (Honduras)

Ex Officio
The Most Reverend Frank Griswold, Presiding Bishop
The Very Reverend George L.W. Werner, President of the House of Deputies
The Reverend Rosemari G. Sullivan, Secretary of the General Convention
Mr. Thomas Hershkowitz, Treasurer of the General Convention

REGISTRAR OF THE GENERAL CONVENTION

From September 23, 2000 to April 5, 2003, 26 Bishops have been ordained and consecrated in and for this Church.

The Rev. Canon Carlson Gerdau, was in attendance as the Registrar at the following consecrations:
The Rev. William Otis Gregg as Bishop of Eastern Oregon
The Rev. David Jung-Hsin Lai as Bishop Coadjutor of Taiwan
The Rev. Katherine Jefferts Shori as Bishop of Nevada
The Rev. Roy Frederick Cedarholm, Jr., as Bishop Suffragan of Massachusetts
The Rev. Don Edward Johnson as Bishop of West Tennessee
The Rev. John Neil Alexander as Bishop of Atlanta
The Rev. William Michie Klusmeyer as Bishop of West Virginia
The Rev. Lloyd Emmanuel Allen as Bishop of Honduras
The Rev. Gladstone Bailey Adams III as Bishop of Central New York
The Rev. Pierre Welte Whalon as Bishop Suffragan-in-Charge of the Convocation of American Churches in Europe
The Rev. James Marshall Adams Jr., as Bishop of Western Kansas
The Rev. Robert Ronald Gepert as Bishop Coadjutor of Western Michigan

Br. Richard Thomas Biernacki, BSG, Canon, served as Deputy Registrar at the following consecrations:
The Rev. Stacy Fred Sauls as Bishop of Lexington
The Rev. James Elliot Curry as Bishop Suffragan of Connecticut
The Rev. Wilfrido Ramos-Orench as Bishop Suffragan of Connecticut
The Rev. James Edward Waggoner, Jr. as Bishop of Spokane
The Rev. Thomas Clark Ely as Bishop of Vermont
The Rev. Philip Menzie Duncan, II as Bishop of the Central Gulf Coast
The Rev. George Wayne Smith as Bishop Coadjutor of Missouri

The Registrar, the Rev. Canon Carlson Gerdau, and the Deputy Registrar, Brother Richard T. Biernacki, BSG, Canon, served jointly at the following consecrations:
The Rev. Carol Joy W.T. Gallagher as Bishop Suffragan of Southern Virginia
The Rev. John Bryson Chane as Bishop of Washington
The Rev. Gayle Elizabeth Harris as Bishop Suffragan Bishop of Massachusetts

Other Deputy Registrars were appointed and served as follows:
The Rev. Canon Anthony Jewiss at the ordination and consecration of the Rev. Mark Handley Andrus as Bishop Suffragan of Alabama; David Booth Beers, Esq. at the ordination and consecration of the Rev. John Bryson Chane as Bishop of Washington and the Rev. James Joseph Shand as Bishop of Easton; the Rev. Canon David L. Seger at the ordination and consecration of the Rev. Alan Scarfe as Bishop of Iowa, and the Rev. Carmen Guerrero at the ordination and consecration of the Rev. Francisco José Duque as Bishop Coadjutor of Colombia.

At each ordination and consecration, Letters of Consecration were signed and sealed in duplicate by the consecrating Bishops, and by other Bishops present and participating. One of the Letters was given in each instance to the newly consecrated Bishop, and the other, duly attested, has been filed with the Archives of the General Convention.

All Journals received from the Secretaries of the Dioceses have been deposited in the Archives of the General Convention, together with the original Minutes of the General Convention, and the papers, documents and reports relating to such Minutes.

THE REGISTRAR SUBMITS HEREWITH THE PARTICULARS OF THE 26 CONSECRATIONS THAT HAVE TAKEN PLACE SINCE THE LAST REPORT.

957: The Reverend William Otis Gregg, consecrated as Bishop of Eastern Oregon, on Saturday, being the twenty-third day of September A.D. 2000, in Calvary Baptist Church, The Dalles, Oregon, by:
    Edmond Lee Browning, D.D., XXIV Presiding Bishop (Seal)
    Rustin Ray Kimsey, D.D., Bishop of Eastern Oregon, Resigned (Seal)
    Robert Louis Ladehoff, D.Min., Bishop of Oregon (Seal)
    Harry Brown Bainbridge, III, D. Min., Bishop of Idaho (Seal)
    Jerry Alban Lamb, D.D., Bishop of Northern California (Seal)
assisted by:
    Sanford Z.K. Hampton, Assistant Bishop of Olympia (Seal)
    John S. Thornton, Assisting Bishop of Spokane (Seal)
    Neff Powell, Bishop of Southwestern Virginia (Seal)
    William B. Spofford, Bishop of Eastern Oregon, Resigned (Seal)
    Gethin B. Hughes, Bishop of San Diego (Seal)
    Paul R. Swanson, Bishop of Oregon Synod, ELCA

958: The Reverend Stacy Fred Sauls, consecrated as Bishop of Lexington, on Saturday, being the thirtieth day of September A.D. 2000, in the Cathedral of Christ the King (Roman Catholic), Lexington, Kentucky, by:
    Robert Hodges Johnson, D.D., Bishop of Western North Carolina (Seal)
    Don Adger Wimberly, D.D., Bishop of Lexington, Resigned (Seal)
    Edwin Funsten Gulick, Jr., D.D., Bishop of Kentucky (Seal)
    Frank Kellogg Allan, Bishop of Atlanta, Resigned (Seal)
    Rogers Sanders Harris, Bishop of Southwest Florida, Resigned (Seal)
assisted by:
    David B. Reed, Bishop of Kentucky, Resigned (Seal)
    Henry I. Loutitt, Jr., Bishop of Georgia (Seal)
    Charels G. vonRosenberg, Bishop of East Tennessee (Seal)

959: The Reverend James Elliot Curry, consecrated as Bishop Suffragan of Connecticut, on Saturday, being the fourteenth day of October A.D. 2000, in, The First Cathedral, Bloomfield, Connecticut by:
    Douglas Edwin Theuner, Bishop of New Hampshire (Seal)
    Andrew Donnan Smith, Bishop of Connecticut (Seal)
    Clarence Nicholas Coleridge, D.D., Bishop of Connecticut, Resigned (Seal)
    Barbara Clementine Harris, D.D., Bishop Suffragan of Massachusetts (Seal)
    Chilton Abbie Richardson Knudsen, Bishop of Maine (Seal)
    Gordon Paul Scruton, Bishop of Western Massachusetts (Seal)
    assisted by:
    David B. Reed, Bishop of Kentucky, Resigned (Seal)
    James A. Kelsey, Bishop of Northern Michigan (Seal)
    M. Thomas Shaw, SSJE, Bishop of Massachusetts (Seal)
    Margaret Payne, Bishop of the New England Synod, ELCA
    Steven Charleston, Bishop of Alaska, Resigned (Seal)
    A. Ervine Swift, Bishop of Puerto Rico, Resigned (Seal)
    Francisco Reus-Froylan, Bishop of Puerto Rico, Resigned (Seal)
    David Andres Alvarez, Bishop of Puerto Rico (Seal)
    Julio C. Holguin, Bishop of the Dominican Republic (Seal)
    George E. Packard, Bishop for the Armed Services, Healthcare and Prison Ministries (Seal)
    Rodney R. Michel, Bishop Suffragan of Long Island (Seal)
    Morgan Porteus, Bishop of Connecticut, Resigned (Seal)
    Paul Moore, Bishop of New York, Resigned (Seal)
    Antonio Ramos-Orench, Bishop of Costa Rica, Resigned (Seal)

960: The Reverend Canon Wilfrido Ramos-Orench, consecrated as Bishop Suffragan of Connecticut on Saturday, being the fourteenth day of October A.D. 2000, in the First Cathedral, Bloomfield, Connecticut, by:
    Douglas Edwin Theuner, Bishop of New Hampshire (Seal)
    Andrew Donnan Smith, Bishop of Connecticut (Seal)
    Clarence Nicholas Coleridge, D.D., Bishop of Connecticut, Resigned (Seal)
    José Antonio Ramos-Orench, Bishop of Costa Rico, Resigned (Seal)
    Francisco Reus-Froylan, Bishop of Puerto Rico, Resigned (Seal)
    Albert Irvine Swift, Bishop of Puerto Rico, Resigned (Seal)
    assisted by:
    M. Thomas Shaw, SSJE, Bishop of Massachusetts (Seal)
    Margaret Payne, Bishop of the New England Synod, ELCA
    Steven Charleston, Bishop of Alaska, Resigned (Seal)
    Morgan Porteus, Bishop of Connecticut, Resigned (Seal)
    Paul Moore, Bishop of New York, Resigned (Seal)
    Chilton R. Knudsen, Bishop of Maine (Seal)
    David B. Reed, Bishop of Kentucky, Resigned (Seal)
    Gordon P. Scruton, Bishop of Western Massachusetts (Seal)

David A. Alvarez, Bishop of Puerto Rico (Seal)
George E. Packard, Bishop Suffragan for the Armed Forces, Healthcare, and Prison Ministries (Seal)
Rodney R. Michel, Bishop Suffragan of Long Island (Seal)
James A. Kelsey, Bishop of Northern Michigan (Seal)
James E. Curry, Bishop Suffragan of Connecticut (Seal)
Julio C. Holguin, Bishop of the Dominican Republic (Seal)
Barbara C. Harris, Bishop Suffragan of Massachusetts (Seal)
Paul Moore, Bishop of New York, Resigned (Seal)

961: The Reverend Canon James Edward Waggoner, consecrated as Bishop of Spokane on Saturday, being the twenty-first day of October A.D. 2000, in The Cathedral of St. John the Evangelist, Spokane, Washington, by:
Jerry Alban Lamb, Bishop of Northern California (Seal)
Robert Poland Atkinson, D.D., Assistant Bishop of Virginia (Seal)
Kenneth Lester Price, Jr., D.D., Bishop Suffragan of Southern Ohio (Seal)
Claude Charles Vaché, D.D., Bishop of Southern Virginia, Resigned (Seal)
Leigh Allen Wallace, Jr., D.D., Bishop of Spokane, Resigned (Seal)
John Raymond Wyatt, Bishop of Spokane, Resigned (Seal)
assisted by:
James S. Thornton. Bishop of Idaho, Resigned (Seal)
Harry S. Bainbridge, Bishop of Idaho (Seal)
Sanford Z.K. Hampton, Assistant Bishop of Olympia (Seal)
Sylvestre Donato Romero-Palma, Bishop of Belize (Seal)
Robert H. Cochrane, Bishop of Olympia, Resigned (Seal)
Robert L. Ladehoff, Bishop of Oregon (Seal)
Robert R. Shahan, Bishop of Arizona (Seal)
Rustin R. Kimsey, Bishop of Eastern Oregon, Resigned (Seal)
Edmond Lee Browning, XXIV Presiding Bishop, Resigned (Seal)

962: The Reverend David Jung-Hsin Lai, consecrated as Bishop Coadjutor of Taiwan on Saturday, being the twenty-fifth day of October A.D. 2000, in St. Timothy's Church, Kaohsiung, Taiwan, by:
Richard Sui On Chang, Bishop of Hawaii (Seal)
John Chih-Tsung Chien, Bishop of Taiwan (Seal)
David Shoji Tani, Bishop of Okinawa (Seal)
Michael C. Ingham, Bishop of New Westminster (Seal)
Thomas Yee-po Soo, Bishop of Western Kowloon (Seal)
John Chew, Bishop of Singapore (Seal)
assisted by:
Robert R. Shahan, Bishop of Arizona (Seal)
Harry B. Bainbridge, Bishop of Idaho (Seal)

963: The Reverend Katherine Jefferts Shori, consecrated as Bishop of Nevada on Saturday, being the twenty-fourth day of February A.D. 2001, in the Alexander Dawson School, Las Vegas, Nevada, by:
>   Jerry Alban Lamb, D.D., Bishop of Northern California (Seal)
>   Robert Louis Ladehoff, Bishop of Oregon (Seal)
>   Carolyn Tanner Irish, Bishop of Utah (Seal)
>
>   assisted by:
>   J. Michael Garrison, Bishop of Western New York (Seal)
>   Rustin R. Kimsey, Bishop of Eastern Oregon, Resigned (Seal)
>   James A. Kelsey, Bishop of Northern Michigan (Seal)
>   William O. Gregg, Bishop of Eastern Oregon (Seal)
>   Harry B. Bainbridge, Bishop of Idaho (Seal)
>   James E. Waggoner, Bishop of Spokane (Seal)
>   Sanford Z.K. Hampton, Assistant Bishop of Olympia (Seal)
>   Chilton Knudsen, Bishop of Maine (Seal)
>   Gethin B. Hughes, Bishop of San Diego (Seal)
>   Bruce Caldwell, Bishop of Wyoming (Seal)
>   George N. Hunt, Bishop of Rhode Island, Resigned (Seal)

964: The Reverend Roy Frederick Cedarholm, Jr., consecrated as Bishop Suffragan of Massachusetts on Saturday, being the twenty-fourth day of March A.D. 2001, in Trinity Church Copley Square, Boston, Massachusetts, by:
>   Douglas Edwin Theuner, Bishop of New Hampshire (Seal)
>   Marvil Thomas Shaw, SSJE, Bishop of Massachuestts (Seal)
>   Barbara Clementine Harris, D.D., Bishop Suffragan of Massachusetts (Seal)
>   Andrew Donnan Smith, Bishop of Connecticut (Seal)
>
>   assisted by:
>   James E. Curry, Bishop Suffragan of Connecticut (Seal)
>   Arthur E. Walmsley, Bishop of Connecticut, Resigned (Seal)
>   Jack M. McKelvey, Bishop of Rochester (Seal)
>   Steven Charleston, Bishop of Alaska, Resigned (Seal)
>   Geralyn Wolf, Bishop of Rhode Island (Seal)
>   Glauco Soares deLima, Primate of Brazil (Seal)
>   John K. Stendahl, New England Synod, ELCA
>   Jubal Pereira Neves, Bishop of Southwestern Brazil
>   Wilfrido Ramos-Orench, Bishop Suffragan of Connecticut (Seal)
>   Walter Righter, Bishop of Iowa, Resigned (Seal)
>   Chilton R. Knudsen, Bishop of Maine (Seal)
>   Gordon P. Scruton, Bishop of Western Massachusetts (Seal)

965: The Reverend Thomas Clark Ely, consecrated as Bishop of Vermont on Saturday, being the twenty-eighth day of April A.D. 2001, in Shapiro Field House, Norwich University, Northfield, Vermont, by:
>Douglas Edwin Theuner, Bishop of New Hampshire (Seal)
>Andrew Donnan Smith, Bishop of Connecticut (Seal)
>Mary Adelia Rosamond McLeod, D.D., Bishop of Vermont, Resigned (Seal)
>Daniel Lee Swenson, D.D., Bishop of Vermont, Resigned (Seal)
>Morgan Porteus, D.D., Bishop of Connecticut, Resigned (Seal)
>Arthur Edward Walmsley, D.D., Bishop of Connecticut, Resigned (Seal)
>
>assisted by:
>Steven Charleston, Bishop of Alaska, Resigned (Seal)
>James E. Curry, Bishop Suffragan of Connecticut (Seal)
>Donald Harte, Bishop of Hawaii, Resigned (Seal)
>R. Stewart Wood, Bishop of Michigan, Resigned (Seal)
>Chilton R. Knudsen, Bishop of Maine (Seal)
>M. Thomas Shaw, SSJE, Bishop of Massachusetts (Seal)
>Barbara C. Harris, Bishop Suffragan of Massachusetts (Seal)
>Roy F. Cedarholm, Bishop Suffragan of Massachusetts (Seal)
>Gordon P. Scruton, Bishop of Western Massachusetts (Seal)
>G. Russell Hatton, Assistant Bishop of Montreal (Seal)
>Wilfrido Ramos-Orench, Bishop Suffragan of Connecticut (Seal)

966: The Very Reverend Philip Menzie Duncan, consecrated as Bishop of the Central Gulf Coast on Saturday, being the twelfth day of May A.D. 2001, in the Pensacola Civic Center, Pensacola, Florida, by:
>Frank Tracy Griswold, D.D., Presiding Bishop and Primate (Seal)
>Charles Farmer Duvall, Bishop of Central Gulf Coast (Seal)
>Barry Robert Howe, Bishop Coadjutor of West Missouri (Seal)
>Catherine Elizabeth Maples Waynick, Bishop of Indianapolis (Seal)
>David Bruce MacPherson, Bishop Suffragan of Dallas (Seal)
>Rogers Sanders Harris, D.D., Bishop of Southwest Florida, Resigned (Seal)
>James Louis Jelinek, D.D., Bishop of Minnesota (Seal)
>Sam Byron Hulsey, D.D., Bishop of Northwest Texas, Resigned (Seal)
>Telesforo Alexander Isaac, Bishop of the Dominican Republic, Resigned (Seal)
>
>assisted by:
>Edward L. Salmon, Jr., Bishop of South Carolina (Seal)
>John B. Lipscomb, Bishop of Southwest Florida (Seal)
>Charles L. Keyser, Bishop of the Armed Forces, Resigned (Seal)
>David B. Reed, Bishop of Kentucky, Resigned (Seal)
>Charles E. Jenkins, Bishop of Louisiana (Seal)
>Henry N. Parsley, Jr., Bishop of Alabama (Seal)
>Stephen H. Jecko, Bishop of Florida (Seal)
>Onell Soto, Assistant Bishop of Alabama (Seal)

967: The Reverend Don Edward Johnson, consecrated as Bishop of West Tennessee on Saturday, being the thirtieth day of June A.D. 2001, in Mississippi Boulevard Christian Church, Memphis, Tennessee, by:
>Frank Tracy Griswold, D.D., Presiding Bishop and Primate (Seal)
>William Evan Sanders, D.D., Bishop of East Tennessee, Resigned (Seal)
>Charles Glenn vonRosenberg, D.D., Bishop of East Tennessee (Seal)
>Duncan Montgomery Gray, III, Bishop Coadjutor of Mississippi (Seal)
>James Malone Coleman, D.D., Bishop of West Tennessee (Seal)
>
>assisted by:
>Onell Soto, Assistant Bishop of Alabama (Seal)
>Clifton Daniel, III, Bishop of East Carolina (Seal)
>Henry I. Louttit, Jr., Bishop of Georgia (Seal)
>Charles E. Jenkins, Bishop of Louisiana (Seal)
>Robert H. Johnson, Bishop of Western North Carolina (Seal)
>Edwin F. Gulick, Jr., Bishop of Kentucky (Seal)
>Dorsey F. Henderson, Jr., Bishop of Upper South Carolina (Seal)
>William J. Skilton, Bishop Suffragan of South Carolina (Seal)
>Bertram Nelson Herlong, Bishop of Tennessee (Seal)
>Philip M. Duncan, Bishop of Central Gulf Coast (Seal)
>Johnn L. Said, Bishop Suffragan of Southeast Florida (Seal)
>Alfred C. Marble, Bishop of Mississippi (Seal)
>John B. Lipscomb, Bishop Suffragan of Southwest Florida (Seal)
>Michael B. Curry, Bishop of North Carolina (Seal)
>Stacy F. Sauls, Bishop of Lexington (Seal)
>J. Gary Gloster, Bishop Suffragan of North Carolina (Seal)
>Larry E. Maze, Bishop of Arkansas (Seal)
>Henry N. Parsley, Jr., Bishop of Alabama (Seal)
>Alex D. Dickson, Bishop of West Tennessee (Seal)
>Ronald B. Warren, Southeastern Synod, ELCA

968: The Reverend John Neil Alexander, consecrated as Bishop of Atlanta on Saturday, being the seventh day of July A.D. 2001, in the Cathedral of St. Philip, Atlanta, Georgia, by:
>Frank Tracy Griswold, D.D., Presiding Bishop and Primate (Seal)
>Frank Kellogg Allan, D.D., Bishop of Atlanta, Resigned (Seal)
>Charles Judson Child, Jr., D.D., Bishop of Atlanta, Resigned (Seal)
>Bennett Jones Sims, D.D, Bishop of Atlanta, Resigned (Seal)
>Michael Bruce Curry, D.D., Bishop of North Carolina (Seal)
>Onell Asiselo Soto, D.D., Assistant Bishop of Atlanta (Seal)
>Ronald B. Warren, Bishop of Southeastern Synod, ELCA
>
>assisted by:
>Robert H. Johnson, Bishop of Western North Carolina (Seal)
>John L. Rabb, Bishop Suffragan of Maryland (Seal)
>Leo Frade, Bishop of Southeast Florida (Seal)

Henry I. Louttit, Jr., Bishop of Georgia (Seal)
Charles E. Jenkins, Bishop of Louisiana (Seal)
Robert G. Tharp, Bishop of East Tennessee (Seal)
Alfred C. Marble, Jr., Bishop of Mississippi (Seal)
Henry N. Parsley, Jr., Bishop of Alabama (Seal)

969: The Reverend Francisco José Duque-Gomez, consecrated as Bishop Coadjutor of Colombia on Saturday, being the fourteenth day of July A.D. 2001, in Iglesia de San Alban, Bogota, Colombia, by:

Frank Tracy Griswold, D.D., Obispo Primado
Bernardo Merino Botero, Obispo de Colombia
Neptali Larrea-Moreno, Obispo de Ecuador, Diócesis Central
James Hamilton Ottley, D.D., Interino de Honduras
Alfredo Morante-España, Obispo de Ecuador, Diócesis de Litoral
Armando Guerra, Obispo de Venezuela

assisted by:
Benito Juarez, Bishop of Southeastern Mexico
David B. Reed, Bishop of Kentucky, Resigned
Leo Frade, Bishop of Southeast Florida
Martín de Jesús Barahona, Bishop of El Salvador

970: The Reverend William Michie Klusmeyer, consecrated as Bishop of West Virginia on Saturday, being the thirteenth day of October A.D. 2001, in Wesley Chapel, West Virginia Wesleyan College, Buckhannon, Virginia, by:

Frank Tracy Griswold, D.D., Presiding Bishop and Primate (Seal)
William Dailey Persell, Bishop of Chicago (Seal)
Robert Poland Atkinson, D.D., Bishop of West Virginia, Resigned (Seal)
Wendell Nathaniel Gibbs, Jr., Bishop of Michigan (Seal)
Claude Charles Vaché, D.D., Bishop of Southern Virginia, Resigned (Seal)
James Winchester Montgomery, D.D., Bishop of Chicago, Resigned (Seal)
Ralph William Dunkin, Bishop, West Virginia Synod, ELCA

assisted by:
James E. Waggoner, Bishop of Spokane (Seal)
Kenneth L. Price, Bishop Suffragan of Southern Ohio (Seal)
Robert Duncan, Bishop of Pittsburgh (Seal)
David C. Jones, Bishop Suffragan of Virginia (Seal)
J. Michael Garrison, Bishop of Western New York (Seal)

971: The Reverend Lloyd Emmanuel Allen, consecrated as Bishop of Honduras on Saturday, being the twentieth day of October A.D. 2001, in Expocentro, San Pedro Sula, Honduras, by:

James Hamilton Ottley, D.D., Bishop of Panama, Resigned (Seal)
Leopold Frade, D.D., Bishop of Southeast Florida (Seal)
Francis Raymond Lyons III, Bishop of Bolivia (Seal)

Julio Murray, Bishop of Panama (Seal)
Sylvestre Donato Romero-Palma, Bishop of Belize (Seal)
assisted by:
Francisco Duque, Bishop of Colombia (Seal)
Martin Barahona, Bishop of El Salvador (Seal)
Armando Guerra, Bishop of Guatemala (Seal)

972: The Reverend Gladstone Bailey Adams, III, consecrated as Bishop of Central New York on Saturday, being the twenty-seventh day of October A.D. 2001, in St. Paul's Cathedral, Syracuse, New York, by:
Jack Marston McKelvey, D.D., Bishop of Rochester (Seal)
David Bruce Joslin, Assisting Bishop of New Jersey (Seal)
Edwin Funsten Gulick, Jr., D.D., Bishop of Kentucky (Seal)
Martin de Jesús Barahona, Bishop of El Salvador (Seal)
David Charles Bowman, Assisting Bishop of Central New York (Seal)
Lee M. Miller, Bishop, Upstate New York Synod, ELCA
assisted by:
Orris G. Walker, Bishop of Long Island (Seal)
O'Kelley Whitaker, Bishop of Central New York, Resigned (Seal)
Daniel W. Herzog, Bishop of Albany (Seal)
Ned Cole, Bishop of Central New York, Resigned (Seal)

973: The Reverend Pierre Welte Whalon, consecrated as Bishop Suffragan-in-Charge of the Convocation of American Churches in Europe on Sunday, being the eighteenth day of November A.D. 2001, in St. Paul with-in-the-Walls, Rome, Italy by:
Frank Tracy Griswold, D.D., Presiding Bishop and Primate (Seal)
John Wadsworth Howe, D.D., Bishop of Central Florida (Seal)
Jeffery William Rowthorn, D.D., Bishop-in-Charge, Convocation of American Churches in Europe (Seal)
Geoffrey Rowell, Bishop of Basingstoke (Seal)
Fernando da Luz Soares, Bishop of Portugal (Seal)
Carlos Lopez Lozano, Bishop of the Spanish Reformed Church (Seal)
Joachim Vobbe, Bishop of Germany, Old Catholic Church (Seal)
assisted by:
Richard Garrard, Anglican Centre in Rome (Seal)
William J. Skilton, Bishop Suffragan of South Carolina (Seal)
C. Christopher Epting, Bishop of Iowa, Resigned (Seal)
George E. Packard, Bishop Suffragan, Armed Services, Healthcare and Prisons (Seal)
J. Michael Garrison, Bishop of Western New York (Seal)
Edward L. Lee, Jr., Bishop of Western Michigan (Seal)

974: The Reverend Mark Handley Andrus, consecrated as Bishop Suffragan of Alabama on Thursday, being the seventh day of February A.D. 2002, in the Cathedral Church of the Advent, Birmingham, Alabama, by:
>Frank Tracy Griswold, D.D., Presiding Bishop and Primate (Seal)
>Henry Nutt Parsley, Jr., D.D., Bishop of Alabama (Seal)
>Peter James Lee, D.D., Bishop of Virginia (Seal)
>David Colin Jones, Bishop Suffragan of Virginia (Seal)
>Creighton Leland Robertson, Bishop of South Dakota (Seal)
>Mary Adelia Rosamond McLeod, D.D., Bishop of Vermont, Resigned (Seal)
>Furman Charles Stough, D.D., Bishop of Alabama, Resigned (Seal)
>Robert Oran Miller, D.D., Bishop of Alabama, Resigned (Seal)
>Ronald B. Warren, Bishop, Southeast Synod, ELCA
>
>assisted by:
>Duncan M. Gray, Bishop Coadjutor of Mississippi (Seal)
>J. Neil Alexander, Bishop of Atlanta (Seal)
>David Colin Jones, Bishop Suffragan of Virginia (Seal)
>Francis C. Gray, Assistant Bishop of Virginia (Seal)
>Onell Soto, Assistant Bishop of Alabama, Resigned (Seal)
>Don E. Johnson, Bishop of West Tennessee (Seal)
>Edwin F. Gulick, Jr., Bishop of Kentucky (Seal)

975: The Reverend George Wayne Smith, consecrated as Bishop Coadjutor of Missouri on Saturday, being the second day of March A.D. 2002, in St. Francis, Xavier College Church, St. Louis, Missouri, by:
>Joseph Clark Grew, D.D., Bishop of Ohio (Seal)
>Hays Hamilton Rockwell, D.D., Bishop of Missouri (Seal)
>Carl Christopher Epting, D.D., Deputy for Ecumenical and Interfaith Relations (Seal)
>Philip Hougen, Bishop, Southeastern Iowa Synod, ELCA
>Warren Freiheit, Bishop, Central/Southern Illinois Synod, ELCA
>
>assisted by:
>Arthur B. Williams, Bishop Suffragan of Ohio (Seal)
>David Alvarez, Bishop of Puerto Rico (Seal)
>Edward S. Little, Bishop of Northern Indiana (Seal)
>Weldell N. Gibbs, Jr., Bishop of Michigan (Seal)
>Russell E. Jacobus, Bishop of Fond du Lac (Seal)
>James A. Kelsey, Bishop of Northern Michigan (Seal)
>William A. Jones, Bishop of Missouri, Resigned (Seal)
>Catherine M. Waynick, Bishop of Indianapolis (Seal)
>William D. Persell, Bishop of Chicago (Seal)
>Roger J. White, Bishop of Milwaukee (Seal)
>Barry R. Howe, Bishop of West Missouri (Seal)
>Peter H. Beckwith, Bishop of Springfield (Seal)

REGISTRAR

976: The Reverend James Marshall Adams, Jr., consecrated as Bishop of Western Kansas on Saturday, being the sixteenth day of March A.D. 2002, in St. John's Military School, Salina, Kansas, by:
  William Edward Smalley, D.Min., Bishop of Kansas (Seal)
  Vernon Edward Strickland, Bishop of Western Kansas (Seal)
  Russell Edward Jacobus, Bishop of Fond du Lac (Seal)
  Roger John White, D.C.L., Bishop of Milwaukee (Seal)
  Dorsey Felix Henderson, Jr., D.D., Bishop of Upper South Carolina (Seal)
  assisted by:
  Robert M. Moody, Bishop of Oklahoma, Resigned (Seal)
  Robert William Duncan, Bishop of Pittsburgh (Seal)
  Gerald L. Mansholt, Bishop, Central States Synod, ELCA
  C. Charles Vaché, Bishop of Southern Virginia (Seal)
  Wallis Ohl, Bishop of Northwest Texas (Seal)

977: The Reverend Carol Joy W.T. Gallagher, consecrated as Bishop Suffragan of Southern Virginia on Saturday, being the sixth day of April A.D. 2002, in St. Paul's College, Lawrenceville, Virginia, by:
  Robert Deane Rowley, D.D., Bishop of Northwestern Pennsylvania (Seal)
  David Conner Bane, Jr., Bishop of Southern Virginia (Seal)
  Barbara Clementine Harris, D.D., Bishop Suffragan of Massachuestts (Seal)
  Donald Purple Hart, Assistant Bishop of Southern Virginia, Resigned (Seal)
  Wayne Parker Wright, Bishop of Delaware (Seal)
  Edmond Lee Browning, D.D., XXIV Presiding Bishop, Resigned (Seal)
  Mark Lawrence MacDonald, TSSF, Bishop of Alaska (Seal)
  assisted by:
  C. Charles Vaché, Bishop of Southern Virginia, Resigned (Seal)
  James M. Adams, Bishop of Western Kansas (Seal)
  Jane Holmes Dixon, Bishop of Washington, Pro-tempore (Seal)
  Robert C. Johnson, Jr., Bishop of North Carolina, Resigned (Seal)
  John L. Rabb, Bishop Suffragan of Maryland (Seal)
  Katharine Jefferts Shori, Bishop of Nevada (Seal)
  Heath Light, Bishop of Southwestern Virginia, Resigned (Seal)
  O'Kelley Whitaker, Bishop of Central New York, Resigned (Seal)
  Peter James Lee, Bishop of Virginia (Seal)
  Frank H. Vest, Bishop of Southern Virginia, Resigned (Seal)
  Clifton Daniel III, Bishop of East Carolina (Seal)
  Catherine S. Roskam, Bishop Suffragan of New York (Seal)
  Walter D. Dennis, Bishop Suffragan of New York, Resigned (Seal)
  Francis C. Gray, Assistant Bishop of Virginia (Seal)

978: The Reverend Ronald Gepert, consecrated as Bishop Coadjutor of Western Michigan on Saturday, being the twenty-seventh day of April A.D. 2002, in Fountain Street Church, Grand Rapids, Michigan, by:
    Arthur Benjamin Williams, Jr., D.D., Bishop Suffragan of Ohio (Seal)
    Edward Lewis Lee, Jr., D.D., Bishop of Western Michigan (Seal)
    James Michael Mark Dyer, D.D., Bishop of Bethlehem, Resigned (Seal)
    Robert Deane Rowley, Jr., Bishop of Northwestern Pennsylvania (Seal)
assisted by:
    J. Michael Garrison, Bishop of Western New York (Seal)
    Edward S. Little, Bishop of Northern Indiana (Seal)
    Russell E. Jacobus, Bishop of Fond du Lac (Seal)
    William W. Wiedrich, Bishop Suffragan of Chicago (Seal)
    George Wayne Smith, Bishop Coadjutor of Missouri (Seal)
    Kenneth L. Price, Bishop Suffragan of Southern Ohio (Seal)
    William D. Persell, Bishop of Chicago (Seal)
    Gary L. Hansen, Bishop of the North West Lower Michigan Synod, ELCA

979: The Very Reverend John Bryson Chane, consecrated as Bishop of Washington on Saturday, being the first day of June A.D. 2002 in The Cathedral of Saint Peter and Saint Paul, Washington, District of Columbia, by:
    Frank Tracy Griswold, D.D., Presiding Bishop and Primate (Seal)
    Jane Holmes Dixon, Bishop of Washington, pro-tempore (Seal)
    Ronald Hayward Haines, Bishop of Washington, Resigned (Seal)
    Joseph Jon Bruno, Bishop of Los Angeles (Seal)
    Gethin Benwil Hughes, Bishop of San Diego (Seal)
    John Shelby Spong, D.D., Bishop of Newark, Resigned (Seal)
    Robert Munro Wolterstorff, Bishop of San Diego, Resigned (Seal)
assisted by:
    James W. Montgomery, Bishop of Chicago, Resigned (Seal)
    Theodore Schneider, Bishop, Metro DC Synod, ELCA
    Robert D. Rowley, Jr., Bishop of Northwestern Pennsylvania (Seal)
    Arthur E. Walmsley, Bishop of Connecticut, Resigned (Seal)
    Carol Joy W.T. Gallagher, Bishop Suffragan of Southern Virginia (Seal)
    J. Michael Garrison, Bishop of Western New York (Seal)
    Michael W. Creighton, Bishop of Central Pennsylvania (Seal)
    Mark Dyer, Bishop of Bethlehem, Resigned (Seal)
    Rodney R. Michel, Bishop Suffragan of Long Island (Seal)
    F. Clayton Matthews, Office of Pastoral Development (Seal)
    Robert C. Johnson, Jr., Bishop of North Carolina, Resigned (Seal)
    Robert W. Ilhoff, Bishop of Maryland (Seal)
    Neff Powell, Bishop of Southwestern Virginia (Seal)
    Walter Righter, Bishop of Iowa, Resigned (Seal)
    Allen L. Bartlett, Bishop of Pennsylvania, Resigned (Seal)
    Nyongankulu Ndungane, Archbishop of Capetown (Seal)

REGISTRAR

Donald P. Hart, Bishop of Hawaii, Resigned (Seal)
Peter Lee, Bishop of Virginia (Seal)
Philip Dunst Baji, Bishop of Tanga in Tanzania (Seal)
Leopold Frade, Bishop of Southeast Florida (Seal)
A. Theodore Eastman Bishop of Maryland, Resigned (Seal)
David Colin Jones, Bishop Suffragan of Virginia (Seal)
Lloyd E. Allen, Bishop of Honduras

980a: The Right Henry W. Scriven, received into the House of Bishops, Assistant Bishop of Pittsburgh.

981: The Reverend Gayle Elizabeth Harris, consecrated as Bishop Suffragan of Massachusetts on Saturday, being the eighteenth day of January A.D. 2003, in Trinity Church, Copley Square, Boston, Massachusetts, by:
    Arthur Benjamin Williams, Jr., D.D., Bishop Suffragan of Ohio, Resigned (Seal)
    Marvil Thomas Shaw, S.S.J.E., D.D., Bishop of Massachusetts (Seal)
    Barbara Clementine Harris, D.D., Bishop Suffragan of Massachusetts, Resigned (Seal)
    Roy Frederick Cederholm, Jr., Bishop Suffragan of Massachusetts (Seal)
    Jack Marston McKelvey, D.D., Bishop of Rochester (Seal)
    Frederick Houk Borsch, D.D., Bishop of Los Angeles, Resigned (Seal)
assisted by:
Willialm Michie Klusmeyer, Bishop of West Virginia (Seal)
Arthur E. Walmsley, Bishop of Connecticut, Resigned (Seal)
Steven Charleston, Bishop of Alaska, Resigned (Seal)
James E. Curry, Bishop Suffragan of Connecticut (Seal)
Katherine Jefferts Shori, Bishop of Nevada (Seal)
Chilton R. Knudsen, Bishop of Maine (Seal)
Gordon P. Scruton, Bishop of Western Massachusetts (Seal)
R. Stewart Wood, Bishop of Michigan, Resigned (Seal)
Thomas C. Ely, Bishop of Vermont (Seal)
Peter James Lee, Bishop of Virginia (Seal)
Andrew D. Smith, Bishop of Connecticut (Seal)
Orris George Walker, Jr., Bishop of Long Island (Seal)
Walter D. Dennis, Bishop Suffragan of New York, Resigned (Seal)
Mark MacDonald, Bishop of Alaska (Seal)
David Colin Jones, Bishop Suffragan of Virginia (Seal)
Michael B. Curry, Bishop of North Carolina (Seal)
Douglas E. Theuner, Bishop of New Hampshire (Seal)
Clarence N. Coleridge, Bishop of Connecticut, Resigned (Seal)
Franklin D. Turner, Bishop Suffragan of Pennsylvania, Resigned (Seal)
Walter Righter, Bishop of Iowa, Resigned (Seal)
John Bryson Chane, Bishop of Washington (Seal)
Chester Talton, Bishop Suffragan of Los Angeles (Seal)

Glauco Soares de Lima, Primate Bishop of Brazil
Catherine S. Roskam, Bishop Suffragan of New York (Seal)
Rodney R. Michel, Bishop Suffragan of Long Island (Seal)
Herbert Thompson, Jr., Bishop of Southern Ohio (Seal)

982: The Reverend James Joseph Shand, consecrated as Bishop of Easton on Saturday, being the twenty-fifth day of January A.D. 2003, in the Hyatt Regency, Chesapeake Bay Resort, Cambridge, Maryland, by:
  Robert Wilkes Ihloff, D.D., Bishop of Maryland (Seal)
  Martin Gough Townsend, D.Min., Bishop of Easton, Resigned (Seal)
  Elliott Lorenz Sorge, Bishop of Easton, Resigned (Seal)
  Robert William Duncan, Bishop of Pittsburgh (Seal)
  Charles Lindsay Longest, Bishop Suffragan of Maryland, Resigned (Seal)
  assisted by:
  F. Clayton Matthews, Bishop Suffragan of Virginia, Resigned (Seal)
  David K. Leighton, Jr., Bishop of Maryland, Resigned (Seal)
  Francis C. Gray, Bishop of Northern Indiana, Resigned (Seal)
  Harry B. Bainbridge, Bishop of Idaho (Seal)
  Gayle E. Harris, Bishop Suffragan of Massachusetts (Seal)
  David B. Joslin, Bishop of Central New York, Resigned (Seal)
  Mark Dyer, Bishop of Bethlehem, Resigned (Seal)
  David C. Bane, Bishop of Southern Virginia (Seal)
  David Colin Jones, Bishop Suffragan of Virginia (Seal)
  Peter James Lee, Bishop of Virginia (Seal)
  Wayne P. Wright, Bishop of Delaware (Seal)
  W. Michie Klusmeyer, Bishop of West Virginia (Seal)
  H. Gerard Knoche, Bishop, Delaware-Maryland Synod, ELCA

983: The Reverend Alan Scarfe, consecrated as Bishop of Iowa on Saturday, being the fifth day of April A.D. 2003, in Polk County Convention Center, Des Moines, Iowa, by:
  James Louis Jelinek, Bishop of Minnesota (Seal)
  Carl Christopher Epting, D.D., Bishop of Iowa, Resigned (Seal)
  Gayle Elizabeth Harris, Bishop Suffragan of Massachusetts (Seal)
  Joseph Jon Bruno, Bishop of Los Angeles (Seal)
  James Arthur Kelsey, Bishop of Northern Michigan (Seal)
  Philip Hougen, Bishop, Southeastern Iowa Synod, ELCA
  assisted by:
  Walter Righter, Bishop of Iowa, Resigned (Seal)
  J. Michael Garrison, Bishop of Western New York (Seal)
  Meshak Mabuza, Bishop of Swaziland (Seal)
  Bruce Caldwell, Bishop of Wyoming (Seal)
  Steven Ullestad, Bishop, Northeastern Synod, ELCA
  James J. Shand, Bishop of Easton (Seal)
  George Wayne Smith, Bishop of Missouri (Seal)

REGISTRAR

Thomas K. Ray, Bishop of Northern Michigan, Resigned (Seal)
Katherine Jefferts Shori, Bishop of Nevada (Seal)
Neville Chamberlain, Bishop of Brechin (Seal)
Barry Howe, Bishop of West Missouri (Seal)
James E. Krotz, Bishop of Nebraska (Seal)
Michael Arthur Last, Bishop, Western Iowa Synod, ELCA

REPORT OF THE RECORDER OF ORDINATIONS

This report covers the years of 2000, 2001 and 2002. It is based on the data contained in the Diocesan Reports which the Bishop of each jurisdiction is required by Canon Law to send to the Recorder of Ordinations each year.

The figures below compare the totals in the current report with those in the report made by the Recorder of Ordinations in 2000.

Additions	2000	2003
Deacons ordained in the USA	1116	1358
Deacons ordained in a Foreign Jurisdiction	24	5
Receptions and Ordinations under Title III, Canon 11, Section 5(a)(1)	43	44
Receptions from other Churches in the Anglican Communion	71	89
Restorations	8	24
Total Additions	**1262**	**1520**
Transfers to other Churches in the Anglican Communion	13	36
Depositions/Renunciations/Releases/Removals	136	125
Deaths	729	769
Total Deletions	**878**	**930**
NET GAIN	384	590
Suspensions	23	36

Report submitted by Michael W. Corney, for The Church Pension Fund in its capacity as Recorder of Ordinations.

Alan F. Blanchard
President, The Church Pension Fund

RECORD OF ORDINATIONS TO THE PRIESTHOOD OF THOSE ORDAINED DEACON BEFORE 2000

(Date shown is that of Ordination to the Priesthood)

Serial Number	Name	Date	Ordaining Bishop
X-37300-A	Aguilar-Rodriguez, C. Z.	06/14/00	Frade, L.
X-37300-B	Aguilar-Rodriguez, N.	06/24/00	Frade, L.
37626	Albergate, Scott P.	06/17/00	Iker, J. L.
36123	Allee, Roger G.	11/03/02	Frade, L.
X-37300-C	Alvarado-Palada, Carlos	07/29/00	Frade, L.
37444	Amaya, Adrian A.	01/13/00	Folts, J. E.
37399	Anderson-Smith, Susan	04/26/00	Haines, R. H.
X-37537	Archer, Melinda G.	08/26/00	Holguin, J. C.
37400	Armstrong, William H.	06/10/00	Vache, C. C. Title III, Canon 9
37592	Aveni, James V., Jr.	10/20/01	Ohl, C. W., Jr. Title III, Canon 9
37351	Bacon, Robert, Jr.	06/03/00	Shaw, M. T., III
37595	Baird, Carolyn M.	06/03/00	Swing, W. E.
37352	Barker, Ann B.	01/29/00	Thompson, H., Jr. for Allan, F. K.
37450	Bartz, James P.	06/23/00	Payne, C. E.
37517	Bass-Choate, Yamily	03/04/00	Marble, A. C., Jr.
37401	Beck, Alma T.	06/10/00	Vache, C. C.
34972	Bennett, Vivian R.	03/25/01	Marshall, P. V.
37440	Berry, Mary H.	03/04/00	Marble, A. C., Jr. for Jecko, S. H.
37452	Bishop, Jeffrey P.	05/31/00	Stanton, J. M.
37453	Bonner, Bruce H.	06/22/00	Payne, C. E.
37558	Boyd, Julia W.	10/28/00	Curry, M. B.
33370	Bradshaw, Council F.	12/16/01	Curry, M. B.
35878	Buchanan, James D.	10/08/00	Schofield, J.-D.
37455	Buck-Glenn, Judith M.	05/20/00	Bennison, C. E., Jr.
37540	Bullard, Carol A.	11/07/01	vonRosenburg, C. G. for Keyser, C. L.
37603	Burmeister, Melissa L.	07/01/00	Brown, J. B. for Persell, W. D.
37641	Bushey, Howard W., Jr.	08/06/00	Jenkins, C. E., III
37456	Byrum, Rick Y.	01/08/00	Borsch, F. H.
36601	Cafferata, Gail L.	04/14/02	Lamb, J. A.

Serial Number	Name	Date	Ordaining Bishop
37457	Caimano, Catherine A.	01/22/00	Johnson, R. C., Jr.
X-37303-E	Chacon-Rodriguez, D.	07/29/00	Frade, L.
X-37303-D	Cartagena, Maria C.	07/22/00	Frade, L.
X-37303-F	Chavez-Chacon, Rafael	07/29/00	Frade, L.
37563	Christian, John M.	03/25/00	MacDonald, M. L.
37354	Cicora, Julia A.	05/27/00	McKelvey, J. M.
34965	Clarke, Charles R.	11/30/02	Caldwell, B. E. Title III, Canon 9
37623	Clodfelter, Jonathan N.	06/25/00	Gloster, J. G. for Lee, P. J.
36408	Conradt, James R.	10/04/01	Jacobus, R. E.
37406	Correll, Ruth E.	02/24/00	Duncan, R. W.
X-37285	Cox, Donald A., Jr.	04/08/00	Duncan, R. W.
37594	Cram, Donald O.	04/25/01	Kelshaw, T.
37624	Crockett, Larry J.	08/10/00	Swenson D. L. for Jelinek, J. L.
37629	Curran, Michael J.	06/18/00	MacDonald, M. L. Title III, Canon 9
37356	Darling, Mary	09/29/00	McKelvey, J. M.
29956	Davidson, Robert P.	12/16/01	Winterrowd, W. J.
37520	DePriest, Sandra M.	02/11/00	Parsley, H. N., Jr. for Marble, A. C., Jr.
37409	Dinoto, Anthony C.	01/08/00	Smith A. D.
37549	Dooling, Thomas A.	04/08/00	Jones, C. I. Title III, Canon 9
37155	Drebert, David A.	12/15/01	Jacobus, R. E.
37358	Duke, Cecilia B.	02/05/00	Allan, F. K.
37410	Dupree, Charles T.	05/02/00	Daniel, C., III
37608	Eades, Susan T.	06/17/00	Jones, C. I.
37359	Eastman, Sarah C. F.	06/03/00	Shaw, M. T., III
31647	Edwards, Roger D.	05/31/02	Ihloff, R. W.
36878	Egerton, Karen C.	06/29/02	Howe, J. W.
37361	Eustis, Patricia A.	06/03/00	Shaw, M. T., III
37551	Fay, Michael J.	04/01/00	Jones, C. I. Title III, Canon 9
37488	Ferrell, Sean D.	02/05/00	Allan, F. K. for Howe, B. R.
37489	Ferrito, Michael L.	06/14/00	Shimpfky, R. L.
37090	Forman, Bernard K.	06/24/00	Warner, V. W., Jr.
32556	Foughty, Donna L.	06/26/02	Jones, D. C. for Lee, P. J.
37462	Friese, Walter E., Jr.	03/02/00	Stanton, J. M.

JOURNAL REPORTS

Serial Number	Name	Date	Ordaining Bishop
37618	Froehlich, Meghan F.	06/11/00	Johnson, R. H.
32176	Funk, Jeffrey L.	09/29/01	Marshall, P. V. Title III, Canon 9
X-37301-B	Galeano-Franco, Gustavo	08/11/00	Frade, L.
X-37301-C	Gamez-Cardona, Rosa A.	06/24/00	Frade, L.
37412	Gates, Mary M.	01/22/00	Smith, A. D.
35755-A	George, Mitzi G. S.	05/12/01	Hargrove, R. J., Jr.
37545	Gilsdorf, John W.	05/24/00	Kimsey, R. R.
X-37393-G	Granados-Arreaga, C. A.	07/22/00	Frade, L.
37515	Grandon, Douglas A.	01/29/00	Ackerman, K. L.
37463-A	Gray, Cathy, J. A. T.	01/06/00	Hughes, G. B.
35038	Guyott, Frederic F., III	12/09/00	Marshall. P. V.
37535	Hadaway, Michael M., Jr.	06/10/00	Vache, C. C.
37630	Hanks, Alexander H., Jr.	06/21/00	Johnson, R. H. Title III, Canon 9
37418	Heathcock, Deborah B.	06/24/00	Warner, V. W., Jr. for Daniel, C., III
37464	Heenan, Craig V.	06/01/00	Stanton, J. M.
37364	Heiligman, Sara E. M.	06/24/00	McKelvey, J. M.
37611	Henderson, Michael J.	06/18/00	Jecko, S. H. Title III, Canon 9
37612	Henderson, Sterling A.	06/18/00	Jecko, S. H. Title III, Canon 9
33471	Hudspeth, Denise W.	06/01/02	Said, J. L.
37254	Hussey, David P.	10/18/00	Robertson, C. L.
22578	Ince, Edgar E., Jr.	01/27/01	Coleman, J. M.
37466	James, C. Jan	06/07/00	Stanton, J. M.
36445	James, Sue C.	12/16/01	Gregg, W. O. Title III, Canon 9
31538	Jekabsons, Wendie S. S.	06/20/01	VonRosenberg, C. G.
35005	Jellison, Mary L.	05/26/01	Ihloff, R. W.
37445	Jerome, Douglas D.	04/03/02	Gregg, W. O.
37366	Johnson-Toth, Louise M.	05/27/00	McKelvey, J. M.
37339	Jones, Rosa L. H.	03/04/00	Marble, A. C., Jr.
37509	Jung, Pamela R.	01/23/00	Chang, R. S. O.
37513	Kennedy, Gary G.	02/15/00	Smalley, W. E. Title III, Canon 9
37495	King, John C.	01/28/00	Roskam, C. S. for Shimpfky, R. L.
35716	Kirking, Kerry C.	06/02/01	Waggoner, J. E., Jr.
37367	Klots, Stephen B.	06/03/00	Shaw, M. T., III

Serial Number	Name	Date	Ordaining Bishop
37302	Kuhr, Elisabeth S.	10/16/00	Thornton, J. S.
34892	Kurtz, James E.	07/30/00	Howe, J. W.
33823	LeBlanc, Ronald J.	05/25/02	Hargrove, R. J., Jr.
37619	LeClaire, Patrick H.	07/16/00	Thornton, J. S. Title III, Canon 9
37145	Lediard, JoAnne	09/16/01	Jefferts Schori, K. Title III, Canon 9
37467	Legge, Don E.	01/05/00	Alard, L. J. for Payne, C. E.
36720	Lewis, John G.	11/15/01	Folts, J. E.
X-37296	Lin, Justin Chun-Min	01/08/00	Chien, J. C. T.
37527	Lindstrom, Justin A.	08/29/00	Payne, C. E.
36863	Linscott, Stephanie	10/18/02	Payne, C. E.
37496	Long, Eric C.	11/15/00	Howe, B. R.
37542	Mackey, Guy L.	03/18/00	Hargrove, R. L., Jr.
34686	Macnab, Alan D.	11/04/01	Herzog, D. W.
33394	Marshall, William S., Jr.	06/24/00	Marshall, P. V.
37614	Martin, Joseph R.	06/24/00	Duncan, R. W.
36590	Marvic, Paula A.	05/20/01	Kelsey, J. A. Title III, Canon 9
36719	Matthew, Stephen A.	02/13/00	MacDonald, M. L. Title III, Canon 9
37498	McAulay, Roderick N.	01/05/00	Shimpfky, R. L. for Warner, V. W., Jr.
37469	McCalister, Van A., II	01/18/02	Schofield, J.-D.
37597	McCloghrie, Kathleen L.	06/03/00	Swing, W. E.
37470	McDonald, Janet S.	05/23/00	Lee, P. J.
32708	McNellis, Kathleene M.	05/23/00	Kelshaw, T.
37499	McQueen, Dale L.	01/8/00	Caldwell, B. E. for Warner, V. W., Jr.
37472	Michelfelder, Susan R.	03/25/00	Hayes, C. W. for Thompson, H., Jr.
37581	Michie, Michael W.	11/02/00	Payne, C. E.
33138	Miller, M. Richard	04/28/02	Little, E. S., II
37500	Moline, Mark E.	02/05/00	Allan, F. K. for Shimpfky, R. L.
X-37302-C	Monge-Mancia Israel	8/11/00	Frade, L.
37222	Monroe, Brenda F.	01/15/00	Haines, R. H. for Persell, W. D.
37260	Moore, Mary N.	02/03/01	vonRosenberg, C. G.
33980	Moore, William H., Jr.	06/29/02	Beckwith, P. H.
X-36095	Morales Perez, Jose	06/06/00	Guerra, A.

Serial Number	Name	Date	Ordaining Bishop
			Title III, Canon 9
37387	Morris, Thomas R.	02/05/00	Allan, F. K. for Hargrove, R. J., Jr.
37338	Mudge, Melanie A.	02/12/00	Gloster, J. G. for Johnson, R. C., Jr.
37328	Murphy, Edward J.	01/15/00	Donovan, H. A., Jr.
37620-A	Murray, Alfonso J., III	06/24/00	Hughes, G. B.
			Title III, Canon 9
37392	Neat, W. Jessee	05/13/00	Creighton, M. W.
34392	Neidlinger, Theodore P.	02/08/02	Little, E. S., II
37370	Nestlehutt, Mark S. G.	06/03/00	Shaw, M. T., III
X-34473	Ochoa-Gonzalez, J. C.	05/13/00	Downs-Higgs, S. W.
37371	O'Connell, Kelly A.	06/03/00	Shaw, M. T., III
36937	Paulson, Diane T.	05/12/01	Bainbridge, H. B., III
			Title III, Canon 9
37553	Pendergraft, Randall S.	04/15/00	Jones, C. I.
			Title III, Canon 9
37622	Petty, Michael W.	06/03/00	Jecko, S. H.
37602	Phelps, Kenneth O., Jr.	06/02/00	Ihloff, R. W.
37640	Pilarski, Terri C.	06/28/00	Persell, W. D.
35553	Piper, Mary E. M.	10/07/00	Jones, C. I.
37424	Pizzonia, Wanda S.	02/12/00	Smith, A. D.
35242	Powell, Vivian G.	06/03/00	Swing, W. E.
36644	Prehm, Katherine A. T.	06/02/02	Waggoner, J. E., Jr.
37303	Price, Susan A.	10/16/00	Thornton, J. S.
37538	Price, W. Wayne	05/11/00	Bane, D. C., Jr.
37554	Purvis, Howard B.	05/30/00	Bane, D. C., Jr.
33530	Rahn, Gaynell E. M.	02/05/00	Allan, F. K.
37620	Ray, Wanda L.	07/23/00	Leidel, E. M., Jr.
37255	Red Owl, Cordelia	06/26/00	Robertson, C. L.
			Title III, Canon 9
37637	Reeves, Diane D.	06/04/00	Jecko, S. H.
			Title III, Canon 9
34012	Reuman, Eugene F.	07/01/01	Howe, J. W.
35974	Roberts, Judith S.	09/15/02	Waynick, C. M.
37373	Roberts, Patricia E.	02/05/00	Allan, F. K.
37297	Robertson, Bruce E.	03/05/00	Kelsey, J. A.
			Title III, Canon 9
37474	Rodriquez, Frankie P.	06/20/00	Payne, C. E.
37394	Rohman, Suzannah L.	03/25/00	Creighton, M. W.
34794	Rosenbaum, Richard L.	06/25/01	Moody, R. M.

RECORDER   APPENDIX

Serial Number	Name	Date	Ordaining Bishop
36084	Rowe, Mary S.	09/14/00	Jones, C. I.
37526	Roy, Robert R.	06/03/00	Jelinek, J. L. Title III, Canon 9
37374	Royalty, Virginia B.	02/05/00	Allan, F. K.
36804	Rudolph, Joan E. F.	05/27/00	Ohl, C. W., Jr. Title III, Canon 9
37306	Ruyak, Mark A.	01/22/00	Marshall, P. V.
37330	Saucedo-Sica, Susan T.	02/05/00	Donovan, H. A., Jr.
37511	Schieffler, Daniel K.	01/15/00	Maze, L. E.
37476	Sehulster, Donald W.	05/20/00	Bennison, C. E., Jr.
37562	Shortt, Mary J.	07/22/00	Leidel, E. M., Jr.
37344	Slaymaker, Lorraine P.	02/02/00	Maze, L. E. for Jones, C. I.
37543	Smith, James C.	03/15/00	Marshall, P. V. Title III, Canon 9
32677	Smith, John P. F.	05/25/02	Ihloff, R. W. Title III, Canon 9
37428	Snickenberger, Patricia	02/02/00	Persell, W. D.
37502	Spina, Frank A.	01/23/00	Warner, V. W., Jr.
33582	Spruhan, Judy B.	06/25/00	Robertson, C. L.
37516	Starr, John A., Jr.	02/21/00	MacDonald, M. L. Title III, Canon 9
37564	Steele, Gary R.	03/26/00	MacDonald, M. L.
32200	Stevenson, Carolyn E.	12/22/01	Theuner, D. E.
37642	Stevenson, Edward M.	08/05/00	Jenkins, C. E., III
37528	Stockton, James V.	08/30/00	Payne, C. E.
37503	Strudwick, Paul A.	05/31/00	Shimpfky, R. L.
35394	Sublett, Gayle P.	09/07/02	Gulick, E. F., Jr.
37505	Taylor, Linda S.	01/22/00	Shimpfky, R. L.
37506	Thiel, Meigan C.	11/01/01	Scantlebury, V. A.
37639	Thomas, Arthur R., Jr.	08/06/00	MacDonald, M. L.
37430	Thompson, Gaea A.	01/16/00	Duncan, R. W.
37560	Towers, Richard A.	06/26/00	McKelvey, J. M.
X-37300	Ubiera, Jose R.	05/13/00	Holguin, J. C.
37512	Van Culin, Thomas A.	03/05/00	Chang, R. S. O.
37477	Varghese, Winnie S.	01/08/00	Borsch, F. H.
37396	Viggiano, Robert P.	01/15/00	Creighton, M. W.
X-37303-C	Villalobos-Matute, F.	08/11/00	Frade, L.
37525	Wake, Virel R.	06/24/00	Irish, C. T.
37507	Wallace, Martha E.	06/22/00	Wood, R. S., Jr.
37433	Walley, Kent R.	01/30/00	Salmon, E. L., Jr.

Serial Number	Name	Date	Ordaining Bishop
37625	Walton, R. Lindsley D.	06/18/00	for Duncan, R. W. Townsend, M. G. for Lee, P. J.
37536	Wayman, Teresa L.	09/20/01	Vache, C. C. Title III, Canon 9
37298	Weston, Myrtle M.	03/05/00	Kelsey, J. A. Title III, Canon 9
37397	Wheatley, Elizabeth H.	03/04/00	Marble, A. C., Jr.
37534	White-Hassler, M. Jane	03/10/00	Smith, A. D.
36803	Whitfield, Mary D.	10/06/01	Ohl, C. W., Jr. Title III, Canon 9
37382	Wiggers, John M.	02/19/00	Duvall, C. F.
37519	Williams, Carolynne J. G.	02/05/00	Allan, F. K.
37508	Williams-Duncan, Stacy	01/18/00	Howe, B. R.
37481	Woody, Robert J.	06/19/00	Payne, C. E
37591	Wulsin, Stockton	06/03/00	Thompson, H., Jr.

BISHOPS CONSECRATED SINCE LAST RECORDER REPORT

Number	Name	Date	Serial Number
950	Gibbs, Wendell Nathaniel, Jr.	02/05/00	32269
951	Packard, George Elden	02/12/00	27187
952	Little, Edward Stuart, II	03/18/00	26119
953	Bruno, Joseph Jon	04/29/00	28302
954	Bena, David John	06/03/00	26914
955	Curry, Michael Bruce	06/01/00	28586
956	Gray, Duncan Montgomery, III	06/01/00	27530
957	Gregg, William Otis	09/23/00	28212
958	Sauls, Stacy Fred	09/30/00	32888
959	Curry, James Elliott	10/14/00	31362
960	Ramos-Orench, Wilfrido	10/14/00	23967
961	Waggoner, James Edward, Jr.	10/21/00	28976
962	Lai, David J. S.	11/25/00	X-27463
963	Jefferts Schori, Katharine	02/24/00	35438
964	Cederholm, Roy Frederick, Jr.	03/24/00	26177
965	Ely, Thomas Clark	04/28/01	29397
966	Duncan, Philip Menzie, II	05/12/01	25705
967	Johnson, Don Edward	06/30/01	27967
968	Alexander, John Neil	07/07/01	32820
969	Duque-Gomez, Francisco Jose	07/14/01	X-33112
970	Klusmeyer, William Michie	10/13/01	29416
971	Allen, Lloyd Emmanuel	10/20/01	X-33143
972	Adams, Gladstone Bailey, III	10/27/01	29274
973	Whalon, Pierre Welte	11/18/01	31404
974	Andrus, Mark Handley	02/07/02	32413
975	Smith, George Wayne	03/02/02	29720
976	Adams, James Marshall, Jr.	03/16/02	29184
977	Gallagher, Carol Joy	04/06/02	33380
978	Gepert, Robert Ronald	04/27/02	31371
979	Chane, John Bryson	06/01/02	26522
980-A	Scriven, Henry William	09/01/02	Rec'd

NECROLOGY

BISHOPS
January 1, 2000 - December 31, 2002

Name	Number	Date of Death
Ashby, John F.	757	05/10/01
Barrett, George W.	594	12/03/00
Burrill, Gerald F.	500	07/17/01
Carral-Solar, Anselmo	686	06/02/02
Cochran, David R.	700	10/30/01
Cole, Ned, Jr.	602	12/16/02
Duncan, James L.	583	07/20/00
Gaskell, Charles T.	689	09/14/00
Gilliam, Jackson E.	634	10/19/00
Gross, Hal R.	612	10/13/02
Haden, Clarence R., Jr.	550	03/11/00
Harris, George C.	759	05/07/00
Jones, Harold S.	670	11/12/02
Lewis, David H., Jr.	739	05/15/02
Marmion, Charles G., Jr.	527	12/07/00
Marmion, William H.	528	05/30/02
Quarterman, George H., Sr.	466	09/07/02
Varley, Robert P.	661	05/02/00

PRIESTS AND DEACONS
January 1, 2000 - December 31, 2002

NAME	NUMBER	DATE OF DEATH
Abbitt, Raymond E.	15631-S	09/20/01
Achuff, Delbert L., Jr.	23005	02/27/01
Acosta, William C.	15569-S	01/28/01
Addington, Lloyd B.	33121	09/26/01
Alden, Vernon	Received	02/16/00
Aldrich, Herbert P.	15954-S	05/05/02
Allaire, Maurice J.	28466	02/02/00
Allen, James B.	25347	09/04/02
Allen, Kenneth J., Jr.	17359	08/16/01
Alleyne, John R.	Received	06/26/00
Amo, David R.	31428	02/08/00
Anderson, J. William	18009	01/16/02
Anderson, Kenneth E.	23310	07/07/01
Anderson, Vincent H.	23115	10/24/00

RECORDER APPENDIX

NAME	NUMBER	DATE OF DEATH
Andresen, Merton W.	28907	08/19/02
Andrews, Jacob L.	19384	06/15/02
Andrews, Sherman W.	15704-S	07/01/00
Anker, Herman	13959-S	05/30/01
Arcacha, Luis O.	X-21605	06/13/01
Armfield, John S.	14886-S	02/26/02
Armstrong, Donald A.	35872	12/23/00
Armstrong, Paul C.	14920-S	11/28/00
Ashey, John P., II	18554	07/27/01
Auer, E. Rugby	16558	11/22/00
Baar, William H.	18893	01/05/02
Babb, Robert J.	22335	07/23/02
Baker, H. Raymond, Jr.	22581	08/20/00
Balch, Leon C.	18645	12/24/01
Balcomb, Sara A.	33493	07/20/02
Bamford, Edwin A., Jr.	23534	09/06/00
Barham, Ethel M.	37163	01/04/00
Barnes, Richard M.	19407	12/27/00
Barnhill, Fredrick A.	20330	10/15/00
Barr, O. Sydney, Jr.	16881	03/19/00
Baskin, William R.	19445	09/18/02
Battin, Robert D.	19502	12/13/02
Bauder, Richard K.	18367	09/05/00
Baur, Robert M.	16942	01/14/01
Becker, Robert T.	14686-S	03/05/01
Beckles, Edward B.	20355	08/30/00
Bedigrew, Marguerite S.	37173	04/01/01
Bel, Ernest F.	21931	06/29/01
Belcher, Barbara F. H.	33623	03/23/02
Belden, Francis R.	14275-S	11/07/00
Berndt, Douglas J.	18332	05/27/01
Bird, Robert M.	14703-S	10/16/01
Blackburn, James P., II	25335	06/04/01
Blackburn, Robert E., Jr.	17970	10/03/00
Blackwelder, Francis W.	14396-S	05/09/02
Blake, Marvin H.	22068	10/14/02
Blankenship, Edward E.	18115	10/19/01
Blankenship, Perry M.	17257	04/18/01
Blanton, Walter P.	27174	10/01/01
Blaxton, Reginald G.	29390	03/11/01
Bliss, Reginald T.	13716-S	06/15/00
Blumenstein, Ted L.	21539	03/03/02

NAME	NUMBER	DATE OF DEATH
Boatwright, Robert W.	33511	06/14/01
Bolger, Joseph R.	18393	02/02/02
Borg, Warren R.	21206	12/12/00
Bournes, Fraser J.	Received	11/15/01
Bowen, Evelyn P.	35661	01/08/01
Bowersox, Glen	Received	01/12/01
Bowles, Robert B., Jr.	23678	12/12/00
Boyd, William D.	16834	12/23/02
Boykin, Elmer M., Jr.	18397	04/06/02
Brace, Charles R.	20899	08/17/01
Bradley, Philip E., Jr.	28682	07/30/02
Brandt, Roger N.	20821	04/08/00
Braun, Harold E.	18662-A	04/08/02
Bray, F. Elwood	19060	08/11/00
Brieant, Charles H.	17704	05/13/01
Brill, Earl H.	19537	09/19/01
Brinkman, Philip T.	20431	01/07/02
Broburg, Anselm	16729	12/07/00
Brock, Pope F., Jr.	18580	01/16/00
Brock, Robert H.	17554	08/01/01
Brockmann, John N.	15803-S	02/16/00
Bromeley, Robert B.	25151	05/11/00
Brown, Byron H., Jr.	22755	04/13/02
Brown, William E.	23312	11/26/02
Brownfield, John C.	20889	01/13/01
Buck, Harvey E.	17904	06/16/02
Budd, Osborne	14716-S	12/07/01
Bull, John H.	17424	12/09/02
Burnett, James C.	29246	11/12/01
Burnworth, Alvin P.	22253	09/02/02
Burrows, Robert V.	24073	02/24/01
Burton H. Robert	25197	09/14/01
Bush, Loren H.	19780	02/22/02
Cafky, William M.	24434	10/26/02
Calder, Jeffrey C.	37486	12/30/00
Callender, Wilfred S.	22756	01/22/02
Calloway, Arthur J.	18116	06/02/02
Camm, Paul A.	25333	02/26/00
Campbell, Edward J., Jr.	23200	09/25/01
Campbell, Eli H., Jr.	32230	02/29/00
Campbell, Harry G., Jr.	16213	05/14/00
Campbell, Walter E., Jr.	20122	01/02/01

RECORDER APPENDIX

NAME	NUMBER	DATE OF DEATH
Campbell, W. Thomas, Jr.	24811	05/09/00
Canepa, Paul C. P.	30173	11/16/02
Canfill, Joseph D.	22917	05/13/01
Carlo, Jose D.	22029	02/19/00
Carpenter, Jerry E.	14951-S	10/29/01
Carr, Edward R.	33971	11/29/00
Carroll, Daniel W.	22929	12/23/01
Carter, John W.	18202	10/19/02
Carter, Junius F., Jr.	19520	10/03/01
Casady, Phineas M.	13804-S	09/22/00
Chaffee, Thomas K., Jr.	17173	10/10/01
Charnock, Arnold	16026	12/15/02
Chatman-Royce, Edgar T.	32416	10/30/01
Cheales, Alan B.	Received	01/02/00
Cheney, Francis X.	16394	01/27/02
Chillington, Joseph H.	13571-S	01/13/00
Clapp, Robert A.	29247	01/02/00
Clarke, Elisha S., Jr.	16999	06/11/01
Cleasby, Clarence S., Jr.	20448	12/27/02
Cline, John E.	21065	05/26/02
Clute, Arden A., Jr.	20773	02/21/02
Chochrane, Frederic J.	21626	10/07/02
Cochrane, R. Scott	21654	07/13/00
Coffin, Baird B.	19762	12/29/00
Colby, Charles E.	19377	12/11/02
Cole-King, Susan M.	32130	03/01/01
Collins, William C.	24200	10/15/02
Colyer, Robert L., Sr.	26663	02/03/00
Comer, H. Hunt	19375	05/14/01
Condron, Thomas W.	38272	12/20/01
Coombs, Maurice A.	27374	03/23/02
Coombs, R. Richard P.	16320	11/20/00
Coomes, Robert L.	29765	08/01/02
Cooper, Austin R.	21592	02/14/01
Corrigan, Thomas A., Jr.	24634	08/05/01
Covey, John B.	17357	07/08/01
Cox, Brice G.	23363	07/01/02
Crain, Clark N.	28498	05/01/01
Cranmer, Chappell	25403	02/18/00
Creech, Robert J.	16445	06/17/01
Crockett, W. David	19361	10/24/01
Crum, Winston F.	18940	05/25/02

NAME	NUMBER	DATE OF DEATH
Cunningham, Robert W.	17595	10/16/02
Cure, Thomas G.	25682	02/13/01
Daniels, G. Earl	15646-S	01/26/00
Davenport, Stephen R., II	15699-S	07/14/02
Davidson, Virginia S.	35051	12/01/00
Davis, Kenneth C.	37541	09/01/02
Davis, Robert N.	23396	09/21/02
Davison, George W.	16907	06/04/01
de Lara, Dionisio	X-20289-B	08/11/02
Denkinger, Marshall E.	21175	09/15/00
Dennis, William R., Jr.	22889	01/17/01
Dent, W. Gilbert, III	21345	09/15/02
Deutsch, William R.	20057	12/21/00
DiBrandi, Herman A.	18152	06/16/00
Dice, Owen J.	20981	10/28/01
Doan, Charles B.	23512	09/19/00
Dodd, Wayne C.	23538	09/04/01
Dodd, William P., Jr.	23134	10/29/02
Donovan, Harlow P., Jr.	19312	10/30/02
Doppler, Albert J.	31178	01/14/02
Dornemann, William E.	32536	01/28/01
Draper, John W. C.	31364	03/02/00
Driver, Edwin T.	33156	09/13/00
Driver, William A.	14103-S	05/13/00
Dugan, Michael H.	20476	10/02/00
Duran, Frank D., Sr.	17403	05/13/02
Eastham, Frederick L.	23808	11/05/01
Eaton, J. Powell	17796	10/27/00
Eckel, Malcolm W.	15740-S	08/11/00
Edson, Diane M.	30912	09/19/00
Ehly, Charles F.	15639-S	12/02/02
Ehmer, Virgilee B.	30829	08/17/02
Eichenberger, Alan J.	22619	07/26/01
Elliott, Joseph M.	23118	11/02/02
Elliott, Joseph W.	25913	08/20/01
Engram, W. Thomas	18904	05/29/01
Etherton, Donald F.	18955	05/26/00
Evans, Alan R.	24218	12/07/02
Evans, Alfred W.	19916	11/11/00
Evenson, L. Franklin	16231	11/03/00
Ewald, Russell V.	18476	03/27/00
Ewan, Henry L.	13407-S	12/12/00

NAME	NUMBER	DATE OF DEATH
Fargher, John S. W.	17568	12/25/01
Farner, John R.	31156	05/27/00
Fera, Mary E.	29557	04/17/00
Ferris, Fred I. E.	18949	03/24/00
Field, George C., Jr.	18153	11/30/02
Fickling, John M.	27110	11/22/01
Fifer, Louis E., III	14336-S	12/02/01
Figenbaum, Ernest K., Jr.	28375	11/18/02
Figge, Federick W.	19063	09/13/02
Finlaw, William W., Jr.	20942	07/27/00
Firth, Katharine R.	33230	09/30/00
Fisher, Charles R.	17391	01/23/00
Fisher, Sandra H.	36879	03/10/01
Fitzpatrick, Veronica A. E.	29871	10/29/02
Foderingham, Noel A.	Received	01/04/02
Forbes, Terry W.	37934	08/26/01
Forrest, Edgar H.	23339	09/28/00
Forsyth, Chiron W.	Received	02/09/00
Fox, Charles H. W.	20584	08/29/00
Fox, John R.	31182	12/25/00
Frank, Warren P.	17785	11/17/00
Frankhuizen, William J.	21962	06/04/02
Fraser, Laura C.	26983	03/02/02
Frederick, Gordon H.	27618	10/26/02
Frieman, Arthur E.	27219	11/12/02
Frieman, Walter E.	15853-S	11/14/00
Fruechtel, Warren B.	25153	08/17/02
Frye, Richard H.	18316	05/06/01
Frye, Roye M.	18937	11/19/00
Gain, H. Clifford, II	25900	03/29/02
Gaither, E. Jesse, Jr.	26247	09/18/01
Gardner, Darwin E.	19742	06/20/01
Gardner, Donald J.	17392	11/30/02
Garlick, Bernard M.	13979-S	10/03/00
Garner, Thomas J.	23840	11/14/00
Gasek, Stanley P.	15856-S	08/06/02
Gast, Stuart F., Jr.	21422	03/18/00
Gatto, Robert B.	19940	02/01/01
Gauffreau, Elliott F.	19723	03/15/00
Gausby, Philip B.	23074	08/23/00
George, Lloyd V.	Received	11/06/01
George, Robert A.	15572-S	12/24/00

NAME	NUMBER	DATE OF DEATH
Gerardi, Barbara A.	32562	09/11/01
Gerety, Sally M. C.	29976	07/15/02
Geyer, Edward B., Jr.	20478	07/24/01
Giles, Frank J.	27528	07/06/00
Gill, John S.	16435	02/08/01
Gillespie, Stephen W.	18465	11/19/02
Gimlin, Jack T.	21906	11/17/02
Goldberg, Jean A.	29898	09/10/01
Gomer, Alvin D.	24760	09/08/00
Good, Jerry D.	36840	09/10/00
Good, William J.	14360-S	06/05/02
Goodfellow, Peter B.	18455	11/01/00
Goodson, Mercer-Logan	19340	12/12/00
Gracie, David M.	22005	05/22/01
Graham, Leo F., Jr.	32631	06/23/02
Gray, Christopher C.	32056	03/19/01
Greaves, Lyman B.	15914-S	09/12/02
Green, James M.	22727	11/22/01
Green, John R. Z.	16828	01/31/00
Greene, Charles R.	19874	04/27/02
Greer, M. Crisler	33974	09/24/02
Grissom, Martin L.	17130	11/19/01
Groton, Erland L.	14287-S	04/06/00
Grumbine, Robert	17631	04/09/02
Guy, George W.	27731	12/15/01
Haas, William J.	17319	12/16/00
Hacke, James E., Jr.	17333	12/09/00
Haddad, Ibrahim F.	Received	10/18/00
Hadden, William J., III	27399	01/27/00
Hall, George J.	14575-S	03/10/02
Hall, Warren	26282	10/06/02
Hammond, Frederick C.	16664	06/28/01
Hand, Chester C., Jr.	17363	08/17/02
Hannaford, Paul E.	18162	06/28/01
Hannan, Burdette F.	26264	04/11/02
Hardin, Durrie B.	13380-S	05/10/00
Harper, John C.	18395	09/12/02
Harper, Melvin H.	27045	01/06/01
Harris, Charles U.	14802-S	09/16/01
Harris, James R.	24122	07/24/01
Harris, Samuel M.	34290	02/21/00
Harrison, Joseph S.	19906	05/04/01

NAME	NUMBER	DATE OF DEATH
Hart, Edna J. C.	32645	08/01/00
Hart, Lois B.	36783	12/18/02
Hartley, Rex J.	26990	08/16/00
Hartman, John K.	21458	06/17/02
Hauan, James W. Jr.	17271	03/21/00
Hay, Albert R.	16137	10/04/00
Hay, Lamar D., Jr.	27385	11/10/00
Haynes, John G.	17429	01/10/00
Healy, Paul E.	16721	02/21/00
Heath, Henry L., Jr.	21990	10/07/00
Hegg, David P., II	22317	01/24/02
Heiligstedt, Patrick C.	21310	12/05/00
Hemm, Richard G.	20523	03/20/02
Henckell, Paul W.	13999-S	11/15/02
Hendricks, Roy J.	20350	10/26/02
Henriques, Edward F.	23872(a)	08/31/02
Herrick, Warren C., Jr.	21924	03/22/00
Hess, W. Lyndon	21637	12/21/00
Hewett, Paul C.	29408	07/10/01
Hiatt, Suzanne R.	27760	05/30/02
Hickey, Howard M.	18214	10/21/00
Higbie, Alanson	14969-S	01/09/01
Hildebrand, John W.	16957	02/03/00
Hill, Fontaine S.	19842	03/28/02
Hill, William R.	18387	12/15/01
Hines, James W., Jr.	33235	07/28/01
Hoard, Gayle F.	22261	10/05/02
Hoch, Carl A.	17110	01/13/01
Hodgkin, Wilfred H.	17061	11/14/00
Hoggard, Robert E.	21660	10/04/02
Holby, Worrell H., Jr.	20904	08/29/01
Holcomb, William S.	16851	02/27/02
Holifield, Loyd W., Jr.	25266	08/20/00
Holloway, Edward F.	23154	07/08/02
Holmes, John A.	17643	03/14/01
Holmes, Robert C.	Received	08/04/00
Holsinger, David N.	23349	12/04/00
Holt, William T., Jr.	15547-S	05/30/01
Hoover, Edwin L.	17151	10/24/01
Horner, Thomas M.	19206	03/10/02
Howard, Carolyn A.	32934	04/17/00
Hudson, Thomas F.	19987	04/09/00

NAME	NUMBER	DATE OF DEATH
Hughes, John D.	17178	04/25/01
Hunter, David R.	15586-S	08/26/01
Huske, Joseph S., Jr.	16313	12/02/02
Hutchinson, Bernice M.	35389	06/19/01
Hutchinson, Dovie M.	32586	12/28/02
Hutton, Ralph E.	18327	06/13/02
Infantino, Stephen S.	27761	03/01/00
Ingraham, Herbert M.	29259	03/26/02
Ireland, Frank G.	14959-S	11/11/02
Irving, C. Elaine	34746	05/04/01
Ismay, R. Robert	20128	04/07/02
Jackson, Jack L.	26168	03/01/01
James, J. Edward	25827	03/09/02
Janke, Richard K.	17826	03/22/02
Jarman, Terence R.	24178	05/17/02
Jarry, Dennis G.	Received	12/27/01
Jelliffe, Robert W.	Received	08/15/01
Jenkins, Schuyler D.	14550-S	09/09/00
Jennings, Helen E.	31229	12/25/00
Johnson, Charles R.	16385	12/09/01
Johnson, Frederick J.	22014	10/14/01
Johnson, Robert F.	19752	06/04/00
Johnson, Robert J.	31552	03/24/02
Johnson, Theodore T.	15950-S	10/10/00
Johnston, James S.	18414	08/14/01
Johnston, John J.	21727	05/09/01
Jones, Cecil B., Sr.	14058-S	11/06/01
Jones, Enoch R. L., Jr.	13875-S	02/26/01
Jones, Harry K.	14742-S	12/30/02
Jones, James L., Jr.	17200	01/04/01
Jones, Roger C.	18960	06/30/00
Jordan, Frances J.	31649	02/05/02
Jordan, Jean P.	18909	07/21/02
Joslin, Allen W.	16376	01/01/00
Juhr, William F. E., Jr.	19136	09/21/01
Kalbacher, Joseph F., Jr.	20063	03/05/01
Katt, William P.	17123	01/18/01
Kauber, Barbara M.	34817	09/01/02
Kauffman, Daniel G.	37738	08/09/01
Keith, Edsel L.	19026	07/12/01
Kellett, Norman L.	15566-S	02/24/01
Kellett, Orme S.	25122	09/14/02

RECORDER APPENDIX

NAME	NUMBER	DATE OF DEATH
Kennedy, Joseph R., Jr.	24357	07/25/00
Kershaw, Alvin L.	16149	11/29/01
Key, William B.	17728	10/24/02
Keys, Colin D.	22077	10/23/00
Kibitz, William G.	14589-S	01/08/02
King, Ware G.	15948-S	06/26/02
Kipnis, Judith R.	32151	03/01/01
Kirk, Richard R.	20980	07/12/01
Kirk, Terrell T.	22082	10/13/00
Kirk, William H.	14324-S	10/19/01
Kishpaugh, Howard B.	19113	01/11/01
Knight, H. Holly	Received	12/29/02
Knight, Richard S.	16255	12/12/01
Kreutzer, S. Knox, Jr.	18017	08/27/02
Lacava, Richard N., Jr.	31017	05/08/01
Laister, Peter	Received	10/24/02
Lampton, Robert K.	21610	09/08/01
Landskroener, Peter A.	25595	04/21/00
Langdon, Bruce A.	25546	01/05/00
Lawrence, Iver G., Jr.	17364	02/21/00
Lawson, LeRoy D.	15786-S	02/17/01
Lawson, William J.	27507	01/07/00
Lazenby, Herbert C., Jr.	17775	06/18/00
Lea, James B.	30795	07/14/02
Lee, Alfred S.	20766	02/20/02
Lefebvre, Frederick P.	21348	10/20/00
Lemmon, Sarah M.	36102	09/28/02
Letteney, Ward H.	30324	05/01/00
Linck, Sandra B.	35099	06/11/01
Lindsey, Sanford C.	17676	09/19/02
Littell, Edward M.	14063-S	03/10/02
Little, Haskin V.	14929-S	06/15/00
Liu, John Y. F.	22246	10/02/00
Livengood, Hugh	22563	01/12/02
Livesay, Alexander E.	19452	12/26/02
Lloyd, Kermit L.	19127	01/28/00
London, Jesse L.	33058	02/18/01
Long, Charles H., Jr.	16520	11/19/00
Long, R. Richard	31673	07/13/02
Lopes, Donald D., II	23987	08/08/02
Lott, Albert O.	23350	07/17/00
Louis, Joseph S.	X-16497-A	05/21/02

NAME	NUMBER	DATE OF DEATH
Ludlow, Ogden R.	19897	09/13/01
Luther, Richard M.	29645	05/05/01
Lynch, G. Ernest, Jr.	17270	11/28/00
Ma, Mark Y. L.	X-19931-B	01/28/00
MacColl, James R., III	16162	12/05/01
MacDonald, Douglas S., Jr.	20906	05/20/00
Mackey, George T.	Received	05/04/48
Maclean, Dougald L.	15859-S	03/01/00
Madden, Wilbur G.	28861	06/14/01
Mahan, Albert L., Jr.	24038	09/19/00
Mahon, Jeannine F.	33577	07/23/00
Maitland, Robert H., Jr.	19242	06/22/00
Malcom, Steve C.	31796	08/24/00
Martin, Gilbert D., Jr.	16410	04/06/00
Martin, James A.	25869	04/01/00
Martin, John S.	X-17318-B	10/14/02
Martins, Josette A. H.	31508	07/18/00
Mason, Ernest J.	14072-S	12/13/00
Mason, Richard E.	22527	03/12/00
Mason, Robroy	20568	09/25/00
Mattes, Alfred L.	16720	05/10/01
Maxey, William M.	18662	09/13/01
McCarty, Chandler H.	16461	11/29/01
McClain, Frank M.	17898	12/15/00
McClaren, George W., Jr.	22644	04/21/01
McClenahan, Helen L.	28703	06/17/02
McCoombe, Lawrence R.	26097	12/17/01
McCord, David	22641	09/07/00
McCracken, Edward R.	19753	07/31/00
McCrary, Robert E.	21884	01/19/01
McDonald Frederick A.	14117-S	03/09/02
McDougall, Bryon D.	33908	12/06/01
McElwain, Harold A.	16685	08/22/00
McFarland, Robert D.	17029	01/09/00
McKee, Hugh C., Jr.	16837	06/13/02
McLain, John A.	35254	11/26/00
McLellan, Herbert B.	25473	11/29/00
McManis, Lester W.	17533	06/16/02
McPhillips, Julian L.	22330	02/11/01
Mead, Alfred	18951	06/02/02
Meagher, Frederic W.	23028	03/06/02
Meginniss, Benjamin A., Jr.	14675-S	06/25/01

NAME	NUMBER	DATE OF DEATH
Merry, Robert E.	14417-S	03/09/01
Mertz, Christine T.	31262	12/07/01
Metz, Robert E.	33119	08/14/00
Metz, Ronald I.	25440	08/25/02
Meyer, R. Charles	26529	11/13/00
Meyer, Warren K.	30094	04/30/02
Mickey, John A.	30063	09/25/02
Miller, Charles M., III	22202	03/12/02
Miller, Dale V.	30779	09/11/02
Miller, Edward O.	15747-S	09/16/00
Miller, John H., III	34506	01/24/01
Miller, Randolph C.	14411-S	06/13/02
Mills, Duane R. S.	22207	08/02/02
Mills, Lewis H.	21935	01/26/02
Miner, Harold E.	34071	02/28/02
Minnerly, Thomas J.	31352	03/12/01
Mitchell, Henry B.	20104	06/15/02
Mitchell, Leonard R.	30409	07/27/01
Moch, Philip H.	32618	06/07/01
Moncure, Charles P.	18385	02/16/00
Moore, Charles B.	27401	10/19/01
Moore, Harry I.	28272	04/04/02
Moore, John F.	29192	05/18/00
Moore, John T., Jr.	26730	08/07/00
Moore, Peter C.	17945	08/25/00
Moore, Robert H.	16012-S	02/10/00
Moore, William J.	21557	02/19/00
Morrill, Douglas M.	25923	06/24/01
Morrill, E. Elbridge, Jr.	25500	10/19/01
Morseberger, James H.	28918	02/14/01
Moulton, John P.	14051-S	12/03/01
Muller, Pamela A. J.	36793	02/25/01
Munroe, Allan H.	25252	03/12/00
Murphy, Charles H., Jr.	22829	08/18/01
Murphy, Edward E., III	20542	06/15/01
Murphy, Frank M.	36176	07/03/02
Murray, David M.	32379	04/05/00
Musson, H. Sheppard, Jr.	14758-S	03/10/00
Neal, William P.	16058	05/09/02
Needham, Grosvenor M.	19324	06/30/00
Nichols, H. Christopher	16404	07/09/00
Nielsen, Charles R.	17741	03/02/01

NAME	NUMBER	DATE OF DEATH
Nikkel, Marc R.	31597	09/03/00
Noll, Joseph E., Jr.	25408	10/04/02
Nolting, Gerald H.	Received	04/20/01
Norcross, Walter G.	23405	06/11/01
Norfleet, Charles W., Jr.	19360	01/02/01
Norman, Alfred E.	16270	05/26/01
Northup, Isaac N.	14648-S	11/30/00
Norton, Howard G.	21299	05/15/01
Noseworthy, Donald W.	Received	03/08/00
Nostrand, George F.	14628-S	01/23/01
Oates, J. F. Titus	Received	04/15/00
Oathout, Edward N.	33185	03/03/02
Ohmen, Audrey F.	34604	03/04/02
Oliveros, Robert L.	17233	03/12/02
Opel, Wayne N.	20019	10/02/02
O'Reilly, Francis P.	Received	12/18/01
Ostrow, Joanne K.	34791	04/19/01
Otwell, Jerry D.	21250	07/11/02
Outtrim, William B.	19858	07/15/01
Ovalle Ruano, Ramon I.	X-34503	12/09/01
Owens, John C.	18994	12/09/02
Page, Louisa	38634	07/23/02
Page, Robert J.	16794	05/26/02
Painter, Earl R.	23354	02/10/01
Parker, Jack D.	17176	12/17/02
Paul, Stephen H.	31335	02/03/00
Paulson, Everett W.	24098	08/03/02
Peabody, John N.	15564-S	09/17/02
Peaks, Granville V., Jr.	16151	02/24/00
Pearson, Barbara M.	36841	09/26/00
Peckenpaugh, Howard D.	24291	08/15/02
Peek, George H.	17300	09/12/00
Peirce, Thomas E.	22853	08/01/00
Pemble, Richard H., II	27076	06/01/01
Penaloza, Elias H.	23429	06/21/01
Pennepacker, Wallace M.	15901-S	12/27/01
Perkins, Kenneth D.	13879-S	01/23/01
Pickens, Henri B.	14634-S	02/23/00
Pierson, Lawrence A.	21401	06/20/01
Poole, James P., Jr.	34606	11/15/02
Postel, James L.	19233	04/06/01
Powell, Bruce T.	17481	02/14/00

RECORDER APPENDIX

NAME	NUMBER	DATE OF DEATH
Poyser, Willis W. H.	27136	03/20/00
Preller, Victor S.	19525	01/19/01
Pratt, Clayton S.	22112	01/05/00
Priest, Kenneth A.	27097	08/29/02
Prior, John	18239	02/06/00
Pritchett, Arthur E.	15274-S	06/29/00
Prunty, Lon M.	17335	11/05/02
Puckett, H. Clay T.	20739	04/21/00
Purdom, Allen B., Jr.	20669	03/23/01
Pyle, John W.	15787-S	11/01/01
Quarles, Althea A.	33405	10/13/01
Raff, Jonathan F.	28406	07/14/01
Rains, Harry J., Sr.	18000	02/05/02
Ramos-Orench, Francisco	22414	03/09/02
Ramsey, John R., Jr.	13855-S	09/14/00
Rankin, Sheldon S.	22153	02/13/01
Rapp, Frederick W.	16950	01/18/02
Rau, Joachim H.	25293	01/24/00
Ray, James G,	31265	10/24/01
Reamy, Harold J., Jr.	26336	07/19/02
Reeves, James A., Jr.	26538	06/23/02
Reeves, Joseph M., III	23465	10/01/00
Regen, Kenneth P.	19914	09/07/02
Reinheimer, John B.	16196	04/16/00
Rementer, Edward P.	18754	11/10/01
Remmel, Norman A.	14162-S	01/06/02
Rice, Quay D., Sr.	20427	11/15/02
Richards, John B.	Received	02/11/01
Ridgway, Maria S.	38522	05/24/02
Riker, Malcolm P.	17810	11/17/02
Roberson, Lemuel G.	18167	08/16/02
Roberts, Thomas D.	21151	01/24/00
Robinson, Bruce M.	18495	10/28/01
Robinson, Paul G.	30496	12/19/02
Robinson, William R.	26237	11/13/02
Rockwood, Frank B.	26468	09/06/01
Rodie, Robert R., Jr.	18859	03/03/02
Rodriguez, Reginald D.	20176	04/14/01
Rogers, Fielding G., Jr.	29100	07/21/00
Rohane, Milton A.	17937	05/29/01
Roller, W. Neil	20937	11/29/00
Rollit, Archibald D.	Received	04/02/02

NAME	NUMBER	DATE OF DEATH
Ross, David F.	X-24329	07/11/02
Ross, Jane W.	35079	04/08/01
Ross-Evanson, R. J.	Received	04/01/01
Rowe, Edward E.	32295	07/19/01
Royster, Robert F.	17924	10/25/00
Ruble, E. Hubert	32516	04/11/02
Rudd, Neilson	26301	04/04/01
Russell, John M.	34302	11/07/00
Rutherford, Reid S.	23059	05/25/02
Ryan, Kathleen	25931	04/01/00
Salman, Donald R.	20302	06/06/00
Samuel, Cynthia K. S.	28326	05/16/00
Samuel, James B., Jr.	25038	08/18/02
Sarles, Dale G.	21778	11/29/00
Schaaf, Donald D.	28519	01/06/00
Schildwachter, Austin E.	16455	07/29/02
Schirmer, Thomas E.	26883	05/27/01
Schlothauer, Lee M.	20943	02/29/00
Schutze, Wilbur R.	16792	08/13/02
Scogin, Alfred F., Jr.	22496	11/27/01
Scott, Conley J.	17854	08/29/00
Scott, Lyle E.	16649	01/08/00
Seabrook J. Allan	Received	07/19/02
Secker, Harry G., Jr.	17244	04/07/02
Sedgwick, Harold B.	14331-S	08/27/00
Seeliger, M. Wesley	23533	05/03/00
Shaw, Don C.	18234	05/24/01
Sheldon, George M.	22427	09/25/01
Sheldon, Joseph L., Jr.	21132	03/14/00
Shelley, Harry E., Jr.	19439	08/30/01
Shelley, Robert E.	25586	05/22/01
Shelton, William W.	21276	02/27/00
Sherrill, Henry W.	17383	03/21/01
Shields, Ellis G.	26064	11/09/01
Shirer, Marie E.	34989-A	06/04/02
Shoemaker, John E.	18658	08/31/02
Shrubsole, Bernard C. M.	35951	03/20/02
Shuffler, Ralph H., II	22812	04/15/01
Shulda, Chester S.	24171	06/22/00
Simmons, Jeffrey T.	26728	03/22/02
Simpson, James B.	24424	03/11/02
Sims, David J.	Received	04/21/00

NAME	NUMBER	DATE OF DEATH
Sims, Rudolph W.	25056	06/11/01
Sine, James H.	26683	11/07/02
Skidmore, William M., Jr.	26782	12/13/02
Skinner, James E. D.	14222-S	10/13/00
Slater, Norman T.	16795	06/26/00
Smiley, Wallace B., Jr.	32096	11/08/01
Smith, David L.	28244	01/24/02
Smith, Harry E.	21948	09/18/00
Smith, Max E.	18521	02/23/00
Smith, Otis	37569	06/06/00
Smith, Russell D.	16411	03/07/01
Smith, William T.	Received	04/04/00
Smolen, Daniel S.	22807	09/14/00
Snider, Hervon L.	Received	11/23/00
Snider, Paul M.	19104	08/05/00
Soutar, James C.	18419	07/26/00
South, Robert W.	25622	12/28/00
Sox, James A.	30165	12/11/01
Spalding, John A.	19440	12/11/01
Spitler, Thomas L.	18765	01/24/01
Stafford, Charles W., II	24924	02/09/02
Stanley, David C.	18584	03/22/00
Steilberg, Robert H.	19672	02/11/00
Steinberg, Willis H.	17590	02/12/01
Stetler, Robert H.	14642-S	03/08/02
Stevens, John F.	16958	08/17/00
Stewart, John R.	17205	02/09/01
Stewart, Reginald G.	Received	05/04/01
Stoll, Thomas F.	23097	03/08/01
Stone, Ellsworth B.	17232	02/07/02
Story, Edward M.	24195	11/26/01
Streett, David C., II	18962	08/12/01
Strickland, Walter R.	16967	01/19/02
Stringer, Warner A., Jr.	23361	10/06/02
Strohsahl, Vincent H.	14789-S	07/28/02
Stube, Edwin B.	20011	02/16/01
Sturm, Raymond L.	21821	01/03/02
Styles, Douglas F.	19121	01/16/02
Sullivan, Thomas V.	21093	03/21/01
Sumners, Thomas W.	13230-S	11/20/00
Sutton, Charles E.	16683	02/09/01
Sutton, Charles R.	16316	02/29/00

NAME	NUMBER	DATE OF DEATH
Swope, J. Gordon, Jr.	19431	01/18/00
Sydnor, C. William	14487-S	05/25/00
Taylor, Frederick E.	18942	01/24/00
Taylor, Meadie A., III	20731	06/14/02
Taylor, Paul J.	23320	12/10/02
Temple, James W.	14219-S	03/27/01
Terry, R. Franklin	27655(a)	02/05/01
Thelin, Harold B.	13233-S	03/01/01
Thomas, Harry N.	18112	08/06/00
Thomas, Robert K.	16775	05/02/00
Thompson, George N.	21744	09/22/01
Thorp, John V.	17142	11/17/00
Tickell, Diane B.	26966	04/24/02
Tickner, Edward H.	21122	04/27/02
Tierney, John C.	17054	02/21/00
Titcomb, James R.	20561	09/23/02
Towne, Page	36570	09/23/02
Townes, Harry R.	27013	05/23/01
Tracy, Manton L., Jr.	29509	01/31/02
Trautwein, James L. P.	18421	03/10/00
Truitt, Laban W.	23426	05/11/00
Truitt, Laban W.	23426	05/11/00
Turley, Douglas C., Jr.	24728	09/10/02
Turner, Robert W., III	16036	12/17/00
Upton, John G.	22313	06/28/01
Urban, Richard G.	13800-S	07/25/00
Urmy, Frank E.	26479	02/01/02
Vail, Alfred	19055	12/18/02
Van Drew, Jerry	24858	09/18/02
Van Ham, Anthony W.	26098	12/27/01
Vaughan, Forrest E.	14955-S	03/02/00
Vere, Harry W.	16997	10/19/02
Vergith, Charles C.	22126	01/30/02
Viverette, Jacob A., Jr.	19376	03/15/00
Wagg, Evarts J., Jr.	19307	12/02/00
Wagner, Robert S.	19974	01/30/03
Wainwright, Robert M.	19083	08/23/02
Wakefield, Victoria E. J.	33459	02/25/00
Walker, William T.	18497	07/30/00
Waller, John E.	19220	12/28/02
Walthall, William S.	16244	12/27/02
Ward, Arthur B.	14797-S	09/24/02

NAME	NUMBER	DATE OF DEATH
Ware, Marshall T.	21901	09/15/02
Washington, Paul M.	16638	10/07/02
Wattley, James C.	18189	07/23/02
Watts, David E.	16540	08/08/00
Wayland, Ellsworth	25492	01/24/02
Weatherly, Theodore L.	18403	08/04/00
Webbe, Gale D.	14371-S	02/03/00
Webber, Roy L.	13150-S	01/01/00
Webster, Ralph K.	16071	07/14/00
Wellford, Thomas D.	18004	04/23/00
Wendt, William A.	17751	07/08/01
Werner, Kenneth C.	18339	08/26/01
Werth, McRae	20022	08/30/00
Wertz, Richard W.	20412	02/22/02
West, Samuel E., Jr.	15666-S	06/25/00
Westhorp, Clifford S.	19244	04/06/02
Weston, M. Moran, Jr.	17394	05/18/02
Whipple, F. Plummer	20786	05/02/02
Whitbread, Arthur C.	Received	05/22/02
White, Hugh C., Jr.	16691	04/14/01
Whiteford, John R.	18489	09/22/00
Whitehead, Bruce E.	20686	11/30/00
Whiting, Eric J.	Received	09/06/02
Whiting, Rodney B.	Received	01/10/02
Whitney, Alden E.	30578	05/20/00
Whitney, Kenneth L.	17905	09/05/02
Wickersham, George W., II	14790-S	09/09/00
Williams, Bernard A.	26292	01/01/00
Williams, Eric B.	30967	06/15/02
Willcox, Jerry M.	23379	02/01/01
Williams, David J.	16522	02/24/01
Williams, Edward T. H., IV	15849-S	10/19/00
Williams, George B.	16576	02/05/02
Williams, John P.	14413-S	12/30/00
Williams, Richard S.	24936	04/11/02
Williams, Turner E.	30433	07/12/02
Williamson, William B.	17278	11/14/00
Willoughby, William D.	20071	02/28/02
Wilmer, Raymond R.	37208	02/27/00
Wilson, David K.	19037	03/30/00
Wing, John D., Jr.	16502	02/16/02
Winslow, Donald F.	19589	09/17/00

NAME	NUMBER	DATE OF DEATH
Winter, Gibson	15750-S	04/03/02
Wise, Robert W.	16311	06/24/00
Withington, Robert W.	18104	11/19/02
Wittlinger, Leonard P.	18565	06/03/00
Wolfe, J. Saxton, Jr.	16615	01/27/00
Wolff-Richards, Richards W.	24712	05/14/01
Woodruff, James E. P.	21519	01/30/02
Woods, Paula V.	28616	01/27/01
Woods, W. Ralph	18596	12/22/02
Worrell, John C.	18566	03/02/01
Worrell, William L.	19373	10/14/01
Wright, Donald L.	25866	01/09/00
Wyatt-Brown, Charles W.	15907	08/13/00
Yasutake, Seiichi M.	17368	12/29/01
Yeoman, Edgar H.	13997-S	04/08/01
Yoho, Clayton W.	23458	08/15/01
Young, Joseph S.	14944-S	01/20/00
Zabriskie, Cornelius A.	18113	11/18/02
Zeller, Paul F.	18275	11/22/00
Zimmerman, John R.	19590	12/02/02
Zinser, Henry A.	16979	01/13/01

DEPOSITIONS/RENUNCIATIONS/RELEASES/REMOVALS
2000–2002

Name	Serial Number	Date	Bishop
Amiott, William K.	31683	03/29/02	Scruton, G. P.
Anthony, Karen L.	35170	06/28/01	Howe, J. W.
Appel, Charles W., Jr.	28575	10/29/01	Duncan, R. W.
Arnold, James O.	35817	01/29/01	Maze, L. E.
Arps, Joseph W. Jr.	26913	08/31/00	Stanton, J. M.
Atkins, John T.	Received	08/10/01	Winterrowd, W. J.
Bailey, William K., Jr.	31355	06/03/02	Henderson, D. F., Jr.
Barbour, Carroll C.	21062	04/17/02	Bruno, J. J.
Behrel, Kenneth K.	28678	09/26/01	Persell, W. D.
Bessette, Theodore A.	16355	05/09/01	Persell, W. D.
Bodishbaugh, C. Conlee	32471	04/20/01	Duvall, C. F.
Bradshaw, Kenneth E.	32763	05/20/02	Curry, M. B.
Brown, J. Robert	26582	04/17/02	Bruno, J. J.
Brown, Robert H.	32344	02/21/01	Bruno, J. J.
Burn, Kathleen D.	30335	03/01/00	Grew, J. C., II
Caridad, Jon A.	24853	05/31/02	Marble, A. C., Jr.
Carroll, Charles P.	21166	07/18/01	Winterrowd, W. J.
Christian, William K., III	31915	06/15/01	Folts, J. E.
Clark, J. David	30527	11/23/02	Irish, C. T.
Clark, Philip G.	24430	02/21/01	Louttit, H. I., Jr.
Clarke, Enrique E.	X-32617	08/01/00	Holguin, J. C.
Cole, Christopher K.	23395	11/09/00	Daniel, C., III
Cole, Mark R.	33210	09/06/00	Herzog, D. W.
Collins, Wayne C.	30140	08/14/01	Stanton, J. M.
Cook, Kenneth R.	31224	12/19/01	Bennison, C. E., Jr.
Davis, M. Scott	29824	04/20/01	Duvall, C. F.
Davis, Patrick M.	30532	06/05/01	Lipscomb, J. B.
Diamond, Daryl E.	28186	02/17/00	Allan F. K.
DiCristina, Mark J.	31806	04/20/01	Duvall, C. F.
Dixon, Don M.	22179	05/03/02	Lee, E. L., Jr.
Dodd, Brian J.	38102	06/28/01	Howe, J. W.
Donlon, Kevin F.	33344	04/22/02	Lipscomb, J. B.
Dowker, John H.	Received	04/17/00	Duncan, R. W.
Dwinell, Michael	24625	02/07/02	Knudsen, C. A. R.
Echols, John D.	23957	02/20/01	Wright, W. P.
Edel, Wilbur H.	25711	12/12/00	Parsley, H. N., Jr.

Name	Serial Number	Date	Bishop
Edwards, Samuel L.	29144	08/19/02	Iker, J. L.
Eleazer, Victor W.	37244	05/16/02	Sauls, S. F.
Erickson, Bonnie J.	37973	10/11/02	Jefferts Schori, K.
Evans, John D.	19171	03/22/02	Kelsey, J. A.
Fisher, W. Bowlyne	23358	08/30/00	Stanton, J. M.
Fowler, Jay D.	32810	11/21/01	Howe, B. R.
Frances, Ricardo L.	31368	04/12/01	Swing, W. E.
Garin, George M., Jr.	31640	12/31/01	Herzog, D. W.
Garrione, Robert M.	Received	09/07/00	Strickland, V. E.
Gibson, Joel A.	27994	11/09/00	Jelinek, J. L.
Gillette, David G.	28312	10/01/01	Herzog, D. W.
Gilman, Charles S., Jr.	31925	06/20/02	Curry, J. E.
Gladstone, John W.	35830	11/09/00	Daniel, C. III
Glenn, Terrell L, Jr.	30538	03/06/00	Salmon, E. L., Jr.
Gough, Richard H.	34851	12/07/00	Jecko, S. H.
Gradone, Elizabeth M.	35056	11/12/02	Scruton, G. P.
Grafe, Robert L., Jr.	36325	04/20/01	Duvall, C. F.
Gray, Douglas A.	36284	07/12/00	Salmon, E. L., Jr.
Grayson, John H.	29452	11/09/00	Daniel, C., III
Gurley, James R.	30459	12/23/99	Shaw, M. T., III
Hall, Robert T.	22711	09/19/02	Joslin, D. B.
Hancock, Norman E., Jr.	32143	03/28/00	Townsend, M. G.
Hanger, Robert B.	34221	11/07/02	Ihloff, R. W.
Hartman, Richard B.	26160	10/30/02	Ladehoff, R. L.
Hesse, Michael E.	26855	04/20/01	Duvall, C. F.
Huerta Garcia, Oscar	X-33155	04/03/00	Espinoza Venegas, S.
Hughes, Robert E., Jr.	34594	09/07/00	Swing, W. E.
Hutchinson, John M.	30333	05/23/01	Rockwell, H. H.
Jackman, Michael J.	23771	05/02/00	Swing, W. E.
Jacobson, Arthur T.	35815	09/13/01	Epting, C. C.
James, Charles W.	33473	09/04/01	Swing, W. E.
Johnson, James P.	35305	02/19/01	Iker, J. L.
Kallstrom, Scott A.	28968	10/10/01	Croneberger, J. P.
Kehayes, Thomas C.	23853	04/01/00	Warner, V. W., Jr.
Kessler, Matthew S.	36327	08/15/01	Payne, C. E.
Kirk, Stephen S.	31992	01/18/00	Wright, W. P.
Kremer, Anna P.	28494	12/04/01	Sauls, S. F.
Lawrence, Raymond Q., Jr.	31491	12/12/00	Powell, F. N.
Lyman, Philip D.	28828	12/19/01	Bennison, C. E., Jr.
Mayes, A. Bernard D.	Received	09/07/00	Swing, W. E.
McAlpine, Laurie A.	32325	08/05/02	Johnson, R. H.

Name	Serial Number	Date	Bishop
McEvers, James M.	23564	04/29/02	Beckwith, P. H.
McKenzie, Jerry B.	22340	08/05/02	Winterrowd, W. J.
McNeeley, William J.	31470	10/03/01	Herlong, B. N.
Meyers, Hal I.	25742	12/05/01	Herzog, D. W.
Miller, Samuel G., Jr.	29540	08/02/00	Hendricks, W. F., III St. Com Pres. for Dio of CNY
Mobley, Forrest C., Jr.	24237	11/29/01	Parsley, H. N., Jr.
Moyer, David L.	Received	09/05/02	Bennison, C. E., Jr.
Murray, Carl C.	Received	02/14/02	Jecko, S. H.
Neller, Wayne A.	33911	08/24/00	Howe, J. W.
Neri, Arthur D.	27998	06/02/01	Waggoner, J. E., Jr.
Parker, John E., III	38083	07/01/02	Salmon, E. L., Jr.
Payne, Veronica I. H.	32593	10/24/00	Frade, L.
Persson, Bernard C.	Received	01/29/02	Rockwell, H. H.
Pettit, Walton S., Jr.	24849	08/29/00	Lee, P. J.
Phillips, Francis A.	36463	12/06/02	Ladehoff, R. L.
Phillips, Michael V.	34184	12/12/00	Caldwell, B. E.
Pollard, Richard A.	18827	06/10/02	Lipscomb, J. B.
Rakoczy, August A.	34019	09/19/01	Shaw, M. T., III
Raulerson, Steven W.	29064	05/25/00	Howe, J. W.
Richer, Victor G.	19982	07/08/02	Keyser, C. L.
Riley, Wayne T.	32388	03/13/02	McKelvey, J. M.
Robison, Ronald L.	34755	07/28/00	Lee, P. J.
Rutledge, Gail L.	37684	10/31/01	Herzog, D. W.
Schmidt, Dennis J. J.	28392	12/09/02	Howe, B. R.
Sharpe, William G.	27623	10/01/01	Howe, J. W.
Shissler, Donald G.	22016	10/21/02	Winterrowd, W. J.
Sisson, Rick L.	35399	09/13/01	Epting, C. C.
Smith, Richard U., Jr.	Received	12/18/01	Bennison, C. E., Jr.
Smith, Timothy R.	31313	04/20/01	Duvall, C. F.
Smith, William G., Jr.	25843	10/08/02	Gepert, R. R.
Stevens, Gregory T.	32549	06/18/01	Grew, J. C., II
Stoudenmire, William W.	35033	10/12/01	Duncan, P. M., II
Strey, Robert J.	32155	07/12/01	Leidel, E. M., Jr.
Strom, John D.	24283	03/18/02	Grew, J. C., II
Stumpf, Stephen E.	31663	05/08/02	Ackerman, K. L.
Sullivan, James S.	29327	02/19/01	Iker, J. L.
Sumrall, Ernie C.	31010	01/14/02	Lipscomb, J. B.
Thorp, Almus M., Jr.	24207	10/19/00	Wood, R. S., Jr.
Towner, James O.	27900	03/29/01	Frade, L.
Twist, Richard L.	30655	01/24/01	Gibbs, W. N., Jr.

Name	Serial Number	Date	Bishop
Walfoort, Michael R.	30789	09/26/00	Jelinek, J. L.
Walker, John D.	30973	08/21/01	Ohl, C. W., Jr.
Ward, Pamela A.	35581	01/25/01	Walker, O. G., Jr.
Weber, Thomas R.	28085	09/16/02	White, R. J.
Westerfield, James A.	36378	05/03/02	Lee, E. L., Jr.
Yeager, Wayne E.	25147	02/18/00	Gulick, E. F., Jr.
Zelaya-Chavez, Otto D.	X-24679	04/14/01	Little, E. S., II

SUSPENSIONS
2000–2002

Name	Serial Number	Date	Bishop
Barker, Kenneth L.	28676	05/01/00	Duvall, C. F.
Bird, John E., Jr.	25185	05/23/00	Joslin, D. B.
Bwechwa, Oswald D.	Received	04/21/00	White, R. J.
Clifton, Stephen G.	30839	06/03/00	Lipscomb, J. B.
Cole, C. King	23395	03/26/00	Daniel, C., III
Coleman, James P.	30813	12/11/00	Howe, J. W.
Cook, Kenneth R.	31224	05/25/01	Bennison, C. E., Jr.
DiNunno, Lisa	37390	06/01/00	Banes, D. C., Jr.
Eleazer, Victor W.	37244	07/01/00	Sauls, S. F.
Evett, Douglas P.	22687	01/14/01	Gibbs, W. N., Jr.
Fitzgibbons, Michael J.	25942	04/17/00	Robison, Thomas J.
Fowler, Jay D.	32810	05/18/01	Howe, B. R.
Gladstone, John W.	35830	03/26/00	Daniel, C., III
Grayson, John H.	29452	03/26/00	Daniel, C., III
Haddix, Theodoree R., Jr.	28234	01/01/01	Lee, P. J.
Hahneman, Geoffrey M.	29439	06/01/00	Bane, D. C., Jr.
Halliwell, Leigh J.	30849	12/13/02	Whalon, P. W.
Harte, John J. M., Jr.	25729	04/09/02	Shahan, R. R.
Hartney, Michael E.	27164	01/01/01	Garrison, J. M.
JONES, CHARLES I. III	28202	06/17/02	Griswold, F. T., III
Kallstrom, Scott A.	28968	02/08/01	Croneberger, J. P.
Keili, Michael S.	Received	10/18/02	Bane, D. C., Jr.
Krumenacker, Gerald W., Jr.	36214	10/24/02	Stanton, J. M.
Lyman, Philip D.	28828	05/25/01	Bennison, C. E., Jr.
McBride, Jerry A.	29458	03/29/00	Marble, A. C., Jr.
Miner, Daniel F.	23698	04/03/01	Shahan, R. R.
Moyer, David L.	Received	03/04/02	Bennison, C. E., Jr.
Nairn, Frederick	Received	07/10/01	Jelinek, J. L.
Pedersen, Charles L.R., Jr.	34027	01/25/01	Winterrowd, W. J.
Sinkler, Wharton, III	23744	04/29/01	Jelinek, J. L.
Slocum, Robert B.	32002	12/21/02	White, R. J.
Snow, Gary N.	33075	12/08/00	Robertson, C. L.
Stoudenmire, William W.	35033	02/19/01	Duvall, C. F.
Sutor, Jack T., Jr.	33724	10/23/01	Klusmeyer, W. M.
Swann, Stuart A.	34717	01/25/01	Lee, P. J.
Trimble, William B., Jr.	25332	05/30/02	Daniel, C., III

RESTORATIONS
2000–2002

Name	Serial Number	Date	Bishop
Adams, David R.	32819	05/23/00	Joslin, J. B.
Allen, Philip C.	23263	03/18/00	Jelinek, J. L.
Andersen, Paul J.	28188	09/23/02	Chane, J. B.
Clark, James D.	30527	07/13/01	Kelshaw, T.
Dalton, William T.	23237	12/13/02	Stanton, J. M.
Hahneman, Geoffrey M.	29439	04/01/01	Bane, D. C., Jr.
Hale, William C.	33448	09/24/02	Gibbs, W. N., Jr.
Horton, Richard L.	25673	02/20/02	Croneberger, J.
Huber, Donald M.	28594	10/31/01	Garrison, J. M.
Jackson, Eric M. C.	Received	03/06/01	Warner, V. W., Jr
Kellerhouse, Dean K.	28266	02/01/01	Duncan, R. W.
Kilfoyle, J. Richard	22395	01/06/00	Scruton, G. P.
Klohn, Franklin J.	16813	02/15/00	Epting, C. C.
Kohn, George F.	27577	02/12/00	Shimpfky, R. L.
Landis, Clifford K.	20566	03/02/00	Borsch, F. H.
McCarthy, B. Anderson	25852	09/12/00	Stanton, J. M.
Merritt, Frederick D.	32715	11/30/01	Krotz, J. E.
Miller, Joseph P.	25905	05/23/01	Borsch, F. H.
Moffat, Alexander D., Jr.	20465	06/29/01	Iker, J. L.
Putman, Richard B.	28077	05/19/02	Parsley, H. N.
Ramos-Orench, Francisco	22414	10/14/01	Smith, A. D.
Spencer, John R.	27069	04/26/00	Winterrowd, W. J.
Stevenson, Carolyn E.	32200	12/16/00	Smith, A. D.
Sullivan, James S.	29327	04/29/02	Iker, J. L.

RECEPTIONS
From Other Churches of, or in Communion with, the Anglican Church
2000–2002

Name	Date	From
Akinkugbe, Felix O.	02/06/01	Church of Nigeria
Albano, Randolph V. N.	06/10/00	Philippines Episcopal Church
Alleyne, Edmund T.	12/19/02	Church of the West Indies, Barbados
Ananshekhar, Joseph	12/11/02	Church of South India, Karnataka
Ayala-Porfil, Eugenio	07/08/02	Church of Mexico
Barrett, S. Dawn	06/03/02	Church of Canada, Montreal
Bawtree, Andrew J.	01/01/00	Church of England, St. Albans
Beauvoir, Oge	03/31/00	Church of Canada, Montreal
Branche, Ronald C. W.	05/10/02	Church of the West Indies, Trinidad & Tobago
Brown-Watson, Rosa M.	07/20/02	Church of Costa Rica
Chaney, John P.	11/16/01	Church of Southeast Asia
Chapman, Hugh W.	07/01/01	Church of the West Indies, Barbados
Clarke, Carlton C.	05/30/01	Church of Jamaica
Clarke, Michael A.	11/01/01	Church of the West Indies, Barbados
Cleeve, Admire W.	10/16/02	Church of England, Oxford
Cook, Paul R.	02/01/00	Church of Australia
Corbett, Ian D.	09/01/01	Church of Canada, Qu'Appelle
Daniel, Wilfred A.	09/01/00	Church of England
den Blaauwen, Edward A.	01/01/00	Church of South Africa, Kimberly & Kuruman
Dickinson, Garrin W.	12/31/02	Church of Kenya, Mount Kenya South
Duraikannu, Yesupatham	03/14/01	Church of India, Madras
Elliott, Paul A.	10/31/00	Church of Australia, Rockhampton
Faust, Andrew S.	09/27/01	Church of Scotland, Glasgow & Galloway
Fenton, Gordon D.	12/11/02	Church of Canada, New Westminster
Frederick, Warren	09/24/00	Church of England, Guildford
Gambling, Paul	05/15/01	Church of Canada, Huron
Gay, Judith S.	11/27/02	Church of South Africa, Lesotho
Goode, Colin	12/01/02	Church of Canada, New Westminster
George, Johannes M. P.	09/27/01	Church of Liberia, Kenema
Halliday, Christopher N. R.	03/01/00	Church of Ireland
Halliday, Paula P.	03/01/00	Church of Ireland, Ferns
Han, Valentine S-G.	02/01/00	Church of South Korea, Pusan
Heidt, Michael L.	04/01/00	Church of England, Oxford
Holder, Anthony B.	03/01/01	Church of West Indies, Barbados

Name	Date	From
Hyde, Jack E. A.	06/20/00	Church of Canada, Ottawa
Iswariah, James C.	08/06/02	Church of Australia, Perth
Jackson, David H.	12/31/02	Church of England, Oxford
Jackson, Peter J. E.	12/31/02	Church of England, London
Jansma, Henry P.	10/01/01	Church of England, Lincoln
Johnson, James M.	10/15/02	Church of Canada, Eastern Newfoundland & Labrador
Joo, Indon P.	05/29/01	Church of Korea, Seoul
Joseph, Winston	10/04/00	Church of the West Indies, Trinidad & Tobago
Kaswarra, George A.	12/19/02	Church of Uganda, Mukono
Kilpatrick, Alan W.	01/04/02	Church of England, London
Kollin, James T.	05/01/01	Philippines Episcopal Church, North Central Philippines
Kowbeidu, Anthony K.	12/01/00	Church of Liberia
Kramer, B. Kristopher	12/01/01	Church of England, London
Lee, Kirk A.	01/01/01	Church of Canada, Toronto
Lewis, Timothy J.	07/24/01	Church of England, Canterbury
MacKenzie, Vanessa M.	01/01/01	Church of South Africa
Martin, William J.	12/27/00	Church of West Indies, Nassau & the Bahamas
Merchant, Wilmot T., II	10/16/00	Church of Liberia
Morehead, James C.	08/08/02	Church of Rwanda, Shyria
Moyer, David L.	09/05/02	Province of Central Africa, Upper Shire
Muldoon, Maggie R. D.	11/05/02	Church of Canada, New Westminster
Mungoma, Stephen M.	07/17/00	Church of Uganda, Mbale
Ndishabandi, William K.	11/01/02	Church of Uganda, South Rwenzori
Newton, Louis K.	02/14/01	Church of England, Chelmsford
Nuamah, Reginald	05/13/02	Church of West Africa, Kumasi
Owen, Petra D.	10/03/01	Church of England, Derby
Pastores, Tancredo R., Jr.	06/10/00	Philippines Episcopal Church
Ponic, Joseph J.	06/26/02	Church of Canada, Saskatoon
Porter, George M.	01/09/01	Church of Canada, Manitoba
Quevedo-Bosch, Juan A.	10/09/00	Church of Cuba
Reece, Nathaniel S. T.	05/07/02	Church of Tanzania, Southern Highlands
Richards, Dennison S.	6/26/02	Church of the West Indies, Windward Islands
Roddam, John W. R.	11/18/00	Church of Canada, New Westminster
Rojas Poveda, Jesus A.	11/27/00	Church of Puerto Rico
Sarkissyian, Sabi K.	09/12/01	Church of Jerusalem
Scriven, Henry W.	09/01/02	Church of England

Name	Date	From
Sey, Reginald F. A.	05/23/02	Church of West Africa, Sekondi
Singh, Prince G.	04/18/00	Church of South India, Madras
Smart, Clifford E. S.	05/04/01	Church of England
Stone, Glenn H.	12/28/01	Church of Canada, Calgary
Stone, Glenn H.	12/28/01	Church of Canada, Calgary
Thompson, Edward H.	11/27/02	Church of Liberia
Thomson, Ian C.	06/04/00	Church of Canada, Quebec
Thurlow, David W. T.	10/16/01	Church of Canada, Saskachewan
Tristram, Geoffrey R.	03/13/02	Church of England, St. Albans
Turton, Neil C.	03/14/02	Church of England
Tyndall, Jeremy H.	08/07/01	Church of England, Birmingham
Villagomeza, Christian	10/12/01	Philippines Independent Church
Waweru, Christine G.	03/26/02	Church of Kenya, Thika
Webster, Thomas H.	02/01/01	Church of Canada, Niagara
Westberg, Daniel A.	06/05/01	Church of Canada, Toronto
Wilson, Christopher R. M.	10/18/01	Church of Canada, Toronto
Wilson, James N., II	01/01/02	Church of Liberia
Wismer, Robert D.	10/24/02	Church of Canada, New Westminster
Wright, Winston A.	10/12/00	Church of Canada, Toronto
Wyld, Kevin A.	07/24/00	Church of England, Durham
Zubieta Gutierrez, Agustin T.	03/31/01	Church of Bolivia

TRANSFERS

Clergy Transferred to Other Churches of the Anglican Communion

Name	Transferred to:
Boardman, William A.	Church of Southeast Asia
Britt, Frances M.	Church of Rwanda
Brodie, R. Gerald A.	Church of Canada, Diocese of Niagara
Brown, Rosalind	Church of England, Diocese of Salisbury
Bryan, David C.	Church of Rwanda
Bryan, Robert J.	Church of Southeast Asia
Calderhead, Christopher C.	Church of England, Diocese of Ely
Doyle, Lawrence E.	Church of Southeast Asia
Eberhart, Philip D.	Church of Rwanda
Feliu-Gonzalez, Candida E.	Church of Puerto Rico
Garrou, Dennis J.	Church of Southeast Asia
Goode, Colin	Church of Canada, Diocese of New Westminster
Greene, Alexander M.	Church of Southeast Asia
Hinson, Paul A.	Church of Rwanda
Jackman, Kathleen R.	Church of Rwanda
Kenney, William C., Jr.	Church of Rwanda
King, Kathy J.	Church of Southeast Asia
Koscheski, Nelson W.	Church of Rwanda
Mollica, Ralph J.	Church of Southeast Asia
Morris, Shirley L.	Church of Southeast Asia
Moyer, David L.	Province of Central Africa, Diocese of Upper Shire
Roberts, Jose F.	Church of Puerto Rico
Ross, Kenneth E.	Church of Rwanda
Sausele, Elizabeth J.	Church of Rwanda
Schnackenberg, Gerald L.	Church of Southeast Asia
Smith, Gregory M.	Church of Southeast Asia
Stansberry, Carmen M.	Church of Canada, Diocese of Calgary
Stone, James F.	Church of Southeast Asia
Sulzenfuss, Alan L.	Church of Southeast Asia
Taylor, Emerson B., Jr.	Church of Rwanda
Titus, David A.	Church of Canada
Toon, Peter	Church of England, Diocese of Lichfield
van Schalkwky, George E.	Church of South Africa, Diocese of Capetown
Welbourne, Jacob A.	Church of West Africa, Diocese of Sekondi
Westin, John-Paul	Church of Canada, Diocese of Eastern NF & Labrador
Wiley, John D.	Church of Southeast Asia
Wolverson, Marc A. M.	Church of England, Diocese of Chester

CLERGY LIST

Serial #	Name	Diaconate Date	Ordaining Bishop	Priesthood Date	Ordaining Bishop
37644	Kilpatrick Madlock, Marcia J.	01/06/2000	Epting, C. C.		
37645	Lovelace, Darin R.	01/06/2000	Epting, C. C.		
37646	Campbell, Karen A.	01/08/2000	McLeod, M. A. R.	10/28/2000	Scruton G. P. for McLeod, M. A. R.
37647	Williams, Edward S.	01/14/2000	Louttit, H. I., Jr. Title III, Canon 6		
37648	Keeler, Charles B.	01/15/2000	Marble, A. C., Jr. Title III, Canon 6		
37649	Tester, Helen W.	01/15/2000	Marble, A. C., Jr. Title III, Canon 6		
37650	Warwick, Eilene R.	01/15/2000	Marble, A. C., Jr. Title III, Canon 6		
37651	Wyatt, Thomas C.	01/15/2000	Marble, A. C. Jr. Title III, Canon 6		
37652	Baker, Susan E.	01/22/2000	Winterrowd, W. J.	07/29/2000	Winterrowd, W. J.
37653	Chambers, Rex N.	01/22/2000	Winterrowd, W. J.	08/05/2000	Winterrowd, W. J.
37654	Engels, Allen R.	01/22/2000	Winterrowd, W. J. Title III, Canon 9	07/29/2000	Winterrowd, W. J. Title III, Canon 9
37655	Fhuere, Brenda L.	01/22/2000	Winterrowd, W. J.	07/29/2000	Winterrowd, W. J.
37656	Griffin, Ronald W.	01/22/2000	Winterrowd, W. J. Title III, Canon 9	08/05/2000	Winterrowd, W. J. Title III, Canon 9
37657	Flexer, Katharine G.	01/23/2000	Warner, V. W., Jr.	09/09/2000	Swing, W. E. for Warner, V.

Serial #	Name	Diaconate Date	Ordaining Bishop	Priesthood Date	Ordaining Bishop
37658	Young, Robert A.	01/25/2000	MacDonald, M. L.	05/14/2000	MacDonald, M. L.
37659	Lethin, Judith L. W.	02/01/2000	MacDonald, M. L.		
37660	Lethin, Kris W.	02/01/2000	MacDonald, M. L.		
37661	Colyn, Robert, Sr.	02/03/2000	Title III, Canon 6 Rath, G. E.		
37662	Johnson, Dennis L.	02/03/2000	Title III, Canon 6 Caldwell, B. E.		
37663	Bond, Michael D.	02/05/2000	Title III, Canon 6 Persell, W. D.		
37664	Brookman, Cathleen A.	02/05/2000	Title III, Canon 6 Persell, W. D.		
37665	Carlson, William A.	02/05/2000	Title III, Canon 6 Persell, W. D.		
37666	Gaede, Lee Ann L.	02/05/2000	Title III, Canon 6		
37667	Logue, Frank S.	02/05/2000	Louttit, H. I., Jr.	08/26/2000	Louttit, H. I., Jr.
37668	Martin, Judy S.	02/05/2000	Caldwell, B. E. Title III, Canon 6		
37669	Shaffer, Michael	02/05/2000	Howe, B. R. Title III, Canon 6		
37670	Stanley, Gordon J.	02/05/2000	Persell, W. D. Title III, Canon 6		
37671	West, John R.	02/05/2000	Louttit, H. I., Jr.		

CLERGY LIST APPENDIX

Serial #	Name	Diaconate Date	Ordaining Bishop	Priesthood Date	Ordaining Bishop
37672	Whelan, Janet K.	02/05/2000	Howe, B. R. Title III, Canon 6		
37673	Everson, Jacquelyn	02/13/2000	Kelsey, J. A. Title III, Canon 9		
37674	Jones, Harriet M.	02/13/2000	Kelsey, J. A. Title III, Canon 9		
37675	Miron, Mary L.	02/15/2000	Kelsey, J. A. Title III, Canon 9		
37676	Pearce, Robert C., Jr.	02/19/2000	Smalley, W. E. Title III, Canon 6		
37677	Van Dyke, Robert H.	02/24/2000	Parsley, H. N., Jr.	09/10/2000	Parsley, H. N., Jr.
37678	Roberson, Keith J.	02/26/2000	Iker, J. L.	09/29/2000	Iker, J. L.
37679	Dandridge, Robert F.	03/01/2000	Hargrove, R. J., Jr.	11/12/2000	Hargrove, R. J., Jr.
37680	Gardner, Carol H.	03/04/2000	Coleman, J. M. Title III, Canon 6		
37681	Gonterman, Maynard C.	03/04/2000	Maze, L. E. Title III, Canon 6		
37682	Turner, John E.	03/04/2000	Chang, R. S. O.		
37683	Bignall, Alton K.	03/05/2000	Kelsey, J. A. Title III, Canon 9		
37684	Rutledge, Gail L.	03/15/2000	Herzog, D. W. Title III, Canon 6		
37685	Corley, Kathryn S.	03/18/2000	Grein, R. F.	09/16/2000	Grein, R. F.
37686	Ekrem, Katherine B.	03/18/2000	Grein, R. F.	09/16/2000	Grein, R. F.
37687	Grab, Virginia L.	03/18/2000	Grein, R. F.	09/16/2000	Grein, R. F.

Serial #	Name	Diaconate Date	Ordaining Bishop	Priesthood Date	Ordaining Bishop
37688	Poisson, Ellen H.	03/18/2000	Grein, R. F.	09/16/2000	Grein, R. F.
37689	Rubinson, Rhonda J.	03/18/2000	Grein, R. F.	09/16/2000	Grein, R. F.
37690	Santiviago-Espinal, Maria I.	03/18/2000	Grein, R. F.	09/16/2000	Grein, R. F.
37691	Synan, Thomas N. J.	03/18/2000	Grein, R. F.	09/16/2000	Grein, R. F.
37692	Hoffman, Robyn R.	03/19/2000	Persell, W. D. for Hargrove, R. J., Jr.	10/28/2000	Scantlebury, V. A. for Hargrove, R. J., Jr.
37693	von Wrangel, Carola	03/24/2000	Herzog, D. W.	09/30/2000	Herzog, D. W.
37694	Guernsey, Justine M.	03/25/2000	Herzog, D. W.		
			Title III, Canon 6		
37695	Kay, Frances C.	03/25/2000	Hargrove, R. J., Jr.		
			Title III, Canon 6		
37696	Osburn, Bernard C.	03/25/2000	Schofield, J.-D.	10/01/2000	Schofield, J.-D.
37697	Kempster, Patricia S.	03/26/2000	Lamb, J. A.	10/28/2000	Lamb, J. L.
37698	Kelly, Dennis P.	03/27/2000	Schofield, J.-D.	09/29/2000	Schofield, J.-D.
37699	Holly, F. Eugene	04/01/2000	Thornton, J. S. for Nevada	09/30/2000	Hunt, G. N. for Nevada
			Title III, Canon 9		Title III, Canon 9
37700	Bianchi, Mary E.	04/02/2000	Thornton, J. S.		
			Title III, Canon 6		
37701	Sims, Richard O.	04/02/2000	Thornton, J. S. for Nevada	11/18/2000	Hunt, G. N. for Nevada
			Title III, Canon 9		Title III, Canon 9
37702	Gleason, Dorothy J.	04/09/2000	Schofield, J.-D.		
			Title III, Canon 6		
37703	Shadow, Burton A.	04/24/2000	Iker, J. L.	11/18/2000	Iker, J. L.
37704	D'Urbano, Faith J.	04/29/2000	Marshall, P. V.	03/26/2001	Marshall, P. V.

CLERGY LIST APPENDIX

Serial #	Name	Diaconate Date	Ordaining Bishop	Priesthood Date	Ordaining Bishop
37705	FitzSimmons, Daniel V.	04/29/2000	Marshall, P. V.	12/02/2000	Marshall, P. V.
37706	Hazen, Susan M.	04/29/2000	Marshall, P. V.		
X-37707	Addison, Orlando J.	05/01/2000	Frade, L.		
37708	Mottl, Christine E.	05/02/2000	Krotz, J. E.	11/05/2000	Krotz, J. E.
37709	Bradley, Patrick J.	05/06/2000	Garrison, J. M. Title III, Canon 6		
37710	McConchie, Leann P.	05/06/2000	Garrison, J. M. Title III, Canon 6		
37711	Brockmann, Sarah J.	05/11/2000	Wright, W. P.	02/02/2002	Wright, W. P.
37712	Lufburrow, Sara D.	05/11/2000	Louttit, H. I., Jr. Title III, Canon 6		
37713	Walter, George A., II	05/12/2000	Wolfrum, W. H. for Montana	11/13/2001	MacDonald, M. L. for Montana
37714	Thompson, Susan M.	05/13/2000	Shimpfky, R. L.		
37715	Seeley, Walter D., Jr.	05/16/2000	Caldwell, B. E. Title III, Canon 9	12/06/2000	Caldwell, B. E. Title III, Canon 9
37716	Close, LeRoy S.	05/20/2000	Grein, R. F. Title III, Canon 6		
37717	Craig, Idalia S.	05/20/2000	Joslin, D. B.		
37718	Dambrot, Donna L.	05/20/2000	Grein, R. F. Title III, Canon 6		
37719	Duval, Linda M.	05/20/2000	Grein, R. F. Title III, Canon 6		
37720	Graham, Joanna D.	05/20/2000	Joslin, D. B.	12/16/2000	Marshall, Paul V. for Joslin, D. B.

Serial #	Name	Diaconate Date	Ordaining Bishop	Priesthood Date	Ordaining Bishop
37721	Hinton, Bradley A.	05/20/2000	Parsley, H. N., Jr.		
37722	Hopper, Edgar W.	05/20/2000	Grein, R. F. Title III, Canon 6		
37723	Keator, Marion K.	05/20/2000	McLeod, M. A. R.	12/02/2000	McLeod, M. A. R.
37724	Lindquist, Mary D.	05/20/2000	Joslin, D. B.		
37725	Oasin, Elizabeth J.	05/20/2000	Joslin, D. B.	04/28/2001	Joslin, D. B.
37726	Size, Patricia B.	05/20/2000	White, R. J.	12/02/2000	White, R. J.
37727	White, Stephen L.	05/20/2000	Joslin, D. B.		
37728	Gerhard, Kurt J.	05/21/2000	Krotz, J. E.		
37729	Kramer, Aron M.	05/25/2000	Jelinek, J. L.	11/30/2000	Swenson, D. L. for Jelinek, J. L.
37730	Balius, Valerie A.	05/27/2000	Howe, J. W.	03/17/2001	Howe, J. W.
37731	Black-Graham, Rebecca L.	05/27/2000	Shaw, M. T., III		
37732	Catania, Jason A.	05/27/2000	Ackerman, K. L.	12/21/2000	Herzog, D. W.
37733	Custer, R. Dale	05/27/2000	Bane, D. C., Jr.	12/07/2000	Bane, D. C., Jr.
37734	Edington, Mark D. W.	05/27/2000	Shaw, M. T. III		
37735	Gough, Frank D., II	05/27/2000	Howe, J. W.	12/09/2000	Howe, J. W.
37736	Guback, Thomas H.	05/27/2000	Lee, E. L., Jr.	11/25/2000	Lee, E. L., Jr.
37737	Jacobs, John R.	05/27/2000	Howe, J. W.	12/09/2000	Howe, J. W.
37738	Kauffman, Daniel G.	05/27/2000	Howe, J. W. Title III, Canon 6		
37739	McCarthy, Jean E. R.	05/27/2000	Epting, C. C.	02/24/2001	Epting, C. C.
37740	Nee, Michael J.	05/27/2000	Ackerman, K. L.	11/29/2000	Ackerman, K. L.
37741	Oldland, William D.	05/27/2000	Johnson, R. C., Jr.	06/09/2001	Curry, M. B.

CLERGY LIST — APPENDIX

Serial #	Name	Diaconate Date	Ordaining Bishop	Priesthood Date	Ordaining Bishop
37742	Rowe, Sean W.	05/27/2000	Rowley, R. D., Jr.	12/02/2000	Rowley, R. D., Jr.
37743	Sholander, Mark E.	05/27/2000	Howe, J. W.	12/09/2000	Howe, J. W.
37744	Sorvillo, James A., Sr.	05/27/2000	Howe, J. W.	12/09/2000	Howe, J. W.
37745	Townsend, M. Clayton, Jr.	05/27/2000	Howe, J. W.	01/13/2001	Curry, M. B. for Howe, J. W.
37746	Jones, Duncan	05/28/2000	Johnson, R. C., Jr.		
37747	Petersen, Barbara J.	05/30/2000	Krotz, J. E.	11/30/2000	Krotz, J. E.
37748	Fowler, William Y., IV	06/01/2000	Folts, J. E.	02/09/2001	Folts, J. E.
37749	Rivetti, Mary E.	06/01/2000	Irish, C. T.	12/07/2000	Irish, C. T.
37750	Stock, David R.	06/01/2000	Irish, C. T.	01/25/2001	Irish, C. T.
37751	Two Bulls, Robert W.	06/01/2000	Irish, C. T.	01/06/2001	Irish, C. T.
37752	Droste, Robert E.	06/02/2000	Ladehoff, R. L.	12/02/2000	Swing, W. E.
37753	Ambler, Michael N, Jr.	06/03/2000	Knudsen, C. A. R.	12/16/2000	Knudsen, C. A. R.
37754	Bevans, Marjorie S.	06/03/2000	Hart, D. P. for MacDonald, M. L.	01/28/2001	Hart, D. P. for MacDonald, M. L.
37755	Carmody, Alison C.	06/03/2000	Parsley, H. N., Jr.		
37756	Clark, Johnny W.	06/03/2000	Hargrove, R. J., Jr.	12/09/2000	Hargrove, R. J., Jr.
37757	Conner, Martha A. H.	06/03/2000	Duvall, C. F.	02/24/2001	Duvall, C. F.
37758	Dailey, Harry E.	06/03/2000	Stanton, J. M. Title III, Canon 6		
37759	DeWees, Herbert R.	06/03/2000	Stanton, J. M.	06/07/2001	Stanton, J. M.
37760	Doherty-Ogea, Kathleen L.	06/03/2000	Hargrove, R. J., Jr.	12/16/2000	Hargrove, R. J., Jr.
37761	Fellows, Jessica H.	06/03/2000	Swing, W. E.	12/02/2000	Swing, W. E.
37762	Ferrel, Artis L.	06/03/2000	Epting, C. C. Title III, Canon 9	12/09/2000	Epting, C. C. Title III, Canon 9

Serial #	Name	Diaconate Date	Ordaining Bishop	Priesthood Date	Ordaining Bishop
37763	Giacobbe, Georgia B.	06/03/2000	Ihloff, R. W. Title III, Canon 6		
37764	Graves, Verna E.	06/03/2000	Jelinek, J. L. Title III, Canon 9	12/08/2000	Swenson, D. L. for Jelinek, J. L. Title III, Canon 9
37765	Gremillion, Dorothy A.	06/03/2000	Hargrove, R. J., Jr.	12/09/2000	Hargrove, R. J., Jr.
37766	Hagen, Amelia A.	06/03/2000	Swing, W. E.	12/02/2000	Swing, W. E.
37767	Harrigfeld, Christopher L.	06/03/2000	Swing, W. E. Title III, Canon 6		
37768	Henderson, Mark W.	06/03/2000	Swing, W. E.		
37769	Hill, Joel G.	06/03/2000	Ihloff, R. W. Title III, Canon 6		
37770	Hornaday, Evelyn W.	06/03/2000	Howe, B. R.	12/09/2000	Howe, B. R.
37771	McDonald, Mark W.	06/03/2000	Duvall, C. F.	02/17/2001	Duvall, C. F.
37772	Meck, Nancy E.	06/03/2000	Howe, B. R.	02/06/2001	Lee, P. J. for Howe, B. R.
37773	Mitchell, Dawn-Victoria	06/03/2000	Howe, B. R.	12/05/2000	Howe, B. R.
37774	Palmerhall, Juanita	06/03/2000	Jelinek, J. L. Title III, Canon 9	12/08/2000	Swenson, D. L. for Jelinek, J. L. Title III, Canon 9
37775	Pruitt, Albert W.	06/03/2000	Duvall, C. F.	02/02/2001	Duvall, C. F.
37776	Rice, Sandra K. E.	06/03/2000	Ihloff, R. W. Title III, Canon 6		
37777	Ross, Sue Ann	06/03/2000	Stanton, J. M. Title III, Canon 6		
37778	Sanders, JoAnne M.	06/03/2000	Swing, W. E.	12/02/2000	Swing, W. E.

CLERGY LIST APPENDIX

Serial #	Name	Diaconate Date	Ordaining Bishop	Priesthood Date	Ordaining Bishop
37779	Smith, Kerry J.	06/03/2000	Ihloff, R. W.		
37780	Thompson, Catherine M.	06/03/2000	Title III, Canon 6 Stanton, J. M.		
37781	Tomlinson, Ruth M.	06/03/2000	Bruno, J. J. for Borsch, F. H.		
37782	Wall, Anne F.	06/03/2000	Swing, W. E. Title III, Canon 6		
37783	Ward, George B. P., Jr.	06/03/2000	Ihloff, R. W. Title III, Canon 6		
37784	Whitebird, George	06/03/2000	Jelinek, J. L. Title III, Canon 9	12/08/2000	Swenson, D. L. for Jelinek, J. L. Title III, Canon 9
37785	Woodle, Thomas F., Jr.	06/03/2000	Salmon, E. L., Jr.	12/12/2000	Salmon, E. L., Jr.
37786	Greer, George H., Jr.	06/04/2000	Gulick, E. F., Jr.	01/13/2001	Gulick, E. F., Jr.
37787	Kennedy, Zelda M.	06/04/2000	Johnson, R. C., Jr.	04/28/2001	Curry, M. B.
37788	Peeples, David H.	06/04/2000	Parsley, H. N., Jr.		
37789	Chappell, Veronica D.	06/09/2000	Creighton, M. W. Title III, Canon 6		
37790	Hallas, Cynthia J.	06/09/2000	Creighton, M. W.	01/31/2001	Persell, W. D. for Creighton, M. W.
37791	Mease, Carole A.	06/09/2000	Creighton, M. W. Title III, Canon 6		
37792	Moczydlowski, Ann L. H.	06/09/2000	Creighton, M. W.	02/25/2001	Dixon, J. H.
37793	Sinnott, Lynn D.	06/09/2000	Creighton, M. W.	01/10/2001	Creighton, M. W.
37794	Barrett, Patricia R.	06/10/2000	Scruton, G. P.		
37795	Betts, Susan E.	06/10/2000	Winterrowd, W. J.		

Serial #	Name	Diaconate Date	Ordaining Bishop	Priesthood Date	Ordaining Bishop
37796	Breyer, Chloe A.	06/10/2000	Haines, R. H.	05/24/2001	Dixon, J. H.
37797	Buettner, Andrea J.	06/10/2000	Duncan, R. W. Title III, Canon 6		
37798	Carlson, Katherine A.	06/10/2000	Haines, R. H.	12/16/2000	Dixon, J. H.
37799	Carr, Spencer D.	06/10/2000	Winterrowd, W. J.	12/16/2000	Winterrowd, W. J.
37800	Chess, Jean D.	06/10/2000	Duncan, R. W. Title III, Canon 6		
37801	Cimijotti, Jerry A.	06/10/2000	Duncan, R. W.	12/10/2000	Leidel, E. M., Jr.
37802	DeYoung, Lily A.	06/10/2000	Croneberger, J. P.	02/24/2001	Croneberger, J. P.
37803	Dougharty, Philip W.	06/10/2000	Croneberger, J. P.	02/10/2001	Croneberger, J. P.
37804	Fierro, John E.	06/10/2000	Duncan, R. W.		
37805	Frantz-Dale, Heidi H.	06/10/2000	Scruton, G. P.		
37806	Gossling, Nancy E.	06/10/2000	Smith, A. D.		
37807	Green, Patricia L. O.	06/10/2000	Winterrowd, W. J.		
37808	Green, Stephanie M.	06/10/2000	Epting, C. C.	01/07/2001	Epting, C. C.
37809	Greenaway, Douglas A. G.	06/10/2000	Haines, R. H.	12/10/2000	Haines, R. H.
37810	Griffith, Shawn L.	06/10/2000	Bane, D. C., Jr.	12/09/2000	Hart, D. P. for Bane, D. C., Jr.
37811	Haddad, Mary E.	06/10/2000	Borsch, F. H.		
37812	Hamer, Donald L.	06/10/2000	Smith, A. D.		
37813	Hardy, Margaret F.	06/10/2000	Plummer, S. T. Title III, Canon 6		
37814	Hess, Howard J.	06/10/2000	Croneberger, J. P.	12/11/2000	Henderson, D. F., Jr. for Croneberger, J. P.
37815	Hines, Caroline V.	06/10/2000	Johnson, R. H.	12/16/2000	Theuner, D. E. for Johnson,

CLERGY LIST APPENDIX

Serial #	Name	Diaconate Date	Ordaining Bishop	Priesthood Date	Ordaining Bishop
37816	Hoffmann, Beth B.	06/10/2000	Duncan, R. W.		R. H.
37817	Irving, Hannah J.	06/10/2000	Croneberger, J. P.	02/24/2001	Croneberger, J. P.
37818	Irwin, Zachary T.	06/10/2000	Rowley, R. D., Jr. Title III, Canon 6		
37819	Johnson, Christopher A.	06/10/2000	Winterrowd, W. J.	12/23/2000	Winterrowd, W. J.
37820	Kennedy, Hilda L.	06/10/2000	Vache, C. C. for West Virginia	06/09/2001	Vache, C. C. for Diocese of West Virginia
37821	Laws, Robert J., III	06/10/2000	Duncan, R. W.	12/12/2000	Louttit, H. I., Jr. for Duncan, R. W.
37822	Malloy, Nancy L.	06/10/2000	Winterrowd, W. J.	01/06/2001	Winterrowd, W. J.
37823	Martin, Russell E. J.	06/10/2000	Hughes, G. B.	12/16/2000	Hughes, G. B.
37824	Martin-Coffey, Nancee L.	06/10/2000	Winterrowd, W. J.		
37825	McIntyre, Moni	06/10/2000	Duncan, R. W.		
37826	Meck, Daniel S., III	06/10/2000	Rabb, J. L. for Ihloff, R. W.	12/09/2000	Ihloff, R. W.
37827	Mouer, Patricia W. E.	06/10/2000	Johnson, R. H.	12/18/2000	Johnson, R. H.
37828	Pegram, Langdon	06/10/2000	Duncan, R. W.		
37829	Porter, Shawn E.	06/10/2000	Duncan, R. W.		
37830	Rachal, Paula C.	06/10/2000	Vache, C. C. for Diocese of West Virginia	05/26/2001	Curry, M. B.
37831	Rawn, Jeffrey A.	06/10/2000	Duncan, R. W.		
37832	Richardson, James D.	06/10/2000	Lamb, J. A.		
37833	Schenck, Timothy E.	06/10/2000	Rabb, J. L. for Ihloff, R. W.	12/08/2000	Rabb, J. L. for Ihloff, R. W.
37834	Smith, Gregory M.	06/10/2000	Duncan, R. W.		

Serial #	Name	Diaconate Date	Ordaining Bishop	Priesthood Date	Ordaining Bishop
37835	Smith, Patsy A.	06/10/2000	Johnson, R. C., Jr.	01/27/2001	Curry, M. B.
37836	Spiers, Linda M.	06/10/2000	Smith, A. D.		
37837	St. Louis, J. Allison	06/10/2000	Haines, R. H.	01/13/2001	Dixon, J. H. for Haines, R. H.
37838	Swan, Craig R.	06/10/2000	Smith, A. D.		
37839	Tafoya, Stacey T.	06/10/2000	Winterrowd, W. J.		
37840	Thomas, Allisyn L.	06/10/2000	Hughes, G. B.	12/14/2000	Hughes, G. B.
37841	Truby, Laura C.	06/10/2000	Lee, E. L., Jr.	12/09/2000	Lee, E. L., Jr.
37842	Tyler, Pamela H.	06/10/2000	Bruno, J. J. for Borsch, F. H.		
37843	Wallace, Tanya R.	06/10/2000	Croneberger, J. P.	12/16/2000	Croneberger, J. P.
37844	Warner, Christopher S.	06/10/2000	Duncan, R. W.		
37845	Wood-Hull, Larry D.	06/10/2000	Smith, A. D.	01/12/2001	Ramos-Orench, W. for Smith, A. D.
37846	Zolner, Eric W.	06/10/2000	Winterrowd, W. J.		
37847	Boline, Travis S.	06/11/2000	Jecko, S. H.	12/10/2000	Jecko, S. H.
37848	Busse, Mary R.	06/11/2000	Jecko, S. H.	12/10/2000	Jecko, S. H.
37849	Dukes, Lynne A.	06/11/2000	Jecko, S. H.	12/10/2000	Jecko, S. H.
37850	Eldredge, Mark R.	06/11/2000	Jecko, S. H.	12/16/2000	Ohl, C. W., Jr. for Jecko, S. H.
37851	Farmer, Charles A.	06/11/2000	Jecko, S. H.	12/10/2000	Jecko, S. H.
37852	Hardwick, Michael E.	06/11/2000	Beckwith, P. H.		
37853	Hobby, Sharon S. E.	06/11/2000	Jecko, S. H.	12/10/2000	Jecko, S. H.
37854	Hopkins, Christine C.	06/11/2000	Beckwith, P. H. Title III, Canon 6		
37855	Lyons, Lorraine B.	06/11/2000	Herzog, D. W.	12/16/2000	Herzog, D. W.
37856	McDowell, Todd S.	06/11/2000	Beckwith, P. H.		

CLERGY LIST APPENDIX

Serial #	Name	Diaconate Date	Ordaining Bishop	Priesthood Date	Ordaining Bishop
37857	Milano, Mary L.	06/11/2000	Beckwith, P. H. Title III, Canon 9		
37858	Schnabl, Emily J.	06/11/2000	Beckwith, P. H.		
37859	Schutz, Christine E.	06/11/2000	Epting, C. C.		
37860	Tofani, Ann H.	06/11/2000	Beckwith, P. H. Title III, Canon 6		
37861	Wolfenbarger, Mary S.	06/11/2000	Beckwith, P. H. Title III, Canon 6		
37862	Ciesel, Barbara "Bitsey"	06/12/2000	Robertson, C. L. Title III, Canon 6		
37863	Jones, Kathleen A.	06/12/2000	Epting, C. C.	05/01/2001	Moody, R. M.
37864	Pearsall, Arlene E.	06/12/2000	Robertson, C. L. Title III, Canon 6		
37865	Vershure, Claude E.	06/12/2000	Robertson, C. L.		
37866	Harrity, Alison P.	06/14/2000	Schofield, C. O., Jr.	12/16/2000	Frade, L.
37867	Knight, Kimberly A.	06/14/2000	Schofield, C. O., Jr.	11/17/2001	Frade, L.
37868	Sims, Mark H.	06/14/2000	Schofield, C. O., Jr.	12/15/2000	Frade, L.
37869	Murdock, Audrey J.	06/15/2000	McLeod, M. A. R.	10/19/2000	McLeod, M. A. R.
37870	Black, Milton E., Jr.	06/17/2000	Payne, C. E.	06/29/2001	Payne, C. E.
37871	Carlson, Carol E.	06/17/2000	Rowley, R. D., Jr.	12/17/2000	Rowley, R. D., Jr.
37872	Civetta, Heath H.	06/17/2000	Persell, W. D.	01/04/2001	Persell, W. D.
37873	Doerr, Nan L.	06/17/2000	Payne, C. E.	06/17/2001	Payne, C. E.
37874	Frens, Mary J.	06/17/2000	Lee, E. L., Jr.	12/16/2000	Lee, E. L., Jr.
37875	Haddox, Jason M.	06/17/2000	Payne, C. E.	06/26/2001	Payne, C. E.

Serial #	Name	Diaconate Date	Ordaining Bishop	Priesthood Date	Ordaining Bishop
37876	Huff, Clark K.	06/17/2000	Payne, C. E.	04/18/2001	Payne, C. E.
37877	Johnson, Robert G.	06/17/2000	Payne, C. E.	06/22/2001	Payne, C. E.
37878	Marcrum, J. Alice	06/17/2000	Persell, W. D.	12/16/2000	Persell, W. D.
37879	Miller, Patrick J.	06/17/2000	Payne, C. E.	06/27/2001	Payne, C. E.
37880	Wojahn, Karen A.	06/17/2000	Talton, C. L. for Borsch, F. H.		
37881	Bird, Peter R.	06/18/2000	Jacobus, R. E.	12/21/2000	Jacobus, R. E.
37882	Schjonberg, Mary F.	06/18/2000	Jones, C. I.	01/18/2001	Jones, C. I.
37883	Stevens, Walter A., III	06/22/2000	Chang, R. S. O.	03/25/2001	Chang, R. S. O.
37884	Proctor, Judith H.	06/23/2000	Rockwell, H. H.	04/17/2002	Rockwell, H. H.
37885	Allen, Barbara A.	06/24/2000	Bennison, C. E., Jr.	05/12/2001	Bennison, C. E., Jr.
			Title III, Canon 9		Title III, Canon 9
37886	Anderson, David T.	06/24/2000	Lee, P. J.	02/06/2001	Lee, P. J.
37887	Andrews, Patricia M.	06/24/2000	Lee, P. J.	02/06/2001	Lee, P. J.
37888	Bailey, David B.	06/24/2000	Thompson, H., Jr.	01/06/2001	Thompson, H., Jr.
37889	Bauman, Dwayne R.	06/24/2000	Maze, L. E.		
37890	Becker, Kimberly L.	06/24/2000	Daniel, C., III	12/13/2000	Dixon, J. H. for Daniel, C., III
37891	Blake, Thomas W., Jr.	06/24/2000	Daniel, C., III		
37892	Brandenburg, Marilyn J.	06/24/2000	Warner, V. W., Jr.		
			Title III, Canon 6		
37893	Brown, Nancy E. N.	06/24/2000	Moody, R. M.		
			Title III, Canon 6		
37894	Brownridge, Walter B. A.	06/24/2000	Grew, J. C., II	06/09/2001	Williams, A. B., Jr.
37895	Carlson, R. Bryant	06/24/2000	Warner, V. W., Jr.	01/07/2001	Ladehoff, R. L. for Warner, V. W., Jr.

CLERGY LIST — APPENDIX

Serial #	Name	Diaconate Date	Ordaining Bishop	Priesthood Date	Ordaining Bishop
37896	Carpenter, Charles M.	06/24/2000	Waynick, C. M.	02/11/2001	Waynick, C. M.
37897	Cunningham, Jeunee J.	06/24/2000	Lee, P. J.		
37898	Deming, Nancy J.	06/24/2000	Bennison, C.E. Jr. Title III, Canon 6		
37899	Domenick, Warren L., Jr.	06/24/2000	Daniel, C., III	02/17/2001	Daniel, C., III
37900	Fox, Deborah	06/24/2000	Daniel, C., III	03/24/2001	Daniel, C., III
37901	Fredrickson, David A.	06/24/2000	Bennison C. E., Jr.	05/12/2001	Bennison, C. E., Jr.
37902	Gott, Jaynne L. C.	06/24/2000	Hampton, S. Z. K. for Warner, V. W., Jr. Title III, Canon 6		
37903	Gracen, Sharon K.	06/24/2000	Waynick, C. M.	06/23/2001	Waynick, C. M.
37904	Grewell, Genevieve M.	06/24/2000	Hampton, S. Z. K. for Warner, V. W., Jr. Title III, Canon 6		
37905	Hillquist, Catherine R.	06/24/2000	Borsch, F. H.	01/06/2001	Borsch, F. H.
37906	Honig-Smith, Julie	06/24/2000	Hampton, S. Z. K. for Warner, V. W., Jr.	01/13/2001	Warner, V. W., Jr.
37907	McConnell, Joyce	06/24/2000	Warner, V. W., Jr.	01/13/2001	Warner, V. W., Jr.
37908	Morrison, Mary K.	06/24/2000	Shimpfky, R. L.		
37909	Newland, Benjamin J.	06/24/2000	Thornton, J. S.		
37910	Novak, M. Anne	06/24/2000	Hampton, S. Z. K. for Warner, V. W., Jr. Title III, Canon 6		
37911	Olson, Anna B.	06/24/2000	Bruno, J. J. for Borsch, F. H.	02/06/2001	Lee, P. J. for Daniel, C., III
37912	Piver, Jane D.	06/24/2000	Daniel, C., III		

Serial #	Name	Diaconate Date	Ordaining Bishop	Priesthood Date	Ordaining Bishop
37913	Pogue, Blair A.	06/24/2000	Lee, P. J.	02/06/2001	Lee, P. J.
37914	Ponce, Jacqueline	06/24/2000	Bennison, C. E., Jr. Title III, Canon 6		
37915	Rahhal, Michele D.	06/24/2000	Moody, R. M. Title III, Canon 6		
37916	Robbins-Penniman, Sylvia B.	06/24/2000	Thompson, H., Jr.	01/06/2001	Thompson, H., Jr.
37917	Scissons, Antoinette M.	06/24/2000	Ladehoff, R. L.	02/17/2001	Ladehoff, R. L.
37918	Shigaki, Jerry M.	06/24/2000	Hampton, S. Z. K. for Warner, V. W., Jr.	01/13/2001	Hampton, S. Z. K. for Warner, V. W., Jr.
37919	Smith, Alan B.	06/24/2000	Thompson, H., Jr.	01/06/2001	Thompson, H., Jr.
37920	Smith, Hilary B.	06/24/2000	Lee, P. J.	02/06/2001	Lee, P. J.
37921	Swanson, Richard R.	06/24/2000	Borsch, F. H.		
37922	Teague, C. Steven	06/24/2000	Daniel, C, III	12/30/2000	Daniel, C, III
37923	Vidmar, Mary B.	06/24/2000	Thompson, H., Jr.	01/06/2001	Thompson, H., Jr.
37924	Westpfahl, Carol E.	06/24/2000	Hampton, S. Z. K. for Warner, V. W., Jr.	01/13/2001	Hampton, S. Z. K. for Warner, V. W., Jr.
37925	Wingert, Anita L.	06/24/2000	Knudsen, C. A. R.	02/17/2001	Knudsen, C. A. R.
37926	Wood, Jan M. S.	06/24/2000	Shimpfky, R. L.	02/10/2001	Shimpfky, R. L.
37927	Brown, Nancy E.	06/25/2000	Talton, C. L. for Borsch, F. H.		
37928	Richardson, Frederick J., Jr.	06/25/2000	Herlong, B. N.	04/22/2001	Herlong, B. N.
37929	Zook-Jones, Jill	06/25/2000	Herlong, B. N.	04/22/2001	Herlong, B. N.
37930	Alexandre, Hickman	06/29/2000	Walker, O. G., Jr.	01/20/2001	Walker, O. G., Jr.
37931	Percival, Michael J.	06/30/2000	Epting, C. C.	01/20/2001	Epting, C. C.
37932	Milian, Mario E.	07/15/2000	Frade, L.	02/10/2001	Shahan, R. R. for Frade, L.

CLERGY LIST APPENDIX

Serial #	Name	Diaconate Date	Ordaining Bishop	Priesthood Date	Ordaining Bishop
37933	McLaren, Christopher T.	07/16/2000	Ladehoff, R. L.		
37934	Forbes, Terrry W.	07/21/2000	Duvall, C. F.	02/03/2001	Duvall, C. F.
37935	Freeman, Diana G. B.	07/21/2000	Duvall, C. F.		
37936	Mayer, Sandra C.	07/21/2000	Duvall, C. F.	02/04/2001	Duvall, C. F.
37937	Ballinger, Kathryn E.	07/22/2000	Thornton, J. S. Title III, Canon 6		
37938	Grady, Ann N.	07/22/2000	White, R. J.	07/28/2001	White, R. J.
37939	Allen, Patrick S.	07/23/2000	Salmon, E. L., Jr.	01/24/2001	Salmon, E. L., Jr.
37940	Howard, Walter W.	08/05/2000	Thornton, J. S. Title III, Canon 6		
37941	Arndt, Cindy L.	08/09/2000	Caldwell, B. E. Title III, Canon 9	08/21/2001	Caldwell, B. E. Title III, Canon 9
37942	Sonderegger, Katherine A.	08/13/2000	McLeod, M. A. R.		
37943	Yarbrough, O. Larry	08/13/2000	McLeod, M. A. R.		
37944	Hoch, Helen E.	08/16/2000	Smalley, W. E.	02/17/2001	Smalley, W. E.
37945	Bowman, Andrea C.	08/20/2000	Thornton, J. S. for Spokane	06/02/2001	Waggoner, J. E., Jr.
37946	Cocke, Reagan W.	08/23/2000	Folts, J. E.		
37947	Dingman, Joel A.	08/23/2000	Caldwell, B. E. Title III, Canon 9	03/17/2001	Caldwell, B. E. Title III, Canon 9
37948	George, Jacob C., Jr.	08/23/2000	Folts, J. E.	02/27/2001	Folts, J. E.
37949	Webb, James W., Jr.	08/30/2000	Gray, D. M, III for Marble, A. C., Jr.		
37950	Eguia Arroyo, Margarita	08/31/2000	Folts, J. E.		
37951	Doctor, Virginia C.	09/02/2000	MacDonald, M. L.	07/15/2001	MacDonald, M. L.

Serial #	Name	Diaconate Date	Ordaining Bishop	Priesthood Date	Ordaining Bishop
37952	Solomon, Mardow, Sr.	09/02/2000	MacDonald, M. L.	12/13/2001	MacDonald, M. L.
37953	Titus, Bessie C.	09/02/2000	MacDonald, M. L.	04/08/2001	MacDonald, M. L.
37954	Boutros, Gail A.	09/09/2000	Smalley, W. E. Title III, Canon 6		
37955	Tracy, Dick B.	09/09/2000	Smalley, W. E. Title III, Canon 6		
37956	Tracy, Rita V.	09/09/2000	Smalley, W. E. Title III, Canon 6		
37957	Wolff, William G.	09/09/2000	Smalley, W. E. Title III, Canon 6		
37958	Butler, Keith W.	09/21/2000	Vache, C. C.	06/09/2001	Vache, C. C.
37959	Kelley, James T.	09/21/2000	Vache, C. C. Title III, Canon 6		Vache, C. C. Title III, Canon 9
37960	Kelley, Theresa M.	09/21/2000	Vache, C. C. Title III, Canon 9	06/09/2001	Vache, C. C.
37961	Tracey, Edward J.	09/23/2000	Henderson, D. F., Jr.	05/18/2001	Henderson, D. F., Jr.
37962	Baker, Joseph S.	09/23/2000	vonRosenberg, C. G.		
37963	Beasley, Nicholas M.	09/23/2000	Henderson, D. F., Jr.	05/22/2001	Henderson, D. F., Jr.
37964	Long, Gail A.	09/23/2000	Henderson, D. F., Jr.	06/08/2001	Henderson, D. F., Jr.
37965	Sullivan, Michael R.	09/23/2000	Jecko, S. H. Title III, Canon 6		
37966	Hemphill, Ann S.	09/24/2000			
37967	Rusling, Julia G.	09/24/2000	Herzog, D. W.	03/24/2001	Herzog, D. W.
37968	Bertolozzi, Michael A.	09/29/2000	Hunt, G. N. for Nevada		

CLERGY LIST — APPENDIX

Serial #	Name	Diaconate Date	Ordaining Bishop	Priesthood Date	Ordaining Bishop
37969	Cage, Stewart B., Jr.	09/29/2000	Title III, Canon 6	11/14/2001	Jenkins, C. E., III Title III, Canon 9
37970	Guerra-Diaz, Juan A.	09/30/2000	Jenkins, C. E., III Title III, Canon 9		
37971	Palagyi, Addyse L.	09/30/2000	Ladehoff, R. L.	06/09/2001	Ladehoff, R. L.
37972	Russell, Kenneth P.	09/30/2000	Ladehoff, R. L. Title III, Canon 6		
37973	Erickson, Bonnie	010/01/2000	Standing Com. of Nevada Title III, Canon 6		
37974	Keating, Julie L.	10/01/2000	Standing Com. of Nevada Title III, Canon 9	05/06/2001	Jefferts Schori, K. Title III, Canon 9
37975	Duncan, Victoria D.	10/06/2000	Garrison, J. M.		
37976	Slanger, George C.	10/08/2000	Fairfield, A. H. Title III, Canon 9	05/25/2001	Fairfield, A. H. Title III, Canon 9
37977	Anderson, Judith K. F.	10/14/2000	Jones, C. I. Title III, Canon 6		
37978	Arnold, Kimball C.	10/14/2000	Shahan, R. R. Title III, Canon 6		
37979	Ashley, Beverley B.	10/14/2000	Shahan, R. R. Title III, Canon 6		
37980	Faure, Susan B.	10/14/2000	Shahan, R. R. Title III, Canon 6		
37981	Kirk, Patricia L.	10/14/2000	Shahan, R. R. Title III, Canon 6		

Serial #	Name	Diaconate Date	Ordaining Bishop	Priesthood Date	Ordaining Bishop
37982	Lee, Vicki Y.	10/14/2000	Shahan, R. R. Title III, Canon 6		
37983	Lindell, Thomas J.	10/14/2000	Shahan, R. R. Title III, Canon 6		
37984	Wilner, Janice M.	10/14/2000	Shahan, R. R. Title III, Canon 6		
37985	Massenburg, Barbara J.	10/15/2000	MacDonald, M. L.		
37986	Landwer, Virginia	10/17/2000	Frade, L. Title III, Canon 6		
37987	Bonadie, L. Rowland	10/21/2000	Joslin, D. B. Title III, Canon 6		
37988	Cavaliere, Denise B.	10/21/2000	Joslin, D. B. Title III, Canon 6		
37989	Elley, Eric M.	10/21/2000	Joslin, D. B. Title III, Canon 6		
37990	Frey, Louane F. V.	10/21/2000	Joslin, D. B. Title III, Canon 6		
37991	Grennan, William J.	10/21/2000	Joslin, D. B. Title III, Canon 6		
37992	Henderson-Johnson, Lynn N.	10/21/2000	Joslin, D. B. Title III, Canon 6		
37993	Holman, Emily C.	10/21/2000	Joslin, D. B. Title III, Canon 6		
37994	Knight, Arthur J.	10/21/2000	Joslin, D. B. Title III, Canon 6		

CLERGY LIST — APPENDIX

Serial #	Name	Diaconate Date	Ordaining Bishop	Priesthood Date	Ordaining Bishop
37995	Lemay, Anne R.	10/21/2000	Joslin, D. B. Title III, Canon 6		
37996	Lilliard, Eddie L, Sr.	10/21/2000	Joslin, D. B. Title III, Canon 6		
37997	May, Frederick B.	10/21/2000	Joslin, D. B. Title III, Canon 6		
37998	Orlando, Helen M. G.	10/21/2000	Joslin, D. B. Title III, Canon 6		
37999	Sanzo, Marie B.	10/21/2000	Joslin, D. B. Title III, Canon 6		
38000	Suruda, Teresa A.	10/21/2000	Joslin, D. B. Title III, Canon 6		
38001	Wichael, Karen L.	10/21/2000	Smalley, W. E. Title III, Canon 6		
38002	Borden, Robert B.	10/22/2000	McLeod, M. A. R. Title III, Canon 9	07/14/2001	Ely, T. C. Title III, Canon 9
38003	Ferneyhough, Dallam G.	10/22/2000	Duncan, R. W.	04/28/2001	Duncan, R. W.
38004	Lee, Robert B.	10/22/2000	McLeod, M. A. R. Title III, Canon 9	08/04/2001	Ely, T. C. Title III, Canon 9
38005	Baird, Gary C.	10/28/2000	Maze, L. E. Title III, Canon 6		
X-38006	Chang, Ling-Ling	10/28/2000	Chien, J. C. T.		
38007	Clausen, Kathryn P.	10/28/2000	Thompson, H., Jr.	06/23/2001	Thompson, H., Jr.
38008	Fribourgh, Cynthia K.	10/28/2000	Maze, L. E. Title III, Canon 6		

Serial #	Name	Diaconate Date	Ordaining Bishop	Priesthood Date	Ordaining Bishop
38009	Jones, Curtis C.	10/28/2000	Maze, L. E. Title III, Canon 6		
X-38010	Lee, Enoch	10/28/2000	Chien, J. C. T.		
38011	Storm, Astrid J.	10/28/2000	Thompson, H., Jr.	06/23/2001	Thompson, H., Jr.
38012	Van Doren, Robert L., Jr.	10/28/2000	Coleman, J. M. Title III, Canon 6		
38013	Williams, Marianne R.	10/28/2000	Coleman, J. M. Title III, Canon 6		
38014	Wiseman, Grant B.	10/28/2000	Thompson, H., Jr.	06/23/2001	Thompson, H., Jr.
38015	Guthkelch, Cynthia A. G.	11/01/2000	Smalley, W. E.	6/28/2001	Smalley, W. E.
38016	Pinnock, Betty L.	11/04/2000	Ladehoff, R. L. Title III, Canon 6		
38017	Burnham, Karen L.	11/11/2000	Winterrowd, W. J. Title III, Canon 6		
38018	Dyer, Susan J.	11/11/2000	Winterrowd, W. J. Title III, Canon 6		
38019	Mutolo, Frances	11/11/2000	Winterrowd, W. J. Title III, Canon 6		
38020	Frances, Martha	11/30/2000	Payne, C. E.	06/29/2001	Payne, C. E.
38021	Seiter, Claudia D.	11/30/2000	Irish, C. T. Title III, Canon 9		
38022	McAdams, Kathleen A.	12/02/2000	Swing, W. E.	06/02/2001	Swing, W. E.
38023	Rogers, Timothy J.	12/02/2000	Swing, W. E.	06/02/2001	Swing, W. E.
38024	Trapani, Kathleen M.	12/02/2000	Swing, W. E.	06/02/2001	Swing, W. E.

CLERGY LIST

Serial #	Name	Diaconate Date	Ordaining Bishop	Priesthood Date	Ordaining Bishop
38025	Carney, Vinnie L.	12/07/2000	Lee, P. J.		
38026	Barfield, DeOla E. J.	12/09/2000	Smith, A. D.		
38027	Cooper, Paul A.	12/09/2000	Title III, Canon 6 Duncan, R. W.		
38028	Duer, Don R.	12/09/2000	Howe, J. W.		
38029	Ellis, Jane F.	12/09/2000	Title III, Canon 6 Smith, A. D.		
38030	Gallian, Paul, V., Jr.	12/09/2000	Title III, Canon 6 Howe, J. W.		
38031	Goglia, Bette M.	12/09/2000	Title III, Canon 6 Howe, J. W.		
38032	Gregory, Loren H.	12/09/2000	Title III, Canon 6 Smith, A. D.		
38033	Griggs, Joel T.	12/09/2000	Title III, Canon 6 Ackerman, K. L.	06/23/2001	Herzog, D. W. for Ackerman, K. L.
38034	Hubbard, Charles H., Jr.	12/09/2000	Ackerman, K. L.	06/24/2001	Ackerman, K. L.
38035	Lewis, Mark W.	12/09/2000	Ackerman, K. L.	09/21/2001	Ackerman, K. L.
38036	Mestre, Jose W., Jr.	12/09/2000	Smith, A. D.		
38037	Raby, Edith G.	12/09/2000	Title III, Canon 6 Howe, J. W.		
38038	Richey, Donald	12/09/2000	Title III, Canon 6 Smith, A. D.		
38039	Sireno, Robert	12/09/2000	Title III, Canon 6 Smith, A. D.		

Serial #	Name	Diaconate Date	Ordaining Bishop	Priesthood Date	Ordaining Bishop
38040	Warley, Dianne G.	12/09/2000	Smith, A. D. Title III, Canon 6		
38041	Juarez-Castro, Francisco	12/12/2000	Shimpfky, R. L.	06/16/2001	Shimpfky, R. L.
38042	Aalan, Joshua C.	12/16/2000	Jacobus, R. E.	07/23/2001	Jacobus, R. E.
38043	Bell, Katherine A.	12/16/2000	MacDonald, M. L.	06/18/2001	MacDonald, M. L.
38044	Cole, Allan H.	12/16/2000	Daniel, C., III		
38045	Coulter, Sherry L.	12/16/2000	Coleman, J. M.		
38046	Jones, Constance R.	12/16/2000	MacDonald, M. L.	07/22/2001	MacDonald, M. L.
38047	Turner, Nancy M.	12/16/2000	Sauls, S. F.	09/06/2001	Sauls, S. F.
38048	Veale, David S.	12/16/2000	Shimpfky, R. L. Title III, Canon 6		
38049	Vietor, Oliver R.	12/16/2000	Hart, D. P. for Bane, D. C., Jr.	07/21/2001	Hart, D. P. for Bane, D. C., Jr.
38050	Hetler, Gwendolyn K.	12/17/2000	Kelsey, J. A. Title III, Canon 9	07/01/2001	Kelsey, J. A. Title III, Canon 9
38051	Livingston, James L.	12/17/2000	Kelsey, J. A. Title III, Canon 9	07/01/2001	Kelsey, J. A. Title III, Canon 9
38052	Glover, Mary E.	12/20/2000	Ohl, C. W., Jr.	06/30/2001	Ohl, C. W., Jr.
38053	Baron, Stephen A.	12/21/2000	Hughes, G. B.	06/09/2001	Hughes, G. B.
38054	Lane, Wendy D.	12/21/2000	Persell, W. D.		
38055	Odom, Robert M.	12/27/2000	Jenkins, C. E., III	09/08/2001	Jenkins, C. E., III
38056	Bradford, Lyman P.	01/06/2001	Marble, A. C., Jr. Title III, Canon 6		
38057	Foncree, Rose M.	01/06/2001	Marble, A. C., Jr. Title III, Canon 6		

CLERGY LIST — APPENDIX

Serial #	Name	Diaconate Date	Ordaining Bishop	Priesthood Date	Ordaining Bishop
38058	Gieseler, Mary M.	01/06/2001	Marble, A. C., Jr. Title III, Canon 6		
38059	Jones, Stephen W.	01/06/2001	Iker, J. L.	07/07/2001	Iker, J. L.
38060	Kellum, Rose A.	01/06/2001	Marble, A. C., Jr. Title III, Canon 6		
38061	Marks, Sharla J.	01/06/2001	Iker, J. L.		
38062	Sisson, Penny R.	01/06/2001	Title III, Canon 6 Marble, A. C., Jr. Title III, Canon 6		
38063	Giacoma, Claudia L.	01/11/2001	Irish, C. T. Title III, Canon 6		
38064	Foster, Kenneth E., Jr.	01/13/2001	White, R. J. Title III, Canon 6		
38065	Pelnar, William D.	01/13/2001	White, R. J. Title III, Canon 6		
38066	Trigleth, John P.	01/13/2001	White, R. J. Title III, Canon 6		
38067	Osborne, William P.	01/14/2001	MacDonald, M. L.		
38068	Keplinger, Stephen J.	01/18/2001	Irish, C. T.	08/04/2001	Irish, C. T.
38069	Wiltsey, Susan A.	01/18/2001	Irish, C. T.		
38070	Binder, Thomas F.	01/20/2001	White, R. J. Title III, Canon 6		
38071	Brauza, Ellen L.	01/20/2001	Garrison, J. M.	08/19/2001	Garrison, J. M.
38072	Schmidt, Kevin L.	01/20/2001	Strickland, V. E. Title III, Canon 9	09/15/2001	Strickland, V. E. Title III, Canon 9

Serial #	Name	Diaconate Date	Ordaining Bishop	Priesthood Date	Ordaining Bishop
38073	Bowers, George F.	02/03/2001	Louttit, H. I., Jr.	11/26/2002	Louttit, H. I., Jr.
38074	Brenmark-French, Regina	02/03/2001	Persell, W. D. Title III, Canon 6		
38075	Menger, J. Andrew	02/03/2001	Louttit, H. I., Jr.	08/23/2001	Louttit, H. I., Jr.
38076	Molony, Roberta D.	02/03/2001	Persell, W. D. Title III, Canon 6		
38077	Braden, Anita L. H.	02/04/2001	White, R. J.	08/04/2001	White, R. J.
38078	Martin, Patricia L.	02/07/2001	Kelsey, J. A. Title III, Canon 9	08/12/2001	Kelsey, J. A. Title III, Canon 9
38079	Slater, Joan B.	02/07/2001	Kelsey, J. A. Title III, Canon 9	08/12/2001	Kelsey, J. A. Title III, Canon 9
38080	Bernacchi, Jacqueline A.	02/09/2001	Fairfield, A. H.	09/07/2001	Fairfield, A. H.
38081	Goldman, Norman C.	02/13/2001	Ladehoff, R. L.		
38082	Bergner, Mario J.	02/15/2001	Ackerman, K. L.	09/17/2001	Ackerman, K. L.
38083	Parker, John E., III	02/21/2001	Salmon, E. L., Jr.	09/08/2001	Salmon, E. L., Jr.
38084	Morgan, Pamela S.	02/22/2001	Maze, L. E.	09/15/2001	Maze, L. E.
38085	McDermott, Gerald R.	02/23/2001	Powell, F. N.		
38086	Morris, Jonathan E.	02/23/2001	Powell, F. N.	09/14/2001	Powell, F. N.
38087	White, Laura D.	02/23/2001	Powell, F. N.		
38088	Steadman, Larry K.	02/24/2001	Strickland, V. E. Title III, Canon 6		
38089	Davis, R. Jonathan	03/03/2001	Howe, J. W.	10/20/2001	Howe, J. W.
38090	Alexander, Patricia A. P.	03/10/2001	Grein, R. F.	09/16/2001	Sisk, M. S.
38091	Barrows, Jennifer E. M.	03/10/2001	Grein, R. F.		

CLERGY LIST APPENDIX

Serial #	Name	Diaconate Date	Ordaining Bishop	Priesthood Date	Ordaining Bishop
38092	Bordador, Noel E.	03/10/2001	Grein, R. F.		
38093	Kendall, Michael J.	03/10/2001	Grein, R. F.	09/15/2001	Sisk, M. S.
38094	Roadman, Betsy J.	03/10/2001	Grein, R. F.	09/16/2001	Sisk, M. S.
38095	Brown, David A.	03/17/2001	Schofield, J. D. Title III, Canon 6		
38096	Davis, Gail E.	03/17/2001	Smalley, W. E.	10/27/2001	Smalley, W. E.
38097	Mason, Samuel A.	03/17/2001	Smalley, W. E.	09/30/2001	Smalley, W. E.
38098	Plummer, Dale W.	03/17/2001	Smalley, W. E.	10/14/2001	Smalley, W. E.
38099	Senuta, Lisa A.	03/17/2001	Smalley, W. E.	10/16/2001	Smalley, W. E.
38100	Smith, Jane C.	03/17/2001	Smalley, W. E.	10/03/2001	Smalley, W. E.
38101	Sweeney, Craig C.	03/17/2001	Smalley, W. E.	09/29/2001	Smalley, W. E.
38102	Dodd, Brian J.	03/31/2001	Howe, J. W.		
38103	McDonald, Karen L.	04/04/2001	Lee, E. L., Jr. Title III, Canon 6		
38104	Adney, John G.	04/07/2001	Epting, C. C. Title III, Canon 6		
38105	Rogerson, George W.	04/07/2001	Epting, C. C. Title III, Canon 6		
38106	Smith, Merle E., Jr.	04/07/2001	Epting, C. C. Title III, Canon 6		
38107	Tripses, Kathleen R. M.	04/07/2001	Epting, C. C. Title III, Canon 6		
38108	Allen, Christopher C.	04/18/2001	Stanton, J. M.	10/27/2001	Stanton, J. M.
38109	Hazen, Alba D.	04/21/2001	Marshall, P. V.	09/29/2001	Marshall, P. V.

Serial #	Name	Diaconate Date	Ordaining Bishop	Priesthood Date	Ordaining Bishop
38110	Mooney, Michelle P.	04/21/2001	White, R. J.		
38111	Perrin, Mary E.	04/22/2001	Title III, Canon 6 Lee, E. L., Jr.	10/27/2001	Lee, E. L., Jr.
38112	Limozaine, Bruce J.	04/28/2001	Maze, L. E. Title III, Canon 6		
38113	Seibert, Joanna J.	04/28/2001	Maze, L. E. Title III, Canon 6		
38114	Jensen, Mary A.	05/08/2001	Joslin, D. B. Title III, Canon 6		
38115	Beshears, Earl D.	05/19/2001	Townsend, M. G.	11/17/2001	Longest, C. L.
38116	Bourhill, John W.	05/19/2001	Grein, R. F. Title III, Canon 6		
38117	Boynton, Caroline C.	05/19/2001	Grein, R. F. Title III, Canon 6		
38118	Clarke, John D. B.	05/19/2001	Grein, R. F. Title III, Canon 6		
38119	Daubert, Sharon A.	05/19/2001	Ackerman, K. L. Title III, Canon 6		
38120	Hardy, Velinda E.	05/19/2001	Curry, M. B. Title III, Canon 6		
38121	Thom, Kenneth S.	05/19/2001	Townsend, M. G.	11/18/2001	Longest, C. L.
38122	Zito, Robert J. A.	05/19/2001	Grein, R. F. Title III, Canon 6		
38123	Foulke, Mary L.	05/20/2001	Borsch, F. H.		
38124	Gonzalez, Antonio	05/20/2001	White, R. J.		

CLERGY LIST APPENDIX

Serial #	Name	Diaconate Date	Ordaining Bishop	Priesthood Date	Ordaining Bishop
38125	Riddle, Jennifer L.	05/20/2001	Title III, Canon 6		
38126	Runge, Phillip D.	05/20/2001	Parsley, H. N., Jr.		
			White, R. J.		
			Title III, Canon 6		
38127	Sipe, Robert B.	05/20/2001	Bainbridge, H. B., III	12/14/2001	Bainbridge, H. B., III
38128	Wils, Duane M.	05/20/2001	Kelsey, J. A.		
			Title III, Canon 9		
38129	Graham, Earnest N., III	05/24/2001	Caldwell, B. E.	12/29/2001	Lee, P. J. for Caldwell, B. E.
38130	Hesse, Alan R.	05/25/2001	Charleston, S.		
38131	Clark, Margaret A. P.	05/26/2001	Fairfield, A. H.	01/26/2002	Sisk, M. S. for Fairfield, A. H.
38132	Frazier, Mark W.	05/26/2001	Coleman, J. M.	12/15/2001	Joslin, D. B.
38133	Green, Gordon G.	05/26/2001	Howe, J. W.	12/08/2001	Duncan, R. W. for Howe, J. W.
38134	Greenwell, Gail E.	05/26/2001	Ladehoff, R. L.	12/01/2001	Swing, W. E.
38135	Peoples, David B.	05/26/2001	Howe, J. W.	11/25/2001	Lipscomb, J. B. for Howe, J. W.
38136	Riddle, Jonathan H.	05/26/2001	Howe, J. W.	12/01/2001	Howe, J. W.
38137	Rosendahl, Mary A.	05/26/2001	Howe, J. W.	12/08/2001	Jecko, S. H. for Howe, J. W.
38138	Weiler, Matthew G. B.	05/26/2001	Howe, J. W.	11/30/2001	Griswold, J. T., III for Howe J. W.
38139	Young, Paul W.	05/26/2001	Howe, J. W.	11/24/2001	Howe, J. W.
38140	O'Connor, Edward F., Jr.	05/27/2001	Gray, D. M, III	01/16/2002	Marble, A. C., Jr.
38141	Roeske, Michael J.	05/27/2001	Whitmore, K. B.		
38142	Simmons, Mary K.	05/27/2001	Kelsey, J. A.		

Serial #	Name	Diaconate Date	Ordaining Bishop	Priesthood Date	Ordaining Bishop
38143	Addiego, Jeffrey C.	05/29/2001	Title III, Canon 9	12/01/2001	Swing, W. E. for Jefferts Schori, K.
38144	Waples, Jan S.	05/29/2001	Jefferts Schori, K.		
			Jefferts Schori, K.		
38145	Meginniss, David H.	05/31/2001	Parsley, H. N., Jr.		
38146	Ueda, Ajuko L. K.	05/31/2001	Chang, R. S. O.		
38147	Abeyaratne, K. Anoma	06/02/2001	Shaw, M. T., III	06/08/2002	Shaw, M. T., III
38148	Arents, Gina	06/02/2001	Ihloff, R. W.		
			Title III, Canon 6		
38149	Bailey, Anne C.	06/02/2001	Swing, W. E.	12/01/2001	Swing, W. E.
38150	Berman, Elizabeth E. S.	06/02/2001	Shaw, M. T., III	06/08/2002	Shaw, M. T., III
38151	Bezilla, Gregory A.	06/02/2001	Joslin, D. B.	01/19/2002	Joslin, D. B.
38152	Brambila, Gerardo E.	06/02/2001	Borsch, F. H.		
38153	Brown, Gregory B. F.	06/02/2001	Lee, E. L., Jr.	12/08/2001	Lee, E. L., Jr.
38154	Carlson-Scholer, Linda M.	06/02/2001	Joslin, D. B.		
38155	Christoffersen, Timothy R.	06/02/2001	Swing, W. E.	12/01/2002	Swing, W. E.
38156	Croom, James	06/02/2001	Swing, W. E.	12/01/2001	Swing, W. E.
38157	Fisher, Margaret J.	06/02/2001	Waggoner, J. E., Jr.	10/26/2002	Waggoner, J. E., Jr.
38158	Fitzhugh, Mark L.	06/02/2001	Soto, O. A. for Parsley, H. N., Jr.		
38159	Glass, Vanessa J.	06/02/2001	Swing, W. E.	12/01/2001	Swing, W. E.
38160	Gonzales, Ricardo, Jr.	06/02/2001	Borsch, F. H.	06/15/2002	Bruno, J. J.
38161	Gray, Patrick T.	06/02/2001	Shaw, M. T., III	06/08/2002	Shaw, M. T., III
38162	Hodges, Michael J.	06/02/2001	Shaw, M. T., III	06/08/2002	Shaw, M. T., III

CLERGY LIST APPENDIX

Serial #	Name	Diaconate Date	Ordaining Bishop	Priesthood Date	Ordaining Bishop
38163	Hornbeck, Jennifer M.	06/02/2001	Swing, W. E.	12/01/2001	Swing, W. E.
38164	Kreamer, Martha H.	06/02/2001	Duncan, P. M., II		
38165	Mathews, Koshy	06/02/2001	Shaw, M. T., III	06/08/2002	Shaw, M. T., III
38166	Mayrer, Jane G.	06/02/2001	Ihloff, R. W. Title III, Canon 6		
38167	McKenzie-Hayward, Renee E.	06/02/2001	Joslin, D. B.		
38168	Penfield, Joyce A.	06/02/2001	Joslin, D. B.		
38169	Raulerson, Aaron D.	06/02/2001	Duncan, P. M., II		
38170	Sanderson, Holladay W.	06/02/2001	Waggoner, J. E., Jr.	12/08/2001	Waggoner, J. E., Jr.
38171	Simple, Margo	06/02/2001	MacDonald, M. L.		
38172	St. Clair, Melinda L.	06/02/2001	Waggoner, J. E., Jr.	12/12/2001	Waggoner, J. E., Jr.
38173	Sterling, Leslie K.	06/02/2001	Shaw, M. T., III	06/08/2002	Shaw, M. T., III
38174	Stoessel, Andrew J.	06/02/2001	Shaw, M. T., III	06/02/2001	Shaw, M. T., III
38175	Werner-Hall, Judith B.	06/02/2001	Swing, W. E. Title III, Canon 6		
38176	White, Nancy A.	06/02/2001	Ihloff, R. W. Title III, Canon 6		
38177	Williams, Charles A., IV	06/02/2001	Johnson, D. E.	06/15/2002	Johnson, D. E.
38178	Feather, Mark R.	06/03/2001	Gulick, E. F., Jr.	06/08/2002	Gulick, E. F., Jr.
38179	Hayler, Andrew J.	06/03/2001	Salmon, E. L., Jr.		
38180	Lawson, Richard T., III	06/03/2001	Parsley, H. N., Jr.	12/04/2001	Parsley, H. N., Jr.
38181	Quigley, James E.	06/03/2001	Gulick, E. F., Jr.	02/02/2002	Gulick, E. F., Jr.
38182	Simmons, David T.	06/03/2001	Gulick, E. F., Jr.	01/12/2002	Gulick, E. F., Jr.
38183	Goodkind, Caroline C.	06/04/2001	Johnson, R. H.	04/06/2002	Curry, M. B. for Johnson, R.

Serial #	Name	Diaconate Date	Ordaining Bishop	Priesthood Date	Ordaining Bishop
38184	Lloyd, Kevin M.	06/04/2001	Johnson, R. H.	11/24/2002	Johnson, R. H.
38185	Smith, Gary M.	06/04/2001	Johnson, R. H.	04/27/2002	Johnson, R. H.
38186	Stevens, Robert E., Jr.	06/04/2001	Johnson, R. H.	12/21/2001	Duncan, R. W. for Johnson, R. H.
38187	Royes, Mary A.	06/05/2001	Gregg, W. O.	06/05/2002	Gregg, W. O.
38188	Weldon, A. Kenneth	06/05/2001	Salmon, E. L., Jr.		
38189	Jillard, Christine L.	06/08/2001	Creighton, M. W.	12/08/2001	Creighton, M. W.
38190	Kerr, Lauri A.	06/08/2001	Creighton, M. W.	12/12/2001	Creighton, M. W.
38191	Moore, Charlotte E.	06/08/2001	Creighton, M. W.	01/23/2002	Creighton, M. W.
38192	Alston, Phyllis M.	06/09/2001	Duncan, R. W.	01/19/2002	Duncan, R. W.
38193	Anderson-Krengel, W. Erich	06/09/2001	Smith, A. D.	02/16/2002	Smith, A. D.
38194	Antoci, Peter M.	06/09/2001	Dixon, J. H.	05/26/2002	Bartlett, A. L., Jr. for Dixon, J. H.
38195	Armstrong, Elizabeth	06/09/2001	Lamb, J. A.		
38196	Babcock, Theodore S.	06/09/2001	Smith, A. D.		
38197	Bassett, John W.	06/09/2001	Herzog, D. W.	01/12/2002	Herzog, D. W.
38198	Bowden, Gloria D.	06/09/2001	Tharp, R. G. for Atlanta		
38199	Bradford, Lawrence J.	06/09/2001	Winterrowd, W. J.	12/23/2001	Winterrowd, W. J.
38200	Brock, Jane C. K.	06/09/2001	Duncan, R. W.	12/19/2001	Duncan, R. W.
38201	Brower, Anne C.	06/09/2001	Bane, D. C., Jr.	12/15/2001	Whitaker, O. for Bane, D. C., Jr.
38202	Brown, Dewey E., Jr.	06/09/2001	Bane, D. C., Jr.	12/18/2001	Daniel, C, III for Bane, D. C., Jr.

CLERGY LIST — APPENDIX

Serial #	Name	Diaconate Date	Ordaining Bishop	Priesthood Date	Ordaining Bishop
38203	Bunyan, Grace V.	06/09/2001	Winterrowd, W. J.		
38204	Bush, Emilie C. H.	06/09/2001	Borsch, F. H.	06/12/2002	Borsch, F. H.
38205	Byers, Mark H.	06/09/2001	Smith, A. D.	12/15/2001	Smith, A. D.
38206	Carrier, Harold D.	06/09/2001	Herzog, D. W.	06/22/2002	Bena, D. J.
38207	Charles, Kathleen J.	06/09/2001	Whitmore, K. B. Title III, Canon 6		
38208	Cook, Catherine E.	06/09/2001	Winterrowd, W. J.	12/23/2001	Winterrowd, W. J.
38209	Critchfield, Margot D.	06/09/2001	Dixon, J. H.	02/09/2002	Dixon, J. H.
38210	Curtin, Anne F.	06/09/2001	Herzog, D. W.	12/08/2001	Herzog, D. W.
38211	Daley, Joy A.	06/09/2001	Stanton, J. M.	05/25/2002	Stanton, J. M.
38212	Danitschek, Thomas K.	06/09/2001	Winterrowd, W. J.	12/29/2001	Winterrowd, W. J.
38213	Davis, Vicki M.	06/09/2001	Smith, A. D.	05/25/2002	Smith, A. D.
38214	Deihle, Lawrence C.	06/09/2001	Duncan, R. W.	12/22/2001	Duncan, R. W.
38215	Durand, Sally E.	06/09/2001	Hughes, G. B. Title III, Canon 6		
38216	Ebert, Bernhard	06/09/2001	Winterrowd, W. J.	12/01/2001	Winterrowd, W. J.
38217	Elliott, Beverley F.	06/09/2001	Tharp, R. G. for Atlanta	01/21/2002	Alexander, J. N.
38218	Estrada, Carolyn S.	06/09/2001	Borsch, F. H.		
38219	Falconer, Virginia P.	06/09/2001	Stanton, J. M.	05/13/2002	Stanton, J. M.
38220	Gorchov, Michael I.	06/09/2001	Herzog, D. W.	12/08/2001	Herzog, D. W.
38221	Gustafson, Mary D.	06/09/2001	Duncan, R. W.	12/17/2001	Duncan, R. W.
38222	Guy, Ronald A.	06/09/2001	Stanton, J. M.	04/08/2002	Stanton, J. M.
38223	Harkins, J. William, III	06/09/2001	Tharp, R. G. for Atlanta		
38224	Hart, Larry D.	06/09/2001	Winterrowd, W. J.	12/15/2001	Winterrowd, W. J.

Serial #	Name	Diaconate Date	Ordaining Bishop	Priesthood Date	Ordaining Bishop
38225	Holland, Eleanor L.	06/09/2001	Dixon, J. H.	02/07/2002	Dixon, J. H.
38226	Houk, David S.	06/09/2001	Duncan, R. W.	12/15/2001	Duncan, R. W.
38227	Huber, Ellen B.	06/09/2001	Smith, A. D.	12/01/2001	Smith, A. D.
38228	Jackson, Connie W.	06/09/2001	Bane, D. C., Jr.	12/15/2001	Powell, F. N. for Bane, D. C., Jr.
38229	Jacobs, Mary L.	06/09/2001	Ihloff, R. W.		
38230	Jenson, Constance L.	06/09/2001	Dixon, J. H.	12/14/2001	Dixon, J. H.
38231	Johnson, Horace S.	06/09/2001	Smith, A. D.	12/15/2001	Smith, A. D.
38232	Kee-Rees, James L.	06/09/2001	Tharp, R. G. for Atlanta		
38233	Kellington, Laurie R.	06/09/2001	Herzog, D. W. Title III, Canon 6		
38234	Knudson, Richard L.	06/09/2001	Herzog, D. W. Title III, Canon 6		
38235	Kostas, George A.	06/09/2001	Vache, C. C. Title III, Canon 9	06/08/2002	Klusmeyer, W. M. Title III, Canon 9
38236	Lebron, Linda R.	06/09/2001	Dixon, J. H.	01/19/2002	Bartlett, A. L., Jr. for Dixon, J. H.
38237	Lehmann, Richard B.	06/09/2001	Herzog, D. W. Title III, Canon 6		
38238	Lehtinen, Erike A.	06/09/2001	Herzog, D. W. Title III, Canon 6		
38239	Lucas, Thomas S.	06/09/2001	Tharp, R. G. for Rabb, R. L.		
38240	Macke, Elizabeth A.	06/09/2001	Tharp, R. G. for Atlanta		
38241	Mayer, Peter W.	06/09/2001	Herzog, D. W.	01/19/2002	Eastman, A. D. for Herzog, D. W.

CLERGY LIST   APPENDIX

Serial #	Name	Diaconate Date	Ordaining Bishop	Priesthood Date	Ordaining Bishop
38242	Milam, David R.	06/09/2001	Hargrove, R. J., Jr.		
38243	Miller, Brian R.	06/09/2001	Duncan, R. W.		
38244	Nelson, Robert A., Sr.	06/09/2001	Hughes, G. B. Title III, Canon 6		
38245	Norman, Curtis K.	06/09/2001	MacPherson, D. B. for Stanton, J. M.	05/18/2002	Stanton, J. M.
38246	Parrish, Judy K.	06/09/2001	Bane, D. C., Jr.	12/21/2001	Said, J. L. for Frade, L.
38247	Puryear, James H.	06/09/2001	Bane, D. C., Jr.	12/16/2001	Lipscomb, J. B. for Bane, D. C., Jr.
38248	Quin, Alison J.	06/09/2001	Dixon, J. H.	12/18/2001	Bartlett, A. L., Jr.
38249	Rambo, Thomas B.	06/09/2001	Sauls, S. F.		
38250	Read, Kathleen	06/09/2001	Waynick, C. M.		
38251	Reed, Glenna J.	06/09/2001	Tharp, R. G. for Atlanta		
38252	Reed, Stephen K.	06/09/2001	Winterrowd, W. J.	12/02/2001	Winterrowd, W. J.
38253	Running, Joseph M., Jr.	06/09/2001	Bane, D. C., Jr.	12/15/2001	Leidel, E. M., Jr. for Bane, D. C., Jr.
38254	Shanks, Margaret R.	06/09/2001	Sauls, S. F. Title III, Canon 6		
38255	Smith, Theophus H.	06/09/2001	Tharp, R. G. for Atlanta		
38256	Sterchi, Margaret	06/09/2001	Stanton, J. M.	05/11/2002	Stanton, J. M.
38257	Tolzmann, Lee A. D.	06/09/2001	Ihloff, R. W.		
38258	Trebbe, Robert S.	06/09/2001	Hughes, G. B.		
38259	Watkin, Robert G.	06/09/2001	Duncan, R. W.	12/29/2001	Duncan, R. W.
38260	Wilcox, Melissa Q.	06/09/2001	Smith, A. D.		

Serial #	Name	Diaconate Date	Ordaining Bishop	Priesthood Date	Ordaining Bishop
38261	Wilson, Linda L.	06/09/2001	Herzog, D. W. Title III, Canon 6		
38262	Barwick, Frederick E., III	06/10/2001	Curry, M. B. Title III, Canon 6		
38263	Horne, Lance C.	06/10/2001	Chang, R. S. O.		
38264	Horowitz, Robert A.	06/10/2001	Jecko, S. H.	12/09/2001	Jecko, S. H.
38265	Needham, James R.	06/10/2001	Jecko, S. H.	12/09/2001	Jecko, S. H.
38266	Adams, Daniel W.	06/16/2001	Henderson, D. F., Jr.		
38267	Barnes, Susan J.	06/16/2001	Payne, C. E.	06/19/2002	Payne, C. E.
38268	Barron, Carol D.	06/16/2001	Frade, L.	04/26/2002	Frade, L.
38269	Bridges, Nancy K.	06/16/2001	Moody, R. M. Title III, Canon 6		
38270	Carr, Dale R.	06/16/2001	Gregg, W. O.		
38271	Clark, Ralph O.	06/16/2001	Daniel, C., III		
38272	Condron, Thomas W.	06/16/2001	Payne, C. E.		
38273	deMontmollin, Dolores A.	06/16/2001	Frade, L.	12/15/2001	Frade, L.
38274	Fico-Brown, Beverly	06/16/2001	Gibbs, W. N., Jr. Title III, Canon 6		
38275	Forest, Elizabeth J. S.	06/16/2001	Gibbs, W. N., Jr.		
38276	Fout, Jason A.	06/16/2001	Persell, W. D.	12/15/2001	Lee, E. L., Jr. for Persell, W. D.
38277	Hensley, Lane G.	06/16/2001	Persell, W. D.	12/15/2001	Persell, W. D.
38278	Hubbard, Carol M.	06/16/2001	Henderson, D. F., Jr.	03/03/2002	Sisk, M. S.
38279	Keedy, Susan S.	06/16/2001	Frade, L.	12/16/2001	Frade, L.

CLERGY LIST — APPENDIX

Serial #	Name	Diaconate Date	Ordaining Bishop	Priesthood Date	Ordaining Bishop
38280	Kirchmier, Anne R.	06/16/2001	Scruton, G. P.	01/02/2002	Lee, P. J. for Scruton G. P.
38281	Lacy, Mary C.	06/16/2001	Persell, W. D.	12/15/2001	Persell, W. D.
38282	Lecroy, Anne K.	06/16/2001	von Rosenberg, C. G. Title III, Canon 6		
38283	Lesesne, William G., Jr.	06/16/2001	Henderson, D. F., Jr.		
38284	Manning, Shannon R.	06/16/2001	Marble, A. C., Jr.	12/16/2001	Gray, D. M, III
38285	McGee, William E.	06/16/2001	von Rosenburg, C. G. Title III, Canon 6		
38286	Moehl, Thomas J.	06/16/2001	Ladehoff, R. L.	12/21/2001	Ladehoff, R. L.
38287	Morris, Julie H.	06/16/2001	Borsch, F. H.		
38288	Ousley, P. Lance	06/16/2001	Payne, C. E.	06/19/2002	Payne, C. E.
38289	Pamatmat, Roberto D. R.	06/16/2001	Persell, W. D.		
38290	Peck, Felicity	06/16/2001	von Rosenberg, C. G. Title III, Canon 6		
38291	Robbins, Janice	06/16/2001	von Rosenberg, C. G. Title III, Canon 6		
38292	Sanders, Marilyn M.	06/16/2001	Gibbs, W. N., Jr.		
38293	Scott, Nolie E.	06/16/2001	von Rosenberg, C. G. Title III, Canon 6		
38294	Sims, Kenneth H.	06/16/2001	Frade, L. Title III, Canon 6		
38295	Swanner, Rhoda J.	06/16/2001	Payne, C. E.	06/20/2002	Payne, C. E.
38296	Treppa, Joyce L.	06/16/2001	Gibbs, W. N., Jr. Title III, Canon 6		

Serial #	Name	Diaconate Date	Ordaining Bishop	Priesthood Date	Ordaining Bishop
38297	Ward, Meredyth W.	06/16/2001	Scruton, G. P.	01/02/2002	Scruton, G. P.
38298	Watton, Sharon L.	06/16/2001	Gibbs, W. N., Jr. Title III, Canon 6		
38299	Wehner, Paul B.	06/16/2001	Payne, C. E.	06/18/2002	Payne, C. E.
38300	Wight, Susan M.	06/16/2001	Henderson, D. F., Jr.		
38301	Yaw, Christopher L.	06/16/2001	Borsch, F. H.		
38302	Young, James O.	06/16/2001	Moody, R. M. Title III, Canon 6		
38303	Bowden, Teresa N. T.	06/17/2001	Chang, R. S. O.		
38304	Deetz, Susan M.	06/17/2001	Jelinek, J. L. Title III, Canon 6		
38305	Hauck, Barbara H.	06/17/2001	Jelinek, J. L. Title III, Canon 6		
38306	Hill, David E.	06/17/2001	Jelinek, J. L. Title III, Canon 6		
38307	Hill, Mary A.	06/17/2001	Little, E. S., II	05/31/2002	Little, E. S., II
38308	Huber, Amy W.	06/17/2001	Jelinek, J. L. Title III, Canon 6		
38309	Olson, Alice I.	06/17/2001	Jelinek, J. L. Title III, Canon 6		
38310	Packard, Nancy L. M.	06/17/2001	Theuner, D. E.	12/22/2001	Theuner, D. E.
38311	Tollefson, Jane C.	06/17/2001	Jelinek, J. L. Title III, Canon 6		
38312	Waggoner, Janet C.	06/17/2001	Ladehoff, R. L.		

CLERGY LIST — APPENDIX

Serial #	Name	Diaconate Date	Ordaining Bishop	Priesthood Date	Ordaining Bishop
38313	Bobo, Melinda D.	06/20/2001	Caldwell, B. E.	12/20/2001	Jelinek, J. L. for Caldwell, B. E.
38314	Johnson, Keith	06/20/2001	Frade, L.	12/20/2001	Frade, L.
38315	Myers, Bruns M., III	06/21/2001	Gray, D. M., III	01/24/2002	Marble, A. C., Jr.
38316	Amburgey, Cristina G.	06/23/2001	Hampton, S. Z. K. for Warner V. W., Jr. Title III, Canon 6		
38317	Bell, Susan E. W.	06/23/2001	Hargrove, R. J., Jr.	01/05/2002	Hargrove, R. J., Jr.
38318	Brackett, Thomas L.	06/23/2001	Knudsen, C. A. R.	12/23/2001	Hughes, G. B. for Knudsen, C. A. R.
38319	Coleman, Kim L.	06/23/2001	Lee, P. J.	12/29/2001	Lee, P. J.
38320	Connelly, Constance R.	06/23/2001	Curry, M. B.	07/10/2002	Curry, M. B.
38321	Conner, Lu-Anne	06/23/2001	Knudsen, C. A. R.	02/02/2002	Knudsen, C. A. R.
38322	Conrads, Alexandra K.	06/23/2001	Lee, P. J.	12/29/2001	Lee, P. J.
38323	Corkern, Matthew T. L.	06/23/2001	Lee, P. J.	12/29/2001	Lee, P. J.
38324	Crane, Susan H.	06/23/2001	Herlong, B. N.	04/21/2002	Herlong, B. N.
38325	Ellis, Elizabeth A.	06/23/2001	Shimpfky, R. L.		
38326	Erickson, Kenneth L.	06/23/2001	Curry, M. B.	01/20/2002	Ladehoff, R. L.
38327	Espeseth, Cynthia A.	06/23/2001	Warner, V. W., Jr.	01/13/2002	Warner, V. W., Jr.
38328	Fichter, Richard E., Jr.	06/23/2001	Lee, P. J.	12/29/2001	Lee, P. J.
38329	Huey, S. Marshall, Jr.	06/23/2001	Salmon, E. L., Jr.		
38330	Jones, Timothy K.	06/23/2001	Herlong, B. N.	04/21/2002	Herlong, B. N.
38331	LaFond, Charles D., II	06/23/2001	Lee, P. J.	12/29/2001	Lee, P. J.
38332	Ledgerwood, Mary J.	06/23/2001	Lee, P. J.	01/26/2002	Rabb, J. L. for Lee, P. J.

Serial #	Name	Diaconate Date	Ordaining Bishop	Priesthood Date	Ordaining Bishop
38333	Lukas, Arlene	06/23/2001	Curry, M. B.	03/16/2002	Johnson, R. H.
38334	Manning, Gene B.	06/23/2001	Herlong, B. N.	04/21/2002	Herlong, B. N.
38335	Midgett, William D.	06/23/2001	Lee, P. J.	12/29/2001	Lee, P. J.
38336	Moore, Nancy L.	06/23/2001	Knudsen, C. A. R.		
38337	Myers, Kira S.	06/23/2001	Lee, P. J.	12/29/2001	Lee, P. J.
38338	Preece, Mark W.	06/23/2001	Bennison, C. E., Jr.	12/23/2001	Bennison, C. E., Jr.
38339	Segal, Danna J.	06/23/2001	Bennison, C. E., Jr.	06/01/2002	Bennison, C. E., Jr.
38340	Sheehan, John T.	06/23/2001	Lee, P. J.	12/29/2001	Lee, P. J.
38341	Smith, Robert C.	06/23/2001	Bennison, C. E., Jr.	06/01/2002	Bennison, C. E., Jr.
38342	Tate, Mary K.	06/23/2001	Bennison, C. E., Jr. Title III, Canon 6		
38343	Thomas, James M., Jr.	06/23/2001	Moody, R. M.		
38344	Toepfer, Laura K.	06/23/2001	McKelvey, J. M.	05/04/2002	McKelvey, J. M.
38345	Torrey, Dorothy E.	06/23/2001	Shimpfky, R. L.		
38346	Varner, Joshua H.	06/23/2001	Curry, M. B.	05/18/2002	Curry, M. B.
38347	Waters, Elliott M.	06/23/2001	Lee, P. J.	12/29/2001	Lee, P. J.
38348	Whitaker, Ann L.	06/23/2001	Marble, A. C., Jr.	01/16/2002	Marble, A. C., Jr.
38349	Whitfield, Deirdre R.	06/23/2001	Bennison, C. E., Jr. Title III, Canon 6		
38350	Wizorek, Julie C.	06/23/2001	Shimpky, R. L.		
38351	Woodliff, Kirk A.	06/23/2001	Moody, R. M.		
38352	Wooliver, Tammy S.	06/23/2001	Moody, R. M.	01/06/2002	Bartlett, A. L., Jr. for Moody, R. M.
38353	Heden, Eileen M.	06/30/2001	Ladehoff, R. L.	01/20/2002	Swing, W. E. for Ladehoff R.

CLERGY LIST — APPENDIX

Serial #	Name	Diaconate Date	Ordaining Bishop	Priesthood Date	Ordaining Bishop
38354	Kleffman, Todd A.	06/30/2001	Waynick, C. M.	01/06/2002	Waynick, C. M.
38355	MacSwain, Robert C.	06/30/2001	Carey, G. L. for Daniel, C., III		
38356	Schatz, Stefani S.	06/30/2001	Borsch, F. H.		
38357	Britton, Judith A.	07/01/2001	Kelsey, J. A. Title III, Canon 9		
38358	Meade, Jean A. M.	07/05/2001	Jenkins, C. E., III	01/19/2002	Jenkins, C. E., III
38359	Taylor, Norman D.	07/07/2001	Warner, V. W., Jr. Title III, Canon 6		
38360	Becker, C. S. Honey	07/15/2001	Chang, R. S. O. Title III, Canon 6		
38361	Sanchez, Alfonso	07/20/2001	Bruno, J. J.		
38362	McClure, William J., Jr.	07/22/2001	Leidel, E. M., Jr.	02/23/2002	Leidel, E. M., Jr.
38363	Anderson, Kenneth E.	07/28/2001	Kelshaw, T. Title III, Canon 6		
38364	Bates, Thomas J.	07/28/2001	Kelshaw, T. Title III, Canon 6		
38365	Chandler, Susan E.	07/28/2001	Kelshaw, T.		
38366	McFarland, Earl E.	07/28/2001	Kelshaw, T. Title III, Canon 6		
38367	Meade, Gary J.	07/28/2001	Kelshaw, T.	02/23/2002	Kelshaw, T.
38368	Noland, Elisabeth H.	07/28/2001	Kelshaw, T. Title III, Canon 6		
38369	Olsen, Robert	07/28/2001	Lamb, J. A.		

Serial #	Name	Diaconate Date	Ordaining Bishop	Priesthood Date	Ordaining Bishop
38370	Orbaugh, Phyllis R. J.	07/28/2001	Title III, Canon 6		
38371	Watson, Charles E.	07/28/2001	Kelshaw, T.		
			Title III, Canon 6		
38372	Wells, Ann L. C.	07/28/2001	Kelshaw, T.		
			Title III, Canon 6		
38373	White, Donald K., Jr.	07/28/2001	Kelshaw, T.	08/18/2002	Duncan, R. W. for Kelshaw, T.
38374	Allen, Diogenes	07/29/2001	Joslin, D. B.		
38375	Hannabass, Katherine	08/12/2001	Kelsey, J. A.		
			Title III, Canon 6		
38376	Hart, Danny R.	08/15/2001	Garrison, J. M.		
			Title III, Canon 6		
38377	Bernardi, Frank A.	08/18/2001	Schofield, J.-D.		
38378	Chavez, Velma	08/28/2001	Caldwell, B. E.		
			Title III, Canon 9		
38379	Hopkins, Vivian L.	09/01/2001	Frade, L.		
			Title III, Canon 6		
38380	Ingraham, Doris W.	09/01/2001	Frade, L.		
38381	Masterman, Brenda P.	09/01/2001	Frade, L.		
			Title III, Canon 6		
38382	Murray, John P.	09/01/2001	Kelshaw, T.	09/21/2002	Kelshaw, T.
38383	Shafer, Samuel H.	09/01/2001	Kelshaw, T.	09/05/2002	Kelshaw, T.

CLERGY LIST — APPENDIX

Serial #	Name	Diaconate Date	Ordaining Bishop	Priesthood Date	Ordaining Bishop
38384	Shoemaker, Eric W.	09/01/2001	Frade, L. Title III, Canon 6		
38385	Short, Margaret I.	09/01/2001	Kelshaw, T.		
38386	Van Dermark, Fayetta	09/09/2001	Herzog, D. W. Title III, Canon 6		
38387	Johnson, David A.	09/12/2001	Salmon, E. L., Jr.		
38388	Bundrock, Bonnie R.	09/14/2001	Garrison, J. M. Title III, Canon 6		
38389	Hilfiker, Gerald M.	09/14/2001	Garrison, J. M. Title III, Canon 6		
38390	Dorsey, Laura M.	09/15/2001	Townsend, M. G.	10/05/2002	Longest, C. L.
38391	Lokey, Michael P.	09/15/2001	Townsend, M. G. Title III, Canon 9	10/05/2002	Longest, C. L. Title III, Canon 9
38392	Nettleton, Jerome P.	09/15/2001	Townsend, M. G. Title III, Canon 6		
38393	Sutherland, Melody P.	09/15/2001	Townsend, M. G. Title III, Canon 6		
38394	Moore, Pamela A.	09/16/2001	Lamb, J. A. Title III, Canon 6		
38395	Sunderland, Douglas C.	09/17/2001	Caldwell, B. E. Title III, Canon 9	04/26/2002	Caldwell, B. E. Title III, Canon 9
38396	Bauer, Lee F.	09/18/2001	Louttit, H. I., Jr.	04/17/2002	Louttit, H. I., Jr.
38397	Bowden, Talmadge A., Jr.	09/18/2001	Louttit, H. I., Jr.	03/31/2002	Louttit, H. I., Jr.
38398	Owen, Charles B.	09/18/2001	Marble, A. C., Jr.	03/20/2002	Gray, D. M, III for Marble, A. C., Jr.

Serial #	Name	Diaconate Date	Ordaining Bishop	Priesthood Date	Ordaining Bishop
38399	Davis-Heller, Lisa	09/20/2001	Vache, C. C.	06/08/2002	Klusmeyer, W. M.
38400	Morris, Patricia	09/29/2001	Ladehoff, R. L. Title III, Canon 6		
38401	Muhlheim, Nancy C. C.	09/29/2001	Ladehoff, R. L. Title III, Canon 6		
38402	Griffin, Jon E.	010/05/2001	Beckwith, P. H. Title III, Canon 9	08/24/2002	Beckwith, P. H. Title III, Canon 9
38403	Bostick-Bearden, Jane G.	10/06/2001	Shaw, M. T., III Title III, Canon 6		
38404	Gaiser, Ted G.	10/06/2001	Shaw, M. T., III Title III, Canon 6		
38405	Noyes, Daphne B.	10/06/2001	Shaw, M. T., III Title III, Canon 6		
38406	Stowe, Barbara E.	10/06/2001	Shaw, M. T., III Title III, Canon 6		
38407	Tibbetts, Ronald C.	10/06/2001	Shaw, M. T., III Title III, Canon 6		
38408	Bennett, Pattiann B.	10/09/2001	Keyser, C. L. for Montana		
38409	Johnson, Marietta	10/09/2001	Keyser, C. L. for Montana Title III, Canon 9		
38410	Sadler, Alice I.	10/16/2001	Lipscomb, J. B.	04/20/2002	Lipscomb, J. B.
38411	Kircher, Kathleen L.	10/17/2001	Lipscomb, J. B.	04/19/2002	Lipscomb, J. B.
38412	Baldwin, Robert E.	10/20/2001	Thompson, H., Jr.	06/01/2002	Thompson, H., Jr.
38413	Bartholomew, A. Gilbert L.	10/20/2001	Thompson, H., Jr.	06/01/2002	Thompson, H., Jr.
38414	Hardin, Nancy H.	10/20/2001	Thompson, H., Jr.	06/01/2002	Thompson, H., Jr.

Serial #	Name	Diaconate Date	Ordaining Bishop	Priesthood Date	Ordaining Bishop
38415	Hitch, Kenneth R.	10/20/2001	Thompson, H., Jr.	06/01/2002	Thompson, H., Jr.
38416	Layden, Daniel K.	10/20/2001	Thompson, H., Jr.	06/01/2002	Thompson, H., Jr.
38417	Templeman, Mark A.	10/20/2001	Thompson, H., Jr.	06/01/2002	Thompson, H., Jr.
38418	Twiggs, Frances R.	10/20/2001	Thompson, H., Jr.	06/01/2002	Thompson, H., Jr.
38419	Shier, Nancy K.	10/21/2001	Borsch, F. H.		
38420	Diely, Elizabeth B. H.	10/23/2001	Marshall, P. V.	10/06/2002	Marshall, P. V.
38421	Heffner, John H.	10/23/2001	Marshall, P. V.	10/06/2002	Marshall, P. V.
38422	Hunt, Hazel B.	10/23/2001	Marshall, P. V. Title III, Canon 6		
38423	Malia, Gregory	10/23/2001	Marshall, P. V.	10/06/2002	Marshall, P. V.
38424	Carlson, Philip L.	10/27/2001	Shahan, R. R.	06/08/2002	Shahan, R. R.
38425	Mills, Byron K.	10/27/2001	Shahan, R. R.	11/09/2002	Shahan, R. R.
X-38426	Miranda Lopez, Neli A.	10/27/2001	Guerra Soria, A. R.		
38427	Ricketts, Marcia C.	10/28/2001	Ohl, C. W., Jr. Title III, Canon 6		
38428	Rose, Roland	10/28/2001	Ohl, C. W., Jr. Title III, Canon 6		
38429	Erickson, Scott E.	11/01/2001	Theuner, D. E.	05/19/2002	Theuner, D. E.
38430	Humphrey, Nathan J. A.	11/01/2001	Rabb, J. L.	05/09/2002	Ihloff, R. W.
38431	Lewis, Philip M.	11/01/2001	Herzog, D. W.	05/01/2002	Herzog, D. W.
38432	Whorton, Jeffrey T.	11/02/2001	Keyser, C. L. for Duncan, R. W.	05/04/2002	Keyser, C. L. for Duncan, R. W.
38433	Heath, Claudia	11/03/2001	Maze, L. E. Title III, Canon 6		

Serial #	Name	Diaconate Date	Ordaining Bishop	Priesthood Date	Ordaining Bishop
38434	McDermott, Nelda G.	11/03/2001	Maze, L. E. Title III, Canon 6		
38435	Seamans, Harry S.	11/03/2001	Maze, L. E. Title III, Canon 6		
38436	Snow, George R.	11/07/2001	Caldwell, B. E. Title III, Canon 9	05/09/2002	Caldwell, B. E. Title III, Canon 9
38437	Dickinson, Garrin W.	11/09/2001	Duncan, R. W.	05/25/2002	Duncan, R. W.
38438	Denton, Marie A.	11/10/2001	Winterrowd, W. J. Title III, Canon 6		
38439	Dykes, Deborah W.	11/10/2001	Winterrowd, W. J. Title III, Canon 6		
38440	Ellis, Karen L.	11/10/2001	Winterrowd, W. J. Title III, Canon 6		
38441	Marsh, Abigail	11/10/2001	Keyser, C. L. for Montana		
38442	Scheeler, Joseph L.	11/10/2001	Lee, P. J.		
38443	Anschutz, Maryetta M.	11/17/2001	Lee, P. J.	05/18/2002	Lee, P. J.
38444	Christopher, E. Kathleen	11/17/2001	Lee, P. J.	05/18/2002	Lee, P. J.
38445	Dickson, Patricia J.	11/17/2001	Lee, P. J.	05/18/2002	Lee, P. J.
38446	Murphy, Joseph P.	11/17/2001	Lee, P. J.		
38447	Hazzard, Richard A., Sr.	11/21/2001	Creighton, M. W. Title III, Canon 6		
38448	Towne, Jane C.	11/23/2001	Fairfield, A. H. Title III, Canon 6		
38449	Lynn, Suzanne M.	11/24/2001	Leidel, E. M., Jr.		

CLERGY LIST — APPENDIX

Serial #	Name	Diaconate Date	Ordaining Bishop	Priesthood Date	Ordaining Bishop
38450	Price, Robert P.	11/27/2001	Title III, Canon 6	05/02/2002	Smith, G. W.
38451	Stewart, William O., Jr.	11/29/2001	Rockwell, H. H.		
38452	Hixson, Mary L.	11/30/2001	Louittit, H. I., Jr.	12/13/2002	Adams, J. M., Jr.
			Strickland, V. E.		Title III, Canon 9
38453	Seaton, Robert D.	11/30/2001	Title III, Canon 9		
			Strickland, V. E.		
38454	Bennett, JoAnne	12/01/2001	Swing, W. E.	06/01/2002	Swing, W. E.
38455	Deleuse, Betsey W.	12/01/2001	Knudsen, C. A. R.		
			Title III, Canon 6		
38456	Drinkwater, Gary G.	12/01/2001	Knudsen, C. A. R.		
			Title III, Canon 6		
38457	Eunson, Lisa K.	12/01/2001	Swing, W. E.	06/01/2002	Swing, W. E.
38458	Klein, Everett H.	12/01/2001	Lee, E. L., Jr.	09/14/2002	Gepert, R. R.
38459	Knowlton, Carroll B.	12/01/2001	Knudsen, C. A. R.		
			Title III, Canon 6		
38460	Leigh-Taylor, Christine H.	12/01/2001	Swing, W. E.	06/01/2002	Swing, W. E.
38461	Powell, Everett	12/01/2001	Swing, W. E.		
			Title III, Canon 6		
38462	Wile, Mary L. H.	12/01/2001	Knudsen, C. A. R.		
			Title III, Canon 6		
38463	Powell, Brent C.	12/02/2001	Johnson, D. E.		
			Title III, Canon 6		
38464	Fornea, Stan W.	12/05/2001	Daniel, C., III	04/10/2002	Daniel, C., III
38465	Craig, Eric J.	12/06/2001	Ackerman, K. L.	12/21/2002	Ackerman, K. L.

Serial #	Name	Diaconate Date	Ordaining Bishop	Priesthood Date	Ordaining Bishop
38466	Murphy, Michael J.	12/06/2001	Ackerman, K. L.	09/01/2002	Ackerman, K. L.
38467	Yost, Martin C.	12/06/2001	Ackerman, K. L.	09/04/2002	Ackerman, K. L.
38468	Bakker, Cheryl A.	12/08/2001	Howe, J. W. Title III, Canon 6		
38469	Bryant, Peter F.	12/08/2001	McKelvey, J. M.		
38470	Cook, Susanna R.	12/08/2001	Duncan, R. W.		
38471	Curl, James F.	12/08/2001	McKelvey, J. M.		
38472	Dominguez, Patrick E.	12/08/2001	Duncan, R. W. Title III, Canon 9		
38473	Hansell, Susan W.	12/08/2001	Howe, J. W. Title III, Canon 6		
38474	Harrison, Elizabeth A.	12/08/2001	Howe, J. W. Title III, Canon 6		
38475	Janikowski, Thomas A.	12/08/2001	Jacobus, R. E.		
38476	Lockett, Tina L.	12/08/2001	Duncan, R. W.		
38477	Murray, Elizabeth A.	12/08/2001	Howe, J. W. Title III, Canon 6		
38478	Natzke, Vicki J.	12/08/2001	Jacobus, R. E.	06/08/2002	Jacobus, R. E.
38479	Rincon, Virginia M.	12/08/2001	Shaw, M. T, III		
38480	Schneider, Marian H.	12/08/2001	McKelvey, J. M.		
38481	Tyo, Charles H., Jr.	12/08/2001	McKelvey, J. M.		
38482	Welty, Terrence A., IV	12/08/2001	Duncan, R. W.	06/09/2002	Duncan, R. W.
38483	Woods, Karen E.	12/08/2001	Duncan, R. W. Title III, Canon 6		

CLERGY LIST APPENDIX

Serial #	Name	Diaconate Date	Ordaining Bishop	Priesthood Date	Ordaining Bishop
38484	Adams, Sheryl L.	12/09/2001	Jecko, S. H.	06/09/2002	Jecko, S. H.
38485	Catinella, Gayle L.	12/13/2001	Krotz, J. E.	06/29/2002	Krotz, J. E.
38486	Burch, Suzanne	12/15/2001	von Rosenberg, C.G. Title III, Canon 6		
38487	Frye, J. Wade, III	12/15/2001	von Rosenberg, C.G. Title III, Canon 6		
38488	Pipkin, Michael R. J.	12/15/2001	Ohl, C. W., Jr.	06/22/2002	Ohl, C. W., Jr.
38489	Lee, Thomas M.	12/16/2001	Herlong, B. N.	06/23/2002	Herlong, B. N.
38490	White, Kathryn L.	12/18/2001	Persell, W. D.	06/18/2002	Persell, W. D.
38491	Clement, Betty C.	12/19/2001	Stanton, J. M. Title III, Canon 6		
38492	Saltzgaber, Jan M.	12/19/2001	Louttit, H. I., Jr. Title III, Canon 6		
38493	Schrimsher, Alyce M.	12/19/2001	Stanton, J. M. Title III, Canon 6		
38494	Ashcroft, Mary E.	12/20/2001	Jelinek, J. L.		
38495	Brown, Lydia A. H.	12/20/2001	Jelinek, J. L.	06/20/2002	Jelinek, J. L.
38496	Delamater, Joan P.	12/20/2001	Jelinek, J. L.	06/20/2002	Jelinek, J. L.
38497	Burns, Deborah S.	12/22/2001	Smalley, W. E Title III, Canon 6		
38498	Clark, Cheryl L.	12/22/2001	Maze, L. E.	06/22/2002	Maze, L. E.
38499	Dinwiddie, Philip M.	12/22/2001	Gibbs, W. N., Jr.	06/26/2002	Gibbs, W. N., Jr.
38500	Ellison, Monique A.	12/22/2001	Gibbs, W. N., Jr.		
38501	Farrey, Shannon C.	12/22/2001	Gibbs, W. N., Jr.	06/27/2002	Gibbs, W. N., Jr.

Serial #	Name	Diaconate Date	Ordaining Bishop	Priesthood Date	Ordaining Bishop
38502	Johnson, Ann L.	12/22/2001	Gibbs, W. N., Jr.	06/29/2002	Maze, L. E.
38503	Stroop, William G.	12/22/2001	Maze, L. E.	07/17/2002	Gibbs, W. N., Jr.
38504	West, Kelly E.	12/22/2001	Gibbs, W. N., Jr.	06/24/2002	Ackerman, K. L.
38505	Mahue, Louis D.	12/23/2001	Ackerman, K. L.		
38506	Hood, Stephen D.	12/27/2001	Jenkins, C. E, III		
38507	Koppel, Mary E.	12/27/2001	Jenkins, C. E, III	07/03/2002	Jenkins, C. E, III
38508	Meaux, Amy D.	12/27/2001	Jenkins, C. E, III	07/10/2002	Jenkins, C. E, III
38509	Papazoglakis, Thomas W.	12/27/2001	Jenkins, C. E, III	06/30/2002	White, R. J. for Jenkins, C. E., III
38510	Zeller, Margaret K.	12/27/2001	Jenkins, C. E, III		
38511	Boone, Connie L.	01/06/2002	Gregg, W. O.		
38512	Sheppard, Patricia S. K.	01/06/2002	Title III, Canon 6		
38513	Blakelock, Douglas P.	01/12/2002	Lamb, J. A.		
			Herzog, D. W.		
			Title III, Canon 6		
38514	Rollins, Belle F.	01/12/2002	Hargrove, R. J., Jr.		
			Title III, Canon 6		
38515	Fenty, Maria	01/13/2002	Herzog, D. W.		
			Title III, Canon 6		
38516	Earle, Richard T, III	01/18/2002	Lipscomb, J. B.		
			Title III, Canon 6		
38517	Griscom, Donald	01/18/2002	Lipscomb, J. B.		
			Title III, Canon 6		
38518	Jamieson, Sandra S.	01/18/2002	Lipscomb, J. B.		
			Title III, Canon 6		

CLERGY LIST — APPENDIX

Serial #	Name	Diaconate Date	Ordaining Bishop	Priesthood Date	Ordaining Bishop
38519	McManis, Dennis	01/18/2002	Lipscomb, J. B. Title III, Canon 6		
38520	Hussey-Bynes, Teddra R.	01/19/2002	Curry, M. B.		
38521	Barber, Grethe	01/20/2002	Warner, V. W., Jr.	08/24/2002	Hampton, S. Z. K. for Warner, V. W., Jr.
38522	Derbyshire, James W.	01/24/2002	Ackerman, K. L.	07/25/2002	Ackerman, K. L.
X-38523	Kuang Yang, Chou Y.	01/25/2002	Lai, D. J. H.		
X-38524	Wen Bin, Tzeng	01/25/2002	Lai, D. J. H.		
38525	Rouse, Albertine C.	01/27/2002	Borsch, F. H.	09/08/2002	Bruno, J. J.
38526	Byer, Martha R.	02/02/2002	Howe, B. R. Title III, Canon 6		
38527	Kitt, Michael	02/02/2002	Persell, W. D. Title III, Canon 6		
38528	Lloyd, Elizabeth A.	02/02/2002	Persell, W. D. Title III, Canon 6		
38529	Lynn, Jacqueline G.	02/02/2002	Persell, W. D. Title III, Canon 6		
38530	Meade, Elizabeth G.	02/02/2002	Persell, W. D. Title III, Canon 6		
38531	Riis, Susan H.	02/02/2002	Persell, W. D. Title III, Canon 6		
38532	Spurlock, Paul A.	02/02/2002	Winterrowd, W. J.		
38533	Ely, James E.	02/03/2002	Payne, C. E.	11/16/2002	Wimberly, D. A. for Payne, C. E.
38534	Gwin, Lawrence P., Jr.	02/03/2002	Payne, C. E.	12/21/2002	Wimberly, D. A. for Payne, C. E.

Serial #	Name	Diaconate Date	Ordaining Bishop	Priesthood Date	Ordaining Bishop
38535	Beecham, Troy C.	02/08/2002	Louttit, H. I., Jr.		E.
38536	Calhoun, Judson J.	02/11/2002	Jefferts Schori, K.	09/08/2002	Jefferts Schori, K.
38537	Edwards, James P.	02/12/2002	Jefferts Schori, K.	09/14/2002	Jefferts Schori, K.
38538	Estes, Jack A.	02/16/2002	Schofield, J.-D.	08/24/2002	Schofield, J.-D.
38539	Kamai, Gordon M.	02/16/2002	Schofield, J.-D.	08/31/2002	Schofield, J.-D.
38540	Longbottom, Robert J. D.	02/16/2002	Schofield, J.-D.	09/21/2002	Schofield, J.-D.
38541	Hale, Douglas J.	02/25/2002	Gregg, W. O.	08/03/2002	Gregg, W. O.
38542	Hale, Patricia A.	02/25/2002	Gregg, W. O.	08/03/2002	Gregg, W. O.
38543	von Grabow, Richard H.	03/03/2002	Lamb, J. A.		
			Title III, Canon 6		
38544	Higgs, Richard H.	03/09/2002	Kelshaw, T.	09/21/2002	Kelshaw, T.
38545	Morrill, Donald P.	03/09/2002	Kelshaw, T.		
			Title III, Canon 6		
38546	Snyder, Belinda A. W.	03/15/2002	Maze, L. E.	09/10/2002	Maze, L. E.
38547	Fox, Carol R.	03/16/2002	Sisk, M. S.	09/21/2002	Sisk, M. S.
38548	Matkin, Timothy M.	03/16/2002	Iker, J. L.	09/23/2002	Iker, J. L.
38549	Mitchell, Patricia S.	03/16/2002	Sisk, M. S.	09/21/2002	Sisk, M. S.
38550	Speeks, Mark W.	03/16/2002	Sisk, M. S.	09/21/2002	Sisk, M. S.
38551	Luck, Jane A.	03/23/2002	Knudsen, C. A. R.		
			Title III, Canon 6		
38552	Ridgway, Maria S.	03/23/2002	Shimpfky, R. L.		
			Title III, Canon 6		
38553	Drury, Joanne C.	04/05/2002	Robertson, C. L.		

CLERGY LIST APPENDIX

Serial #	Name	Diaconate Date	Ordaining Bishop	Priesthood Date	Ordaining Bishop
38554	Spear, Leslie E.	04/05/2002	Title III, Canon 6 Robertson, C. L.	10/23/2002	Robertson, C. L. Title III, Canon 9
38555	Tate, Donald S.	04/05/2002	Title III, Canon 9 Robertson, C. L.		
38556	Burkett, William V.	04/06/2002	Lipscomb, J. B.		
38557	Dagg, Margaret K.	04/06/2002	Smalley, W. E.	10/05/2002	Smalley, W. E.
38558	Gunn, Daniel C.	04/06/2002	Marshall, P. V.	10/06/2002	Marshall, P. V.
38559	Huntington, Carol L.	04/06/2002	Marshal, P. V. Title III, Canon 6		
38560	Mendoza, Loretta J.	04/06/2002	White, R. J.		
38561	Murray, George R., Jr.	04/06/2002	Longest, C. L. Title III, Canon 6		
38562	O'Connor, Mary C. M.	04/06/2002	White, R. J.	10/06/2002	White, R. J.
38563	Papanek, Nicolette	04/06/2002	Smalley, W. E.	10/12/2002	Smalley, W. E.
38564	Peterson, Iris E.	04/06/2002	Marshall, P. V. Title III, Canon 6	10/06/2002	Marshall, P. V.
38565	Trygar, Earl P., Sr.	04/06/2002	Marshall, P. V. Title III, Canon 9	10/06/2002	Marshall, P. V. Title III, Canon 9
38566	Wenner, Rachel E.	04/06/2002	White, R. J.	10/17/2002	White, R. J.
38567	Dunlap, Eunice R.	04/10/2002	Daniel C., III		
38568	Peterman, Lynn C.	04/10/2002	Daniel C., III	10/19/2002	Daniel, C, III
38569	Findlen, Beth	04/13/2002	Knudsen, C. A. R. Title III, Canon 6		
38570	Matarazzo, Laura R.	04/13/2002	Croneberger, J. P.		

Serial #	Name	Diaconate Date	Ordaining Bishop	Priesthood Date	Ordaining Bishop
38571	Petroccione, James V.	04/13/2002	Brome, R. T. for Croneberger, J. P.		
38572	Thompson, Wanda J.	04/13/2002	Knudsen, C. A. R. Title III, Canon 6		
38573	Hartzog, Howard G.	04/14/2002	Folts, J. E.		
38574	LeSueur, John T., II	04/14/2002	Knudsen, C. A. R. Title III, Canon 6		
38575	Isaacs, James S.	04/18/2002	Longest, C. L.		
38576	Baxter, Donald L.	04/19/2002	Rowley, R. D., Jr.	11/17/2002	Rowley, R. D., Jr.
38577	Ryan, Matthew W.	04/20/2002	Rowley, R. D., Jr.	11/17/2002	Rowley, R. D., Jr.
38578	Thomas, Franklin B., Jr.	04/23/2002	Louttit, H. I., Jr. Title III, Canon 9	12/02/2002	Louttit, H. I., Jr. Title III, Canon 9
38579	Moreno-Richardson, Mary	04/26/2002	Bruno, J. J. Title III, Canon 6		
38580	Bradshaw, Tommy J.	04/27/2002	Maze, L. E. Title III, Canon 6		
38581	Gibson, Earl D.	04/27/2002	Bruno, J. J.		
38582	Kozak, Janet M.	05/01/2002	Gregg, W. O. Title III, Canon 9		
38583	Mahon, Laurence F.	05/01/2002	Gregg, W. O. Title III, Canon 6		
38584	Warner, Janet L.	05/01/2002	Gregg, W. O. Title III, Canon 6		
38585	Porter, Elizabeth J. S.	05/03/2002	Fairfield, A. H.	11/23/2002	Fairfield, A. H.
38586	Delaney, Mary T. K.	05/04/2002	Leidel, E. M., Jr.	11/02/2002	Leidel, E. M., Jr.

Serial #	Name	Diaconate Date	Ordaining Bishop	Priesthood Date	Ordaining Bishop
38587	Montague, Cynthia R.	05/04/2002	Shimpfky, R. L.		
38588	Wells, Mary B.	05/04/2002	Title III, Canon 6 Frade, L.		
38589	Stuart, Judith L.	05/09/2002	Title III, Canon 6 Leidel, E. M., Jr.	11/03/2002	Leidel, E. M., Jr.
38590	Anderson, Ann J.	05/10/2002	Fairfield, A. H.		
38591	Brothers, Christy F.	05/10/2002	Title III, Canon 9 Kelshaw, T.		
38592	Crupi, Hilary	05/10/2002	Jacobus, R. E.	12/21/2002	Jacobus, R. E.
38593	Garcia, Margaret J.	05/10/2002	Kelshaw, T.		
38594	Gokey, Mary J.	05/10/2002	Title III, Canon 6 Fairfield, A. H.		
38595	Grabner-Hegg, Linnae M.	05/10/2002	Title III, Canon 6 Fairfield, A. H.		
38596	Williams, G. T. Duffy	05/10/2002	Title III, Canon 9 Fairfield, A. H.		
38597	Cass, Nancy	05/11/2002	Title III, Canon 9 Jefferts Schori, K.		
38598	Wilkinson, Joyce A. M.	05/11/2002	Title III, Canon 6 Maze, L. E.	11/16/2002	Maze, L. E.
38599	Bates, Steven B.	05/16/2002	Parsley, H. N., Jr.		
38600	Auchincloss, R. Anne	05/18/2002	Sisk, M. S.		
38601	Boyle, GeorgeAnne	05/18/2002	Title III, Canon 6 White, R. J.		
38602	Duncan, Daniel L.	05/18/2002	Rowley, R. D., Jr.		

Serial #	Name	Diaconate Date	Ordaining Bishop	Priesthood Date	Ordaining Bishop
38603	Peterson, Frank L., Jr.	05/18/2002	Title III, Canon 6 Sisk, M. S.		
38604	Rowe, Richard C.	05/18/2002	Title III, Canon 6 Rowley, R. D., Jr. Title III, Canon 9	11/17/2002	Rowley, R. D., Jr. Title III, Canon 9
38605	Barker, Lynn K.	05/25/2002	Gray, D. M., III	12/07/2002	Gray, D. M., III
38606	Keene, Ruth C.	05/25/2002	vonRosenberg, C. G.		
38607	Kirkland, Robert G.	05/25/2002	Salmon, E. L., Jr.	12/07/2002	Rowley, R. D., Jr. for Salmon, E. L., Jr.
38608	Parsons, Martha L. T.	05/25/2002	vonRosenberg, C. G.		
38609	Snyder, Gregory A.	05/25/2002	Salmon, E. L., Jr.	12/14/2002	Salmon, E. L., Jr.
38610	Durren, Paula E.	05/26/2002	Lee, E. L., Jr.		
38611	Guinta, Denise G.	05/26/2002	MacDonald, M. L.		
38612	Knight, James D.	05/26/2002	Gray, D. M., III	12/14/2002	Gray, D. M., III
38613	Carey, Thomas P.	05/27/2002	Walker, O. G., Jr.		
38614	Curry, Glenda S.	05/29/2002	Parsley, H. N., Jr.		
38615	Fleming, Philip B., II	05/31/2002	Ackerman, K. L. Title III, Canon 6		
38616	Grotke, Mark D.	05/31/2002	Bruno, J. J.		
38617	Jaynes, Ruth L. M.	05/31/2002	Krotz, J. E.		
38618	Benson, J. Brad	06/01/2002	McKelvey, J. M.		
38619	Brock, Laurie M.	06/01/2002	Duncan, P. M., II		
38620	Bushee, Grant S.	06/01/2002	Swing, W. E. Title III, Canon 6		

CLERGY LIST — APPENDIX

Serial #	Name	Diaconate Date	Ordaining Bishop	Priesthood Date	Ordaining Bishop
38621	Calhoun, Joseph W., Jr.	06/01/2002	Gray, D. M., III	12/28/2002	Gray, D. M., III
38622	Graham, Shirley E. S.	06/01/2002	Lamb, J. A.		
38623	Greene, Margaret C.	06/01/2002	Swing, W. E.	12/07/2002	Swing, W. E.
38624	Harper, Helen O.	06/01/2002	Croneberger, J. P.		
38625	Hoover, Joshua A.	06/01/2002	McKelvey, J. M.		
38626	Hunt, Edward W.	06/01/2002	McKelvey, J. M.	12/07/2002	McKelvey, J. M.
38627	Jensen, Julia K.	06/01/2002	Swing, W. E. Title III, Canon 6		
38628	Kirkley, John L.	06/01/2002	Swing, W. E.	12/07/2002	Swing, W. E.
38629	Kuhlmann, Martha C.	06/01/2002	Swing, W. E.	12/07/2002	Swing, W. E.
38630	Miller, M. Elizabeth S.	06/01/2002	Knudsen, C. A. R.	12/08/2002	Knudsen, C. A. R.
38631	Nefstead, Eric M.	06/01/2002	Swing, W. E.		
38632	Nicholson, Wayne P.	06/01/2002	Swing, W. E.		
38633	Otterburn, Margaret K.	06/01/2002	Croneberger, J. P.	12/07/2002	Brome, R. T. for Croneberger, J. P.
38634	Page, Louisa	06/01/2002	Knudsen, C. A. R.		
38635	Reed, Jeffrey B.	06/01/2002	Swing W. E.	12/07/2002	Swing, W. E.
38636	Sanborn, Calvin F. L.	06/01/2002	Knudsen, C. A. R.	11/24/2002	Knudsen, C. A. R.
38637	Servetas, Linda A.	06/01/2002	Bena, D. J. Title III, Canon 6		
38638	Sever, Cynthia A.	06/01/2002	McKelvey, J. M.	12/14/2002	McKelvey, J. M.
38639	Sloan, Ellen M.	06/01/2002	Croneberger, J. P.	12/07/2002	Croneberger, J. P.
38640	Stiegler, Mark A.	06/01/2002	McKelvey, J. M.		
38641	Tierney, Dennis S.	06/01/2002	Swing, W. E.	12/07/2002	Swing, W. E.

Serial #	Name	Diaconate Date	Ordaining Bishop	Priesthood Date	Ordaining Bishop
38642	Tuttle, Margaret C.	06/01/2002	Croneberger, J. P.		
38643	Vreeland, James L.	06/01/2002	Herzog, D. W.	12/01/2002	Bena, D. J. for Herzog, D. W.
38644	Weber, Dean A.	06/01/2002	Brome, R. T. for Croneberger, J. P.		
38645	Willis, Ronnie W.	06/01/2002	Swing, W. E.	12/07/2002	Swing, W. E.
38646	Anderson, Jon R.	06/02/2002	Bruno, J. J.	12/14/2002	Bruno, J. J.
38647	Cole, Suzanne L.	06/02/2002	Bena, D. J.	12/08/2002	Herzog, D. W.
38648	Hopkins, John L.	06/02/2002	Herzog, D. W.	11/30/2002	Bena, D. J. for Herzog, D. W.
38649	Lewis, Katherine A.	06/02/2002	Bruno, J. J.		
38650	Ridgill, Michael	06/02/2002	Salmon, E. L., Jr.		
38651	Scalise, Margaret M.	06/02/2002	Parsley, H. N., Jr.	12/03/2002	Parsley, H. N., Jr.
38652	Wolfe, Dorothy	06/02/2002	Krotz, J. E. Title III, Canon 6		
38653	Cormeny, Geroge F., III	06/03/2002	Salmon, E. L., Jr.	12/15/2002	Salmon, E. L., Jr.
38654	Lauer, Daniel D.	06/04/2002	Folts, J. E.		
38655	Hurley, Janet	06/06/2002	Bruno, J. J.	12/19/2002	Bruno, J. J.
38656	Allport, William H., II	06/08/2002	Creighton, M. W.		
38657	Anderson, Marilyn L. C.	06/08/2002	Smith, A. D.		
38658	Angerer, John D., Jr.	06/08/2002	Wright, W. P.	12/21/2002	Wright, W. P.
38659	Barrett, John H.	06/08/2002	Stanton, J. M.		
38660	Biggs, Carolyn K.	06/08/2002	Howe, J. W.	12/07/2002	Howe, J. W.
38661	Bowersox, Sally A.	06/08/2002	Winterrowd, W. J.	12/21/2002	Winterrowd, W. J.
38662	Boxill, Lois E. C.	06/08/2002	Alexander, J. N.		
38663	Burnett, Matthew K.	06/08/2002	Winterrowd, W. J.		Winterrowd, W. J.

CLERGY LIST — APPENDIX

Serial #	Name	Diaconate Date	Ordaining Bishop	Priesthood Date	Ordaining Bishop
38664	Cabana, Denise E.	06/08/2002	Smith, A. D.		
38665	Cole, Brian L.	06/08/2002	Johnson, R. H.	12/07/2002	Johnson, R. H.
38666	Cope, Marie S.	06/08/2002	Johnson, R. H.	12/21/2002	Johnson, R. H.
38667	Dalton, Harlon L.	06/08/2002	Smith, A. D.		
38668	D'Anieri, Margaret C.	06/08/2002	Grew, J. C., II	12/14/2002	Williams, A. B., Jr. for Grew, J. C. II
38669	Danson, Michelle A.	06/08/2002	Winterrowd, W. J.		
38670	Dawson, Adrien P.	06/08/2002	Rabb, J. L.		
38671	Dixon, Valerie W.	06/08/2002	Smith, A. D.		
38672	Drennen, Zachary P.	06/08/2002	Klusmeyer, W. M.		
38673	Fleischer, Scott R.	06/08/2002	Howe, J. W. Title III, Canon 9	12/07/2002	Salmon, E. L., Jr. for Howe, J. W. Title III, Canon 9
38674	Frey, Matthew V.	06/08/2002	Winterrowd, W. J.	12/08/2002	Winterrowd, W. J.
38675	Greene-McCreight, Kathryn	06/08/2002	Smith, A. D.		
38676	Grimball, Richard B., Jr.	06/08/2002	Johnson, R. H.	12/14/2002	Johnson, R. H.
38677	Helmer, Richard E.	06/08/2002	Howe, B. R.	12/07/2002	Swing, W. E.
38678	Hofer, Christopher D.	06/08/2002	Williams, A. B., Jr. for Grew, J. C., II	12/11/2002	Grew, J. C., II
38679	Jarrell, Robin C.	06/08/2002	Creighton, M. W.		
38680	Jarvis, Kendron D.	06/08/2002	Alexander, J. N.		
38681	Johnson, Malinda M. E.	06/08/2002	Smith, A. D.	12/14/2002	Smith. A. D.
38682	Jones, Andrew B.	06/08/2002	Rabb, J. L.		
38683	Jones, Jeffrey T.	06/08/2002	Sauls, S. F.		

Serial #	Name	Diaconate Date	Ordaining Bishop	Priesthood Date	Ordaining Bishop
38684	Jones, Jennifer S. H.	06/08/2002	Title III, Canon 9 Stanton, J. M.		
38685	Kennedy, Ellen K.	06/08/2002	Title III, Canon 6 Smith, A. D.		
38686	Kern, Roy A.	06/08/2002	Creighton, M. W.		
38687	Leslie, Joanne	06/08/2002	Title III, Canon 6 Talton, C. L. for Bruno, J. J. Title III, Canon 6		
38688	Lively, James W.	06/08/2002	Howe, J. W.	12/07/2002	Howe, J. W.
38689	McCone, Susan J.	06/08/2002	Smith, A. D.		
38690	McGuire, Mark A.	06/08/2002	Howe, B. R.	12/07/2002	Howe, B. R.
38691	Meroney, Anne E.	06/08/2002	Alexander, J. N.		
38692	Mindrum, Alice A.	06/08/2002	Smith, A. D.	12/14/2002	Smith, A. D.
38693	Mollard, Elizabeth M.	06/08/2002	Creighton, M. W.		
38694	Morley, Richard M.	06/08/2002	Rabb, J. L.		
38695	Motz, Larry L.	06/08/2002	Williams, A. B., Jr. for Grew, J. C., II		
38696	Munroe, Sally G.	06/08/2002	Winterrowd, W. J.	12/14/2002	Winterrowd, W. J.
38697	Musselman, Barbara M.	06/08/2002	Winterrowd, W. J.		
38698	Nusser-Telfer, Hiltrude M.	06/08/2002	Grew, J. C., II	12/18/2002	Grew, J. C., II
38699	Reed, Poulson C., Jr.	06/08/2002	Smith, A. D.		
38700	Rehberg, Gretchen M.	06/08/2002	Creighton, M. W.		
38701	Reynolds, James R.	06/08/2002	Iker, J. L.	12/21/2002	Iker, J. L.
38702	Richards, Emily B.	06/08/2002	Sauls, S. F.		

CLERGY LIST — APPENDIX

Serial #	Name	Diaconate Date	Ordaining Bishop	Priesthood Date	Ordaining Bishop
38703	Schwend, Amy F. P.	06/08/2002	Bruno, J. J.	12/08/2002	Montgomery, J. W. for How. B. R.
38704	Shakespeare, Lyndon C.	06/08/2002	Howe, B. R.		
38705	SmithGraybeal, Felicia S.	06/08/2002	Winterrowd, W. J.		
38706	Speck-Ewer, Nathan S.	06/08/2002	Smith, A. D.		
38707	Spicer, John M.	06/08/2002	Howe, B. R.	12/07/2002	Howe, B. R.
38708	Sten, Pamela V.	06/08/2002	Lee, E. L., Jr.	12/21/2002	Persell, W. D. for Gepert, R. R.
38709	Swiedler, Anne E.	06/08/2002	Alexander, J. N.		
38710	Tennant, Paul J.	06/08/2002	Stanton, J. M. Title III, Canon 6		
38711	Tenny, Claire M.	06/08/2002	Winterrowd, W. J.	12/08/2002	Winterrowd, W. J.
38712	Terry, Eleanor A.	06/08/2002	Smith, A. D.		
38713	Weglarz, Eileen E.	06/08/2002	Creighton, M. W.	12/08/2002	Bena, D. J. for Creighton, M. W.
38714	Weidman, Hal J.	06/08/2002	Lamb, J. A.		
38715	Zifcak, Patricia	06/08/2002	Shaw, M. T., III Title III, Canon 6		
38716	Manning, Gary B.	06/09/2002	Jecko, S. H.	12/14/2002	Gallagher, C. J. for Jecko, S. H.
38717	Ritchie, Harold L.	06/09/2002	Jecko, S. H.		
38718	Barrett, Timothy	06/13/2002	Croneberger, J. P.		
38719	Glover, Beth F.	06/13/2002	Croneberger, J. P.		
38720	Wickham, Jonathan W.	06/13/2002	Folts, J. E.		
38721	Abrahamson, Wendy K.	06/15/2002	Lee, P. J.	12/16/2002	Lee, P. J.

Serial #	Name	Diaconate Date	Ordaining Bishop	Priesthood Date	Ordaining Bishop
38722	Altopp, Whitney F.	06/15/2002	Adams, G. B., III		
38723	Avery, Daniel T.	06/15/2002	Bane, D. C., Jr.		
38724	Baillie, Ronald J.	06/15/2002	Duncan, R. W.	12/23/2002	Duncan, R. W.
38725	Barron, Scott W.	06/15/2002	Persell, W. D.	12/21/2002	Persell, W. D.
38726	Breckenridge, Ella H.	06/15/2002	Hargrove, R. J., Jr.		
38727	Brown, Clifford R.	06/15/2002	Shaw, M. T., III		
38728	Cogill, Richard L.	06/15/2002	Jelinek, J. L.	12/17/2002	Jelinek, J. L.
38729	Conley, Patricia A.	06/15/2002	Persell, W. D.	12/21/2002	Persell, W. D.
38730	Elliott, R. Neil	06/15/2002	Jelinek, J. L.	12/17/2002	Jelinek, J. L.
38731	Famulare, Joseph A.	06/15/2002	Bena, D. J. Title III, Canon 6		
38732	Ferrell, Nathan W.	06/15/2002	Lee, P. J.	12/16/2002	Lee, P. J.
38733	Fiske, Thomas W.	06/15/2002	Jelinek, J. L.	12/17/2002	Jelinek, J. L.
38734	Franklin-Vaughn, Robyn E.	06/15/2002	Shaw, M. T., III		
38735	Gardner, John B.	06/15/2002	Bane, D. C., Jr.	12/15/2002	Gallagher, C. J. for Bane, D. C., Jr.
38736	Gilchrist, Ramsey D.	06/15/2002	Lee, P. J.	12/18/2002	Lee, P. J.
38737	Griffin, Christopher E.	06/15/2002	Persell, W. D.	12/21/2002	Persell, W. D.
38738	Hutchinson, John F., Jr.	06/15/2002	Shaw, M. T., III		
38739	Inscoe, Laura D.	06/15/2002	Lee, P. J.	12/16/2002	Lee, P. J.
38740	Jenkins, Kathryn E.	06/15/2002	Bane, D. C., Jr.	12/18/2002	Gallagher, C. J. for Bane, D. C., Jr.
38741	Kapurch, Linda M.	06/15/2002	Lee, P. J.	12/18/2002	Lee, P. J.
38742	Kennedy, Anne C.	06/15/2002	Adams, G. B., III		

CLERGY LIST APPENDIX

Serial #	Name	Diaconate Date	Ordaining Bishop	Priesthood Date	Ordaining Bishop
38743	Keyse, Andrew C.	06/15/2002	Persell, W. D.	12/21/2002	Persell, W. D.
38744	Koehler, Norman E., III	06/15/2002	Duncan, R. W. Title III, Canon 6		
38745	Lander, Stephen K.	06/15/2002	Jelinek, J. L.	12/17/2002	Jelinek, J. L.
38746	Lawlor, Jay R.	06/15/2002	Shaw, M. T., III		
38747	MacPhail, Alexander D.	06/15/2002	Lee, P. J.	12/16/2002	Lee, P. J.
38748	McCaskill, James C.	06/15/2002	Duncan, R. W.		
38749	Meengs, John R.	06/15/2002	Lee, E. L., Jr. Title III, Canon 6		
38750	Miller, Charles B.	06/15/2002	Bane, D. C., Jr.		
38751	Monson Lutes, Kathleen	06/15/2002	Jelinek, J. L.		
38752	Morris-Kliment, Nicholas M.	06/15/2002	Shaw, M. T., III		
38753	Murray, William M.	06/15/2002	Lee, P. J.	12/18/2002	Lee, P. J.
38754	Neal, Deonna D.	06/15/2002	Chane, J. B.		
38755	Oh, KyungJa	06/15/2002	Persell, W. D.	12/21/2002	Persell, W. D.
38756	Olsen, Christiana	06/15/2002	Shaw, M. T., III		
38757	Reddig, Michael D.	06/15/2002	Lee, P. J.		
38758	Rimer, Kathleen P.	06/15/2002	Shaw, M. T., III		
38759	Russell, Daniel S.	06/15/2002	Duncan, R. W.		
38760	Seles, Deborah G.	06/15/2002	Persell, W. D.	12/21/2002	Persell, W. D.
38761	Shepherd, Stephen G.	06/15/2002	Lee, P. J.	12/18/2002	Lee, P. J.
38762	Siwek, Peter C.	06/15/2002	Persell, W. D.	12/21/2002	Persell, W. D.
38763	Stephens, Paul J.	06/15/2002	Marble, A. C., Jr.		
38764	Walsh, Eileen P.	06/15/2002	Bane, D. C., Jr.		

Serial #	Name	Diaconate Date	Ordaining Bishop	Priesthood Date	Ordaining Bishop
38765	Ward, Mary C. M.	06/15/2002	Persell, W. D.	12/21/2002	Persell, W. D.
38766	Werntz, Pamela L.	06/15/2002	Shaw, M. T., III		
38767	Wheatley-Dyson, Elizabeth	06/15/2002	Shaw, M. T., III		
38768	Wilkinson, Hazel L.	06/15/2002	Duncan, R. W.		
38769	Wilson, Dennis M.	06/15/2002	Duncan, R. W. Title III, Canon 6		
38770	Wong, Diane C. K.	06/15/2002	Shaw, M. T., III		
38771	Wright, Martin L., III	06/15/2002	Duncan, R. W.		
38772	Beebe, Jeffrey S.	06/16/2002	Frade, L.	12/21/2002	Frade, L.
38773	Carling, Paul J.	06/16/2002	Ely, T. C.		
38774	Garwood, Martha J.	06/16/2002	Robertson, C. L. Title III, Canon 6		
38775	Gay, Jean R.	06/16/2002	Frade, L.		
38776	Mesteth, Rhoda Y.	06/16/2002	Robertson, C. L.		
38777	Sweeney, Peter H.	06/16/2002	Bena, D. J. for Herzog, D. W. Title III, Canon 6		
38778	Todd, Christopher H.	06/16/2002	Frade, L. Title III, Canon 9	12/21/2002	Frade, L. Title III, Canon 9
38779	Trainor, Helen C.	06/16/2002	Frade, L. Title III, Canon 6		
38780	Bledsoe, Faith E.	06/18/2002	Ladehoff, R. L.		
38781	Sedlacek, Wesley H.	06/19/2002	Ladehoff, R. L.	12/28/2002	Ladehoff, R. L.
38782	Brown, Scott J.	06/20/2002	Folts, J. E.		
38783	Blaine, Carol M.	06/22/2002	Payne, C. E.		

CLERGY LIST APPENDIX

Serial #	Name	Diaconate Date	Ordaining Bishop	Priesthood Date	Ordaining Bishop
38784	Boyd, Samuel L.	06/22/2002	Payne, C. E.		
38785	Brandon, Miles R., II	06/22/2002	Payne, C. E.		
38786	Britt, T. Diane	06/22/2002	Curry, M. B.		
38787	Butcher, Gerald A.	06/22/2002	Moody, R. M. Title III, Canon 6		
38788	Chrisman, Dale L.	06/22/2002	Payne, C. E.		
38789	Code, David A.	06/22/2002	Joslin, D. B.		
38790	Cooke, Barbara J.	06/22/2002	Curry, M. B.		
38791	Crompton, Sherry A.	06/22/2002	Bennison, C. E., Jr.		
38792	Doar, Katherine B.	06/22/2002	Shimpfky, R. L.		
38793	Garland, John G., III	06/22/2002	Payne, C. E.		
38794	Hawley, Elizabeth L.	06/22/2002	Shimpfky, R. L.		
38795	Himes, John M.	06/22/2002	Payne, C. E.		
38796	James, Edmund L.	06/22/2002	Moody, R. M. Title III, Canon 6		
38797	Jensen, Jan D.	06/22/2002	Payne, C. E.		
38798	Johnson, Janet H.	06/22/2002	Joslin, D. B.	12/21/2002	Joslin, D. B.
38799	Kennedy, Matthew M.	06/22/2002	Payne, C. E.	12/22/2002	Adams, G. B., III
38800	Koonce, Kelly M.	06/22/2002	Payne, C. E.		
38801	Malia, Linda M.	06/22/2002	Garrison, J. M.		
38802	Mettler, Garrett M.	06/22/2002	Shimpfky, R. L.		
38803	Mitchell, Karin R.	06/22/2002	Joslin, D. B.	12/21/2002	Joslin, D. B.
38804	Morales-Dennis, Chantal B.	06/22/2002	Curry, M. B.		
38805	Morehouse, Timothy L.	06/22/2002	Bennison, C. E., Jr.		

Serial #	Name	Diaconate Date	Ordaining Bishop	Priesthood Date	Ordaining Bishop
38806	Nunez, Carlos E.	06/22/2002	Ladehoff, R. L.	12/22/2002	Ladehoff, R. L.
38807	Parker, Dennis J.	06/22/2002	Ladehoff, R. L.		
38808	Phillips, A. William, III	06/22/2002	Payne, C. E.		
38809	Potts, Kathleen K.	06/22/2002	Marble, A. C., Jr.		
38810	Schutte, Christopher M.	06/22/2002	Shahan, R. R.		
38811	Scott, C. Sue M.	06/22/2002	Payne, C. E.		
38812	Smedley, Walter, IV	06/22/2002	Bennison, C. E., Jr.		
38813	Watson, Suzanne E.	06/22/2002	Shimpfky, R. L.		
38814	White, R. Ellen	06/22/2002	Powell, F. N.		
38815	Williams, John F., II	06/22/2002	Shimpfky, R. L.		
38816	Wilson, Gregory M.	06/22/2002	Bennison, C. E., Jr.		
38817	Wilson, Jill M. L.	06/22/2002	Bennison, C. E., Jr.		
38818	Wratten, Kenneth B.	06/22/2002	Shimpfky, R. L.		
38819	Meister, Deborah A.	06/23/2002	Bruno, J. J.	12/14/2002	Bruno, J. J.
38820	Robinson, Sybil C. F.	06/23/2002	White, R. J. Title III, Canon 6		
38821	Nelson, Benjamin H., III	06/24/2002	Folts, J. E.		
38822	Baker, Kim T.	06/26/2002	Folts, J. E.		
38823	Allen, John M.	06/29/2002	Warner, V. W., Jr.	12/07/2002	Swing, W. E. for Warner, V. W., Jr.
38824	Armstrong, Warren B.	06/29/2002	Moody, R. M.		
38825	Back, Nathaniel L.	06/29/2002	Moody, R. M.		
38826	Bessler, Jeffrey L.	06/29/2002	Waynick, C. M.		
38827	Cona, Robin P.	06/29/2002	Beckwith, P. H.		

CLERGY LIST — APPENDIX

Serial #	Name	Diaconate Date	Ordaining Bishop	Priesthood Date	Ordaining Bishop
38828	Dean, Susan C.	06/29/2002	Hampton, S. Z. K.		
38829	Doherty, Maureen C.	06/29/2002	Moody, R. M.		
38830	Dyche, Bradley C.	06/29/2002	Moody, R. M.		
38831	Feltner, Allan L.	06/29/2002	Beckwith, P. H.		
			Title III, Canon 6		
38832	Hudson, Kimberly	06/29/2002	Curry, M. B.		
			Title III, Canon 6		
38833	Kenney, Christine S.	06/29/2002	Moody, R. M.		
38834	King, Karen L.	06/29/2002	Waynick, C. M.		
38835	Moon, Mary L.	06/29/2002	Warner, V. W., Jr.		
			Title III, Canon 6		
38836	Morris, Cecelia G.	06/29/2002	Warner, V. W., Jr.		
			Title III, Canon 6		
38837	Newman, Ryan D.	06/29/2002	Bruno, J. J.		
38838	Ousley, David K.	06/29/2002	Herzog, D. W.		
			Title III, Canon 6		
38839	Peppler, Connie J.	06/29/2002	Waynick, C. M.		
38840	Poirier, Esther H.	06/29/2002	Hampton, S. Z. K.		
38841	Randall, Paul R.	06/29/2002	Lamb, J. A.	12/21/2002	Lamb, J. A.
38842	Reddall, Jennifer A.	06/29/2002	Bruno, J. J.		
38843	Rozendaal, Jay C.	06/29/2002	Hampton, S. Z. K.		
38844	Smith, Steven R.	06/29/2002	Bruno, J. J.		
38845	Walthall, Charles L.	06/29/2002	Beckwith, P. H.		
38846	Way, Gary L.	06/29/2002	Beckwith, P. H.		

Serial #	Name	Diaconate Date	Ordaining Bishop	Priesthood Date	Ordaining Bishop
38847	LaVine, Patricia I.	06/30/2002	Herzog, D. W.		
38848	Austin, Henry W.	07/05/2002	Title III, Canon 6 Krotz, J. E.		
38849	Arnold, William S. M., Jr.	07/07/2002	Title III, Canon 6 Jefferts Schori, K.		
38850	Warner, John S.	07/09/2002	Louttit, H. I., Jr.		
38851	Anderson, Carolyn K.	07/10/2002	Louttit, H. I., Jr. Title III, Canon 6		
38852	Adams-Riley, Gena D.	07/11/2002	Irish, C. T.		
38853	Sunderland, Melanie J.	07/11/2002	Irish, C. T.		
38854	Winter, Brian W.	07/11/2002	Irish, C. T.		
38855	Rose, Joy A.	07/13/2002	Whitmore, K. B.		
38856	Koskela, Robert N.	07/20/2002	White, R. J.		
38857	Koskela, Ruth A.	07/20/2002	White, R. J.		
38858	Montes, Elizabeth	07/27/2002	Kelshaw, T.		
38859	Rohlff, Deborah L.	07/29/2002	Strickland, V. E. for Caldwell, B. E. Title III, Canon 9		
38860	Tweedale, David L.	07/31/2002	Winterrowd, W. J.		
38861	Windsor, Janice R.	07/31/2002	Winterrowd, W. J. Title III, Canon 6		
38862	Jones, Kevin H.	08/02/2002	Strickland, V. E. for Caldwell, B. E.		
38863	Abbott, Gary L., Sr.	08/03/2002	Louttit, H. I., Jr.		
38864	Butin, John M.	08/03/2002	Louttit, H. I., Jr.		

CLERGY LIST APPENDIX

Serial #	Name	Diaconate Date	Ordaining Bishop	Priesthood Date	Ordaining Bishop
38865	LeFavi, Robert G.	08/03/2002	Louttit, H. I., Jr.		
38866	Thompson, Elena	08/03/2002	Louttit, H. I., Jr.		
38867	Campbell, Linda J. M.	08/10/2002	Lamb, J. A.		
X-38868	Lee, Daniel C. J.	08/24/2002	Lai, D. J. H.		
38869	Grabher, Jerald	08/28/2002	Howe, B. R.		
			Title III, Canon 6		
38870	Findley, Christopher G.	08/29/2002	Herlong, B. N.		
38871	Gilson, Christine M. W.	08/31/2002	Adams, J. M., Jr.		
38872	Wills, Edwin F., Jr.	08/31/2002	Maze, L. E.		
38873	Hacker, Craig A.	09/07/2002	Herzog, D. W.		
38874	Hupf, Jeffrey L.	09/07/2002	Bena, D. J. for Herzog, D. W.		
38875	North, Jay	09/08/2002	Bena, D. J. for Herzog, D. W.		
38876	Wilde, Glenn H.	09/08/2002	Smalley, W. E.		
			Title III, Canon 6		
38877	Allen-Herron, Dawn	09/14/2002	MacDonald, M. L.		
38878	Childs, Julie B.	09/14/2002	Salmon, E. L., Jr.		
			Title III, Canon 6		
38879	Gadden, James J.	09/14/2002	Ackerman, K. L.		
			Title III, Canon 6		
38880	Holmes, William H.	09/14/2002	Salmon, E. L., Jr.		
			Title III, Canon 6		
38881	Tata, Suzanne	09/14/2002	Salmon, E. L., Jr.		
			Title III, Canon 6		
38882	Hoster, Elizabeth M.	09/19/2002	Klusmeyer, W. M.		

Serial #	Name	Diaconate Date	Ordaining Bishop	Priesthood Date	Ordaining Bishop
38883	Miller, Eric L.	09/19/2002	Klusmeyer, W. M.		
38884	Moyer, Laureen M. H.	09/19/2002	Klusmeyer, W. M.		
38885	Mulford, Marie L.	09/19/2002	Klusmeyer, W. M.		
38886	Brunson, Catherine E. F.	09/21/2002	Title III, Canon 9		
38887	Byrer, Johnine V.	09/21/2002	Joslin, D. B.		
38888	Clark, Frances M. A.	09/21/2002	Title III, Canon 6		
38889	Clarke, Debra M.	09/21/2002	Joslin, D. B.		
38890	Krieger, Kristen S.	09/21/2002	Title III, Canon 6		
38891	Marques, Judith L.	09/21/2002	Joslin, D. B.		
38892	Spoor, Cornelia P.	09/21/2002	Title III, Canon 6		
38893	Sweeny, Thomas E.	09/21/2002	Joslin, D. B.		
38894	Zimmerschied, Jill W.	09/21/2002	Title III, Canon 6		
38895	Barker, Christine D.	10/05/2002	Caldwell, B. E.		
38896	Haake, Gilbert M.	10/05/2002	Title III, Canon 9		
			Shahan, R. R.		
			Title III, Canon 6		
			Shahan, R. R.		

CLERGY LIST APPENDIX

Serial #	Name	Diaconate Date	Ordaining Bishop	Priesthood Date	Ordaining Bishop
38897	Johnson, Ann E. S.	10/05/2002	Title III, Canon 6 Shahan, R. R.		
38898	Meyers, Michael W.	10/05/2002	Title III, Canon 6 Shahan, R. R.		
38899	Rowles, S. Paul	10/05/2002	Title III, Canon 6 Lee, P. J.		
38900	Smith, James A.	10/05/2002	Shahan, R. R.		
38901	Symington, Ann P.	10/05/2002	Title III, Canon 6 Shahan, R. R.		
38902	Morrigan, Johanna V. S.	10/06/2002	Title III, Canon 6 Swenson, D. L. for Jelinek, J. L.		
38903	Carlson, Carl B.	10/09/2002	Title III, Canon 6 Kelsey, J. A.		
38904	Colbert, Paul A.	10/11/2002	Title III, Canon 9 Jefferts Schori, K.		
38905	Erquiaga, Trudel N.	10/11/2002	Jefferts Schori, K.		
38906	Loya, Craig W.	10/11/2002	Robertson, C. L.		
38907	Banks, Patricia A.	10/12/2002	Iker, J. L.		
38908	McCown, Sandra W.	10/12/2002	Title III, Canon 6 Iker, J. L.		
38909	Monastiere, Sally M.	10/12/2002	Title III, Canon 6 Bruno, J. J.		
38910	Slaughter, Susan E.	10/12/2002	Iker, J. L. Title III, Canon 6		

Serial #	Name	Diaconate Date	Ordaining Bishop	Priesthood Date	Ordaining Bishop
38911	Smith, Betty	10/13/2002	Kelsey, J. A. Title III, Canon 9		
38912	Maloney, Linda M.	10/15/2002	Jelinek, J. L.		
38913	Monson, Scott B.	10/15/2002	Jelinek, J. L.		
38914	Waters, Margaret H.	10/19/2002	Wimberly, D. A.		
38915	Platt, Gretchen M.	10/20/2002	Leidel, E. M., Jr. Title III, Canon 6		
38916	Daly, Joseph E.	10/26/2002	Herzog, D. W.		
38917	Denton, Edna M.	10/26/2002	Thompson, H., Jr. Title III, Canon 6		
38918	Heller, Richard C.	10/26/2002	Thompson, H., Jr.		
38919	Kramer, Katherine F.	10/26/2002	Thompson, H., Jr.		
38920	Lubin, Gary R.	10/26/2002	Thompson, H., Jr. Title III, Canon 6		
38921	Maree, Donna L.	10/26/2002	Thompson, H., Jr.		
38922	Reade, John M., IV	10/26/2002	Thompson, H., Jr.		
38923	Schisler, Richard T.	10/26/2002	Thompson, H., Jr. Title III, Canon 6		
38924	Schisler, Sallie C.	10/26/2002	Thompson, H., Jr. Title III, Canon 6		
38925	Stewart-Sicking, Megan E.	10/26/2002	Thompson, H., Jr.		
38926	Talk, John G., IV	10/26/2002	Thompson, H., Jr.		
38927	Thompson, Owen C.	10/26/2002	Thompson, H., Jr.		
38928	Tierney, Bridget K.	10/26/2002	Thompson, H., Jr.		

CLERGY LIST — APPENDIX

Serial #	Name	Diaconate Date	Ordaining Bishop	Priesthood Date	Ordaining Bishop
38929	Burns, Thomas	10/27/2002	Ohl, C. W., Jr. Title III, Canon 6		
38930	Byrd, Janice L.	10/27/2002	Ohl, C. W., Jr. Title III, Canon 6		
38931	Fowler, Conetta B.	10/27/2002	Ohl, C. W., Jr. Title III, Canon 6		
38932	Marshall, John H.	10/27/2002	Ohl, C. W., Jr. Title III, Canon 6		
38933	Robertson, Karen S.	10/27/2002	Wimberly, D. A.		
38934	Vaughn, Jessie H.	10/27/2002	Ohl, C. W., Jr. Title III, Canon 6		
38935	Seitz, Philip A.	11/2/2002	Leidel, E. M., Jr.		
38936	Hoekstra, Robert B.	11/07/2002	Whitmore, K. B.		
38937	Johnson, Ronald A.	11/07/2002	Whitmore, K. B.		
38938	Beecher, Josephine C.	11/09/2002	Warner, V. W., Jr.		
38939	Perdue, Thomas H.	11/09/2002	Jones, D. C. for Duncan, R. W.		
38940	Shecter, Teri A.	11/09/2002	Winterrowd, W. J. Title III, Canon 6		
38941	Stockton, Marietta G.	11/09/2002	Adams, J. M., Jr.		
38942	Weir, Silas M.	11/09/2002	Winterrowd, W. J. Title III, Canon 6		
38943	Slakey, Anne-Elisa M.	11/16/2002	White, R. J.		
38944	Muller, Thomas G.	11/17/2002	Whalon, P. W.		
38945	Fuller, Steven G., Sr.	11/19/2002	Ely, T. C.		

Serial #	Name	Diaconate Date	Ordaining Bishop	Priesthood Date	Ordaining Bishop
38946	Horvath, Victor J.	11/19/2002	Title III, Canon 9 Ely, T. C.		
38947	Barry, Eugenia C. M.	11/23/2002	Title III, Canon 9 Johnson, R. H.		
38948	Beschta, Gerald T.	11/23/2002	Title III, Canon 6 Johnson, R. H.		
38949	Calloway, N. Laine	11/23/2002	Title III, Canon 6 Johnson, R. H.		
38950	Fritschner, Ann R.	11/23/2002	Title III, Canon 6 Johnson, R. H.		
38951	Hilliard, Robert G.	11/23/2002	Title III, Canon 6 Schofield, J.-D.		
38952	Jones, Blandford B., II	11/23/2002	Title III, Canon 6 Schofield, J.-D.		
38953	Kovach, Gary D.	11/23/2002	Title III, Canon 6 Johnson, R. H.		
38954	Loudenslager, Samuel C.	11/23/2002	Title III, Canon 6 Maze, L. E.		
38955	McDaniel, Elna I.	11/23/2002	Title III, Canon 6 Whitmore, K. B.		
38956	Neckels, Arlen G.	11/23/2002	Title III, Canon 6 Schofield, J.-D.		
38957	Williams, Jane R. F.	11/23/2002	Title III, Canon 6 Hughes, G. B. for Schofield, J.-D.		

CLERGY LIST APPENDIX

Serial #	Name	Diaconate Date	Ordaining Bishop	Priesthood Date	Ordaining Bishop
38958	Darmour, Myron T.	11/24/2002	Title III, Canon 6		
38959	Haase, Sylvia A.	11/30/2002	Winterrowd, W. J. Title III, Canon 9		
38960	Hall, Mavis	11/30/2002	Hampton, S. Z. K. Title III, Canon 9		
38961	Henault, Rita L.	11/30/2002	Krotz, J. E.		
38962	Logan, Christie L.	11/30/2002	Smalley, W. E. Hampton, S. Z. K. Title III, Canon 9		
38963	Neal, James F.	11/30/2002	Hampton, S. Z. K. Title III, Canon 9		
38964	Trees, Thomas H.	11/30/2002	Bena, D. J. for Herzog, D. W.		
38965	Bunting, Michael A.	12/6/2002	Frade, L. for Henderson, D. F., Jr.		
38966	Benesh, Jimi W. B.	12/07/2002	Swing, W. E.		
38967	Ekstrom, Ellen L.	12/07/2002	Swing, W. E.		
38968	Heron, Marsha S.	12/07/2002	Swing, W. E. Title III, Canon 6		
38969	Kwiatkowski, Janet M.	12/07/2002	White, R. J. Title III, Canon 6		
38970	Pain, Mary R.	12/07/2002	White, R. J. Title III, Canon 6		
38971	Ross, David J.	12/07/2002	Swing, W. E. Title III, Canon 6		

Serial #	Name	Diaconate Date	Ordaining Bishop	Priesthood Date	Ordaining Bishop
38972	Williams, Christina H. E.	12/07/2002	Swing, W. E.		
38973	Bousfield, Nigel J.	12/14/2002	Title III, Canon 6		
38974	Carroll, Roland W.	12/14/2002	Ackerman, K. L.		
38975	Dorn, James M., III	12/14/2002	Henderson, D. F., Jr.		
38976	Ewing, Judith L.	12/14/2002	Henderson, D. F., Jr.		
38977	Granger, Nancy W.	12/14/2002	Henderson, D. F., Jr.		
			Title III, Canon 6		
			Howe, J. W.		
38978	Gwyn, Lewis R., III	12/14/2002	Title III, Canon 6		
38979	Harres, Elisa P.	12/14/2002	Howe, J. W.		
38980	Hazel, Dorothy M.	12/14/2002	Title III, Canon 6		
			Duncan, R. W.		
			Henderson, D. F., Jr.		
38981	Johnson, Shirley M.	12/14/2002	Title III, Canon 6		
			Howe, J. W.		
38982	Mill, John W.	12/14/2002	Title III, Canon 6		
			Henderson, D. F., Jr.		
38983	Parlier, Susan T.	12/14/2002	Title III, Canon 6		
			Henderson, D. F., Jr.		
38984	Pemberton, Barbara L.	12/14/2002	Title III, Canon 6		
			Howe, J. W.		
38985	Ray, Andrew M.	12/14/2002	Title III, Canon 6		
38986	Spencer, Patricia A.	12/14/2002	Duncan, R. W.		
			Howe, J. W.		
			Title III, Canon 6		

Serial #	Name	Diaconate Date	Ordaining Bishop	Priesthood Date	Ordaining Bishop
38987	Thompson, Carol A.	12/14/2002	Howe, J. W. Title III, Canon 6		
38988	Reger, Timothy S.	12/15/2002	Adams, G. B, III		
38989	Wiesner, Kurt C.	12/15/2002	Williams, A. B, Jr. for Grew, J. C, II		
38990	Billman, Sharon L.	12/21/2002	Smalley, W. E. Title III, Canon 9		
38991	Dieter, David D.	12/21/2002	Gibbs, W. N., Jr.		
38992	Parris, Cheryl A. E.	12/21/2002	Garrison, J. M.		
38993	Salles, Stacy D.	12/21/2002	Gibbs, W. N., Jr.		
38994	Jones, Irene C.	12/27/2002	Smith, G. W.		
38995	Rectenwald, Marion B.	12/27/2002	Smith, G. W.		
38996	Rhodes, Robert R.	12/27/2002	Smith, G. W.		
38997	Easterling, Richard B., Jr.	12/28/2002	Jenkins, C. E., III		
38998	Heine, William A. J., Jr.	12/28/2002	Jenkins, C. E., III		
38999	Smith, Vickie M.	12/28/2002	Jenkins, C. E., III		
39000	St. Romain, John B.	12/28/2002	Jenkins, C. E., III		
39001	Terry, William H.	12/28/2002	Jenkins, C. E., III		

ALPHABETICAL LISTING OF CLERGY INCLUDED IN THIS REPORT

Note: *All serial numbers prior to 37644 are ordinations to the Priesthood; others are to the Diaconate. An "X" before a number indicates an ordination to a foreign jurisdiction. An "A" after a number indicates late notification of an Ordination.*

Bishops' names are in full capitals and their numbers refer to their order of consecration. Other section references are:

Dep:	Deposition/Renunciation/Release/Removal
Rec'd:	Reception
Rest:	Restoration
Susp:	Suspension
Trans:	Transfer

A

Aalan, Joshua C. 38042
Abbott, Gary L., Sr. 38863
Abeyaratne, K. Anoma 38147
Abrahamson, Wendy K. 38721
Adams, Daniel W. 38266
Adams, David R. 32819 Rest
Adams, Sheryl L. 38484
Adams-Riley, Gena D. 38852
Addiego, Jeffrey C. 38143
Addison, Orlando J. 37707
Adney, John G. 38104
Akinkugbe, Felix O. Rec'd
Albano, Randolph V. N. Rec'd
Alexander, Patricia A. P. 38090
Alexandre, Hickman 37930
Allen, Barbara A. 37885
Allen, Christopher C. 38108
Allen, Diogenes 38374
Allen, John M. 38823
Allen, Patrick S. 37939
Allen, Philip C. 23263 Rest
Allen-Herron, Dawn 38877
Alleyne, Edmund T. Rec'd
Allport, William H., II 38656
Alston, Phyliss M. 38192
Altopp, Whitney F. 38722
Ambler, Michael N., Jr. 37553
Amburgey, Christina G. 38316
Amiott, William K. 31683 Dep
Ananshekhar, Joseph Rec'd
Andersen, Paul J. 28188 Rest
Anderson, Ann J. 38590
Anderson, Carolyn K. 38851
Anderson, David T. 37886
Anderson, Jon R. 38646
Anderson, Judith K. F. 37977
Anderson, Kenneth E. 38363
Anderson, Marilyn L. C. 38657
Anderson-Krengel, W. Erich 38193
Andrews, Patricia M, 37887
Angerer, John D., Jr. 38658
Anschutz, Maryetta M. 38443
Anthony, Karen L. 35170 Dep
Antoci, Peter M. 38194
Appel, Charles W., Jr. 28575 Dep
Arents, Gina 38148
Armstrong, Elizabeth 38195
Armstrong, Warren B. 38824
Arndt, Cindy L. 37941
Arnold, James O. 35817 Dep
Arnold, Kimball C. 37978
Arnold, William S. M., Jr. 38849
Arps, Joseph W., Jr. 26913 Dep
Ashcroft, Mary E. 38494
Ashley, Beverley B. 37979
Atkins, John T. Rec'd Dep
Auchincloss, R. Anne 38600
Austin, Henry W. 38848
Avery, Daniel T. 38723
Ayala-Porfil, Eugenio Rec'd

B

Babcock, Theodore S. 38196
Back, Nathaniel L. 38825
Bailey, Anne C. 38149
Bailey, David B. 37888
Bailey, William K., Jr. 31355 Dep
Baillie, Ronald J. 38724
Baird, Gary C. 38005
Baker, Joseph S. 37962
Baker, Kim T. 38822
Baker, Susan E. 37652
Bakker, Cheryl A. 38468
Baldwin, Robert E. 38412
Balius, Valerie A. 37730
Ballinger, Kathryn E. 37937
Banks, Patricia A. 38907
Barber, Grethe 38521
Barbour, Carroll C. 21062 Dep
Barfield, DeOla E. J. 38026
Barker, Christine D. 38895
Barker, Kenneth L. 28676 Susp
Barker, Lynn K. 38605
Barnes, Susan J. 38267
Baron, Stephen A. 38053
Barrett, John H. 38659
Barrett, Patricia R. 37794
Barrett, S. Dawn Rec'd
Barrett, Timothy 38718
Barron, Carol D. 38268
Barron, Scott W. 38725
Barrows, Jennifer E. M. 38091
Barry, Eugenia C. M. 38947
Bartholomew, A. Gilbert L. 38413
Barwick, Frederick E., III 38262
Bassett, John W. 38197
Bates, Steven B. 38599
Bates, Thomas J. 38364
Bauer, Lee F. 38396
Bauman, Dwayne R. 37889
Bawtree, Andrew J. Rec'd
Baxter, Donald L. 38576
Beasley, Nicholas M. 37963
Beauvoir, Oge Rec'd
Becker, C. S. Honey 38360
Becker, Kimberly L. 37890
Beebe, Jeffrey S. 38772
Beecham, Troy C. 38535
Beecher, Josephine C. 38938
Behrel, Kenneth K. 28678 Dep
Bell, Katherine A, 38043
Bell, Susan E. W. 38317
Benesh, Jimi W. B. 38966
Bennett, JoAnne 38454
Bennett, Pattiann B. 38408
Benson, J. Brad 38618
Bergner, Mario J. 38082
Berman, Elizabeth E. S. 38150
Bernacchi, Jacqueline A. 38080
Bernardi, Frank A. 38377
Bertolozzi, Michael A. 37968
Beschta, Gerald T. 38948
Beshears, Earl D. 38115
Bessler, Jeffrey L. 38826
Bessette, Theodore A. 16355 Dep
Betts, Susan E. 37795
Bevans, Marjorie S. 37754
Bezilla, Gregory A. 38151
Bianchi, Mary E. 37700
Biggs, Carolyn K. 38660
Bignall, Alton K. 37683
Billman, Sharon L. 38990
Binder, Thomas F. 38070
Bird, John E., Jr. 25185 Susp
Bird, Peter R. 37881
Black, Milton E., Jr. 37870
Black-Graham, Rebecca L. 37731
Blaine, Carol M. 38783
Blake, Thomas W., Jr. 37891
Blakelock, Douglas P. 38513
Bledsoe, Faith E. 38780
Boardman, William A. 16278 Trans
Bobo, Melinda D. 38313
Bodishbaugh, C. Conlee 32471 Dep
Boline, Travis S. 37847
Bonadie, L. Rowland 37987
Bond, Michael D. 37663
Boone, Connie L. 38511
Bordador, Noel E. 38092
Borden, Robert B. 38002
Bostick-Bearden, Jane G. 38403
Bourhill, John W. 38116
Bousfield, Nigel J. 38973
Boutros, Gail A. 37954
Bowden, Gloria D. 38198

Bowden, Talmadge A., Jr. 38397
Bowden, Teresa N. T. 38303
Bowers, George F. 38073
Bowersox, Sally A. 38661
Bowman, Andrea C. 37945
Boxill, Lois E. C. 38662
Boyd, Samuel L. 38784
Boyle, GeorgeAnne 38601
Boynton, Caroline C. 38117
Brackett, Thomas L. 38318
Braden, Anita L. H. 38077
Bradford, Lawrence J. 38199
Bradford, Lyman P. 38056
Bradley, Patrick J. 37709
Bradshaw, Kenneth E. 32763 Dep
Bradshaw, Tommy J. 38580
Brambila, Gerardo E. 38152
Branche, Ronald C. W. Rec'd
Brandenburg, Marilyn J. 37892
Brandon, Miles R., II 38785
Brauza, Ellen L. 38071
Breckenridge, Ella H. 38726
Brenmark-French, Regina 38074
Breyer, Chloe A. 37796
Bridges, Nancy K. 38269
Britt, Frances M. 34451 Trans
Britt, T. Diane 38786
Britton, Judith A. 38357
Brock, Jane C. K. 38200
Brock, Laurie M. 38619
Brockmann, Sarah J. 37711
Brodie, R. Gerald A. Rec'd Trans
Brookman, Cathleen A. 37664
Brothers, Christy F. 38591
Brower, Anne C. 38201
Brown, Clifford R. 38727
Brown, David A. 38095
Brown, Dewey E., Jr. 38202
Brown, Gregory B. F. 38153
Brown, J. Robert 26582 Dep
Brown, Lydia A. H. 38495
Brown, Nancy E. 37927
Brown, Nancy E. N. 37893
Brown, Robert H. 32344 Dep
Brown, Rosalind 36727 Trans
Brown, Scott J. 38782
Brown-Watson, Rosa M. Rec'd

Brownridge, Walter B. A. 37894
Brunson, Catherine E. F. 38886
Bryan, David C. 30625 Trans
Bryan, Robert J. Rec'd Trans
Bryant, Peter F. 38469
Buettner, Andrea J. 37797
Bundrock, Bonnie R. 38388
Bunting, Michael A. 38965
Bunyan, Grace V. 38203
Burch, Suzanne 38486
Burkett, William B. 38556
Burn, Kathleen D. 30335 Dep
Burnett, Matthew K. 38663
Burnham, Karen L. 38017
Burns, Deborah S. 38497
Burns, Thomas 38929
Bush, Emilie C. H. 38204
Bushee, Grant S. 38620
Busse, Mary R. 37848
Butcher, Gerald A. 38787
Butin, John M. 38864
Butler, Keith W. 37958
Bwechwa, Oswald D. Rec'd/Susp
Byer, Martha A. 38526
Byers, Mark H. 38205
Byrd, Janice L. 38930
Byrer, Johnine V. 38887

C

Cabana, Denise E. 38664
Cage, Stewart B., Jr. 37969
Calderhead, C. C. 37024 Trans
Calhoun, Joseph W., Jr. 38621
Calhoun, Judson J. 38536
Calloway, N. Laine 38949
Campbell, Karen A. 37646
Campbell, Linda J. M. 38867
Carey, Thomas P. 38613
Caridad, Jon A. 24853 Dep
Carling, Paul J. 38773
Carlson, Carl B. 38903
Carlson, Carol E. 37871
Carlson, Katherine A. 37798
Carlson, Philip L. 38424
Carlson, R. Bryant 37895
Carlson, William A. 37665
Carlsono-Scholer, Linda M. 38154
Carmody, Alison C. 37755

Carney, Vinnie L. 38025
Carpenter, Charles M. 37896
Carr, Dale R. 38270
Carr, Spencer D. 37799
Carrier, Harold D. 38206
Carroll, Charles P. 21166 Dep
Carroll, Roland W. 38974
Cass, Nancy 38597
Catania, Jason A. 37732
Catinella, Gayle L. 38485
Cavaliere, Denise B. 37988
Chambers, Rex N. 37653
Chandler, Susan E. 38365
Chaney, John P. Rec'd
Chang, Ling-Ling X-38006
Chapman, Hugh W. Rec'd
Chappell, Veronica D. 37789
Charles, Kathleen J. 38207
Chavez, Velma 38378
Chess, Jean D. 37800
Childs, Julie B. 38878
Chrisman, Dale J. 38788
Christian, William K., III 31915 Dep
Christoffersen, Timothy R. 38155
Christopher, E. Kathleen 38444
Ciesel, Barbara (Bitsey) 37862
Cimijotti, Jerry A. 37801
Civetta, Heath H. 37872
Clark, Cheryl L. 38498
Clark, Frances M. A. 38888
Clark, J. David 30527 Rest/Dep
Clark, Johnny W. 37756
Clark, Margaret A. P. 38131
Clark, Philip G. 24430 Dep
Clark, Ralph O. 38271
Clarke, Carlton C. Rec'd
Clarke, Deborah 38889
Clarke, Enrique E. X-32617 Dep
Clarke, John D. B. 38118
Clarke, Michael A. Rec'd
Clausen, Kathryn P. 38007
Cleeve, Admire W. Rec'd
Clement, Betty C. 38491
Clifton, Stephen G. 30839 Susp
Close, LeRoy S. 37716
Cocke, Reagan W. 37946
Code, David A. 38789

Cogill, Richard L. 38728
Colbert, Paul A. 38904
Cole, Allan H. 38044
Cole, Brian L. 38665
Cole, Christopher K. 23395 Susp/Dep
Cole, Mark R. 33210 Dep
Cole, Suzanne L. 38647
Coleman, James P. 30813 Susp
Coleman, Kim L. 38319
Collins, Wayne C. 30140 Dep
Colyn, Robert, Sr. 37661
Cona, Robin P. 38827
Condron, Thomas W. 38272 Dec
Conley, Constance R. 38320
Conley, Patricia A. 38729
Conner, Lu-Anne 38321
Conner, Martha A. H. 37757
Conrads, Alexandra K. 38322
Cook, Catherine E. 38208
Cook, Kenneth R. 31224 Susp/Dep
Cook, Paul R. Rec'd
Cook, Susanna R. 38470
Cooke, Barbara J. 38790
Cooper, Paul A. 38027
Cope, Marie S. 38666
Corbett, Ian D. Rec'd
Corkern, Matthew T. L. 38323
Corley, Kathryn S. 37685
Cormeny, George F., III 38653
Coulter, Sherry L. 38045
Craig, Eric J. 38465
Craig, Idalia S. 37717
Crane, Susan H. 38324
Critchfield, Margot D. 38209
Crompton, Sherry A. 38791
Croom, James 38156
Crupi, Hilary 38592
Cunningham, Jeunee J. 37897
Curl, James F. 38471
Curry, Glenda S. 38614
Curtin, Anne F. 38210
Custer, R. Dale 37733
D
Dagg, Margaret K. 38557
Dailey, Harry E. 37758
Daley, Joy A. 38211
Daly, Joseph E. 38916

Dalton, Harlon l. 38667
Dalton, William T. 23237 Rest
Dambrot, Donna L. 37718
Dandridge, Robert F. 37679
Daniel, Wilfred A. Rec'd
D'Anieri, Margaret C. 38668
Danitschek, Thomas K. 38212
Danson, Michelle A. 38669
Darmour, Myron T. 38958
Daubert, Sharon A. 38119
Davis, Gail E. 38096
Davis, M. Scott 29824 Dep
Davis, Patrick M. 30532 Dep
Davis, R. Jonathan 38089
Davis, Vicki M. 38213
Davis-Heller, Lisa 38399
Dawson, Adrien P. 38670
Dean, Susan C. 38828
Deetz, Susan M. 38304
Deihle, Lawrence C. 38214
Delamater, Joan P. 38496
Delaney, Mary T. K. 38586
Deleuse, Betsey W. 38455
Deming, Nancy J. 37898
DeMontmollin, Dolores A. 38273
den Blaauwen, Edward A. Rec'd
Denton, Edna M. 38917
Denton, Marie A. 38438
Derbyshsire, James W. 38522
DeWees, Herbert R. 37759
DeYoung, Lily A. 37802
Diamond, Daryl E. 28186 Dep
Dickinson, Garrin W. 38437
Dickson, Patricia J. 38445
DiCristina, Mark J. 31806 Dep
Diely, Elizabeth B. H. 38420
Dieter, David D. 38991
Dingman, Joel A. 37947
DiNunno, Lisa 37390 Susp
Dinwiddie, Philip M. 38499
Dixon, Don M. 22179 Dep
Dixon, Valerie W. 38671
Doar, Katherine B. 38792
Doctor, Virginia C. 37951
Dodd, Brian J. 38102 Dep
Doerr, Nan L. 37873
Doherty, Maureen C. 38829

Doherty-Ogea, Kathleen L. 37760
Domenick, Warren L., Jr. 37899
Dominguez, Patrick E. 38472
Donlon, Kevin F. 33344 Dep
Dorn, James M., III 38975
Dorsey, Laura M. 38390
Dougharty, Philip W. 37803
Dowker, John H. Rec'd Dep
Doyle, Lawrence E. 37587 Trans
Drennen, Zachary P. 38672
Drinkwater, Gary G. 38456
Droste, Robert E. 37752
Drury, Joanne C. 38553
Duer, Don R. 38028
Dukes, Lynne A. 37849
Duncan, Daniel L. 38602
Duncan, Victoria D. 37975
Dunlap, Eunice R. 38567
Duraikannu, Yesupatham Rec'd
Durand, Sally E. 38215
D'Urbano, Faith J. 37704
Durren, Paula E. 38610
Duval, Linda M. 37719
Dwinell, Michael 24625 Dep
Dyche, Bradley C. 38830
Dyer, Susan J. 38018
Dykes, Deborah W. 38439
E
Earle, Richard T., III 38516
Easterling, Richard B., Jr. 38997
Eberhart, Philip D. 35528 Trans
Ebert, Bernhard 38216
Echols, John D. 23957 Dep
Edel, Wilbur H. 25711 Dep
Edington, Mark D, W, 37734
Edwards, James P. 38537
Edwards, Samuel L. 29144 Dep
Eguia Arroyo, Margarita 37950
Ekrem, Katherine B. 37686
Ekstrom, Ellen L. 38967
Eldredge, Mark R. 37850
Eleazer, Victor W. 37244 Susp/Dep
Elley, Eric M. 37989
Elliott, Beverley F. 38217
Elliott, Paul A. Rec'd
Elliott, R. Neil 38730
Ellis, Elizabeth A. 38325

RECORDER APPENDIX

Ellis, Jane F. 38029
Ellis, Karen L. 38440
Ellison, Monique A. 38500
Ely, James E. 38533
Engels, Allen R. 37654
Erickson, Bonnie J. 37973 Dep
Erickson, Kenneth L. 38326
Erickson, Scott E. 38429
Erquiaga, Trudel N. 38905
Espeseth, Cynthia A. 38327
Estes, Jack A. 38538
Estrada, Carolyn S. 38218
Eunson, Lisa K. 38457
Evans, John D. 19171 Dep
Everson, Jacquelyn 37673
Evett, Douglas P. 22687 Susp
Ewing, Judith L, 38976

F

Falconer, Virginia P. 38219
Famulare, Joseph A. 38731
Farmer, Charles A. 37851
Farrey, Shannon C. 38501
Faure, Susan B. 37980
Faust, Andrew S. Rec'd
Feather, Mark R. 38178
Feliu-Gonzalez, Candida 34132 Trans
Fellows, Jessica H. 37761
Feltner, Allan L. 38831
Fenton, Gordon D. Rec'd
Fenty, Maria 38515
Ferneyhough, Dallam G. 38003
Ferrel, Artis L. 37762
Ferrell, Nathan W. 38732
Fhuere, Brenda L. 37655
Fichter, Richard E., Jr. 38328
Fico-Brown, Beverly 38274
Fierro, John E. 37804
Findlen, Beth 38569
Findley, Christopher G. 38870
Fisher, Margaret J. 38157
Fisher, W. Bowlyne 23358 Dep
Fiske, Thomas W. 38733
Fitzgibbons, Michael J. 25942 Susp
Fitzhugh, Mark L. 38158
FitzSimmons, Daniel V. 37705
Fleischer, Scott R. 38673
Fleming, Philip B., II 38615

Flexer, Katharine G. 37657
Foncree, Rose Mary I. 38057
Forbes, Terry W. 37934 Dec
Forest, Elizabeth J. S. 38275
Fornea, Stan W. 38464
Foster, Kenneth E., Jr. 38064
Foulke, Mary L. 38123
Fout, Jason A. 38276
Fowler, Conetta B. 38931
Fowler, Jay D. 32810 Susp/Dep
Fowler, William Y., IV 37748
Fox, Carol R. 38547
Fox, Deborah 37900
Frances, Martha 38020
Frances, Ricardo L. 31368 Dep
Franklin-Vaughn, Robyn E. 38734
Frantz-Dale, Heidi H. 37805
Frazier, Mark W. 38132
Frederick, Warren Rec'd
Fredrickson, David A. 37901
Freeman, Diana G. B. 37935
Frens, Mary J. 37874
Frey, Louane F. V. 37990
Frey, Matthew V. 38674
Fribourgh, Cynthia K. 38008
Fritschner, 38950
Frye, J. Wade, III 38487
Fuller, Steven G., Sr. 38945

G

Gadden, James J. 38879
Gaede, Lee Ann L. 37666
Gaiser, Ted G. 38404
Gallian, Paul V., Jr. 38030
Gambling, Paul Rec'd
Garcia, Margaret J. 38593
Gardner, Carol H. 37680
Gardner, John B. 38735
Garin, George M., Jr. 31640 Dep
Garland, John G., III 38793
Garrione, Robert M. Rec'd Dep
Garrou, Dennis J. 35642 Trans
Garwood, Martha J. 38774
Gay, Jean R. 38775
Gay, Judith S. Rec'd
George, Jacob C., Jr. 37948
Gerhard, Kurt J. 37728
Giacobbe, Georgia B. 37763

Giacoma, Claudia L. 38063
Gibson, Earl D. 38581
Gibson, Joel A. 27994 Dep
Giesler, Mary M. 38058
Gilchrist, Ramsey D. 38736
Gillette, David G. 28312 Dep
Gilman, Charles S., Jr. 31925 Dep
Gilson, Christine M. W. 38871
Gladstone, John W. 35830 Susp/Dep
Glass, Vanessa J. 38159
Gleason, Dorothy J. 37702
Glenn, Terrell L., Jr. 30538 Dep
Glover, Beth F. 38719
Glover, Mary E. 38052
Goglia, Bette M. 38031
Gokey, Mary J. 38594
Goldman, Norman C. 38081
Gonterman, Maynard C. 37681
Gonzales, Ricardo, Jr. 38160
Gonzalez, Antonio 38124
Goode, Colin Rec'd Trans
Goodkind, Caroline C. 38183
Gorchov, Michael I. 38220
Gossling, Nancy E. 37806
Gott, Jaynne L. C. 37902
Gough, Frank D., II 37735
Gough, Richard H. 34851 Dep
Grab, Virginia L. 37687
Grabher, Jerald 38869
Grabner-Hegg, Linnae M. 38595
Gracen, Sharon K. 37903
Gradone, Elizabeth M. 35056 Dep
Grady, Ann N. 37938
Grafe, Robert L., Jr. 36325 Dep
Graham, Earnest N., III 38129
Graham, Joanna D. 37720
Graham, Shirley E. S. 38622
Granger, Nancy W. 38977
Graves, Verna E. 37764
Gray, Douglas A. 36284 Dep
Gray, Patrick T. 38161
Grayson, John H. 29452 Susp/Dep
Green, Gordon G. 38133
Green, Patricia L. O. 37807
Green, Stephanie M. 37808
Greenaway, Douglas A. G. 37809
Greene, Alexander M. 26111 Trans

Greene, Margaret C. 38623
Greene-McCreight, Kathryn 38675
Greenwell, Gail E. 38134
Greer, George H., Jr. 37786
Gregory, Loren H. 38032
Gremillion, Dorothy A. 37765
Grennan, William J. 37991
Grewell, Genevieve M. 37904
Griffin, Christopher E. 38737
Griffin, Jon E. 38402
Griffin, Ronald W. 37656
Griffith, Shawn L. 37810
Grigg, Joel T. 38033
Grimball, Richard B., Jr. 38676
Griscom, Donald 38517
Grotke, Mark D. 38616
Guback, Thomas H. 37736
Guernsey, Justine M. 37694
Guerra-Diaz, Juan A. 37970
Guinta, Denise G. 38611
Gunn, Daniel C. 38558
Gurley, James R. 30459 Dep
Gustafson, Mary D. 38221
Guthkelch, Cynthia A. G. 38015
Guy, Ronald A. 38222
Gwin, Lawrence P., Jr. 38534
Gwyn, Lewis R., III 38978

H

Haake, Gilbert M. 38896
Haase, Sylvia A. 38959
Hacker, Craig A. 38873
Haddad, Mary E. 37811
Haddix, Theodore R., Jr. 28234 Susp
Haddox, Jason M. 37875
Hagen, Amelia A. 37766
Hahneman, Geoffrey M. 29439 Term
Hale, Douglas J. 38541
Hale, Patricia A. 38542
Hale, William C. 33448 Rest
Hall, Mavis 38960
Hall, Robert T. 22711 Dep
Hallas, Cynthia J. 37790
Halliday, Christopher N. R. Rec'd
Halliday, Paula P. Rec'd
Halliwell, Leigh J. 30849 Susp
Hamer, Donald L. 37812
Han, Valentine S-G. Rec'd

Hancock, Norman E., Jr. 32143 Dep
Hanger, Robert B. 34221 Dep
Hannabas, Katherine 38375
Hansell, Susan W. 38473
Hardin, Nancy H. 38414
Hardwick, Michael E. 37852
Hardy, Margaret F. 37813
Hardy, Velinda E. 38120
Harkins, J. William, III 38223
Harper, Helen O. 38624
Harres, Elisa P. 38979
Harrigfeld, Christopher L. 37767
Harrison, Elizabeth A. 38474
Harrity, Alison P. 37866
Hart, Danny R. 38376
Hart, Larry D. 38224
Harte, John J. M., Jr. 25729 Susp
Hartman, Richard B. 26160 Dep
Hartney, Michael E. 27164 Susp
Hartzog, Howard G. 38573
Hauck, Barbara H. 38305
Hawley, Elizabeth L. 38794
Hayler, Andrew J. 38179
Hazel, Dorothy M. 38980
Hazen, Alba D. 38109
Hazen, Susan M. 37706
Hazzard, Richard A., Sr. 38447
Heath, Claudia 38433
Heden, Eileen M. 38353
Heffner, John H. 38421
Heidt, Michael L. Rec'd
Heine, William A. J., Jr. 38998
Heller, Richard C. 38918
Helmer, Richard E. 38677
Hemphill, Ann S. 37966
Henault, Rita L. 38961
Henderson, Mark W. 37768
Henderson-Johnson, Lynn N. 37992
Hensley, Lane G. 38277
Heron, Marsha S. 38968
Hess, Howard J. 37814
Hesse, Alan R. 38130
Hesse, Michael E. 26855 Dep
Hetler, Gwendolyn K. 38050
Higgs, Richard H. 38544
Hilfiker, Gerald M. 38389
Hill, David E. 38306
Hill, Joel G. 37769
Hill, Mary A. 38307
Hilliard, Robert G. 38951
Hillquist, Catherine R. 37905
Himes, John M. 38795
Hines, Caroline V. 37815
Hinson, Paul A. 33648 Trans
Hinton, Bradley A. 37721
Hitch, Kenneth R. 38415
Hixson, Mary L. 38452
Hobby, Sharon S. E. 37853
Hoch, Helen E. 37944
Hodges, Michael J. 38162
Hoekstra, Robert B. 38936
Hofer, Christopher D. 38678
Hoffman, Robyn R. 37692
Hoffmann, Beth B. 37816
Holder, Anthony B. Rec'd
Holland, Eleanor L. 38225
Holly, F. Eugene 37699
Holman, Emily C. 37993
Holmes, William H. 38880
Honig-Smith, Julie 37906
Hood, Stephen D. 38506
Hoover, Joshua A. 38625
Hopkins, Christine C. 37854
Hopkins, John L. 38648
Hopkins, Vivian L. 38379
Hopper, Edgar W. 37722
Hornbeck, Jennifer M. 38163
Hornaday, Evelyn W. 37770
Horne, Lance C. 38263
Horowitz, Robert A. 38264
Horton, Donald M. 28594 Rest
Horvath, Victor J. 38946
Hoster, Elizabeth M. 38882
Houk, David S. 38226
Howard, Walter W. 37940
Hubbard, Carol M. 38278
Hubbard, Charles H., Jr. 38034
Huber, Amy W. 38308
Huber, Ellen B. 38227
Hudson, Kimberly 38832
Huerta Garcia, Oscar X-33155 Dep
Huey, S. Marshall, Jr. 38329
Huff, Clark K. 37876
Hughes, Robert E., Jr. 34594 Dep

Humphrey, Nathan J. A. 38430
Hunt, Edward W. 38626
Hunt, Hazel B. 38422
Huntington, Carol L. 38559
Hupf, Jeffrey L. 38874
Hurley, Janet 38655
Hussey-Bynes, Teddra R. 38520
Hutchinson, John F., Jr. 38738
Hutchinson, John M. 30333 Dep
Hyde, Jack E. A. Rec'd
I
Ingraham, Doris W. 38380
Inscoe, Laura D. 38739
Irving, Hannah J. 37817
Irwin, Zachary T. 37818
Isaacs, James S. 38575
Iswariah, James C. Rec'd
J
Jackman, Kathleen R. 36063 Trans
Jackman, Michael J. 23771 Dep
Jackson, Connie W. 38228
Jackson, David H. Rec'd
Jackson, Eric M. C. Rec'd Rest
Jackson, Peter J. E. Rec'd
Jacobs, John R. 37737
Jacobs, Mary L. 38229
Jacobson, Arthur T. 35815 Dep
James, Charles W. 33473 Dep
James, Edmund L. 38796
Jamieson, Sandra S. 38518
Janikowski, Thomas A. 38475
Jansma, Henry P. Rec'd
Jarrell, Robin C. 38679
Jarvis, Kendron D. 38680
Jaynes, Ruth L. M. 38617
Jenkins, Kathryn E. 38740
Jensen, Jan D. 38797
Jensen, Julia K. 38627
Jensen, Mary A. 38114
Jenson, Constance L. 38230
Jillard, Christine L. 38189
Johnson, E. S. 38897
Johnson, Ann L. 38502
Johnson, Christopher A. 37819
Johnson, David A. 38387
Johnson, Dennis L. 37662
Johnson, Horace S. 38231

Johnson, James M. Rec'd
Johnson, James P. 35305 Dep
Johnson, Janet H. 38798
Johnson, Keith 38314
Johnson, Malinda M. E. 38681
Johnson, Marietta 38409
Johnson, Robert G. 37877
Johnson, Ronald, A. 38937
Johnson, Shirley M. 38981
Jones, Andrew B. 38682
Jones, Blanford B., II 38952
JONES, CHARLES I., III Susp
Jones, Constance R. 38046
Jones, Curtis C. 38009
Jones, Duncan 37746
Jones, Harriet M. 37674
Jones, Irene C. 38994
Jones, Jeffrey T. 38683
Jones, Jennifer S. H. 38684
Jones, Kathleen A. 37863
Jones, Kevin H. 38862
Jones, Stephen W. 38059
Jones, Timothy K. 38330
Joo, Indon P. Rec'd
Joseph, Winston Rec'd
Juarez-Castro, Francisco 38041
K
Kallstrom, Scott A. 28968 Susp/Dep
Kamai, Gordon M. 38539
Kapurch, Linda M. 39741
Kaswarra, George A. Rec'd
Kauffman, Daniel G. 37738 Dec
Kay, Frances C. 37695
Keating, Julie L. 37974
Keator, Marion K. 37723
Keedy, Susan S. 38279
Keeler, Charles B. 37648
Keene, Ruth C. 38606
Kee-Rees, James L. 38232
Kehayes, Thomas C. 23853 Dep
Keili, Michael S. Rec'd Susp
Kellerhouse, Dean K. 28266 Rest
Kelley, James T. 37959
Kelley, Theresa M. 37960
Kellington, Laurie R. 28233
Kellum, Rosa A. 38060
Kelly, Dennis P. 37698

Kempster, Patricia C. 37697
Kendall, Michael J. 38093
Kennedy, Anne C. 38742
Kennedy, Ellen K. 38685
Kennedy, Hilda L. 37820
Kennedy, Matthew M. 38799
Kennedy, Zelda M. 37787
Kenney, Christine S. 38833
Kenney, William C., Jr. 35409 Trans
Keplinger, Stephen J. 38068
Kern, Roy A. 38686
Kerr, Lauri A. 38190
Kessler, Matthew S. 36327 Dep
Keyse, Andrew C. 38743
Kilfoyle, J. Richard 22395 Rest
Kilpatrick, Alan W. Rec'd
Kilpatrick Madlock, Marcia J. 37644
King, Karen L. 38834
King, Kathy J. 34230 Trans
Kircher, Kathleen L. 38411
Kirchmier, Anne R. 38280
Kirk, Patricia L. 37981
Kirk, Stephen S. 31992 Dep
Kirkland, Robert G. 38607
Kirkley, John L. 38628
Kitt, Michael 38527
Kleffman, Todd A. 38354
Klein, Everett H. 38458
Klohn, Franklin J. 16813 Rest
Knight, Arthur J. 37994
Knight, James D. 38612
Knight, Kimberly A. 37867
Knowlton, Carroll B. 38459
Knudson, Richard L. 38234
Koehler, Norman E., III 38744
Kohn, George F. 27577 Rest
Kollin, James T. Rec'd
Koonce, Kelly M. 38800
Koppel, Mary E. 38507
Koscheski, Nelson W. 25754 Trans
Koskela, Robert N. 38856
Koskela, Ruth A. 38857
Kostas, George A. 38235
Kovach, Gary D. 38953
Kowbeidu, Anthony K. Rec'd
Kozak, Janet M. 38582
Kramer, Aron M. 37729
Kramer, B. Kristopher Rec'd
Kramer, Katherine F. 38919
Kreamer, Martha H. 38164
Kremer, Anna P. 28494 Dep
Krieger, Krisen S. 38890
Krumenacker, Gerald W. 36214 Susp
Kuang Yang, Chou Y. X-38523
Kuhlmann, Martha C. 38629
Kwiatkowski, Janet M. 38969

L

Lacy, Mary C. 38281
LaFond, Charles D., II 38331
Lander, Stephen K. 38745
Landis, Clifford K. 20566 Rest
Landwer, Virginia 37986
Lane, Wendy D. 38054
Lauer, Daniel D. 38654
LaVine, Patricia I. 38847
Lawlor, Jay R. 38746
Lawrence, Raymond Q., Jr. Dep
Laws, Robert J., III 37821
Lawson, Richard T., III 38180
Layden, Daniel K. 38416
Lebron, Linda R. 38236
Leckrone, Walter T. 24204 Dep
Lecroy, Anne K. 38282
Ledgerwood, Mary J. 38332
Lee, Daniel C. J. 38868
Lee, Enoch X-38010
Lee, Kirk A. Rec'd
Lee, Robert B. 38004
Lee, Thomas M. 38489
Lee, Vicki Y. 37982
LeFavi, Robert G. 38865
Lehmann, Richard B. 38237
Lehtinen, Erike A. 38238
Leigh-Taylor, Christine H. 38460
Lemay, Anne R. 37995
Lesesne, William G., Jr. 38283
Leslie, Joanne 38687
LeSueur, John T., II 38574
Lethin, Judith L. W. 37659
Lethin, Kris W. 37660
Lewis, Katherine A. 38649
Lewis, Mark W. 38035
Lewis, Philip M. 38431
Lewis, Timothy J. Rec'd

Lillard, Eddie L., Sr. 37996
Limozaine, Bruce J. 38112
Lindell, Thomas J. 37983
Lindquist, Mary D. 37724
Lively, James W. 38688
Livingston, James L. 38051
Lloyd, Elizabeth A. 38528
Lloyd, Kevin M. 38184
Lockett, Tina L. 38476
Logan, Christie L. 38962
Logue, Frank S. 37667
Lokey, Michael P. 38391
Long, Gail A. 37964
Longbottom, Robert J. D. 38540
Loudenslager, Samuel C. 38954
Lovelace, Darin R. 37645
Loya, Craig W. 38906
Lubin, Gary R. 38920
Lucas, Thomas S. 38239
Luck, Jane A. 38551
Lufburrow, Sara D. 37712
Lukas, Arlene 38333
Lyman, Philip D. 28828 Susp/Dep
Lynn, Jacqueline G. 38529
Lynn, Suzanne M. 38449
Lyons, Lorraine B. 37855

M

Macke, Elizabeth A. 38240
MacKenzie, Vanessa M. Rec'd
MacPhail, Alexander D. 38747
MacSwain, Robert C. 38355
Mahon, Laurence F. 38583
Mahue, Louis D. 38505
Malia, Gregory 38423
Malia, Linda M. 38801
Malloy, Nancy L. 37822
Maloney, Linda M. 38912
Manning, Gary B. 38716
Manning, Gene B. 38334
Manning, Shannon R. 38284
Marcrum, J. Alice 37878
Maree, Donna L. 38921
Marks, Sharla J. 38061
Marques, Judith L. 38891
Marsh, Abigail 38441
Marshall, John H. 38932
Martin, Judy S. 37668

Martin, Patricia L. 38078
Martin, Russell E. J. 37823
Martin, William J. Rec'd
Martin-Coffey, Nancee L. 37824
Mason, Samuel A. 38097
Massenburg, Barbara J. 37985
Masterman, Brenda P. 38381
Matarazzo, Laura R. 38570
Mathews, Koshy 38165
Matkin, Timothy M. 38548
May, Frederick B. 37997
Mayer, Peter W. 38241
Mayer, Sandra C. 37936
Mayes, A. Bernard D. Rec'd Dep
Mayrer, Jane G. 38166
McAdams, Kathleen A. 38022
McAlpine, Laurie A. 32325 Dep
McBride, Jerry A. 29458 Susp
McCarthy, B. Anderson 25852 Rest
McCarthy, Jean E. R. 37739
McCaskill, James C. 38748
McClure, William J., Jr. 38362
McConchie, Leann P. 37710
McCone, Susan J. 38689
McConnell, Joyce 37907
McCown, Sandra W. 38908
McDaniel, Elna I. 38955
McDermott, Gerald R. 38085
McDermott, Nelda G. 38434
McDonald, Karen L. 38103
McDonald, Mark W. 37771
McDowell, Todd S. 37856
McEvers, James M. 23564 Dep
McFarland, Earl E. 38366
McGee, William E. 38285
McGuire, Mark A. 38690
McIntyre, Moni 37825
McKenzie, Jerry B. 22340 Dep
McKenzie-Hayward, Renee G. 38167
McLaren, Christopher T. 37933
McManis, Dennis 38519
McNeeley, William J. 31470 Dep
Meade, Elizabeth G. 38530
Meade, Gary J. 38367
Meade, Jean A. M. 38358
Mease, Carole A. 37791
Meaux, Amy D. 38508

Meck, Daniel S., III 37826
Meck, Nancy E. 37772
Meengs, John R. 38749
Meginniss, David H. 38145
Meister, Deborah A. 38819
Mendoza, Loretta J. 38560
Menger, J. Andrew 38075
Merchant, Wilmot T., II Rec'd
Meroney, Anne E. 38691
Merritt, Frederick D. 32715 Rest
Mesteth, Rhoda Y. 38776
Mestre, Jose W., Jr. 38036
Mettler, Garrett M. 38802
Meyers, Hal I. 25742 Dep
Meyers, Michael W. 38898
Midgett, William D. 38335
Milam, David R. 38242
Milano, Mary L. 37857
Milian, Mario E. 37932
Mill, John W. 38982
Miller, Brian R. 38243
Miller, Charles B. 38750
Miller, Eric L. 38883
Miller, Joseph P. 25905 Rest
Miller, M. Elizabeth S. 38630
Miller, Patrick J. 37879
Miller, Samuel G., Jr. 29540 Dep
Mills, Byron K. 38425
Mindrum, Alice A. 38692
Miner, Daniel F/ 23698 Susp
Miranda-Lopez, Neli A. X-38426
Miron, Mary L. 37675
Mitchell, Dawn-Victoria 37773
Mitchell, Karin R. 38803
Mitchell, Patricia S. 38549
Mobley, Forrest C., Jr. 24237 Dep
Moczydlowski, Ann L. H. 37792
Moehl, Thomas J. 38286
Moffat, Alexander D., Jr. 20465 Rest
Mollard, Elizabeth M. 38693
Mollica, Ralph J. 25754 Trans
Molony, Roberta D. 38076
Monastiere, Sally M. 38909
Monson, Scott B. 38913
Monson Lutes, Kathleen 38751
Montague, Cynthia R. 38587
Montes, Elizabeth 38858

Moon, Mary L. 38835
Mooney, Michelle P. 38110
Moore, Charlotte E. 38191
Moore, Nancy L. 38336
Moore, Pamela A. 38394
Morales-Dennis, Chantal B. 38804
Morehead, James C. Rec'd
Morehouse, Timothy L. 38805
Moreno-Richardson, Mary 38579
Morgan, Pamela S. 38084
Morley, Richard M. 38694
Morrigan, Johanna V. S. 38902
Morrill, Donald P. 38545
Morris, Cecelia G. 38836
Morris, Jonathan E. 38086
Morris, Julie H. 38287
Morris, Patricia 38400
Morris, Shirley L. 37100 Trans
Morris-Kliment, Nicholas M. 38752
Morrison, Mary K. 37908
Mottl, Christine E. 37708
Motz, Larry L. 38695
Mouer, Patricia W. E. 37827
Moyer, David L. Rec'd/Trans/Susp/Dep
Moyer, Laureen M. H. 38884
Muhlheim, Nancy C. C. 38401
Muldoon, Maggie R. D. Rec'd
Mulford, Marie L. 38885
Muller, Thomas G. 38944
Mungoma, Stephen M. Rec'd
Munroe, Sally G. 38696
Murdock, Audrey J. 37869
Murphy, Joseph P. 38446
Murphy, Michael J. 38466
Murray, Carl C. Rec'd Dep
Murray, Elizabeth A. 38477
Murray, George R., Jr. 38561
Murray, John P. 38382
Murray, William M. 38753
Musselman, Barbara M. 38697
Mutolo, Frances 38019
Myers, Bruns M., III 38315
Myers, Kira S. 38337
N
Nairn, Frederick Rec'd Susp
Natzke, Vicki J. 38478
Ndishabandi, William K. Rec'd

Neal, Deonna D. 38754
Neal, James F. 38963
Neckels, Arlen G. 38956
Nee, Michael J. 37740
Needham, James R. 38265
Nefstead, Eric M. 38631
Neller, Wayne A. 33911 Dep
Nelson, Benjamin H., III 38821
Nelson, Robert A., Sr. 38244
Neri, Arthur D. 27998 Dep
Nettleton, Jerome P. 38392
Newland, Benjamin J. 37909
Newman, Ryan D. 38837
Newton, Louis K. Rec'd
Nicholson, Wayne P. 38632
Noland, Elisabeth H. 38368
Norman, Curtis K. 38245
North, Jay 38874
Novak, M. Anne 37910
Noyes, Daphne B. 38405
Nuamah, Reginald Rec'd
Nunez, Carlos F. 38806
Nusser-Telfer, Hiltrude M. 38698

O

Oasin, Elizabeth J. 37725
O'Connor, Edward F., Jr. 38140
O'Connor, Mary C. M. 38562
Odom, Robert M. 38055
Oh, KyungJa 38755
Oldland, William D. 37741
Olsen, Christiana 38756
Olsen, Robert 38369
Olson, Alice I. 38309
Olson, Anna B. 37911
Orbaugh, Phyllis R. J. 38370
Orlando, Helen M. G. 37998
Osborne, William P. 38067
Osburn, Bernard C. 37696
Otterburn, Margaret K. 38633
Ousley, David K. 38838
Ousley, P. Lance 38288
Owen, Charles B. 38398
Owen, Petra D. Rec'd

P

Packard, Nancy L. M. 38310
Page, Louisa 38634 Dec
Pain, Mary R. 38970

Palagyi, Addyse L. 37971
Palmerhall, Juanita 37774
Pamatmat, Roberto D. R. 38289
Papanek, Nicolette 38563
Papazoglakis, Thomas W. 38509
Parker, Dennis J. 38807
Parker, John E., III 38083 Dep
Parlier, Susan T. 38983
Parris, Cheryl A. E. 38992
Parrish, Judy K. 38246
Parsons, Martha L. T. 38608
Pastores, Tancredo R., Jr. Rec'd
Payne, Veronica I. H. 32593 Dep
Pearce, Robert C., Jr. 37676
Pearsall, Arlene E. 37864
Peck, Felicity 38290
Pedersen, Charles L. R. 34027 Susp
Peeples, David H. 37788
Pegram, Langdon 37828
Pelnar, William D. 38065
Pemberton, Barbara L. 38984
Penfield, Joyce A. 38168
Peoples, David B. 38135
Peppler, Connie J. 38839
Percival, Michael K. 37931
Perdue, Thomas H. 38939
Perrin, Mary E. 38111
Perrson, Bernard C. Rec'd Dep
Peterman, Lynn C. 38568
Petersen, Barbara J. 37747
Peterson, Frank L., Jr. 38603
Peterson, Iris E. 38564
Petroccione, James V. 38571
Pettit, Walton S., Jr. 24849 Dep
Phillips, A. William, III 38808
Phillips, Francis A. 36463 Dep
Phillips, Michael V. 34184 Dep
Pinnock, Betty L. 38016
Pipkin, Michael R. J. 38488
Piver, Jane D. 37912
Platt, Gretchen M. 38915
Plummer, Dale W. 38098
Pogue, Blair A. 37913
Poirier, Esther H. 38840
Poisson, Ellen H. 37688
Pollard, Richard A. 18827 Dep
Ponce, Jacqueline 37914

Ponic, Joseph J. Rec'd
Porter, Elizabeth J. S. 38585
Porter, George M. Rec'd
Porter, Shawn E. 37829
Potts, Kathleen K. 38809
Powell, Brent C. 38463
Powell, Everett 38461
Preece, Mark W. 38338
Price, Robert P. 38450
Proctor, Judith H, 37884
Pruitt, Albert W. 37775
Puryear, James H. 38247
Putman, Richard B. 28077 Rest
Q
Quevedo-Bosch, Juan A. Rec'd
Quigley, James E. 38181
Quin, Alison J. 38248
R
Raby, Edith G. 38037
Rachal, Paula C. 37830
Rahhal, Michele D. 37915
Rakoczy, August A. 34019 Dep
Rambo, Thomas B. 38249
Ramos-Orench, Francisco 22414 Rest
Randall, Paul R. 38841
Raulerson, Aaron D. 38169
Raulerson, Steven W. 29064 Dep
Rawn, Jeffrey A. 37831
Ray, Andrew M. 38985
Read, Kathleen 38250
Reade, John M., IV 38922
Rectenwald, Marion B. 38995
Reddall, Jennifer A. 38842
Reddig, Michael D. 38757
Reece, Nathaniel S. T. Rec'd
Reed, Glenna J. 38251
Reed, Jeffrey B. 38635
Reed, Poulson C., Jr. 38699
Reed, Stephen K. 38252
Reger, Timothy S. 38988
Rehberg, Gretchen M. 38700
Reynolds, James R. 38701
Rhodes, Robert R. 38996
Rice, Sandra K. E. 37776
Richards, Dennison S. Rec'd
Richards, Emily B. 38702
Richardson, Frederick J., Jr. 37928
Richardson, James D. 37832
Richer, Victor G. 19982 Dep
Richey, Donald 38038
Ricketts, Marcia C. 38427
Riddle, Jennifer L. 38125
Riddle, Jonathan H. 38136
Ridgill, Michael 38650
Ridgway, Maria S. 38552 Dec
Riis, Susan H. 38531
Riley, Wayne T. 32388 Dep
Rimer, Kathleen P. 38758
Rincon, Virginia M. 38479
Ritchie, Harold L. 38717
Rivetti, Mary E. 37749
Roadman, Betsy J. 38094
Robbins, Janice 38291
Robbins-Penniman, Sylvia B. 37916
Roberson, Keith J. 37678
Roberts, Jose F. 30300 Trans
Robertson, Karen S. 38933
Robinson, Sybil C. F. 38820
Robison, Ronald L. 34755 Dep
Roddam, John W. R. Rec'd
Roeske, Michael J. 38141
Rogers, Timothy J. 38023
Rogerson, George W. 38105
Rohlff, Deborah L. 38859
Rojas Poveda, Jesus A. Rec'd
Rollins, Belle F. 38514
Rose, Joy A. 38855
Rose, Roland 38428
Rosendahl, Mary A. 38137
Ross, David D. 38971
Ross, Kenneth E. 35493 Trans
Ross, Sue Ann 37777
Rouse, Albertine C. 38525
Rowe, Richard C. 38604
Rowe, Sean W. 37742
Rowles, S. Paul 38899
Royes, Mary A. 38187
Rozendaal, Jay C. 38843
Rubinson, Rhonda J. 37689
Runge, Phillip D. 38126
Running, Joseph M., Jr. 38253
Rusling, Julia G. 37967
Russell, Daniel S. 38759
Russell, Kenneth P. 37972

Rutledge, Gail L. 37684 Dep
Ryan, Matthew W. 38577
S
Sadler, Alice I. 38410
Salles, Stacy D. 38993
Saltzgaber, Jan M. 38492
Sanborn, Calvin F. L. 38636
Sanchez, Alfonso 38361
Sanders, JoAnne M. 37778
Sanders, Marilyn M. 38292
Sanderson, Holladay W. 38170
Santiviago-Espinal, Maria I. 37690
Sanzo, Marie B. 37999
Sarkissyian, Sabi K. Rec'd
Sausele, Elizabeth J. 36342 Trans
Scalise, Margaret M. 38651
Schatz, Stefani S. 38356
Scheeler, Joseph L. 38442
Schenck, Timothy E. 37833
Schisler, Richard T. 38923
Schisler, Sallie C. 38924
Schjonberg, Mary F. 37882
Schmidt, Dennis J. J. 28392 Dep
Schmidt, Kevin L. 38072
Schnabl, Emily J. 37858
Schnackenberg, Gerald L. 28465 Trans
Schneider, Marian H. 38480
Schrimsher, Alyce M. 38493
Schutte, Christopher M. 38810
Schutz, Christine AE. 37859
Schwend, Amy F. P. 38703
Scissons, Antoinette M. 37917
Scott, C. Sue M. 38811
Scott, Nolie E. 38293
SCRIVEN, HENRY W. Rec'd
Seamans, Harry S. 38435
Seaton, Robert D. 38453
Sedlacek, Wesley H. 38781
Seeley, Walter D., Jr. 37715
Segal, Donna J. 38339
Seibert, Joanna J. 38113
Seiter, Claudia D. 38021
Seitz, Philip A. 38935
Seles, Deborah G. 38760
Senuta, Lisa A. 38099
Servetas, Linda A. 38637
Sever, Cynthia A. 38638

Sey, Reginald F. A. Rec'd
Shadow, Burton A. 37703
Shafer, Samuel H. 38383
Shaffer, Michael 37669
Shakespeare, Lyndon C. 38704
Shanks, Margaret R. 38254
Sharpe, William G. 27623 Dep
Shecter, Teri A. 38940
Sheehan, John T. 38340
Shepherd, Stephen G. 38761
Sheppard, Patricia S. K. 38512
Shier, Nancy K. 38419
Shigaki, Jerry M. 37918
Shissler, Donald G. 22016 Dep
Shoemaker, Eric W. 38384
Sholander, Mark E. 37743
Short, Margaret I. 38385
Simmons, David T. 38182
Simmons, Mary K. 38142
Simple, Margo 38171
Sims, Kenneth H. 38294
Sims, Mark H. 37868
Sims, Richard O. 37701
Singh, Prince G. Rec'd
Sinkler, Wharton, III 23744 Susp
Sinnott, Lynn D. 37793
Sipe, Robert B. 38127
Sireno, Robert 38039
Sisson, Penny R. 38062
Sisson, Rick L. 35399 Dep
Siwek, Peter C. 38762
Size, Patricia B. 37726
Slakey, Anne-Elisa M. 38943
Slanger, George C. 37976
Slater, Joan B. 38079
Slaughter, Susan E. 38910
Sloan, Ellen M. 38639
Slocum, Robert B. 32002 Susp
Smart, Clifford E. S. Rec'd
Smedley, Walter, IV 38812
Smith, Alan B. 37919
Smith, Betty 38911
Smith, Gary M. 38185
Smith, Gregory M. 37834 Trans
Smith, Hilary B. 37920
Smith, James A. 38900
Smith, Jane C. 38100

Smith, Kerry J. 37779
Smith, Merle E., Jr. 38106
Smith, Patsy A. 37835
Smith, Richard U., Jr. Rec'd Dep
Smith, Robert C. 38341
Smith, Steven R. 38844
Smith, Theophus H. 38255
Smith, Timothy R. 31313 Dep
Smith, Vickie M. 38999
Smith, William G., Jr. 25843 Dep
SmithGraybeal, Felicia S. 38705
Snow, Gary N. 33075 Susp
Snow, George R. 38436
Snyder, Belinda A. W. 38546
Snyder, Gregory A. 38609
Solomon, Mardow, Sr. 37952
Sonderegger, Katherine A. 37942
Sorvillo, James A., Sr. 37744
Spear, Leslie E. 38554
Speck-Ewer, Nathan S. 38706
Speeks, Mark W. 38550
Spencer, John R. 27079 Rest
Spencer, Patricia A. 38986
Spicer, John M. 38707
Spiers, Linda M. 37836
Spoor, Cornelia P. 38892
Spurlock, Paul A. 38532
Stanley, Gordon J. 37670
Stansberry, Carmen M. Rec'd Trans
St. Clair, Melinda L. 38172
Steadman, Larry K. 38088
Sten, Pamela V. 38708
Stephens, Paul J. 38763
Sterchi, Margaret 38256
Sterling, Leslie K. 38173
Stevens, Gregory T. 32549 Dep
Stevens, Robert E., Jr. 38186
Stevens, Walter A., III 37883
Stevenson, Carolyn E. 32200 Rest
Stewart, William O., Jr. 38451
Stewart-Sicking, Megan E. 38925
Stiegler, Mark A. 38640
St. Louis, J. Allison 37837
Stock, David R. 37750
Stockton, Martha G. 38941
Stoessel, Andrew J. 38174
Stone, Glenn H. Rec'd

Stone, James F. 25087 Trans
Storm, Astrid J. 38011
Stoudenmire, William 35033 Susp/Dep
Stowe, Barbara E. 38406
Strey, Robert J. 32155 Dep
St. Romain, John B. 39000
Strom, John D. 24283 Dep
Stroop, William G. 38503
Stuart, Judith L. 38589
Stumpf, Stephen E. 31663 Dep
Sullivan, James S. 29327 Dep/Rest
Sullivan, Michael R. 37965
Sulzenfuss, Alan L. 37242 Trans
Sumrall, Ernie C. 31010 Dep
Sunderland, Douglas C. 38395
Sunderland, Melanie J. 38853
Suruda, Teresa A. 38000
Sutherland, Melody P. 38393
Sutor, Jack T., Jr. 33724 Susp
Swan, Craig R. 37838
Swann, Stuart A. 34717 Susp
Swanner, Rhoda J. 38295
Swanson, Richard R. 37921
Sweeney, Craig C. 38101
Sweeney, Peter H. 38777
Sweeny, Thomas E. 38893
Swiedler, Anne E. 38709
Symington, Ann P. 38901
Synan, Thomas N. J. 37691
T
Tafoya, Stacey T. 37839
Talk, John G., IV 38926
Tata, Suzanne 38881
Tate, Donald S. 38555
Tate, Mary K. 38342
Taylor, Emerson B., Jr. 35914 Trans
Taylor, Norman D. 38359
Teague, C. Steven 37922
Templeman, Mark A. 38417
Tennant, Paul J. 38710
Tenny, Claire M. 38711
Terry, Eleanor A. 38712
Terry, William H. 39001
Tester, Helen W. 37649
Thom, Kenneth S. 38121
Thomas, Alisyn L. 37840
Thomas, Franklin B., Jr. 38578

Thomas, James M., Jr. 38343
Thompson, Carol A. 38987
Thompson, Catherine M. 37780
Thompson, Donald F. Rec'd
Thompson, Edward H. Rec'd
Thompson, Elena 38866
Thompson, Owen C. 38927
Thompson, Susan M. 37714
Thompson, Wanda J. 38572
Thomson, Ian C. Rec'd
Thorp, Almus M., Jr. 24207 Dep
Thurlow, David W. T. Rec'd
Tibbetts, Ronald C. 38407
Tierney, Bridget K. 38928
Tierney, Dennis S. 38641
Titus, Bessie C. 37953
Titus, David A. Rec'd Trans
Todd, Christopher H. 38778
Toepfer, Laura K. 38344
Tofani, Ann H. 37860
Tollefson, Jane C. 38311
Tolzmann, Lee Ann D. 38257
Tomlinson, Ruth M. 3778
Toon, Peter Rec'd Trans
Torrey, Dorothy E. 38345
Towne, Jane C. 38448
Towner, James O. 27900 Dep
Townsend, M. Clayton, Jr. 37745
Tracey, Edward J. 37961
Tracy, Dick B. 37955
Tracy, Rita V. 37956
Trainor, Helen C. 38779
Trapani, Kathleen M. 38024
Trebbe, Robert S. 38258
Trees, Thomas H. 38964
Treppa, Joyce L. 38296
Trigleth, John P. 38066
Trimble, William B. Jr. 25332 Susp
Tripses, Kathleen R. M. 38107
Tristram, Geoffrey R. Rec'd
Truby, Laura C. 37841
Trygar, Earl P., Sr. 38565
Turner, John E. 37682
Turner, Nancy M. 38047
Turton, Neil C. Rec'd
Tuttle, Margaret C. 38642
Tweedale, David L. 38860

Twiggs, Frances R. 38418
Twist, Richard L. 30655 Dep
Two Bulls, Robert W. 37751
Tyler, Pamela H. 37842
Tyo, Charles H., Jr. 38481
Tyndall, Jeremy H. Rec'd
U
Ueda, Ajuko L. K. 38146
V
Van Dermark, Fayetta 38386
Van Doren, Robert L., Jr. 38012
Van Dyke, Robert H. 37677
van Schalkwky, George E. Rec'd Trans
Varner, Joshua H. 38346
Vaughn, Jessie H. 38934
Veale, David S. 38048
Vershure, Claude E. 37865
Vidmar, Mary B. 37923
Vietor, Oliver R. 38049
Villagomeza, Christian Rec'd
von Grabow, Richard H. 38543
von Wrangel, Carola 37693
Vreeland, James L. 38643
W
Waggoner, Janet C. 38312
Walfoort, Michael R. 39789 Dep
Walker, John D. 30973 Dep
Wall, Anne F. 37782
Wallace, Tanya R. 37843
Walsh, Eileen P. 38764
Walter, George A., II 37713
Walthall, Charles L. 38845
Waples, Jan S. 38144
Ward, George B. P., Jr. 37783
Ward, Mary C. M. 38765
Ward, Meredyth W. 38297
Ward, Pamela A. 35581 Dep
Warley, Dianne G. 38040
Warner, Christopher C. 37844
Warner, Janet L. 38584
Warner, John S. 38850
Warwick, Eilene R. 37650
Waters, Elliott M. 38347
Waters, Margaret H. 38914
Watkin, Robert G. 38259
Watson, Charles E. 38371
Watson, Suzanne E. 38813

Watton, Sharon L. 38298
Waweru, Christine G. Rec'd
Way, Gary L, 38846
Webb, James W., Jr. 37949
Weber, Dean A. 38644
Weber, Thomas R. 28085 Dep
Webster, Thomas H. Rec'd
Weglarz, Eileen E. 38713
Wehner, Paul B. 38299
Weidman, Hal J. 38714
Weiler, Matthew G. B. 38138
Weir, Silas M. 38942
Welbourne, Jacob A. Rec'd Trans
Weldon, A. Kenneth 38188
Wells, Ann L. C. 38372
Wells, Mary B. 38588
Welty, Terrence A., IV 38482
Wen Bin, Tzeng X-38524
Wenner, Rachel E. 38566
Werner-Hall, Judith B. 38175
Werntz, Pamela L. 38766
West, John R. 37671
West, Kelly E. 38504
Westberg, Daniel A. Rec'd
Westerfield, James A. 36378 Dep
Westin, John-Paul Rec'd Trans
Westpfahl, Carol E. 37924
Wheatley-Dyson, Elizbeth
Whelan, Janet K. 37672
Whitaker, Ann L. 38348
White, Donald K., Jr. 38373
White, Laura D. 38087
White, Kathryn L. 38490
White, Nancy A. 38176
White, R. Ellen 38814
White, Stephen L. 37727
Whitebird, George 37784
Whitfield, Deirdre R. 38349
Whorton, Jeffrey T. 38432
Wichael, Karen L. 38001
Wickham, Jonathan W. 38720
Wiesner, Kurt C. 38989
Wight, Susan M. 38300
Wilcox, Melissa Q. 38260
Wilde, Glenn H. 38876
Wile, Mary L. H. 38462
Wiley, John D. X-29596 Trans

Wilkinson, Hazel L. 38768
Wilkinson, Joyce A. M. 38598
Williams, Charles A., IV 38177
Williams, Christina H. E. 38972
Williams, Edward S. 37647
Williams, G. T. Duffy 38596
Williams, Jane R. F. 38957
Williams, John F., II 38815
Williams, Marianne R. 38013
Willis, Ronnie W. 38645
Wills, Edwin F., Jr. 38872
Wilner, Janice M. 37984
Wils, Duane M. 38128
Wilson, Christopher R. M. Rec'd
Wilson, Dennis M. 38769
Wilson, Gregory M. 38816
Wilson, James N., II Rec'd
Wilson, Jill M. L. 38817
Wilson, Linda L. 38261
Wiltsey, Susan A. 38069
Windsor, Janice R. 38861
Wingert, Anita L. 37925
Winter, Brian W. 38854
Wiseman, Grant B. 38014
Wismer, Robert D. Rec'd
Wizorek, Julie C. 38350
Wojahn, Karen A. 37880
Wolfe, Dorothy 38652
Wolfenbarger, Mary S. 37861
Wolff, William G. 37957
Wolverson, Marc A. M. Rec'd Trans
Wong, Diane C. K. 38770
Wood, Jan M. S. 37926
Wood-Hull, Larry 37845
Woodle, Thomas F., Jr. 37785
Woodliff, Kirk A. 38351
Woods, Karen E. 38483
Wooliver, Tammy S. 38352
Wratten, Kenneth B. 38818
Wright, Martin L., III 38771
Wright, Winston A. Rec'd
Wyatt, Thomas C. 37651
Wyld, Kevin A. Rec'd
Y
Yarbrough, O. Larry 37943
Yaw, Christopher L. 38301
Yeager, Wayne E. 25147 Dep

Yost, Martin C. 38467
Young, James O. 38302
Young, Paul W. 38139
Young, Robert A. 37658
Z
Zeller, Margaret K. 38510
Zelaya-Chavez, Otto D. X-24679 Dep
Zifcak, Patricia 38715
Zimmerschied, Jill W. 38894
Zito, Robert J. A. 38122
Zolner, Eric W. 37846
Zook-Jones, Jill 37929
Zubieta Gutierrez, Agustin T. Rec'd

INDEXES

INDEX OF RESOLUTION ACTIONS

Note: This index references the consideration of all resolutions by original, amended, and final text. For those resolutions that died with adjournment, page numbers are given for the last mention of an action taken. Page numbers follow the sequence of the consideration; the final action is in boldface.

Key

Concur:	Resolutions **concurred** were adopted by both Houses.
Concur/a:	Resolutions **concurred with amendment** were adopted by both Houses.
Concur/s:	Resolutions **concurred with substitute** were adopted by both Houses.
Adopt:	Resolutions **adopted** were considered in one House only.
Reject:	Resolutions **rejected** failed to pass by a House vote.
Reject/d:	Resolutions that **died with adjournment**.
Refer:	Resolutions **referred** to a Standing Commission by both Houses.
Discharge:	Legislative Committee was **discharged** from further consideration.
No Action:	Legislative Committee did not report the resolution to the House floor.
Non-Concur:	Resolutions with final status of **non-concurrence** because both Houses did not concur on the same text or action.

Resolution/Title		Action	Page Numbers
A001	Appropriation for the Archives	Discharge	601 (See D086.)
A002	Appropriation for Church Deployment Board	Discharge	601 (See D086.)
A003	Appropriation for GBEC	Discharge	601 (See D086.)
A004	General Ordination Exam Fee	Discharge	601 (See D086.)
A005	Continue Forward Movement Publications	Concur	**238**, 469
A006	Employment Policies Task Group	Concur/a	**341**, 444
A007	Aging Task Force	Concur/a	110, **476**
A008	Repeal Mandatory Federal Sentencing Guidelines	Concur/a	**126**, 370
A009	Amend Canon I.4.2(b)	Concur	**125**, 366
A010	Continue Anti-Racism Mandate	Concur/a	**173**, 412
A011	Ethical Guidelines for Gene Transfer and Germline Interventions	Concur/a	**254**, 481
A012	Caring for Children and the New Genetics	Concur/a	**209**, 485
A013	Biomedical Ethics Counseling and Education	Non-concur	111, 476
A014	Approve Research on Human Stem Cells	Concur/s	174, 414, **613-614**
A015	Jubilee Ministry Thanksgiving	Concur	**315**, 406
A016	Food Security	Reject/d	677
A017	Conversation on Women's Ordination	Concur/a	**222**, 449
A018	HIV/AIDS Drugs Full Inclusion	Reject/d	464
A019	Continue HIV/AIDS Stdg. Committee	Concur/a	**216**, 409

A020	HIV Medications Availability	Reject/d	463
A021	Broadening HIV Prevention Methods	Concur/a	155, **610**
A022	Nathan Network Funding	Non-concur	218, 688
A023	Institutional Wellness and the Prevention of Sexual Misconduct Task Force	Concur/a	**216**, 451
A024	Support for CEDAW	Discharge	412
A025	Trafficking of Women, Girls and Boys	Concur/s	**320**, 508
A026	Baptismal Parity	Concur/a	**182**, 400
A027	Use of Titles	Concur/s	**181**, 400
A028	Palestinian and Afghani Women Support	Concur/s	**327**, 566
A029	Open Dialogue on Difficult Issues	Concur/a	113, 118, **630**
A030	21st Century Survey Resources	Concur/a	112, **476**
A031	A Multicultural, Multiracial Church	Discharge	694 (See A076.)
A032	Youth Study	Reject/d	551
A033	Just and Unjust Wars	Concur/a	**317**, 503
A034	UN Millennium Development Goals	Discharge	593 (See D006.)
A035	Implement Humanitarian Goals in Africa	Concur/a	**340**, 436
A036	Korean Peninsula	Reject/d	510
A037	Status of Forces Agreement with Korea	Concur/a	**328**, 564
A038	Peace and Justice Studies and Training	Concur	110, **477**
A039	Amend Constitution Article II.2	Concur/a	80, **430**
A040	Amend Canon I.1.2(n)(6)	Concur	**133**, 367
A041	Ratify Actions of SCLM	Concur	81, **450**
A042	Amend Canon I.1.9	Concur	**316**, 470
A043	Amend Canon I.6.1	Discharge	480 (See A072.)
A044	Amend Canon I.17.1(c)	Concur/a	193, **637**
A045	Amend Canon I.17.2	Concur	84, **431**
A046	Amend Canon III.22.1(e)	Concur/a	106, **675**
A047	Amend Canon IV.14.13	Concur/s	160, 165, **636**
A048	Amend Canon IV.4.16(d)	Concur/s	107, **674**
A049	Amend Canon IV.2(A)(2)	Concur	83, **431**
A050	Amend Canon IV.2(B)(10)	Concur	84, **432**
A051	Amend Canon IV.4.14	Concur/s	166, **671**
A052	Amend Canon IV.4.48	No action	(See A051.)
A053	Amend Canon IV.5.29	No action	(See A051.)
A054	Amend Canon IV.6	No action	(See A051.)
A055	Amend Canon IV.12.9	No action	(See A051.)
A056	Amend Canon IV.12.11	No action	(See A051.)
A057	Amend Canon IV.13.1	No action	(See A051.)
A058	Amend Canon IV.13.5	No action	(See A051.)
A059	Design New Resources	Concur/s	202, **676**
A060	Contemporary Language Competency	Concur/s	103, 323, 489, 495, **689**

RESOLUTIONS INDEX

A061	Continuing Education Scholarships	Discharge	203 (See A059.)
A062	Diversity in Leadership Recruitment	Discharge	219
A063	Ethnic Specific Discernment Committees	Concur/a	127, **688**
A064	Seminarian Expenses	Concur/s	109, **475**
A065	Leadership Programs for 18-30 Year-Olds	Concur/s	156, **609**
A066	Campus Ministry Allocation	Concur/s	172, **669**
A067	Fund for Theological Education	Concur/s	219, **687**
A068	Episcopal Church Website	Discharge	597 (See A080.)
A069	Spanish Music Resources	Discharge	137 (See A092.)
A070	Creative Worship Resources	Discharge	137 (See A092.)
A071	Mission-based Prayers	Discharge	136 (See A092.)
A072	Amend Canon I.6.1	Concur/a	**215**, 433
A073	Plant New Churches	Concur/a	**312**, 416
A074	Congregational Annual Study	Concur/a	**335**, 555
A075	Diocese Mission Perspective	Concur/a	**336**, 554
A076	Transformation Resources	Concur/a	**334**, 580
A077	Trained Leadership	Concur/s	**313**, 524
A078	Next Generation Mentoring	Discharge	597 (See A080.)
A079	General Convention Deputies	Concur/a	**337**, 535
A080	Episcopal Church Website	Concur/s	**324**, 526
A081	National Ad Campaign	Concur/a	**252**, 417
A082	Multilingual Publications	Concur/s	**181**, 399
A083	Articulate Faith Story	Concur/a	**187**, 398
A084	20/20 Vision Reporting	Concur/s	**218**, 487
A085	ELCA Member Reception	Concur/s	104, 117, **638**
A086	Lutheran Ordination Bylaw	Concur/a	130, **592**
A087	Interim Eucharistic Sharing with the Moravian Church	Concur	123, **591**
A088	Response to Gift of Authority	Concur	159, **610**
A089	"Open Communion"	Non-Concur	159, 544
A090	Christian-Muslim Dialogue	Concur/a	105, **477**
A091	Continue Enriching Our Worship 1 & 2	Concur	95, **445**
A092	Enriching Our Worship Work	Concur/s	135, **594**
A093	Approve Liturgical Calendar Commemorations	Concur	96, **445**
A094	Church Year Calendar Inclusions	Concur	96, **445**
A095	Authorize Trial Use of Commemorations	Concur	97, **446**
A096	Inclusion in the Church Year Calendar	Concur	98, **447**
A097	Authorize Trial Use of Commemoration	Concur	98, **448**
A098	Church Year Calendar Inclusion	Concur	107, **488**
A099	Authorize Trial Use of Commemoration	Concur	108, **488**
A100	Revise Lesser Feasts and Fasts 2000	Concur/s	134, **593**
A101	Church Planting Liturgies	Concur/a	153, 158, **322**

JOURNAL

A102	Culturally Sensitive Rites	Discharge	137 (See A092.)
A103	Adopt the Revised Common Lectionary	Concur/s	188, **354**, 635, 639, 667
A104	Facilitate Worship with Evangelism Focus	Discharge	137 (See A092.)
A105	Resources for Liturgical Education	Discharge	137 (See A092.)
A106	Liturgical Development and Episcopal Authority	Concur/s	268, **685**
A107	Renewal and Enrichment of Common Worship	Discharge	211 (See A092.)
A108	Amend Constitution Article X	Reject	78
A109	International Anglican Liturgical Consultation	Concur/s	211, **678**
A110	Complete Title III Revisions	Concur	238, **685**
A111	Title III Proposed Canons	Concur/s	273, 635, **641**
A112	Amend Constitution Article I.4	Reject	79
A113	Amend Canon I.1.2(a)	Reject	202
A114	Amend Canon I.2.5	Reject	82
A115	Amend Canon I.4.1(c)	Reject	201
A116	Amend Canon I.4.3(d)	Reject	201
A117	Amend Canon I.9.7	Reject	201
A118	Amend Canon IV.3.27	Reject	200
A119	Role of Deacons	Concur/a	100, **444**
A120	Theological Education Committee	Concur/a	217, 395
A121	Clergy and Lay Professional Education	Concur/a	101, **489**
A122	Improving Health Care for Children	Reject/d	462
A123	Diocesan Alcohol and Drug Dependency Policies	Concur/a	**340**, 453
A124	Standing Commission on Health	Concur/s	204, 251, 371, **689**
A125	Ministry to Prisoners and Their Families	Concur/a	**253**, 517
A126	Youth Charged and Convicted as Adults	Concur/a	**255**, 519
A127	Mandatory Sentencing Guidelines	Discharge	406
A128	Ministering to "At Risk" Youth	Concur/s	**321**, 548
A129	Dismantling Racial Profiling	Reject/d	514
A130	Establish Living Wage	Concur/a	**341**, 465
A131	Worker's Prayer	Reject	211
A132	Christian Responses to Warfare	Concur/a	**320**, 502
A133	Adopt "Expanding Mission and Vitality in Small Congregations"	Concur/a	95, **435**
A134	Implement Alleluia Fund	Concur/a	121, **668**
A135	Holy Habits	Concur/a	119, **588**
A136	National Annual Report	Concur/a	158, **633**
A137	Accountability Of Mission Partners	Concur/s	170, **634**
A138	50/50 Outreach for Congregations	Concur/a	122, **589**
A139	Affirm the Work of TENS	Concur/a	128, **589**

RESOLUTIONS INDEX

A140	Mission Funding	Concur/a	129, **590**
A141	Admit Diocese of Puerto Rico	Concur/a	151, **389**
A142	Admit Diocese of Venezuela	Concur/a	**236**, 433, 493
A143	Amend Constitution Article I.7	Concur/s	79, **339**, 407, 501
A144	Amend Canon I.1.14	Concur/a	82, **350**, 432, 556
A145	General Convention Model	Concur	**216**, 396
A146	Provincial Coordinators Funding	Concur	**215**, 409
A147	Legislative Committee Membership	Concur/s	**317**, 408
A148	Amend HDRO Article VI	Reject	369
A149	Special Legislative Committees	Reject	366
A150	World Mission Vision	Concur/a	191, **634**
A151	World Mission Funds	Concur/a	126, **452**
A152	Episcopal Partnership for Global Mission	Concur	85, **435**
A153	HB Committee on Pastoral Development Appropriation	Discharge	601 (See D086.)
A154	75th General Convention Site	Concur	191, **249**, 402
A155	76th General Convention Site	Concur	**315**, 407
A156	2003 General Convention Daily Agenda	Concur/a	**73**, 360
A157	Program, Budget and Finance	Discharge	601 (See D086.)
A158	Title IV Appropriation	Discharge	601 (See D086.)
B001	Historic Anglican Doctrines and Policies	Reject	130
B002	Amend Canon III.16.5	No action	
B003	The Reuilly Accord	Concur/a	122, **590**
B004	Mission Funding Task Force	Concur/s	171, **632**
B005	Amend Constitution Article I.2	Concur/s	204, **669**
B006	Reformed Episcopal Church Dialogue	Concur	123, **591**
B007	Facilitate Emergence of Consensus	Discharge	250
B008	Protect Children and Youth from Abuse	Concur	**255**, 512
B009	Faith and Order Commission	Reject	182, 250, 689
B010	Continue Leadership Program for Musicians Serving Small Congregations	Concur/a	134, **486**
B011	Amend Rules pertaining to 2/3rds Votes	Adopt	76
B012	Amend House of Bishops Rule XXIV	Adopt	76
B013	Amend House of Bishops Rule II	Adopt	76
B014	Amend House of Bishops Rule VI	Adopt	77
B015	Amend House of Bishops Rule X	Adopt	77, **78**
B016	Human Rights in Afghanistan and Iraq	Discharge	693
B017	Fresh Start	Concur/a	219, **687**
B018	Families of Clergy United in Support	Concur/a	220, **686**
B019	Crisis on Korean Peninsula	Discharge	693
B020	Family Survivors of Murder Victims	Concur	189, **686**
B021	Title III Revision	No action	
B022	Celebrate African Martyrs	Concur	164, **669**

JOURNAL

B023	Change Consent Process to Provinces	Refer	214, **671**
B024	Task Force on Christian Education and Formation	Concur	170, **631**
B025	Criminal Justice Committee	Discharge	692 (See B026.)
B026	Criminal Justice Committee	Concur/a	**338**, 537
B027	Pastoral Letter from the Bishops	Adopt	184, **258**
B028	Gratitude to the Presiding Bishop	Adopt	**349**
C001	Oppose Reparative/Conversion Therapy	Discharge	614 (See C004.)
C002	Violence in the Name of Religion	Discharge	692
C003	In Support of H.R. 40	Reject	517, 540, 590
C004	Reparative Therapies	Concur/s	**261**, 515
C005	Rites for Committed Relationships	Discharge	251 (See C051.)
C006	Evangelism to the New Majority	Concur/s	**210**, 474
C007	Ending the Cycle of Violence	Discharge	692
C008	ECIM Funding	Concur/a	**209**, 473
C009	Commemorate Tikhon	Refer	**99**, 448
C010	Commemorate King Charles the Martyr	Reject	99
C011	ELCA Ordination Policy Change	Discharge	214 (See A086.)
C012	Ethnic Desks and 20/20	Discharge	445 (See C015.)
C013	Commemorate the Rev. Dr. John Roberts	Refer	100, **449**
C014	Reaffirmation of Faith and Purpose	Refer	**352**, 637
C015	Ethnic Desks at the National Church Office	Concur/a	**187**, 416
C016	Integrated Pest Management	Discharge	633, 692 (See C026.)
C017	Conservation for Church Headquarters	Reject/d	427
C018	A045 Task Force Report	No action	
C019	Direct Ordination	Reject	127
C020	Stem Cell Research	Discharge	468 (See A014.)
C021	Stem Cell Research	Discharge	468 (See A014.)
C022	AIDS Epidemic Explosion	Reject/d	412
C023	Direct Ordination	Reject	199
C024	Nonviolent U.S. Foreign Policy	Concur/a	**330**, 545
C025	Ministry of the Baptized in Ordinations	Concur/s	267, **684**
C026	Reduce Use of Toxic Chemicals	Concur/a	**338**, 398, 535
C027	AV Materials of the Episcopal Church	Concur	**181**, 399
C028	Immigrant Workers Freedom Ride	Concur	**326**, 579
C029	Spanish and French Translations	Concur/s	**190**, 421
C030	The Working Poor	Concur/a	**262**, 520
C031	Waging Reconciliation	Concur	103, **477**
C032	Direct Ordination to the Priesthood	Reject	200
C033	Immigration and Undocumented Workers	Concur/s	**319**, 509
C034	General Convention Length	Discharge	435 (See A145.)
C035	Lectionary for Lesser Feasts and Fasts	Reject	212

RESOLUTIONS INDEX

C036	Spirituality of Food Production	Concur/a	**318**, 507
C037	Episcopal Church International Communications	Concur/s	221, **681**
C038	Stigmatization and Spiritual Abuse	Discharge	694
C039	Consent to the Election of The Rev. George Edward Councell as Bishop	Concur	93, **102**, 370
C040	Consent to the Election of The Rev. Joe Goodwin Burnett as Bishop	Concur	93, 102, **113**, 369
C041	Consent to the Election of The Rev. Samuel Johnson Howard as Bishop Coadjutor	Concur	116, **128**, 397
C042	Consent to the Election of The Rev. C. Franklin Brookhart, Jr. as Bishop	Concur	116, 118, **128**, 397
C043	Consent to the Election of The Rev. Canon Johncy Itty as Bishop	Concur	149, **159**, 410
C044	Consent to the Election of The Rev. Steven A. Miller as Bishop	Concur	149, 151, **161**, 410
C045	Consent to the Election of The Rev. Canon V. Gene Robinson as Bishop Coadjutor	Concur	209, **222**, 440, 454
C046	Consent to the Election of The Rev. Rayford B. High as Bishop Suffragan	Concur	234, **239**, 501
C047	Consent to the Election of The Rev. Robert John O'Neill as Bishop Coadjutor	Concur	234, **239**, 502
C048	Consent to the Election of The Rev. Dean E. Wolfe as Bishop	Concur	234, **239**, 502
C049	Declining U.S. Aid to Developing Nations	Discharge	692
C050	Family Planning	Discharge	693
C051	Committed Same-Gender Relationships	Concur/s	239, 242, 608, **615**
C052	Transfer of Diocesan Territories	Concur	**337**, 555
D001	Funding Implications of a 10% Tithe	Discharge	190 (See A136, B004.)
D002	International Peace Zone for Jerusalem	Reject	637
D003	Revision of the Catechism	Refer	212, **679**
D004	ELCA Ordination Practices	Discharge	214 (See A086.)
D005	Amend Canons I.2.4(c) & I.4.3	Reject	480
D006	Supporting International Relief and Development	Concur/a	**265**, 505
D007	Episcopal Election Reform	Reject/d	410
D008	Demolition of Palestinian Homes	Concur/a	**320**, 546
D009	Support 2008 Anglican Gathering	Concur	169, **611**
D010	Amend Canons I.1.2(n)(5)	Concur/a	179, **680**
D011	Append "Anglican Communion"	Concur	**334**, 581
D012	Amend Canons I.13, IV.3.42, 43, IV.14.2	Refer	264, **682**

1005

JOURNAL

D013	Annotated Constitution and Canons	Concur/a	132, **675**
D014	Japanese-American Internment in WW II	Concur/s	**326**, 565
D015	COSE Materials on the Web	Concur/a	**262**, 518
D016	Protect Animals from Cruel Treatment	Concur/s	**253**, 483
D017	Promote Reconciliation and Minimize Schism	Refer	**333**, 582
D018	Amend Canon I.6.1	Reject	124
D019	Amend Canon III.17	No action	
D020	Opposition to Sharia Law	Concur/s	207, **677**
D021	Church Publishing Inc.'s Revised Strategy	Concur	165, **680**
D022	Rites Supporting Life-long Relationships	Discharge	251 (See C051.)
D023	U.S. Support for Liberia	Concur/a	**266**, 510
D024	Ministry of ECVA Thanksgiving	Concur	**315**, 443
D025	Efforts to End Racism	Concur/a	**343**, 547
D026	Commend www.ExploreFaith.org	Discharge	252
D027	Amend Constitution Article II	Concur	206, **670**
D028	Amend Constitution Article X	Discharge	124 (See A108.)
D029	Reparative Therapy	Discharge	614 (See C004.)
D030	Reg. Ministry vs Pol. Advocacy	Reject	612
D031	Culture of Nonviolence	Concur/a	**325**, 558
D032	Gail Courtney Rittgers	Concur	**316**, 372
D033	Encourage Financial Teaching	Concur/s	203, **676**
D034	Sex Trafficking	Concur/a	**330**, 561
D035	Harriet Tubman Commemoration	Refer	213, 679, **680**
D036	Marriage	Concur/s	**333**, 568
D037	Pregnant Women Support	Discharge	694 (See 1994-A054.)
D038	Resolution on Liberia	Discharge	694 (See D023.)
D039	Priorities for Triennial Budget	Concur	**152**, 407
D040	Housing for the Poor	Concur/a	**332**, 569
D041	Service Animals Welcome	Concur	183, **681**
D042	Amend Canon I.8.2	Reject	157, 638
D043	Elimination of Barriers	Reject/d	550
D044	Election Clarification	Concur/a	**344**, 478
D045	Rel. Coal. for Reproductive Choice Withdrawal	Reject	332, 569
D046	Stewardship of Water	Concur	**314**, 469
D047	Post-Abortion Healing Service	Concur/s	192, **684**
D048	Committee Vote Hearings	No action	
D049	First Communion on the Moon	Refer	213, **679**
D050	Cuba–Honor Commitments	Concur	309, **683**
D051	General Convention Accessibility	Concur/a	**337**, 527, 534
D052	Rescind Policy of Disinvest. in Defense Contractors	Reject	331, 587

RESOLUTIONS INDEX

D053	Honor John Kemper Cannon	Adopt	**419**
D054	Keep America's Promise to Africa	Concur/s	327, 563
D055	Transitional Diaconate as an Option	No action	
D056	Canons on Court for Trial of a Bishop	Reject/d	570, 571
D057	Convention Technology Use	Concur/a	353, 551
D058	Assisted Hearing Devices	Discharge	593
D059	Justice For Juveniles	Discharge	613
D060	Ordained and Licensed Ministries Education	Concur	189, **688**
D061	Jubilee Ministry Funding	Reject	250, 546
D062	Amend Constitution Article IX	Concur	206, 570, **571**
D063	Civil Liberties and the USA Patriot Act	Concur/a	325, 561
D064	Amend Canon III.22.3 (a)	Discharge	693 (See D072.)
D065	Funding for Global Engagement	Discharge	694 (See A150, A151.)
D066	Declaration on Sustainable Development	Concur/a	329, 559
D067	Amend Canon 2.2	Concur/a	263, **683**
D068	Response to New War Situations	Concur/s	329, 560
D069	Stdg. Com. on Church Communications	Concur/a	336, 578
D070	Water Policy	Concur	331, 567
D071	Federally Sponsored Marriage Promotion	Concur/s	332, 567
D072	Amend Canon III.22.3 (a)	Concur/a	352, 479, 556
D073	Formation of Episcopal Community Services In America	Concur	331, 580
D074	Name Change for SCER	Discharge	325 (See D010.)
D075	Christian Education Study	Discharge	171 (See A065, B024.)
D076	Oppose USA Patriot Act	Discharge	693 (See D063.)
D077	Post 9/11 Racial Hatred and Incarcerations	Concur/a	342, 522
D078	David Hegg	Adopt	**699**
D079	CPF Board of Trustees	Adopt	698, **699**
D080	Alan Blanchard	Adopt	552, **552**
D081	Israeli Security Wall	Concur/a	328, 558
D082	Gratitude to Minneapolis	Adopt	**700**
D083	The Very Rev. George L. Werner	Adopt	**699**
D084	Listserve Appreciation	Concur	348, 603
D085	Gratitude to Church Periodical Club	Concur	348, 603
D086	Episcopal Church 2004–2006 Budget	Concur	269, 598
D087	Evening of Conversations	Concur	346, 606
D088	Ministry to the Deaf	Concur	345, 605
D089	Thanks to Bishop Jelinek and the Diocese of Minnesota	Concur	347, 604
D090	Nancy Piatkowski	Concur	347, 604
D091	Chaplain Brian Prior	Adopt	**698**

JOURNAL

D092	Greetings to the Archbishop of Canterbury	Concur	**346**, 604
D093	Honoring Sonia Francis	Concur	**353**, 695
D094	Appreciation of Platform Party	Adopt	**695**
D095	Thanks for Worship	Adopt	**696**
D096	Thanks for MYP Cluster Programs	Adopt	**696**
D097	Thanks to Convention Volunteers	Adopt	**697**
D098	Behind the Scenes	Adopt	**697**

INDEX

18–30 year olds, leadership programs for, *(A065)* 156, **609–10**, 840
2008 Anglican Gathering, *(D009)* 169, **611**
20/20 initiative
    ethnic desks *(C012)* 445
    new programs, *(A059)* 202–3, **676**
    presentation, 395
    resolutions in budget, 840–45
    vision reporting, *(A084)* **218**, 487
    youth study, *(A032)* 551
21st Century Survey Resources, *(A030)* 112, **476**, 839
50/50 outreach for congregations, *(A138)* 122, **589**

- A -

A028 Task Force, prevention of sexual misconduct, *(A023)* **216**, 451, 452, 839
abortion, post-abortion healing service *(D047)* 192–93, **684**, 846
Action Alerts, *(D030)* 612–13
ad campaign, *(A081)* 252–**53**, 417–19, 841
Afghani women, *(A028)* **327**, 566–67
Afghanistan, *(B016)* 693
Africa
    humanitarian goals in, *(A035)* **340**, 436, 839
    martyrs, celebration of, *(B022)* 164, **669**
African Chaplaincy Program, 768
Aging Task Force, *(A007)* 110–11, **476**, 838
AIDS, continuing epidemic, *(C022)* 412. *See also* HIV, HIV/AIDS
alcohol and drug dependency policies, diocesan, *(A123)* **340**, 453–54
Alleluia Fund–Build My Church, *(A134)* 121, **668**
Anglican and International Peace with Justice Concerns, Standing Commission on, 6
    report to GC, *BB* 96-103
    supporting international relief and development *(D006)* **265-66**, 505
    water policy, *(D070)* **331**, 567
Anglican Communion Office
    Gift of Authority, response to, *(A088)* 159, **610-11**
"Anglican Communion" wording, *(D011)* **334**, 581
Anglican Consultative Council
    theological issues related to human sexuality, *(B009)* 182-83, 250, 689
    2008 Anglican Gathering, support of, *(D009)* 169, **611**
Anglican Environmental Network, *(D066)* **329**, 559–60
Anglican Gathering, *(D009)* 169, **611**
Anglican heritage, reaffirming, *(C014)* **352**, 637
Anglican Province of America, dialogue with, *(B006)* 123, **591**
animals
    protect from cruel treatment, *(D016)* **253**, 483–85
    service, *(D041)* 183–84, **681–82**
Anti-Racism, EC Committee on, 768
    baptismal parity, *(A026)* 400–401
    continue anti-racism mandate, *(A010)* **173–74**, 412–14, 838
    difficult issues, open dialogue on, *(A029)* 113, 118, **630-31**
    members, 26-27
    racial profiling, dismantling *(A129)* 514–15
    racism, continuing efforts to end, *(D025)* **343**, 547–48, 846
    report to GC, *BB* 59-62
APA. *See* Anglican Province of America
Archbishop of Canterbury, greetings to, *(D092)* **346**, 604–5

1009

Archives of the Episcopal Church, 17
appointments to, 72, 616
repository for proceedings of
courts *(A051)* 166,
671-74
report to GC, BB 3-9
ARCIC, Gift of Authority, response to,
(A088) 159, **610–11**
Arctic oil exploration, 746–47, 770
assisted hearing devices, providing,
(D058) 593, 846
audio-visual materials of The Episcopal
Church, *(C027)* **181**, 399, 845

- B -

baptismal parity, *(A026)* **182**, 400–401,
839
Bible translations, *(D067)* 263–64, **683**
biomedical ethics, church's role, *(A013)*
111–12, 476, 838
Bishop Suffragan for Chaplaincies
aging task force, *(A007)* 110–11,
476
just war *(A132)* 320, 502
Bishops. *See also* Bishops, House of;
Rules of Order
age of bishops, Constitution
Article II.2, [First
Reading], *(A039)* 80,
430–31
change in status, 722, 732
consent process for, *(B023)*
214–15, **671**
consent to election of, *(C039)* 93,
102, 370; *(C040)* 93,
102, **113**, 369; *(C041)*
116, **128**, 397; *(C042)*
116, 118, **128**, 397;
(C043) 149, **159**, 410;
(C044) 149, 151, **161**,
410; *(C045)* 209, **222**,
440, 454; *(C046)* 234,
239, 501; *(C047)* 234,
239, 502; *(C048)* 234,
239, 502

election of, Canon III.22.1 &
Canon III.22.3(a),
(D072) **352**, 479–80,
501, 556; Canon
III.22.1(e), *(A046)*
106–7, **675**;
Constitution Article
II.1, [Second Reading]
(D027) 206, **670–71**
necrology, 70, 716, 732, 760, 777,
874
newly consecrated, 713-715,
730-732, 755-758, 776
newly received, 759
Ordained and Consecrated,
849-63
resignation of, 94–95, 707, 715,
732, 744, 759, 777
trial court of, Constitution Article
IX, [Second Reading],
(D062) 206, 570–**71**
Bishops, House of. *See also* Bishops;
Rules of Order
appointment of assistant
secretaries, 69
election of PB nominating
committee, 243
election of Secretary, 349
election of Vice-Chair, 70, 349
interim meetings, bishops present
at, 711–12, 728–29,
739–41, 753–54,
774–75
legislative committee members,
87–92
make-up of, 86
officers of, 40
Pastoral Development
Committee, 31
protecting children and youth
from abuse *(B008)* **255-57**, 514
report to GC, BB 327-28
pastoral letter from, *(B027)*
184–87, **258–61**
Planning Committee, 32

INDEX

Presiding Bishop's Council of
  Advice, 32–33
Religious Communities, 33
seat and voice, Constitution
  Article I.2, *(B005)* [First
  Reading], 204–5,
  224–28, 669–70
roll call votes, 131, 139-146, 205,
  224-228
roster of (Minneapolis), 41–44
Theology Committee, 34
  baptismal parity, *(A026)* **182**,
  400–401
  response to new war situations,
  (D068) **329**, 560
  visiting bishops, 69–70, 93, 124,
  149
black colleges, funding for, 847
Black, Cynthia, *(D091)* **698**
Blanchard, Alan, *(D080)* 552–**53**
Board for Church Deployment, *See*
  Church Deployment Board
Brookhardt, C. Franklin, Jr.,
  consecration of, *(C042)* 116,
  118, **128**, 397
budget for The Episcopal Church
  enabling Resolution, *(D086)*
  269-72, 598
  presentation of budget document,
  541
  printed report, 791-848
  triennial priorities, *(D039)* **152–53**,
  407–8
Burnett, Joe Goodwin, consecration of,
  (C040) 93, 102, **113**, 369–70

- C -

Calendar of the Church Year. *See also*
  Lesser Feasts and Fasts
  inclusion, *(A098)* 107, **488**
campus ministry allocation, *(A066)*
  172–73, **669**
Cannon, John Kemper, honoring
  (D053) **419**
Canon

annotated constitution and
  canons, *(D013)* 132,
  675, 845
complete revisions to III.10, 11,
  12, and 22–32, *(A110)*
  237, 685–**86**
ratify actions of Liturgy and
  Music, Standing
  Commission on *(A041)*
  81, 450–**51**
Canon, Title I, amendments to
  I.1.2(n)(5), Standing Commission
    on Ecumenical and
    Interreligious Relations
    (D010) 179–80, **680**
  I.1.2(n)(6), Standing Commission
    on Liturgy and Music,
    (A040) **133**, 367–68
  I.1.2(n)(13), Standing Commission
    on Health, *(A124)* 204,
    251, 371, **689**
  I.1.2(n)(12), Standing Commission
    on Episcopal Church
    Communication, *(D069)*
    336, 578
  I.4.2(b), Executive Council
    members, *(A009)* **125**,
    366–67
  I.1.9, General Convention
    treasurer, *(A042)* **316**,
    470
  I.1.9.1, admit Puerto Rico to
    PECUSA, *(A141)*
    151-52, **389-91**
  I.1.14, General Convention site
    selection, *(A144)* 82–83,
    350–51, 432, 556–58
  I.6.1, annual parochial reports,
    (A072) **215**, 433
  I.17.1(c), faith affirmation and
    reception of adult
    members, *(A044)*
    193–94, **637–38**
  I.17.2, communicants definition
    (A045), 84, 428–30, **431**

Canon, Title I, unsuccessful amendments to
  I.1.2(a), "confirmed" language, *(A113)* 202; I.4.1(c), *(A115)* 201; I.4.3(d), *(A116)* 201; I.9.7, *(A117)* 201
  I.2.4(c), officers' roles at GC, *(D005)* 480–81
  I.2.5, Chancellor to the Presiding Bishop, *(A114)* 82
  I.6.1, ethnic origin of clergy on staff, *(D018)* 124–25
  I.8.2, Church Pension Fund trustees, *(D042)* 157, 638

Canon, Title I, referred to Standing Commission
  I.13, IV.3.42, 43, IV.14.2, resort to secular courts, *(D012)* 264-65, **682–83**

Canon, Title II, amendments to
  amend II.2, Bible translations, *(D067)* 263–64, **683**

Canon, Title III, amendments to
  III.1-9, revision of Title III canons, *(A111)* 273-308, **641–667**
  III.22.1(e), election of bishops, *(A046)* 106–7, **675**
  III.22.1 & III.22.3(a), election of bishops, *(D072)* **352**, 479–80, 501, 556

Canon, Title III, referred to Standing Commission
  III.22.4(a), (b), consent process for bishops, *(B023)* 214–15, **671**

Canon, Title IV, amendments to
  IV.4-6, 14-15, repository for proceedings of courts *(A051)* 166, **671–74**
  IV.2(A)(2), sentencing of priests and deacons, *(A049)* 83–84, **431–32**
  IV.2(B)(10), sentencing of bishops, *(A050)* 84–85, **432**
  IV.14.13, disqualification in proceedings, *(A047)* 160, 165, **636**
  IV.4.16(d), sentencing if respondent fails to appear, *(A048)* 107, **674**

Canon, Title IV, unsuccessful amendments to
  court for trial of bishop, *(D056)* 571–72, 575
  IV.3.27, "confirmed" language, *(A118)* 200

Casey, Rayelenn, *(D088)* **345**, 605–6
catechism, revision of, *(D003)* 212–13, **679**
Causey, J. P., Jr., appreciation of, *(D094)* **695–96**
CEDAW, support for, *(A024)* 412
Chase, Philander *(A096, A097)* 98–99, **447–48**
Chew, Matt, *(D084)* **348**, 603
child abuse, protection of children and youth from, *(B008)* **255**, 512–14
child sexual abuse, 768–70
children
  caring for, face of new genetics, *(A012)* **209**, 485–86
  leadership training for, *(A077)* **313**, 524–25, 841
A Children's Charter for the Church, **255–57**, 512
Christian-Muslim dialogue, *(A090)* 105–6, **477–78**
church, multicultural and multiracial, *(A031)* 694, 839
Church Building Fund, 19-20
  report to GC, *BB* 30-31
Church Deployment Board, 18
  appointments to, 72, 344, 442
  report to GC, *BB* 10-13
Church Deployment Office, Fresh Start, *(B017)* 219–20, **687**

INDEX

church headquarters, national, energy conservation for, *(C017)* 427–28, 845
Church Insurance Corporation, 769
Church Pension Fund, 18-19
   amend Canon I.8.2, election of Church Pension Fund trustees, *(D042)* 157, 638
   appreciation for board of trustees, *(D079)* 698–**99**
   report to GC, *BB* 15-25
   search for new president, 373
   seminarian expenses, *(A064)* 109, **475**
   trustees, election of, 157, 368–69, 395, 412, 427, 440, 459, 472, 638
   work with Diocese of Puerto Rico, *(A141)* 151-52, **389**
   work with Diocese of Venezuela, *(A142)* **236-37**, 433, 493-94
Church Pension Group, 769
Church Periodical Club, gratitude to, *(D085)* **348**, 603
church planning liturgies, *(A101)* 153, 158, **322**, 525–26, 841
Church Publishing, revised strategy, *(D021)* 165, 680–**81**
Churches Uniting in Christ, 548
civil liberties, *(D063)* **325–26**, 561
Clergy. *See also* Recorder of Ordinations
   continuing education, *(A121)* 101–2, **489**, 842
college students, leadership training for, *(A077)* **313**, 524–25, 841
commemoration. *See Lesser Feasts and Fasts*
Committee on Anti-Racism. *See* Anti-Racism, EC Committee on
Committee on National Concerns. *See* Executive Council Committees
Committee on Sexual Exploitation. *See* Sexual Exploitation, Committee on
Committee on Social Responsibility in Investments. *See* Executive Council Committees
Committee on the State of the Church. *See* Deputies, House of; Committee on the State of the Church
Committee on the Status of Women. *See* Women, Committee on the Status of; *See also* Executive Council Committees
Committees, Commissions, Agencies and Boards, 3, 6-38
common worship
   renewal and enrichment of, *(A107)* 211, 842; *(A108)* 78–79
communicants definition, Canon I.17.2,*(A045)* 84, 428–30, **431**
Companion Diocese Committees
   "Companions in Transformation: The Episcopal Church's World Mission in a New Century," *(A150)* 191–92, **634**
   world mission vision, *(A150)* 191, **634–35**
"Companions in Transformation: The Episcopal Church's World Mission in a New Century," *(A150)* 191-92, **634–35**
"confirmed" language, *(A113, 115, 116, 117, 118)* 200–2
congregational annual study, *(A074)* **335**, 555
Congregational Development, 600
Congregational Development, Office of
   evangelism to the new majority, *(C006)* **210**, 474–75

"Expanding Mission and Vitality in Small Congregations: A Framework Affirming and Strengthening the Ministry of Small Churches," *(A133)* 95, **435–36**
  planting new churches, *(A073)* **312–13**, 416
  transformation resources, *(A076)* **334**, 580, 581
Congregational Development Unit, *See* Congregational Development, Office of
congregations
  50/50 outreach for, *(A138)* 122, **589**
  annual study, *(A074)* **335**, 555
Consecration of Bishops,. *See also* Bishops, consent to elections
  Election Reform, *(D007)* 410–11
consensus, affirmations for facilitating *(B007)* 250
Constitution and Canons, Standing Commission on, 7 *(A051)* 166, **674**
  annotated Constitution and Canon, *(D013)* 132, **675**
  liturgical development and episcopal authority, *(A106)* 268–69, **685**
  open communion, *(A089)* 159-160, 544
  report to GC, *BB* 104-111
Constitution, amendments to
  amend Article I.2, *(B005)* bishops, seat and voice [First Reading], 204–5, 224–28, 669–**70**
  amend Article I.7, GC site selection [First Reading], *(A143)* 79–80, **339–40**, 407, 501
  amend Article II.1, election of bishops [Second Reading], *(D027)* 206, **670–71**
  amend Article II.2, age of bishops [First Reading], *(A039)* 80, **430–31**
  amend Article IX, Trial Court of Bishops [Second Reading], *(D062)* 206, 570–**71**
Constitution, referred to Standing Commission
  Article II.2, consent process for bishops, *(B023)* 214–15, **671**
Constitution, unsuccessful amendments to
  Book of Common Prayer [Second Reading], *(A108)* 78–79; *(D028)* 124
  confirmed adult communicants, *(A112)* 79
constitution and canons, annotated, *(D013)* 132, **675**, 845
contemporary language competency, *(A060)* 103, 236, 323–24, 489, 495, **689**
continuing education
  clergy and lay professionals, *(A121)* 101, **489**, 842
  scholarships, *(A061)* 203, 840
conversations, evening of, *(D087)* **346–47**
COSE. See Committee on Sexual Exploitation
Councell, George Edward, consecration of, *(C039)* 93, **102**, 370
Council of Advice, 778–79, 38
Court for the Trial of a Bishop
  amend Canons on, *(D056)* 570, 571–78
  records of proceedings, *(A051)* 166-67, 671, **672–74**

INDEX

Court of Review for the Trial of a Bishop, 38
Crew, Louie, *(D084)* **348**, 603
Criminal Justice Committee, *(B026)* **338–39**, 537–38, 844; *(B025)* 640, 692. *See also* Executive Council Committees
Cuba, honoring commitments to, *(D050)* 309, 683–**84**
Currie, Vincent, Jr., *(D094)* appreciation of, **695–96**

- D -

Daily Agenda, General Convention *(A156)* **73–76**, 360
deacons
    canon revisions, *(A111)* 277–82, **645–50**
    role of, *(A119)* 100–101, **444**
deaf, ministry to, *(D088)* **345**, 605–6
death penalty, *(B020)* 189, **686**
Decade of Remembrance, Recognition, and Reconciliation, 210
Declaration on Sustainable Development, *(D066)* **329–30**, 559
defense contractors, disinvestment policy, *(D052)* 331, 587–88
Depositions, 893–86
Deputies, House of
    address by ECW, 364, 598
    address by Mayor of Minneapolis, 373
    address by Youth Presence, 373
    address of the President, 364, 427, 493, 628
    appointment of assistant secretaries, 359
    appointment of Chaplain, 358
    appointment of Chancellor to President, 363
    appointment of Parliamentarian, 358
    appointment of special assistant to President, 363
    appreciation to president, *(D083)* **699**
    Committee on the State of the Church, 35
    Mission Funding Task Force, *(B004)* 171-72, **632**
    report to GC, BB 337-54
    ecumenical visitors, 470-72
    election of president, 389–91, 427
    election of secretary, 359
    election of vice-president, 439, 472
    legislative committees of, 374-87
    necrology, 701
    officers of, 45
    President's Council of Advice, 34–35
    roster of members, 46-63
    thanks to chaplain, *(D091)* **698**
    thanks to GC staff, *(D098)* **697**
    thanks to platform, *(D094)* **696**
    thanks to volunteers, *(D097)* **697**
    thanks to worship, *(D095)* **696**
    vote by orders, 441, 454, 571, 609, 615, 635, 639, 668
Diener, Nancy, *(D088)* **345**, 606
difficult issues, open dialogue on, *(A029)* 113, 118–19, **630–31**, 839
diocesan alcohol and drug dependency policies, *(A123)* **340–41**, 453–54
diocesan territories, transfer of, *(C052)* **337–38**, 555–56
Diocese of Minnesota, thanks to, *(D089)* **347**, 604
Diocese of Puerto Rico admitting, (A141) 151–52, **389–91**
Diocese of Venezuela, admitting, *(A142)* **236**, 433–44, 493–95
dioceses, mission perspective of, *(A075)* **336**, 554–55
direct ordination, *(C019)* 127
discernment, *(A111)* 273, 635, **641-42**
Disciplinary Policy and Procedures, Task Force on, 36

1015

preventing sexual misconduct task
force, *(A023)* **216**
report to GC, *BB* 355-68
response teams for, *(D015)*
262-63, 518, 845
disinvestment in defense contractors,
(D052) 331, 587
disqualification of bishop, judge, or
member of review
committee, *(A047)* 160–61,
165–66, **636**
diversity in leadership recruitment,
(A062) 219
Domestic and Foreign Missionary
Society. *See also* Episcopal
Church Center; General
Convention
50/50 outreach for congregations,
(A138) 122, **589**
accounting records, *(A137)* 170,
634
budget for, *(D086)* **269**, 598–601
facilitating internal
communications,
(C037) 221-22, **681**
Mission Funding Task Force,
(B004) 171–72, **632**
mission partners, accountability
of, *(A137)* 170, **634**
national mission narrative/annual
report, *(A136)* 158, **633**
translations, French and Spanish,
(C029) **190–91**, 421-22,
845
website for, *(A080)* **324**, 526
Domestic, Mission and Evangelism,
Standing Commission on, 8
evangelism to the new majority,
(C006), **210**, 474–75
report to GC, *BB* 112-35
trained leadership for youth and
adults *(A077)* **313–14**,
524–25
20/20 Vision Reporting, *(A084)*
218, 487

- E -

EC. *See* Executive Council
Ecclesiastical court
disqualification in proceedings,
(A047) 160, 165, **636**
repository for proceedings, *(A051)*
166, 168, **671–74**
Ecumenical and Interreligious
Relations, Standing
Commission on, 8-9
dialogue with Reformed Episcopal
Church, *(B006)* 123, **591**
Gift of Authority, response to,
(A088) 159, **610–11**
interfaith worship services, *(C031)*
103-4, **477**
Lutheran ordination bylaw,
(A086) 130, **592**
name change for, *(D010)* 179–80,
680; *(D074)* 325
open communion, *(A089)* 160,
544
report to GC, *BB* 136-156
study and present the Reuilly
Accord, *(B003)* 122-23,
590
Ecumenical guests, 177–78, 470–72
Ecumenical Relationships
Christian-Muslim dialogue, *(A090)*
105, **477–78**
waging reconciliation, *(C031)* 103,
477
ECVA. *See* Episcopal Church and
Visual Arts
ELCA. *See* Evangelical Lutheran
Church in America
election clarification, *(D044)* **344–45**,
478
Election of the Presiding Bishop, Joint
Nominating Committee for
the
election of committee, 243,
629–30, 635
members, 36-37

INDEX

election reform, consecration of bishops, (D007) 410–11
Employment Policies Task Group, (A006) **341**, 444, 838
Enmegahbowh, *(A093)* 96, **445**
Enriching Our Music
  further development of, *(A092)* 135–36, **594**, 841
  reauthorizing, *(A092)* 135, **594**, 841
Enriching Our Worship, 240, 245
  1 & 2, *(A091)* 95–96, **445**
  further development of, (A092) 135–36, **594**, 841
  reauthorizing, *(A092)* 135, **594**, 841
EPGM. See Episcopal Partnership for Global Mission
Episcopal Church Center
  Anglican and Global Relations, Anglican Gathering, *(D009)* 169, **611**
  Communications, ad campaign, *(A081)* **252-53**, 417-18
  Congregational Development, planting new churches, *(A073)* **312**, 416–17
  energy audit at, *(C017)* 427-28
  ethnic ministries desks, *(C015)***187**, 416; *(A076)* **334-35**, 580
  multilingual publications, *(A082)* **181**, 399
  national mission narrative/annual report, *(A136)* 158, **633**
  Officer for Criminal Justice Reform, *(B026)* **38-39**, 537–38
  Program and women's desk, ordination process, removing barriers from, *(D043)* 550
  world mission vision, *(A150)* 191, **634–35**
Episcopal Church Communications, Standing Commission on
  establish, *(D069)* **336**, 578–79, 847

members, 6-7
Episcopal Church Foundation
  Fresh Start, *(B017)* 219–20, **687**
  seminarian expenses, *(A064)* 109, **475–76**
Episcopal Church and Visual Arts, thanks to, *(D024)* **315**, 443
Episcopal Colleges, Association of
  report to GC, BB 26-29
Episcopal Community Services in America, formation of, *(D073)* **331**, 580
Episcopal Conference of the Deaf, recognition of, *(D088)* **345**, 605–6
Episcopal Council of Indigenous Ministries, funding, *(C008)* **209–10**, 473–74, 845
Episcopal Ecological Network, spirituality of food production, *(C036)* **318–19**, 507
Episcopal Evangelical Education Society, seminarian expenses, *(A064)* 109, **475–76**
"Episcopal Formation News," 723
Episcopal Life
  congregations, transformation resources, *(A076)* **334-35**, 580, 581
  holy habits, *(A135)* 119-20, **588–89**, 618
  Spanish translations, *(C029)* **190–91**, 421
Episcopal Network for Economic Justice, housing assistance programs, (D040) **332-33**, 569-70
The Episcopal Network for Stewardship. See TENS
Episcopal News Service, baptismal parity, *(A026)* **182**, 400–401
Episcopal Partnership for Global Mission, *(A152)* 85, **435**

1017

"Companions in Transformation: The Episcopal Church's World Mission in a New Century," *(A150)* 191–92, **634**
Episcopal Relief and Development, 20, 81, 459
  celebration of African martyrs, *(B022)* 164, **669**
  "Companions in Transformation: The Episcopal Church's World Mission in a New Century," *(A150)* 191–92, **634–35**
  granting allocations, *(D061)* 250, 546-47
  report to GC, BB 32-33
Episcopal Urban Caucus, Religious Coalition for Reproductive Choice, *(D045)* 332, 569
Episcopal Women's Caucus, Religious Coalition for Reproductive Choice, *(D045)* 332, 569
Ethnic Congregational Development, Office of
  baptismal parity, *(A026)* **182**, 400
  ethnic desks and 20/20*(C012)* 445
  national church office, *(C015)* **187**, 416
  open dialogue on difficult issues (A029) 113, 118–19, **630-31**
  Spanish and French translations, *(C029)* **190–91**, 421
ethnic desks, *See* Ethnic Congregational Development, Office of
ethnic-specific discernment committees, *(A063)* 127–28, **688**
eucharistic sharing, Moravian Church, *(A087)* 123–24, **591–92**
Evangelical Lutheran Church in America
  member reception, *(A085)* 104–5, 117–18, **638**
  ordination bylaw, *(A086)* 130, **592**

ordination practices, *(C011)* 214; *(D004)* 214
relationship with, 722
Evening of Conversations, *(D087)* **346**, 606
Examining Chaplains, General Board of, 21-22, 722
  election for, 178–79, 190, 544
  report to GC, BB 34-36
executions, impact of, on healing and pastoral care, *(B020)* 189, **686–87**
Executive Council, 25–26
  election of, 159, 495, 516, 533
  nominations for, 430
  report to GC, BB 47-93
  terms of office, *(A009)* **125**, 366–67
Executive Council Committees, 4
  20/20 Task Force, report to GC, BB 77
  A045 Task Force, report to GC, BB 78-81
  Anti-Racism. *See also* Anti-Racism, EC Committee on, 26-27
  Audit, 27
  Criminal Justice. *See also* Criminal Justice Committee, 27
  Economic Justice Loan, 28
    report to GC, BB 62-63
  Episcopal Council of Indigenous Ministries, 28–29
    report to GC, BB 70
  Ethics and the New Genetics, report to GC, BB 63-69
  HIV/AIDS, 28
    continuation of, *(A019)* **216**, 409–10, 839
    report to GC, BB 81-85
  Investments, 29
  Jubilee Advisory. *See also* Jubilee Advisory Committee, 29
    report to GC, BB 71

INDEX

National Concerns, post 9/11
    racial hatred, *(D077)* **342**, 522
Science, Technology and Faith, 30
    report to GC, *BB* 72-75
Social Responsibility in
    Investments, 30
    food production*(C036)* **318-19**, 507–8
    report to GC, *BB* 76
Status of Women. *See also* Women, Committee on the Status of, 31
    report to GC, *BB* 87-93
"Expanding Mission and Vitality in Small Congregations: A Framework Affirming and Strengthening the Ministry of Small Churches," *(A133)* 95, **435–36**, 843

- F -

faith affirmation, Canon I.17.1(c) *(A044)* 193-94, **637-38**
faith story, articulating, *(A083)* **187**, 398
Families of Clergy United in Support, *(B018)* 220–21, **686**, 844
family planning, international, (C050) 693
Ferguson, Erin, 81
financial teaching, encouraging, *(D033)* 203–4, **676–77**
FOCUS. See Families of Clergy United in Support
Fontaine, Ann, *(D084)* **348**, 603
food production, spirituality of, *(C036)* **318–19**, 507–8
food security, (A016) 677–78
Forward Movement Publications, 499
    Executive Committee, 21
    continuing, *(A005)* **238**, 469-70
    report to GC, *BB* 37-39
Francis, Sonia, *(D093)* **353–54**, 695
French, translating, (C029) **190**, 421-22, 845
Fresh Start, *(B017)* 219–20, **687**

Fund for Theological Education, *(A067)* 219, **687**, 840

- G -

gene transfer, ethical guidelines for, *(A011)* **254–55**, 481–83
General Board of Examining Chaplains. *See* Examining Chaplains, General Board of
General Convention. *See also* Bishops, House of; Deputies, House of; Rules of Order
    adoption of agenda, *(A156)* **73-75**, 360-63
    CCAB's, 34
    electing bishops prior to, *(D072)* **352**, 479, 556
    election of secretary, 360
    election of treasurer, 360
    full accessibility at, *(D051)* **337**, 527, 534–35
    length of, *(C034)* 435
    meeting sites, *(A144)* 82–83, **350–51**, 432, 556–58
    meetings of, *(A143)* 79–80, **339**, 407, 501
    model, *(A145)* **216**, 396
    nominating deputies, *(A079)* **337**, 535
    officers of, 5
    sites for 2006, *(A154)* 191, **249–50**, 402
    sites for 2009, *(A155)* **315**, 407
    thanks to GC staff, *(D098)* **697–98**
    thanks to volunteers, *(D097)* **697**
    treasurer, *(A042)* **316**, 470
    timing of, *(A143)* 79, **339**, 407, 501
    use of technology at, *(D057)* **353**, 551–52
General Ordination Exam Fee, budget appropriation for, *(A004)* 601-02, 838

General Theological Seminary, Trustees of the
election of, 178, 472, 586, 602, 629, 691
members, 22–23
report to GC, *BB* 40-42
genetic advances, caring for children in face of, *(A012)* **209**, 485–86
germline interventions, ethical guidelines for, *(A011)* **254–55**, 481–83
Getz, Pauline, appreciation of, *(D094)* **695–96**
Gift of Authority, response to, *(A088)* 159, **610–11**
Gitari, David, 721-22
Gleason, Ted, 499
Global Anglican Congress of the Stewardship of Creation, declaration on sustainable development, *(D066)* **329-30**, 559-60
global engagement, funding for, *(D065)* 694
Global Mission Network, "Companions in Transformation: The Episcopal Church's World Mission in a New Century," *(A150)* 191–92, **634–35**
global warming, *(C017)* 427–28, 845
Gnat, Thomas, 207
Government Relations, Office of
advocating for needy families, *(D071)* 332, 567-68
civil liberties and the USA PATRIOT Act, *(D063)* **325-26**, 561
health care for children, *(A122)* 462–63
HIV/AIDS relief for Africa, *(D054)* **327**, 563
housing assistance programs, *(D040)* **332-33**, 569-70
mandatory federal sentencing guidelines, *(A008)* **126–27**, 370
post 9/11 racial hatred and incarcerations, *(D077)* **342,** 522
spirituality of food production, *(C036)* **318–19**, 507–8
stem cell research, *(A014)* 174, 414, **613–14**
youths charged and convicted as adults, *(A126)* **255,** 519–20
Griswold, Frank T., *(B028)* 349, *(D095)* **696**
GTS. *See* General Theological Seminary, Trustees of the
Guernsey, John, 395
Gwi'chin peoples, 723, 746–47, 770

- H -

Hanson, Mark, 176
Hart, Christopher, *(D084)* **348**, 603
HB. *See* Bishops, House of
HD. *See* Deputies, House of
Health, Standing Commission on, 9
establish, *(A124)* 204, 251–52, 371–72, 689–**91**, 843
health care
improving, for children, *(A122)* 462–63
staff position in, *(A124)* 204, 251–52, 371–72, **689–91**, 843
Hegg, David, appreciation for, *(D078)* **699–700**
Hernandez, Aña, *(D091)* **698**
High, Rayford B., consecration of, *(C046)* 234, **239**, 501–2
historic Anglican doctrines and policies, *(B001)* 130–31, 139–46
Historical Society of the Episcopal Church, 23-24
report to GC, *BB* 43-46
Historiographer

INDEX

election of The Rev. Dr. Robert Wright, 72, 442
HIV
  availability of medications for, *(A020)* 463–64
  broadening education of prevention methods, *(A021)* 155–56, **610**
HIV/AIDS
  continuing Standing Committee on, *(A019)* **216**, 409–10, 839
  drug clinical trials, full inclusion, *(A018)* 464
  relief to Africa, *(D054)* **327–28**, 563–64
  statement on solidarity with initiative of Council of Anglican Provinces in Africa, 748–49
holistic Christian education study, *(D075)* 171, 847
holy habits, *(A135)* 119–21, 147–48, **588–89**, 618–25
homosexuality, theological perspective, 781–82
House of Bishops. *See* Bishops, House of
House of Deputies. *See* Deputies, House of
housing for the poor, investing in, **332–33**
Howard, Samuel Johnson, consecration of, *(C041)* 116, **128**, 397
HR40, *(C003)* 517, 540, 590, 597–98
human rights, Afghanistan and Iraq, *(B016)* 693
human sexuality, study of theological issues, *(B009)* 182-83, 250, 689
human stem cells, approve research of, *(A014)* 174, 414, **613–14**

- I -

Immigrant Workers Freedom Ride, *(C028)* **326–27**, 579–80
immigration, *(C033)* **319**, 509
incarcerations, post 9/11, *(D077)* **342**, 522–24, 847
Institutional Wellness and Prevention of Sexual Misconduct Task Force, *(A023)* **216–17**, 272, 451–52, 839
interfaith worship services, *(C031)* 103-04, **477**
Interim Eucharistic Sharing, *(A087)* 123-24, **591**
International Anglican Liturgical Consultation, *(A109)* 211, **678**, 842
international communications, in the Episcopal Church, *(C037)* 221–22, **681**
International Development Fund, 724
international relief and development, supporting, *(D006)* **265-66**, 505–7
Ionnitiu, Lori, *(D098)* **697–98**
Iraq, human rights in, *(B016)* 693
Israeli Security Wall, *(D081)* **328–29**, 558–59
Itty, Johncy, consecration of, *(C043)* 149, **159**, 410
IWFR. See Immigrant Workers Freedom Ride

- J -

Japanese-American internment in World War II, accountability, *(D014)* **326**, 565–66
Jelinek, James L.
  thanks, *(D089)* **347**, 604; (D095) **696**
  welcome from, 69
Jerusalem, International Peace Zone for area, *(D002)* 637
Joint Nominating Committee for the Election of the Presiding Bishop. *See* Election of the Presiding Bishop, Joint Nominating Committee for the

Joint Standing Committee on Planning and Arrangements. *See* Planning and Arrangements, Joint Standing Committee on
Joint Standing Committee on Nominations. *See* Nominations, Joint Standing Committee
Joint Standing Committee on Program, Budget and Finance. *See* Program, Budget and Finance, Joint Standing Committee on
Joint Standing Committees, 3
Jubilee Ministry Advisory Committee, 29
    housing assistance programs, *(D040)* **332-32**, 569-70
    funding of, *(D061)* 250, 546–47, 847
    report to GC, *BB* 71-72
    Thanksgiving, *(A015)* **315–16**, 406
justice studies training, *(A038)* 110, **477**
juveniles, justice for, *(D059)* 613

- K -

King Charles the Martyr, *(C010)* 99
Korea
    crisis in, *(B019)* 693
    relations with *(A036)* 510
    Status of Forces Agreement (SOFA) with, *(A037)* **328**, 564–65

- L -

language competency, *(A060)* 103, 323, 489–90, 495–96, **689**
Lawton, Sarah, 395
lay professionals, continuing education *(A121)* 101, **489**, 842
leadership, trained for evangelism, *(A077)* **313–14**, 524, 841

Leadership Program for Musicians Serving Small Congregations, continuing, *(B010)* 134, **486–87**, 844
leadership training, for youth, children, and college students, *(A077)* **313**, 524–25, 841
legislative committee membership, *(A147)* **317**, 408, 480
Lesser Feasts and Fasts,
    lectionary for, *(C035)* 212, 845
    new commemorations in, *(A093)* 96, **445**
    proposed commemorations in, *(A094, A095)* 96-97, **445-46**; **446-47**; *(A096, A097)* 98-99, **447–48***(A098, A099)* 107-08, **488–89**
    refer for consideration, *(C009)* 99–100, **448–49**; *(C013)* 100, **449**; *(D035)* 213, 679–**80**; *(D049)* 213, **679**
    reject, *(C010)* 99
    revising, *(A100)* 134–35, **593**, 841
Lewis, Clive Staples, *(A094, A095)* 96-97, **445-46**
Liberia, support for people of, *(D023)* **266–67**, 510–12; *(D038)* 694, 846
Lifelong Christian Education and Formation, task force on, *(B024)* 170–72, **631-32**, 844
listserv, appreciation, *(D084)* 348, 603
liturgical development and episcopal authority, *(A106)* 268–69, **685**, 842
Liturgy. *See also* Book of Common Prayer; Calendar of the Church Year; Church Music; *Enriching Our Worship*; *Enriching Our Music*; *Lesser Feasts and Fasts*; Liturgy and Music; Revised Common Lectionary

INDEX

church planting, *(A101)* 153–55, 158, **322–23**, 841
education resources, *(A105)* 137, 842
Liturgy and Music, Standing Commission on, 9-10
  actions ratified, *(A041)* 81, 450-**451**
  baptismal parity, *(A026)* **182**, 400–401
  commemorations. *See Lesser Feasts and Fasts*
  Criminal Justice Committee, *(B026)* **338-339**, 537–38
  Enriching Our Worship and *Enriching Our Music*, *(A092)* 135–36, **594**
  Lesser Feasts and Fasts 2000, revision of, *(A100)* 134–35, **593**; *(C035)* 212
  liturgical development and episcopal authority, *(A106)* 268–69, **685**
  liturgies supplemental to "Burial of a Child," *(D047)* 192, **684**
  ministry of the baptized in ordination, *(C025)* 267–68, **684**
  moon, first communion on, *(D049)* 213, **679**
  open communion, *(A089)* 159, 544
  report to GC, *BB* 157-215
  Revised Common Lectionary, *(A103)* 188, **354**, 635, 639, 667
  transfer Harriet Tubman, *(D003)* 212-213, **679**
  rites supporting life-long relationships, *(D022)* 251
  structure of, *(A040)* **133**, 367–68
  "Worker's Prayer," *(A131)* 211–12
living wage, establishing, *(A130)* **341–42**, 465–66

Luwum, Janani, *(A094, A095)* 96-97, **445-46**
Lutheran ordination bylaw, *(A086)* 130, **592**
Lynch, Diane, *(D088)* **345**, 605-06

- M -

Magar, Priscilla, *(D085)* **348**, 603
mandatory sentencing guidelines *(A008)* **126–27**, 370–71; *(A127)* 406
"Manifesto to the Church," 724
Mann, Barbara, *(D084)* **348**, 603
marriage
  enrichment and renewal, *(D036)* **333**, 568–69, 846
  federally sponsored promotion of, *(D071)* **332**, 567–68
McFarland, Cynthia, *(D084)* **348**, 603
McKendree, Fran, *(D091)* 698
mentally ill, against stigmatization and spiritual abuse of, *(C038)* 694
Miller, Steven A., consecration of, *(C044)* 149, 151, **161**, 410
minimum wage, *(C030)* **262**, 520–22
ministries, *See* ministry
Ministries with Young People Cluster
  18–30 year olds, leadership programs for, *(A065)* 156, **609–10**
  ministering to at-risk youth, *(A128)* **321**, 548-49
  thanks for, *(D096)* **696–97**
  trained leadership, *(A077)* **313**, 524–25
ministry
  canon revisions, *(A111)* 273-308, **641–67**
  of the baptized, in ordination, *(C025)* 267–68, **684**, 845
  ordained and licensed, education about, *(D060)* 189, **688**, 846
Ministry Development, Office of
  aging task force, *(A007)* 110, **476**, 838

1023

Families of Clergy United in Support, *(B018)* 220–21, **686**
Fresh Start, *(B017)* 219–20, **687**
planting new churches, *(A073)* **312–13,** 416–17
Ministry Development, Standing Commission on, 10-11
clergy and lay professional continuing education, *(A121)* 101, **489**
contemporary language competency, *(A060)* 103, 323-24, 489, 495, **689**
education about ordained and licensed ministries, *(D060)* 189, **688**
Episcopal election reform, *(D007)* 410–11
liturgical development and episcopal authority, *(A106)* 268–69, **685**
report to GC, *BB* 217-251
revisions to Title III, *(A111)* 273-309, 635, **641-67**
role of deacons, *(A119)* 100–101, **444**
seminarian expenses, *(A064)* 109, **475–76**
task force on preventing sexual misconduct, *(A023)* **216,** 451, 452
theological education committee, *(A120)* **217–18,** 395–96
Minneapolis, gratitude to, (D082) **700**
mission
diocese perspective, *(A075)* **336,** 554
funding, *(A140)* 129, **590,** 843
priorities for, *(D039)* **152-53,** 407
mission-based prayers, *(A071)* 136, 840
Mission Funding Office, *(A140)* 129–30, **590**
Mission Funding Task Force, *(B004)* 171, **632,** 844

mission narrative/annual report, *(A136)* 158, **633,** 843
mission partners, accountability of, (A137) 170, **634**
Missioner for Rural and Small Communities, "Expanding Mission and Vitality in Small Congregations: A Framework Affirming and Strengthening the Ministry of Small Churches," *(A133)* 95, **435–36**
moon, first communion on, *(D049)* 213, **679**
Moravian Church in America, *(A087)* 123–24, **591–92**
multilingual publications, *(A082)* **181,** 399, 841; *(C027)* 181, **399**
murder victims, survivors of, *(B020)* 189, **686–87,** 844
musicians, leadership program for, *(B010)* 134, **486,** 844

- N -

Nathan Network, *(A022)* 218, 272, 688, 839
National Concerns EC Committee, marriage, *(D036)* **333,** 568–69
National Concerns, Standing Commission on, 11-12
report to GC, *BB* 252-62
rites supporting life-long relationships, *(D022)* 251
National Dialogues on Anti-Racism methodology, *(A010)* **173,** 412, 838
National Network of Episcopal Clergy Associations, task force on prevention of sexual misconduct, *(A023)* 216-17, 451, 452

INDEX

National Network of Lay Professionals, task force on prevention of sexual misconduct, *(A023)* **216-17**, 451, 452, 839
Native Peoples, *(C008)* 209-**10**, 473
necrology. *See* Bishops; Deputies, House of; clergy, necrology
Neer, Harriett, 239
neurological disorders, against stigmatization and spiritual abuse of persons with, *(C038)* 694
new churches, planting, 416–17, 840, *(A073)* **312–13**
new majority, evangelism to, *(C006)* **210**, 474–75, 844
next-generation mentoring, *(A078)* 597
Nightingale, Florence, *(A093)* 96, **445**
Nominations, Joint Standing Committee, 15
  report to GC, *BB* 293-94
nonviolence, culture of, *(D031)* **325**, 558, 846
North American Association of the Diaconate, *(A119)* 100–101, **444**

- O -

Office of the Bishop of the Armed Services, Health Care and Prison Ministries. *See* Bishop Suffragan for Chaplaincies
Office of the Bishop Suffragan for Chaplaincies. *See* Bishop Suffragan for Chaplaincies
Office of Communication. *See* Episcopal Church Center, Communications
Office of Congregational Development. *See* Congregational Development, Office of
Office of Ethnic Congregational Development. *See* Ethnic Congregational Development, Office of

Office of Government Relations. *See* Government Relations, Office of
Office of Ministry Development. *See* Ministry Development, Office of
Office of Pastoral Development, *See* Pastoral Development, Office of
Office of Peace and Justice. *See* Peace and Justice Ministries
Office of Social Justice. *See* Peace and Justice Ministries
Office of Stewardship. *See* Stewardship, Office of
Office of Youth Ministries. *See* Ministries with Young People Cluster
O'Neill, Robert John, consecration of, *(C047)* 234, **239**, 502
On Waging Reconciliation, 735–36
open communion, *(A089)* 159–60, 544, 841
ordination
  general provisions, *(A111)* **644–45**
  process, removing barriers from, *(D043)* 550
  sexuality related to, 786
Ordinations. *See* Recorder of Ordinations
Ott, Connie, *(D084)* **348,** 603

- P - Q -

pain, alleviation of, *(C021)* 468
Palestinian and Afghani Women Support, *(A028)* **327,** 566–67
Palestinian homes, demolition of, *(D008)* **320–21,** 546
parishes and congregations, reports of, *(A072)* **215**, 433
parochial reports, Canon I.6.1, *(A072)* **215**, 433
Pastoral Development, Office of, 778
Pastoral Leadership Search Effort, *(A067)* 219, **687**
pastoral letters, 184–87, 718–19

1025

Peace and Justice Ministries
   continue anti-racism mandates, *(A010)* **173**, 412-13
   difficult issues, open dialogue on, *(A029)* 113, 118–19, **631**
   ministry to prisoners and their families, *(A125)* **253-54**, 517–18
   nonviolence curriculum, *(D031)* **325**, 558
   ordination process, removing barriers from, (D043) 550
   protecting animals, *(D016)* **253**, 483
   spirituality of food production, *(C036)* **318–19**, 507
   "Surviving Loved Ones of Murder Victims: The Impact of Executions on Healing and Pastoral Care," *(B020)* 189-90, **686–87**
peace and justice studies and training, *(A038)* 110, **477**
Peace Cranes, 208
peace training, *(A038)* 110, **477**
Peers, Michael G., 93
pest management, integrated, *(C016)* 633, 692, 845
Philip the Deacon, *(A093)* 96, **445**
Piatkowski, Nancy, *(D090)* **347**, 604
Pitts, David, 373
Planning and Arrangements, Joint Standing Committee on, 15-16
   full accessibility at, *(D051)* **337**, 527, 534
   meeting sites, *(A144)* 82–83, **350–51**, 432, 556–58
   model, *(A145)* **216**, 396
   report to GC, *BB* 329-32
   timing of, *(A143)* 79–80, **339**, 407, 501
political advocacy, funding, *(D030)* 612–13

poor, investing in housing for, *(D040)* **332**, 569–70
pregnant women, support for, *(D037)* 694
pre-marital counseling, *(D036)* **333**, 568-69, 846
Presiding Bishop
   appointments by, 72, 442–43
   Council of Advice, members of, 32-33
   election of Nominating Committee, 243, 629–30, 635
   gratitude to, *(B028)* **349**
   nominations by, 72
   members of Nominating Committee, 36-37
   Official Acts of, 114-115
   statement on Robinson, from Presiding Bishop, 195
Presiding Bishop's Fund for World Relief. *See* Episcopal Relief and Development
priesthood, direct ordination to, *(C023)* 199–200; *(C032)* 200
priests
   life and work of, *(A111)* **657–67**
   ordination of, *(A111)* **650–57**
Prior, Brian, *(D091)* **698**
prisoners, ministry to, and their families, *(A125)* **253–54**, 517–18
Program, Budget and Finance, Joint Standing Committee on, 16–17
   Mission Funding Task Force, *(B004)* 171–72, **632**
   report to GC, *BB* 333-336
   support Anglican Gathering, *(D009)* 169, **611**
   world mission funds, *(A151)* 126, **452–53**
provincial coordinators funding, *(A146)* **215**, 409, 843
Provincial Presidents and Vice-Presidents, 39

INDEX

Puerto Rico admission to PECUSA, *(A141)* 151-52, **389-91**
Pulse Project, *(A067)* 219, **687**

- R -

racial hatred, post 9/11, *(D077)* **342,** 522–24, 847
racial profiling, dismantling, *(A129)* 514–15
racism, continuing efforts to end, *(D025)* **343,** 547–48, 846
RCRC. See Religious Coalition for Reproductive Choice
reaffirmation of faith and purpose, *(C014)* **352,** 637
REC. See Reformed Episcopal Church
reception of adult members, Canon I.17.1(c), *(A044)* 193-94, **637-38**
Receptions, 899–901
reconciliation
  promoting, *(D017)* **333–34,** 582–83
  waging, *(C031)* 103, **477**
Recorder of Ordinations
  election of the Church Pension Fund, 72, 443
  report of, 863-996
Reflective Framework to Guide the House of Bishops in Our Vocation as Teachers, 733–34
Reformed Episcopal Church, dialogue with *(B006)* 123, **591,** 844
regional ministry, funding, *(D030)* 612–13, 846
Registrar
  election of The Rev. Canon Carlson Gerdau, 72, 443
  report of, 847-861
Reid, Brian, *(D084)* **348,** 603
Releases, 893–86
Religious Coalition for Reproductive Choice, withdrawal from, *(D045)* 332, 569

Removals, 893–86
Renton, Nigel, *(D084)* **348,** 603
Renunciations, 893–86
reparative therapy, *(C001)* 614; *(C004)* **261–62** , 515; *(D029)* 614
resolutions and memorials, *(A148)* 369
resources, designing new, *(A059)* 202–3, **676**
Respondent's refusal or failure to appear, *(A048)* 107, **674–75**
Restorations, 898
Reuilly Accord, *(B003)* 122–23, **590–91**
review committees, disqualification in Ecclesiastical proceedings, *(A047)* 160, 165, **636**
Revised Common Lectionary, *(A103)* 188, **354,** 635, 639, 667–68
rites, *See also* same-gender relationships; same-sex
  committed relationships, for *(C005)* 251
  culturally sensitive, *(A102)* 137, 842
Rittgers, Gail Courtney, courtesy for, *(D032)* **316–17,** 372
Roberts, John, *(C013)* 100, **449**
Robinson, V. Gene, 195, 196, 209, 222–23, 229-31, 232, 466, 516, 528, 533
  consecration of, *(C045)* 209, **222,** 428–30, 431, 439–41, 454 , 466
Rockwell, Hays, *(D021)* 165, 680-**81**
Roskam, Catherine, *(D095)* **696**
Rules of Order, House of Bishops, amendments to
  Rule II–First Day, *(B013)* **76–77**
  Rule VI–First Day, *(B014)* **77**
  Rule X, *(B015)* 77, **78**
  Rule XXIV, *(B012)* **76**
  rules pertaining to 2/3 votes, *(B011)* **76**
Rules of Order, House of Deputies, unsuccessful amendments

1027

Article VI, Rule 21(e), resolutions
    and memorials, *(A148)*
    369
Rules of Order, Joint, amendments to
    election clarification, *(D044)*
    344–45, 478
Rybak, R. T., *(D082)* 365, **700**

- S -

same-gender relationships, *(C051)*
    239–42, 244–45, 607–9,
    615–16
same-sex
    blessings, 785–86
    unions, 745
Scarfe, Donna, *(D088)* **345,** 605–6
SCDME. *See* Domestic Mission and
    Evangelism, Standing
    Commission on
schism, minimize, *(D017)* **333–34,**
    582–83
Schori, Katharine Jefferts, *(D095)* **696**
secular courts, *(D012)* 264–65, **682–83**
seminarian expenses, *(A064)* 109,
    475–76
Seminary Deans, Council of
    seminarian expenses, *(A064)* 109,
    475–76
    task force on preventing sexual
        misconduct, *(A023)*
        216, 451, 452
September 11, 2001, 735–36, 761
service animals welcome, *(D041)*
    183–84, **681–82**
sex trafficking, *(A025)* **320,** 508–9, 839;
    (D034) **330,** 561–63, 846
sexual abuse of children, 768–70
Sexual Exploitation, Committee on
    materials on the Web, *(D015)*
    262–63, 518–19, 845
    report to GC, *BB* 85-87
    task force on prevention of sexual
        misconduct, *(A023)*
        216, 451-52
sexual misconduct

pastoral letter from Bishops
    regarding, *(B027)*
    184–87, **258–61**
preventing, establishing task force,
    (A023) **216,** 451–52,
    839
sexual orientation, as gift from God,
    (C004) **261,** 515–16
sexuality
    gift of, theological perspective,
        780–88
    study of theological issues, *(B009)*
        182-83, 250, 689
Sharia law, opposition to, *(D020)* 207,
    677
Simrill, Spenser, thanks, *(D089)* **347,**
    604
slavery reparations, *(C003)* 517, 540,
    590, 597–98
Small Congregations, Standing
    Commission for, 12
    "Expanding Mission and Vitality
        in Small Congregations:
        A Framework
        Affirming and
        Strengthening the
        Ministry of Small
        Churches," *(A133)* 95,
        435
    report to GC, *BB* 263-67
Smith, T. D., 373
Social Justice Department. *See* Peace
    and Justice Ministries
Society for the Increase of the Ministry,
    seminarian expenses, *(A064)*
    109, **475–76**
Solomon Islands, death of Anglican
    missionaries in, 632
Spanish language
    music resources, *(A069)* 137, 840
    translating documents into, *(C029)*
        190, 421–22, 845
special legislative committees, *(A149)*
    366
Standing Commissions, 3, 6–14. *See also*
    listings of individual commissions

INDEX

Standing Commission for Small Congregations. *See* Small Congregations, Standing Commission for...
Standing Commission on Anglican and International Peace with Justice Concerns. *See* Anglican and International Peace with Justice Concerns, Standing ...
Standing Commission on Church Communications. *See* Episcopal Church Communications, Standing...
Standing Commission on Constitution and Canons. *See* Constitution and Canons, Standing...
Standing Commission on Domestic Mission and Evangelism. *See* Domestic Mission and Evangelism, Standing...
Standing Commission on Ecumenical and Interreligious Relations. *See* Ecumenical and Interreligious Relations, Standing...
Standing Commission on Ecumenical Relations. *See* Ecumenical and Interreligious Relations, Standing...
Standing Commission on Health. *See* Health, Standing...
Standing Commission on Liturgy and Music. *See* Liturgy and Music, Standing...
Standing Commission on Ministry Development. *See* Ministry Development, Standing...
Standing Commission on National Concerns, *See* National Concerns, Standing...
Standing Commission on Stewardship and Development. *See* Stewardship and Development, Standing...
Standing Commission on Structure of the Church. *See* Structure of the Church, Standing...
Standing Commission on World Mission. *See* World Mission, Standing...
Standing Committee on HIV/AIDS. *See* Executive Council Committees
Status of Forces Agreement with Korea, (A037) **328**, 564
stem cell research, *(A014)* 174, 414–15, **613-14**; *(C020, C021)* 468
Stewardship and Development, Standing Commission on, 12-13
  Mission Funding Task Force, *(B004)* 171–72, **632**
  report to GC, *BB* 268-74
Stewardship, Office of, encouraging financial teaching, *(D033)* 203–4, **676–77**
"Stop the Hate" Campaign, *(A010)* **173**, 413
Straub, Gregory, appreciation of, *(D094)* **695–96**
Structure of the Church, Standing Commission on, 13
  General Convention model, *(A145)* **216**, 396
  report to GC, *BB* 275-281
Sullivan, Rosemari, *(D057)* **353**, 551–52; *(D094)* **695–96**
"Surviving Loved Ones of Murder Victims: The Impact of Executions on Healing and Pastoral Care," *(B020)* 189, **686–87**
Suspensions, 897
sustainable development, *(D066)* **329**, 559–60
Swan, Sandra, 81, 459

- T -

Task Force on Disciplinary Policy and Procedures. *See* Disciplinary Policy and Procedures, Task Force on
Temple, William, *(A094, A095)* 96-97, **445-46**
Temporary Workers Program, *(C033)* **319**, 509
TENS (The Episcopal Network for Stewardship), *(A139)* 128–29, 130, **589–90**
theological calling, 717
Theological Education Committee, *(A120)* **217–18**, 395–96
Theology Committee of the House of Bishops. *See* Bishops, House of,
Tikhon, *(C009)* 99–100, **448–49**
Tim-Oi, Florence Li, *(A098, A099)* 107-08, **488–89**
tithing, *(D001)* 190
Title IV Revision Task Force. *See* Disciplinary Policy and Procedures, Task Force on
titles, use of, *(A027)* 181–**82**, 400
"Toward Reconciliation in the World," 761–62
toxic chemicals, reducing use of, *(C026)* **338**, 398, 535–37
trafficking of women, girls, and boys, *(A025)* **320**, 508–9, 839
Transfers, 902
transformation resources *(A076)* 334–**35**, 580–81, 840
treasurer. *See* General Convention. Canon, Title I, amendments to
Trial of Bishops, establishing courts for, *(D062)* 206, 570–**71**
Tubman, Harriett, transfer date for, *(D035)* 213, 679–**80**

- U -

undocumented workers, *(C033)* **319**, 509
United Nations Millennium Development Goals, *(A034)* **265–66**, 593; (D006) **265–66**, 505; *(A035)* **340**, 436
United States
foreign aid to developing nations, *(C049)* 692–93
foreign policy, nonviolent, *(C024)* **330**, 545–46
United Thank Offering, "Companions in Transformation: The Episcopal Church's World Mission in a New Century," *(A150)* 191–92, **634–35**
USA PATRIOT Act, *(D063)* 325–26, 561
opposition to, *(D076)* 693

- V -

Venezuela, admitting Diocese of, *(A142)* **236**, 433, 493
violence
ending cycle of, *(C007)* 692
in name of religion, *(C002)* 692

- W -

waging reconciliation, *(C031)* 103–04, **477**
Waiver and Voluntary Submission, *(A049)* 83–84, **431–32**; *(A050)* 84–85, **432**
war
bishops' letter to Congress, 763–64
Christian responses to, *(A132)* **320**, 502–3
just and unjust, *(A033)* **317–18**, 503–5, 538–40
response to new situations, *(D068)* **329**, 560, 847

INDEX

war-torn areas, support for women and children in, *(A028)* **327**, 566
water, stewardship of, *(D046)* **314–15**, 469
water policy, *(D070)* **331**, 567
website, *(A068)* 597; *(A080)* **324–25**, 526–27
Werner, George L., *(D057)* **353**, 551–52; *(D083)* **699**; *(D095)* **696**
Williams, Rowan, greetings to, *(D092)* **346**, 604–5
Williamson, Jan, *(D088)* **345**, 606
Wilson, Sandye, thanks, *(D089)* **347**, 604
Wolfe, Dean E., consecration of, *(C048)* 234, **239**, 502
women
    dioceses not ordaining, visiting, 722
    support for, in war-torn areas, *(A028)* **327**, 566–67
Women, Committee on the Status of. *See also* Executive Council Committees
    baptismal parity, *(A026)* **182**, 400–401
    trafficking of women, girls, and boys, *(A025)* **320**, 508, 839
    youth study, *(A032)* 551
Women's Ministries Office, open dialogue on difficult issues *(A029)* 113, 118–19, **630-31**
women's ordination conversation, *(A017)* **222**, 449–50, 838
worker's prayer, *(A131)* 211–21
working poor, *(C030)* **262**, 520–22
World Council of Churches' Decade to Overcome Violence, *(C024)* **330**, 545
World Mission, Standing Commission on, 14
    2008 Anglican Gathering, support of, *(D009)* 169, **611**

"Companions in Transformation: The Episcopal Church's World Mission in a New Century," *(A150)* 191–92, **634**
    report to GC, *BB* 282-290
world mission funds, *(A151)* 126, **452–53**
world mission vision, *(A150)* 191, **634–35**
world mission funds, *(A151)* 126, **452–53**
world mission vision, *(A150)* 190–91, **634–35**
worship. *See also Enriching Our Worship*; *Lesser Feasts and Fasts*; Liturgy
    resources, creative, *(A070)* 137, 840
    thanks for, *(D095)* **696**
    with evangelism focus, *(A104)* 137, 842
www.ExploreFaith.org, commendation of, *(D026)* 252

- X - Y - Z -

Young Adult Service Corps, 771
youth
    at-risk, ministering to, *(A128)* **321**, 548–49
    charged and convicted as adults, *(A126)* **255**, 519–20, 843
    leadership training for, *(A077)* **313**, 524–25, 841
    protection from abuse, *(B008)* **255**, 512–14
Youth Ministries Cluster. *See* Ministries with Young People Cluster
youth study, *(A032)* 551, 839

CD-ROM Instructions

System Requirements

Windows

Pentium-class processor
Microsoft Windows 98 Second Edition, Windows Millennium Edition, Windows NT 4.0 with Service Pack 5 or 6 (Service Pack 6 recommended), Windows 2000, Windows XP Professional or Home Edition
64MB of RAM
30MB of available hard-disk space (an additional 60MB is needed temporarily during installation)

Web browser support
The Web browsers within which Adobe PDF files may be viewed are:
Internet Explorer 5.0
Netscape Navigator 4.5 to 4.77, 6.1
America Online 6.0

Macintosh

PowerPC processor
Mac OS 9.1, 9.2, or 9.2.2, or Mac OS X v.10.1.3, 10.1.5, 10.2 or 10.3
64MB of RAM
30MB of available hard disk space (an additional 60 MB is needed temporarily during installation)

Web browser support
The Web browsers within which Adobe PDF files may be viewed are:
Internet Explorer 5.0
Netscape Navigator 4.5 to 4.77, 6.1
America Online 6.0

Windows Users

1. Insert the Journal CD-ROM into your CD-ROM drive.
2. Follow the prompts for the Adobe Acrobat installer (should the automatic installation fail to run, please open the CD-ROM directory and double-click the autorun.exe file).
3. Once you have completed the Acrobat installation process, double-click on the Journal PDF document contained on the CD-ROM. You may also save this onto your hard drive, by using the "Save As" feature on your computer. Please, however, read the instructions for this below.
4. For help using Acrobat Reader, select Reader Guide under the Help menu.

Macintosh Users

1. Insert the Journal CD-ROM into your CD-ROM drive.
2. Open the folder named Acrobat Reader and double-click the Reader Installer icon. Follow the instructions on your screen.
3. After installation of Acrobat Reader is complete, you may open the Journal by double clicking the Journal PDF icon that appears on your screen.
4. For help using Acrobat Reader, select Reader Guide under the Help menu.

Note: If you copy the Journal PDF file to your hard drive from the CD-ROM, be sure to copy the index.pdf, and the index folder to the same folder as the Journal PDF. This file and folder add to the searching capabilities of Acrobat Reader.

Note also: Journal is a heavily formatted technical document. If you are performing a COPY/PASTE, choosing copy as graphics may help to retain the formatting, while copying as text will not.